ILLINOIS:
POLITICAL PROCESSES AND GOVERNMENTAL PERFORMANCE

EDGAR G. CRANE, JR.
Northern Illinois University

with the assistance of
ROBIN M. CRANE

Sponsored by the
Illinois Political Science Association

Library of Congress Catalog Card Number: 79-91029

ISBN 0-8403-2141-4

Printed in the United States of America

B 402141 01

this book is
doubly dedicated

to
my parents
for their early sacrifices on my behalf
and
for their continuing encouragement

and to
W. Russell Arrington
formerly Majority Leader of the Illinois Senate (1965 – 1970),
one whose intelligence, dedication and tenacity,
spanning three decades of service in the Illinois General Assembly,
exemplify the high caliber of political leadership
from which Illinois has benefitted
and which inspires future generations of public servants

Contents

Preface

This book fills a gap in the available literature on Illinois government and politics. It is not the first general text on the subject, but it is comprehensive, original and current. It draws extensively upon the outstanding group of practitioners and academics who operate, study and improve the Illinois political system.

The book is officially sponsored by the Illinois Political Science Association. It is their intention, and mine, that the book be revised regularly, on the order of every two or three years, and become a mainstay of courses on Illinois state and local government. We anticipate that the volume will be highly compatible with the *Illinois Issues Annual,* the annual always being slightly more up-to-date and the book providing a more comprehensive background.[1]

The volume has as its primary audience undergraduate college and university classes. It is also suitable for secondary school and public libraries. At the same time, it will be invaluable to scholars and researchers in state and local government, by synthesizing the literature and identifying areas where further research is needed—a major objective of the Illinois Political Science Association in sponsoring this volume is to provide a vehicle for the promotion of research and analysis on Illinois government and politics. Finally, the focus on issues, changes, reforms and the future will make it ''must'' reading for active participants in the Illinois political process.

We take particular pride in the high academic and practical qualifications of contributors to this volume. Authors include many individuals whose work benefits from the combination of their advanced training in political science and other disciplines and from extensive practical experience in Illinois politics. They include delegates and staff to the Sixth Constitutional Convention, legislators and staff, Governor's staff, agency directors, city council members and governmental consultants. Many received their academic training at Illinois institutions of higher education and are or have been affiliated with a diversity of community colleges, liberal arts colleges and state universities.

Space limitations have inevitably prevented inclusion of other excellent authors and material, for which we apologize to both authors and readers. It seems appropriate to mention here some of the major literature. Probably the most comprehensive single-authored text is David Kenney's *Basic Illinois Government.*[2] William K. Hall edited an earlier reader on *Illinois Government and Politics.*[3] Sam Gove is chief author of the frequently revised *Illinois Legislature,* with Richard J. Carlson and Richard F. Carlson.[4] Allan P. Dionosopoulos has edited *Governing Illinois Under the 1970 Constitution,* which analyzes the impact of the new Constitution on many facets of State government and politics.[5] Rollin Posey has authored a primer on *The Constitution of Illinois.*[6] Kopecky has written on *Legal Issues in Illinois Government.*[7]

Any discussion of prominent supplemental resources would also have to mention the 1979 reports and working papers of the State-oriented Illinois Futures Task Force[8] and of the private sector-oriented Illinois 2000 Foundation,[9] which provide an important background for any consideration of future alternatives and the choices we make among them. Among the numerous State documents and reports, one would turn first to the Governor's annual budget and state of the State messages; the Executive Budget Document and its appendices;[10] the reports of the Comptroller,[11] the Auditor,[12] the Illinois Economic and Fiscal Commission, the Illinois Legislative Council and the Intergovernmental Cooperation Commission; and the annual reports of State agencies. The Illinois Department of Local Government Affairs has published a *Guide to Illinois State Services,*[13] and the Secretary of State publishes the *Handbook of Illinois Government.*[14] Neal Peirce has presented the most extensive journalistic perspective on Illinois.[15]

The generous efforts of many people have made this book possible; in many respects the book is a product of the public service commitment of Illinois political scientists. The officers of the Illinois Political Science Association for 1978 and 1979 have consistently encouraged our efforts. In 1978, Sam Sarkesian of Loyola University was President and Tony Fusaro of Northern Illinois University was Secretary-Treasurer. In 1979, Margaret Soderberg of Eastern Illinois University moved up to the Presidency, with Hibbard

Roberts of Illinois State as Vice-President and Rob McIntyre of Millikan University as Secretary-Treasurer. Members of the IPSA advisory committee to the project have been immensely helpful: Sam Sarkesian (Loyola), Chairman; James M. Banovetz (Northern Illinois University); Richard J. Carlson (Governor's Office); Sam Gove (Institute of Government and Public Affairs, University of Illinois at Urbana); Dave Kenney (Southern Illinois University and Illinois Department of Conservation); John Wenum (Illinois Wesleyan); and Paula Wolff (Governor's Office and Governors' State University). Bob Agranoff, Director of Northern Illinois University's Center for Governmental Studies, was instrumental in crystalizing the idea for the book, and made available Center resources without which it would have been impossible to produce the book. Jim Banovetz, my Department Chairman, has characteristically lent his encouragement when it was most needed. Mike Lennon, publisher of *Illinois Issues* magazine, has been a consistent source of good editorial advice. Finally, the editorial assistance of my wife, Robin M. Crane, has improved the style and substance of this first edition in numerous ways large and small!

We welcome reader comments and suggestions on the book as a whole or any part of it. Each chapter has already had the benefit of review by several expert readers. However, in a project of this scope it seems appropriate to view a first edition as being ''out to reviewers.'' The editor and individual authors would appreciate comments on gaps in coverage, matters of perspective and questions of accuracy and readability. We look forward to hearing from our readers and to improving future editions.

To this end it may be useful to summarize the general objectives of the book:

1. *Balance of description* (legal, institutional, structural, process, actors, programs, policies) and *analysis* (political dynamics, power relationships, problems of policy formulation/implementation/evaluation/impacts/revision; change/innovation/reform; success/failure; future implications);
2. *Balance of political* (power, influence, action) and *administrative* (bureaucratic; productivity) considerations;
3. Recognition of current *knowledge limits* (research, data, methodology), and consideration of the extent to which more knowledge may affect the structuring of issues and alternatives—what are the unresolved political issues and the related future research opportunities?
4. Placement of Illinois government and politics in a *comparative* setting—what is most striking and significant about Illinois politics and government? its difference from or similarity to other states?
5. Use of *key events* and available *case material;* and
6. Treatment of *cross-cutting themes:* changing patterns of political power/influence; the linkage among public/voters/elected officials/bureaucrats; the role of interest groups and parties aggregating the political process to formal political institutions; changes in political style; and problems of identifying and achieving the public interest.

These are appropriate objectives, yet they are ambitious ones. We hope that future editions will more fully realize them, and we solicit the help of our readers in this common enterprise!

Ed Crane
Geneva, Illinois

NOTES

[1]Illinois Issues. *Illinois Issues Annual* (Springfield: Sangamon State University, published annually since 1975–76 edition). The journal, *Illinois Issues* is published monthly.

[2]David Kenney, *Illinois Government* (Carbondale: Southern Illinois University Press, 1974).

[3]William K. Hall, ed., *Illinois Government and Politics* (Dubuque, Iowa: Kendall-Hunt, 1974).

[4]Samuel K. Gove, Richard J. Carlson and Richard F. Carlson, *The Illinois Legislature* (Urbana: University of Illinois Press, 1976).

[5]Allan P. Dionosopoulos, ed., *Governing Illinois Under the 1970 Constitution* (DeKalb: Northern Illinois University, Center for Governmental Studies, 1978).

[6]Rollin E. Posey, *The Constitution of Illinois/1970 Revised Edition* (New York: Harper and Row, 1971).

[7]Frank Kopecky, *Current Illinois Legal Issues* (Springfield: *Illinois Issues Magazine,* 1977).

[8]Illinois Futures Task Force, in care of the Illinois Department of Local Government Affairs, 160 N. LaSalle St., Chicago, Illinois 60601.

[9]Illinois 2000 Foundation, in care of the Illinois State Chamber of Commerce, 2040 Wacker Drive, Chicago, Illinois 60606.

[10]Illinois Bureau of the Budget, *Executive Budget* and *Appendices,* State House, Springfield, Illinois 62703.

[11]Illinois Office of Comptroller. *Annual Report.* State House, Springfield, Illinois 62703.

[12]Illinois Auditor General, *Staff Development Course on State Government,* training manual, Stratton Building, Springfield, Illinois 62706, 1977.

[13]Illinois Department of Local Government Affairs, *Guide to Illinois State Services* (Springfield, Ill.: The Department, periodically revised).

[14]Illinois Secretary of State, *Handbook of Illinois Government* (Springfield, Ill.: Office of the Secretary of State, periodically revised).

[15]Neal R. Peirce, "Illinois and the Mighty Lakeside City: Where Clout Counts," in *The Megastates of America: People, Politics and Power in the Ten Great States* (New York: Norton, 1972), pp. 341–402.

Contributors

John Ahlen: Staff Scientist, Illinois Legislative Council; was legislative science intern; helped develop plan for state science policy at Institute of Government and Public Affairs.

James H. Andrews: private consultant in community planning processes; served as Assistant to the Speaker, Illinois House of Representatives, and as Research Director, House Democratic Caucus.

James M. Banovetz: Director, Public Administration Division and former Chairman, Political Science Department, Northern Illinois University; has published widely on municipal management and consulted with the International City Management Association, the Illinois City Management Association, the Illinois Muncipal League and the Illinois Department of Local Government Affairs; author, *Managing the Modern City*.

Jesse C. Brown: Instructor, Political Science Department, Southern Illinois University at Carbondale.

Martin Burlingame: Political scientist and Professor, School of Education, University of Illinois (Urbana); Director of Administration and Policy Studies.

Richard J. Carlson: Assistant to Governor James R. Thompson for reorganization and management; served as staff assistant, Illinois Senate, Coordinator of Research, Sixth Illinois Constitutional Convention and Director of Research, Council of State Governments.

Peter Colby: Professor, College of Business and Public Affairs, Governors State University; co-author of political parties articles, *Illinois Issues*.

Raymond F. Coyne: Comptroller, City of Chicago; was Executive Director, Illinois Economic and Fiscal Commission; former staff, Illinois Senate Democratic Appropriations Committee.

Edgar G. Crane, Jr.: Assistant Professor of Political Science and Public Administration, Northern Illinois University; served as Director, National Legislative Conference and Director of Legislative Services, Council of State Governments; was Assistant to the Majority Leader, Illinois State Senate; also served legislatures of California and New York; author, *Legislative Review of Government Programs* (1977); *State Government Productivity* (1976).

Robin Morris Crane: governmental consultant; was management analyst, New York State Budget Division; criminal justice planner and office administrator, Kentucky Law Enforcement Commission; day care grant administrator, Illinois Department of Children and Family Services.

Stephen Daniels: Assistant Professor of Political Studies and Public Affairs in the Center for Legal Studies, Sangamon State University.

J. Dixon Esseks: Associate Professor of Political Science and Public Administration, Northern Illinois University; chairs interdepartmental Land Use Task Force; developing extensive program of applied research and public service in local growth management.

Samuel K. Gove: Director, Institute of Government and Public Affairs and Professor, Political Science Department, University of Illinois (Urbana); served on numerous federal, state and local study or advisory commissions; staff member of the Commission to Study State Government (1950); Commission on State Personnel Administration (1953); reorganized office of Auditor of Public Accounts after Hodge scandal (1957); Governor's appointment to Commission on State Government (1965); with respect to the 1970 Constitution, served as Staff Director and member, Constitution Study Commission; also Chairman, Governor-appointed Citizens Task Force on Constitutional Implementation; author, *The Illinois Legislature*.

Paul Green: Professor, College of Business and Public Affairs, Governors' State University; co-author of political parties articles, *Illinois Issues*.

William K. Hall: Chairman, Political Science Department, Bradley University; editor, *Illinois Government and Politics* (1974); member, Kansas House of Representatives (1965–67).

Robert E. Hartley: editor, Lindsay-Schaub newspapers; author, *Charles H. Percy: A Political Perspective* (1975) and *Big Jim Thompson of Illinois* (Rand McNally, 1979).

A. James Heins: Professor, Economics Department and Institute of Government and Public Affairs, University of Illinois (Urbana); authored major economic studies for Illinois State Chamber of Commerce and various state commissions.

Boyd R. Keenan: Professor, Political Science Department, University of Illinois (Chicago Circle) and Institute of Government and Public Affairs; was Science Advisor to Governor Richard B. Ogilvie; active in intergovernmental science relations as consultant to National Science Foundation; directing study of power plant impacts on Ohio River Basin; author, *Energy and Environment: An Intergovernmental Perspective* (1978).

David Kenney: Director, Illinois Department of Conservation; Professor, Political Science Department, Southern Illinois University (Carbondale); delegate, Sixth Illinois Constitutional Convention; author, *Basic Illinois Government* (Southern Illinois University Press, 1974).

Richard Kolhauser: Deputy Director, Illinois Bureau of the Budget; economist.

Frank J. Kopeckey: Director, Legal Studies Center, Sanagamon State University; author, *Current Illinois Legal Issues* (Illinois Issues Magazine, 1978).

Mary Lee Leahy: Springfield attorney; was Assistant and Counsel to Governor Dan Walker, Acting Director of Illinois Environmental Protection Agency, Director of Illinois Department of Children and Family Services, and Delegate, Sixth Illinois Constitutional Convention.

Thomas Littlewood: Dean, School of Journalism, University of Illinois (Urbana); was correspondent, *Chicago Sun Times*.

Ann Lousin: Associate Professor, John Marshall College of Law; Chairman, Illinois Civil Service Commission; was Parliamentarian of Illinois House of Representatives and Staff of Sixth Illinois Constitutional Convention.

Kevin McKeough: Associate Professor, Political Science Department, Northern Illinois University; and Social Science Research Coordinator, Graduate School; author of publications on election finance.

Marvin W. Mindes: Oklahoma City University School of Law; former Chicago attorney and faculty member, Kent College of Law; Research Director, gubernatorial campaign of Otto Kerner (1960); advised Kerner on credit reform; was Chairman of the Illinois Unemployment Compensation Board of Review and of the Urban Affairs Committee of the Chicago Bar Association.

Alan Monroe: Associate Professor, Political Science Department, Illinois State University; author, *Public Opinion in America* (1975); current research on relation between public opinion and public policy.

Michael Schneiderman: Chicago attorney; service under Governor Richard B. Ogilvie (first Director, Illinois Institute for Environmental Quality; Executive Secretary, Environmental Quality Cabinet; first Chairman, Illinois Industrial Pollution Control Financing Authority; Member, Illinois Commission on Atomic Energy, Commission on Organization of the Illinois Department of Transportation, and Governor's Task Force on Public Transportation in Northeastern Illinois); service under Governor James R. Thompson (member, Governor's Science and Technology Task Force; counsel, Task Force on the Future of Illinois).

Dick Simpson: Associate Professor, Political Science Department, University of Illinois (Chicago Circle); was independent alderman in Chicago City Council and has been a leading organizer of Chicago's independent Democrats; author, *Chicago's Future*.

John Steinke: Professor, Political Science Department, College of Lake County.

Jack Van der Slik: Dean, Trinity Christian College; was Professor, Political Science Department, Southern Illinois University (Carbondale); was staff, Illinois Legislative Council; author, *American Legislative Processes* (Crowell, 1975).

John Wenum: Chairman, Political Science Department, Illinois Wesleyan University; Delegate, Sixth Illinois Constitutional Convention and member, Local Government Committee.

John A. Williams: Assistant Professor, Political Science Department, Loyola University.

Richard Wiste: Associate Director of Budget and Planning, Northern Illinois University; also Adjunct Professor of Political Science; research on legislative behavior and electoral systems.

Paula Wolff: Director, Policy Staff, Office of Governor James R. Thompson; was Professor, College of Business and Public Affairs, Governors State University; Delegate, Sixth Illinois Constitutional Convention.

CHAPTER 1

Illinois Government and Politics: An Overview

Edgar G. Crane, Jr.

Illinois government and politics, like its people, is rich in its diversity. By the nature of democratic politics it touches the lives of many Illinoisans. Depending on the circumstances, it may provoke a wide range of responses: curiosity, fascination, confusion, insight, satisfaction, frustration, disgust, enthusiasm, rejection, acceptance or reform. The objective of this chapter is to present an overview of Illinois politics which will help bring it into focus for the students, citizens, leaders, teachers and researchers of the 1980's, while serving as a useful introduction to this book.

Since this book attempts to combine the findings of scientific study with the lessons of practical experience, the chapter begins with a discussion of the dual nature of politics, as both science and art, theory and practice. Scientific, comparative study of state government has challenged the independent influence of political institutions. Although it has been able to explain policy outcomes partially in terms of non-political factors such as economics, it is necessary to study political factors if we are to understand the impact of government, society and the economy on our lives. Moreover, it is of increasing, not decreasing, importance to understand the role of state government in making the federal system work. Our understanding at the state level or any other can benefit from an integrated view of the entire policy cycle and from an understanding of the interplay of politics with policy through the phases of that cycle. It is in this context that we can best understand the legislative, executive, judicial and bureaucratic institutions of state government. They play an active, not a passive, role in linking political demands to policy responses. The intergovernmental, constitutional, economic and political environments of state government, together with the institutional "rules of the game," combine to determine State policy. As Illinois State government enters the 1980's, its major problem will be creating the institutional "policy management" capability required to identify the combination of policies on energy, environment, growth and human resources which will equitably promote a healthy State economy and an attractive quality of life for Illinois citizens.

The Science and Art of Politics

We live in an age and in a society where important dimensions of human life have been transformed by science and technology. The success of physical science and engineering has encouraged serious efforts to develop a social and political science, with its corresponding engineering applications. It may well be that the American federal system represents the most successful effort to apply a set of "scientific" principles to the solution of classic political problems (liberty and order, power and justice), through the design of a political system (federalism, checks and balances, separation of powers).

The contemporary discipline of political science carries on its enterprise partly in that tradition of successful practicing scientists who integrated empirical comparative study with normative Lockeian political philosophy and goals. Modern political science and other social science disciplines are developing a substantial body of useful knowledge and a variety of useful conceptual frameworks for interpreting and applying that knowledge. At the same time it is clear that by itself scientific study does not generate answers or tell us which course of action is preferred. It does perform the invaluable function of identifying alternatives and improving our ability to anticipate their various consequences. Ultimately, however, political decisions require the strong guidance of values and the prudent use of judgment by the multitude of political actors who populate our pluralistic system. To that extent, government and politics, though subject to scientific influences, are ultimately art, not science.

Politics and the Comparative Study of State Government

There is a body of growing and useful national research on state political systems. It looks at certain broad cross-cutting themes, including the influence of political institutions; the distribution of political power; the nature and effects of competition for political power; who is best and least represented; the technical competency of state government to make, implement, evaluate and improve public policy; and the strength and nature of movements for modernization and reform.

The most fundamental question raised by contemporary comparative study of state political systems is highly susceptible to scientific methods of analysis, yet full of practical implications: do political actors and institutions have an independent impact on public policy outcomes, or are they of relatively minor consequence compared with other influences? Until the 1950's, political scientists simply assumed the importance of politics and attempted to identify which political variables were most important to the performance of a political system, for example, the level of two-party competition, or the basis of legislative apportionment.[1] A second phase began in the 1960's, when new techniques of statistical analysis permitted the raising of broader questions about the impact on state policy of economic as well as political influences. Initial findings suggested that economic factors could explain policy variations from state to state better than political factors. For example, the single most important explanation of high state spending is high state personal income.[2] We are now in a period where further research has made it clear that even the economic variables are only modestly explanatory. It remains highly likely that political factors and political action are crucial in determining the shape of public policy at the state level.[3] Therefore it is important to examine political factors, and, at the same time, it is important to analyze a political system in its economic setting.

State Political Systems: Understanding and Importance

How well do we understand state political systems, and how much better are we likely to understand them? It seems that we understand quite a bit that is useful. At the same time important considerations suggest that we can improve our current understanding immensely. First, the "state of the art" in political science is improving rapidly—new analytic tools increase our ability to observe and understand. Second, recent decades of rapid progress in political science have been characterized by a primary focus of attention on international and national levels, not on state and local phenomena, nor on intergovernmental relations.

How much difference does this relative inattention to state and local government make? Are the federal principles established in the United States Constitution still valid in today's world? A chief principle of the federal design is the non-centralized exercise of shared powers by separate institutions, with the provision for checks and balances among levels and branches of government. The intention was to create a system of "ordered liberty," permitting majority rule while preventing majority tyranny. To this end the Constitution protects the states and confers co-equal status with the national government. Yet for fully half or more of our national history we have been experiencing a powerful tide of centralization, starting with industrialization and the rise of the large corporation, and culminating with the still-prevailing "New Deal" era initiated in 1932 by Franklin D. Roosevelt. This trend may have reached its peak in Lyndon Johnson's "Great Society" of the mid-1960's. The depression of the 1930's was the catalyst for the birth of a dominant political coalition based upon the principle that American society and economy had become so complex and interdependent that state and local government, together with the private sector, could no longer be expected to manage the economy and deliver the bulk of public services; and, instead, national goals, financing and administration would be necessary. More recently we have been learning an equally painful counterbalancing lesson—if the public sector is to perform at its best, every element of the federal system must be fully utilized, and its capacity strengthened.[4]

Parallel to the emergence of a new appreciation for the federal system and its capabilities has been the development of the disciplinary distinction between political science and public administration. Efforts to understand and improve state government are profoundly affected by the transition of public administration from an academic subfield of political science to an interdisciplinary superfield which integrates applications from many disciplines, including not only political science, but economics and the other social sciences. A third area of "policy studies" has emerged to link the pure and applied branches of political science. The focus is on policy as a dependent and independent variable—what causes policy and what impact policy has. The three areas together constitute the heart of contemporary political science. They lend renewed emphasis to the role of the discipline in "making the system work." These parallel developments reflect the fact that one of our major challenges is to clarify public purposes and control the role of bureaucracy in contemporary society, purposes and bureaucracy which increasingly cut across the federal system via intergovernmental policy and programs.[5]

Toward an Integrated View of the Policy Cycle

The organization of this book reflects the broadening scope for study, operation and improvement of the political system. To the extent permitted by space limitations, publishing costs and the state of existing research on Illinois, the book is organized to reflect upon the broad, interactive process depicted in Figure 1-1. Not so long ago political scientists defined the scope of their interests as policy formulation, with emphasis on formal description of policy, and the institutions established in law to make that policy. Correspondingly, administration would in all likelihood be viewed as a neutral, impartial, apolitical instrument for the implementation of public policy. The contemporary study of politics and government seeks to develop a more comprehensive understanding of the interplay of actors representing formal, legal institutions of Illinois State government (legislature, executive, judiciary) with others who have a profound impact on the political process (interest groups, professions, political parties, media). Together they make and implement (1) policy in various areas (educa-

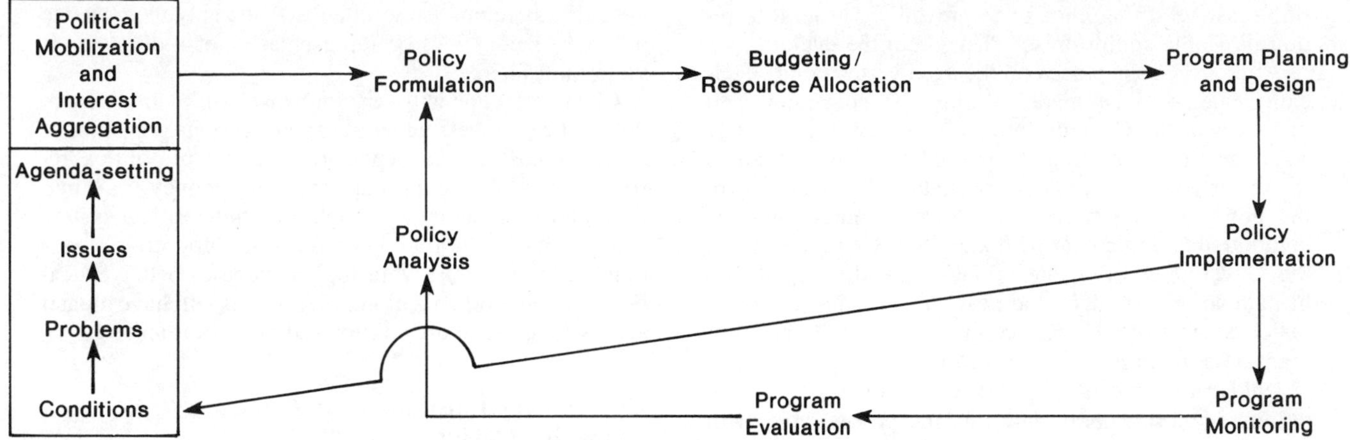

Figure 1-1. POLITICS AND POLICY: AN INTEGRATED FRAMEWORK OF ANALYSIS

tion, land use and growth management, energy and environment, human resources) and (2) "metapolicy," or policy on policy-making (State organization and policy management capability). They are constrained or given impetus by broad "environmental" influences (political culture, condition of the economy, changing demographic patterns and their effect on partisan and regional conflict, available technology, intergovernmental relations, the State Constitution and other "rules of the game").

"Policy management" may be defined as the application of the policy cycle concept to governmental operations in such a way that they become better integrated (coordinated), with a resultant improvement in performance across levels of government, phases of the policy cycle, and state programs. Improved policy management capability seems to be a requirement if State government is to "get its act together" in the 1980's.[6]

The Interplay of Politics and Policy

"Politics" can be defined in various ways. At root it refers to matters affecting the polity, or the citizenry. A very practical definition of politics which fits Illinois well is: "who gets what, when, how, and why."[7] More abstractly, politics has been defined as "the authoritative allocation of values" (rights, goods, status, quality of life).[8]

"Policy" can also be defined in various ways. Narrowly, policy is the official declaration of public goals by representative institutions. More broadly, it is whatever governmental or quasi-governmental institutions *do* over any period of time. Policy can be viewed as the output of the political process. It has been suggested that there are different kinds of politics for different kinds of policies. Policy may *distribute* public goods relatively evenly, or it may target resources in a *redistributive* manner, or it may be *regulatory* of business activity in the interests of free competition, economic efficiency or consumer protection.[9] Achieving a policy objective, that is, getting government to act, or to refrain from action, requires power, the proverbial "clout" of Illinois political lingo—the ability to influence others to endorse and implement a course of action, regardless of what those others might have decided independently. Key political actors mobilize power by commanding institutional resources and guiding political processes. Generally, however, we find the origins of power in a broad set of social and economic conditions. Someone must perceive that those conditions are causing problems which permit or require public action. The issue must be raised in such a way that it can be placed on the agenda of political institutions. As Figure 1 illustrates, in reality the political process is a continuous, highly interactive series of events. However, it is analytically useful to begin consideration at the point where conditions have been perceived as problems and where issues are being pushed onto the agenda.

The dispersion of ability to formulate an issue and place it on the agenda for serious consideration is the first test of whether a political system provides for effective representation and an equitable distribution of power.[10] Political competition must be sufficient to provide adequate opportunity for dissatisfied groups to enter into new coalitions through which they can advance their views. Political parties have traditionally been the key instrument of coalition-building and have somewhat protected elected officials from the leverage of interest groups, particularly in states which have a balance of diverse interests, like Illinois. However, the decline of parties has been accompanied by the rise of interest group influence and, quite probably, the reduction of wide and equitable representation.[11] Any political system can be evaluated in terms of how well it provides for such interest aggregation, or political mobilization.

But this is only the beginning, rather than the end, of such questions. They must be asked at each point of the political process and the policy cycle. A group or coalition must be strong enough to prevail, or at least to require a viable compromise, throughout the cycle.

After an issue is placed on the agenda, the policy decision remains to be made. Within the constraints and mandates of the Constitution, as interpreted by the State Supreme Court, the Legislature and the Governor share the major powers of policy formulation. They also share the power to determine what State resources will be committed to implementing that policy. On major issues, the Governor is often the initiator, but the Legislature has ample opportunity to impose its own views through majority votes of whatever coalitions happen to be dominant on a given issue at a given time.

Until rather recently, political scientists have come perilously close to assuming that the process ends with "the decision," ignoring its cyclical nature and the remaining components. The growth of public programs and their attendant bureaucracies has forced a refocusing of attention to what happens next—program planning, design, implementation, monitoring, evaluation and the crucial closing of the "feedback loop" as the cycle repeats. Without this crucial element of memory and learning, the political system would be unable to profit from the lessons of experience, a deficiency which too often prevails in practice.[12]

Throughout the cycle, political and technical components must be jointly planned for and monitored, if today's complex programs are to work and be improved. To assure that this is done, governments have invested increasing resources in policy analysis and program evaluation.[13] "Policy analysis" involves defining a problem, identifying alternative programmatic responses to it, clarifying the consequences (costs and benefits) of implementation, and presenting the trade-offs (pros and cons) of the alternatives in such a way that decision-makers are aided. Policy analysis looks to the future. Program evaluation, one of its components, looks to the past and asks "how well did we use our resources and to what extent did we achieve our policy goals?"

As these twin activities have been institutionalized, or built into government, they have had a modest—sometimes substantial and sometimes negligible—impact on the nature of the political process, shifting it more in the direction of a long-range, public-interest, comprehensive planning approach to the policy cycle. Yet experience makes it evident that analysis and evaluation, like science in general, are only aids to decision, not substitutes for the human values and judgments of political actors. It has been persuasively argued that the principle of checks and balances designed into the political system so thoughtfully by our founding political scientists, remains applicable to these new quasi-scientific inputs to the political process. That is, it is crucial that these appropriately named "policy management" capabilities not be concentrated at one point in the political system, but be widely dispersed, like other resources of political power. This means that the public would do well to support policy management and analytic capability not only at all levels and branches of government, but also outside of government, in universities and free-standing institutes as well, to improve the chance that analytic inputs to policy decisions will be representative of a diversity of views and interests.[14]

Clearly, groups will vary immensely in their access to the political process generally and to various points in the cycle. Access and influence are functions of political resources available to a group, including money, information relevant to an issue, insight into the political system and potential for joining or forming supportive coalitions. Clearly, those with higher income, better education and wider organizational affiliations will have greater access than the poor, uninformed and unorganized.

Governmental Institutions in Politics and Policy-Making

Illinois political institutions mirror the principles and structures established by the federal Constitution for the national government. The basic principle is that of checks and balances, with sharing of powers by separated institutions. The core structures are the chief executive (Governor), the legislature (General Assembly), and the court system (with the Illinois Supreme Court at its apex). Despite the strength of interest groups and partisanship in Illinois politics, the Office of Governor and the Legislature are formidable independent actors in the system—neither is the simple resultant of the group process, or of economic forces, or of political party direction. Their active importance in all phases of the Illinois political process will be evident throughout this chapter and the entire book.

In Illinois the Office of Governor, though enjoying powers which compare favorably with any other state and, in form at least, with the Presidency, also experiences important limitations by design. In all his major formal powers—appointment, budgeting, veto, and reorganization—the Governor can be checked, reversed and modified by the Legislature. The 1970 Constitution followed a national trend by strengthening the powers of both the Governor (veto, budget) and the Legislature (post-audit; annual sessions; calling itself into session). Important statewide constituencies have confidence in and work through both branches. Thus constitutionally and politically Illinois enjoys the basis for a "strong" State government, one which has the authority to take responsive action, and where a strong Governor and strong Legislature may check and balance each other. Importantly, the private sector in Illinois continues to support a politically strong and technically competent State government, as evidenced by the work of the Chamber of Commerce-affiliated Illinois 2000 Foundation.

Crane finds that post-World War II Illinois Governors have set high standards of success for future Governors and that some clear guidelines for success emerge from their experience as a group. If there is one key to success, it is building effective political coalitions in support of policy goals and their implementation. When this is not done, the Legislature with its shared powers becomes a major barrier to effective administration, as well as to the Governor's policy leadership. The Hartley chapter suggests that Governor Thompson has met the requirements for political effectiveness but has not yet mobilized his power to implement a full program.

The Illinois Legislature has been modernized greatly since 1965, yet preserves many of its political traditions. The modernization has made it a stronger institution by establishing a full-time professional staff to provide an independent basis for policy-making and by streamlining numerous procedures to make action easier, more orderly, and more open to public scrutiny. Much of this progress can be traced to the continuing work of the Commission on Organization of the General Assembly (COOGA), created in 1965 by the ''orange ballot'' Legislature elected statewide as a result of its predecessor's inability to agree on the specifics of a court-ordered reapportionment plan. The improved information and procedures continue to serve the traditional purposes of the various factions represented in the Legislature.

In his chapter, Gove focuses on four key features which determine legislative impact on State policy: representation, constitutional powers, partisan politics and legislative-executive relations. Van Der Slik/Brown and Wiste examine voting patterns and the impact of the unique cumulative voting system. All three shed further light on the complex of actors and motives which drive the legislative appropriations process, discussed by Coyne. The Legislature will continue to be a frustration to deal with and a fascination to study, because it is a complex body undergoing continuous change—the reality is a far cry from the stagnant, passive body imagined by outmoded myths about state government!

Together, the Legislature and the Governor can employ great power in the service of Illinois. Both institutions have reached a significant level of maturity and competency. As Gove observes, the Legislature will continue to evolve, and some important issues remain to be resolved along the way. It seems reasonable to conclude that if State government is to play its fullest role in making the federal system work, both institutions must develop ways of better utilizing their impressive resources. This means each must strengthen the package of activities which come under the heading of ''policy management'' by elected officials.

The Illinois courts, like any major institution, may be viewed from a variety of perspectives. Kenney looks at the courts in the context of checks and balances by examining the politics of the Sixth Constitutional Convention. Daniels and Kopecky examine the workload and function of the courts, which leads them to focus attention more on the lower courts than on the Illinois Supreme Court. Mindes reminds us that the courts and the legal profession do not necessarily operate in conformance with formal design or norms, because they are affected by a complex set of realities beyond effective policy control. This is a realistic perspective which can readily be applied to other institutions as well—political realities are always more complex than our attempts to control them or even describe them might suggest. A major theme of this volume is that recognition of our limited ability to *control* events simply establishes the context for our efforts to improve governmental *response* to events through better *management* of policy-making and implementation.

Intergovernmental Relations: Role of Illinois in the Federal System

Under the dominant ''New Deal'' coalition assembled by Franklin D. Roosevelt, the federal government has played an increasing role during the past fifty years in domestic policy and programs which have traditionally been the province of state and local government. The federal bureaucracies established to implement the New Deal programs have tended to dominate their state and local counterparts, severely weakening state and local elected officials in the ''battle of expertise.'' It is important to recognize, however, that the federal-state relationship has seldom been a one-way street with federal officials giving the orders. State and local bureaucrats have played a major role in persuading Congress to enact new programs and fund them from the superior revenues generated by the progressive federal income tax as the economy expanded. Recently it has become evident that, with the expansion of higher education and the improvement of state and local salaries, state and local bureaucrats are as able as their federal counterparts. Together with recent lessons on the limitations of solely federal problem solving efforts, these changes create a new set of circumstances for the conduct of federal-state relations.[15] At one time it was common for state administrators of intergovernmental programs to place their loyalties first with the federal bureaucrats. In the future it is more likely they will look to priorities set by state and local elected officials. The states can no longer be seen as negative opponents of the rights of citizens, but as key partners in making the federal system work. Their relationship with local governments is crucial in this enterprise.

Because the federal Constitution provides for the states, but not for local governments, the latter are constitutionally and legally ''creatures of the states.'' State constitutions and statutes enacted by state legislatures determine the form of local government and establish the conditions under which local governments are created, have their boundaries, operate, levy and collect taxes, cooperate with each other, or consolidate with other local governments. One might anticipate, therefore, that local governments would also be extensions of the state. However there is a great variation among the states in the extent of state supervision and control, as well as in the extent to which local governments depend on taxes collected by the state or serve solely as delivery systems for state mandated programs. In many states coalitions of local elected officials or dominant cities exercise great power in state policymaking. Even state legislators or members of Congress may feel that they are local representatives. The national trend is toward more flexibility for local self-government through ''home rule'' provisions. Those incorporated in the 1970 Illinois Constitution are among the strongest. Ironically, however, this increasing freedom from state supervision for local government comes at a time when available local revenue sources are becoming less adequate and when the importance of intergovernmental cooperation among local governments has become paramount.

In this context, the 1960's and 1970's have seen an increasingly direct federal-local relationship focused not only on the large cities like Chicago, but also on substate regional planning districts covering the entire state. During the 1960's the federal emphasis was on innovative processes to revitalize the central cities. While the emphasis on innovation and reform has declined, the aging central cities of the Midwest and Northeast continue to be the recipients of increasing direct federal financial aid.[16] Urban areas, which now receive two-thirds of federal revenue sharing—general purpose financial aid to state and local governments initiated in 1972—are now seeking to gain the one-third state share to revitalize the declining central cities.

During the 1970's a new dimension of the increasing federal role in state-local relations has emerged. Congress has required that, as a condition of funding many intergovernmental programs, the states establish regional substate districts. In effect this is a new level of government between the state and local levels. These districts cover the State, with a set for each of various functions such as criminal justice, economic development, community development and transportation. They play a key role in planning and data collection for local governments within their boundaries; they review and comment on all local applications for federal funding. In Illinois the best known are those in the Chicago metropolitan area: The six-county Northeastern Illinois Planning Commission (NIPC) and the Regional Transportation Authority (RTA), a special-purpose government which not only plans but subsidizes and even delivers transportation services and levies taxes. Although the role of the national government in providing for these entities as a condition of aid has been crucial, substate districts, like local governments, are creatures of the State.

For the 1980's, a major challenge to state governments will be to find better ways of solving the twin problems of fiscal imbalance and the need for government services which spill over local boundaries. It will be necessary to provide for more effective interlocal cooperation and for a stronger state role in assuring that substate districts—for which the public elects no officials—are made both accountable and effective. The value of NIPC services and the efficiency of RTA operations will be crucial to public confidence in any future metropolitan-scale solutions to metropolitan-scale problems.

The partisanship and sectionalism which have characterized Illinois politics are focused with particular intensity on relations with the City of Chicago. Traditionally, bargaining has taken place around the interests of Chicago and "downstate," dominated respectively by the Democratic and Republican parties. Currently it is more accurate to think of three major divisions—increasingly Democratic Chicago, the Republican suburbs, and pivotal downstate voters who may lean to either party. The decreasing population of Chicago may give the Republicans a long-term advantage for statewide and legislative offices, though at this writing there are Democratic majorities in both houses of the Legislature, and as McKeough and Steinke observe, Democrats may be making suburban inroads. If State policies are to deal equitably with all the people of Illinois, it will be necessary to continue the prevailing practice of bipartisan accommodation.

Five chapters in the book deal with various aspects of the crucial state-local relationship. Banovetz and Wenum present an overview of local government in Illinois—it is diverse and changing, and it faces important problems of modernization which need to be addressed. Within this context, the important differences in the politics of Chicago, suburbia and downstate are highlighted.

Simpson challenges the ability of "machine politics" to address the problems of Chicago. He presents reform proposals which require wider participation at both the neighborhood and metropolitan levels. It is natural and respectable for reformers, like other advocates, to equate their proposals for change with the public interest. The Simpson proposals clearly do present the issues of metropolitan governance in terms which our founding political scientists would understand—Who is represented? How can the excesses of faction be controlled? For his reform proposal, as for any which affects interest groups, political parties or the structure of government, serious consideration must be given to the question whether the public interest would be better served by the suggested changes in representation, influence and power. Such a judgment requires an ability to anticipate the likely consequences of change.

Simpson's reform proposals clearly illustrate that, powerful as the City of Chicago and its allies in the Cook County Democratic organization are and will remain, the ability of Chicagoans to choose the kind of future he envisages is dependent on the City's relations with suburbia and with the State of Illinois. The Williams analysis of suburban politics, with its strong commitment to the autonomy of a multitude of smaller governments, demonstrates the strength of the barriers to establishing the kind of metropolitan government Simpson envisages.

There is a painful irony in the situation for blacks and Latinos who represent an increasing proportion of Chicago's declining population. Neither group has been able to mobilize political power in relation to its numbers. This reflects their lack of resources—education, money, political skills—and their difficulties in forming effective political coalitions. Even if one or both were able to dominate Chicago politics at some time in the future, the alternatives could be bleak indeed: either an "independent" Chicago starved for financial resources or a Chicago limited in its independence in an uneasy governmental and financial partnership with the suburbs.

The dilemma which faces the State of Illinois is that if it takes no effective action to promote such a partnership, the federal government is likely to continue to strengthen its direct relationship with the City, and over a period of time the role of the State in key matters within its boundaries will erode. The idea that the federal government deals with major (urban) problems and the State is left to cover the ''balance of state'' has already begun to emerge in federal programs, for example the manpower program. In the 1980's and beyond, the Chicago metropolitan problem is likely to worsen, and the Illinois response will help determine the role of the states in the federal system. Elsewhere Murray and Kustra have presented progress reports on the Illinois response. The message is clear—there is a continuing need for review and action; responses of the past are inadequate to needs of the future.[17]

The concept of ''power structure'' is an important one in political science, the subject of continuing debate as to the extent of elite versus pluralistic control of a political system—to what extent do we find the existence of multiple channels of access and the opportunity for new groups to form and to influence policy? The extent of elitism or pluralism varies greatly, depending on circumstances which are now being researched by political scientists.[18] The concept can be applied to all levels—local, state and national. The issue posed by Simpson is whether the Chicago power structure equitably meets the needs of its citizens for participation, integrity and services. Hall's chapter on voting blocs in the Peoria City Council is a partial study of power structure in Peoria, a city known for its large corporations (e.g., Caterpillar) and their civic involvement. While the power structure of Peoria is not fully addressed, Hall makes it clear how difficult it can be for new community groups to maintain coherence even when they appear to win major electoral victories. The road to basic reforms is rocky indeed. Success requires immense commitments of time, the ability to build and preserve coalitions and a demonstration of the necessity for change. Such obstacles may well be more difficult to overcome than any ''power structure.'' Furthermore, examination of community politics makes it clear that the State must play a crucial role in local problem solving.

State Constitutions

State constitutions have been a major limiting factor on the state role in the federal system and on states' responses to urban problems. They have historically not been as effective in setting forth a fundamental framework as the federal Constitution. On the whole they have been immensely more detailed, subject to frequent amendment, in need of occasional major revision and vulnerable to the workings of special interests. State constitutions have broadly reflected shifting currents of public confidence in, and demands on, state government. At the turn of the century, state constitutions were widely amended to restrict flexibility to levy taxes and enter into debt as a remedy against their capture by economic interests. By the 1960's it had become evident that yesterday's solutions were contributing to today's problems—these and other restrictions were preventing elected officials from responding to the problems of complex twentieth century society and forcing citizens to turn to a more responsive and flexible federal government.

Illinois was no exception. Its 1870 Constitution, riddled with special interest provisions, prevailed for a century. Despite 1954 measures to ease the amendment process, only seven of 26 amendments submitted by the Legislature were adopted. Finally the Legislature and the voters provided for the Sixth Annual Constitutional Convention in 1969, and the voters adopted a new Constitution in 1970. Politically, the key factor may have been the failure of the Legislature to reapportion, resulting in the statewide ''orange ballot'' election of 1964. An unusual number of ''good government''-oriented amateur politicians were elected. They proved unusually susceptible to the case for comprehensive constitutional revision. In general the Constitution of 1970 increased the flexibility of State government to respond to the problems of an urban society, incorporated strong protection of citizen rights and substantially avoided special interest provisions. However, it may not have gone far enough in its largely permissive provisions for intergovernmental cooperation among local governments, as Banovetz and Wenum indicate here, and Sherbenou suggests elsewhere.[19]

Key provisions of the 1970 Illinois Constitution are discussed throughout this book, but two chapters focus on it. Lousin presents an overview, augmented by in-depth discussion of key features not discussed elsewhere. Kenney demonstrates that the Sixth Constitutional Convention incorporated the same kinds of political processes and forces we find elsewhere in Illinois government. Elsewhere, Dionosopoulos assesses the positive contribution of the 1970 Constitution to constitutionalism generally, and to the safeguarding of constitutional liberties.[20]

State Government and the Economy

Comparative study of state government makes it clear that the wealth of a state and the productivity of the state economy are major determinants of the state's ability to afford, and therefore to implement, public purposes. Elsewhere Banovetz has concluded that the 1970 Constitution gives the legislature the flexibility to raise needed taxes and to borrow, while providing adequate safeguards in the expenditure of State funds. The constitution does not seek to alleviate the regressive impact of the Illinois tax structure, but this was apparently a condition of gaining acceptance for the document. Chapters of this book examine the size of the State public sector, the intended and unintended impact of State activities on the State's private sector and the politics of the legislative appropriations process.

States differ not only in their ability to raise taxes but in their tax effort—the extent to which they utilize this ability. In this context, Illinois has traditionally been a relatively low tax state and its tax effort continues to be modest. Kolhauser's analysis suggests a reason why there has been heightened concern about tax levels in Illinois—the State share of personal income has roughly doubled in the 1970's, from five to ten percent. The same analysis, as presented here and elaborated elsewhere, explains in economic terms at least, why the "taxpayers' revolt" has not, and perhaps will not, affect Illinois in the dramatic manner of California, with its Proposition 13 and massive property tax roll-back—after the spurt of State government growth, there has been a reversal of direction, with a relative shrinkage in State government's share of the Illinois economy. Some interpretation is in order here. It is probably not appropriate to attribute the spurt in State government growth to the political chaos of the Walker years, although that may have been a contributing factor. For nearly two decades (1952–1968), Governors Stratton and Kerner had been forced to oppose an income tax and were limited to stop-gap adjustments in the revenue system. When Governor Ogilvie took office in 1969, it had not been possible for some time to meet growing demands for State services. Enactment of the income tax in 1969 provided a new revenue source and made it possible to catch up. This was also a period of peak demands for State services which may not be equalled in the forseeable future: higher education, a greater State share in funding elementary and secondary education, rising welfare costs and a new State role in funding metropolitan transportation (RTA).

It may be that Illinois politicians have a reasonably good feel for the net result of the conflicting desires of Illinois' diverse citizenry. Some like Governor Ogilvie have paid the price for resolving the ambivalence about taxes (less) and services (more). The Ogilvie and Walker years (1969–1976) were ones of service expansion. The Thompson years have been ones of response to rising taxpayer concern. More radical forces have been preempted by Thompson's 1978 reelection year advisory referendum on a tax limitation. Because the State share of the economy is already on the downtrend, it may well be possible to satisfy taxpayer concerns by establishing a tax limitation, without requiring citizens to do without the public services they continue to desire.

The economic and political impact of State spending is not limited to the electoral relationship between individual taxpayers and public officials. It extends also to the health of the corporate economy and to the controversial, often elusive, concept of the business climate. Just as there are consulting firms which specialize in statewide efficiency studies for incoming governors (Warren King), there are also those which specialize in comparing and rating states on their hospitality to business (Fantus). In his chapter, Heins presents an overview of the State impact on business, in which he summarizes the results of studies conducted for the Illinois State Chamber of Commerce. What aids business may or may not be equated with the public welfare, but it is highly useful to know the impact of State activity on business. Heins makes it clear that existing research does not permit us to fully gauge that impact. Where analysis has been conducted, the impact appears to be quite diverse. Not surprisingly, we find that increased State expenditures in certain areas like transportation (highways) and education apparently promote economic growth. State activities to promote business may have little impact; and, as one might expect, State regulatory activities may have a negative impact. It is possible that the most negative impact on economic growth may be the relatively generous welfare programs (public assistance, unemployment compensation, workmen's compensation), which may reduce the opportunity of marginally profitable firms to find employees at a price they can afford.[22] In all likelihood, more definitive analysis of State impact on the economy will be called for as the public continues to question the role of government in the economy.

In any such assessment, it is imperative that the roles of the Governor and the Legislature be understood. While the Governor may often be instrumental in focusing attention and promoting a comprehensive analysis, the Legislature is ultimately the arena, or marketplace, within which the political feasibility of policy is tested. The Legislature plays a key role in the revenue and expenditure decisions which determine the State impact on the economy. Sometimes the Legislature accedes to the recommendations of the Governor, but sometimes it acts independently, forcing a compromise or imposing its own will. Coyne presents an insider's perspective on why, under what conditions and in what ways the Legislature chooses to exercise its authority independently.

Non-Governmental Groups and State Policy

Illinois is a state with a strong, diverse economy which could permit substantial public expenditure, as in New York or California. At the same time, Illinois political culture is characterized by a substantial degree of skepticism and cynicism regarding both the integrity of public officials and the efficacy of public spending. Thus in Illinois political culture is more of a constraint on government than is resource availability. Public opinion, however, is not translated directly and automatically into policy. Non-governmental groups play an important role in mobilizing public opinion, providing access to the political process and determining who has influence in each phase of the policy cycle. These mediating structures include interest groups, coalitions, political parties, elections and the mass media.

American political parties have traditionally been loose shifting coalitions, unlike the tightly organized, centralized, programmatic and ideological political parties of Europe. Nevertheless they have lent an important element of stability to American politics between the "crucial elections" which tend to realign American political coalitions every generation or two. As individual candidates replace parties and the role of the centralized news media in defining issues grows, the system is likely to become more volatile. Since each state party system is largely autonomous, we can observe considerable variation in their evolving roles.[23]

If the role of State political parties in coalition formation is declining, what does this mean for elections? Will election results and turnover of elected officials, with possible changes in party control, continue to be the central means for achieving representative and accountable government? Or will new institutions emerge, with heavier reliance on the investigative role of the media in conjunction with citizen watchdog groups, or creation of ombudsman systems to cut through bureaucratic red tape? While these and other innovations are likely to continue, the electoral process will remain the key to responsive and accountable government.

For this reason, the decline in voter turnout suggests something important. Despite the continuing expansion of voting rights, the proportion of citizens who regularly choose to make government accountable to them is declining. It is by no means simple to interpret this trend. In principle, it could reflect a range of attitudes, from satisfaction or indifference to apathy or disgust. However, public opinion surveys suggest the latter. Elsewhere, Dubin assesses the impact of the 1970 Constitution on Illinois political parties. He concludes that although the Constitution has helped bring needed uniformity to the conduct of Illinois elections by providing for a State Board of Elections, ''changes in Illinois politics . . . have been mainly the consequence of socioeconomic factors, the national enfranchisement of eighteen year olds, and judicial opinions permitting citizens to switch party affiliation at will, reducing residency requirements, limiting patronage, and establishing the paramountcy of national party rules.''[24]

Political parties, though declining in influence, remain highly competitive electorally. A major factor in their competitiveness is the common practice of ''ticket-splitting,'' rather than voting a straight party ticket, by Illinois voters. A result is that control of the Legislature and the governorship are rarely in the hands of the same party and are subject to frequent change as well. The frequency with which Illinois experiences ''divided government'' has resulted in a high degree of competitive accommodation by the two parties on major issues. (Where there is no competition, there is no need for accommodation.) At the State level the strategy of compromise tends to be successful and, especially where distribution of resources is involved, a substantial minority coalition is seldom frustrated for long. Illinois political parties outside of the legislative process appear to have declined as independent forces for recruitment and control of elected officials, as cadres of professional politicians who dominate elections and as the primary channels for hiring of State employees. Comparative study strongly suggests that, where parties are weaker, interest groups are more able to dominate the political process.[25] Illinois has traditionally had a diversity of politically active interest groups. This diversity, together with the continued strengthening of the Legislature, may compensate for the weakening of the parties, serving as a constraint on the dominance of any one interest group and preserving the informal non-governmental complements to Illinois' formal governmental system of checks and balances. Even if this is the case, Illinois remains a state whose people and politicians on the whole are comfortable with the idea that the public interest is best achieved by, and probably amounts to no more than, the policy resulting from active advocacy by those special interests which are able to gain access to, and influence in, the political process. Illinois politicians have reacted with particular skepticism to the new type of ''public interest group'' (Common Cause, Businessmen for the Public Interest, Public Citizen, the Urban Coalition) which has supplemented more traditional groups (Taxpayers Federation and the Better Government Association (BGA)]. Clearly these organizations are unique in that they represent broad membership on a variety of issues. Whether they can speak for the public interest is open to serious debate, but Illinois government is designed so that the Legislature has the final word.

Five chapters cover extra-governmental components of State politics. Green places Illinois political parties in their historical and comparative context. Colby compares current party operations with the ideal of ''responsible party government'' advocated by some and concludes that, even though they fall considerably short of this ideal, they continue to perform important functions in our political system. Monroe examines the diverse political cultures of Illinois which constrain the parties, candidates and incumbents as they seek to represent their constituencies or to shape public opinion. Andrews examines the role of interest groups and finds that, despite the widely perceived element of corruption in their efforts to influence State officials, they perform the indispensable function of helping provide and test information which serves as the basis of policy. Finally, Littlewood raises the question of whether the media are an objective constraint on interest groups or merely a different type of interest group.

These characteristics of the State political system have their effects on policy. Over the long run, Illinois has been a low tax state, reflecting its political culture. But it has used its strong economic base to finance welfare programs at a relatively high level, reflecting a compromise between the evenly matched dominant adversary interests of Illinois politics, ''labor'' and ''management.'' Traditionally the balance of forces between the two groups has resulted in a Legislative practice of insisting on, and acting favorably upon, ''agreed bills'' which have already been compromised by the interested parties. Recently however, we have seen the rare coincidence of Democratic (pro-labor) majorities in both houses of the General Assembly and in the Governor's office (1972–76). This resulted in a change in the rules, ignoring the ''agreed bill'' principle, and passage of legislation which gave Illinois the highest workmen's benefits in the nation. This case illustrates the conditions which contribute to both the continuity and the changeability of Illinois politics.

Political Issues and Policy Outcomes

Policy may be viewed as the central outcome of the political process, as structured and constrained by governmental insitutions and the ''rules of the game.'' Since this process is not capable of continually and systematically reviewing policy and programs in all areas, it must be selective. A key to understanding State politics is identifying those policy areas which are selected as priorities at any given time and examining the impetus for this selection.

Space does not permit coverage in this book of every major policy area. Those selected should permit the reader to appreciate the generic complexity of state policy issues and to explore some major current problem areas. The organization of State government and implementation of policy have a profound impact on the performance of every state program. Gove and Carlson review the recent history of attempts to improve state government through reorganization. It is doubtful that administration can be freed of political influence in any system of government, but it is especially clear in Illinois that politics and administration are inextricably intertwined, as illustrated by the politics of administrative reorganization.

Given the interdependence of organizational structure and policy goals, it is not surprising to find that reorganization is part of every major policy-making episode. When Governor Kerner wanted to focus attention on promoting business, he created the Department of Business and Economic Development; likewise, Governor Ogilvie established the Department of Local Government Affairs and the environmental agencies; Governor Walker created the Office of Collective Bargaining. Governor Thompson has systematically reorganized a number of existing agencies and has under consideration major new initiatives in growth management and human resources programs.

If government is to be effective, the setting of broad policy goals and establishment of an appropriate organizational structure for achieving those goals must be only the beginning. The bulk of public expenditure is required for the implementation of policy—for the design of programs which actually work, and the hiring, organization and direction of personnel. Just as the State employs central control systems for budgeting and accounting for its fiscal resources, it also employs a central Personnel Department to prepare or authorize job definitions, set salaries and process hiring by State agencies. The quality of State personnel is universally recognized as a major factor in the performance of State programs. Public personnel systems must maintain a balance between technical merit and responsiveness to policy direction by elected officials. After placing primary emphasis on merit for almost a century at the federal level, emphasis has been shifted somewhat to responsiveness by the creation of the Presidential Office of Personnel Management and associated reforms. Despite Illinois' historic tradition of patronage, one which has declined rapidly in recent years, patronage is no guarantee of responsiveness to policy direction, and Illinois may be ripe for a corresponding set of personnel system revisions. A future edition of this book might well present a chapter on the fiscal and personnel control systems crucial to policy implementation.

The chapter by Wolff presents a much broader view of policy implementation in Illinois government, illustrating some of the many pitfalls involved, and indirectly reflecting on the condition of Illinois public administration.

The State role in promoting or regulating science and technology has traditionally been secondary to the dominance of the federal government in this area. Despite the pervasive impact of science on state economies and programs, only recently have the states begun to play an active role in intergovernmental science relations. In the past decade governors and legislatures have begun to institutionalize science advisors and science staffs to help them do three things: (1) promote and regulate science; (2) utilize scientific information in state policy-making; and (3) improve productivity by introducing new technological applications. The states have been inconstant in these efforts, and ironically the most constant source of support has been a small, underfunded program in the National Science Foundation, the Intergovernmental Science Program. This state passivity and dependency are now doubly ironic because in 1978 Congress decided to terminate implementation funding for a promising new State Science, Engineering and Technology (SSET) program. Governors and legislatures had already prepared plans under this program—it will be interesting to observe what, if any, independent implementation occurs. The significance of the SSET program is that it comes as close as anything yet has to a federal program of building policy management capacity for state government. The Congressional action to terminate reflects the dilemma of the federal government—despite wide acceptance of the idea that if the federal system is to perform at its best, state and local capacity must be enhanced, there is a reluctance at the federal level to undermine hard-won power. The parallel irony for state and local government is that on the whole they have not yet found the commitment to invest in modernizing their own policy-management capability.

In this book, Keenan reviews the growing role of Illinois state government in attracting the facilities of "big science," starting with a negligible role in bringing Argonne National Laboratory in 1946 and culminating with the major political orchestration of Fermilab in 1966. Since then, Governors have employed some type of formal science advisory mechanism. Ahlen reviews the corresponding development and use of a scientific staff by the Legislature. While its applications are limited by the highly politicized environment, the Legislature now has an important independent capacity to generate scientific information relevant to policy issues and to assess the validity of such information supplied by others.

This relatively new policy capacity of State government will be tested in the years to come by a reassessment of Illinois' substantial energy requirements and the need to balance those requirements against environmental considerations in the selection of an appropriate mix of energy sources. Should Illinois cut back on its growing commitment to nuclear power? Should Illinois increase its commitment to using its substantial coal resources? And, if so, how will it deal with the environmental problems resulting from the sulfur content of that coal?

Hot policy issues have a way of cooling off and then resurfacing in a different form or under new circumstances. The central issues of the recent past have included highway systems (1950's), urban problems, human equity and opportunity (1960's), and energy and the environment (1970's). In the 1980's, all will still be with us, interacting with each other, as the focus shifts to the role of the public sector in the economy and to related concerns with the quality of life. We are warned that the economy will suffer unless a substantial long-term commitment is made to renovating the State transportation (highway) system. The success of our search for energy systems adequate to support a dynamic economy, yet compatible with environmental protection needs, will be a major determinant of future quality of life. The underlying problem is whether a partnership of state and local government can create a workable growth management policy and implement it: where will people live, where will business locate, and what services will be provided at what cost to whom? Within this economic and physical framework, the problem of our valuable human resources, juxtaposed against ineffective service delivery systems and limited opportunities for many, continues to beg for more tangible progress.

In this book, Schneiderman reviews a wide range of environmental problems and the powerful State agencies which have sought to deal with them in the 1970's. Illinois environmental agencies have been strongly supported by Governors and notably effective in resisting attempts to undermine their powers through the Legislature. This does not make them "apolitical"—it simply means they have been successful in defending a particular policy orientation. There may be a need for a stronger State role in growth management, but State leaders manifest a marked reluctance to take the lead in areas traditionally viewed as local turf. Once again we may face the prospect of federal action in the absence of effective state action. Esseks focuses on current local experience in implementing growth management policies and finds a modest basis for hope in an evolving state-local partnership.

Leahy assesses the continuing fragmentation of Illinois human resource programs at a time when many other states have chosen to establish "umbrella" comprehensive agencies as a means of better policy formulation and improved service delivery coordination. Leahy argues that in an umbrella agency the clientele (interest) groups with the greatest clout would dominate funding and priorities. For example, the adequacy of children's services would suffer under such a system, in comparison with their fate, still far from ideal, under the Illinois Department of Children and Family Services. Elsewhere Pattakos and Agranoff approach the problem from a different perspective, emphasizing the importance of integrated organization and policy management if there is to be any substantial improvement in the effectiveness of our human services.[26]

To understand the human resources problem it is useful to distinguish between three broad sets of objectives: maintenance (helping people survive at an acceptable level, in their current condition); rehabilitation (people function at a higher level, e.g. self-support); and prevention (providing developmental opportunities which help avoid either temporary or permanent dependence). Education is the prime example of preventive/developmental programs, although health is another, and neglected, area where such efforts can have substantial pay-off. Illinois invests in elementary-secondary education at a relatively higher level than it does in most programs. Though Illinois students continue to perform above the national average, Illinois like other states has become skeptical about the quality of teaching and learning and has begun to move toward systematic evaluation of teacher and student performance, as the State has funded an increasing share of elementary-secondary education.

Burlingame assesses the development of governance and policy-making, specifies the basic features of educational performance and examines their linkage with educational policy-making. He finds that major policy actors continue to have fundamental conflicts over the appropriate measures of educational performance, creating the likelihood of continuing conflict over basic State policy in this area.

Illinois has not been as generous in supporting its system of public higher education as it has with elementary-secondary education. This long-term deficiency has recently been compounded by the effects of declining enrollment, which has had a greater impact on higher education budgets. Higher education politics and policy are not covered in this edition. Some major issues of governance are addressed elsewhere by Keenan, of research management by Murray, and of policy formulation by Nowlan.[27]

Other major policy areas of State government are not covered in this edition because of space limitations, including transportation, agriculture, and public and private sector labor/management relations. Energy is a major policy area which is only touched upon and will surely merit more extensive treatment in a later edition. All these topics receive careful analysis in the 1979 reports of the Illinois Futures Task Force and the Illinois 2000 Foundation.

Conclusion

Illinois is widely known for a political tradition which relies heavily on short-term, self-interested, back-room partisan bargaining among a few key professional politicians as the basis of policy-making. As a corollary Illinois politics has historically been "job-oriented" and has cultivated one of the largest patronage systems of any state. All of this has contributed to a common image of Illinois politics as corrupt and lacking in vision.

However, there appears to be a moderate but significant trend toward a greater measure of long-term, public-interested planning and analysis involving a wider range of public interest groups and experts. As a corollary, patronage is beginning to lose its appeal, especially to Republican political leaders. An increasing number of elected officials create their own volunteer political organizations and media campaigns. They have less need of patronage jobs. In fact, their key supporters disapprove. Furthermore, as State programs become more complex they require professionals whose loyalty is to the program rather than the elected official.

If we are witnessing a change from "politics" to "planning," it is a modest one at best. Recent efforts to improve State budget systems, planning and management capacity and accounting and evaluation have encountered significant setbacks or made only slow progress. The traditional mood of skepticism toward "gimmicks" aimed at rationalizing the system continues to prevail. To the extent that it does, it may impose its own self-fulfilling prophecy on the success or failure of future initiatives.

Clearly there is a need for balance here. The experts can rationalize the system only so much before they encounter the conflicting values inherent in Illinois' diverse structure of interests. Beyond that point, partisan bargaining and personal judgment take over. Ultimately, then, the political system must rely on the art of compromise, with important help from planning and scientific analysis.

But there is a reason for recent sporadic movements toward professionalizing and rationalizing State government, a reason which suggests these developments will and should continue. For all the diversity of interests, Illinois appears to be experiencing a broad, emerging consensus, not that the State should be weak or that taxes should radically be reduced. Rather, there is support for a competent State government, one which can analyze major policy issues confronting the State, make balanced policy, implement it effectively and determine where improvements need to be made. Policy areas where such needs clearly exist are energy and environment, the State link with the private economy, land use and growth management, local government relations and federal relations.

Recently study groups at many levels have recommended that a key to the effectiveness of the federal system is enhanced state "policy management" capability. Illinois' efforts in this area are shaky, faltering and ambivalent. We have a long way to go. But some progress has been made, and more can be anticipated.[28] Whether it will be enough will depend on the vision, competency and persuasiveness of Illinois political leaders. In the past, we have done tolerably well by them.

NOTES

[1]V.O. Key, *American State Politics* (New York: Crowell, 1956).

[2]Thomas R. Dye, *Politics, Economics and the Public: Policy Outcomes in the American States* (Chicago: Rand McNally, 1966); Ira Sharkansky, *Spending in the American States* (Chicago: Rand McNally, 1968); and Richard I. Hofferbert and Ira R. Sharkansky, *State and Urban Politics* (Boston: Little, Brown, 1971). Dye periodically updates the findings in *Understanding Public Policy* (Englewood Cliffs, N.J.: Prentice-Hall, 1971, 1974, and 1978); for the most recent review, see "Symposium on Determinants of Public Policy: Cities, States and Nations," *Policy Studies Journal* 7:4 (Summer 1979).

[3]The variety of comparative analysis is immense. It has appeared widely in the political science journals and in papers at professional meetings. An early synthesis was done by Richard I. Hofferbert, "State and Community Policy Studies: A Review of Comparative Input-Output Analysis," in *Political Science Annual*, ed. by James A. Robinson 3 (Indianapolis: Bobbs-Merrill, 1973). Also see American Political Science Association, *Political Science and State and Local Government* (Washington, D.C.: 1973); and M. Kent Jennings and L. Harmon Zeigler, "The Salience of American State Politics," *American Political Science Review* 64 (June 1970), 523–35. A good textbook synthesis of the literature may be found in Kenneth T. Palmer, *State Politics in the United States* (New York: St. Martin's, 1977). A reform approach to comparison may be found in L. Harmon Zeigler and Harvey J. Tucker, *The Quest for Responsive Government* (North Scituate, Mass.: Duxbury, 1978). For readers, see Donald P. Sprengel, ed., *Comparative State Politics* (Columbus, Ohio: Merrill, 1971); and Herbert Jacob and Kenneth N. Vines, eds., *Politics in the American States* (Boston: Little, Brown, 1966, 1971 and 1978 editions).

[4]Milestones in efforts to balance and strengthen the federal system include creation of the U.S. Advisory Commission on Intergovernmental Relations (ACIR) in 1959, enactment of general revenue sharing (1972), the work of the Office of Management and Budget Study Committee on Policy Management Assistance (1974) and the study of improving intergovernmental management by the American Society for Public Administration (Improving Intergovernmental Management, 1979). Unfortunately, in many areas recognition of need has not been followed by adequate implementation. See Allen K. Campbell (ed.), *The States and Urban Problems* (New York: American Assembly, Columbia University, 1968); Richard Nathan, *Revenue Sharing: the Second Round* (Washington, D.C.; Brookings Institution, 1977); Roy Bahl, *The Fiscal Outlook For Cities: Implications of a National Urban Policy* (Syracuse: Syracuse University Press, 1978).

[5]For a contemporary policy approach see Charles O. Jones and Robert D. Thomas, *Public Policy Making in a Federal System* (Beverly Hills: Sage, 1976); also Jeffrey Pressman and Aaron Wildavsky, *Implementation* (Berkeley: University of California Press, 1974); Kenneth Hanf and Fritz W. Scharpf, eds., *Interorganizational Policy-Making: Limits to Coordination and Central Control* (Beverly Hills: Sage, 1978); and Judith V. May and Aaron B. Wildavsky, *The Policy Cycle* (Beverly Hills: Sage, 1978).

[6]"Policy Management," Symposium, *Public Administration Review* (Special Issue; December 1975); National Governors' Association, *State Policy Management* (Washington, D.C.: The Association, 1976); American Society for Public Administration, *Improving Intergovernmental Management* (Washington, D.C.: The Society, 1979).

[7]Harold Lasswell, *Politics: Who Gets What, When, How* (New York: McGraw-Hill, 1936).

[8]David Easton, *A Framework for Political Analysis* (Englewood Cliffs, N.J.: Prentice-Hall, 1965).

[9]Theodore Lowi, *End of Liberalism* (2d ed.; New York: Norton, 1979).

[10]Roger W. Cobb and Charles D. Elder, *Participation in American Politics: The Dynamics of Agenda-Building* (Baltimore: Johns Hopkins, 1972).

[11]Malcolm E. Jewell and David M. Olson, *American State Political Parties and Elections* (Homewood, Ill.: Dorsey, 1978).

[12]Karl Deutsch, *Nerves of Government* (New York: Praeger, 1964).

[13]Harry Hatry, *Practical Program Evaluation for State and Local Government* (Washington, D.C.: Urban Institute, 1974); and Harry Hatry, *Program Analysis for State and Local Government* (Washington, D.C.: Urban Institute, 1976); Edgar G. Crane, Jr., *Legislative Review of Government Programs* (New York: Praeger, 1977); and Edgar G. Crane, Jr., *State Government Productivity* (New York: Praeger, 1976).

[14]James S. Coleman, "Policy-Related Research on Controversial Issues" (Ft. Worth: Texas A & M University, published Lecture Series, April 1976); Edgar G. Crane, Jr., "Program Evaluation in a

System of Shared Powers," *Journal of Health and Human Resources Administration* 1:3 (March 1979), pp. 293–306.

[15]Jones and Thomas, *op. cit.*

[16]Richard Nathan, *Revenue Sharing: The Second Round* (Washington, D.C.: Brookings Institution, 1977) and Roy Bahl, ed., *The Fiscal Outlook for Cities; Implications of a National Urban Policy* (Syracuse: Syracuse University Press, 1978) emphasize the current importance of states in addressing urban problems, but the failure of federal urban policy to include them.

[17]These issues are further developed by William G. Colman in *Cities, Suburbs and States* (New York: Free Press, 1975). The author is a former Director of the Advisory Commission on Intergovernmental Relations (ACIR). For an Illinois perspective, see Michael A. Murray, ed., *The States and the Urban Crisis* (Urbana: Institute of Government and Public Affairs, University of Illinois, 1971); and Robert W. Kustra, "Illinois Reshapes Urban Role," *Illinois Issues* 4:5 (May 1978), pp. 22–25.

[18]The classic case for elite power is Floyd Hunter, *Community Power Structure* (Chapel Hill: University of North Carolina Press, 1953). Robert A. Dahl makes the case for the presence of pluralism in *Who Governs?* (New Haven: Yale University Press, 1958). We are beginning to understand how power structure varies with more recent studies such as Terry N. Clark, *Community Structure and Decision-Making: Comparative Analyses* (San Francisco: Chandler, 1968).

[19]Edgar L. Sherbenou, "Social and Constitutional Change: A Commentary," in *Governing Illinois Under the 1970 Constitution*, ed. by P. Allan Dionosopoulos (DeKalb: Center for Governmental Studies, Northern Illinois University, 1978), pp. 53–58.

[20]P. Allan Dionosopoulos, "Constitutions and Constitutionalism: The Illinois Experience," and "Safeguarding Constitutional Liberties," in Dionosopoulos, *op. cit.*, pp. 1–3, 4–7.

[21]James M. Banovetz, "Revenue and Finance," in Dionosopoulous, *op. cit.*, pp. 31–37.

[22]Arthur Okun, *Efficiency and Equity: The Big Trade-Off* (Washington, D.C.: Brookings Institution, 1972).

[23]Jewell and Olson, *op. cit.*

[24]Martin David Dubin, "Illinois Politics and the 1970 Constitution," in Dionosopoulos, *op. cit.*, pp. 38–44.

[25]Harmon Zeigler, *Interest Groups in American Society* (Englewood Cliffs, N.J.: Prentice-Hall, 1964); Harmon Zeigler and Michael Baer, *Lobbying: Influence and Interaction in American State Legislatures* (Belmont, Calif.: Wadsworth, 1969).

[26]Robert Agranoff (ed.), *Coping With the Demands for Change Within Human Services Administration* (Washington, D.C.: American Society for Public Administration, 1977); Robert Agranoff and Alex Pattakos, *Dimensions of Service Integration* (Rockville, Md.: Department of Health, Education and Welfare, Project SHARE Monograph Series, 1979).

[27]Boyd R. Keenan, "Higher Education in Illinois: A 'System of Systems' Manages the Knowledge Industry," *Illinois Issues* 1:1 (January 1975), 4–7; Boyd R. Keenan, *Governance of Illinois Higher Education* (Urbana: Institute of Government and Public Affairs, University of Illinois, 1975); Michael A. Murray, *The Role of Higher Education in Meeting Public Service Needs in Illinois* (Urbana: Institute of Government and Public Affairs, University of Illinois, 1973); Michael A. Murray, "The State, Academia and Cooperative Research," ??? ; James R. Nowlan, *Making Higher Education Policy in Illinois* (Urbana: University of Illinois Press, 1974).

[28]See the 1979 reports and recommendations of the Illinois Futures Task Force, a State body; of the Illinois 2000 Foundation, an affiliate of the Illinois State Chamber of Commerce; and of Illinois Today and Tomorrow, a project of the University of Illinois Cooperative Extension Service. The first Illinois Futures Task Force publication was *A Working Paper on the Future of Illinois* (January 1979), based on a series of Resource Statements in various areas. At this writing, Illinois 2000 has published *Alternative Economic Futures for Illinois: Executive Summary* (December 1978); *The Illinois Economy Today: Trends and Statistics* (January 1978); *Alternative Economic Futures for Illinois: First Year Report* (December 1978); *Conference Report: Goals for Illinois' Economic Future* (March 1979). Illinois Today and Tomorrow has published *Community Problems: The Citizens' Perspective* (September 1978), a statewide study of public concerns.

PART I

THE CONSTITUTIONAL FRAMEWORK

CHAPTER **2**

The Impact of the 1970 Constitution

Ann Lousin

On July 1, 1971, a new constitution became effective in Illinois, following approval at the referendum held in December, 1970. After a decade, one may fairly ask whether the Constitution has had an impact on the people of Illinois. Has it enabled the citizens and their public officials to solve problems that have arisen in the 1970's? Will it help solve the problems of the 1980's? Should it, and will it, be amended?

This chapter defines the nature of a state constitution, particularly in Illinois. It describes several major innovations, or attempted innovations, in the Constitution and assesses their impact upon Illinois. It does not attempt to describe each constitutional provision or even all of the major new provisions; neither does it attempt to compare these major innovations with provisions in other state constitutions or suggest ways in which the Constitution ought to be amended. It does, however, consider whether some important problems of the 1970's would have been solved, or at least solved as well, if the Constitution had not been adopted.

The Role of Constitutions in Illinois

It is not easy to define the role of an American state constitution or to ascertain its impact on the public and private lives of that state's citizens. Samuel W. Witwer, who served as President of the constitutional convention which drafted the 1970 Illinois constitution, defined a constitution as

> an accepted body of organic laws which structures the government of a state; limits the powers of the legislative, executive, and judicial branches; and guarantees the rights, immunities, and liberties of the people.[1]

Benjamin N. Cardozo, a great jurist and an Associate Justice of the United States Supreme Court, spoke more generally when he warned that "a constitution states, or ought to state, not rules for the passing hour but principles for an expanding future." Witwer and Cardozo would agree that a constitution should not contain provisions on the rights of the people and powers of the government which are so detailed and so limited to current problems that they trivialize the constitution, at best, or hamstring future generations, at worst.[2]

There are, however, two great obstacles in the path of those seeking to write a constitution containing only "principles for an expanding future." First, it is much easier to ascertain the problems of "the passing hour" and to write rules to solve those problems than it is to forecast the problems of the future and establish guidelines to avoid or remedy them. Second, a modern state constitution must be submitted to the electorate for ratification. The voters, of course, are likely to be more interested in the proposed constitution's solutions to the concrete problems of today than in its guidelines for solving the potential problems of tomorrow. The pressure groups, political parties and other organizations whose support is necessary to muster most of the voter support for a proposed constitution insist upon a constitution which fulfills the felt needs of those organizations as favorably as possible.

Consequently, a modern state constitution really must meet two tests. It must contain enough rules for the passing hour to gain acceptance by the generation of voters voting on its adoption, and it must also contain enough principles for an expanding future to enable future generations to solve their problems.

The 1970 Illinois Constitution is the fourth basic charter of Illinois. The 1818 Constitution yielded to the 1848 Constitution, which in turn yielded to the 1870 Constitution. This charter, which was operative for a century, was a typical late-nineteenth century charter. Created during the economic and moral depression caused by the Civil War, it was designed to limit the powers of the state and local governments. The chief characteristic of this constitution was its long lists of restrictions on the institutions of government, particularly the General Assembly.[3] In fact, the limits it placed on governmental powers to raise taxes and incur debt were so restrictive that they invited evasion by government officials almost immediately.

During the first seven decades of the Twentieth Century, combinations of citizens' groups, scholars and interest groups fought a long campaign to reform the Constitution, but they were only partially successful. In 1968, however, their efforts culminated in a successful campaign to call a constitutional convention.

The stories of the call for the Sixth Illinois Constitutional Convention, of the election of the 116 delegates to the convention, of the proceedings of the convention and of the climactic day when the voters adopted the Constitution proposed by the delegates have all been told well elsewhere and do not warrant lengthy repetition

The author gratefully acknowledges the editorial assistance of Daniel A. Richman and the research assistance of James M. Nicholas in the preparation of this article.

here.[4] It suffices to note that in November, 1968, the people voted to call a convention; that they elected two delegates from each of the 58 State Senatorial districts in November, 1969; that the convention met from December 8, 1969, through September 3, 1970; that the people adopted the new Constitution on December 15, 1970; and that virtually all of the Constitution became effective on July 1, 1971.

This chapter discusses ten major features of that Constitution and the extent to which they have contributed to addressing the State's problems: provision for future revision; official disclosure of personal economic interests; free and equal elections; freedom from discrimination; legislative-executive relations; the judiciary; taxes and state debt; local home rule; education; and branch banking.

Future Constitutional Revision

The first major constitutional issue considered by the delegates to the constitutional convention helped determine whether they would write a ''fundamental charter'' or a ''fundamental statute.'' This was Article XIV, ''Constitutional Revision,'' the article that establishes the manner by which the people may later amend their constitution. The delegates knew that any game must have rules, but that the players must have the right to change the rules from time to time. The delegates also knew that the 1870 Constitution's inadequacy was due in great part to the inflexibility of its amending article and that the voters now wanted a constitution which could be amended more easily.

Illinois has traditionally provided for constitutional amendment by one of two methods: the calling of a constitutional convention or the General Assembly's submission of an amendment to the electorate for ratification. Under the 1870 Constitution, there were only two successful attempts to call a convention: the one calling the 1920–1922 convention, which drafted a constitution soundly defeated at the polls, and the one calling the 1969–1970 convention. The record of legislatively-submitted amendments was erratic and largely unsuccessful.

The 1970 Constitution departs from traditional ways of amending the Illinois Constitution in three major respects. The first is the facilitation of the system of proposing and adopting amendments submitted by the General Assembly to the electorate. Many observers thought that the 1870 Constitution's requirements for approval of an amendment were too stringent.[5] The delegates lowered the majority needed to propose an amendment from two-thirds of each house of the General Assembly to three-fifths of each house. They also lowered the majority of votes needed to approve the amendment at the polls.[6]

The three-fifths requirement seemed reasonable in both instances, because the 1970 population of Illinois fell into three almost equal groups: Chicago; the suburbs (suburban Cook and the five ''collar'' counties); and Downstate (the 96 other counties). A two-thirds requirement would have enabled one segment of the state's population, or their representatives, to frustrate the will of the other two, whereas a three-fifths requirement requires the opposing third to secure the cooperation of some of the residents of another part of the state.

Since 1970, the Legislature has submitted three proposed amendments. In 1974, it proposed an amendment to restrict the Governor's power to use an amendatory veto; in 1978, it submitted two amendments on property taxes. None passed. At first glance, these failures seem somewhat surprising in view of the lowered majority now needed. However, the three amendments submitted thus far have been ''low profile'' issues—relatively non-controversial as far as most voters and the press were concerned. It is difficult to galvanize 60% of the electorate into voting for a constitutional amendment. The real test of the efficacy of the lowered voting requirements will come only when a truly controversial amendment, such as one providing for the appointment of judges, is about to be approved by the Legislature for submission to the voters.

The second major change in the amending process concerns amendments proposed by constitutional conventions: if the question of a convention call is not submitted for twenty years, the Secretary of State must submit that question to the people at the next November election.

Because twenty years have not yet passed since the constitution's adoption, and because there is no current pressure to call a convention, it is impossible to say whether this change is salutary. Clearly, however, the mandate to submit the question every other decade could become extremely important in the late 1980's. If the Legislature, which controls the other avenue to constitutional revision, perceives that the public wants a convention in 1992, the General Assembly may forestall a campaign to approve a call by initiating a spate of constitutional revision on its own. Potentially, therefore, this change could be one of the most important provisions in the entire document.

The third major change in the amending process is the establishment of a limited initiative and referendum method of amending the state constitution. In a state which has the ''initiative,'' proponents of a constitutional amendment may solicit signatures of voters on a petition asking that the amendment, called a ''proposition,'' be submitted to the electorate for adoption or rejection. If enough voters sign the petition, the proposition is placed on the ballot.[7] The key to this method of popular control over the legislature is the complete bypass of the legislature.

The 1970 Illinois Constitutional Convention rejected the argument that the unlimited initiative is an effective way to amend a constitution. The Convention chose instead to write a Constitution which they hoped would provide for a legislature so open and responsive to the needs and will of the public that the initiative procedure would be unnecessary.

The Convention also realized, however, that some aspects of the legislative process are so dear to legislators' hearts that the General Assembly, by itself, would never change them. The delegates remembered the recent battles over Congressional and state legislative reapportionment, which were fought in the federal courts because the state legislatures were unwilling to give up the power to determine the boundaries of the election districts—and thus the power bases—of Congressmen and the state legislators.

The convention also realized that one of the issues dearest to Illinois legislators' hearts was the so-called "cumulative voting vs. single-member districts" controversy. This issue involved the unique manner in which Illinois has elected the members of its state House of Representatives since 1870. Because the Kenney and Wiste chapters in this book[8] and another part of this chapter[9] describe in depth this method and the controversy surrounding it, there is no need to discuss it at length here. It suffices to say that many delegates, politicians and observers felt very strongly that the traditional cumulative voting system should be retained, while many other delegates, politicians and observers felt equally strongly that the system should be replaced by a single-member districts system of electing state representatives.

The incumbent members of the Illinois House were virtually unanimous and vociferous in their opposition to any change in the elective system which enabled them to hold office. Like most incumbents, they favored the status quo. These legislators and several influential newspapers in the State threatened to oppose any draft constitution which proposed a single member districts system.

Faced with this formidable political combination, the Convention agreed upon a two-part compromise. The first part was the submission of the issue of how the state representatives were elected to the people as one of the four "side-elections" held at the constitutional referendum. These side-elections, called "separate propositions," concerned four extremely controversial constitutional issues. Besides election of state representatives, these were the method by which judges were to be selected (election or appointment), whether the death penalty should be abolished and whether eighteen- through twenty-year-olds should be allowed to vote. Both sides of all four issues commanded support among the delegates and the voters. Several delegates and interest groups threatened to oppose any draft constitution which proposed the view opposite their own on that issue. In order to avoid fracturing the convention itself on these issues and insuring defeat of any draft constitution which proposed a solution not amenable to a substantial part of the electorate, the Convention agreed to remove these four controversies from the main draft of the constitution and submit them as four separate issues to the people.

This happy solution defused these four issues at the Convention and transferred the battles over them to the public arena. The people were free to adopt or reject each of the four proposed departures from the traditional Illinois posture as four separate issues—separate from each other and separate from the main body of the proposed constitution.

The second part of the compromise was the creation of a limited initiative and referendum procedure for amending the Legislative article of the Constitution. The Convention decided that the aspects of the legislative process which the General Assembly was least likely to change were those relating to "structural and procedural subjects contained in Article IV" (the article on the legislative branch). The term "structural and procedural subjects," found in Article XIV, Section 3, clearly extends to the obvious controversies—reapportionment, bicameralism, the method of election to the House and the size of the General Assembly. It is not clear, however, whether the Convention intended to include more than those four issues or, if it did, how many other issues it intended to include. In guessing the Convention's intent, however, one must always remember that the initiative and referendum method of amending the Constitution was totally new to Illinois constitutional philosophy.

The first test of the new method came in 1976. An organization called the Coalition for Political Honesty, claiming authority under Article XIV, Section 3, circulated a petition calling for a referendum on three amendments to the Legislative article. When it became apparent that the petition had received enough signatures, five former delegates and a former staff member of the Convention filed suit to prevent the submission of the amendments at the November 1976 election. In deciding *Coalition for Political Honesty v. State Board of Elections,*[10] the Illinois Supreme Court held that any proposed amendment must meet two tests: (1) the amendment must relate to "subjects contained in Article IV," eliminating, for instance, the possibility of an amendment on taxes being grafted onto Article IV; and (2) the amendment must be *both* "structural" *and* "procedural." Because none of the amendments was *both* structural and procedural, none of the amendments was proper under Article XIV, Section 3.

In the case of these three amendments, the crucial issue was whether the "and" in "structural and procedural" meant that any proposed amendment must meet the test of being structural as well as the test of being procedural. Neither the opinion of the court nor the dissenting opinion defined either "structural" or "procedural." Presumably, "structural" would mean "pertaining to the structure of the General Assembly" and include the issues of bicameralism, method of election of the House and size of each chamber. Perhaps it would also include reapportionment.

The adjective "procedural" is more difficult to define. If one assumes that means "pertaining to the manner (procedure) by which the General Assembly takes action," one is including a potentially large number of provisions of Article IV in the term "procedural." Indeed the Illinois Supreme Court opinion concluded that every provision of Article XIV is at least structural or at least procedural.[11] Consequently, said the Court, allowing the initiative to be used for *either* structural *or* procedural subjects would be tantamount to allowing the initiative to be used for the entire Legislative article. The Convention history obscure as it was, did clearly show that the delegates did not propose an initiative so broad that it would extend to all of Article IV.

The three amendments in question were (1) a proposal to prevent a legislator from receiving compensation "from any other governmental entity" during his legislative term; (2) a proposal to prevent a legislator from voting on a bill in which he had "a conflict of interest as a result of a personal, family, or financial interest;" and (3) a proposal to prevent a legislator from receiving his salary "in advance of performance of duties" as a legislator. Because clearly none of the three was both a "structural and procedural" amendment, none was the proper topic for an initiative. The dissent suggested, however, that Proposition 2 was "procedural" in character, apparently because it concerned the manner by which bills become law.[12] This conclusion is the only hint we have on any justice's definition of the key adjective "procedural;" we have no hint at all on the definition of "structural."

Regardless of how one might feel about the merits of the three amendments or even about the reasoning of the Court, it is clear that this is one of the most significant decisions yet on the 1970 Illinois Constitution. The two tests established by the Court are so difficult to meet that very few, if any, controversies other than those specifically mentioned by the delegates could now be the subject of a constitutional amendment initiated by citizen petitions. The overall impact of the 1976 case is that, except for those relatively well-defined matters for which the initiative method is appropriate, constitutional amendments will now be made in a simple, two-step process: (1) either a constitutional convention or the General Assembly will write an amendment; and (2) the electorate will either reject or adopt it.

Amending the Constitution is now somewhat easier, because the votes needed to propose or adopt an amendment are easier to achieve than previously. It is also easier to call a constitutional convention, because the question of a call will arise at least five times in a century. It is also easier to achieve substantial changes in those aspects of the legislative branch which are clearly both "structural and procedural" in character, because there is now a limited citizens' initiative for that type of change.

Indeed, in 1974 a coalition of organizations circulated a petition to submit the single-member districts issue to the voters. Although they were unable to obtain sufficient signatures then, the coalition has reorganized and is now seeking to place the issue on the November 1980 ballot.[13]

In short, amending the Illinois Constitution is now theoretically easier than before, but no amendment has been successful since the new Constitution took effect in 1971.

Disclosure of Economic Interests by Public Officials

One of the salient themes of the 1969–1970 Convention was the delegates' perception that the people wanted a new constitution that would insure, or at least promote, honesty in government. The scandals of corruption in public life were almost at their peak—this was three years before the Watergate Crisis—and the scandals in Illinois had even reached into the Illinois Supreme Court in 1969.[14] Largely in response to the demand for honesty in government, the Convention proposed three "ethics sections," Article XIII, Sections 1, 2 & 3.

These three sections seek to establish high standards of conduct for public officials. Section 3 establishes a modern form of the traditional oath of office taken by holders of state offices or positions created by the Constitution. Section 1 strengthens the similar provision of the 1870 Constitution, declaring a person convicted of a felony or another serious crime to be ineligible to hold an office created by the Constitution. Although it allows the Legislature to restore a convict's eligibility to hold office, the General Assembly has not done so. The State officials convicted of bribery in recent years are thus still ineligible to hold constitutional office again.

The most innovative of the three "ethics" provisions is Section 2, which had no counterpart in the 1870 Constitution. It requires every State officer or holder of an office created by the Constitution to file a statement of his economic interests. If the officeholder fails to file this report on his or her finances, he or she forfeits office. Section 2 also allows any branch of government to establish ethical standards for that branch and gives the General Assembly authority to require financial disclosure reports of local government and school district officers.

Section 2 is a strong provision which could be of great use to citizens seeking to know whether their public officials hold financial interests that could conflict with their public duties. Nonetheless, it can also be a source of abuse, because it may force candidates for even minor offices to divulge the personal holdings of their families, even though these holdings do not create any ethical problems. This inherent conflict between the public's right to know and the individual officeholder's right to privacy became critical when the General Assembly passed a bill to implement Section 2: the Illinois Governmental Ethics Act. The Illinois Supreme Court resolved the conflict in favor of the public when it upheld the Act's constitutionality.[15]

After the basic constitutional issue had been settled, problems arose because of attempts by the Governor to enforce the Section 2 standards. The first conflict evolved from an executive order issued by Governor Daniel Walker which required most employees of agencies subject to him to file separate statements of financial disclosure and copies of their income tax returns with a Board of Ethics appointed by the Governor. In *Illinois State Employees' Ass'n. v. Walker,*[16] the Illinois Supreme Court held that Walker, as head of the executive branch, could require such extensive disclosure from his employees, because the income tax records were for the use of the Governor in assigning people to sensitive positions and were not made public.[17]

A second problem arose from another executive order requiring regulated businesses and those seeking to sell goods or services to agencies of the State responsible to the Governor to disclose their political campaign contributions. Here the court drew the line by holding that the Governor had no power to require this type of disclosure from people outside state government.[18]

It is difficult at present to assess the impact of Article XII, Section 2 and the three decisions interpreting it. There is no evidence that good citizens have refused to hold public office because of the economic disclosure requirement. On the other hand, there is some evidence that the citizens and press are not interested in the contents of public officials' disclosure statements.[19] There is also no way to determine whether the disclosure requirement has caused office holders to refrain from unethical practices. After nine years, Article XIII, Section 2 seems to be a requirement which has neither cleansed the State of corruption nor driven the best people from office.[20]

Free Equal Elections

There were really two basic questions concerning elections: (1) who should have the right to vote? and (2) how should elections be regulated? The most-debated aspect of the first question was also one of the most controversial issues of the Convention: that of lowering the voting age for state and local elections to 18. After eight years, it is hard to remember the apprehension over allowing "the kids" to vote. It suffices to note that the delegates submitted the issue to the voters as one of the four separate propositions voted upon at the constitutional referendum on December 15, 1970. The proposal failed. Ironically, the United States Supreme Court upheld the Congressional act lowering the voting age for federal elections[21] only a week later. Further, the 26th amendment to the United States Constitution, lowering the voting age for state and local elections as well, was adopted a few months later. Whether the Illinois electors would have voted for extending the franchise to eighteen through twenty-year-old Illinoisans if they had known of either of these developments must remain an historical "if"—in any case, the issue was taken out of their hands.

Compared to the youth vote issue, the other questions of suffrage were relatively uncontroversial. The most interesting of these subsidiary provisions is the automatic restoration of the right to vote upon the completion of a criminal sentence.[22] Formerly, only a gubernatorial pardon could restore suffrage to an ex-convict. Although it is impossible to know whether ex-convicts have made use of their new right, it may help some of them in their efforts at rehabilitation. This provision is apparently still well ahead of its time, because the United States Supreme Court has held that there is no federal Constitutional right to re-enfranchisement after the completion of a penal sentence.[23]

Another change made by the elections article is also related to federal Constitutional law. The delegates thought that the former requirement of a year's residence in Illinois before one could vote[24] was unnecessarily long in an era when the average American moves at least every two years. They shortened it to a maximum of six months, but allowed the General Assembly to establish an even shorter period of durational residence.[25] The United States Supreme Court held just two years later that a state could not require a person to live in the state for longer than 30 days before he could vote.[26] Thus, the Convention's decision, which many observers considered radical, was conservative in comparison to United States Supreme Court standards.

The second basic question about elections was how elections should be regulated. The issue was particularly important to the delegates, because several of them had experienced what they considered unfair treatment in their campaigns for the Constitutional Convention. Many delegates had never run for office before and were unfamiliar with the intricacies of filing procedures. They quickly discovered that many aspects of "election law" were not written precepts published in the Illinois Revised Statutes, but unwritten, informal "rules" administered by local election officials who sometimes served the interests of the candidates and voters. Because the Convention races were officially non-partisan, many candidates were not in the mainstream of either party and a few were even non-partisan.

The most outlandish treatment of candidates came at the hands of Paul Powell, who was Secretary of State in 1969 when the Convention elections were held. Powell, who by virtue of his office was the chief administrator of state elections, openly placed the names of candidates he favored most first on the ballot and those he favored least last on the ballot. Because both the primary and general elections for the convention attracted little public attention, most voters knew less about the candidates than usual and presumably were more likely to vote for candidates whose names appeared at the top of the ballot. Powell's actions and total lack of remorse over them sharpened the delegates' perception that one person had too much discretion in running elections.[27]

Their solution to these problems was to create a State Board of Elections to oversee the voter registration and elections in the whole state. Although the delegates left the number, compensation and manner of selection of the Board members to the Legislature, they specified that no political party could have a majority of members on the Board.

After two years of bitter wrangling over these issues, in 1973 the General Assembly passed a bill creating the State Board of Elections. The Board was to have four members selected by a two-step process: each of the four party leaders in the General Assembly nominated two people, and the Governor appointed one of each pair to the Board. From the beginning, the Board was in constant turmoil. Virtually every decision it made, even on the forms of ballots, created controversy and litigation.[28]

Two 1976 decisions, *Lunding v. Walker*[29] and *Walker v. State Board of Elections*,[30] helped establish the basic constitutional status of the Board. In *Lunding* the precise question was whether the Governor could remove a member of the Board. Governor Walker, relying upon the decision in *Illinois State Education Association v. Walker* holding that he had the power to require some employees responsible to him to file financial disclosure reports,[31] insisted he could remove Lunding, a member of the Board, for failing to file such a report. The underlying issue, however, was whether the Board was basically part of the executive branch of State Government.

After prolonged, complicated litigation, the Illinois Supreme Court held that, even though the Governor had appointed members of the Board and even though the Board is part of the executive branch, of which the Governor is the head, he could not remove them in the same way he could remove the heads of ordinary agencies. The Board of Elections, said the Court, is a very special part of the executive branch—it is independent and nonpartisan. Not even the Governor, the holder of "the supreme executive power,"[32] could remove a member of the Board unless he could show that there was very good cause for the removal.[33]

The Court's holding that the Board, although a unique, highly independent body, is a part of the executive branch, was crucial to its consideration of the constitutionality of the two-step selection of Board members. In *Walker v. State Board of Elections,* the Supreme Court held that selection procedure unconstitutional. It pointed out that the Constitution forbids the Legislature, whose four leaders nominated the four pairs of people from whom the Governor appointed the four members of the Board, to "elect or appoint officers of the Executive Branch."[34]

As a consequence of these cases, it is clear that the State Board of Elections is a part of the executive branch, but that it has a unique constitutional status which protects its independence and integrity from encroachment by the members of the executive and legislative branches. The General Assembly cannot take part in the selection of Board members, and the executive officer appointing them cannot remove them unless he can show a very good reason for doing so.

In another section of *Walker* the court invalidated the "tie-breaker" provision of the bill establishing the Board. This statutory provision allowed the Board to break a tie among is four members by having one member, to be chosen by lot, abstain from voting. The Court said that the Board's decisions on elections, which affect the basic constitutional rights of every candidate and voter in Illinois, are too important to be left to "a lottery."

In January, 1978, the General Assembly passed another bill creating a new State Board of Elections. The new Board has eight members. The Governor appoints two from members of his political party who live in Cook County and two from co-partisans who live outside Cook County. The next highest-ranking state executive officer[35] who belongs to the major political party other than the Governor's nominates twelve members of his party, three for each of the four remaining positions. The Governor then appoints one of the three nominees for each post. This procedure is an attempt to insure a Board made up of four Democrats and four Republicans, all selected from varied geographical and political areas and all appointed (at least in form) by the Governor.[36]

It is too early to tell whether the new Suffrage and Elections article will have much impact. If the electorate had rejected the 1970 Constitution, or if the electorate had adopted Separate Proposition 4 at the constitutional referendum, the practical results would have been the same. Recent unofficial surveys suggest that citizens under twenty-one know less about political issues and vote less regularly than do citizens over twenty-one. There is no evidence that the facilitation of registration and voting by ex-convicts and new residents in Illinois has resulted in greater voter participation by those citizens.

Similarly, it is too early to tell whether the new Board of Elections will succeed either. Certainly it is less controversial than its predecessor. In the few months of its existence it has kept a very low profile and has only attempted to handle the day-by-day administrative tasks of supervising registration and elections. The county clerks and Boards of Election Commissioners remain powerful local election officials; the Board does not seem to want to challenge their local hegemony. In short, the provisions establishing the Board, like the rest of the article on suffrage and elections, simply offers an opportunity to promote free and equal elections in Illinois. So far it is largely an unrealized opportunity.

Freedom from Discrimination

When we speak of the rights of an individual, we usually mean his rights vis-a-vis the government–rights which the courts will enforce. The 1970 Constitution contains many provisions on individual rights, some of them traditional, some daringly new. Article One, the Bill of Rights, contains most of these provisions, but other individual rights are granted in Article XI, which guarantees a clean, healthful environment, and in Article XIII, Section 5, which confers a contractual status on membership in public employee retirement plans and bars any impairment of earned benefits under those plans.

The Bill of Rights itself retains many rights traditional in both American and Illinois constitutional history.[37] However, twelve sections of the twenty-four in the Bill of Rights are either substantial revisions of traditional rights or are completely new.[38]

Of these, by far the most striking innovations are Sections 17, 18 and 19, the attempts to combat discrimination. Both the United States and Illinois constitutions guarantee due process and equal protection of the laws.[39] Where governments are involved, an equal protection clause is the traditional means of preventing discrimination, particularly racial discrimintion. The Convention decided, however, that three additional provisions, each attacking discrimination in its own way, were necessary reinforcements of the principle of equality.

The most important of the three provisions is Article I, Section 17, which prohibits discrimination based upon "race, color, creed, national ancestry and sex in the hiring and promotion practices of any employee or in the sale or rental of property.'' The Convention decided to attack only employment and property discrimination primarily because jobs and housing are the two most critical needs of racial, religious and ethnic minorities. A mere glance at the section shows why some observers have called it the broadest civil rights provision in any state constitution. It provides that the right to be free of discrimination is not limited to the public sector, but extends to private employment and private property as well. There are no exemptions from this broad grant except for those ''reasonable exemptions'' which the General Assembly may set. The rights are self-executing, *i.e.*, not dependent upon legislative action, but the General Assembly may add remedies to those usually given by a court.

For the first few years after the constitution became effective, no one petitioned a court for a remedy under Article I, Section 17. Finally, two noteworthy cases arose. In *Walinski v. Morrison*[40] the plaintiff alleged discrimination by a private employer. She sought damages from an accounting firm that had refused to hire her, allegedly because of her sex. The Illinois Appellate Court held that Article I, Section 17 created a private right of action, allowing a victim of discrimination to obtain any damages a civil court could grant, including money damages, instead of having to proceed through an administrative process.

In the other case, *Davis v. Attic Club,*[41] one man and several women contended that several clubs in downtown Chicago violated Article I, Section 17 by selling ''property''—liquor and food—to a membership whose ranks were not open to women. Over a strong dissent, the majority of the Illinois Appellate Court held that the clubs had not violated the Constitution. The case held that, although food and liquor are ''property'' for purposes of Article I, Section 17, the General Assembly had created a permissible ''reasonable exemption'' for ''private clubs,'' including businessmen's clubs. It also held that the clubs' membership policies were protected by the members' right of privacy.

Although the Illinois Supreme Court refused to hear the plaintiffs' appeal, the case attracted much attention for two reasons. First, the Appellate Court extended the right of privacy beyond that established by the marital and sexual privacy cases decided by the United States Supreme Court[42] and the economic disclosure cases decided by the Illinois Supreme Court.[43] The Court thereby suggested that one constitutional right, the right of privacy, may conflict with another constitutional right, the right to be free of discrimination. Second, the Court based its finding of a ''reasonable exemption'' upon a 1949 statute concerning the sale of alcoholic beverages. Obviously, the General Assembly sitting in 1949 could not have been creating an exemption to a constitution adopted in 1970. Nobody knows how many other statutes passed years ago can now be considered retroactive ''exemptions'' to Article I, Section 17. If, in the future, the Illinois courts declare many statutes to be exemptions, the effect may vitiate Section 17. If that occurs, the General Assembly will have to consider repealing the statutes. Ironically, the effect of the *Davis* case is to allow the Legislature to limit the scope of Article I, Section 17—precisely the result the delegates wanted to avoid when they drafted the section.

To summarize, the future of Article I, Section 17, lies chiefly in civil actions brought in court for civil damages. After *Walinski,* employees who are dissatisfied with their administrative remedies under the Illinois Fair Employment Practices Act[44] and the United States Equal Employment Opportunity Commission[45] may seek more certain, if not speedier, relief in the courts. On the other hand, *Davis* has reduced the deterrent value of Article I, Section 17. The chief value of an anti-discrimination provision lies in its threat that the courts will enforce it against an offender. *Davis* has removed some of that threat.

The second of the three new anti-discrimination provisions is Article I, Section 18. Cast almost in the words of the standard equal protection clause and of the proposed Equal Rights Amendment to the United States Constitution, the section seeks to prohibit sex discrimination ''by the State or its units of local government and school districts.'' As the Convention debates clearly show, the Convention intended to make sex a ''suspect classification.'' This means that if a law treats males and females differently, the Legislature must prove to the court that there is a compelling reason for the law to treat them differently. If sex were not a ''suspect classification,'' the person being discriminated against would have to prove that the distinction drawn between males and females was improper. This difference in who bears the burden of proving inequality is crucial to many equal protection cases.

The first Illinois Supreme Court case on Article I, Section 18 was *People v. Ellis,*[46] in which a 17-year-old boy claimed that the statute on criminal trials of juveniles was unconstitutional. The act said that females under 18 years old and males under 17 years old were to be tried as juveniles, rather than as adults. Ellis claimed that being tried in juvenile court was more favorable to a defendant than being tried in adult court. The Supreme Court agreed and said the act violated Article I, Section 18. Most important, it held that the section made sex a ''suspect classification.'' Because the state could not show that it had a very good reason, called a ''compelling state interest,'' for distinguishing between males and females for the trial of juvenile offenses, the court said that the sexes had to be treated equally for this purpose.

Under the ''compelling state interest'' test, not every classification by sex is unconstitutional. For example, several Illinois courts struggled with the incest statutes, which until 1977 imposed a heavier penalty upon a father who had sexual relations with his daughter than upon a mother who had sexual relations with her son.[47] The Illinois Supreme Court refused to decide whether the incest statute was a ''sex-based classification,'' but it held that even if the statute had created a sex classification, the state could impose a heavier penalty on the fathers, partly because this action can result in pregnancy, whereas the actions of the mothers cannot.[48] Thus, the cases on Article I, Section 18 show that it can be a powerful tool to invalidate governmentally-related sex discrimination, but that it does not automatically invalidate all classifications based on sex.

Ironically, although many observers regard both Section 18 and its close relative, the Equal Rights Amendment, as "women's rights provision," none of the Section 18 cases in Illinois has involved discrimination against women. All of the plaintiffs have been men.[49] One reason for this is that, although about 75% of the Illinois statutes that might have been found to be discriminatory under Section 18 discriminated against women, most of those statutes have been amended by the legislature since 1971 to conform to the requirements of the new constitution. Thus, one result of Section 18 has been to reduce litigation. The potential of the section in litigation is obviously still great, but it is still an unrealized potential.

The third anti-discrimination provision, Article I, Section 19, prohibits discrimination against the mentally or physically handicapped. The prohibition extends only to discrimination in the sale or rental of property and to discrimination "unrelated to ability in the hiring and promotion practices of any employer," because the handicapped face more obstacles from discrimination in those areas than in others. One of the key questions in this section is the definition of "handicapped." The only case interpreting the section specifically addresses this question. In *Advocates for the Handicapped v. Sears, Roebuck & Co.*,[50] the Illinois Appellate Court held that "handicap" meant "a class of physical and mental conditions which are generally believed to impose severe barriers upon the ability of an individual to perform major life functions."[51]

In this case Sears denied employment to a nephritis victim whose kidney transplant prevented his lifting heavy weights, apparently solely because he was an uninsurable risk under Sear's self-insurance program. The court held that, in the employment context, "the question of whether a person is handicapped turns upon whether the character of the disability is one which is generally perceived as one which severely limits the individual in performing work-related functions."[52] Under this definition, said the court, a mere restriction "from lifting heavy weights" was not a severe enough physical disability to constitute a handicap.[53]

A difficulty with this opinion is its failure to discuss why, if the employee's disability was not that severe, the insurance carrier (who in this case is also the employer) denied him membership in the program. The insurance carrier apparently did not deny him coverage because he could not lift weights, but because he had kidney disease. If kidney disease is not a handicap, are cancer, heart trouble and diabetes handicaps? May a business refuse to hire a diabetic if he cannot pass an examination for insurance coverage?[54] May the Legislature create "reasonable exemptions" to the rights of the handicapped, as it my in regard to those covered by Article I, Section 17? As yet, no court has addressed these questions, and Section 19 remains one of the great enigmas of the constitution. In company with the other two anti-discrimination provisions, it offers hope, but not a guarantee.

The General Assembly and the Executive Officers

The State government of Illinois, like that of every American state, consists of three branches, each patterned on the corresponding branch of the federal government. The legislative and executive branches operate jointly to a great extent; together, they formulate policy and make laws. For the purpose of understanding the impact of the 1970 Constitution upon government, however, it is necessary to know only the basic constitutional framework of the two branches.

The General Assembly

The legislative power of the state is vested in a bicameral General Assembly consisting of a 59-member Senate and a 177-member House of Representatives. At the Constitutional Convention the two most controversial questions concerning the legislature were (1) the method by which the members of the House are elected—the cumulative voting vs. single member districts question; and (2) the method by which the entire legislature is redistricted.

The history of the "cumulative voting" system, which is unique to Illinois, the convention debates over it, and its effects on legislative decisions, are the subject of other chapters.[55] Briefly, the system prescribes that the people of each district elect three state representatives. This is the "multi-member district" feature of the system. Each voter may cast up to three votes for any one of the field of candidates running for the three seats. This is the "cumulative voting" feature which gives the system its nickname. The three candidates in each district with the highest vote totals are the winners.

It is not the purpose of this chapter to analyze the arguments for and against this system or the arguments for and against the likeliest alternative, election of a single representative from each district, with each voter being able to cast only one vote for only one candidate. It suffices to remember each system had many strong supporters, both in and out of the Convention.

As a result, the Convention decided that, for the first time in a century, the people should be able to vote on whether to retain cumulative voting or adopt the single-member district system. It submitted both a clarified cumulative voting system and the single-member district system to the voters as a separate proposition at the constitutional referendum. The people voted to retain cumulative voting.

The debate, however, has not ended. In 1974, several groups organized into a coalition called the Committee for Legislative Reform tried to place the issue on the ballot again. They did not obtain enough signatures on their petitions to meet the requirements of Article XIV, Section 3 for an initiative and referendum attempt to amend the constitution.[56]

But this is precisely the type of constitutional issue for which the Convention drafted Article XIV, Section 3. In 1979 the coalition renewed its efforts to place the issue on the ballot in 1980. If it is successful, and the voters approve the amendment, the legislature will undergo a radical change in 1981: a change in the method of electing the House, and perhaps also a reduction in size of one or both chambers. This would be in addition to the inevitable trauma caused by the undergoing of reapportionment after the Federal Decennial Census.

Reapportionment was the other great controversy concerning the General Assembly faced by the Convention. In an effort to provide for an orderly reapportionment every ten years and to avoid the specter of an at-large election of each house of the legislature,[57] the Convention established a detailed procedure to be followed every ten years.

According to this provision, the General Assembly must redistrict itself in the year following each Federal Decennial Census. If it cannot agree upon a reapportionment map, each of the four party leaders of the legislature (Speaker of the House, Minority Leader of the House, President of the Senate and Minority Leader of the Senate) appoints one legislator and one non-legislator to form an eight-member redistricting commission. The commission then tries to find an acceptable compromise map.

This provision had its baptism by fire in 1971, when the legislature had to redistrict itself. Three of the four leaders appointed themselves and one of their legislative aides to the commission. The fourth, who was ill, appointed his party's leader in his absence and a former Governor. In *People ex rel. Scott v. Grivetti,*[58] the Illinois Supreme Court held that the three leaders should not have appointed themselves; neither should they have appointed their aides, because the intent of the delegates in framing the provision had been to include the views of "the public" in the legislative redistricting process. The aides, quite predictably, had simply voted with their bosses on the commission.

Eventually the General Assembly was able to use the map on a provisional basis for the 1972 elections. Pursuant to the court's order, the General Assembly properly adopted a permanent map in 1973. It was identical to the 1971 map.

In 1981 the General Assembly will have to redistrict itself again. If the members cannot agree, there will be another commission. It is difficult to imagine a person who would represent "the public interest" rather than "the legislature's interest," and yet would be appointed by a legislative leader. Presumably, past activity in partisan politics is no barrier, because the *Grivetti* court held valid former Governor William G. Stratton's appointment as a non-legislator member.

The two great controversies over the Legislative branch are still very much alive. The cumulative voting vs. single-member districts issue may be on the November 1980 ballot. Even if it is not, or if the people vote to retain cumulative voting, the supporters of single-member districts will surely not surrender. Reapportionment will certainly be a dominant issue in the 1980 campaign, for the party which controls the General Assembly in 1981 will have an excellent opportunity to draw the map which will determine the partisan nature of the Legislature all during the decade of the 1980's.

The Executive Officers

In 1848, Illinois began the practice of electing at least a half-dozen officers of the executive branch. But by 1969 it had become almost conventional wisdom that principles of good public administration required only a few elected officers. There was general agreement at the Convention, for example, that the Superintendent of Public Instruction, an elected officer, ought to be replaced by a chief state education officer appointed by a State Board of Education. The delegates also agreed that the Illinois Supreme Court ought to appoint its own clerk instead of having to deal with one elected by the public on a partisan basis.

Ultimately the delegates chose to retain the election of a Governor and a Lieutenant Governor (to be elected jointly); an Attorney General; a Secretary of State; a Comptroller (who replaced the Auditor of Public Accounts); and a Treasurer, all to be elected for four-year terms. Because the process by which the Convention arrived at this decision is the subject of the Kenney chapter,[59] it will not be discussed here.

At the same time the Convention decreased the number of elected executive officers, it strengthened the powers of those retained. Foremost among the delegates' intentions was to concentrate power in the chief executive officer, the Governor. He retains the "supreme executive power," the basis of his authority to issue executive orders.[60] Among the Governor's most significant new powers are the newly-created power to issue an executive order reorganizing state government;[61] a wide arsenal of vetos;[62] and new budgeting responsibilities.[63] Because the Crane chapter analyzes the Governor's powers in depth, there is no need to discuss them here.[64]

In comparison to the powers of the Governor, those of the Secretary of State, Comptroller and Treasurer changed very little. The Secretary of State remains essentially the chief administrator of a variety of State services from the granting of corporate charters to the issuance and revocation of driver's licenses. The Comptroller is—or at least has been so far—essentially a modern reincarnation of a previous officer, the Auditor of Public Accounts, the chief fiscal officer of the State. The Treasurer continues to be the State's banker; his primary duty is to invest the State's funds.

The powers of the Attorney General are now second only to those of the Governor. It is unclear whether this stature is due to an assumption of new powers or to the exercise of long-dormant ones by an incumbent, William G. Scott, who takes an activist view of his role.

Pre-convention case law suggested that the Attorney General was the only person who could act as lawyer for the State, or at least was able to prevent anyone else from acting as lawyer for the State.[65] Since 1970, a series of court decisions have confirmed a broad interpretation of the powers of the Attorney General. The most important decision is *People ex rel. Scott v. Briceland,*[66] which establishes the power of the Attorney General to represent State agencies, if he so chooses. Two other decisions allow him to choose which State agency he wants to represent, if two agencies are adverse parties to a court proceeding.[67]

With these impressive victories, it is clear that the position is now second only to the governorship in power. Indeed, in a world in which no public official can move without consulting a lawyer, "the legal officer of the State" can influence virtually every aspect of State government.[68] Between them, the Governor and the Attorney General now share or influence virtually all of the powers of the executive branch.

The Judiciary

The third branch of government is the judicial branch. Although judges obviously have an impact on the political life of Illinois, their official role is not that of policy-makers, but of dispute-settlers. They decide issues of law which others have brought before them. In order to perform this role optimally, judges should be free from outside influences, especially partisan considerations.

The nature of the judiciary, particularly the method by which judges ought to be selected for their offices, was one of the most divisive issues of the Convention. Indeed, if the Convention had ever disintegrated over one issue, that one would have been either the selection of judges or the abolition of the *ad valorem* personal property tax. Because the Kenney, Kopecky-Daniels and Mindes chapters describe the process of writing the Judicial article at the Convention and the nature of the court system,[69] there is no need to discuss those topics in depth here.

The 1970 Constitution has had the greatest impact upon three aspects of the judiciary: the selection of judges, the retention or removal of judges and the discipline of judges.

One of the most controversial issues in Illinois government is the method of selecting judges. Should they be elected or appointed? In either case, how? Should they have party affiliation or not? Essentially the debate centered around those favoring retaining the elective system ("let the people choose their judges") and those favoring appointment by the Governor ("merit selection"). In the end, the Convention submitted the issue to the voters as a separate proposition at the constitutional referendum, the first time that the public had the opportunity to vote on the issue. This was the most-debated of the four propositions. Even though "merit selection" commanded 46 percent of the vote, the people decided to retain the elected-judges system.

This result dismayed, but did not defeat, proponents of the appointive system. Like proponents of single-member districts for the House, they continue to strive for a constitutional amendment. Every year the Legislature considers a variation of the gubernatorial judicial-appointment system designed at the 1970 Convention. So far, it has not passed a constitutional amendment on judicial selection, although presumably that will continue to be one of the major issues facing it during the 1980's. Furthermore, if neither the single-member districts nor the merit selection advocates are successful by 1990, the two groups will probably combine forces to promote the calling of a constitutional convention in 1990.[70] Should they succeed, they will attempt to use the convention as a means of obtaining the constitutional amendments they were unsuccessful in obtaining by legislative proposal (or, in the case of single-member districts, by popular initiative). By 1990 these two issues may be the dominant constitutional questions.

Even though the people voted to retain an elective system, it would be wrong to assume that the constitution had absolutely no impact upon the procedure for selecting judges. Under the old constitution, judicial candidates were nominated by a party convention; under the new one, they are to be nominated at a primary (whether it is partisan or non-partisan) or by petition. It is thus now possible for lawyers who are not slated by a party to be nominated by their party's primary electors and become the party's nominees. The most successful examples of this phenomenon are two Illinois Supreme Court justices, James A. Dooley and William C. Clark, who were nominated over their party's "slated" candidates in 1976.

The second great change made by the Judicial article has been in the retention of judges. At the end of a judge's term, he or she may "run for retention," i.e., the voters are asked simply whether the judge should be retained in office. If the judge receives a sufficiently favorable vote, he or she is re-elected; if not, he or she is removed and there is a vacancy in the judiciary. Once elected, a judge may be removed from office more easily than before, because the Convention raised the percentage of favorable vote needed to retain office from 50 percent to 60 percent. Since 1972, this increase has made a crucial difference in six retention elections. In 1974, the people of Cook County voted not to retain a circuit court judge in office.[71] In 1976 they voted not to retain an influential circuit court judge, the Chief of the Criminal Division,[72] and in 1978 they voted not to retain the Chief Judge of the Circuit Court of Cook County.[73] Also in 1978, Downstaters voted not to retain three resident circuit judges.[74]

All of the non-retentions were the result of concerted campaigns by the press, citizens' groups and the bar. In effect, Illinois judges are still elected, but they are subject to a "recall vote" at the end of their terms.

The third major impact of the Judicial article may alter the nature of the judiciary more than the institution of appointment of judges would. This is the creation of the Illinois Judicial Inquiry Board, which supervises judicial conduct. Incumbent judges, regardless of how they were selected, may become unable to serve or may commit unethical acts. The phrase "judicial discipline" sounds harsh, but it conveys the requirement that judges conform to certain standards of conduct. If they do not conform, the bar and the public suffer.

In order to give those two groups a role in enforcing standards of judicial conduct, the Convention established the Board as the first step in investigating the fitness of a judge. The Governor appoints four nonlawyers and three lawyers to the Board, and the Supreme Court appoints two circuit judges. The nine members hear and investigate charges of unfitness. If they find that the judge is probably unfit, they file a complaint with the Illinois Courts Commission, a panel of five judges who have had the responsibility for judicial discipline since 1964. If the Commission agrees with the Board, it can remove or discipline the judge.

Although the Commission thus far continues to regulate judicial discipline, a recent Illinois Supreme Court case has called into question the scope of the Judicial Inquiry Board's power to file complaints. In 1977 the Court held in *People ex rel. Samuel G. Harrod, III, Judge, Petitioner v. The Illinois Courts Commission,*[75] that the Supreme Court could define, and therefore restrict, the Board's jurisdiction. It also held that the Board could certify to the Commission "only conduct violative of the Supreme Court Rules of Judicial Conduct."[76]

The *Harrod* decision means that the Illinois Supreme Court, which promulgates the rules of judicial conduct,[77] will now also define the role of non-judges in disciplining judges. Certainly, judges should be insulated from outside influence so that they can judge disputes fairly and well. The question is, who will judge the judges? *Harrod* suggests that the answer may be—the judges.

Taxes and State Debt

Apart from funds disbursed by the federal government, there are three major sources of revenue available to the Illinois State government: the income tax, which the State government imposes, although both the State and local governments share in the benefits; the 5% sales tax, which the State collects, although it splits the collection with municipalities and counties; and debt incurred by the State. Apart from federal and State funds, there are three major sources of revenue available to local government: the *ad valorem* real property tax, and the *ad valorem* personal property tax, both of which only the local governments impose; and local debt.

Although each source of revenue was the subject of heated convention debate, the Constitution has probably had the greatest impact upon two local sources—the *ad valorem* real property tax and the *ad valorem* personal property tax—and on state debt.

Property Taxes

Long the mainstay of local governments and school districts in Illinois, *ad valorem* taxes on real and personal property were the subject of two of the most turbulent debates at the Convention. The chief controversy over the real property tax was whether real property could be classified, so that owners of some types of real property paid taxes at a higher rate than others paid. The controversy over the personal property tax was simply whether the constitution should abolish the tax on businesses.

At the time of the Convention, Cook County "classified" real property by its use. The county assessor first established the market value of the real property—the price it could fetch at an open market—and then established the "assessed valuation" of the real property. The "class" of single-family homes, for example, had an "assessed valuation" of about one-third of the home's market value. The class of shopping centers, on the other hand, had an "assessed valuation" of about 80 percent of the center's market value. This was "classification." When real property taxes were levied, they were imposed upon the assessed valuation of the real property, e.g., "$3.00 per each $100 of assessed valuation." Although both the homeowner and the shopping center owner each paid a "3 percent tax," and even though their properties had identical market value, their tax bills were vastly different. Although only Cook County openly admitted it classified real property, there were strong indications that other counties also classified to a certain extent.

At the 1970 Convention almost all the delegates from Cook wanted to retain Cook County's power to classify real property. The regular Democratic organization made it clear that they would not support a constitution which did not allow Cook County to classify. Although the "official" Downstate position was against classification, some Downstate delegates admitted privately that their counties also wanted the power to classify. As a compromise, the delegates decided to allow the counties with more than 200,000 people to classify, but forbid smaller counties to do so. Although the Illinois Supreme Court has said that this distinction between large and small counties is constitutional,[78] no county except Cook has taken advantage of the power to classify real property. Therefore, so far the real impact of the Constitution has been to remove any doubts about the validity of the Cook County classification system.

A less controversial aspect of real property taxation has been that of exemptions from the tax. For over a hundred years, Illinois constitutions have allowed the legislature to exempt property used for county fairs and ". . . for school, religious, cemetery and charitable purposes." In the past fifty years there has been a movement towards extending exemptions to the elderly and others unusually hard-pressed by real estate taxes. The General Assembly enacted a homestead exemption for senior citizens in 1970, but the Illinois Supreme Court held that the 1870 Constitution prohibited the exemption.[79] Because the new constitution specifically allows the legislature to "grant homestead exemptions or rent credits,"[80] the General Assembly re-passed the bill under the new constitution. The Illinois Supreme Court held it constitutional under the new provision.[81] This is a specific instance of which it can be said that the new constitution has certainly made a difference.

The *ad valorem* personal property tax has been even more controversial than the real property tax. The delegates knew that in November 1970, the General Assembly would submit a proposed amendment to the 1870 Constitution which abolished that tax as it applied to individuals. They also assumed that the amendment would be adopted. To ensure that the result of this amendment would carry over into the new constitution, they drafted Article IX, Section 5(b), which forbids the reinstatement of an *ad valorem* personal property tax abolished before the effective date of the new constitution.

The delegates further realized that the personal property tax was the most unpopular, least-collected and most unevenly-administered tax in Illinois. They decided to abolish it by constitutional fiat. Opponents of the abolition, however, demanded that the local governments and school districts be guaranteed a new source of the revenues they would thereby lose. The compromise between the two forces is Article IX, Section 5(c), which gave the General Assembly a deadline of January 1, 1979, to abolish the remaining personal property tax. It also required the Legislature to enact concurrently a replacement tax, to be imposed only upon the taxpayers relieved of the burden of paying the tax by this second abolition—in short, businesses. (Businesses are the primary "non-individuals" in Illinois.)

Section 5(c) has caused untold confusion in the Legislature and the courts. The Legislature was unable to abolish the tax, because it could not agree upon a workable, constitutional replacement for the revenues lost. In 1973, ruling on an attempt at partial abolition of the tax, the Illinois Supreme Court said that any time the Legislature attempted even a partial abolition, it must replace the revenues thereby lost.[82] The Court also said that the abolition is not self-executing: if the General Assembly did not pass a bill abolishing the tax and replacing revenues, the tax would continue in effect. Most observers thought that the Court also meant that, in the absence of legislative action, the tax would continue beyond 1979.

In 1978, the General Assembly submitted a proposed constitutional amendment which would have eliminated the 1979 deadline and made the abolishment language permissive instead of mandatory. In effect, it would have withdrawn the mandate to abolish the remaining *ad valorem* personal property taxes. The issues were complex, the public found these constitutional nuances difficult to understand and business groups and the press were split on the issue. The proposal received 56 percent of the vote, four percent less than the 60 percent approval needed for adoption. No one was surprised when the General Assembly adjourned in December 1978 without abolishing the tax.

In March 1979, however, the Illinois Supreme Court surprised virtually everyone by announcing that the *ad valorem* personal property tax could not be imposed after January 1, 1979. In *Client Follow-up Co. v. Hynes*[83] the Court held that its previous statements applied only to abolition before 1979 and that the constitutional convention intended the tax to expire no later than 1979. It is now the General Assembly's responsibility to reimburse local governments for the revenues they have lost. At least, neither business taxpayers nor local officials can claim that the 1970 Constitution has not had any effect.

State Debt

Debt is a proper way to finance the construction of capital improvements, such as buildings, as long as the term of the debt does not exceed the "useful life" of the improvements. Under the 1870 Constitution, the State could not incur more than $250,000 in debt without voter approval at a referendum.[84] This unrealistic limit soon spawned many quasi-state agencies which were actually, although not officially, under the control of the State government. For example, the Illinois Armory Board built the State armory and still runs it under the direction of the State, but the debt it incurred is not part of the State debt. When the General Assembly failed to separate a quasi-state agency sufficiently from the state to evade the debt limit, the courts found the bonds issued by the agency unconstitutional. The last such failure occurred in 1970 when the Illinois Supreme Court invalidated a bill creating an agency to issue road construction bonds.[85] The Convention, which was meeting at the time, abolished the debt limit, but substituted a requirement that three-fifths of each house must approve a bill incurring state debt.[86] Although the approval of three-fifths of each house is difficult to obtain, the state Legislature has occasionally passed a debt bill. For example, in 1971 it re-passed substantially the same highway debt bill declared unconstitutional a year earlier. The Illinois Supreme Court later found the new bill constitutional under the new Constitution.[87]

When one considers the abolition of the personal property tax, the extension of homestead exemptions to the elderly and the improved bonding procedure, it seems likely that the Revenue article has had as much impact as any in the Constitution.

Home Rule

Perhaps the most startling innovation in the Constitution is the grant of home rule powers to certain counties and municipalities. Indeed, it is often said that Illinois now has the strongest home rule provision in the country.[88] This situation is all the more striking because, until 1970, Illinois probably had less local self-government than any state.

Until the adoption of the new Constitution, the Illinois courts followed a principle of local government law called "Dillon's Rule."[89] According to this rule, a local government has only those powers "granted in express words," powers "implied in or incident to" the expressly-granted powers and powers "essential to the accomplishment" of the purposes of the local government.

The Illinois courts interpreted "Dillon's Rule" so strictly that observers often said that no local government could take any action unless it could point to specific statutory authority to take the action. This interpretation had devastating results upon counties, townships and municipalities. The large counties, especially Cook, and the large cities, especially Chicago, sometimes had the political power base from which they could launch new programs to meet the growing urban and suburban ills of the twentieth century, but they first had to obtain enabling legislation from the General Assembly. The Legislature soon found itself passing bills to meet the purely local needs of counties and cities in different parts of the state.

In a sense, the entire Local Government article is a many-faceted response to this challenge. Because the Banovetz/Wenum chapter deals with local government under the new Constitution, there is no need to discuss the article in depth here.[90] The most important facet of this response is home rule, however, and it does warrant some analysis here.

An Illinois home rule unit may, subject to enumerated exceptions, "exercise any power and perform any function pertaining to its government and affairs including, but not limited to, the power to regulate for the protection of the public health, safety, morals and welfare, to license; to tax; and to incur debt."[91] Under the new Constitution, more units of local government receive home rule powers automatically than they do in most states; moreover, the powers they receive are stronger than those in other states.

Only two types of local governments can obtain home rule status: municipalities and counties. Presumably because the Convention had faith in the stability and judgment of the officials of the larger cities, they gave automatic home rule status to every municipality with more than 25,000 people. Thus, in 1971, over 70 cities automatically obtained home rule. By 1979, about 90 cities enjoyed that status, either because of population growth or by approval of the people at a special referendum. When the delegates considered county home rule, they thought primarily of Cook County and, to a certain extent, of the five "collar counties" surrounding Cook and a few of the largest Downstate counties. The convention decided that the key to the effectiveness of county government was not the population of the county, but its form of government. It decided that only a county which elected a chief executive officer had the administrative structure to manage home rule powers wisely. In 1970 only Cook County had such an officer. Although the General Assembly passed a county executive act enabling other counties to elect a county executive and thereby to obtain home rule status,[92] no other county has chosen to acquire that form of government and home rule, and referenda have failed in seven counties.

The threshhold issue in any home rule case is whether the home rule unit's ordinace falls within the scope of "its government and affairs." It is an indication of the complexity of home rule that even this one issue is broad enough to have spawned over two dozen appellate cases in eight years. The key to the cases is the word "its." In several cases the courts have made it clear that, while home rule units have great powers, no home rule ordinance can unduly interfere with the "government and affairs" of the State, of other local governments or of school districts. Five of these cases illustrate the court's viewpoint and the problems of home rule particularly well.

The first is *Ampersand Co. v. Finley,*[93] in which the Illinois Supreme Court considered a Cook County ordinance requiring each party filing a civil action in the Circuit Court of Cook County to pay a $2 filing fee. The Clerk of the Circuit Court was to deposit the fee in a fund for the maintenance of a law library. The Court held that the fee imposed a burden on the court system, which is regulated by Article VI of the Constitution. In spite of their names, the Circuit Court of Cook County and the Cook County Law Library were really part of the judicial branch of State government and thus part of the *State's* "government and affairs."

In the second case, *Bridgman v. Korzen,*[94] the Illinois Supreme Court held invalid Cook County's attempt to collect real estate taxes four times a year, not just twice, as provided by statute. The Court reasoned that the collection of taxes, although performed by the county, was an action taken on behalf of all the taxing units in the county, including other local governments or school districts. This action, which in fact would have produced revenue for those units at a faster pace, pertained not simply to Cook's government and affairs, but also to all the taxing units' governments and affairs.

By contrast, in *Rockford v. Gill*[95] the Illinois Supreme Court allowed the City of Rockford to levy a tax "for library purposes" in excess of the pre-1970 Constitution property tax rate limits. Apparently the chief distinction between the units of local government and school districts in *Bridgman* and the Rockford Public Library in *Rockford* is that the former are entities clearly separate from Cook County, while the library board is not separate from the city's corporate entity.

The courts relied upon the separateness and peculiar status of school districts in the last two cases. In *Board of Education of School District No. 150 v. City of Peoria,*[96] a court held that Peoria's fair employment practices ordinance did not extend to employees of the school district. The court noted that Article X of the Constitution makes education primarily a State concern and that a school district is not only a "mere creature of the state," but a creature which performs a particularly significant constitutional role.

In a later case of the same name,[97] the Illinois Supreme Court held that Peoria could not require the same school district, as owner of a facility dispensing food or alcohol, to collect its tax "upon the privilege of purchasing food or alcohol" from consumers. The Court clearly relied upon the peculiarly state-supported function of school districts in holding the ordinance invalid, for it held the tax was applicable to the "Pleasure Driveway and Park District of Peoria," a "special district." Both "special districts" and "school districts" are creatures of the State, but the latter enjoy a specially-protected status because of their State-supported function under Article X of the Constitution.

As these cases indicate, a home rule unit must take care not to be so zealous in promoting and protecting its own government and affairs that it interferes with the State's, other local governments' and school districts' governments and affairs. This is true, even if the interference is arguably really for the benefit of those other governments. If the ordinance does not impinge upon the powers of other governments, however, the home rule may regulate and raise revenue to a great extent.

These are but five cases on but one aspect of Illinois home rule. Their complexity and variety give only a hint of the potential of Illinois home rule, despite judicial limitation.

Education

Article X "Education" is one of the shortest articles in the 1970 Constitution, but it is potentially one of the most important. Each of the three sections has already had a telling effect on Illinois education. In considering this article, one must remember that the delegates met when both school finance and aid to parochial schools were still hotly-debated constitutional and political issues. Moreover, scandals in the office of the Superintendent of Public Instruction, an elected officer loosely charged with supervision of education, had recently brought the state-level administration of Illinois education into question.

Section 3 bans the use of "public funds for sectarian purposes," thus apparently forbidding "parochiaid" (aid to parochial private schools), one of the most volatile issues in the nation in 1970. Indeed, the division of New Yorkers over this issue was usually considered a major reason for the defeat of the product of the 1967 New York Constitutional Convention. The Illinois Convention, in a decision both politically cunning and statesmanlike, left intact the exact language of the 1870 prohibition.[98] This left any change in the constitutional status of parochiaid to the federal courts deciding cases on First Amendment grounds. After the United States Supreme Court decided the first major case against grants to parents of children in non-public schools in 1971,[99] the Illinois Supreme Court followed suit and invalidated the Illinois statutes.[100] Thus, this issue, so volatile in 1970, has become virtually a non-issue.

Although the question of aid to parochial schools is not dead, the battle over aid to non-public schools has since shifted to another front: the issue of financing elementary and secondary education. Section One of Article X is based on language simply lifted from the 1870 Constitution. It adds three significant sentences, however. The first establishes that "[a] fundamental goal of the People of the State is the educational development of all persons to the limits of their capacities." A court recently held that this language requires that a statute providing for special education cannot set a dollar limit on the amount of funds spent to aid a handicapped child.[101] This may mean that if a school district cannot or does not provide aid for the handicapped, the state must do so.

Another sentence provides, "Education in public schools through the secondary level shall be free." In 1970, almost half the adult Illinois population did not have a high school diploma. If they were all suddenly to demand a free high school education, the schools could not accommodate them either physically or financially. As yet, however, these adults seem satisfied to attend high school equivalency classes at local junior colleges. Because under-education is a cause of unemployment, the education of adults may become a serious issue in the 1980's. At that point free education may well become a financial burden on the state.

The last sentence of the section is the most controversial. It reads, "The State has the primary responsibility for financing the system of public education." One question of its interpretation was whether the language is hortatory, merely stating a goal, or whether it is mandatory and judicially enforceable. In *Blase v. State,*[102] the Illinois Supreme Court held that it was only hortatory. The second problem of interpretation is the meaning of "primary responsibility." According to *Blase,* it apparently means that the State should provide at least 50 percent of the financial support for public schools. Without judicial enforcement, however, the definition of "primary responsibility" is probably nothing more than an intellectual exercise.

Section Two of Article X provided what many hoped would be the most radical change in the Education article. It replaced the elected executive officer called the Superintendent of Public Instruction with a State Board of Education. Here the wishes of the delegates and the public coincided almost exactly: almost everyone favored "taking politics out of education and education out of politics." The members of the Board are appointed from geographical areas by the Governor, subject to the advice and consent of the Senate.

Their main accomplishment to date has been the fulfillment of their constitutional duty to appoint a chief state educational officer.[103] This officer is the general supervisor of Illinois education below the university level. Beyond that, the Board has simply not had much impact so far. The highly political issues of school funding and de-segregation are still decided by the General Assembly, the courts and the school districts, as they were before. The only difference that the Board has made is that state education policy is no longer officially under a partisan elected executive officer. Education policy is still, however, very much a part of politics.

Branch Banking

Almost every state constitution has at least one provision which has assumed great importance in that state, but not in most other states. In Illinois that issue was branch banking—whether one financial institution ought to have more than one place at which it could transact business.

The issue of branch banking divided Downstate bankers from Chicago bankers, as well as the Convention delegates from those areas, almost on an exact regional basis. Since the nineteenth-century, locally-owned Downstate banks have feared that, if Chicago banks were permitted to establish branches there, they would drive the Downstate banks out of business. Even in 1970, the issue called forth deeply-rooted regional prejudices and antagonisms which consumed a disproportionate share of the Convention's time.

Finally, the Convention decided that branch banking was primarily a matter for the Legislature. Its sole concession to the anti-branch-banking forces was the inclusion in the Constitution of a unique majority requirement for approval of branch banking by the Legislature: "three-fifths of the members voting on the question or a majority of the members elected, whichever is greater, in each house of the General Assembly."[104] Although the Downstate bankers thought this vote requirement would make it more difficult for the Legislature to approve branch banking, the efficacy of this device has yet to be tested. No bill has reached a final vote in the Legislature.

Ironically, after all that dissension, the issue has become almost moot, for several reasons. Most Chicago banks have decided they do not want far-flung branches. The Legislature has allowed banks so many "service centers" that the need for true full-service branches is reduced. And Downstate banks have discovered that their real competition is federally-chartered and regulated savings and loan associations—which are immune from State prohibitions on branch banking. In short, the post-Convention history of branch banking illustrates why constitutional conventions ought not preoccupy themselves with solving the problems of the present, at the expense of failing to help future generations to solve the problems of the future.

Conclusion

Cardozo's statement that "a constitution states, or ought to state, not rules for the passinghour but principles for an expanding future" provides a standard against which we can judge the eight-year-old Illinois Constitution. Although the delegates to the 1969–1970 Convention found it necessary to try to solve problems of the "passing hour" in order to obtain the voters' approval of their constitution, they also tried to write a constitution suitable for "an expanding future".

The experience so far demonstrates the wisdom of Cardozo's statement. As the example of branch banking shows, some of the most controversial issues of 1970 have diminished in importance or virtually disappeared. Additionally, United States Supreme Court decisions and the 26th Amendment have rendered almost moot other issues, such as suffrage for those under 21 years old and aid to parochial schools. Even if Illinois voters had rejected the 1970 Constitution, federal action would have effected these changes anyway.

In two instances, the separate propositions concerning appointment of judges and election of state representatives from single-member districts, failure has bred hope for future success. Their strong showing in 1970 has encouraged their advocates, who continue to try to win approval of their plans. The threat of those two alternative plans constantly challenges the defenders of an elected judiciary and a House elected by cumulative voting to prove that the people did not err in approving those judicial and legislative systems. Even though they failed to become part of the Constitution itself, these proposals have become part of the continuing examination of the Constitution in practice.

In at least three specific cases one can discern the decisive impact on the Constitution. The 1971 bills granting homestead exemptions to senior citizens and incurring state debt for building highways are substantially identical to bills passed under the 1870 Constitution and declared invalid by the Illinois Supreme Court. The Court declared both 1971 bills valid under the new Constitution. Third and most important, the abolition of the *ad valorem* personal property tax would almost certainly never have occurred under the old constitution.

It is too early to tell if the three major administrative innovations, the Judicial Inquiry Board, the State Board of Elections and the State Board of Education, will fulfill their promise. All three were responses to felt needs of the "passing hour" of 1970 Illinois. The needs are still here and are still felt. Whether they—or the other new constitutional provisions—will meet the needs of an expanding future is a question which awaits future generations for an answer.

NOTES

[1]J. Cornelius, *Constitution Making In Illinois, 1818–1970* xi (1972).

[2]Indeed, Witwer quoted Cardozo's statement in his inaugural address as president of the Convention on December 9, 1969. 2 *Proceedings,* Sixth Illinois Constitutional Convention 31.

[3]See e.g., Ill. Const. Art. IV, Sec. 22, (1870), which seeks to prevent passage of special and local laws.

[4]See particularly J. Cornelius, *supra* note 1; S. Gove & T. Kitsos, *Revision Success: The Sixth Illinois Constitutional Convention* (1974).

[5]The drafters of the 1870 Constitution did not intend to make it so difficult to amend their constitution. For a good account of the historical accidents which resulted in a restrictive amending article, see Bergstrom, "The Amending Process," in *Con Con: Issues for the Illinois Constitutional Convention*, ed. by S. Gove and V. Ranney, 465 (1970).

[6]Ill. Const. Art. XIV, Sec. 1 (1970).

[7]California is the leader in using this device. The two most famous California constitutional amendments initiated and adopted without legislative approval are Proposition 14, the 1968 attempt to ban open housing laws which the United States Supreme Court declared unconstitutional in *Mulkey v. Reitman,* 387 U.S. 369 (1967), and Proposition 13, the 1978 attempt to limit ad valorem real property taxes imposed by local governments.

[8]See "Constitutional Politics: Writing the Executive, Legislative and Judicial Articles of the 1970 Illinois Constitution" by David Kenney at page 59.

[9]See "The General Assembly and the Executive Officers" in this chapter.

[10]65 Ill.2d 453, 359 N.E.2d 138 (1976). The author was one of the plaintiffs.

[11]65 Ill.2d 466, 359 N.E.2d 144 (1976).

[12]65 Ill.2d 476, 359 N.E.2d 149 (1976).

[13]A member of the 1979 coalition is the Coalition for Political Honesty.

[14]See discussion of this in the Daniels and Kopecky chapter and "The Judiciary," below in this chapter.

[15]*Stein v. Howlett,* 52 Ill.2d 570, 289 N.E.2d 489 (1972). The U.S. Supreme Court dismissed an appeal contending that the Illinois constitutional requirement violated officeholders' rights to privacy and to seek office. 412 U.S. 925 (1973).

[16]57 Ill.2d 512, 315 N.E.2d 9 (1974).

[17]Again, the U.S. Supreme Court refused to hear an appeal based on federal constitutional rights. Cert. denied, 419 U.S. 1058, (1974).

[18]*Buettel v. Walker,* 59 Ill.2d 146, 319 N.E.2d 502 (1974).

[19]*Illinois Issues* 3:16 (January 1977).

[20]The author should acknowledge that she, in her capacity as Chairman of the State Civil Service Commission, files statements of economic interest pursuant to both the Illinois Government Ethics Act and gubernatorial executive order.

[21]*Oregon v. Mitchell,* 400 U.S. 112 (1970).

[22]Ill. Const. Art. III, Sec. 2 (1970).

[23]*Richardson v. Ramirez,* 418 U.S. 24 (1924).

[24]Ill. Const. Art. VII, Sec. 1 (1870).

[25]Ill. Const. Art. II, Sec. 1 (1970).

[26]*Dunn v. Blumstein,* 405 U.S. 330 (1972).

[27]A federal court later held that Powell had violated the delegates' constitutional rights, see *Weisberg v. Powell,* 417 F.2d 388 (7th Cir. 1969).

[28]For a good history of the Board, see Bernardini, *"The Illinois State Board of Elections: A History and Evaluation of the Formative Years,"* 11 J. Mar. J. 321 (1977–78).

[29]65 Ill.2d 516, 359 N.E.2d 96 (1977).

[30]65 Ill.2d 543, 359 N.E.2d 113 (1976).

[31]*Supra,* note 16.

[32]Ill. Const. Art. V, Sec. 8 (1970).

[33]Because the case was appealed from a temporary injunction issued by a circuit court, the Supreme Court did not reach the question of whether Lunding's failure to file a financial disclosure report was sufficient "cause" for discharge.

[34]Ill. Const. Art. V, Sec. 9(a) (1970).

[35]The rank of the State executive officers is Governor, Attorney General, Secretary of State, Comptroller and Treasurer. Ill. Rev. Stat. Ch. 46, Sec. 1A-3(2) (1977–1978 Supplement).

[36]In 1978 Governor James R. Thompson appointed four Republicans. He also appointed four of the twelve Democrats nominated by Secretary of State Alan J. Dixon, the highest ranking non-Republican officer.

[37]Indeed, twelve sections are virtual carryovers from the 1870 constitution. Ill. Const. Art. I, Secs. 1, 3, 4, 5, 8, 9, 10, 13, 15, 16, 21 & 23 (1970).

[38]Ill. Const. Art. I, Secs. 2, 6, 7, 11, 12, 14, 17, 18, 19, 20, 22 & 24 (1970).

[39]U.S. Const., Amendments V and XIV; Ill. Const. Art. I, Sec. 2 (1970).

[40]60 Ill.App.3d 616, 377 N.E.2d 242 (1978).

[41]56 Ill.App.3d 58, 371 N.E.2d 903 (1977). For a good discussion of Article I, Section 17 and the *Davis* case, see Gertz, "The Unrealized Expectations of Article I, Section 17," 11 J. Mar. J. 283 (1978).

[42]*Griswold v. Connecticut,* 381 U.S. 479 (1965), *Roe v. Wade,* 410 U.S. 113 (1973).

[43]*Stein v. Howlett,* 52 Ill.2d 570, 289 N.E.2d 489 (1972); *Illinois State Employees' Ass'n v. Walker,* 57 Ill.2d 512, 315 N.E.2d 9 (1974); *Buettel v. Walker,* 59 Ill.2d 146, 319 N.E.2d 502 (1974).

[44]Ill. Rev. Stat., Ch. 48, Sec. 851 (1977).

[45]42 U.S.C.A. 2000-E-4.

[46]57 Ill.2d 127, 311 N.E.2d 98 (1974).

[47]Ill. Rev. Stat., Ch. 38, Secs. 11-10, 2-7 (1977). *See* also Linton, "Sex Discrimination Under Article I, Section 18 of the 1970 Illinois Constitution," 66 Ill. Bar J. 450 (1978). The legislature equalized the penalties in 1977, Ill. Rev. Stat., Ch. 38, Sec. 11-10 (1977).

[48]*People v. Boyer,* 63 Ill.2d 433, 349 N.E.2d 50 (1976).

[49]See Linton article, note 47, *supra.*

[50]67 Ill.App.3d 512, 385 N.E.2d 39 (1978).

[51]67 Ill.App.3d 517, 385 N.E.2d 43 (1978).

[52]*Ibid.*

[53]67 Ill.App.3d 518, 385 N.E.2d 44 (1978).

[54]The Illinois Attorney General has advised Tazewell County that it may not refuse to hire an employee "who cannot pass the required physical examination and who refuses to waive his coverage under the insurance plan." Op. Atty. Gen. No. S-435, 1972 Op. Atty. Gen. 69.

[55]See "Constitutional Politics: Writing the Executive, Legislative and Judicial Articles of the 1970 Illinois Constitution" by David Kenney at page 59.

[56]See the discussion of the initiative method at notes 7–13, *supra.*

[57]The at-large election of the House in 1964 was remembered as a debacle no one wished repeated.

[58]50 Ill.2d 156, 277 N.E.2d 881, *cert. denied* 407 U.S. 921 (1971).

[59]See "Constitutional Politics: Writing the Executive, Legislative and Judicial Articles of the 1970 Illinois Constitution" by David Kenney at page 59.

[60]Ill. Const. Art. V, Sec. 8 (1970).

[61]Ill. Const. Art. V, Sec. 11 (1970).

[62]Ill. Const. Art. IV, Sec. 9 (1970).

[63]Ill. Const. Art. VIII, Sec. 2 (1970).

[64]*See* Edgar G. Crane, Jr., "The Office of Governor" at page 99.

[65]*Fergus v. Russel,* 270 Ill. 304, 110 N.E. 130 (1915).

[66]65 Ill.2d 485, 359 N.E.2d 149 (1976).

[67]*Scott v. Cadagin,* 65 Ill.App.2d 477, 358 N.E.2d 1125 (1976) and *Environmental Protection Agency v. Pollution Control Board,* 69 Ill.2d 394, 372 N.E.2d 50 (1977).

[68]The potential for conflict between the Attorney General and his fellow-officers increases with the amount of legal work in which the state is involved, and is further heightened by different political affiliations. From 1973 to 1977, when the Attorney General and Governor were of different political parties for the first time in Illinois history, the conflicts were frequent and open. Only time and the personalities of the officeholders involved will decide if those conflicts will recur.

[69]See "Constitutional Politics: Writing the Executive, Legislative and Judicial Articles of the 1970 Illinois Constitution" by David Kenney at page 59 and 59 by Frank Kopecky.

[70]See discussion of Art. XIV, Sec. 2 in part 1 of this chapter, *supra.*

[71]Judge David Lefkovits received a 59.8 percent favorable vote. The United States Supreme Court upheld the validity of the extraordinary majority vote requirement for retention in *Lefkovits v. State Bd. of Elections,* 424 U.S. 901 (1975).

[72]Judge Joseph A. Power received a 58.8 percent favorable vote.

[73]Judge John Boyle received a 59.1 percent favorable vote.

[74]Judge William A. Ginos, Jr., resident circuit judge of Montgomery County (fourth judicial circuit), received a 58.4 percent favorable vote; Judge Albert Pucci, resident circuit judge of Putnam County (tenth judicial circuit), received a 59.8 percent favorable vote; and Judge Charles W. Iben, resident circuit judge of Peoria County (tenth judicial circuit), received a 50.9 percent favorable vote.

[75]69 Ill.2d 445, 372 N.E.2d 53 (1978).

[76]69 Ill.2d 470, 372 N.E.2d 64 (1978).

[77]Ill. Const. Art. VI, Sec. 13 (1970).

[78]*People ex rel. Kutner v. Cullerton,* 58 Ill.2d 266, 319 N.E.2d 55 (1954).

[79]*Hoffman v. Lenhausen,* 48 Ill.2d 323, 269 N.E.2d 465 (1971).

[80]Ill. Const. Art. IX, Sec. 6 (1970).

[81]*Doran v. Cullerton,* 51 Ill.2d 553, 283 N.E.2d 865 (1972).

[82]*Elk Grove Engineering Co. v. Korzen,* 55 Ill.2d 393, 304 N.E.2d 65 (1973).

[83]Ill. Sup. Ct., No. 51598 (January, 1979).

[84]Ill. Const. Art. IV, Sec. 18 (1870).

[85]*Rosemont Bldg. Supply, Inc. v. Illinois Highway Trust Authority,* 45 Ill.2d 243, 258 N.E.2d 569, *appeal after remand* 51 Ill.2d 126, 281 N.E.2d 338 (1970).

[86]Ill. Const. Art. IX, Sec. 9 (1970).

[87]*People ex rel Ogilvie v. Lewis,* 49 Ill.2d 476, 274 N.E.2d 87 (1971).

[88]Ill. Const. Art. VII, Sec. 6 (1970). For a good discussion of the development of the Local Government article, particularly of the home rule section, see Anderson and Lousin, "From Bone Gap to Chicago: A History of the Local Government Article of the 1970 Illinois Constitution," 9 J.Mar.J. 697 (1976). For a good discussion of the case law on home rule, see Michael & Norton, "Home Rule in Illinois: A Functional Analysis," 1978 U.Ill.L.F. 559.

[89]J. Dillon, *Law of Municipal Corporations* 237 (5th ed. 1911).

[90]See Banovetz & Wenum, chapter 17.

[91]Ill. Const. Art. VII, Sec. 6(a) (1970).

[92]Ill.Rev.Stat., Ch. 34, Sec. 701 et seq. (1977).
[93]61 Ill.2d 537, 338 N.E.2d 15 (1975).
[94]56 Ill.2d 74, 295 N.E.2d 9 (1972).
[95]75 Ill.2d 334, 388 N.E.2d 384 (1979).
[96]48 Ill.App.3d 1051, 363 N.E.2d 648 (1977).
[97]*Board of Education of School District No. 150 v. City of Peoria,* Ill.Sup.Ct. No. 51239 (March, 1979).
[98]*Cf.* Ill. Const. Art. VIII, Sec. 3 (1870); Ill. Const. Art. X, Sec. 3 (1970).
[99]*Lemon v. Kurtzman,* 403 U.S. 602 (1971).
[100]*People ex rel. Klinger v. Howlett,* 56 Ill.2d 1, 305 N.E.2d 129 (1973).
[101]*Eliot v. Board of Education of the City of Chicago,* 64 Ill.App.3d 229, 380 N.E.2d 1137 (1978).
[102]55 Ill.2d 94, 302 N.E.2d 46 (1973).
[103]Ironically, the appointed chief holds the same title as the elected officer the Board replaced: Superintendent of Public Instruction.
[104]Ill. Const. Art. XIII, Sec. 8 (1970).

SUPPLEMENTAL READINGS

For an indexed bibliography of books, law review articles and other publications on the Sixth Illinois Constitutional Convention and the 1970 Illinois Constitution, please write to The Library, The John Marshall Law School, 315 South Plymouth Court, Chicago, Illinois, 60604.

CHAPTER **3**

Constitutional Politics: Writing the Executive, Legislative and Judicial Articles of the 1970 Illinois Constitution

David Kenney

In spite of the great importance of such matters as revenue, the Bill of Rights and home rule, the real core of the 1970 Constitution lay in other areas. The basic arrangements for the three branches of government—executive, legislative and judicial—are certain to be of paramount importance in any state constitution. While there was much in these articles that proved to be uncontroversial in the 1970 Illinois Convention, there were certain other matters which the delegates contested fiercely. Among these were the schedule for electing executive officers, the practice of cumulative voting for state representative and the issue of whether judges should be appointed or elected. The latter was probably the crucial contest of the Convention. In the pages which follow, an effort is made to describe the most controversial aspects of the three central articles and to explain the political forces bearing on them.

Mention will often be made of the delegates from Chicago, allied with the dominant political organization there, the "regular Democrats." No meaningful analysis of the events of the Sixth Illinois Constitutional Convention could do otherwise. The regular Democrats were a highly coherent group, well led and well disciplined, which came to the Convention with a clear cut set of goals and priorities. As professional politicians, they looked upon the Convention as an exercise in professional politics and were often perplexed when less professional delegates took other points-of-view. It was inevitable that the whole Convention should turn upon the central pivot provided by the goals and strategies of the Chicago regular Democrats.

There was a relatively even balance of Republicans and Democrats among the Convention's delegates. Objective analysis has shown that, overwhelmingly, the party factor explains more variation in Convention voting than does any other. This is the case even though the nomination and election of Convention members was by a non-partisan process. As experience in other settings has indicated, to superimpose a non-partisan election upon a partisan system often does little to reduce the partisanship of the officials who are selected. This was the case in the Illinois Convention. It must be recognized, however, that the non-partisan nature of the process by which delegates were selected made it possible for a certain type of individual—partisan, yet often somewhat independent of formal party organization—to be chosen. The element of independence so introduced often made a very great difference in the Convention's work.

The Convention had to cope with many of the urgent problems of its time. The questions of 18 year old vote, abortion, the death penalty, equal rights for women, the funding of education, both public and private, and discrimination in housing and employment were among the hazards through whigh the Convention was compelled to find its way. Any one of them could have been the rock upon which the venture foundered. All were successfully dealt with. That this was so is strong testimony to the sensitivity and political skill of the Convention's members.

Delegates came to Springfield with very little by way of a fixed agenda. There were few non-negotiable positions. Legitimation of the classification of real property for tax purposes was an imperative for the Chicago regular Democrats. They were most reluctant to give up the personal property tax levied on corporations and partnerships. They were intent on retaining the election of judges, and this became the primary issue of the Convention. Among others, feeling for the appointment of judges was strong, and the struggle continued to the very end. Having gained property classification, it was not likely that the Chicago regular Democrats would have withdrawn their support of the total document, even if they had lost election of judges; but that decision never became necessary due to the fact that their political skills in vote-trading allowed them to retain the election process.

Deeply involved in that vote trading were the issues of cumulative voting versus single-member districts and the limitation of branch banking. The Chicago regular Democrats employed great finesse in offering support for cumulative voting—an issue on which they felt they had little to lose—and the obstruction of branch banking—finally in a form so weak as to be ineffective—in exchange for support for election, rather than appointment, of judges—an issue crucial to the organization. It is worthwhile here to describe the series of events in which the final shape of Convention decisions in these matters was determined.

Early on, the Convention invited each of the elected executive officials to speak before it. Governor Ogilvie did so, of course, on the ceremonial opening day, and the others soon followed him to the rostrum of the Convention. Within their addresses could be discerned the seeds of matters soon to be controversial among the delegates. Each executive spoke from the point of view of his office and his personal situation.

After the Governor, Attorney General William J. Scott was the first to appear. He offered the straightforward plea that the Convention retain his office as an elective one, rather than have it filled by appointment by the Governor. He described the Attorney General as "the people's lawyer," a role that officer hardly could carry out well if appointed by the chief executive. General Scott stressed his independent role in regard to problems of consumer fraud and pollution. "The lessons of history and governmental experience," he concluded, "should teach us that to deprive the Attorney General of his independent status by giving the Governor the power to appoint him is not only unnecessary, but dangerous."[1]

At least no one could say that the Attorney General did not come directly to the point. He obviously was at odds with Governor Ogilvie over the question of shortening the ballot so far as his own office was concerned. Once political allies, the two had become less compatible. "I know that the Governor has recommended that the Attorney General be an appointed office rather than an elected office," Scott said, but "I think that is hs mistaken in that position."[2] The Attorney General's point of view eventually prevailed in the Convention.

Lieutenant Governor Paul Simon, once a youthful prodigy of the Democrats of the State, as Attorney General Scott had been of its Republicans, offered a persuasive, well-reasoned address in which he made many suggestions of needed constitutional change.[3] Unlike the Attorney General, he did not confine himself to his own office and functions but ranged widely over the whole scope of State and local government. Professor-like in appearance, earnest and spectacled, he seemed unable to resist offering the Convention a scholarly lecture. His address went considerably deeper into the subject than had Governor Ogilvie's.

A major concern of Lieutenant Governor Simon was for strengthening the authority of the chief executive, a fact perhaps explained in part by his obvious intention to run for the top job in 1972. He recommended teaming the Governor and Lieutenant Governor for election purposes, even though, he insisted, "the present governor and I have a good working relationship . . ."[4] Simon may have been anticipating some future time when as Governor he would not have wished to have a Republican as his Lieutenant Governor.[5]

In contrast to Lieutenant Governor Simon's broad approach, Auditor of Pulbic Accounts Michael Howlett confined his remarks to two areas—his own office and duties and local government. He recommended merging the offices of Auditor and Treasurer in that of an elected Comptroller.[6] For local governments, Auditor Howlett recommended simply a greater flexibility, which would lead to increased fiscal strength and consolidation. In the role of "everyone's friend," in contrast to Simon's "earnest professor," Howlett apparently felt little need to offer a comprehensive review of constitutional problems. He too displayed a ready ability to turn a witty phrase, as the question period following his talk revealed:

> MR. FRIEDRICH: We have a lot of creatures of the legislature, taxing bodies, airport districts, fire protection districts . . . and so on . . But now we find ourselves in the position of adding taxation without representation, in that the people who run those taxing bodies are appointed by a judge that you can't reach . . . actually, that is what the Revolutionary War was fought about and I am about ready to fight another one on the same ground. Do you want to make a comment on that?
>
> MR. HOWLETT: Well, Dwight, I am not in favor of judges you can reach. (Applause)[7]

Next, it was Secretary of State Paul Powell's turn to caution the Convention to take care not to make any significant changes, especially where his own office was concerned. Upon the basis of nearly two generations spent in State office, he counseled the necessity of frequent compromise. Then after much rhetoric, he came to the core of his concern: "There has been much talk about doing away with the election of state officials. . . . Let me warn you that this could be a most dangerous error. . . ."[8] Secretary Powell was concerned that the appointment of such officers would weaken the parties and reduce citizen interest in government. Checks and balances among State officials were desirable, he said, and he referred to an equal division of such officers between the parties as one calculated to keep those parties strong. When he listed the executive officers he felt should be elected, it surprised no one that the list was identical with the arrangement provided by the 1870 Constitution.

Then, after another flight of rhetoric, Secretary Powell came directly to the point: ". . . bear in mind, that in December of 1969, the voters of New Mexico rejected a new state constitution . . . that would have made the post of . . . Secretary of State . . . appointive."[9] The implication for Illinois in 1970 was obvious. Moments later he ended, and then, in response to a question from the floor by John Parkhurst, Mr. Powell replied, "No, I do not know of any 'serious' proposals to make the secretary of state appointive. I just like to be prepared."[10]

He must have been the only person in the chamber unaware that elimination of the elective office of Secretary of State had been often and seriously proposed. Perhaps he was confusing seriousness with practicability. There was no doubt that with all the patronage available to his office and his influence within his party, Mr. Powell could have been a formidable foe of a proposed new constitution. If his death and attendant circumstances had come a year earlier, in 1969 rather than 1970, it is quite likely that the office of Secretary of State would have been made appointive.

The Convention also heard from State Treasurer Adlai Stevenson III, a candidate for his party's nomination for United States Senator, who undertook a statesmanlike address. He began with a reference to the writing of the national Constitution in 1787, which he compared to the efforts of the Illinois Convention. He urged adherence to principle and recognition of political realities. He recommended a shortening of the state-wide ballot. "The executive branch," he declared, "is not so much an executive as a chorus. When something goes wrong, seven state officials are likely to point fingers at each other. When something goes right, seven state officers hold press conferences to emphasize their contributions to the commonwealth."[11] To lessen such divisive performances, the ballot should be shortened by providing for appointment, rather than election, of Trustees of the University of Illinois, the Superintendent of Public Instruction, Clerk of the Supreme Court and Treasurer.

Mr. Stevenson ranged broadly over other issues likely to confront the Convention—voting age, debt limitation, reapportionment, selection of judges, home rule, the environment and economic disclosure. His was the best of the speeches made to the Convention by any of the elected State officials. Perhaps as a candidate for the United States Senate, Mr. Stevenson was freer to speak his mind than were others.

The last of the elected executive officers to address the Convention was State Superintendent of Public Instruction Ray Page. He limited his remarks to problems of education. Mr. Page called for a greater State—as distinguished from local—share in the costs of public education, and for the deletion of constitutional restrictions, which hampered the Legislature in dealing with the problems of State aid to private schools. There should be a State board of education, with members elected by region, which would appoint the chief state school officer, he recommended. Thus, Page joined Howlett and Stevenson in recommending abolition of the elected offices they held. He felt that a State board of education should have jurisdiction over all levels of education. "There seems to be little reason for the continuation of the six separate boards which deal with higher education . . . and all the others . . . [I] recommend . . . the coordination of all education . . . under the jurisdiction of an all-encompassing state board. . . ."[12] Although the Convention did eventually authorize a State board of education, which would appoint the chief State school officer, it stopped short of mandating the inclusion of higher education under such a board's jurisdiction, as Page had urged. The politics of higher education in Illinois made this a very touchy subject.

The man whom Page had succeeded as Superintendent of Public Instruction, George Wilkins, also felt that the office should be filled by appointment by a board. He recommended to the Convention's Education Committee, in contrast to Page's views, that the board should be appointed by the Governor and that its authority should be limited to pre-college education. Wilkins stressed the importance of freeing the chief school officer from political activities, and his staff from patronage ties, as well as the greater professional merit in both chief and staff which might be obtained through appointment.

A Guide to the Action

Jockeying for position on the major issues contended in the Convention was typically complex. On some issues, the positions of major factions and the outcome of the votes on various readings shifted dramatically. To one who was not there, keeping it all straight can be a problem. The chart below records changing positions on the major items of contention. It should help the reader follow the discussion of the motives and complex machinations of the various Convention facts. Tracing the changes over time can lead to interesting insights.

Some of the Convention's fundamental procedures differed significantly from those of the Legislature, despite the use of similar terminology. A bill is introduced into the Legislature by giving it a First Reading, whereupon it is referred to a standing committee for review. The bill is then reported back to the House or Senate and the body receives the committee, report, debates and takes action on amendments sponsored by the committee or by other members. A Third Reading is reserved for final vote after sufficient time for final deliberation, usually at least three days. In the Convention, proposals were initiated directly by standing committees, with the effect of allocating both a first and a second reading for debate and amendment. Thus, the Convention placed a greater premium on debate and reconsideration than does the Legislature, an appropriate feature, given the more profound nature of constitutional matters. An important consequence of this feature was that there was not only more occasion for deliberation, but for more complex political bargaining processes as well. While the Convention limited debate on Third Reading, it did provide important opportunities for implementing or revising political strategy, as we shall see. In view of the rocky history of constitutional amendment in Illinois, the additional opportunity for achieving political acceptability with the voters—a trickier business than the more self-contained legislative bargaining—would likely prove helpful.

The Executive Branch

When late in May the Convention as Committee of the Whole took up the Executive Article on first reading, it found itself confronted immediately with the issue of a shorter ballot, the question of election versus appointment of such officers as the Treasurer and Secretary of State. In the proposal coming from the Committee on the Executive the number of elected officers was reduced from seven to six. The superintendent of public instruction was to be appointed. The number of election contests was further reduced to five through the specification that the Governor and Lieutenant Governor should be elected as a team. From seven elected positions to five represented a substantial shortening of the ballot, yet there were those who wished to do more.[13]

Dawn Clark Netsch and Frank Cicero moved that the Treasurer be omitted from the list of elected officials. That office was considered to be the most vulnerable of all to conversion to appointed status. If the Treasurer could be made appointive, then other offices would face the same challenge; if the Convention were unwilling to change the status of the Treasurer, there would be little

	Judicial Inquiry Board	Judicial Selection		House Election		Branch Banking	
		Appt.	Elec.	Single-Member	Cum. Vot./ Multi-Memb.	Limit.	No Limit
Initial Self-Intersts of Factions							
Chi. Reg. Dems.							
Ind. Dems.							
Lib. Reps.							
"Good Gov't. Forces"							
Chi. Papers							
Other Reg. Party Ldrship.							
Comm. Major. Rept.							
1st Reading							
2nd Reading							
3rd Reading							
Referendum:							
Statewide							
Cook Co.							
Downstate Univ.							
Other							

hope that any other office could be so altered. The question was ably debated, especially so by Netsch and Dwight Friedrich; and then in roll call the motion lost 50 to 55.[14]

The prevailing side was comprised of Chicago's regular Democrats and the more conservative of the downstate delegates of both parties.[15] It was a powerful coalition, one which was to reappear time after time on later questions. This vote meant that there was little chance that any other elective office could be made appointive. Some held that such allegiance to the status quo was necessary in order to insure public support for the new constitution, yet it is doubtful that public demand for the election of the Treasurer was so great as to make much difference in the eventual referendum. There was no doubt that the professional politicians cared a very great deal about such matters.

Motions to make other offices appointive failed by much greater margins (Lieutenant Governor, 18 to 71; Comptroller, 29 to 62; Secretary of State, 20 to 74; Attorney General, 6 to 74). Clearly Treasurer was the most vulnerable office. There was a second reading effort, early in August, to provide for the appointment of the Treasurer. It failed in roll call 51 to 56,[16] almost precisely the vote taken over two months before on the same question. Since no minds had been changed, the other elected offices were not challenged on second reading. The ballot was as short as the Convention was willing to make it:

Off Year Election

The Executive Committee recommended in its report to the Committee of the Whole that the election of the Governor and other executive offices occur in the off-year rather than the presidential year. This arrangement was to begin in 1978, with a two-year term starting in 1976 to put it on schedule.

Apparently Chicago's regular Democrats didn't like the idea, for Martin Tuchow moved to amend to retain the traditional arrangement and spoke persuasively for his proposal. James Kemp argued for the Tuchow amendment on the ground that it would give blacks a greater chance to participate in the political system; while Al Raby spoke against it with the idea that the majority proposal would offer blacks opportunity for more meaningful participation. After a substantial debate, the Committee of the Whole voted down the Tuchow amendment 36 to 71 in roll call.[17] The minority was composed of the Chicago regulars plus a few downstate Democrats.

This was one of the more sharply contested issues in the Executive Article. Apparently the Chicago regulars, sound professionals that they were, didn't wish to have a major campaign every second year if once in four years would do. They knew how expensive such campaigning could be. The amateurs among the delegates were more concerned with the greater emphasis which might be placed on State issues in the off-year, and with avoiding the coat-tail effect, which the presidential contest invariably has on an accompanying State race. When the Chicago regulars tried again on second reading to keep the traditional schedule, they were met with even greater resistance.[18] Apparently the idea of off-year elections was generally approved within the Convention.

Other matters of change in the Executive Article were remarkably noncontroversial. Such significant matters as election of the Governor and Lieutenant Governor as a team, change in the order of succession to the gubernatorial chair, authority for the Governor to reorganize executive agencies and reassign their functions subject to legislative veto and the reduction and amendatory vetoes were all approved with little controversy. It was probably a lingering dislike for off-year elections which caused Richard Daley to pass when the entire Executive Article came up for approval on second reading. After his abstention, ten other Chicago Democrats followed suit.[19]

Some delegates were deluded by the ease of approval of the Executive Article to anticipate that change in the legislative and judicial branches would come as readily. How wrong that estimate proved to be!

The Judicial Branch

Central issues of the judicial system surfaced before the Convention was many days old. When Chief Justice Robert C. Underwood addressed the delegates on January 20, it was apparent that he favored leaving the discipline of judges to the judges themselves through the Courts Commission already in existence. He was aware that recent instances of judicial misconduct[20] might cause some to institutionalize the disciplining of judges by persons not members of the bench or bar.

> Improvement in our judicial system ought always to be eagerly sought [Chief Justice Underwood stated], but change is not necessarily improvement, and to embody in a document as permanent as a Constitution is designed to be, changes which impair the integrity or changes which lessen the independence of the judicial branch of our government would in my judgment be an abdication of the responsibility of the delegates to this Convention.[21]

When Chief Justice Underwood appeared before the Judiciary Committee in mid-February, the matter of disciplining judges came up again. He preferred to have the sole power to discipline judges reside in the Courts Commission, which was comprised totally of judges. Delegate Clarence Yordy challenged Chief Justice Underwood: " 'You said you've got things pretty well contained—the judges can take care of it. We've travelled around the state and we get just the other viewpoint.' " When Underwood answered that he was interested in the best possible system, Yordy pressed him further: " 'Are you talking about best for the people or for the judges? Your . . . point is that things are just right the way they are.' " Underwood replied that common practice among other states was for only judges to discipline judges.[22]

From that exchange, Committee members went on to express their concern over the fact that a circuit judge in Chicago, recently suspended, continued to draw his full salary. Both Chief Justice Underwood and Roy Gulley, Administrator of the Illinois Courts, hastened to explain that there was no legal authority within their reach, nor within that of the Supreme Court of Governor, which would allow any of them to suspend the judge's pay. Apparently the Judiciary Committee had come away from recent hearings around the State with the idea that the public was distrubed about judicial conduct.

When he addressed the Convention in January, Chief Justice Underwood did not discuss the selection of judges, an issue which became the chief point of contention within the Convention so far as the Judicial Article was concerned. Perhaps this was among the subjects upon which members of the Court did not agree, for the Chief Justice had said at the start of his address, ". . . there are differences of opinion among us . . . upon which I shall not dwell."[23] The matter of judicial selection was not long in appearing, however, for when Supreme Court Judge Walter V. Schafer appeared before the Judiciary Committee on the following day, he recommended that appellate and supreme court judges be appointed rather than elected.

The controversial nature of the means of selecting judges came more clearly into focus early in February with the presentation of a report, from the Joint Committees on the Judicial Article of the Chicago and Illinois Bar Associations, to the Convention's Judiciary Committee. It called for appointment of judges by the Governor from a list of three names presented to him for each position by a Judicial Nominating Commission. Other matters relating to the courts were treated in some detail, but it was the critical issue of the selection of judges which received greatest attention. Patronage-oriented partisans generally regarded the so-called election of judges, which often amounted to party appointment, as essential to the continued well-being of the parties and their chieftains. That was especially true in Chicago, where the regular Democratic organization felt that any challenge to party welfare had to be strenuously resisted. That was also the view of professional and near-professional partisans of both parties downstate.

Opposition within the Convention to the appointment of judges had become apparent late in January—just after details of the Bar Associations' plan had been announced—when Dwight Friedrich made from the floor what one account held to be a "brutal verbal assault" on Professor Rubin Cohn of the University of Illinois College of Law. Earlier Professor Cohn had indicated, in response to a question from a member of the Judiciary Committee before which he was appearing, that he favored the appointment of judges.[24] Thereafter he was appointed counsel to the Judiciary Committee, and on January 27 Freidrich rose to complain in plenary session that a certain committee counsel was in fact "lobbying" within the committee to which he was assigned. It was at a time when it appeared the Convention might overspend its appropriation, and Freidrich asked how much the committee counsels were being paid, implying that whatever the amount, it was more than "inside lobbyists" should receive or the Convention could afford. On the advice of the acting parliamentarian, President Witwer ruled the inquiry out of order. Whereupon Friedrich addressed his next remark to the parliamentarian: "I am sorry you ruled that way, since the question was about you, Professor Cohn." The President acted quickly to cut Friedrich off, but it was apparent that controversy over the manner of selecting judges was going to be severe. While Chief Justice Underwood had not mentioned judicial selection when he addressed the whole Convention, inevitably the matter came up when he appeared before the Judiciary Committee. He expressed the opinion there that, while appointment of judges might be necessary in the more urban areas, election should be retained elsewhere. That, of course, was precisely the arrangement which the Chicago Democrats wished to avoid.

Judicial Discipline and Selection in Committee of the Whole

When by mid-April reports from the Judiciary Committee[26] were taken up by Committee of the Whole, it was clear that the great battles of the Judicial Article were to be fought over the selection and disciplining of judges. It was apparent from divisions within the Judiciary Committee that selection was an issue which the Convention as a whole would have to decide. In the Committee, Chicago's regular Democrats were lining up solidly for election, with the support of certain conservative Republicans, while more liberal Republicans, a downstate Democrat, and a suburban independent favored appointment. Thus, the stage was being set for the most bitter battle of first reading, soon to come. But first the Convention had to consider the matter of the disciplining of judges.

In regard to the disciplining of judges the Judiciary Committee submitted a majority and a minority report. "Public concern," the Committee stated, "in the subject of judicial discipline is very great, largely as a result of recent disclosures and charges of judicial impropriety. . . ."[27] The Committee had sought to integrate that concern with preservation of the integrity of the judiciary in both majority and minority versions. Essentially the majority proposed a "two tier" structure in which a Judicial Inquiry Board, including persons who were not judges, would receive and hear complaints against judges, and if it found those complaints justified, would file them with the Courts Commission. The minority would employ the Courts Commission, composed entirely of judges, as the sole means of disciplining judges, as in the 1870 Constitution as amended. The desire for change and an attachment to the *status quo* were in conflict.

When the minority, which felt that the Courts Commission had been working well, presented its views, the questioning got rather sharp. Some excerpts follow:

> DELEGATE FOSTER: Am I correct in understanding the position of the minority that of the 11,000,000 citizens of this state there do not exist four laymen with the sophistication, knowledge, wisdom, independence, and integrity to determine whether or not a judge has been guilty of impropriety?
>
> DELEGATE NICHOLSON: No. We don't say that at all.
>
> DELEGATE FOSTER: Well, I don't really understand the apparent objection you have to laymen on the investigatory commission. Could you explain it more fully, please?
>
> DELEGATE NICHOLSON: We say that we reject the principle totally of laymen serving on such a commission involving the judiciary.
>
> . . . .
>
> DELEGATE FOSTER: . . . with regard to lawyers, is it inconceivable that there could exist lawyers with sufficient independence so that they wouldn't worry about the possibility of facing the judge that they had asked to be investigated?
>
> DELEGATE NICHOLSON: . . . I wouldn't want to serve on such a Commission . . . you would be hard put . . . to find a lawyer who would want to serve on such a commission. Only a lawyer who had some axe to grind . . . would want to serve. . . .[28]
>
> . . . .
>
> DELEGATE COLEMAN: I would like to ask Delegate Nudelman a question. . . . What is the profession of the people who serve on the grievance commissions for attorneys and lawyers?
>
> DELEGATE NUDELMAN: As you well know, Mr. Coleman, they're all lawyers.
>
> DELEGATE COLEMAN: All lawyers?
>
> DELEGATE NUDELMAN: All Lawyers.
>
> DELEGATE COLEMAN: Thank you.
>
> DELEGATE NUDELMAN: And further, Mr. Coleman, as you . . . know, jurors are all lay people.[29]
>
> . . . .
>
> DELEGATE GERTZ: Mr. Nudelman, I was rather intrigued by a comment you made about . . . the commission . . . working so well, why did it become necessary to have a special commission appointed?
>
> DELEGATE NUDELMAN: . . . the point that I was trying to make, Mr. Gertz, was that it is adaptable. . . .[30]
>
> . . . .
>
> DELEGATE CICERO: . . . I wonder, Delegate Nudelman, if you would review for us exactly what the Courts Commission did last summer that you view as an example of the success of it as it operates at the present time . . .
>
> DELEGATE NUDELMAN: . . . the Courts Commission . . . in fact, did create the Greenberg Commission. . . .
>
> DELEGATE CICERO: . . . did the Courts Commission give reasons why it was creating the Greenberg Commission?
>
> DELEGATE NUDELMAN: My personal opinion, sir, is that it was a mistake.
>
> DELEGATE CICERO: . . . I'm even more confused now, because you cited what you now call a mistake as an example of its working properly. . . .
>
> DELEGATE NUDELMAN: It works, the system works, whether they had done it themselves or . . . created the Greenberg Commission, it works.[31]
>
> . . . .
>
> DELEGATE FOSTER: Mr. Nudelman . . . would you expect them [Courts Commission members] to be less responsive to the desires of the supreme court than, say, the Chicago Board of Education is to the desires of the mayor?
>
> DELEGATE NUDELMAN: I'm not going to grace that supercilious question with an answer, Mr. Foster.[32]

The Chicago regular Democrats were almost alone in opposition to a Judicial Inquiry Board which would play a role in the discipline of judges. Perhaps they feared the impact of such a body on Democratic judges in Chicago. Or perhaps as one of them, Odas Nicholson, argued persuasively, allowing non-judges a role in disciplining judges would be a violation of separation of powers and the integrity of the judiciary. The question was decisively settled in roll call, 29 to 73,[33] and the proposal for a Judicial Inquiry Board was approved on first reading. An attempt to delete it on second reading met with no success.

Selection of Judges on First Reading

The matter of judicial selection was far more controversial than discipline. A majority of the Judiciary Committee recommended that supreme and appellate court judges be appointed and circuit judges elected, and that the question of appointing the latter, as well, should be separately submitted to the voters. This was the Committee compromise of the controversy over judicial selection. The Committee divided 6 to 5, with independent Democrats Wayne Whalen and Anne Willer joining four Republicans to form the majority and Republican Helen Kinney and four Chicago regular Democrats dissenting.[34] After members of the Committee's majority explained their proposal on July 7, the Chicago regulars immediately moved to the attack, and with questions challenged the appointment or "merit" plan. Thomas McCracken led off:

> MR. McCRACKEN: . . . Delegate Whalen and Delegate Ladd, you both used the term "merit." Were you referring to the elective or the appointive system when you used the word "merit?"
>
> MR. WHALEN: The appointive system.
>
> MR. McCRACKEN: The appointive? And what is there that differentiates and makes it appropriate to use that term?
>
> MR. LADD: We think that the appointive system will result in a substantial increase in the quality of judges. . . .[35]

This went on hour after hour. The opponents of appointment seemed to be staging a delaying tactic—or was it simply that they wished to question every detail of the majority proposal? Their argument appeared to be that appointment is an "elitist" system in contrast to the more democratic election. It was claimed that few members of minority groups would go to the bench if appointment prevailed.[36]

Then in turn the Committee minority made its case for continued election of judges at all levels. It stressed the "openness" of its plan. It suggested the provision that, if appointment should prevail, then no member of the Convention should be eligible for such appointment for twenty years. The purpose was apparent; it was to bludgeon the body away from the merit idea. Immediately, of course, the obvious question was asked: Why not make the same prohibition if the Convention went for election? Some interesting exchanges followed. For example:

> MR. WEISBERG: Do you think we should . . . protest against such inferences [of conflict of interest] only where personal benefit might result from change and not personal benefit result from . . . the status quo?
>
> MR. NUDELMAN: I think you and I have a lot of problems with language. (Laughter)
>
> MR. WEISBERG: I think we understand each other pretty well.
>
> MR. NUDELMAN: Sometimes we do and sometimes we don't. If something is not changed, I don't think you can say that it is not changed to somebody's benefit. . . .
>
> MR. WEISBERG: In other words, you can't retain it to your benefit?
>
> MR. NUDELMAN: Well, again, I don't quite follow you.[37]

The fact that the argument could be turned caused it promptly to be dropped, and the central discussion continued.

A fringe issue vote found the regular Democrats almost alone on the losing side, with a scattering of downstate Democrats and the Republicans Samuel Martin and Henry Hendren. It was ironic that Hendren had gone to the Convention convinced that the Chicago monster would have to be slain every day, and then, because of the conservatism of many of his views, had ended up in bed with the Chicago Democrats on issue after issue. Consistently the postures of the most conservative Republicans were similar to those of Chicago's regular Democrats.

When at last on July 8 there was a motion to approve the majority proposal, a storm of amendments followed. Some were genuinely meant to perfect while others had sabotage as their aim. Motions of this latter sort caused William Fay, Chairman of the Judiciary Committee, to observe: ". . . the help that we have been getting . . . to perfect the majority report is mainly coming from those . . . in support of the minority position, and it is a far cry from perfection. It really is . . . emasculation."[38]

Other amendments on the matter were more complex. Paul Elward moved that the General Assembly be given authority to change the method of selection of judges at all levels, from appointment to election or vice versa with approval in a popular referendum. "What's fair is fair," Elward declared, taking a favorite line of Charles Coleman's. "This should not be a one way street . . . from election to appointment . . . the people should have the right . . . to come back from . . . appointment . . . to . . . election."[39] To agree was tempting, until the realization struck home that this was simply a way in which a merit system specified in the constitution could be abandoned through less than the usual procedure for constitutional change. This oddity actually was approved, in roll call, 56 to 52.[40] Its opponents resolved to delete it later on, and eventually did.

As it became more and more apparent that the appointment of supreme and appellate court judges had majority support, the advocates of election became increasingly dilatory and their motions less substantial. Now and then the demand for a roll call was thrown in, in most cases simply to delay.[41] With the filibuster in full flower, Richard Daley moved that the minimum age for members of the judicial nominating commissions be 18. That was truly a nonsense amendment, and evidence that the supply of dilatory motions was running short. (Later when charges of delay were made, however, Daley denied that he had any intention of obstructing the work of the Convention. "I took time . . . to read the whole judicial article. I asked a number of questions . . .

I was sincere about it. . . .''[42] No doubt Daley *was* sincere in his purpose.) That sort of thing went on until dinner time, with much rambling speech making, and tempers grew shorter as the frivolous nature of much of what was offered, and the viciousness of some it it, became apparent.

And it was no better when the delegates came back after dinner. The principal effort then was to impose restrictions upon service with the judicial nominating commissions. One after another, a series of motions toward that end were rejected, often in roll calls intended to delay. The Convention was obviously getting nowhere, and the frustration level mounted on both sides. Finally the flash point was reached and the explosion came.

Helen Kinney offered an amendment which would have deleted the prohibition of judicial nominating commission service on the part of officials of State and local governments and of political parties. The interest of Chicago's regular Democrats in such an amendment was obvious. Several delegates spoke to the question. When Elbert Smith moved that the Committee of the Whole rise, as prelude to adjournment, President Witwer seemed to welcome the idea. He called for a voice vote and then, apparently wishing to bring the long day to a close and not hearing a sufficient number of ''ayes,'' called for a show of hands, even though it seemed to some that the chorus of ''nays'' had been the louder. Immediately the chamber was in great disorder. Delegates were on their feet, shouting and cursing at the chair. It was a wild scene, and it was several minutes before order was restored. Then the recriminations began. Witwer was accused of bias in hearing the voice vote—'' 'You call them the way you want them,' '' John Knuppel had shouted at him over the earlier din[43]—and of inefficiency in handling the whole long day's discussion. Thomas McCracken charged that the debate had been prolonged because ''you have imposed upon us the necessity of producing in the majority report a document which is most to our liking in the event it becomes the Convention's proposal.''[44] Others joined in the chorus of criticism.

President Witwer then erred in going on the defensive. His conduct in the chair had been without fault throughout the day. He had insisted, properly, that perfection of the majority proposal be concluded before the minority view could be offered in substitution for it. That had consistently been the procedure in earlier debates. In appraising the voice vote on the Smith motion to rise from Committee of the Whole, he could have announced that the ''ayes'' had prevailed and attempted to gavel that decision through. Instead he had taken the fairer route of asking for a show of hands, and, ironically, that was the action which had precipitated the storm. It was idle to charge as some did that the ''nays'' had obviously been in the majority in the voice vote, for such procedures are notoriously poor measures of voting strength, truly useful only in situations where near unanimity prevails or when a presiding officer indeed wishes to discriminate.

Witwer was blameless in this matter and should have behaved accordingly. But it had been a long and frustrating day for him as well, in the face of an obvious tactic of delay and obstruction directed against a position which he favored.[45] Thus he became angry and defensive, charged that ''games had been played'' all day (giving Paul Elward a chance to admonish him to credit others with his own sincerity) and insisted that his conduct during the day had been according to advice rendered by parliamentarian Richard Murphy. He should have stopped there, but could not resist adding, since it was the Chicago regulars in the main who were taunting him, that Murphy was eminently qualified and had in fact been parliamentarian for the 1968 Democratic National Convention in Chicago. This drew derisive laughter, for that convention had of course been notoriously disorderly. Witwer's remarks produced angry replies, and it was some minutes before cooler and wiser delegates, such as Elbert Smith and Edward Jenison, could with their remarks help resotre a degree of order.[46]

Then Smith withdrew the motion that had set off the whole uproar. The Committee of the Whole voted to approve the Kinney motion, deleting the prohibition of public and party officials serving on judicial nominating commissions, by a 59 to 27 roll call vote.[47] If it had been voted on before the shouting match had taken place, it would probably have been defeated, but Witwer's apparent desire to adjourn before the vote was taken had gained it a degree of additional support.

Was the whole tumultuous episode a planned or spontaneous affair? Probably some of both. Coming when and as it did, it was largely spontaneous, but systematic harassment of the chair was already an obvious strategem. There can be no doubt that to ''break'' the President was then and thereafter a conscious goal for some. The regular Democrats were so totally committed to preserving the advantages which a system of so-called election of judges conferred upon them, both personally and in terms of their party, that they were apparently going to go all out to oppose appointment in any way they could. Some of their tactics were brought into play again on the following day, when Maurice Scott took the floor to plead for reconciliation of the Convention's warring factions. He ended by saying, ''. . . we are in the home stretch. Let's work hard; let's fight hard; but above all, let's be fair to our fellow delegates and to our leader.''[48] With their applause, the delegates seemed to endorse Scott's views.

But with the first amendment of the morning, offered by Wendell Durr and Paul Elward, it was apparent that there was to be more of the previous day's obstruction. After an hour and fifteen minutes and fifteen speakers, one of them, Elward, having risen four times, the President pleaded for greater speed. That prompted a speech from Thomas Lyons and another from James Strunck. At last the vote, with roll call demanded, and the amendment was beaten 66 to 40.[49]

Attacks upon President Witwer began again in mid-afternoon. A dramatic roll call made it apparent that the majority for the appointment of supreme and appellate court judges was holding firm.[50] Chicago Democrats Elward and Lyons then laid a trap for the President by offering an amendment that was clearly out of order. When Witwer ruled it so, the Chicago regulars immediately launched a storm of verbal abuse upon him. This had none of the spontaneity of the previous evening's brawl, but instead appeared to be a carefully planned maneuver to disrupt proceedings and harass the chair. The opponents of an appointed judiciary, especially at the circuit court level, realized they did not have the strength to substitute the minority proposal. Vote after vote on related issues had made that clear, and thus they chose disruption instead.[51]

Thomas McCracken and Thomas Lyons took the lead in abusing the President. Several days earlier, Lyons had said of judicial appointment, " 'It's not a merit plan; it's a Czarist plan' " in which the Governor would control all appointments and the newspapers and bar associations would have undue influence.[52] The grossness of much of this can be judged from the following exchanges:

> PRESIDENT WITWER: . . . You [responding to Elward] didn't object this morning when I accepted an interpretation from the Parliamentarian that you liked.
>
> VICE-PRESIDENT LYONS: Sometimes he's right.
>
> PRESIDENT WITWER: . . . Nobody has to take that abuse, Mr. Lyons, from a vice president or a member of this Convention. . . . You withdraw that, I hope. . . . I am sorry you don't. . . .
>
> DELEGATE McCRACKEN: Can you ever be wrong up there, Mr. President?
>
> PRESIDENT WITWER: . . . it will be up to this body to decide when the president is wrong, and if you want to appeal him, you have had the opportunity, and you'll have it again. . . .[53]
>
> . . . .
>
> PRESIDENT WITWER:. . . You do not have the floor, Mr. Elward. Mr. Tomei. . . .
>
> DELEGATE KNUPPEL: Mr. Tomei always gets it when he wants it.
>
> PRESIDENT WITWER: No, he doesn't always get it, Mr. Knuppel. (General laughter)[54]

Next Lyons moved to appeal the President's ruling. In debating the appeal, Leonard Foster observed:

> . . . . I think we have finally come face to face with the problem of the integrity of this convention
>
> . . . .
>
> I have seen people today setting traps for the Chair, and I must gently rebuke the Chair for falling into most of them. (General laughter)
>
> . . . .
>
> I am sickened by the sight of people sitting around here shouting at the Chairman without any due regard for order, without any due regard for this body. We are a Constitutional Convention, and we have a mandate to write a constitution; and regardless of how you interpret the activities of this week, they haven't been very much along the line of writing a constitution.
>
> This is not the House of Representatives where people can shout, "Shame, shame, dummy, dummy" (reference to Elward's recent behavior in the House). . . . I urge all members to . . . support the Chair. . . . (Applause)[55]

After some further blustering on the part of McCracken and Elward, the vote was 35 to 65 against the appeal. This whole episode was an unbelievably crude and heavy-handed one, and if anything cost, rather than gained, strength for those who favored the election of judges.[56]

After perfection of the majority recommendation, the Committee of the Whole turned its attention to the minority report which called for election of judges at all levels. Many earlier arguments were repeated. Against the claim by James Kemp, Thomas Hunter and Samuel Patch that blacks would be less favored by an appointed judiciary, Al Raby observed:

> As I was coming down here with my friend, Victor Arrigo, on the train, he . . . said, "Al . . . which of these two systems [appointment or election] do you believe in?" I told him, "Neither." And I tell this convention today, "Neither."
>
> I don't think that it will make a great deal of difference. . . . Any systems can be subverted if men are . . . not willing to make them work. . . .
>
> . . . I have found . . . that black people do not, in fact, get justice under the elective system—have not and I suspect will not for a long time to come.
>
> . . . .
>
> I support the majority report hecause . . . I think that the arm of justice must be separated from the political process. . . .[57]

Finally, after much debate, wrangling, shouted charges and motions to adjourn, in a key vote the coalition for appointed supreme and appellate court judges held firm, 62 to 43.[58] By an identical vote the Committee's recommendation to submit separately the question of appointing circuit judges as well was sustained.[59]

There was considerable unhappiness with these decisions, however, and predictions that further negotiation of the issue occur. John Knuppel asserted that the Convention was on "a mission of destruction" if it did not compromise the matter. And Thomas Lyons called the vote "an expression of lack of confidence in the electorate of this state." If supporters of the ". . . majority proposal . . . think . . . the voters are too ignorant to govern themselves, I wish they would have the grace to say so [illegible] [Appointed] judges [will be] picked by . . . the well born, the well fixed, and the well connected."[60] One wonders how Lyons would have described the manner of selection of judges in Chicago in the process called "election?" Certainly it was by the "well fixed" and "well connected" if not necessarily the "well born."

The fact that final approval of the controversial sections on first reading was by a vote of 62 to 33,[61] only three votes beyond the necessary 59 was an indication that the question was far from finally settled. If the controversy had taught anything, it was that the Chicago regular Democrats were going to be intransigent on the question of electing judges. They would yield to the point of separate submission to the voters of the entire question, from top to bottom of the court structure. In retrospect, that appeared to be a fair compromise of the matter, and, of course, that is what in the end the Convention did. It was not ready on first reading to do so, however, for the necessary trading for positions had not yet occurred.[62]

Consideration on first reading of other aspects of the Judicial Article brought little controversy and were memorable chiefly for a comment by James Kemp to Ralph Dunn. Dunn had moved that circuit court clerks be elected, instead of leaving the choice between election and appointment to the General Assembly. After the motion was lost, Kemp offered an observation which was to become a favorite slogan of the Convention: "If I might be permitted to cite to my good and warm friend, Delegate Dunn, an admonition taught to me by my grandmother, 'If you play with a puppy, it will lick you in the mouth.' "[63] Dunn had been doing some trading for votes for an anti branch banking provision, and Kemp's implication was that some, who had been trading with Dunn, had opposed him on this motion.

Selection of Judges on Second Reading

It was mid-August before the Judicial Article came before the Committee of the Whole on second reading. Since it was vacation time, there were many tourists in the city, and every day they appeared in the gallery. Many who were from other states were in Springfield primarily to see the Lincoln shrines. They entered the Old Capitol without any idea that an historic event was taking place within. What a surprise they must have gotten when they looked over the gallery rail at the strife going on below. On the day the judicial article was taken up on second reading, one woman, when leaving the gallery, asked the doorkeeper when the "next performance" would be. She thought the delegates were a group of public spirited citizens, reenacting a previous convention.

With second reading, it was apparent that certain earlier decisions of the Judicial and Legislative Articles were likely to be altered. This writer, as a delegate, noted in his diary on the day the Judicial Article was taken up on second reading that:

> It has become apparent in the last few days, that a group of more conservative Republicans are making common cause with the Chicago regulars in order to favor . . . elected judges (at all levels) *and* cumulative voting. This move has a good chance of success. It has been in formation for months, as gradually the way conservative and liberal lines are drawn in the convention become clear. Thus in the last analysis we are going to see the great questions of revenue, judiciary, and legislative structure, decided *not* by party but by *philosophy*—which is probably the way it should be.[64]

The shape of the central coalition on second and third reading was already apparent.

After several minor changes in the Judicial Article were approved, next came the move which many had anticipated. As approved on first reading, the Judicial Article provided for the appointment of supreme and appellate court judges with the question of appointing Circuit judges, as well, to be separately submitted.[65] That arrangement had commanded a solid majority at the time. But now, Helen Kinney moved, with David Linn seconding, a series of changes which would put election at all levels in the proposed constitution, and appointment at all levels in the disadvantaged posture of a separately submitted item.

The issue was clear and debate proceeded at a high level and at length. President Witwer made one of his better speeches for the merit principle and against the motion. James Kemp was especially effective in speaking for election. The whole morning was spent in discussion. It was noteworthy that the Chicago regular Democrats felt so confident of victory that they took relatively little part in the debate.[66]

The arguments of first reading were heard again. But the alignments were different now, and, when at last the roll call came, the Kinney motion was approved 58 to 49, with 7 passing.[67] The fact that 114 responded to this roll call indicated the interest which the issue aroused. Chicago regular and downstate Democrats and the more conservative Republicans made up the winning side. It was clearly a triumph for the status quo. Fourteen downstate Republicans came over to favor election of judges on this vote, from the opposit position on first reading.[68] Republican leaders in this reversal were Charles Young, Dwight Friedrich and Arthur Lennon. According to one newspaper,

> Young reportedly told some delegates the night before the vote on judicial selection that he had 18 signed defections. . . .
>
> One delegate from the . . . suburbs said he changed his vote on judicial selection because Mayor Daley told his supporters that if they lost the judicial article, they could kiss the whole constitution goodbye. That delegate believed it, although on other occasions he has called Chicago's bluff.[69]

At this juncture, this writer noted; "And so we will have election of judges in, and merit separate. This is in one sense a defeat, in another a victory, and should lead to an interesting campaign, bringing a lot of money and attention to bear which would not otherwise be the case."[70] Apparently others felt the same way, for after several minor changes in other parts of the Judicial Article, it was approved on second reading by a vote of 103 to 3. Most of the delegates felt that they had done the best they could with it at that stage. Third reading changes are detailed in a later section.[71]

The Legislative Branch

In February, ideas which were portents of later controversy were heard in meetings of the Legislative Committee. Philip Sorensen, at one time president of the Nebraska unicameral Legislature, described that legislative structure for the Committee. Few believed that the unicameral idea had any chance of adoption in Illinois. Yet it received surprising support on first reading. From then on, however, the unique electoral arrangements in the House of Representatives claimed center stage.

On February 24, significant testimony was heard in the Legislative Committee from Secretary of State Paul Powell and House Majority Whip Arthur Telcser. Both strongly favored the retention of the combination of multi-member districts and cumulative voting in the election of members of the House of Representatives. That was not surprising, for cumulative voting had made it possible for Secretary Powell to spend 30 years in the House almost without an election contest; while Representative Telcser, a Republican from a Democratic district in Chicago, currently owed his position to this unique electoral arrangement. The latter was so strong in praise of cumulative voting as to say that " 'every state should adopt' " it. This was a rather unusual judgment, since in the last century no other state had done so. Both also declared firm opposition to unicameralism; and Secretary Powell expressed the feeling that with such an arrangement " 'things would be terrible' " in the General Assembly.[72] Apparently, both felt that little change in the legislature was needed.

Somewhat different views were expressed by W. Russell Arrington, majority leader and president *pro-tem* of the Senate, when he addressed the Convention late in March. First he invited the delegates, in case they wished to ". . . learn some partisan-body techniques . . . as a matter of self-defense. . . .," to visit the General Assembly, where "some of the finest partisans in Illinois will be . . ." in action.[73] Not surprisingly, he felt that the Senate should elect its own presiding officer. The General Assembly, he believed, should be little changed in its basic structure and procedures. Its behavior patterns had been developing over a century and should not be altered by ". . . superficial structural change."[74] The effective date for legislation to become law should be revised to allow greater time for the public to be informed. The General Assembly should meet annually and should be able to convene itself in special session. The Legislature should have the power to impeach and remove judges.

In response to a question about the wisdom of cumulative voting, Senator Arrington claimed not to know, though he did feel that a system, which in many districts consistently produced only three candidates for three positions, was unsound.[75] Such a limitation of candidacies, he declared, ". . . is effected by cozy little arrangements between present holders of office and the local political authorities—in many cases. . . . It is not a popular election."[76] In spite of such views, in early April the Legislative Committee voted decisively to retain cumulative voting.

Cumulative Voting on First Reading

Recommendations of the Legislative Committee were taken up by the Committee of the Whole on first reading in mid-July. They included no great changes, but instead a number of lesser ones. Reduction in the size of House and Senate, annual sessions, elimination of the Lieutenant Governor as presiding officer of the Senate and addition of the popular petition for initiating amendments to the Legislative Article were the most significant of the changes recommended. It was not a very bold program, but it was to gain considerably in that regard before the Committee of the Whole was finished with it at first reading.

Dissension over cumulative voting surfaced early in discussion of the Legislative Article.

Illinois is unique among all the states in employing a system of multimember districts with cumulative voting for the House only—voters in 59 three-member districts may vote for either one, two or three candidates. This has had the general effect of strengthening the minority party in most districts, producing a 2-to-1 partisan split, and resulting in narrow House majorities. It is of special importance in Chicago, where it allows the election of Republicans and independent Democrats, and in the suburbs, where it allows election of Democrats who would not otherwise be elected. Malcolm Kamin poked some gentle fun at the practice of cumulating voting during discussion of the Johnson amendment described below, by reading a parody of Vachel Lindsey's poem "Lincoln Walks at Midnight:"

SOMEBODY WALKS AT MIDNIGHT
(With apologies to Vachel Lindsay)

Is it pretentious in a thing of state,
That here at midnight in our little town
A mourning figure walks and will not rest
In this old court house pacing up and down.
It is the ghost of Joe Medill
Who haunts this place at hours late
Who strives to keep his dream alive
That each his votes must cumulate.
That each shall cast one, two or three
Or one for three, or three for one,
So when the casting all is through,
The judges' work is just begun.
And thus in lessons from the past
We learn and study histories
How we held intact our splintered state
And shielded all minorities.
Has not at last the time arrived,
When we can shake his ghostly power
When Representatives can be chosen straight
When Joe won't haunt throughout this state
But only haunt the Tribune Tower?[77]

The debatable impacts of cumulative voting on the Illinois political system are discussed in the chapters by Gove, Wiste, Lousin and Colby. Not surprisingly, this became one of the most complex issues of the Convention: (1) Even if cumulative voting were eliminated, should multi-member districts be retained? (2) If one or both were deleted, would the provision be incorporated in a package with the entire new Constitution, or would it be submitted as a separate referendum question, or as some combination of both? Tactics in the Convention varied at each phase, depending on the prospects for linkage to other referendum issues, of which the more important by far was the election/appointment of judges.

Behind these tactical shifts lay the overriding objectives of the regular Democrats to preserve election of judges and to provide for one simple instruction to voters, that is, either "yes" or "no" on all separate submissions.

Early in the discussion on perfection of the Legislative Committee's majority report, Stanley Johnson moved to abolish the practice of cumulative voting. Such a measure had already been anticipated by certain members of the Convention, and action had been taken to combat it. At a July 10 press conference in Chicago, Representatives Arthur Telcser, Harold Katz, Robert Mann, Henry Hyde and Daniel Pierce, and Dr. Bruce Douglas, a candidate for the House, expressed the unwarranted view that the movement in the Convention to eliminate cumulative voting was a plot by both party organizations to reduce the number of representatives inclined to be independent. " 'In the House we have real debate,' said Mann, 'and all opinions are expressed. If Con-Con should abandon cumulative voting, we will have the same type of staid situation that exists in the Senate.' " Dr. Douglas warned that to delete cumulative voting would be to endanger a new constitution.[78] Each of these persons had an intense personal interest in preserving the cumulative vote.

Johnson's motion to abolish cumulative voting was opposed by the independent Democrats of Chicago and Cook County as had been expected. Several weeks earlier, the Independent Voters of Illinois had been sounded out and found to be solidly for cumulative voting. Their purpose was clear, of course; it was to preserve a practice with which they could flail the major parties, especially the Cook County Democrats, and which was their only way to win an election in areas of strong party control. President Witwer also was opposed to Johnson's motion. Apparently, he was going to be strong for cumulative voting/multi-member districts. Could it be for the same reason that he had supported continuation of the personal property tax; that he wished to pacify a particular bloc in the Convention with a pro-cumulative voting point of view?

When the vote came on the Johnson motion, it carried 64 to 40 in roll call.[79] The Chicago regulars went with the majority on this question, to the surprise of some. Regular Democrats undoubtedly enjoyed seeing the independents and liberal Republicans at odds, after the success of their coalition of the previous week on the Judicial Article. It may be, further, that they saw cumulative voting as a means the independents had of beating them occasionally and thus opposed it here.[80] However, it seems more likely from a review of the entire process that the regular Democrats threw their support with the opponents of cumulative voting simply to establish a credible threat with proponents, thereby setting up the proponents for a trade—regular Democrats would "shift" their votes to support restoration of cumulative voting in return for downstate Republican support for judicial election.

Johnson's motion had called for the abolition of cumulative voting, but not multi-member districts. Perhaps his strategy was to bring the independents over to the single-member district plan as their best hope of winning elections if the cumulative vote were done away with.[81] Those who opposed cumulative voting also hoped that the Chicago regular Democrats would join them in order to deny the independents the advantage which the system offered them. It was a complex situation with almost any outcome possible.

After much debate, the traditional system of cumulative voting and multi-member districts was rejected 42 to 59.[82] Then, after much more wrangling, the choice was for single- rather than multi-member districts. The Chicago regular Democrats divided here, and the independents generally voted for single-member districts. It appeared that the strategy to drive them over to the single-member side had succeeded,[83] but they appeared unhappy about it. For the time, the issue appeared to be settled and the Committee of the Whole went on to other aspects of the legislative article.

Cumulative Voting on Second Reading

When the Legislative Article came up for second reading in mid-August, it was apparent that the central issue was cumulative voting. An early vote ended at 51 to 49,[84] suggesting that opinion was evenly divided. Later in the day, the vote in a similar question was 51 to 48.[85] While the delegates seemed to be playing a numbers game, in reality they were jockeying for position. Then Lucy Reum and Samuel Martin offered the motion, cosponsored by George Lewis, James Perona and Mary Pappas, that many had known was in store, the deletion of single-member districts in favor of three-member districts with cumulative voting, the traditional arrangement. The motion seemed a sure winner. It had certain Republicans and, after a switch, the Chicago regular Democrats on its side, and that combination alone had been enough to tilt the scales in favor of the election of judges only a day or so earlier. What was more, cumulative voting also had the support of the Chicago independents, who seldom could be found voting with the regular Democrats or the "19th century" Republicans. The independents favored cumulative voting for the striking power it gave them in behalf of single candidates, district by district, in Chicago. So it appeared that the amendment and cumulative voting would surely win.

But when the delegates voted at last on roll call, the verdict went the other way, 52 to 56.[86] A number of Republicans held firm for single-member districts, but more significantly the Chicago regular Democrats had four of their stalwarts missing—Brown, Cooper, Lennon and Tuchow. Fennoy and Kelleghan, who were often with them on questions of this sort, also did not respond to this roll call. So it was a decision by default. How ironic it seemed that when a showdown came, the Chicago regular Democrats should lose through the kind of weakness that non-attendance represented! After eight months of delay, so that their superior discipline and resources might prevail after salary money had run out and the amateurs had suffered attrition, they were beaten at their own game. At least beaten temporarily. It was rumored that orders were going out for the absent ones among the Chicago Democrats to be back in the fold the next day.

At first, this writer found it hard to understand why the Chicago regular Democrats were so strong for cumulative voting, when on first reading they seemed either indifferent or in opposition to it. Then, slowly, he came to the realization that they had "traded" their support for cumulative voting, which they could live with very well in any case—even though it did allow the independents to torment them from time to time—for the election of judges. This helped to explain why the Committee of the Whole had reversed itself on judicial choice between first and second reading and appeared now to be so close to doing so on cumulative voting.

Also, having incorporated election of judges in the package and appointment on separate submission, the Chicago Democrats could now see merit in getting cumulative voting in and single-member districts out, so that they could approach the referendum with orders to their followers to vote "yes" on the package and "no" on everything else! How much easier that would be than to be obliged to explain that one separate submission item should be favored and another opposed, and how to tell the two apart. Also, they knew that the Chicago newspapers were going to be strong for cumulative voting, and thus they feared the effect on the voters if that matter *and* the appointment of judges (which the Chicago press also favored) were equally at separate submission. It was a complex matter, but in any case, after having traded support for cumulative voting for support for elected judges, they were stuck with the bargain and obliged to make the most of it.

The matter came up again later in the day, when independent Democrat Bernard Weisberg moved separate submission for multi-member districts with cumulative voting. The independents keenly wanted to retain cumulative voting so that they could win a seat from time to time from the organization; and the Chicago regular Democrats definitely did not want it submitted separately in the company of the appointment of judges, on which they would have to instruct followers to vote "no," so a long dispute ensued. Finally, in roll call the Weisberg motion for separate submission was approved, 67 to 31.[87] The regular Democrats voted "no" or "pass" and soon moved again to adjourn. The decision was to go on, and there was a motion to approve the whole Legislative Article on second reading. Immediately there were requests for dividing the question. It was obvious that the strategy of the Chicago regulars was to delay action until the next day, so that overnight they might get their absentees back and then attempt to reverse the placement on the ballot of the single-member district idea and cumulative voting. Finally, late at night, the Committee of the Whole adjourned without finally approving the article.

When the group convened the next day, there was some feeling that the dilatory tactics of the Chicago regular Democrats had weakened their case. There were those in the chamber who had been in favor of cumulative voting during the previous day, but who now opposed it. The regulars had their strength up for the battle, however—Madison Brown was back, from Jamaica it was said, and Martin Tuchow was present, delaying a vacation trip to Florida. Rumor had it that he had gotten as far as the airport when the order to return to Springfield caught up with him. Richard Cooper and William Lennon were also back in the regular's fold, and it appeared that they might have enough strength to turn things around so far as cumulative voting was concerned. But when the crunch came, on a motion to reconsider, the margins for single-member districts (56 to 52) and against cumulative voting (45 to 57) were even greater than they had been the day before.[88] Apparently there was even greater certainty, with the second vote, that single-member districts belonged in the constitution package, with cumulative voting on separate submission.

Before the vote on final approval of the Legislative Article was taken, Paul Elward threatened dire results if the Committee of the Whole approved single-member districts for inclusion in the body of the constitution. His argument was that traditional arrangements should be left in, while anything new should be separately submitted. "I want to tell you," Elward scolded, "that this kind of system [single-member districts] is going to be anathema to the regular politicians . . . in both political parties."[89] The Committee seemed to accept his warning with equanimity. The professionals favored cumulative voting for the very reasons which made it a system not in the public interest.

Elward's threat had little effect, apparently, for on the motion to approve the article, the roll call went 74 to 30. The Chicago regulars were almost alone on the losing side, and during the roll call, as they explained their votes and vented their frustration, they figuratively cried like children. Just a few examples:

> MR. ARRIGO: . . . [if] I . . . vote yes, I would turn my back to the friendships and to the men that I have learned to admire and respect. And I may add, my respect and admiration for my [legislative] colleagues has grown to monumental proportions, especially since my service in the Constitutional Convention. . . .
>
> MR. ROSEWELL: This is a sad day. In my district we will elect three Democrats. I think it's a shame, I think it's a crime. . . .
>
> I am sorry, I am indeed sorry, it makes me feel very, very bad. . . .
>
> MR. PATCH: . . . though this (single-member districts) would be an advantage to me, to my people and to my district, especially my party, I have to vote no.[90]

The Chicago Democrats genuinely hated to see cumulative voting on separate submission with the appointment of judges. The two issues would then form a package, which the Chicago newspapers would gladly support, as would the Chicago independents. The regulars' rage was thus not over the single-member district idea itself, but because of the effect the ballot placement of its alternative might have on the electoral success of appointment for judges. They persisted in opposing separate submission of cumulative voting to the final second reading vote on the Legislative Article. They were not successful, however, and thus second reading ended, so far as the issue of cumulative voting was concerned, with only half the bargain struck by Chicago Democrats and certain downstate Republicans accomplished. The coalition had succeeded in getting election of judges in the constitutional package and appointment on separate submission, but as yet it had failed to do the same for cumulative voting and its alternative. Still, everyone knew the battle was not over and that third reading remained.

On the following day, John Alexander rose to offer in jest the proposal that a system of cumulative voting be introduced for electing members of the Chicago City Council. With a fine irony, he repeated all of the arguments which had been heard in behalf of cumulative voting. Each of them, he pointed out, was applicable to the Chicago situation. With tongue-in-cheek, he suggested that if single-member districts were approved for the General Assembly, there would be a number of Chicago Republicans turned out of legislative posts who would be naturals for serving on the City Council as minority representatives from three-member wards. This was turning the argument around with a vengeance, and the Chicago regulars were not amused. Apparently, what was good in Springfield was not necessarily good in Chicago.

Redistricting

In most respects there was little controversy at first reading over recommendations of the Legislative Committee. The matter of the effective date of legislation was troublesome and time consuming, but not highly divisive. The provision that amendments to the Legislative Article might be proposed by popular petition was challenged and narrowly escaped deletion. The only issue other than cumulative voting to become highly controversial, however, was that of how best to accomplish the periodic redrawing of legislative district lines. In the first round of action on redistricting, Odas Nicholson moved to delete the prohibition that district lines not cut across Chicago or Cook County boundaries. This was a highly partisan matter. The motion, if approved, would allow a given district to lie in part in Chicago and in part in the County, and this possibility seemed to make the County Republicans nervous. Lucy Reum (Oak Park) pointed out that suburban people feared ". . . that apportioners will join a substantial portion of suburban Cook County to Chicago, thereby denying this geographical section the representation to which it is justly entitled." Joseph Tecson (Riverside Township) predicted "bowling alley" districts which would stretch from within the city completely across the County. And ". . . the Republican Party . . . could get badly burned here," Jeffrey Ladd (Crystal Lake) added.[91] The amendment was debated at length and then approved in roll call 65 to 37.[92] The requirement of sets of districts, which would not cut city and county lines, seemed to be an impossibly artificial one, which would make realization of one person, one vote standards in redistricting very difficult.

With the process of periodic redistricting itself, the principal controversy was over the procedure to be followed in case the General Assembly could not agree. The history of the matter indicated that legislative agreement upon a new map of districts would often not be easy to accomplish. The organization Democrats favored arrangements which might end in the at-large election of all legislators, as had been the case for the House in 1964. They felt that, given the size of the vote in Chicago and the quality of discipline there, they could bring about overwhelming Democratic victory in any at-large election of legislators, as they had in '64. Republicans were much less confident that at-large election was a desirable alternative to redistricting by the Legislature.

After much debate and parliamentary maneuvering, there finally was agreement by a roll call vote of 61 to 41[93] upon a redistricting plan. It provided that if both the General Assembly and then a bipartisan commission should fail to redistrict on schedule, one person out of two named by the Supreme Court should be added by lot to the commission as a "tie breaker," and if the commission still should fail, the whole matter would go to the Supreme Court. Thus an at-large election would be avoided. During debate, the interesting conjecture was made that in 1963 the Democrats had resisted redistricting (the Democratic Governor had vetoed a redistricting act passed by both houses) in Legislature *and* Commission, hoping for an at-large election with the expectation that the Republicans would nominate Senator Goldwater for President, as they did, and that 1964 would thus be a Democratic year and they could sweep the House. This they did, winning two-thirds of the seats. In any case, it appeared that at-large election would not be as likely to occur again, if the scheme favored by the Committee of the Whole were finally adopted, as eventually it was.

The organization Democrats resisted abandonment of the at-large possibility, calling the "tie breaker" scheme a game of Russian roulette. Illustrative of their position were these remarks by Frank Stemberk:

> . . . if you want to go to a bingo system, if you want to go to a lottery system, if you want to settle our problems of government, not by agreement, not by the parties getting together, not by the will of the people being served, let's get a great big bingo card, set it up over there in the legislature, and every one of the issues that are difficult to settle, we'll just have a guy calling out the numbers.[94]

But that argument was not effective. The "tie breaker" idea prevailed at first reading and was not seiously challenged at second. It represented the last substantial controversy of the legislative article during first reading.

Getting It All Together: Third Reading

During the interval in August between second and third reading, when most delegates were at their homes, rumors to the effect that a determined effort would be made to reverse the positions of single-member districts and cumulative voting, placing the latter in the package and the former on separate submission, were heard about the State. This was disturbing to those who felt that the single-member district idea was the most significant reform of the entire document. To submit it separately would almost certainly be to lose it. For that reason others sought such action.

The first solid indication of a concerted campaign by the Chicago press in behalf of cumulative voting came on August 20 in an editorial in *Chicago Today*. It was full of error, both interpretive and factual, including the statements that the Convention "thoughtlessly threw out" cumulative voting (it didn't, of course; it discarded it only after careful thought and a series of votes on the matter) and that "normally" the voters had a choice among four candidates for the three representative positions from each district (they didn't, of course, nor had they had since at least the turn of the century). The editorial went on to suggest that single-member districts could result only in a House which would be heavily Republican (another error—witness the 12–12 division in 1970 of the State's single-member congressional districts, and the 29–29 division of its single-member Senate districts) and that if the single-member idea were left in the voters would flock to vote against the idea and thus defeat the Constitution (still another error, for referendum results later in the year showed that downstate, where the Chicago press and the Chicago regular Democratic organization were of less influence, the voters in fact preferred the single member idea to cumulative voting when the two were offered equally to them). The *Chicago Today* editorial was the first round in a carefully planned barrage that eventually was to include blasts in the leading Chicago and Springfield newspapers as well as statements by the Governor, the Mayor and Convention President Sam Witwer.

As delegates gathered again in Springfield on August 26, there was much discussion of the move to put cumulative voting back in the package. In response to a direct question, a consultant to the President, Dick Lockhart, replied that there was to be an effort to restore the status quo in that regard.[95] During the evening of the 26th, delegates Wayne Whalen, Betty Ann Keegan and Dawn Clark Netsch, among others, discussed possible strategies which might be employed in behalf of the single-member district idea. Already Whalen was struggling to develop the concept of equal separate submission for the alternatives, and in connection with that, of a similar arrangement for the alternatives of judicial election and appointment. As yet, no clear-cut plan for action had been developed.

On August 27, the *Sun-Times* delivered another round in the editorial barrage being laid down in the Chicago press in behalf of cumulative voting. It was less in error than the blast fired the previous week by *Chicago Today*, but still substantially faulty and thoroughly wrong-headed throughout. By this time, it was clear that the movement to reverse the positions of cumulative voting and single-member districts was a formidable one.

How To Elect Legislators? How To Choose Judges?

Third reading began on August 27, with consideration of recommendations from the Committee on Style, Drafting and Submission on matters of style and certain substantive changes, plus the Adoption and Transition Schedule, separate submission proposals and form of the ballot.[96] Throughout the explanation of stylistic changes, there was an undercurrent of criticism directed at Wayne Whalen, Chairman of the Committee, by the Chicago regular Democrats on the ground that matters of substance had also been changed. It almost seemed to be a prearranged attempt to harass Whalen to the point where his critical role in third reading would be impaired. Perhaps the regulars knew of his plan for equal separate submission of the alternatiges of the election and appointment of judges.

Delegates were keenly aware that changes could be introduced during third reading only with suspension of the rules, which required a simple majority of 59 votes. Consequently, when Mary Lee Leahy moved that the ban on discrimination in housing and employment on account of physical or mental handicap be moved from separate submission status into the bill of rights, some were amazed to hear the President declare it to be a proper amendment, requiring no suspension of the rules. It was a bad ruling, since substantive change was clearly called for.

Witwer was attempting, not too artfully, to set the stage for later action in moving cumulative voting into the constitutional package and single-member districts out. The Chicago regular Democrats supported him. Quickly, his ruling was appealed by William Sommerschield and Charles Shuman, both stout defenders of the single-member idea. ". . . When we move from one side of this imaginary line [between the package and separate submission] to the other side," Shuman pointed out, "we *are* making a substantive change. . . ."[97] The Convention voted 55 to 52, on roll call, to support the appeal.[98] This was a critical vote, for action of this kind without suspension of the rules would have facilitated all kinds of changes throughout third reading. As James Thompson observed, ". . . we could be here for a long, long time if we can move things around with less than fifty-nine votes, . . ."[99]

Review of the newspapers of the day emphasized the probability that the cumulative voting forces were moving in for the kill. On the previous day, the *Daily News* had joined the editorial chorus, and now the *Tribune* added its bit. Both repeated the traditional faulty arguments for cumulative voting, and both predicted voter wrath unless it were restored to the package. The *Illinois State Register* took a similar tack. In a news article in the *Register,* Charles Scolare flatly predicted that "The attempt [would] be made to include the cumulative voting section in the main body of the new constitution, and take the single-member district plan now in the proposed main text and submit it separately." The *Illinois State Journal* reported that Governor Ogilvie had come out in support of such action, joining President Witwer in that view. Apparently there was a careful plan to have all this appear in the newspapers at just that time.

On August 28, Coleman Mobley reported in the Lindsay-Schaub newspapers, which continued editorially to support single-member districts,[100] in refreshing contrast to the unanimity of the Chicago papers on the other side, that Mayor Daley was in accord with the Governor on the cumulative vote issue. Mobley wrote:

> That seems to spell the end for supporters of single-member districts. . . . Charles R. Young of Danville, a Republican, was seen in conference with Democratic leader Thomas G. Lyons in Chicago Thursday. Young was buttonholing delegates for tete-a-tetes throughout the day.
>
> He told newsmen that he was seeking votes to restore multimember districts (cumulative voting) to the main document. . . . He claimed at noon Thursday to have the necessary 59 votes to do it.[101]

At least one journalist wrote that disagreement over cumulative voting and other disputed matters might yet doom the Convention's work. Ken Watson headed his remarks in the *Illinois State Journal,* "Blowup Eyed in Con-Con." He reported that

> . . . some of the most knowledgeable Statehouse politicians would . . . be surprised if Con-Con concluded in smooth and friendly fashion. . . .
>
> There are several key issues which could throw the Convention into prolonged debate and deadlock (revenue, cumulative voting, choice of judges, and homerule). . . .
>
> Some students of Con-Con feel the ballot is going to end up so complicated and confusing the voters will reject it out of pure frustration. . . .
>
> Absenteeism has become an increasing problem in recent weeks [not so—113 answered roll call on the 27th, 115 on the 28th, and 114 on the 29th]. . . .
>
> A complete collapse of Con-Con . . . is a possibility which cannot be ruled out.[102]

When on August 28, the Convention turned again to the Legislative Article, Bernard Weisberg moved to defer consideration of it and the Judicial Article until the following day, and to take up the Executive and Local Government Articles instead. His purpose was to gain additional time for development of the idea of equal separate submission for the alternatives of single-member and multi-member legislative districts and election and appointment of judges. The Chicago regulars reacted typically as they sensed that someone might be trying to outmaneuver them and found enough allies to carry the vote decisively against any variation in the order of procedure. Thus the Convention took up next the Legislative Article.

After the approval of several minor changes, came the moment many had anticipated. Charles Young and Thomas Lyons moved a suspension of the rules in order to admit a motion to exchange the places of cumulative voting and single-member districts. The roll call vote on suspension was 67 to 34 with 10 passes.[103] This told all that one needed to know—the coalition for cumulative voting had the votes necessary to get the job done. From the array of affirmative votes it seemed likely that this majority had come about through a trade involving the branch banking question and the recently decided matter of choosing judges, as well as the issue at hand.

When the vote for suspension of rules was at 55, with a number of passes still standing, Samuel Martin (strong for a banking referendum) was seen to signal to Henry Hendren, much against branch banking, Helen Kinney, a leader in the fight for elected judges, and Stanley Klaus that the time had come for them to switch from "pass" to "yes." Hendren and Kenney ended up in the "yes" column, though Klaus did not. Apparently the supporters of cumulative voting, limitation of branch banking and elected judges had put together a winning coalition. Just what the payoff on the banking issue would be remained to be seen. It was clear what it would be on judges.

Then Lucy Reum moved the switch—cumulative voting to be in the package with single-member districts on separate submission. Her second came from Thomas Miller, and her cosponsors were an interesting assortment, Charles Young, Joseph Tecson, Harlan Rigney, Ted Borek, Mary Pappas and Thomas Lyons. The debate which followed was conducted on a high level and at length. Most of the speakers were opposed to the motion. Its proponents knew that they had the votes. Reum urged the delegates not to "unduly jeopardize the product over which we have labored hard and long,"[104] by retaining single-member districts in the main package, while William Sommerschield commented bitterly, "we have been sold down the river by individuals who find it more important to pass a constitution no matter what's in . . . [it] rather than [put] something in . . . [it] that is good for the people. . . ."[105] John Alexander expressed the opinion that ". . . the only significant institutional reform in the package was . . . single-member districts."[106]

Stanley Johnson was unhappy about this proposed surrender to the status quo and suggested that on the next day an editorial item might read "breakfast as usual on August 28. Eggs on the menu, very appropriate, for this was the day that courage flew the coop and Con-Con chickened out on legislative reform."[107] David Davis pointed out that with both the appointment of judges and single-member districts on separate submission, ". . . then we are in a position where Chicago can urge its voters to support the . . . package . . . and vote no on every separately submitted issue . . ." with the result that all such issues would lose.[108]

But no amount of argument could overcome the solid coalition in favor of cumulative voting. At last the vote, despite an effort by Dwight Friedrich and Wayne Whalen to adjourn, and the Reum amendment prevailed on roll call 60 to 41, with 13 answering "present" or "pass."[109] Nine Republicans and three Democrats had changed from their second reading positions to make this majority. Some of the "winners" in this vote seemed strangely saddened over its result. Mary Lee Leahy displayed that attitude and also heaped scorn on those who had reversed earlier positions, when she said:

> I have long understood why I do not consider myself a regular Democrat. I think now I understand why I could never be a Republican . . . they are just not tough enough.

> Tonight I should be happy because I favor cumulative voting, and . . . it's going in the package [but] . . . I am very sad. . . .[110]

Perhaps she realized that cumulative voting was contrary to the public good in the long run, and thus her sadness was over seeing the single-member idea lose, when it had seemed before so likely to prevail. Shortly after the vote was taken, the Convention adjourned, because the Witwers were entertaining the delegates at a reception and already the appointed hour was past. The President was understandably anxious to adjourn; and no effort was made to give final approval to the Legislative Article on third reading.

Before the session began the following day, a small group met with President Witwer in his office. The purpose of the visit was to inform the President that his callers were ready to abandon support of the whole document, if the two great reforms of appointment of judges and single-member districts were left on separate submission, where their chances of adoption would be slight. Witwer was inclined not to believe them and to doubt too that the League of Women Voters would reject the product for the same reason, though there was reason to believe that it might. This was obviously a critical moment in the course of the Convention, but Witwer seemed to take it lightly. It must have given him pause, however, to hear such able delegates as Stanley Johnson, Jeffrey Ladd, Charles Shuman and William Sommerschield announce that they had come to the end of the line so far as yielding to the status quo was concerned.

Then as the plenary session got underway, George Lewis moved to approve the Legislative Article on third and final reading. This might have been done the previous day, if the delegates had not been in some haste to adjourn in order to attend the Witwer's reception. Approval of the Lewis motion would for all practical purposes have locked up the whole Article against further change.

The roll call began. With the first responses—Alexander, "no," Anderson, "no;"—it was apparent that this was onc vote on final approval which was *not* to be a matter of form. As the call proceeded, a ripple of excitement spread over the chamber. Yesterday's switch of cumulative voting and single-member districts had been so professional, so cooly and competently done that it had been a trifle dull. But now the delegates appeared to be departing from the script, and interest mounted as the total of "no" and "pass" votes and failures to respond increased. Fifty-nine votes were needed for approval. The roll call concluded—Wilson, "no;" Woods, "no;" Wymore, "no;" Yordy, "yes;" Young, "no!"[111] Zeglis, "yes;" Witwer, "yes."

There were not 59 votes in favor of the motion, and at once a delaying action set in, before the vote was announced, with the hope that late arrivals would appear to swell the affirmative total. One of the delegates who sat in the back row and was a member of the Chicago regular organization, went flying out of the chamber, perhaps to round up all of the absentees he could find. The wife of one delegate, who was in her room at the State House Inn, told later that at about this time the paging system suddenly came alive, calling over and over for certain delegates.

On the Convention floor, the request was to poll the absentees, and this was done, slowly. An explanation of votes began and continued at length. Delay was the obvious goal, and the explanations became blatantly irrelevant. Suddenly Samuel Martin, who had voted on the affirmative side, rose to announce his disgust with such proceedings and changed his vote to "pass." This made it apparent to advocates of the motion that further delay might be counter-productive. Explanations and other stalling tactics ended, and at last the totals were announced—yes, 53; no, 24; and pass, 23.[112] The motion to approve the Legislative Article had failed. The meaning of this action was clear—47 who had voted "no" or "pass" had no intention of approving the Legislative Article as it stood.

But 47 was far from a majority. What kept the affirmative side from obtaining the necessary votes? The reason was plain. A number of delegates were not in their seats, and of special significance, due to their strong third reading stance in favor of cumulative voting and of the Article as amended, was the absence of eight of the Chicago regulars. Six of their votes would have given the motion to approve the necessary majority. And where were the errant eight? Who knows? Perhaps they had celebrated the previous day's victory too well, after a start at the Witwer reception, and were still in their beds when the vote was taken. They hardly could have anticipated that their amateur opponents would do so professional a thing as refusing to vote the formality of approving the Legislative Article. But so they had, and now the whole issue was again up for debate instead of being safely locked away, it might have been, had every delegate been present.

As a consequence, the Legislative Article was left lying on the table, and the Convention went on to the Executive. With only minor changes it was approved with 100 votes. By then the absentees of earlier in the morning were on hand, and Thomas Lyons and Paul Elward moved to take Article IV from the table. There was an air of "now we will set this mischief straight" in the Chamber. And it appeared that the Article might be approved, for the vote to take it from the table passed on roll call 75 to 16, with 13 voting pass or present.[113] Elward and Harold Nudelman moved to approve, and the professionals were in full gear, grinding away at their task.

Then Wayne Whalen rose to move a suspension of the rules. His purpose was to amend both the Legislative *and* Judicial Articles in order to put *both* cumulative voting and single-member districts, from the one, and *both* election and appointment of judges, from the other, *equally* on separate submission, with neither alternative in either case in the package. This was the compromise which Whalen had been struggling to perfect for several days. Elward objected on the ground the Whalen motion was out of order. The chair ruled it was not. Elward requested a division of the motion. Agreed. Arthur Lennon asserted that the Whalen motion was out of order. Again the chair held that it was not. Elward requested that the Whalen motion be submitted in writing, and the Convention recessed for 20 minutes to allow that to be done. Those who had thought they had elected judges and cumulative voting safely locked away, seemed to be in shock.

The brief recess ended, and Whalen's motion was offered in writing. Elward requested a further division as to rules 43 and 49, which were to be suspended if the motion passed. Agreed. Lennon requested still a different further division, but it was ruled out of order. He appealed and the appeal lost. This was all just ''parliamentary gimmickery,'' as Whalen put it, and finally when the Convention voted on his motion as to rule 49, it carried on roll call 68 to 39, with three passing. On suspended rule 43, the vote was 62 to 46, with three passing.[114]

The drama continued to unfold after a brief break for lunch. Betty Ann Keegan, with Wayne Whalen and Lewis Wilson as cosponsors and Clifford Downen to second, moved that, for both the Legislative and Judicial Articles, the two major alternatives be put out equally on separate submission, with the one in each case receiving a majority of the vote to become a part of the constitution. If neither alternative in either case should be approved by the electors, then the applicable provisions of the 1870 Constitution should remain in effect. That seemed to some to be as fair and equitable an arrangement as could be made, giving everyone an equal run for his money, but much consternation followed. A great sotrm of objection was raised, centering among the Chicago regular Democrats. It appeared that there was a coalition, one more by instinct at this stage than by design, of Cook Countians and downstaters of both parties plus Chicago independents, which was large enough, if it should hang together, to put the Keegan amendment through. The chair seemed to appreciate the fairness of the proposal, whether it was President Witwer or Vice President Smith presiding.

The rest of the day was consumed in debate of the Keegan motion. Helen Kinney moved an amendment, which would have provided explicitly that an item on separate submission would have to receive a majority of all voting in the election, in order to be adopted. That, of course, would have established the maximum difficulty for approval on separate submission, and if the Keegan proposal were adopted, it would make it more likely that the ''applicable provisions'' of the 1870 Constitution (election of judges and cumulative voting) would continue in effect, even if the 1970 Constitution were approved.

A long and tedious discussion followed. At one point, Lewis Wilson remarked, ''in forty years in the practice of law I have never seen such a persistent and consistent effort to confuse what is a very simple issue. . . . The question is whether we should write in here our construction of what the 1870 Constitution requires in the way of a majority, or whether we should not.''[115] Apparently some felt that the Convention should. The Kinney amendment was divided, and the first part was beaten 44 to 62.[116] The coalition was holding. The other parts then went down on division. Arthur Lennon moved to delete the parts of the Keegan motion which referred to the Judicial Article and was ruled out of order. He appealed and was beaten on roll call, 46 to 59.[117] As a victory for the Keegan amendment came nearer, there was much consternation among the Chicago regular Democrats and their allies. Finally, in the vote on the Keegan motion in roll call, it was approved 70 to 39.[118]

It is quite possible that this was the crucial day of the Convention. Earlier, the Convention had appeared to be ready to approve the Legislative Article with cumulative voting in and single-member districts out. If that had been accomplished (and only a quirk of fate prevented it), it might later have been impossible to reverse that action and to alter the arrangements of the Judicial Article previously agreed to on second reading. And if that combination of circumstances had developed, some important elements of support of the final product might have been permanently forfeited. By day's end, the Convention had reached a basic compromise which kept all important elements in a supportive stance, so far as the new basic document was concerned.[119]

The day that followed saw much delay on the part of those who opposed equal separate submission for the principal alternatives of the Legislative and Judicial Articles. Amendments which had the purpose of dividing the dominant coalition were offered, but none was approved. One had come very close, a proposal by Charles Young for appointment of judges by the Governor with the advice and consent of the Senate, rather than following nomination by a Judicial Nominating Commission. Fifty-eight delegates voted to suspend the rules in order to consider that proposition, only one short of the necessary majority.

The Judicial Article was taken up while further wording relating to the Legislative was being prepared. Frank Dove moved with 63 cosponsors that the requirement of a vote of ⅔ to retain a judge running on his record for re-election and without an opponent be reduced to ⅗. The Convention voted 62 to 38 to suspend the rules. Then the Dove motion was approved 67 to 24. After much more delay, in a critical roll call the Judicial Article, as amended, was approved 71 to 35.[120] That vote indicated that the coalition was holding fast. Another decisive moment in the development of a new constitution had come and gone.

"Bankers Last Stand"

After consideration of other matters, on August 31, it became clear what the payoff was for the support which the opponents of branch banking had given to the election of judges and cumulative voting. Ralph Dunn moved suspension of the rules so that an additional section of the General Provisions Article might be considered. Suspension was approved with votes to spare. Dunn offered his motion, with regular Democrat Leonard Miska seconding, to add the provision that branch banking could be authorized only by a three-fifths vote on the question in each house of the General Assembly or a majority of the members elected, whichever was greater. This was no deterrent at all to authorization of branch banking, for it would require an extraordinary ''majority'' so thin as to be almost non-existent. To pass *any* legislation, of course, required a majority of all members elected in each house. And often that figure would be greater than three-fifths of those voting on the question. For example, with 50 of the 59 senators voting, three-fifths would be 30, precisely the same vote required for passing any act. The thinness of this provision was recognized at once, as Dwight Friedrich called attention to it. Dunn agreed that this was

> . . . a watered down version, I admit Mr. Friedrich.
>
> MR. FRIEDRICH: . . . It certainly is. I think the puppy licked you on this one. (Laughter)
>
> MR. DUNN: Thank you. I have been licked so much during this Convention, I am beginning to feel right at home. Different colored puppies every once in a while, though, or different spots on them. . . .[121]

Later Ronald Smith stressed the same point:

> I suppose you could characterize this as a ''just in case'' provision. Just in case anybody asks, ''Did you do anything for banks,'' you can point to it. It isn't worth anything. It is kind of like nipples on a man—just in case. (Laughter)[122]

After long discussion the Dunn motion was approved in roll call, 68 to 19, with 20 passing.[123]

Why such a meaningless provision? A glance at the record reveals the difference between earlier votes on limiting branch banking and this one. Here the Chicago regulars were in favor as they were not before. This was the ''payoff'' for part of the support which they received for the election of judges and cumulative voting. And if those two arrangements had been safely in the package and their alternatives out on separate submission, the quid pro quo perhaps would have been more substantial, such as a requirement of approval by three-fifths of all members for any authorization of branch banking. But having received less than the bargain called for, the Chicago regulars delivered less. ''If you play with the puppy,'' as James Kemp earlier had remarked to Ralph Dunn, ''he'll lick your face.''

Before adjournment, Leonard Foster got in a parting shot at the Chicago blacks who had voted ''yes'' on the branch banking provision. Foster had repeatedly stressed the importance of branching in providing banking services to black communities. Now he said,

> When I walk through my neighborhood and your neighborhoods, when I look at the vacant land where there has been no new construction for the last ten or fifteen years, and when I look at people in raggedy old $9,000 houses they paid $18,000 on for up to 34 percent interest on contract because they couldn't get a mortgage . . . and you ride by those houses in your Cadillacs and Buicks, and you only go into them on the day before an election—don't come down to this hall and talk about the pulse of the people, and for God's sake don't dare talk about the little people, because you haven't seen them.[124]

A moment later Madison Brown rose to speak:

> THE PRESIDENT: For what purpose do you rise, Mr. Brown?
>
> MR. BROWN: I rise on a point of personal privilege. I'm a Cadillac driver. (Applause)[125]

With that the Convention recessed for the day.

Defining the Majority: A Clever Strategy Which Failed

It was late on the following day when Dawn Clark Netsch moved approval of the provision, which would become effective if neither of the separately submitted alternatives for the Legislative and Judicial Articles received majority approval. These were the applicable provisions of the constitution of 1870'' as Netsch had put them in coherent constitutional language. Thomas McCracken moved to specify that approval of separately submitted items could be only by a majority of those voting in the referendum, as distinguished from a majority of those voting on the question of the separately submitted item itself, in each case. McCracken's motion was ruled out of order as repetitive of one rejected earlier. He appealed the ruling and was beaten on roll call 31 to 65.[126] The coalition which had come together only days before was holding.

The question of the majority to be required to carry separate submission items meant a great deal to the Chicago regulars. They would have liked nothing better than to be able to tell their followers to ignore the legislative and judicial alternatives on separate submission and vote yes on the package. That would have insured the defeat of both alternatives in each case, were a majority of all voting in the referendum to be required to carry such an item. Then it would be the applicable provisions of the 1870 Constitution which would have continued in force, a result which would have greatly pleased the Chicago regulars, wedded as they were to the status quo. But they could not afford to instruct their troops to ignore the separately submitted items so long as there was the possibility that only a majority of those voting on the issue was required, for that would mean they would be conceding defeat on the all-important question of selecting judges. Thus they felt obliged to press hard to get the Convention to declare its interpretation to be in favor of the larger majority. This no rational person, interested in carrying either alternative of the legislative and judicial pairs, would have consented to do.

Finally, the Convention voted on the all important Netsch proposal. It carried in roll call 69 to 27.[127] Here the Chicago regulars held off completely, anxious to deny the sections, which they opposed, the necessary 59 votes. But enough others were there to see them through. The regulars' strategy of nine months to delay until salaries had run out and enough of the amateurs had gone home to allow them to have their way, at last had failed. After the vote there seemed to be a general lessening of tension, as if the die finally were cast. Only mechanical details such as the form of the ballot remained to be decided. However, these took much time, and it was 3:25 a.m. when adjournment finally came. The substantive work of the Convention had ended.

The Referendum Vote

As the referendum campaign went into December, the media gave more and more attention to the substance of the proposed constitution, and especially to the four issues which were to be separately submitted. As the campaign went on, the wisdom of separate submission became more apparent. It served to defuse much controversy so far as the main body of the document was concerned. In addition, disagreement over the method of selecting judges, which was in some measure a struggle between the parties, or at least between their leaderships—there was much crossing over on this issue—had the effect of greatly increasing popular interest. Both sides found it imperative to turn out their troops in the greatest possible numbers in order not to be beaten at the polls—and neither could risk opposing the package, for fear the other would favor it and thus have its preference prevail. To a lesser extent the same was true of the struggle over single- and multi-member legislative districts. The other two items on separate submission—the 18 year old vote and the death penalty—did not share this characteristic, but the fact that each *was* separate kept opposition to the entire package from compounding.

The Basic Constitutional Package

Referendum vote totals revealed some interesting insights into the distribution around the State of opinion on the basic constitution and the separately submitted items, as well. First let us look at the vote on the "package," in the State as a whole, in Cook County, and downstate, as shown in Table 3-1. Casual inspection of these vote totals indicates that while the affirmative margin in the whole State was narrow (55.6% of all ballots cast showed affirmative votes), in Cook County it was better than 2 to 1. In the other 101 counties together (downstate) only 44.9% of those who went to the polls voted yes. Thus, it is clear that, as expected, it was Cook County which held the key to the adoption of a new constitution. The affirmative percent in Cook was a full 20 points above that of downstate, with the state-wide total falling midway between the two extremes. As one analyst put it, ". . . the overwhelming support by Cook County voters carried the election in an otherwise lukewarm to negative environment. Downstate could not withstand the 350,000 Cook County plurality."[129]

TABLE 3-1
The Vote on the Basic Package[128]

	Yes	No	Totals
Statewide	1,122,425	838,168	1,960,593
	(55.6%)	(41.5%)	(97.1%)
Cook County	696,026	332,242	1,028,268
	(65.1%)	(31.1*)	(96.2%)
Downstate	426,399	505,926	932,325
	(44.9%)	(53.5%)	(98.2%)

The main package carried in only 30 of the State's 102 counties, including Cook. However, the 30 contained more than 75% of the people of the State. Many of the earlier patterns of voting on questions of constitutional change were repeated in this referendum. Most of the counties which had traditionally been opposed to change did not approve the proposed constitution as they had not approved the Convention call two years earlier. Jackson County was one of the few exceptions to this rule. Although it had been strongly opposed to constitutional change in 15 referenda from 1950 to 1966, it responded affirmatively—65.1%—in 1970 as it had done on the question of the Convention call in 1968. Union County, just to the south of Jackson, also returned an affirmative majority—51.8%. No other counties in the southern third of the State did so, except Crawford—60.9%, Edwards—65.9%, and Wabash—65.9%. These were in delegate Henry Hendren's home grounds, especially the latter two counties, which responded at precisely the same level to his attention. These three are very similar counties, in population as well as social and economic characteristics. Edwards and Wabash are adjacent and in fact once were one county. That they went so strongly for the proposed new Constitution is evidence of Hendren's influence, for other rural counties of southern Illinois behaved quite differently. The result in Crawford was probably due in part to its Mayor, Carl Zimmerman, then newly elected president of the Illinois Municipal League.

And what about the rest of the State in terms of the vote on the central constitutional package? Cook, of course, made the difference. With its 60 delegates, there is no point in attempting to identify those supportive of the new document. But its level of approval, while high—it was tied with Jackson at 65.1%—was exceeded not only by Edwards and Wabash, but also by the affirmative vote in Morgan County—70.6%! What was there about Morgan which was so different? Intuition would say that a long liberal tradition going back before the Civil War, its role as an educational center, the fact that it had an active chapter of the League of Women Voters and other active civic groups, and that it was the home of delegate William Fay, were the factors which allowed it to lead the State in support of the new Constitution. This analysis was endorsed by a person who was very much involved in the Morgan County campaign. But she added, "Bill was in Europe when we voted equally well in '68, so perhaps his presence in '70 wasn't a critical factor after all." It is probable that Bill Fay made a great difference in both campaigns, even from a European base!

Gross inspection indicates that similar counties returned similar affirmative votes for the new Constitution. In fact the persistence of certain characteristics across county lines is impressive. The two counties which in addition to Jackson are the location of large universities—Champaign and DeKalb—voted affirmatively almost exactly at the same level as did Jackson. With Jackson at 65.1%, DeKalb was at 64.5 and Champaign at 63.9. Thus this writer's pride in Jackson's performance was tempered by the thought that perhaps his efforts had not made much difference, that it was the nature of the county which was determinative. Still, Stanley Johnson had been busy in DeKalb, and Henry Green in Champaign, so perhaps active support, such as this writer had tried to provide in Jackson, did make a difference as well.

While state-wide election returns are reported by county and not by city—except for Chicago—it is possible to learn of city totals. One study of five university towns, and for each one a somewhat similar community located nearby, showed that Carbondale returned an "amazing" vote of 83% for the new Constitution. The other university communities and their vote levels were DeKalb, 75%, Champaign-Urbana and Bloomington-Normal, each at 67%, and Charleston, 51%. The writer was pleased that Carbondale was substantially in the lead in this group. Many months of hard work and dozens of public personal and radio appearances seemed to have paid off.[130]

It is interesting to note the differences in voting behavior exhibited by the university communities and in each case the nearby non-university community. For Carbondale in Jackson County and Marion in adjoining Williamson, the support levels were 83 and 54% respectively. For Champaign-Urbana and Decatur they were 67 and 53%; for Bloomington-Normal and Kankakee 67 and 34%; for Charleston and Mattoon 51 and 31%; and for DeKalb and Ottawa, 75 and 47%.[131] Apparently the cultural differences between university and other communities did make a great difference in this regard.

Carroll County, at a 63% level of support, was another like Edwards and Wabash which seemed to be deviant in its voting behavior. It was a rural county but didn't behave as most rural counties did. In the period 1950–66 Carroll had a record of support for constitutional change which placed it among the top ten counties in the State in that regard. It was the seat of Shimer College; and in the district represented in the Convention by Harlan Rigney and Wayne Whalen. Perhaps those factors made the difference. Beyond Carroll County in the ranking of affirmative votes we can generalize that it was the suburban collar counties, large downstate industrial counties not dominated by the AFL-CIO, and large university counties which returned maximum support for the new Constitution. Thus, adjoining Peoria and Tazewell counties, seat of Caterpillar with its United Auto Worker affiliation, performed almost identically at 61.3 and 61.4%, respectively. We cannot overlook the influence of delegates David Connor and John Parkhurst in Peoria and Clarence Yordy and William Fogal in Tazewell, each a strong supporter of the new document. McLean County, with Illinois State University and delegates David Davis and Paul Mathias, followed close after at 59.6%.

Then after McLean came a group of collar counties with almost identical performances—Kane, 57.5%; McHenry, 57.3%; Lake, 56.5%; and DuPage, 54.3%. Apparently the similar characteristics of these counties resulted in a similar vote. Also there were in these counties such staunch supporters of the new document as John Wenum and Mary Pappas in Lake, Jeannette Mullen and Jeffrey Ladd in McHenry and Lake; Stanley Johnson and Maxine Wymore in McHenry and Kane; and William Sommerschield, Helen Kinney, James Brannen, Betty Howard and Anthony Peccarelli in DuPage and Kane. Rock Island County ranked along with the collar counties, at 56.1% affirmative. Like them it was populous and suburban, and it had strong supporters for the new Constitution in William Armstrong and Lewis Wilson. It is worth noting that the remaining collar county adjoining Cook, Will County, fell far below its class with an affirmative vote of 44.8%. Perhaps the fact that it was more industrial, with a consequent greater degree of AFL-CIO influence, is explanatory. Each of these counties mentioned above performed in the 1970 referendum in a way consistent with its performance in regard to constitutional change in the period 1950–66, and in the Convention call referendum in 1968.[132]

Aggregate voting data by county tell us nothing about voting behavior *within* counties, and in the case of Cook the internal patterns are important. Chicago wards voting most strongly for the package were the "black" 4th, 24th, 27th, and 29th, and the North Side 49th and 50th in the district represented in the Convention by Peter Tomei and Paul Elward. The affirmative vote for the package was better than two to one in 34 of the City's 50 wards. In only two was the decision negative—the 25th and the 32nd. These were essentially low income and blue collar wards, and the AFL-CIO influence was probably significant. Generally opposition in Chicago seemed to center in such low income and blue collar neighborhoods. There seemed to be a meaningful correlation between opposition to the package and support for George Wallace in the 1968 presidential election. In suburban Cook County support for the package was strongest in the north and less in the more industrial south and west. As in the City, County areas favoring Wallace in 1968 tended to be opposed to the proposed Constitution.[133]

What, one might ask, were the characteristics of the downstate counties voting most negatively in the 1970 referendum, so far as the central constitutional package was concerned? Generally they were counties influenced by delegates who were neutral or negative, or they were industrial, or rural, or in the southern half of the State, or exhibited any combination of those characteristics. Thus the industrial southern counties of Madison and St. Clair yielded only 21.6 and 18.4% affirmative votes. AFL-CIO influence there was undoubtedly important. Elsewhere rurality seemed to be the compelling factor: Bond, 20%; Clinton, 15.3%; and Montgomery, 12.5% (these three rural counties were in delegate Dwight Friedrich's district); Cumberland, 19%; Hamilton, 18.6%; Hardin, 13.6%; Jefferson, 15.4%; Macoupin, 15% (John Alexander's home county); Perry, 25.9%; and Wayne, 20.4%. Sentiment in the rural portion of the State simply was not favorable to constitutional change, as had been the case for many years.

Cumulative Voting Vs. Single-Member Districts

When we turn from the vote on the package to the questions which were separately submitted, we find voting patterns which are quite different. As JoAnna Watson observed, among the separate submission items

> most striking was the support, measured in terms of number of counties, for reform [she intended no normative judgment by use of the word reform] of the selection of representatives to lower house. . . . Option 1-B, single-member districts for state representatives, a complete reversal of the cumulative voting, multi-member district formula (Option 1-A), was approved at this election by seventy-six Illinois counties.[134]

This was a startling reversal of form, in comparison to voting on the package, and also in regard to traditional attitudes toward constitutional change, including change in the Legislature. The vote on this question by area is shown in Table 3-2.

TABLE 3-2
The Vote on Option 1
(Legislative Districts)[135]

	1-A (multi-member)	1-B (single-member)	Totals
State-wide	1,031,241	794,909	1,826,150
	(51.1%)	(39.4%)	(90.5%)
Cook County	630,920	349,792	980,712
	(59%)	(32.7%)	(91.7%)
Downstate	400,321	445,117	845,438
	(42.2%)	(46.9%)	(89.7%)

Here we see that the multi-member plan received just over half of the total vote cast in the referendum, state-wide, but substantially more than did single-member districts. Cook County favored the traditional arrangement almost two-to-one, but downstate the preference was for the innovation. This behavior seems to reverse the traditional roles of the two regions in voting upon questions of constitutional change. Counties downstate in which single-member districts received over 50% of the total vote were: Peoria, 63.9%; Tazewell, 62.8%; DeKalb, 62.4%; Woodford, 57.1%; Marion and Marshall, each at 56.4%; Edwards, 55.5%; McLean, 55.2%; Morgan, 54.1%; Jackson, 54.1%; Wabash, 53.6%; Fulton, 52.5%; Lee, 52.7%; Henderson, 52.5%; Stark, 52%; Kendall, 51.6%; Champaign, 51.5%; Jo Daviess and Kane, each at 51.4%; Stephenson, 50.7%; and Macon and McHenry, each at 50.2%. Thus the greatest support for single-member districts came from the large industrial (UAW) counties, certain collar counties and certain rural counties. A mixed bag, this; and it is evident that another variable or other variables—probably including delegate influence—was operative. In addition to Cook, the counties giving greatest support to multi-member districts were Crawford, 53.9%; Lake, 52%; and Will, Vermilion and Warren, all at 49.7%. Again a mixed bag, with two collar counties, one urban and two tending to be rural. Again delegate or legislator influence is probable, especially in Vermilion, delegate Charles Young's county.

It is remarkable that the single-member district idea did as well as it did. Clearly the margin of defeat was in Cook County. There the Democratic organization, the four major newspapers, and the IVI were all for multi-member districts. If only the Chicago newspapers, or the Republican leadership, or the IVI, or any combination thereof, could have supported single-member districts, this significant reform might have been achieved. And it was one over which Chicago Democrats probably would not have abandoned the basic package, as they might have in their desire to avoid the appointment of judges.

The view that the editorial support of the Chicago newspapers, or Republican or IVI support, might have turned the trick for single-member districts is supportable because of the vote on the second separate submission item, the question of the manner of the selection of judges.

Selection of Judges: Fortuitous Victory for the Regulars

This issue was presented on the ballot as Options 2-A and 2-B, respectively for election and appointment. This was the question which is generally credited with bringing out a relatively sizable vote in Cook County. It tended there to be a partisan issue, and in addition there was an ad hoc Committee for Merit Selection which adopted a precinct style organization in order to advance the cause of appointment. The Cook County Democratic organization put major emphasis on election as evidenced by a brochure which its precinct workers circulated. It stressed retaining election of judges and only on page three did it get around to recommending a "yes" vote on the whole package.[136]

In spite of the major effort which Cook County Democrats made in behalf of the election of judges, they lost the County to the proponents of appointment. The state-wide and regional votes on this issue are shown in Table 3-3. It is apparent that in this matter the usual domination of the electoral process in Cook County by the Democratic organization did not apply. The combination of Republican effort in the County, the work of a

TABLE 3-3
The Vote on Option 2 (selection of judges)[138]

	2-A (Election)	2-B (Appointment)	Totals
State-wide	1,013,559	867,230	1,880,789
	(50.2%)	(43%)	(93.2%)
Cook County	466,217	535,034	1,001,251
	(43.6%)	(50.1%)	(93.7%)
Downstate	547,342	332,196	879,538
	(57.7%)	(35%)	(92.7%)

Committee for Merit Selection which utilized portions of the Cook and collar county organization which had worked for the election of Adlai Stevenson in November,[137] and the editorial support of the leading Chicago newspapers, was sufficient to gain the advantage for the appointment of judges.

Of course, the state of public opinion when the campaign began was also an important variable. It has been suggested that the highly political nature of elected judges was more evident in Cook County than downstate. Thus downstate voters were more willing to continue to elect judges. It is paradoxical that it was Republican downstate which carried the day for election of judges, when appointment would have done so much to reduce the power of the Cook County Democratic organization and thus Democratic power in the State generally.

In all, seven counties preferred judicial appointment—Cook, five collar counties—Lake, DuPage, McHenry, Kane and DeKalb—and downstate McLean. In the rest, voting ran heavily against appointment and for election. The preference for election was essentially rural, as is evidenced by the list of counties returning the greatest proportion for that option: Marion, 79.7%; Wayne, 77%; Montgomery, 75.9%; White, 75.7%; Jasper, 74.5%; Vermilion, 74.1%; Clay, 74%; Union, 73.7%; and Alexander, 73.5%. Aside from the seven counties where appointment was preferred, strongest support for that option was found in Champaign, 45.8%; Stephenson, 43.7%; Will, 41.1%; Peoria, 40.9%; Rock Island, 40.4%; and Jo Daviess, 40%. Thus it appears that support for appointment, downstate as well as in Cook and its suburban ring, was found in university counties and in counties that were more urban than rural.

Constitutional Politics: A Summary

In the pages above we have traced the resolution of the crucial issues of the Executive, Legislative and Judicial Articles in the Sixth Illinois Constitutional Convention. In summary of the core of the matter:

On first reading the group favoring the appointment of judges—a group comprising the independent Democrats of Chicago, many of the suburban Republicans and more idealistic downstaters of both parties—was able to prevail by a narrow margin. In regard to the issue of the plan for election of representatives, it was the downstate reformers and the Chicago regular Democrats who joined forces to throw out cumulative voting and install the single-member district plan it its place. The Chicago independents wished to retain cumulative voting because they could use it from time to time to beat the organization, and the regular Democrats were willing to let it go for that very reason. At this stage the Convention was firmly against any constitutional prohibition of branch banking, with the regular Democrats joining in that position.

Before second reading, however, the Chicago regular Democrats realized that election of judges was genuinely threatened. Therefore they cast about for votes which could be traded. They didn't feel strongly about cumulative voting—in fact, they had mixed feelings about it—so they were quite willing to give up their anti-cumulative voting stance of first reading in order to gain votes for the election of judges. Thus, on second reading there was a carefully designed move to replace the first reading vote—for appointment of supreme court and appellate judges and separate submission of the question of appointment at the circuit level—with the specification of election at all levels and appointment to be separately submitted. The move succeeded, but the quid pro quo was not fully deliverable, and instead of reversing positions of cumulative voting and single-member districts, the best the coalition could do on second reading was to put cumulative voting on separate submission. Thus as second reading ended, it was election of judges in, appointment on separate submission; and single-member districts in, cumulative voting on separate submission. Still the Convention was resolved not to continue any constitutional impediment to branch banking.

The Chicago regular Democrats were very uneasy about the situation as it stood prior to third reading. True, election of judges was in, as they felt it must be, but on separate submission were appointment of judges *and* cumulative voting, each an arrangement favored by the Chicago press, the independent Democrats, and a number of other influential persons and organizations. Indeed, the very bargain which put election of judges in the package compelled the regular Democrats themselves to support cumulative voting on separate submission in the forthcoming referendum. Thus they faced the difficulty of attempting to tell their followers to vote "yes" on one separately submitted item, "no" on another, and how to tell the two apart. They also faced the danger of the two separate items reinforcing one another to the point where both might carry, giving them cumulative voting, which they did not feel strongly about in any case, and denying them the election of judges, which they cared very much about, indeed. What were the poor regular Democrats to do?

What they did was to look about before third reading and find another trade. The proponents of branch banking limitation were the logical target. They were brought into the coalition and, with third reading, the regulars systematically orchestrated the switch on cumulative voting and single-member districts. At last they had the arrangement of alternatives as they wished it to be—election of judges and cumulative voting in the package and their alternatives on separate submission. Thus the regulars could instruct their troops to vote "yes" on the package and "no" on everything else. They also did not have to risk the mutual reinforcement of separately submitted items both supported strongly by the press. The status quo was in the saddle and the finish line loomed just ahead.

But by now one new hazard had appeared. With the switch on cumulative voting, the reformers had taken all they could and more. They made it known that if it was to be the traditional arrangements for selecting judges and representatives, they were bowing out. The new constitution would have to win approval without their support, and even against their opposition. Few seemed to take their threat seriously, yet this writer at least, who was one of the disaffected, believes that a crisis had been reached and the whole document was in danger of going down the drain. The critical moment of the Convention was at hand.

The crisis was overcome by means of a combination of good luck, creative thinking, and much hard work. Sheer chance delayed final third reading approval of the Legislative Article long enough to allow development of the concept of *equal separate submission* of the principal alternatives for choosing judges and representatives. The Chicago regular Democrats resisted stoutly, but enough delegates felt that equal separate submission was fair to all sides to cause it to be adopted.

Equal separate submission kept all significant factions in postures of support for the proposed constitution. The Chicago regular Democrats were "hooked" by classification and home rule. They could not afford to ignore the separately submitted items for fear of losing the election of judges. Independent Democrats and progressive Republicans were committed to the many improvements which they saw in the package, as well as to various alternatives on separate submission. Thus maximum strength was brought to the campaign for approval of the proposed document.

Emerging Issues and Future Research Needs

It is interesting to note that the primary issues of the Sixth Illinois Constitutional Convention—the selection of judges, cumulative voting and single member districts, and replacement of the personal property tax—are just as timely in 1979 and '80 as they were ten years earlier. They continue to be primary issues of Illinois politics.

The question of how best to select judges in the Illinois context has not received adequate research attention. There are many opinions about the matter, but very few of them are based upon objective evidence having to do with the quality of judges chosen and their performance upon the bench.

The effects of cumulative voting in Illinois have been far too little studied. The extent of competition for House seats with a cumulative voting system needs attention, as does the effect of the system in alienating candidates from a given political party who are in a sense fishing in the same partisan pool for cumulated votes.

Elimination of the personal property tax and an appropriate substitute therefor is a controversial matter as deliberations of the Illinois General Assembly in 1979 indicated. This issue is part of the whole question of the proper structure of the system for State and local revenue in Illinois. This system must be viewed as a whole.

In the coming decade, some attention should be paid to the success of constitutional changes introduced in 1970 and remaining constitutional defects. No later than 1988, the voters of the State will again be offered the question, "Should a Convention be called?" and a sound scholarly foundation should in the intervening years be laid so that the public will have assistance in responding to that question.

NOTES

[1]News release, Attorney General William J. Scott address to the Convention, p. 5.

[2]*Record of Proceedings,* January 7, 1970, p. 149.

[3]*Kenney Diary* (Committee of the Whole), January 14, 1970, p. 15.

[4]*Journal of the Sixth Illinois Constitutional Convention,* January 14, 1970, p. 8. Due to separate election of the two officers, Governor Ogilvie and Lieutenant Governor Simon were of different political parties. This was a situation which might have occurred at any time. It did not, as a result of election, until 1968.

[5]*Record of Proceedings,* January 14, 1970, p. 217. In spite of his earnestness, Lieutenant Governor Simon showed his capacity for the humorous response when in taking questions he heard Victor Arrigo state:

> I think you ought to make . . . clear that by action of the General Assembly the name is no longer ombudsman but its proper name, Tribune of the People. (The Lieutenant Governor had been serving unofficially as ombudsman.)
>
> MR. SIMON: With my political affiliation, "tribune" doesn't seem like quite the right word.

[6]*Journal,* January 14, 1970, pp. 13–17. The fact that the person then Treasurer, Adlai Stevenson, was constitutionally ineligible to run for reelection may have made it easier for his fellow Democrat to recommend abolition of the Treasurer's office. State officials wishing to run again for the offices they held seemed to find it difficult to recommend appointment as a means of filling other state offices occupied by incumbents who were also interested in continuing. Thus a mutual "herding together" occurred, with reinforcement of mutual points-of-view. In contrast, after Ray Page, Superintendent of Public Instruction, let it be known that he felt his office should be an appointive one, everyone seemed to be in agreement with him.

[7]*Record of Proceedings,* January 14, 1970, p. 220.

[8]*Journal,* January 20, 1970, pp. 24–25.

[9]*Ibid.,* pp. 29–30.

[10]*Record of Proceedings,* January 20, 1970, p. 238. Events following Powell's death several months later, including the discovery of three-quarters of a million dollars in cash and other negotiables in his hotel room, made it clear that he did indeed follow that motto.

[11]*Journal,* January 21, 1970, p.7.

[12]*Ibid.,* p. 15.

[13]The League of Women Voters of Illinois, for example. In a letter to delegates dated May 26 and signed by its President, Mary Helen Robertson, the League expressed general satisfaction with the proposed Executive Article, but would have preferred a shorter executive ballot, especially by removing from it the treasurer and comptroller.

[14]*Journal,* May 26, 1970, p. 8.

[15]*Kenney Diary* (Committee of the Whole), May 26, 1970, p. 62.

[16]*Journal,* August 7, 1976, p. 5.

[17]*Ibid.,* May 27, 1970, p. 5.

[18]*Ibid.,* August 7, 1970, p. 7.

[19]*Ibid,* p. 11.

[20]See Rubin Cohn, *To Judge with Justice: History and Politics of Illinois Judicial Reform* (Urbana: University of Illinois Press, 1973), pp. 28–29.

[21]*Journal,* January 20, 1970, p. 5.

[22]*Southern Illinoisan,* February 18, 1970.

[23]*Journal,* January 20, 1970, p. 4.

[24]*Southern Illinoisan,* February 6, 1970.

[25]*Record of Proceedings,* January 27, 1970, p. 280.

[26]On the Judiciary Committee generally see Cohn, *op. cit.,* Ch. IV.

[27]Sixth Illinois Constitutional Convention, Committee on Judiciary Proposal Number 2, p. 1.

[28]*Record of Proceedings,* May 19, 1970, p. 1099.

[29]*Ibid.*

[30]*Ibid.*, p. 1100.
[31]*Ibid.*, p. 1101.
[32]*Ibid.*, p. 1102.
[33]*Journal*, May 22, 1970, p.4.
[34]On the formation of these groupings, see Cohn, *op. cit.*, Ch. V.
[35]*Record of Proceedings*, July 7, 1970, p. 2297.
[36]*Kenney Diary* (Committee of the Whole), July 7, 1970, p. 96.
[37]*Record of Proceedings*, July 7, 1970, p. 2351.
[38]*Ibid.*, July 8, 1970, p. 2409.
[39]*Ibid.*, p. 2375.
[40]*Journal*, July 8, 1970, p. 10.
[41]*Kenney Diary* (Committee of the Whole), July 8, 1970, p. 98.
[42]*Record of Proceedings*, July 8, 1970, p. 2409.
[43]*Illinois State Register*, July 9, 1970; *Illinois State Journal*, July 9, 1970. See also the *Southern Illinoisan* for that date.
[44]*Record of Proceedings*, July 8, 1970, p. 2432.
[45]According to the *Illinois State Register* (July 2, 1970), Witwer had said that "judicial nominations and election 'is dictated by the party bosses.' " He suggested judicial candidates are often slated because of their loyalty to a political party.

" 'I am tired of being forced to appeal cases because this kind of person sits on a bench,' Witwer . . . said.

"He predicted the appointive system . . . would 'bring about a higher performance and a higher degree of responsibility' in the state's judicial branch."

[46]See *Illinois State Journal* and *Illinois State Register*, July 9, 1970. Also see the *Record of Proceedings*, July 8, 1970, pp. 2431–34; Kenney Diary (Committee of the Whole), July 8, 1970, pp. 99.
[47]*Journal*, July 8, 1970, p. 26.
[48]*Record of Proceedings*, July 9, 1970, p. 2437.
[49]*Journal*, July 9, 1970, p. 5.
[50]*Ibid.*, p. 9.
[51]*Kenney Diary* (Committee of the Whole), July 9, 1970, p. 101.
[52]*Illinois State Register*, July 2, 1970.
[53]*Record of Proceedings*, July 9, 1970, p. 2493.
[54]*Ibid.*, p. 2494.
[55]*Ibid.*, p. 2495.
[56]The *Chicago Sun-Times*, July 10, 1970, described this incident accurately. See also *Illinois State Register*, July 10, 1970.
[57]*Record of Proceedings*, July 10, 1970, p. 2534.
[58]*Journal*, July 10, 1970, p. 9.
[59]*Ibid.*, p. 11.
[60]*Record of Proceedings*, July 10, 1970, p. 2562.
[61]*Journal*, July 11, 1970, p. 11.
[62]On the merit plan on first reading see Cohn, *op. cit.*, pp. 93–100.
[63]*Record of Proceedings*, July 14, 1970, p. 2640.
[64]*Kenney Diary* (Committee of the Whole), August 11, 1970, pp. 151–52. See Cohn, *op. cit.*, p. 102. Professor Cohn's analysis is somewhat different. He states that "the switch in most cases was tied to the bitterly controversial branch banking issue which the Chicago Democrats adroitly exploited."
[65]Sixth Illinois Constitutional Convention. Committee on Style, Drafting and Submission Proposal Number 7.
[66]See the analysis by Robert Hartley in the *Southern Illinoisan*, August 23, 1970.
[67]*Journal*, August 11, 1970, p. 64.
[68]*Chicago Sun-Times*, August 12, 1970. See also the *Southern Illinoisan*, August 12, 1970.
[69]*Southern Illinoisan*, August 16, 1970.
[70]*Kenney Diary* (Committee of the Whole), August 11, 1970, p. 152.
[71]See p. 47.
[72]*Illinois State Register*, February 24, 1970. See also the *Chicago Sun-Times*, February 25, 1970.
[73]*Journal*, March 25, 1970, p. 3.
[74]*Ibid.*, p. 11.
[75]*Kenney Diary* (Committee of the Whole), March 25, 1970, p. 28.
[76]*Record of Proceedings*, March 25, 1970, p. 515.
[77]*Record of Proceedings*, July 16, 1970, p. 2765.
[78]*Chicago Tribune*, July 11, 1970.
[79]*Journal*, July 16, 1970, p. 11.
[80]See Charles Scolare's analysis in the *Illinois State Register;* also Coleman Mobley's in the *Southern Illinoisan;* Charles Wheeler's in the *Chicago Sun-Times;* and Caryl Carstens' in the *Illinois State Journal*, all of July 17, 1970.
[81]*Kenney Diary* (Committee of the Whole), July 16, 1970, pp. 109–10.
[82]*Journal*, July 17, 1970, p. 5.
[83]See the *Chicago Sun-Times*, July 18, 1970.
[84]*Journal*, August 12, 1970, p. 33.
[85]*Ibid.*, p. 36.
[86]*Ibid.*, p. 38.
[87]*Ibid.*, p. 51.
[88]*Ibid.*, August 13, 1970, p. 6.
[89]*Record of Proceedings*, August 13, 1970, p. 4110.
[90]*Ibid.*, pp. 4111, 4112.
[91]*Ibid.*, July 21, 1970, pp. 2938, 2939, 2943.
[92]*Journal*, July 21, 1970, p. 16.
[93]*Ibid.*, July 22, 1970, p. 15.
[94]*Record of Proceedings*, July 22, 1970, p. 2982.
[95]On August 26 the *Illinois State Register* reported that Sam Witwer had recommended to the Convention's Committee on Style, Drafting and Submission, meeting in Chicago, that single-member districts should be on separate submission with the appointment of judges. His reasoning was that in this way the package would not be endangered by such innovations. The same, of course, could be said of any significant change.
[96]Committee on Style, Drafting and Submission, Report No. 15.
[97]*Record of Proceedings*, August 27, 1970, p. 4268.
[98]*Journal*, August 28, 1970, pp. 219–220.
[99]*Record of Proceedings*, August 27, 1970, p. 4268.
[100]See for example the *Southern Illinoisan*, August 9, 1970.
[101]*Ibid.*, August 28, 1970.
[102]*Illinois State Journal*, August 27, 1970.
[103]*Journal*, August 28, 1970, p. 17.
[104]*Record of Proceedings*, August 28, 1970, p. 4330.
[105]*Ibid.*, p. 4325.
[106]*Ibid.*, p. 4320. See the *Chicago Sun-Times*, August 29, 1970. See also the analysis by Caryl Carstens in the *Illinois State Journal*, August 29, 1970.
[107]*Record of Proceedings*, August 28, 1970, p. 4317.
[108]*Ibid.*, p. 4321.
[109]*Journal*, August 28, 1970, p. 20.
[110]*Record of Proceedings*, August 28, 1970, p. 4328.
[111]This surely must have been a *Journal* error. Charles Young was chief architect of the successful move to put cumulative voting out of the package and on separate submission.
[112]*Journal*, August 29, 1970, pp. 2–3.
[113]*Ibid.*, p. 5.
[114]*Ibid.*, pp. 9–10.
[115]*Record of Proceedings*, August 29, 1970, p. 4386.
[116]*Journal*, August 29, 1970, pp. 18–19.
[117]*Ibid.*, p. 20.
[118]*Ibid.*, pp. 21–22.
[119]See Coleman Mobley's analysis in the *Southern Illinoisan*, August 30 and 31, 1970; Edith Herman's in the *Chicago Tribune*, August 30, 1970, and Caryl Carsten's in the *State Journal-Register*, August 30, 1970.
[120]*Journal*, August 30, 1970, pp. 11–12.
[121]*Record of Proceedings*, August 31, 1970, p. 4520.
[122]*Ibid.*, p. 4523.
[123]*Journal*, August 31, 1970 p. 7.
[124]*Record of Proceedings*, August 31, 1970, p. 4528.
[125]*Ibid.*
[126]*Journal*, September 1, 1970, pp. 33–34.
[127]*Ibid.*, p. 39.
[128]State of Illinois, *Official Vote, General Election 1970*, etc, John W. Lewis Secretary of State. Following data generally are also from this source. Percentages do not sum to 100 because not every person taking a referendum ballot voted on the package.
[129]JoAnna M. Watson, "Analysis of the Vote at the Election for the 1970 Illinois Constitution," *Illinois Government* (Institute of Government and Public Affairs: Urbana), No. 34 (February, 1971), unnumbered [1].
[130]Joan Severns, "Voter Survey Champaign-Urbana Fall 1970 Proposed 1970 Constitution" unpublished paper, 1971, p. 71.

[131]*Ibid.*

[132]The analysis above is primarily my own. The reader may wish to see Charles Wheeler's analysis of the vote in the *Chicago Sun-Times,* December 20, 1970.

[133]*Ibid.*

[134]Watson, *op. cit.* p. 2.

[135]State of Illinois, *Official Vote . . . 1970,* p. 106. Percentages do not sum to 100 because not all voters expressed an opinion on this question.

[136]Watson, *op. cit.,* p. 2.

[137]*Ibid.,* p. 3.

[138]State of Illinois, *Official Vote . . . 1970, op. cit.,* p. 108. The percentages do not sum to 100 because not all voters expressed an opinion on this question.

SUPPLEMENTAL READINGS

Principal materials used in the preparation of materials in this chapter include the verbatim *Record of Proceedings* and the *Journal of the Sixth Illinois Constitutional Convention.* In addition, the writer drew upon his personal diary, compiled as a member of the Convention, of the activities of its Committee of the Whole. The principal newspapers of the State were extensively used. For other useful materials, attention is drawn to the writer's book *Basic Illinois Government* (Southern Illinois Press, 1974), especially chapter 9, and the series of monographs on the Sixth Illinois Constitutional Convention published by the University of Illinois Press, especially the volume by Professor Rubin Cohn, *To Judge with Justice: History and Politics of Illinois Judicial Reform* (University of Illinois Press, 1973).

PART II

STATE GOVERNMENT: SHARED POWERS IN SEPARATE INSTITUTIONS

CHAPTER **4**

The Office of Governor

Edgar G. Crane, Jr.

State governments have been designed as part of a federal system of checks and balances which permits effective partnership of pluralistic political forces. The majority can rule, yet the liberties of minorities and individuals are given significant protection. In addition to being part of this larger system of checks and balances, each state establishes a similar system internally. In short, the federal system is designed to prevent any one person or group from controlling it at the expense of others.

Yet at the same time, a common statewide public interest requires a strong voice, a central point of political leverage, a focus of public attention and a source of efficiency in the implementation of public purposes. It is for these reasons that the states have established the elected position of governor.

Given these principles of our political system and the manner in which the system has been structured to implement those principles, the state governor becomes a center of creative tension between political forces of state and local, and long-term and short-term, interests. This chapter examines the Office of Illinois Governor in this broad context. Is the Office evolving in a clear direction, or does its use depend entirely on the peculiarities of the Governor's personality, the existing political forces and the nature of the problems faced by the State at a given time? To what extent does the Office of Governor in Illinois enable an incumbent to have the impact his "mandate" and judgment would suggest? Correspondingly, how effective is the Office of Governor in addressing long-term and state-wide interests or in achieving accountability to the citizens of Illinois? How do the formal powers of the Governor—constitutional and legal—interact with his informal political powers to provide a basis for effective leadership? Do these different sources of power regularly reinforce each other or do they occasionally conflict and undermine each other? Does an examination of recent Governors lead to the conclusion that there are, at least tentatively, identifiable formulas for gubernatorial success? What can the people of Illinois expect of future Governors? Are the roles and the criteria for success changing in some way?

These questions are explored by placing Illinois in the context of national trends. Then the contemporary Office of Governor in Illinois is described, and an analytic framework is suggested for examining its impact. Finally, the careers of Illinois Governors since World War II are examined as a means of exploring the issues in a flesh and blood context. The author is grateful for discussions with the former holders of that office and for the openness with which they presented their views.

In the opinion of the author, Illinois Governors during this period have represented the people with a high degree of integrity and success. As a group they have contributed immensely to preserving and strengthening the political and economic health of the State. On the record, Illinois voters have a right to hold high expectations of future Governors. As a corollary, citizens of Illinois can work in the better interests of the State with the expectation that the person sitting in the Governor's office will be a source of support, within the limits of what is possible.

Roles of the Governor

A governor uses his formal and informal powers in order to fulfill a variety of roles which are sometimes complementary and sometimes in conflict. The major roles of a governor include policy development, legislative leadership, party leadership, coalition building, management of the executive branch, intergovernmental relations and ceremonial functions. Each governor places different emphasis on these roles, depending on background, personal styles the problems confronting the state and the nature of the state political system. Each governor makes a conscious or unconscious trade-off between survival considerations and the wider merits of any issue.

A 1976 national survey of governors identified the following as the most difficult and demanding elements of the job in order of importance: working with the legislature (23), interference with family life (20), ceremonial demands on time (16), invasion of privacy (14), long working hours (13), tough decisions (11), working with the federal government (11), squabbles inside of state government (11), day-to-day management of state government (10), working with the press (8) and building and keeping a staff (7).[1]

In this context, future Illinois Governors may find the advice of their peers from other states useful and interesting. They were asked, "If you had to provide only three pieces of advice to a new Governor, what would they be?" The most consistent suggestions were (1) appoint and retain good people in key positions; (2) avoid crisis mentality and don't panic; (3) be yourself, be in command and make your own decisions; (4) highlight the importance of image and press relations; (5) monitor carefully your own personal work schedule and level of work effort; (6) establish appropriate general management approaches to assure an adequate flow of advice, goal selection, priority setting and delegation; (7) establish contingency plans or defensive strategies; (8) avoid isolation; and (9) keep an open door to the legislature.[2]

As state government grows in size and complexity, governors are giving greater importance to their management role, to its intergovernmental dimension and to integrating the management role with the other roles. It seems clear that a major challenge to future governors will be to combine strong roles of both political and managerial leadership. This will be difficult not only because of the potential conflicts between political responsiveness and managerial effectiveness, but because of the other demands on a governor's time which seem to crowd out management.[3] Clearly the individual governor's commitment to and competence for his managerial role are crucial. But equally clearly, successive generations of governors must work together to strengthen the state's systems and procedures for management, and the governor's staff for policy, budgeting, planning, management, personnel and information systems.

It is instructive to note the major topics of the National Governors Association *Handbook for New Governors;*[4] the experience of being governor; improving transition from the incumbent to his successor; organization and staffing of the governor's office in support of his major functions; selecting the cabinet and other state officials for managerial performance and political effectiveness; policy development; an approach to management which promotes effective staff-line relationships and a balance between daily routines and responsiveness to crisis; scheduling the governor's time to reflect priorities; dealing with constituent contacts and the media; using the budget as a tool for policy, planning, management and spending control; legislative relations; state-federal relations; reorganization; ethics; and the governor and his family.

Clearly, the office makes a multitude of demands on the incumbent. In large part his effectiveness will depend on how well and how quickly he establishes an approach which addresses these demands. For this reason, the period of transition to office is crucial. The major challenges of transition include setting policy priorities; identifying what is controllable, in principle; assessing the limitations imposed by other political actors and by partisan considerations; and making appointments which will maximize policy goals. Recent Illinois Governors vary greatly in this regard, and some represent outstanding models.

The Office: Its Power and Limits[1]

In the current *Handbook of Illinois Government,* the Office of Governor is described as follows:[5]

> The Governor of Illinois is the chief executive of the state and generally is responsible for administration of the government exclusive of other constitutionally-elected officials. The Civil Administrative Code establishes clear lines of authority between the Governor and the code departments, and gives him general administrative responsibility over a large number of semi-independent boards, commissions and agencies. He appoints hundreds of key administrators, including department directors, subject to approval by the Illinois Senate.
>
> The Governor's powers include granting of pardons and repireves, calling special legislative sessions, submitting annual budgets to the General Assembly, approving or vetoing thousands of bills, approval of state construction contracts, and Commander-in-Chief of the state's military and naval forces.
>
> He issues certificates of election and commissions to members of Congress, judges and clerks of courts, members of the General Assembly and certain other elective offices. Under certain circumstances the Governor's appointment power is extended; he may fill vacancies in the office of the Secretary of State, Treasurer, Attorney General and Comptroller. He also fills vacancies in the United States Senate until the next congressional election. Although the Governor does not exercise direct administrative control over other elected state officers, the Constitution empowers him to require information on any subject relating to the condition, management or expenses of these offices.
>
> The Lieutenant Governor shall perform the duties and exercise the powers in the Executive Branch that may be delegated to him by the Governor and that may be prescribed by law. He may be called upon to represent the Governor at State and public functions and, in case of the death or resignation or any event of a vacancy in the office of Governor, he becomes Chief Executive.

Any such listing of the formal powers and responsibility of the Illinois Governor risks both exaggerating that power and underestimating it. The formal powers may be likened to a bag of tools provided by the people, through Constitution and statute, so the Governor can effectively exercise leadership in the political process without imposing tyranny upon it.

Executive Power: Historical Doctrines, Analytic Measures and the 1970 Constitution

During the course of American history, several normative doctrines of executive power have emerged.[6] Each has influenced Illinois politics, government and constitution-making. First, reflecting colonial fear of tyranny exercised via executive power, the initial Constitution of 1818 required legislative appointment of all executive positions other than Governor and Lieutenant Governor. Second, reflecting Jacksonian democracy's faith in direct popular election of public officials, the 1848 Constitution adopted a long ballot, making the Secretary of State, Auditor and Treasurer elective. The 1870 Constitution further lengthened the ballot by adding the Attorney General and Superintendent of Public Instruction. Two other themes emerged during the long period of relative constitutional inactivity in Illinois. It has been considerably less affected than its neighboring State of Wisconsin by the theme of "anti-politics"—the nonpartisan progressivism of the early Twentieth Century. Nationally proponents of a fourth doctrine of "administrative efficiency and accountability'' have sought to control expenditures and improve government services through centralized gubernatorial control of executive agencies.

The Constitutional changes made in 1970 strongly reflect this final theme. At the same time the Governor's political and administrative powers were enhanced, however, the Legislature was also given new tools, reflecting the view that state government works best when both branches have the capacity to perform their respective, and shared, functions. It remains to be seen whether a workable balance has in fact resulted.

In practice, a governor's leadership efficacy depends upon the interplay between his formal powers, protected by constitution and statute, and his informal powers, derived from his popularity, party and legislative politics, and patronage. Schlesinger has developed a useful index of the governor's *formal* authority, based on an aggregate of budget, veto, appointment and tenure. Even prior to the constitutional changes of 1970, the Governor of Illinois rated as ''strong'' overall, by virtue of a four-year term, the prerogative of succeeding himself in office, recourse to an ''item'' veto, broad powers of appointment and removal and the power to prepare an executive budget. Even before constitutional revision, the Governor of Illinois ranked second with New Jersey's, behind only that of New York State.

The more informal, and political, sources of gubernatorial power, however, are less easily measured. Illinois history under the 1970 Constitution affords a classic illustration of the way in which political factors may undermine or test formal powers, vis-a-vis the Legislature. In the preceding decade, both branches had strengthened themselves in significant ways. Under the leadership of such men as Senate Majority Leader W. Russell Arrington and through such vehicles as the 1965 Commission on the Organization of the General Assembly, the Legislature had created a professional bipartisan staffing system, developed continuous standing committees for policy development as well as oversight, and initiated annual and other interim sessions in 1968. Under Governors Kerner and Ogilvie, substantial improvements in the budget system as a tool of executive policy were sought. The two branches agreed to strengthen the executive budget by eliminating the budget-making role of the Illinois Budgetary Commission.

Such were the realities when Con-Con convened in 1970. Separate committees were established on the Legislature and the Executive. Explicit attention was given to the balance and sharing of powers. The 1970 Constitution, in fact, promoted a stronger Legislature in several significant ways: it established a constitutional basis for the annual sessions already under way; it gave the Legislature tools for coping with the enhanced veto powers of the Governor; and it brought the rapidly broadening post-audit power fully under legislative direction by creating the constitutional office of Legislative Auditor General. While the latter development gave legislative oversight an important new tool, it did nothing directly to enhance the Legislature's formal tools for coping with the executive veto.[7]

While there is a useful measure of formal executive power, no comparable composite measure of legislative power exists, nor, consequently, of the relation or balance between legislative and executive power in a given state system. One national study has ranked legislatures on a multiple scale, reflecting function, accountability, information, independence and representativeness. Illinois ranked third in 1971, behind California and New York.[8] A more recent observation suggests it has more than held its own.[9] Thus, one might expect, if it could be measured, to find a large degree of parity between the two branches.

In view of Con-Con's modest work on the executive article, and of the anticipation of the political scientists who served it, it is not surprising that in 1971 an observer would conclude:

> The changes from previous practice were but minor modifications rather than dramatic shifts and, though all tended to enhance the Governor's power, they did so in slight increment.[10]

At the end of 1979, after nine years and parts of three regimes, this assessment still seems to hold true for tenure, unity of executive power, the role of chief executive and that of ''keeper of the purse.'' But there remains a serious, and as yet unresolved, question regarding the impact of the expanded veto powers upon the Governor's role as ''chief legislator'' and upon the balance of legislative-executive relations.

Unity of the Elected Executive

The Convention considered more radical steps, but finally limited itself to three actions, only one of which deleted an elected executive. Thus, the Governor remains only one of a number of elected executive officials with an independent base of political power.

First, the new Constitution provided that the Governor and Lieutenant Governor be elected jointly, rather than as individuals, on the premise that this would maximize compatability and continuity—in 1968, Paul Simon, a Democrat, had been elected Lieutenant Governor when Richard B. Ogilvie, a Republican, was elected Governor. It was anticipated that, as a result of the change, there would be ''increased utilization of the Lieutenant Governor as an aide to the Governor.'' Though of the same party, political differences suggest it would be inappropriate to consider the first incumbents under this provision, Governor Walker and Lieutenant Governor Hartigan, to be a team. Nevertheless, Hartigan did take on some major responsibilities for the aged. The team concept is more applicable to Governor Thompson and David O'Neal elected in 1976. Yet the latter's responsibilities have been more political than managerial or policy-oriented. Both Walker and Thompson appointed others as ''Deputy Governors.'' In all likelihood, Lieutenant Governors will continue to function in this political capacity, reflecting (1) the ticket-balancing process by which they were selected; and (2) the Governor's desire to maintain clear lines of authority within his administration.

Second, the previous position of Auditor of Public Accounts was replaced by the new office of Comptroller, with the goal of concentrating fiscal accountability, to assure "the maintenance of central accounts in accordance with sound practice" and the reduction of "non-productive duplication in handling the state's financial transactions." As a result of these changes, the position has rapidly become visible and may now be considered a potential stepping-stone to gubernatorial candidacy, since it affords the best single platform for an alternative to the fiscal picture presented by the Governor and his Budget Bureau.[11]

Finally, the Convention did approve the elimination of one elective post, the Superintendent of Public Instruction. Under the terms of Article X, Section 2, a chief State educational officer is appointed by the State Board of Education. This does not significantly further executive unity. To a large extent, this feature retains the principle of separating elementary and secondary education, a major State program, from direct management by the Governor. In practice, the appointed educational officer has continued to be an independent spokesman and administrator. In the short time since it began operating in January 1975, the Board and its chief have undertaken an only partially successful struggle to establish "its independent status as a nonpartisan constitutional agency, free from outside bureaucratic controls."[12]

A 1974 controversy between Governor Walker (Independent Democrat) and Attorney General Scott (Republican) illustrates the inherent conflict potential of multiple elected executive officers. The issue was which of them would control lawyers employed by executive agencies. In order to assert control, the Governor used his line-item veto on an appropriation which would have made these officers responsible to the Attorney General. Despite expert opinion that "neither the judicial precedents nor the constitutional history supports the categorical positions of either,"[13] it appears the Attorney General's position has been supported by the Courts.[14]

Tenure Potential

The 1970 Constitution did not alter the "tenure potential" of the Governor. He and all other executive officials serve four-year terms, without restraint on re-election. However, all executives are to be elected in non-presidential years beginning in 1978, in order to increase the visibility and independence of major State political races. In order to implement this change, it was necessary to provide for two-year rather than four-year terms in 1976–78. Politically a two-year term increases the risks of defeat for an incumbent by structuring a dilemma—he is faced with losing votes, either by bold action resulting in well-remembered resentments, or by excessive caution exposing him to the charge of inaction and incompetence. Governor Thompson's actions during this term may be assessed as an effort to evade this dilemma.

The Governor: Protector of the Purse?

Traditionally, the legislature has exercised the "power of the purse." State constitutions typically assign the power over revenues and appropriations to the legislature and mandate a balanced budget. Current controversy regarding the power to control executive use of federal funds through legislative appropriation has made it clear this is a legislative power. However, for a century, state constitutions have sought to restrain legislative spending powers, and the emergence of the "executive budget" has in practice made the governor the "protector of the purse."

In Illinois, the performance of these roles shifts between the two branches, depending in part on which party dominates and on the condition of State revenues. Despite enactment of a State income tax in 1969, the State has faced fiscal crises, and the last three Governors have been highly conscious of their role as "protector of the purse." All have substantially enhanced the capability and responsibilities of their Bureau of the Budget, a unit created by Ogilvie in 1969 with legislative approval.[15]

The 1970 Constitution also modifies and makes explicit the budgetary powers of the Governor. Section 2 of Article VII, "Finance," clearly spells out the Governor's authority to prepare an annual budget for:

> . . . every department, authority, public corporation and quasi-public corporation of the State, every State college and university, and every other public agency created by the State.

This provision, however, does not so much represent a change of direction as it does a securing of the constitutional authority for practices which had already been developing. Thus, it is natural that Governors since 1970 have expressed no awareness that this provision reflects any increased powers.

The constitutional tool most instrumental to the Governor's role as "protector of the purse" is a dual aspect of his diverse veto power: the "line-item" and "reduction" veto. In addition to vetoing an entire appropriation bill, the Governor may either veto (delete) a line-item in its entirety or reduce it to any amount. He may not, however, increase a line item. Addition of the reduction veto to the existing line item veto was intended, not so much to augment executive power, as to "update" the item veto. Con con's Committee on the Executive noted that trends in appropriations practices had eliminated many of the details from appropriations bills in favor of a more programmatic approach to budgeting. They foresaw that if this trend were to continue, it would limit the applicability of the line-item veto alone, thus vitiating the effectiveness of what had previously been an important power.[16]

The three Governors who served since 1970 have made extensive use of the leverage on the budget process afforded by the option of exercising a line or reduction veto. Hanley reports that Governor Ogilvie initiated the practice on July 13, 1971, twelve days after its effective date, by using the reduction veto to reduce appropriations by the unprecedented amount of $146.3 million, involving 141 line items in sixteen appropriation bills.[17] In a special message to the General Assembly, the Governor stated:

> . . . the General Assembly passed appropriations from the General Revenue Fund at a level $259 million more than the budget. There are no revenues available to pay for the additional appropriations.

None of the reductions was restored when the Legislature reconvened in October, despite the requirement of only a majority vote to do so.

Subsequently, Governor Walker has made equally extensive use of the new reduction veto power, including but not limited to the 1974 "recession session" when revised revenue projections necessitated a cut. Of necessity, the Legislature left the Governor with the final responsibility for an adjustment.

The reduction veto has not become a source of controversy comparable to the amendatory veto. Yet, this does not eliminate the necessity of closer examination of its effects on the balance of both power *and* accountability between the Legislature and Executive. Clearly this device has swung the balance in favor of the Governor on both counts, and in the process has opened the door to, if not made inevitable, a legislative budgetary politics of lessened responsibility. The reduction veto increases the legislative opportunity to treat appropriations actions as "funny money" ultimately to be made real by the Governor. The legislator can say "I voted for it—the Governor took it away," but needn't be responsible for actual expenditures.[18]

Johnson reports on a major constraint on the reduction veto.[19] In 1973, the Attorney General ruled that this power does not extend to reduction of a flat grant formula vote for State aid to junior colleges because it is not an item of appropriations, but instead is established elsewhere in the statutes.[20]

Executive Orders and Reorganization Powers

The provisions of Section 11 also increase the Governor's powers as chief executive by granting him greater authority over the structure of the State's administrative apparatus. The Governor is empowered to reassign functions or reorganize executive agencies by executive order, subject only to "legislative veto" by majority vote of either house, within sixty days. The Committee on the Executive noted that in the absence of such a power, "inertia" and disinterest on the part of the General Assembly could permit worthwhile measures to "die by inaction." The Committee reported that nine other states utilize a similar device.

The reorganization powers were not extensively used until 1977. Governor Ogilvie made no attempt to use them in the remainder of his term, 1970–72, but in all likelihood would have undertaken extensive reorganization had he been reelected to a second term.[21]

Despite speculation that he would use the new powers extensively, in view of his earlier service with the Schaefer Commission to Study State Government, Walker took no such initiatives.[22] First, this experience led him to be skeptical, rather than optimistic, regarding the importance of organizational structure—to him, top appointments and gubernatorial leadership were the keys to improved performance. Second, Walker judged that, as an Independent Democrat, his complicated relations with the Legislature would require more effort than it was worth—political realities rendered use of this particular formal power impractical. Walker also recognized that the new powers had not, in fact, evaded the necessity of positive legislative action. To be implemented, any major reorganization would require the enactment of numerous companion bills.

Had circumstances been more favorable, Walker might well have created an umbrella "housekeeping" department inclusive of the then Departments of Finance, General Services, and Personnel.

Thus, the reorganization powers had not been tested by the first two Governors to whom they were available. Evidence that this would probably change came when the 1976 Republican and Democratic gubernatorial candidates jointly created the Illinois Task Force on Governmental Reorganization, which submitted recommendations to Governor-elect Thompson and his staff.[23] In his first three legislative sessions Thompson successfully submitted a number of proposals.

Together the Walker and Thompson experiences illustrate the effect of legislative and party politics on the practical utility of formal powers of executive reorganization. Every Governor must, in effect, conduct an assessment of the political costs and benefits before determining how such powers will be employed. Each Governor has available a unique set of political resources and confronts a unique set of political constraints. See the chapter by Gove and Carlson for an in-depth study of reorganization.

The Amendatory Veto: Unintended Powers?

The governor's role as "chief legislator" has been prominent during nearly a century of increasing support for the doctrine of executive government at the state level. A new era of legislative reform and strengthening, triggered in 1963 when the U.S. Supreme Court required reapportionment on the basis of "one man, one vote" has not brought any corresponding diminution of support for executive power. Rather, the prevailing view seems to be that the states are best served by the interplay of stronger legislatures with stronger executives. Because of the manner in which the new amendatory veto has been implemented and might be implemented in the future in Illinois, there is considerable question as to whether it swings the balance of power too much in favor of the Executive.[24]

Illinois Governors: Uniqueness and Continuity

Within the context of the powers, roles and evolution of the Office, this section examines some of the most salient features of the experience of Illinois Governors since World War II. The choice of contemporary Governors is based on the assumption that their experience is sufficient to illustrate the major dimensions of the Office. Earlier Illinois Governors, however, have had a demonstrable impact on the shape of Illinois government and the style and goals of Illinois politics. In various ways contemporary Governors have been shaped by their predecessors. Although the Office continues to evolve in important ways, the continuity of this evolution can be seen by examining recent developments in light of the 1962 Assembly on the Office of Governor. Background papers for the conference focused on such enduring themes as issues and styles, as well as important fiscal, planning and intergovernmental limits on the effectiveness of the Office. Participants approved a summary statement on the Office, emphasizing (1) continuing attention to the powers, prestige and importance of the Office; (2) strengthening the executive budget and budget staff; (3) revising the civil service system to permit more effective administrative action, e.g., by raising the salary structure; (4) centralizing the authority of the Office through appointment of then-elected statewide officials, as well as of commission chairmen; (5) shifting elections to non-presidential years; (6) eliminating earmarked State taxes; (7) strengthening the interdependent roles of legislative and public opinion leader, as well as manager of the economy; and (8) conferring the power to initiate reorganization, subject to legislative disapproval.[25] Clearly the 1970 Constitution addressed a number of these matters. The following section reflects on the manner in which post-War Governors have addressed them, and on the implications of experience for a strategy of governing within this framework.

Adlai Stevenson II
Democrat, 1948–1952

Adlai Stevenson II served one term as Governor. He was an idealist in politics, whose primary concerns were national and international in scope. Stevenson's major impact on Illinois politics was to increase the plausibility of the belief that political leadership which is consistently committed to noble and selfless ideals can have not only a short-term but a long-term impact on the quality of political leadership and governmental administration.

In all likelihood, his service has increased the concern of subsequent Governors with such matters and has influenced their decisions to some extent in these directions. Stevenson does not stand alone in this regard. In its history Illinois is fortunate to have had the services of a number who have stood visibly as models for what a Governor should strive for, even when that may appear to call for something beyond the pragmatic ''art of the possible.''

The Stevenson legacy of idealism and reform, like any other, must be given shape in the circumstances of the times. It may be of particular interest to consider the extent to which the independent Dan Walker lies within the Stevensonian legacy and what the ramifications might be for the future of idealism and reform in Illinois politics.

To be understood, the Stevenson legacy must be seen as a continuing family saga of aristocratic public service. It began with the grandfather, Adlai I of Bloomington, who served as Vice-President of the United States with Grover Cleveland in 1893–1897. It has continued with Adlai III, who served in the General Assembly, as State Treasurer, and as U.S. Senator since 1968. The Stevensons have been classic ''amateurs'' in politics, focusing on politics as an instrument of public benefit, as distinct from the ''professionals'' for whom politics is a permanent career to be pursued with personal survival or partisan benefit foremost.

The depth of this family orientation to politics helps explain Adlai II's temporary and limited alliance with the Illinois Democratic political organization. He had been instrumental in the design of the United Nations while working in the State Department. His idealism appealed to well-heeled political reformers and independents. For different but equally valid reasons it appealed to the organization as a way of selling its ticket. Stevenson was more interested in the U.S. Senate, but the organization selected Douglas for that position, and after some deliberation Stevenson agreed to be the candidate for Governor. Stevenson's term has been characterized as follows:[26]

> Adlai Stevenson became governor in 1949 and promptly set out to take politics out of Illinois state government. Despite a plurality of half a million votes, he greeted the politically divided General Assembly as follows:
>
> > Political parties and party principles are essential to our system of government, but economic and social principles upon which a healthy electorate divides diminish in importance as government descends from the national to the local level. Basic divisions between Democrats and Republicans on national issues have little bearing upon state or municipal problems.
>
> With this, Stevenson made a major assault on the state's personnel system. He asked that the position classification function be made a responsibility of the Civil Service Commission, that the administration of conservation laws be lodged in a ''nonpolitical commission form'' of administrative unit, that the state police be reorganized, and that a state police merit system be established. He would have lengthened and staggered the terms of members of the major regulatory commission, the Illinois Commerce Commission, and increased their salaries, all by way of diminishing political influence. Arguing for a career service, Stevenson alleged, ''The patronage system of the past is inefficient because effective administration is impossible when employees owe their allegiance and responsibility not to their supervisors but to their political sponsors. And I know that the system is even of diminishing political value as the electorate finds it more and more distasteful.''
>
> Although he had no real financial problem to overcome, Stevenson tied economy and fiscal conservatism to the problems of cold war. ''I think we must put first things first. Our job is to aid wherever possible in shoring up the nation's defenses.'' He would spend nothing that could be saved, build nothing that could be deferred, use no manpower that could be conserved. And yet, $53 million of the surplus accumulated during the war years was spent during 1949–1953. Stevenson indicated his system of priorities in his farewell message when he pointed out that 98 per cent of the

increases in general revenue expenditures during that period had been for education and public welfare. He characterized new money for the common schools as part of putting "first things first" and found that "public welfare is perhaps our most moving and urgent problem." Stevenson's preoccupation with nonpolitics in state government did not lead him into a dewy-eyed approach to all state problems. Pointing out some of the inadequacies of the Illinois Constitution of 1870, he pinpointed a fear of reapportionment and a fear of an income tax as major impediments to a constitutional convention, and "realistically" sought to eliminate both questions as issues. Acknowledging that the constitutional requirement for reapportionment "would give control of both houses of the General Assembly to Cook County," Stevenson invited downstate support by stating, "I do not believe that Cook County wants legislative dominance in both houses." As for an income tax, he would have frozen the ambiguity of the old constitutional language in a new document: "Rather than risk the rejection of a new constitution because of this apprehension, I would urge the convention to leave the income tax problem precisely where it stands at present."

In general, the Stevenson technique was to discuss a relatively limited number of subjects, to make his proposals in the areas covered specific as to goals, but less specific as to how to achieve the goals unless he was transmitting the findings of a study group. He discussed the problem of public higher education and saw the most urgent need "to establish a better overall administration" in order to "attack disorder and disintegration boldly and decisively." He noted in both state of the state messages that racial and religious prejudice damaged the national image in a critical time, urged fair employment practice legislation, and expressed concern about discriminatory practices of labor unions.

Stevenson transmitted an air of deadly seriousness for all of his well-known ability to turn a phrase. He used a relatively selective approach in making legislative suggestions. There were aspects of legislative and state business that he was determined to have a hand in like any other governor. But unlike Green, he did not approach the legislature with a soft, amiable front; unlike Horner, he did not push his ideas with the prospect of "making Illinois a leader"; unlike Stelle, he did not overstate his case. Stevenson seemed to play the professor-politician. He kept his distance, sought to build up his strength by emphasizing the righteousness of his cause and the good taste of his concerns: "the amenities of life on the farm" and "the human problem of inactive older people" appear to be concerns shared by no other recent governor. And again and again the return to nonpolitics and personnel practices appear as a kind of legacy of purity. Personnel practices and policy headed the list of items by which he wished history to judge the worth of the administration. "Of all the things I have tried to do during my term as Governor nothing is more important than the progress which has been made in bringing to and retaining in the State service capable men and women without regard to politics."

As governor, Adlai Stevenson hammered on one principal idea, improving the quality of the state service by eliminating political considerations. Stevenson never became part of the state's state political elite, spoke for reform (and accomplished a good bit in the way of administrative reorganization), and chose both his ideas and his associates from outside the mainstream of Illinois political life.

A recent biography review addresses the question of how Stevenson rated as governor:[27]

How did Stevenson rate as a governor? His son, Adlai III, now a U.S. senator, said in an interview with Martin that if his father "had had more experience in politics and he had better understood the dimensions of his power, he might have done more to reform the government and his party." Carl McGowan, his closest staff member and now a federal judge, thought his weakness was his failure to spend enough, to ask for a sales tax increase: "he didn't think in terms of spending enough money." (But he did obtain a gas tax increase.) Congressman Abner J. Mikva, drawn into politics by Stevenson, blames Paul Powell for the "myth" that Stevenson was "an ineffective governor," arguing on the contrary that "the truth is that to this day you can't turn anywhere in Illinois without seeing his mark." Martin himself concedes Stevenson was less successful in his legislative program than his Republican successor, William G. Stratton, but points out that Stevenson had to deal with a Republican Senate during two sessions and a Republican House during one session. Nor was he outstanding as a political leader, Martin says, except for slating Schaefer for the Illinois Supreme Court (certainly a high mark there!). Still, Martin concludes, "by bringing good men into government, he did improve the tone . . . of state government. This, in a state as big and corrupt as Illinois, is no small accomplishment."

In summary, Stevenson set high standards for future Governors, but left many important practical questions of political leadership and managerial implementation to be worked through by others.

William G. Stratton
Republican, 1952–1960

William G. Stratton served two terms as Governor at a crucial time for the development of the Illinois economy. His effective administrative and political leadership contributed significantly to an important role for State government in developing the institutions, public services and economic infrastructure required for the growth of the Illinois economy. At the same time he was able to implement a fiscal philosophy of tight budgets, small surpluses and administrative cost control. Stratton's good working relationships with a Republican-controlled Legislature were instrumental to these achievements.[28]

Of all the post-war Governors, Stratton had the most extensive familiarity with State Government when he took office. He had already served as the youngest member of Congress, as well as two terms as State Treasurer. The Congressional experience led to a continuing concern with federal-state relations; he was the only Illinois Governor to serve as Chairman of the National Governor's Conference. The experience as Treasurer prepared him with an intimate knowledge of the State's financial condition and led to a uniquely direct involvement in budget preparation. Stratton, a political scientist, is also unique among post-war Governors in being the only non-lawyer.

Political Leadership When Stratton took office, he encountered a State administration which he felt had been run at arms length by the highly principled Stevenson. Stratton intended to govern differently, by managing and conducting legislative relations in a very direct and intimate manner. John Bartlow Martin, a prominent journalist and backer of Stevenson, had written that needed legislative reapportionment and highway financing were politically impossible. Stratton proved him wrong.

Legislative reapportionment had begun to emerge as a fundamental political issue after the war. Population movements had concentrated the people of Illinois and other states in cities, but rural-dominated Legislatures districted in earlier times had no inclination to redistrict. It appeared that urban interests were not being fairly represented. It was not until the U.S. Supreme Court intervened in 1963 that state legislatures were compelled to implement the equal representation principle of "one man, one vote". In 1952 the barriers to reform seemed insuperable. But Stratton tackled the problem immediately. He obtained legislative support for a compromise which included four additional seats for suburban Cook County.

Financial Leadership Like other states during World War II, Illinois had postponed capital improvements which would be necessary to support the infrastructure of a growing postwar economy. In his election campaign Stratton responded to wide support for such improvements by promising extensive highway construction, bridge repairs and new facilities for mental health and education.

Building on his experience as State Treasurer, Stratton devised a proposal for the sale of bonds through which the projects could be funded without requiring a tax increase. The proposals included massive highway projects at a time when the federal highway program had not yet been initiated; therefore funding would be entirely a State responsibility. The states to the east had established turnpikes, but none yet existed in Illinois. By 1954 construction had begun on a system of Illinois toll roads. Within two years 185 miles had been completed. In order to accelerate the projects and assure financial control, Stratton limited each contractor to a maximum of ten miles and opened the bidding process to contractors from other states.

Stratton's predecessor, Adlai Stevenson, had vetoed a $240 million authorization for highway bonds, which would have been guaranteed by Cook County property tax receipts. Stratton worked with the Legislature to obtain a new authorization and agreed to a $19 million annual allocation of the State gas tax, permitting work to proceed on the major Chicago area expressways, now named after Dan Ryan, John F. Kennedy and Dwight D. Eisenhower.

Programmatic Leadership At the time, the package prepared by Stratton to fund the State highway system was the largest bond issue ever presented at one time outside the federal government. The package was successfully sold on the grounds that the tollway system would be self-financing. Stratton takes great pride in the fact the bonds are being paid off ahead of schedule.

In addition to highways, Stratton also provided leadership for extensive funding of educational, mental health and correctional facilities. A $325 million bond issue would be required, split equally between mental health and higher education. The initial proposal failed, but a prospectus specifying projects in detail was approved in 1959. The capital construction momentum developed under the Stratton Administration was carried over for much of its implementation to the Kerner Administration. This illustrates the substantial degree of continuity as successive Governors provide leadership in State problems. Each Governor can affect direction and priorities, but each is also constrained by the commitments of predecessors. For example, Kerner completed and accredited a dozen new mental hospitals funded under Stratton initiatives, but he also rechanneled a substantial portion of the funds into a new zone center concept. The mental health policies of all recent Illinois Governors have been affected by new drugs and community-based care programs which permit reduction in the population of large institutions. Kerner's mental health director Dr. Francis Gerty proposed the new zone center concept to facilitate the reorientation of patient flow to the community rather than to unnecessary long-term inpatient care at large institutions. Under Stratton, the first State-run training and research facility was created at the Illinois Psychiatric Institute, and a new minimum security prison was started.

The post World War II baby boom had produced a wave of increasing enrollment which would clearly move through elementary, secondary and higher education. Major expansion was undertaken at the Carbondale campus of Southern Illinois University and the Edwardsville campus was begun. Funding for the Chicago Circle campus was also arranged.

Managerial Leadership Stratton's direct and intimate style of managing State agencies appears to be unique among recent Illinois Governors. It was possible in part because of his detailed familiarity with State agencies, his professional interest in administrative regulation and the relatively smaller size of the State's administrative apparatus at the time. The last factor alone may render such an approach impractical in the future and may necessitate instead the "institutionalization" of the Governor's staff and cabinet which appears to be emerging. A closer look at Stratton's approach may help illustrate the difference.

Stratton consciously chose to have few staff assistants so he could maintain direct contact and control of State agencies. In a step which foreshadowed more recent "ombudsman" ideas, Stratton conducted regular Thursday meetings in the hall outside his office for the purpose of improving agency response to citizen problems. He would spend a few minutes discussing problems with anyone in line. Two secretaries were present to record his commitments for follow-up. In one case, a farmer who had been unable for years to get remedial action for problems caused by laying a nearby highway found State crews working to remedy the situation when he returned to his farm that day. Stratton feels such practices kept his department heads and their organizations alert. In fact, agency directors occasionally got in line themselves!

Budget Leadership In like manner, Stratton personally developed each of the four biennial budgets and budget messages delivered during his two terms, by isolating himself with all the detail for several days without interruption. This occasionally involved working straight through the night. He would then immediately brief top agency personnel on his decisions. During these years, the Legislative Budgetary Commission was generally uninvolved despite its statutory role in the process. This probably reflects the harmonious relation between Stratton and the Republican Legislature. In order to assure that the spending which actually took place was consistent with his tight budgets, Stratton personally scrutinized a detailed monthly financial report which department heads were required to present at cabinet meetings. If they were overspending, Stratton required that full written explanations be submitted in red ink! Stratton believes that the final construction cost of $12 milliion for the State Office Building which now bears his name came in $1.5 million under estimates because of attention to detail resulting directly from his involvement. Stratton is inclined to feel that the contemporary budget process creates far too much distance between the Governor and State operations.

Overcoming Constraints: Finance, Chicago, State Officials Stratton, like all governors, experienced important constraints on his leadership. It is clear that the shape of his revenue strategy and the success of his tactics were substantially constrained by opinion within the GOP.[29] He found it necessary to oppose a State income tax. In the last year of his term he advocated a comprehensive national tax study, but ironically vetoed the appropriation for a State tax study.

Stratton found in the governorship adequate powers to work effectively with the other independently elected statewide officials. He established the unique practice of involving them regularly in his cabinet meetings and maintaining regular communication. This led to tangible cooperation, especially in matters of business management; for example, he negotiated an agreement with the Secretary of State for joint publication of road maps with the Highway Department.

In matters of State finance, Stratton consistently worked toward a balanced budget by reducing the postwar surplus. The basic shape of an emerging fiscal crisis became relatively clear during the Stratton years. The existing tax base would not permit State government to respond to the service demands of a growing, young and increasingly urban population. Stratton initiated what was to become the interim strategy for raising revenue by pushing through a $100 million increase in the sales tax, earmarked for the schools.

Stratton also established a pattern of cooperation by Republican Governors in a State role to help the City of Chicago solve its problems. Mayor Daley took office in 1955. The two encountered no serious problems in arriving at agreement on issues. Stratton's comand of the diverse tools of public finance permitted him to take the lead in tailoring special State solutions to major problems of urban finance. For example, he played a major role in the joint public-private financing of McCormick Place, the giant convention center on the lake front, for which the State secured $30 million in bonds.

Stratton's interests extended to substantive innovation, and many of his fiscal strategies were created for the purpose of promoting the State's programmatic impact. The Illinois Youth Commission (IYC) was created with his support to permit separate handling of juvenile delinquents and keep them from exposure to more hardened adult criminals in the prison system. At the time this was a controversial concept implemented in only three other states: New York, California and Minnesota.

Despite constraints, Stratton substantially succeeded in achieving his goals. It may be that a major contributing factor was his conciliatory approach to rivals. Within the Republican Party he contested 18 primary elections and emerged with few enemies, despite the fact that his opponents were serious candidates. For example, in 1952 he faced five major opponents, including the incumbent Secretary of State, a member of the Cook County Board and a member of the University of Illinois Board of Trustees. He would typically organize a congenial campaign caravan for the convenience of all primary candidates, including his opponents. His gubernatorial appointments were not limited to those who supported him in the primary.

Aftermath Since his departure from office in 1960, Stratton has served as Director of Corporate Relations for the Canteen Corporation, including government relations and charitable contributions. He has been active in the Restaurant Association and served in 1979 as President of the National Institute for the Food Service Industry. He has been active with the State Chamber of Commerce and served on numerous boards of college trustees and corporate directors. Stratton served as President of the Chicago Rotary Club in 1979. He has retained his interests in the field of education and mental health, including service on the board and as President of the Mental Health Association of Greater Chicago.

Otto Kerner and Samuel Shapiro Democrats, 1960–1968

The administration of Otto Kerner and his running mate and successor, Samuel H. Shapiro, amply illustrates the difficulty of fully and objectively assessing any Illinois Governor. Kerner was a popular Governor who promoted humanitarian causes, led an important presidential commission and resigned office to accept a federal judgeship. In his short term, Shapiro distinguished himself as a worthy successor to Kerner and it seemed clear that if he had been elected in 1968, Shapiro would have continued in similar directions. The passage of time has preserved Shapiro's good reputation, but Kerner was convicted of major improprieties in office, sentenced and imprisoned. For these reasons alone it is important to deal carefully with these years, yet the scope of this chapter does not permit full justice. One thing is clear however, the Kerner conviction is in no way a full verdict on his governorship.

Otto Kerner came from one of Chicago's leading political families. His father served as Illinois Attorney General and as a Cook County judge. Young Otto married into another prominent political family, that of Anton Cermak, the Chicago Mayor who was the first to create a Democratic organization of the broad base and efficiency later to epitomize the Daley years. Kerner was clearly marked for success. He established an outstanding military record as an artillery officer. Prior to serving as Governor, he was U.S. Attorney for the Northern district of Illinois. He was elected Cook County Judge in 1954 and 1958. Thus he had served both as judge and prosecutor. Kerner entered the governorship with an outstanding reputation for competence and integrity; he was humane, sincere and consciencious.

Running Mate Kerner's running mate for Lieutenant Governor, Samuel H. Shapiro, was a Kankakee attorney who had served fourteen years in the Illinois House of Representatives. He and Kerner had worked closely since Young Democrat days in the 1930's. Shapiro illustrates the impact that Illinois Governors have had on the growth and development of budding younger politicians. Shapiro's idol as Governor was Henry Horner, who served in the Depression days of the 1930's. Shapiro had been deeply impressed with Horner's fairness on the bench and later with his sacrifice of his own health as a highly consciencious Governor. At the same time, Shapiro worked on another wavelength—his political mentor was Jake Arvey, the legendary kingmaker of Chicago Democratic politics.

The Kerner-Shapiro ticket proved to be popular with the voters in both the 1960 and 1964 elections. At the time Illinois still elected the Governor and Lieutenant Governor separately, but in 1960, Kerner made it clear he expected a Kerner vote to be a Shapiro vote as well. Kerner and Shapiro, opposing Stratton's attempt to win an unprecedented third term as Governor, overwhelmed him by a margin of better than half a million votes. In a hard-fought 1964 campaign, they defeated Charles H. Percy, then a rising GOP star who went on to be elected U.S. senator in 1966, 1972 and 1978.

Perspective: A Democrat and His Party Perspectives on Kerner's Administration depend in part on an appreciation of the differences in organization between the Democratic and Republican parties. Stratton wrote after leaving office that a Governor must exercise independent leadership, but it is clear that his comments were most applicable to a Republican Governor.[30] The Republican Party performs well the functions of recruiting and supporting candidates, but it is not organized to have an extensive influence on governing. The incumbent Republican Governor dominates the Party. In all likelihood, a Governor who depended on the Party would not do justice to his responsibilities. In contrast, the Democratic Party is organized to control governance as well as election. Candidates have been slated by the "organization" rather than contesting for the nomination in a Party primary. Democratic Party officials, particularly those representing Cook County and the City of Chicago, play a major role, partly through the Legislature, in the formulation of policy, the making of appointments and the implementation of policy.

In this context, Kerner was a home-grown product of the Chicago organization. The system was in his blood. It was clear that Daley, not Kerner, would be the Party boss. Furthermore, Kerner's political objectives did not require establishing a statewide organization—the Democratic Party was a perfectly serviceable vehicle.

Transition Problems: A Weak Beginning Illinois Governors have not uniformly or wholeheartedly assisted each other in transition. According to Stratton: "When I came in I didn't ask Stevenson for anything but the key to the mansion and the key to the office. I wouldn't expect to do any more than that for any other governor."[31] Stratton put these sentiments into practice when he left office. Kerner failed to anticipate this; as a result his first months in office were understaffed and poorly organized. At a crucial time, the image of gubernatorial impotence became widespread.[32]

> The somewhat checkered history of Governor Kerner's first budget demonstrated quite clearly that the governor, though universally respected as an honest and upright man, was beyond his depth in a political system dominated by veterans whose rules of behavior were unfamiliar to him. Since his closest advisors were also outsiders . . . there was no alternative but a long and sometimes painful period of on-the-job training marked by hesitation, vacillation and inconsistency.[33]

There are two differing but related views on Kerner's style of leadership. The positive side perceives an excellent Governor who faced all problems without fear or difficulty, one who benefitted the State by administering ably and impartially, if without flair. Kerner's critics take the view that he delegated too much, including important aspects of policy, budgeting and legislative relations, while devoting too much of his time and energy to the ceremonial functions of the governorship. From the latter view, it is a short step to speculation that excessive readiness to delegate and to trust key colleagues, entrapped him in the race track stock scandal which was to undo him after he left office.

An Effective Partnership: The Lieutenant Governor The strengths in his willingness to delegate are evident in the uniquely effective partnership which developed between Kerner and Shapiro in matters of mental health care. Substantial improvements in Illinois mental health care had been underway before Kerner took office. These improvements were not simply a result of gubernatorial leadership. Rather, important support came from a bipartisan effort centered in the House, where then-Representative Shapiro had teamed with GOP Representative Bernice Vandervrieze to initiate and promote the required statutes and appropriations.

When Kerner took office in 1961, he established mental health as a major policy concern, and he soon became known for his advocacy of the program. Even prior to the 1960 election, Kerner had recruited the nationally prominent Dr. Francis J. Gerty to direct the Mental

Health Department. He also delegated responsibility for political strategy and legislative relations in that area to Lieutenant Governor Shapiro.

Other Governors have attempted to delegate responsibilities to their Lieutenant Governors, but none have been as successful as Kerner and Shapiro in implementation. Under Ogilvie, such an arrangement was unlikely, since the voters elected Democrat Paul Simon as Lieutenant Governor. In view of the partisan split, Ogilvie and Simon enjoyed an amicable relationship. Simon was quietly laying the groundwork for being slated in 1972. Since 1972 Illinois voters have selected the Governor and Lieutenant Governor as a team. Walker's Lieutenant Governor, Neil Hartigan, was an organization Democrat, a fact which destined the gap between them to be even greater than that between Ogilvie and Simon. Hartigan took independent initiatives in several areas foremost of which was policy on aging. Thompson's Lieutenant Governor David O'Neal, formerly Sherriff of St. Clair County (East St. Louis), appears to fit the traditional Republican mold, serving primarily to balance the ticket by increasing appeal to downstate voters. The fact that he has occasionally taken independent positions may actually enhance the downstte appeal of the ticket.

Some observers of American politics have suggested that the Office of Lieutenant Governor be given more substantive responsibilities and in effect, converted into that of a deputy governor in the direct chain of command. Illinois experience suggests that, with the possible exception of the Kerner-Shapiro relationship, the inherent rivalry involved in the primary function of replacement for the Governor is incompatible with such delegation. In fact, the institutionalization of the Governor's office has been proceeding in a different direction with the evolution of a staff position of Deputy Governor.

Political and Finance Leadership Some observers use Kerner's relationship to State finance and budgeting, as well as legislative relations, to illustrate their belief that he lost effectiveness as a Governor by remaining too distant from the political process and from the inner workings of State policy and operations. In 1963, Kerner promoted a budget reform program which would have required an extensive effort to restructure the Illinois budget process by shifting attention from the "what" of line items (personnel, supplies, travel, data processing) to the "why" of programs, objectives and plans. The initiative had little impact.[34] In fairness, it was attempted even before the well-known 1965 executive order by President Johnson requiring implementation of a program planning and budgeting system (PPBS) throughout the federal government. Wherever these budget reforms were attempted, there was a failure to anticipate how the immense paper-work and data problems would divert attention from the policy decisions they were intended to improve. These problems were encountered in Illinois, as elsewhere, but the reforms involved other important pitfalls as well. In Illinois the budget process was not clearly divided into executive preparation and legislative disposition. The General Assembly had preserved a role in budget preparation through the Joint Budgetary Commission, a body which received and reviewed agency requests before passing them on to the Governor with its own recommendations. The Governor then formulated his executive budget and resubmitted it to the Legislature with his recommendations. Program budgeting would have required more involvement by the Governor and would have confronted the Legislature with a different kind of budget than it was accustomed to dealing with. Even with Kerner's substantial involvement, the program budgeting effort may have been frustrated, but, without it, the effort was clearly doomed to failure from the beginning.

As Ray Coyne has suggested, the shifting role of the Budgetary Commission during the 1950 to 1970 period probably illustrates the dominance of partisan (Democratic-Republican) considerations over institutional ones (legislative-executive). During the Stratton years the Commission had taken little independent action, but during the Kerner years it proved to be a major factor in oversight as well as appropriations, mental health being a particularly prominent example. Not surprisingly, the Republican majority which persisted throughout most of this period, and thus controlled the Budgetary Commission, was much more independent in reviewing Kerner, a Democratic Governor than Stratton, a Republican.

However, there are two complicating considerations to this view of the primacy of partisanship. First, Stratton was both more knowledgeable and aggressive than Kerner in financial matters. To some extent, Kerner left a vacuum to be filled. Second, it was Ogilvie who prevailed upon his Republican legislative colleagues to weaken and then abolish the Commission in preference to his centralized Bureau of the Budget.

Kerner entered office in an atmosphere of fiscal crisis.[35] By June 1961, the General Fund was projected to be in deficit by $12,000,000.[36] There had been stormy debate in the 1959 General Assembly on a wide range of tax issues, including not only the State revenue gap, but the equity of local property tax systems. Recall that Governor Stratton had recognized the revenue gap but opposed any move toward an income tax. He proposed a national study of tax structure, but vetoed a bill appropriating funds for a State tax study commission. In 1961 Kerner sought to establish a gubernatorial revenue study commission but it was crippled by legislative opposition and lack of funds. Kerner in turn vetoed a proposed legislative study commission. Finally a compromise became law in the 1961 Special Session. A commission was organized under the chairmanship of Robert Cushman, a prominent tax attorney. The composition of the commission almost guaranteed difficulty in arriving at agreement. Kerner did not actively support its recommendations to the 1963 General Assembly, which did not act on them. Kerner desired a new and flexible revenue article, but he, like Stratton, was in a bind because he had pledged to oppose an income tax. Fisher reports that "at no time did he provide forceful leadership in fiscal matters."[37] Kerner did successfully negotiate his priorities into a legislative proposal for constitutional amendment, but did not actively campaign. It failed in 1966 to receive voter approval. At the 1967 Session, Kerner opposed an increase in the sales tax rate as inequitable and urged broadening of the tax base as an alternative. After immense agony and with little involvement from Kerner, the Legislature enacted a tax package in which rate increases domited.

Legislative Leadership Observers of Kerner's relationship with the Legislature, and of his inability to overcome the opposition of GOP Senate Majority Leader W. Russell Arrington, typically find that Kerner:

> . . . endured frustrating encounters with legislators that still defy easy analysis. Although he won legislative approval for a number of his programs . . . Kerner . . . whose political demeanor was always cool and detached . . . seldom battled publicly for his proposals.
>
> Like many governors, Kerner admittedly had little knowledge of legislative workings when he took office in 1961. His aides insisted though, that he became much more adept at maneuvering with lawmakers in his record second term than his first. Still, his troubles with Republican legislative leaders, his most consistent critics, never ceased.[38]

Yet a more substantive review of his legislative record demonstrates it is filled with major accomplishments, including creation of a substantial group of new State agencies, such as Business and Economic Development.[39] It is not clear whether this suggests that critics have been looking at the wrong considerations, that Kerner's style was effective, that even a governor as "ineffective" as Kerner will do well with good proposals, or that the Legislature has a propensity to enact which surpasses usual impressions.

A National Role and a Federal Judgeship The Kerner years were ones of unprecedented pressures on and hope for government to address itself to the racial and urban problems then coming to a head. They were years of "war" on poverty, intense struggle for equal rights and of frightening urban riots. In 1967 President Johnson asked Governor Kerner to serve as chairman of the National Advisory Commission on Civil Disorders. During the remainder of his term, Kerner's attention was heavily committed to the work of the Commission. It became best known as the "Kerner Commission." Its final report outlined the dangers of "two societies," divided largely along racial lines, one affluent and white, the other poor and black. Because of the report's timing, it fell to the succeeding administration of Richard B. Ogilvie to pursue a corresponding urban agenda for Illinois.

In recognition of Kerner's service on the Commission, President Johnson appointed him to a federal judgeship, and Shapiro became Governor in May 1968. Shapiro had already served as Acting Governor for more than 100 days, but not under circumstances which allowed him to take full responsibility for State policy-making and administration. It was Shapiro who mobilized the National Guard to maintain order in Chicago following the tragic assassination of Martin Luther King, Jr. in April 1968; who had to deal with the prison revolt at Chester where six were killed; and who confronted the safety implications of a coal mine disaster.

Shapiro as Governor: Fiscal Statesmanship During his brief term as Governor, Sam Shapiro continued to pursue his and Kerner's major policy concerns with mental health and helped focus the political process on the State's fiscal problems. During the campaign and the transition that followed, he joined with the victor Richard B. Ogilvie in acting for the benefit of the State as they both saw it.

It is in the nature of Illinois politics to experience a continuing fiscal problem, but Shapiro perceived that the situation was proceeding, without adequate leadership, to a major crisis. Public demand for services had clearly outstripped the ability of the existing tax base to meet that demand. Recent Illinois Governors of both parties had followed the conservative strategy of not taxing more than necessary to meet current obligations. They had not maintained a substantial surplus or reserve from year to year. When Shapiro took office it had become evident that at the end of fiscal year 1967–68, the State of Illinois would be at least $50 million in the red (roughly one percent of the total State budget). Shapiro took decisive action in two areas which exemplify bipartisan cooperation during the postwar years. He obtained the support of Republican legislative leaders for an emergency measure and created machinery which could develop a more long-term solution.

Instead of letting the newspapers solve the problem, Shapiro met privately with James Ronan, his Finance Director; Adlai Stevenson III, the elected Democratic State Treasurer; and the Republican legislative leaders, Senate Majority Leader W. Russell Arrington and House Speaker Ralph Smith. The GOP leaders agreed to put through the Governor's program, albeit with the expected criticism of the Administration in public for letting the situation develop. The stop-gap measures were three. First, work was halted on all capital improvements under way, and no new ones were to begin. Second and much lesser in magnitude, the rate of operating expenditures of State agencies would be slowed. Finally and crucially, the State Legislature would authorize a transfer from the earmarked highway fund to the general fund. Rather than floating trial balloons to gauge public support, the decision was announced at a joint press conference in which the key figures identified above participated.

Shapiro also set in motion the mechanics of a more long-term solution by establishing the Illinois Revenue Study Commission. He appointed as chairman Simeon E. Leland, Dean of the Graduate School of Northwestern University.

The Campaign The timing of Kerner's resignation left Shapiro with little time to organize an election campaign. He was doubly disadvantaged by the impact on Illinois voters of the riotous 1968 Democratic Convention in Chicago, which depressed and demoralized his own campaign. The Democratic presidential campaign for Hubert Humphrey began to close ground at the end, but Humphrey strategists wrote off Illinois and declined to run a Shapiro-suggested campaign train through Southern Illinois. In the face of these difficulties, Shapiro took the "high road" during the campaign, as further discussed in the section on Ogilvie.

Aftermath After leaving office, Shapiro practiced law in Chicago and Kankakee. He remained active in the Democratic Party and in the field of mental health.

Richard B. Ogilvie
Republican, 1968–1972

In any assessment of Illinois Governors by informed observers, Richard B. Ogilvie would undoubtedly rank at or near the top, and was, in fact, widely recognized as one of the best in the nation at the time. Ogilvie combined the roles of policy innovator and administrator with his role as political leader. He had not placed so much emphasis on "getting results" and solving problems, he would almost certainly have been re-elected and continued in the same style. In a very real sense, Ogilvie was a Governor whose style *was* his substance. A review of his annual Budget and State of the State messages, and of the action which followed, suggests that his own self description is accurate—he meant what he said and he did it.

Ogilvie's political career demonstrates a remarkable degree of continuity. His long-standing interest in electoral politics led to a stint with the U.S. Attorney's office. There he became deeply involved in the investigation of organized crime. He was waiting to run for State's Attorney when an opportunity to run for Cook County Sheriff emerged. Ogilvie anticipated a serious risk of ruining his reputation and assumed he would be unable to run for any other office. He felt that to do the job right he would have to alienate some GOP strongholds in Cook County, for example, Cicero. As sheriff, Ogilvie felt law enforcement was not receiving the budget allocations needed. This concern projected him into a successful run for the President of the Cook County Board, a four-year term beginning in 1966. During his service there, Ogilvie developed strong views on the need for a more cooperative State-local relationship, particularly in addressing urban problems. Law enforcement, State-local cooperation, and urban problem-solving received Ogilvie's concentrated attention as Governor.

As Republican President of the Cook County Board in a heavily Democratic county, Ogilvie offered to consult with Mayor Daley on minority appointments to boards and commissions. Though he was turned down, this foreshadowed a future willingness to cooperate across party lines, even under highly partisan circumstances.

The Campaign The close party competition and shifting political alignments characteristic of Illinois make it likely that a Governor of one party will be succeeded by one of the other party. The chances may have been improved when the popular incumbent Otto Kerner resigned in 1968 to accept a federal judgeship. The Republican nomination was a valuable one. Ogilvie was pitted in the primary election against former Governor William G. Stratton and John Altorfer of Peoria. He early assembled a coalition of supporters and a team of aides which would continue through the general election and into the governorship. A key element was the strong support he received from Senate Majority Leader W. Russell Arrington, who assigned his outstanding legislative staff to work with the Ogilvie team.

In the general election, Ogilvie faced the newly promoted incumbent Governor Shapiro, who had little time to organize a statewide campaign or to mobilize the political resources usually available to an incumbent. The campaign was waged on a remarkably high level. The two candidates agreed not to make an issue of the major problem confronting the State—the crisis of a widening gap between revenues and expenditures. If the issue were joined, both would have to repudiate the income tax alternative, yet both were convinced the alternative would have to be left open. Previous campaigns had forced Stratton and Kerner to enter office on records flatly in opposition to an income tax. Throughout the primary and the general election, Ogilvie strove to communicate his awareness of public opposition to a tax, while avoiding any personal commitment to oppose it.

A Successful Transition Recent renewed attention to the importance of state governors in the American system has focused in part on the importance of transitions from one administration to another. In many, if not all, respects, recent Governors of Illinois have maintained a degree of mutual confidence, but this has not always led to a productive transition. The Shapiro-Ogilvie transition may have been exemplary. Ogilvie organized a group of transition task-forces which thoroughly assessed existing policies and administration. As a result, when he took office in January, he was well prepared with perspective and specific suggestions for next steps. During this process Ogilvie continued to work with the Republican legislative leadership and their staffs, a mutually beneficial element of influence and cooperation across branches and within the GOP. A key element in the success of the transition was the active cooperation of Governor Shapiro, who made space and State funds available for the transition staff. He also instructed agency personnel to cooperate, and they did.

Financial Crisis Leadership: Senator Arrington and Mayor Daley When Ogilvie took office in Janury 1969, he faced a major financial crisis. In the interim period following the election he had received the report of the Revenue Study Commission to Governor Shapiro. It was clear that the gap between revenues and expenditures was growing. The public was clearly demanding more, not less services. At one of his first regular breakfast meetings with the Republican majority leadership of both houses, Ogilvie announced his proposal for an income tax and requested their support. Senator Arrington immediately quipped, ". . . and who's the dummy that's going to sponsor the bill in the Senate?'' Ogilvie's rejoinder was equally quick: ''You are, Russ!'' Arrington, who had been a staunch opponent of the tax, was persuaded of its necessity and became one of the key backers. But the support of Democrats, and that meant Chicago Democrats, would be necessary for enactment.

The viability of Ogilvie's relationship with the Chicago Democratic organization had been immediately cast in doubt, for the public at least, on the day after his election when newspaper headlines quoted his pledge to ''dismantle the machine.'' In fact, Ogilvie had communicated to Mayor Daley during the campaign that as Governor of Illinois, he would cooperate with the City of Chicago. Earlier, as President of the Cook County Board, he had even tried to consult the Mayor on appointments. The newspaper headlines reflected Ogilvie's momentary irritation with Democratic officials who were holding back the ballot returns, a situation for which the GOP had no remedy other than to reciprocate in suburban areas. Ogilvie had spoken in an understandable language, however; and the delays were quickly rectified.

Mayor Daley had a strong interest in passage of the income tax, so it became possible to handle the issue in the bipartisan mixture of cooperation and conflict so typical of Illinois politics. Clearly, an income tax would be enacted—the major question became which legislators, and how many from each party, would become the potential sacrifical lambs who would have to vote for it! The Democrats insisted that since the Republicans were in the majority in both houses, they should contribute a majority of the votes. The Senate presented more of a problem in this regard than the House. Senate Majority Leader W. Russell Arrington had been persuaded that the time had come for an income tax, but despite his best efforts, it proved impossible to obtain the needed Republican votes. Ogilvie then obtained the cooperation of Minority Leader Arthur McGloon, who sent two Democratic Senators to the Governor's office, and Ogilvie was able to obtain their support.

Urban Leadership Ogilvie's concern for local and urban government was reflected in his incorporation of a revenue-sharing feature in the State income tax three years in advance of the well-known federal revenue-sharing plan. As a result, local governments receive 12.5 percent of the income tax revenue, now about $200 million annually, for unrestricted use. In addition to providing local governments with additional funds, Ogilvie took the lead in establishing a new Department of Local Government Affairs to perform a double administrative and political function. The administrative function was to provide technical assistance and training to local governments too small to fund their own. The political function was to provide local officials with effective channels within the executive branch through which they could communicate their needs. Local government has traditionally enjoyed excellent access to the Legislature, so Ogilvie was attempting to bring the relationship of the two branches with local government into better balance. Ogilvie also backed the creation of the Illinois Housing Development Authority (IHDA) with State guarantees of bond funding for needed low and middle-income housing in communities throughout the State.

Federal Initiative Ogilvie's concern with local government was matched by his awareness of the impact of the national government on the State. He took steps to strengthen the Illinois office in Washington, D.C., appointing as director Tom Corcoran, then an Arrington aide, now U.S. Congressman (15th). Through this office, Ogilvie carried on high level negotiations with the Department of Health, Education, and Welfare (HEW) and the office of Management and Budget (OMB) for substantially increased federal matching funds under the social services program (Title XX, Social Security Act). Before the negotiations were completed, it became necessary to go over the heads of federal bureaucrats to the GOP White House, and Ogilvie did this effectively. A major consideration at the time was that the new funds would permit a balanced budget in an election year, improving GOP changes of carrying Illinois for Ogilvie and Nixon in 1972.

Managerial Leadership Ogilvie has a deserved reputation as an excellent manager of State government. The illustrations below give some insight into the reasons as well as the costs of that particular management style. Ogilvie implemented his desire for results (effective, well managed programs) largely by modernizing the budget office, careful non-partisan appointments of agency heads and letting managers manage. Ogilvie set out to have the best cabinet in the history of the State, and believes that will prove to be the case. Contrary to partisan urgings, he retained a number of agency heads from the previous Administration. He was exceptionally successful in recruiting top-level business and federal executives. Apparently, Ogilvie maintained a strict principle of non-intervention in agency management, fully aware of the risks. Having recruited able independent leaders, he knew they would stay only under those conditions. Ogilvie spoke with the head of the Environmental Protection Agency (EPA) only once after appointing him, to suggest that a member of the public relations staff be replaced. Ogilvie had also implemented the Judicial Inquiry Board required under the 1970 Constitution. He was subsequently placed under great pressure to protect a judge, but refused to intercede—again, he had appointed individuals who wouldn't stand for it. Ogilvie also appointed some well-known politicians, for example John Lewis in the Department of Agriculture, which was perceived to have a particularly challenging constituency with which Lewis was well equipped to deal.

A key element in Ogilvie's approach to management, and one of his major innovations, was the new Bureau of the Budget, created in 1969 with the reluctant support of the Legislature. Up to this time Governors had relied heavily on a largely clerical staff, under the perennial direction of Ted Leth, to assemble agency budget requests, submit them for review to the Legislative Budgetary Commission and then prepare the Governor's Budget. The involvement of individual Governors in the budget process had varied considerably. Ogilvie persuaded the Legislature to remove the Budgetary Commission from the process of formulating the executive budget and to create a Bureau of the Budget (BOB) to be consciously modeled after the federal Office of Management and Budget. Throughout his term, Ogilvie's BOB and the often intimidating "whiz kids" who ran it were usually at the center of, and the source of, major controversies over State expenditures and their policy implications. For the first time Illinois had an executive budget process, and a staff to run it, which could accommodate serious analysis of issues, alternatives, spending levels and finances. For the first time, the Governor's staff incorporated substantial planning and management improvement capabilities in close connection with the budget process. Without the acceptance of the Legislature, however, grudging it may have been, these new capabilities could never have been installed. Legislative cooperation in these initiatives reflected the close working relationship cultivated by both Ogilvie and the Republican majority leadership of both houses.

Organizing the Governor and His Office Ogilvie's managerial consciousness extended to his own office operations. A major objective was to maintain the free flow of communication to him, avoiding the tendency of the boss to receive highly selective and biased messages from staff. Ogilvie made sure all his staff had access to him, rather than letting the natural instincts of his top staff control him by restricting access. The most thorough analysis of the Ogilvie staffing experience concludes that the staff would have been more productive if each key assistant had clearly understood the precise nature of his responsibility, had been given a clear grant of authority vis-a-vis agency directors, and had been held more firmly accountable for results.

A political scientist serving on Ogilvie's staff analyzed the use of the Governor's time for 24 working days during the month of June 1971, with the results presented below:

Analysis of a Monthly Schedule
of the Governor of Illinois
June 1971

Category	Hours	Percent
I. Public Relations	67	27
II. Management of State Government	48	19
III. Invitations to Private Functions	44	18
IV. Legislative Relations	39	16
V. Political Leadership	27	11
VI. Intra-Office Responsibilities	14	6
VII. Out-of-State Travel	12	5
	251	100

Source: Ronald D. Michaelson, *Public Affairs Bulletin* (Carbondale: Southern Illinois University, September/October 1971), 1–6.

This analysis highlights the intense competition for a governor's time. Even a governor as substantively oriented as Ogilvie may spend only 25 percent of his time on matters of substantive policy and management (including intra-office responsibilities) although these undoubtedly spill over into related promotional activities required to generate support for policy and management initiatives.

Legislative Leadership Ogilvie's relations with the legislature fall into two distinct phases. From the beginning, he clearly recognized the necessity of cooperation and took advantage of the cooperation offered by the Republican majority leadership of both houses. However, relations were never to be as good for Ogilvie as they were in 1969, the first session of his term. Immense energy was unleashed in behalf of common programs. But fiscal measures such as the income tax and numerous innovations and reforms, some of which are identified here, took their toll in hostilities. There is some evidence that Ogilvie sought without success to purge several GOP legislators who had failed to support his program, by running candidates against them in the 1970 elections. They returned to the Legislature even less favorably disposed to cooperate. Also, the 1970 elections brought the loss of a Republican majority in the Senate, undermining a base of legislative support. Ogilvie rewarded House Speaker Ralph Smith for his labors by appointing him to the U.S. Senate when Everett Dirksen died.

The 1970 Constitution: Implementation of Precedent—Setting Powers Ogilvie was Governor when the Constitutional Convention was in session and when the voters of Illinois enacted a new Constitution in 1970. He established an implementation task force under Sam Gove of the University of Illinois Bureau of Government and Public Affairs. Ogilvie personally implemented key new veto powers which may have altered the balance of power between the Governor and the Legislature. Prior to 1970 the Governor had the power to veto an entire piece of substantive legislation and to strike any item from the Legislature's line item appropriation bills. Under the new Constitution, Ogilvie had additional powers of the "amendatory" veto and the "reduction" veto—in addition to eliminating a line item he could reduce it to any amount. These new veto powers were compensated somewhat by a legislative power to call itself into session for the purpose of overriding vetoes, but questions have been raised as to whether the new features create an incentive to legislative fiscal irresponsibility. More weighty questions have been raised regarding Ogilvie's conversion of the amendatory veto from a purely technical corrective device to a major tool of substantive amendment, a practice which has been enthusiastically followed by his successors.

Ogilvie's new Bureau of the Budget, under Director John McCarter, Deputy George A. Ranney, Jr. and Assistant John Cotton, contributed to Illinois' often fickle experimentation with improved budget systems by selectively implementing "zero-base" budgeting concepts long before more systematic and publicized efforts by states like Georgia and Texas. While the technical proficiency of these exercises was unquestioned, the implications of the analyses were overwhelmed by more intense political considerations, and the anticipated savings were seldom realized. For example, the BOB recommended the closing of the Chicago Tuberculosis Sanitarium, which was successfully resisted by Democrats in the Legislature.

The 1970 Constitution gave Ogilvie one power which he didn't use, though he intended to do so in his second term. Toward the end of his first term Ogilvie commissioned a reorganization task force under the direction of his informal "czar of management improvement," John Briggs. The task force worked on the assumption that Ogilvie would be reelected and submitted its report at the end of his term.

Gubernatorial Style and Re-Election Chances By many standards Ogilvie was a conspicously successful Governor. If that is the case, it is worth trying to explain why he was not reelected in 1972, a year in which a GOP President carried Illinois by a substantial margin. Could Ogilvie have done anything about it? And, if so, would he do it differently if he could? Or does the explanation lie more in the nature of the times or in the effectiveness of the Walker campaign?

A simple and popular explanation is that Ogilvie lost because he pushed through an income tax in 1969, against general public opposition, which was strongest within the Republican Party. It had been clear in advance that this would be a liability. A poll taken immediately following enactment indicated only 30 percent of Illinois voters approved the job he was doing. And since the margin of defeat in 1972 was narrow, it is plausible that a decisive number of Republican voters may have declined to vote for Ogilvie. A supreme irony of the campaign according to Ron Michaelson was that Ogilvie Republican's had crossed over to the Democratic primary and voted for Walker, thinking he would be easier to defeat than Simon.

Ogilvie himself thinks a more crucial factor was that even during the campaign he allowed his managers to manage irrespective of political considerations. A number of actions with serious political consequences were taken. In mid-campaign, the Environmental Protection Agency and the Pollution Control Board, Ogilvie creations, took action to prohibit agricultural feed-lot run-off, arousing the farmers, and to institute a statewide ban on leaf burning, arousing many small town rural downstate Republicans and symbolizing their fears of the powers these agencies had been given. Ogilvie himself had instructed the State Police to remove illegal slot machines from east central Illinois. Apparently the Police, who had to live with neighbors who were upset by this, fixed the blame squarely on the Governor. Ogilvie had made and kept a campaign commitment on extension of the East-West Tollway beyond Aurora, resulting in opposition by the Illinois Agricultural Association. Characteristically, Ogilvie states he wouldn't do differently if he could. He governed in a style which suited him, confident that he could return to a successful law practice and that history would be kind.

Retrospect Despite Ogilvie's remarkable success in achieving his objectives as Governor, he has witnessed substantial alterations under two successors, one from his own party. A prime example is the Department of Local Government Affairs, scheduled for consolidation into a larger agency with a broader mission under Governor Thompson's systematic reorganization of State government. Ogilvie had strongly felt that local governments needed "their department" to represent their needs to the governor. Similarly, Ogilvie had created the Illinois Bureau of Investigation to focus resources and attention on crime problems with which local governments were unable to cope; as Cook County Sheriff Ogilvie had been burnt by inadequate investigative resources. One of Thompson's first acts was to consolidate the "IBI", thought by many to have been "politicized" under Governor Walker, into a more comprehensive law enforcement agency. Finally, one of Ogilvie's overall objectives for State government improvement had been to bring professionals in at all levels, reduce total employees and increase individual salaries. He feels Governor Walker fired many of the professionals in unprotected staff positions, an action Walker views as removing excess middle management personnel.

Aftermath Since his departure from office in 1972 Ogilvie has rejoined the prominent Chicago law firm of Isham, Lincoln and Beale, where he remains active in governmental as well as corporate matters. He was seriously considered for appointment to several federal cabinet positions under the Nixon and Ford administrations, including the FBI. One of Ogilvie's most intriguing activities during this period was his service on the advisory board to the model committee project of the Citizens' Conference on State Legislatures, a recognition of the breadth of his commitment to strong state government.

Dan Walker
Independent Democrat, 1972–76

In many important respects Dan Walker was unique among Illinois Governors—in the way he came to office, his primary goals, his approach in seeking to achieve those goals and the nature of the opposition he encountered—and all were characteristic. Walker came to office through a primary election victory over fellow Democrat Paul Simon, who had been slated by the Democratic State Central Committee.

A Unique Objective and its Consequences His primary concern as a candidate and as Governor was to reform State politics by opening up the Democratic Party to better representation for suburban and downstate, as distinct from Chicago, interests. He consciously sacrificed many opportunities for compromise agreements in order to preserve the independent stance he felt was essential to open up State politics. As a consequence, other key actors in both parties, particularly in the Legislature, confronted with an unfamiliar and essentially alien style of governing, rather early took the position of a 'disloyal opposition." Walker's politically disadvantageous position proved to be a constant drain on his political resources.

In effect, Walker tested both the viability of a particular strategy of reform and what a Governor can accomplish by exercising his formal powers and by appealing to the people, but often without the cooperation of key actors in either political party. Against his wishes, Walker became widely known in political circles as a "confrontation Governor." The reason for this unfortunate situation may lie in the fact that Walker was never able to reconcile his comitment to independence in policy-making and administration with his objective of opening up the Democratic Party. Together they placed unmanageable strains on his relationship with both political parties in the legislature. Walker is still inclined to the view that it is not only possible, but necessary, for a good Governor to resist accommodation with the Legislature or with the Mayor of Chicago, because that would not be moral, open and honest—that is, it would require too much compromise at objectives.

Route to the Governorship Dan Walker served in the Navy, graduated from law school, served on Governor Adlai Stevenson's reorganization study group and became an immensely successful corporation counsel for Marcor, which controls Montgomery Ward and other companies. Walker, like Ogilvie, had a special interest in management, one which he applied with some success and some frustration as Governor. For a long period Walker had been aligned with the "independent" Democratic movement of Chicago and suburban politics. He was to draw substantial support from that group of political activists in the 1972 campaign, and a number of key lieutenants were drawn from the group, the foremost being his Deputy Governor Victor DeGrazia.

Walker achieved national political visibility in 1968, when President Johnson asked him to head a study of the civil disturbances which defamed the 1968 Democratic Convention in Chicago. The "Walker Report" made quite a splash when it was released, because it diagnosed a large part of the problem in terms of a "police riot." Mayor Daley's response was apoplexy. While this lack of accommodation typified their relationships as Governor and Mayor, it should not be assumed that future problems were therefore inevitable. A deeper source of the problems to come was the "independent" commitment to transform and open up Democratic politics.

When Walker entered the Democratic primary in 1972, reform politics had reached its height in the National Democratic Party, led by U.S. Senator George McGovern who was to emerge as the Party's presidential candidate. There was a strong aura of populism in the air, blurring the usual liberal and conservative distinctions. Campaign styles were affected. Lawton Childs had been elected to the U.S. Senate by walking all over Florida. Walker did the same in Illinois, with great success. However Walker may have over-estimated the potential of similar tactics for generating political power by using the media to go over the heads of the "politicians" to the people. Perhaps no governor in any state has made the effort Walker did to use television and flie-ins to "town meetings" as a means of overcoming resistance to his proposals. Probably at least one other governor, Ronald Reagan of California, a movie actor, has used the media more effectively.

Changing Circumstances By the time Walker took office in 1972, he faced a very different situation from that faced by Ogilvie in 1968, and the situation was to change radically during his term. Ogilvie walked into a revenue crisis of massive proportions and resolved it by pushing through an income tax. Revenues generated were sufficient not only to close the gap and restore money borrowed from earmarked funds, but to create new State programs and expand State services. By the end of his term, however, Ogilvie was encountering difficulty in balancing the budget, and he was impelled to negotiate for new federal matching funds. The Ogilvie years had seen increasing and undeniable demands for funds from increasing welfare rolls and from commitments by the Governor and many other political actors to increase State support for all levels of education. A 1970–71 recession had compounded matters by reducing expected revenues and increasing necessary expenditures for income security programs. As a consequence, Walker felt he had entered office without benefit of any large "bulge" from the new income tax. As he saw it State revenues were already fully committed. The validity of this view has been a continuing point of contention.

Achievements and Burdens of Independence Democratic majorities in both houses of the Legislature were of no aid to Walker. His legislative priority was not to work out accommodations necessary to get a program through, but to realign key legislative power blocks toward a more open process where issues could be discussed on their merits. For Walker this strategy required simultaneous strengthening of downstate Democrats and avoidance of gubernatorial cooperation with the Chicago organization. Only with the Governor on their side could the downstate Democrats become a viable and independent force. Independent Democrats needed better access and a Governor they could rely on for support. Walker intended to meet that need.

Walker feels this strategy achieved an important degree of success which has continued beyond his term. In league with independent Democrats he played a major role in denying the House Speakership to Clyde Choat of Carbondale, viewed as a Chicago ally. After over 100 ballots in the House it eventually became possible to elect Rep. William Redmond of suburban DuPage County as Speaker, a move Walker felt advanced the quality of downstate representation substantially. Walker takes credit for providing crucial support to the independent Democrats in the Senate, who became known as the "Crazy Eight" for their unprecedented solidarity vis-a-vis the Chicago group. A result of this cohesiveness was that they were able to obtain an Assistant Majority Leader position and several chairmanships.

However, the downstate and Chicago independents whom Walker was committed to strengthening represented a small block in the Legislature. On many occasions Democrats and Republicans combined to thwart him. Traditionally the Legislature allows the Governor substantial leeway in budgeting, staffing and organizing his office to reflect his priorities. In Walker's case, the traditional practices were not observed. With legislative cooperation, Governor Ogilvie had established a Governor's Office of Human Resources (GOHR) and an Office of Manpower. The Illinois Information Service had been operated by several Governors. Walker wanted funding for similar activities, including Governor's action offices, an Office of Collective Bargaining, and a special investigation unit. These were attacked as "pet agencies" in the Legislature and special funding requests were denied, although Walker found other ways of operating them.

In order to achieve his primary reform goals, Walker had, in effect, voluntarily relinquished the traditional tools of accommodation with the dominant political forces in the Legislature. In compensation, he used his formal powers to the hilt. For example, a study of the use of the veto power shows that Walker substantially expanded its use as a means of achieving budget and policy objectives. The Legislature, in turn, enacted a number of items such as highway appropriations which Walker perceived as intentional challenges. Even extensive use of the veto power, however, was insufficient to compensate for the absence of accommodation.

Perhaps the issues which most typify Walker's role in the political process are those where the City of Chicago came to the Legislature for its transportation needs. These involve the crosstown expressway, aid to the Chicago Transit Authority (CTA) and the Regional Transportation Authority (RTA). Mayor Daley was strongly committed to installing a north-south "crosstown" expressway on the west side of Chicago. He needed State approval to obtain federal matching funds. Community opposition was intense and very well organized. Walker flatly refused to deal with the City on the matter and became the chief public opponent. Early in the debates on State aid to the Chicago Transit Authority, Walker sent a message to Daly in which he made it clear that he would not continue to play the game of progressively increasing the State share. Walker felt it necessary to demonstrate that he was willing to fight, and could not be intimidated, even at the risk of an override of his veto.

In retrospect, Walker suggests that he did not actively seek confrontation politics, but that it was imposed on him as the only alterntive to giving in. Varying interpretations are possible. It may be that the single-mindedness of Walker's reform commitments necessitated confrontation politics. However, Walker felt the other side could have negotiated but chose not to. This may illustrate a classical zero-sum game where each side prefers to pursue a high risk/high gain strategy. The value of such a game may be different for the professional politicians than for the people of Illinois; it depends heavily on the importance of the reforms being sought, a matter on which judgment will differ. In Walker's opinion, the most disappointing development since he left office is the resumption of "business as usual"—private accommodations between the Governor of Illinois and the Mayor of Chicago. Walker remains convinced that "cutting deals" is not the way the system is supposed to work.

Managerial Leadership Walker entered office with a definite philosophy of managerial leadership derived from his corporate experience. His straightforward view of the job and its authority did not lend itself to ready adoption to the inevitable machinations and indirectness of the political process. By Illinois tradition, more than in many states, public administration has been very much a part of the political process.

As a Governor must, Walker chose management systems congenial to his style and rejected approaches he found uncongenial. He rejected reorganization as a major strategy. His experience under Stevenson had led him to be skeptical of what can be accomplished by reorganization. In view of the difficulties with the Legislature which prevailed throughout his administration, it may be that an attempt to exercise these powers would have been thwarted in any case. Walker also doubted the usefulness of the substantial State planning capability established by Ogilvie in the BOB and proceeded to largely dismantle it. Nevertheless, Walker's strong criticism of inadequate funds flowing into Illinois was based on a study done by the Planning Office.

Walker chose to establish a dual system for budgeting and management. He committed himself to the systematic implementation of "zero-base-budgeting" (ZBB) and to a system of "management by objectives" (MBO) which he would personally direct in his capacity as chief executive. Despite Walker's serious commitment to these systems, they were vitiated or pushed aside during his term, in ways from which broader lessons may be drawn.

ZBB was undermined by a combination of factors largely beyond control: difficulties in the national economy and traditional legislative indifference to executive budget innovation. The national energy crisis of 1973 triggered a period of intense "stagflation"—a combination of economic stagnation and increased unemployment with double-digit inflation and reduced purchasing power. Once again the State entered a period in which actual revenues were less than anticipated and income security payments were greater than anticipated. This new State fiscal crisis broke after Walker submitted his budget, while the Legislature was still acting on it. The Legislature responded, as it could be expected to, by making substantial across-the-board cuts which obliterated the ZBB rationale. Nevertheless, it appears that Walker's extension of ZBB, implemented by budget directors Harold Hovey and Leonard Schaeffer, did move the State toward a greater capability for fundamental examination of current expenditures, in contrast to exclusive focus on additional increments of spending.

The system of management by objectives (MBO) was somewht more sheltered, but it too proved vulnerable to the political process. Walker anticipated that he would have the time, energy and attention to work closely with his cabinet over a period of years in setting clear objectives for State agencies, measuring how well they were doing and taking corrective measures as needed. A small staff was created within the BOB to handle the paper work and details, but as Walker realized, his full attention was necessary for the system to work. Walker is proud of initial accomplishments in clarifying the objectives of the Departments of Public Health and Conservation and linking them more closely to gubernatorial leadership. Quantitative goals were set for the disease control and innoculation program. Nevertheless, before the end of the term Walker's attention was so diverted by political battles that the MBO system fell into virtual disuse. BOB staff were unable to operate the system without the Governor's extensive attention.

It was Walker's observation that Ogilvie had a practice of allowing his liaison assistants and key people in the Bureau of the Budget to speak for him on matters of program and policy within individual departments and agencies. Walker felt this practice of staff control would be counterproductive by generating line manager resentment. He established a firm policy that the staff were to help solve problems and achieve financial accountability, but under no circumstances were they to speak for him or to make decisions on matters of program and policy.

Policy Continuity, Leadership and Frustration- Walker takes pride in his support of continued progress for programs already under way when he took office, for example mental health and public housing. Ogilvie had created the Illinois Housing Development Authority (IHDA) to guarantee bonds for low and middle-income housing. During Walker's term, conventional mortgage money became unavailable, and IHDA emerged as a major source of housing finance. A comparable New York agency had just experienced a financial crisis, and Illinois legislators feared they also might become responsible for making good on implied guarantees. Walker persisted for several years and finally obtained legislative approval for an increase in the IHDA bond ceiling, permitting more housing to be funded. Under Walker IHDA also became a partner in developing dispersed housing for the retarded.

More on Management Because certain problems in the Department of Mental Health were not being resolved, Walker instituted a regular monthly meeting in which he and the Director met with persons representing the major statewide interests. From these meetings emerged a concept of "Specialized Living Centers" for the retarded, with "turnkey" financing. The first centers were opened in 1979.

Some of Walker's major impacts and frustrations as a manager were in the area of personnel. He experienced considerable success in a major objective of reducing the number of middle management personnel and in improving the productivity of those who remained. He continued the trend toward reducing the total number of State personnel, by 10 percent, while increasing the salaries of the professionals needed to operate increasingly complex State programs. Police in the Department of Conservation were removed from patronage causing some resentment, and possibly leading to retaliation via Walker's subsequent arrest by federal officials for illegal hunting!

In the absence of an Illinois collective bargaining law, Walker issued an executive order providing for State employees and established an Office of Collective Bargaining within the Governor's Office, over legislative opposition. The prevailing view of executive orders is that they do not require any particular basis in statute as long as they do not contradict legislative policy. Despite unhappiness in the Legislature, the Walker order stood, and with some difficulty he was able to fund the staff.

One of Walker's most important and most frustrated initiatives involved a mixture of policy conflict and personnel controversy. Walker was committed to the reform of institutional programs serving dependent, delinquent and disturbed youths. Under previous Governors Illinois, like other states, had begun a massive transition from long-term care in large institutions to short-term community-based care. As the transition proceeded, the need for better quality control of voluntary sector service providers became evident. Walker nominated candidates to direct the related State agencies (Children and Family Services, Corrections, and Mental Health) who were committed to protecting the clients. The Senate found these nominations an excellent opportunity to exercise its powers of approval. It denied several Walker appointments entirely and made others an ordeal.

The Walker candidate eventually approved for the Department of Children and Family Services, Jerome Miller, had administered a similar program in Massachusetts so aggresively that opposing interests were able to mobilize in the Legislature and chase him out. A remarkably similar sequence of events followed his appointment in Illinois. When Miller proceeded to implement the Walker policy of improving quality control and placing children more selectively with voluntary institutions, the institutions demonstrated unanticipated political clout by mobilizing their prestigious boards of directors. The battle which ensued was not won by the Governor, and Miller moved on to join the faculty at the Loyola University School of Social Work. Despite the rocky experience, Walker feels much was accomlished. In this case, he concedes a mistaken approach, to the extent of trying to do too much at once.

Retrospect In retrospect, Walker feels his management strengths and contributions were among his most substantial ones. He fought to give that part of the job the time it deserved. He made improvements and got results. Yet he left with the feeling that few people in or out of State government cared.

Gubernatorial Style and Re-Election Chances In the 1976 primary elections, the regular Democratic organization selected popular Secretary of State Mike Howlett to run against Walker, and Howlett won. Why? Some informed observers judge a wide disaffection with "confrontation politics," even among the core suburban, independent Walker supporters of 1972. The congenial noncontroversial Howlett was an ideal opponent. Walker sees it as more complex. He admits he did not fully appreciate the disaffection. Opinion polls indicated that 52 percent of Chicago voters favored him, but they did not turn out as well as the anti-Walker voters. This reinforces the common impression that a significant element in voting behavior is negative, and it underlines the importance of organization in turning out the vote. Walker had a media problem in Chicago, partly because the media did not wish to alienate the Mayor. Several key commentators were personally opposed to Walker, one because Walker had failed to appoint a person the commentator recommended. Also, at a crucial time the national television networks refused to run Walker commercials on the grounds they were "governmental advertising." Walker does not feel the economic problems faced by Illinois and the nation during his term hurt him politically.

Perspective on a Unique Administration Walker's term was unique and can be assessed differently depending on one's viewpoint. Dan Walker felt a change of procedures and access were crucial to Illinois politics. It was this which set the tone for his campaign, his style as Governor and the problems on which he focused. Of almost equal importance, Walker saw himself as a manager. The net result was that Walker's political goals resulted in political resistance, which in turn required herculean efforts to preserve time and attention for management. Walker's willingness to sacrifice himself and his colleagues for these ideals resulted in an image of the "confrontation Governor," one which he feels was not his normal style, nor his choice. Rather, it was a consequence of insisting that decisions be made, not in the traditional personal deals between Illinois Governors and Chicago Mayors, but in the open where the public interest could be debated. The Illinois political system has reverted to its prior style of bipartisan accommodation, but Walker has left a more idealistic, and perhaps more politically costly, alternative example for those in the Democratic Party who might wish to follow it. If suburban and downstate Democrats continue to gain power in the Party, Walker may become known for his chosen role of changing the posture of Democratic Governors and the nature of representation in the Illinois Democratic Party. For additional perspective on the partisan changes which affected the style of gubernatorial leadership in the seventies, see the Colby and Green discussions of the 1970 Constitutional changes and court decisions which have led to more cross-overs in primary elections and increased ticket-splitting in general elections.

Aftermath Since his departure from office in 1976, Walker has established a statewide law practice with headquarters in suburban Oak Brook and offices in a number of downstate cities. He may very well return to the political arena, but he has passed up the opportunity to contest Secretary of State Alan Dixon in the 1980 primary which will determine the Democratic Party's candidate to succeed the retiring incumbent, Adlai Stevenson III. Walker has expressed the view that he may be more naturally suited to a chief executive job, with an emphasis on management, than to a legislative position, with its emphasis on the compromise of policy-making. In this context, it is noteworthy that at the 1979 conference of the Midwest Political Science Association, Walker expressed the view that management is the central but neglected function of governors and that relations with the legislature are an unfortunate, and largely unimportant, diversion. Perhaps an excessively simple interpretation would be that Walker has moved very close to the view that legislatures make policy and governors implement it, a view which clearly distinguishes him from other recent Governors of Illinois.

James R. Thompson

By almost any standard of practical politics, the incumbent Governor, James R. Thompson, has been highly successful thus far in achieving his goals and in obtaining public support. Thompson's future problems may derive largely from his current successes and from the common perception that he aspires to the GOP presidential nomination as early as 1980. Like each of his predecessors, Thompson's handling of his responsibilities adds a new dimension to our perception of the office and its requirements. Any assessment of Thompson's performance to date must be undertaken in the context of his unique first term, which lasted only two years and required special attention to the problem of reelection.

Route to Office "Big Jim" Thompson was elected Governor while still a young man, at the age of 38. An attorney, he had served as a member of the law faculty at Northwestern University. He projected himself into Illinois politics as U.S. Attorney for the Northern District of Illinois, where he directed the prosecution of elected officials of both parties in unprecedented numbers, including members of the State Legislature.

Thompson has done well by the electoral process, despite the uncertainties of his unique two-year first term. He was elected by a record margin of 1.5 million votes in 1976 and improved on his winning percentage in 1978. A major feature of the 1970 Constitution had been the provision for shifting the election of Illinois governors from the presidential election year to "off-years." This required either a two-year or six-year term, and the Convention opted for the former, to occur in 1976–78. Any person contemplating a run for the office would have to consider the risks or gains in such a short term. It may be that some who declined to run were deterred by the short term, but it is more likely that other considerations prevailed. A major consideration would have to be the anticipated fiscal crisis which the victor would have to confront. As it developed, there was no shortage of candidates.

Predictably Dan Walker sought reelection and equally predictably, the regular Democratic organization sent forth a challenger. The man selected was Mike Howlett, the genial and popular Secretary of State, who had also served as State Comptroller. Howlett won a hard-fought contest in which the organization backed him to the hilt, but Walker supporters gave Howlett little support in the general election. In addition to the divisive nature of the campaign and of the relationships which had preceded it, Thompson himself was a key factor.

Thompson's prosecution of corrupt politicians had immense public appeal and was conducted in a highly visible manner. He obtained the support of most major figures in the Illinois GOP, including Ogilvie. No major candidate opposed him in the primary. The Thompson campaign achieved a momentum—carrying over into the general election—which Howlett was unable to match. Thompson had little difficulty in appealing to the substantial number of independent voters and obtained the endorsement of the Independent Voters of Illinois (IVI).

Ironically, but not uniquely to Illinois politics, Thompson and Howlett were old friends. They followed the Shapiro/Ogilvie precedent of subordinating campaign competition to shared views on the needs of the State by jointly commissioning the blue-ribbon "Bonniwell Report" on reorganization. Each committed himself to implementing the recommendations if elected. The shift of emphasis from 1968 to 1976 is noteworthy. In 1968, the cooperation of the candidates had been aimed at meeting a financial crisis by generating more revenue. In 1976, cooperation was aimed instead at saving money without reducing services by introducing greater efficiency into State government. At the same time, State Comptroller Michael Bakalis was making similar proposals for comprehensive State productivity improvement. The rhetorical response to public concerns was clear in its direction—what remained to be seen was the degree of practical implementation which would result.

Favorable Conditions In many respects, other than the short term, Thompson entered office under ideal circumstance. He enjoyed broad public support and had made few commitments to other politicians or business leaders. There would be a clear "bottom line" for the first term. Thompson would have to demonstrate prudent fiscal management, and he would have to follow through on his law enforcement reputation. Then, to preserve his options for a run at the Presidency, he would have to win big again in 1978. The subsequent requirements are subject to differing personal judgments, but it seems reasonable to suggest that Thompson must continue to do two things he did well in his first term: demonstrate prudent fiscal management and actively cooperate with members of both parties. He would also have to do at least two other specific things which were not conspicuous in his first term: demonstrate leadership in addressing substantive policy problems and project his interest in foreign policy.

Legislative Leadership: Working Things Out In his first term, Thompson demonstrated that his ability to obtain broad electoral support was equalled by his ability to work with both parties in the Legislature. That is, Thompson was able to push hard for his priorities and to resist Legislative priorities without undermining his working relationships. Some have referred to his style of working with the Legislature as "clubbish." The opposite might have been expected in view of the fact that he had put a number of legislator colleagues behind bars in his prosecutorial days! A cynic, or even a realist, might be inclined to speculate that some information from those days might still be used in bargaining with the Legislature! Be that as it may, it is all the more crucial that a major factor in Thompson's relations with the Legislature has been the general sense of relief at a return to the normal style of bargaining following the mutual frustration of the Walker years.

An index of the increase in mutual tolerance has been the use of the veto. Walker used the amendatory veto with much greater frequency than Ogilvie, and the necessity of using it appeared to reflect the lack of legislative-executive cooperation. Surprisingly, Thompson initially employed that power with even greater frequency than Walker, yet without incurring any of the rancor evident during the Walker years. A contributing factor may be the improvement of communication with legislators whose bills might be vetoed, provided for in the consultation procedures followed by Thompson's legislative liaison staff.

Dealing for the Big Ones A major element in Thompson's successful management of the fiscal squeeze is his 1977 bargain with Chicago Democrats on the crosstown expressway. Thompson had opposed the expressway in his campaign against Howlett, but agreed to support a revised proposal in exchange for Democrat cooperation in the budget process. Governor Walker's view of his responsibilities clearly did not permit him to undertake such a bargain, nor would it have permitted him the benefits which accrued to Thompson.

The crosstown illustrates how Governors are major factors in the revision of basic political bargains as circumstances change. At the end of the 1979 Session, Thompson and Chicago's new Mayor, Jane Bryne, announced their major deal of the Session. By agreement, the crosstown would be dropped, along with a planned subway extension, in order to free $2 billion for other metropolitan transportation subsidies and improvements in the area served by the Regional Transportation Authority (RTA). Ordinarily when a Governor of Illinois and a Mayor of Chicago get together and make an announcement, legislative forces have been committed to the bargain in advance. However in this case the two apparently failed to get their ducks in line—the 1979 Legislature adjourned its regular session without taking action. This probably reflected the new Mayor's shakedown process in the Legislature and would prove to be the beginning, not the end, of this particular episode in transportation policy-making. It is clearly one case where non-legislative party leaders were unable to control the Legislature, and it suggests that Governor Walker's problems may be reflective at least in part of the growing difficulty of "controlling" the Legislature from inside or outside.

Although Thompson's legislative relations have generally been immensely successful, they have also involved other serious conflicts. The most extensive conflict on any one issue was probably over the "Class X" legislation to reform criminal sentencing. The main objective was to restore determinate sentencing and make it clear how long individuals would be imprisoned. The bill Thompson introduced into the Legislature was complex, and the Democrats in the House wanted some changes. Before the matter was resolved, there was some public name-calling on both sides, involving speaker Redmond. In the end, Thompson gave up some key features in order to assure that any reforms would be enacted under *his* "Class X" label. Subsequent analyses of the provisions as enacted raise serious questions as to whether the original objectives will be achieved.

Several of Thompson's vetoes have been overridden by the Legislature in its Fall "veto sessions". Thompson's handling of one is typical of how a Governor must make difficult decisions in which his values and judgment are the ultimate factors. In 1977 the Legislature followed a national trend, in response to strong pressures, and passed legislation denying Medicaid payments for abortions of poor women. The national ramifications of the issue, and the deep divisions of Illinois voters on it, called for careful consideration. Expert political consultants were brought in from Washington to back up the judgment of Thompson's own advisors. All seemed to be in agreement—about 60 percent of the voters of Illinois supported the Legislature's action. To veto the bill would be to undermine his prospects of reelection in 1978. Yet Thompson decided to veto the bill, on the grounds that it would be unfair to deny to the poor an option available to others. The veto was cast, but the story doesn't end here. In an unanticipated development, following Thompson's explanation of his veto, his mail clearly showed that a significant number who supported the legislation respected Thompson for acting according to his judgment. Subsequently the Legislature overrode the veto and was in turn reversed by a federal court which found the particular provisions unconstitutional, further illustrating the complexity of the political environment within which Illinois Governors must operate.

State Government: Means or End? Among recent Illinois Governors, Stratton, Ogilvie and Walker have been deeply committed to their responsibility for managing State government. At this writing Thompson's commitment to the managerial role is somewhat less clear. A variety of sources suggest that he has committed a significant amount of his time to out-of-state travel in pursuit of presidential ambitions. Although the comparison with previous governors is not documented, Thompson's *opportunity* to do so is undeniable. New faces are emerging in the GOP, and it is not clear that familiar ones will dominate. At such a time, one when there are relatively few Republican governors, it is natural to sense an opportunity in GOP national politics.

Yet the officials and apparatus of State government are primarily focused on the State's problems. In such circumstances, there is a risk of morale problems among the staff, and some did occur during the first term. The experience of other Governors makes it clear that Illinois makes more than enough demands to fully occupy the time of any Governor. At the same time, a Governor and his administration must be judged in the broader terms of total organizational effort and performance. This requires a review of Thompson's staff arrangements and of his approach to managing the executive branch.

Institutionalizing the Office Thompson has continued the gradual trend of expanding the Governor's office staff, including distinct staff groups for scheduling, patronage and other appointments, budgeting, program and policy, subcabinet management, legislative liaison, legal counsel and intergovernmental relations. In contrast with Ogilvie and Walker, Thompson has chosen to limit staff access to him by creating a more hierarchical staff structure, with substantial delegation of authority to one or more Deputy Governors. Under Ogilvie there had been no Deputy; his top assistants, Brian Whalen and Jerry Marsh, had several peers; none were delegated substantial authority to speak for the Governor or to control intra-office communications. The difficulty of controlling staff is reflected in the perception of others, including Walker, that the staff did indeed speak for Ogilvie on many occasions, whether or not they were directed to do so. Walker centralized his staff somewhat by appointing Victor DeGrazia Deputy Governor and delegating extensive responsibilities for political and managerial matters. But Walker was fiercely committed to maintaining open channels and checking staff people against other sources and ideas in the manner of Franklin Roosevelt. Thompson has developed a much more orderly, hierarchical and bureaucratized system with extensive delegation of authority. This is clearly helpful in managing the competing demands on his attention. It may reflect a trend in large states toward institutionalizing the Office of Governor along a presidential model.

The trend toward institutionalization in Illinois can be illustrated by expenditures and staffing for the Governor's Office. Under Stevenson and Stratton, actual expenditures were stable or even declining at $150,000 to $125,000 annually. In 1957 the State Budget exceeded $1 billion for the first time. Governor Kerner served in a period of rapid governmental expansion, with the annual figure exceeding $2 billion for the first time during his term. By 1967, under Kerner, the expenditures of the Governor's Office had also increased to $1 million annually, with a staff of 44. The Office budget remained stable under Ogilvie and Walker, though staff increased to over 60. During this period (1969–1976), the State budget continued to rise to over $10 billion annually, without a corresponding increase in the Office. Under Thompson the Office of the Governor has resumed its growth and now exceeds $2 million annually with a staff of about 100.

Party Leadership and the Decline of Patronage Thompson has probably accelerated the recent trend to a reduction of the role of patronage in Illinois politics. A major activity of his transition to office was a professional, nationwide search for top appointments, conducted under the auspices of the Continental Illinois Bank's personnel department. Neither party background nor Illinois experience were major considerations, although most appointments were Illinoisans. Illinois has traditionally been known as a leading patronage state, with up to 15,000 jobs (about 20 percent) potentially available, mostly in unskilled or trades positions at large institutions and in the Highway Department. The attraction of patronage to elected officials, particularly Republicans, has declined as their dependence on a State party apparatus has declined. Increasingly, elected officials create their own volunteer organizations, people who, unlike party professionals, do not depend on patronage jobs as incentives for campaign activity. Thus, the recent splits between elected officials, for whom patronage struggles become a distraction, and their county chairmen, for whom patronage remains a key element of political operations. From the beginning, GOP county chairmen have urged Thompson to open up the patronage jobs, but without avail. Another key factor in the decline of patronage has to be the greater complexity of State programs, requiring unprecedented technical expertise and professionalism. As a result, the focus of gubernatorial attention has shifted from maximizing the number of patronage jobs to reducing total State employment and increasing salaries of remaining positions to improve the chances of recruiting competent individuals. Correspondingly, these individuals tend to see the basis of their employment as a programmatic commitment, not a political one.

The Bottom Line: Top Priority Given Thompson's priorities the budget office has dominated the Governor's staff. Thus far the bottom line has been the balanced budget, with relatively little concern for improving the planning, programming and managerial aspect of budgeting. This can be interpreted as a matter of focusing on what is important, and as a simple reflection of the prevailing skepticism in Illinois government on the worthwhileness of such systematic improvements. Thompson has freely retained the services of a number of Walker budgeteers, despite some GOP protests of this traditional practice. There are some signs that Thompson's second term will see a low key but significant restoration of the impressive planning capacity introduced under Ogilvie but eliminated by Walker. If these developments materialize, the Thompson years may well see a move toward the institutionalization of specialized capabilities in the BOB which until now have been temporary.

Managing the State Management improvement of the executive branch under Thompson has been distinctive in an emphasis on task forces and study groups, combined with an unprecedented use of the reorganization powers. Midway through the first term Thompson received the task force report on efficiency in State government. It had been underwritten by business executives who also supplied manpower working under the direction of the Governor's staff and the firm of Warren King and Associates. The numerous detailed recommendations of the report added up to the conclusion that the State could save $500 million a year, roughly five percent of the State budget. In the 1978 elections, Thompson's opponent, Comptroller Michael Bakalis, unsuccessfully attempted to raise the issue of implementation. Selective implementation plans are reflected in the executive budget document for fiscal year 1979–80.

Shortly after Thompson took office, he also received the "Bonniwell Report" on executive branch reorganization, which he and Howlett had jointly commissioned. It was a counterpart to the "Briggs Report" submitted to Ogilvie too late for action in his term. Walker's skepticism had led him to do little in that area. In this context, the succession of systematic reorganization plans submitted by Thompson and approved by the Legislature is highly visible as an unprecedented use of the reorganization powers conferred under the 1970 Constitution. A special staff in the Governor's Office has prepared several major reorganization proposals for submission to the Legislature in each session Thompson has been in office. Reorganizations have been approved and implemented in law enforcement, finance and administration, human rights, energy and economic development/local affairs.

The constitutional procedure for reorganization requires that the Governor submit a plan to the Legislature. It is clear that in Illinois, the administrative organization of government is a political matter of great interest to the Legislature and to various groups which might be affected. The plans are closely reviewed, and legislative suggestions are made for revision. For example, as a result of legislative politics, the State Fire Marshal's office was excluded from the law enforcement reorganization to satisfy the Democrats. See the chapter by Gove and Carlson for an in-depth analysis of reorganization.

Politics of Public Finance: Crisis or Paper Tiger? The politics of public finance in Illinois is dynamic and evolving. Each Governor confronts a different situation, has a major influence during his term and leaves his successor facing a different situation. Thompson has experienced several important challenges to his leadership in this area and has thus far combined good financial management with adroit politics to emerge at best with substantial credit for real achievements, and at worst with some skepticism about his handling of key issues.

When Thompson took office there was so much controversy over the State's fiscal condition that he established a private sector task force of business and labor, which largely confirmed his view that the State's cash reserves were dangerously low. In an atmosphere strongly affected by the specter of bankruptcy and shame in New York, the establishment of a healthy fiscal condition in Illinois would clearly be a prerequisite to other policy initiatives. It is to Thompson's credit that the analytic resources of BOB and the political cooperation of Democrats in the Legislature were effectively mobilized to this end. However it is important to recognize that, just as economic forces of "stagflation" beyond control undermined Walker's ability to manage State finances, such forces enhanced Thompson's ability to do so. In addition to a strong economy during his early years, Thompson benefitted from a continued leveling off in the demand for State resources from major programs such as public assistance and education.

Through the "taxpayers' revolt," Illinois politics has continued to generate challenges to fiscal policy which go beyond the question of a balanced budget to that of the appropriate size of the State's public sector. At issue are the values of public services, the individual taxpayer's fight against inflation and the health of the State's private sector economy. In June 1978, California voters utilized their initiative powers, nonexistent in Illinois, to roll back local property taxes by up to one-half, creating the prospect of tremendous strains on both State and local government. California developments gave impetus to the taxpayers' revolt nationally and in Illinois, where a number of legislators introduced proposals which emphasized State tax limitation rather than rollback, together with reforms in local finance.

Thompson's response to the "taxpayers' revolt" in Illinois was two-fold. First, he established a Revenue Study Commission to tap the considerable expertise of Illinois citizens. The Commission proceeded to hold hearings throughout the State and submitted its recommendations in February 1979, permitting the Governor to submit recommendations for action at the 1979 session of the Legislature. Perhaps ironically, its principal responsibility was to reform local, rather than State, taxation.

While the Commission was doing its work, California voters enacted Proposition 13 in the midst of the 1978 Illinois gubernatorial campaign. Thompson responded immediately, some said cynically, by proposing that the Legislature place on the 1978 ballot an "advisory referendum" through which the voters could express a desire for tax limitation. Enough valid petitions were obtained to place the "Thompson proposition" on the ballot, and it was approved by a margin even more overwhelming than Thompson's reelection. The voters of Illinois didn't punish Thompson for the vagueness of the proposition's wording, but general skepticism was evident.

Pay Raise: Tempest in a Teapot? Before the 1979 tax package could be assembled, an unanticipated issue arose, and its full impact remains unclear at this writing. One of the many citizen study commissions during Thompson's first term reviewed State salaries and recommended substantial increases. The Governor immediately concurred, but legislative awareness of substantial public resistance prevented quick and dramatic action, at least for a time. From the perspective of legislative tacticians, the time for such action arrived in December 1978, after the November elections but prior to the taking of office in January. Legally, this "lame duck" legislative session could act to raise salaries, taking effect in January, to the benefit of many incumbents who would continue in office. Thompson was in a position to veto such action, in such a way as not only to embarass the Legislature, but also to make it impossible for the legislation to take effect, by holding the bill until the current term ended. Thompson chose to veto the bill immediately after enactment, permitting the Legislature to remain in session and immediately override the veto, thus implementing an immediate pay raise.

The depth of the public rage which ensued was apparently unanticipated. Feelings were reinforced when President Carter's chief inflation fighter Alfred Kahn stated flatly that the action set a poor example by breaking the voluntary wage-price guidelines. The resulting heat was more than Illinois officials could take. In his inaugural address, Thompson sought to appease the public with a direct apology for poor judgment. The Legislature enacted a revised plan which delayed the full raise. What is most noteworthy about this event is that the level of political sophistication among Illinois citizens was high enough to make it transparent that Thompson's veto was an effort to appear to resist while actually accommodating. Walker's judgment on the limits of accommodation may have been too strict, but the public clearly felt that in this case accommodation was occurring at their expense. The manner of doing it had created the appearance of self-seeking to which Thompson became a party. One result was diversion from the primary issue of adequate compensation for Illinois public servants. The pay incident is clearly the most serious threat to Thompson's credibility, trust and support. While it is too early to judge, it may represent a gubernatorial decision where, to obtain future legislative cooperation, public support was lost. An over-all judgement, fair to Thompson, will have to take account, not only of the substantive merits of the pay raise issue, but also other 1979 steps which were only possible through similar accommodation with legislative forces, and which have public support, such as the earlier "Class X" legislation.

At this writing it is not easy to put the pay issue in perspective. Ogilvie's support for an income tax was not forgotten three years later despite his outstanding service. Thompson will have ample opportunity to make voters forget, and to impress them with further evidence not only of sound fiscal management but of effective support for the step beyond, a credible, but not overly restrictive limitation on the public sector's share of the Illinois economy. The 1979 legislative session made it clear that in Illinois politics, although tax limitation and tax reduction have gained new appeal to which Governors must respond, they have not dominated the process, for reasons Kohlhauser and Heins discuss in their chapters.

Challenge of the Future There are also signs that Thompson is beginning to turn to areas as yet left untouched, but which must be addressed if his leadership is to demonstrate the balance helpful to a presidential candidate and necessary for recognition as a great Governor. Thompson has established a number of efforts which address themselves to the future of Illinois and to the adequacy of our planning for that future. These include the work of the legislatively established Illinois Futures Task Force and its private sector partner, the Illinois 2000 Foundation, as well as the Committee to Strengthen Local Economies. These efforts may well be laying the ground work for major policy and program initiatives in a wide range of areas including State planning and capability, energy and the environment, land use, urban revitalization and State stimulation of the private sector economy. If these proposals are developed and win the Governor's support, his proven ability to work with the Legislature and the political forces represented there may become a crucial factor in their adoption, and in the emergence of a broader gubernatorial leadership role for Thompson.

Conclusion

No simple judgments about the success or failure of Illinois governors are warranted. Each term is characterized by unique features—the personal goals of the Governor, the acumulation of commitments and constraints, the set of problems faced by the State and the agendas of other key political actors. Above all, there is no single model of success:

> Governors are individuals, they have each achieved an important degree of political success, and they play their roles according to their individual perceptions of what constitutes success.[4]

Yet, there are important patterns. A collective and favorable judgment can reasonably be made. Recent Illinois Governors have used their constitutional and legal powers, together with their political resources, to provide effective leadership in getting the major problems of the State on the agenda, marshaling the public and private sector resources of the State to develop workable solutions, pushing on for the adoption of those solutions and overseeing their implementation.

As a group, Illinois Governors have identified a broad formula for success, demonstrated its workability and tried some alternatives which appear less successful. The core of the successful strategy seems to feature the following components: (1) working within and achieving full access to the two-party system for their programs; (2) utilizing the various roles of the office, particularly political and managerial leadership, to reinforce each other; (3) establishing an atmosphere of consultation and cooperation with a Legislature which has grown in power as it has modernized itself; (4) seeking an accommodation, rather than confrontation, among the major interests and coalitions of Illinois politics—particularly with the City of Chicago, the expanding metropolitan suburbs and the pivotal downstate forces; and (5) seeking the good of the entire State rather than of sections or groups or even their own political parties.

Governors who pursue this broad strategy seem to have an excellent opportunity to see their efforts to guide the State come to fruition and to leave a legacy upon which future leaders can build. The legacy of a successful Governor is clearly not to be measured in terms of permanency. Rather, a Governor can hope, and the people of Illinois should expect, to lay a foundation for future adaptations to changing circumstances, not only in his policies and programs, but in an atmosphere and a set of working relationships which promotes a bipartisan problem-solving partnership.

There is less basis for confidence in alternative strategies. The Walker alternative may be identified as a particular approach to reform. The primary objective was to open up the Democratic Party to greater influence by suburban and downstate Democrats and to redistribute State resources accordingly. The major consequence of adhering to this objective appears to have been the diversion of the Governor's political resources and managerial attention to a continuing, and ultimately frustrating, confrontation with other forces of Illinois politics. Even the substantial powers of the office were insufficient to achieve so basic and rapid a change in traditional methods of doing business. This experience, at least, seems to tell us that the risks of this "high risk/high gain" strategy of reform did indeed outweigh the gains. For it can be argued that the accomplishments of managerial leadership envisaged were thereby made impossible and that cooperation in financial management was impaired. Clearly, however, the results of such a strategy are not the sole responsibility of a Governor, but of all the major power centers of State politics. To establish as a Governor's primary goal a fundamental change in the structure of political power itself is to risk much.

However, to identify elements of short-run failure and frustration in a strategy of reform is not to discount either its possible indirect effect or reform in general. Clearly the history of Illinois politics, and of Illinois Governors, is a history of continuing and significant reform. The complex and ambiguous nature of the political process makes it ever a battleground of reform and corruption, of excellence and mediocrity. Every Illinois Governor must and does have a reform agenda, based on ever-present areas of policy, program, management, procedure and power, where corrective and responsive action are overdue. It may well be that the greatest measure of success can be obtained, not by strategies of overt reform, but by judicious use of current political processes and by careful meshing of the many powers and roles of the Governor's Office.

Research Needs

The office of Illinois Governor is an important one for many reasons, including its remarkable yet limited resources for influencing Illinois politics, policy and administration. If Illinois Governors function well, it is not only the State polity and economy which benefit, but the federal nation of which Illinois is so vital a part. Yet little serious research has been done on the Governor and his increasingly extended office. A better perspective on how Illinois Governors compare with each other, compare with governors of other states, or with Presidents, each in their respective settings, could provide a better basis for reflection on future governors and on the continuing evolution of the office as the focal source of leadership in Illinois State government. Some key research areas would surely include the following:

1. What is at stake in a Governor's choice of priorities and approaches?
2. What have been the various strategies of reform adopted by Illinois Governors, how can their success be evaluated, and what have the concommitants or side effects been? What are the key trade-offs of various reform strategies?
3. What are the various patterns of integrating the multiple roles of Governor so they reinforce, rather than undermine, each other?
4. What is the impact of increasing emphasis on the managerial and intergovernmental roles? How responsive has the evolution of the Office been to these new requirements?
5. What is the nature and effectiveness of agenda development (policy and management), together with the coalition-building (politics) needed to promote the agenda, in an era of declining party organization, rising interest group activity and limited salience of State politics in the mass media? How does this affect the trade-offs of addressing State problems versus getting reelected?
6. What are the extent and limits of gubernatorial power, vis-a-vis (a) the various choices made by individual Governors; (b) the condition of institutional checks and balances of State government, e.g., legislative-executive relations, and (c) intergovernmental relations?
7. To what needs is the continuing institutionalization (specialized staffs) of the Office responding? How does this institutionalization affect the impact of the Office? What alternatives do Governors employ in organizing, leading and controlling their staffs?

NOTES

[1]National Governors' Association, *Governing the American States: A Handbook for New Governors* (Washington, D.C.: National Governors' Association, 1978), pp. 4–9.

[2]Thad L. Beyle, "Governor's Views on Being Governor," Political Science Department, University of North Carolina, Chapel Hill, April 1979. (Mimeographed.) This updates the *Handbook for New Governors*.

[3]Ronald D. Michaelson, "An Analysis of the Chief Executive: How the Governor Uses His Time," *State Government* 65 (Summer 1972).

[4]National Governors' Association, *op. cit.*

[5]Illinois Secretary of State, *Handbook of Illinois Government* (Springfield: Office of the Secretary of State, 1977), p. 12.

[6]This discussion builds from that by Andrew L. Case, "The Executive," in *Governing Illinois Under the 1970 Constitution,* ed. by David R. Beam (1st ed.; DeKalb: Northern Illinois University, Center for Governmental Studies, 1971) and, in turn, on the scholarship of Joseph A. Schlesinger, "The Politics of the Executive," in *Politics in the American States,* ed. by Herbert Jacob and Kenneth N. Vines (Boston: Little, Brown and Company, 1965), pp. 217–32.

[7]The impact of the Constitution on the Legislature—and the Legislature's ambivalence about the product—resulted in limited enthusiasm for legislative action required to implement the Constitution. See Ann Louisin, "The General Assembly and the 1970 Constitution," *Illinois Issues* 1:5 (May 1975) pp. 131–34.

[8]Citizens Conference on State Legislatures, *The Sometimes Governments* (New York: Bantam Books, 1971).

[9]Samuel K. Gove, *et al., The Illinois Legislature* (Urbana: University of Illinois Press, 1976).

[10]Case, *op. cit.*

[11]Roger C. Nauert, "The Comptroller: Illinois Chief Fiscal Control Officer," *The John Marshall Journal of Practice and Procedure* 8:2 (Winter 1974–75).

[12]Laurie Joseph Wasserman, "New State Education Board's Fight to Assert Independent Role," *Illinois Issues* 2:5 (May 1976).

[13]Rubin G. Cohn, "Attorney General and Governor Fight Over Control of Lawyers," *Illinois Issues* 1:1 (January 1975).

[14]"Attorney General Vindicated," *Illinois Issues* 1:2 (February 1975).

[15]Robert W. Kustra, "BOB, State Agencies Struggle Over Program vs. Line Item Budgets," *Illinois Issues* 1:3 (March 1975).

[16]*Ibid.*

[17]William S. Hanley, Legislative Counsel to the Governor, "The 1970 Illinois Constitution and the Executive Veto," *Public Affairs Bulletin,* a publication of Southern Illinois University at Carbondale, 5:1,2 (January/February and March/April 1972).

[18]This strengthens a preexisting characteristic of legislative budgetary politics noted by Thomas Anton in *The Politics of State Expenditure in Illinois* (Urbana: University of Illinois Press, 1967).

[19]Stanley M. Johnson, "The Legislative Process Under the 1970 Constitution," *John Marshall Journal of Practice and Procedure* 8:2 (Winter 1974–75).

[20]Ill. Op. Atty. Gen., 5-630 (October 11, 1973).

[21]The "Briggs Report" on Executive Organization, 1972.

[22]Arvid Hammers, "Walker's Chance to Rearrange State Government to His Liking," *Illinois Issues* 1:3 (March 1975).

[23]Illinois Task Force on Governmental Reorganization, *Orderly Government: Organizing for Manageability* (November 1976). See also "The State of the State: Reorganizing Executive Agencies," *Illinois Issues* 3:4 (April 1977); and Richard E. Favoriti, "Executive Power Under the New Illinois Constitution: Field Revisited," *The John Marshall Journal of Practice and Procedure* 6:21.

[24]For an extensive analysis of Illinois experience with the amendatory veto see Edgar G. Crane, "The Executive" in *Governing Illinois Under the 1970 Constitution,* ed. by Alan P. Dionosopoulos (2d ed.; DeKalb: Northern Illinois University, Center for Governmental Studies, 1978), pp. 16–23; also Raymond Coyne, "Gubernatorial Power," Political Science Department, Northwestern University, Evanston, 1973 or (Mimeographed).

[25]The University of Illinois, Institute of Government and Public Affairs *The Office of Governor* (Urbana: University of Illinois, The Institute, 1963).

[26]*Ibid.*, pp. 42–44.

[27]William L. Day, "Adlai E. Stevenson: Portrait of a Collector, Patrician, Candidate, Political Strategist and Governor," review of *Adlai Stevenson of Illinois,* by John Bartlow Martin (Garden City, N.Y.: Doubleday, 1975), in *Illinois Issues* 2:7 (July 1976), 24.

[28]Steiner and Gove, *op. cit.*, pp. 44–47.

[29]Glenn W. Fisher, *Taxes and Politics: A Study of Illinois Public Finance* (Urbana: University of Illinois Press, 1969), pp. 186, 190–91.

[30]William G. Stratton, "A Former Governor Views the Office," in *The Office of Governor, op. cit.*

[31]Anton, *op. cit.*, p. 120.
[32]*ibid.*, p. 123.
[33]*Ibid.*, p. 126.
[34]*Ibid.*, pp. 127ff.
[35]Fisher, *op. cit.*
[36]Anton, *op. cit.*, p. 120.
[37]Fisher, *op. cit.*, p. 199.
[38]Taylor Penseneau, "Walker, Ogilvie and Kerner Used Different Techniques in Dealing with the Legislature," *Illinois Issues* 1:2 (February 1975), pp. 51–53.
[39]"Legislative Record of Governor Kerner's Years," *Illinois Issues* 2:7 (July 1976), 25.
[40]Ronald D. Michaelson, *Gubernatorial Staffing—Problems and Issues: The Ogilvie Experience* (DeKalb: Center for Governmental Studies, Northern Illinois University, 1974).
[41]Steiner and Gove, *op. cit.*, p. 47.

SUPPLEMENTAL READINGS

Anton, Thomas J. *The Politics of State Expenditure in Illinois*. Urbana: University of Illinois Press, 1966.

Benjamin, Gerald. "Executive Powers and State Fiscal Policy." New Paltz: Political Science Department, State University of New York, 1978.

Beyle, Thad L. "The Governor and the Public." *State Government* 51:3 (Summer 1978), 180–86.

———. "The Governor as Chief Legislator." *State Government* 51:1 (Winter 1978).

———. "The Governor's Formal Powers: A View From the Governor's Chair." *Public Administration Review* 28 (November/December 1968), 540–45.

———, Harold A. Hovey and Kenneth C. Olson. "Intergovernmental Relations in the Governor's Office." *State Government* 50:2 (Spring 1977).

Beyle, Thad L., and Charles H. Williams. "The Gatekeeper Function on the Governor's Staff." *Western Political Quarterly* (forthcoming).

Beyle, Thad L., and J. Oliver Williams. *The American Governor in Behavioral Perspective*. New York: Harper and Row, 1972.

Council of State Governments. *The Governor: The Office and Its Powers*. Lexington, Ky.: The Council, 1972.

———. *Staffing the Office of the Governor*. Lexington, Ky.: The Council, 1971.

Coyne, Raymond. "Gubernatorial Powers". Evanston: Political Science Department, Northwestern University, 1973.

Crane, Edgar G. "The Executive." *Governing Illinois Under the 1970 Constitution*. Edited by Alan P. Dionosopoulos. 2d ed. DeKalb: Northern Illinois University, 1978, pp. 16–23.

Davis, S. Kenneth. *Adlai Stevenson: The Politics of Honor*. New York: Putnam, 1957.

Elazar, Daniel J. *The Office of Governor in Illinois: 1818–1933: A Case Study of Gubernatorial Roles and Styles*. Philadelphia: Center for the Study of Federalism, 1976.

Fisher, Glenn W. *Taxes and Politics: A Study of Illinois Public Finance*. Urbana: University of Illinois Press, 1969.

Gove, Samuel K. "Why Strong Governors?" *National Civic Review* (March 1964), pp. 131–134.

Governor's Cost Control Task Force. *Report*. Chicago: Warren King and Associates, 1978.

Illinois Bureau of the Budget. *Papers in Public Finance: The Ogilvie Years*. Springfield: Illinois Bureau of the Budget, 1972.

Key, V. O., Jr. and Corinne Silverman. "Party and Separation of Powers: A Panorama of Practice in the States." *American State Politics*. Edited by Frank J. Munger. New York: Crowell, 1966.

Martin, John Bartlow. *Adlai Stevenson of Illinois*. New York: Doubleday, 1976.

McCally, [Morehouse] Sarah. "The Governor and His Legislative Party." *American Political Science Review* 60 (December 1966), 933–41.

———. "The Governor as Political Leader." *Politics* in the American States: A Comparative Analysis. Edited by Herbert Jacob and Kenneth N. Vines. 3d ed. Boston: Little, Brown, 1976, pp. 196–241.

———. "The State Political Party and the Policy-Making Process." *American Political Science Review* 67 (March 1973), pp. 55–72.

Michaelson, Ronald D. "An Analysis of the Chief Executive: How the Governor Uses His Time." *State Government* 65 (Summer 1972), pp. 156–158. Also in *Public Affairs Bulletin* Public Affairs Research Bureau, Southern Illinois University at Carbondale. 4 (September/October 1971) pp. 1–6.

———. "Gubernatorial Staffing—Problems and Issues: The Ogilvie Experience," Center for Governmental Studies, Northern Illinois University, DeKalb, 1974. (Mimeographed.)

———. "The Illinois Executive and Urban Problems." *The States and the Urban Crisis*. Urbana: Institute of Government and Public Affairs, University of Illinois, 1970.

Muchmore, Lynn. "Policy Management as an Approach to Gubernatorial Decision-Making," National Governors' Association, Washington, D.C., 1979. (Mimeographed).

National Governors' Association. *The Critical 100 Days: A Handbook for the New Governor*. Washington, DC: National Governors' Association, 1975.

——. *The Governor's Office*. Multi-volumes. Washington, D.C.: The Association, 1976.

———. *The New Governor's Handbook*. Washington, D.C.: The Association, 1979.

———. *Gubernatorial Transition: A Guide*. Washington, D.C.: The Association, November 1976.

"The Office of Governor." Mini-symposium. *Public Administration Review* 36 (1976).

Ogilvie, Richard B. "Illinois' Response to the Urban Crisis." *The States and the Urban Crisis*. Edited by Michael A. Murray. Urbana: Institute of Government and Public Affairs, University of Illinois, 1970.

Olson, Kenneth C. "The States, Governors and Policy Management: Changing the Equilibrium of the Federal System." *Public Administration Review* 35 (December 1975), pp. 764–70.

Pensoneau, Taylor. "Walker, Ogilvie and Kerner Used Different Techniques in Dealing with the Legislature." *Illinois Issues* 1:2 (February 1975), pp. 51–53.

Ransone, Coleman B., Jr. "The American Governor in the 1970's." Symposium. *Public Administration Review* 30 (January/February 1970).

Sabato, Larry. *Good-Bye to Good Time Charlie: The American Governor Transformed, 1950–1975*. Lexington, Mass.: Lexington Books, 1978.

Schlesinger, Joseph A. "The Politics of the Executive." *Politics in the American States*. Edited by Jerbert Jacob and Kenneth N. Vines. 2d ed. Boston: Little, Brown, 1971, pp. 210–38.

Sharkansky, Ira. "Agency Requests, Gubernatorial Support, and Budget Success in State Legislatures." *American Political Science Review* 62 (December 1968), pp. 1220–31.

"Should the Amendatory Veto Power Be Curbed?" *Illinois Issues* 3:9 (September 1977), pp. 10–12.

Sprengel, Donald P. *Gubernatorial Staffs: Function and Political Profiles*. Iowa City: University of Iowa, 1969.

Steiner, Gilbert Y., and Samuel K. Gove, eds. *The Office of Governor*. Urbana: Institute of Government and Public Affairs, University of Illinois, 1963.

Tucker, Joseph B. "Administration of a State Patronage System: The Democratic Party in Illinois." *Western Political Quarterly* 23 (March 1969), pp. 79–84.

Weinberg, Martha Wagner. *Managing the State*. Cambridge, Mass.: Massachusetts Institute of Technology Press, 1976.

Wright, Deil S. "Executive Leadership in State Administration." *Midwest Journal of Political Science* (February 1967), 1 ff.

Wyner, Alan J. "Governor-Salesman." *National Civic Review* 66:2 (February 1967), p. 86.

CHAPTER **5**

The Administration of Governor James R. Thompson

Robert E. Hartley

This chapter conducts a critical examination of the major issues which reflect on the Administration of Governor James R. Thompson in his first (two-year) term (1976–78): dealing with Chicago Mayors, balancing the budget, responding to the taxpayers' revolt, asserting policy leadership and asserting party leadership. It concludes with a mid-stream assessment of the Thompson Administration and poses some issues for the remainder of his second term, issues which might well confront any Governor.

Dealing With Chicago Mayors

Beginning in the late 1890s the fate of Illinois Governors increasingly turned on relationships with Mayors of Chicago. That was in recognition of the political facts of life as dictated by an emerging metropolis on Lake Michigan. Even the strongest Governors—among them those who have lingered in history as remarkable public servants—could not escape the reality of influence from Chcago's City Hall.

John Peter Altgeld, Governor from 1893 to 1897, was drawn into a head-to-head clash with Mayor Carter Henry Harrison Jr. and lost. The failure cost Altgeld his reputation and his health. Frank O. Lowden, Governor from 1917 to 1921, might have been the Republican nominee for President of the United States in 1920, but his quarrels with Mayor William "Big Bill" Thompson could not be overcome. Henry Horner, Governor from 1933 to 1939, warred until his dying day with the stubborn Kelly-Nash political organization in Chicago. Adlai E. Stevenson II, Governor from 1949 to 1953, was denied support for the 1960 presidential nomination by his old associate Richard J. Daley. And so the tale goes, down to the days of Gov. James R. Thompson.

To fathom the relationship of a Governor of Illinois and Mayor of Chicago requires an understanding of practicality, accommodation and communication. Talk has been cheap throughout Illinois political history. Most Governors before Thompson delighted in an occasional attack on the City's reigning monarch as a means of declaring independence. The true test of making the relationship work, however, was in being available for a telephone conversation or a dinner meeting where the two could settle affairs of state. Most Mayors accepted an occasional public outburst from the Governor for the privilege of accessibility. Before he became Governor in January, 1976, Thompson planned to be accessible, and, if necessary, accommodating, and he communicated that to Daley.

What Thompson did not know late in 1976 was that he would have the rare treat of accommodating three different Mayors of Chicago, an unheard of experience. Actually, as Governor, Thompson never confronted Daley, because the Mayor died on December 20, 1976. But Daley's ghost turned out to ge as formidable as the Mayor would have been in the flesh, for the City and the political structure were stamped in Daley's image. Whether dealing with Daley, or his successor Michael Bilandic, or his successor Jane Byrne, Thompson knew what came first: Chicago. More than any other presence, that fact dictated the performance of Thompson in his first years as Governor.

The earliest accommodation of Thompson's administration resulted from political needs in Springfield and Chicago created by Daley's death. Bilandic faced a primary election in April and a general election in June, and he needed to prove he could fill Daley's shoes. Chicago leaders of the House and Senate in the General Assembly were new and needed to assert themselves. Further, Thompson faced a hostile Legislature, overwhelmingly Democratic and determined to teach the upstart Governor a lesson. All individuals needed a victory to establish themselves as legitimate leaders with their constituencies.

From this mixture of needs came an agreement on the crosstown expressway, a subject readymade to fulfill the demands of new leaders.

Daley had proposed the crosstown expressway to run north and south through the western portion of the City several years before Thompson's candidacy for Governor. He had bi-partisan support including Governor Richard B. Ogilvie, until Governor Daniel Walker took office. Claiming the expressway would displace too many citizens in its path, Walker refused to work out a deal with Daley. Crosstown became a symbol of the tug-of-war between Daley and Walker. Daley did not give up.

Daley was used to bargaining arrangements with Governors, whether Republican or Democratic. If a Democratic Governor played ball the benefits were obvious. No strong opposition would confront the incumbent within the Party, and he would end up with a nice retire-

Portions of Mr. Hartley's narrative about the administration of Gov. James R. Thompson are from *Big Jim Thompson of Illinois,* by Rand McNally & Company, Chicago.

ment job. Daley would get essentially what he wanted for Chicago to keep State money flowing.

But Walker resisted. The Mayor could offer little that attracted the Governor. He had beaten Daley in the 1972 elections, so coalitions weren't useful. Walker was able to neutralize Chicago Democrats in the Legislature by using the veto and aligning himself with dissident Democrats and Republicans. So Crosstown became larger than life. To Daley it was an example of Walker's recalcitrance. To Walker it was a case of Daley's pervasive power. A Republican Governor might have been more understanding, and certainly a friendly Democrat would have seen the "wisdom" of Crosstown. In that context the 1976 gubernatorial alternatives to Walker looked good to Daley.

Prior to the 1976 primary election, Michael Howlett, soon-to-be Democratic candidate for Governor, announced support of a modified Crosstown, but Thompson opposed Howlett and Daley's plans, leaving the door open for another arrangement. In January, 1977, Thompson told the Economic Club of Chicago that Crosstown "is an idea whose time has gone" and State funds should be used for other projects. That was a come-on. Thompson knew Chicago didn't plan to give up on Crosstown even with Daley dead. Public statements notwithstanding, Thompson and Bilandic began talking about an expressway arrangement. Announcement of an agreement came on May 12 in the middle of both the legislative session and Bilandic's campaign for Mayor.

In agreeing to Crosstown, Thompson had reversed his field slightly. "I felt a certain amount of discomfort," Thompson said, "because I had condemned Howlett's half-a-crosstown, as I called it, pretty strongly during the campaign. . . . Some people have pointed out that [Crosstown] bears a remarkable resemblance to Howlett's proposal which I attacked. To that extent, it appears I'm going against my campaign position."

The package of highway projects, of which Crosstown was one, totaled $1.5 billion in State and federal money. A deal had been cut and everyone knew it. So, Thompson spoke of the agreement openly. It became clear that legislative cooperation was part of the bargain. "Democrats organized the House and Senate. They had the votes; they had the horses. You have to accommodate them to get your program passed. So you have to make agreements that give them some of what they want to get some of what you want," Thompson told an interviewer.

Until the agreement, the Legislature had dawdled and refused to accept Thompson's budget requests. After the agreement most appropriations fell in place with Chicago impetus, and Thompson got his balanced budget. The tradeoff meant Thompson could campaign for re-election in 1978 having made good on a promise to balance the budget. Crosstown gave Bilandic a needed boost in the mayoral campaign, and he ultimately ran up huge margins of victory. Legislative leaders looked good by bringing order to a potentially chaotic session.

The practical side of Thompson prevailed and set a theme for his Administration. "Where we can't get along, we'll fight . . . But that doesn't mean that I refuse to recognize that an entity called the Chicago city hall exists; because it certainly does."

Routinely, Chicago Democrats come to a legislative session with an agenda of special interest bills, especially those dealing with money. Much of the session is spent haggling over the bills and trading votes with downstate interests. In 1978, Thompson's second legislative session, Chicago-interest legislation looked skimpier than usual. After getting Crosstown funds the year before, Chicago decided not to be too greedy. Or so it seemed. In reality, the subject of most interest to Chicago in 1978 was off-track-betting, or OTB as it was called. The lure was an estimated $21 million in revenue for the City if OTB were legalized. Accordingly, the full force of the Democratic organization was behind an effort to pass legislation. However, the action occurred off-stage.

Legal betting on horseracing away from the tracks was permitted in a few locations across the nation, mostly notably New York State and Atlantic City, New Jersey. Proponents in Illinois cited as its virtue its convenience to the thousands of persons who like to wager on horse races but are not able to reach the track.

Opponents attacked from two sides. One—epitomized by the Methodist churches in Illinois—called the proposal immoral and an encouragement for families with minimum income to squander money that otherwise would be spent on necessities. The other viewpoint was represented by private and public law enforcement agencies. They raised the specter of organized crime moving in on OTB and bringing with it an across-the-board increase in all crime in Illinois cities.

Chicago politicians have tried for decades to legalize betting in the City. The subject has taken several disguises, but the proposal always was clear: Take advantage of the public desire to bet on horse races to raise revenues for the City. Governors and Mayors quarreled over the years, as early as 1934 when Henry Horner was Governor and Edward J. Kelly was Mayor. Horner, a Democrat and associate of Kelly, vetoed a bill that would have permitted bookies to be licensed in Chicago. Kelly wanted the law for its potential licensing revenue and the opportunity for patronage and payoffs. Emphasizing the high-stakes nature of the subject, the veto cost Horner Kelly's support in the 1936 elections.

Quite naturally then, OTB came up in political negotiations between Thompson and Bilandic in 1977. Crosstown was the centerpiece in 1977, and OTB was to be the same in 1978. As a means of obtaining supporting evidence on which to base public acceptance, Thompson named the "Governor's Revenue Study Commission on Legalized Gambling," with a reporting date coinciding with the 1978 legislative session. He named Thomas A. Reynolds, Jr., as chairman. Reynolds had been chairman of Citizens for Thompson and was a partner in the law firm of Winston and Strawn in Chicago.

The public heard of the Commission's report in April 1978, just as the Legislature warmed up and Democrats submitted a bill to legalize off track betting. The Commission supported OTB. Bilandic endorsed the proposal.

Thompson insisted he had not taken a position on OTB. "I don't know what bill, if any bill, is going to get out. I object to people saying I'm making early legislative judgments . . . The bill may be radically different when it comes to me." His "non-position" was in conflict with statements made during the 1976 gubernatorial campaign when he had opposed OTB. Newspapers reminded him of the switch.

As a vote neared in the House late in May, Thompson came out of his corner. He appeared before a Republican caucus and asked fellow party members to vote to keep OTB alive and send it to the Senate for further study. Despite press speculation that supporters were several votes short of passage, OTB cleared the House by a single vote on May 26, the deciding ballot cast by a Republican.

Passage sounded alarm bells across the State. The Chicago Crime Commission began a systematic campaign to arouse editorial opposition, counting as allies the two major Chicago newspapers. The Commission's argument against OTB rested on an alleged link with organized crime.

While the bill languished in the Senate through June, short of votes needed for passage, other events occurred which affected consideration of OTB. The combination of issues, pressure against OTB from Chicago interests and Thompson's own second thoughts, resulted in adjournment of the Legislature without action. Thompson and legislative leaders vowed to consider it anew during the fall session.

In the meantime OTB became entwined with Thompson's campaign for re-election. During the public outcry Thompson and his political aides had worked to obtain endorsement of the Illinois AFL-CIO. As they came close to getting the endorsement, Michael Bakalis, Thompson's opponent for Governor, entered the picture with an appeal to Bilandic to salvage AFL-CIO support for the Democrats. Bilandic's intervention in behalf of Bakalis miffed Thompson, and he felt betrayed. In mid-August he declared opposition to OTB. "If the people of Illinois want off-track-betting they'll have to elect someone else as their governor. I will neither support an OTB bill nor sign one."

Thompson's behavior on OTB characterized the first years of his Administration. There were no bold strokes of genius or great successes, nor were there failures or demonstrations of shocking weakness. Most issues settled down somewhere between.

Balancing the Budget

In the first six months of his term Thompson made it clear he understood what the people wanted. They wanted a rest, and he had the medicine. "Save money and get off the people's back. I think maybe that is the issue. Give us a little peace and quiet," he said. "I said maybe the mood of the people of Illinois—after four years of Walker, fighting and confrontation—was to have two years with nothing happening to them."

He added a balanced budget but little more; he believed the public didn't want much more. The Thompson Administration began with symbols and contrasts, as if the Governor had a set of mirrors left over from the campaign. He began at his inauguration with a speech devoid of specifics and full of slogans. An example:

"There will be no jobs bought; there will be no favors sold."

As appealing as the generalities sounded to a weary electorate, Thompson did not stop there. He had to be visible, and that is where the politics of personality came in. While doing as little as possible, he sold the image of a physically-fit, mentally sharp young Governor wrestling with the complexities and frustrations of government. He had another campaign for office to begin immediately and that left little time for more than imagery and dealing with the basic business of government.

Thompson's greatest concern was the budget and Democratic acceptance of a balanced budget. Immediately after the election Thompson began calling for a "year of sacrifice" to restore the State's financial security. No other projects exceeded the budget in importance, Thompson later told columnist Neal Peirce. "We had been deficit spending in the state for three years. Our financial rating was in jeopardy. If we had another year of deficit spending, we would have been bankrupt . . . So I submitted the first balanced budget in four years. It attended to the needs of the people of Illinois, but may not have met everybody's expectations."

What had actually happened? Walker had inherited a small surplus of funds from the Ogilvie administration. By 1974, half way through Walker's term, the State still enjoyed a comfortable cash surplus of $453 million. But the recession of 1974–75 reduced State revenues below a normal yield, while increasing the demand on the State Treasury. It would clearly be too simplistic to blame the ensuing fiscal squeeze on Walker—conditions beyond his control were a major factor.

The term "balanced budget" as used by Thompson was a bit of political rhetoric. His intent was to point up the reckless manner in which Walker had spent tax revenue and used the State's bonding authority. In fact, Walker had submitted "balanced budgets" too. In that sense, the planned expenditures did not exceed the projected income. But Walker did resort to floating bonds to finance some routine State expenses. In that sense he spent more than was collected in tax revenues. The bonds, however, would not have to be repaid from general revenue funds of the State until a later date, so the funds did not appear to be spent from current revenues.

Whatever the difficulties faced by Walker, Thompson took a very different tack. In March 1977, Thompson submitted a "conservative" $10 billion budget to the Legislature. Thompson and his budget director, Robert Mandeville, determined the State would have about $300 million in new revenues for spending in the fiscal year beginning July 1, 1977. If the Legislature followed Thompson's spending suggestions there would be a small surplus to bridge the gap from one fiscal year to another.

Thompson allocated about $100 million of the amount to pay debt service and other commitments. Of the remaining $200 million Thompson gave $125 million to education, backing up his pledge to make education a top budget priority. That left only $75 million for all other agencies and departments of government, far from enough to keep up with the erosion of inflation.

Asserting Policy Leadership

In the weeks preceding adjournment of the General Assembly on June 30, Thompson carefully declared his position on a handful of issues. Rather than provide light as to the philosophical direction of his Administration, they were random pronouncements and did little to reveal a coherent Thompson program. He reaffirmed support of the Equal Rights Amendment, although the Legislature again refused to ratify. (He would support it again in 1978 and in 1979). He also said he would not work the legislative aisles for the amendment because it was an issue for the Legislature, not the Governor.

He signed a new capital punishment law which complied with U.S. Supreme Court guidelines, thus reaffirming his law-and-order leanings. The deteriorating condition of Illinois roads and a rapidly diminishing road fund inspired Thompson to support a State gasoline tax increase. It was not until 1979, however, that he proposed legislation for consideration by the General Assembly. He vetoed legislation legalizing the so-called cancer drug Laetrile and a bill prohibiting use of State funds for abortions. Both were overridden by the Legislature. Thompson made little attempt to find votes to uphold his vetoes.

Thompson made one attempt during the first year to meet criticism that he had no legislative program beyond the budget. The Governor brought two specific subjects before the Legislature: ethics and criminal justice. Neither was a new subject, but Thompson had talked at length about them during the campaign and on one occasion unveiled a specific ethics program. A proposal related to criminal justice was a natural outgrowth of his background and experience. On familiar ground he could be a tenacious fighter, as the Legislature learned. He wanted changes in the criminal code more than improved ethical standards, but early in the session he called an ethics bill his second priority after a balanced budget.

In April Thompson dropped an ethics proposal on the Legislature. His press release said it would "plug loopholes and add teeth to existing conflict of interest laws and strip the secrecy from lobbyist spending to influence public officials." Legislative leaders demolished the plan verbally. After that Thompson backed away and did not press for consideration. His unwillingness disappointed ethics advocates. Later Thompson explained, "People have asked me why I didn't try to arouse public opinion on that. Well, sometimes a Governor can successfully arouse public opinion in support of a legislative proposal, but it has to be done carefully, deliberately."

If ethics legislation didn't excite the public, Thompson knew an issue that would. About his package of crime bills Thompson said, "This is one I'm willing to go to the people on. They can understand it. It's very simple, it's tough. It's what they want." And he wanted it, too, to maintain the image of a two-fisted prosecutor and deliver on the promises he made to put more criminals behind bars.

The crime package didn't sprout from Thompson's brow. For two years Democrats had worked on a package of bills that addressed the subject of flat-time sentences for all crimes. Authors of the legislative package introduced bills about the time Thompson introduced his.

The Governor's package included eight crime bills involving a number of issues ranging from authorization of the Attorney General to convene statewide grand juries to creation of a new category of crimes called Class X. He proposed that seven heinous crimes such as rape and use of a weapon in the commission of a felony be subject to sentences of at least six years each in prison without parole.

Various pieces of the package died in committee before adjournment, but Thompson wanted only to have Class X. He spent an enormous amount of personal and staff time on the plan, making it clear he intended to fight. His behavior on Class X revealed a determination not previously seen in the Governor. Dedicated to the crime package, Thompson called a Special Session of the Legislature in the Fall to deal with the subject.

The Special Session became a free-for-all. The necessary compromises did not cause as much trouble as Thompson's determination to label it Class X and take credit for passage. After public and private wrangling, a bill emerged and passed. Its main provisions included:

—Creation of a category of ten serious crimes, labeled Class X. Class X crimes carried a mandatory minimum six-year jail sentence, with the maximum ranging from 30 to 60 years in some cases. The ten crimes were aggravated kidnapping, rape, deviate sexual assault, heinous battery, armed robbery, aggravated arson, treason, armed violence, hard narcotics transactions and conspiracy to sell, produce or distribute hard drugs.

—A three-time-loser provision, under which persons convicted three times of Class X crimes would be sentenced to a mandatory life in prison with no chance of parole.

—Elimination of the Parole and Pardon Board and the system of parole. Prisoners would get a specific release date instead of having to take a chance on persuading the Parole Board to release them.

—A system of determinate sentencing, with fixed terms for defendants and less discretion by judges in sentences.

Although Thompson sensed correctly that the public wanted toughter crime laws—public opinion polls on the death penalty were a tipoff—murmurs continued after passage that the Administration's crime fight had narrow dimensions. Sociologists, criminologists and some newspaper editorial pages expressed their lack of enthusiasm for Class X by calling for a crime fight that tackled the causes not the results.

Asserting Party Leadership

While legislative matters occupied much of Thompson's time, political developments required his attention, too. Having been on the "outs" in Springfield since 1972, Republicans grumbled as Thompson played ball with legislative Democrats, cut deals with Chicago Democrats, appointed Democrats to key cabinet posts and romanced Democratic leaders, such as Secretary of State Alan Dixon. Thompson put down the rebellions saying, "Politicians just love to grouse . . ." But the critics weren't easily discouraged. Republicans at the local level throughout Illinois expected to reap a harvest of jobs when Thompson moved into the mansion, and they wanted action. Thompson warned them he didn't have as many jobs as party officials thought.

Republican anger never subsided during the first two years. Appointments of Democrats to key cabinet posts, including the Department of Transportation which dispenses hundreds of patronage jobs, prompted much of the anger. Thompson inherited Langhorne H. Bond as Director of the Department after Walker's departure. Bond later left to join the Carter Administration as head of the Federal Aviation Administration. Serving Bond as deputy was John D. Kramer, 28, a Democrat appointed by Walker.

Thompson wanted Kramer for the position, despite his youth and party credentials. With a Democratic administration in Washington and Bond in the federal Department of Transportation, Kramer had the connections Thompson wanted for a variety of State projects. He intended to announce Kramer's appointment early in June 1977. Republicans heard of the plan and forced Thompson to postpone it while they tried to change his mind. They argued against the appointment on political grounds and cited Kramer's inexperience.

Finally, after a month's delay Thompson announced Kramer as his choice. Republicans howled across the State. Thompson's support of Kramer never sagged. About the Republican sentiment the Governor said, ". . . I understand that feeling and I'm not putting it down. Republicans have a right to expect that when they nominate and elect a governor that some of their people will be put into sensitive policy-making positions . . . And it's been very frustrating for the Republicans of Illinois to see so many holdovers . . . I thought John Kramer was the best person available to me in the nation." A year later, with party criticism no less intense, Thompson said, "Kramer's appointment has not cost the Republicans jobs."

Jim Thompson didn't raise the expectations of Illinoisans much in 1977, and he continued into his second year with the same approach. He had a modest wish list for 1978. He hoped for a quiet legislative session and another balanced budget. He prayed for tranquility in the relationship with Chicago. He envisioned a pay increase. He expected no scandals; and he wished it all would end with re-election in a landslide. Remarkably, the major events of 1978 affecting Thompson occurred pretty much according to order.

The Illinois Legislature pondered the Governor's budget and Democrats wondered how they could help Democratic candidate Bakalis without disturbing their priorities and the arrangements made between Bilandic and Thompson. The best they did was present Bakalis with a property tax rebate bill, but otherwise Thompson got much of what he asked for in the budget. The legislative session ranked as one of the least exciting and most unproductive in recent history. Democrats were unable to disrupt Thompson's strategy for his second budget, the priorities of which were: Give as much new money to education as possible; balance the budget; declare no need for higher taxes. If that sounded like 1977, it didn't bother Thompson, because 1977 had been a success in political terms.

Balancing Taxpayer Complaints and Service Needs

Thompson's rhetoric played on the public sensitivity to taxes, as he had done in the 1976 campaign and his first year as Governor. In a continuation of the theme, he said, "The wolf is still at the door, but at least we have closed that door in his face."

The Thompson priority for education funds—a second year in a row—not only recognized a need but served a sound political purpose as well. Bakalis's background as Superintendent of Public Instruction from 1971 to 1975 gave him a readymade constituency among faculty and administrators of the State's elementary and secondary schools. Also as a former professor at Northern Illinois University he had close ties with higher education. If Bakalis had been successful in accusing Thompson of slighting education, the entire legislative session might have turned out differently, and maybe the election. But Thompson anticipated the Bakalis moves. He recommended that higher education receive $79 million more than the previous year, or 85 percent of the requested amount of $94 million. That satisfied higher education officials and removed one potential Bakalis appeal.

The other was more difficult. Elementary and secondary officials requested $185 million more than the previous year and Thompson budgeted $103 million, accompanied by an explanation that he differed with the needs as expressed by officials. Thompson gave Bakalis an opening, but the problem was where to find additional money in the budget for use in education. The Democrats spun their wheels on that issue for the entire session, shifting money around from one pot to another and threatening bodily harm to the budget.

The Democrats finally pushed through a bill calling for an expenditure of $26 million over Thompson's recommendation, the funds coming from a federal windfall. Thompson avoided a fight and signed the bill, taking credit for the total and denying Bakalis the issue.

Thompson continued his practice of singling out education for large pieces of budget increases in his budget for 1979–80. These were not enough to quiet education forces on the campuses and in the elementary and secondary schools, but Thompson's attention to education priority was one continuing thread of his Administration.

The Thompson budget as approved by the Legislature ignored a growing list of needs for the State. Despite priority spending for education many educators feared funds were insufficient to curb an erosion of quality in higher education and to prevent increasing pressure on local property taxes for secondary and elementary school funding. The Thompson budget offered in 1979 did little to alleviate the fears. The less spent at the State level, the more property taxes had to make up the difference.

Recipients of public aid received a five per cent increase in payments, but neither the Governor nor the Legislature indicated any interest in a systematic program of increases over time to ease the blow of inflation. Public employee pension programs continued to be inadequately financed. A deteriorating road system received little official attention, and questions of an increase in state gasoline taxes were postponed again. The subject arose in 1979 when Thompson proposed a gas tax increase, regardless of stiff legislative opposition. The Governor and legislative leaders correctly assessed no willingness on the public's part to develop programs to ease those problems or to support the tax increase that would be necessary to finance corrective measures.

The Pitfalls of Office and the Taxpayers' Revolt

Thompson avoided major scandals but was plagued by pecadillos that caused him embarrassment. There was the time he took a trip to the Kentucky Derby at the expense of a railroad firm. Reporters wrote about large entertainment expenses at the Executive Mansion. Thompson's membership in private clubs that excluded minorities and women from membership received considerable coverage. But nothing raised the public ire until late in 1978. Thompson learned the hard way that the public had a low tolerance level for shenanigans when it came to officials feathering their own nests.

From the time of his election in 1976, Thompson had complained about his $50,000 annual salary. The last ballot hardly had been counted when he called for a pay raise for members of the cabinet and himself. In the first few months of the Administration Thompson persisted, leading himself to some discoveries. One was the deep-rooted sensitivity of the public toward pay increases for public officials. Open criticism and hostility to the suggested increases silenced the Governor and paralyzed the Legislature. Thompson kept the pay raise subject alive later in the year by appointing former Governor Samuel Shapiro, a Democrat, chairman of a commission to study state pay levels and report to him in 1978. He said the recommendations would form a proposal to the Legislature.

The Shapiro Commission recommended a salary of $75,000 for the Governor, an increase of 50 per cent, and similar percentage boosts for other elected officials, judges and legislators. A public outcry followed, focusing on the large percentages.

As weeks passed the issue became too hot for Thompson. At a meeting of broadcast journalists, he said, "I just think government salaries have been too low, but it's not a message you can get through to people in an election year." On May 19 Thompson announced he would veto any pay raise bill passed by the Legislature. The Legislature took no action on the bill to raise salaries, carrying the issue over to the fall legislative session which was to occur after the elections.

The period after an election and before the seating of a new Legislature has been a favorite for consideration of government pay increases. Anticipating action on salaries by a lameduck Legislature, Thompson had earlier said he wouldn't sign a bill passed during that period.

After the election Thompson left Illinois for a Republican Governors' Conference in Williamsburg, Virginia, and a vacation afterward in South Carolina. The pay raise action occurred during his absence but with his knowledge. After legislative approval, including a legislator salary increase from $20,000 to $28,000 annually, Thompson issued a veto message from South Carolina making good on his earlier pledge. Within hours the House and Senate overrode the veto, and the salaries went into effect.

The public expressed its outrage with great vehemence, but legislators and Thompson had expected the explosion and waited for the cry to abate, as it had done other times after pay increase action. Public criticism, spurred by editorials in dozens of newspapers and headline news treatment on television, mounted. But the Legislature adjourned its fall session without reconsidering.

The uprising gathered momentum. Individuals organized a "tea bag" protest symbolic of the Boston Tea Party and thousands of tea bags arrived at the Governor's mansion and his office in the State House. Thompson responded by conferring with legislative leaders to see if they would reconsider. The answer was "no." After two years of playing ball with Thompson on budgetary matters, the Legislature stood its ground while the Governor perspired.

Thompson called a special legislative session for January 5, 1979, saying, "I'm convinced that an overwhelming majority of the people of Illinois favor a rollback and phase-in of salary increases . . ." After 18 hours of wrangling, they agreed to implement $5,000 of the $8,000 raise in the first year and the rest in the second. The same plan applied to Thompson. There was no reduction in the amounts of the raises.

Three days later, Thompson stunned the State by spending about a quarter of his 13-minute second inaugural speech apologizing to the citizens for his errors on the pay raise matter. He said, "I did veto them, but many people concluded that the manner in which I did so, to paraphrase MacBeth, kept the word of promise to your ear and broke it to your hope. And you were right, and I apologize."

The Thompson Administration had a brush with the national phenomenon of public outrage at taxes and attempts at corrective measures in 1978. The issue arose because of the gubernatorial campaign, not because

Thompson was interested in further restricting revenues available on which to run State government. Thompson would just as soon have ignored the matter.

On June 6 when California residents approved Proposition 13, a reduction in property taxes that created tax cut hysteria and a so-called "tax revolt," Bakalis saw an opportunity to become the Illinois tax-cut champion. Thompson was indifferent toward the subject, reflecting a disinterest in any plan that would interrupt the orderly flow of State business. With cooperation from the Democratic-controlled Legislature, Bakalis took over a tax rebate plan that had languished in the General Assembly's committee system and called it "The Bakalis Tax Rebate Plan."

Thompson resisted panic in the wake of California's vote. He said Illinois was not California and the Proposition 13 proposal had no place in his programs. He misjudged the intensity of the feeling. The bill passed the House and Senate, giving the Democrats and Bakalis a major campaign issue. Bakalis said rebates would cost $33 million in the first year, and Thompson set the figure at about $90 million, thus making an issue over drain on the General Fund.

After passage Thompson threatened a veto, but agonized over the need for tax reform. Saying "rebates aren't reform" Thompson vetoed the bill on July 27, despite lobbying by consumer groups and Bakalis, who promised to make the veto a campaign issue.

In California, after passage of Proposition 13, Gov. Jerry Brown embraced the proposition, performing one of the most successful acrobatic moves of the year. Before June 6 Brown had opposed the proposition and worked to defeat the measure. Afterward, Brown became the proposition's champion and almost immediately outran Republican opposition in preference polls.

After announcing he would veto the property tax rebate bill, Thompson took a leaf from the Brown notebook. On the morning of July 18, the Governor conceived the "Thompson Proposition" and unveiled it publicly. The proposition, to be placed on the November ballot, asked, "Shall legislation be enacted and the Illinois Constitution be amended to impose ceilings on taxes and spending by the state of Illinois, units of local government and school districts?" Thompson had proposed a purely advisory referendum, but worded it in such a way as to raise expectations of action. To get the "Thompson Proposition" on the ballot Thompson undertook a campaign to obtain nearly 600,000 signatures on petitions to meet requirements for placing it on the ballot.

Outside his circle of supporters and staff, Thompson's proposition took a bruising. Editorial pages across the State ridiculed the proposition as meaningless; a waste of time, energy and money, and too blatantly political. Thompson never blinked, and defended the proposition as a means of giving expression to public feelings and drawing from it some direction for the future. Having snatched the tax issue to his side of the board, Thompson spent much of the remaining time before August 21—petition filing deadline—touring the State for signatures.

The quest went down to the wire with a last minute media blitz and airplane trips by Republican officials to collect petitions. The final count showed 43,020 petitions bearing 607,410 signatures or about 18,000 more than the minimum needed. They would be handy, though, when challenges surfaced. Attackers waited in the wings, for there hadn't been much they could do to stop the petition-signing juggernaut. But Thompson beat back all challenges and by early in September the proposition had been verified for the ballot by the State Board of Elections, despite accusations of fradulent signatures on petitions.

On November 7, the Thompson proposition passed with 83 per cent approval. Hardly a mention was made in the newspaper reports that two months earlier the issue had nearly become a major scandal in the Thompson Administration. Thompson, undaunted by continuing ridicule of the proposition, pledged a ceiling on taxes and spending. In March, 1979, he proposed a series of constitutional amendments designed to place a ceiling on taxes and give citizens a greater voice over taxing levels.

Conclusion

Although Thompson often appeared in the first two and a half years to treat his job as if it were one continuous taffy pull, he proved to be an astute politician with a careful eye for public opinion. Regardless of media criticism and the potshots of political opponents he won elections in 1976 and 1978 by exceptional margins. In spite of slippage on such issues as the salary increase, he retained public support well into 1979. The continuing question was whether or not Thompson's reading of the public interest in less government activism would remain accurate and carry him through a full four years.

His statements and actions indicate he intends to offer modest programs and initiatives while doing all he can to balance the budget and prevent increases in the income tax. His insistence on austere budgets ignores the cracks caused by several years of neglect in such areas as mental health, public aid, children and family services, and fair employment. Although he maintained education as a budget priority, officials in higher education and elementary and secondary education fretted that his allocations were not maintaining quality services.

The effect of Thompson's first years was a sense of calm. Is the relentless storm on its way?

CHAPTER **6**

The Illinois General Assembly

Samuel K. Gove

The Illinois General Assembly has had a long and colorful history. Like other legislative bodies, its character has changed frequently. Some of the most marked changes came about as a result of legislative reform movements in the 1960's. Many of these changes are still with us. More are bound to come. All of them do, and will continue to provide material for writers and scholars. This was not always so, although there are a number of studies that do give the flavor of the Legislature in earlier days. Congressman Paul Simon relates an early experience of one of Illinois's illustrious citizens. During the Special Session of 1840 Abraham Lincoln took a drastic step to prevent a quorum in the General Assembly—he jumped out of the window.[1] In later years it was an episode he hoped people would forget.

Over the years, the General Assembly has been involved in numerous incidents that did little to enhance its image. For example in the late 1930's a State Senator writing anonymously in the *American Mercury* charged widespread bribery in the Legislature.[2] In late 1953, the Illinois General Assembly was the subject of an in-depth study by John Bartlow Martin.[3] While Martin was gathering material for the article late in the 1953 session, a Chicago legislator was kidnapped; he has not been seen since. The article highlighted this incident. For the image of the Legislature and for the legislators involved, the timing of the article was unfortunate. The reader could hardly dismiss the fact that a legislator had been kidnapped, even though the 1953 Session did have some accomplishments for which it could be justifiably proud; the following year Illinois was one of the first states to pass a constitutional amendment on legislative reapportionment, a change that was to influence both the legislative process and the legislative image.

More recently Paul Simon and Alfred Balk wrote an article covering ten years of the legislature's history.[4] The article described many alleged payoffs and political deals. The authors concluded by quoting an American Political Science Association report that "modernization of American state legislatures is considered by many to be the most important piece of unfinished business in the area of government reorganization." Simon added: "From my experience in Illinois and my knowledge of other legislatures, I would consider that an understatement."[5]

After this article appeared, a number of other articles were published in various periodicals, all with the common theme of how bad legislatures were across the country. Illinois was one of the main targets in an article by Trevor Armbrister. In the best muckraking tradition, Armbrister seemed bent on painting the worst possible picture of the Illinois Legislature. The opening sentence of his section on this State gives an indication of his approach: "In no state do so many of the body sores afflicting state government fester quite so appallingly as they do in Illinois."[6] Again the State Legislature was the victim of bad timing. Late in the 1965 Session, which Armbrister was visiting, an unknown person planted a tape recorder in the Springfield hotel room of a lobbyist for currency exchanges. On the 15 rolls of tape were devastating statements about legislators being offered various sums of money for their votes. The names of 61 legislators mentioned on the tapes, not all cast in derogatory roles, were published in a Chicago newspaper.

Interestingly, since the mid-1960's, there have been no national articles attacking the Illinois General Assembly. The image of the Legislature seems to have improved, although in a 1972 public opinion survey, 52.5 percent of the respondents said that the Legislature did a fair job, while only 28.2 percent said that the body did a good job.[7]

But the 1979 increase in legislators' salaries and the way that was accomplished, caused the biggest public furor in recent history. Once again negative attention was focused on the legislative institution.

In addition to all these changes in its image and character, the Illinois General Assembly has undergone a number of specific changes as well. Illinois lawmakers today play a different game, and the legislators themselves appear to be different from their counterparts ten or twenty years ago—as a group they are younger, better educated and harder working. Their facilities and surroundings are greatly improved, as are their perquisites. The Illinois Legislature is quite well-staffed now—at least compared to fifteen years ago, when research and technical staff was nonexistent. The impact of these changes on the public policies of the state is debatable; certainly the impact is not readily quantifiable.

The changes in Illinois are in line with national trends to strengthen the State legislative institution. Developments in Illinois have been looked upon favorably by persons outside the State. In fact, as early as 1971, the Citizens Conference on State Legislatures ranked Illinois as having the third best legislature in the nation. The same (if not a higher) ranking would probably be found if another survey were made today using the same criteria.

This chapter is a description of the Illinois General Assembly. We do not attempt to discuss the legislative product. Another caution: we do not necessarily think that all is well with the legislative system, but our self-designated role is not to suggest reorganization or reforms. What we do want to do is suggest some of the more salient aspects of the General Assembly which must be recognized and thought about if one hopes to understand this very complex and important legislative body. To this end, we have chosen four areas to concentrate our discussion on: the representative role of the Illinois Legislature, the constitutional powers of the Legislature, the Legislature and partisan politics, and executive-legislative relations.

The Representative Role of the Illinois Legislature*

Most, if not all, of the prevailing political interests in Illinois emerge with the convening of each session of the General Assembly. At least once each year there is a mass influx of lobbyists, reporters and politically interested citizens into the State's capital city. There is, in fact, no other activity which swells the population, the economy, even the pace of life in Springfield as much. Why all this excitement and turmoil? Probably because those who follow the Illinois General Assembly have learned that when the Legislature is not itself initiating a change in public policy, it can assert its power to check, frustrate, delay, reject, modify or adopt the policy initiatives of the Governor, the Mayor of the City of Chicago, one of the other elected State officials, or various interest groups.

There are in Illinois 236 men and women with varying degrees of experience who have sought and won election by the people of one of the fifty-nine legislative districts. Each district elects one Senator and three Representatives. As the General Assembly, they assert their role in making the policy of State government. They review and evaluate the conduct of State administration and the effects of State programs. Even when they are not in the State capital, these legislators maintain contacts with and work for constituents, month in and month out. In the interim periods when the Legislature is recessed, legislators are also kept busy by committees and commissions which continue to function during the entire biennium.

Constituents—the people back in the district—expect their legislators to act for them, to be their instruments for getting things done. In these terms representation may be defined as a kind of activity, a way of acting, or an expectation about how a representative ought to act in place of or in behalf of his constituents.

Among legislators and political philosophers alike there remain clearly divergent views as to how a legislator should act in representing the people of his district. Regardless of how they view their role, most legislators do endeavor to represent their constituents in two ways: by initiating and supporting legislation that confers advantages in their districts and by performing personal services or running errands for constituents. How much time a legislator devotes to these functions is probably dependent on his perception of his role and the margin by which he won election. There are probably many Illinois legislators who spend a majority of their time handling the "casework" of their constituents, although this situation is gradually changing as legislators have started to receive more staff help and clerical assistance.

Almost as important as the duties of the legislators after they are elected is the question of how they are elected in the first place. Apportionment and the drawing of legislative district lines are important techniques of representation which have become especially controversial in recent years. No method of representation extends equally to all individuals, and none is politically neutral.

Reapportionment

The legislative article of the 1970 Illinois Constitution requires that the General Assembly redistrict the fifty-nine legislative districts in the year following each federal decennial census year. The districts are to be "compact, contiguous and substantially equal in population." The redistricting plan must be approved and effective by June 30 of that year, or, as happened in 1971, a legislative redistricting commission must be formed within ten days. With conterminous districts, both Senate and House members are vitally concerned with how the lines are redrawn. Coupled with stringent requirements for population equality, redistricting means that one change made in a proposed map may ripple across the entire map, affecting literally dozens of incumbents in both houses. With the Republicans holding a narrow edge in the House in 1971, and neither party alone able to pass a bill in the Senate, it was not totally surprising then that as of July 1, 1971, dawned the Legislature was still without a new apportionment plan.

In situations such as this, the new Constitution provides that "a Legislative Redistricting Commission shall be constituted not later than July 10." The Commission is to consist of eight people, no more than four of whom may be of the same political party. The Speaker and the Minority Leader of the House as well as the President and the Minority Leader of the Senate each appoint one member from among his own legislative ranks and one member from outside the General Assembly. The Commission then has thirty days in which to organize and file a redistricting plan. A simple majority, or five members, is required for a plan to be approved.

The failure of five members of the Commission to agree on a plan by the end of this period results in the random choice of a tie breaker (one of two persons of different political parties named by the Supreme Court and drawn by the Secretary of State). Thus, one political party or the other should gain a majority on the Commission by luck of the draw. This step was not utilized in 1971 as the Commission succeeded in filing a plan approved by a vote of 6 to 2 with the Secretary of State prior to the August 10 deadline.[8]

*This section is a condensation and revision of the author's *The Illinois Legislature: Structure and Process* co-authored with R.W. and R.J. Carlson.

Every even-number year at the general election in November, between 19 and 39 of the Senate's 59 members and all of the House's 177 members are up for election. In 1972 two-thirds of the Senators up for election were running for four-year terms, the other third for two-year terms. They had to stand for election again in 1974, only this time for four year terms and the other half for two-year terms. Thus, during the decade in which each redistricting plan is supposed to be applicable, each seat comes up for election three times, twice for four-year terms, once for a two-year term.

Under a system of cumulative voting unique in Illinois, three members of the House of Representatives are elected from each of the State's fifty-nine legislative districts for two-year terms. Designed to give the minority party in each district one of the three seats, cumulative voting allows a voter to cast three votes for one candidate or to distribute his or her votes among two or three candidates. By "plumping" three votes for one of its candidates, the minority party can ordinarily insure the election of at least one member of its party from that district. The new Constitution prohibits a political party from limiting its nominations to fewer than two candidates in each district. Since 1930 the minority party has only once held less than 42 percent of the seats.[9] In contrast, minority representation in the Senate has dropped as low as 25 percent.

Cumulative voting plays a crucial role in the election of members to the House of Representatives. It was first adopted as part of the 1870 Constitution, and the voters of Illinois have twice rejected attempts to do away with this system of minority representation. Both the proposed 1922 Constitution, which would have abolished cumulative voting, and a separate proposition submitted along with the 1970 Constitution, providing for single-member districts, were defeated. The latter went down to defeat by better than a four-to-three margin on December 15, 1970.

Those who successfully fought for the retention of cumulative voting in the new Constitution argued that the system gives people accessibility to their representatives and a choice of political opinion even in the staunchest one-party district. Members of the minority party have an elected member of the government around whom the local party can rally. The conflict that results from this system helps create interest in both the future of the party and the government. Cumulative voting has been credited with channeling conflict of opinion into the legislative process because it provides representation from all sections of the State. Since both parties contain members from areas where their party is not dominant, diverse opinions have a chance to reach both party caucuses and proceedings in committee and on the floor. With the majorities in the House historically small, the party leaderships have been forced to listen to these opinions and attempt to reconcile them so that their legislative programs can be passed.

While the partisan division in the House has been extremely close over the years, the Republican Party has clearly had the edge. Since 1920, the Democrats have had a majority in only six biennia. During this same period the Republicans have also dominated the Senate. Before 1971–72, when a 29–29 split occurred, the Democrats had been in control for only four sessions (1933–39) during the preceding half century. The period of Republican dominance seems to be at an end, however, as the Democrats have made inroads into traditionally Republican downstate districts.

Having dealt with the representative role of the General Assembly, we can now turn to the constitutional powers granted to this body as a collective entity.

Constitutional Powers of the Illinois Legislature

The State Constitution (both the 1870 and 1970 versions) channels the power of the State into three branches—the legislative, the executive, and the judicial—and expressly prohibits any one branch from exercising powers allocated to either of the others. Although the lines separating each of the three branches of State government have never been completely clear, the essential responsibility of the General Assembly has always been that of enacting statute law. The General Assembly and the legislative branch are located in the Constitution ahead of the executive and judiciary.

The General Assembly, in both a constitutional and a democratic sense, represents all the people of Illinois. The elected legislators exercise the sovereign power of the State in the name of the people. This is the basis for some of the great powers vested in the Legislature and for some aspects of its procedure.

Statute Law

Most enactments of the General Assembly become part of the statute law. These statutes may affect virtually every activity involving individuals, groups, and corporations in the State, a situation that has led to the enormous quantity of bills and resolutions that have been introduced in recent years. Although many involve fundamental matters usually only a few major bills command virtually all the media attention devoted to legislation. The bills of greatest concern to the general public usually involve revenue, appropriations, education, or judicial matters. No issue can be settled for all time,and each time a new law is added to the statutes, a strong possibility exists that subsequent General Assemblies will be required to rework it through amendatory bills. A heavy proportion of all the bills introduced and adopted are of this nature. While they have general relevance for the system, they usually have only slight relevance for the public. To give the flavor of the current workload over 5,000 bills plus resolutions were considered in the 1977–79 biennium.

The Governor shares in this lawmaking process at many stages, notably in his power either to recommend changes to the legislature or to veto a bill, his authority to reorganize the executive branch of government subject to a legislative veto, and the longstanding tradition that the chief executive proposes his own legislative program. The Illinois Governor, by constitutional powers, is one of the strongest in the nation.

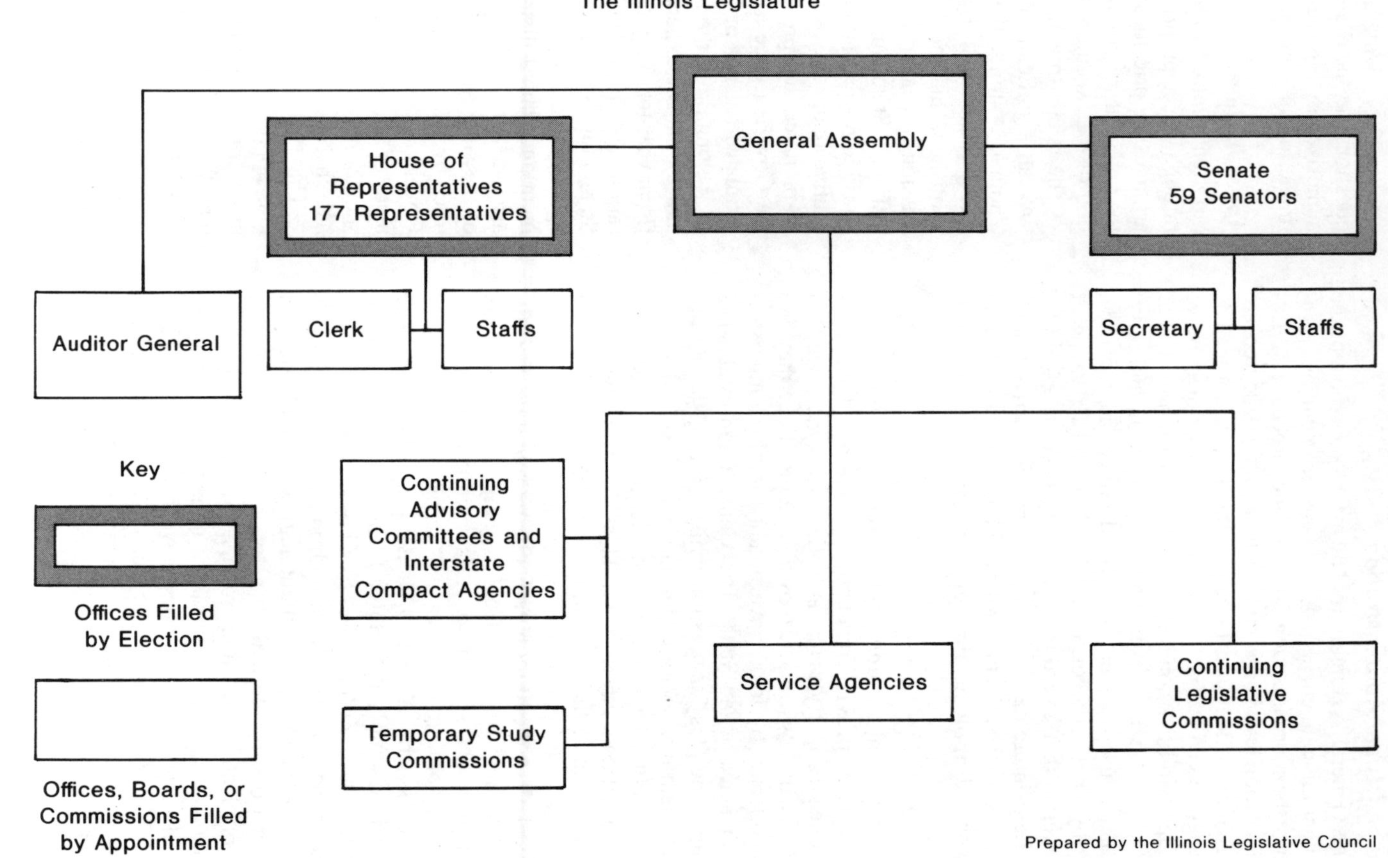

Figure 6-1. THE ILLINOIS LEGISLATURE

State and Local Administration

The General Assembly by law establishes most of the administrative agencies of State government and prescribes their organization, duties, and procedures. Excepted from legislative control to a limited degree are those State offices mentioned in the Constitution. The Legislature cannot by statute abolish offices or impinge on responsibilities controlled by the Constitution. Under the Governor's new executive reorganization authority, if either house does not specifically reject an executive order by a majority vote on a roll call within sixty days of its receipt, that executive order will become effective. The Legislature has insisted in playing a positive role in executive reorganization plans submitted thus far and has enacted implementing legislation.

Revenue

An important constitutional power of the General Assembly is to provide revenue for State and local governments. Property taxes and other taxes are levied on the basis of laws enacted by the Legislature; they are then collected by local governments and by administrative agencies of the State. The Constitution establishes certain principles for taxation while the Legislatture develops them into specific measures. In this way the General Assembly shapes the way monies are collected by all levels of Illinois government. This is a critically important power since the availability of fiscal resources often determines how government meets its responsibilities.

The 1970 Constitution grants home rule units (mostly larger municipalities and Cook County) the power to tax and incur debt subject to certain limitations. For instance, a home rule unit cannot license for revenue unless the General Assembly should grant this right. The General Assembly by a three-fifths vote of each house may deny or limit the power of a home rule unit to tax.

The imposition of new or additional taxes to raise additional local revenue without legislative authorization has been one of the main uses of these new home rule powers. Hotel and motel rooms, cigarettes, factories, and businesses have been taxed; municipal utility taxes as well as new parking taxes have been imposed. The City of Chicago in particular has made strong use of this authority, and the Illinois Supreme Court has thus far upheld its authority to impose among others a cigarette tax, a parking tax, a wheel tax, a transaction tax on the transfer of real property and the rental or leasing of personal property and an employer's expense tax (''head tax''). Hotel and motel taxes have been imposed in Chicago as well as in several other suburban and downstate cities without any legal challenges.[10]

The Legislature may also limit the amount of debt a home rule municipality can incur without referendum. Such limitations, if enacted, can limit nonreferendum debt only when it exceeds a set percentage of the home rule municipality's total assessed valuation.

Otherwise, the incurring of debt by State and local governments is subject to legislative authorizations within new, less restrictive, constitutionally prescribed limits. Under the 1970 Constitution, the General Assembly may, without a statewide referendum on the question, put the State's full faith and credit behind debt authorized by a three-fifths majority of each house. The impact of this change has already been profound.

Appropriations

Often referred to as the ''power of the purse,'' it is through the appropriations process that the Legislature arranges the priorities of State government and possesses the potential for controlling or restricting the administration of the executive branch.

The budget-making process in Illinois has undergone several significant changes since the publication of Thomas Anton's then-authoritative book on the subject.[11] The old Budgetary Commission has been abolished, and the Illinois Economic and Fiscal Commission has taken its place. As part of the Governor's Office, a State Bureau of the Budget is now totally responsible for preparation of what can be called a true executive budget. Constitutionally, the State budget must be prepared and presented to the General Assembly by the Governor once a year. His budget must set forth an estimated balance of funds available for appropriation at the beginning of the fiscal year, an estimate of receipts, and a plan for expenditures and obligations during the fiscal year for every department, authority, public corporation, and quasi-public corporation of the State, every State college and university and every other public agency created by theState except units of local government and school districts. The Governor's budget must also set forth the indebtedness and contingent liabilities of the state and such other information as may be required by law. Finally, the Constitution mandates that the Governor's proposed expenditures not exceed his estimate of funds to be available for the coming year. A statute requires that this all be done on or before March 1.

The Governor's budget document is then translated into appropriation bills which often spell out the purposes for which the money may be used by specifying both the internal organization of an agency and the type of operating expenditure (e.g., personal services) in separate line items. Under the Constitution all expenditures of public funds must be appropriated by the General Assembly, and the sum of these appropriations for a given fiscal year must not exceed the Legislature's own estimate of the funds that will be available during that year.

All appropriation bills traverse the legislative process like other bills. Upon passage they become temporary parts of the body of statute law. Committee deliberations have become more important to the process with the addition of professional staff for both the majority and minority members of the Appropriations Committee in each chamber. Subcommittees are now the scene of the intensive review and bargaining. Their recommendations almost always prevail in their own chamber, and the members of these subgroups are usually their chamber's representatives in the many conference committees that often develop.

Postaudit Review of Expenditures

In another change brought about by the new State Constitution, the General Assembly now appoints its own Auditor General, who serves a ten-year term and is to audit, or cause to be audited, the obligation, receipt, and use of public funds of the State. The first Legislative Auditor General was confirmed by the required extraordinary majorities in both houses of the General Assembly after his appointment had been recommended by the Legislative Audit Commission.

This legislative agency replaced the Department of Audits, which had been part of the executive branch; it is responsible for conducting a financial audit of each State agency at least once during every biennium. The Auditor General works in cooperation with the Legislative Audit Commission, which may authorize him to conduct either a management or program audit of a state agency. The Audit Commission may authorize the Auditor General to make certain investigations. The Auditor General also has jurisdiction over local government agencies and private agencies as to the use of State funds which were granted with specific limitations or conditions imposed by law. Finally, the Auditor General may initiate and conduct an efficiency audit of any State agency or program whenever the findings of a postaudit indicate that such an audit is advisable.

Home Rule

The 1970 Illinois Constitution has a great deal more to say about local government than its predecessor did, with an entire article devoted to these governments. Under the new Constitution, home rule units are not dependent on the General Assembly to enact legislation affecting their powers and functions. The State-local relation in effect was reversed by the new Constitution. Qualifying for home rule status are those municipalities over 25,000 population, smaller municipalities which elect by referendum to become home rule units counties with an elected chief executive officer. (Currently Cook County is the only Illinois county in this category.) A home rule unit may also revert to its former non-home rule status by referendum.

With certain specific limitations, a home rule unit may "exercise any function pertainining to its government and affairs including, but not limited to, the power to regulate for the protection of the public health, safety, morals and welfare; to license; to tax; and to incur debt." There are specific limitations to this broad grant of power. They relate to limitations on the taxing power of home rule units. These local governments cannot (1) license for revenue, (2) impose taxes upon or measured by income or earnings, or (3) tax occupations, unless the Legislature grants these powers.

The "preemption" provisions of the new Constitution, subsections (g), (h), and (i) of Article VII, section 6, constitute the second group of limitations on home rule powers. These spell out the most important ways in which the Legislature palys a role in Illinois home rule. In general, they give the General Assembly vehicles to restrict the broad powers of the local governments.

The late Professor David C. Baum, who was the counsel for the local government committee at the 1970 convention, explained the intent of the pre-emption sections this way: "The design of Section 6 places great responsibility upon the legislature to ensure that home rule does not degenerate into provincialism which could injure the people of the state. This emphasis on legislative authority to limit home rule, plus the specification of ways in which the legislature must act to assert its authority, makes the Illinois home rule provision unique."[12]

By the end of 1978 there were ninety-two home rule municipalities in Illinois. Twenty-nine of these units, with populations under 25,000, had adopted home rule by referendum; thirteen municipal home rule referenda had been defeated. Cook County was the only home rule county. Nine other counties had tried to attain home rule by adopting the elected chief executive officer form of government by referendum; all were unsuccessful.[13]

Constitutional Changes

The General Assembly is also responsible for initiating changes in the state constitution although the current charter provides alternative methods for change should the General Assembly not act.

The question of whether to call a constitutional convention to consider reworking the document as a whole can be submitted to the voters at any general election, provided at least three-fifths of the members elected to each house approve an enabling resolution at least six months prior to the election.

Specific amendments to the constitution may be proposed by the General Assembly directly, again by a three-fifths vote of the members elected if, at the general election next occurring at least six months after such legislative initiative, the amendment is approved by either three-fifths of those voting on the question or a majority of those voting in the election.

The 1970 constitution provides several changes that have the effect of allowing the initiative for certain changes to come from outside the legislature. (Illinois does not have the open-ended constitutional initiative and referendum found in some states.) Private citizens can by petition initiate a referendum on changes in structural and procedural subjects in the legislative article of the constitution if 8 percent of the vote cast in the preceding gubernatorial election is obtained on such petitions. To date several initiated amendments have been proposed but none have reached the ballot.

Constitutional change without legislative action may occur in yet another way: the question of whether to call a constitutional convention must automatically appear on the ballot at the general election in the twentieth year following the last submission. Thus the electorate will be voting on a constitutional convention call at least every twenty years regardless of what action the General Assembly does or does not take.

The General Assembly may be called upon by the Congress to consider amendments to the federal Constitution, for ratification either by legislatures or by conventions in the several states. The new Illinois Constitution requires the affirmative vote of three-fifths of the members elected to each house for the General Assembly to petition Congress to call a federal constitutional convention, to ratify a proposed amendment to the U.S. Constitution,[14] or to call a State convention to ratify a proposed amendment to the federal Constitution.

Investigations

Although bill consideration may involve questioning or testimony in the nature of an inquiry, the General Assembly conducts investigations of governmental or other matters on a limited basis. But it has general power to make investigations appropriate to the legislative function, and on occasion a special inquiry is authorized. Perhaps one of the more common of these relates to contested elections to the General Assembly. Since each house has complete constitutional discretion in determining the qualifications of its members, election disputes in Illinois have not been settled in court but by the chamber involved. Inquiries into how state and local governments conduct their affairs are also possible, and even the behavior of private persons or business may have a sufficient relation to existing or needed legislation to permit detailed inquiries.

The distinguishing feature of an investigation is probably the power to compel by subpoena both the attendance and testimony of witnesses and the production of books, records and papers. As provided in the State Constitution, this power may be exercised by either house of the General Assembly or any committee thereof. Statutes allow these bodies to administer oaths and otherwise search out desired information rather than be content with what is offered as volunteered information, arguments, and answers to questions. The General Assembly established by law in 1971 the Illinois Legislative Investigating Commission, which is empowered to conduct any investigation authorized by statute or established by a specific resolution of either or both houses of the General Assembly. A 1957 statute sets down various procedural requirements designed to protect the rights of those affected by any investigative hearings conducted apart from the operations of the legislature's standing committees.

Confirmation of Appointments

The Senate alone is given the power by the constitution of "advice and consent" to gubernatorial appointments to a number of State administrative offices. The Senate must act within sixty session days of its receipt of a nomination, and a majority of all the elected Senators is necessary for confirmation.

Subject to confirmation, according to the Constitution, are "all officers whose election or appointment is not otherwise provided for." Under existing laws this entails a long list ranging from department heads directly subordinate to the Governor to nonsalaried members of various local and regional boards and commissions. In recent years the Senate has begun expending more time and resources on this function with the upper chamber now being in recess for no longer than about four months at any time.

Impeachment

The legislature may remove executive and judicial officers from office, an extreme action that is seldom taken. Such action can be threatened, however, as in 1974, when a resolution seeking the impeachment of a code department director "for failure to enforce the . . . law" was introduced in the House. No action was taken on it. Prior to the Watergate scandal the use of the impeachment power was almost unheard of in Illinois.

Educating the Public

The most easily overlooked function of the Legislature is that of informing and instructing the public. The business of the Legislature on the floor and in committee is carried out in full public view to develop the dialogue essential to popular government. The Illinois Legislature and its committees historically have been very open bodies. Floor debate and committee investigations are vital in stimulating the people's awareness of major public issues, and the Illinois General Assembly has been in the forefront among the nation's state legislatures in opening both its floor sessions and committee deliberations to the public. In accordance with both the State Constitution and legislative rules, all legislative committees and commissions are required to give public notice of their meetings at least six days in advance.

Limitations

The 1970 Illinois Constitution does provide the General Assembly with considerably fewer restrictions than did the 1870 version. Gone are the extremely restrictive provisions for incurring state debt and the prohibitions against lotteries and changes in the general banking statutes. Sovereign immunity has been abolished. A laundry list of prohibitions against special legislation has been replaced by a general provision prohibiting such laws.

Yet, there still are a number of restrictions in the present constitution. Carried over from the old document are prohibitions against enacting ex post facto laws, laws impairing the obligation of a contract, or any special legislation (the new Constitution simply provides that the question of what is special legislation shall be judicially determined). New restrictions on the type of legislation the General Assembly can enact are found principally in the local government and revenue articles of the new constitution. As discussed earlier, home rule powers granted certain municipalities and counties impose certain limitations on the Legislature.

The new revenue article represents one of the real ironies in this area—it is probably more restrictive than the article it replaced in the 1870 constitution. For many years it was believed that the old revenue article prohibited an income tax. One of the major reasons for calling a convention in the late 1960s was this supposed prohibition and the problems inherent under the old article with classifying property, particularly in the large urban counties like Cook, DuPage, Lake and St. Clair. After the

Convention call had been approved, the Illinois Supreme Court ruled in *Thorpe v. Mahin* that an income tax was constitutional under the old article.[15] The new article, while lacking the old uniformity clause, provides some very tight parameters within which the General Assembly can legislate in both the property and the income tax areas.

The new Constitution also imposes several constitutional limitations on how individual legislators can conduct both their public and private lives by requiring that they file according to law a verified statement of their economic interests with the Secretary of State. The penalty for failing to file, as set by the Constitution, is forfeiture of, or ineligibility for, office. A person convicted of a felony, bribery, perjury or other heinous crime also becomes ineligible to hold office.

Finally, the Legislature cannot delegate its lawmaking power to the people, so there is no general power to pass a statute of statewide impact and submit it to the people for acceptance or rejection as in some other states. Advisory referenda such as the 1978 "Thompson Proposition" are, of course, a different matter. The Legislature may not encroach on the powers of other branches of government, and citizens are protected from its power by the bill of rights. It may not deny equal protection of the laws of due process of law.

Having set the constitutional basis for the organization and the powers of the General Assembly, we now turn to two of the most important influences on the Illinois Legislature—the political parties and the executive. Partisanship plays such an important role in the legislative process primarily because Illinois is a sharply divided state politically. Insight into this division as well as into how the individual parties function is vital to a clear understanding of the legislative process in this State.

The Legislature and Partisan Politics

The most pervasive and, at the same time, the most elusive of all the elements that influence legislative behavior is membership in a political party. American political life is organized on the basis of party. Entrance to politics and subsequent success are achieved through the two-party system. Regardless of the level of involvement—precinct, township, county, state, or national—from the outset a political career is usually intertwined with one of the two major political parties. The contribution of party affiliation to political success is likely to vary greatly. The national parties themselves are merely aggregates of state and local organizations of varying efficacy. Within the states party effectiveness often runs the gamut from highly organized, tightly disciplined local party organizations whose support is essential for electoral success to loosely knit organizations whose support is completely unrelated to individual success at the polls. This is certainly true in Illinois, where the Democrats and Republicans are relatively evenly matched at the statewide level but where local organizations are often quite unevenly matched and competition is frequently nonexistent.

The categories used most frequently in any discussion of Illinois politics are "Cook County" and "Downstate." "Cook County" refers simply to Chicago and surrounding suburban areas while "Downstate" refers to the rest of the State outside Cook County. This distinction enjoys official status since legislation applying only to Cook County or Chicago has been commonly passed by the Legislature. A number of laws have also enabled Cook County and the City of Chicago to conduct elections in a manner somewhat different from Downstate. In addition, the two political parties are organized differently in Cook County and Downstate. The distinction between the two areas does make sense. Slightly over half the State's population is concentrated in Cook County, and a majority of the people there live in the City of Chicago. Even more significant, however, is the difference between these two geographic areas in voting behavior. Cook County, and Chicago in particular, constitute one of the state's most consistently Democratic areas. If a Democratic candidate for statewide office is to win, he must roll up substantial majorities in Cook County to overcome the traditionally Republican vote Downstate. A statewide election in Illinois is essentially a contest between Republican Downstate and Democratic Cook County. Within Cook County the contest is between the Republican suburbs and the Democratic city, where the Democrats need a large vote to carry the county by a margin sufficient to carry the State.

The division of the State into two partisan strongholds, however, tends to obscure some important enclaves of minority party strength. Major Republican strength tends to be concentrated in suburban Cook County as well as in the central and northern parts of the state outside the county. Democratic strength is found in the City of Chicago and in the southern third of the State. The relative importance of the Downstate Democratic vote is overshadowed by the huge party plurality in the city. In addition, the cumulative voting system used to elect members of the state House of Representatives regularly permits a party that is permanently in the minority in a particular area to elect a member of the Legislature, with all the perquisites and prestige attendant to holding major public office. If he has the requisite qualities, such a person can become a powerful leader in the State party despite the fact that he comes from an area where his party is far in the minority.[16] This accounts for the existence of a large number of Democratic legislators from Downstate and a significant bloc of Republican legislators from Chicago. Such a situation might not be expected in light of the solidly Republican nature of much of Downstate Illinois and the equally solid Democratic character of Chicago.[17]

Generally, the Democratic party is less fragmented than its counterpart, although this certainly was not the case in the 1975–76 biennium. With control of the Governor's Office and both houses of the General Assembly, the Democrats went through an unprecedented ninety-three ballots before finally electing a Speaker of the House with some Republican help. Two years later the

Democrats took 186 ballots to elect the Senate President. The usual cohesiveness of the Democrats is directly attributable to the existence of a large power base in Chicago, where most Democratic strength is concentrated. It is too early to speculate on the impact of the death of Mayor Daley and the upset win by Mayor Jane Byrne will have on the Democratic party in Chicago, or in the legislature.

Members of the Legislature, then, are likely to be associated with their party in a variety of ways depending upon their party's standing statewide and within their home districts. Party loyalty can take on a wide range of meanings. Election to the Legislature also means membership in a new form of party organization—the legislative party. The demands and responsibilities of party membership in the General Assembly are likely to be quite different from those back home. The nature of this relationship again depends generally upon the conditions under which a legislator is elected and the position of his party within the statewide political system. Equally important is the nature of the leadership within the legislative party itself. Differences within the parties do exist and factions sometimes develop, but the tugs of party loyalty are strong and conflicts between the two parties are often intense. Beyond participation in differences that periodically split each party, party membership also means an association that will determine a legislator's friends, the nature of his social relationships, the issues he will become involved with, and occasionally the advancement of his career. In this ambiguous way party affiliation takes on a significant role in the legislative process.

The Leaders

The Republican and Democratic parties play the major role in organizing the Legislature, conducting its business, and providing much of the dynamic force behind the legislative process. The majority party in each chamber assumes control of committee assignments, committee chairmanships, bill referrals, and the scheduling of floor activity. These powers are exercised by the leadership of each party, particularly the majority party. In the Senate the President serves as both presiding officer and leader of the majority party. He is assisted by four assistant majority leaders, who help carry floor debate and also act as whips for their party. The President's counterpart, the Minority Leader, is usually assisted by three assistant minority leaders. Although party leaders in both houses are officially elected on opening day, usually their election is carried out at party caucuses prior to the convening of the General Assembly.

Certainly the President's most important power is as the leader of the majority party in the Senate. On the surface his role may appear somewhat perfunctory, since most of the significant responsibilities are delegated elsewhere. Actually, however, those powers which are not formally delegated to him accrue to him informally. For instance, the President is not autorized to make committee assignments; that power is delegated to the Committee on Committees. In reality the President does make the assignments or has the final word in assigning members to a committee because his caucus will almost always support his choices for the chairman and majority party members of that committee. Thus, having determined the composition of the Committee on Committees, the President's decisions on committee assignments are likely to be affirmed by that committee. Assignment of bills, another important source of influence, is formally allocated to the Committee on the Assignment of Bills. Normally, the Chairman (who for more than a decade now has been one of the assistant majority leaders) is responsible for this daily chore. But here again, the President has a considerable amount of influence and can exert his will on those few occasions during a session when the assignment of a bill to committee assumes critical significance. The Senate Operations Commission is a third major repository of influence which actually accrues to the President. This Commission is technically responsible for the hiring and firing of Senate employees and for the assignment of office quarters. These decisions, however, are almost always made by the leader of the majority party, except in the case of minority party employees, who come under the direct supervision of the minority leader.

As a party leader, the President has a number of other significant duties. On major issues he frequently leaves the chair to articulate his party's position from his desk on the floor. He presents party positions to other political figures and to the press. He schedules legislative business, setting the time, length and pace of each daily session. On occasion he lends his prestige to other members, particularly by cosponsoring legislation. He mends party fences, informally or through the caucus, and distributes rewards according to established traditions. Finally, he keeps the membership informed on the "big picture." In carrying out these responsibilities, the President is clearly the single most influential member of the Senate.

In practice the office of President closely resembles that of Speaker of the House. However, the Speaker has more formal control of the legislative machinery. He, like the Senate President, also is allowed to vote and occasionally he may speak out on issues from the floor, although he customarily maintains as much impartiality as possible when presiding over floor activities.

Since the Speaker is usually on the rostrum presiding, the majority leader assumes the general responsibility for leading partisan activities on the floor. He is nominally the number two man in the chamber's majority leadership. The nature of the relationship between the Speaker, his majority leader, his assistants, and his whips, however, varies considerably with changing circumstances and personalities. Together they run the House much as the President and his leadership team run the Senate. They maintain the same kinds of control in a slightly different way over committee assignments, committee chairmanships, bill referrals, the scheduling of floor activity and partisan responsibilities.

The minority party leaders in each house generally play a much more muted role in the legislative process.

They are usually consulted on matters concerning the operation of the chamber and the scheduling of activity simply as a matter of courtesy, while the authority for such decisions rests entirely with the majority party. The minority party and its leaders find their authoritative responsibilities confined mostly to internal party matters. One of the most important powers they have is that of making minority party appointments to various committees and commissions. They are also their party's spokesmen on the floor and in the press room.

The Legislative Party

In Illinois the Democratic party is relatively homogeneous and well organized. The major source of Democratic strength lies in the City of Chicago, where a very effective Democratic political organization controlled the city administration and regularly insured impressive Democratic pluralities at the polls. There exists within the party, however, a group of downstate Democratic legislators who constitute an increasingly more numerous and significant bloc in the Illinois House. Their presence stems from the cumulative voting system and they tend to moderate the Chicago orientation of the House Democrats. The situation is intensified by a sense of mistrust between those from Downstate and those from Chicago.

The cumulative voting system insures a sizable bloc of Republican legislators from the Democratic stronghold of Chicago, although the GOP legislators from the City have never been in such direct conflict with their Downstate colleagues as have the Chicago Democrats from time to time. The presence of a large number of GOP legislators from Chicago seems to result instead in increased conflict with Chicago Democrats. Indeed much of the partisan conflict in the Legislature finds the Chicago Democrats, who control the City administration, pitted against Republicans from within the City and those situated in the adjoining suburbs.

Over in the Senate, the traditional Republican majority that dominated that chamber for over thirty years evaporated following the 1970 election. Thus, the competition that characterizes relations between the parties in the House, and which had been absent in the Senate, has been very much in evidence during the current decade. In spite of this the Senate is basically a much more stable environment than the House. Smallness in size (fifty nine as contrasted to 177 in the House), longer terms of office and frequent intercameral movement from House to Senate all contribute to the creation and maintenance of a well-ordered and predictable legislative operation.

For most Chicago Democrats election and reelection to the General Assembly are party rather than personal accomplishments. Accordingly, the concerns of party are likely to be crucial to these members in formulating a broad range of legislative positions. The power base is in Chicago, not Springfield. This is particularly true in the Senate, where at least three-fifths, and as many as four-fifths, of the Democrats who have served during the last several General Assemblies have come from Chicago. In every session the Democratic floor leader also came from the City. Thus, it is not hard to see why the Chicago political organization exerts a more effective influence over Senate Democrats than over House Democrats, proportionately more of whom usually come from Downstate.

For most Republican legislators, on the other hand, election to the General Assembly is largely a personal accomplishment, since the statewide party has little influence over individual success at the polls. Consequently GOP legislators tend to emphasize political power within the General Assembly more heavily than do their Democratic counterparts. The Republican legislator who regularly returns to Springfield generally depends more on himself and his colleagues for direction on issues than on the statewide party. Efforts have been made under past Republican governors and other State officials to provide some centralizing influence on the legislative party. Even in the presence of this kind of influence, however, the Republican party in the Legislature has remained a fairly autonomous body, although somewhat less so than in the absence of such influence.

In addition to the differences between the legislative parties that reflect their relative orientations (Chicago or suburban-Downstate) in the statewide political system, there are also differences within each party that generally reflect some basic differences between the House and the Senate. As suggested above, the cumulative voting system under which House members are elected insures a sizable bloc of downstate Democrats that tends to dilute the Chicago orientation among House Democrats as a whole. (It has been argued that cumulative voting serves to insure competition between the two parties in the House.) Every two years majority control is determined by the results in a handful of seriously contested districts in which two Democrats run against two Republicans for three seats. Under this system, the minority party in a district, with only a slight hope of winning two of the three seats, may find it has two candidates competing against each other rather than against the candidates of the majority party. The system can also result in deflating or inflating a party's share of representation in the House relative to its total statewide vote.

Party Issues

The vase majority of issues that come before the General Assembly do not result in serious differences between the parties. There is, however, a small but persistent number of issues that do cause intense rifts between Republicans and Democrats. Perhaps the most obvious category of bills creating partisan conflicts are those dealing with elections and party organization. They are bills which seem to confer an advantage on one party at the expense of the other. Occasionally the party responsible for the administration of the State or the City of Chicago is subject to harassment by the opposite party. This is a case of the "outs" trying to embarrass the "ins." Another category includes disagreements over broad programmatic issues which are keyed to the traditional differences between the two parties. These are issues of "principle" which are particularly evident in the parties at the national level but which can also become important sources of division at the state and local levels.

In addition to these three broad kinds of issues there is a tendency for partisan splits to occur over bills that seem totally unrelated to party. One former Republican leader in the House related the phenomenon this way: "Only a small portion of the total bills are really partisan issues, but early in the session a sort of fraternal or 'gang' feeling within the parties develops. Members become very gung-ho for the party as the two parties compete against one another. As a consequence many bills with no partisan significance will find the two parties lining up against each other." This particular kind of party split is difficult to predict, since it seems to be mostly a matter of chance and personality reather than design. Occasionally members of the opposite party will refrain as a group from supporting legislation which would be politically beneficial for the sponsor if he is from a marginal district and must stand for reelection in the immediate future. Events of this nature indicate that party affiliation can be rather important in the Legislature.

There are several specific sources of party issues or legislation that come to be identified with one party or the other. Each session the Governor's party in the Legislature is responsible for passage of his legislative program. The administration program is the largest and most significant set of measures the General Assembly considers; it includes most of the plans and aspirations of State government for the succeeding biennium. Various portions of the Governor's program do become sources of partisan dispute, but it is not accurate to say that an administration bill inevitably becomes a hot party issue. Quite often this is not the case. Most larger cities have home rule and have limited legislative programs as a result. Non-home rule school districts and special districts must still seek legislation to embark on new programs or meet financial crises. Home rule units are on guard to protect any erosion of their home rule powers. Each of the independently elected state officials usually has various bills introduced in the Legislature. The Secretary of State has been particularly active during the last several sessions since the responsibilities of that office have increased very rapidly in recent years. Practically all of the major political officeholders in the state, then, introduce some kind of program for legislative consideration and in varying degree these programs become identified with one party or the other, although they do not automatically become objects of partisan conflict.

Occasionally the party which does not control the Governor's Office has submitted a legislative program which has served as that party's counterpart to the administration program. These attempts to commit either party to a specific program have met with mixed success even though by now much of the legislation proposed in the earlier programs has become law. In the past neither party has consistently attempted to commit itself formally on a broad range of legislative items. Major leadership in this area has come from the governor and other officers within the executive branch. However, as the Legislature has become better equipped with staff and other resources the development of issues and party programs has become a more significant part of the legislative process. This was especially true recently when the Governor and both houses of the Legislature were of opposite parties. Even if the same party controls both houses of the General Assembly and the governor's office, the pursuit of a legislative program developed independently of the governor is, in some cases, still likely to occur.

Party issues become known to the membership in different ways, depending upon their importance to the party. On some bills, such as those dealing with elections and party organization, the leaders do not have to do much to stimulate party members' awareness of the significance of the issue, since it obviously hits close to home. On many issues, however, the partisan element is not always explicit and a number of devices are employed to communicate party positions. The caucus is the most obvious device; it is reserved for the more significant issues. Sometimes a less direct procedure is used in which the chairman or minority spokesman voices an opinion on particular bills as they are heard in committee and is then supported by the other members of his party on that committee. Members of the Governor's staff, who attend committee hearings and have the privilege of the floor, keep their party members informed of the governor's position on pending legislation. An additional cue is the bill sponsor code. If a bill is sponsored by the party leadership, the names of the leaders will appear as sponsors and cosponsors in the *Digest* and on the printed bill itself. As one House member remarked, "With any member, if the speaker's name is listed as a cosponsor on a bill, he will think twice before voting against it." Generally the identification of party issues has been less difficult among the Democrats because of the higher level of discipline and organization found there, but that is also changing. Communicating party positions is easier in the Senate because it is a much smaller and more stable body and information is consequently easier to channel.

Party Discipline

There are a number of ways in which each party in the Legislature generates allegiance among its members. As stated above, the vase majority of bills are not generally considered party matters, but many do have some partisan significance. On these bills the commitment of either party is likely to vary greatly, and the pressures that each member feels to vote with his party will depend upon the importance to the party of the issue in question. Obviously, the most severe threat that a party can use to guarantee the support of a legislator is the denial of renomination. This sanction is at the disposal of only the Democratic party in Chicago, which contribures a majority of the Democrats in each house. The situation is summed up by a Republican legislator: "The Democrats are a much better organized and better disciplined party than we are. They can get at their men outside the legislature and keep them from being reslated.'' And a Democrat concurs: ''The Republicans use their caucus as their principal instrument of party control. We don't have to—we can discipline our men both in and outside the legislature. Denying a member nomination is a rare form of party discipline.'' Republicans as well as Democrats effectively utilize a number of other pressures within the legislature to insure discipline. Perhaps the most frequent punishment for irregular party support is the denial of a committee or commission appointment, as the following comment illustrates:

> ''The discipline for party irregularity depends on the types of issues involved. One member was kept off committees he wanted for several sessions, but he finally became chairman of the Judiciary Committee. You'll note, however, that this was a committee which is in a position to do the least bit of harm to the party. A member who has left the party at times may be trusted to handle some issues but he will never be trusted to handle something like party organization because of his past irregularities.''

This story also illustrates the subtle form party discipline often takes.

The pressures that form around irregular party support are informal and highly personal, and they are not necessarily generated by the party leadership.

Sometimes a legislator can avoid party sanctions for leaving the party on a particular bill if his vote would endanger his position within his district. The party leadership is inclined to accept this situation as an excuse if it is genuine and is not used with great frequency. As one Republican House leader explains: ''We will usually accept an excuse based on a man's district. However, we usually know the composition of a man's district pretty well and we usually know whether he is telling the turth about what his district is going to do to him if he votes a certain way.''

The relative independence of Republican legislators, all coming from somewhat diverse local organizations, helps explain why GOP caucuses are held so often. If a member is not going to vote with most of the group, the caucus is the place for him to alert both the leadership and his colleagues. In the process of ''counting noses'' a member may be talked or cajoled into switching sides or, alternatively, he may succeed in winning enough votes to his point of view to carry the day on the floor. Occasionally the manner in which a member votes against his party determines the reaction of his leaders and colleagues. A member of the Senate prompted the following remark by one of his fellow senators: ''He leaves the party more than anyone else, but he does so quietly, and he's such a nice likable guy that he usually gets away with it.''

In many aspects of the legislative process in Illinois, personality and reputation are often crucial determinants of individual accomplishment. They often outweigh even such factors as party in determining personal success or failure.

We turn now to the role of the Governor. Illinois's governors have strong contitutional power, and as a result governors have been an important influence in the legislative decisions.

Executive-Legislative Relations

One important reason for Legislatures to attend closely to the executive branch is that governors and legislators, as politicians elected to represent the people, have similar stakes in controlling professionals in the administrative departments and agencies of State government. Too often, the professional bureaucracies are responsive neither to the Governor nor to the Legislature. On the other hand, as chief executive, chief legislator, and usually the leader of his party, the Governor's actions and decisions weigh heavily upon how the Legislature performs and what it produces.

Growth of Gubernatorial Supremacy

Historically, the first State constitutions gave the Legislatures supreme power while severely circumscribing the powers of State Governors. Today, the positions of the Legislature and the Governor are almost completely reversed, and constitutional limitations, which once applied to the Governor, now work to restrict the Legislature. A number of circumstances and powers can be linked to the emergence and development of the Governor as a legislative leader. For example, administration bills—a Governor's legislative program—are usually the principal bills of almost any session of almost any state legislature. They occupy a major portion of the legislator's time and their success or failure is used as the chief yardstick by which sessions are evaluated.

An important constitutional power of the Governor's which allows him to direct the Legislature's energies is his ability to call special sessions. The Governor's call specifically limits the Legislature's workload to consideration of his proposals. Threats of a special session are also an effective weapon for the governor to use in prodding legislative action.

A Governor's major constitutional power is his right to veto any legislation passed by the General Assembly and, thus, to stop it from becoming law (if the veto is not subsequently overriden). In Illinois, the 1970 Constitution added the line-item reduction and amendatory veto powers to the governor's arsenal.

A further source of power for the Governor is his ability to lead the legislature through his authority over budget making. In Illinois he also has the authority now to take the initiative in executive reorganization.

Gubernatorial Action

The constitutional power of the Governor to veto legislation passed by the General Assembly has always been a critical element in the legislative process. Although students of Illinois politics generally advocate a strong executive, they also seek a strong Legislature. These goals are not mutually exclusive, although they may necessarily conflict at times.

The members of the 1970 Constitutional Convention evidently agreed with this assessment of the relationship between the chief executive and Legislature. One of the delegates, in an article published prior to the Convention, noted: "In Illinois the governor's veto is virtually absolute, and the question is whether it is desirable to leave it that way. Knowledge of the finality of the governor's action may lessen the legislature's acceptance of responsibility for its action; if so, that may be a serious impediment to the development of a strong legislative branch—which is equally a goal of constitutional revision."

In the Convention itself it appears that most of the delegates subscribed to the view that it was time for the Legislature to stop taking a "back seat" to the Governor. The majority of the Committee on the Legislative Article, in explaining their proposal to the entire Convention, argued as if they believed that the balance of power was unbalanced and that it was desirable to expand the potential power of the General Assembly: "Every effort must be made . . . to restore a proper balance of power in our tri-partite separation of powers among the executive, legislative and judicial branches, and this provision represents at least a small opportunity to place confidence in the General Assembly. . . ."

In the end, the constitutional framers broadened the Governor's veto powers while at the same time they lowered the numerical requirement for overruling the governor. Formerly, when a bill passed by the General Assembly was presented to the Governor, he had three choices in every case except appropriation bills. He could approve it, veto it or allow it to become law without his signature. In the case of appropriation bills he had the additional option of an item veto. Under the 1970 Constitution the governor retains all of these options while acquiring two more. At the same time the vote required to override a gubernatorial veto is now a three-fifths majority rather than two-thirds.

Item-Reduction Veto

The Con-Con delegates expanded the Governor's "fine-tuning" control over the "throttle" of State expenditures by giving him an item-reduction veto power subject to a legislative override by a simple majority vote. The line-item veto, subject to the regular three-fifths majority needed to override, was retained in the document. In recommending the proposed reduction veto to the entire convention, the Committee on the Executive argued: "Modern appropriation practices have rendered the existing item veto virtually obsolete because it is no longer common to have appropriation bills so detailed that a veto could strike an entire item without being destructive of the program of the agency."

Thus, the Convention reversed a landmark 1915 Illinois Supreme Court decision so as to "revitalize the intent of the 1884 addition to the constitution of the item veto." With this change the Governor is no longer faced with the necessity of accepting or rejecting an appropriated amount in toto. A line-item reduction veto may be restored to its original amount by a record vote of a majority of the members elected to each house.

After the new Constitution went into effect, Governor Richard Ogilvie wasted little time applying this new authority. On July 13, 1971, twelve days after the Constitution's effective date, he used this power in reviewing appropriation bills passed by the General Assembly for fiscal year 1972. By the time he had finished acting on these bills, the Governor had reduced the 141 line items in sixteen bills for total reductions of $146,253,791. Despite this unprecedented cut in appropriations for a single fiscal year, and the fact that only a simple majority was needed to restore the original amounts, the Governor's actions held in every case. Following the 1974 session, Governor Daniel Walker used this device to remove an entire series of "retirement amendments" which provided for a higher level of funding State pension systems than the Governor had recommended. As a result he exercised his item-reduction veto in signing forty-four bills, and his line-item veto as well as the reduction veto on another twenty-six bills. This pattern was continued in 1979, when the Governor reduced and/or line-item vetoed the appropriations in twenty-six bills.

Amendatory Veto

The delegates also added "a flexible tool of government to be used by both the lawmakers and the governor" which is commonly referred to as an amendatory veto. Instead of having to either approve or veto a bill in its entirety, the Governor may now return a bill with specific recommendations for change to the house in which it originated. These specific recommendations for change may be accepted by a vote of the majority of the elected members of each house. The Legislature also has the option of overriding an amendatory veto, as it has for any kind of veto. Such bills in which gubernatorial changes are accepted by the General Assembly must be presented again to the Governor for his certification that the final products conform with his recommendations, whereupon they become law. If the Governor refuses to certify a bill, he returns it to the originating house as a vetoed bill.

The amendatory veto was designed to save time and money while enabling State government to function more smoothly, more efficiently, and more effectively. As one delegate explained: "It is not our intention to change the separation of powers with respect to the Legislative Article. It is to make certain that it remains historically the way we now understand it to be."

Yet, this new gubernatorial power has already evoked considerable controversy centering on the question of how much flexibility the delegates intended the Governor to have in making changes in legislation presented for his signature. Many an incumbent legislator might attribute the adage "the road to hell is paved with good intentions" to the amendatory veto. It has been charged with upsetting the balance of power between the two branches of government, destroying the viability of the separation of powers and enabling the Governor to dominate the legislative process. There are also those who believe the problem has been caused by the way individual governors have used the amendatory veto rather than the veto authority itself. The central question in this controversy has been whether it was intended that this veto be used by the governor to change only technical errors or whether he was meant to be able to go so far as to completely strike the substance of the bill presented to him and substitute an entirely new bill.

The Legislature's first experience with the amendatory veto in 1972 ended with two joint resolutions proposing a constitutional amendment limiting the amendatory veto power being introduced in the Senate. Those particular resolutions died with the end of the biennium, but in 1973 the General Assembly did approve an amendment which put the question of whether to limit the scope of the amendatory veto before the voters in the 1974 general election. The proposed amendment would have changed the language to "The Governor may return a bill together with specific recommendations for change to the house in which it originated;" the words "specific recommendations for the correction of technical errors or matters of form" would have replaced the words "specific recommendations for change."

The proposed amendment cleared both houses by large margins, but in the absence of an organized campaign in favor of ratification it is not surprising that the voters rejected the measure. The major argument in favor of the amendment was that the amendatory veto gives the governor too much power and amounts to a distortion of the normal legislative process; the argument against (and in favor of retention of the amendatory veto) was the value of the flexibility it affords and also the fact that the General Assembly can always decline to accept the governor's changes if it feels he has gone too far.

Despite the failure of the 1974 referendum, the use of the amendatory veto has been restricted somewhat by a 1972 Illinois Supreme Court decision which held that the Governor may not use this power to substitute in form and substance completely new bills. It is interesting to note, however, that in the first session after the defeat of the proposed constitutional amendment the Governor returned 79 bills to the General Assembly. This compares with a total of 119 amendatory vetoes in all of the preceding four years. In 1977, 82 vetoes were certified by the General Assembly and another 16 were not, thus dying.

Although the Governor has gained significant new authority and flexibility in dealing with legislation passed by the General Assembly, the legislative branch has also gained added power in the dynamic relationship between two branches of State government. Because the General Assembly usually passed most of its legislation during the last month of the session and then adjourned *sine die*, almost invariably the Governor's action was final; the Legislature rarely had any further opportunity to challenge his decision. The old constitutional requirement that a two-thirds majority of the members elected was necessary to override the Governor also contributed to the finality of his veto. The close partisan division in the House resulting from the cumulative voting system made it difficult, if not impossible, to muster the required majority since the Governor needed only to secure the support of a portion of his party to sustain his veto.

As mentioned earlier, under the new Constitution the majority needed to override has been relaxed from two-thirds to three-fifths. Thus, although it remains difficult to override the Governor's veto, it is no longer virtually impossible, particularly now that the Legislature is in session more often. In January 1972, for example, the General Assembly successfully overrode the Governor twice in one day. This set the trend for an increasing number of successful overrides in each succeeding year, with three overrides in 1972, five in 1973, thirteen in 1974, seventeen in 1975 and ten in 1977. This is in sharp contrast to the history of legislative attempts to override the Governor under the 1870 Constitution. During the one-hundred-year life span of the old Constitution, gubernatorial vetoes were successfully challenged on only four occasions—in 1871, 1895, 1936 and 1969.

Unresolved Issues and Further Research Opportunities

A great deal has been written about the Illinois General Assembly. The interested reader is urged to look at the list of selected readings at the end of this chapter for an idea of some of the topics covered in earlier publications. Since this body, like all legislative bodies, is constantly changing, much of the literature is dated and may have greater historical than contemporary value. Clearly, a great deal remains to be learned. The following questions are designed to help the student begin the difficult task of thinking critically and productively about the Illinois Legislature. The questions by no means cover the entire array of researchable areas, in some instances they touch on topics not covered in this chapter, and throughout there are issues for which no definitive answer may be possible.

1. Are we moving inevitably to a full-time professional legislature? Is the citizen-legislature a thing of the past? What are the consequences of this movement on public policy, and on the characteristics of the membership? What effect will the recent development for members to resign in mid-term to accept other governmental positions have, if any, on the legislative institution?

2. Although Governors still have strong veto powers in the legislative process, is the decline of their political powers recently only a temporary phenomenon?

3. If continued in the constitution, will the impact of cumulative voting change as more districts elect "independents" who are in reality another member of the majority party? On the other hand, if the opponents of cumulative voting are able to get the question of abolishing the unique system on the ballot and passed, what will be the impact of this change on the legislative system?

4. Lastly, what will be the impact of the post-Daley era on the system? Will the Chicago Democratic organization be able to maintain a strong relatively unified front in the legislative halls?

NOTES

[1]Paul Simon, *Lincoln's Preparation for Greatness: The Illinois Legislative Years* (Norman: University of Oklahoma Press, 1965), p. 224.

[2]A State Senator, "Crooks in the Legislature," *American Mercury* 41 (July 1937), pp. 269–75.

[3]John Bartlow Martin, "Backstage at the Statehouse: What Those Politicians Do to You," *Saturday Evening Post,* December 12, 1953, pp. 20–21; December 19, pp. 30–31; December 26, p. 28.

[4]Paul Simon and Alfred Balk, "The Illinois Legislature: A Study in Corruption," *Harper's,* September 1964, pp. 74–78.

[5]*Ibid.,* p. 78.

[6]Trevor Armbrister, "The Octopus in the State House," *Saturday Evening Post,* February 12, 1966, pp. 25–29.

[7]Charles W. Dunn and Samuel K. Gove, "Legislative Reform Vacuum," *National Civic Review* 61 (1972), 441–46.

[8]Subsequently the Illinois Supreme Court invalidated this plan on the ground that the commission was illegally constituted. The court ruled that three of the legislative leaders violated the intent of Art. IV, sec. 3(b), when each appointed a member of their staff to serve as their non-General Assembly member on the commission. The court also held that the same three leaders improperly appointed themselves to the commission. The commission's work product was approved by the court as a provisional redistricting plan for the election of members of the General Assembly in 1972. An amended opinion mandated the 1973–74 General Assembly to adopt a permanent plan in 1973, which it did by reenacting the same map. See *People ex rel. Scott V. Grivetti,* 50 Ill. 2d 156, 277 N.E. 2d 881 (1971).

[9]After an unprecedented at-large election in 1964, the Republicans occupied only one-third of the seats in the House.

With the close party division, it should be noted that the General Assembly is a very partisan body—on most important decisions party considerations are uppermost in the final vote results. This is not to say that there are not divisions within the parties as illustrated by the 1975 election of the Speaker (93 ballots) and the 1977 election of the Senate President (186 ballots).

[10]*Home Rule Newsletter* no. 7, Institute of Government and Public Affairs, University of Illinois, Urbana, May 1974; and Jerry DeMuth, "Home-Rule Power Used Mainly for Revenue," *Chicago Sun-Times,* May 26, 1974.

[11]Thomas J. Anton, *The Politics of State Expenditure in Illinois* (Urbana: University of Illinois Press, 1966).

[12]David C. Baum, "A Tentative Survey of Illinois Home Rule (Part I): Powers and Limitations," *University of Illinois Law Forum* 1972, No. 1, p. 157.

[13]Illinois Department of Local Government Affairs, *Home Rule for Small Municipalities in Illinois,* 1979.

[14]This requirement has been much debated in the courts and the legislature in regard to the adoption of the Equal Rights Amendment.

[15]43 Ill. 2d 36, 250 N.E. 2d 633 (1969).

[16]Since 1960, three House speakers—from both parties—have come from districts where their parties were in the minority.

[17]The partisan composition of the Senate more closely reflects the political makeup of the state than does that of the House. The usual Republican majority comes primarily from central and northern Illinois and from the Chicago suburbs. All but a few Senate Democrats have come from Chicago, although since the 1971 reapportionment the ranks of the downstate Democrats have grown.

SUPPLEMENTAL READINGS

For a comprehensive bibliography on the Illinois General Assembly, the reader can review the "Bibliographic Essay" in Gove, Carlson and Carlson, *The Illinois Legislature . . ., at pages 171*–181. Listed here are some of the key items, especially those that are more recent. Many other shorter articles can be found in *Illinois Issues.*

Anton, Thomas J. *The Politics of State Expenditure in Illinois.* Urbana: University of Illinois Press, 1966.

Baum, David C. "A Tentative Survey of Illinois Home Rule (Part I): Powers and Limitations." *University of Illinois Law Forum,* 1972, No. 1:137–57.

———. "A Tentative Survey of Illinois Home Rule (Part II): Legislative Control, Transition Problems, and Intergovernmental Conflict." *University of Illinois Law Forum,* 1972, No. 3:559–88.

Blair, George S. *Cumulative Voting: An Effective Electoral Device in Illinois Politics.* Urbana: University of Illinois Press, 1960.

Braden, George D. and Rubin G. Cohn. *The Illinois Constitution: An Annotated and Comparative Analysis.* Urbana: Institute of Government and Public Affairs, University of Illinois, 1969.

Citizens Conference on State Legislatures. *The Sometimes Governments: A Critical Study of the 50 American Legislatures.* New York: Bantam, 1971.

Fishbane, Joyce D., and Glenn W. Fisher. *Politics of the Purse: Revenue and Finance in the Sixth Illinois Constitutional Convention.* Urbana: University of Illinois Press, 1969.

Fisher, Glenn W. *Taxes and Politics: A Study of Illinois Public Finance.* Urbana: University of Illinois Press, 1969.

Gove, Samuel K. "The Implications of Legislative Reform in Illinois." *Legislative Reform and Public Policy.* Edited by Susan Welch and John Peters. New York: Praeger, 1977.

———. *Reapportionment and the Cities: The Impact of Reapportionment on Urban Legislation in Illinois.* Chicago: Center for Research in Urban Government, Loyola University, June 1968.

Illinois. General Assembly. Commission on the Organization of the General Assembly. *Improving the State Legislature.* Urbana: University of Illinois Press, 1967.

Lousin, Ann. "The General Assembly and the 1970 Constitution." *Illinois Issues* 1:5 (May 1975), 131–34.

McDowell, James L. *The Politics of Reapportionment in Illinois.* Carbondale: Southern Illinois University Press, 1967.

McGriggs, Lee. *Black Legislative Politics in Illinois: A Theoretical and Structural Analysis.* Washington, D.C.: University Press of America, 1977.

Steiner, Gilbert Y., and Samuel K. Gove. *Legislative Politics in Illinois.* Urbana: University of Illinois Press, 1960.

CHAPTER 7

Legislators and Roll Call Voting in the 80th General Assembly

Jack R. Van Der Slik and Jesse C. Brown

The purpose of our chapter is to provide an overview of voting behavior in the Legislature. We shall focus upon the 80th General Assembly whose members were elected in 1976 and who acted on legislation during 1977 and 1978. Most of our attention is on how the legislators voted on final passage of bills into law. The analysis focuses on the question of whether legislative voting is chaotic or shows meaningful patterns related to the basic alignments of Illinois politics. Are partisan, sectional, or individual factors more determinate of legislative behavior?

Data for the Study

We gathered two kinds of information to serve as the basis of our analysis. The first deals briefly with the characteristics of the legislators. Each biennium the State of Illinois publishes the *Illinois Blue Book*. A regular feature of each *Blue Book* is the biographies of state officials, including members of the General Assembly. These brief biographies, supplied by the members themselves, indicate partisan affiliation, sex, race, and previous service in the General Assembly.

The second kind of information we have is a sample of the roll call votes of the members. The reason for choosing a sample is simply because the Illinois General Assembly votes so often. There are thousands of bills, accompanied by thousands of amendments; final adoption requires action on both houses. Because of the volume of votes and the way the General Assembly reveals its own voting records, systematic study of all its votes is extremely time consuming.[1] Our research strategy was to limit our attention to the roll calls on final passage (third reading) in each chamber between January 1977 and December 1, 1978, on all regular legislation (excluding constitutional resolutions, motions to recall, veto overrides and the like) in which not more than 80 percent of the members voted on the prevailing side. It should be recalled that in Illinois final passage requires a constitutional majority in each chamber (89 in the House and 30 in the Senate). To vote "present" is, in effect, to vote "nay." We identified all the roll calls fitting these criteria: 412 in the Senate and 556 in the House. Using a computerized random selection process, one fourth of these contested roll calls in each chamber (103 in the Senate and 139 in the House) were coded for further analysis. The roll call analyses that follow draw upon these samples of contested votes.

Characteristics of the Members

There is diversity in the membership of the two chambers, but the legislators are no random sample of the population. Most are male (90 percent in the House and 95 percent in the Senate) and white (91.5 percent in the House and 95 percent in the Senate). The mean age in the House for those about whom data is available is 49 years, with 28 percent under forty and only 7 percent at age 60 or older. In the Senate mean age is also 49, with 24 percent under 40 and 14 percent at age 60 or older.

The occupational backgrounds of the legislators are reported in Table 7-1. The largest categories in both the House and Senate are lawyers and persons in business and real estate. It is noteworthy that in Illinois, as in other states where data are reported separately for the House and Senate,[2] the percentage of lawyers is higher in the upper house. The third largest occupational category is government employment. This reflects a long standing practice in Illinois which allows "double dipping." That is, members may hold salaried positions in local governments in addition to holding office as a legislator. In Congress and in some states, legislators may not serve in more than one paying governmental position. (It should be noted, however, that for days served in the legislature, such members are not paid for services in their other position.)

There is a partisan bias in occupations. Democrats are disproportionately the educators, government employees and labor union officials. Republicans dominate among business and real estate people, farmers and other professionals.

Most members of the 80th General Assembly have legislative experience. About one-fourth of the Senators (27.1 percent) and one-fifth of the Representatives (21.5 percent) were serving their first session in their respective chambers. Compared to other states this is a low percentage of newcomers. In fact, about one-third of the

The authors are grateful to John H. Baker, Chairperson of the Department of Political Science at Southern Illinois University, Carbondale, for providing the research resources that were needed to complete this study. We thank K. Chou for coding data and R. Damron for assistance in processing the data.

TABLE 7-1
Legislators' Occupations (Percentages)

House Members	Democrats	Republicans	All
Lawyers	23.4	24.4	23.7
Business or Real Estate	26.6	39.0	32.2
Educators	16.0	3.7	10.2
Farmers	0.0	4.9	2.3
Government employees	23.4	14.6	19.8
Labor union officials	5.3	0.0	2.8
Other professionals	2.1	6.1	4.0
Unreported	3.2	7.3	5.1
Totals	100.0	100.0	100.1
Senate Members			
Lawyers	47.1	36.0	42.4
Business or Real Estate	11.8	36.0	22.0
Educators	8.8	0.0	5.1
Farmers	2.9	8.0	5.1
Government employees	20.6	12.0	16.9
Labor union officials	0.0	0.0	0.0
Other professionals	5.9	8.0	6.8
Unreported	2.9	0.0	1.7
Totals	100.0	100.0	100.0

members (30.5 percent in the Senate and 33.3 percent in the House) were serving their 4th session or more in that chamber. Those figures do not include service in the other chamber. It is commonplace for persons to have moved from the House to the Senate. In the 80th General Assembly 24 Senators (40.7 percent) had previously served in the House. Traffic is not entirely in one direction; four Representatives (2.3 percent) had previously served in the Senate. Partisan balance was close in both chambers with 34 Democrats in the Senate (57.6 percent) and 94 in the House (53.1 percent). The House had one self-identified independent from Cook County who usually voted with the Democrats.

Roll Call Voting

Participation

Members may respond to the roll call by voting yea or nay; by voting present (which, in effect, counts as a nay vote on final passage); or they may simply not vote. Presumably no absentees vote; however, it is not unknown for members to be physically absent and have a colleague operate the electronic vote switch at the member's desk. Sometimes members are physically present, but they simply choose not to be recorded on a roll call. The data reported here are taken from the House and Senate Journals.

Voting "present" is not commonplace on contested votes. The percentage of times it was done by Senators ranged from 0 to 13, with an average of 3.3. Representatives varied from 0 to 22 percent, with an average of 5.8.

Absence from roll calls varies substantially among the members. Every Senator was absent at least once. Five members were absent for forty percent or more of the votes. On the average Senators failed to vote on 17 percent of the roll calls. In the House no one participated on all roll calls. On the average Representatives failed to vote on 17 percent of the votes. Eight representatives missed forty percent or more of the roll calls. See Table 7-2.

Participation by members on final passage is actually quite high. On the average, members of the Senate participate with a yea or nay vote on 79 percent of the roll calls. In the House the figure is about 77 percent. Nearly one out of five Senators has been on the record with a yea or nay vote on 90 percent or more of the roll calls. The proportion is slightly smaller in the House, with about

TABLE 7-2
A. Absenteeism: Percent of Roll Calls for which the Member is not Reported Voting (40% or more)

Senate			House		
Sangmeister	(D)	66%	Kornowicz	(D)	81%
Smith	(D)	58	Stearney	(R)	63
Ozinga	(R)	45	Dunn	(R)	46
Savickas	(D)	45	Hoffman	(R)	46
Soper	(R)	44	Kucharski	(R)	45
			Bianco	(D)	45
			Madison	(D)	43
			Laurino	(D)	41

B. Participation: Percent of Roll Calls for which the Member is Reported Voting Yea or Nay (90% or more)

Senate			House		
McMillan	(R)	96%	Matijevich	(D)	98%
Buzbee	(D)	94	McClain	(D)	97
Davidson	(R)	93	Birchler	(D)	95
Hall, H.	(R)	93	Mulcahey	(D)	95
Rock	(D)	93	Georgi	(D)	94
Vadalabene	(D)	93	Lechowicz	(D)	94
Berning	(R)	92	McLendon	(D)	94
Carroll	(D)	92	Stuffle	(D)	94
Sommer	(R)	92	Anderson	(R)	93
Bloom	(R)	90	Kelley	(D)	93
Rupp	(R)	90	McPike	(D)	93
			Neff	(R)	93
			Madigan	(D)	92
			Pechous	(D)	92
			Robinson	(D)	92
			Dawson	(D)	91
			Edgar	(R)	91
			Mahar	(R)	91
			Pouncey	(Ind)	91
			Reilly	(R)	91
			Taylor	(D)	91
			Vitek	(D)	91
			Cunningham	(R)	90
			Doyle	(D)	90
			Matejek	(D)	90
			McMaster	(R)	90

The letter in parenthesis indicates party affiliation: D, Democrat, R, Republican; and Ind., Independent one member in seven voting yea or nay on 90 percent or more of the roll calls. Curiously, among the high participators in the House, more than two-thirds of them are Democrats. Probably this is best explained by the close party balance in the House. Usually contested votes pit the Democrats against the Republicans. The majority party, in this case the Democrats, has the upper hand. But to win it must have 89 yea votes. To get those the majority needs its members present and voting. For the opposition an "absent" member counts as much against a bill as does one who votes "nay." Thus, the pressure to be present and voting was stronger for Democrats than Republicans. The participation scores suggest the House Democrats responded to that pressure.

Party Voting

Illinois politics is noted for its partisan flavor.[3] That partisanship is conspicuous in legislative voting. Our analysis of the Senate revealed that 58 roll calls, 56 percent of the contested votes in our sample, were party votes. A "party vote" roll call is one in which a majority of Democrats voted the opposite of a majority of the Republicans.[4] In the House there were 83 party votes, 60 percent of the contested roll calls included in our analysis.

Party loyalty takes shape in the members' party loyalty scores, which are fully reported in Table 7-3 along with participation and faction support scores. The party loyalty score is the percentage of times the member voted with his or her party's position on party votes. Party loyalty was more consistent among the Democrats than the Republicans. The average score for Senate Democrats was 88 percent. Republican Senators averaged 73 percent. In the House, Democrats averaged 86 percent, while Republicans scored 71. This is a dramatic party difference.

TABLE 7-3
Members of the 80th General Assembly: Participation and Support Scores

SENATE District Number	Member Name	Party	Percent Absent	Percent Present	Percent Yea or Nay	Party Support Score		Cook versus Downstate		Cook and Collar vs. Downstate	
						Dem	Rep	Cook	Down	C & C	Down
11	Berman	D	15	1	84	96		86		87	
32	Berning	R	8	0	92		76		79	53	
46	Bloom	R	7	3	90		73		96		100
41	Bowers	R	14	6	80		74		95	24	
54	Bruce	D	12	2	86	76			47		57
58	Buzbee	D	4	2	94	74			41		50
15	Carroll	D	7	1	92	100		95		100	
29	Chew	D	23	1	76	93		91		94	
17	Clewis	D	11	4	85	93		96		100	
53	Coffey	R	1	12	87		68		88		82
21	Collins	D	12	4	84	81		64		50	
23	Daley	D	38	2	60	97		100		100	
20	D'Arco	D	20	0	80	100		100		100	
50	Davidson	R	5	2	93		62		71		71
49	Demuzio	D	6	8	86	72			55		67
55	Donnewald	D	23	0	77	91			11		7
16	Egan	D	18	2	80	91		90		93	
1	Glass	R	17	6	77		75	27		27	
2	Graham	R	13	4	83		90	14		31	
38	Grotberg	R	15	5	80		77		91		81
19	Guidice	D	16	1	83	94		95		100	
44	Hall, H.	R	3	4	93		84		91		82
57	Hall, K.	D	13	3	84	94			12		19
34	Hickey	D	14	3	75	78			88		77
28	Hynes	D	12	0	88	96		100		100	
59	Johns	D	12	1	87	89			27		27
43	Joyce	D	11	5	84	87			32		43
48	Knuppel	D	10	4	86	94			20		20
10	Lane	D	32	0	68	97		88		100	
25	Lemke	D	21	0	79	93		95		94	
31	Leonard	D	11	3	86	81			55	46	
30	Maragos	D	14	4	82	96		100		100	
47	McMillan	R	4	0	96		89		100		87
12	Merlo	D	20	4	76	96		95		100	
39	Mitchler	R	11	4	85		71		82	50	
9	Moore	R	20	10	70		63	36		63	

TABLE 7-3 Continued

District Number	Member Name	Party	Percent Absent	Percent Present	Percent Yea or Nay	Party Support Score		Cook versus Downstate		Cook and Collar vs. Downstate	
						Dem	Rep	Cook	Down	C & C	Down
SENATE continued											
13	Netsch	D	9	8	83	75		57		43	
24	Newhouse	D	38	1	61	87		73		90	
4	Nimrod	R	8	13	79		87	25		41	
8	Ozinga	R	45	0	55		68	36		70	
40	Philip	R	24	4	72		80		83	47	
3	Regner	R	18	5	77		85	27		41	
6	Rhoads	R	6	9	85		80	26		38	
18	Rock	D	6	1	93	87		86		94	
35	Roe	R	21	1	78		72		95		94
51	Rupp	R	5	5	90		55		82		71
42	Sangmeister	D	66	6	28	67			88	40	
27	Savickas	D	45	0	55	97		100		100	
33	Schaffer	R	9	3	88		67		83		71
37	Shapiro	R	18	2	80		83		86		67
22	Smith	D	58	2	40	100		100		88	
45	Sommer	R	6	2	92		66		91		94
7	Soper	R	44	4	52		67	39		69	
56	Vadalabene	D	7	0	93	91			7		12
5	Walsh	R	17	5	78		76	27		43	
26	Washington	D	19	3	78	90		68		73	
52	Weaver	R	22	2	76		70		74		69
36	Wooten	D	13	7	80	66			65		80
14	Ziomek	D	16	2	82	86		86		93	
HOUSE											
14	Abramson	R	6	17	77		83	25		26	
35	Adams	R	12	9	79		96		100		100
45	Anderson	R	6	1	93		65		85		91
19	Antonovych	R	11	9	80		40	48		56	
29	Barnes, E.	D	23	4	73	95		95		94	
8	Barnes, J.	R	19	7	74		49	38		38	
49	Bartulis	R	22	17	61		74		86		89
27	Beatty	D	20	1	79	92		84		90	
51	Bennett	R	24	17	59		73		82		81
25	Bianco	R	45	6	49		49	36		33	
58	Birchler	D	1	4	95	88			25		13
5	Bluthhardt	R	26	6	68		70	19		25	
6	Boucek	R	12	8	80		84	23		23	
11	Bowman	D	12	14	74	66		60		64	
44	Bradley	D	14	5	81	93			13		10
11	Brady	D	17	3	80	96		96		95	
14	Brandt	D	23	1	76	96		92		90	
38	Breslin	D	15	11	74	87			20		20
54	Brummer	D	12	11	77	73			52		50
55	Brummet	D	20	6	74	88			17		24
55	Byers	D	11	4	85	72			32		38
24	Caldwell	D	31	9	60	90		84		82	
53	Campbell	R	10	6	84		67		88		89
16	Capparelli	D	19	4	77	93		86		89	
22	Catania	R	10	22	68		47	58		62	
3	Chapman	D	22	2	76	90		83		89	
43	Christensen	D	10	14	76	81			24		15
30	Collins	R	24	12	64		80	18		18	
18	Conti	R	15	9	76		69	39		33	
54	Cunningham	R	9	1	90		80		88		95
40	Daniels	R	24	5	71		72		86	24	
36	Darrow	D	4	8	88	80			33		36
22	Davis, C.	D	17	1	82	99		96		95	
42	Davis, J.	R	25	4	71		66		80	25	
30	Dawson	D	8	1	91	95		89		91	
44	Deavers	R	32	4	64		64		76		88
32	Deuster	R	22	4	74		63		85	25	

TABLE 7-3 Continued

HOUSE continued District Number	Member Name	Party	Percent Absent	Percent Present	Percent Yea or Nay	Party Support Score		Cook versus Downstate		Cook and Collar vs. Downstate	
						Dem	Rep	Cook	Down	C & C	Down
18	Di Prima	D	16	2	82	96		92		90	
20	Domico	D	27	3	70	94		95		94	
18	Doyle	D	9	1	90	96		96		95	
51	Dunn, J.	D	17	17	66	79			23		35
58	Dunn, R.	R	46	4	50		80		94		92
41	Dyer	R	14	9	77		50		45	61	
37	Ebbesen	R	14	3	83		84		88		90
53	Edgar	R	6	3	91		77		93		91
24	Epton	R	16	0	84		59	30		28	
29	Ewell	D	35	4	61	92		95		94	
38	Ewins	R	18	10	72		84		91		89
14	Farley	D	15	3	82	91		93		90	
57	Flinn	D	14	2	84	85			21		16
2	Friedland	R	17	7	77		63	35		42	
55	Friedrich	R	31	6	63		76		76		86
29	Gaines	R	23	5	72		25	55		63	
19	Garmisa	D	13	1	86	95		88		89	
31	Geo-Karis	R	9	5	86		32		59	50	
10	Getty	D	15	8	77	73		59		67	
30	Giglio	D	24	1	75	95		95		94	
34	Giorgi	D	3	3	94	88			26		23
15	Grieman	D	18	3	79	88		88		95	
31	Griesheimer	R	21	4	75		81		92	5	
33	Hanahan	D	16	4	80	86			23		14
59	Harris	D	10	1	89	86			27		24
59	Hart	D	24	4	72	79			30		24
40	Hoffman	R	46	9	45		79		86	20	
17	Holewinski	D	10	4	86	82		82		83	
28	Houlihan, D.	D	8	4	88	93		89		87	
13	Houlihan, J.	D	17	3	80	83		91		89	
38	Hoxsey	R	14	9	77		84		93		91
41	Hudson	R	10	14	76		94		92	11	
20	Huff	D	21	3	76	86		92		89	
8	Huskey	R	24	15	61		68	24		15	
36	Jacobs	D	10	6	84	79			29		25
4	Jaffe	D	10	4	86	76		69		71	
52	Johnson	D	17	12	71	37			62		55
28	Jones, D.	D	19	6	75	86	88	88		85	
50	Jones, E.	R	16	9	75		61		78		79
50	Kane	D	13	6	81	55			57		70
1	Katz	D	32	9	59	61		57		65	
1	Keats	R	15	5	80		83	11		14	
9	Kelly	D	4	3	93	90		81		86	
39	Kempners	R	12	10	78		72		80	29	
48	Kent	R	14	1	85		92		96		95
7	Klosak	R	30	4	66		69	26		31	
25	Kornowicz	D	81	1	18	88		89		88	
16	Kosinski	D	11	12	77	86		92		90	
23	Kozubowski	D	19	1	80	94		92		95	
27	Kucharski	R	45	1	54		55	23		13	
15	Laurino	D	41	3	56	98		94		93	
17	Lechowicz	D	4	2	94	99		100		100	
42	Leinenweber	R	15	9	76		83		86	18	
5	Leverenz	D	13	13	74	81		73		77	
12	Levin	D	17	7	76	90		88		90	
56	Lucco	D	12	4	84	95			14		9
45	Luft	D	12	9	79	83			33		32
3	MacDonald	R	2	9	89		65	21		26	
27	Madigan	D	7	1	92	96		93		91	
21	Madison	D	43	14	43	84		81		83	
9	Mahar	R	6	3	91		61	23		29	
24	Mann	D	35	2	63	85		87		89	
23	Margalus	R	17	13	70		55	33		31	
12	Marovitz	D	22	4	74	94		96		95	

TABLE 7-3 Continued

HOUSE continued District Number	Member Name	Party	Percent Absent	Percent Present	Percent Yea or Nay	Party Support Score		Cook versus Downstate		Cook and Collar vs. Downstate	
						Dem	Rep	Cook	Down	C & C	Down
34	Martin, L.	R	22	4	74		76		87		84
26	Martin, P.	D	23	11	66	94		100		100	
10	Matejek	D	6	4	90	92		81		91	
31	Matijevich	D	1	1	98	83			32	74	
7	Matula	R	27	10	63		75	17		21	
37	Mautino	D	14	6	80	78			38		35
16	McAuliffe	R	20	2	78		60	32		36	
43	McBroom	R	24	6	70		76		88		95
48	McClain	D	1	2	97	89			25		26
11	McCourt	R	10	4	86		75	20		25	
47	McGrew	D	24	1	75	84			32		19
22	McLendon	D	5	1	94	98		96		95	
47	McMaster	R	6	4	90		84		96		95
56	McPike	D	5	2	93	90			19		18
28	Meyer	R	37	6	57		47	50		42	
10	Miller	R	9	8	83		92	11		13	
21	Molloy	R	23	6	71		39	44		50	
46	Mudd	D	18	2	80	90			19		18
2	Mugalian	D	13	8	79	71		76		76	
35	Mulcahey	D	4	1	95	63			57		70
39	Murphy	D	11	6	83	91			9	100	
19	Nardulli	D	22	2	76	94		90		88	
47	Neff	R	4	3	93		81		93		96
13	O'Brian	D	19	6	75	93		95		94	
7	Pechous	D	5	3	92	95		89		95	
15	Petes	R	26	6	68		71	21		21	
32	Pierce	D	17	3	80	85			22	82	
36	Polk	R	17	6	77		65		88		86
1	Porter	R	18	3	79		70	20		30	
26	Pouncey	Ind.	8	1	91	***	***	89		87	
4	Pullen	R	15	7	78		93	14		18	
40	Redmond	D	25	1	74	95			5	94	
32	Reed	R	14	6	80		73		88	20	
49	Reilly	R	4	5	91		63		85		86
58	Richmond	D	6	6	88	80			24		15
35	Rigney	R	12	4	84		84		88		95
50	Robinson	D	4	4	92	73			26		32
43	Ryan	R	6	8	86		81		81		86
13	Sandquist	R	11	13	76		38	42		53	
52	Satterwaite	D	14	11	75	82			30		22
48	Schisler	D	20	4	76	80			27		35
4	Schlickman	R	35	6	59		81	24		29	
41	Schneider	D	36	4	60	60			50	13	
39	Schoeberlein	R	24	2	74		83		82		89
37	Schuneman	R	15	2	83		85		83	53	
49	Sharp	D	14	4	82	79			42		42
21	Shumpert	D	9	4	87	91		93		91	
34	Simms	R	7	8	85		81		92		90
33	Skinner	R	6	17	77		56		61		57
2	Stanley	R	12	9	79		49	48		52	
20	Stearney	R	63	5	32		67	31		11	
9	Steczo	D	7	9	84	84		79		85	
56	Steele	R	9	6	85		74		88		89
56	Stiehl	R	11	3	86		77		92		95
53	Stuffle	D	4	2	94	81			43		35
46	Sumner	R	6	11	83		95		93		91
26	Taylor	D	8	1	91	93		89		86	
12	Telcser	R	9	11	80		59	23		24	
25	Terzich	D	16	2	82	95		92		95	
51	Tipsword	D	15	14	71	83			24		24
3	Totten	R	5	8	87		94	4		5	
46	Tuerk	R	12	7	81		88		87		89

TABLE 7-3 Continued

HOUSE continued District Number	Member Name	Party	Percent Absent	Percent Present	Percent Yea or Nay	Party Support Score		Cook versus Downstate		Cook and Collar vs. Downstate	
						Dem	Rep	Cook	Down	C & C	Down
42	Van Duyne	D	14	11	75	82			15	90	
44	Vinson	R	23	5	72		72		81		94
23	Vitek	D	4	5	91	93		96		96	
45	Von Boeckman	D	18	1	81	94			0		0
33	Waddell	R	15	3	82		91		92		90
54	Walsh, R.	D	9	2	89	68			44		40
6	Walsh, W.	R	9	9	82		87	35		29	
52	Wikoff	R	17	7	76		75		73		76
6	Willer	D	14	6	80	80		85		91	
5	Williams	D	9	6	85	84		92		95	
59	Winchester	R	25	1	74		69		82		89
17	Wolf	R	18	11	71		79	26		32	
57	Younge	D	10	2	88	95			8		5
8	Yourell	D	15	1	84	89		85		86	

Table 7-4 identifies the members of the party who were at the extreme ends of party loyalty. A quick scan of the numbers reinforces the meaning of the differences in the party support score averages. The five high Senate Democrats range from 100 to 97, but the five high Republicans vote with much less unity, scoring from 90 to 84. Among low party scorers in the Senate, Republican scores are substantially lower than those of low-scoring Democrats. Differences in House scores are similar, except that the range among Republicans is even greater.

The lists of high and low scoring Democratic legislators vividly indicate that the core of party loyalty is among the Chicago Democrats. All the five high Democrats in the Senate are Chicagoans and all the low scorers are from outstate. Results are nearly the same in the House. Only two of the top fifteen Democrats in the House are downstate Representatives—Redmond, the Speaker, and Lucco, from Edwardsville. The low scorers include only five from Cook County—Katz, Bowman, Mugalian, Getty and Jaffe—and only Bowman's district includes much of the City. All these legislators, by the way, come from districts also represented by two Republicans.

Not only is Republican party loyalty lower, it does not have as homogeneous a constituency base as the Democratic party does. According to Gove, Carlson and Carlson,[5] "much of the partisan conflict in the legislature finds the Chicago Democrats . . . pitted against Republicans from within the city and those situated in the adjoining suburbs." Among high scoring Republican Senators, Graham, Nimrod and Regner are from suburban Cook County. The others are downstate Republicans from the northern half of the State. Among highly loyal House Republicans are Totten, Pullen, Miller, W. Walsh, and Boucek from suburban Cook County. They are joined by members from suburban "collar county" districts, those adjacent to Cook, represented by legislators such as Hudson and Waddell. The rest of the high scoring Republicans are from the northern half of the State. However, the voting patterns are mixed by what can be seen among low scoring Republicans. Two of the low scoring Senators, Moore and Schaffer, are from the suburbs. Among lowest scoring Republicans twelve come from districts that include part of Chicago. The remaining low scorers, Geo-Karis, Dyer and Skinner, all come from collar county suburban districts. Thus Cook and collar county suburban Republican representatives support the Republican position with markedly varying voting records on partisan issues.

Regional Coalitions

One traditional way of looking at Illinois conflicts is to contrast Cook County legislators with those from "Downstate."[6] We identified Cook vs. Downstate roll calls as previously, finding all in which a majority of the Cook County delegation voted together in opposition to a majority of Downstate members, and then worked out the factional loyalty scores as the percentage of times each person voted with his or her coalition ("present" counting as "nay," and absences ignored). Another possible coalition is that of Cook and "collar counties"[7] versus Downstate. Again we identified roll calls in which a majority of Cook and "collar" legislators opposed a majority from Downstate and identified factional loyalty scores.

The results of these analyses impress us again with the significance of party conflict. Using the Cook vs. Downstate criterion, there were 24 roll calls (23 percent) in the Senate index and 28 (29 percent) in the House. Using Cook and Collar vs. Downstate, there were 17 roll calls (17 percent) in the Senate index and 23 (17 percent) in the House. Moreover, with few exceptions

TABLE 7-4
Party Support Scores: High and Low Scorers by Chamber and Party (District)

SENATE					
High Scoring Democrats			High Scoring Republicans		
1. Carroll	(15)	100	1. Graham	(2)	90
2. D'Arco	(20)	100	2. McMillan	(47)	89
3. Smith	(22)	100	3. Nimrod	(4)	87
4. Lane	(10)	97	4. Regner	(3)	85
5. Daley	(23)	97	5. Hall, H.	(44)	84
Low Scoring Democrats			Low Scoring Republicans		
1. Wooten	(36)	66	1. Rupp	(51)	55
2. Sangmeister	(42)	67	2. Davidson	(50)	62
3. Demuzio	(49)	72	3. Moore	(9)	63
4. Hickey	(34)	73	4. Sommer	(45)	66
5. Buzbee	(58)	74	5. Schaffer	(33)	67
HOUSE					
High Scoring Democrats			High Scoring Republicans		
1. Lechowicz	(17)	99	1. Adams	(35)	96
2. Davis, C.	(22)	99	2. Sumner	(46)	95
3. Laurino	(15)	98	3. Hudson	(41)	94
4. McLenden	(22)	98	4. Totten	(3)	94
5. Madigan	(5)	96	5. Pullen	(4)	93
6. Doyle	(18)	96	6. Miller	(10)	92
7. Brady	(11)	96	7. Kent	(48)	92
8. DiPrima	(18)	96	8. Waddell	(33)	91
9. Brandt	(14)	96	9. Tuerk	(46)	88
10. Barnes, E.	(29)	95	10. Walsh, W.	(10)	87
11. Redmond	(40)	95	11. Schuneman	(37)	85
12. Giglio	(30)	95	12. McMaster	(47)	84
13. Pechous	(7)	95	13. Ebbesen	(37)	84
14. Dawson	(30)	95	14. Ewing	(38)	84
15. Lucco	(56)	95	15. (Boucek	(6)	84
			(Rigney	(35)	84
Low Scoring Democrats			Low Scoring Republicans		
1. Johnson	(52)	37	1. Gaines	(29)	25
2. Kane	(50)	55	2. Geo-Karis	(31)	32
3. Schneider	(41)	60	3. Sandquist	(13)	38
4. Katz	(1)	61	4. Molloy	(21)	39
5. Mulcahey	(35)	63	5. Antonovych	(19)	40
6. Bowman	(11)	66	6. Meyer	(28)	47
7. Walsh, W.	(54)	68	7. Catania	(22)	47
8. Mugalian	(2)	71	8. Bianco	(25)	49
9. Byer	(55)	72	9. Barnes, J.	(8)	49
10. Brummer	(54)	73	10. Stanley	(2)	49
11. Getty	(10)	73	11. Dyer	(41)	50
12. Robinson	(50)	73	12. Margalus	(23)	55
13. Jaffe	(4)	76	13. Kucharski	(27)	55
14. Mautino	(37)	78	14. Skinner	(33)	56
15. Dunn	(51)	79	15. Epton	(24)	59

the roll calls in the factional indices are also in the party loyalty index. It is also the case that most of the roll calls in the Cook and Collar vs. Downstate index are also in the Cook vs. Downstate index. Lower coherence in the factions compared to that in the parties is evident in averages for each coalition. The Senate Cook faction averages 71 while Downstate is 66, and the House Cook faction averages 64 to the Downstate average of 58. Looking at the Senate Cook and Collar faction reveals an average of 72 against Downstate's 62 and the House Cook and Collar average is 62 versus Downstate's 58. In short, these alternative ways of looking for coherent voting do not reveal unique and contrasting patterns. There are very few contested roll calls which are regionally explained when compared to those explained by party.

Of course, factionalism can be important in the voting of particular members of the Legislature. We looked for that sort of evidence for factionalism in Table 7-5. We searched the membership for legislators whose factional scores were 15 or more points higher than their party support scores. The results indicate several things. There are practically no factionalists among the Democrats. Sangmeister, a suburban Democrat, is one of the least loyal Democrats in the Senate and votes proportionately more often with Downstaters than with his party. (Recall, however, his absenteeism means that these scores are derived from relatively few votes.) Two downstate Democrats, Johnson and Kane, the least loyal members in their party, show greater loyalty to "Downstate" factions.

TABLE 7-5
Legislators with a Factional Support Score that Exceeds their Party Support Score by 15% or More

MEMBERS, by Party (District)		Party Support	Cook Versus Downstate		Cook and Collar vs. Downstate	
			Cook	Down	C & C	Down
SENATE, Democrat Factionalists						
Sangmeister	(42)	67		88	40	
SENATE, Republican Factionalists						
Bloom	(46)	73		96		100
Bowers	(41)	74		95	24	
Coffey	(53)	68		88		82
Roe	(35)	72		95		94
Rupp	(51)	55		82		71
Schaffer	(33)	67		83		71
Sommer	(45)	66		91		94
HOUSE, Democrat Factionalists						
Johnson	(52)	37		62		55
Kane	(50)	55		57		70
HOUSE, Republican Factionalists						
Anderson	(45)	65		85		91
Antonovych	(19)	40	48		56	
Bartulis	(49)	74		86		89
Campbell	(53)	67		88		89
Catania	(22)	47	58		62	
Cunningham	(54)	80		88		95
Deavers	(44)	64		76		88
Deuster	(32)	63		85	25	
Edgar	(53)	77		93		91
Gaines	(29)	25	55		63	
Geo-Karis	(31)	32		59	50	
Jones	(50)	61		78		79
McBroom	(43)	76		88		95
Neff	(47)	81		93		96
Polk	(36)	65		88		86
Reed	(32)	73		88	20	
Reilly	(49)	63		85		86
Sandquist	(13)	38	42		53	
Steele	(56)	74		88		89
Stiehl	(57)	77		92		95
Vinson	(44)	72		81		94
Winchester	(59)	69		82		89

Factionalism is much more commonplace among Republicans. The most typical factionalists are downstate Republicans with average or below average party loyalty who more consistently oppose the "Cook" faction in Cook-versus-Downstate votes. This is illustrated, for example, by Senators Coffey and Roe, and House members Edgar and Polk. Other Republicans are similar except that their higher factional scores are with Downstate against the Cook and Collar supporters. These include Senators Bloom and Sommer and House members such as Anderson, Campbell and Winchester.

Other factionalists among Republicans are those from Cook County. Several Cook County Republicans were previously noted as scoring low on party loyalty. Antonovych, Catania, Gaines and Sandquist all register their highest scores in support of "Cook and Collar" versus Downstate. Suburbanite factionalists, such as Senator Bowers and House members Deuster and Reed, vote proportionately more for the Downstate faction against Cook than for any other grouping.

It is evident that Republicans are more factionalized and cross-pressured in their voting than Democrats. Ten House Republicans vote with their own party on party votes less than half the time. All of them except Geo-Karis, who represents a Collar district, are from Cook County, and most of them are more consistently in the Cook and Collar faction against Downstate than elsewhere. But none of their scores are high in any alignment. Their voting is more particularistic than that of most other members.

Concluding Observations on Legislative Voting

Our study has focused upon only a small part of the roll call votes taken in the 80th General Assembly. However, we chose a sample of votes on the final passage of bills which were contested. Among those roll calls more than half pitted a majority of Republicans against a majority of the Democrats. These findings indicate that the Legislature lives up to its reputation of being a strongly partisan political arena.

Studying the votes of individual legislators reveals that Democrats vote with a good deal more unity than Republicans. This finding reflects the very solid and cohesive core of Democratic party loyalists in Chicago. Suburban and downstate Democrats are not as devoted to their party. Republicans vote with substantially less unity than Democrats. The Republican loyalists reside in the northern half of the State, but several Chicago Republicans and a few suburbanites have rather low party support scores.

Regional factionalism is not strongly evident in legislative voting. The "Cook versus Downstate" and "Cook and Collar versus Downstate" categories for analysis indicate that factions actually overlap with party voting. Analyzing the factional and party support scores we find that partisan loyalties are regularly higher and more comprehensive than factional alignments.

On roll call voting participation it seems to us that General Assembly members do rather well in their participation. Substantial nonparticipation occurs among only a few members, some of whom may have been affected by illness or personal circumstances. The General Assembly rules allow the "present" vote which functions as a "nay," but is usually not understood that way by citizen observers. There is not heavy use by the legislators of the "present" vote. Our findings show that about one-seventh of the House members and nearly one-fifth of the Senators cast "yea" or "nay" votes on 90 percent or more of the roll calls.

The Illinois General Assembly is not always a model of decorum. The occasional gallery visitor may find it bewildering, or even chaotic, and go away thinking, "No man's life, liberty or property are safe while the Legislature is in session." In fact, however, there is a great deal of structure and order in the roll call votes that legislators cast. The basis of that regularity is interparty competition and partisan loyalty.

NOTES

[1]We have long been convinced that voting records in the General Assembly are obscure because Illinois legislators want them to be so. The votes are published in the House and State Journals. However, because there are so many roll calls and because members are listed alphabetically by yeas, nays and "present" for each roll call, coding these votes for analysis by computer is very time consuming. Ironically, the votes are taken mechanically in each chamber and could easily be preserved in a computerized record for convenient analytical use. Up to now the General Assembly has prevented such access to the roll call data.

[2]William J. Keefe and Morris S. Ogul, *The American Legislative Process: Congress and the States* (4th ed.; Englewood Cliffs, N.J.: Prentice-Hall, Inc., 1977), p. 119.

[3]David Kenney, *Basic Illinois Government: A Systematic Explanation* (rev. ed.; Carbondale: Southern Illinois University Press, 1974), pp. 95–110.

[4]In identifying party votes, a member voting "present" was counted as having voted "nay." This fits the rules which require a constitutional majority for passage of a bill. Absentees, however, were ignored in our calculations, even though absence can work to one's advantage or disadvantage, depending on the circumstances.

[5]Samuel K. Gove, Richard W. Carlson and Richard J. Carlson, *The Illinois Legislature: Structure and Processes* (Urbana: University of Illinois Press, 1976).

[6]See David R. Derge, "Urban-Rural Conflict: The Case in Illinois," in *Legislative Behavior: A Reader in Theory and Research,* ed. by John C. Wahlke and Heinz Eulau (Glencoe, Ill.: The Free Press, 1959).

[7]Cook County includes districts 1 through 30. Districts from the "collar counties" are 31, 32, 39, 40, 41, and 42.

CHAPTER **8**

Cumulative Voting and Legislator Performance

Richard Wiste

Illinois has a unique method of electing members to the lower house of its State Legislature. Cumulative voting provides each voter with three votes and allows him to distribute them among one, two, or three candidates. A primary concern in devising this system after the Civil War and retaining it in the 1970 Constitution was the effects of this system on the party composition of the House. These effects are rather easy to guage. However, there also may be subtle effects on the performance of legislators as they become aware of vulnerability to changes in nominating practice by the other party and competition from fellow incumbents of their own party and district.

This article will outline the basic mechanics of cumulative voting, its effects on composition and representation and some possible effects on legislator performance.

Composition

Minority Representation

Cumulative voting was implemented in Illinois at a time when the State was divided basically along north-south lines in such a way as to provide large, essentially one-party areas in the State.[1] Under these conditions, it was thought desirable to provide for some form of minority representation within each of the dominant one-party areas. This was expected to not only mitigate conflict between areas but also insure that, for example, a Democrat in a predominantly Republican area could find someone of similar party views representing his area.

In the basic respect of providing minority representation, cumulative voting has turned out more or less as anticipated. Since 1920 only about one-and-a-half percent of district elections have produced a 3–0 split. Thus the overwhelming share of major party supporters in Illinois have had a member of their party representing their district in the lower house of the State Legislature.

Majority Margin

A second major effect on lower house composition is the moderation of majority margins in the Legislature. The most commonly used American method of legislative elections—simple plurality, single-member district—is widely recognized as increasing the advantages in seats of the majority party. Thus a party receiving fifty-five percent of its total vote in all districts of a legislature would normally receive more than fifty-five percent of the seats. Indeed several studies have suggested that the ratio of votes received by two parties across all districts can be cubed to provide the ratio of seats won in the entire legislature. Thus a party winning twice as many votes (2/1 ratio) might be expected to obtain eight times (2/1 cubed or 8/1) as many seats. More realistically, a party receiving twenty percent more votes might receive seventy-three percent (1.2/1 cubed or 1.728) more seats.

Thus, the full impact of cumulative voting in moderating majority margins can best be appreciated in the light of the fact that the normal method of American legislative elections works in the opposite direction—to exaggerate the margin. The figures in Table 8-1 provide an illustration of this tendency. In none of the 24 elections did the Illinois lower house majority (elected by cumulative voting) exceed that of the Illinois Senate (elected by standard single-member district methods). In the omitted 1964 election the lower house was elected at large.

Restricted Choice

Two aspects of cumulative voting, minority representation in geographically distinct areas, and minority representation at the aggregate level, have worked more or less as anticipated by early proponents of cumulative voting. A third aspect, the degree to which electoral competition in districts was encouraged, did not. As a consequence, nominating procedures used in cumulative voting were changed somewhat in the 1970 Constitution.

Under cumulative voting, party leaders soon learned that they could lose seats by nominating too many candidates and dividing their strength too many ways. This can best be illustrated with simple numerical examples.

In a district with 12,000 Democrats and 8,000 Republicans, the Democrats might be expected to comfortably win most normal elections. Indeed, if each party nominated three candidates, typical results might be as follows:

Republicans		Democrats	
A	8,500	D	12,500
B	8,000	E	12,000
C	7,500	F	11,500

TABLE 8-1
(Percentage Distribution)
Division of Votes Cast and Legislators Elected by Republican and Democratic Parties, 1920–1966

Election Year	Illinois House of Representatives		Illinois Senate	
	R	*D*	*R*	*D*
1920	62.1	37.9	84.3	15.7
1922	57.5	41.8	82.4	17.6
1924	61.4	38.6	72.5	27.5
1926	60.1	39.2	78.4	21.6
1928	59.5	40.5	78.4	21.6
1930	52.9	47.1	64.7	35.3
1932	47.7	52.3	35.3	64.7
1934	45.1	54.9	31.4	68.6
1936	43.1	55.6	33.3	62.7
1938	51.6	48.4	39.2	60.8
1940	51.6	48.4	54.9	45.1
1942	54.9	45.1	54.9	45.1
1944	51.6	48.4	66.7	33.3
1946	57.5	42.5	74.5	25.5
1948	47.1	52.9	64.7	35.3
1950	54.9	45.1	60.8	39.2
1952	56.2	43.8	74.5	25.5
1954	51.6	48.4	62.7	37.3
1956	53.1	46.9	65.5	32.8
1958	48.6	51.4	58.6	41.4
1960	50.3	49.7	53.4	46.6
1962	50.8	48.5	60.3	39.7
1966	55.9	44.1	65.5	34.5
1968	53.7	46.3	63.8	32.8

SOURCE: Illinois Constitutional Convention Legislative Committee Report, an Appendix.

However, if the Republicans were to nominate only two candidates while the Democrats nominated three, the results might easily resemble the following:

Republicans		Democrats	
A	12,300	D	13,000
B	11,700	E	11,500
		F	11,500

As a result, the Republicans would win two-thirds of the seats with only two-fifths of the vote. Thus, even when the majority party has a fifty percent edge in voting strength, they can easily lose two of the three seats in a district. Moreover, the ability of the majority party to win two of the three seats depends not only on the size of its margin, but also on the evenness with which the voters distribute their votes among the three majority party candidates. This situation is aggravated by the fact that those races which were in the most doubt provided candidates with the greatest incentive to urge their supporters to "plump" all three of their votes for them.

The result of all this was a great reluctance on the part of district majority party leaders to nominate three candidates. Moreover, the two incumbents, who typically dominated the district committees making this decision, often found their enthusiasm for a third candidate restrained by the knowledge that, even if the party was assured of two seats, one of the two might be the new third candidate rather than either of them. Furthermore, even if the majority party ran only two candidates, and thus could not shut out the minority party no matter how it splintered its vote, the single incumbent would realize that it might be the newcomer rather than he who walked off with the only seat.

District minority party leaders found themselves facing a similar set of considerations. If they nominated two, rather than one candidate in a district, they might fragment their support and get no seats at all.

The result of all these considerations was that the voters usually found themselves with little in the way of options in the Illinois lower house district contests. Thus, in 1970 a minority report of the Constitutional Convention Committee on the Legislative Article reported:

> In *not a single district election* of the 1,790 held since 1902 have the voters been given a choice among full slates of three candidates from both parties. Even more incredibly, there have been five nominees on only seventeen occasions, and on forty-six occasions have there been three nominees by one party and one by the other.

Although calculation of electoral advantage or self-interest by district nominating committees nearly always resulted in only three or four candidates for three seats, the three candidates for three seats arrangement in particular seemed to many to be incompatible with basic democratic electoral principles. Sentiment of this sort led to the adoption of a Legislative Article in the 1970 Constitution which provided that no party should "restrict" its number of candidates to less than two. Since the parties do not have an obligation to find a second candidate if none presents himself, this provision has reduced, but not eliminated, the number of three-candidate elections since that time.

In summary, it can fairly be said that the effect of cumulative voting on legislative composition in partisan terms has been as anticipated on two of three counts: provision of minority party representation in large one party dominant areas; reduction of overall majority margins in the lower house; and partial reduction of electoral competition by providing an average of substantially less than two major party candidates per seat.

Legislator Performance

While the effects of cumulative voting on legislative composition in gross party terms are relatively easy to guage—we can count votes, seats, candidates, and nominees—the ultimate effects of cumulative voting on legislator performance or representational relationships are more difficult to measure and analyze. They are also probably more important. If party plays little role in determining how legislators actually behave, there is not much value in analysis centered on effects in terms of party composition.

One group of legislators owes its very incumbency to cumulative voting—those elected from districts where the opposing party won more than seventy-five percent of the vote but failed to nominate three candidates. In a four candidate (3–1) race, the minority party can assure itself of a seat if it concentrates one vote more than twenty-five percent of the total on a single candidate. However, with less than twenty-five percent of the vote, the minority party can be shut out by the majority party. Legislators representing such districts might be expected to display differences in their voting behavior.

Roll Call Voting

In an effort to determine the consequences of cumulative voting on the behavior of these and other individual representatives within the legislative context, one hundred roll call votes[2] from the 1966, 1968 and 1970 legislative sessions were randomly selected. This data was examined for evidence of a relationship between legislators' electoral treatment by cumulative voting and subsequent roll call behavior.

Although cumulative voting might affect individual legislator performance in a variety of ways, a logical place to begin looking for such effects would be in the area of party discipline. At a minimum, one might expect those persons receiving a seat through grace—failure of the other party to nominate three candidates in areas where they had more than seventy-five percent of the vote—to be more responsive to requests for legislative support from the opposite party. In general this might be reflected in lowered party loyalty scores for "free ride" representatives.

Dissents

Table 8-2 contains a comparison of the number of party dissents as a proportion of positions taken by "free ride" and other representatives. From the standpoint of party regularity across all roll calls, there is clearly little to divide "free ride" representatives from others. Although the difference was substantial in the 1966 Assembly, it was insignificant in 1968 and in the opposite direction from that expected in 1970. In 1966 "free ride" representatives dissented from their party majorities slightly more than twenty-three percent of the time, while the remainder of the legislature averaged only twelve percent dissention on the roll calls sampled. The analysis of variance indicates that such a pattern could be expected to appear less than one time in a thousand as a result of random variation in the data. However, the other years presented no such pattern. In 1970 the dissention rate was slightly lower within the "free ride" group than among others. Thus a simple comparison of party regularity among "free ride" and "non-free ride" legislators showed little evidence that "free ride" aspects of election circumstances were of any predictive value with regard to party regularity on roll call voting.

No Position

A simple alternative hypothesis might be that "free ride" representatives avoided offending their district's majority party on many issues by abstaining or being recorded as absent. Thus, receptivity to demands from opposing parties might be manifested in higher absence or abstention rates among "free ride" representatives.

Table 8-3 gives a comparison of absence rates among both groups. Here the differences are all in the anticipated direction and statistically significant at no less than the .001 level in two of the three time periods. Thus absence rates ranged from 26.56 percent to 36.27 percent in the "free ride" group and from only 21.05 percent to 25.00 percent in the "non-free ride" group.

TABLE 8-2
Dissents

Year		Free Ride	Non-Free Ride	Marginal
1966	Means	23.67	12.51	13.01
	Count	(8)	(169)	(177)
	Significance	0.000		
1968	Means	14.85	14.08	14.12
	Count	(9)	(166)	(175)
	Significance	0.704		
1970	Means	14.21	16.93	16.76
	Count	(11)	(166)	(177)
	Significance	0.260		

TABLE 8-3
No Position

Year		Free Ride	Non-Free Ride	Marginal
1966	Means	35.25	21.05	21.69
	Count	(8)	(169)	(177)
	Significance	0.001		
1968	Means	26.56	22.15	22.38
	Count	(9)	(166)	(175)
	Significance	0.196		
1970	Means	36.27	25.00	25.70
	Count	(11)	(166)	(177)
	Significance	0.000		

Taken as a whole, the results for all three time periods are highly suggestive of a relationship between treatment by cumulative voting and party regularity. Yet the pattern is neither as consistent nor as sharply delineated as might be anticipated. For this reason, an attempt to sharpen these relationships was made by adjusting for two muddying influences: the large number of non-party issues arising in the General Assembly; and the heterogeneous nature of the "non-free ride" group.

Party Issues

Many of the roll call votes in the Illinois General Assembly concern issues which are either noncontroversial or do not cause cleavages along party lines. On votes of these types, there would be less reason to expect any differential levels of party loyalty by the two types of legislators. On the other hand, when parties were relatively cohesive and on opposite sides, opposite party influences on "free ride" representatives might be expected to manifest themselves. If, for example, Democratic party leaders in overwhelmingly Democratic districts looked on with equanimity as the third seat went to

TABLE 8-4
Dissent on Party and Non-Party Issues

Year		Free Ride	Minority	Majority	Marginal
1966	Means				
	Party Issues	13.45	1.64	1.62	2.16
	Non-Party Issues	29.54	18.36	18.31	18.83
	Marginal	21.50	10.00	9.96	10.49
	Count	(8)	(49)	(120)	(177)
	Analysis of Variance				
	Group	Significance 0.000			
	Interaction	Significance 0.981			
1968	Means				
	Party Issues	3.82	1.26	0.87	1.13
	Non-Party Issues	19.95	22.48	19.01	20.03
	Marginal	11.88	11.87	9.94	10.58
	Count	(9)	(49)	(117)	(175)
	Analysis of Variance				
	Group	Significance 0.038			
	Interaction	Significance 0.050			
1970	Means				
	Party Issues	4.52	2.31	1.41	1.85
	Non-Party Issues	16.07	23.10	19.39	20.19
	Marginal	10.29	12.70	10.40	11.02
	Count	(11)	(48)	(118)	(177)
	Analysis of Variance				
	Group	Significance 0.037			
	Interaction	Significance 0.009			

a Republican by default because of confidence that that vote could be delivered when needed, "free ride" Republicans would show a distinctive pattern on party issues. During all three time periods, the party margins were sufficiently close to allow a few dissenters to swing the balance.

For these reasons, the roll calls within each time period were divided into two categories: those in which the parties were on opposite sides with minorities of less than ten percent in each party were considered party issues; those roll calls with more than ten percent dissention in either party or with both parties on the same side were considered non-party issues. This procedure produced 31, 27 and 17 party issue roll calls in the three time periods.

Minority Representatives

A second muddying factor might result from the inclusion of minority representatives (those elected in districts where their party won only one of the three seats, but with more than twenty-five percent of the vote) along with majority members (those elected as one of two representatives elected by their party to the legislature). One might expect minority members representing districts dominated by the other party to also be subject to a variety of influences different from those in tune with the majority of voters in their district.

Interaction-Dissents

The results of an analysis of variance test reflecting both of these considerations are presented in Table 8-4. Readers not of a statistical bent may find it easiest to look only at the proportions. Thus, in 1970, the eleven "free ride" representatives dissented 4.52 percent of the time, the forty-eight "minority" members 2.31 percent, and the one-hundred-eighteen majority members 1.41 percent of the time on party issues. This pattern held across all time periods on party issues; there was no such pattern on non-party issues. The significance levels can be looked upon as summaries of the figures and an indication that, despite the small number of legislatures involved, the results far exceeded those which were likely to occur as a result of random variation. The model used was a two-way analysis of variance involving three groups and two repeated measurements (proportions of two types of roll calls). Since trial differences in dissent levels were guaranteed by the distinction between the trials, no significance levels are reported for roll call difference in dissents.

In general, the figures indicate a very clear relationship between group and tendency to dissent on party issues. Moreover, no such strong relationship is apparent on non-party issues. This is reflected in the high significance levels for both groups and interaction across the three time periods. Only in the 1966 Legislature, when extremely high differences between groups were observed on both sets of roll calls was the interactive significance level insignificantly low.

The tripartite group division revealed an intermediate level of discipline among minority representatives on party issues, but again showed no pattern on non-party issues.

TABLE 8-5
No Position on Party and Non-Party Issues

Year		Free Ride	Minority	Majority	Marginal
1966	Means				
	Party Issues	27.82	15.67	10.08	12.43
	Non-Party Issues	38.59	24.67	25.50	25.86
	Marginal	33.20	20.17	17.79	19.14
	Count	(8)	(49)	(120)	(177)
	Analysis of Variance				
	Group	Significance 0.001			
	Roll Call	Significance 0.000			
	Interaction	Significance 0.000			
1968	Means				
	Party Issues	12.76	10.13	8.67	9.29
	Non-Party Issues	31.66	25.92	27.42	27.22
	Marginal	22.21	18.02	18.05	18.25
	Count	(9)	(49)	(117)	(175)
	Analysis of Variance				
	Group	Significance 0.489			
	Roll Call	Significance 0.000			
	Interaction	Significance 0.345			
1970	Means				
	Party Issues	39.04	20.59	15.45	18.31
	Non-Party Issues	35.71	24.66	27.48	27.23
	Marginal	37.37	22.62	21.47	22.77
	Count	(11)	(48)	(118)	(177)
	Analysis of Variance				
	Group	Significance 0.000			
	Roll Call	Significance 0.012			
	Interaction	Significance 0.000			

Interaction-No Position

Table 8-5 presents a similar analysis for difference in proportion of those who failed to take a position on the two types of issues. Inasmuch as the variable classifications were independent of the number of absences, significance levels are included for roll calls. In all three time periods, there was a significantly greater tendency on the part of all groups to take a position on party issues. The group differences and interaction effects were in the expected direction on all three time periods but only in the second time period failed to reach normally acceptable significance levels. Thus while absence rates most probably also reflected a high volume of effectively random, genuine absences, there appeared to be unmistakable evidence of a distinctive pattern of behavior on the part of "free ride" and minority representatives. Once again there was reason to believe that those representatives elected to the Legislature through cumulative voting's minority representation effect tended to act in a less partisan manner on the most partisan issues. Moreover, this effect was most noticeable with the group that was most uniquely affected by cumulative voting.

Summary and Conclusion

Cumulative voting is Illinois' relatively unique contribution to the world's legislative election systems. It has certain obvious effects on legislative composition and more subtle effects on legislator performance. The effect on composition has been to break up homogeneous areas by electing Republican representatives from heavily democratic Chicago areas and Democratic representation from heavily Republican downstate areas. Over the years, it has consistently narrowed the margin between minority and majority party in the lower house as a whole. Normal electoral calculations under cumulative voting have also severely limited the number of nominees among which the voters have been allowed to choose.

The unique mode of elections may be presumed to have some effect on legislator behavior as well as legislative composition. In particular, party ties might be expected to be weakened as many legislators face their real general election competition from other members of their own party and district. These ties might be even weaker among those who received their seats less as a result of their own party's strength than from failure of the opposing party to run three candidates.

Analysis of roll call voting results showed that party ties were indeed weakest among the "free ride" group but that these differences manifested themselves primarily on crucial party issues. "Minority" members occupied an intermediate position. These differences occurred not only on actual dissents, but also with absences or abstentions on key party issues.

Thus the willingness of party leaders in essentially one-party districts to tolerate the capture of one seat by a member of the opposing party may be partially based on the realization that such votes cannot be reliably delivered on the most crucial partisan roll call issues.

From the standpoint of representational efficiency, the case for cumulative voting is mixed. On one hand, the voter has a restricted set of candidates to choose from in the general election. Moreover, the frequent struggle between two minority party candidates to see which will obtain the third seat tends to focus conflict on intra-party issues in a manner which contributes little to programmatic politics and meaningful party choices at the statewide level.

On othe other hand, cumulative voting not only tends to blur regional cleavages, represent political minorities, and provide more proportionality than is typical of single member districts, but also seems to provide further gradations of partisan division than is apparent from party composition alone. Thus, representatives from districts dominated by the other party tend to dissent from their own party more than others; those minority members classified as ''free-ride'' dissent most of all.

It is unlikely that the effects of cumulative voting on legislator performance are confined to those described here. More study is needed of such issues as perceptions of competition from fellow incumbents among majority members and of effects on variables other than partisanship. In addition, as the effects of the 1970 Constitution begin to affect nominating practice more consistently, there will be fewer and fewer ''free ride'' representatives who owe their election solely to failure of the other party to nominate a third candidate. Most of them may have to defeat a second candidate from their own party as well.

These changes, as well as other unexplored effects of cumulative election on legislator performance should continue to make Illinois cumulative voting a worthwhile object of further study.

NOTES

[1]Various aspects of cumulative voting are discussed in Blair, *Cumulative Voting: An Effective Electoral Device in Illinois Politics,* University of Illinois Press, 1960; C.S. Hyneman and J.D. Morgan, ''Cumulative Voting in Illinois,'' *Illinois Law Review,* 1937; B.F. Moore, ''The History of Cumulative Voting and Minority Representation in Illinois, 1870–1919.'' *University of Illinois Studies in the Social Sciences,* 1919.

[2]Roll calls with a level of unanimity greater than 90% were excluded from the universe sampled.

CHAPTER **9**

The Illinois Judicial System

Stephen Daniels and Frank J. Kopecky

Many definitions of politics have been suggested, some with their origins in ancient Greece. But perhaps the most adequate definition offered by a student of American politics is Harold Lasswell's: who gets what, when, and how.[1] Government is intimately involved in the process of authoritatively deciding who gets what, when and how.[2] Making such decisions unavoidably results in conflicts and disputes. Governmental institutions are called upon to resolve disputes in an acceptable way. The courts perform a unique function in this process.

Most Illinoisans have only the vaguest notion of the nature of their State courts. If they are familiar with any court, it most likely will be the United States Supreme Court which attracts the attention of the news media more than other courts. This emphasis is perhaps misplaced since 90 percent of the court business in this country takes place in the state trial courts. Consequently, our emphasis here will be more on Illinois' lower courts than upper courts. We hope to avoid the bane of most discussions about Illinois and federal courts ". . . the myth that upper courts are the heart of court-house government."[3] This "upper court" myth induces the mistaken idea that what occurs in the lower courts is of no importance. It is the rare view of the Illinois judicial system which looks much beyond the Supreme Court and its politics to the politics of the lower courts.

Illinois Courts: A Political Perspective

Perhaps for many people law is some mysterious, brooding omnipresence in the sky with judges as demigods. Nonetheless, our starting point is the fact that courts, as other governmental institutions, are political institutions and that judges, as other political officials, are political actors. The reason for this approach is simple: courts are the authoritative interpreters of laws and constitutions. Such interpretations involve choices among competing positions. In a very real sense, the law is what the judges say it is.[4] As a result, many fundamental public policy issues come before them. This makes judges more similar than different from other public officials. Along with legislators, bureaucrats and city council members, judges help make the political decisions of government. The courts of Illinois, then, are an integral part of the State's governmental structure, and ". . . they are inevitably drawn into . . . the state's . . . political life."[5]

Without an understanding of the political nature of judicial behavior and the role of courts, one's understanding of the Illinois political system will be incomplete. Courts in Illinois and elsewhere are political because of what they do. Court decisions, whether of the Supreme Court or the most obscure trial court, are not neutral; all have some political effect. Court decisions resolve conflicts, enforce community norms, stigmatize people, legitimize (or deny legitimacy to) decisions made elsewhere in the government and make law. In short, for ". . . many people litigation is another way of waging a partisan political battle."[6]

Although all of us have strong feelings about law and courts, there is a paradox in those feelings. Without a common heritage or religion we have turned to law as a secular religion—as something transcedent. Yet, at the same time, our beliefs in self-governance and individualism say that law and courts should be viewed pragmatically, as things instrumental and within our control. Historian Daniel J. Boorstin describes this paradox in the following way:

> We wish to believe both that our laws come from a necessity beyond our reach, and that they are our instruments, shaping our community to our chosen ends. We wish to believe that our laws are both changeless and changeable, transcendental and pragmatic.[7]

Law and courts have an unusual yet powerful position. Their importance in the Illinois political system should not be underestimated. We revere, at times almost worship, law and courts, yet we use them for the most mundane and political purposes. As a highly legalistic people we are prone to viewing the law as a set of moral precepts. Nonetheless, we see law used instrumentally to determine how much a homeowner can receive for his condemned house which lies in the path of a new highway; to extract large sums of money from doctors and other professionals whose performance is adjudged substandard; or, by management, to prevent striking workers from picketing.

The power allowed courts is illustrated by what we expect courts to do, resolve the most controversial issues of the day—often those which legislatures and executives have not resolved—from capital punishment to the environment to allocating the powers of state and local government. In no other nation do courts have such power and responsibility. Over 140 years ago Alexis

DeToqueville noted: "Scarcely a political question arises in the United States which is not resolved, sooner or later, into a judicial question."[8] When Nazis wanted to march in Skokie, a predominately Jewish suburb of Chicago, and village officials refused to issue a permit, the Nazis went to court. When the citizens of downstate Wilsonville in Macoupin County wanted to stop Earthline, Inc., from dumping toxic wastes in their town, they went to court.[9] In each case, important political issues were involved. In these cases, courts were asked to resolve complex problems of free speech and environmental protection.

Courts as Governmental Institutions

Under the principle of separation of powers, courts have been given the Constitutional authority to resolve disputes, but they have extremely limited powers to carry out their orders and judgements—courts have to rely on the executive branch to carry out their orders. They have no power over the budget—from a practical viewpoint, the judiciary is dependent upon the appropriation of funds from the Legislature. This interdependence creates the potential for political leverage on the courts by the other branches.

The Constitutional doctrine of separation of powers has been raised in several recent court cases. The courts have become increasingly vigilant concerning encroachment upon their constitutional authority. In 1975 in the case of *People v. Cunningham,*[10] the Supreme Court declared the capital punishment statute unconstitutional. Interestingly, the Court never resolved the issue as to whether capital punishment itself violated the Constitution but decided the case on the ground that the statute violated the doctrine of separation of powers. The court ruled that the Legislature had improperly interfered with judicial activities by requiring a special tribunal to hear capital punishment cases.

In *People v. Jackson,*[11] the Court once again declared a statute unconstitutional on grounds of violation of the separation of powers doctrine. In this case, the Legislature enacted a law which attempted to regulate the process of selecting jurors. The Court felt that this statute interfered with its inherent power to make rules governing trial procedure. Since separation of powers is a constitutional issue, courts under the doctrine of judicial review have the final word on when the Legislature or executive is overreaching. This, of course, gives great power to the courts, countervailing the legislature and executive.

An instance where the separation of powers doctrine may have been abused, however, occurred in 1978 when the Supreme Court refused to allow the Illinois Auditor General (who is appointed by the Legislature to audit State agencies) to audit the books of the Board of Bar Examiners and the Attorney Registration and Discipline Commission. Both organizations regulate attorneys and are supported entirely by attorney's fees which the Auditor claims are public funds subject to the legislative audit. The Court argued that the Auditor General did not have the authority to audit these entities because the Court itself has the inherent and exclusive right to regulate lawyers. The Court argued that a legislative audit would be in derogation of separation of powers. The Court was willing to compromise with an audit by a private firm, but doubts remain as to whether the private audit fulfills the Legislature's version of the compromise or the public interest. The possibility of a constitutional confrontation has been raised by the audit issue, but in any argument with the Court about its own rules, the challenger is at a great disadvantage.

The controversy between the Legislature and the Illinois Supreme Court over the Auditor General's claims for constitutional mandate to audit the Court's two commissions is illustrative of the network of tension which links all three branches. Within the network each branch continually exerts pressure, altering power relationships. The other branches, with countervailing powers, work to check and balance.

Courts as Law-Making Institutions

It is often said that the function of the legislature is to make law; the function of the executive is to implement the law; and the function of the judiciary is to enforce the law. While such a view of the role of the branches of government may be adequate for an elementary understanding of government, the more sophisticated student of government is aware that all three branches of government make law. The legislative law-making function is easy to understand. Executive agencies make laws primarily by enacting administrative rules and regulations. Courts make law by deciding cases. The function of the courts is to resolve disputes in society. The dispute may be between individuals, between individuals and government, or between governmental entities. If a dispute arises which cannot be resolved by mutual agreement, a court may be asked to decide the issue. Courts are increasingly regarded as the final arbiters of rights and responsibilities in American society.

In resolving a dispute, courts not only decide cases in favor of one side or the other. They also issue opinions or holdings giving reasons for decisions. A decision becomes precedent for other judges to follow. It is a critical part of the Anglo-American legal tradition for judges in similar cases to follow the decisions reached in previously decided cases. The tradition of following the legal reasoning of previous decision (known as the doctrine of *stare decisis*) is quite strong. Most courts will follow previous cases unless there are extremely compelling reasons to do otherwise.

The body of law which develops as a result of the judicial decision making process is known as the common law. In the past, courts in England, the United States and other countries influenced by the English legal system relied quite heavily on court-made common law. The decisions of judges, particularly appellate judges, are recorded in law books known as "reporters."

Over the years, state law governing such areas as poverty, contracts and personal liability has evolved through the common law process. Decisions of courts and the law they have created reflect dominant political views and values of the times, or at least the views and values of those who have controlled the legislature. The law governing landlord-tenant relations illustrate this point. Judges as a group have tended to come from the property owning class. Law which has evolved from the courts has strongly favored landlords. In more recent times courts, largely as a result of the growing political influence of renters, have begun to favor the rights of tenants. The Illinois Supreme Court in the case of *Jack Spring, Inc. v. Little*[12] ruled that, in at least some limited circumstances, a landlord must warrant the habitability or fitness of the property rented. Prior to this decision, the renter was under a legal obligation to pay the full amount of rent unless the property was virtually uninhabitable. Law involving the consumer has demonstrated similar evolution. The Illinois Supreme Court has followed laws that have developed in virtually all states which hold manufacturers responsible for damages caused by carelessly produced products.[13] This trend has reversed the previous doctrine of caveat emptor, "let the buyer beware." The doctrine of sovereign immunity, preventing suits against local government units, was abolished in the case of *Molitor v. Kaneland Community Unit District*[14] overruling a precedent which had been maintained for centuries. In all three examples, law has changed as a result of court opinions which reflect society's current sense of justice and fairness.

The legislature's role in law-making has steadily grown over the last century. Legislatures are primary sources of law in our governmental structure. Except when prohibited by constitutional restraints, legislatures can supercede judge-made law by enacting statutes. There is virtually no substantive area of the law which remains exclusively governed by common law decisions. Courts, nevertheless, still play an important law-making role as the interpreters of statutes. It is impossible to pass a statute sufficiently detailed to cover every situation which will arise or one which cannot be subject to a variety of interpretations. For example, does a statute which defines armed robbery as the taking of property from the person of another with a dangerous weapon include a robbery with an unloaded gun? Illinois courts have ruled that such is armed robbery.[15] Courts can declare a student a "minor in need of supervision" if the "minor under 18 years of age is beyond the control of his parents" or grant a divorce if a spouse has been guilty of "cruel and repeated mental cruelty." Courts must interpret these statutes to determine if they apply to factual situations in cases before them. Decisions interpreting these statutes are recorded and become a part of the governing law.

Courts also make law through their power of review over final decisions of administrative agencies. The area of administrative law is becoming increasingly important as administrative agencies continues to expand their functions. Administrative agencies such as the Pollution Control Board, the Illinois Commerce Commission and the Fair Employment Practices Commission conduct administrative hearings and render decisions. These hearings are subject to review by the courts of the State. Additionally, most State agencies are authorized by statutes to issue regulations. These regulations are found in the *Illinois Register* published weekly by the Secretary of State. Courts will review agency adjudicatory or rulemaking decisions to determine if they meet constitutional standards and are consistent with the legislative grant of authority.

"Judicial review," the final arena of law making, is the law-making power of the courts which has been most frequently analyzed by political scientists. Judicial review refers to the power of any court to declare unconstitutional and hence *unenforceable* any law, any act based upon law, or any other official action which the court determines to be in conflict with the relevant constitution—state or federal.[16]

John Marshall, Chief Justice of the United States, enunciated the doctrine of judicial review in the famous case of *Marbury v. Madison.*[17] Since this case, the judiciary's authority for final decisions in determining whether statutes or administrative actions are constitutional has become an accepted part of the American system of law and government. Although most writing about judicial review has been about the United States Supreme Court, all courts engage in the practice of judicial review. In recent years, the Illinois Supreme Court has interpreted the Illinois Constitution in such a manner that statutes enacted by the Illinois General Assembly providing for capital punishment and no-fault automobile insurance have been declared unconstitutional.

Legal Culture

In many respects the Illinois court system is different from those of the other 49 states. For instance, not all states choose their judges or even structure their systems as Illinois does. However, if we take a few steps back and give ourselves some perspective, we see that Illinois shares one important thing with all other state systems and the federal system, as well—a common legal culture. An understanding of this common legal culture shows that, while there are differences between Illinois and other states, those differences are not fundamental. Rather, they are variations on a single theme, a theme set by the legal culture. Our perspective, then, is that while Illinois' court system may differ from other U.S. systems in many respects, fundamentally they are all alike.

To understand legal culture, we must start with the concept "culture" itself. The concept "culture" refers to the beliefs, knowledge, customs and skills that distinguish one society from another. Culture is the ". . . distinctive way of life of a group of people, their complete design for living."[18] This concept has found its way into the study of politics through what is called "*political* culture." Political culture refers to ". . . the set of attitudes, beliefs, and sentiments which give order and meaning to a political process and which provide the underlying assumptions and rules that govern behavior in the political system. It encompasses both the political ideals and the operating norms of a polity.''[19]

From the concept of political culture it is a small step to the concept of ''legal culture.'' Legal culture is the set of attitudes, beliefs and sentiments which give order and meaning to the legal process and which provide the underlying assumptions and rules which govern behavior within the system. It is the set of enduring beliefs, symbols, and values which help to distinguish the American judicial system from all others; which help to define how the system functions; and which makes the judicial systems of the 50 states much more similar than different. According to political scientist Joel B. Grossman, four aspects of legal culture are particularly important: constitutionalism, legalism, professionalism and the adversary process.[20]

Constitutionalism

Constitutionalism refers to the belief in government according to a constitution usually, though not necessarily, written. A constitution sets out the design and organization of government—its offices and structure—along with the powers *and* limitations of government. It incorporates the basic values of a polity; it defines the place of the individual in the political community and his sphere of autonomy (his rights). Constitutionalism, then, is the belief in limited government. It is ''. . . the practice of politics according to rules of the game, which insure effective restraints upon governmental and other political action . . .''[21]

While constitutionalism may not be strong in many parts of the world, it is particularly strong in the United States. The federal Constitution is the premier political and legal symbol in our political system.[22] We have, in fact, a uniquely constitutional approach to governance. Constitutions legitimize not only governments but governmental actions as well. ''The Constitution provides principled legal standards for judging political actions . . .''[23] The federal government and each of the 50 state governments are based upon written constitutions. Illinois has had four different State Constitutions, established in 1818, 1848, 1870, and 1970.

Legalism

Legalism goes hand-in-hand with constitutionalism. ''It is the ethical attitude that holds moral conduct to be a matter of rule-following, and moral relationships to consist of duties and rights determined by rules. Like all moral attitudes—it expresses itself not only in personal behavior but also in political ideologies and in social institutions.''[24] Legalism is reflected in the elaborate systems of courts, at least 16,000 of them, in this country! It is reflected in the idea of the ''rule of law'' and the sentiment often uttered in frustration that there ''ought to be a law.''

Legalism is also evident in our use of the courts and the tendency toward ''overcriminalization.'' Americans have turned to the courts in increasing numbers. Between 1964 and 1976, there was an overall increase of 55 percent in litigation in Illinois trial courts.[25] Between 1962 and 1972, there was a 70 percent increase in litigation in the federal district courts.[26] Increasingly, we see the courts being used to settle social and political controversies. Legalism is also evident in our tendency to pass laws against those things we do not like. Examples are plentiful, particularly in the area of ''victimless crimes'' such as prostitution or gambling. Law is used frequently to regulate individual behavior which is felt to be immoral even though that behavior harms no one else and may even be done in private.

Professionalism

Professionalism refers to the fact that most activity in the court system involves experts—lawyers and judges. The ordinary citizen plays only a minor role in the system, primarily as a member of a petit or grand jury.[27] In Illinois, as in the other 49 states, it is illegal for the ordinary citizen to practice law. In fact, he would be hopelessly lost in a court proceeding without a lawyer. Special expertise is needed to understand and deal with the elaborate rules and proceedings required to conduct a trial or even to negotiate a settlement. Only lawyers have the expertise needed to be successful in the system. Lawyers have traditionally worked on a ''fee for service'' basis, which usually has meant that those with the most money have received the best legal services.[28] In a very real sense how much ''justice'' one gets often depends upon how much justice one can afford.[29]

Whatever role there may have been for popular—or at least non-laywer—participation, it has been decreasing. The judicial system has become increasingly professionalized. In most states, including Illinois, all judicial officers must be ''learned in the law.'' Offices which in the past were often held by non-lawyers, such as justices of the peace and police magistrates in Illinois, have been rapidly disappearing. In 1964 the offices of justice of the peace and police magistrate were abolished in Illinois. The trend towards professionalism has found its way into other aspects of the judicial system with the professionalization of offices such as court clerk and with the increased use of professional court administrators. For instance, the Association of Clerks of the Circuit Court of Illinois in 1974 voted to recommend that the position of Clerk be made appointive instead of elective, the first step toward professionalization.[30] The overall move toward professionalism in such areas is a part of the legacy of the Progressive Movement earlier in this century and lives on today as a part of the court reform movement. Whether increased professionalization has improved the delivery and quality of justice remains to be empirically shown.

Adversary Process

A traditional part of our legal culture is the adversary process, which plays a crucial role in structuring court activity. We think of judicial decisions as being made on the basis of a courtroom confrontation between two opposing sides. The adversary process is a conflictual approach to determining the facts of a matter in dispute and the appropriate legal rule for resolving that dispute. The approach emphasizes conflict so much that the late Judge Jerome Frank called it the "fight" theory of justice, ". . . a theory which derives from the origin of trials as substitutes for private out-of-court brawls."[31]

According to Marian Neef and Stuart Nagel, the American adversary process assumes:

> . . . that the fairest decision can be obtained when the two parties to the immediate conflict argue in open court according to carefully prescribed rules and procedures. The confrontation of witnesses in open court is at the heart of the American legal system since it is thought that the best result is obtained when the parties face each other as adversaries in a kind of constrained battle procedure. The adversary theory of justice is premised on the assumption that the truth can best be determined if each side strives as hard as it can, in a keen partisan spirit, to bring to the court's attention the evidence favorable to its own side.[32]

Of course, for the "battle procedure" to work effectively, there must be a professional group of champions—lawyers—who know the rules of the fight.

As Frank noted, this "fight theory" is a type of laissez-faire theory of justice.[33] Given this approach, courts are passive. In other words, judges must wait for disputes to be brought to court. Additionally, the approach assumes that individuals can identify their own legal problems and that they will have sufficient resources to protect their interests. Unfortunately, both of these assumptions are often inaccurate.

It is important to realize that while the adversary approach is an integral part of the legal culture, it is not always an accurate reflection of what actually happens. Organizational and practical constraints, such as court overload, have led to the development of ways to avoid the full-blown courtroom trial, ways such as plea-bargaining in criminal cases and out-of-court settlements in many civil matters.

The Structure of the Illinois Judicial System

The structure of the judicial system can be most meaningfully discussed in the context of its special role in the political process and its relation to federal and other state systems, as well as to the history of reform.

Relation to Federal and Other State Systems

The Illinois Court system exists along with 50 other court systems—those of the federal government and the 49 other states. Within its own realm the Illinois system is independent of those of the other states. Over 90 percent of this country's court business begins and ends in the state courts.

Illinois' system is largely, though not entirely, beyond the reach of the federal government, as well. Nonetheless, state courts are subservient to the federal government in one special way. Article VI, Section 2 of the federal Constitution (the "supremacy clause") says that the Constitution itself and all laws and treaties made under its authority are the supreme law of the land. Judges in every state are bound to follow the supreme law of the land, state laws and constitutions notwithstanding. The Illinois judicial system can do anything so long as it is within the supreme law.

Background: The History of Reform

The Illinois judicial system has been "reformed" a number of times since Illinois entered the Union in 1818. Under the 1818 Constitution, Illinois had a system designed to serve a rural state in which the population was sparse and largely limited to the southern third of the state. It consisted of a Supreme Court that ranged in number from 4 to 9 and, at the varying whims of the General Assembly, as many as nine circuits courts and judges. During those periods when the General Assembly did not allow for circuit courts and judges, the Supreme Court justices actually "rode circuit" throughout the State hearing cases individually as trial judges. Between 1818 and 1848, when the second Illinois Constitution was adopted, the circuit courts were legislated in and out of existence three times. During the 1818 to 1848 period, the General Assembly also established justice of the peace courts in each county with trial jurisdiction in minor matters.

The 1848 Constitution created a three-man Supreme Court and nine circuit courts and judges. Subsequent legislation pursuant to the Constitution established a county court in each county. In addition, each county had two justices of the peace ". . . to sit with county judges in all cases in the county courts."[34] The county courts had jurisdiction in minor matters and concurrent, or shared, jurisdiction with circuit courts in some areas. During the next twenty years there was a great population increase in Illinois as the sparsely populated north attracted more settlers. To deal with the added burden on a judicial system designed for a rural state whose population was centered in the south, the General Assembly created the position of police magistrate in each city and town. The General Assembly called for ". . . one in towns and cities of less than 6,000 inhabitants; two in towns and cities of 6,000 to 12,000 inhabitants; and three in towns and cities of more than 12,000 inhabitants."[35] These magistrates had jurisdiction over all minor ordinance cases and the same jurisdiction as justices of the peace. Nonetheless, the structure of 1848 could not adequately deal with a state whose character was rapidly changing.

In 1870, Illinois adopted its third constitution, one which radically altered the judicial system. Unfortunately, the changes resulted in a jurisdictional chaos. The Supreme Court now consisted of seven justices, and for the first time, a middle tier of appellate courts was established. There were four appellate courts, each one responsible for and sitting in a different part of the State. Each had three judges. The circuit courts were kept, but now there were 17 plus Cook County which was a separate circuit. Trial courts were allowed some appellate jurisdiction in cases arising from inferior courts. By the turn of the century, a number of inferior courts had been established by the General Assembly under the authority of the 1870 Constitution. Each county had a court plus justices of the peace and police magistrates. In some matters the circuit and county courts had concurrent jurisdiction, but the circuit courts had appellate jurisdiction over the county courts. In addition, the county courts had concurrent jurisdiction in some matters with the justices of the peace and police magistrates but had appellate jurisdiction over those same courts in other matters. By 1881, the General Assembly had established probate courts in counties withover 70,000 people (taking that jurisdiction from the county courts). Finally, under the 1870 Constitution, an almost separate judicial system was developed to meet the growing urban needs of Chicago. In spite of this succession of changes, the 1870 Constitution still ". . . was not flexible enough to cope with a growing population and the need for an expandable judiciary."[36] Nonetheless, this system was in effect until the 1960's when the judicial system was completely overhauled!

The problems of the 1870 system are perhaps best exemplified by Cook County.

> In 1962, Cook County had 208 courts: the Circuit Court, the Superior Court, the Family Court, Criminal Court, Probate Court, County Court, Municipal Court of Chicago, 23 city, village, town and municipal courts, 75 justices of the peace courts, and 103 police magistrate courts. Many of these courts had overlapping jurisdiction which increased the already great organizational problems. Pehaps more serious was the fact that there was no administrative authority to unify, coordinate and supervise them.[37]

In addition, many of the inferior courts, not only in Cook County, were staffed by non-lawyers (particularly justices of the peace and police magistrates). The results of these shortcomings were often corruption, overloads and lengthy delays.

Despite the complications, expense, and confusion created by the 1870 judicial system, an amendment to the Illinois Constitution was not proposed until 1961. Modernization of the court system was achieved when the amendment went into effect on January 1, 1964.

A Three-Tiered Judicial System

The 1964 Judicial Article, as it is called, created a streamlined, unified court system. This reform created, according to Rubin G. Cohn of the University of Illinois Law School ". . . perhaps the most efficiently structured state judicial system in the country."[38] Cohn continued:

> The single unified trial court in each judicial circuit absorbing and abolishing all prior constitutional and statutory courts of limited jurisdiction (e.g. county, probate, municipal, city, village and town courts, Superior Court of Cook County, justice of the peace and magistrate courts), the independent and intermediate appellate court, and the supreme court—the totality of the judicial structure in this state—constitute a remarkably concise and simplified organizational concept of judicial administration.[39]

This new system consisted of three tiers: first, a seven-member Supreme Court with complete administrative authority over the rest of the system. Second, an Appellate Court divided into five judicial districts of substantially equal population. Third, the 21 circuit courts which are the trial courts of general jurisdiction. Most circuits consist of two or more contiguous counties. The exceptions are DuPage County, which is itself an entire circuit, and Cook County which, as before, is still almost a separate system unto itself. There is at least one circuit judge sitting in each of the 100 other counties.

The 1970 Constitution, Illinois' fourth, made only minor alterations in the judicial system. The three-tiered Illinois system parallels that of the federal judicial structure—a supreme court, a middle tier of appellate courts, and trial courts of general jurisdiction.[40] Of the 49 other states, 25 now have some kind of three-tiered system although some are quite different than that of Illinois. For example, Alabama, Oklahoma, Tennessee and Texas each have a separate appeals court for just criminal matters operating alongside an appeals court for civil matters.[41] The Illinois Appellate Court hears both civil and criminal matters. The remaining 24 states have only a two-tiered system; trial court and supreme court. One point must be made clear. Even though 25 states have a three-tiered system as does Illinois, there are as many variations as states.

Circuit Courts

In Illinois, most issues, though not all, enter the judicial system in a circuit court sitting in one of the 102 counties. The State is divided into 21 judicial circuits by statute.[42] Two circuits, Cook County and the 18th Circuit (DuPage County), each consist of one county. The 1964 Judicial Article and the 1970 Constitution set Cook County as a separate, unnumbered circuit.[43] The composition of the other circuits is set by statute, and it is by virtue of statute that DePage County comprises the entire 18th Circuit. "The other 19 judicial circuits are composed of two or more contiguous counties as provided by law. Each judicial circuit has but one, unified Circuit Court."[44] There are no longer inferior trial courts sharing jurisdiction with the circuit courts, such as justice of the peace, police magistrate or county courts. However, as we shall see shortly, the circuit courts may be divided into specialized divisions.

Where do these circuit courts sit? Where are trials held? Under present State law the circuit courts hear cases in each of the 102 counties. For example, legal disputes arising in Montgomery County would normally be settled in the Fourth Circuit Court sitting in Montgomery County. The law states that there must be at least one circuit court judge elected from each county. Tradition holds that each county should have a judge holding court there, but the 1970 Constitution gives the General Assembly authority to change this.[45] "Practical as well as political considerations, however, will assure that this legislative power will not be exercised except in the smallest of counties."[46]

Jurisdiction The circuit courts in Illinois are the trial courts of general jurisdication. Jurisdication refers to the legal authority to hear and decide cases. General jurisdi-

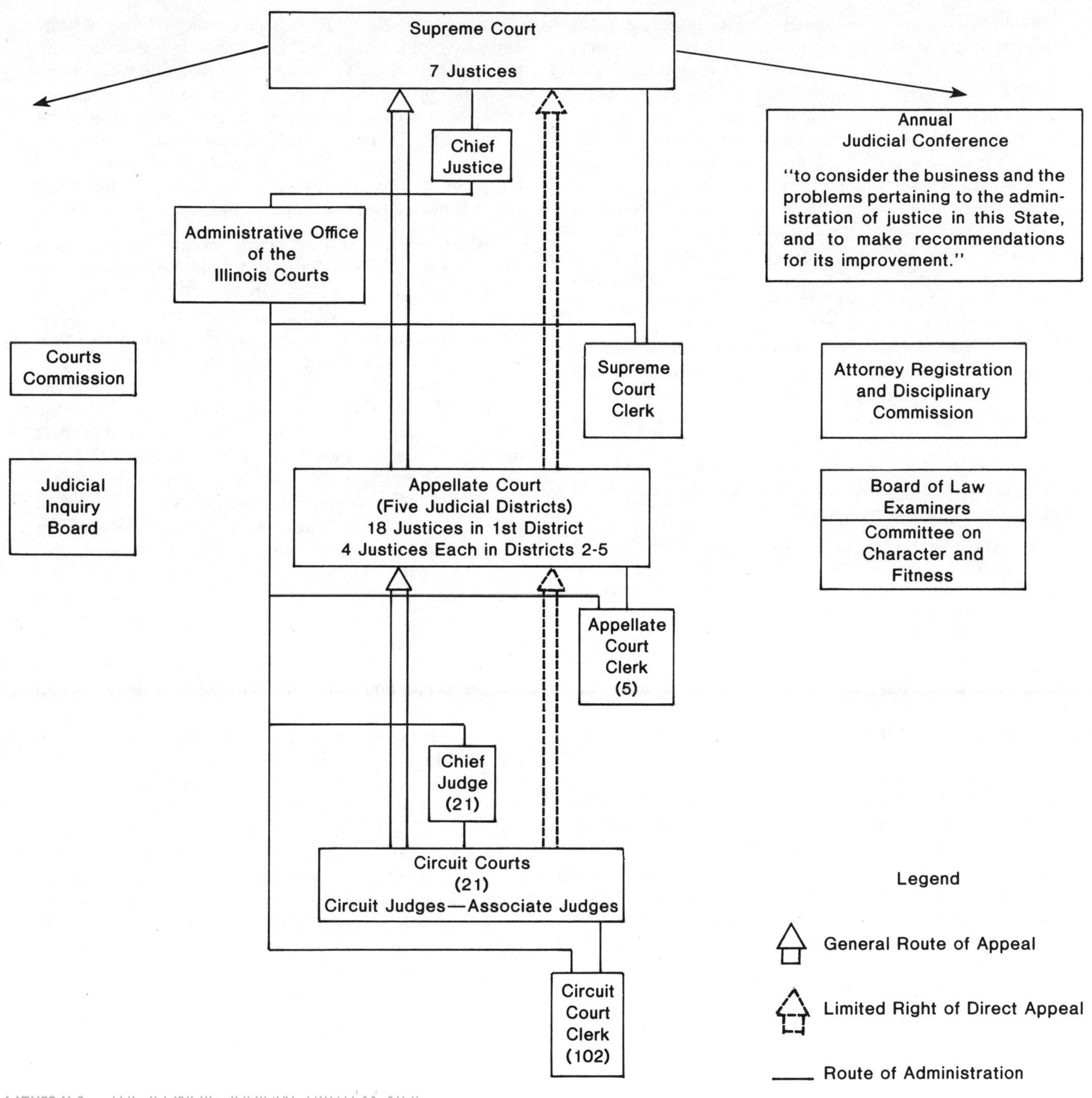

Figure 11.1 THE ILLINOIS JUDICIAL SYSTEM, [illegible]

cation refers to the circuit court's authority to hear cases in almost all areas (the exceptions will be noted later) both civil and criminal arising under State and local law, and in rare instances, even under federal law. Circuit courts have *only* original jurisdiction, meaning that these are courts with no appellate jurisdiction. Appellate jurisdiction is the authority vested in a superior court to hear cases involving questions of error in inferior courts and to revise their decisions accordingly. Only in courts of first instance, such as the circuit courts, ". . . is evidence, written and oral, introduced, tested by cross-examination and extensive oral argument, and a full record of court proceedings made."[47] When the inferior courts were abolished their respective jurisdictions were given to the unified circuit courts. "The jurisdictional problems (the overlaps and resulting confusion) which had frequently plagued the pre-existing system of fragmented trial courts were completely eliminated by the integrated circuit concept. . . ."[48]

There are three exceptions to the circuit courts' general jurisdication. Cases cannot be heard in the circuit courts in the following areas:

> . . . (1) in matters relating to redistricting of the General Assembly and the ability of the Governor to serve or resume office; (2) where the Supreme Court exercises its discretionary original jurisdiction in cases relating to revenue, mandamus, prohibition or habeas corpus: (3) by statute, the review of orders of the Pollution Control Board and certain orders of the Pollution Control Board and certain orders of the State Board of Election.[49]

Jurisdiction in the first area was turned over to the Supreme Court by the 1970 Constitution.

In the circuit courts, ". . . flexibility in subject matter jurisdiction was assured by authorization for administrative establishment of generalized and specialized divisions within each circuit court."[50] This means that instead of separate probate, divorce, etc., courts each working independent of the other, there is one administrative structure in which there may be a number of specialized divisions. The 1970 Constitution grants to the Chief Judge of each circuit the authority to provide for such specialized divisions, subject to the Supreme Court's ultimate administrative authority. Again, this is one of the important aspects of a unified system. The idea of organized divisions within a circuit especially applies to larger industrialized counties—particularly Cook.

The Circuit Court of Cook County is by far the largest and busiest in Illinois. The problems of such a court require specialized treatment. The court is divided into two departments, County and Municipal. The latter deals with minor cases in the county. The department is further divided into six geographical districts, and each district is divided into civil, criminal, traffic and ordinance sections. The County Department hears major cases. It is divided into functional rather than geographical divisions. There are seven divisions: Criminal, Juvenile, County, Probate, Divorce, Chancery and Law. The jurisdictions of the Criminal, Juvenile and Divorce divisions are self-evident. The County Division hears cases involving adoptions, inheritance tax, election contests, real estate taxes, municipal organizations and mental health proceedings. The Probate Division is responsible for matters involving wills and administration of estates. The Chancery Division hears matters involving injunctions, construction of wills and trusts and mortgage forclosures. Finally, the Law Division hears suits for the recovery of damages in excess of $15,000.[51]

Judges After all trial courts except circuits were abolished by the 1964 Judicial Article, only two groups of trial judges were left—circuit and associate. The judges of all the abolished courts automatically became either circuit or associate judges. The Article also provided for magistrates to be appointed by circuit judges. "The circuit judges of all circuit courts, the judges of the Superior Court of Cook County, the chief justice of the Municipal Court of Chicago, and the county and probate judges of the County and probate courts of Cook County, respectively, became circuit judges of their respective circuit courts."[52] The pre-Article associate judges ". . . of the Municipal Court of Chicago, the judges of the several municipal, city, village and unincorporated town courts, and unincorporated town courts, and county and probate judges in all counties other than Cook became associate judges of the circuit court into which they were absorbed."[53]

The 1970 Constitution further refined the State court system. It combined the 1964 Judicial Article circuit and associates into a single classification of circuit judge. An entirely new category of associate judge, comprised of the 1964 Judicial Article magistrates, was created by the Constitution. It was intended by the framers of the 1964 Article that this class of magistrates be a group of younger jurists just entering judicial service; that they would gain experience at this level and then serve as a pool for candidates who might then become circuit and associate judges. However, the work of these magistrates consisted largely of the dregs of the system, the type of cases previously handled by justices of the peace and police magistrates. The magistrate's position carried virtually no professional prestige. Magistrates were appointed by the circuit judges of each circuit without any assured tenure, serving at the pleasure of the circuit judges. Their image was that of "inferior" judicial officers. As a result, it was difficult to attract highly qualified people to the position. The 1970 Constitution remedied this problem by eliminating the magistrates' position and making the 1964 Judicial Article magistrates the new associate judges with a fixed term of office.

Under the 1970 Constitution the circuit courts, then, are staffed by circuit and associate judges. Circuit judges are elected to six-year terms. Associate judges are appointed by the circuit judges of each circuit for four-year terms. Both circuit and associate judges must be lawyers.[54] "Both categories of judges have the full constitutional jurisdiction conferred on the Circuit Courts, however, the Supreme Court by rule provides for the matters to be assigned to Associate Judges. At the present time, under Supreme Court Rule 295, the Chief

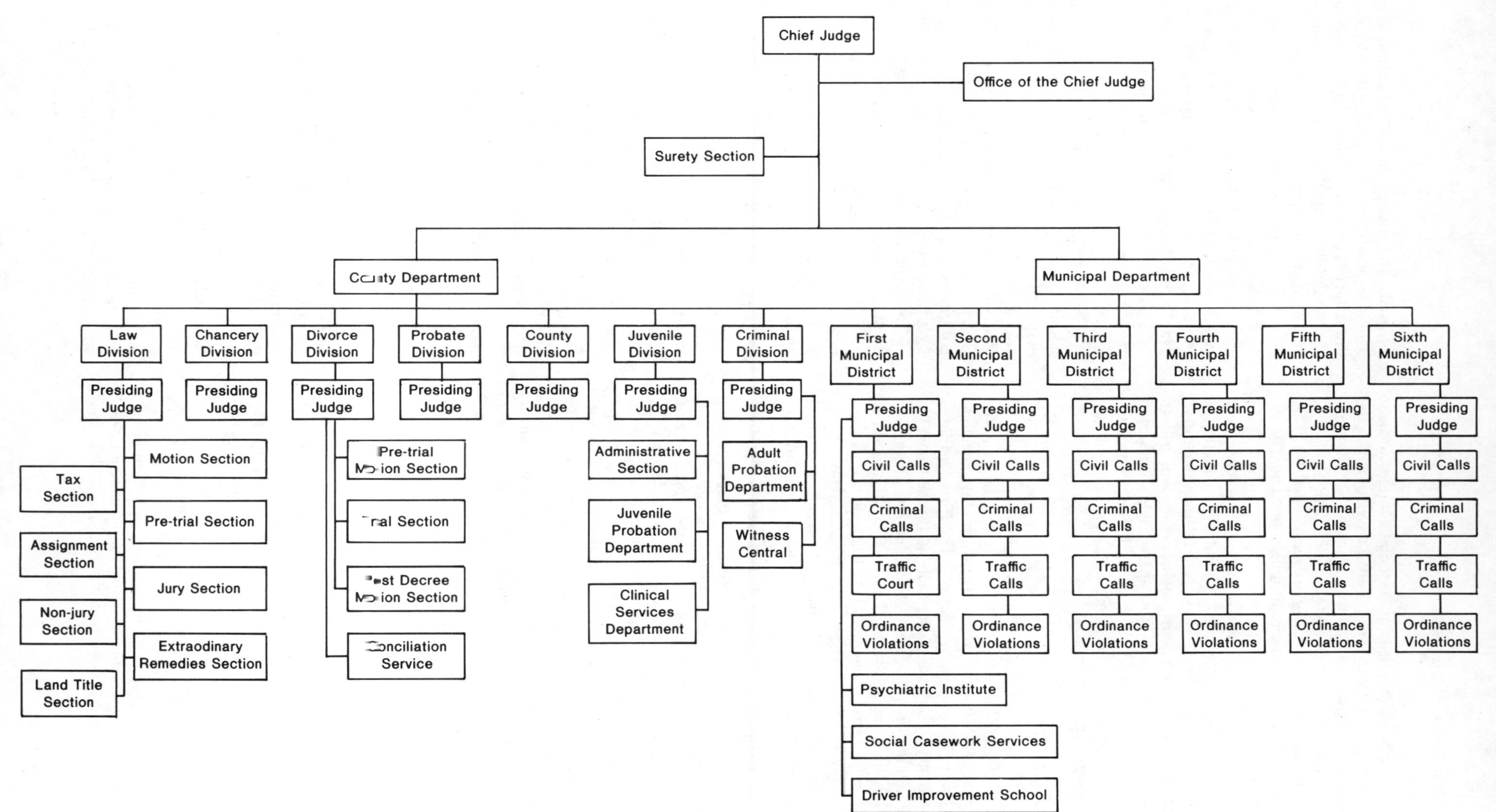

Figure 9-2. CIRCUIT COURT OF COOK COUNTY

Judge of a circuit may assign Associate Judges to hear any matters except the trial of criminal cases in which the defendant is charged with an offense punishable by imprisonment for more than one year."[55] The number of both circuit and associate judges is set by law. In 1977, there were 386 authorized circuit judgeships and 279 authorized associate judgeships.[56]

The circuit judges in each circuit elect from among themselves a Chief Judge of the circuit. The balloting is secret. The Chief Judge has general administrative authority over the circuit court, including the authority to provide for divisions and for appropriate times and places for holding court.[57] The Chief Judge's authority, however, is limited by the Supreme Court's overall administrative authority.

Appellate Court

The State is divided into five judicial districts for the selection of appellate and Supreme Court judges and for the organization of the Appellate Court. An appellate court sits in each of the five districts. The First District is Cook County. The rest of the State is divided into the four remaining districts, each of the districts being substantially equal in population. The exact configuration of these four districts is set by law.[58] Each district is then divided into divisions. There must be at least one division in each district. The authority to create additional divisions lies with the Supreme Court. Each division must have at least three appellate judges. Assignment of judges to divisions within a district is made by the Supreme Court which also sets the time and place for each of the divisions to hear appeals. When deciding cases, a majority of a division constitutes a quorum and a vote of a majority of the division is necessary for a decision.[59]

There are 34 authorized appellate judgeships. Judges are elected for ten-year terms. Eighteen of the judgeships have been allocated to the First District. Each of the other four districts has four judgeships each. Under its administrative authority the Supreme Court has promulgated Rule 22 which states that the divisions will sit in panels of three. The First District is divided into five divisions, all of which sit in the City of Chicago. In the Second District, there are two divisions, both sitting in the City of Elgin. The remaining three districts have one division each. The Third District court sits in Ottawa, the Fourth in Springfield and the Fifth in Mount Vernon. Rule 22 also requires that the judges in each division elect one of their number to serve a one-year term as presiding judge. Together, the presiding judges constitute the Executive Committee of the Appellate Court which exercises general administrative authority. In addition, there is a separate Executive Committee for the First District with five members, one elected from each of the divisions.

Jurisdiction One of the important changes made by the 1964 Judicial Article and retained by the 1970 Constitution was in the appellate jurisdiction of the Supreme Court. The Court's mandatory appellate jurisdiction was cut drastically and its discretionary jurisdiction increased. The result was an expansion of the Appellate Court's jurisdiction. Accordingly, all final judgements from the circuit courts can be appealed to the appropriate division of the Appellate Court as a matter of right. This means that the Appellate Court *must* hear all appeals. The only exceptions are those frew areas in which appeal lies directly to the Supreme Court. There is no appeal from an acquittal in a criminal case.[60] Such an appeal is prohibited by the Double Jeopardy clause of the Fifth Amendment of the United States Constitution and Article 1, Sec. 10 of the Illinois Constitution. Illinois is ". . . one of a few states that provides for appeal as a matter of constitutional right in the intermediate court of review."[61]

The Appellate Court also has jurisdiction to review administrative actions as provided by law. The General Assembly has provided for such appellate jurisdiction in two areas: 1) final decisions and orders of the Illinois Pollution Control Board; and 2) decisions of the State Board of Elections concerning disclosures of campaign contributions and expenditures.[62] Finally, the Appellate Court has some very restricted original jurisdiction.[63]

This expanded jurisdiction caused a ". . . steady and dramatic increase . . ." in caseload between 1964 and 1976.[64] According to the Administrator's Report, 1,211 new appellate cases were filed in 1964, but there were 3,973 new cases filed in 1976.[65] This represents an increase of over 228 percent. As one might expect, the First District is the busiest. In 1976, 1,731 new cases were filed there, over 48 percent of the total filed in 1976.[66]

Supreme Court

Sitting figuratively and administratively atop the Illinois judicial system is the Supreme Court. The Court has seven members, all elected for ten-year terms. According to the Constitution, three justices are elected from the First District. The remaining four justices are elected from the other four districts, one from each district. Four justices constitute a quorum, and a majority of four is needed for a decision. Unlike the Chief Justice of the United States, who is nominated by the President and confirmed by the Senate, the Illinois Chief Justice is a member of the Court chosen by his colleagues to serve a three-year term.

The Court holds five terms per year during January, March, May, September and November. It sits in Springfield, and during the Court's sessions the Justices actually reside in the Supreme Court building. The Court also has quarters in the Civic Center in Chicago where it also meets on a regular basis. It is during these sessions that the Court does its business—judicial as well as administrative and budgetary.[67]

Jurisdiction The Supreme Court has a unique combination of original and appellate jurisdictions. It may exercise original jurisdiction in cases dealing with revenue, mandamus, prohibition or habeas corpus. In saying that the Court *may* exercise original jurisdiction in these areas means that the Court may also delegate to the circuit courts concurrent—or shared—jurisdiction.[68] The Court has exclusive original jurisdiction in cases involving the redistricting of the General Assembly and the ability of the Governor to serve or resume office.[69] This was one of the specific changes made by the 1970 Constitution.

As the "court of last resort" in Illinois, the Supreme Court also possesses appellate jurisdiction. Appeals from decisions of the circuit courts imposing the death penalty are directed to the Supreme Court as a matter of right.[70] The Court may provide for direct appeal in other areas by rule, this being an entirely discretionary decision on the Court's part. Appeals from the Appellate Court to the Supreme Court are a matter of right in two areas: 1) if a question arises under the Illinois *or* the United States Constitution for the first time in and as a result of appellate court action; and 2) if an appellate division certifies that a case it has decided involves a question of such importance that the case should be considered by the Supreme Court. In all other areas, appeal to the Supreme Court is at the Court's discretion.[71] This represents a major change in the Court's appellate jurisdisdiction from that under the 1870 Constitution. The most important result of the change is that the Court now has discretionary control over most of its appellate jurisdiction. Of the 918 petitions filed during 1977, only 138 or 15 percent were accpeted.[72] In spite of the lower acceptance rate, the number of petitions for leave to appeal to the Supreme Court has been steadily increasing since the early 1960's.[73]

As the highest court in Illinois' unified judicial system, the Supreme Court possesses general administrative and supervisory authority over the entire system. This authority is exercised by the Chief Justice in accordance with Supreme Court rules.[74] The Constitution allows the Court to appoint an administrative director and staff to assist the Chief Justice in exercising administrative and supervisory authority.[75] The present administrator is the Honorable Roy O. Gulley. (The Administrator's Office and the details of the Court's administrative authority will be discussed in a later section.)

Court of Claims

The final part of the court structure is the Court of Claims. Its jurisdiction is unique, and its mandate does not stem from the State Constitution. Before the 1970 Constitution, the Court was an administrative body and not a part of the judiciary. This was because the 1870 Constitution included within its provisions the doctrine of sovereign immunity which meant that the State could not have been sued without its permission. As an administrative court, the Court of Claims could not itself award money damages. It could only make recommendations to the General Assembly to appropriate the necessary funds. The General Assembly made the final decision as to whether the award would be paid, and there was no appeal to another court. The 1970 Constitution abolished sovereign immunity except as the General Assembly may provide.[76]

Under the 1970 Constitution, the Court of Claims is an administrative court created by the General Assembly. As such, it can act only if all other possible remedies, both judicial and administrative, have been exhausted. The Court consists of three judges which, unlike judges of constitutional courts, are appointed by the Governor with the advice and consent of the Senate. They serve for six-year terms, one of the three being specifically appointed as the Chief Judge. In addition, nine appointed hearing officers sit throughout the State. The initial hearing for a claim is heard by one of these hearing officers, and a recommendation is forwarded to the Court of Claims. The Court holds regular sessions on the second Tuesday of January, May and November of each year in Springfield. The Secretary of State is the ex officio clerk of the Court, but he appoints a deputy to act for him in this capacity.

By statute the Court of Claims has jurisdiction in eight areas: claims against the State based upon State law or regulation, other than under the Workmen's Compensation Act or the Workmen's Occupational Diseases Act; claims based upon contracts with the State; damage suits for wrongful incarceration; tort actions against the State; claims for recoupment made by the State against any claimant; claims pursuant to the "Law Enforcement Officers and Firemen's Compensation Act;" claims pursuant to the "Crimes Victims Compensation Act;" and claims pursuant to the "Illinois National Guardmen's and Naval Militiaman's Compensation Act."[77]

The General Assembly appropriates funds for the Court to award as damages in these areas at its own discretion. However, claims over $10,000 are usually cleared through the Legislature before an award is made. Because of the unique status of the Court as a legislative and not a constitutional court, appeals from its decisions are not to the Supreme Court, but to the General Assembly. A legislator from the appellee's district may introduce legislation to reverse the Court's decision. Of approximately 3,200 cases filed in 1978, only two were successfully appealed in this way.

Administration

The 1964 reforms had created a unified court structure placing the Supreme Court atop that structure both figuratively and administratively. This position was reaffirmed and strenghthened by the 1970 Constitution. "General administrative and supervisory authority over all courts is vested in the Supreme Court and shall be exercised by the Chief Justice in accordance with its rules."[78] In addition the Court is given the authority to appoint an administrative director and a staff to assist the Court in the exercise of its administrative duties.[79] The Court delegates subordinate administrative authority to the Chief Judge of each appellate district and the Chief Judge of each judicial circuit. The administrative authority of the Court over the remainder of the system is unrestricted. The rationale behind this grant of power is that it is necessary if the Illinois judicial system is to be an efficient mechanism for the administration of justice.

Even though the Court's administrative authority is unrestricted, the Constitution does note in various places some of the specific powers. According to the 1977 Administrator's Report, they are: prescribing the number of Appellate Divisions in each Judicial District; assignment of judges to Appellate Divisions; prescribing the time and place for Appellate Divisions to sit; providing for the manner of appointing Associate Judges; providing for matters assignable to Associate Judges; in the absence of a law, filling judicial vacancies by appointment; prescribing rules of conduct for judges; assignment of retired judges to judicial review; appointment of an administrative Director and staff; temporary assignment of judges; providing for an annual Judicial Conference and reporting thereon annually in writing to the General Assembly; and appointment of the Supreme Court Clerk and other non-judicial officers of the Court.[80] The General Assembly may also provide for other administrative duties by statute. The Court also has the authority to appoint committees to study and suggest amendments in substantive and procedural matters, Supreme Court rules, and other matters affecting the system.[81]

The Supreme Court's administrative authority also includes fiscal matters. General revenue funds are appropriated to the Court by the General Assembly. These funds are administered and monitored by the Court with the aid of the Administrative Office's accounting division. The funds cover salaries for all judges, appellate law clerks, court reporters, clerks of the Supreme and Appellate Courts and related personnel. There are also appropriations for day-to-day operational costs for the upper courts, Administrative Office, Judicial Conference, Impartial Medical Program, travel for judges and court reporters, transcription fees and other miscellaneous accounts.[82] "There are forty-two separate appropriations which, in Fiscal Year 1978, totaled $49,375,561. Of this figure, $36,398,644 was appropriated for judicial and related personnel salaries and $7,630,885 for the operational costs of the previously identified judicial divisions."[83]

Obviously, the Chief Justice cannot handle the Court's administrative duties alone; the Administrative Office exists to help. Since the Court's administrative authority is unrestricted, it is not possible to list all of the Administrative Office's functions. In general, these functions include the following: personnel, fiscal management, continuing judicial education, records and statistics, secretarial, liaison with the legislative and executive branches, management of court facilities and equipment, and research and planning.[84] The Administrative Office has two sites, the headquarters in Springfield and an office in Chicago which is especially concerned with Cook County. As of 1977, the Office employed 28 people.[85]

Non-Judicial Personnel

An understanding of the Illinois judicial system requires an awareness that it relies heavily on "non judicial" ancillary personnel who bring it business and help process cases: the state's attorney, public defenders, circuit court clerks, court administrators, court services personnel, court reporters, sheriffs and private attorneys.

State's Attorney Each county elects a State's Attorney for a four year term. Additional assistant state's attorneys are appointed according to caseload requirements and the availability of funds. The primary function of the State's Attorney's office is to represent the State or the "people" in criminal prosecutions. Additionally, the State's Attorney represents the county government unit in a variety of civil cases involving quasi-criminal matters such as non support, mental health commitments and juvenile violations. The State's Attorney is given a great deal of discretion concerning the types of criminal actions which will be filed in the county. The authority to decide whether or not to prosecute for criminal action is known as prosecutorial discretion.

Public Defender The Public Defender provides legal counsel for persons without sufficient funds to pay for an attorney in criminal and juvenile court matters. Counties over 35,000 population must appoint a Public Defender. This may, depending on the volume of cases, be a full or part-time office. Counties smaller than 35,000 may provide legal counsel for indigents by appointing private attorneys from a rotating list. Two or more counties in the same judicial circuit may join together to appoint a public defender. The Public Defender must be an attorney and is appointed by a majority vote of the circuit judges of the circuit. In most instances, Public Defenders' salaries are paid from county funds.

Circuit Court Clerks Circuit Court Clerks are elected for four year terms at the county level. The Clerk keeps the records of the court. Legal papers necessary for a law suit are filed with the Clerk. There are several persons working in the Clerk's Office. Under the Constitution of the State of Illinois, the Legislature may provide for the appointment of Circuit Court Clerks. Although there is interest in changing to this procedure, there has been no organized effort to allow the appointment of Clerks. Clerks of the five appellate courts and of the supreme court are appointed.

Court Administrators In larger counties, such as Cook and DuPage, the position of Court Administrator is being used more extensively. Court Administrators assist presiding judges in managing court systems. They help in budget, personnel management, scheduling cases, and in dealing with the communications media. Many Court Administrators have degrees in public administration or in the specialized field of court management.

Court Services Personnel Many courts have social services staff members assigned to the court. In Illinois, the provision of probation services is a judicial function. Both juvenile and adult probation are administered by the court. Probation officers are employed by county governments, but State funds help support a portion of their salaries. Court services personnel also investigate adoptions, attempt reconciliations in family matters, and they may become involved in non-support matters.

Court Reporter In Illinois, all courts are considered courts of record. A verbatim record should be made in all cases. Court Reporters keep these records. The salaries of Court Reporters are paid by the State. Court Reporters are appointed by the Chief Judge of the Circuit and serve for an indefinite term. They may be assigned to clerical and secretarial work for judges.

Sheriffs Sheriffs are elected officials of county government. They serve a four year term. In addition to their duties as law enforcement officials, they have many duties associated with the court system. Sheriffs serve summons, writs and other legal documents on parties involved in litigation. They may be ordered by the court to carry out the court's judgements. For example, it is the Sheriff who is ordered to evict a tenant. The Sheriff is responsible for the county jail and is the caretaker of the courthouse. Sheriff's personnel, known as bailiffs, are often present in courtrooms to maintain order.

Private Attorneys In addition to the above public officials, many private attorneys work in the court system, representing clients who bring cases to court. Most civil litigation involves private attorneys. To promote responsibility and accountability, private attorneys are considered officers of the court.

Although Courts are now entirely part of State government, they still have an important relationship to local governments. Judges are elected or appointed at the local level and have been generally active in local political affairs prior to assuming the bench. Since less than one percent of all the cases filed in Illinois are appealed, the local judge in virtually all cases becomes the final arbiter. Additionally, the judiciary has varying, and often indirect degrees of control over many of the officials who work in the county courthouses. The sheriff, state's attorney, circuit court clerk, bailiffs, probation officers, public defenders, and private attorneys all should be conscious of the judge's attitudes on certain matters. The chapter by Mindes explores important issues which involve the role of the legal profession in the system of justice.

Courts at Work

We now have a picture of the structure of the Illinois court system and its place in State government, but our picture requires more. We must also have some understanding of how cases are processed—the business of courts. Since we do not accept the "upper court" myth mentioned at the outset, our discussion on the business of courts will emphasize lower courts, where the trial process and the business of Illinois trial courts is most clearly observed. We begin with the simple but valuable distinction between two broad categories of cases: civil and criminal. While there are many similarities, there are important differences in substance and form. Above all, the major difference is that, in a criminal case, one may be deprived of liberty and even life. Because of this important distinction, the processing of civil and criminal cases is discussed separately.[86]

The Civil Process

Both civil and criminal courts of this country use adversary proceedings. Each side is allowed to give its version of the facts, product favorable witnesses, present legal arguments and criticize the other side's case. The party beginning a lawsuit is called the "plaintiff," and the party against whom action is brought is called the "defendant." The plaintiff's first step is to choose a court with jurisdiction, that is, with legal power to hear the case. The plaintiff then files a complaint outlining the nature of the suit and naming the defendant. The court notifies the defendant, and the lawsuit is on its way. This notification is usually done with a document known as a "summons."

The defendant has a number of options after notification: (1) he may admit the claim and settle it out of court; (2) he may take no action ("default"), in which case the court will enter a judgement in favor of the plaintiff; (3) the defendent may also file an "answer," which states his position on the plaintiff's complaint; (4) finally, the defendant may file a "counterclaim." The legal papers filed in court are known as "pleadings."

Either the defendant or the plaintiff may file a "motion to dismiss" after both pleadings have been submitted to the court. The "motion to dismiss" challenges the legality of a pleading, not the facts contained in the pleadings. The judge then rules on the issues raised without a trial. Cases in which the facts are disputed generally bypass this method and go to trial either with or without a jury.

Modern trial courts have virtually eliminated the Perry Mason-type element of surprise in jury trials. The idea behind the modern code of legal procedures is that both sides should be as fully informed about the opposition's case as possible. It is assumed that truth and justice are better served if both sides are informed about the opposition's facts and arguments. "Pre-trial conferences" between the judge and opposing attorneys serve this purpose by clarifying issues and establishing facts which are not in dispute. "Discovery" procedures also aid in eliminating surprise. Through discovery, parties may require information about the case which the other side possesses. Lists of witnesses and statements of witnesses may also be obtained.

If the suit involves what is essentially a question of law, rather than fact, the trial will probably be held before a judge only. If facts are disputed, the suit may be heard before a jury. Lawyers representing both parties have a role in choosing the jury. Once the jury has been selected, each attorney makes an opening statement summarizing what he or she intends to prove during the trial. During the trial, both parties are allowed to call witnesses and cross-examine opposition witnesses. Finally, each attorney makes a summary statement trying to persuade jury members in favor of his or her client. The judge summarizes evidence that has been presented and explains to the jury the law or laws which apply to the case. Following instructions by the judge, the jury retires to decide on a verdict. The final decision of the court is called a "judgment."

The party which loses at the trial level may appeal to a higher court if an error has been made by the trial court. The appellate court does not stage another trial; instead it reviews the record or transcripts of the trial court to determine the legality of the trial court's decision. If the appellate court disagrees with the law applied by the trial court, it can reverse or modify the trial court's judgment and render its own. Alternatively, the appellate court may order that the case be returned ("remanded") to the trial court for further hearing. The appellate court generally will not reverse or modify a trial court's decision if the issue on appeal involves only an interpretation of facts heard by the trial court.

The Criminal Process

A criminal case generally enters the court system after police arrest of a person accused of violating a law. The "prosecution" (attorney representing the State) then files a complaint. Police and prosecutors often exercise a great deal of discretion at these primary stages, and many accused offenders are released.

In criminal cases, the prosecutor gathers evidence, sometimes calling upon the investigative powers of local or State police in order to demonstrate that the accused is guilty as charged. As in civil cases, discovery rules apply, and the prosecutor must disclose all evidence including that which is beneficial to the defense.

After arrest, the defendant is brought before a judge for hearing. This initial hearing is commonly known as an "arraignment." The court advises the defendant of the charges and of his rights. Bail is then set. "Bail" is an amount of money which is deposited with the court to assure that the defendant will appear for trial. It is forfeited if the defendant does not appear. The court must set bail in all cases except those which are punishable by death. Bail is generally very high for serious crimes.

At a criminal trial the State attempts to demonstrate that the defendant violated a law and deserves punishment. The defendant is presumed innocent until proven guilty and the court must follow a prescribed set of rules. Unless he knowingly waives the right, the defendant must be represented by legal counsel. Innocence or guilt is determined by a jury of the defendant's fellow citizens, unless the right to jury is waived.

In "felony" cases (more serious crimes), the defendant comes before a judge for a preliminary hearing to determine if there is "probable cause" to go to trial. If there is, the judge sets a trial date. The prosecution may, in some instances, use a "grand jury." The grand jury, composed of 23 citizens chosen randomly from voter registration lists, decides whether probable cause exists to believe that the defendant has committed a felony.

At any time during the criminal process, the prosecution and the defendant may attempt to "plea bargain." This is an agreement between the prosecution and defense whereby the defendant agrees to plead guilty to a lesser charge in exchange for a lighter sentence. Nationally, more than 90 percent of criminal cases are settled in this manner.

Sentencing, the final step in the criminal court process differs from civil procedures. The judge has the power to sentence the defendant within the minimum and maximum limits set by the criminal code for the crime in question. A probation officer supplies the judge with a presentence report outlining the defendant's personal and family background, prior record, education and employment. The report also makes a recommendation on how good a risk the defendant would be on probation. As in civil cases, there is a right to appeal.

Probation is the most frequently imposed sentence. The convicted offender is released under the supervision of a probation officer for a period of time set by the court. Violation of probation (which may include leaving the state, quitting a job, using drugs or an excessive amount of alcohol) may mean commitment to prison to serve the original sentence.

The Business of Trial Courts

Most of the day-to-day business of the Illinois court system takes place at the trial level, in the circuit courts. It is here that the average citizen is most likely to come into contact with the system. During 1977, 3,524,456 cases were filed or reinstated in the circuit courts,[87] up from 3,484,572 during 1976.[88] As a point of comparison, fewer than 200,000 cases have been initiated in the federal trial courts in any recent year. Few of the cases begun in the circuit courts are appealed. In 1977, only 4,381 cases were filed in the Appellate Court[89] (in 1976, only 3,973 were appealed[90]). Of course, the caseload of the circuit courts is not evenly distributed throughout the State. During 1977, 2,328,654, or about 66 percent, of 3,524,456 cases initiated were in Cook County. In some downstate counties, fewer than 1,000 cases were filed or reinstated. For instance, in Hardin County near the southern tip of Illinois, only 379 cases were begun in 1979, and in Scott County in west-central Illinois, only 619 were begun.[91] The statewide average (for the 101 counties aside from Cook) is about 11,840 cases per county. The wide variations in caseloads seem to be a result of the combined influences of population, urbanization-industrialization and affluence.

We generally tend to think that trial courts function as institutions for the resolution of genuine controversies. Our model is often akin to courtroom dramatizations on television, stage and screen. However, this view is far from accurate. Courts today seldom settle genuine controversies. Increasingly, the function of trial courts in Illinois and other states has shifted to the administrative processing of routine cases where there is little controversy.[92] Criminal cases in which the defendant pleads guilty or cases where the decisions are made out of court require only court legitimization—such as in many divorce cases.

Circuit courts in Illinois find most of their business in the processing of routine cases. This is perhaps best illustrated by the fact that the largest single category of cases heard by the circuit courts are traffic violations. In 1977, 2,342,770 traffic cases were begun or reinstated.[93] This

TABLE 9-1
Total Circuit Court Caseload by Area: 1977

Law Over $15,000		Law $1000 to $15,000							
Jury	Non-Jury	Jury	Non-Jury	Small Claims	Tax	Eminent Domain	Misc. Remedies	Chancery	Divorce
25,652	9665	13,484	140,099	172,792	113,005	504	6604	24,282	67,025

Mental Health	Municipal Corporation	Probate	Juvenile	Family	Misd.	Ordinance Violations	Conservation Violations	Felony	Traffic
8,290	147	33,929	25,686	20,188	422,954	57,525	7192	31,663	2,343,770

TOTAL
3,524,456

figure represents 66 percent of the circuit courts' business and the percentage holds even without the Cook County cases. Anyone who has ever experienced a traffic court hearing in Illinois knows that trials, when they occur, are perfunctory; large numbers of cases are processed quickly with verdicts rendered and fines paid in rapid succession. Such proceedings are more like "assembly line justice" rather than like traditional stereotyped versions of courtroom confrontations.

The second largest category of cases are those involving ordinance and misdemeanor violations. In 1977, there were 480,479 such cases.[94] These are relatively minor criminal matters, often processed without a formal trial through bargained pleas of guilty. Third, are small claims cases, of which there were 172,792 in 1977.[95] Many of these cases are also routine and quickly processed. Often, small claims courts are little more than bill collection agencies for creditors. Cases are handled quickly since many times debtors never appear. Even when they do, resolution is swift and usually in the creditor's favor. The remaining distribution of caseload is included in Table 9-1.

Participants in the Judicial System

The judiciary is staffed by judges. A variety of professional and support personnel work in the court system. By far, the largest percentage of persons work at the trial level. They work in county courthouses throughout Illinois, in Cook County, Chicago's Daley Center and in the suburban branches of the Circuit Court of Cook County. Although the judiciary is a branch of State government, a significant portion of the cost of maintaining the court system is borne by county government units.

Judicial Personnel

There are two types of judges in Illinois' lower courts; circuit judges and associate circuit judges. With the exception of serious criminal cases, associate circuit judges have the same authority to hear cases as circuit judges. The chief judge of each judicial circuit assigns cases to various judges in the circuit. In larger counties where specialization is possible, classes of cases, such as probate, divorce, and traffic, are assigned to certain judges. Generally, circuit judges are assigned to more important or prestigious cases. Most felony cases, jury trials and probate and estate matters will be heard before circuit judges. Routine cases tend to be heard by associate circuit judges. The circuit judges elect one of their number as Chief Judge of the Circuit for each county. These judges have additional administrative duties. Circuit judges are paid higher salaries than associate circuit judges. Having two levels of judges provides an opportunity for younger lawyers to obtain judicial experience before seeking election as circuit judges. Since 1964, all judges elected or appointed to the bench are required to be attorneys. Circuit judges are elected to six year terms in partisan elections. At the end of their terms, they may stand for re-election in "retention elections." When a candidate makes his or her initial run for a judgeship, he or she is placed on the ballot as a result of a partisan primary or by petition and is generally run with party identification and party support. Once elected, however, judges are prohibited from engaging in political activities; therefore, when they seek reelection, it is on a "nonpartisan" basis. To remain in office, a judge must receive an affirmative vote from 60 percent of the voters.

Merit Selection vs. Political Election of Judges The method of selecting judges is an issue which has been debated for several decades. The two basic methods used for judicial selection in the United States are election and appointment. Elective methods may be either partisan or nonpartisan. In partisan elections the judicial candidate is nominated by a party and runs with a party identification. In nonpartisan elections the judicial candidate is generally nominated in a nonpartisan primary and runs in the general election without a party label.

Proponents of the different plans for judicial selection disagree about allocating authority for nominations. Most states use a combination of elected and appointed systems. Nominations, under different plans, can be made either by the governor, legislature or by a judicial nominating commission. The method which uses a judicial nominating commission is generally referred to as merit selection or the Missouri plan. Missouri uses merit selection for its state appellate and supreme court judges and its trial judges in the counties of St. Louis, Jackson (Kansas City), Clay and Platte, but election is used to select trial judges in the rest of the state.[96] Executive and legislative appointment plans are popular principally among the original thirteen states. In many of these states, appointments by the governor must have the advice and consent of at least one of the houses of the State legislature.

In recent years, there has been a trend toward the use of merit selection.[97] Twenty-seven states now select some of their judges through a merit selection process. No state has changed to any plan other than merit selection during the last 25 years. A state is considered a merit state if some judges are appointed by merit plan or if some element of a merit selection process is found within the state. Currently, the federal judiciary is selected by executive appointment. The President makes all judicial appointments with the advice and consent of the Senate, but significant roles are played in the selection process by the senator of the President's party from the state in which the vacancy exists, the Justice Department and the American Bar Association.[98] In 1978 President Jimmy Carter took the first step in selecting U.S. judges on merit by establishing the U.S. Circuit Court Judge Nominating Commission to propose candidates for the U.S. Court of Appeals.

A merit selection plan generally has three key elements: (1) a list of qualified candidates (usually three) developed by a nonpartisan judicial nominating commission consisting of lawyers and nonlawyers; (2) appointment of the judge by the governor from a list developed by the nominating commission; and (3) a short probation period for the judge followed by a retention election in which the judge has no opponent but must receive enough "yes" votes to be retained.

The major variation in merit selection states is found in the membership of the nominating commission. In some states, the majority of the commission consists of lawyers; in others, nonlawyers constitute the majority. The number of commission members selected by the governor or bar association also varies. In Missouri, the nominating commission for appointing trial judges consists of two lawyers who practice in the district, two nonlawyers appointed by the Governor and the presiding judge of the appellate court. In theory, these members vigorously screen candidates and nominate three qualified individuals. The governor must appoint one of the three. The commission is designed to represent several interests: the interests of the bar by lawyers, the judiciary by chief appellate judges, and the general public by members appointed by the governor. The authority to choose one out of the three candidates nominated gives the governor a significant role in the selection process.

Proponents of merit selection contend that higher quality, more independent judges are placed on the bench through merit selection. The qualifications of judicial candidates are thoroughly reviewed by a panel whose members have the expertise necessary to evaluate characteristics of a good judge. It is also contended that lawyers with exceptional judicial talents are more likely to seek judicial office through merit selection than through the political nominating process. With merit selection, lawyers no longer have to develop political support within a political party in order to obtain a judicial nomination. Theoretically, political influence is minimized, and independence of the judiciary is insured because judges no longer seek party support. The partisan election system is criticized on the grounds that political influence dominates, because (1) a majority of the voters do not know the candidates in a judicial election; (2) judicial campaigns usually attract little attention; and (3) the general public has no criteria for determining which candidate will make a good judge.

Defenders of the election system generally begin with an impassioned plea for democracy. They argue that judges make law and that the public must have a voice in the lawmaking process. It is contended that members of racial and ethnic minority groups have a better opportunity to become judges through the local political processes than through a merit selection process. Furthermore, it is argued that politics are not removed from the "merit" selection process; that gubernatorial and bar association politics are merely substituted for local politics, and the general public is left out of the system.

The history of how Illinois developed its current system of judicial selection is a history of political controversy. Prior to 1964, when the Judicial Article went into effect, Illinois' court system was totally disorganized. There was no centralized court administrative office, and there were courts with overlapping jurisdiction in counties and towns. In the early 1950's, the Illinois Bar Association and the Chicago Bar Association, with the support of several civic organizations, began a campaign for court reform. The reform had dual goals to establish a unified court system and to enact a merit selection plan. Generally, this plan had the support of Republican Governor William G. Stratton and the Republicans in the Legislature, but it was opposed by the Democrats, particularly Democrats from Chicago. In 1957, a compromise reached in the Legislature took the form of a proposal for a constitutional amendment to unify the court system. No change in the system of electing judges was included. The proposed amendment was defeated by a slim margin in the statewide vote.

Determined to succeed, proponents for court reform almost immediately began another campaign for a constitutional amendment, but the Chicago Democrats continued opposition to changes relating to partisan election of judges. The need for court reorganization was pressing, and the Legislature tackled it again, finally reaching a compromise similar to the 1957 plan. The Legislature proposed a constitutional amendment to create a unified court system. Finally, in 1962 voters ratified an amendment, and by 1964 Illinois courts were reorganized.

Although judges were still subject to election, there were two significant changes. First, judges no longer had to be reelected in a partisan election campaign. This was accompanied by the prohibition that judges could not actively participate in political activities. Second, the appointment system for associate circuit judges was created.

The issue of merit selection surfaced again during the Constitutional Convention of 1969. It was vigorously debated, and the Convention deadlocked over the issue. Finally, the Convention reached a compromise which placed the issue before the general public on the ballot as a special question. In addition to voting on the entire con stitution, voters had the option of selecting either election or appointment of judges. The campaign over the options was vigorous. Mayor Richard J. Daley and the Cook County regular Democrats actively supported election. Chicago newspapers, bar associations and civic groups generally favored appointment. In the final tally, 50.2 percent of the voters statewide approved election. The chapter by David Kenney analyzes this entire episode in depth.

Another significant reform was included in the adopted constitution and eliminated the selection of judicial candidates by party convention. The effect of these changes was to weaken the role of political party leaders in judicial elections. For example, in 1976, two candidates for Supreme Court Judge's positions, James Dooley and William Clark, defeated candidates backed by the Cook County Regular Democratic Organization in the judicial primary, and they won in the general election. Although the party primary is the principal vehicle through which judges are nominated for the general election, the Constitution also provides for being placed on the ballot by citizen petition.

Removal of Judges One of the most difficult policy issues involving the judiciary is the issue of removing judges from office. There are two separate issues involved in removal: first, misconduct and physical or mental incapacity; second, decisions inconsistent with the views of the majority of the electorate.

This latter issue is extremely difficult to resolve. A judge should be independent of direct political influences, yet the judge's decisions should reflect the general consensus of the law held by the society. The federal system has resolved the issue clearly in favor of an independent judiciary. Federal judges are appointed for life. With the exception of impeachment proceedings which have rarely been used, federal judges cannot be removed from office. The majority of the states, on the other hand, have opted for some degree of voter control. There are 41 states where the judiciary must face some type of retention process.[99]

All states have methods for removing incompetent judges and judges who have engaged in misconduct. There is a definite trend to the development of a judicial disciplinary commission to review charges against the judiciary. Thirty-one states now have judicial discipline commissions.[100]. The discipline commission is usually made up of judges. However, lawyers and non-lawyers are often put on these commissions.

Illinois uses three methods of removing judges: (1) the retention election cited above, (2) mandatory retirement, and (3) a judicial discipline commission.

The retention election gives the voters some voice in the decision process. Yet, at the same time, it does not force a sitting judge to become involved in a partisan political election. Critics point out that the general population does not have sufficient knowledge to evaluate the judge. The lack of an election opponent diminishes the possibility that any issues will be raised during the election. Since 1964, when the retention system was first used, of the 524 judges running for election, only six have not been retained.[101] Illinois' two bar associations, the Illinois State Bar Association and the Chicago Bar Association, rate judges as qualified or unqualified. This information is released to the public. However, of the 33 judges rated as unqualified by the bar associations between 1970 and 1978, thrity-one were elected.[102] The retention election, nevertheless, does afford some degree of judicial accountability to the general public. Judges must be conscious that at some point in the future they will have to face reelection. The retention election is an effort to strike a balance between the conflicting goals of popular control and an independent judiciary.

By statute, all judges in Illinois must retire during the year in which they reach their seventieth birthday. Mandatory retirement has eliminated most problems caused by judges who are physically or mentally incapable of continuing to serve. Judges have a generous pension system which encourages judges to voluntarily retire before the mandatory age. Retired judges can be assigned to the bench for a temporary period to fill vacancies and meet special needs.

Illinois has developed an elaborate system of judicial discipline. The Illinois Constitution created two independent agencies, the Judicial Inquiry Board and the Illinois Courts Commission, to investigate and hear cases of judicial wrongdoing. The problems of judicial discipline attracted much attention during the 1970 Constitutional Convention because two Illinois State Supreme Court judges resigned following an investigation of judicial misconduct shortly before the start of the Convention. Public attention was focused on the need for judicial discipline. The weaknesses of the Illinois system were widely discussed. Under the system which now exists, the Judicial Inquiry Board has the responsibility to investigate allegations of judicial wrongdoing or incapacity and to recommend action to the Illinois Courts Commission. The Illinois Courts Commission hears cases and applies remedial actions ranging from censure to removal from office. The decisions of the Courts Commission can be appealed to the Illinois Supreme Court.

The Judicial Inquiry Board consists of nine members—two judges appointed by the Supreme Court, four non-lawyers and three lawyers. The lawyers and non-lawyers are appointed by the Governor. The Judicial Advisory Board also has an executive director and an investigative staff. The Courts Commission consists of five judges—one Supreme Court judge, two Appellate judges, and two Circuit judges. During the first six years of its investigations, the Board investigated 605 cases. The large majority of these cases, 506, were closed following only minimal screening investigation. Seventy-eight were closed following a thorough investigation and twenty-one were referred to the Courts Commission. Through 1976, the Courts Commission took some form of disciplinary action in nineteen of the cases.[103]

Conclusion

Three trends in the Illinois judicial system foreshadow future developments. First, there has been a steady increase in the demand placed upon the system—more and more cases. There is every indication that the trend will continue. This increasing caseload has led, in part, to the consideration of alternative ways of handling these ever-growing demands *and* of enhancing the quality of the process. This leads us to the other two trends, increased professionalization and increased centralization, which raise the most perplexing questions. Each is seen as a way of improving the operation of the Illinois judicial system. Increased professionalization has come in many forms, such as the constitutional requirement that all judges be lawyers or the rise of specially trained court administrators. In general, this is a trend toward having experts as the only official actors in the judicial process along with making the choice of many such experts the responsibility of other experts and not the citizenry. Increased centralization has come primarily in the form of a unified court structure, meaning that the Supreme Court has administrative authority over the entire state judicial system. Centralization is pursued as the way of improving the system's efficiency—handling the most cases for the least possible money.

These two trends pose for the people and policymakers of the State difficult and sensitive questions concerning their courts. Increased professionalization moves control of the system farther and farther away from the average citizen, making the accountability of these experts tenuous at best. At some point, a balance must be struck between the reliance upon so-called experts and self-government. This problem is aggravated by the trend toward centralization which decreases local control and may eventually decrease local services. Some have suggested, in the interest of cost-efficiency, that circuit courts discontinue the current practice of sitting in every county. Instead, the suggestion is made for circuit courts to sit only in regional centers. This means, of course, that most counties would not have their own courts. The availability of court services would be farther removed from the local community, raising questions of public accessibility. Again, a balance must be struck between cost-efficiency on the one hand and local control and ease of accessibility on the other.

Both professionalization and centralization have been the mainstays of the court reform movement in Illinois and other states. Such "reforms" have been supported by people of good intentions, but whether these "reforms" actually result in an improved system is debatable. Maintaining an efficient, yet responsive judicial system within a complex society offers many challenges. How to achieve balance between desirable but often conflicting goals continually raises crucial questions of policy. We can only leave you with the vexing questions, but we remind you that answers to judicial policy questions will ultimately come through the political process.

QUESTIONS FOR FURTHER RESEARCH

1. What role do courts play in our society? Is knowledge of the courts necessary to understand the system of government?
2. Why can it be said that courts are political institutions?
3. Can law be separated from the political system?
4. Are trial courts or appellate courts more important?
5. What were the principal changes made in the Judicial Amendments which went into effect in 1964?
6. Trace the history of judicial reform in Illinois for the last twenty-five years. Describe the dominant trends.
7. To what extent should judges be independent of politics?
8. It is almost certain that the issue of merit vs elected judges will again surface in Illinois. Which do you favor? Why?
9. Court reformers are advocating that circuit court clerks become appointed rather than elected and that court administrator positions be developed. Do you favor their suggestion? Why?
10. If a plan were developed to consolidate the courts into one large circuit court closing several of the courthouses in counties with small populations, would you favor this plan? Why?

NOTES

[1]Harold Lasswell, *Politics: Who Gets What, When, How* (New York: McGraw Hill, 1936).

[2]See David Easton, *The Political System* (New York: Knopf, 1960), especially Chapter V in which Easton defines politics as the authoritative allocation of values or valued things.

[3]Jerome Frank, *Courts on Trial: Myth and Reality in American Justice* (Princeton: Princeton University Press, 1949), p. 222.

[4]In a May 3, 1907 speech, Charles Evans Hughes, later Chief Justice of the United States, made the following statement: "We are under a Constitution, but the Constitution is what the judges say it is," quoted in William B. Lockhart, *et al., The American Constitution: Cases and Materials* (St. Paul: West Publishing Co., 1975), p. 7.

[5]Herbert Jacob, *Justice in America: Courts, Lawyers, and the Judicial Process,* (3d ed.; Boston: Little, Brown, 1978), p. 4.

[6]Jacob, *op. cit.*, p. 6.

[7]Daniel J. Boorstin, "The Perils of Indwelling Law," in Robert Paul Wolff, ed., *The Rule of Law* (New York: Simon and Schuster, 1971), p. 76.

[8]Alexis de Tocqueville, *Democracy in America,* ed. by Richard D. Heffner (New York: New American Library, 1956), p. 126.

[9]For an account of the Wilsonville suit, see Harold Hendersen's four part series in the *Illinois Times:* ''Wilsonville's War on Waste,'' October 13–19, 1978; ''Earthline Company of Wilsonville,'' October 20–26, 1978; ''Wilsonville: Politics and the EPA, October 27–November 2, 1978; and ''Living.''

[10]336 N.E. 2d 1, 61 Ill. 2d 353 (1975).

[11]37 N.E. 2d 602, 69 Ill. 2d 252 (1977).

[12]280 N.E. 2d 208, 50 Ill. 2d 351 (1972).

[13]*Sovada v. White Motor Co.,* 210 N.E. 2d 182, 33 Ill. 2d 612 (1964).

[14]163 N.E. 2d 89, 18 Ill. 2d 11 (1960).

[15]*People v. Webber,* 362 N.E. 2d 399, 47 Ill. App. 3d 543 (1977).

[16]Henry Abramson, *The Judicial Process* (2d ed., New York: Oxford University Press 1968), p. 283.

[17]1 Cranch 137 (1803).

[18]Clyde Kluckhohn, ''The Study of Culture,'' in *The Policy Sciences,* ed. by Daniel Lerner and Harold Lassell (Stanford: Stanford University Press, 1951), p. 86.

[19]Lucien Pye, ''Political Culture,'' in *International Encyclopedia of the Social Sciences* 12 (1968), 218.

[20]See Grossman's Chapter 6 ''The Legal System,'' in *American Politics: The People and the Policy,* ed. by Peter K. Eisinger, *et al.* (Boston: Little, Brown, 1978). Most of our discussion of legal culture is based upon Grossman's idea of legal culture.

[21]Carl J. Friedrich, ''Constitutions and Constitutionalism'' in *International Encyclopedia of the Social Sciences* (1968), Vol. 3, pp. 319–20.

[22]See Stuart Scheingold, *The Politics of Rights: Lawyers, Public Policy, and Political Change* (New Haven: Yale University Press, 1974), Chapter 2, ''Law as Ideology: An Introduction to the Myth of Rights.''

[23]Scheingold, *op. cit.,* p. 25.

[24]Judith N. Sklar, *Legalism* (Cambridge: Harvard University Press, 1964), p. 1.

[25]*1976 Annual Report to the Supreme Court of Illinois* (Springfield: Administrative Office of the Illinois Courts, 1977), p. 33.

[26]See Joel B. Grossman and Austin Sarat, ''Litigation in the Federal Courts: A Comparative Perspective,'' *Law and Society Review* 9:2 (Winter 1975), 336.

[27]*Black's Law Dictionary,* 4th ed., defines a petit jury as an ordinary jury for the trial of civil or criminal matters. A grand jury is defined as a jury of inquiry summoned for a fixed period of time to receive complaints and accusations in criminal cases, hear the evidence presented by the state, and issue bills of indictment in those cases where they feel a trial should be held. It is called a grand jury to distinguish it from the petit jury. Usually a petit jury will have from 6 to 12 members, and a grand jury will usually have from 12 to 23 members. The exact numbers will vary from state to state. In Illinois it is 23 for the grand jury and 12 for the petit jury. Ill. Rev. Stat. Ch. 78, Sec. 16 and Ill. Rev. Stat. Ch. 78, Sec. 20.

[28]For an interesting and provocative discussion of the American legal profession see Jerold S. Auerbach, *Unequal Justice: Lawyers and Social Change in Modern America* (New York: Oxford University Press, 1976).

[29]See Abraham Blumberg, ''The Practice of Law as a Confidence Game,'' in *Law and Society Review* 1:2 (June 1967).

[30]*1976 Annual Report,* p. 43.

[31]Frank, *op. cit.,* p. 80.

[32]Marian Neef and Stuart Nagel, ''The Adversary Nature of the American Legal System from a Historical Perspective,'' *New York Law Forum* 20 (1974), 123–24.

[33]Frank, *op. cit.,* p. 92.

[34]David F. Rolewick, *A Short History of the Illinois Judicial Systems,* (1971 rev. ed.; Springfield: Administrative Office of the Illinois Courts), p. 11.

[35]*Ibid.,* p. 12.

[36]*Ibid.,* p. 19.

[36]*Ibid.*

[38]Rubin Cohn, ''The Illinois Judicial Department: Changes Effected by the Constitution of 1970,'' *Illinois Law Forum* 1971:3 (1971), 356.

[39]*Ibid.*

[40]See Henry Glick and Kenneth Vines, *State Court Systems* (Englewood Cliffs: Prentice-Hall, 1973), pp. 28–33.

[41]Kenneth Vines and Herbert Jacob, ''State Courts and Public Policy,'' in *Politics in the American States: A Comparative Analysis,* ed. by Herbert Jacob and Kenneth N. Vines (3d ed.; Boston: Little, Brown, 1976), p. 247.

[42]Ill. Rev. Stat., Ch. 37, Sec. 72.1.

[43]1970 Constitution, Article VI, Sec. 7a.

[44]*1976 Annual Report,* p. 32.

[45]1970 Constitution, Article VI, Sec. 7b.

[46]Cohn, *op. cit.,* p. 364.

[47]Samuel Gove, ''The Judicial Function in Illinois State Government,'' in *Workbook on Illinois State Government,* ed. by Samuel Gove (Springfield: Auditor General's Office, 1978), p. 7.

[48]Cohn, *op. cit.,* p. 356.

[49]*1976 Annual Report,* p. 32.

[50]Cohn, *op. cit.,* p. 356.

[51]Rolewick, *op. cit.,* Chapter VII.

[52]Cohn, *op. cit.,* p. 365.

[53]*Ibid.,* pp. 365–66.

[54]1970 Constitution, Article VI, Sec. II.

[55]*1976 Annual Report,* p. 32.

[56]*1977 Annual Report to the Illinois Supreme Court,* (Srpingfield: Administrative Office of the Illinois Courts, 1978), p. 64.

[57]1970 Constitution, Article VI, Sec. 7c.

[58]*Ibid.,* Sec. 2.

[59]*Ibid.,* Sec. 5.

[60]*Ibid.,* Sec. 6.

[61]*1976 Annual Report,* p. 27.

[62]*Ibid.,* pp. 26–27.

[63]1970 Constitution, Article VI. Sec. 6.

[64]*1976 Annual Report,* p. 27.

[65]*Ibid.*

[66]*Ibid.,* p. 96.

[67]*Ibid.,* p. 15.

[68]1970 Constitution, Article VI, Sec. 4a.

[69]*Ibid.,* Sec. 9.

[70]*Ibid.,* Sec. 4b.

[71]*Ibid.,* Sec. 4c.

[72]*1977 Annual Report,* p. 14.

[73]*Ibid.,* p. 106.

[74]1970 Constitution, Article VI, Sec. 16.

[75]*Ibid.*

[76]*Ibid.,* Article XIII. Sec. 4.

[77]Ill. Rev. Stat. Ch. 37, Sec. 439.8.

[78]1970 Constitution, Article VI, Sec. 16.

[79]*Ibid.*

[80]*1977 Annual Report,* p. 13.

[81]*Ibid.,* p. 14.

[82]*Ibid.,* p. 78.

[83]*Ibid.*

[84]*Ibid.*

[85]*Ibid.*

[86]This discussion is taken from Frank Kopecky, ''Introduction,'' in *Current Illinois Legal Issues* (Springfield: *Illinois Issues Magazine,* 1978), pp. 2–3.

[87]*1977 Annual Report,* p. 163.

[88]*1976 Annual Report,* p. 139.

[89]*1977 Annual Report,* p. 35.

[90]*1976 Annual Report,* p. 28.

[91]*1977 Annual Report,* p. 135 and p. 145.

[92]This pattern has been found in California, see Lawrence Friedman and Robert Percival, ''A Tale of Two Courts: Litigation in Alameda and San Benito Counties, ''*Law and Society Review*'' 10 2 Winter 1976.

[93]*1977 Annual Report*

[94]*Ibid.*

[95]*Ibid.*

[96]See Richard Watson and Ronald Downing, *The Politics of the Bench and Bar: Judicial Selection Under the Missouri Nonpartisan Court Plan* (New York: John Wiley, 1969).

[97]This discussion is based upon Frank Kopecky, "Should Judges be Elected or Appointed? *Illinois Issues* 3:12 (December 1977).

[98]See Joel B. Grossman, *Lawyers and Judges* (New York: John Wiley, 1965).

[99]Edward S. Schoenbaum, "A Historical Lack of Judicial Discipline," *Chicago-Kent Law Review* 54 (1977), 10.

[100]Schoenbaum, *op. cit.*, p. 21.

[101]Paul Lermack, "Illinois Judges: Too Much Retention and Too Little Selection," *Illinois Issues* 5:6 (June 1979), 9.

[102]*Ibid.*

[103]Frank Greenberg, "Illinois' Two-Tiered Judicial Discipline System," *Chicago-Kent Law Review* 54 (1977), 115.

SUPPLEMENTAL READINGS

Blumberg, Abraham. "The Practice of Law as a Confidence Game." *Law and Society Review.* 1:2 (June 1967).

Cohn, Rubin. "The Illinois Judicial Department: Changes Effected by the Constitution of 1970." *Illinois Law Forum* 1971:3 (1971).

Jacob, Herbert. *Justice in America: Courts, Lawyers, and the Judicial Process.* 3d ed. Boston: Little, Brown, 1978.

Jerome, Frank. *Courts on Trial: Myth and Reality in American Justice.* Princeton: Princeton University Press, 1949.

Kopecky, Frank. "Introduction." *Current Illinois Legal Issues.* Springfield: Illinois Issues Magazine, 1978, pp. 2–5.

1977 Annual Report to the Illinois Supreme Court. Springfield: Administrative Office of the Illinois Courts, 1978.

1976 Annual Report to the Supreme Court of Illinois. Springfield: Administrative Office of the Illinois Courts, 1977.

Rolewick, Davie F. *A Short History of the Illinois Judicial Systems.* 1971 rev. ed. Springfield: Administrative Office of the Illinois Courts, 1971.

CHAPTER **10**

Courts, Lawyers and the Realities of the Law

Marvin W. Mindes

This chapter explores the relationship of the formal law and legal system to real human behavior. It begins with a preliminary examination of the relationship and its consequences, via a brief history of recent legal thinking. It introduces issues of law impact with special emphasis on the limits of our court system. Finally, some emerging systemic stresses and related issues are identified.

On both surface and underlying levels the legal enterprise in America deals with the distribution of values—and thus is directly political. Courts are specifically focused on handling conflicts between opposing parties, either for quantities of jointly valued goods or for alternative values. They also intervene robustly in other political processes. We have an adversarial legal profession which has a power and reach unique throughout the world. This factor, buttressed by the market system and our frontier heritage, has given strong adversarial and distributive orientations to all law-type activities. This includes the non-court work of lawyers (which constitutes most of their activity) and much work in government and in law-related institutions (e.g., title companies, insurers, CPAs)—in fact, it extends to the reciprocal and related activity of practically everyone! We increasingly rely on legal institutions to resolve private conflicts.

Law As Behavior

The law is sometimes spoken of by lawyers and others as an abstract body of rules, appearing partly in books of statutes, ordinances and regulations and, in our system, partly in case law handed down by judges. Not only is this formal law a human product, but also, it can only be given effect by human *actors*. The behavior of these actors may be looked at in various ways: it is channeled and habituated in various roles—lawyers, litigants, administrators, legislators, police, arrestees and beneficiaries. These roles are played in, and by, various *institutions*—courts, legislatures, bar associations, state houses and government agencies. Behavior is also shaped by (and reflected in) beliefs, feelings, reactions, thoughts, values and knowledge more or less commonly held—in other words, a *legal culture*. Moreover, all of these elements—rules, roles, institutions and culture—are not in any fixed relationship with each other. Rather they exist in numerous interchanges or dialectics, each with the others and with various other human arrangements and systems—private business, labor, the family, housing, welfare, schools, etc. The most important aspects of the Illinois legal system consist not of the formal rules, but rather of their reflection of our national legal culture and its associated dominant patterns of behavior.

A clear illustration of this is in the basic *theoretical* differences between the so-called common law states, such as Illinois (along with most northern, midwestern and eastern states) and those states, such as Florida, Louisiana and California, whose laws descend from civil law systems of Continental Europe. Examination of these two types of legal systems shows that the *practical* impact of civil law origins is almost nil in most cases and that even in areas which are matters of state and local governance, the substance of the institutions and roles is by and large the same as in the common law states.

Thus, Illinois case law regarding damages from auto accidents is largely similar to that of most other states, as a result of national professional communication processes rather than formal authority. Admittedly this incremental evolution of legal behavior can at times be overridden by major policy initiatives such as the current wave of no-fault legislation, whereby several states have removed smaller accident cases from the courts. Because of the strength of our judiciary under the 1970 Illinois Constitution, a rudimentary and limited auto no-fault bill was invalidated by the Illinois Supreme Court. Despite these important exceptions, most legal behavior is shaped by incremental informal adaptation.

There are variations even in the underlying phenomena on which this chapter focuses. Behavior and problems differ somewhat based on type of community—metropolitan, suburban or rural; southern vs. northern influences; ethnic and racial origin; degree and nature of wealth or impoverishment. By and large, however, such variations within Illinois are not unique but representative of national variations.

Dissonance Between Formal Law and Law As Behavior

Focusing on the distinction between law as a set of formal rules, on the one hand, and law as behavior on the other, is particularly important because of the pervasive tendency—embodied in our thought and language—to ignore it. Thus newspapers almost daily titillate and shock us with stories that government agencies, corporations and others "break" the law, that legal rules are not "working" or do not accomplish their "intent." The underlying notion often appears to be that there is, can or should be an underlying reality or efficacy about legal rules as such, a version, perhaps, of the primitive belief in the magical powers of words! One consequence of this belief is a tendency to overuse laws and courts to the exclusion of other approaches. Another is that public discourse is all too often simplistic or illusional. Kenneth Culp Davis[1] points out how the legal dogma prohibiting delegation of legislative discretion prevents us from recognizing when such delegation exists—such as discretion in the police, prosecutors and others—and dealing rationally to govern it. The popular version of this is the quixotic notion that the police should have no discretion as to which laws they enforce. Another consequence of unreal expectations is that individuals and groups may become cynical, disillusioned and alienated when they discover the difference between myth and reality. Finally, such a belief blocks perception of experience so that those holding it are wrapped in a mist as to the real nature of their legal problems and situation.

From the descriptive point of view our formal law is but one partial map covering limited aspects of the territory of behavior. Some of the other maps are political science, sociology, psychology, economics, science, technology, history, fiction and popular song. Moreover, as a map law is often smudged, torn, contradictory, unreadable and inaccurate to such an extent as to be highly treacherous unless supplemented by substantial quantities of other general and expert knowledge. For example, a standard Illinois form lease, until recently in general use and still having some currency, provided for landlord "self-help" in evicting tenants, i.e., throwing or locking them out himself. This created substantial civil liability for the landlord who used it.

Actual practices vary locally and situationally: some local courts will turn a deaf ear to tenant grievances; police may refuse to help a "deadbeat" who is a stranger to the community; related landlords and tenants may work out problems peacefully or engage in the bitterest of lawsuits. Other factors are the assertiveness or influence of landlord and tenant and a host of interacting rules and circumstances including knowledge of the law and availability of attorneys. For another example, divorce by mutual consent rather than for cause is theoretically illegal but practically allowed. Even under Illinois law prior to 1977 (when this was somewhat easted), in DuPage County one spouse with consent of the other could file a complaint, have a "trial" and a final decree signed on the same morning. In Cook County, because of court congestion and public relations concerns the same process took from 60 to 90 days. An internationally renowned scholar, Max Rheinstein[2] of the University of Chicago Law School, pointed out that no law against divorce can force people to live together against their will—and no country tries to do so. A "tough" divorce law merely prevents people from entering new legally recognized marriages.

The law conflicts and interacts with other normative or expectational systems—those imposed by religion, internalized moral code, family, peer group and organizational loyalties, as well as the various imperatives of biological and even situational needs as they vary from time to time. The impact of other demands is illustrated by protest of unjust laws for reasons of conscience, breaking the speed law to keep a date, and by ceremonial murder as initiation into a street gang. "Other demands" also include some urban groups' customary use of public sidewalks as social gathering places in violation of local laws against loitering. The impact of extra-legal factors is recognized by the police who may ignore not only the loitering and curfew violations, as in the last case, but also marijuana smoking or low-level dealing in harder drugs. In reality, stringency of enforcement depends largely on police interpretation of the situation: Is this a real threat? What activities are being planned? What is the danger of a general confrontation?

Indeed, honest and effective policemen will often ignore violations of the law which they or the public regard as quite serious. They may do this in order to secure needed information or evidence, to prevent or detect worse crimes, or to avoid what they perceive to be substantive injustice in the literal application of the law. Less desirably, policemen, like lawyers, students, industrial employees or physicians, when confronted with rule violations by their peers, will often look the other way or cover up.

The point of the above discussion is not that laws have no effect, or that many laws are not in fact accurately communicated and carried out (such as the criminal prohibition against counterfeiting the currency) or that there is not harmony between some laws and the group, individual and cultural norms that buttress them (the law against killing one's mother is in most instances a clear, obeyed and enforced dictate). Nor do we argue that our law should not be much simpler, clearer and more consistent than it is. The point is that the impact of a legal rule, its correspondence with behavior, and its enforcement are dependent upon its interplay with numerous other factors and circumstances in the culture and in the environment.

American Legal Thought

However, not only was this simple fact of legal life denied in the American legal theory of the last century, but the prevailing legal culture and juristic philosophy took the position that law itself was not a social product subject to social causes and inputs. Rather, judges derived our public law from the "eternal principles" of the natural law via constitutionalism, and our civil law from the immutable principles of the common law as discovered and applied by judges who were said to apply these rules mechanically to determine specific cases. Reinforcing this special role concept of the judiciary was the unique power and autonomy of the American legal profession, of which the judges were a special part. Taken together these made possible the general position and attitude of law as an isolated body of rules and principles standing apart from society and having a theoretically automatic impact upon it in a one-way flow.

This concept was further buttressed and rationalized with the rise of the modern American law school at Harvard in 1870. Dean Christopher Columbus Langdell conceived law to be a science composed of rational principles to be learned empirically from the study of appellate court decisions. The Harvad pattern has come to be, with variations, the national model of American legal education. While the model has since evolved theoretically, the Socratic dialogue Langdell introduced still plays a central role in law schools. Similarly, although formally prevailing theory has changed substantially, the general legal enterprise still reflects many of the patterns of decision, language and thought of the old order.

The first major critics of the traditional position, beginning in the late 19th Century, were Holmes and Thayer. These writers emphasized law as an historical process and argued that the course of the law was a developing one determined by matters generally not considered in judicial opinions, particularly social and political pressures and conflicts. The early 20th Century saw the rise of sociological jurisprudence led by men such as Brandeis, Pound and Frankfurter. These scholars emphasized the way in which the law responded to nonlegal facts such as economic factors, working conditions and the actual operation of the criminal justice system. They went on to suggest how the law might implement its higher ideals by recognizing and relating to these aspects of the real world—including by social experiment. It was a third generation of thinkers, starting in the 1920s, who argued that not only should law take cognizance of facts outside of the legal system, but that extralegal facts, values and viewpoints had strong relevance to the legal system itself. This group included such men as Judge Jerome Frank,[3] Karl Llewellyn,[4] Thurman Arnold[5] and others—the iconoclasts who pointed out the myths, images, pretenses and masks of the formal legal rules and systems. These were the legal realists who, together with the sociological jurists who had preceeded them, were the American forerunners of the interdisciplinary, generally empirical or reality-oriented view of law taken here. (The use of the term "reality" in this chapter simply indicates the quality of phenomena that have an independent existence. As defined by Berger and Luckmann,[6] "reality" is "a quality pertaining to phenomena that we recognize as having a being independent of our own volition [we cannot wipe them away].")

The sociology of law has developed broadly as an independent field but has had limited impact. Rather, earlier popular and professional concepts of the law have in general retained their primacy. The thought of the legal realists, together with the work of the growing group of empirical researchers, has begun to give us useful understandings regarding (1) the impact of formal institutions, procedures and rules and (2) the actual workings of the formal legal system. These will be the subjects of the next two sections.

The Impact of the Law

A few still largely open questions and some emerging possible answers can be briefly set forth here.

Do Criminal Sanctions Deter?

One specific area that has been the subject of numerous studies and which is still unresolved is the deterrent effect of criminal sanctions. The rational utilitarian concept voiced by Bentham is that the greater the penalty, the stronger the deterrent. Though still popularly assumed, this relationship is far from direct and in some situations may not operate at all. The hackneyed example is 17th Century England, where they hanged pickpockets while pickpockets were plying their trade in the crowds near the gallows. One factor that obviously intervenes in deterrence is the probability, as perceived by the potential lawbreaker, that sanctions will be applied to him. Another factor that a Skinnerian behaviorist would emphasize is the amount of delay between the initial crime and the punishment.

It is clearly demonstrable that in our system legal penalties often tend to be both too uncertain and too remote in time to adequately deter law violation. Among the causes of this indeterminancy are the complexities and delays of our criminal court system, uncertainties of detection and the strong prejudice in our system in favor of the accused. In Western Europe, where there is no such presumption and rules of evidence are far simpler, trials are swifter and the outcome perhaps more certain. Yet there are costs for this, just as improved detection would require substantial outlays for more police or the loss of freedom implied in closer surveillance. Possibly the main limiting effect on sanctions is that they do not enter into the criminal's decision-making process. Rather he or she is concerned almost entirely with situational factors and other meanings attaching to the act. Sometimes these other meanings are shared with a deviant group or sub-culture which imposes its own pressures and unofficial sanctions which offset any effect from the law.

Humans sometimes behave rationally—with a view to consequences—but observation, report, detection, arrest and punishment are but one range of factors that impinge on their behavior.

Certain criminal acts have been described as expressive rather than instrumental, which is to say they are not primarily based upon a utilitarian calculation. These include matters of life style such as drug use, consensual sexual acts or intra-family violence. It also includes some irrational emotional acts such as rape, most nonprofessional murder and amateur shoplifting. It seems clear that increasing penalties beyond a certain level (sometimes called a "saturation point") for a given crime will not deter any significant additional numbers of potential lawbreakers. On the other hand, there are instrumental acts such as illegal parking where the curve is highly responsive within a given range. In addition, such increase may lead to a lessening of enforcement as police refuse to arrest, prosecutors to indict, and judges and juries to convict. For this reason a reduction in penalties for marijuana to the status of a misdemeanor may have the effect of substantially increasing arrests, prosecutions and convictions, as resistance by authorities and by the lawbreakers themselves to the application of the law is decreased.

Obviously many other characteristics of an act affect the impact of setting criminal penalties for it, such as whether the act is public or private. Non-public behavior, such as private sex, gambling, drug use and violence within the family, is considerably harder to police and therefore to discourage than are public acts such as bank robbery or wrongful formal acts of government employees.

An even more important factor has to do with the feelings and attitudes of potential lawbreakers. Individuals have broad discretion to obey or disobey the law and subsequently to avoid, evade or even invite the official penalties. Their voluntary obedience to law, or to the moral, rational, cultural or personal norms that the law expresses, is the central fact in determining whether their behavior will be lawful or unlawful. Sykes[7] shows that even in prisons and prison camps the consent of the inmates is the chief fact relied upon for governance: force can accomplish a very limited range of objectives, and threats have limited efficacy, since the prisoners have no privileges of which to be deprived and they hold the preponderance of physical power.

Courts and Litigation

Realism about our legal institutions requires a recognition that often the courts do not reach their decisions in the manner formally prescribed and that most court cases are not even decided by the courts.

How Courts Reach Their Decisions

The legal realists observed that on a less visible level than Supreme Court decisions there are severe inherent limitations on the real life meaning of legal rules. The first of this group of criticisms (called "rule-skepticism") is that prior cases and *stare decisis* really do not determine cases, at least not any difficult case. When judges disagree, opinions of majority and dissenters both state in categorial terms that, based on prior decisions, only their view can apply. Thus the U.S. Supreme Court in the Ellsburg/Pentagon Papers Case[8] characterized the issue as a First Amendment Freedom of the Press problem rather than as a property rights case involving stolen documents. Llewellyn[9] and other realists pointed out that there are always alternative precedents among which a judge may choose in deciding a case, using a tool kit of alternative ways of using precedents (e.g., "narrow" or "broad" interpretation). In addition, legal language is vague. Facts are unique and complex and the assumed social reality continually changing. As a result, judges are really free within a broad range to decide cases based on their own political, economic, cultural or visceral perceptions and preferences.

In practice this point may be limited to the difficult or highly contested matters that go to formal court hearings, trial or appeal. Many legal rules and factual situations are subject to customary or agreed understandings so that the cost or effort to have them re-examined is not usually available. Legal doctrine as enunciated by judges and others is also a special cultural tradition and a vehicle for other social and cultural values and, as Llewellyn showed[10] such doctrine is a significant factor influencing appellate case outcome. However, the realists' analysis serves to emphasize that judges are policy determinors rather than simple appliers of pre-existing rules.

Judge Jerome Frank, looking at the trial court level, focused on a much more pervasive cause of uncertainty under the term "fact-skepticism."[11] Court testimony involves non-verbal expressions, nuances of timing and emphasis and is viewed only by the triers of fact who determine the credibility of witnesses. Therefore, findings of fact by judge and jury are, under the rules and for practical purposes, non-reviewable in most instances. Frank went on to point to the reality of *faulty* observations, recollections and testimony of witnesses and the frequent occurrence of missing documents and testimony. He noted, further, that judge and jury are subject to the same human limitations as witnesses based on their own known and unknown biases. Consequently, said Frank, "facts are guesses." And it is these guesses that determine which legal rules can apply.

Other criticism has been directed at the rules of evidence. According to this point of view, represented by James Marshall, when trial proceedings are viewed as truth finders the law of evidence presents major flaws. Protracted, confusing, often out of date, and contrary to both ordinary sense and science, a comparable set of rules does not exist in any Western European legal system. They lengthen trials inordinately, confuse and impede witnesses and often block consideration of the data that would be most helpful in determining the truth. Yet the rules of evidence are vigorously supported by the professional ideology of trial lawyers, and the Illinois Supreme Court recently refused to adopt the moderate reforms contained in the new Federal Rules of Evidence.

Once again, like legal rule indeterminancy, the direct impact of factual uncertainty is limited in practice to issues that can actually be tried. The social construction of many human situations is stereotyped within the legal establishment. It thus takes a major effort to obtain a real hearing in local Illinois courts of facts bearing on borrowers' equities, welfare recipients' interests, fathers' custody rights or consumer defenses. The only cost effective means of accomplishing such consideration is often a long expensive court fight to change procedural rules or to expand substantive rights. However, the basic unpredictability of outcome that Frank raised is a factor impinging on most legal disputes. Uncertainty, difficulty of proof, long delays and high costs combine so that a credible threat of real contest or even delay may induce settlement or discourage lawsuits both "good" and "bad."

To this must be added the fact that only one out of 17 felony cases and one out of 250 civil cases are appealed and reviewed at all by a higher court, so that decisions of the trial level court are usually final.

According to official records,[12] the number of cases filed in the Circuit Courts in Illinois during 1977 was 3,500,000 (up 57 percent from 1964). The number of cases filed in the Appellate Courts for the same year was 4,400 (up 266 percent from 1964.) Less than half of Appellate Court decisions were accompanied by full opinions—explanations of the legal basis for the decision. During the same period the seven Justices of the Illinois Supreme court disposed of 1,150 cases, only 219 of them by full opinions.

Most Court Cases Are Not Decided by Courts

A further limitation on the determination of facts and the application of legal rules to them by courts is that less than five percent of cases that are filed in court actually go to trial. For example, in 1977, law jury cases terminated in the Illinois Circuit Courts numbered 33,158. Only 1,419 of these were terminated by actual verdicts. In downstate Illinois, for this category the average delay between filing and verdict was 24 months; in Cook County 40.7 months—and verdicts were involved in 8 percent of downstate cases compared to only 2 percent of Cook County law jury cases. Statewide only 10 percent of persons charged with a felony were actually tried—but over 60 percent of those charged were convicted of a felony or lesser charge.[13]

Only the United States and Eastern Europe base almost all of their criminal convictions on confessions. In Western Europe, where the rules of evidence are simpler and trials less cumbersome, they can afford to try their criminals rather than confess them. Professor Langbein[14] has compared the plea bargaining process with confession by torture, in the threat of heavier penalty being used to "compel" a guilty plea. Blumberg[15] pointed out that defense attorneys are locked into the position of pressuring their clients to comply with this demand of the court/prosecution bureaucracy.

Except for accident cases, where insurance companies are usually involved, the largest number of civil cases go to judgment by default; that is to say, no defense is offered. And so the matter is settled on the basis of *assertions* of the plaintiff, sometimes with a "prove-up"—a perfunctory one-sided trial. The next largest category of civil cases—like the bulk of criminal cases—are "settled" (brought to conclusion) by an agreement of the contending parties which receives little or no examination by a judge. This may be theoretically based on anticipation as to what the results would or might be if the case were tried. A settlement may also be based on one or both parties' financial, administrative, professional or emotional limitations or on knowledge of those limitations possessed by the other side (e.g., a plaintiff might accept a small settlement in a "big" case because he was pessimistic about being able to collect a large judgment from a defendant of limited income).

Settlements are generally compromises rather than the all-or-nothing result the law calls for. For example, an accident case with tenuous liability will be discounted appropriately.

The fact remains that the vast majority of matters that come into our adversarial system are not determined by formal adversary procedures. Some may be settled by mock confrontation in conferences involving partially accurate disclosure, arguments, bluffs and threats, depending on the resources available to pay for laywers and other time involved. But in most cases the adversary system fails to function simply because there is only one adversary. Caplovitz's study of Illinois consumer collection cases,[16] for example, showed that 91 percent of cases result in judgments by default with "appearance" (participation) by neither the defendant nor a lawyer on his behalf. In other cases the defendant may show up without a lawyer and be directed by the judge to sit down with the plaintiff's lawyer to "work things out." In eviction cases the percentage of defaults is even greater; and the chance of winning is almost non-existent for the tenant who cannot pay or is holding out on his rent, or whose lease is expired, provided that the landlord has obeyed the technicalities. The tenant has no practical chance to raise other issues which the Illinois Supreme Court has said are relevant. However the judge may typically give the tenant a week or two to move. If the tenant is hard-nosed enough to stay put it may take the landlord 30 to 60 days, during which the tenant pays no rent, to get the sheriff to make an actual eviction. The sheriff may be sensitive to the human and political costs of putting people's belongings out on the streets and in Cook County will send the tenant a warning letter. Events thus center on practical, non-legal factors as does the judicial act. Eviction cases resemble the vast majority of business in the modern local trial court in being chiefly ministerial, administrative or pragmatic rather than adhering to the adversarial trial model.

What Doesn't Go Into the Court System

Very few matters that are theoretically subject to court disposition or application of law ever come into the formal court system to begin with. Both quantitatively and qualitatively this is the most significant deviation of the world from the lawyer's formal precedent and trial model. Courts are by their nature reactive rather than pro-active: someone outside the court system has to take the initiative by filing criminal charges or a civil suit.

Macauley's study of the purchasing behavior of a group of Wisconsin manufacturers[17] indicated that to a large extent they did business without enforceable contracts, and when there were enforceable contracts and one party wanted to get out, this was generally allowed—possibly with some adjustment for tooling costs. In general, litigation only takes place between strangers, or between persons whose relationships have been severed and are no longer in the same community. For example, the largest category of commercial cases in the federal district courts was found to be franchise termination cases, just as consumer collection cases are the bulk of contract litigation in the local courts. People in a smaller community or those who have continuing business relations are likely to know why one does not live up to a contract, and an accommodation is more likely to be reached based on the non-legal realities of the situation. By contrast, there is evidence that consumer collection is extremely costly and counter-productive, not only to society but, as Caplovitz and Leff have charged,[18] even to the creditors bringing the action.

Sociologist Jerome Skolnick[19] has pointed out that the out-of-court decision of the policeman *not* to arrest generally has a final non-appealable exonerative effect on the potential arrestee. A decision *to* arrest subjects the arrestee to substantial and potentially crippling costs ranging from legal fees and loss of time to loss of job or business and social stigmatization, even if he is later proven innocent of the charge. Similarly, a suit by an individual fighting dismissal may have the effect of immobilizing for weeks key personnel of the government agency or private business firm for whom he worked; in addition, the agency or firm bears the costs of legal fees and the publicity which may cause irreparable damage. A Securities and Exchange Commission restraining order, even if eventually upset, can put a brokerage firm out of business; and a suit by the Currency Exchange Association against the State of Illinois delayed for years the imposition of State curative legislation limiting their fees. This law was recently voided on technical grounds by the Illinois Supreme Court, and the Legislature is beginning the entire process again.

To these costs of litigation may be added the uncertainty costs described above which are inherent in court proceedings. Other costs include the sheer abrasiveness and disruption of relationships that formal legal proceedings entail. In this situation it would seem predictable that no one who has a choice or does not see a substantial possibility of gain will subject himself to the formal justice system. However, some parties are litigation prone—and large numbers of lawyers find employment there.

By far the largest amount of activity by lawyers is not in the courts—or even the behind-the-scenes preparation, drafting, research, discovery and investigation that "major' litigation involves. Rather, most lawyers' work—including that of the most prestigious—is routine paper shuffling and people handling: drafting, negotiating, counselling, researching (seeking law and facts), corresponding and drafting. This is the intermediary world between the business behavior Macauley describes and the work of the courts.

Problems and Trends

The major problems and trends of the legal system profoundly affect the public but are not easily manageable by public policy—they are the "litigation explosion" and the derivative growth of the legal profession. The consequences create significant economic and social costs which need to be more widely recognized.

The Litigation Explosion

There is theoretically no limitation on the amount of lawyer's time—that must be somehow paid for—to be used in any court case. A lawsuit is a kind of war in which an escalation of the conflict by one side compels the other to escalate. Moreover, there is always the likelihood that the litigant who is the more organized, who has the largest resources or the greatest flexibility using or threatening to use greater firepower than the other side can afford, thereby, in effect, "buys" justice as a rich man "buys" a no-limit poker game. Thus, it is very hard for the individual litigant to fight City Hall, General Motors or the Teamsters Union. Recent studies, however, tend to indicate that a key factor in litigation success is organization—the organized litigant has a very substantial probability of victory as compared to the unorganized and solitary litigant. Thus public interest law firms, with their sustained effort for general social concerns, can potentially bring about broad systemic changes.

All this is influenced by institutional arrangements. It can easily be shown that the prevalence of automobile liability insurance combined with the contingent fee arrangement (whereby lawyers in this country, in contrast to Britain, can accept a contingent portion of the recovery for payment of their services) has substantially increased the volume of litigation.

It is a common observation that people are more litigous, that is to say, more willing to sue. Certainly in urban America there is much less of the social disapproval of lawsuits which restrains potential litigants in England, nor do we possess the monolithic community power structure that has checked the growth of litigation in Canada. Yet a number of studies have shown that the use of legal services by individuals is highly correlated with whether they are acquainted with or have contact with lawyers, or with lay intermediaries having such contacts. Thus the availability of lawyers is a major factor in determining how much legal work is done and how many potential legal claims mature into lawsuits. Such availability is also a major determinant of how much lawyers' time will be expended on these lawsuits or other representation—thereby commanding roughly equivalent increases in lawyer's time spent on the other side of the transaction or lawsuit.

Growth of the Legal Profession

Milton Friedman reports that the organized lawyers' associations have never been successful in seizing control over professional training of lawyers and entry to the legal profession.[20] In contrast, organized medicine accomplished such control in the second and third decades of this century, control which they then used in the '30s to reduce the supply of physicians and protect their income. Law had no such apparatus, and, when there was a substantial increase in the number of applicants for law school in the 1960s, there was expansion in the legal education apparatus. All law schools could be more selective and almost all law students were now completing law school and passing their bar exams.

As a result, the number of attorneys has risen sharply. Since 1973 all Illinois attorneys have been required to register annually with the Attorney Registration and Disciplinary Commission of the Illinois Supreme Court. On June 30, 1973, 22,866 lawyers were registered. On December 31, 1978 the comparable figure was 33,090 lawyers—an increase of 45 percent in five years. Looking at the number of lawyers admitted to the bar less than six years, on June 30, 1974 the figure was 4,363; the number registered on December 31, 1978 was 9,566, an increase of 119 percent![21] Since these proportions closely parallel national statistics, the following figures from the Bureau of Census may be applicable here: the national proportion of female lawyers went from 3.8 percent in 1972 to 9.5 percent in 1977; the proportion of Black and other minority lawyers from 1.9 to 3.2 percent. Law school enrollment figures indicate that this expansion in the profession will continue, resulting in an expected doubling of the number of lawyers between 1979 and 1986.

The only unmet demand (as opposed to the theoretical need that the ABA sees) is for qualified minority law graduates seeking corporate and government jobs. Otherwise, because of the strongly hierarchical nature of the bar, graduates of the less prestigious law schools will be competing for a declining number of small law firm jobs—and many will end up in essentially independent practice, using excess time, energies and abilities to create new law work. Many will end up as employees for banks, title companies, insurance companies, real estate operations and others; there, they will tend to do the most complex tasks they can—which will involve escalating the formal legal structure of the activities they touch. (Rawls[22] calls this the "Aristotelian principle" motivation.)

Other factors have substantially increased the availability of legal services and can be expected to continue to do so. One such factor is the U.S. Supreme Court cases permitting advertising by attorneys. Since what is involved here are the First Amendment constitutional rights (the right of lawyers to speak and of clients to know), advertising by attorneys is spreading in Illinois despite considerable opposition by the Illinois Bar. Also spreading are legal clinics, some of them sponsored by bar associations in more or less elaborate experiments and others set up by individual lawyers or groups of lawyers in Chicago neighborhoods. One of the notable trends, as the number of lawyers has increased, has been the substantial dispersion of traditional law practices throughout urban neighborhoods, the outlying communities and the smaller towns of Illinois. Another institutional change has been the introduction of group legal services, a trend that was fought by the Illinois State Bar Association in the courts on the basis of the lawyers' code of ethics. This issue was settled by the U.S. Supreme Court as a matter of establishing the rights of citizens to petition the government, which included the right to be represented on a group basis in small legal matters as well as large. This possibility of concentrating legal representation and firepower on special issues of interest to segments of the middle-class has as much potential for escalation of legal rights and position as had the onset in the 1950s of federally financed legal assistance for the poor.

Further Consequences: The Costliness of Expansion

Major factors making the cost of litigation particularly ungovernable are the rule and fact indeterminancy introduced by the legal realists. Although these points are generalizable to foreign settings, they apply particularly in America. Many years ago, Max Weber pointed out that the common law tradition and the professional autonomy of lawyers are the factors preventing simplification, clarifiction and systematization of laws and legal procedures. In England, a separate group of non-adversary lawyers (solicitors) handle the out-of-court and lower court law work; contingent fees are not allowed; and the extension of the adversary system into new areas and rights has not occurred.

In America we also have Congress plus 50 state legislatures and 51 court systems and bars, theoretically separate but actually interacting in numerous formal and informal ways. Thus the mass of precedent, statute and other writings produced by courts, legislators and private lawyers, with potential nationwide impact, has been growing for years. This accumulation started during Colonial days and today is itself increasing exponentially. One result is a large body of latent rules which an expanded lawyer population is now able to use to expand rights and to actualize claims which had previously been only theoretical. Thus medical malpractice and product liability suits have increased many-fold. Under the particularly strong judicial independence (or supremacy) rules in the Illinois Constitution of 1970, a mild attempt by the Legislature to constrain growth of malpractice litigation was struck down by the Illinois Supreme Court. Meanwhile, the development of complexities and specializations has combined with the increasing litigation in older fields, such as anti-trust law, to add further to the growing law explosion.

Another notable escalation has been the growth of regulatory effort on federal, state and local levels as more and more licensure and other special laws are added to the total pattern each year. Illinois is reported to license more trades and occupations than any other state, in arrangements often controlled by the group being regulated.

As with other states, Illinois regulatory patterns and interventions are generally puny when compared to the new federal regulatory schemes dealing with air pollution, the environment, job safety, disclosure of credit terms and real estate closings. These have been productive of new lawyer specialties, litigation and increased business courts.

On a less visible level the same escalatory factors have been functioning to expand the world of law works outside of litigation.[22] Even in drafting a will, an American lawyer works with a mind to the potential adversary: sometimes an excluded relative, generally the Internal Revenue Service. Thus the document and the work involved grow. In a larger real estate sale, we see extended technical negotiations, draftsmanship and counter-draftsmanship, bluff and counter-bluff. Documentation of corporate deals grows by the hundreds of clauses and thousands of pages of exhibits. The body of legal hazards, ambiguities and problems that must be protected against is theoretically without limit. Formalization and legalization are like ravenous animals, as lawyers continue to make work for other lawyers.

An issue for the future is to what extent growth of law activity will continue and for how long the present spectacular curve can last. Counterpressures in the form of anti-regulatory efforts, sunset laws, constitutional amendments to limit spending and simplification of public and private legalese are sweeping the country and beginning to have impact in Illinois. The effect of specific measures is often unclear: federal pension law reform (ERISA) introduced complex new rules, but is taming and reducing an impenetrable thicket of private contractual arrangements—probably a net gain for simplification. The situation is further muddied by distributive issues; much new law and law expansion consist of liberal reforms which restrict private interests. Thus the business community is in the forefront of many anti-regulatory movements: the drive for elimination of barnyard watchdogs is often led by foxes! All of these law reduction efforts are national movements to which Illinois shows above average resistance. They run counter to the interests of lawyers and to the institutional habits and thought processes of all that are involved—law-expanding is a national tune to which we all dance.

Moreover it is doubtful if such efforts will provide much succor unless combined with broad-scale recodification, delegalization (including measures "delawyering" numerous routine transactions) and other more basic reforms which limit and transform the adversary process itself.

Conclusion

What then is the bottom line of the legal enterprise for Illinois citizens—beyond work for lawyers and unwanted and often artificially expanded problems for laymen? Fifty years ago Huizinga wrote that law (together with religion, language, war and indeed all culturally derived activities) was a play activity, self-defining and self-contained. In a sense all human activities are their own purpose, but the question remains, whether and to what extent law activities are particularly humanizing or productive of grace. This chapter has raised some critical issues as to the impact they have on other aspects of human life.

The case is strong for substantial improvements in our system of private and public justice, including the role and functioning of lawyers. We should also ask critical questions about the basic assumptions of that system. One issue always present is: what are the available alternatives? For example, most would agree that lawsuits are a better mode of settling disputes than force or violence. But direct compromise, mediation or inaction are often better than either. And there is a powerful case for leaving more decisions to popularly elected executives and legislators rather than judges.

In principle, the purpose of our legal system is justice. A *sense* of justice is intimately connected to the morale of our social system and therefore to the maintenance of that fabric which underlies society. But justice as a value is infinitely more complex and pluralistic than, for example, health. There are many "justices"; individuals and groups frequently differ as to what is just, depending on their specific relationship to an issue and its outcome. The legal realists, rather than being value free, were passionately concerned with reform of our legal system in the direction of greater rationality, the alleviation of human hardship and other important values. Thus they insisted on viewing law as reality rather than as a self-contained body of eternal principals. So viewed, judges have the task of balancing divergent values in relationship to emergent facts; rules are seen not as *controlling* behavior but rather as having *influence* within and between complex and interacting social realities.

When we focus on behavioral approaches, it is important to remember that culture is central to human life and is a major determinate of behavior. Thus the critical elements of social reality include the intangible and the non-rational—such as the felt need for maintenance of the generally shared sentiments that are referred to as the "ideal of legality" or the "rule of law." Selznick[23] describes the ideal of legality as absence of arbitrariness. Like many who start from the conservative theory of Anglo-American legal development, he focuses on restriction of official power. But it is also important that powerful private organizations, groups and individuals affecting the lives of citizens be restricted. However, parties have wide disparity in their power to litigate, and the courts are imperfect and cumbersome at this task of controlling private power. This is a central public problem for which the primary solution is unlikely to be found in the courts. However, the concept of legality is appropriate *not* as a description but rather as an ideal or aspiration.

Political scientist Theodore Becker, after extensively examining the question of the consequences of having courts, states as follows:[24]

> (T)he fact that [the judicial structure] *apparently* dispenses justice, just by its peculiar decision-making process, may have substantial political effect.
>
> The most enduring function of the court—indeed of the judicial structure—seems best described as the appeasement of the outrage felt in the soul and mind of man at the instability, tedium, amorphousness, and basic arbitrariness of our national environment and our mortality. Whether man's mind should be eased of worry over these aspects of the human condition is a question that both social and political philosophers should discuss, at least as to whether such pacification should be a political function. . . .
>
> The thinking of those who see courts as a social structure that helps procreate existing social values and which serves some very deep psychic need of individuals within society seems sound.

Behavioral research has shown the strong effect of legal processes such as criminal justice "labelling" and other formal declarations of value. These are social facts of immense importance—together with the ceremonial, the artistic and the ritualistic—that embody, express and create shared social meanings. Laws as well as courts are the focus of many such shared meanings.

Thus the major operational reality of the law is not force, but rather a process that persuades, socializes and educates. Like the actions of private citizens, many laws are symbolic rather than instrumental. Prohibition and the rules against marijuana, gambling, homosexuality and prostitution are declarations of the moral superiority of some groups and ways compared to others. Criminal trials and punishments may be viewed as symbolic rites that affirm the official values of the general community. A verdict or judgment, like a legislative act, or even the filing of a suit can be a victory, a vindication or a defeat. The law thus can legitimate, stigmatize or celebrate. Many legal acts have different degrees of such meaning interlaced with instrumental or rational consequences or intent. Many of these phenomena raise severe and difficult ethical issues, which in some instances such as capital punishment are now under debate. But the existence of this set of meanings does not mean that we should not be critical about the law *per se,* or the law as it exists in any particular context or embodiment. Rather, they give a deeper perspective to scrutiny of the law both scientifically and in day-to-day life.

This chapter began by saying that human behavior gives reality to laws and legal structures; to the extent that those laws and structures are invested with intangible values it can be said that they give *meaning* to life. One very basic problem in thinking on this level is that we have very little systematic, non-intuitive understanding of symbolic reality. According to general systems theory, symbolic systems are of the highest, most complex order of systems. This is the far frontier of the growth of scientific understanding. It embodies critical issues for the human condition.

Law is felt to pertain in some part to what is sacred. Sacred areas are traditionally protected by their guardians against systematic examintion from external points of view. (A more modern method is to compartmentalize or ignore criticism.) But even sacred symbols should be critically examined to the end that they might augment life and other human values. The Church of the 15th Century took the position that an empirical view of the solar system and particularly heliocentrism threatened religion itself. We still have a similar feeling that our essential legality and public order are dependent on a basic sense of obligation to law that is threatened by objective understanding. By way of example, the belief that others are punished for violation of a rule has been suggested as necessary in order that each of us maintain the balance between our social and anti-social instincts and thus ourselves obey the law. Yet Piaget,[25] Kohlberg[26] and others have indicated that as children develop moral thinking the reward/punishment orientation only applies to an early stage of individual development; mature adults finally come to obey rules through an ethical sense of obligation. Research in this critical area is only beginning.

To those concerned with achieving a decent society, needed law reform seems distressingly slow. Often a legal malfunctioning, the related social problems and the resistance to change seem like different sides of the same problem. Central to all three are issues of perception and attitude. With a greater appreciation of the realities of our legal system, we will be more able to react appropriately and effectively as individuals and citizens. In addition, we may then anchor our belief systems in firmer and less vulnerable grounds, including tolerance for the ambiguity and complexity that characterize the real world.

NOTES

[1]Kenneth Culp Davis, *Discretionary Justice* (Urbana: University of Illinois Press, 1971).

[2]Max Rheinstein, *Marriage Stability, Divorce and the Law* (Chicago: University of Chicago Press, 1972).

[3]Jerome N. Frank, *Courts on Trial: Myth and Reality in American Justice* (Princeton, N.J.: Princeton University Press, 1949).

[4]Karl N. Llewellyn, *The Bramble Bush: On Our Law and Its Study* (New York: Oceana, 1960).

[5]Thurman W. Arnold, *The Folklore of Capitalism* (New Haven: Yale University Press, 1937).

[6]Peter L. Berger and Thomas Luckmann, *The Social Construction of Reality: A Treatise in the Sociology of Knowledge* (Garden City, N.Y.: Doubleday/Anchor, 1967).

[7]Gresham M. Sykes, *The Society of Captives: A Study of a Maximum Security Prison* (New York: Atheneum, 1970).

[8]*New York Times Co. v. United States* 403 U.S. 713 (1971).

[9]Llewellyn, *op. cit.*

[10]Karl N. Llewellyn, *The Common Law Tradition: Deciding Appeals* (Boston: Little, Brown, 1960).

[11]Frank, *op. cit.*

[12]Administrative Office of the Illinois Courts, *1977 Annual Report to the Supreme Court of Illinois* (Springfield, Illinois: 1978).

[13]*Ibid.*

[14]John A. Langbein, "Torture and Plea Bargaining," *University of Chicago Law Review* 46 (1978), 3.

[15]Abraham S. Blumberg, "The Practice of Law as a Confidence Game: Organizational Cooptation of a Profession," *Law and Society Review* 1 (1967), 15.

[16]David Caplovitz, *Consumers in Trouble: A Study of Debtors in Default* (New York: Free Press, 1974), p. 221.

[17]Stewart Macaulay, "Non-contractual Relations in Business: A Preliminary Study," *American Sociological Review* 28 (February 1963), p. 55.

[18]Caplovitz, *op. cit.;* Arthur Leff, "Injury, Ignorance and Spite—The Dynamics of Coercive Collection," *Yale Law Journal* 80 (November 1970), p. 1.

[19]Jerome H. Skolnick, *Justice Without Trial* (New York: John Wiley & Sons, 1966).

[20]Milton Friedman, "Occupational Licensure" in *Capitalism and Freedom* (Chicago: University of Chicago Press, 1962), pp. 137–60.

[21]Attorney Registration and Disciplinary Commission of the Supreme Court of Illinois, *Annual Reports* (Chicago: 1974–79).

[22]John Rawls, "The Aristotelian Principle," *A Theory of Justice* (Cambridge: Belknap/Harvard University Press, 1971), Section 65, pp. 424–33.

[23]Philip Selznick, *Law, Society and Industrial Justice* (New York: Russell Sage Foundation, 1969).

[24]Theodore L. Becker, *Comparative Judicial Politics: The Political Functioning of Courts* (Chicago: Rand McNally, 1970).

[25]Jean Piaget, *The Moral Judgment of the Child,* 1932, trans. by M. Gebain (New York: The Free Press, 1965).

[26]Lawrence Kohlberg, "Development of Moral Character and Moral Ideology," *Review of Child Development Research,* ed. by M. L. Hoffman and L. W. Hoffman (Vol. 1; New York: Russell Sage Foundation, 1964); and Lawrence Kohlberg, "The Child as a Moral Philosopher," *Psychology Today* 25 (September 1968).

SUPPLEMENTAL READINGS

Aubert, Vilhelm, ed. *Sociology of Law: Selected Readings.* Baltimore: Penguin, 1969.

Barnsley, John H. *The Social Reality of Ethics.* London: Routledge and Keegan Paul, 1972.

Becker, Theodore L. *Comparative Judicial Politics: The Political Function of Courts.* Chicago: Rand McNally, 1970.

Berger, Peter L., and Thomas Luckmann. *The Social Construction of Reality: A Treatise in the Sociology of Knowledge.* Garden City, N.Y.: Doubleday/Anchor, 1967.

Chambliss, William J. "Types of Deviance and the Effectiveness of Sanctions," *1967 Wisconsin Law Review,* 703.

Curran, Barbara A. *The Legal Needs of the Public: The Final Report of a National Survey.* Chicago: American Bar Foundation, 1977.

Frank, Jerome N. *Courts on Trial: Myth and Reality in American Justice.* Princeton, N.J.: Princeton University Press, 1949.

Friedman, Lawrence M. *The Legal System: A Social Science Perspective.* New York: Russell Sage Foundation, 1975.

——— and Steward Macauley, eds. *Law and the Behavioral Sciences.* Indianapolis: Bobbs-Merritt, 1959.

Gardiner, John A. *Traffic and the Police: Variation in Law Enforcement Policy.* Cambridge: Harvard University Press, 1969.

Johnstone, Quentin, and Dan Hopson, Jr. *Lawyers and Their Work: An Analysis of the Legal Profession in the United States and England.* Indianapolis: Bobbs-Merrill, 1967.

Llewellyn, Karl N. *The Common Law Tradition: Deciding Appeals.* Boston: Little Brown, 1960.

Macaulay, Stewart. "Non-contractual Relations in Business: A preliminary Study." *American Sociological Review* 28 (February 1963), p. 55.

Maru, Olavi. *Research on the Legal Profession: A Review of Work Done.* Chicago: American Bar Foundation, 1972.

Piaget, Jean. *The Moral Judgment of the Child.* 1932. Translated by M. Gebain. New York: The Free Press, 1965.

Rheinstein, Max, ed. *Max Weber on Law in Economy and Society.* Cambridge: Harvard University Press, 1966.

Schwartz, Richard D., and Sonya Orleans. "On Legal Sanctions," *University of Chicago Law Review* 34 (1967), p. 274.

Schwartz, Richard D., and Jerome H. Skolnick, eds. *Society and the Legal Order.* New York: Basic Books, 1970.

Simon, Rita J., ed. *The Sociology of Law.* Scranton, Pa.: Chandler, 1968.

Skolnick, Jerome H. "Coercion to Virtue: The Enforcement of Morals." *Southern California Law Review* 41 (1968), p. 588.

———. *Justice Without Trial.* New York: John Wiley & Sons, 1966.

Suchar, Charles S. *Social Deviance: Perspectives and Prospects.* New York: Holt Rinehart & Winston, 1978.

PART 

ENVIRONMENT: THE INFLUENCE OF NON-GOVERNMENTAL ENTITIES

CHAPTER **11**

Elections: Political Culture, Public Opinion, Sectionalism and Voting

Alan D. Monroe

The outcome of electoral decisions in Illinois is a topic of considerable interest both to residents of the State and to observers across the nation. The State is politically important at the national level, because of both its size and the closeness of competition between the parties. It is also a very typical state on many dimensions of political behavior. Yet this aggregate pattern of close competition is a product of cultural diversity. As will be seen in this chapter, there are many different factors, both historical and contemporary, which have drawn the political map of Illinois. This chapter will attempt to describe the distribution of voting patterns throughout the State and to determine their antecedents.

The Cultural Basis of Illinois Politics

When one seeks to explain why one community has a different pattern of partisan preference or political style than another, the explanation is often in terms of some sort of historical factors, e.g., Civil War loyalties, the strength of certain ethnic groups, the presence of certain religious denominations. While such explanations are persuasive for individual cases, it is difficult to put them all together into an integrated analysis of many communities. There are so many potentially relevant groups as to be quite bewildering in total. However, there is at least one theory which seems capable of organizing this array of background factors into a unified explanation.

Elazar's Theory of Political Culture

Daniel Elazar has advanced an interesting theory of cultural variations in American politics.[1] His formulation rests upon the idea of cultural streams which are made up of the various groups who settled the American frontier (including the contemporary "urban frontier") throughout the last two centuries. These groups are defined by their *regional* origin (e.g., Yankees, Southerners), their *national* origin (e.g., Germans, Italians), their *religion* (e.g., Lutherans, Catholics), their *race* (e.g., blacks), or even their *language* (e.g., Chicanos, French Canadians). Given the variety of classifications and their possible permutations, it would be impossible to sort out the effects of these variables were it not that Elazar has discovered a way to aggregate these groups into three different streams. This aggregation is based on the principle that the various components of each stream tend to share a common pattern of orientations to politics, an arrangement assisted by a tendency of the groups to have settled in the same areas as other groups in the same cultural stream.

Elazar defines three major streams and three corresponding political cultures. First of all, there is the *Northern* stream which includes those original settlers who came from New England (i.e., the Yankess) plus later migrants directly from several European countries, especially the Scandinavian nations. The Northern stream, according to Elazar, is the bearer of the *Moralistic* culture which sees government as a "commonwealth" and the political process as a way of bettering society. This emphasis on government as a means, rather than as an end in itself has resulted in support by people in Moralistic areas for many of the great "crusades" in American history, such as the abolition of slavery, the prohibition of alcohol and the nonpartisan reforms and Progressive movement of the early Twentieth Century.

The *Middle* stream is the dominant one in American politics. It is made up of areas settled by people from the middle Atlantic states and from a number of foreign nations, including England, Germany, and Ireland. The middle stream is said to carry the *Individualistic* political culture which sees the political process as a "marketplace" in which individuals can advance their own interests. It is therefore much more tolerant than the Moralistic culture of a reasonable amount of political corruption and tends to value strong political party organizations which are often based upon job patronage.

The *Southern* stream is composed, not suprisingly, of those settlers who came originally from the slave states on the Eastern seaboard. Elazar also includes in this stream the later immigrants to the U.S. from various Southern and Eastern European nations (Italy, Poland, etc.), though these people rarely settled in the same places as the native Southerners. Also included are what Elazar calls the "excluded streams" of black and Spanish-speaking Americans who were largely kept out of participation in American politics until very recently.

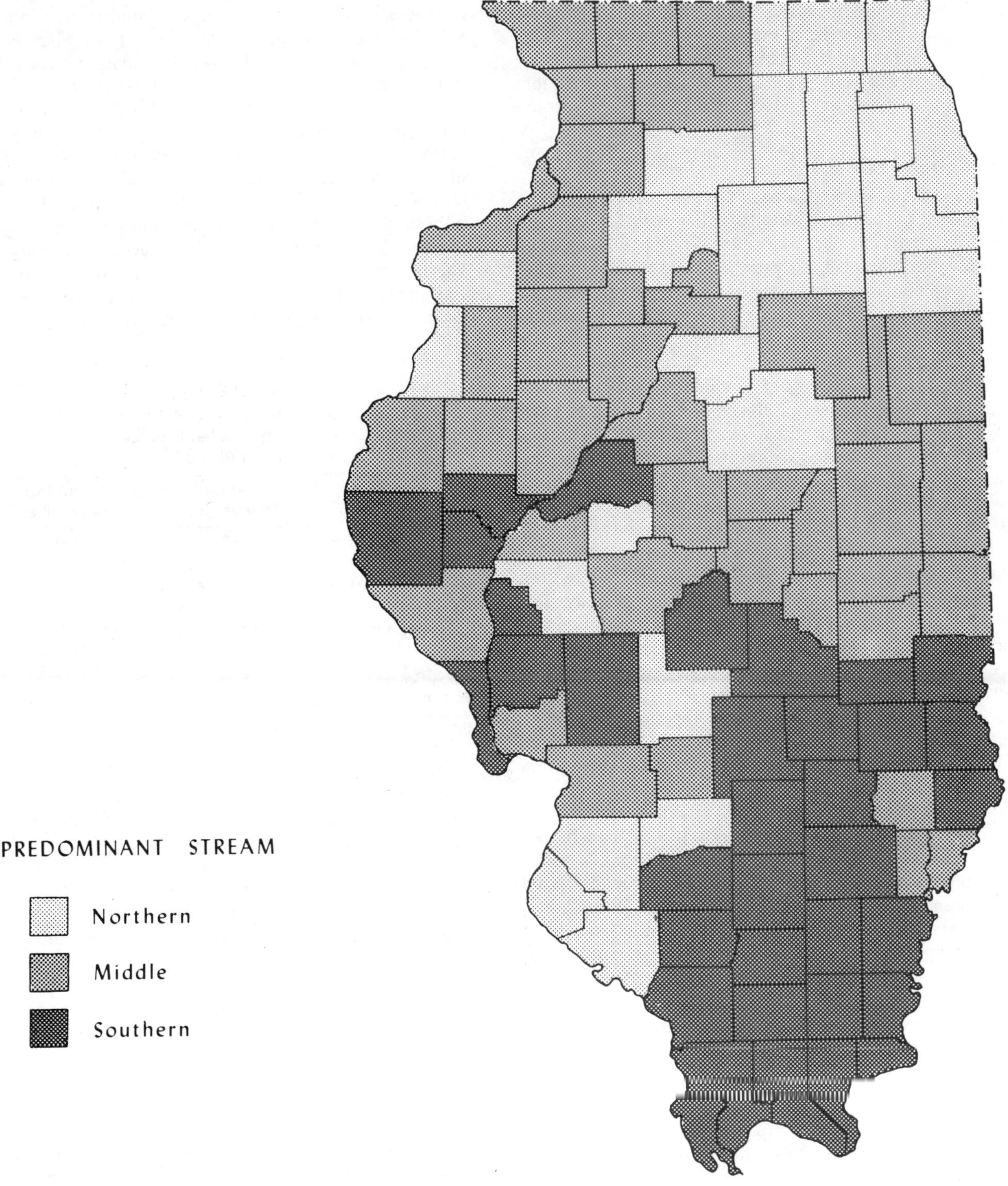

Figure 11-1: RELATIVE STRENGTH OF CULTURAL STREAMS IN ILLINOIS COUNTIES

Source: Data as reported in Alan D. Monroe "Operationalizing Political Culture: The Illinois Case," *Publius* 7 (1977), 113.

The Southern stream carries the *Traditionalistic* political culture which sees the main purpose of government as the preservation of established values and institutions. Political parties are not particularly appreciated by this culture and mass political participation is not encouraged.

The Cultural Mix In Illinois

Elazar suggests a number of contemporary manifestations of these cultural patterns and various researchers have found his attribution of cultural types to the states of some value in explaining variations in public policy and governmental arrangements.[2] But we are concerned with the utility of this theory in explaining variations within the State of Illinois. Happily, Elazar's theory seems particularly applicable to this state, even though the original inquiry, *Cities of the Prairie,* which led to the theory, was based upon a study of eleven communities, none of which are located in Illinois. All three political cultures are strongly represented within the state, a circumstance shared only by Ohio. Elazar argues that Illinois "in its social structure and its pattern of political response . . . is very likely the nation's most representative state."[3]

The important point is that each of the three streams is dominant in some parts of the State. Figure 1 shows the pattern of distribution as derived from a factor analysis of Nineteenth Century indicators of migration, religion and politics. It should be emphasized that Figure 11-1 is based solely on mid-Nineteenth Century migrational patterns. Where there have been considerable amounts of later immigration—as is the case for Cook County—there has been considerable cultural change. But for most of the counties in the State, the fundamental parameters of political culture were set a century ago.

As Elazar's research indicates, a number of variations in local government and policy in Illinois can be accounted for by differences in cultural background.[4] The quantitative measures of the cultural background of each county in Illinois upon which the map in Figure 11-1 is based also demonstrate the utility of Elazar's theory in explaining the geographical distribution of various indicators of contemporary political behavior, such as support for the adoption of the 1970 Constitution.[5] Of more direct interest to this chapter are the relationship of these cultural streams to partisan voting and turnout.

Voting Patterns in Contemporary Illinois

Cook County Versus Downstate: Some Common Myths

Among casual observers of Illinois politics, some common misconceptions about the distribution of partisan strength within the State have become so well entrenched that they might be called "myths." Like most such mistakes, these myths have some basis in fact, but represent fundamentally inaccurate generalizations. Myth 1: Cook County is almost all Democratic, while the rest of the State is all Republican. True, the City of Chicago typically turns in heavy majorities for most Democratic candidates, but these pluralities are largely offset by the Republican tendencies of suburban communities. Cook County is more than marginally Democratic in its habits, but it is never the most Democratic county in the State. Similarly, "Downstate" turns in vote totals which are, on the average, quite evenly divided among the parties. In fact, survey data indicate that slightly more Downstate residents identify with the Democratic party than the Republican, though the typically higher turnout and loyalty among Republicans combine to give that party a slight electoral advantage. The first part of Table 11-1 presents the division of the vote in the two areas for the 1976 presidential race; the same relative pattern would appear for any other election.

TABLE 11-1
Cook County and Downstate Illinois in the 1976 Presidential Election*
Division of the Vote

	% Voting Democratic	% Voting Republican
Cook County	55%	45%
Rest of Illinois	44%	56%

Contribution to the Party Vote

	% of Democratic Votes Coming From	% of Republican Votes Coming From
Cook County	52%	41%
Rest of Illinois	48%	59%

*Major party votes only

Another way of looking at the Cook/Downstate division results is Myth 2: Most of the Democratic votes come from Chicago. As the second part of Table 1 indicates, this is a misleading interpretation. True, slightly over half of Carter's support in Illinois came from Cook County, but over forty percent of Ford's votes did also. The fact is that Cook County contains almost half of the State's population and therefore accounts for almost half of everything, including votes for Democratic candidates.

Myth 3 is that in Illinois, urban residents vote Democratic while rural people vote Republican. The inaccuracy of this assumption can be seen by looking at counties displaying strong partisan tendencies. The most Democratic counties in most elections include both the Downstate urban concentrations of Madison and St. Clair counties (both in the St. Louis metropolitan area) as well as a number of heavily rural counties in Southern Illinois such as Gallatin, Franklin, Jefferson and Union. Areas which are the most Republican typically include not only predominantly rural counties such as Ford, Iroquois and Livingston, but also heavily urbanized suburban counties such as McHenry and DuPage. In fact, many of the metropolitan areas outside of the Chicago area tend toward the Republican side, e.g., Rockford, Bloomington-Normal and Champaign-Urbana. Overall, there is typically a very low correlation between the degree of urbanization of a county and its partisanship.[6]

Why have these myths endured? Perhaps it is because of the failure to recognize that the City of Chicago is only a part of the whole Chicago metropolitan area. Indeed, if we include the other five counties which are part of the Chicago Standard Metropolitan Statistical Area (SMSA), we find that they balance off the Democratic votes of Cook County. In the 1976 presidential election, the Republican plurality in DuPage County alone was over half the size of Cook's Democratic margin. It may also be that politicians occasionally find it advantageous to exaggerate the political differences between Chicago and the rest of the State. Former Governor Daniel Walker was known to point out that he was from a little Downstate town (the affluent Lake County suburb of Deerfield), while Governor Richard Ogilvie was from Cook County. (In fact, Walker's home was only about ten miles from Ogilvie's residence in Glenview.)

Party Voting and Candidate Voting

The outcome of any election can be thought of as the product of long-term and short-term forces. By "long-term" forces we mean those patterns which are fairly stable over a period of years and give a constant partisan tendency. These can be largely measured by the distribution of party identification within any geographic social group, because most people tend to have a particular partisan loyalty (i.e., they consider themselves to be Republicans, Democrats or Independents) which seldom changes. "Short-term" forces, on the other hand, represent the sum of all of those factors relevant to a particular election which cause deviations away from established party patterns. These factors would include the mood of the times, events, the effects of campaigning and the appeal of the individual candidates.[7]

It is necessary to distinguish these two forces in order to identify election patterns in Illinois. Elections for some offices obviously tend to generate much more voting on the basis of short-term forces, especially the popularity of the individual candidates. This is typically the case, in Illinois, for Governor and U.S. Senator and, at least in the 1970's, for Attorney General and Secretary of State. If we were to map the distribution of party strength by using one of these races, we could show the whole State as supporting the Republican or the Democrat, depending on which office in which year we chose. On the other hand, some of the less visible State offices seem to attract votes almost entirely on the basis of party loyalty. This is not surprising because very few voters have any knowledge of who the candidates for an office such as Comptroller are or what is involved in the working of that office. The extreme example of such an office is that of Trustee of the University of Illinois, a statewide elective post. Voters are called upon to choose three trustees at each general election and the similarity of vote totals for all three candidates from the same party indicate that there must be almost no attempt to distinguish individuals.

Table 11-2 presents some examples of recent elections illustrating the different types of office. The important thing to note is that while "candidate-centered" elec-

TABLE 11-2
Results of Statewide Elections in the 1970's*

Year	Office	Democratic Candidate and % of the Vote		Republican Candidate and % of the Vote	
1970	U.S. Senator	Stevenson	58	Smith	42
	Treasurer	Dixon	51	Kucharski	49
	Supt. Public Instruction	Bakalis	57	R. Page	43
	U. of I. Trustees	—	54	—	46
1972	President	McGovern	41	Nixon	59
	U.S. Senator	Pucinski	38	Percy	62
	Governor	Walker	51	Ogilvie	49
	Attorney General	Lyons	36	Scott	64
	Secretary of State	Howlett	52	Kucharski	48
	Comptroller	Barringer	49	Lindberg	51
	U. of I. Trustees	—	53	—	47
1974	U.S. Senator	Stevenson	58	Burditt	42
	Treasurer	Dixon	65	H. Page	35
	U. of I. Trustees	—	57	—	43
1976	President	Carter	49	Ford	51
	Governor	Howlett	35	Thompson	65
	Attorney General	Partee	38	Scott	62
	Secretary of State	Dixon	65	Harris	35
	Comptroller	Bakalis	52	Lindberg	48
	U. of I. Trustees	—	53	—	47
1978	U.S. Senator	Seith	46	Percy	54
	Governor	Bakalis	40	Thompson	60
	Attorney General	Troy	35	Scott	65
	Secretary of State	Dixon	75	Sharp	25
	Treasurer	Cosentino	53	Skelton	47
	Comptroller	Burris	50	Castle	50
	U. of I. Trustees	—	51	—	49

*All percentages based upon the two-party vote. Votes listed for President are actually votes for presidential electors. Percentages for University of Illinois Trustees are based on total votes for three candidates from each party.

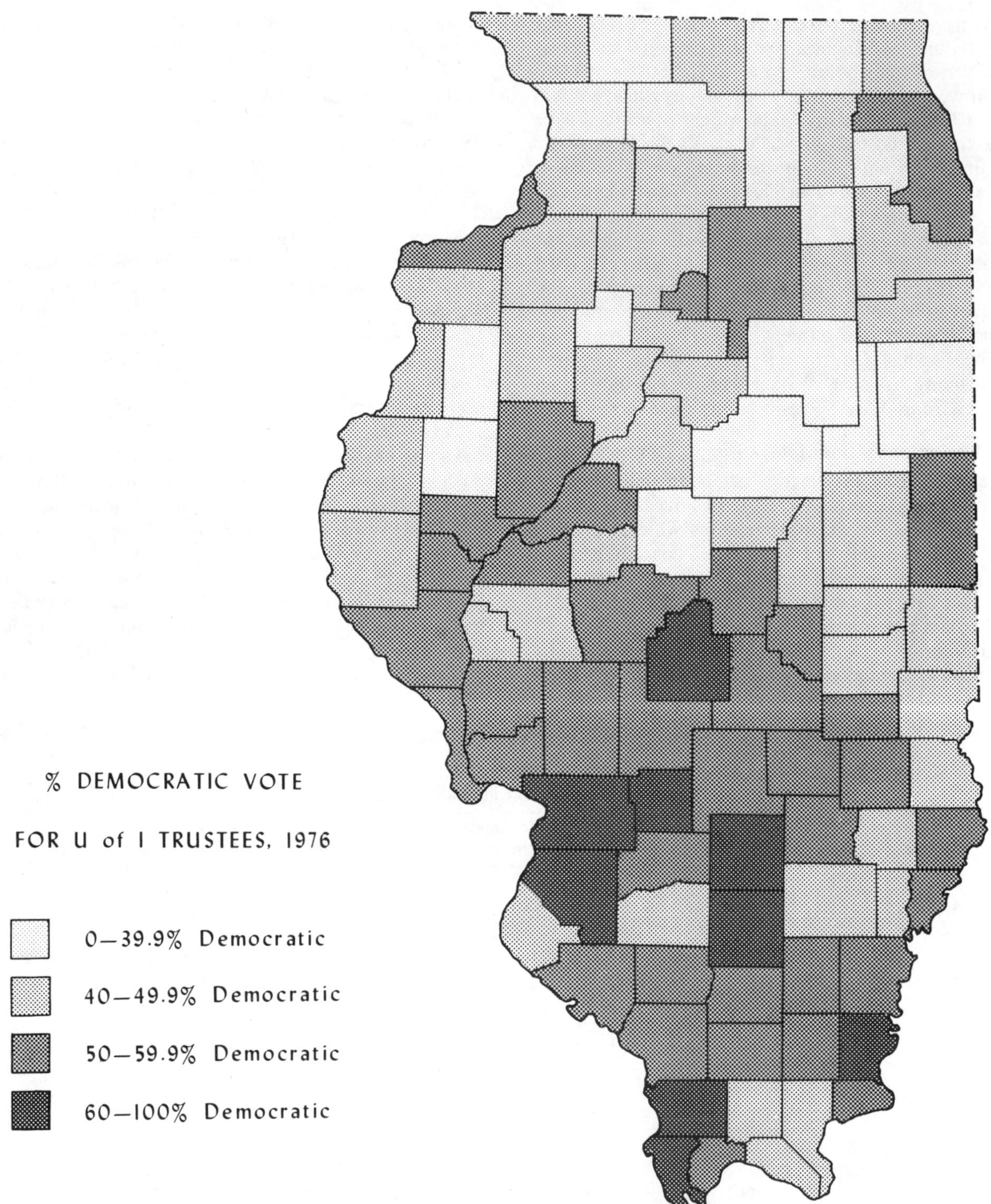

FIGURE 11-2: DISTRIBUTION OF PARTISAN VOTING IN ILLINOIS COUNTIES: 1976 VOTE FOR UNIVERSITY OF ILLINOIS TRUSTEES

tions, such as those for Governor and Senator, vary widely in their partisan outcomes, "party-centered" races almost always resulted in very close elections. This latter circumstance reflects the fact that the parties in Illinois are closely divided in their strength among voters. Indeed, an estimate of the "normal vote" in Illinois (i.e., the division of the vote between the parties if everyone voted according to party loyalty, taking into account normal rates of defection and turnout), is that it would be about 52.5 percent Democratic. (See the chapter by Green for a discussion of trends.)

The party centered offices therefore provide useful indicators of party strength. Figure 11-2 shows the distribution of the partisan vote for University of Illinois Trustees in 1976. This is a particularly good example because the total vote in that race was almost exactly the 52.5 percent Democratic figure cited above. Any possible local attraction to particular candidates was further diminished by adding together the votes for the three candidates for each party.

The Distribution of Partisanship in Illinois

The map in Figure 2 indicates that there is a definite pattern in the distribution of party strength throughout the State. Basically, the further south one goes in Illinois, the greater the tendency to vote for Democratic candidates. Most of the counties south of the center of the State (i.e., south of Springfield) are Democratic and all of the counties giving more than sixty percent of their vote to the Democrat's in 1976 were found there. Conversely, most of the counties in the northern half of the State were Republican, and all of the most heavily Republican counties were there.

The most obvious explanation for this distribution is the historical cultural pattern outlined at the start of this chapter. This can be seen by comparing the maps in Figures 1 and 2. Statistical analysis of the relationship between measures of the strength of the different cultural streams of migration into county and partisan voting in elections of the past two decades indicate that there are definite tendencies for the *Northern* and, especially, *Middle* stream areas to vote Republican and *Southern* stream-dominated areas to vote Democratic.[8] Furthermore, the three streams collectively are capable of explaining significant amounts of variation in the distribution of the vote, over and above that attributable to other socio-economic factors. Data for one recent election is presented in Table 3 and is discussed below. The patterns of historical culture and contemporary partisanship are not identical by any means, but they are similar enough to suggest that the differences in politics from one part of Illinois to another are largely a result of influences from the past century.

Historical patterns of party loyalty are not the only reason for some groups of people to vote differently from others. As almost four decades of survey-based studies of individual voting behavior have demonstrated, a number of socio-economic characteristics are associated with partisanship. While research into those relationships is best conducted with data on individuals, we can still look to see whether the distribution of demographic attributes within counties explains their partisanship. Table 3 presents the results of a multiple regression analysis of voting in the 1976 presidential election by Illinois counties, including the effects of both the cultural stream factors and a number of common demographic indicators.[9]

TABLE 11-3
Multiple Regression Analysis of Democratic Voting in the 1976 Presidential Election by Illinois Counties

Independent Variable	Beta Weight
Southern Stream	.589
Middle Stream	−.225
% Black	.235
Northern Stream	−.189
Southern Ethnicity	.196
% in Professional/Managerial Jobs	−.241
% in Urban Places	.282
Middle Ethnicity	−.162
Median Education	−.121
Median Family Income	−.215
Farm Income	.156
Northern Ethnicity	.110

R=.81 N=102

The coefficients in Table 11-3 illustrate the impact of the historical stream factors discussed above, *Southern* predominance being associated with support for the Democratic party and prevalence of the other two streams being associated with non-Democratic (i.e., Republican) voting. The most powerful demographic variable is the proportion of the population which is black, this of course being associated with Democratic support. This is consistent with national survey data which has shown blacks to have voted very heavily for democratic candidates in national elections since 1960. Several indicators of social status—education, employment in professional or managerial occupations, and income are all negatively associated with Democratic voting, a not suprising consequence of the general tendency for higher status individuals to be Republican. Farm income, however, has the reverse relationship, though it is a relatively weak one. Finally, controlling for the other factors, we see that there is some tendency for counties with higher levels of urbanization to be more Democratic in their voting habits. The data analyzed here are for only one election, but other years and offices yield highly similar patterns. When the explanatory impact of the cultural and the socio-economic variables are combined, we can explain almost two thirds of the variance in the partisanship of Illinois counties.

Issues and Candidates

Our discussion of election outcomes has thus far ignored the "short-term" forces which cause deviations from established patterns of partisanship. These forces would seem to be largely a question of the effects of voter's perceptions and preferences on the issues and their reactions to the candidates involved in a particular election. Research into this topic necessarily involves the collection of survey data on a large scale, and that has almost always been done for the whole nation rather than a particular state, so it would be difficult to talk only about the "Illinois Voter" as distince from the "American Voter." All indications are that the behavior patterns of the Illinois electorate are quite similar to those for the nation as a whole,[10] however, and that we may therefore draw upon the broader literature on this topic.

As a number of analyses of American voting behavior have demonstrated, both an individual's perception of a candidate's merits and his judgement about which party and candidate best represents his point of view on major issues are good predictors of the voting choice.[11] People strongly tend to vote for the candidate whom they feel is the better in both issue and personal terms. However, this fact does not rule out the importance of established patterns of party identification. Not surprisingly, a person's party loyalty has a definite impact on his judgement as to which candidate seems most qualified. And there is definite evidence that voters sometimes distort the issue position taken by presidential candidates so as to attribute their own positions to the candidate of their party.[12] Hence, it would be questionable to assume that consistency between issue preferences and candidate choice proves that voters are issue-oriented. However, as a number of sophisticated analyses have demonstrated, voter preferences on issues as well as judgements about the candidates have a significant independent impact on the voting choice. Indeed, there is much evidence that voters have been becoming somewhat more issue-oriented and somewhat less dependent on party identification over the past two decades. Hence, short-term forces are capable of producing substantial deviations in election results from the outcomes expected on the basis of long-term forces.

The preceding conclusions are almost all based upon research into voting in presidential elections. There is little doubt that it would be applicable to the presidential choices of Illinois voters. But what of all of the lesser offices for which voters in this state must make a decision? In general, it might be said that the less visible an office is to the voter, the more important party identification will be and the less important any short-term factors. Elections for Governor and Senator in Illinois are highly visible, and one could probably conclude that the candidate and issue components of the vote are about as strong as they are for the presidential choice.[13] But as argued earlier in this chapter in our discussion of candidate-centered versus party-centered offices, the lower the office, the more dominant the party forces. Not only are such offices as State Comptroller less visible and the candidates for them less well known, there is also less basis for meaningful issue divisions, for the policy questions over which these officials have jurisdiction are fewer. The occasional exception comes when a particular candidate has managed to achieve considerable popularity in these lesser offices and therefore is able to attract additional votes to his personal candidacy.[14] What is true of these lesser statewide offices is undoubtedly applicable to elections for smaller jurisdictions. Most voters lack knowledge of their U.S. Representatives[15] and this would be even more true of their State legislators. Similar statements could probably be made about the variety of county and judicial offices filled by popular elections in Illinois.[16] In short, the distribution of party identification in a particular electorate is likely to be the key factor in determining who will win an election—with an occasional adjustment for those years when one party as a whole does much better or worse as a result of national trends and events.[17]

Voting Turnout

Another aspect of voting behavior is the frequency with which citizens choose to participate in elections. Variations in the turnout rate are of interest to the political scientist because the proportion of people voting in the United States is frequently less than half. And American turnout, already lower than that of most other Western nations, has been dropping even further since 1960. We will examine levels of electoral participation in Illinois as compared to the rest of the nation and in terms of variations within the State.

Illinois: Higher than Average Turnout

Table 11-4 reports turnout figures for Illinois and the nation as a whole since 1960. Note that these figures (and all turnout statistics reported in this chapter) are expressed as a proportion of the population of voting age—not as a proportion of registered voters. There are two reasons for using the total voting age population as a base. From a theoretical standpoint, we are interested in what part of the population chooses to participate and the decision to register to vote is the biggest part of that process. As a practical matter, statistics on voter registration are typically very poorly kept, if they are kept at all. In a number of Illinois counties, the number of registered voters reported by local officials exceeds the number of people of voting age according to the U.S. Census! This is not necessarily an indicator of any malfeasance of office by those in charge of voter registration, but simply a consequence of the fact that people who are once registered remain on the rolls for at least four years after they have died or moved away.

TABLE 11-4
Turnout Rates for Illinois and for the U.S. in Presidential (P) and Congressional (C) Elections 1960–1976

Year	Office	% of Voting Age Population Illinois	U.S.
1960	P	76	63
1962	C	59	45
1964	P	73	62
1966	C	57	45
1968	P	69	61
1970	C	51	44
1972	P	63	56
1974	C	37	36
1976	P	61	50

TABLE 11-5
Voter Turnout in Categories of Illinois Counties, 1972

	Mean % Turnout	Range	Number of Counties
No urban population*	84	72–96	13
Largest Town Less Than 10,000*	77	65–92	50
Largest City 10,000 to 19,999*	71	65–78	10
Largest City 20,000 or Greater*	66	62–74	8
S.M.S.A. Counties	65	56–78	10
Suburban Counties (Chicago S.M.S.A. only)	69	60–77	5
"College" Counties	62	53–66	6
ALL COUNTIES	74	53–96	102

*Non-S.M.S.A. Counties

As Table 11-4 indicates, turnout in Illinois is always somewhat above the national average. Like the nation as a whole, turnout figures have dropped for both presidential and Congressional elections since 1960. When compared to other states individually, Illinois always ranks above average, but never at the top. Ranney finds that Illinois ranked ninth among all states in average turnout from 1962 through 1972.[18] All of the states ranking above Illinois were less urbanized and industrialized (e.g., Utah, South Dakota, Idaho, etc.). This rank represented a slight gain for Illinois since the 1952–1960 period when it ranked fifteenth, though the general alignment of states has not changed very much.[19]

Why does Illinois rank above the national norm in turnout? First of all, it is not a Southern state. This is significant because it is the states of the deep South which have had much lower rates of participation due to a number of legal and extralegal restrictions which for many years prevented most blacks and some whites from registering and voting. While these restrictions have largely been removed by federal action in the last ten years, the South still pulls down the national average somewhat. Secondly, Illinois has a high degree of competition between the political parties. This is significant because a number of studies have shown that the greater the inter-party competition, the higher the turnout.[20] Related to this is the nature of the legal requirements and procedures for registration and voting. Longer residency requirements, literacy tests and other restrictive devices lead to lower turnout rates, while provisions for absentee ballots, registration within the precinct and other facilitative devices tend to increase participation. Some of these factors are no longer relevant, as federal laws and judicial decisions have banned poll taxes, literacy tests and residency requirements longer than thirty days. Illinois does facilitate participation somewhat more than some other states with some provision for door-to-door registration, ease of obtaining absentee ballots and the like. Finally, one might note that residents of Illinois tend to be somewhat above the national norms on socioeconomic variables such as education, income and occupational status. As these variables are positively associated with participation by individuals, their higher level for the State as a whole might explain the higher turnout level. However, as the analysis of Kim, Petrocik and Enokson indicates,[21] the factors of competition and electoral laws are much more important in the case of Illinois. And as the following discussion of turnout variations within the State indicates, those individual relationships may not hold for geographic areas.

Variations in turnout from one type of election to another are also significant. The higher the office to be elected, the higher the turnout for that election is likely to be. As Table 11-4 illustrated, turnout typically is ten to twenty percent higher in presidential contests than in "off-year" Congressional elections. It is more difficult to generalize about municipal, primary and other elections held at other times, but these typically have even lower levels of turnout, rates of ten percent or less not being unheard of. Illinois seems to be no different than the rest of the nation in this regard.

Turnout Variations within Illinois[22]

If we were to seek an answer to the question of what areas in Illinois have the lowest and the highest levels of voter participation, the conventional wisdom would be that rural areas have lower turnout, while the highest levels should be found in those suburban counties where education and income are the highest. Such generalizations, however, would be completely erroneous. When turnout figures are calculated for Illinois counties and compared to the proportion of the population living in urban areas, the result is a rather strong negative correlation. In other words, the more urban a county, the lower the turnout rate. This is illustrated by the data in Table 11-5 in which counties are divided into categories of urbanization based on the size of the largest city as well as some other considerations.[23] The highest levels of turnout are recorded by those counties which were completely rural, the leader being Hardin County, a small rural area on the Ohio River where 96 percent of the residents of voting age participated in the 1972 election! As the level of urbanization increases, turnout drops. The suburban counties around the Chicago area do have a slightly higher rate than some less populous categories, but hardly what would be expected in view of their economic and educational levels.

What can account for this pattern? One possibility would be the cultural background of different parts of the State. Elazar's cultural theory described at the start of the chapter would predict that voter participation would be the lowest in the *Southern* stream and highest in those counties settled by the *Northern* stream. However, analysis of the data reveals that this is not the case. Indeed, those rural counties with high turnout prove to be almost entirely *Southern*-settled areas in the southern half of the State.[24] Nor does the distribution of socio-economic variables explain why rural areas have higher turnout. The less urban counties typically have lower levels of education, income and white-collar employment. Therefore, their demographic composition means they should have had lower turnout, not higher. Two variables which do correlate with turnout in a manner one would have expected are age and party competition. The higher the median age in a county, the higher the turnout rate, as one would expect from what is known about individual behavior. And more competitive counties tend to have higher turnout. But these two factors are not sufficient to explain away the urban-rural pattern by any means. Until more discriminating research is done, the conclusion must be simply that people in rural areas are more disposed to participate in electoral politics.

Changing Electoral Patterns in Illinois

While this chapter has emphasized the existence of a relatively stable geographic pattern of politics in Illinois, there are some potential changes underway which bear scrutiny. In this section we will examine two such possible trends.

Cultural Realignment?

The traditional regional pattern of southern support for the Democratic party and northern Republicanism is hardly a phenomenon limited to Illinois, for it has represented the basic geographic pattern for the whole nation for a century. Yet that national pattern has been altered in recent years, at least for presidential voting. In 1964, 1968 and 1972, the states of the Deep South gave much more support to the Republican candidate for President than they did to the Democrat. At the same time, what had been the most firmly Republican states, e.g., the Yankee-settled areas of upper New England, the Midwest and the Pacific Northwest shifted toward the Democrats. In short, the geographic alignment which had prevailed since the advent of the New Deal was not only destroyed, but somewhat reversed.[25] The parties have still largely retained their older electoral bases for lesser offices, but there have been more Republicans elected in the South and more Democrats in the Yankee-influenced states. The pattern established in 1964 was clearly maintained in the next two presidential elections, but the contest of 1976—perhaps because of the candidacy of Carter, a Southerner—saw a substantial return to the pattern of the 1940's and 1950's.[26] These changes, at least that of 1964, can be easily argued to be a product of the cultural streams in American political behavior in combination with the changing nature of political issues in contemporary society.[27]

Have these shifts in the alignment of cultural background with partisanship occurred within the State of Illinois? If we expect to find the critical reversal of past patterns which occurred on a national level in 1964 and 1976, the answer must be in the negative. The *Southern* settled areas continued to be the most Democratic in the State for all offices, with the *Northern* and *Middle* areas more Republican. But there have been somewhat more moderate changes. The correlation between cultural stream factors and partisanship for Illinois counties had been decreasing slowly since the 1952 election. But as was the case with the whole nation, there was an increase in the strength of this older regional pattern in voting for Carter in 1976.[28] Therefore, the traditional pattern of party strength in Illinois might be said to be generally back to where it was two decades ago. However, it should be noted that since the counties with the most identifiable cultural patterns (i.e., southern Illinois counties and rural counties in the central and northern parts of the State) have been declining in population, the impact of cultural background upon the outcome of the vote is necessarily being diminished.

Growth of the Suburbs[29]

An unavoidable fact of political life in Illinois over several decades has been the change in the distribution of population throughout the State. While the State as a whole increased in population by 46 percent from 1930 to 1970, the City of Chicago actually suffered a slight decline, the suburbs grew by 326 percent and the rest of the State experienced a moderate 29 percent increase.[30] These differential rates of growth have produced a marked shift in potential political power as illustrated in Table 11-6. Whereas the City of Chicago once had more people than either the suburbs or the remainder of the State, they now find themselves in third place among these three "regions." The beneficiary of this change is, of course, the suburban area, which now holds a full third of the State's population. And since the suburban areas tend to have somewhat higher levels of voter turnout than the City of Chicago, their electoral votes would be even greater than what the table suggests. This trend has continued since 1970 and will undoubtedly be continued in future years.

What is the political impact of these changes? There is a temptation to conclude that since the Democratic stronghold of Chicago is losing importance and the Republican-dominated suburbs are rapidly expanding, the Republican proportion of the vote should be greatly

TABLE 11-6
Population Change in Illinois, 1930–1970

Area	Percentage of Population				
	1930	1940	1950	1960	1970
City of Chicago	44	43	42	35	30
Suburban	14	15	18	27	33
Rest of State	42	42	40	38	37

increased. But such a conclusion would not be an accurate one. First of all, as a number of studies have shown, people usually do not change their party loyalties when they change their location.[31] If the suburbs are Republican, it is because people with Republican sympathies move into them. Secondly, it should be noted that the suburban areas around Chicago, while predominantly Republican, do contain a substantial number of Democratic voters and that this tendency is probably increasing. Thirdly, the City is becoming even more solidly Democratic and will continue to do so as the proportion of blacks and Latins in the electorate increases. On the other hand, it should be remembered that there has also been a relative population loss outside the Chicago SMSA. This has probably taken votes from both the Democrats and the Republicans downstate, but perhaps somewhat more from the Democratic strongholds of southern Illinois which (except for the Madison-St. Clair County complex) have been losing population for many years.

The upshot of all of this is that the political balance probably has not been much changed over the years. If anything, the relative number of Republican identifiers may have decreased slightly, just as it has nationally. What has changed is the basis of party strength. The Republican Party is quite dependent on the suburbs for political support. One would expect that the Democratic Party will become somewhat more dependent on the suburban areas also. This suggests a loss of some political influence for the Chicago Democratic organization, as well as for the Democratic leaders from the far southern part of the State, and the corresponding growth of a more reform-oriented Democratic Party in Illinois.

Unresolved Issues and Future Research Opportunities

In many ways, voting behavior in the United States is a subject which has received more extensive and sophisticated research than any other in political science—if we are interested only in presidential elections. One area where there is a need for more research is that of voting for lesser offices, both State and local. Is the role of party identification greater here? What kind of issues are important? Are voters more or less aware of the identity of candidates for the most local offices? These are the sort of questions to which previous research, largely based upon national sample surveys, has offered only very tentative answers. More research, such as that conducted by the Comparative State Election Project in 1968 using large scale surveys in a number of different states, would seem to be what is needed. Perhaps some return to the studies of voting behavior in single communities, which in the 1940's initiated the scientific study of the electoral process, should also be attempted.

While there is a large and diverse literature relevant to the role of region, migration, religion and ethnicity in American politics, that material is extremely heterogenous and disorganized. Daniel Elazar's theoretical formulation offers a promising paradigm for future research, but one which undoubtedly could be further refined. The method of quantitatively operationalizing the strength of the three cultural streams for Illinois counties cited in this chapter could obviously be extended to other states and perhaps to the nation as a whole. And these measures of cultural background probably have explanatory value for many other measures of political behavior and policy today.

While few will be likely to be able to engage in original survey research on any large scale (though they may well be able to use existing survey data), the analysis of aggregate voting data, i.e., voting returns for cities, counties, etc., offers a source of data which is readily available. It is also appropriate for the analysis of many questions raised in this chapter, e.g., patterns of turnout, the role of historical forces and the possibility of geographic realignment over the years. State by state results for presidential elections throughout American history are available in countless reference books. Returns for other elections and for smaller units, mainly counties, are also available if one knows where to look. Since 1952, Richard Scammon's *America Votes* series has given county-by-county results for elections for President, Governor and U.S. Senator. For the Nineteenth Century, W.D. Burnham's *Presidential Ballots* covers the years 1828 through 1892. For Illinois in particular, Samuel Gove, *Illinois Votes,* 1950–1958, gives county results for President, Governor, and Treasurer. The original source for Illinois results are the "Official Vote" reports published by the Secretary of State of Illinois (since 1974 by the State Board of Elections). These reports, which go back well into the last century, vary in their specificity, but in recent decades have included county-by-county results of all statewide general elections and state legislative races and, since 1954, reports by wards for Chicago.

Those researchers who are interested in analysis of voting for units smaller than the county, e.g., the precinct, face a much more difficult task, as there is no comprehensive publication reporting these figures. For smaller communities, local newspapers often publish at least the unofficial returns for some offices just after the election. And statistics for at least recent elections should be available from local election officials, though the format of the data and the cooperativeness of the officials will vary greatly.

NOTES

[1] Daniel J. Elazar, *Cities of the Prairie: The Metropolitan Frontier and American Politics* (New York: Basic Books, 1970); and *American Federalism: A View from the States* (2d ed.; New York: Corwell, 1972).

[2] E.g., Ira Sharkansky, "The Utility of Elazar's Political Culture: A Research Note," *Polity* 2 (1969), 66–83; Leonard G. Ritt, "Political Cultures and Political Reform: A Research Note," *Publius* 4 (1974), 127–33; and Charles A. Johnson, "Political Culture in American States: Elazar's Formulation Examined," *American Journal of Political Science* 20 (1975), 491–509.

[3] Elazar, *Cities, op. cit.,* p. 282. Also see Austin Ranney, *Illinois Politics* (New York: New York University Press, 1961), p. 1.

[4] See Elazar, *Cities, op. cit.,* Chapter 7 on "Competing Political Cultures in Illinois," for a summary.

[5]Alan D. Monroe, "The Cultural Basis of American Politics: Testing Elazar's Theory," Paper presented to the Southern Political Science Association, Atlanta, November 9–11, 1978.

[6]Note that we are using "urban" here in the same way that the Census Bureau does, i.e., any place with a population of 2,500 or more (recently raised to 5,)000).

[7]This discussion is based upon the ideas formulated in Philip E. Converse, "The Concept of a Normal Vote," in *Elections and the Political Order*, ed. by Angus Campbell, *et al.* (New York: Wiley, 1966), pp. 9–39.

[8]See Monroe, "The Cultural Basis," *op. cit.*, pp. 17–19 and Alan D. Monroe, "Operationalizing Political Culture: The Illinois Case," *Publius* 7 (1977), 115–16.

[9]For a complete explanation of the operationalization of these variables, see *Ibid.* The "Stream" variables are the result of a factor analysis of 53 variables for Illinois counties in the period 1840–1870. The "Ethnicity" variables are based upon the frequency of various immigrant groups as of 1910. Other variables are drawn from the 1970 Census. "Beta Weights" are standardized partial regression coefficients.

[10]In addition to all of the customary arguments which can be made as to Illinois being a representative state, the Comparative State Election Project data indicate that the effects of various influences on the voting decision are the same in Illinois as they are for the nation as a whole. See Gerald C. Wright, Jr., *Electoral Choice in America: Image, Party, and Incumbency in State and National Elections* (Chapel Hill: University of North Carolina, 1974), pp. 67–68, 104–11, and 155–56.

[11]This section draws upon such works as Angus Campbell, *et al.*, *The American Voter* (New York: Wiley, 1960); Gerald M. Pomper, *Voter's Choice: Varieties of American Electoral Behavior* (New York: Dodd, Mead, 1975); and Norman H. Nie, Sidney Verba and John R. Petrocik, *The Changing American Voter* (Cambridge: Harvard University Press), 1976.

[12]See, for example, the case of distorted perceptions regarding candidate perceptions of the Taft-Hartley Act in the 1948 election in Bernard R. Berelson, Paul F. Lazarsfeld and William N. McPhee, *Voting: A Study of Opinion Formation in a Presidential Campaign* (Chicago: University of Chicago Press, 1954), pp. 215–33; and of the Viet Nam war question in 1968 in Benjamin I. Page and Richard A. Brody, "Policy Voting and the Electoral Process; The Viet Nam War Issue," *American Political Science Review* 66 (1972), 979–95.

[13]This was the finding on a national basis in 1968. See Barbara C. Hinckley, Richard Hofstetter and John H. Kessel, "Imformation and the Vote: A Comparative Election Study," *American Politics Quarterly* 2 (1974), 131–58.

[14]The outstanding example in the 1970's would be Alan Dixon.

[15]Donald E. Stokes and Warren E. Miller, "Party Government and the Saliency of Congress," *Public Opinion Quarterly* 26 (1962), 531–46.

[16]And Illinois, which has more local governmental units (over 6,000) than any other state, also has more elected officials (approximately 36,500).

[17]The last clear case of an overall national trend which affected less visible offices was in 1974 when the post Watergate reaction worked against the Republicans. But in general, there has been little evidence of much "coat tail" effect in Illinois in recent years.

[18]Austin Ranney, "Parties in State Politics," in *Politics in the American States*, ed. by Herbert Jacob and Kenneth N. Vines (3d ed.; Boston: Little, Brown & Co., 1976), p. 54.

[19]Lester W. Milbrath, "Political Participation in the States," in Jacob and Vines, *op. cit.*, p. 40.

[20]*Ibid.*, p. 52; also see Stanley Kelley, Jr., Richard E. Ayres and William G. Bowen, "Registration and Voting, Putting First Things First," *American Political Science Review* 61 (1967), 359–79.

[21]Jae-On Kim, John R. Petrocik and Stephen H. Enokson, "Voter Turnout Among the American States: Systemic and Individual Components," *American Political Science Review* 69 (1975), 107–23.

[22]This section is largely based upon analysis reported in Alan D. Monroe, "Urbanism and Voter Turnout: A Note on Some Unexpected Findings," *American Journal of Political Science* 21 (1977), 71–78.

[23]In Table 11-5, the "SMSA Counties" include Cook County as well as the core counties for other metropolitan areas in the state as defined by the Census. The "College Counties" are those which have large state Universities in them and suffer a reduced turnout record as most students are registered elsewhere.

[24]For a complete analysis on this point, see Monroe, "The Cultural Basis," *op. cit.*, pp. 11–13.

[25]For a more detailed analysis of this change see Gerald M. Pomper, *Elections in America: Control and Influence in Democratic Politics* (New York: Dodd, Mead, 1968), Chapter 5; and Walter Dean Burnham, *Critical Elections and the Mainsprings of American Politics* (New York: Norton, 1970), Chapter 6.

[26]Gerald M. Pomper, *The Election of 1976: Reports and Interpretations* (New York: David McKay, 1977), pp. 79–81.

[27]Kevin P. Phillips, *The Emerging Republican Majority* (Garden City: Doubleday, 1969) makes essentially this argument, though not using Elazar's terminology. See also Elazar, *American Federalism, op. cit.*, pp. 135–9.

[28]See Monroe, "The Cultural Basis," *op. cit.*, pp. 17–19 for analysis on this point.

[29]For a more detailed presentation of relevant data on this topic, see Peter W. Colby and Paul Michael Green, "Downstate Holds the Key to Victory," *Illinois Issues* 4:2 (February 1978), 7–11.

[30]In this discussion and in Table 11-6, "Suburbs" refers to that part of Cook County outside the City of Chicago plus the six surrounding counties: Lake, McHenry, DuPage, Kane, Kendall and Will.

[31]E.g., Jerome G. Manis and Leo C. Stine, "Suburban Residence and Political Behavior," *Public Opinion Quarterly* 22 (1959), 483–89 and Frederick M. Wirt, "The Political Sociology of American Suburbs: A Reinterpretation," *Journal of Politics* 27 (1965), 647–66.

SUPPLEMENTAL READINGS

On Elections Generally

Asher, Herbert. *Presidential Elections and American Politics: Voters, Candidates and Campaigns Since 1952*. Homewood, Ill.: Dorsey, 1976.

Campbell, Angus, *et al. The American Voter: An Abridgement*. New York: Wiley, 1964.

Flanigan, William H. and Nancy H. Zingale. *Political Behavior of the American Electorate*. 3d ed. Boston: Allyn & Bacon, 1975.

Nie, Norman H., Sidney Verba end John R. Petrocik. *The Changing American Voter*. Cambridge: Harvard University Press, 1976.

Pomper, Gerald M. *Elections in America: Control and Influence in Democratic Politics*. New York: Dodd, Mead, 1968.

———. *Voter's Choice: Varieties of American Electoral Behavior*. New York: Dodd, Mead, 1975.

Sundquist, James L. *Dynamics of the Party System: Alignment and Realignment of Political Parties in the United States* Washington: Brookings Institution, 1973.

On Illinois

Elazar, Daniel J. *Cities of the Prairie: The Metropolitan Frontier and American Politics*. New York: Basic Books, 1970.

——— and Joseph Zikmund II, eds. *The Ecology of American Political Culture: Readings*. New York: Crowell, 1975.

Fenton, John H. *Midwest Politics*. New York: Holt, Rhinehart & Winston, 1966.

Kleppner, Paul. *The Cross of Culture: A Social Analysis of Midwestern Politics, 1850*–1900. New York: The Free Press, 1970.

MacRae, Duncan, Jr. and James A. Meldrum. "Critical Elections in Illinois: 1888–1958." *American Political Science Review* 54: 3 (September 1960), 669–83.

Ranney, Austin. *Illinois Politics*. New York: New York University Press, 1960.

Richard Jenson, Winning of the Midwest

Anton, Tom,

CHAPTER **12**

History of Political Parties in Illinois

Paul M. Green

Historians and political scientists generally concur that the history of American political parties can be divided into four periods: 1800–1828—a one party era of good feelings; 1828–1860—the resurgence of two party politics with Democratic Party domination; 1860–1932—the industrialization of America under Republican Party leadership; 1932–present—Franklin D. Roosevelt's New Deal coalition attempts to keep its diverse factions inside the Democratic Party. This chapter analyzes Illinois political party history and compares its development with trends across the rest of the nation.

The United States Constitution makes no provision for political parties. This decision of the founding fathers followed the established pattern of previous colonial assemblies, the Continental Congress and the ill-fated Articles of Confederation. In 1789 George Washington became the newly established country's first President, but as history would soon prove he also became the nation's last non-party President.

Any real hopes for an "a-party" America disappeared early in Washington's Presidency. According to Arthur Schlesinger Jr., "Disagreements over both domestic and foreign policy brought the first parties . . . the Federalists and the Republicans into existence."[1] In broad terms the Federalists, led by Washington, Alexander Hamilton and John Adams, advocated a strong central government and were heavily supported by the eastern seaboard merchants and commercial interests. The Republicans, led by Thomas Jefferson and James Madison, wanted a weak central government and found their best supporters among artisans, frontier farmers and southern planters.

Thomas Jefferson's 1800 victory over John Adams ended the early Federalist presidential domination and started that party down the road to eventual extinction. Never again would a Federalist occupy the White House, and by 1814 the country would be left with only one major party. It was in this national political climate that Illinois achieved statehood and began its own political party development.

1800–1828: Illinois Party Politics in the "Era of Good Feelings;" Factionalism and Individualism Dominate

In 1804 Illinois was set off as a separate territory. In 1812 it elected its own territorial legislature and in 1818 Illinois achieved statehood. Throughout this period and the subsequent decade, no organized political party appeared in Illinois. Instead, Illinois political leadership was exercised by individuals who led shifting alliances with little regard to party structure or formal political organization.

Ninian Edwards was the key figure in this chaotic political environment. Edwards, a former chief justice in Kentucky, was Governor of the Illinois Territory from 1809 to 1818. His two able lieutenants, also former Kentuckians, were Nathaniel Pope and his son-in-law, Daniel Pope Cook. Edwards and his allies never organized into a party even though they controlled most important jobs during territorial days as well as the early statehood period.

Allied against Edwards was a faction of former easterners headed by Shadrach Bond, Elias Kent Kane and John McLean. Bond had been Illinois' first territorial delegate in Congress, and he would also serve the State as its first Governor. Like the Edwards group, Bond and his allies were not a political party but a loose coalition of men interested in public office.

The high desire for public employment can be best illustrated by the fact that after statehood in 1818 *all* the old territorial factional leaders received public office.[2] One might call it statesmanship or blind luck, but more likely a deal was struck instituting a tradition in Illinois politics.

Jeffersonian philosophy dominated Illinois politics in its territorial days. The Federalists were perceived as tight money advocates and anti-farmer and thus, all Illinois politicians huddled under a loose Jeffersonian Republican label.[3] When General Andrew Jackson and his allies changed the Republican Party's name nationally to Democrat, Illinois leaders moved along with Old Hickory.

Presidential politics heightened political interest during this period. Without structured party organization, national presidential candidates entered into the individualistic politics of Illinois and in their efforts developed political parties. The 1824 presidential battle between Andrew Jackson and his three main rivals, John Quincy Adams, Henry Clay and William Crawford, set the stage for the establishment of political party organizations. In this election Illinois voters made their presiden-

The author would like to acknowledge the assistance of Martin Dubin Al Manning, Ron Michaelson and former Governor Samuel Shapiro who read and commented on an earlier draft of this chapter.

tial choice by selecting electors [by district][4] pledged to a particular candidate. In a surprisingly close contest Adams, Jackson and Clay received the most popular votes.[5] Since no candidates nationwide received a majority of electoral votes, the election was thrown into the U.S. House of Representatives. Daniel Pope Cook, Illinois' sole congressman and Edwards-faction leader, cast his crucial vote for Adams sending the State's electoral votes into the Adams column. Illinois Jacksonians cried fraud and set their guns on destroying Cook and the Edwards faction. Cook's House vote caused his political demise and, in former Governor Edward Dunne's words, "closed out the Edwards dynasty in Illinois politics."[6]

This election also left three distinct political groupings in Illinois with men now eager to enter party politics. One group was called the "ultra or whole hog party" led by Elias Kent Kane and William Kinney. This political branch was based in the populated southern part of the State and was extremely favorable to Andrew Jackson. From this band of Jacksonian politicians would come the nucleus of the Democratic party of Illinois.[7] Another group called the "milk and cider" faction favored Jackson but not to the degree of the "whole hogs." "Milk and cider" men were moderates with heavy representation in the center of the State around Sangamon and Morgan counties. This political wing had some Edwards supporters who along with the rest of the group's members would split between the emerging two parties in the State. The third group was simply labeled "anti-Jackson." They were clustered mainly in the northern counties and were made up of many Edwards and Cook supporters. This group would become the keystone of the soon-to-be-formed Whig Party of Illinois. And, though they would be overwhelmed by the Democrats in 1828 and every subsequent presidential and gubernatorial election until the middle 1850's, they would hold their organization solidly against the principles and personality of Andrew Jackson.

Race also entered Illinois Party politics in 1824. In August, Illinoisans voted for the first and last time on whether slavery should be introduced into the State through a constitutional convention. The debate over slavery gave added impetus to political organization and indicated the future geographical distribution of political party membership. Pro-slavery advocates came largely from the State's southern counties. They had been outraged by Illinois Governor Edward Coles' strong anti-slavery statements to the General Assembly. Migration had filled the lower part of Illinois with many former southerners. These individuals were pro-Jackson, pro-Democrat and pro-slavery. Early on they demonstrated the sectionalism which would afflict Illinois politics and make political unity so difficult in this elongated state. Anti-slavery forces achieved victory in the August constitutional convention referendum on the slave issue. The State voted by sections—the southern counties favored holding a "pro-slavery" convention; in the south central and north central counties the vote was fairly even; and in the northern counties the anti-convention supporters produced such overwhelming numbers that it defeated pro-convention forces statewide.[8]

The 1824 presidential election and convention referendum vote were harbingers of political party fortunes for the rest of the century. Democratic downstate southern counties along with some mid-state county allies would dominate Illinois Politics for another quarter of a century. The national era of good feelings or single party domination would continue in Illinois, though with obvious ironies. The newly formed Whig party which challenged the Democrats nationwide created more smoke than fire in Illinois. The political incompetence and lack of party organization of Illinois Whigs kept this State consistently in the Democratic column during the second party stage. However, the population growth in northern Illinois, especially Chicago, combined with the uncompromising reality of the slave issue, would eventually shatter downstate Democratic hegemony over Illinois politics and leave the State in Republican hands for the rest of the century.

1828–1860: Illinois in the Era of Resurgent Party Politics—Democrats Out-Organize the Whigs but Fall to the New Republican Party

In 1828 Andrew Jackson could not be denied the Presidency. He and his Democratic supporters re-energized American party politics by bringing a new equalitarianism to the political process. The Jacksonian appeal broadened the electorate, and the efforts of Jackson's with chief lieutenant Martin Van Buren of New York, modernized the political apparatus in states across the country. Illinois was no exception to the national Jacksonian trends. In the 1828 Presidential election Jackson clobbered Adams by better than a 2 to 1 margin. His adoring "whole hog" supporters dominated the Illinois General Assembly, and politicians throughout the State cloaked themselves with Jackson's mantle.

Illinois was a fast growing frontier state. From 1820 to 1840 its population increased sixfold, the number of counties in the State rose from 19 to 88 and its congressional districts increased from one to three.[9] Other than race, there were two key political issues in Illinois. At the national level, there was the debate over the country's banking policy; and statewide there was the sectional dispute over internal improvements.

For the purpose of this article, we will summarize the complex banking issue by simply stating that most Illinois residents wanted more paper money and currency in circulation. Farmers, land developers and various types of speculators also wanted extended credit to expand their business interests. These entrepreneurs, as well as the average frontier settler, viewed the fiscally conservative U.S. Bank as their enemy. When Jackson vetoed the U.S. Bank recharter bill on grounds that it was a monopoly controlled by a few easterners and foreign investors, he hit the political bull's-eye in Illinois.

"Internal improvements" was a catch-all phrase used to describe economic development projects. In the

1830's and '40's they were mostly transportation related, as all parts of Illinois fought for roads, canals and railroads to boost their local land values, commercial and farming prospects, and the business growth of area cities. The increased population concentration in northern Illinois made the issue of internal improvements a heated sectional battle. Downstate fears multiplied when ground was broken for the construction of an Illinois-Michigan Canal linking the newly incorporated City of Chicago with the Mississippi River. Illinois Democrats vainly sought compromise on improvement projects but in the end were unable to reconcile their southern county supporters with the burgeoning northern county newcomers.

While the issues were being debated, some Democratic leaders began the task of consolidating their party into a more cohesive entity. Led by a young Morgan county attorney, Stephen A. Douglas, these men used the party convention system as their vehicle to achieve greater party discipline. The Democrats had held their first party convention in Baltimore in 1832 to select a new running mate for President Andrew Jackson. Though these efforts were less than spectacular,[10] Illinois Democrats adopted the convention plan in 1835 following a divisive gubernatorial campaign between two men each claiming to be the true Jacksonian Democrat. The Democratic convention plan consisted of four basic principles. First, each election district would elect delegates to a county, state or national convention. Second, at the appropriate convention a declaration of principles would be adopted. Third, the convention delegates would select a single candidate for each public office. Fourth, the candidate would then receive a pledge of individual support from all party members on election day.[11] It took the Democratic convention proponents over two years to convince enough fellow Illinois Democrats before they were able to hold the first convention. The Democrats met at Vandalia in December 1837 and chose their Governor and Lieutenant Governor candidates.[12] A fifteen-man central committee was selected, and Illinois had its first modern political party.

Though the Democratic Convention did not end individualistic politics in the State, it did signal the future of political organization in a growing and heterogeneous Illinois. According to Walter Townsend, Illinois Democratic Party historian, "prior to the convention system anyone who desired might announce himself as a candidate for office, choose his party affiliation, and begin his campaign."[13] However, the establishment of a convention system produced the ideas of party regularity, a party creed and a party platform. By 1838, recalcitrant Democrats, mainly in the southern counties, accepted the convention system. What the convention system produced was far from a well oiled machine. However, it did engender enough discipline to produce an unbroken string of Democratic statewide victories over Whig opponents for almost two decades.[14] It also gave the Democrats the ability to organize on strict party lines for leadership positions in the Illinois House and Senate. Finally the Whigs, despite their early anti-convention denunciations also adopted the convention system, but their futile cause was beyond any procedural political redemption.

Not all Illinoisans were Democrats and Jackson devotees during this period. Opposition to the dominant Democrats came from varied sources. First were supporters of Henry Clay of Kentucky who believed in his "American system" plan for internal improvements. Unlike Jackson, Clay advocated federal government expenditures in the construction and maintenance of improvements. Second were disgruntled Democrats who like the old Edwards faction saw themselves being bypassed in Illinois by the diehard Jacksonians. Third the old Federalist party types who were shocked at Jackson's common man appeal and were angered over his hardnose views on political organization. Finally, a small but vocal band of anti-slavery exponents known as abolitionists who pushed the Jacksonians hard on the moral issue of slavery and eventually ended the Democrats' dominance in Illinois.

This diverse Democratic opposition was loosely allied with the Illinois branch of the National Whig party. However, in the 1830's Illinois Whigs did *not* believe political parties should have a central authority, hold political conventions and organize a central committee. Instead, they relied on a group of young Springfield and Sangamon County politicians led by Abraham Lincoln to direct their party's fortunes. This "Springfield Junto" selected Whig state candidates and directed the party's presidential campaign every four years, but it was unable to organize county and congressional races. In short, the Whigs were no match for the better disciplined Democrats.

In desperation, Illinois Whigs adopted their foes' convention system in 1839, but by 1842 they disbanded this plan as unworkable. Democratic victories continued in Illinois and on the surface it looked like their reign would continue in the State. However, once again the slavery problem reappeared, and this time Democrats nationally and in Illinois could not compromise the issue away.

By the late 1840's some Illinois Democrats were near revolt against the southern county pro-slavery wing of their party. However, due to the personality and leadership of Stephen Douglas and the desire to keep its winning tradition, the party stayed politically unified. Many Whigs saw this potential Democratic split over slavery as the key to a political turn-around in Illinois. Not that the Democratic Party foes were pro-Negro; rather they played up the national North-South dispute over this issue by attacking the Democrat's patriotism, faith in the Constitution and lack of geographical pride. Before this sectionalism could break up the union, it spawned a new northern political party which in a short period of time would dominate Illinois as well as the rest of the country.

Congressional passage of the 1854 Kansas-Nebraska Act accelerated political opposition to Democratic leadership. This bill sponsored by Stephen Douglas as a member of the U.S. Senate, divided the Nebraska territory into two states. Citizens in each new state would vote ("popular sovereignty") on whether to allow slavery legally inside their borders. The Kansas-Nebraska Act outraged many northerners who saw it as a possible extension of slavery beyond the boundaries established by the 1820 Missouri Compromise. In March 1854, an anti-K-N group met in Ripon, Wisconsin, and, in July 1854, a new Republican Party was born in a Jackson, Michigan, state convention.

Illinois lagged behind its midwest neighbors in establishing a state Republican Party. In October, 1954, an anti-Kansas-Nebraska meeting took place in Springfield but its abolitionist-dominated membership did not use the Republican name. This Springfield group named a state central committee headed by Abraham Lincoln, but Lincoln refused to attend any meetings and declined to serve on the committee.[15]

The impetus of an organized Illinois Republican party began in February 1856, when Paul Selby, editor of the *Morgan Journal* in Jacksonville, Illinois, issued a formal call for a conference of anti-Kansas-Nebraska newspaper editors. Twelve influential editors plus Abraham Lincoln, the only non-editor admitted to the meeting, met in Decatur. They put together a platform advocating the restoration of the Missouri Compromise by protesting the introduction of slavery into territory already free.[16] The excitement engendered by this platform moved a coalition of anti-Kansas-Nebraska Democrats, Whigs, Abolitionists and others to call for a state convention.

On May 27, 1856, the first Illinois State Republican Convention was held in Bloomington—though nowhere in the recorded proceedings does the name Republican appear. John M. Palmer, a future political kingpin in Illinois, presided over the Convention. William Bissell, a Mexican War hero and former Democratic Congressman, was nominated for Governor,[17] but the star of the Convention was Abraham Lincoln. Lincoln, acting as chairman of the selection committee, brought the Convention to its feet with a rousing, emotional speech against the Kansas-Nebraska Act. Exhibiting his vast but sometimes overlooked practical political ability, Lincoln was also the behind-the-scenes organizer.

The upstart Republican Party made a remarkable showing in its first statewide election. Though Democratic presidential candidate James Buchanan beat Republican John Fremont in Illinois the entire GOP state ticket swept Illinois. The Republican State sweep was no one-time fluke; it would be almost forty years before Illinois would have another Democratic Governor. The Republican Party, unlike their Whigs predecessors, accepted party organization as a way of life. They quickly set up a complete county organization in every county in the State, and their party's central committee mandated that there be biennial conventions.

Besides riding the crest of the slavery issue, initial Republican Party efforts were aided by two other factors. First, migration patterns were filling up the GOP northern areas of the State faster than the Democratic southern areas. Chicago's population in 1860 would top 100,000, and though some Republicans complained about the Democratic proclivity of the City's new Irish and German immigrants, by-and-large Chicago was reliably Republican in state and national elections. Second, Republicans at the outset of their existence faced a badly divided State Democratic Party. By 1860 there were at least two Democratic parties in Illinois, one loyal to President Buchanan, the other devoted to its own Senator Douglas.

The second party stage ended on the eve of America's great civil war. In Illinois Democrats were divided and dispirited over the breaks in their ranks and their inability to settle the slavery issue. The newly formed Republican Party, led by its old mentor and the country's new President, Abraham Lincoln, was flexing its muscles westward and southward from its northern and north-central county base. Political organization was now accepted in Illinois, even if party dicipline and structure were still somewhat haphazard. The democratization of American politics had taken place during the second party system. In Illinois it meant a wider and more heterogeneous electorate seeking greater involvement in the political process.

1860–1932: Illinois in the Era of Industrialization—Republicans in Control

From the Civil War to the coming of the New Deal the Republican Party dominated the nation's politics. In this period only two Democrats, Grover Cleveland and Woodrow Wilson, were able to break the GOP's hold on the White House. Under Republican Party leadership the country's economy was industrialized, its transportation system was expanded from coast to coast, the nation underwent a technological revolution and America became the dream destination of millions of immigrants.

The Republicans were the party of union and progress. Nationally they reflected the country's desire for glory and gold. The Republicans dominated the urban vote, the business vote, the labor vote and the black vote. The Democrats were a country party, concentrated in the rural south and west, with Irish enclaves in northern cities.[18]

The Republican Party also prevailed in Illinois during the third party system period. State politics reflected the national mood, as GOP candidates outdistanced their Democratic opponents. From 1860 to 1932 Illinois Democrats elected only three U.S. senators, two Governors, three Attorney Generals, two Secretaries of State and two Auditors of Public Accounts. The Democratic resurgence in Illinois and the nation would come about only when the Republicans proved unable to solve the social and economic problems unleashed by America's rapid industrialization.

Following the Civil War, Illinois gained approximately one million new residents every decade. Chicago alone saw its population rise from 100,000 in 1860 to over 1,000,000 by 1890. The State's changing demographics, its economic growth and simple political reality demanded that Illinois' basic law be changed. In 1868 the voters approved a constitutional convention which convened in late 1869 and lasted until May, 1870.[19] This convention had vast impact on the future political party development of Illinois because it presented to the voters of the State the concept of cumulative voting.[20] (See Chapters by Gove, Wiste and Kenney.)

Leading exponents of cumulative voting at the 1870 Constitutional Convention, like *Chicago Tribune* editor Joseph Medill, argued "that the purpose of minority representation was to destroy the sectional feeling that prevailed in the state."[21] The Civil War was over but the State's geographical divisions were mirrored in the relative political party strength at both ends of the State. The North was Republican territory, Democratic strength resting mainly with the new immigrants in some larger city neighborhoods. The southern part of the State was Democratic turf, its residents resenting the party of Lincoln and its reconstruction policies. Since 1854 neither party had been able to win legislative seats in the other party's strong area. Thus, the allure of cumulative voting was to give minority interests elected representation in districts where it was impossible for them ever to achieve victory.

The long range effect of cumulative voting and minority representation has been detrimental to political party discipline in Illinois. It has created personal fiefdoms for minority representatives who have often fought or ignored their own party leaders. In recent times, Republican house representatives elected from heavily Democratic Chicago have been largely outside of the mainstream of their party. Likewise their Democratic counterparts from strong Republican downstate and suburban areas have often not reflected their party's philosophy. At times this has produced progressive Chicago Republicans and independent suburban Democrats who have bravely fought for the public good. However, it has also given Illinois the alleged criminally-connected Republican "West Side Bloc" in Chicago and some downstate Democrats, like Paul Powell, whose conduct and behavior were beyond any party apparatus control.

Cumulative voting has given Illinois minority representation but in doing so has given individuals power bases immune from partisan competition, public debate, and party philosophy. Often minority representatives work hard to prevent other members of their party from contesting house races thereby insuring their own reelection while delegating their party to permanent minority status. Finally cumulative voting has not diminished sectionalism, because minority representatives seldom vote on sectional issues differently from their majority colleagues.

The GOP completely dominated Illinois politics from 1870 to 1892. Illinois Democrats unable to field a respectable state ticket often combined their efforts with several "third" or fusion parties. Liberal Republicanism, the Granger Movement and the Greenback at one time or another were aligned with the state Democrats. "The enduring fiber of the Illinois Democrats" writes Townsend, "was never more convincingly shown than in the days of the 80's . . . [Illinois] had become one of the most dependable Republican strongholds."[22]

Despite their election shellackings, Illinois Democrats continued to hold state party conventions every two years. Unlike today these state conventions had the power to make nominations of candidates for State office. Starting in the 1870's a gradual power shift towards Chicago began within the Democratic hierarchy. In 1872 Cyrus McCormick became the first Chicago Democrat to head the central committee. By 1878 Cook County Democrats elected M.W. Robinson as permanent chairman of the state convention. One year later Carter Harrison I started his first of five terms as Chicago's Mayor and local Democratic kingpin.

Harrison and his son Carter II, who would also be elected Chicago Mayor five times, reflected the general image of Democratic leaders in Chicago and Illinois. Both men were cultured and sophisticated gentlemen who in their critics eyes were too close to the City's lower elements—especially the saloonkeepers, gamblers and vice providers. Though successful in Chicago, they and their fellow Democrats were unable to expand their following to win many statewide contests. Their negative image throughout the rest of the State can be seen in the reports concerning the 1896 Democratic Cook County Convention. Approximately 700 delegates attended this convention and their occupational breakdown (in part) read as follows:

265 saloonkeepers
148 political employees
84 ex-prisoners
43 penetentiary convicts

540 or 77%[23]

Downstate Democrats were not overjoyed at the prospect of Chicago or Cook County Democrats[24] taking over the party. Many were frightened at the party's growing ethnic composition and were appalled at the rough and ready factional rivalries emerging within Chicago Democratic ranks. Thus, downstate Democrats turned to a national Democrat, William Jennings Bryan, and a national issue, free silver, to regain their status within the state party.

In the 1890's Bryan became a national figure espousing free and unlimited coinage of silver. As in the 1830's, hard-pressed farmers wanted more money in circulation and easier credit. Bryan, a Nebraskan, had his early roots in downstate Illinois. He had been born in Marion County and educated in Jacksonville (Morgan County) and was married to a woman from a prominent Pike County family.[25]

Bryanism in Illinois enabled John Peter Altgeld in 1892 to break a forty year dry spell and become the State's first Democratic Governor since Joel Matteson. Altgeld, a Cook County resident, was not a typical Chicago Democrat, because he was not a member of any competing City faction and because he fully supported Bryan's monetary politics. He also was unable to bind the sectional wounds inside the Democratic Party.

From 1896 until the 1920's Chicago and downstate Democrats battled for the heart and soul of the Illinois Democracy. Despite the City's incredible population growth (over 2,000,000 in 1910 and over 3,000,000 in 1930), Chicago's Democratic strength was dissipated by the bitter factionalism inside the local party. Five-time Mayor Carter Harrison II and his followers brawled ferociously with the troops of party boss Roger Sullivan and former Chicago Mayor John Hopkins for political control. Also engaged in this battle were reform City Democrats led by Edward Dunne, who was elected Mayor in 1905 and in 1912 became the State's second Democratic Governor since the Civil War.

Downstate Democrats leaned towards Harrison but his association with the politically ambitious newspaper tycoon William Randolph Hearst cooled their ardor. State conventions turned into political riots and contending factions always brought a large group of thugs and sluggers for lobbying purposes.

The passage of Democratic control firmly into Chicago's hands was not accomplished until the City Democrats solidified into a single organization. This deed was accomplished by a series of brutal Sullivan-faction victories and some slick political horse trading by Sullivan's chief lieutenant George Brennan. Also aiding Chicago Democratic organization efforts was state legislation allowing the City to do away with elected precinct committeemen and replace them with precinct captains who were appointed by ward committeemen. This change added stability to the Chicago party apparatus by eliminating thousands of elected party offices and allowing regulars to concentrate on only the ward committeeman contests.

Another factor helping Chicago Democrats organize was the desire for direct primaries. Reform elements believed the convention nominating system fostered boss rule, political confusion and a stacked selection process. Illinois passed a series of direct primary laws and, though several were declared unconstitutional, the primary system consolidated the nomination process and gave party regulars a better chance to marshal their forces for a few primary elections instead of several nominating conventions. Thus, efforts to curtail political chaos were detrimental to reform, because they limited the number of political battles and thereby gave Democratic regulars in Chicago the opportunity to level their guns on fewer election contests.

Illinois Republicans enjoyed a remarkable string of triumphs following the Civil War. Strong in almost every area of the State, the GOP did not suffer from party sectionalism to the extent of its Democratic counterpart. However, following the turn of the century, Chicago Republicans began flexing their muscles inside the party by demanding greater political recognition. Chicago's large population made confrontation almost inevitable in both parties.

The Republican 1904 State Convention was a political "donnybrook" that illustrated the contending forces working inside the state GOP. Until 1904 Republican political good fortune in state races seldom benefitted Republicans north of Peoria County. The office of Governor had usually gone to a central Illinois resident. South and central Illinois also received a major share of the other offices, with Cook County at best getting the Lieutenant Governor slot. In 1904 two Cook County Republicans, Colonel Frank Lowden, the National Committeeman for Illinois and George Pullman's son-in-law, and Charles Deneen, Cook County State's Attorney, challenged incumbent Governor Richard Yates of Morgan County for the gubernatorial nomination.

The marathon convention needed 79 ballots and almost three weeks of balloting including an 11-day recess to nominate Deneen.[26] This Cook County Republican muscle shocked many GOP downstaters who, like their Democratic bretheren, feared future Chicago domination of their party. However, unlike the Democrats, Cook County Republicans were unable to take over their party. Out-migration of Republicans to suburban and collar county areas moved from a trickle to a flood in the next three decades; downstate Republicans had a much stronger political base than downstate Democrats; and finally within one decade local, state, and national Republicans felt the fury and imagination of William Hale "Big Bill" Thompson.

Few men have played a larger role in determining the political party structure of Illinois than did Thompson. He was a political showman who had few political or ethical scruples and only one major goal—winning elective office. In 1915 "Big Bill" was elected Mayor of Chicago—he then turned unsuccessfully to the U.S. Senate primary in 1918, he was re-elected Mayor in 1919 and entertained thoughts of the Presidency in 1920. When he refused to run for a third term in 1923, due in part to several pending indictments, most experts thought his career was over. However, in 1927, he made a miraculous comeback, aided immeasurably by Al Capone, and once again captured the Mayor's office. His re-election defeat by Anton Cermak finally ended his career, but when his political smoke had cleared the Chicago Republican Party was in shambles and state party power had returned once again to the downstaters.

The Republican ascendancy in Illinois came to a crashing conclusion in 1932. Unable to solve or understand the economic deprivations of the Great Depression, frustrated and shocked by the public actions of Thompson in Chicago, and unable to organize state-wide into a single political entity like their Democratic foes, Illinois Republicans were ripe for picking by Democrats Franklin D. Roosevelt, Henry Horner and Anton Cermak. The political initiative had passed to the Illinois Democrats who were producing new and exciting leaders, while the GOP resorted to old Civil War slogans, the memory of Teddy Roosevelt and worn out reform cliches.

Illinois Republicans were pushed back into the position of the old Whig Party prior to the Civil War. They condemned the Democrats' organizing ability and questioned their political methods, while inwardly wishing their party could do likewise. On the other hand, Illinois Democrats solidly controlled by Anton Cermak's Cook County organization were determined to recapture state government. The Republicans of necessity became the party of individual leaders and personal factions, denouncing Machine rule while the Democrats moved easily into a chain-of-command political structure which channeled activity through slating committees and was characterized by strong organization leadership.

1932 to Present: Illinois Welcomes F.D.R.'s New Deal but Refuses to be a One-Party State

The fourth party period starts with Franklin D. Roosevelt's landslide presidential victory over Herbert Hoover in 1932. FDR forged a Democratic alliance of farmers, labor unions, intellectuals, old and new immigrants and the vast number of unemployed into a New Deal coalition. He also made huge inroads with traditional Republican voting groups like the blacks and middle class urban dwellers. This coalition gave FDR four consecutive presidential terms, and it also gave Democrats in Illinois and other states new life with which to take on their entrenched Republican opponents.

Henry Horner, a former Cook County Probate Court Judge, latched onto FDR.'s coattails and became the third Democratic Governor in Illinois since the Civil War. Though Horner was a product of Chicago's notorious First Ward, the scholarly Horner was depicted as a man above politics, honest and a friend of the working man.

Horner's two terms as Governor illustrate the problems of a Democrat holding the top job in Springfield. Almost immediately Horner was at odds with powerbrokers inside the Cook County Democratic organization. His relationship with the Machine further deteriorated following the assassination of his friend and mentor Mayor Anton J. Cermak. In his 1936 renomination bid Horner defeated a Chicago-backed primary challenge by denouncing his own Party's single, most powerful political entity—the Cook County Democratic organization.

Horner's plight illuminates the key issue in Illinois party politics since 1932—the emergence, growth and power of Chicago's Democratic organization. Republicans throughout Illinois at all political levels have made this organization their number one campaign issue. People who have not traveled within 100 miles of Chicago have been warned by GOP candidates that unless they voted Republican the Chicago Machine would swallow them up.

On the other hand, countless Democrats in Chicago have brushed aside Republican Party attacks and independent Democratic challenges to swear fidelity and allegiance to the Cook County Democratic organization. Moreover, they have convinced enough Chicagoans almost all the time, enough Cook County residents most of the time, and enough Illinois voters some of the time, that their organization had the best candidates and that they could win. The dichotomy between these divergent views can be understood only by a short description of Chicago's Democratic organization, and from that analysis one can better understand the rhythm of Illinois political party development during the last five decades.

Anton Cermak's 1931 mayoral victory coupled with the victories of FDR and Horner in 1932 capped the construction of the Democratic Machine in Chicago. Cermak, a survivor of previous intra-party factional wars, "intertwined political and governmental processes and made them almost inseparable."[27] Professor Milton Rakove has compared this organizational structure to the Politburo of the Soviet Union,[28] because the true wielders of governmental power were not the elected public officials but the local party committee. Thus, the Cook County Democratic Central Commitee, like the Political Bureau of the Central Committee of the Communist Party, acted as the true legislative and administrative decision-making body, superceding any governmentally structured separation and balance of powers.

Control of the Chicago organization passed from Cermak to Edward Kelly and Pat Nash in 1933. In the late 1940's Colonel Jacob Arvey took party command and shifted the organization slightly towards a more business-oriented approach to government. In 1953 Richard J. Daley was elected party chairman and two years later completed his takeover by being elected Mayor. Daley ruled Chicago for over two decades and he raised the Machine's dominance and control to a level that will never be reached again.

Democratic power in Chicago turned the Illinois Democratic Party into a seldom used political satellite. Non-Chicago Democrats were helpless to prevent the big city boys from dominating all aspects of the state organization. In slatemaking sessions the Chicago state central committeemen voted as a bloc, and because votes were weighted according to party primary turnout, Chicagoans completely controlled this party organ. Except for a few isolated examples (Horner in 1936 and Dan Walker in 1972), primary challenges to Chicago-backed candidates were useless. Raw population figures, the huge number of Democrats concentrated in the City, and the impact of a cohesive vote-producing political organization gave Chicago a near monopoly over the nomination process.

Statewide political reaction to the Chicagoizing of the Illinois Democratic Party was mixed. Election results reveal that though the Democrats were better organized than their Republican counterparts, voters shifted back and forth in their support of party candidates. In presidential and statewide contests, Illinois voters evenly divided their support between both major parties following Roosevelt and Horner's 1936 victories. This movement towards party competition accelerated in the 1940's and became a political fact of life by the century's mid-point.

The 1950's saw Illinois and the nation move away from the aura and excitement of Roosevelt's New Deal. The politically potent New Deal coalition had been formed to rescue America's industrial and agricultural order. Ironically the 1952 landslide election of American war hero Dwight Eisenhower, a Republican, reflected the successful accomplishment of those goals. The 1930's unemployed were now gaining economic rewards, job security and middle-class status. According to Arthur Schlesinger, Jr., "the more successfully they (the Democrats) pursued New Deal policies the more deeply they undermined the political basis of the New Deal."[29] In short, Schlesinger argues, the Democrats ran out of poor people.

The American odyssey of people journeying from old city neighborhoods to the surrounding suburbs was a national phenomenon, and in Illinois it impacted the political party structure. Formerly sleepy towns or old cornfields around Chicago in a short time sprouted thousands of new suburban voters who represented neither rural nor urban interests. Successful post World War II Democratic and Republican politicians in Illinois have reflected the new suburban constituency. The last three elected Democratic Governors, Adlai Stevenson (1948), Otto Kerner (1960 & 1964) and Dan Walker (1972), were suburban-based candidates whose political careers were not tied to the Chicago Machine. During this same period Republican-elected Governors were two suburbanites, William Stratton (1952 & 1956) and Richard Ogilvie (1968), and a Chicagoan James Thompson (1976 & 1978) who, though geographically a city dweller, is politically the ultimate suburbanite.

The suburbanization of American life gave Illinois Republicans new hope and new supporters. Republicans believed the suburban desire for political independence and grassroots involvement was perfectly suited to their party's philosophy. On the whole these Republican politicians were correct—Cook County's suburbs and the five collar counties (Lake, McHenry, DuPage, Kane, and Will) have become the bedrock of the GOP vote and their influence has dominated the Party's basic framework.

Today, Illinois Republicans hold no slatemaking sessions—their state central committee makes no official endorsements (though individual powerful Republicans make their primary choices known) and their Party's organizational structure resembles a tandem bicycle instead of a machine. State Republican candidates pay lip service to downstate demands, talk bravely about resurrecting the Party in Chicago, but in the final crunch make sure they address the needs and concerns of their suburban constituency. In short, Cook County's suburbs and the five surrounding collar counties provide the Illinois GOP and their presidential candidates an increasing portion of the statewide vote.[30]

Recently some political observers like independent political activist Don Rose have suggested the Demorats have made substantial inroads against the Republicans in the suburbs. According to Rose, "The Republican majority in Cook County suburbs has shrunk to a point where we may never see a GOP candidate elected to a countywide office."[31] A similar view has been voiced by Larry Hansen, an aide to Illinois Senator Adlai Stevenson, who believes that suburban Democrats are on the march because of recent party gains at the township and county level and because of some impressive returns for individual Democratic candidates.[32]

The Rose-Hansen analysis establishes only some increased party competition and ticket splitting in the suburbs and not any major dimunition of GOP power in the five and a half counties. To be sure in 1978 Cook County Republicans were badly beaten by better known and better financed Democratic county candidates. However, at the same time Republican candidates at the top of the ticket were wiping out their Democratic foes and GOP state legislative candidates were winning back traditional Republican suburban seats lost during the Watergate elections. Moreover, recent state Democratic candidates' victories in the five and a half suburban counties have been achieved almost entirely by two popular individuals, Alan Dixon and Adlai Stevenson. Furthermore, no Democratic presidential or gubernatorial candidate has carried any part of the suburban county area since 1964, and in 1976 Jimmy Carter ran nearly 3 percent behind John Kennedy's 1960 suburban vote total.

The Illinois Republican Party's loose political structure and suburban orientation has made the party personality- and not organizationally- oriented. Today Republican superstars like Governor Jim Thompson, U.S. Senator Charles Percy and State Attorney General William Scott, are suburban-type officeholders whose party support and backing has traditionally been less important to them than their own personal following. Percy's brutal 1978 re-election campaign against Democrat Alex Seith is a case of the exception proving the rule. The Senator had to eat humble pie and race around the State trying to convince regular Republicans that he was sorry for his Party indifference and that indeed he had gotten the message. Thus, the Party whose roots go back to the cohesive, issue-oriented 1856 Bloomington convention has become a loose alliance of individual strong state leaders who view themselves as being above or beyond organizational politics.

An analysis of the Illinois Democratic Party structure in 1979 reveals two crucial points. First, Chicago's decreasing population will reduce the City's political muscle to elect statewide candidates. Second, Jane Byrne's upset primary victory over incumbent Chicago Mayor Michael Bilandic and her subsequent mayoral election has shaken the internal workings of the Democratic Machine in Chicago and thus, some party power may shift outside the City's boundaries.

In 1948 Chicago with its population of over 3,500,000 people cast 46 percent of the statewide vote for President. The Chicago Democratic organization had enough of the State's voters living within its city borders to give Harry Truman the Illinois electoral votes. In 1976 the City's population had dropped to around 3,000,000 and Chicago cast only 26 percent of the State's total presidential vote. Moreover, Chicago Democrats gave their presidential candidate Jimmy Carter over 2/3 of the city vote, but unlike previous elections it was not enough to overcome Republican strength in the suburbs and downstate.

The new geography of Illinois politics confronts state Democrats with a perplexing problem. For decades non-Chicago Democrats have grudgingly accepted the City's dominance over the Party structure, because Chicago had the numbers to win elections. Today Chicago can no longer carry Democrats to state victory, but it can still dictate the Party's nominee. In recent years Chicago has grown far more Democratic than the rest of the State Demographic changes have brought more pro-Democratic, poor minority groups into the City while potential Republican, middle class whites and blacks have fled to suburbia.

This political imbalance makes Chicago organization-backed candidates almost unbeatable in state primary elections. However, primary control is a means to party success and political power, not an end. Thus, Democratic leaders, located mainly in Chicago, must make their party election-oriented and not settle for primary control. In short it is in the Chicago organization's interest to open up the political party structure to suburbanites and downstaters and to give Illinois voters "population-proportionate slates based on where the voters live or are moving and not political-proportionate slates based on traditional strength inside the party."[33]

Jane Byrne's takeover of City Hall has produced a volatile political climate inside the Chicago Democratic organization. Her triumph over Bilandic, the continuing confrontations with political ward lords Ed Kelly (47th ward), Ed Burke (14th ward) and Ed Vrdolyak (10th ward), and her pumping up of county chairman George Dunne have unsettled the Chicago political system. Not since the defeat of Carter Harrison II in the 1915 Chicago mayoral primary has the power structure within the City's Democratic Party been so politically fluid. A Byrne Administration in itself does not change the political deck but it certainly suggests a shuffling of the cards.

Unlike the Republicans, the Chicago-dominated Illinois Democratic Party had maintained its tight organizational structure. Recent independent and reform efforts at taking on the controlling Chicago Democratic organization have had limited results. The Independent Voters of Illinois, formed in 1944, and the Democratic Federation of Illinois (later named Committee on Illinois Government), organized in 1957, have pecked for years at the Machine.[34] However, Ms. Byrne's frontal assault has the potential of opening up the party to new constituent groups while rekindling ties with old party loyalists.

Much has been written about the political genuis of the late Richard J. Daley, but sometimes overlooked was his ability to maintain alliances with divergent interests in Chicago. Like Roosevelt, Daley won over labor, brought the blacks completely into the party, played ethnic politics better than anyone in history, and moved his organization into the middle class periphery wards of the City. However, Daley was largely unsuccessful in attempts to extend his influence into the suburbs by such means as legislative redistricting. In many respects he wrote off the rest of the State to the Republicans.

A new invigorated Illinois Democratic Party would most likely find fertile political ground outside the City. (See the McKeough Chapter.) It would also free itself from its 11th Ward "Bridgeport" mentality and recognize the political merit of party inclusion instead of party exclusion from the ruling circles. In short, the shake-up from the 1979 mayoral primary may be a blessing to the Democratic party fortunes, not only in Chicago but in Illinois as well.

Conclusion

Political parties in Illinois and the nation may be evolving into a fifth political period: "The Era of Voter Apathy." In Illinois both parties are suffering from a lack of citizen involvement within the party structure and from a decreasing number of voters willing to go to the polls. According to David Everson and Joan Parker, "recent studies of voter turnout document the significant decline in voter participation in local, statewide, and national elections . . . what has been overlooked . . . is the weakening of traditional party allegiances. . . . Parties are losing their clout, and this loss has significantly affected voter turnout and election results."[35]

It is indeed ironic that after 160 years of political party organization efforts and at a time when technology can send party messages instantly across the State, voters are turning away from the political process. Perhaps modern news communication, slick television campaign commercials and sophisticated polling techniques have lessened the candidate's need for a structured party organization—however, the old fashioned political party apparatus with its cadre of workers at the precinct, county, and state level may have been the most effective method of producing voter participation in our State and nation.

NOTES

[1]Arthur Schlesinger Jr., ed., *History of U.S. Political Parties,* (4 vols.; New York: Chelsea House, 1973) p. xxxv.

[2]Charles Manfred Thompson, *The Illinois Whigs Before 1846* (Urbana: University of Illinois Press, 1915), p. 11.

[3]Theodore C. Pease, *Illinois Election Returns 1818–1848* (Springfield: Illinois State Historical Library, 1923) pp. xviii and xix.

[4]Illinois had three districts.

[5]Theodore C. Pease, *The Frontier State 1818–1848* (Springfield: Illinois Centennial Commission, 1918) p. 107.

[6]Edward F. Dunne, *Illinois: The Heart of the Nation,* Vol. I (Chicago: Lewis Publishing, 1933), p. 304. According to Dunne, "Cook's greatest reward was to have his name given to what is today (1933) the most populous and powerful county in the northwest and possibly the western Hemisphere." Besides being a former Illinois Governor, Dunne was also a former Chicago Mayor and though he was an independent-minded Democrat, he admired the political direction of his home county.

[7]Thompson, *op. cit.,* p. 31.

[8]David Kenney, *Basic Illinois Government: A Systematic Explanation* (Carbondale: Southern Illinois University press, 1970), p. 42.

[9]Richard P. McCormick, *The Second American Party System: Party Formation in the Jackson Era* (Chapel Hill: University of North Carolina Press, 1966), p. 278.

[10]The vice presidential contest produced a bitter feud between the leading contenders Martin Van Buren and Richard Johnson. Their V.P. fight spilled over into Illinois and split the local Democrats. Van Buren's popularity in Illinois never recovered from this bruising battle.

[11]Dunne, *op. cit.,* p. 312.

[12]The 1818 Constitution provided that only Governor and Lieutenant Governor would be elected statewide offices. All other state officers were either appointed by the Governor or the Legislature. The 1848 Constitution added Secretary of State, Auditor of Public Accounts and State Treasurer as elected statewide offices.

[13]Walter A. Townsend and Charles Boeschenstein, *Illinois Democracy* (Springfield: Democratic Historical Association Inc., 1935) pp. 105–06.

[14]McCormick, *op. cit.,* p. 285.

[15]Charles A. Church, *History of the Republican Party in Illinois 1854–1912: With a Review of the Aggressions of the Slave Power* (Rockford: Wilson Brothers, 1912) p. 20.

[16]*Ibid.*, p. 31.

[17]Green G. Raum, *History of Illinois Republicanism* (Chicago: Rollins Publishing Company, 1900) p. 35.

[18]Schlesinger, *op. cit.*, pp. xlii–xliii.

[19]Kenney, *op. cit.*, p. 66.

[20]There have been instances where a dominant party ran two candidates under its label and another party member under the independent label. However, generally both major parties hve respected the two-candidate limit for each representative district.

[21]*Constitution of the State of Illinois* (Springfield: Edward J. Hughes) p. 12. *Journal of the Constitutional Convention of the State of Illinois* (Springfield: State Journal Printing Office, 1870), pp. 412–415.

[22]Townsend, *op. cit.*, p. 141.

[23]Ernest Ludlow Bogart and John Mabry Mathews, *The Modern Commonwealth 1893–1918* (Chicago: A. C. McClurg & Co., 1922), p. 359.

[24]Chicago or Cook County Democrats represented at this time almost the same people since most of Cook County residents lived inside Chicago's boundaries.

[25]Peter W. Colby and Paul M. Green, "Voting Patterns in the 96 Downstate Counties," *Illinois Issues* 4:8 (August 1978), p. 17.

[26]See J. McCan Davis, *The Breaking of the Deadlock* (Springfield: Henry O. Shepard Co., 1904).

[27]Peter W. Colby and Paul M. Green, "The Consolidation of Clout," *Illinois Issues* 5:2 (February 1979), p. 13.

[28]Milton Rakove, *Don't Make No Waves, Don't Back No Losers* (Bloomington: Indiana University Press, 1975), p. 94.

[29]Schlesinger, *op. cit.*, p. xlv.

[30]Peter W. Colby and Paul M. Green, "Downstate Holds the Key to Victory," *Illinois Issues* 5:2 (February 1978), p. 9.

[31]*Chicago Sun-Times,* December 12, 1978.

[32]Lawrence N. Hansen, "Mayor Daley and the Suburbs," *Illinois Issues* 5:1 (January 1978) pp. 14–17 and 5:2 (February 1978) pp. 12–14. Hansen's views were originally expressed at a Lombard Democratic Club meeting August 19, 1977.

[33]Colby and Green, "Downstate Holds the Key to Victory," p. 11.

[34]James Q. Wilson, *The Amateur Democrat* (Chicago: The University of Chicago Press, 1962) p. 74.

[35]David H. Everson and Joan Parker, "Voter Turnout Decline," *Illinois Issues* 5:6 (June 1979), p. 4.

SUPPLEMENTAL READINGS

Bogart, Ernest Ludlow and Charles Manfred Thompson. *The Industrial State 1870–1893* Springfield: Illinois Centennial Commission, 1920.

Bogart, Ernest Ludlow and John Mabry Mathews. *The Modern Commonwealth 1893–1918*. Chicago: A. C. McClurg, 1922.

Brinkley, Wilfred. *American Political Parties: Their Natural History*. New York: A. A. Knopf, 1964.

Church, Charles A. *History of the Republican Party in Illinois: 1854–1912* with a Review of the Agressions of the Slave Power. Rockford: Wilson Bedhers, 1912.

Cole, Arthur C. *The Era of the Civil War 1848–1870*. Springfield: Illinois Centennial Commission, 1919.

Davis, J. McCan, *The Breaking of the Deadlock*. Springfield: Henry O. Shepard Co., 1904.

Dodd, Walter F. *Government in Illinois*. Chicago: University of Chicago Press, 1923.

Dunne, Edward F. *Illinois: The Heart of the Nation*. 5 volumes. Chicago: Lewis Publishing Company, 1933.

Flanigan, William H. and Nancy Zingale. *Political Behavior of the American Electorate*. Boston: Allyn Bacon, Inc., 1979.

Ford, Thomas. *A History of Illinois*. 2 volumes. Chicago: R. R. Donnelly & Sons, 1945.

Illinois Major Party Platforms. Compiled by James Nowlan. Urbana: Institute of Government and Public Affairs, 1966.

Journal of the Constitutional Convention of the State of Illinois. Springfield: State Journal Printing Office, 1870.

Kenney, David. *Basic Illinois: A Systematic Explanation*. Carbondale: Southern Illinois University Press, 1970.

McCormick, Richard P. *The Second American Party System: Party Formation in the Jackson Era*. Chapel Hill: University of North Carolina Press, 1966.

Minor, Henry. *The Story of the Democratic Party*. New York: The MacMillan Company, 1928.

O'Connor, Len. *Clout: Mayor Daley & His City*. Chicago: Regnery & Co., 1975.

Pease, Theodore C. *Illinois Election Returns 1818–1848*. Springfield: Illinois State Historical Library, 1923.

Pease, Theodore C. *The Frontier State 1818–1848*. Springfield: Illinois Centennial Commission, 1918.

Rakove, Milton. *Don't Make No Waves—Don't Back No Losers*. Bloomington: Indiana University Press, 1975.

Ranney, Austin. *Illinois Politics*. New York: New York University Press, 1960.

Royko, Mike. *Boss: Richard J. Daley of Chicago*. New York: E. P. Dutton, 1971.

Schlesinger, Arthur Jr., ed. *History of United States Political Parties,* 4 vols. New York: Chelsea House, 1973.

Thompson, Charles Manfred. *The Illinois Whigs Before 1846*. Urbana: University of Illinois Press, 1915.

Townsend, Walter A., and Charles Boeschenstein. *Illinois Democracy*. Springfield: Democratic Historical Association, 1935.

Wilson, James Q. *The Amateur Democrat*. Chicago: University of Chicago Press, 1962.

CHAPTER **13**

Illinois Politics and the Ideal of Responsible Party Government

Peter W. Colby

Traditionally, most scholars have portrayed political parties as crucially important components in democratic political systems—today, this is no longer the case. It is perhaps symptomatic of the loss of confidence in political and governmental institutions which characterizes our times that scholars are now raising the most fundamental questions about the functions and value of parties. For example, Frank J. Sorauf argues that political parties are not easily distinguished from other organizations, and that many party functions may be performed by other political organizations.[1] William J. Keefe states that parties "are less what they make of themselves than what their environment makes of them."[2] James Q. Wilson notes that the political party in the United States "is a conspicuous exception to the general tendency for society to become increasingly organized, rationalized, and bureaucratized."[3] Frank B. Feigert and M. Margaret Conway ask if political parties are relevant to politics.[4]

Given this climate of opinion, any examination of parties today cannot take their existence and purposes as given, but instead must begin with consideration of the roles parties may or do perform in society. This paper on Illinois political parties will, therefore, open with a discussion of what political partes are, what they do and how they do it. The discussion will next center on the ideal model of a responsible two-party system. Subsequently, we will look closely at parties in Illinois in terms of this model, and, finally, conclude with some observations on the likely future of our State's political party system.

Defining Political Parties

A useful approach to the understanding of politics and government is to view political life as an ongoing system of activity. This approach, popularized by David Easton,[5] defines the political process as being concerned with "the authoritative allocation of scarce values." In other words, government makes decisions about who gets what, when, how and why. Those governmental decisions are binding on society. The systems approach suggests that government functions as a conversion process, evaluating the various and conflicting demands made upon it and producing policies intended to respond to these demands.

When examining political parties in terms of the systems model, it becomes obvious that their function is to link the people together and to the government, to serve as a means for 220,000,000 Americans or 11,000,000 Illinoisans to communicate their needs to public officials in a manner that will assist our society in producing policies that are reasonably satisfactory to most citizens. (See Figure 13-1) As Everett Carl Ladd, Jr. points out, in a society as large and complex as our own, some mechanism is needed for "aggregating the preferences of the mass public for political leadership and policy choice, and converting what was incoherent and diffuse to specific, responsive public decisions."[6]

In the United States and in Illinois, the primary method by which parties link citizens and government is by means of elections. Each party attempts to organize citizens to elect its candidates to office and then to shape the decisions that successful candidates make once in office. In this way, parties help voters communicate their preferences by offering candidates and platforms which voters can support or reject. Political parties can be distinguished from other types of political organization by their breadth, their emphasis on winning elections and their permanent organization. In contrast, a "faction" is a sub-group of party members who support one issue, ideology, leader or interest; an "interest group" is primarily concerned with advancing a particular economic or philosophic goal; and a "movement" is a temporary, unorganized response of people who share a common interest in a particular political objective. Only parties, among all political organizations, have the potential to link citizens and government on many issues over a long period of time.

The Responsible Party Model

The recognition of the need for linking citizens to elected officials and the awareness that only political parties can meet this need in a comprehensive, lasting manner led to the doctrine of responsible parties. The doctrine has derived its greatest support from American political scientists with a fascination for the British system. The most influential statement of these ideas came in the 1950 Report of the Committee on Political Parties of the American Political Science Association, entitled *Toward a More Responsible Two Party System.*[7] The

The author would like to acknowledge the assistance of Martin Dubin, Al Manning, Ron Michaelson and former Governor Samuel Shapiro who read and commented on an earlier draft of this chapter.

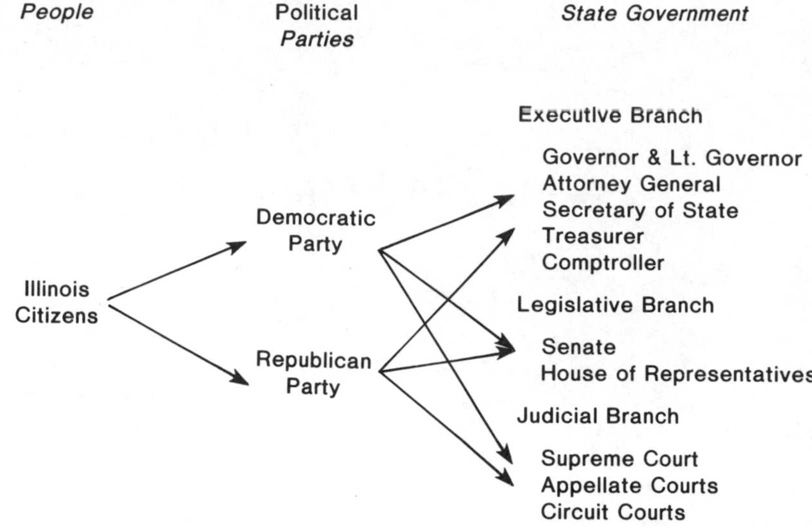

Figure 13-1 POLITICAL PARTIES LINK CITIZENS TO GOVERNMENT IN ILLINOIS

report sets forth a model of how parties can best serve by defining their role and how they can best carry it out.

The argument of the responsible party model is that government can best function under the direction of a set of officeholders working as a team. Government officials must have the power to act, but their actions must always be visible to the citizens who select the officeholders and provide broad guidelines to policy decisions. Thus, as Austin Ranney explains the model:

> In a modern community, therefore, the only way to achieve government that is both efficient and democratic is to establish responsible party government: put a major party in control of the government for a fixed period of time; let the people judge how well or how badly the party has used its power; and, according to the people's judgment as expressed at the polls, let the party continue in power or be replaced by the opposition party. In short, efficient and democratic government can be achieved only by establishing collective *party* responsibility rather than a series of isolated, disconnected individual responsibilities of particular officeholders to their local constituencies.[8]

For the responsible party model to actually function, each party must stake out distinctive positions on major issues which are supported by all its candidates for office. The winning party in an election then takes office and carries out its policies. The losing party "watchdogs" the party in power and develops alternative policies for the next election. Voters thus have a chance to express their opinions of the performance of the party in power as weighed against their opinion of the opposition party. The model works best when two parties compete, so that each party must strive to adopt policies representative of the wishes of the citizens and to carry out those policies once in power in an effective and efficient manner—or risk losing the next election.

In sum, the responsible two party model is an effort to describe a way of making democracy work in a large complex modern society by means of making political parties responsible for developing and implementing policies reflective of citizen preferences. As Everett Carl Ladd, Jr. summarizes:

> Only parties can so organize the issues that mass publics are enabled to speak effectively upon them . . . If they make elected officials in some sense collectively—rather than individually—responsible to the electorate, parties enormously expand the level of meaningful public control over government.[9]

Our purpose in introducing the model here is not to emphasize it as a normative ideal, but, to use it as a frame of reference for clarifying the actual functions of Illinois political parties.

The Three Components of a Political Party

Political parties consist of three more or less distinct components: the party-in-the-electorate, the party organization and the party in government. (See Figure 13-2.) The party-in-the-electorate may be defined in several ways: as anyone who declares himself a party member, as anyone who votes in a party primary election, or as anyone who supports a party's candidates in a general election. By any definition, it is extremely easy to become a part of the party-in-the-electorate—anyone can "join" or "resign" at any time. The party organization is what most people would identify as the political party, since it consists of the officers of the party and others who actively work to preserve and promote the party machinery. Finally, the party in government includes the public officials who won office as candidates of the party and those appointed by the elected officials.

For a party to fulfill or even approach fulfilling the role set for it by the responsible two party model, it must successfully integrate these three components of the party. The party organization, the party voters, and the

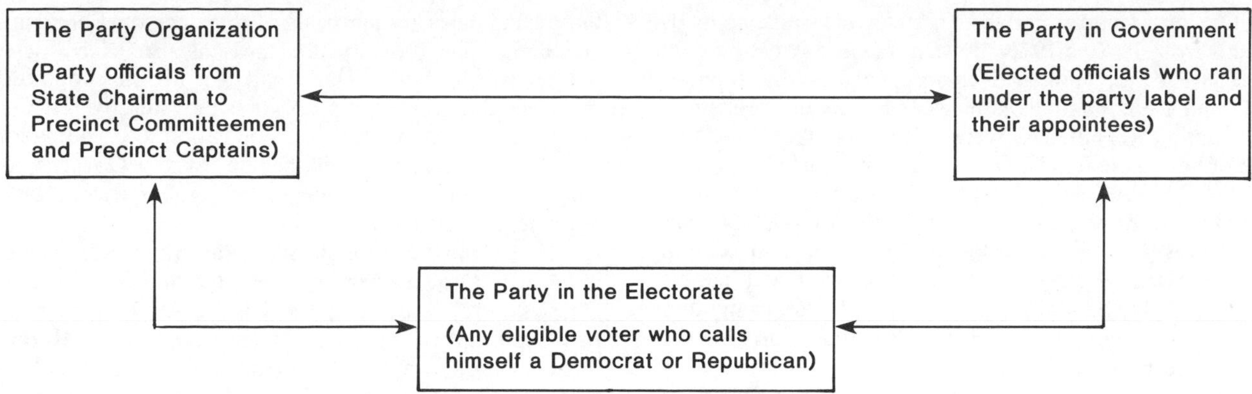

Figure 13-2 POLITICAL PARTIES HAVE THREE DISTINCT COMPONENTS

party's elected officials all have their own interrelated responsibilities in order to perform successfully. For instance, voters must support one party, the party organization must select candidates and issue positions which truly represent the wishes of its supporters in the electorate, and elected officials must support the party position on issues. It is now appropriate to turn our attention directly to the political parties and the party system of Illinois.

The Party in the Electorate

The responsible two party model leads us to two questions about the electorate in Illinois. First, how competitive are the two parties? Do voters have a real chance to choose between parties which both have a good chance at winning? Second, do voters make their decisions on the basis of party affiliation or do they "split their tickets," voting for some candidates of both the Democratic and Republican Parties? Only if the parties represent something, are closely competitive and if the electorate makes its voting decisions on the basis of a candidate's party label can the benefits of a responsible two party system be achieved.

Party Competition To evaluate party competition in Illinois, we can observe past election returns. For instance, in voting for Governor in six elections from 1952 through 1972, the Republicans won three and the Democrats three. Only one of the six elections was won by a margin greater than 52 percent to 48 percent. During those same years, the Illinois Congressional delegation was nearly equally divided, and in eight of 20 years was perfectly split, 12–12.

It is interesting to compare party competition in Illinois to party competition in other states. Austin Ranney has developed an index,[10] which gives equal weight to four factors: the average Democratic percentage of the gubernatorial votes; the average Democratic share of seats in the state Senate and in the House, and the percentage of terms the Democrats controlled the governorship and each legislative branch. Under this index, Illinois ranks as a competitive two party state, tied for 36th on a scale from "most Democratic" to "most Republican." (See Table 13-1)

TABLE 13-1
Competitiveness of State Political Parties

Democratic Dominant States	—	7
Democratic Majority States	—	12
Competitive Two Party States	—	25
Republican Majority States	—	6
Republican Dominant States	—	0

It is also of note that Illinois is one of the most stable states politically based on an analysis of gubernatorial election results and Congressional election results from 1946 through 1974—the support for Republican and Democratic candidates does not vary greatly from year to year. However, as Gove points out:

> On a national basis there is a reasonably effective two party system, although in some areas competition between the two parties is practically nonexistent. Similarly in Illinois, two highly competitive parties exist on a statewide basis, although the degree of competition varies in different areas and at different levels of government.[11]

Looking at Presidential elections from 1900–1956, Gove identified the extent of party competition within Illinois' 102 counties: 17 always Republican, 48 usually Republican, 14 doubtful Republican, 12 usually Democratic and 11 doubtful Democratic counties. However, the Democrats regularly carry the more populous counties. A study by Thomas Kitsos[12] provides additional evidence for the notion that Illinois is a two party state made up of one party areas. Using a standard of elections closer than 60 percent to 40 percent as competitive, Kitsos looked at elections for Clerk, Sheriff, Treasurer and Superintendent of Schools in 1966 for all 102 counties. He found that less than half of all races were competitive even within his rather generous standard. In fact in 20 of the races, there was no opposition to the winning candidate.

Our own analysis of the 16 statewide contests in Illinois from 1970 to 1976 allows us to classify counties on the basis of the number of times carried by the Republican and Democratic candidates.[13] Statewide, 9 Democrats and 7 Republicans were victorious. We found that 52 of the 102 counties were carried by nearly 70 percent of the Republican candidates, while only about a dozen counties were carried that often by the Democratic candidate. Again, this indicates that even in the succession of one-sided wins by popular candidates of both parties like Alan Dixon, Adlai Stevenson, Bill Scott and Jim Thompson, over 60 percent of the counties nearly always supported the same party.

Therefore, Illinois as a state may be considered an example of the kind of two party competition necessary to meet the criteria for a responsible two party system. However, it is important to note that the two party competition that characterizes statewide politics is a result of one party dominance by Democrats and Republicans in many of the cities and counties of Illinois. Thus, while Illinois as a whole is competitive, many parts of Illinois are not.

A competitive two party system like that of Illinois is a necessary but not sufficient condition for achieving responsible party government. The basis of competition is also important—do the parties compete on the basis of issues and personalities, or patronage and preferments? Illinois is generally thought to have a political system based on patronage and preferments—or, as John Fenton calls it, a "job-oriented" two party system.[14] According to Fenton, in Illinois "people who participate in politics on a day-to-day basis do so out of desire for jobs and contracts rather than because of a concern for public policy."[15] The extension of merit personnel hiring and court decisions barring patronage firing has moderated but not changed the nature of Illinois politics.

In a job-oriented state, the prevailing politicial culture regards politics as a profession for politicians, rather than a civic duty for all citizens. People within the system are generally expected to reward their friends, and often politicians of both parties are happy to cooperate in slicing up the pie. Another cause of job-oriented politics is the presence of individuals within political parties who are sharply divided on issues. In Illinois, the rural, suburban and big city elements of each party can rarely agree on anything except a division of jobs and favors—some for you and some for me. (Sometimes, they can't even agree on this!) Politicians are rarely elected to office in Illinois on the basis of issues.

The 1970s have, however, seen the rise of personality politics in Illinois. Outsiders to established party organizations like Dan Walker and Jim Thompson, (and even in Chicago, Jane Byrne who was at least temporarily an outsider), have been elected to major offices by means of media politics, which is a great equalizer of party organizational strength. These successful personality candidates ran campaigns against what they portrayed as a corrupt system of job-oriented politics. None really ran issue-focused campaigns however, and voters supported these candidates on the basis of their personal charisma and their opposition to "business as usual" by party politicians. Many of Dan Walker's liberal supporters deserted him, for example, when they discovered that their only common bond was opposition to organization Democrats. Moreover, one person, even a Governor or Mayor, can do little to change an ongoing system without extensive support.

Aside from these media-superstars (and a few other very well-known personalities like U.S. Senators Charles Percy and Adlai Stevenson, Attorney General Bill Scott and Secretary of State Alan Dixon), Illinois remains a state whose politics can be summarized as "To the victor belongs the spoils." This is not, of course, what the philosophers behind the responsible party model had in mind.

Party Loyalty Turning to the second requirement, that voters choose to vote on the basis of party preference, the evidence is strong that in Illinois, like in most of the nation, the number of independent and ticket-splitting voters is high enough to swing many elections, even if most voters do in fact regularly support the candidates of one party over those of the other.

Twenty years ago, Gove could write that:

> Generally, in each election for state and national offices, Illinois voters choose all candidates from the same party. From 1900–1956, split party tickets were elected in only four of 29 election years. (1930, 1940, 1944, 1954).[16]

Today, this is clearly not true. In the eleven election years since 1958, split party tickets have been elected six times. (See Table 13-2.) Of the 50 races, 30 have been won by Democrats and 20 by Republicans. However, Illinois Republicans have won control of the House in 6 of 11 elections, and of the Senate in 7 of 11, again showing the closely-balanced competition between the parties. Moreover, Illinois voters have been prone to select a Governor of one party and a Legislature of the other during the past 20 years. After the 11 elections from 1958 through 1978, control of the Governorship and the House of Representatives had been in the same hands only four times, control of the Governorship and the Senate had been combined only four times. In addition, party control of the House and Senate have differed on two occasions.

The result of all this ticket splitting and voter independence is that one party rarely receives control of the government with a clear mandate to implement its policies. It is not unusual to see a Democratic Comptroller arguing with a Republican Governor about the budget, or a Democratic Governor and a Republican Attorney General differing on the law, or a Democratic Governor trying to persuade a Republican Legislature to enact his proposals into law. Under these conditions, the breakdown of the responsible two party model becomes complete. Neither party has sufficient control of government to do much, and can always blame the other party for its failure to act. The voter cannot reward or punish the party in power or the party in opposition, because both parties are simultaneously in power and in opposition.

TABLE 13-2
Ticket-Splitting in Illinois
1900–1978*

Year	Democratic Victories	Republican Victories	Year	Democratic Victories	Republican Victories
1900	0	7	1940*	2	6
1902	0	2	1942	0	3
1904	0	7	1944*	3	4
1906	0	2	1946	0	2
1908	0	7	1948	8	0
1910	0	2	1950	0	3
1912			1952	0	7
1914	0	2	1954*	1	2
1916	0	7	1956	0	8
1918	0	3	1958	2	0
1920	0	8	1960*	6	1
1922	0	2	1962	0	3
1924	0	8	1964	6	0
1926	0	3	1966*	1	2
1928	0	8	1968*	3	4
1930*	2	1	1970	3	0
1932	8	0	1972*	2	4
1934	2	0	1974	2	0
1936	8	0	1976*	2	3
1938	3	0	1978*	3	3

*Includes all elections for President, U.S. Senator, Governor, Lieutenant Governor (except 1972 and 1976), Attorney General, Secretary of State, Auditor of Public Accounts/Comptroller, Superintendent of Public Instruction.

The Party As Organization[17]

The major characteristics of State party organizations is decentralization. Illinois, like most other states, has detailed laws concerning party structure and powers at the precinct, ward or township, county and State levels. However, the effect is not to establish a hierarchy of power centralized in the State Chairman and State Central Committee; rather it is to divide power among a series of largely autonomous individuals and committees from the State level through precincts.

It is important to keep in mind that political parties in this country developed as completely voluntary, private groups, operating without legal standing or authority. In Illinois, parties were totally unregulated until 1891 when the Ballot Act was passed stating (among other things) that candidates' names would appear on the ballot in columns under the name of their respective political party. In order to implement this provision, parties were established as legal institutions operating under various regulations. This legislation set the pattern for legal regulation of political parties in Illinois—the law really only concerns how candidates are selected to run under the party label. Therefore, most legal regulation concerns the primary elections now held in March of even-numbered years to select party nominees for the general election in November.[18]

Several features of this legal regulation are worthy of attention.[19] First, in primary elections, any legally qualified person may appear on the ballot by filing petitions with the signatures of a certain number of registered voters. However, party organizations often meet prior to the primary to endorse certain candidates. This endorsing or "slate-making" is an informal, extra-legal process which parties may or may not engage in. In recent years at the State level, the Democratic Party has utilized an elaborate slate-making process to select candidates for Governor and other State elective offices, while the Republican Party has not, although Governors Richard Ogilvie and James R. Thompson have promoted favored candidates. In elections for the Illinois General Assembly, the practice differs in each of the 59 districts from year to year. Endorsed candidates rarely lose—in 1972, Dan Walker was the first non-endorsed statewide Democratic primary winner since the 1930s. On the other hand, party organizations may shy away from making endorsements unless they feel they can guarantee victories to those they slate. This may explain why the Republican Party does not slate candidates for State offices.

Second, Illinois primary voters must declare their party preference, that preference is recorded, and the voter then votes in the appropriate party's primary election. In states with "open" primaries, voters do not have to declare their party preference in order to vote in a primary. However, under the Illinois system there are no limits on the voter switching parties at any subsequent primary election. Illinois voters do not choose a party when they register to vote, nor do they get assigned to a party as a result of their primary participation. This is as "open" as a "closed" primary system (voter reveals party preference) can be. Therefore, Illinois voters can and do participate in the party primary which features the most exciting contest. Normally Democratic or Republican voters may "cross-over" to vote for a weak candidate in the other party's primary so that their own party nominee will have a better chance in the general election. It is commonly believed that many Republicans crossed-over to the Democratic Gubernatorial Primary in 1972 to vote for Dan Walker, on the assumption that he would be a weak opponent in the general election for

Republican Governor Ogilvie. In fact, Walker won the primary and also defeated Ogilvie.

Third, a plurality of votes is all that is required to win an election in Illinois.[20] Since there are usually only two major candidates in the November elections, a Democrat and a Republican, this presents little problem. However, in a primary election there may be many candidates and the victorious nominee of the party may possess a plurality over each of his individual opponents which is far less than a majority of the total votes cast. This means that it is possible for a candidate with very limited appeal within a party to become that party's nominee.

In sum, nominees to represent Illinois political parties are selected in primary elections in which virtually anyone can run and anyone can vote. Whichever candidate receives one vote more than any other single candidate is the winner. Obviously, this is not a system designed to win the hearts of advocates of responsible party government, because a party organization which cannot even control its own nominations for public office cannot begin to assume collective responsibility for the performance of its elected officials. Parties can beat the system when they can endorse candidates and then boost these people to victory in the primary. In Illinois, the Democratic Party generally has been successful. The Republicans do not engage in a formal slate-making process.

Turning to the issue of politicial party organization, the basic unit is the precinct. A precinct is a voting district in which all qualified voters (usually between 500 and 800) vote at the same polling place. There are 11,657 precincts in Illinois, 5,404 in Cook County and 6,153 in the Downstate 101 other counties. Outside Cook County, the 6,153 precinct committeemen in each party are elected for two-year terms at the primary election. The precinct committeemen in turn form a county central committee and elect a county chairman and other officers. In larger counties, an Executive Committee is also elected to help run party affairs; in smaller counties the precinct committeemen serve in that role.

In Cook County, 50 Ward Committeemen are elected in Chicago, and 30 Township Committeemen in the suburbs, for four-year terms. Each Ward and Township Committeeman appoints precinct captains who serve at the pleasure of the Committeeman. These 80 elected Committeemen form the Cook County Central Committee and elect the County Chairman from their ranks.

Power within the party is based on party performance in a party official's own area. For instance, when precinct committeemen elect a county chairman, each committeeman casts the same number of votes as there were party votes cast in his or her precinct in the last party primary election.[21]

The legal requirements of the State of Illinois have given the Democratic and Republican Parties identical formal organizations. The duty of these elected and appointed officials (who except for the Republican State Chairman receive no compensation for their services) is to represent the party in their area and to attempt to persuade voters to support the party candidates. In a legal sense, their most important role is to fill vacancies when primary election winners are unable or unwilling to be candidates in the general election due to death, ill health or personal reasons.

The State Central Committee, made up of one member elected from each of Illinois' 24 Congressional Districts, selects a State Chairman and operates the party on a statewide basis. There is a "paper" hierarchy of State-county-precinct (Downstate) or state-county-ward or township (Cook County) organization in the party, but in fact each unit operates autonomously of the others. When party organization has become hierarchical such as in the Cook County Democratic Party under County Chairman Richard J. Daley, it has been largely in spite of the formal rules and regulations, rather than because of them.[22]

On an informal level, there are some substantial differences between the Republican and Democratic Parties. Since the Republicans have relatively strong organizations in a large number of Downstate counties, the Republican County Chairmen have always been an important force in party affairs. In terms of statewide leadership, the Republican State Chairman and Central Committee have always taken a back seat to Republican Governors. If the Governor is a Democrat (which was rarely the case before 1960), past or future Governors or other high elected Republican officeholders provided what little leadership the party had. A Republican Governor's power over State jobs, grants and contracts often enable him to gain the support of the county chairmen. In turn, the Governor can usually select nominees for other State offices who will get the party's support in primaries. In 1978 for instance, Governor Thompson's candidate for Comptroller won the Republican primary election against a better-known opponent, former House Speaker W. Robert Blair. The Republican Party is *not* a strong hierarchical organization; it is rather a decentralized alliance of county organizations with political rivalries common at every level.

The Democratic Party is somewhat more unified because its vote is concentrated in a few large cities, particularly Chicago. In 1976, for example, 45.6 percent of the statewide Democratic Primary vote was cast in Chicago, and 59.8 percent of that vote was cast in Cook County including Chicago and suburbs. In fact, in a primary election, the Chicago Democratic Organization has been able to provide its favored candidates with a large enough margin to carry the entire State. The Chicago Party dominated slate-making for this reason, and few candidates even challenged the endorsed candidates. Centralized control of nominations and resulting party discipline may be less important in the future as a result of recent primary losses by endorsed candidates for Governor (Paul Simon defeated by Dan Walker, 1972), U.S. Congress (Erwin France defeated by Ralph Metcalfe, 1976) and Mayor (Michael Bilandic defeated by Jane Byrne, 1979). Moreover in 1978, the first Democratic slate-making proceedings since Mayor Daley's death were marked by chaos and controversy. Nevertheless, all the 1978 endorsed candidates were victorious in the primary.

Party-in-Government

According to the responsible party model, the party platform is the crucial link between the party organization, the voters and the party in government. The platform should result from extensive intra-party debate and discussion, be written in specific terms explaining what the party will do if its candidates are elected and be communicated to the voters so that they may decide which party's nominees deserve the voters' support.

In fact, according to James D. Nowlan who made an extensive study of the subject, the platforms of the Democratic and Republican Parties in Illinois meet none of these criteria.[23] Platforms are drafted by committees, approved by a few party leaders and adopted by party members who are rarely familiar with its content. The platforms are deliberately vague and general so as not to offend any segment of the party. Finally, the platforms are rarely publicized, and most voters are never aware of their existence. The only purpose of platforms in Illinois, according to Nowlan, is to give party leaders a chance to discuss major issues and determine areas of agreement and disagreement for future reference in the campaign or later sessions of the General Assembly. As one Illinois party leader quoted by Nowlan summarized it, "No candidate has ever been elected because of our party's platform."[24] Thus, even if an elected official wanted to follow his party's position on an issue, the party platform might provide little or no guidance.

Another important factor in the responsible party model is a party's ability to exercise discipline over its elected officials. In the British system, upon an idealized version of which the model is largely based, party leaders determine who will run for Parliament, the district from which they will run and the finances available for the campaign. Thus a member of Parliament must respond to party needs. In Illinois, as in the United States generally, legislators win office either as individuals or with the support of the local rather than the State political party organization. Richard E. Dunn and Martin D. Glista conducted a survey of the winners and losers of 1972 legislative elections in Illinois and found that both groups reported only "slight" help from the legislative leaders of the candidates' party. As Dunn and Glista point out, "In all probability, it would seem that no legislator feels obligated to his legislative leader for his election . . ."[25] Once in office, legislators will then likely support their party's position only if it coincides with their own views or with the needs of their particular legislative district, although much of the bargaining and compromise that marks the legislative process takes place within parties, so that it is usually in the best interests of party members to vote with their party. In recent years, the legislative leadership of each party has attempted to support party candidates with financial help. However, this trend has not yet had a very significant impact on legislative behavior.

The same tendency is even greater for elected officials in the executive and judicial branches of government. Illinoisans elect a Governor and Lieutenant Governor, Attorney General, Secretary of State, Treasurer and Comptroller. Except for the necessity to earn the approval of a Republican Governor or Democratic slatemakers prior to running for office for the first time, successful candidates for these offices run and finance their own campaigns. Once in office, they seem to build a personal following via media coverage as well as jobs and contracts. They are the leading lights of their political party, but they are able to make decisions in a fairly independent manner if they wish.

As in many states, Illinois citizens elect all the important members of the judiciary at the trial, appellate and Supreme Court levels. Candidates run as Republicans or Democrats in contested elections for their first term of office, but thereafter run only on a retention ballot where they need to obtain 60 percent approval to remain in office. Only rarely does a judge fail to win retention. In fact, since the system was adopted in 1962, 518 of the 524 judges who sought retention were successful.[26] Coupled with the tradition of an independent judiciary and our ideal about the rule of law, political party control over judges is generally weak outside of Chicago and Cook County. However, judges are people, and instances where a judge's personal party loyalties seem to influence his actions are not unknown. Certainly, the use of partisan popular elections to select judges make the judiciary "an important part of the party patronage system."[27]

In summary then, elected officials in Illinois are at least as likely to follow the dictates of their conscience, the needs of their constituents or the chances for advancement of their own political career as they are to support a unified political party to decision-making.

Conclusion

If Illinois' political party system does not provide the kind of responsible party government discussed here, what do political parties contribute to the governance of the State?

First, the Democratic and Republican parties provide vehicles for both professional politicians and activist amateurs to participate in politics. Although candidate-centered campaign organizations are becoming prominent and various civic organizations also exist for those interested in public affairs, parties remain the major means of organizing political activity.

Second, parties provide voters with labels identifying candidates as Republicans, Democrats or members of some third party. Although the label does not mean that a candidate supports a specific set of public policies in the form of a party platform, the label does convey some general information about the policy preferences of the prospective officeholder. In Illinois, Democrats are more likely to support labor union views while Republicans tend to advance the interests of business. As Keefe states, in terms of public policy, "while party members may be marching to different drums, most of them are playing the same tune."[28] Moreover, particularly in the

General Assembly, party members must work together as much as possible to get anything done; thus, voters can also consider a candidate's party label as a guide to the personal relationships he or she will have as part of the "party team" in Springfield.

Third, the Democratic and Republican parties do offer candidates for all major executive offices and nearly all legislative and judicial posts in State government. Without political parties to assist in the recruitment of individuals to run for office, many races would never be contested. Thus, while many complain about the quality of candidates, at least the parties insure that Illinois voters have some choice in elections.

Finally, as discussed briefly above, party membership provides a rough guide to friends and enemies for elected officials. While instances of alliances across party lines and rivalries within party ranks are common, Republicans generally work together, as do Democrats. To some degree this reflects common social backgrounds and personal policy views of party members. More important though, it demonstrates the need for some principle or organization to hold government together. Republicans then pursue their political, governmental and career objectives as part of the Republican team, and the Democrats act in like fashion.

In sum, then, while the political parties of Illinois do not provide responsible party government, they do make substantial contributions to the governance of the State. It is not likely that our political parties will become more responsible in the future. The trends in recent years are toward personality politics and candidate-specific campaign organizations, voter independence and ticket-splitting, emphasis on reform which tends to lessen the power of party organizations, and a decline in party prestige. All point to a future in which Illinois political parties will be fortunate to maintain their current status.

Further Research

Illinois presents many fruitful opportunities for research into political parties and their future role in the political system. If present trends continue and the role of parties and party leadership declines further, how will the whole process of interest aggregation and linking government to the people be affected? Will a strengthened Legislature be able to substitute its own activities for maintaining active two-way communication with the citizens? Alternatively, will the emerging role of the media create a substantially different one-way process of communication with the public on major issues, and can the political system function even minimally under such circumstances? Or will interest groups fill the vacuum, and will we see the continued rise of "single-interest" groups, and the polarization of the public around individual issues? Will the trend toward "open primaries," with their diluting effect on party identity continue? Will new leadership generate viable proposals for the renewal of such party functions as developing issues, recruiting candidates and implementing election strategies?

NOTES

[1]Frank J. Sorauf, *Party Politics in America* (3d ed.; Boston: Little, Brown and Company, 1976), pp. 4–5.

[2]William J. Keefe, *Parties, Politics, and Public Policy in America* (2d ed.; Hinsdale, Illinois: Dryden Press, 1976), p. 1.

[3]James Q. Wilson, *Political Organizations* (New York: Basic Books, 1973), p. 95.

[4]Frank B. Feigert and M. Margaret Conway, *Parties and Politics in America* (Boston: Allyn and Bacon, 1976), p. 2.

[5]David Easton, *A Framework for Political Analysis* (Englewood Cliffs, New Jersey: Prentice-Hall, 1965).

[6]Everett Carll Ladd, Jr., *Where Have All the Voters Gone?* (New York: W. W. Norton, 1978), p. xvii.

[7]Committee on Political Parties, American Political Science Association, *Toward a More Responsible Two-Party System* (New York: Holt, Rinehart and Winston, 1950).

[8]J. Austin Ranney, "The Concept of Party Responsibility," in *Illinois Political Parties,* ed. by Lois M. Pelekoudas (Urbana: University of Illinois, Institute of Government and Public Affairs, March, 1960), p. 15.

[9]Everett Carll Ladd, Jr., *Where Have All the Voters Gone?* (New York: W. W. Norton, 1978), p. xvi.

[10]Austin Ranney, "Parties in State Politics," in *Politics in the American States,* ed. by Herbert Jacob and Kenneth N. Vines (3d ed.; Boston: Little, Brown, 1976), p. 61.

[11]Samuel K. Gove, "Inter-Party Competition," in Pelekoudas, *op. cit.,* p. 29.

[12]Thomas Kitsos, "The 1966 County Elections," *Illinois Government,* No. 30 (April 1968).

[13]Peter W. Colby and Paul Michael Green, "Voting Patterns in the 96 Downstate Counties," *Illinois Issues* 4:8 (August, 1978), pp. 15–21.

[14]John Fenton, *Midwest Politics* (New York: Holt, Rinehart and Winston, 1966), pp. 194–218.

[15]*Ibid.,* p. 115.

[16]Gove, *op. cit.,* p. 33.

[17]For a more detailed description, see Martin David Dubin, "Illinois Politics and the 1970 Constitution," especially pp. 41–44, in *Governing Illinois Under the 1970 Constitution,* Revised Edition, *P. Allan Dionisopoulos, ed.* (DeKalb: Center for Governmental Studies, Northern Illinois University, 1978).

[18]Clarence A. Berdahl, "Some Problems in the Legal Regulation of Political Parties in Illinois," in Pelakoudas, *op. cit.,* p. 19.

[19]For complete reference to the laws regulating parties see the compilation of Election Laws by the State Board of Elections, effective January 2, 1978 (especially Articles 7 and 8).

[20]An exception is Illinois' unique process of cumulative voting which is used to electe the 177 State Representatives, three from each of the 59 legislative districts. For description and analysis of the process and its impact on political parties, see George S. Blair, "The Case for Cumulative Voting in Illinois," *Northwestern University Law Review,* 47: 3 (July/August 1952), pp. 344–357; George S. Blair, *Cumulative Voting: An Effective Electoral Device in Illinois Politics* (Urbana: University of Illinois Press, 1960); James Kuklinski, "Cumulative and Plurality Voting: An Analysis of Illinois' Unique Electoral System," *Western Political Quarterly,* XXVII: 4 (December 1973), pp. 726–746; Jack Sawyer and Duncan MacRae, Jr., "Game Theory and Cumulative Voting in Illinois: 1902–1954," *American Political Science Review,* 56:4 (1962); Michael C. Maibach, "Illinois Cumulative Voting System: Ingenious or Inane?" unpublished Master's Thesis, Sangamon State University, Springfield, Illinois, Spring 1976.

[21]A good readable description of political party organization in Illinois may be found in League of Women Voters of Illinois, *Illinois Voters Handbook* (Chicago: League of Women Voters of Illinois, 1973).

[22]For a superb account of the Daley organization well beyond the scope of this paper, see Milton Rakove, *Don't Make No Waves Don't Back No Losers* (Bloomington: Indiana University Press, 1975).

[23]James D. Nowlan, *Illinois Major Party Platforms: 1900–1964* (Urbana: University of Illinois Institute of Government and Public Affairs, 1966).

[24]James D. Nowlan, "Illinois Party Platforms: An Analysis," *Illinois Government*, 24 (October 1966), p. 2.

[25]Richard E. Dunn and Martin D. Glista, "Illinois Legislative Races: Separating the Winners From the Losers," *Southern Illinois University Public Affairs Bulletin*, VI: 1 (January/February 1973), p. 2.

[26]Paul Lermack, "Illinois Judges: Too Much Retention and Too Little Selection," *Illinois Issues*, 5: 6 (June 1979), p. 9.

[27]L. Peter Schultz, "The Judiciary," pp. 24–27, in *Governing Illinois Under the 1970 Constitution*, Revised Edition, ed. by P. Allan Dionisopoulos, (DeKalb: Center for Governmental Studies, Northern Illinois University, 1978).

[28]Keefe, *op. cit.*, p. 51.

SUPPLEMENTAL READINGS

Political Parties

Chambers, William Nisbet and Walter Dean Burnham. *The American Party Systems: Stages of Political Development.*. 2d ed. New York: Oxford University Press, 1975.

Feigert, Frank B. and M. Margaret Conway. *Parties and Politics in America*. Boston: Allyn and Bacon, 1976.

Jewell, Malcolm E. and David M. Olson. *American State Political Parties and Elections*. Homewood, Illinois: Dorsey, 1978.

Keefe, William J., *Parties, Politics, and Public Policy in America*. 2d ed. Hinsdale, Illinois, Dryden, 1976).

Ladd, Everett Carll Jr. *Where Have All the Voters Gone?* New York: W. W. Norton, 1978.

Rossiter, Clinton. *Parties and Politics in America*. Ithaca, New York: Cornell University Press, 1960.

Illinois

Banfield, Edward C. *Political Influence*. New York: Free Press of Glencoe, 1960.

Fenton, John H. *Midwest Politics*. New York: Holt, Rinehart and Winston, 1966, especially Chapter 7, "Political Clout in Illinois," pp. 194–218.

Gove, Samuel K. *Illinois Legislature: Structure and Process*. Urbana, Illinois: University of Illinois Press, 1976.

Kenney, David. *Basic Illinois Government*. Carbondale, Illinois: Southern Illinois Univesity Press, 1974.

Pelekoudas, Lois M., ed. *Illinois Political Parties*. Institute of Government and Public Affairs, University of Illinois, March, 1960.

Rakove, Milton. *Don't Make No Waves, Don't Back No Losers*. Bloomington, Indiana: Indiana University Press, 1975.

Ranney, Austin. *Illinois Politics*. New York: New York University Press, 1960.

Steiner, Gilbert Y. and Samuel K. Gove. *Legislative Politics in Illinois* Urbana: University of Illinois Press, 1960.

Wilson, James Q. *The Amateur Democrat*. Chicago: University of Chicago Press, 1962.

Wilson, James Q. *Negro Politics*. New York: Free Press of Glencoe, 1960.

CHAPTER **14**

Recent Political Developments in the Chicago Suburban Crescent

Kevin L. McKeough and John Steinke

Several recent analyses of Illinois voting patterns in statewide elections (including presidential races) have underscored the significance of Chicago's suburban "crescent."[1] The five suburban counties—DuPage, Kane, Lake, McHenry and Will—which are part of Chicago's Standard Metropolitan Statistical Area (SMSA) have, in recent years, been dubbed the "collar" counties. Added to the collar counties for analytical purposes is the suburban portion of Cook County outside the City of Chicago. These six areas (which we will refer to as the "suburban crescent" or, simply, the "suburbs") now have a combined population of nearly 3.9 million (approximately 35 percent of the Illinois total) and cast 35 percent of the vote in statewide elections.[2] Examination of presidential voting in the "suburbs" suggests that the Republican dominance of the area now balances the vote produced in Chicago for Democratic candidates. This is a result of the declining population and total vote in Chicago and the rising population and total vote in the suburbs. Given the historical Republicanism of "downstate" Illinois—the 96 counties beyond Cook and the collar have only supported one Democrat for the presidency (LBJ in 1964) since 1936—the ability of the suburban crescent to balance Chicago's Democratic margins does not bode well for future Democratic candidates in statewide races.[3]

While we recognize that attempts to project future events based on the past—and limited past data at that—is a hazardous undertaking, we believe that recent developments suggest the potential for increased Democratic voting in the suburbs. Coupled with Chicago's Democratic pluralities, such suburban votes could be sufficient to sustain Democratic candidates for President and other statewide offices in the 1980's and beyond. We will set forth the major outlines of recent suburban political developments in the following sections.

Changing Patterns in Suburban Voting

The pervasive Republicanism of Chicago's suburbs can be seen in their voting history. In the 11 election years 1948–1968 there were 54 contests for major state executive offices, U.S. Senator and President. Thus, there were 324 opportunities[4] for Démocratic candidates to achieve pluralities (i.e., "carry") in the six suburban areas under examination. But Democrats carried suburban areas only 16 times. Fourteen of these victories were achieved in Will County,[5] the other two in Lake County. This record of futility illustrates the long-standing Republican dominance of the suburbs, but the exceptions also suggest that the suburbs are not all of one piece. Obviously, Will and Lake Counties showed a slight tendency to support Democratic candidates, but the remaining suburbs stayed solidly Republican. Analysis of elections in the 1970's—both State and county contests—reveals the growing political variety and competition in Chicago's suburban crescent.

State Elections in the Seventies

Separate analyses of voting in the six suburban SMSA counties outside Chicago uncover differences which are otherwise masked by summaries of election results. Although the remainder of the suburban crescent was solidly Republican in voting for all statewide candidates in the five elections of the 1970's, Will County was reasonably competitive. Indeed, Democratic candidates carried Will in six of the twenty-two statewide contests of the decade. Moreover, Democratic statewide candidates carried each of the six suburban counties at least twice in the twenty-two contests, and Democratic pluralities were achieved in 23 of the 132[6] total suburban races. This represented a marked increase in Democratic electoral successes compared to the two previous decades.

However, the total number of Democratic suburban "carries" in the Seventies was collected by three candidates—Alan Dixon in his second race for State Treasurer (1974) and two contests for Secretary of State (1976 and 1978), Adlai Stevenson III in two races for U.S. Senator (1970 and 1974) and Mike Bakalis in his campaign for State Comptroller (1976). In order to adjust somewhat for the personal popularity of some Democratic candidates, Table 1 averages the vote for all statewide Democratic candidates in each election, 1970–78.

As is immediately clear from the data in Table 14-1, Democratic candidates received a larger share of the suburban vote in non-presidential years, and had their lowest levels of support in DuPage and McHenry counties, in each of the five elections. Data on straight party and split-ticket voting in the suburbs help to explain this pattern. (See Table 14-2.)

Although data were not available for all counties in all elections, certain patterns are visible in Table 14-2. First, the elections of 1970–76[7] show a lower straight Republican vote surplus in mid-term years (1970 and 1974) and an increased surplus in presidential years.[8] This upsurge in the Republican straight ticket advantage is the result of a decrease in straight Democratic ballots combined with an increase in straight Republican ballots from mid-term to presidential elections.

The second pattern revealed in Table 14-2 is the overall suburban increase in split-ticket voting in each successive election, although the proportion of split tickets does not rise continuously in every county. Nevertheless, the combination of increased split-ticket voting and reduced straight Republican vote margins in mid-term elections produced pluralities for Democratic State candidates in several suburban counties in 1970 and 1974.[9] Additional understanding of suburban electoral change in the Seventies is provided by a review of voting for county offices.

County Elections: Guide to the Future?

As the decade of the 1970's began, no political pundit was likely to have forecast a Democratic breakthrough in Chicago's suburban crescent. With the exception of Will County, which elected four Democrats to county office in the 1964 LBJ landslide,[10] none of the other suburban areas had produced county level Democratic pluralities since 1936. Indeed, McHenry County had not elected a

TABLE 14-1
Average Democratic Vote in Statewide Elections
Chicago Suburbs, 1970–1978

Suburban Area	Year 1970	1972	1974	1976	1978	1970-78 County Total
Cook County	45.9%	33.9%	56.4%	37.9%	40.0%	39.2%
DuPage County	39.5%	29.2%	46.2%	30.5%	34.4%	32.8%
Kane County	42.3%	33.9%	50.5%	35.7%	38.9%	37.4%
Lake County	46.1%	36.2%	55.8%	36.0%	38.7%	39.0%
McHenry County	39.4%	29.0%	49.4%	29.3%	33.1%	31.5%
Will County	49.0%	40.2%	62.2%	43.9%	44.8%	44.6%
Suburban Total	45.6%	33.6%	54.0%	36.6%	39.1%	38.2%

TABLE 14-2
Straight Party and Split-Ticket Voting in Chicago's Suburbs—1970–1978

Suburban Area	Election Year 1970 Surplus Straight Republican Votes[a]	Split Tickets (%)	Election Year 1972 Surplus Straight Republican Votes	Split Tickets (%)	1974 Surplus Straight Republican Votes
Cook County	NA[b]	NA	NA	NA	NA
DuPage County	NA	NA	NA	NA	+13,885
Kane County	+4,646	(70.4%)	+19,535	(60.4%)	+ 2,415
Lake County	+9,515	(50.0)	+23,629	(63.5)	+ 1,597
McHenry County	+3,739	(54.9)	+11,302	(61.7)	+ 1,051
Will County	− 817	(39.6)	+10,410	(57.6)	− 7,012
Totals	+17,083 (4 counties)	(53.1)	+64,876 (4 counties)	(61.0)	+11,936 (5 counties)

[a] Surplus Straight Republican Votes = Straight Republican Ballots − Straight Democratic Ballots
[b] NA = Data not available from election authorities

Suburban Area	1974 Split Tickets (%)	Election Year 1976 Surplus Straight Republican Votes	Split Tickets (%)	Election Year 1978 Surplus Straight Republican Votes	Split Tickets (%)
Cook County	NA	NA	NA	+ 59,309	(67.4%)
DuPage County	(57.0%)	+52,558	(67.2%)	+ 24,016	(76.1)
Kane County	(66.5)	+12,268	(72.5)	+ 3,377	(81.8)
Lake County	(66.8)	+18,825	(67.4)	+ 10,125	(79.9)
McHenry County	(71.8)	+ 5,347	(73.1)	+ 3,447	(81.6)
Will County	(53.4)	+ 917	(79.2)	+ 2,732	(75.2)
Totals	(61.4) (5 counties)	+89,915 (5 counties)	(70.5) (5 counties)	+103,006 (6 counties)	(71.7) (6 counties)

Democrat since 1832![11] Democrats elected in Lake and Kane counties in 1934—the only Democratic victories in this century—were promptly dispatched from office in the next election.[12]

A variety of factors contributed to the Republican solidarity of the suburbs. Among them were: (1) their small town-rural heritage; (2) loyalties to the GOP dating back to the Civil War; (3) fear of being dominated by Chicago's Democratic "Machine;" and (4) the Republican character of the local press, combined with the massive circulation and influence of the fiercely partisan Chicago *Tribune* in the heyday of the late Colonel Robert McCormick.[13] Added to these factors was the population explosion of the 1950's which transformed the suburbs from basically farmland into mainly suburban communities. During the 1950's the population of suburban Cook County increased by almost 80 percent; in DuPage County the increase was 103 percent; the Lake County population rose by 64 percent; Will County by 43 percent; Kane County by 40 percent and McHenry by 66 percent.[14] This population boom also brought even larger Republican vote totals in the suburbs—and predictions of doom for the Democratic Party due to the ostensible conversion of former urban Democrats into suburban Republicans.[15] Republican control of county offices in the collar counties generally continued during the decade of the Sixties; that decade even saw a total of five GOP victories in the Cook County elections of 1962 and 1966![16]

The Democratic Surge

And then came 1970. With it came the election to Lake County office of only the third Democrat since the Civil War and the first Democratic McHenry County officer in 138 years.[17] Will County voters elected Democrats to the offices of Sheriff and County Treasurer. In 1974 Lake County elected its first Democratic Sheriff since the turn of the century and Grace Mary Stern retained the County Clerk's office she had won four years earlier, becoming the first Democrat ever re-elected to office in Lake County's history. In McHenry County Sheriff Art Tyrrell replicated Mrs. Stern's feat when he became the first Democratic official ever re-elected there. Democrats were also re-elected as Will County Sheriff and Treasurer, and a third Democrat was successful in his bid for School Superintendent. In Kane County David Pierce became the first Democratic County Clerk in history and the first major county officer of his party in 40 years.[18]

The elections of 1976 continued the Democratic insurgency. Lake County elected the first Democratic State's Attorney in its history. In Kane County a registered nurse, Mary Lou Kearns, became the first distaff Democrat and the first Democratic Coroner in the county's history. And in Will County a Democrat was elected Auditor.

Election year 1978 extended the run of Democratic breakthroughs. Cook County's "country towns" gave pluralities to candidates for County Clerk and Assessor. Kane County re-elected its Democratic County Clerk and added a Sheriff to the ranks of Democratic county offices. Art Tyrrel was re-elected to this third term as McHenry County Sheriff and Grace Mary Stern to her third term as Lake County Clerk. In Will County Kent Bosworth was re-elected to his third term as County Treasurer and Matthew Raich to his second term as Schools Superintendent.

But 1978 also witnessed the first break in the Democrats' string of successes. Lake County Sheriff "Chick" La Magdeleine was defeated for re-election[19] and Will County Democrats lost their grip on the Sheriff's office when two-term incumbent Joseph Trigna did not seek re-election. The Democratic nominee lost a close race in his attempt to retain the office. Table 14-3 presents a summary of suburban county elections in the 1970's.

Democratic candidates across the nation fared well in 1974,[20] and those in the suburban crescent followed the trend. The sharp decline in surplus straight Republican votes[21] was undoubtedly the result, in part, of the entire range of events captured under the umbrella of "Watergate"—the Agnew affair, the impeachment inquiry and Nixon resignation, the Ford pardon. Added to these factors was suburban opposition to the Regional Transportation Authority (RTA) which contributed to the Republican voter apathy marking the November 1974 elections. Buoyed by these favorable circumstances, and with a party ticket led by popular candidates Adlai Stevenson III and Alan Dixon, suburban Democrats retained the four offices originally won in 1970. They also captured three new offices and came close to victory in still other races. These events encouraged additional Democratic efforts in the 1976 elections and produced still further county-level gains despite an increased suburban Republican vote which garnered Illinois majorities for President, Governor and Lieutenant Governor and Attorney General.

In the 1978 elections, suburban Democrats enjoyed the advantages of incumbency in six contests for county office and retained five. Three other county contests were won, and the Democratic share of the vote for all contested county offices in the suburbs reached its peak—44.8 percent. What do these developments suggest for the future?

Suburban Politics in the 1980's

Data presented in Table 14-1 above revealed the rise in split-ticket voting and reduced surplus straight Republican ballots. By the end of the 1970's these trends reduced the GOP's straight ballot advantage to less than 10 percent of the total vote (Table 14-5). The rise in ticket-splitting[22] in the suburbs provided sufficient "slack" in voting behavior to allow Democrats to overcome the Republican straight ballot surplus. Only in DuPage

TABLE 14-3
Results of Suburban Voting for
Contested County Offices, 1970–1978

Year	Total Contests in Six Counties	# of Democratic Victories	% Democratic Victories
1970	22	4	18
1972	27	0	0
1974	28	7	25
1976	28	3	11
1978	25	8	32
TOTAL	130	22	17

TABLE 14-4
Average Democratic Vote for Contested[a] County Offices,
Chicago Suburbs, 1970–1978

Suburban Area	1970	1972	Year 1974	1976	1978	County 1970-78 Total
Cook County	38.3	38.7	41.9	40.5	46.6	41.2
DuPage County	34.9	34.0	42.1	35.2	35.6	36.2
Kane County	38.9	37.2	46.1	41.8	51.2	42.3
Lake County	45.7	39.9	52.8	46.1	43.2	44.6
McHenry County	58.6[b]	32.2	50.3	33.6	48.9	39.6
Will County	49.8	46.0	55.2	49.3	45.4	48.7
Suburban Total	39.0	38.4	43.6	40.5	44.8	41.1

[a]A total of 12 offices were not contested by Democrats: 9 in McHenry County, 3 in Kane County and 1 in Lake County.
[b]This percentage is for a single contest, the successful Democratic campaign for Sheriff. Three other offices had no Democratic candidates in McHenry County, 1970.

TABLE 14-5
Surplus Straight Republican Ballots and Split-Tickets
Chicago Suburbs, 1978

Suburban Area	Total Vote	Split Tickets	% Splits	Surplus Straight Republican	% Surplus Straight Republican
Cook County	685,294	461,566	(67.4)	+ 59,309	(8.7)
DuPage County	173,867	132,245	(76.1)	+ 24,016	(13.8)
Kane County	66,587	54,464	(81.8)	+ 3,377	(5.1)
Lake County	109,920	87,833	(79.9)	+ 10,125	(9.2)
McHenry County	36,508	29,774	(81.6)	+ 3,447	(9.4)
Will County	78,409	58,940	(75.2)	+ 2,732	(3.5)
Six County Total	1,150,585	824,822	(71.7)	+103,006	(9.0)

County, the lone suburban area which did not elect a single Democrat to county office in the Seventies, was the GOP advantage too great to overcome. Not even Republican Party divisions resulting from primary contests have been sufficient for DuPage Democrats to claim victory in the last bastion of solid Republicanism in the suburbs.[23]

Looking toward the elections of the 1980's, we can identify areas of potential Democratic gains as well as problem areas. As Tables 14-1 and 14-4 revealed, DuPage and McHenry counties were most staunchly Republican in the decade just ended. And as the Seventies came to a close, the lone Democrat to win county office in McHenry in this century had resigned, leaving behind limited prospects for those who would match his success. Democrats in DuPage County face perhaps a greater hurdle. Party activists, seeking to gain from the prominence of their county chairman, William A. Redmond, Speaker of the Illinois House of Representatives, have mounted aggressive fund-raising efforts aimed at establishing a financial base for party organization-building. The task ahead, however, is substantial. Yet Democratic voting strength is growing in several DuPage County townships which are contiguous to Cook County. Even if DuPage Democrats fail to capture county office in the near future, Alan Dixon's sweeping victories in 1976 and 1978 indicate that attractive Democratic candidates can carry this heartland of suburban Republicanism.

Elsewhere in the suburbs—Cook, Kane, Lake and Will counties—a base Democartic vote of 42–48 percent provides a foundation for future growth and success. In Cook County, Democrats should be able to secure sufficient financial support to contest aggressively in the "country towns." There are indications that some Chicago Democrats are seeking electoral bases in the suburbs in order to do so.[24] In Lake County, two Democratic county officials and the Mayor of Waukegan may lead further Democratic advances. Will County's Democratic base is in the industrial areas of Joliet and Lockport. Given the State and county Democratic majorities in Will County even prior to the Seventies, we expect continued Democratic success there in the 1980's. Democratic victories in three successive Kane County elections, along with Secretary of State Alan Dixon's majorities, demonstrate that attractive candidates and aggressive campaigns can be successful. A new party chairman with imaginative approaches to fund-raising and organizational development also enhances the future Democratic prospects in Kane County.

Conclusion

We have reviewed political developments in Chicago's suburban crescent during the 1970's in order to assess the contention that

> . . . Suburban Republicanism now effectively balances Chicago's base of support for the Democratic party. This means that the two parties now can be considered evenly matched in the six-county metropolitan area. [Thus] the balance of power [in statewide elections] is Downstate, where the other 96 counties have regularly produced small deviations in favor of the Republicans.[25]

While presidential election data for the entire suburban crescent may support the view of a Chicago-suburban "balance," we believe the disaggregation of electoral results, presented here, including county-level contests, point towards a brighter future for Illinois Democrats in the suburbs and elsewhere. Tables 14-1 and 14-4 above show that Democrats contesting for county offices did better in the suburbs in the Seventies than did their ticket mates for statewide office. We view the county office gains as significant, pointing toward a stronger vote for state-level Democratic candidates in the future. The elections of Roland Burris as Comptroller and Jerome Cosentino as Treasurer of Illinois in November 1978 may be instructive. Both lost the Downstate 96 counties by substantial margins, yet won by over 150,000 votes statewide. They achieved such success because they pulled 77 percent of the vote in Chicago *and* more than 41 percent of the suburban vote. Yet both were Chicago-based candidates, neither was an incumbent and neither waged highly visible media campaigns. We suspect that their suburban vote share is a reasonable benchmark for Democrats in the future.

Rather than focus on the 96 Downstate counties, we believe Illinois elections in the 1980's will be decided in the suburbs. Continued Democratic gains there can only enhance the party's fortunes.[26]

NOTES

[1]Peter W. Colby and Paul M. Green, "Downstate Holds the Key to Victory," *Illinois Issues* 4:2 (February 1978), 7–11; Peter W. Colby and Paul M. Green, "Vote Power: Suburbs Up, Cities Down," *Illinois Issues* 4:11 (November 1978), 16–22; Peter W. Colby and Paul M. Green, "Voting Patterns in the 96 Downstate Counties," *Illinois Issues* 4:8 (August 1978), 15–21; Lawrence N. Hansen, "Mayor Daley and the Suburbs," *Illinois Issues* 4:1 and 4:2 (January and February 1978), 14–17 and 12–14.

[2]Colby and Green, "Downstate," *op. cit.*

[3]*Ibid.;* Colby and Green, "Vote Power," *op. cit.;* Colby and Green, "Voting Patterns," *op. cit.*

[4]This total (N = 324) results from multiplying the number of offices contested (54) by the number of suburban counties (6, with the suburban portion of Cook County considered as a unit here). Thus, 54 × 6 = 324.

[5]FDR also carried Will County in 1932 and 1936 and lost narrowly in 1940 and 1944. But he failed to carry any other suburban areas in his four Illinois presidential victories.

[6]This total was derived, as in number 4 above, by multiplying the number of contests (22) by the number of counties (6).

[7]Pursuant to the 1970 Illinois Constitution, all five of the state's elected executive offices—Governor/Lt. Governor, Attorney General, Secretary of State, Comptroller and Treasurer—were on the ballot in 1978. This altered the electoral dynamics of earlier years and 1978 is, therefore, excluded from trend analyses.

[8]Careful examination of Table 14-2 will show that this upswing in surplus straight Republican votes in 1976 is not due to the inclusion of DuPage County data, which was unavailable for 1972 comparison. Deducting the GOP surplus in DuPage from the 1976 total still shows a net Republican straight ballot surplus of +37,357 votes. That is above the 1974 surplus, but well below the comparable four-county surplus for 1972.

[9]Although the various elements in the 1978 election were less clear, the proportion of split tickets rose from the 1976 level. Secretary of State Alan Dixon swept all six suburban areas enroute to carrying all 102 Illinois counties and a record Democratic margin of 1,516,986 votes.

[10]The entire statewide Democratic ticket carried Will County in 1964, pulling four of five county candidates into office with them. Democrats did win one county office in 1948 and two in 1962.

[11]Chicago *Sun-Times,* November 5, 1970, p. 18.

[12]*Ibid.*, and Waukegan *New-Sun,* November 9, 1974, p. 14A.

[13]Colby and Green, "Voting Patterns," *op. cit.;* and Michael Barone, Grant Ujifusa and Douglas Mathews, *The Almanac of American Politics* (New York: Dutton, 1972), pp. 214–15.

[14]Barone, Ujifusa and Mathews, *op. cit.*, pp. 214–15; and Hansen, *op. cit.,* 4:1 (January 1978), p. 15.

[15]Samuel Lubell, *Revolt of the Moderates* (New York: Harper, 1956), pp. 112–14; and Robert C. Wood, *Suburbia: Its People and Their Politics* (Boston: Houghton Mifflin, 1958), pp. 135–41.

[16]Republicans had been elected to county office in Cook County in prior years, most notably in 1946–1956. Chicago's late Mayor Richard J. Daley suffered his only electoral defeat in his race for Cook County Sheriff in 1946. See Hansen, *op. cit.* 4:1 (January 1978).

[17]Waukegan *News-Sun,* November 4, 1976, p. 10A and Chicago *Sun-Times,* November 5, 1970, p. 18.

[18]Waukegan *News-Sun,* November 4, 1976, p. 10A and Chicago *Daily News,* November 6, 1974, p. 7.

[19]Despite his defeat La Magdeleine was again Sheriff in early 1979, but in neighboring Lake County. Sheriff Tyrrell resigned his recently-retained office and it was necessary to appoint a Democrat to succeed him. La Magdeleine, who had become Chief of Police in a Lake County municipality was chosen to fill Tyrrell's post.

[20]The Republican National Committee reported that GOP candidates received only 41.1% of the total vote for the U.S. House of Representatives in 1974. Not since 1936 had Republican Congressional candidates fared so badly. See Republican National Committee, "Selected Tables from a Report on the 1976 National Elections," (Washington, D.C.: January 1972). (Mimeograph), Table 15, p. 26.

[21]See Table 14-2 above.

[22]On the general topic of declining partisanship, see Norman Nie, Sidney Verba and John Petrocik, *The Changing American Voter* (Cambridge: Harvard University Press, 1976).

[23]Divisive primary battles contributed to the 1970 election of Democratic Sheriff Art Tyrrell in McHenry County and Democrats David Pierce (County Clerk, 1974) and Mary Lou Kearns (Coroner, 1976) in Kane County.

[24]Hansen, *op. cit.,* 4:2 (February 1978), p. 14.

[25]Colby and Green, "Downstate," *op. cit.,* p. 10.

[26]Since this article was prepared Colby and Green have concurred in "Patterns of Change in Suburban Voting", *Illinois Issues* 5:10 (October, 1979), 17–23.

SUPPLEMENTARY READINGS

Barone, Michael, Grant Ujifusa and Douglas Mathews. *The Almanac of American Politics.* New York: Dutton, 1972.

Colby, Peter W., and Paul M. Green. "Downstate Holds the Key to Victory." *Illinois Issues* 4:2 (February 1978), 7–11.

———. "Vote Power: Suburbs Up, Cities Down." *Illinois Issues* 4:11 (November 1978), 16–22.

———. "Voting Patterns in the 96 Downstate Counties." *Illinois Issues* 4:8 (August 1978), 15–21.

Hansen, Lawrence N. "Mayor Daley and the Suburbs." *Illinois Issues* 4:1 and 4:2 (January and February 1978), 14–17 and 12–14.

Lubell, Samuel. *Revolt of the Moderates.* New York: Harper, 1956.

Nie, Norman, Sidney Verba and John Petrocik. *The Changing American Voter.* Cambridge: Harvard University Press, 1976.

Republican National Committee. "Selected Tables from a Report on the 1976 National Elections." Washington, D.C., January 1977. (Mimeographed.)

Wood, Robert C. *Suburbia: Its People and Their Politics.* Boston: Houghton Mifflin, 1958.

CHAPTER **15**

Interest Groups in Illinois Government

James H. Andrews

This chapter is about representation that exists alongside and in addition to representation by political parties, elected officials and bureaucrats. It is about representation provided by organized interests or interest groups, those associations in whose behalf representatives lobby in Springfield, on the telephone or by mail. Lobbyists may be volunteers or paid executives, employees or counselors of an organization. Their identifying badge is that they have no *official* badge. They represent a special interest; they plead a special cause. Public officials may do the same, but a public official participates as an official and is authorized by law to do so. The lobbyist participates as a citizen whose right it is to petition the government, and because he wants to influence those who have the legal authority to make decisions in behalf of the people generally. To lobby is of course not illegal; indeed it is constitutionally protected. But the lobbyist is not required to lobby. He does so because he seeks government policy that favors his interest or cause.

Lobbyists exist because elections and political parties do not comprehend, represent, express or communicate particular interests strongly enough. Even an active party member, a voter in every election, may call or write a legislator about a matter about which she or he feels very strongly. It is this tendency to go beyond party and elections that accounts for interest groups in politics and the array of activities to be discussed in this chapter.

There is a theme in American thinking about politics that finds the idea of interest groups reprehensible. Interest groups are known as "the interests" or "pressure groups." A 1978 *Time* magazine cover story about national government ran under the heading, "The Swarming Lobbyist."[1] It attributed the loss of a number of the President's proposals in Congress to "the startling increase in the influence of special interest lobbyists." Congressional actions are explained by interest groups' skill and money.

Many people believe that Illinois government can be understood most accurately in terms of the influence of "special interests" and the vulnerability of public officials to their pressure. Indeed, it is almost impossible to talk about interest group politics in Illinois without talking about sin. The history of Illinois is characterized by a continuing battle between those people and institutions that characterize themselves as the leaders of good—of the public interest—and those whom they describe as the forces of evil.

In Dan Elazar's terms, this is a struggle between different political cultures.[2] The political culture of Illinois is divided; the *individualistic* and the *moralistic* are in constant tension with each other. In an *individualistic* state, politics is perceived to be a market place, characterized by bargaining among interests rather than a search for the public good. Most citizens accepting the *individualistic* point of view see politics in terms of jobs, as a business, rather than as a worthy enterprise, a higher calling, demanding dedication and impartiality from citizens as well as officials. The art of government is practiced in terms of mutual obligations based on personal relationships.

In an *individualistic* culture, the kinds of people attracted to political life are those who seek a job rather than a calling, who often accept and expect corruption. Public officials in the *individualistic* state typically initiate few changes or policies themselves, but respond to strong and specific demands. The guide to policy making is the maxim, "Give the public what it wants."

In the *moralistic* culture, on the other hand, political leaders and public officials feel obligated to the public at large, particularly in terms of honest use of public funds. The view of *moralists* toward politics is reflected in the news media. Many people would say that the view is not supported by reality: events, lawsuits, exposes and other evidence over the years show public officials guilty of bribery, conflicts of interest or otherwise doing the bidding of pressure groups, political organizations, business firms or unions who seek advantage for themselves at the expense of the public.

Given conflicting attitudes and beliefs, it is not surprising that reform has long been one of the principal issues in Illinois politics. The "reform" candidate has not always won in the race for Governor or other posts in State government, but one candidate in most statewide elections has usually argued that he would clean up the State, while election of his opponent would lead to the influence of improper interests and organizations or even corruption.

However, to talk about interest group politics and lobbying in terms of corruption and reform alone is to obscure much of the reality of Illinois government. Those are emotion-laden terms, rallying cries for change. In addition, the multitude of interests in the State of Illinois is so vast, the points of view so diverse and the organizations that support and advance this diversity so many and so varied that to use "the interests" as a term of criticism is to deny legitimacy to almost every point of view held by the citizens of Illinois. If one interest or point of view were inevitably correct or representative of the general public, there would be no need for three branches of government, or two houses of the legislature, or representation by legislative and judicial districts. It is because of the different circumstances and interests that exist within a state and the difficulty of deciding what is best that democratic government is desirable and necessary.

A Diversity of Interests

When diversity and complexity are mentioned, it is clear why Illinois has incessant conflict among interests themselves and among diffeent ideas about how such conflicts should be dealt with. Illinois is a large state, in area and in population. It is a northern state, an industrial state, but also an agricultural state and in parts much like neighboring Kentucky and Missouri. It possesses natural resources such as coal and oil. The wealth of its families and communities varies greatly. It is as religiously diversified as any state in the Union. The State was settled by people coming from New England and the South at various times in its history and by immigrants from Asia, the Americas and different parts of Europe.

In Illinois the interests are many, and the number of organized groups is countless. Every local newspaper reports the activities of groups organized for social, religious, patriotic, educational and political purposes. Our attention here is directed to groups with an interest in the policies of the State of Illinois. Even this smaller focus encompasses innumerable organizations and interests.

One indication of the number and variety of groups seeking to influence government on a regular basis is the list of lobbyists who register each year. The Lobbyist Registration Act of 1969 applies to "persons who undertake to promote or oppose the passage of legislation by the General Assembly, or its approval or veto by the Governor." Persons covered by the act are those who undertake to promote or oppose legislation for compensation, or as an employee of someone else, or "on behalf of any person other than himself."

Many people are explicitly excluded from requirements of the law. They include persons who appear as unpaid witnesses before legislative committees, experts who occasionally testify for compensation at the request of legislators, news reporters and editors (unless they lobby), lawyers and other professional persons who draft bills or render opinions on the effects of legislation, employees of state government, employees of religious organizations seeking to protect the right of their members, and members of the General Assembly itself.

Because of the vagaries of the law, a number of people who might be regarded as lobbyists do not register. For example, in the 1978 and early 1979 lists of registrations, one looks in vain for the name of Phyllis Schlafley, identified in one newspaper poll as one of the ten most powerful people in Illinois. In her active campaign against the Equal Rights Amendment to the U.S. Constitution (ERA), Mrs. Schlafley has become a familiar figure in Springfield, testifying before legislative committees and leading rallies in the State House rotunda. Among those supporting ERA in recent years by visits to the State House have been Carol Burnett and Marlo Thomas; Alan Alda testified before a Senate committee. None registered as a lobbyist.

The number of people who do register varies from year to year. When the first Lobbying Registration Act took effect in 1959, some 541 persons registered. The number has since declined; between 300 and 450 have registered in the years since. The number of persons registered in November 1978 was 446.

Representation by Registered Lobbyists

Registered lobbyists speak for labor unions, public employee organizations, business and trade associations, utility and insurance companies, financial institutions, chambers of commerce, civic groups, professional associations, political subdivisions, civil rights, agriculture, education, welfare, veterans and fraternal groups.

In any one year business firms and associations employ about half the lobbyists. Registration lists for 1961 and 1973 suggest that the proportion of lobbyists representing different types of organizations changed little during that period, even though 485 lobbyists registered in the former year, only 308 the latter. (See Table 15-1).

Businesses and business associations accounted for 56 percent of the registered lobbyists in 1961, 49 percent in 1973. Labor groups, including public employees' associations, constituted 17 percent in the first year, 15 percent in the latter. The same slight downward change occurred in the proportion of lobbyists representing civic groups and local governments.

The only category with larger share of lobbyists in 1973 than 12 years earlier was a miscellaneous group of veterans, religious, educational, fraternal, humanitarian and agriculture groups. These interests were represented by nine lobbyists or two percent of the total in 1961. There were 35 registered lobbyists representing such groups in 1973, or 11 percent of the total.

How many organizations are represented? Inspection of several lobbyist registration lists showed 289 groups in 1963, 175 groups 10 years later, and more than 200 groups by April 2 of 1979. (The number always grows throughout the year.)

Lobbyists for the Government

The private sector is not the only part of Illinois that is represented in Springfield. Even though not registered, nor required to be, many people engage in lobbying in behalf of the public sector—public employees, public officials, state and local agencies and local governments themselves.

Representatives of local governments and their officials are on hand whenever the Legislature considers a measure affecting the multitude of rules and regulations under which they exist. Municipalities, park districts, councils of governments, sheriffs, city clerks, coroners, townships, county boards—all have registered lobbyists

TABLE 15-1
Registered lobbyists, 1961 and 1973, by type of group represented.

Type of Group	1961 Number	1961 Percent	1973 Number	1973 Percent
Businesses & business assns.	270	56%	152	49%
Civic & local government	85	17	45	15
Labor organizations	84	17	47	15
Professional groups	37	8	29	9
Agriculture, education, fraternal, humanitarian, religious, veterans groups	9	2	35	11
TOTAL	485	100%	308	99%

Sources: Hedlund & Patterson 1966; Maple 1976.

in Springfield who are well known to the local government committees of the General Assembly. Also well-known are the lobbyists for Cook County and the City of Chicago, who keep track of every piece of legislation that affects their jurisdictions and home rule generally. Their jobs are important ones: the principal lobbyist for the City of Chicago in 1979 resigned a seat in the House to take the job.

The public schools are also represented in all the complexity of the interests involved—school boards, principals, parent-teachers associations, teachers organized in the Illinois Education Association and the Illinois Federation of Teachers, and the State Board of Education.

The several public university systems also send lobbyists to Springfield, as does the Illinois Association of Community College Boards (and the Federation of Independent Illinois Colleges and Universities, representing private institutions). Student groups occasionally send representatives to testify and follow legislation and budgets affecting the institutions they attend.

The legislature receives special attention from representatives of both the executive and judicial branches. Official positions of state departments and other agencies are presented to the legislature by staff members known as legislative liaison. One representative of each executive agency is given access to the floor of the House and the Senate so that the legislative liaison may talk to legislators while sessions are going on. The number of House of Representatives floor passes for executive liaison persons in 1979 was 60.

The Governor maintains a legislative liaison office of his own. In recent sessions of the General Assembly the office has included two or three individuals assigned to each house, in addition to a director. In early 1979 a member of the House of Representatives, elected twice, resigned his seat to serve as Director of Legislative Liaison for the Governor. One of the tasks of the office is to keep track of lobbyists for individual departments, for there is a tendency for executive agencies to pursue their own interests without co-ordination with the Governor. Other elected state officials, such as the Secretary of State, the Comptroller and the Attorney General, also assign persons to perform legislative liaison duties.

Judges also present their views to the General Assembly. The Administrative Director of the Illinois Courts is consulted and advises on matters of administration and budget. In late 1978, when salary increases for officers of all three branches were under consideration, the Illinois Judges Association paid the expenses of two Chicago judges to lobby in Springfield in behalf of pay raises for judges. The Association was represented by two experts—both judges of the Cook County Circuit Court, one a former member of the House, the other principal lobbyist for the Cook County Board for 20 years before taking the bench.

Because some interests are well-organized, it should not be concluded that all interests are represented by lobbyists in Springfield. Some are not organized at all. Among the unorganized who are affected by decisions of state government are consumers of all kinds of goods and services: buyers of insurance, goods sold in stores, hotel service, electric power, gas for heating. The interests of the sellers are represented by registered lobbyists; to the extent that the interests of buyers are different, they are usually not represented in this way.

Some interests are represented mainly by public bodies or volunteer and charitable groups that try to speak *for* them. For example, the Department of Insurance tries to represent the interest of policyholders as well as companies selling insurance. The interests of beneficiaries, present and future, of various kinds of public assistance programs may be defended by United Way, for example, or the Illinois Association for Retarded Citizens, or the State Department of Children and Family Services, or the Illinois Catholic Conference. Some of these groups employ paid lobbyists, but multitudes of persons whom government programs affect directly are themselves not part of any lobbying organizations.

"Public Interest Groups" and the Press

Lobbyist registrations do suggest some changes in the nature of interest group representation in Illinois. In 1978 and 1979 lobbyists registered in behalf of organizations such as the Illinois Public Action Council, the Coalition for Political Honesty, Common Cause and the Alliance to End Repression—groups of relatively recent origin. Spokespersons for the League of Women Voters did not register lobbyists 20 years ago; a number of League representatives have actively lobbied in the last two years.

Such organizations as these are sometimes identified as "public interest groups." They are said to represent the general public interest as opposed to narrower, more special interests. In a general way the existence of the new organizations and their taking up lobbying as a means of influence suggest the expansion of the interest group system to comprehend points of view that 20 years ago might have been expressed either by elected legislators and officials directly, through political parties, or not at all. The existence of any organization engaged in the business of political influence is a sign that its members and followers find other channels of power inadequate and want to express their own position more directly and precisely.

A characteristic strategy of public interest groups is to arouse the citizenry to public action in behalf of their program. The news media are usually part of this strategy. Even though news media are excluded from the requirements of the Lobbyist Registration Act, legislators and other decision makers often consider them to be part of the system of special interests. Most voters know that Governors use the media to enhance their positions; legislators too are learning to arrange hearings, call bills and hold news conferences in ways that will increase the chances of television and newspaper coverage.

News organizations share with public interest and public action groups the position that they act, not in their own interest, but in the interest of the general public. So these groups and the press often share positions and, intentionally or otherwise, join together in campaigns to affect public decisions.

Interest group and news media collaboration is not new. The Better Government Association of Chicago—which registers no lobbyists—has worked for many years with Chicago newspapers, investigating and reporting government inefficiency and corruption. The Committee on Courts and Justice is a coalition of individuals and groups working in recent years for a constitutional amendment to replace the election of judges with a system for appointment to office. As with other constitutional change efforts in the past, this campaign involves alerting the general public as well as lobbying in Springfield for adoption of a particular amendment to be placed on the ballot. Newspapers and television stations are drawn into this campaign, as in the past.

Similarly, public interest groups work with the press to increase public attention and influence. Probably no issue of State government has received more attention in recent years than the salary increase for judges, legislators and some executive officers that was passed by the General Assembly over the Governor's veto in the fall of 1978. Public opposition to the matter was considerable; it was undoubtedly sustained and increased by continuing and repeated attention to the issue by newspapers and radio stations, especially downstate.

All of the attention came after the bill had become law. An amended bill passed both houses, was vetoed by the Governor, then passed over his veto in less than 24 hours. For many weeks newspapers repeated in editorials that the bill should be repealed and discussed in their news columns the chances of repeal actually taking place. The issue was the topic for numerous radio talk and call-in programs.

The communications media were joined in the issue by the Coalition for Political Honesty. The Coalition leader said that the whole process of adopting the legislation had been unfair; it was done too quickly and before the newly-elected Legislature took over. He was reminded, he said, of taxation without representation and the Boston Tea Party protest. So he called on Illinois citizens to signify their protest by sending tea bags to the Governor. Governor Thompson received 30,000 tea bags; some legislators received them, too.

As a result, the Governor felt called upon, when he was inaugurated for his second term in January, 1979, to apologize for placing his veto on the bill so quickly, an action that permitted the General Assembly to override the veto before public opinion could be altered and its message conveyed to the General Assembly.

In this case, widespread popular opposition to a new law was expressed by and through the news media, an organization with little visible structure or membership, and thousands of momentarily aroused citizens—who had just reelected most members of the Legislature and the Governor whom they now chastised for their actions. If one wonders if this lobbying effort can be described as in the general interest—and thus not a special interest—one should note that several newspapers supported the pay raise, as had three-fifths of the elected representatives in each house of the General Assembly. There was more than one respectable side to the issue. Ultimately the Legislature did amend the law as it applied to legislators, the Governor and some other executive officers (though the increase for judges remained), reducing the size of increases and making them effective in several steps rather than all at once.

Who Are the Lobbyists?

The popular picture of the lobbyist tends to emphasize money, deals and back-room arm-twisting. Labor bosses and power-hungry capitalists are sometimes envisioned; occasionally swarms of long-haired radicals come in view, or out-of-touch do-gooders or tight-fisted Neanderthals.

Whatever pictures our minds may conjure, whatever attitudes that may lurk in the heads of lobbyists, in social and economic terms and political orientation lobbyists in Illinois look very much like members of the American middle class.

The most detailed profile of the lobbying corps in Illinois is provided by surveys of lobbyists registered for the 1963 and 1973 legislative sessions.[3] In each case the proportion of lobbyists responding to the survey reflected roughly the distribution of all registered lobbyists among different types of groups and organizations. For example, about half the respondents each year represented business groups, about the same as the proportion of all lobbyists in the same year. There are limits to the reliability of both studies, however. The proportion of lobbyists providing usable questionnaires in the 1963 study was 57 percent; for 1973 it was 39 percent.

The 1973 study, done by Robert C. Maple, describes the typical lobbyist as

> middle-aged (60 percent age 31 to 55), white (more than 95 percent), Protestant (almost 60 percent), and male (over 90 percent). Almost half have law or graduate school backgrounds. Over three-quarters reside in Springfield or Chicago, and half work mainly at the Capitol. While there is a strong underlying pattern of careerism among the lobbyists, reflected in the fact that two-thirds report entering the field before age 40 it should also be noted that more than two-thirds report being in lobbying for less than nine years. . . .
>
> Lobbyists are . . . recruited most commonly from law or business, and, especially among business lobbyists, are likely to have had background experiences similar to the legislators themselves. Business and trade association lobbyists are most likely to have been lawyers, and corporation spokesmen to have been government officials, though less than one-third of the lobbyists overall had held government positions. Other groups such as trade unions, education, and professional associations typically drew their representatives from within their own ranks.
>
> More than two-thirds of the lobbyists work for only one group, and the great majority are on salary. . . . Illinois lobbyists as a group are career professionals, well paid, highly educated, believing themselves hired for their skills and educational backgrounds, . . .[4]

Maple also finds that lobbyists tend to be somewhat more Republican than either the general Illinois population or the General Assembly. Republicans are most likely to be found representing business, trade associations and farmers. Democrats are more likely to be found representing labor unions. Self-designated independents are more likely to be found representing professionals and civic and veterans groups.

These surveys and more recent data on Illinois suggest that lobbyists in this state are somewhat more professional and better educated than state house lobbyists generally.[5]

Many lobbyists seeking to influence decisions in Illinois spend as much time in Springfield as legislators, whether they live there or not. Many spend time away from Springfield working with members of their organizations in educational and other public affairs-related activities. A number of long-time, mostly business lobbyists are informally organized as "the third house" and elect a "Speaker" to lead the group each year.

Not many former legislators become lobbyists after they leave the Illinois General Assembly and they are a small proportion of the entire lobbying corps. In recent years the number of former legislators registered as lobbyists has ranged between 10 and 20. Several of these are lobbyists of considerable importance, however, representing organizations and firms with substantial stakes in State government decisions.

Legislative staffs, which hardly existed 20 years ago, are also recruiting grounds for lobbyists today. In 1978 and 1979, some 12 to 15 former members of leadership and committee staffs were registered. In addition, State departments often recruit legislative liaison people from majority and minority staffs. Legislative staff jobs provide training in bill drafting and analysis, the legislative process and budget review, as well as knowledge of substantive fields (such as health, corrections, conservation) that are useful to groups which want to influence legislative decisions.

In recent years more women have registered as lobbyists than in the past. In April, 1979, forty women constituted 10 percent of the total number of persons registered. The range of organizations represented by women was considerable. Eleven women represented business and labor groups—bankers, truckers, realtors, the State Chamber of Commerce and unions, especially teachers and other public employees. Other women lobbyists represented a variety of professional, civic, humanitarian and reform organizations. Both women and men registered for organizations whose principal goal was passage of ERA; no one registered for ERA opposition groups.

Interest Groups and the Legislature

Interest groups and the lobbyists who represent them perform four major functions in the legislative process: knowing the territory, crystallizing issues, resolving conflict and providing information.

Knowing the Territory

How do lobbyists influence the Legislature? The first task of a lobbyist is to know what is going on—to know when bills affecting his or her group are introduced (sometimes to know that they *will* be introduced), what they provide, where they are in the legislative process and what their chances are. Influence is not likely without knowledge of the situation. It helps to understand how the Legislature operates and who holds power in various situations; and to know legislators personally, so that the lobbyist can talk with them easily. He or she should also know his or her client or employer, what the group's interests are, what its officers and members support and oppose; it may help to understand its interests and operations in some depth and detail.

But the role of interest groups in the legislative process is more fundamental than the skills and competence of individual lobbyists. The influence of groups can be seen in almost everything the General Assembly does. Fifteen years ago is could be said that "private groups perform tasks for the legislature that few other agencies do."[6] This is still the case, but the Legislature and its members perform some of these tasks themselves more often than in years past. It is worth noting the functions that groups serve in the Legislature in relation to changes in the process.

First, private groups provide the initiative and impetus for a large share of the legislation that moves through the General Assembly. When the Governor, executive departments and local governments are added to private groups, the impact of groups outside the Legislature is even more substantial. Most bills have their origins in organizations, public and private.

Nevertheless, as the Legislature has developed more substantial staffs, legislative leadership in shaping legislation has become more frequent, sometimes under strong party leaders, sometimes through imaginative and diligent committee work. In 1976, for example, the State made significant changes in the criminal code, moving to determinant rather than flexible sentencing and adopting a new category of felonies known as Class X. The legislation was the result of two years of careful work, chiefly by a subcommittee of the Judiciary II Committee of the House. The committee did not serve as a "sieve" for bills on the subject—a term that used to be applied with some accuracy to describe committees years ago. The committee wrote a bill of its own and put its name on it. The bill passed the House with substantial bipartisan support. It was amended in the Senate to include the Class X provisions recommended by the Governor, yet the final product was inescapably a *legislative* bill, a product of careful, informed, sustained attention by legislators who examined the need themselves and fashioned a remedy.

Crystallizing Issues

A second function served by groups is to establish and indicate the clash of issues out of which the Legislature determines its course in many areas of public policy. Groups create issues and identify them.

The Illinois legislator is inclined to support any bill that its sponsor brings to a vote in committee or on the floor, unless someone else makes a point of opposing it. The Governor and party leaders organize opinion on only a small share of the bills considered each session. In the past the typical legislator and even his party leaders usually did not know what issues were in a bill until they were identified by lobbyists, the only people who systematically kept track of what was going on. This is no longer the case. The majority and minority staffs each provide an analysis of almost every bill heard in committee; the analysis is usually in the hands of the legislator before the committee hearing. In many cases issues are now raised by legislators and their staffs, who are no longer dependent on lobbying groups for knowledge of the possible effects of proposed legislation.

Resolution of Conflict

A third function performed by groups is resolution of conflict. Having initiated many proposals and indicated their opposition and support for others, groups are often the key to the resolution of differences. However, this is probably the case less often than in the past. One reason may be that legislators are more independent of their leaders, designated or otherwise, than they used to be. Richard Icen has noted that

> for years lobbyists for such favored special interests as racing and trucking industries transmitted their business by whispering in the ears of a few powerful legislative leaders.
>
> There's still plenty of that. But to be successful these days a lobbyist has to spend time with the committee chairmen, staff, and influential opinion leaders among rank-and-file legislators.[7]

Another reason may be that legislative proceedings are more open and better recorded than they used to be, and so groups and legislators find themselves more publicly committed to one position or another. Sometimes it is more difficult to compromise.

At the same time, the General Assembly itself has taken more initiative in recent years to turn aside the specific demands of conflicting groups and to develop common positions that provide resolution of disagreements, with the Legislature itself taking a significant role in shaping their form and content.

An example of the powerful role played by groups in earlier years is the process once called "legislation by collective bargaining."[8] The Legislature ratified agreements made between representatives of management and labor. An example of a more recent kind of conflict resolution is the action of the General Assembly on the problem of product liability in 1978.[9]

The product liability case is worth noting because it required highly technical legislation, with little public concern or attention, yet involved decisions of considerable importance to manufacturers, insurance companies, some lawyers and legislators concerned about business conditions in the State.

The issue was raised in the Spring of 1977, when a coalition of Illinois businessmen, led by the Illinois Manufacturers Association, drafted a Product Liability Reform Bill designed to reduce manufacturers' liability for defective products and thereby reduce the large increases in insurance rates that had occurred in the previous five years. When the bill was introduced, legislators received a barrage of letters from irate businessmen, demanding relief from the high rates they said were threatening their businesses.

The bills were assigned to subcommittees in each house, and it was in those committees that the bill that passed was drafted. The House Judiciary I subcommittee held five hearings between June 1977 and May 1978, with the first hearing set up explicitly to let worried business people know that the Legislature was undertaking a serious investigation of the problem. With meticulous, professional staff work supporting every step, the subcommittee systematically arranged to hear from Illinois manufacturers and distributers who wanted change, insurance companies who wrote product liability coverage, and plaintiffs' and lawyers' groups familiar with the legal issues involved.

Among the committee's findings were that high insurance rates were a serious problem for manufacturers. However, in the entire country there were no data on product liability insurance profits and losses. So the committee staff, with the assistance of the Department of Insurance, undertook a study, producing for the committee's report the first published information describing the profitability of product liability as a line of insurance.

In the Spring of 1978, the Legislature adopted new product liability legislation with only three negative votes in the House and none in the Senate. It was the result of demanding and careful negotiation over several weeks. Among the groups involved were representatives of manufacturers, insurers, trial lawyers, Chicago and State bar associations and the State Chamber of Commerce. Presiding at the several meetings were subcommittee chairmen and legislative sponsors, assisted by committee staff. The final negotiating meeting was held in the office of the Speaker of the House, with his participation. A published account of the two-year effort reports that, "predictably, none of the participants in the negotiations were [sic] entirely satisfied . . ." Yet the crisis, as the manufacturers had called it, was averted; helpful legislation passed; and with the aid of interested groups, the Legislature had led the way to resolution of the problem.

Tangible Service: Information

A fourth function served by interest groups in Illinois is to provide a number of tangible services. Most prominent of these is information. One lobbyist for the insurance industry likes to think of himself as a "walking library," with facts available for any legislator. "After a while I can answer almost any question on insurance legislation that is asked," he was quoted as saying. "I don't pressure legislators to vote our way. I just try to present the pros and cons and let them make the decision. I'm sure a lobbyist is helpful, regardless of how a legislator votes."[10]

Groups probably provide more information to legislators today than ever before; legislators probably seek more information to develop and defend their positions on issues. Yet it can no longer be said that interest groups are the only or even the major source of knowledge for the General Assembly. Interest groups occasionally even cite studies made by legislative staffs, as did the president of the Mental Health Association of Illinois, who recently quoted a report by the staff of the House Human Resources Committee to make his point in a letter to the Chicago Tribune (May 29, 1978).

Lobbyists are still important; they now provide information to legislative staff as well as Representatives and Senators. The increasing complexity of government and the problems it faces and the independence of many legislators have increased the need for substantive knowledge, in addition to knowledge of who's for and against particular provisions of a bill.

Entertainment and hospitality are other ways in which lobbyists have traditionally established relationships with legislators. Much of this continues, although the prolonged legislative year and the lack of confinement to central Springfield hotels have dissipated the sense of comradeship that used to unite lobbyists and legislators. Many lobbyists find they can do their jobs in the offices and halls of the State House complex.

Money as a Source of Influence

On the other hand, the growing cost of winning elections to legislators has added to the resources that interest groups may be able to provide. Money is probably more important to legislators than ever before, and quite legitimately so. There are more legislative contests, more organized campaigns, more turnover in membership in House and Senate, and more expenses for sitting legislators and candidates.

Large amounts of money are raised and spent by legislative candidates. Candidates for the 40 State Senate seats filled in the 1976 election raised a total of $1.5 million in the period July 1975 through December 1976. The average amount for each of the 63 candidates filing reports with the State Board of Elections was $24,000.[11] During the 1978 election year, candidates for State Representative and State Senator were said to have raised $2.2 million. During 1977 when there were no legislative elections, House and Senate members were said to have raised $2 million.[12]

Despite the large amounts of money involved, little is known about the financing of legislative campaigns in Illinois. However, the list of registered lobbyists is a prime invitation list for fund-raising events. Some lobbyists attend and many more contribute to dinners, receptions, golf days, barbecues and testimonials sponsored by campaign committees for individuals and the majority and minority parties of each house.

The need for funds to finance election campaigns complicates the always serious problem of bribery in Illinois. It is sometimes difficult to distinguish a campaign contribution from payment made to a legislator in exchange for assistance in obtaining favorable legislative action.[13]

It seems likely that bribery itself as a means of influencing legislation is used by lobbyists less frequently now than in the past. Moreover, while bribery may be a crucial factor in deciding some issues, it does not determine the role of interest groups in the Legislature generally. That role rests on two qualities that groups possess. One is their possession of specific and often technical knowledge of their own fields of interest. The other quality is their representative character. They represent people and interests, and the General Assembly respects both.

Interest Groups and the Executive

Legislators and groups communicate most often through lobbyists, and much of this activity is highly visible in the corridors and committee rooms of the General Assembly. This is not true of the relationship among private groups and non-legislative branches of government. In executive departments conversation between lobbyists and government officials is more likely to take place in closed offices. For this reason many people believe it does not take place at all.

The popular belief that lobbying takes place only in the Legislature also rests on the notion that State policy is made by the Legislature alone, that only the Legislature legislates, while the executive executes and the judiciary judges. This is not the case, as the constitution suggests and other chapters of this book make clear. Agencies outside the Legislature have considerable legal authority and play a considerable role in determining the actual consequences of public policy.

This is only the beginning of extra-legislative power, however, because a variety of offices actually influence the making of State policy. Some agencies hold direct authority; some exercise power because they advise the Governor, or, more often, because he does not pay close attention to what they do. Some have become independent of the Chief Executive, because interest groups have made the effort to separate them. Some agencies influence policy by lobbying in the Legislature themselves. Wherever public decisions are made, there will be private groups working to see that such decisions are not adverse to their interests.

Of all participants in policy-making in Illinois, the Governor has the most power if he chooses to use it. He has formidable constitutional authority, usually the leadership of his party, and sometimes effective leadership of the whole State. Because of this, the Governor is not apt to be useful to interest groups unless he wants to be. His commitments and responsibilities are to the state at large, to a party at large, to a substantial majority within his party or public opinion more generally. Only a group with large membership or considerable public influence can really deal with the Governor unless he is willing to take a group's advice. He does not normally need interest groups so much as they need him. This suggests a question: Under what circumstances will the Governor be willing to cooperate with a private group?

The Governor is willing to cooperate with a private group if he has no reason not to—that is the general rule. Most of the time a Governor has no reason not to sign a bill from the Legislature or, by the same reasoning, to acquiesce in the administration of State policy by his subordinates.

The Governor's main concern is major questions of State policy. No matter what is called "major," vast areas of State action are beyond the normal vision—one is tempted to say interest—of the Chief Executive. When broad general agreement on policy has been achieved (and in many areas it was achieved years ago), the Governor tends to lose interest in the subject; interest groups do not.

The interests of groups are specific and particular. Except for seeking his help in passing or defeating a bill or appointing a friend to office, private groups do not often need the Governor. They set their sights on the offices that administer programs that affect them directly and watch those offices closely. Groups are especially happy if they can bring their influence to bear without having to seek interference from party politicians or elected officials. They prefer that their demands be taken "out of politics" or considered "above politics." As a general rule, the farther an issue or subject—such as highway construction or licensing of physicians—is removed from control of elected officials, the greater the influence of those groups with special interest in those matters. If executive agencies are far removed from political control, they are highly susceptible to capture by private interest groups. Under a kind of agency syndicalism, the private group may in fact exercise power in the name of government.

It may be, however, that groups are not satisfied working within the broad general agreement that established the conditions of their influence. They sometimes try to change the character of the decision-making authority. Relocating an agency in the structure of State government and changing the direction of an agency from a single cabinet member to a commission are both devices that can change the character of decision-making and the nature of the decisions that are made. (See the Gove and Carlson chapter on reorganization.)

Interest Groups and Reform

A discussion of lobbying moves very easily into discussion of what can be done to reduce the influence of special interests. Illinois is particularly vulnerable to charges of undue influence by forces working against the public interest. One Governor went to prison for illegal acts, based essentially on the belief that he accepted undervalued race track stock in return for favorable consideration of racing interests. Another Governor was found not guilty of income tax evasion, but not before a trial and detailed public attention to his campaign gifts and personal expenses. In 1979 the Attorney General of the State was indicted by a federal grand jury on charges growing out of similar circumstances—confusion of campaign contributions and expenditures and personal gifts and expenses.

Legislators, too, have been indicted, found guilty, and sent to prison. In July, 1976, the *Springfield-Journal* Register summarized the record of the previous 18 months: "Courtroom Boxscore: Seventeen State Legislators Accused—Eleven Convicted."[14] Not all of these cases involved bribery or related charges; several were based on misuse of public funds in one way or another.

There is no question but that such events undermine the faith of the people in their government. They also foster the belief that actions taken by the government can be explained in large part by the influence of special interests who use money and other tangible rewards to buy favorable treatment.

But the issue of special treatment is more complicated than bribery and campaign contributions. The question is, under what circumstances can a public official accept or even possess things of value that can somehow be identified with the authority she or he exercises as a public official?

For example, who can legitimately support a campaign for public office and under what circumstances? Or further, who can employ a public official to work or advise in a non-official capacity? And what kinds of employment should a public official accept?

The last is an especially difficult problem for public officials who do not spend full-time working as officials. Legislators are notably vulnerable on this matter, since for generations members of the House and Senate have practiced law, sold insurance, taught school, held union offices, engaged in farming and so forth. In Cook County, it is traditional that some legislators work for the City of Chicago and other governmental bodies.

The term "double dipping" has been used in recent years to criticize legislators who have two jobs. The complaint is voiced against the control that the Chicago Democratic organization is believed to exercise over legislators who work for the City and other Democratically-controlled governments in Cook County. The term is also used to castigate teachers employed by the public schools and lawyers employed by local governments of various kinds.

When a public official is employed by a private organization or client, the more general term is used—conflict of interest. The term is also used sometimes to refer, in addition to employment, to possession of investments or property or business somehow related to public decisions or policy. Public officials who are active in or own shares of banks, farming businesses or automobile agencies are criticized for having a conflict between their private interests and public obligations.

In order to meet the criticism of these circumstances, several kinds of efforts have been made. One is to add to and specify conduct and actions that are prohibited. A second is to require public disclosure of information about income and campaign support for public officials and sources of financial support for lobbying groups.

The Illinois Governmental Ethics Act was passed in 1967. It applies to executive, legislative and judicial branches of State government and to certain members of local governmental bodies. It is designed to restrict the extent to which legislators may represent interests outside the Legislature, to limit the opportunities to use public office for personal economic advantage and to require public officials and employees to disclose economic interests and relationships that could tend to bring their public responsibilities and private concerns into conflict.

The last section of the law requires public officials and candidates to file with the Secretary of State statements disclosing their broad economic interests in relationships "likely to create conflicts of interest." The annual ethics statements are open to public inspection and are a source of occasional interest to the news media and by reform organizations.

Another attempt to deal with ethical questions and to shed light on the financing of campaigns is the Campaign Financing Disclosure Act, which became effective in 1974. Candidates and political committees that accept contributions or make expenditures of more than $1000 in a year must file financial reports with the State Board of Elections annually and during and following elections.

In 1976 there was a petition drive to place on the ballot an amendment to the Illinois Constitution that would prohibit "double-dipping" and also prohibit a member of the General Assembly from voting on a bill on which he had a "conflict of interest."

It is of course impossible to eliminate "interests" from representative government. Legislatures exist in order to represent interests in their diversity and variety. Yet they are at the same time agencies of the State, of all the people, and so have a larger and broader responsibility as well.

There is a paradox in the efforts to eliminate special interests from government. The reforms and changes that have weakened political parties over the years have probably strengthened interest groups and private interests against public interests. The anti-government bias in the reform movement that this represents tends to undermine the general public power that is necessary if special interests are to be managed in the interest of all. This reflects a more general pattern—too often "reforms" either have effects opposite those intended or fail to achieve their objectives.

The Problem of the Present and the Future

There is a sense in which "the interests" and popular concern about them can be accurately defined as the problem of contemporary American government. It has been widely reported that there is dissatisfaction and lack of confidence in political institutions. Illinois surely shares in this disillusionment; its citizens have doubts about the legitimacy of its government. The two most recent victors in election for Governor have campaigned in opposition to organized politics, to politics as usual.

In a sense, the distrust of political institutions is distress with society itself and the difficulties that seem to be presented to government by the multitude of interests, organized and unorganized, changing from month to month and year to year, all—in the view of many people—seeking special treatment at the expense either of the general interest or of one's own interest.

The challenge of our time is to adjust or adapt the institutions of governance in such a way that interests can be represented and taken account of in ways that are legitimate and acceptable to the people.

The problem of the future for Illinois is the resolution of conflict. There must be admission and acceptance of diversity, but also encouragement of the values and interests that are shared. Beyond that, there must be development of structures to cope with diversity realistically and positively.

A concern with ethics alone, with exposing wrongdoing, will not help the State to deal with its other problems. For example, prohibiting anyone from voting in the Legislature on an issue in which he has some interest or even a concern is not a solution to the problem of interests in conflict. An important part of the problem is the lack of confidence in the institutions and arrangements that do in fact serve to resolve "conflicts of interest."

The objective should be to enable people who represent a variety of interests to get together in a situation in which those interests can be resolved or accommodated to the benefit of all. The need is to find ways in which well-intentioned public officials, private citizens and organized interests can work together with reasonable ease, find rewards for enlightened understanding of eachother's positions and develop a competence to define a public agenda that is in the public's interest.

Research Opportunities

The concept of interest groups is useful in the study of politics. Questions about group activity and influence easily lead to examination of any one of the several branches of government and particular agencies within each branch, as well as political parties, elections and voting behavior. The focus can be broad enough to encompass a whole political system—for example, the State of Illinois—so far as this is possible in the complex federalism of the United States. As this chapter is intended to suggest, attention to interest group politics leads easily to consideration of a whole government or a whole state. Group politics raise some of the most fundamental questions of all, those concerning relations between society on one hand and government on the other.

Despite the potential rewards of studying interest groups, they have received little attention in recent years. Very little scholarship treats the balance of public and private interests or group influence as a situation to be described. When interest group influence is discussed, it is rarely treated as a dependent variable, a situation to be explained. The importance of politics compared to social and economic factors is often analyzed without attention to interest groups at all. For interest group politics generally, most scholarly work relies on hypotheses proposed over 20 years ago, before many changes in state government, especially legislatures. Except for the work cited in this chapter, there has been little study of interest groups in Illinois in the last 15 years.

There is a need for deeper understanding of the constraints on the major functions of interest groups. For example, how effectively is their information evaluated? What is the quality of legislative memory or of legislative examination of the consequences of acting on such information? Against what other sources can such information be tested? How effective are the incentives to provide full and accurate information? Also, as the Legislature changes, do interest groups functions alter? As the Legislature becomes a more independent policy-maker, is it less responsive to being handed interest group compromises for enactment, as under the traditional "agreed bill" process?

Several kinds of study are worthwhile. One is the case study, long out of fashion, but much needed now if we are to understand contemporary institutions and further develop general knowledge. One kind of case begins with a particular policy area—gun control, child abuse, abortion clinic regulation, the Equal Rights Amendment. Another starts with a particular group or cluster of groups. Another looks closely at a legislative committee or executive agency. Because of more complete record-keeping, all of these subjects are more accessible to the researcher now than in years past.

A second kind of inquiry examines the largely unexplored and unevaluated data on interest group activity that are now part of the public record. The files of the State Board of Elections now contain extensive records of campaign expenditures and contributions. The annual ethics statements of large numbers of State officers and employees are on file in the office of the Secretary of State. These are largely untapped, except occasionally by lobbying groups themselves; they can shed light on the complex relationships between the public and private sectors.

A good way to begin to study groups is to examine one or several of the published studies of Illinois government and politics and extract from them hypotheses about the behavior of groups. Some of the respected studies of Illinois are cited in this book. Among those most worth examining are *Legislative Politics in Illinois* by Steiner and Gove, *The Illinois Legislature* by Gove, Carlson, and Carlson and *The Politics of State Expenditure in Illinois* by Anton.

Other good sources of hypotheses are the articles about Illinois politics published regularly by Illinois newspapers, especially those with Springfield correspondents, and by magazines such as *Illinois Issues* and *Chicago*. Another source of questions to guide the study of groups is a day or two of observation of the Legislature. If one observes the Legislature in committee or in session on the floor, does it seem to be what one expected—either from casual knowledge or from a careful reading of some of the materials mentioned here? Can one see any signs of interest group activity?

The student can, looking at any of these sources, ask to what extent the hypotheses derived from books, newspapers or observation hold true in another situation, at a different time, in a particular case of decision-making, or in comparison to the vast literature on other states, other countries and the American national government. In each instance, one can ask, to what extent is Illinois similar? different? In what particulars—and why?

NOTES

[1]"The Swarming Lobbyist," *Time,* August 7, 1978.

[2]Daniel Elazar, *American Federalism: A View from the States* (2d ed.; New York: Thomas Y. Crowell Company, 1972.)

[3]Ronald D. Hedlund and Samual C. Patterson, "Personal Attributes, Political Orientations, and Occupational Perspectives of Lobbyists: The Case of Illinois," *Iowa Business Digest,* 37 (November 1966), 3 –11; and Robert Charles Maple, "Role Orientations of Registered Lobbyists: Illinois 78th General Assembly Session" (unpublished Master's dissertation, Illinois State University, 1976).

[4]Maple, *op. cit.*, pp. 102–03.

[5]Herbert Jacob and Kenneth N. Vines, eds., *Politics in the American States* (3d ed., Boston: Little, Brown and Company, 1976), pp. 113–17.

[6]James H. Andrews, *Private Groups in Illinois Government* (Urbana: Institute of Government and Public Affairs, University of Illinois, 1965), p. 21.

[7]Richard Icen, *Decatur Sunday Herald and Review,* February 19, 1978.

[8]Gilbert Y. Steiner, *Legislation by Collective Bargaining: The Agreed* Bill in Illinois Unemployment Compensation Legislation (Urbana: Institute of Labor and Industrial Relations, University of Illinois, 1951). Andrews FN—p. 2.

[9]Margarent Hunter Eldredge and Daniel L. Houlihan, "Limitations of Action: Strict Liability in Tort—The Legislature Has Intervened," *Illinois Bar Journal* (December 1978), 214–21.

[10]*Chicago Tribune,* June 22, 1975.

[11]James H. Klein, "Campaign Funds: Who Gets Them?" *Illinois Issues* 3:11 (November 1977), pp.4–8.

[12]State Board of Elections, State of Illinois, *Report, 1979,* cited in *Homewood-Flossmoor Star,* April 29, 1979.

[13]Mike Lawrence, "Cement Bribery Trial: Corruption in the Legislature," *Illinois Issues* (December 1976), reprinted in *Illinois Issues Annual* (1976–77), pp. 10–16.

[14]Cited in *Ibid.*

SUPPLEMENTAL READINGS

Andrews, James H. *Private Groups in Illinois Government.* Urbana: Institute of Government and Public Affairs, University of Illinois, 1965.

Elazar, Daniel. *American Federalism: A View from the States.* New York: Thomas Y. Crowell Company, 1966; 1972.

Eldredge, Margaret Hunter, and Daniel L. Houlihan. "Limitations of Action: Strict Liability in Tort—The Legislature Has Intervened." *Illinois Bar Journal* (December 1978), 214–21.

Gove, Samuel K., Richard W. Carlson and Richard J. Carlson. *The Illinois Legislature: Structure and Process.* Urbana: University of Illinois Press, 1976.

Hedlund, Ronald D., and Samuel C. Patterson. "Personal Attributes, Political Orientations, and Occupational Perspectives of Lobbyists: The Case of Illinois." *Iowan Business Digest* 37 (November 1966), 3–11.

Jacob, Herbert, and Kenneth N. Vines, eds. *Politics in the American States.* 3d ed. Boston: Little, Brown and Company, 1976.

Klein, James H. "Campaign Funds: Who Gets Them?" *Illinois Issues* 3:11 (November 1977) 4–8.

Lawrence, Mike. "Cement Bribery Trial: Corruption in the Legislature." *Illinois Issues* (December 1976). Reprinted in *Illinois Issues Annual* (1976–77), 10–16.

Maple, Robert Charles. "Role Orientations of Registered Lobbyists: Illinois 78th General Assembly Session." Unpublished Master's thesis, Illinois State University, 1976.

Steiner, Gilbert Y. *Legislation by Collective Bargaining: The Agreed Bill in Illinois Unemployment Compensation Legislation.* Urbana: University of Illinois, Institute of Labor and Industrial Relations, 1951.

Steiner, Gilbert Y., and Samuel K. Gove. *Legislative Politics in Illinois.* Urbana: University of Illinois Press, 1960.

"The Swarming Lobbyist." *Time,* August 7, 1978.

CHAPTER **16**

Impact of the Media: Analyst or Interest Group?

Thomas B. Littlewood

In a state where sectional differences have been so pronounced for so many years and the political parties so evenly matched, it is not surprising that the news media play an important role in the political system of Illinois. As elsewhere, newspapers and broadcasters are sifters and conveyors of information; setters of the public agenda; careful mixers of what their consumers want to know and what they need to know; monitors of government performance; searchers after corruption in public office; and influential voices in the formulation of public policy. What sets Illinois news media apart from those in many other states is, first, their variety: big-city dailies backed by millions of dollars of corporate wealth; ethnic neighborhood weeklies; prosperous suburban publications; chain-owned operations downstate; other newspapers still run by stubbornly independent country editors; powerful network-affiliated television and radio stations; and tiny stations grinding out country music in southern Illinois.

The regional antagonisms that have persisted for decades in Illinois—between metropolitan Chicago and the ''downstate'' counties (meaning all but Cook County); and between central city and suburb—place an added responsibility on the news media. This responsibility to look beyond the sectionalism and discern statewide values and interests is seldom satisfied as thoroughly as it should be in Illinois. Though there are media with statewide influence, true statewide perspective is lacking most of the time in most of the coverage of government and politics. There is no one ''Illinois'' newspaper or broadcasting voice to provide leadership and a sense of unity for the entire state.

Two publications that clearly wield statewide influence in public affairs are the two Chicago morning dailies, both part of wealthy corporations with lucrative investments in non-communications fields as well. In mid-1978 the *Chicago Tribune* was selling 793,600 copies daily and 1,139,000 on Sundays; the rival *Chicago Sun-Times* 683,500 daily and 719,500 on Sundays.

Although the legendary Paul Powell, House speaker and later Illinois Secretary of State, liked to express his contempt for the Chicago papers by hurling their pages, one by one, out the window of his speeding car as he was being driven back to southern Illinois, the Chicago papers make their presence felt in Springfield—and in deepest southern Illinois.

In this era of syndication, supplemental news services, increasing concentration of ownership and cooperative agreements of various sorts, news media competition is much less than it used to be. But the competition between the Chicago dailies is genuine and it is fierce. In turn, the news coverage and judgments made in the editorial offices of the Chicago papers tend to set both the pace and the tone for public affairs reporting and commentary throughout the State. In the same way that Washington developments don't become major news until they are recognized by as such by the *New York Times* or the *Washington Post,* a State scandal isn't a scandal and a big story in Illinois until it has come to the attention of the Chicago dailies. Similarly, the Chicago television market commands priority attention of State candidates and officeholders. About 70 percent of the state population resides within the 65-mile viewing radius of the 10 Chicago television stations.

It seldom takes long for the Chicago media to pick up on a scandal. Just as the network news departments in New York and Washington tend to follow the lead of the most influential newspapers and columnists, so most Illinois television newscasters look to the Chicago newspapers for their day-to-day judgments about what is major news. In the competitive Chicago market, print and electronic media emphasize personalities, scandal and what critics regard as fluffy sensationalism. With some exceptions (Charles N. Wheeler III, the *Sun-Times'* excellent Springfield correspondent, and the Lindsay-Schaub news service are notable examples), the Chicago media and the Illinois press as a whole are less concerned with substantive reporting of complex State issues than academicians would prefer. Downstate editors comment profusely on State affairs in their editorials, and some of their news staffs are increasingly attempting to expose corruption in State government, but the basic decisions about which topics deserve emphasis still are made in the Chicago newsrooms.

Compared to its neighboring states, Illinois has a rich tradition of public corruption. There doubtlessly are cultural reasons which help explain that, but the muckraking zeal of Chicago journalism contributes to the perception of corruption. For many years a private investigative agency, the Better Government Association of Chicago, has cooperated with the Chicago newspapers in the exposure of governmental wrongdoing, some of it in Springfield. In 1979 the BGA opened an office in

Springfield and hired a former newswoman Peggy Boyer as the director of that office.

This emphasis on sensationalism and scandal over substantive analysis of public affairs that might appeal to only a small segment of the readership is directly attributable to the competition in Chicago. Media monopolies feel more comfortable about giving their audience the information needed for good citizenship instead of the scintillating trivia and entertainment that is thought to "sell newspapers." Chicago is one of the few remaining cities with newspaper competition for the same market. Even in most other large cities with more than one remaining newspaper (e.g., New York, Los Angeles), the publications are aimed at different socioeconomic segments of the metropolitan market. The competition between the *Tribune* and *Sun-Times* affects Illinois government and politics in many ways.

Publishers and Politics

The tradition of partisan political involvement by owners and editors of newspapers lasted longer in Illinois than in many other states. Until quite recently, publishers were also party leaders and sometimes officeholders. An example is the Smalls of Kankakee, who were both newspaper proprietors and Republican party leaders (Len Small was Governor from 1921 until 1929). Ward Just was publisher of the *Waukegan News-Sun* and Lake County Republican "boss" at the same time. Well into the 20th Century, it was not uncommon for the same man to run both the most successful newspaper and the dominant political party in a county. In a fictional version of his ancestors' Waukegan experience, Ward Just's grandson of the same name describes the newspaper as being[1]

> to the town as a dictionary is to the language. The people, most of them, believed the newspaper because it did not surprise them; it was not extraordinary . . . the secret was not to reveal facts but to withhold them. Elections became contests between men and ghosts. Unsuitable candidates for public office would look in vain for their names. In a contest between a man and a ghost, the ghost would lose, and this experience led the editor to a hard conclusion: embarrassments were not disclosed, they were concealed. Embarrassments would be dealt with by the men who knew the facts and were dependable. Dement [the fictitious Waukegan] in that way was an ossuary, skeletons sealed away in closets forever.

Not all editors were Republicans. V.Y. Dallman, editor of the "Democratic newspaper" in the State capital, the *Illinois State Register,* was named district director of internal revenue by President Roosevelt in the 1930's. Adlai E. Stevenson II, Governor from 1949 until 1952, and twice the Democratic nominee for President, inherited partial ownership of the *Bloomington Pantagraph*. The family interest in the newspaper was retained by his sons, among them Sen. Adlai E. Stevenson III.

The best known of these political publishers was the flamboyant Col. Robert R. McCormick, who presided over the *Chicago Tribune* for 45 years until his death in 1955. Briefly an appointed trustee of the Chicago Sanitary District, McCormick made the *Tribune* available to the Republican Party as its unswerving beacon light. The Colonel's heritage is embarrassing to the present management of the *Tribune,* which deliberately tries now to maintain a low profile of moderation and restraint. Though continuing its conservative editorial policy, the *Tribune* no longer colors the news, is much more reasonable about its pronouncements, and gives space willingly to contradictory views. It comes closer than any other to being a Midwestern newspaper with regional impact.

During the McCormick era and in the years immediately following his death, the *Tribune* exerted enormous influence throughout the State. Political Editor George Tagge wore several hats in Springfield, as reporter, ex officio lobbyist for his newspaper, and as "a kind of father confessor of the Republican party," to borrow Neal Peirce's characterization.[2] Tagge could interview a Republican legislator for a news story, lobby in behalf of a bill to increase legal advertising rates and offer counsel on campaigning tactics, all at the same time. Because it never hesitated to connect a legislator's support for *Tribune* causes with its news interpretations, the newspaper was listened to and feared. Probably the most prodigious of Tagge's many feats was his steering through the Legislature of a bill diverting a share of race track betting taxes for the construction of a convention hall in Chicago that was later named McCormick Place for the departed Colonel.[3]

Marshall Field's *Sun-Times,* the only other surviving Chicago downtown daily, was born in 1941 as the *Chicago Sun*. The present Marshall Field's grandfather founded the *Sun* because he thought Chicago deserved a liberal Democratic morning newspaper, a feeling understandably shared by President Franklin Roosevelt. In 1959, the present publisher's father acquired the afternoon *Chicago Daily News* from John S. Knight. But the changing living and working habits of urban Americans—and particularly the competition from evening television news—turned most afternoon papers into money-losing ventures. The third of the publishers Field folded the *Daily News* in 1978, transferring the best reporters and editors onto the staff of the *Sun-Times*.

Ironically, the newspaper that came into being as a reaction to the partisan zeal of the *Tribune* has itself become a strenuous political force in the State (sometimes in behalf of Republicans) at the very time the *Tribune* is trying to live down its activist background. In 1978, for example, after the paper's straw poll sampling of voter opinion showed Senator Charles Percy to be trailing his Democratic opponent Alex Seith the *Sun-Times* pulled out all the stops to help rescue Percy. Field and his father before him had been friends and supporters of the Senator from the beginning of his political career in the early 1960's. Commentary of *Sun-Times* columnists attacking Seith was reprinted by Percy's staff and distributed to 23,000 Republican workers all over the State; or, in the case of a series of slashing anti-Seith columns by Mike Royko, reprinted as paid political advertisements in newspapers downstate, and in St. Louis, Missouri, and Gary, Indiana. Seith's campaign manager also accused the *Sun-Times* of slanting the "straight" news of the campaign, a charge the editors denied. That Percy had apparently fallen behind only three weeks before the election came as a surprise to political reporters who had written off Seith as hopelessly out of the running. Seith's manager Gary South said the press therefore had a subconscious institutional interest in guarding against a Seith upset for which their readers were unprepared. This, according to South, accounted for what he saw as slanted reporting in the final days of the campaign.[4] When the press initially misinterprets conditions, some scholars contend that reporters are likely to color their subsequent reporting so as to make the original misguided prophecy come true. For whatever the reasons, Percy overcame Seith's apparent lead and was reelected. The campaign demonstrated the *Sun-Times'* willingness to involve itself in ways that were once identified with the *Tribune* and Colonel McCormick. The episode also was a vivid illustration of the personal effectiveness of columnist Royko—not just in the metropolitan area but all over the State. One newspaper, the *Danville Commercial-News,* refused to run the anti-Seith ads on ground of possible libel; that normally Republican county (Vermilion) was carried by Seith on election day.

Although it has considerably more Illinois circulation outside the Chicago retail trading area than does the *Sun-Times,* the *Tribune* has de-emphasized its Springfield-based coverage in recent years, possibly a reaction to the Tagge era when Col. McCormick's newspaper cast an ever-present shadow over the State House dome. The *Sun-Times* team of Wheeler and bureau chief Robert Hillman is generally thought to be superior to the *Tribune* lineup in the capital.

McCormick's heirs were not the only owners who became convinced that bitter partisanship is seldom good newspaper business. With the spread of chain ownership, the ranks of the partisan editors have thinned all over the State. V.Y. Dallman's *Illinois State Register* is now owned by the California-based Copley chain. With some exceptions, newspapers in Illinois as in other states are deliberately less politically influential after being acquired by an absentee group owner for whom community good will is more profitable than political power. This policy of "de-politicization" by chain-owned newspapers downstate, [illegible] in Illinois [illegible] the influence of the Chicago dailies, especially that of the *Sun-Times*.

Newspaper Influence In Springfield

There are two important media centers for the coverage of public affairs in Illinois. Chicago, obviously, is one. The State House at Springfield is the other. The *Sun-Times* maintains a year-round two-person bureau in Springfield; the *Tribune* has one resident correspondent in the capital. When the Legislature is in session, the Chicago papers augment their State House bureaus with additional personnel.

Smaller newspapers that cover State government and politics with their own Springfield reporters are influential in varying degrees. They can be categorized generally in the order of their statewide significance as follows:

St. Louis area: Both St. Louis dailies have correspondents based in the Illinois capital and considerable circulation in southern Illinois. Historically, the *Post-Dispatch* is the more influential of the two, but the *Globe-Democrat* devotes more attention to Illinois news. The industrial metropolitan area across the Mississippi River from St. Louis is a competitive market. Since being acquired by Capital Cities Communications, a communications conglomerate headquartered in New York, the *Belleville News-Democrat* has improved its public affairs reporting and now has a resident correspondent in Springfield. The *Alton Telegraph* is the best of several other newspapers also battling for advertising and readers in the area.

Lee newspapers (formerly Lindsay-Schaub): In 1979, Lee Enterprises Inc., a publicly owned company based in Davenport, Iowa, acquired three Illinois newspapers from the family-owned Lindsay-Schaub group. The three were the *Decatur Herald and Review,* the *Southern Illinoisan* (published in Carbondale), and the *Edwardsville Intelligencer*. Lindsay-Schaub had a reputation for providing more in-depth analytical treatment of State government issues than any other comparable newspapers. Operating out of Decatur, the group editor, Robert Hartley, directed a staff of public affairs specialists who sent thoughtful and relatively lengthy articles to the member newspapers. On Sundays the editorial page sections of Lindsay-Schaub newspapers often featured the type of "dope story" or "think piece" on some political or governmental topic that is lacking in most other Illinois publications.

Gannett: The largest of the national newspaper chains, the Gannett group, includes the *Rockford Morning Star and Register Republic* and the *Danville Commercial-News* among its 79 properties.

Peoria: *The Journal-Star* is a prosperous independently-owned newspaper whose political editor, William O'Connell, is regarded as an authoritative downstate reporter of Illinois politics.

Quad-Cities: Rock Island, Moline, East Moline and Davenport, Iowa, make up the Quad Cities. Although the *Quad-City Times* is published in Davenport, it does a more thorough job of reporting on Illinois government and politics than the two principal Illinois-based papers, the *Moline Dispatch* and the *Rock Island Argus*.

Copley: The Copley group with headquarters in La Jolla, Calif., is especially significant in Illinois because of geography. Copley owns the *State Journal-Register* in Springfield and four strategically located dailies on the fringe of the Chicago metropolitan area—the *Elgin Courier-News, Aurora Beacon-News, Joliet Herald-News,* and *Wheaton Journal*.

Suburban dailies: There are several hundred neighborhood weeklies in Chicago and community weeklies or semi-weeklies spread across the suburban area. Most concentrate on local news. Insofar as they devote space to State affairs, they are likely to print the flattering news releases issued by their local representatives without the critical investigation and analysis expected of the bigger papers. However, the Paddock Publications established a Springfield bureau to service its daily morning paper editions of the *Arlington Heights Daily Herald* and ten other localized daily editions distributed in the northwest suburbs. Paddock's Springfield report began showing how State government decisions affect the lives of suburban residents. After the demise of the *Chicago Daily News,* Paddock experimented with a downtown Chicago edition specially aimed at northwest suburban commuters. Gradually, Paddock's Springfield report began competing directly with the *Tribune* and *Sun-Times,* emphasizing exclusive stories of general interest more and suburban news less.

Other independents: Among other downstate dailies, the *Bloomington Pantagraph,* the *Waukegan News-Sun,* and the *Quincy Herald-Whig* are probably the most respected for their State political coverage and commentary.

How influential are the media? According to Wheeler of the *Sun-Times* many legislators view what newspapers and broadcasting stations report in print and on the air, as well as their editorializing, as "the most direct lobby in Springfield." This influence is most pervasive, Wheeler says, in the agenda-setting function, which calls legislative attention to concerns that must be addressed. "Media influence is less a factor in how the legislature reacts once a problem is before it, although the media become more effective to the degree an issue can be characterized as a good guy vs. bad guy confrontation. And lawmakers from districts in which either party has lopsided control seem less susceptible to media suasion."[5]

As a general rule, legislators who run in closely contested districts or who presented themselves as reform or "good government" candidates, particularly in a suburban district with a well-educated, highly literate electorate are more likely to be responsive to media influence. Representatives of strong Democratic organization districts in Chicago or veteran members from rural districts downstate may be totally disdainful of media opinion.

In most marginal districts, the tendency of the press to impugn the motives of legislators who vote the "wrong" way on certain kinds of bills (e.g., having to do with the regulation of race tracks or currency exchanges), makes them more cautious than usual. If, months after the Legislature adjourned, a scandal developed over the passage of a bill, even innocent legislators would have to be prepared to explain their voting decisions.

Television and Radio

Included in the 34 television channel allocations in Illinois (eight of them for public broadcasting stations), are 10 major markets: Chicago; St. Louis; Springfield-Decatur-Champaign; Peoria; Quad-Cities; Rockford; Paducah, Kentucky/Cape Girardeau, Missouri/Harrisburg; Quincy/Hannibal, Missouri; and two in Indiana, Terre Haute and Evansville.

When the Legislature is in session, Chicago television stations WBBM-TV, WMAQ-TV, WLS-TV and WGN-TV assign camera crews and reporters in Springfield, as do WCIA (Champaign), WAND (Decatur) and WICS (Springfield). Radio stations with their own accredited correspondents in the State House are WBBM and WIND, Chicago; and WCVS, WMAY and WSSR, Springfield. WBBM-TV, WMAQ-TV and WLS-TV are owned and operated by the CBS, NBC and ABC national networks. Independent of the networks, WGN-TV is owned by the Tribune Co. through its subsidiary, Continental Broadcasting.

Working facilities at the State House are luxurious for both print and broadcast reporters, compared to pressrooms in most public buildings. Some observers feel this keeps them in their quarters when they should be out developing independent stories. The remodeled press quarters include a large room for television interviews and news conferences. Television has changed the behavior of both the Governor and the Legislature in addition to that of the print reporters. Able to command the instant attention of the visual medium, chief executives are more style conscious; image is at least as important as the substance of their programs and policies. Some students of political journalism see a parallel between the press corps print-broadcasting split and the split of the government branches, executive versus legislative. "The governor can present a single face, a single voice," said Alan Rosenthal, director of the Eagleton Institute of Politics at Rutgers University. "So the governor is bound to be favored by the broadcasters, since the executive style is tailored so neatly to their needs. The intricate dealings and debaters' points of the legislators are left to the pencil press."[6]

In the 1978 gubernatorial campaign, Democratic candidate Michael Bakalis accused the press of preoccupation with photogenic "gimmicks" staged by his opponent, Governor James R. Thompson. According to Bakalis, the news media were more interested in pictures of Thompson on the racquetball court or with his Irish setter than they were with details of his performance in office.

Most of the work of the Legislature is complicated, dull and inherently difficult for television to dramatize visually. Time constraints, combined with the fact that the Legislature is not usually a very good "picture story", mean that TV coverage of the State House is seldom thorough or in depth. It is the nature of the medium. TV reporters generally are content with a 30-second "talking head" or "stand up" interview with a legislator based on news already known. Broadcasters are attracted by simple, controversial and colorful stories that can be summarized in a few seconds of air time. Legislators complain that TV caters to "showhorse" legislators (President Lyndon Johnson divided members of Congress into "showhorses" and "workhorses"). Critics allege that television sensationalizes and makes superficial the complicated business of the legislative branch. Unquestionably, one of the effects has been to increase the public exposure of the showhorse legislator, those who are attractive and glibly articulate sources of quotable remarks. Another effect probably has been to reduce the clowning and other end-of-the-session antics that once were typical of legislative behavior.

Most politicians are on the lookout constantly for controlled television opportunities. In Illinois, broadcasting outlets without reporters or other facilities in Springfield can use the radio "newsfeeds" or TV tapes distributed by the tax-supported State Information Service. Pretaped excerpts from the Governor's speeches to the Legislature are made available, for example, to any TV station that wants them. "Canned news" of this sort makes it possible for the Governor to disseminate a certain amount of propaganda, but it is better than no State government news at all.

The Wire Services

Newspapers and broadcasting stations too small to afford their own Springfield reporters rely on one or both of the wire services for their news of State government and politics. Even some of the bigger organizations depend on the Associated Press and United Press International for their routine coverage, assigning their own reporters to special projects, investigations and news analysis. Competition from television has forced the newspapers to do more than report the surface news. If the Governor's "State of the State" speech is being televised, the print reporter's task is to put the speech in perspective and explain what it means.

AP and UPI, the two wire services, each operate with three reporters and one photographer in Springfield. Wire service bureaus in all state capitals tend to be understaffed, under-experienced and overworked. On newspapers and wire services, state capital assignments do not enjoy the professional prestige they deserve, and the best reporters are eager to move on to Washington.[7] Just as the isolated location of some state capitals (e.g., Springfield, Illinois; Jefferson City, Missouri; Albany, New York) affects the performance of the Legislatures in those big-city states, it also has an effect on the journalistic coverage. It is not unheard of for staff members on Chicago area newspapers to decline transfers to Springfield because they don't want to move to central Illinois.

Until recently, the Springfield bureaus had other responsibilities besides covering the Governor, the Legislature, the State Supreme Court, and the administrative agencies of the State government. They kept tabs on the high school football and basketball scores and ratings for the entire State, handled the "interior Illinois" livestock market, wrote about fatal highway accidents and other spot news happenings in the central Illinois region, and responded to the special service requests of clients for coverage of events such as the tedious rate hearings before the State regulatory agencies. Although the wire service bureaus have wisely been divested of most of their non-State government related coverage responsibilities, the nature of their operation leaves little time for in-depth coverage.

Having to please countless faceless editors, wire service coverage of a political campaign stresses standard news formulas, "hard" angles, especially controversy. This cliche-ridden story from the AP report of October 18, 1978, is typical:

> Oak Brook, Ill.—Gov. James R. Thompson and his Democratic challenger Michael Bakalis traded heated name-calling Tuesday and kept rhetorical gloves on for another round.
>
> Thompson called Bakalis a demagogue and accused him of flipflopping on the issues of abortion as well as on the cost of his plan to cut property taxes.
>
> Bakalis, in turn, called Thompson the "biggest hypocrite and phony we've ever had as governor of Illinois."
>
> Each used the names to describe the other to reporters *after* they jointly appeared before a voters gathering sponsored by the League of Women Voters of Illinois.

(Italics mine. In other words, the joint appearance of the two candidates failed to produce the expected heated name-calling, so the AP encouraged a more lively—and newsworthy—post-debate gloves-on rhetoric.)

Beginning in the early 1970's, the editors who buy and own the AP (the service is cooperatively owned by its customers) requested that Springfield news be more searching, more interpretive, more digestible; in short, more interesting. Consequently, both services are more selective now with their coverage of routine legislative news. Stories are shorter. AP reporters are turned loose on time-consuming investigations, the type of scandal-seeking that the AP once avoided for fear of offending some politically involved client editor. Instead of assigning reporters to cover only the House or the Senate, AP now expects its reporters to follow an important bill from one house to the other and to become an expert on that subject, whether it be unemployment insurance or crime. Endeavoring to satisfy the tastes of many different editors and broadcast news directors, the wire services cannot be expected to duplicate the depth analysis of the major newspaper bureaus. But their reportage is much less bland than in the past.[8] In the end they may be caught on the horns of a dilemma. Editors without their own reporters in Springfield want and expect a deeper and more interpretive report from the wire services, but this invariably involves value judgments on the part of the wire service reporters—judgments that may not be shared by all client editors.

The Legislature and the Press

Modern political activity revolves around the need for news media exposure. Always thinking of the next campaign, members of the Illinois General Assembly are necessarily engaged in a competition for attention. Because power is dispersed among many individuals, it is more difficult for the Legislature to present a neat, coherent institutional image to the public, than it is for the

Governor. By a variety of means individual legislators are clamoring for the attention, understanding and approval of the press.

This process of courtship works in both directions. No bureau has enough staff to cover all the floor sessions, committee hearings and party caucuses, even if the key decisions were being made there instead of behind the closed doors of the leaders' offices and at restaurant tables later in the evening. Because there is much more going on than the available journalistic personnel can keep up with—and much of that is likely to be secret or very complicated or both—reporters cultivate their sources of information. Particularly in the case of newspapers with a single reporter focusing primarily on the activities of the district legislative delegation, this can result in an incestuous relationship between a reporter who is spoonfed hard-to-get information in return for favorable treatment of news involving the source.

Most State House reporters, however, make a conscientious effort to report what is happening. Although the working facilities are comfortable, there is never enough time. A reporter's typical day may begin with a press conference by the Governor or the handing down of opinions by the State Supreme Court, opinions that must be digested, translated into English and, if possible, made sense of. It is not uncommon for a sitting grand jury to be considering some transgression of general political interest that must be followed by the press. New bills introduced once the day's legislative session begins must be screened and evaluated as to their importance. The action on the floor of the Legislature must be covered. Stories are written or someone else may call from the home office with questions. In the afternoon, if the reporter has any stamina left, there are committee sessions. These are often the most significant of the day's activities. But their prospective importance is difficult to judge in advance. Along with the endless stream of news releases—which, unfortunately, often try to obscure the meaning of the news—there may also be voluminous reports from some administrative agencies or State commissions to scan. In the evening, if there are no obligatory social events, a good reporter "bar hops," chatting informally with legislators and establishing relationships of mutual trust. At the end of it all, if the reporter works for an afternoon newspaper, is the "overnight" he files—a story composed in the middle of the night for use the next day.[9] Especially in the final days of the session, when most of the vital decisions are being made, there is little time for reflection. With hundreds of bills at various stages of final action, "there is just no time for the reporter, even if he wishes, to sit back and contemplate the significance of the activity whirling around him."[10]

Ithiel de Sola Pool has written of the symbiotic relationship—the "relation between cronies"—that exists between reporter and politician in Washington.[11] The same can be found in Springfield, possibly even more exaggerated because of the previously mentioned geographic isolation of the capital.

> . . . The politician is the newsman's *raison d'etre*. His daily work and nightly gossip concern the foibles, fights, and policies of politicians. His gratifications include both secret knowledge of the frailities of the mighty and opportunities to cavort in their penumbra.
>
> A bright young journalist who is sent to Washington by his medium can hardly not be titillated when a senator hops to his table, slaps him on the back, and calls him by first name. . . . Reporters are persons whom high officeholders treat with deference and attention.
>
> In this process friendships develop over the years and more importantly, so do working relationships. Ever since Lincoln Steffens' *Autobiography,* it has been a truism in the literature on journalism that reporters are engaged in tacit bargaining with the "pols" they cover. By holding back some of the embarrassing things they know, they keep their contacts in debt. It is a gentle and more unconscious blackmail that keeps the reporters' channels open for more information to come and, at the same time, tames the reporter from going the last mile in his exposes.

Pool says the reporter's adversarial skepticism is "a reaction to the very compromises and concessions that he must make, a brave assertion that wards off guilt. It is the newsman's proof to himself and to society that he has not been bought. It is his way of saying, 'Look not at how I must cohabit with the system; for in fact I am its foe.' "

In Springfield, where the pressures for cohabitation (and for co-option into the "system") are even greater, reporters are compelled to demonstrate their independence periodically.

Good reporters develop a multiplicity of sources, lobbyists as well as legislators. Some legislators acquire a reputation as "media politicians," being available at almost any time for broadcast and print media interviews both on and off the record. A few others (a minority to be sure) are disdainful of the press. These tend to be Cook County regular organization Democrates who rely more on party organization and less on media publicity for their success.

With the weakening of the party structures, most candidates are more conscious of their media-nurtured images. This is especially true of Republicans in Cook County, who lack a strong patronage-based precinct-level organization. No Republican has been elected to major statewide office in Illinois since Senator Everett M. Dirksen without a distinctive, very positive media-created image.

The general impression is that Republicans and "reform Democrats"—that is, those running without regular organization support—work harder at maintaining good media relations. Former Governor Daniel Walker accused his successor Governor Thompson of "subverting what should be an adversary relationship with the press by excessive socializing with reporters."[12] A news report said Walker was referring to "Thompson's practice of occasionally dropping into the Capitol press room for a beer and to chat with reporters."

Replied Thompson:

> I doubt that my occasional trips to the press room for a beer or sitting down with a reporter subverted the free press in any sense. And I don't know what is meant by adversary relationship between a public official and someone in the press. I think that's really a wrong term. An adversary relationship might develop on the editorial page, and if so that would be a proper function over issues, policy and philosophy. But if an adversarial relationship develops on the front page, then something's wrong with the relationship on the press side.

Candidates who run and are elected as media politicians (as contrasted with party organization politicians) must be sensitive about their media image at all times. Thus, in the Winter of 1979, when Thompson and his wife embarked on a long-planned vacation to Palm Beach, Florida, just when much of Illinois was buried by a horrendous blizzard, the Thompsons returned to the State rather than be hounded by the embarrassing questions of reporters.

Chicago may be unique: a large city without a Republican Party organization of any significance. A succession of metropolitan Republicans who achieved statewide success chose to concentrate on the Chicago media instead of organization building—most recently, Percy and Thompson. This, too, has tended to intensify Chicago media influence on public affairs in Illinois.

A related factor that helps explain media influence in legislative affairs is the cumulative voting system for election to the Illinois House of Representatives. As a practical matter, to be elected as the one Republican in a strong Democratic organization Chicago district—a district without an effective Republican organization of any kind—the minority member must either be a good media politician, or have ties to the Democrats, or both.

Are public affairs reporters biased? Most publishers are probably conservative Republicans, but reporters come in all political persuasions. As a group they are probably more liberal than the population at large. Whatever bias they have, younger journalists especially, is likely to be towards reform independents and away from old-style organization politicians often characterized as "machine" politicians. Many younger reporters lack an understanding of the legitimate role of patronage and compromise and constituent service in the political process.

Despite their shared needs and interests, legislators and the reporters who cover their activities often come together in an atmosphere of acrimony. Nerves are frayed after months of involuntary interaction.

> The same reporter may find himself courted, feared, avoided, reviled and denounced from the floor of the Senate, by the same legislator, all within a few days. It's sort of a game. On the one hand, a lot of them hate reporters, and most of them don't think they get a fair shake. But on the other hand, they couldn't get along without (reporters) because if we weren't there, no one would ever know what these guys do. "They would prefer it if the press would not criticize them," said Randy Thomas of the State Journal Register.[13]

Legislators complain that too much legislative reporting is simplistic and episodic, by reporters who have neither the time nor the inclination to comprehend the subtle shadings and political nuances of the legislative arena. Reporters tend to separate the actors into good guys and bad guys without an appreciation of the proper function of a legislative body to reconcile conflict and negotiate compromises. This lack of mutual understanding can[14]

> . . . profoundly affect popular understanding of public issues. A certain level of conflict is inevitable and healthy, but when antagonisms build to the point where the public sees only a distorted and confusing picture of government, some revisions would seem to be in order.

After all is said and done, Al Rosenthal of Rutgers University suggests that[15]

> The legislative process in the states is messy—really, it defies all of the American instincts for order—and extremely subtle. At times, it may be impossible to report it clearly and consistently, since it's not always clear and consistent itself.

Media As Lobby

George Tagge is no longer in the pressroom lobbying for the *Tribune,* but the news media *do* influence State government collectively and directly through the lobbying activities of the Illinois Press Association (IPA) and the Illinois Broadcasters Association. Representing most of the State's newspapers, the IPA employs a full-time Springfield lobbyist who protects the interests of the smaller newspapers particularly. (The big ones are usually powerful enough to protect themselves.) Sometimes the big and little ones clash in the political arena. An example is the competition for public notice advertising revenue. There are several thousand references in the Illinois statutes to public notice advertising, often referred to as "legal notices." Municipalities and other units of government would prefer not to have to pay for the publication of many of these voluminous lists of tax assessments, bidding invitations, notices of election and other items of public business. In 1976 the *Chicago Tribune* challenged the legality of a requirement in Illinois law that these notices must appear in newspapers published in the township or other local jurisdiction. The *Tribune* claimed a share of this advertising revenue for the nine zoned supplemental editions that are produced under the title of "Suburban Trib" and inserted in copies of the regular *Tribune* sold in the suburbs. The State Supreme Court denied the Tribune's contention that this provision violated the First Amendment. Then the battle moved to the State Legislature where it is still being waged, pitting the statewide influence of the *Tribune* against that of the community newspapers. So seriously did the *Tribune* view the controversy that it, the largest newspaper in Illinois withdrew from the Illinois Press Association.

Summary

How well the news media report and clarify the news of State government and politics has a great deal to do with the quality of that government. A press that provides thorough coverage and responsible interpretation of State issues is a more constructive force than newspapers and broadcasters who cater to the lowest tastes of their readers and listeners. Public support of government and of the political parties is related to the images transmitted by the news media.

Although individual legislators often enjoy friendly relationships with their local editors, the media are often critical of the Legislature as an institution. Proposals to raise the salaries of legislators and to increase their allowances for travel, staff and office facilities are opposed on most editorial pages. A repetitive picture of the State House as a den of corruption and selfish partisanship contributes to the public cynicism about politics.

News media influence over public affairs can only be expected to grow in Illinois. The strong one-man domination of the Democratic Party of Chicago, Cook County and Illinois during the reign of Mayor Richard J. Daley is no more. No longer will the Democratic Party be able to draw up its "slate" of candidates in secret with no mind to news media reaction, as was done during the Daley years. Old-style politics is on its way out, even in Chicago.

Regular organization Democrats in Chicago blamed the media for the organization's first big defeat of the post-Daley period in 1979. Mayor Michael Bilandic, the organization candidate, was upset by Jane Byrne in the primary election. Regular Democrats accused the television stations and newspapers of exaggerating Bilandic's bureaucratic blunders in failing to deal with a gigantic snow storm that crippled the City shortly before the election. Thereafter, organization Democrats would be more mindful of their image.

Professional management of political campaigns, developed to a fine art in California, was slow coming to Illinois. But the era of skilled manipulation of the media is here now. More sophisticated attempts to "condition" the press are part of this professionalization of political management. This is a natural development. The role of the news media, and particularly of television, can be expected to increase in Illinois politics. As Americans rely more on television for their news, citizens not only receive less information about State and local government, but the information they receive about all politics comes in shorter spurts and tends, for many reasons, to be more negative and not as consensus-building.

A recent study by two political scientists propounds this as one of the reasons for the decline of voting participation in State and local elections. The number of small newspapers has declined. More people limit themselves to the purchase of one newspaper, which the authors say is likely to be a regional newspaper such as the *Chicago Tribune* or the *St. Louis Post-Dispatch* instead of a community newspaper.

Television, moreover, has had a nationalizing influence, according to the authors of this study.[16]

> Of course, both newspapers and television give primary play to happenings at the national level, but whereas newspapers may carry stories of local politics on the second and third page, television news seldom goes beyond the first page. Politically relevant news on national television, then, tends to be of a national variety.

Newspaper editors have always had to weigh carefully how much "good citizen" information could be force-fed readers without driving them away. In a period when public confidence in politics and government have waned, the public responsibility of media decisionmakers and the skill of the journalists who undertake to report the news of public affairs may have as much as anything else to do with the level of political activity and responsiveness of State and local government in Illinois.

Unresolved Issues and Further Research Opportunities

Only recently have political scientists begun devoting serious attention to the role of the news media in the political system. *Race for the Presidency: The Media and the Nominating Process,* edited by James David Barber (Prentice-Hall, 1978) is an example of the literature now emerging in the study of national politics. If the past is any guide, it will be years before this scholarly interest in the effect of the media on the political processes seeps down to the level of state government. Although there have always been a great many assumptions about the significance of news coverage in the way a state legislature goes about its business or an election campaign is conducted, there was never much solid data to support these assumptions.

In Illinois, specifically, very little is known about the relationship between the State House press corps and the work product of the General Assembly. Very little is known about the sociology of the State House reporters, as a group or interacting with the legislators they cover. Or the effectiveness of the media manipulations of the executive branch of the government. (Governor Thompson's media strategies and tactics are an excellent case to be studied.) Or the extent to which media interest in and coverage of an election campaign affect voter participation and how the candidates campaign.

Where do the people of Illinois get their images of the Legislature? Of the Governor? Of the insurance lobby? How are central city-suburban relations influenced by the news coverage of Chicago dailies? Chicago television? The suburban press? How will the media affect the post-Daley evolution of the Democratic Party of Illinois? How has the image of Chicago been shaped by the media? And how will it change in the post-Daley era?

These are only a few of the almost unlimited supply of research opportunities for students interested in the news media and the political system in Illinois. The opportunities are all the greater because of the heterogeneity of the media and their personnel as well as the political figures struggling for power in big and little communities all over Illinois.

NOTES

[1]Ward Just, *A Family Trust* (Boston: Little, Brown and Co., 1978), pp. 24–25.

[2]Neal R. Peirce, *The Megastates of America: People, Politics and Power in the Ten Great States* (New York: W.W. Norton and Company, 1972), p. 393.

[3]Political scientist Edward Banfield wrote a published case study of the *Tribune*'s sponsorship of this legislation. See Edward Banfield, *Political Influence* (New York: The Free Press of Glencoe, 1961), Chapter Seven, "The Exhibition Hall," p. 190.

[4]Tom Littlewood, "Polls and Politics—the Percy-Seith Race," *Illinois Issues* 5:2 (February 1979), p. 32.

[5]Charles N. Wheeler, III., "News Media's Influential, Too" *Chicago Sun-Times,* May 21, 1978, "Views" Section, p. 4.

[6]Ralph Whitehead, Jr. and Howard M. Ziff, "Statehouse Coverage: Lobbyist Outlast Legislators," *Columbia Journalism Review* (January/February 1974), p. 11.

[7]Al Hester, "The Journalistic Stepchild," Working Paper on Public Affairs Reporting, Englewood, Colorado: Citizens Conference on State Legislatures, 1975.

[8]Tom Littlewood, "The Wire Services and State News," *Illinois Issues* 4:2 (February 1978), p. 33.

[9]———, "The Trials of State House Journalism," *Saturday Review,* December 10, 1966, p. 82.

[10]Douglas N. Kane, "Illinois: Good Guys and Bad," *Columbia Journalism Review* (Fall 1967), p. 57.

[11]Ithiel de Sola Pool, "Newsmen and Statesmen: Adversaries or Cronies?" *Aspen Notebook on Government and the Media* (New York: Praeger, 1973), p. 12.

[12]"Thompson's Good Press Questioned by Rivals," Associated Press story in *Daily Illini,* Urbana, Illinois, October 25, 1977, p. 7.

[13]Jessica Weber, "Statehouse Reporters: Their Unofficial Role in the Governmental Process," *Illinois Issues* 1:4 (April 1975), p. 120.

[14]Samuel Gove, *et al. The Illinois Legislature: Structure and Process* (Urbana: University of Illinois Press, 1976), p. 130.

[15]Whitehead and Ziff, *op. cit.*, p. 12.

[16]Oliver Walter and Albert Karnig, "Illinois Municipalities: Where Have All the Voters Gone?" *Illinois Government Research,* No. 47 (Urbana: Institute of Government and Public Affairs, University of Illinois, November 1978).

SUPPLEMENTAL READING

Alexander, Carol. "The Influential Editor of the Chicago Sun-Times." *Urbana Morning Courier,* December 17, 1978, p. 37.

Cater, Douglas. *Fourth Branch of Government.* Boston: Houghton, Mifflin, & Co., 1959.

Gove, Samuel K., *et al.* "Relations with the Press." *The Illinois Legislative Structure and Process.* Urbana: University of Illinois Press, 1976, pp. 129–132.

Hatch, Richard H. "Reporters and Legislators in Illinois: Their Roles and How They Interact." Ph.D. dissertation, University of Illinois, Urbana, 1969.

Hester, Al. "The Journalistic Stepchild." Working paper on public affairs reporting. Englewood, Colorado: The Citizens Conference on State Legislatures, 1975.

Kane, Douglas N. "Illinois: Good Guys and Bad." *Columbia Journalism Review* (Fall 1967), p. 57.

———. "Newspaper Portraits of the Illinois General Assembly." Master's thesis, University of Illinois, Department of Journalism, Urbana, 1967.

Littlewood, Thomas B. "The Trials of State House Journalism." *Saturday Review* (December 10, 1966), 82–83.

———. "What's Wrong with State House Coverage." *Columbia Journalism Review* (March/April 1972), pp. 39–45.

Sigale, Merwin K. "Press Coverage of the Illinois Legislature." Master's thesis, University of Illinois, Urbana, 1960.

Simon, Paul. "Better News Coverage of the Legislatures Needed to Vitalize State Government." *The Quill,* March, 1957.

Walter, Oliver and Albert Karnig. "Illinois Municipalities: Where Have All the Voters Gone?" Illinois Government Research Report No. 47, Institute of Government and Public Affairs, University of Illinois, November, 1978.

Weber, Jessica J. "Statehouse Reporters: Their Unofficial Role in the Governmental Process." *Illinois Issues* 1:4 (April, 1975), 118–21.

Wheeler, Charles N., III. "News Media's Influential, Too." *Chicago Sun-Times,* May 21, 1978, "Views" Section, p. 4.

Whitehead, Ralph, Jr., and Howard M. Ziff. "Statehouse Coverage: Lobbyists Outlast Journalists." *Columbia Journalism Review* (January/February 1974), p. 11.

PART **IV**

CREATURES OF THE STATE: LOCAL AND URBAN GOVERNMENTS

CHAPTER **17**

Illinois Local Government

James M. Banovetz and John Wenum

Illinois is unique: the State has more units of local government than any other state in the United States and more than many foreign nations. The most recent federal census of governments reported that Illinois had 6,620 units of local government, including 102 counties, 1,274 cities and villages, 1,436 townships, 1,063 school districts, and 2,745 other special districts of all kinds.[1] Overall, such a multiplicity of local governments makes Illinois the most diversely governed, although not necessarily the best governed, state in the union.

This chapter will describe the system of local government in Illinois, beginning with an overview of its general design, history and evolution; discuss the structure and administration of Illinois local government; briefly examine local government politics; and conclude with a description of the relationship between Illinois local governments and agencies of the Illinois state government.

The Design of Illinois Local Government

Local governments in Illinois can be grouped into two broad categories on the basis of diversity of function. *General purpose* governments include municipalities, counties, and to a lesser degree, townships. *Special or limited purpose* governments have been established to provide a particular service to a particular geographic area; these include school, fire protection, mosquito abatement and other types of districts, as well as authorities organized to operate exposition halls, airports, and mass transit systems. Both general and special purpose governments have their roots in forms developed long before Illinois became a state—adaptation of established and tested forms made more sense than trying to invent new ones.

General Purpose Governments

There are two distinctly different kinds of general purpose local governments in Illinois. The first of these, counties and townships, are designed to provide general governmental services in the rural areas of the State. The second are the municipalities, individually known as cities, villages and towns, which were developed to provide governmental services in the State's urban areas.

Governments for Rural Illinois Counties and townships were the two forms of local government initially established in the State of Illinois, and both were designed for the rural culture that then existed throughout the settled portions of the State. These two units of local government continue today to be the essential providers of local government services in rural areas, although they also continue to exist and provide services in those portions of their areas which have subsequently become urbanized. Thus, for example, Cook County, Illinois, continues to provide some services, such as courts, election administration, and real estate records, for all of the area within its boundaries, including the City of Chicago and Cook County suburbs, but many other of its services, such as police protection and zoning, are provided only to those portions of the County lying outside the boundaries of cities and villages.

Counties are clearly the most important of these rural local government units, and serve two distinctly different functions. On the one hand, they are units of local government and, as such, are empowered to provide for the general health, welfare and safety of all land and property within their boundaries. In addition, counties are also viewed as administrative subdivisions of the State. As such, they are responsible for the performance of certain State functions on a local basis, such as the maintenance of state highways and conduct of State elections. The entire State of Illinois is divided into 102 counties in such a manner that each parcel of property in the State is located in a particular county.

Eighty-four Illinois counties contain townships as an additional, smaller unit of local government. Like counties, townships serve a dual function. They provide local government services to their own residents, such as the construction and maintenance of town roads and the operation of cemetaries, and also serve as subdivisions of the county and State for certain administrative purposes, such as the conduct of elections. The functions of townships vary in different parts of the State and, with the development of modern transportation and communication which makes access to county seats easy, many now consider township government in Illinois to be all but obsolete.[2]

Urban Government As Illinois grew, new units of local government were established to provide the higher levels of public services required by the more congested conditions of urban life. Called incorporated places or municipalities, such governments in Illinois have been labeled cities, villages and incorporated towns. As distinguished from rural counties and townships, these *incorporated* municipalities have been:

> designed to give their inhabitants such services as are necessary to urban life: police and fire protection, water supply and sewage disposal, streets and traffic control, for example.

In the eyes of the law, these local units are known as municipal corporations for they are given full corporate powers and those of a local, rather than a state-wide nature. Furthermore, they come into being only after a petition on the part of people desiring such incorporation.[3]

Illinois municipalities are superimposed on the rural counties and townships which proceded them into existence. As a result, counties and townships continue to exist and operate within the boundaries of cities and villages. City and village boundaries need not, however, conform to the boundaries of counties and townships. In fact, some Illinois cities and villages have boundaries which extend accross, and include land within, the boundaries of several townships and counties.

Special Districts

In addition to units of general purpose rural and urban government, Illinois law has provided for the establishment of a multitude of special local governments designed to provide a single service to a specified geographic area. School districts, for example, are units of local government established by the State for the specific purpose of providing public education to the people of school age residing within a particular geographic area. School districts, however, are unique among special districts in Illinois, for virtually all portions of the State fall within the boundaries of one or more school districts. This is not the case with other special districts which are established only in particular areas which desire to use the special district for the provision of a particular service.

Special districts have been established to provide a vast variety of services, including street lighting, mosquito abatement, sanitation, and establishment and maintenance of parks, libraries and forest preserves. Such districts are operated by their own governing board, which may either be elected by the people or appointed by other public officials, and are responsible only for the provision of the service for which the district was created. The boundaries of special districts need not conform to the boundary lines of existing cities, villages, counties or townships.

Special or limited purpose government first appeared in England in the early Seventeenth Century, mainly to meet demands for services resulting from urbanization.[4] Existing units of local government either lacked authority and initiative or were not coextensive with areas requiring additional services and these new, limited purpose jurisdictions were seen as the answer. Special district government spread rapidly and was known throughout the colonies by the time of the Revolutionary War.

The first special districts in Illinois, other than those organized to provide common school education, were created in Chicago and several adjoining townships in 1869.[5] The number of special district governments increased slowly until the depression years of the 1930's, when the inability of states and other forms of local government to meet citizen needs brought on a period of rapid growth. Post-World War II suburbanization also contributed to the increase, so much that by 1977 almost 60 percent of the 6,620 units of government in Illinois were special districts (2,745) or school districts (1,063).[6]

The Total Picture: An Overview

Illinois thus is served by many different kinds of local governmental units and, for reasons which are detailed in the next section of this chapter, the number of such governments has proliferated faster than in any other State. Such governmental proliferation has been criticized repeatedly and severely by scholars and local government study commissions at the national level.[7] The problems caused by such proliferation, including division of responsibility for the provision of local government services, disparities in the tax base resources available to finance such services, weakening of citizen control over local government and difficulties in dealing with regional problems on a regional scale, are most evident in Illinois. They became primary concerns of the 1970 Constitutional Convention and of the Commission on Urban Area Government which advanced a number of legislative recommendations for structural change in Illinois local government to ameliorate them.[8] Despite such attempts, however, Illinois continues to have an excessive number of local government units competing with each other for authority, resources and support in providing services to their residents.

Local Government Under the 1870 Constitution

Illinois local government under the constitutions of 1818 and 1848 was structured to serve a rural and small-town society. Counties and townships were the dominant forms, with municipalities increasingly important in the years immediately before the Civil War. Units of government, which were manifestations of Thomas Jefferson's "republics in miniature," were well suited for the modest administrative burdens and participatory democracy of rural Illinois.[9] They were seriously deficient, however, when confronted by the pressures of increasing urban population, a rapidly growing industrial sector, and the related demands for urban services.

The inadequacy of local government structures to meet new problems was complicated by the lack of administrative expertise and, in some cases, corruption on the part of public officials. The dominance of the Jacksonian view that any citizen could do the work of government, coupled with the spoils system of public employment, led to amateurism in the public service.[10] Moreover, election of large numbers of local administrative officers resulted in a lack of central direction, both in policy development and implementation. Finally, rapid urbanization and industrialization brought on demands for expansion of urban services. This brought about competition among would-be vendors of such services, with the result that the right to do business in and with the city often went to the highest bidder. The problem was that the highest bidder frequently made his payment into the pockets of public officials instead of into the public treasury. William Marcy Tweed, infamous boss of Tamany Hall and New York City, symbolizes the ultimate corruption of local politics and governance during this era.[11]

When the Constitutional Convention met in December of 1869 to draft what would become the Illinois Constitution of 1870, the mood was one of disillusionment.

> . . . The grave abuses of the power of special legislation and the extravagance of municipalities in giving aid to enterprises of internal improvements led Illinois to follow the example of sister states where similar conditions had prevailed and seek a remedy in a reform of the fundamental law.[12]

The Early Years

Although the 1870 Constitution provided some improvement for the organization and operation of local governments, reaction against the excesses noted above led to the imposition of restrictions, the ill effects of which linger on today. The 1870 Constitution was not replaced for a century.

Structure A major accomplishment of the 1870 Convention was the abolition of the practice of enacting special legislation relating to local government. Prior to 1870, for example, municipalities were incorporated under special charters granted by the legislature. This had resulted in a lack of uniformity among municipal governments and a lack of flexibility within individual units. The 1870 Constitution prohibited special legislation related to local governments in several ways. Article IV, Section 22 prohibited special legislation in the following areas related to local government:

> Locating or changing county seats;
> Regulating county and township affairs;
> Incorporating cities, towns, or villages, or changing or amending the charter of any town, city, or village;
> Providing for the election of members of the board of supervisors in townships, incorporated towns or cities;
> Providing for the management of common schools;

Of even greater importance in this section was a statement that "In all other cases where a general law can be made applicable, no special law shall be enacted."

The "general law" provision noted above was probably more important for local governments than the numerous prohibitions that preceded it. Drawing upon it and upon its inherent law-making powers, the Legislature was able to make optional forms of government available to local units during the next century. When the commission and council manager forms of city government were developed early in this century, Illinois could (but in the latter case did not until 1953) make them available.[13] When the need for strong executive leadership became apparent in larger Illinois cities, adoption of the strong-mayor form of government was also provided as a local option.[14]

Attempts at Change Change is a difficult concept as it relates to government. It can entail anything from a substantial modification in the basis of governance to an incremental adjustment in organization or operation. In the case of Illinois after 1870, change in local government was incremental. The theories of Jefferson (local units with a large degree of participatory democrary) and Jackson (a large number of elected officers with no requirement of job-related skills) continued to operate, although the intent embodied in the 1870 Constitution had been to eliminate the worst effects of the earlier era. Despite substantial improvements in the array of options available in state statutes, few changes came about. Those which did occur tended to reflect nationwide trends in local government reform; adoption of commission and, after World War II, council-manager government among mid-size and suburban communities, and some use of merit systems for municipal staffing.

County and township government remained substantially the same as before 1870. In all counties the long ballot tradition of the Jacksonian era was continued, with election of a county judge, clerk, sheriff, treasurer, coroner, clerk of the circuit court, and in counties over 60,000 population, a recorder of deeds.[15] At the township level provision for governmental officers, their duties, and the mode of organization was left to legislative discretion. Little change occurred and the major offices of Supervisor of General Assistance (poor relief) and Road Commissioner continued to exist. In addition, the role of Township Supervisors in constituting the county governing body was continued.

No provision was made regarding special districts but the "general law" statement in Article IV, Section 22 of the 1870 Constitution made it possible for the legislature to continue and expand on the trend begun in 1869.[16] As noted earlier, creation of special district governments occurred at a slow and sporadic pace until the 1930's, when the number of such units began to increase rapidly. The number of special districts eventually created in Illinois, more than in any other state in the nation, reflects the difficulty faced by multi-purpose units attempting to adjust to new conditions.

The Impact of Dillon's Rule In the decade and one-half prior to adoption of the Constitution of 1870, a new judicial doctrine had begun to emerge. By 1870 a number of cases had been decided which embodied restrictive interpretations of the powers of local governments. In 1872 Chief Justice John F. Dillon of the Iowa Supreme Court published his works, *Commentaries on the Law of Municipal Corporations,* in which he drew together the established case law relating to local governments and arrived at the conclusion that municipal corporations (by which he meant all local governments) possessed only those powers explicitly granted by law or constitution and those essential to the performance of functions assigned or permitted by the state.[17]

The consequences of Dillon's "rule" were not long in coming to Illinois. A combination of courts pursuing a doctrine of strict legal construction on the powers of local governments and a legislature unwilling to come to grips with the new urbanization and industrialization led to severe constraints on local authority. The 1870 Constitution had already imposed limits on county tax rates (Article IX, Section 8), mandated uniformity of municipal taxes on all classes of persons and property (Article IX, Section 10), placed a ceiling on the amount of debt which could be incurred by any local government (Article IX, Section 12), and set forth in detail provisions relating to county organization, boundary adjustment and governance (Article X). So far-reaching were the consequences of Dillon's "rule" that by 1917 the Illinois Supreme Court could state that:

> Municipal corporations are purely the creatures of the legislative will . . . and may be created or annuled at the pleasure of the body creating them and their property turned over to some other municipal corporations and their powers and duties conferred upon such body.[18]

A restrictive constitution, detailed statutory provisions and a rigid judicial doctrine had all worked to place limits on local governments such that they had difficulty meeting even the needs, much less the desires, of their constituencies.

Government in the Post-War Era: Adapting to Rapid Growth and Urbanization:

The period following World War II saw rapid expansion of the national economy, a rise in the number of family formations and, most important for our purposes, a marked increase in the number and proportion of people living in urban areas. Table 17-1 illustrates this trend in Illinois, beginning in 1940. However, most of the population growth in Illinois during the period from 1940 to 1970 occurred in suburbs, small and intermediate downstate cities, and in unincorporated urban areas. The larger cities grew more slowly and Chicago lost population after 1950.[19] Areas which were not organized to provide urban services on a large scale bore the brunt of the population increase and often failed, for reasons which are discussed below, to meet the demand.

TABLE 17-1

Population of Illinois, by Urban and Rural: 1940–1970

	1940	1950	1960	1970
Population (000)	7,897	8,712	10,081	11,114
Urban	5,810	6,759	8,140	9,230
Urban as % of state	73.6	77.6	80.7	83.0
Rural	2,088	1,953	1,941	1,884
Rural as % of state	26.4	22.4	19.3	17.0

Source: Adapted from U.S. Bureau of the Census, *Census of the Population: 1970,* Vol. I, Part 15, Illinois, Sec. 1, Table 3.

The Rise of Optional Forms As noted earlier, local units of government generally were limited by the 1870 Constitution and statute law as to form and powers. Counties continued to be limited to the governmental forms of the Nineteenth Century. Townships also lacked both structural options and authority to offer a full array of urban services. The only local governments given a range of optional forms were municipalities.

As noted earlier, municipalities in Illinois were given authority to adopt the commission and strong-mayor forms of government prior to World War II. Not until the 1950's, however, was council-manager government made available. Although it can provide more professional administration, the manager form does not carry with it more authority to act, so all Illinois municipalities continued to be limited by the effects of Dillon's rule during the post-war years of rapid growth.

Tax and Debt Restrictions If limits on structure and functional authority made it difficult for local governments to cope with new problems caused by rapid growth, limits on the power to tax and incur debt made the problems even worse. The 1870 Constitution (Article IX, Section 8) limited counties to a tax rate ". . . the aggregate of which shall never exceed seventy-five cents per one hundred dollars' valuation, . . . unless authorized by a vote of the people of the county." All units of local government were limited as to the power to incur debt in an amount exceeding ". . . five per centum on the value of the taxable property therein, to be ascertained by the last assessment for state and county taxes, . . ." (Article IX, Section 12). Municipalities possessed more latitude regarding tax rates but were subject to statutory limits. Requirements that tax rate increases be approved by popular referendum in many cases placed local policy officers in the anomolous position of having responsibility to act without authority to raise revenue necessary for their actions.

The greatest single constraint imposed by law on local governments was excessive reliance on forms of taxation which were (and are) often regressive in nature, i.e., having their greatest impact on those least able to pay. The property tax was, and continues to be, the largest single source of revenue for general purpose governments. The sales tax, available only to cities and counties in Illinois, is particularly important as a revenue source for cities. Both of these forms of taxation are regressive, with the sales tax as it operates in the State particularly so.[20]

Table 17-2 shows the major sources of revenue available to general purpose governments in Illinois. Their reliance on the more regressive property and sales taxes is impressive: almost 40 percent for counties, almost 50 percent for cities, and over 50 percent in the case of townships. We now find a growing but still limited reliance on more progressive sources. Federal general revenue sharing makes up a modest part of local revenues, except in the case of townships. This source did not exist prior to 1972 and is subject to periodic Congressional review and possible termination. State shared income tax is also modest in amount, limited to cities and counties, and did not exist prior to 1969. Motor fuel tax is another form of shared State revenue, but its use is limited mostly to highway-related activities such as construction and maintenance. The miscellaneous category includes a variety of sources (at least 19 for counties and cities), encompassing a variety of fees for services, fines, grants, vehicle taxes, licenses and so on.[21]

Local general purpose governments in Illinois continue to lack sufficient authority to meet their revenue needs from local sources, even in the case of home rule

TABLE 17-2
Major Sources of Revenue for Counties, Municipalities, and Townships, by Amount and Percent: 1976

Source	Counties $(000)	Counties % of Total	Municipalities $(000)	Municipalities % of Total	Townships $(000)	Townships % of Total
Property Tax	158,944	33.8	310,045	27.7	53,993	50.7
Sales Tax	28,186	6.0	244,410	21.8	—	—
Federal Revenue Share	26,918	5.7	63,032	5.6	29,936	28.1
State Income Tax Share	18,278	3.9	70,131	6.3	—	—
Motor Fuel Tax	41,161	9.8	69,786	6.2	—	—
Investment Income	17,610	3.8	—	—	2,120	2.0
Miscellaneous[1]	173,499	36.9	362,297	32.4	20,369	19.1
Total[2]	469,679	100.0	1,119,582	100.0	106,420	100.0

[1]Category includes revenue from licenses, fees for services, sale of debt instruments, grants, etc.
[2]Totals may vary due to rounding.
Source: Aggregated from summary reports prepared by the Comptroller, State of Illinois, and published as a series by type of local government. Example: *1976 Statewide Summary of Municipal Finance in Illinois,* Fiscal Year Ended in 1976 (1977 in the case of counties).

TABLE 17-3
Local Governments in Illinois, by Type of Unit: 1942–1977

Type of Unit	1942	1952	1957	1962	1967	1972	1977
Total Units	15,854	7,723	6,510	6,453	6,454	6,386	6,620
Counties	102	102	102	102	102	102	102
Municipalities	1,137	1,157	1,181	1,249	1,253	1,264	1,274
Townships	1,436	1,436	1,436	1,436	1,436	1,436	1,436
Special Districts	1,042	1,546	1,800	2,126	2,313	2,407	2,745
School Districts	12,138	3,484	1,993	1,540	1,350	1,177	1,063

Source: Adapted from U.S. Bureau of the Census, *Census of Governments, 1952; 1957; 1962; 1967; 1972; 1977;* and *Statistical Abstract of the United States, 1946,* all issued by the U.S. Government Printing Office, Washington, D.C.

units (see above). In some cases local resources are not sufficient to support a full array of needed services even without legal constraints on the power to tax. Ironically, however, even the wealthiest areas in the State lack the legal authority to use their resources to fully meet the needs and desires of their citizens. The heavy hand of Justice Dillon and the restrictions of law linger on.

Proliferation of Special Districts Although the trend had begun much earlier, the rapid increase in population and related urbanization after World War II brought on a crisis for local governments in Illinois. Confronted by demands for increased urban services, existing local governments could often give only a partial response. There were several interrelated reasons for this failure but one major consequence: a steady increase in the organization of new non-school special districts. Reduction in the number of school districts followed a national trend related to urbanization and consolidation of rural districts.
Table 17-3 illustrates the trend which ensued and continued, albeit at a slower pace, into the 1970's.

The major reasons for the increase in the number of special districts between 1942 and 1977 are three-fold. First, legal and constitutional restrictions on functional authority and on the power to tax and incur debt made it difficult for general purpose governments to meet the demands of the new urbanization. Neither counties nor townships had the range of general authority necessary and these units, as well as municipalities, were limited as to total general obligation debt [22] by the 1870 Constitution (Article IX, Section 12). With total debt authority limited to five percent of the assessed value of all real and personal property, the need for new capital facilities such as parks, fire stations, city halls, etc., exceeded the money available. The result was that new or increased service needs remained unmet in many jurisdictions.

Related to legal and constitutional restrictions was the adherence to Dillon's rule of narrow interpretation of the powers of local governments. Governments which sought to meet new problems by innovative actions were frustrated unless they could find provision in the law which gave specific or clearly implied authority to act. The combination of legal and constitutional limits, compounded by Dillon's rule, made the task of general purpose governments difficult and sometimes impossible in the face of the new growth.

A separate but equally important problem resulting from the post-war urbanization was that new population concentrations frequently did not fall wholly within a single jurisdiction. Where this did happen, local governments could often respond to critical needs, if not to all of them. Where population and jurisdiction did not match, there was no unit of government capable of meeting new demands for services. Unincorporated subdivisions could, and often did, reach across township, school district and even county boundaries, thereby making all jurisdictions responsible for some sub-area and its people, but no jurisdiction responsible for the whole.

As indicated in Table 17-3 municipalities did increase in number in response to population growth. Many annexed areas of high growth and extended urban services to them. By far the greatest increase in number was among non-school special districts, however, a phenomenon which can be accounted for by several factors. First, the special district could be granted such taxing authority as the Legislature deemed fit. The Constitution did not prohibit the creation of such units by the State (Dillon's rule applied only to local governments). Although the five percent debt limit contained in the constitution still applied, a new government had its own debt authority, separate and in addition to other local units. Not all special districts are authorized to incur debt up to the five percent limit but lower limits were of little consequence when the unit was responsible for a single function such as providing parks or fire protection.[23]

An important reason for the increase in special districts was the fact that one could be organized on the basis of some population and a needed service with or without regard to existing jurisdictional boundaries. For example, a city which needed a public library or park but had exhausted its debt limit might find a coterminus special district a ready answer. In the case of an unincorporated subdivision needing fire protection, an appropriate district could be organized, even if it crossed township or county boundaries. Where a group of citizens decided they wanted one form of urban service (sewers and a treatment plant) but did not want another (drainage), they could organize a district to provide one service and do without the other.

From the foregoing it is obvious that there were advantages in special district government for the new urbanites. The rate of organization of such units, more than 48 per year from 1942 to 1977, gives credence to this argument. There were also disadvantages, however, and their effects have become more evident as the number of governments increased. By evading tax and debt limits, the use of special districts created an illusion. Instead of a specific tax imposed by a general purpose government, there were multiple taxes imposed by several governments on the same property. Local debt was compounded as two, three, four or more special districts added their obligations onto those of county, township and, in some cases municipality. The result was that the total public debt apportioned against a parcel of property might be three or four times the constitutional limit of five percent for a single unit of government.

Although there are as many disadvantages as advantages to the extensive use of special district government found in Illinois, only two more will be noted here. The first is the rather abstract but real problem of diseconomies of scale. Long recognized by economists and public finance experts, some units of government (or private businesses) are too small to take advantage of bulk purchasing of goods and services. Special districts are particularly vulnerable in this regard because of their limited function and, related thereto, the need for small quantities of a narrow range of purchased items. Also, small special districts often lack the resources to purchase needed items to perform their assigned function. This is particularly true with respect to sophisticated and expensive equipment which may be needed as much in a small district with a low tax base as in a large and wealthy one.

The most important failure of the special district was in its failure to implement the democratic theory espoused by Jefferson and the representative theory of Jackson. With few exceptions, the policy officers (commissioners or board members) were appointed by the judges of the circuit court in which the district was located. With passage of the 1970 Constitution, appointment was by the chairmen of county boards.[24] In neither case do the citizens in the district have a voice, except indirectly, in the appointment process. Special districts, uniquely local in their provision of a single service to a specific group of citizens, implement a system which violates the basic assumptions of the popular theory of local government.

Growing Professionalism

During the period after World War II there was a marked increase throughout the nation in the employment of professional and technical personnel (trained administrators, engineers, specialists in personnel and fiscal management and others). While employment in the federal civil service was relatively stable after 1953, ranging from 2.4 to 2.8 million persons, employment by the states increased from 1.1 to 2.9 million and that of local governments from 3.6 to 6 million by 1972.[25] Illinois shared in the rapid increase in public employment generally and in the proportionately larger professional-technical component.

Expansion of existing units of government and creation of new ones to cope with population growth accounted for much of the increase in the number of professional and technical personnel employed by local governments. This was directly related to the increasing complexity of new and expanding levels of service. Implementation of urban renewal and public housing programs called for new administrative expertise, as did growing local staffs and budgets.

The advent of the council-manager form of government in the 1950's gave impetus to professionalism, especially among the more than ninety municipalities which eventually adopted it. Because city managers are usually trained in public administration, often at the graduate level, they tend to recruit a larger proportion of their staffs from among persons with professional or technical training. The result is a higher concentration of admininstrative expertise than might be found in non-manager municipalities of comparable size.

Special district governments also tended to recruit at least part of their staffs on the basis of professional or technical expertise. This is is particularly true of those districts delivering services, such as sewage disposal and water treatment and distribution, or providing park and recreation facilities. With the increase in the number of special districts noted earlier, plus the technical complexity of many of the services delivered, the demand for trained professionals rose steadily.[26]

Counties and townships lagged behind in the trend toward more professional and technical staffing. Part of the reason was that they did not increase the array of services offered to include the newer and more complex ones. Lacking tax and debt authority necessary to meet capital and operating costs of new services, counties remained much as they had been in the Nineteenth Century. Not until the 1970's, with a new form of organization in the eighty-four "township" counties, was there expansion in the use of professional or technical experts. Even then, it occurred among a limited number of counties and mainly took the form of data processing experts (computers are being widely adopted as an adjunct to county records maintenance, payroll preparation, etc.), appointed fiscal managers, and, in several counties, an administrator to coordinate the functions overseen by county boards.[27]

Townships, lacking the range of functional authority of cities and counties, have made little use of professional and technical personnel as employees. Like counties, they held on to a Nineteenth Century form and function. In addition, most townships related more to a rural than to an urban setting, and the need for expertise was not as great. Some effort is underway in the 1970's to require specific skills in certain township functions, particularly with respect to the assessment of property for taxation.[28] So long as this unit retains its traditional form and function, however, there is little reason to expect much increase in the use of professional or technical personnel.

Local Government Under the 1970 Constitution

The 1970 Illinois Constitution made a number of provisions intended to alleviate problems created for local governments by the previous document. As noted by Professor Gove and others,[29] the new Constitution broke some new ground but was more a document of political reality and compromise than a radical charter for a new future. Its many provisions relating to local government will not be enumerated here but those which relate to the problems of limits on local authority to act, the weakness of county organization, and the proliferation of units will be addressed.

Home Rule Prior to 1970 no local units in Illinois were granted home rule powers. Home rule, the ability of a local unit of government to take action pertaining to its internal affairs without finding specific authority in state law or constitution, did not exist. As noted earlier, Dillon's rule of strict interpretation of local powers had dominated judicial thinking since the late Nineteenth Century. The 1970 Constitution, at Article VII, Section 6(a), made home rule available to municipalities and counties under certain conditions. Any city over 25,000 population automatically received home rule powers on the effective date of the Constitution. Any city under 25,000 could exercise home rule powers upon approval by the local voters at referendum. Counties were the most constrained, receiving home rule powers only upon condition that a "chief executive officer" be elected. Cook County was granted home rule by declaration that the President of the County Board "shall be elected from the County at large and shall be the chief executive officer of the County" (Article VII, Section 4(b)). Nine counties attempted to adopt home rule in 1972 but the issue failed at referendum. Two of the same counties repeated the effort in 1976 but again the issue was lost.[30]

By 1974 approximately 6.7 million, over half the people in Illinois, lived in home rule jurisdictions.[31] Slightly more than 1.2 million out of the total lived in "downstate" cities, i.e., not located within the six-county Chicago Standard Metropolitan Statistical Area (SMSA).[32] Cook County contained about 5.5 million citizens within its home rule jurisdiction but more than 3 million of those lived within the City of Chicago. It is reasonable to assume that by 1980 as much as sixty-five percent of the population of Illinois will live within a home rule unit.

The home rule powers granted, and in substantial degree sustained by the courts in cases decided to date, have meant a variety of things to those local governments possessing them. In Cook County home rule meant passing a wheel (motor vehicle) tax to supplement local revenues. In Bloomington it meant adopting a simplified municipal budget and tax levy instead of a more complex procedure previously required by law. Chicago implemented an employer's expense tax, also known as a "head tax," one of twenty-five nonproperty taxes suggested in the report of the Chicago Home Rule Commission.[33] Many other examples could be cited with respect to new-found powers to tax, to regulate various activities, to incur debt without referendum approval and to engage in functions and deliver services not permitted by State law.

Home rule powers provided in the 1970 Constitution have had the effect of repealing Dillon's rule in substantial measure for the one county and nearly eighty municipalities which possess them. Home rule has not proven to be a panacea for all of the ills of local governments, but it has given more latitude in terms of internal organization and operation and has reduced local dependency upon the whim and caprice of the Legislature. In effect, home rule has made it possible for units possessing it to decide what they want to do within their jurisdiction and then to do it, so long as the State has not specifically prohibited the activity and it pertains to local affairs. Under the Dillon rule, the local unit had to find specific authority to act or seek legislative action to provide it. Home rule units may now act unilaterally, within limits, without being supplicants before the State Legislature each time they wish to do something which hasn't been done before.

County Modernization Although counties generally fared well in the new Constitution, they did not gain as much new power as home rule cities. Counties may only gain home rule by electing a chief executive officer

(Article VII, Sections 4 and 6(a)), whereas municipalities of the required size receive it automatically. After adopting home rule, counties are not given quite the latitude in incurring non-referendum debt that home rule cities possess (Article VII, Section 6(j) and (k)). Nonetheless, adoption of home rule would provide counties with substantial new powers which they may not now exercise.

Despite the difficult requirement for obtaining home rule, counties gained significant new authority under the 1970 Constitution. All elected county administrative offices may be abolished by referendum and new offices created by ordinance (Article VII, Section 4(c)), public improvements may be made using special assessments (Article VII, Section 7), and new forms of government may be adopted as provided by state law (Article VII, Sections 4 and 7). Although they remain creatures of the State in the full sense of Dillon's rule, counties have gained substantial new authority as a result of the new Constitution and they are beginning to use it. For example, at least three downstate counties have established an appointed office to provide administrative support to the county board in overseeing activities.[34]

Although any of the several elected county administrative offices may be abolished by referendum, efforts to accomplish this have met with limited success. Several small downstate counties did abolish the elected office of coroner in 1972. Similar efforts to abolish this and other offices have failed in recent years, although Lake County did abolish the elected County Auditor in 1978. Public reluctance to make these offices appointive instead of elective seems to be rooted in vestiges of the Jacksonian belief that any citizen can serve and that elected administrators are more accountable than their appointed counterparts. Although counties gained much under the new constitution, many nineteenth century traditions continue to be enshrined in the law and in the public mind.

Dealing With Proliferation The 1970 Constitution did not provide directly for the elimination of a single unit of local government in Illinois. Indeed, the general tone of compromise which pervaded the Convention is also evident in the Local Government Article.[35] There is potential for future reduction in the number of units, however, even though proliferation of special districts actually accelerated between 1972 and 1977 (see Table 17-3 above). The possibility lies in several provisions of Article VII.

Townships are often criticized as an archaic remnant of the Nineteenth Century and of Jeffersonian thinking. Whether this is true or not, and there are good arguments on both sides of the issue, Section 5 offers more potential for abolition, consolidation and dissolution of townships than existed before. The Transition Schedule to the Constitution, at Section 5(c), assured the continuing existence of all townships extant at the time of adoption, but took note of the options available in Article VII, Section 5. Reduction of the number of units was dependent upon local initiative and public referenda, however, not on constitutional fiat.

Special districts may be replaced by "special service areas" authorized in Article VII, Section 7. Counties and municipalities are empowered to:

> . . . levy or impose additional taxes upon areas within their boundaries in the manner provided by law for the provision of special services to those areas and for the payment of debt incurred in order to provide those special services.

The effect of this provision is to make it possible for a city or county to provide a service instead of a special district being organized to do so. By use of the differential taxing authority, a city or county may provide the needed service to an area, tax only those benefited, and avoid creation of yet another unit of government. The evidence to date, however, indicates that while special service areas are being created, they have not been used to displace existing special districts.

Article VII, Section 10, grants extensive authority to local governments to cooperate with each other to accomplish tasks which might otherwise necessitate the creation of special districts. Indeed, intergovernmental cooperation may be the sleeping giant of the 1970 Constitution in that it allows all types of local government to engage in virtually any type of mutual activity ". . to obtain or share services and to exercise, combine, or transfer any power of function, in any manner not prohibited by law or ordinance." This authority has been used in various parts of the State to enable cities to obtain water service, by counties to provide police services to small municipalities, in several counties in southern Illinois to share emergency ambulance facilities, and in other areas to develop plans for orderly urban area growth and development.[36]

Effective use of intergovernmental cooperation depends on mutual good will and trust among the units engaged in the joint effort. Section 10 allows local units to jointly use their personnel or taxing powers, and to incur debt related to the cooperative activity. Because use of resources is involved, a formal agreement or contract becomes necessary and it is at this point that good will and trust become essential. There are, of course, many areas of cooperation where only information is exchanged between units. In such cases, a contractual agreement is seldom needed. Obviously, however, intergovernmental cooperation, whether substantive or informational, involves good will and mutual trust among the parties involved. To date, it is working well and its use is increasing.

As is the case with the use of special service areas, there is no evidence that intergovernmental cooperation has resulted in dissolution of any special districts. It is reasonable to infer, however, that cooperative ventures may have prevented creation of new special districts. In any event, there is now a set of constitutional provisions providing for governmental change by referendum, delivery of services without creation of special districts, and cooperative use of resources to solve shared problems. Although efforts to date are modest and incremental, Illinois now has a constitutional basis for halting or even reversing governmental proliferation in the years ahead.

The Administration of Local Government

Prior to the passage of the 1970 Constitution, the organizational structure of Illinois local government was fixed by State law. The statute provided four different optional forms of government for cities and villages and two different forms for counties, and described the organizational structure to be used in townships and special districts. The new Constitution authorized cities and counties to "adopt, alter, or appeal" their forms of government and "to provide for its officers, their manner of selection and terms of office" subject to approval by referendum and any other applicable State law (Article VII, Section 6F and Section 7). Subsequent use of this authority to amend the structure of local government has been limited, but noteworthy. The City of DeKalb, for example, has changed the office of city treasurer from an elective to an appointive office, and the City of Aurora has required that all candidates for elective city office run on a nonpartisan ballot.

While it is true that the form or structure of local government offers no assurance that any particular government will be either effective, efficient, or responsive to citizen demand, the structure within which a local government is organized and operated is nonetheless important. Local government structure establishes the "rules of the game" within which public policies are made and implemented and helps to determine who will be influential in those processes. It defines the respective roles of elected and appointed officials and can have a very significant effect on governmental effectiveness, efficiency and responsiveness.

Forms of Municipal Government

There are four basic, classical forms of organization for municipal government which are in use throughout the United States: the weak mayor/council form, the strong mayor/council form, the commission form and the council/manager form. Each of these forms has been made available for use by Illinois cities and villages in the Illinois Municipal Code. Each is described below.

The Weak Mayor/Council Form The vast majority of Illinois' 1,274 cities and villages are organized under the weak mayor/council form of government. Designed principally for use in small cities and villages located in rural areas, this form is used overwhelmingly by such communities. It is also used by some of the State's medium size and larger communities and is technically the form still used by the State's two largest cities, Chicago and Rockford, although each use it now in a substantially modified form.

There are two different variants of this form used in Illinois. The first, used in Illinois cities, is called the "aldermanic-city form." Under it, the legislative body normally consists of two aldermen from each ward within the city, with the number of wards depending upon the population of the city. Aldermen serve a four year term, with this term staggered so that one alderman is elected from each ward every two years. Provisions exist under which the number of aldermen can be reduced to one per ward and terms of office may be shortened to two years. In addition to the aldermen, the aldermanic-city form also provides for the election of a mayor, a city clerk, and a city treasurer.

Illinois villages use an alternative form of the weak mayor council structure called the "trustee-village form." Under this format, each village elects six trustees who, together with the village president, constitute the legislative body of the village. Voters also elect a village clerk, but the treasurer is appointed. Villages of over 25,000 population may have each of the six trustees elected by district instead of from the village at large.

This form of government is labeled the "weak mayor/council form" because the mayor or village president, while designated the chief executive officer by statute, is vested with relatively few powers under State law. Since, as a consequence, the administrative powers of the mayor are subject to determination by the city council or village board, the community's chief executive officer must thus share executive and administrative authority with the legislative body. Executive authority is further weakened by the provisions requiring the separate election of the clerk and, in cities, the treasurer. A graphic description of the weak mayor/council form is presented in Figure 17-1. This form of government is provided to cities and villages in Artricle III of Illinois Statutes, Chapter 24.

The Commission Form Although 23 of the 389 Illinois cities and villages over 2500 population still use the commission form of government, it is now generally considered to be obsolete. Under it, the voters elect at large a mayor and four commissioners who, collectively, serve as the city or village council. Individually, each heads an administrative department of the city. The mayor serves as the commissioner of public affairs and a member of the council is designated to be the commissioner, or head, of one of the following departments: accounts and finances, public health and safety, streets and public improvements, and public property. In some communities, each commissioner is elected to head a specific department, in others, the commissioners are elected at large and then by majority vote at the first regular meeting of the council after each election, the council designates each member to head one of the departments. The council also appoints the clerk and treasurer.

The number of Illinois cities and villages using this form of government has steadily declined in recent years. This decline in usage has been attributed to the following:

> Among (the commission form's) disadvantages are that all of the elected commissioners may reside in the same section of the city and that each commissioner has near absolute power over the department he heads. As government becomes more complex, municipalities require greater coordination between departments which is not easily achieved under the commission form.[37]

Figure 17-2 contains a graphic description of the commission form of government, which is made available to Illinois cities and villages under Illinois Statutes, Chapter 24, Article IV.

The Council/Manager Form Called the "manager form" in the Illinois Statutes, the council/manager form of government first appeared in Illinois in the city of Glencoe in 1914, but it was not until 1953 that the Illinois Statutes were amended to provide this form of government as an option to all of the State's cities and villages. Since that time, the number of municipalities utilizing this form has increased substantially:

> Only a handfull of communities had adopted the council manager form by 1951, but since that date the growth of the form has been phenomenal. As of October, 1977, no fewer than 104 Illinois communities were recognized by the International City Management Association as having adopted a managerial form of government. An unknown number of other communities in the state had employed persons in a professional, administrative capacity to oversee daily municipal operations and the number of such communities continues to increase. Currently, over half of Illinois' communities over 15,000 population have adopted a form of government employing a professional administrator in a managerial capacity.[38]

Under this form of government, the voters elect a mayor, a city or village council, a clerk and a treasurer. The mayor and council collectively serve as the council or legislative body and employ a professional municipal administrator to direct the city's administrative activities.

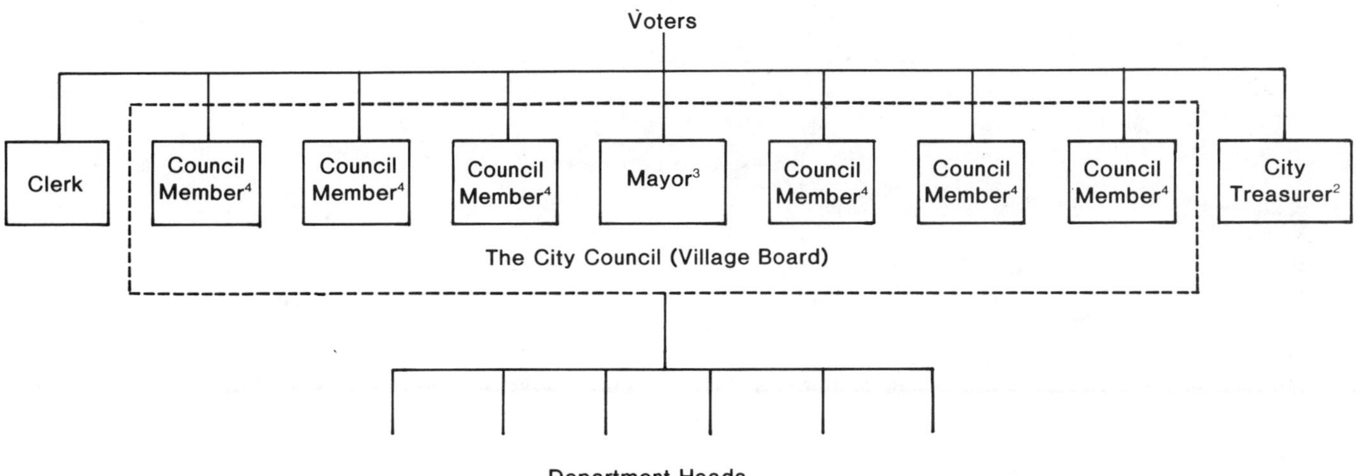

1. Called the Aldermanic-city form in cities and the Trustees-village form in villages.
2. The Treasurer is appointed in villages.
3. The Mayor is called President in villages.
4. Members of the council are called aldermen in cities, trustees in villages.

Figure 17-1. THE WEAK MAYOR–COUNCIL FORM[1]

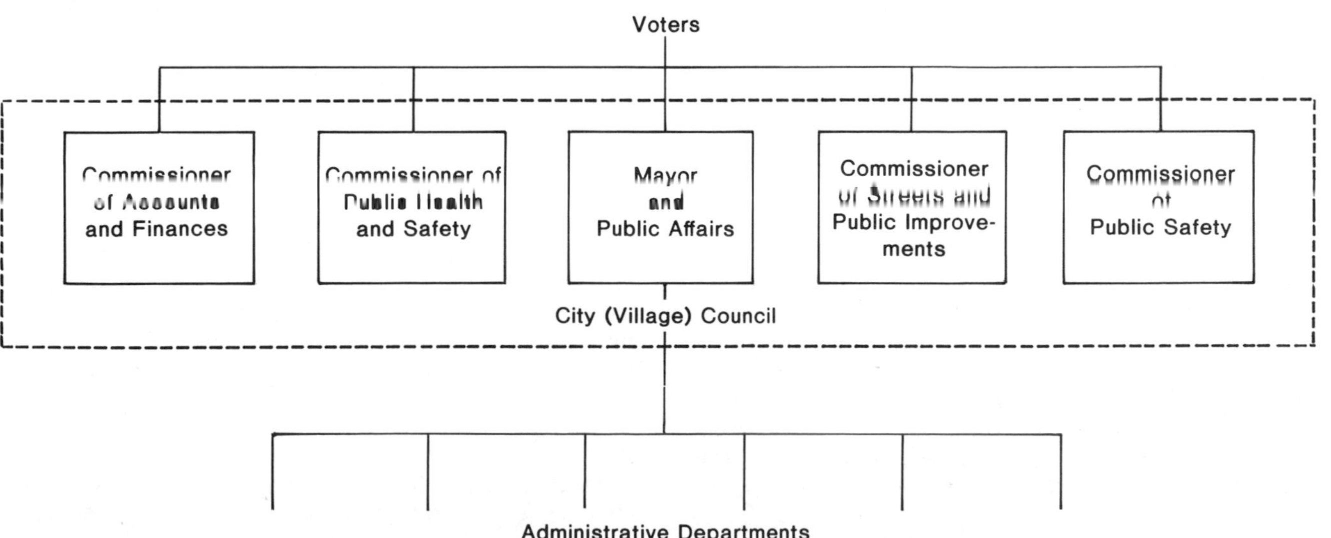

Figure 17-2. THE COMMISSION FORM

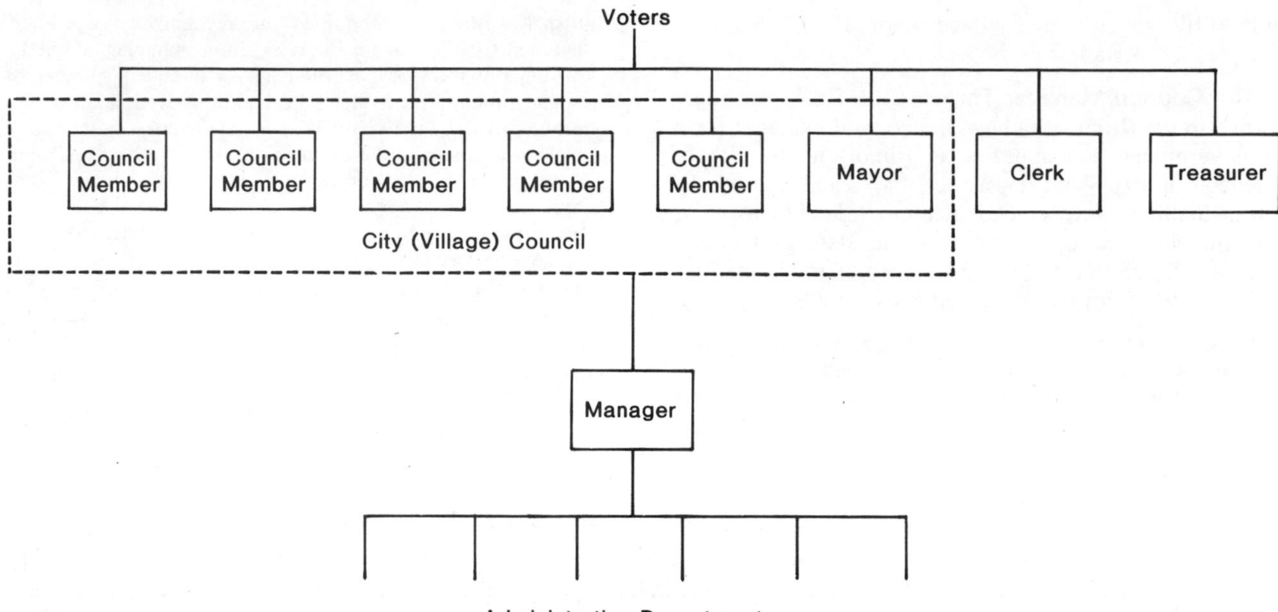

Figure 17-3. THE COUNCIL-MANAGER FORM

The administrator, or manager, appoints and removes all administrative officers and employees of the city, subject to applicable provisions of state law. He also serves as an advisor to the council on matters of policy and legislative concern. The council, in turn, has sole authority to pass ordinances, make municipal policy, and approve all expenses and liabilities of the municipality.

Although vested with considerable executive and administrative authority, city managers work as employees of the council, are subject to the supervision and direction of the council and may be removed by the council at any time. They do not serve fixed terms of office. Typically, persons are recruited to city manager positions who have had professional training and experience in the field of city management and administration.

The council manager form of government is graphically depicted in Figure 17-3, and is set forth in Illinois Statutes, Chapter 24, Article V.

The Strong Mayor/Council Form The strong mayor/council form of government is made available to Illinois cities and villages under Illinois Statutes, Chapter 24, Article VI. To date, no Illinois municipalities have chosen to organize themselves under these statutory provisions. In brief, the statutes provide a form of government under which the voters elect a mayor to be the chief executive and administrative officer of the city, a number of persons to the city council which exercises legislative authority, and an elected clerk and treasurer. The mayor, who may appoint a professional administrative officer as his assistant, has sole responsibility for the direction of the administrative activities of the city. The council, in turn, is responsible for policy making and for the approval of all municipal expenditures and liabilities.

Although they are legally organized under Article III, and thus under the weak mayor/council form of government, a number of Illinois cities have increased the administrative and executive powers of the mayor to the point at which these cities might more properly be said to be organized under the strong mayor/council form. Such strengthening of the mayor's position has been the intent, for example, of a number of State laws passed which apply exclusively to the city of Chicago. It was also the expressed intent of the city of Aurora when it utilized home rule powers to establish its present form of government shortly after voters decided in 1976 to abandon the commission form of government.

Administrative Departments Once the form of government has been established which provides for a structure for the exercise of legislative and executive authority, Illinois cities and villages are free to establish their own departmental structures for the administration of their affairs. Practices in the State vary widely, depending upon the services offered by a particular municipality, the form of government being used and the local preferences of individual municipalities. Departments are usually provided, however, to provide for police protection, fire protection street construction and maintenance, and water and sewer services. Other administrative departments commonly found in cities include parks, library, human resources, cival defense, planning, urban renewal, finance, personnel and health.

Forms of County Government

There are three different formats available to Illinois counties for the organization of their legislative and executive functions. These are the county board form, the county commission form and the county executive form. Each of these are described below. In addition, Cook County has its own, unique form of government prescribed by the Illinois Constitution. This is described in the next subsection of this chapter.

These differences in legislative/executive structure do not carry over into variations in county administrative organization. The administrative structure is usually provided through a combination of elected county administrative officers and special county boards and committees. Variations in such administrative practice from county to county are functions of population size and local choice rather than form of county government. Accordingly, these administrative practices are summarized after the description of the three alternative forms of county government.

The County Board System This is the most common form of county government utilized in Illinois. Eighty-four of the State's 102 counties currently utilize this system for the organization of their legislative/executive functions.

Under this form, the legislative and executive functions of the county are vested in a county board which, in turn, is composed of individuals elected from districts within the county. Prior to 1969, Illinois townships comprised the electoral districts for the county board. Each township in the county sent one or more representatives to serve on the county board. The result was that county boards became very large, and not all persons in the county were equally represented on the county board.

Since 1969, county boards have been limited to a maximum of 29 members, and county board districts must be as nearly equal as possible in population in order to conform to the "one man-one vote" principle of representation laid down by the United States Supreme Court. As a result, county boards are now smaller and more equally apportioned, but the typical county board in Illinois is still extraordinarily large in size, with 15 to 29 members.

The chairman of the county board is elected from among the membership of the board by the members of the board. As a result, the county board form has no elected executive officer chosen at large by the voters of the county. The county board chairman presides at meetings of the board, but has few other executive or administrative functions. The county board's administrative duties are usually handled through board committees.

County Commission Plan The second alternative form available to Illinois counties is the county commission plan. This form is currently used by 17 counties in Illinois. With few exceptions, these counties are located in the southern part of the State and along the southern portions of the Mississippi and Illinois. These are areas which were initially settled by migrants from the southern part of the United States who brought with them a nontownship form of government.

In the county commission, or non-township form, the county board consists of three commissioners elected at large. One commissioner is elected each November for a three year term. The county board, known as the board of commissioners, annually elects one of its members as chairman. This office is usually rotated among the three members of the board. As in the county board form, the board of commissioners holds all legislative/executive powers in the county and is responsible for all county administrative function not otherwise asigned to elected county administrative officers.

County Executive Form This form of government was made available to Illinois counties by statute after the adoption of the 1970 Illinois Constitution. It was designed to meet the constitutional requirements for county home rule, so that any county which adopts this organizational format would simultaneously be empowered to exercise home rule powers. As of late 1979, however, none had yet adopted this form of organization, although it had been submitted to the voters for approval in nine counties.

Under this organizational format, legislative and executive powers are divided. Legislative powers are vested in a county board elected either at large or from districts as in the other alternative forms, but all executive powers are vested in a single county official, called the county executive, who is elected at large by the voters of the county.

The county executive officer serves a four-year term and is not a member of the county board. Among his powers are the following: (1) administer all county departments except those under the jurisdiction of other elected officers; (2) prepare an annual budget and submit it to the county board for approval; (3) appoint members to county boards and commissions, to special districts located within the county, and all other county employees, with the approval of the county board; (4) preside over county board meetings, but without the power of voting on business that comes before the board; and (5) approve or veto ordinances passed by the county board (such vetoes can be overridden by a three-fifths vote of the county board).

County Administration Delegates to the 1970 Illinois Constitutional Convention set the adoption of the county executive form of government as a precondition for the bestowal of home rule powers upon a county government for two reasons. First, the delegates sought to encourage the modernization of county government which had not been substantially altered or changed during the State's history and which was not designed to provide effective government in heavily populated, urbanized areas. Second, the delegates wanted some assurance against the grant of home rule powers to governmental units which lacked the organizational capacity to exercise such powers effectively. Specifically, the delegates wanted an organizational structure for county government which would provide clear lines of executive and administrative authority in county government, and maximize the potentials for coordination among the units of county government.[39]

Counties organized under the county board and county commission format are hampered by the absence of clearly defined lines of administrative authority and by difficulties in securing coordination among operating departments. Part of the difficulty stems from the large number of elected county officers. The Constitution requires that each county elect a sheriff, a county clerk and a county treasurer. Since it was required under the previous constitution, most counties elect also a coroner, a clerk of the circuit court and a state's attorney. Counties over 60,000 elect a county recorder. Many counties also elect an assessor, an auditor and a county superintendant of schools. Finally, some counties also elect officials to one or more of the following: board of assessors, board of review, county board of school trustees. Since such elected officials are not subject to the supervision and jurisdiction of the county board, problems of the coordination of county government operations quite obviously increase as the number of such elected county officials increases.

County administrative departments which do not fall under the jurisdiction of a separately elected official, such as the county highway department or the county welfare department, are generally administered in county board counties by a committee of the county board. Some county institutions, such as a tuberculosis sanitorium or a public library, are managed by separate boards, appointed by the county board. Thus, county administration in most Illinois counties is administered by a haphazard, disjointed collection of elected officials, county board committees, separately elected boards and appointed boards. It is this administrative diversification that has led to widespread criticism of county government in Illinois, and to the 1970 Constitutional Convention's insistance that home rule be given only to those counties which established elected executive administration of county affairs.

Government in the Chicago Area

Because its population, size and density makes it so totally different from any other part of the State, the Chicago area has unique, individualized arrangements for its local government system. These unique arrangements apply both to the City of Chicago and to Cook County in which the city is located.

According to the U.S. Census Bureau, the Chicago area is made up of six Illinois counties: Cook, DuPage, Kane, Lake, McHenry and Will. Governments in the other five counties and all Chicago-area local governments except the City of Chicago itself operate under the same governmental laws, forms and structures applicable in the rest of the State. Because of their distinctiveness, however, the governments for the City of Chicago and Cook County are described briefly below.

The City of Chicago The large size and, for Illinois at least, the unique problems of local government in Chicago have long given rise to demands from the city for specialized treatment in Illinois law. Thus, for example, the Illinois General Assembly has passed many laws applicable only to "cities over five hundred thousand in population." Obviously applying only to Chicago, this legal terminology has enabled the legislature to pass laws specifically applicable to the city without running afoul of the constitutional restriction against statutory enactments which apply to individual cities rather than to an entire class of cities. This special treatment of large cities is not unique to Illinois; New York State, for example, handles special legislation for New York City in a similar manner.

More importantly, these demands for specialized treatment have, for many years, given rise to efforts within the city to achieve home rule. Home rule in this context has meant for Chicago freedom from domination by the Illinois General Assembly and authorization to establish through local legislative action specialized laws, rules and regulations applicable only to the city. Home rule demands upon the Legislature were made frequently during the first six decades of this century, including an unsuccessful 1922 constitutional convention proposal which did reach the referendum stage. The Chicago Home Rule Commission had a long history of efforts to secure home rule for Chicago and published a major conpendium of its findings in 1954.[40] Chicago, along with all other municipalities in the State with a population of more than 25,000, finally achieved home rule status with the adoption of the 1970 Illinois Constitution.[41]

Chicago's city government is divided between a legislative and an executive branch. The legislative branch, the Chicago City Council, is composed of fifty aldermen elected for four-year terms on nonpartisan ballots. Each alderman represents one of the city's 50 wards. The council exercises all powers not conferred on other officials of the city government, including the power to enact local laws or ordinances, to amend and pass an annual appropriation ordinance, to borrow funds, to levy taxes, to provide city services, to approve mayoral appointees and to investigate all matters relating to the use of its legislative power in conducting city government business. A great deal of the council's work is accomplished through eighteen standing committees and special committees appointed by the mayor with the consent of the council (See Figure 17-4).

The City's executive authority resides in a mayor, city clerk, and city treasurer, each of whom are elected for four year terms on a partisan ballot. The chief executive officer is the mayor, who is responsible for directing city departments, appointing the heads of city departments and other agencies, presiding over meetings of the city council, and exercising a veto power over ordinances passed by the council.[42]

The office of Mayor of Chicago became perhaps the most powerful municipal office in the country during the 22-year tenure of the late Mayor Richard J. Daley. By combining the office of mayor with the office of chairman of the Cook County Democratic Central Committee, a combination of offices never previously experienced in Chicago history, Mayor Daley was able to gain

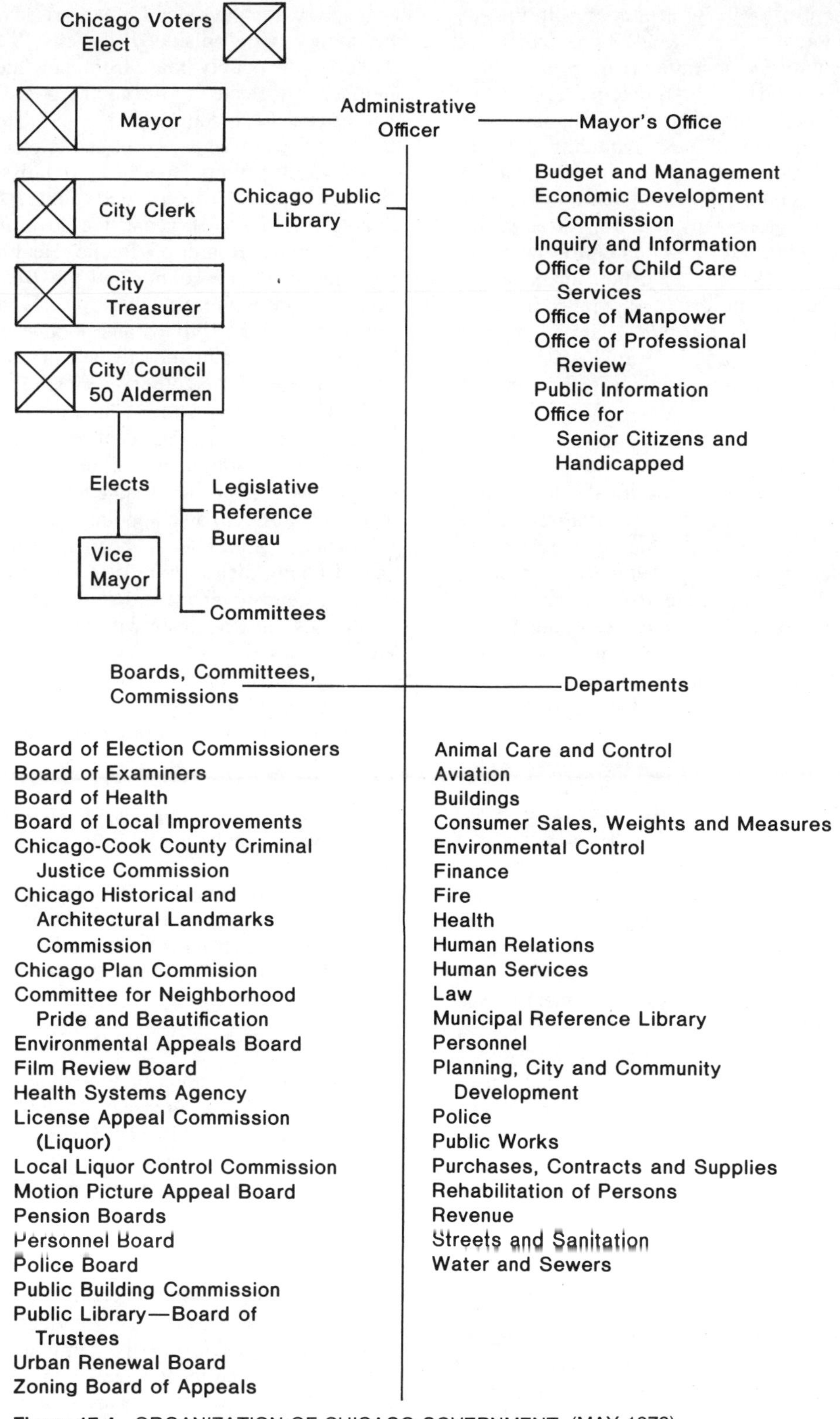

Figure 17-4 ORGANIZATION OF CHICAGO GOVERNMENT (MAY 1978)

Source: Illinois League of Women Voters, *The Key to Our Local Government* (Chicago: Citizens' Information Service of Illinois, 1978).

nearly complete control over the affairs of both the city and the local Democratic Party. Since Daley could use his power in the county Democratic organization to control the slating of candidates for municipal and county offices, and since the Democratic Party regularly won the vast majority of such offices, including approximately 80 percent or more of the city's aldermanic posts, Daley was able to maintain substantial control over elective officers in the city. Furthermore, through the mayoral office Daley was also able to control the political patronage jobs necessary to give him unchallenged control over the Democratic Party apparatus from his post as county chairman. As a result, Daley's power to enact ordinances, direct the administrative affairs of the city, and fashion the city's public policies was never publicly disputed.[43]

The jobs of mayor and Cook County Democratic Party chairman were given to separate individuals after Daley's death in 1976. Since local political leaders claim that the two jobs will not again be centralized in the hands of one person, it is unlikely that any single political leader will ever again attain Daley's power in the City of Chicago. The Democratic Party's candidate to succeed Daley was subsequently defeated in the Democratic primary election of 1979 by an independent Democrat. As a result, as of late 1979, it was still too early to determine what the extent of the mayor's power will be in the post-Daley era.

Chicago's clerk and treasurer have been largely ministerial positions, with little or no apparent public impact on the formation of public policy or the exercise of governmental authority in the city. The functions of the city clerk are: (1) to act as parliamentarian and recordkeeper for the city council and (2) to supervise the issuance of licenses after they have been granted by the mayor.

The city treasurer's job is to serve as the custodian of the city's funds and as ex officio treasurer for the Chicago Board of Education.

Chicago has a vice mayor, a member of the Council who holds that designation and serves as interim mayor in the event that a vacancy occurs in the mayor's office. The city also has an official known as a deputy mayor who, together with five other administrative assistants, serves as the assistant to the mayor. The deputy mayor is expected to supervise the daily operations of all city departments, boards, commissions and other agencies.[44]

The Government of Cook County Cook County is governed by the county board president, a county board composed of sixteen members or commissioners and by eight other elected administrative officers. Voters must elect circuit court judges and two members of the county's tax appeal board. In addition to the county board president, the elected administrative officers are: sheriff, county clerk, treasurer, assessor, superintendant of educational service region, state's attorney, recorder of deeds and clerk of the circuit court.

For electoral purposes, the county is divided into two districts. The first district is comprised of the City of Chicago, while the second is comprised of that portion of the county lying outside of the city. Ten members are elected to the county board from the Chicago district; six members are elected to the county board from the suburban district. Each county board candidate runs at large in the district from which he or she is elected.

The Cook County Board of Commissioners exercises the legislative powers of the county. In addition, the County Board also serves as the governing board of the Cook County Board of Public Health, the planning commission of the county and the Board of the Cook County Forest Preserve District. Finally, the Board levies taxes and approves and adopts the budget of the Cook County Health and Hospitals Governing Commission, but exercised no other responsibility over the affairs of the Commission from 1970–1979.

The County Board President serves as the chief executive officer and administers all departments of the county except those under the jurisdiction of other elected officers. The president also appoints the heads of county departments, commissions, boards, committees and all special taxing district boards in the county whose jurisdiction extends over more than one township. These appointments must be made with the consent of the county board.

The president of the county board may or may not choose to run as a commissioner. In any event, the board president has the same voting privilege as other members of the board, but cannot vote a second time as presiding officer. The president also has the power to veto ordinances, resolutions or motions passed by the board, but can be overridden by a four-fifths vote of the members of the board.

Since the County Board President is elected at large in the county, Cook County qualifies as a home rule unit under the 1970 Illinois Constitution. The county has made liberal use of its home rule powers.[45]

Local Political Systems

Structural discussions of governmental and administrative systems do not present a complete picture of the operational realities of local government. Equally important, some would say more important, are the systems within which political forces operate to determine who holds elective office, who will exercise the powers of government on a daily basis and what influences will be brought to bear upon the determination of public policy and the delivery of governmental services. To a considerable degree these forces are described in other chapters of this book. Because of their importance, and to emphasize their essential linkages with administrative systems, these political systems are summarized in an overview fashion in the following paragraphs, with this caveat: any attempt to summarize, in a few paragraphs, the operating political system of over six thousand units of local government must necessarily be based upon a high degree of generalization. This is particularly true in a state as large and diverse as Illinois: the observer of local politics in Illinois can find examples of virtually any kind of political system and every kind of political practice. The description below is a generalized summation of the typical patterns and most common practices which can be found throughout the state.

It is also important to note that the generalizations which follow do not apply to the City of Chicago or to Cook County. As already noted, these governmental units, by their vast population size and complex service demands, are a case apart which bear little resemblance to other local government units in the state. Generalizations about government and politics in Illinois local government which are based upon either Chicago or Cook County are necessarily bound to be in error. Since the political systems of these units are well discussed elsewhere in this book, the descriptions which follow in this section of this chapter will not be based upon the realities or experiences in either of these two governmental jurisdictions.

Partisanship in Local Government

With very few exceptions, elections for political office in Illinois local governments are legally partisan in nature. That is to say, the statutes under which Illinois local governments are established contemplate, and provide for, partisan elections to fill elective offices. Most county government elections run true to this form, with candidates for office indicating on the electoral ballot whether they are identified with the Republican or Democratic Party. Most Illinois counties are "one party" counties, however. Thus, while both parties can, and usually do, run candidates for political office, the candidates of one party win election to most offices in nearly all cases. In such counties, then, one must identify with the majority party to have any substantial prospect for election to public office.

Most Illinois city and village elections are essentially nonpartisan in nature. That is to say, most candidates for elective city or village office do not identify themselves with one of the major national political parties. In such instances, they will file for office as independents. In other words, even though they may be identified with one of the major political parties, such identification will not show on the election ballot. Further, in such instances, these candidates usually receive neither support nor backing from a national or state political party organization. Even if such candidates' party identifications are generally known publicly, they are considered to be nonpartisan candidates if a party affiliation is not given for them on the ballot.

In other instances, candidates for municipal office affiliate with a local political organization established solely for the purpose of sponsoring candidates for office in that locality. Operating under such names as "Citizens Party" or "People's Party," these local parties may be organized and operated by several candidates who run together as a slate, or in many instances they are organized and operated by a coalition or caucus of local citizens who use such a local party structure as a vehicle for influencing the outcome of local elections. Sometimes such parties are organized just for particular elections, and then dissolved. In other communities, however, such parties have operated over a period of many years, sometimes using the same name and sometimes using the same structure but different names in different elections. While elections involving such parties are, legally and strictly speaking, partisan in nature, they tend effectively to be nonpartisan since national party labels, and hence national party identifications and loyalties, are not involved.

In some few cases—such as elections for aldermen in Chicago, elections of the mayor and commissioners in cities operating under the commission form, and elections for mayor and councilmen in Aurora—municipal elections are legally required to be nonpartisan. In such instances, neither national party nor local party affiliations may be mentioned on election ballots.

In general, then, elections to Illinois county offices are legally partisan in nature. With the exception of mayoral elections in the larger cities, however, most elections for municipal office are effectively, although not legally, nonpartisan in nature.

Political Actors

While local political systems vary greatly from community to community, the kinds of people who are influential in local affairs tend to be similar. These include elected officials; politicians; interest groups, such as business, labor, industry, developers, neighborhood organizations, and others with special concerns; the media; and local government employees.

A local government's elected officials are an obvious element of political influence. The amount of influence exercised by any particular official, however, varies widely. Some locally elected officials are bright, active and enthusiastic in the fulfillment of their public obligations, while others see their elective office as a civic duty to be performed, and maintain as low a profile in local affairs as possible. Other factors affecting the amount of power and influence exercised by any particular local official include the individual official's ability, extent of contact in the community, length of tenure in office, and time and effort devoted to official duties. In many communities, one or two elected officials will have held office for many years. Such persons often assume a high degree of political influence simply because they become the source of local expertise on "how we solved this problem the last time we had it."

Interestingly, however, locally elected officials tend not to play politically influential roles in the affairs of area local governments other than the one on which they serve. That is to say, elected county officials tend to have little involvement or influence in the affairs of municipalities within the county, and vice versa. Similarly, elected members of park boards and school boards tend to have little influence in municipal affairs, and municipal officials similarly tend to maintain a "hands off" attitude toward the affairs of special districts in the area. This is not to say that there is necessarily little cooperation between units of local government serving the same area, although frequently a lack of cooperation is the rule. It is to say, rather, that such cooperation and coordination as does exist is usually carried out by administrative and executive officers rather than by elected members of governing bodies.

Politicians should be considered as a separate group of influentials in local government affairs because most locally elected officials do not perceive themselves to be "politicians." That term, rather, is usually perceived to apply to those persons who are active, on a continuing basis, in the local affairs of national political parties. The term "politicians," then, would refer to such persons as officers in the local county party organization, ward and precinct captains, elected members of the Illinois General Assembly, and persons holding patronage appointments in county and State government agencies. Because of their role in legislative activity, members of the General Assembly can be influential, if they choose, in the affairs of local governments within their legislative districts. More typically, however, they prefer to remain aloof from involvement in local political matters. Behind the scenes, however, they can be influential, particularly in the community in which they reside. Otherwise, politicians tend to be influential in those local governments which elect their officers on a partisan basis. This, as already noted, applies primarily to counties and to larger cities where the mayors are elected on partisan ballots. In nonpartisan communities, however, local politicians rarely seek to play much of a role in local affairs, and frequently will find that their efforts to do so are resented by locally elected officials who prefer to maintain their nonpartisan image.

The relative power and influence of different interest groups varies widely from community to community. In some communities, business groups, such as the chamber of commerce, have extraordinary influence. In other communities, however, neighborhood groups or other special interest organizations may tend to play a dominant role. Most studies of community power and influence find that interests tend to be influential on the resolution of issues in which they are directly interested and involved, but tend to have very little influence on other kinds of issues. Thus, for example, business groups tend to play a very influential role in questions of business regulation, industrial expansion and business zoning, but tend not to become involved or influential in questions relating to matters such as the development of park facilities, residential zoning or the design of service programs for juvenile and senior citizens. Similarly, local religious leaders might attempt to exert influence on matters relating to juvenile and senior citizen programs, but would not become involved in questions of industrial development.

A local source of political pressure of major importance, particularly in suburban communities and larger cities in out-state areas, is the land developer. Regardless of whether their primary interest is related to residential, commercial or industrial development, developers tend to have a major economic stake in local government policies and are a constant source of pressure on county boards and municipal councils for decisions that will increase the profitability of their developmental efforts. As a result, they frequently put substantial amounts of time and money into their efforts to influence the outcome of local policy deliberations.[46]

The mass media—local newspapers and radio stations—have a substantial influence on local government affairs. Such an influence, of course, is exercised only in those communities systematically covered by the media; many small communities are not regularly covered by interpretative radio or newspaper reporters. Sometimes the media influence stems from the media's effectiveness in influencing public opinion. More frequently, media influence appears to stem from the respect which local government officials have for the images which the media portrays of them. Local officials are, consequently, highly sensitive to the professional abilities of local reporters and tend to pattern their behavior accordingly.

Finally, because they deliver local government service and because they help to shape the perspective of local officials on problems, local government employees play a substantial role in decisions affecting local policies and service delivery. The more closely a local government employee works with the city council, the more influential he or she tends to become in local government affairs. Thus, city managers or administrators, where they are employed, tend to be highly influential. Department heads, similarily, tend to have a high degree of influence.

Local employees tend to be of two kinds: professionals and locals. Professionals are those persons whose primary attachment is to a career in local government. Such persons are typically characterized by specific training for their profession, continuing involvement in training for professional advancement, a close identification with professional associations, and a commitment to continue in their present profession whether in the community currently employing them or in some other community. These persons, when they change jobs, are most likely to find a similar position, or an advanced position in the same profession, in another community. Locals, on the other hand, tend to be persons whose primary identification is with employment in a particular community or geographic locale, and who work for local government because that is the best career opportunity available to them at the moment. If their employment with the local government is terminated, such persons typically look for employment in another job or occupation in the community, rather than looking for a similar professional opportunity in another local governmental unit elsewhere. Such persons may be highly trained, but typically are less concerned with professional development than they are with the maintenance of their personal life style in the community. Professionals are very influential in some communities; locals have more "political clout" in others.

Political Systems

As noted earlier, these sources of political influence tend to blend together differently in different communities. Several common types of combinations can be identified, and these are described in the following paragraphs. It should be noted at the outset, however, that not every community in any particular environment necessarily manifests all, or even any, of the traits generally described for that environment.

The Small Town System Local elected officials in small communities are able to devote only a small portion of their time to municipal affairs, as their obligations to their professional employment and their families take priority. While well meaning and hard working, such officials typically have little background or expertise in local government, and have only a very limited amount of time which they can devote to training sessions, conferences and other ways of acquiring more knowledge and information about their professional obligations.

Because small communities typically have nonpartisan elections, local politicians tend to play a relatively insignificant role in local public affairs. Similarly, local interest groups tend to be headed by part time, volunteer leaders who lack professional staff. As a result, interest group activities also tend to be handled on an amateurish and "time available" basis. Public employees, too, tend to be of the local variety, especially since salary levels are not high enough to attract persons with a career orientation to professional local government. In such an environment, developers, because they are full time, professional persons whether working in large or small communities, are frequently more knowledgable about local government policies, procedures and methods than are the local government officials with whom they are dealing. In such a situation, developers are frequently more successful in influencing public policy outcomes in their own favor.

Essentially, then, the small town local government, characteristically found in most rural counties as well as in most small communities, is a governmental pattern based upon the efforts of dedicated, hard working, but part time, volunteer laymen. In many respects, government at this level may be more hard-pressed to achieve optimum levels of operational efficiency, but clearly this system typifies "grass roots" democracy.

The Suburban System Many suburban communities in Illinois present a rather sharp contrast to the small town system. While the public officials are similarly part-time laymen, many of them are persons who are employed in managerial or executive positions with local business or industry, either in the community, in an adjacent community or in the central city to which the suburb is economically attached. As a result, even though they lack a background of knowledge in local government affairs, they bring with them a substantial, relevant frame of reference in organizational management. Such officials, too, are more likely to employ city or village managers and other professionally oriented local government employees since they are accustomed, in their business lives, to seeking out professionally skilled and competent persons for managerial positions. The expertise of local government employees, accordingly, tends to be relatively high.

Interest group participants in the suburban milieu may be of two different varieties. Neighborhood and special interest spokespersons tend to be, as in the small town system, part time laypersons who are able to apply only limited time and skill to their efforts to influence local government. Because of the larger scale of business and economic enterprise in metropolitan areas, however, many business, industry, labor, and other interest groups have access to full time, professional consultants which they employ in their dealings with local governments. Developers, too, employ highly paid professional consultants to assist them in their dealings with the municipality, particularly since suburban developments tend to offer the promise of substantial financial profits.

Because of the influence of the metropolitan press, which gives little coverage to suburban local government activities, the major media influences tend to be less in suburban areas. Nonetheless, suburban government officials remain highly sensitive to the reports on their activities which are contained in their neighborhood and community newspapers, so that press influence continues to be a substantial consideration.

The typical suburban political system, then, is one characterized by a high degree of professional expertise, even though many of the participants are part time laypersons. Further, since suburban residents tend to have a weak identification with the community in which they live, and thus pay less attention to community affairs, the influence of pressure groups and other interested parties tends to be proportionately stronger in suburban government than is usually the case in "out-state" local governments.

The Out-State City System Out-state cities, communities with populations in excess of approximately 20,000, tend to represent a middleground between the small town system and the suburban system. In such communities, elected officials are also predominantly part time and most public employees are of the local variety, but enough of them have developed professional associations to give a higher level of professional identification and competence to the ranks of public employees. Some interest groups, such as chambers of commerce and labor organizations, do have professional staffs which develop a substantial measure of competence in dealing with local government officials and policies. Politicians, too, tend to take a higher degree of interest in the larger out-state communities, with the result that they are more apt to exercise influence in local government affairs. Finally, most larger out-state communities have local news media which provides close and continuing coverage of local government affairs.

As a result, the typical pattern in out-state communities is one in which the affairs of government tend to place very heavy time demands upon part time local officials, severely limiting the amount of time such officials can spend on any particular issue. The persons with whom such officials must deal tend to be a blend of professionals and locals among their public employees, with a substantial number of skilled professionals bringing

TABLE 17-4
State-Local Administrative Relations, by Selected Functions and Source of Primary Funding

Source of primary funding	State mandates function, local unit provides service	State permits function, local unit provides service
Substantial State funding[1]	State's Attorney Circuit Court Adult and Juvenile probation Elementary and secondary education	Nursing Home care for indigent Shelter care for indigent
Little or no State funding[2]	Sheriff's department Property assessment Elections administration County Board of Health	Municipal police Fire protection Waste disposal County Health Department Municipal Health Department

[1]Levels of State funding vary from one function to another and, in the case of public education, from one unit to another.
[2]Small grants are available to law enforcement agencies through the Illinois Law Enforcement Commission. The State pays one-half of the salary of County Supervisors of Assessment but provides no other support for this function (*IRS*, Chapter 120, Section 464b).
Source: *Illinois Revised Statutes (1977)* and interviews with local officials.

pressure to bear upon them from local public interest groups. Frequently caught in a cross fire between their own public employees and local interest groups, and with too little time to devote to any one issue, public officials in such communities are less likely than their suburban counterparts to follow the advice and direction of their own employees. Furthermore, because there tends to be a relatively high degree of citizen interest in, and identification with, local affairs, these public officials tend to be highly sensitive to media coverage and to public perceptions of their performance in office.

As a result, the out-state city system tends to be a form of political environment which places tremendous pressures on the part time, locally elected officials. Public interest and concern for their behavior tends to be high, both quantitatively and qualitatively. Pressures from interest groups tend to be severe, well planned and well executed. Support from their local employees tends to be less grounded in professional expertise and less compelling in any event. As a result, the burdens upon such officials are immense, and the performance of government is affected.

Conclusion Obviously, such models are ideal types. Few communities exemplify totally the traits described above for any one community type; most communities will exhibit the traits of two or three of these models. The models do suggest, however, that local political systems are a composite of many variables, that these variables interact differently in different settings, and that individual communities do tend as a result to develop highly idiosyncratic cultures within which their local governing systems operate.

State-Local Administrative Relationships

Local Units as Administrative Subdivisions

Local units of government in Illinois are often seen as mere subdivisions of the State, linked by law and tradition in a superior (State)-subordinate (local unit) relationship. In terms of the legal right to exist and function, this is true. All units derive their existence and function from State law and constitution. Even the home rule municipality or county may find its powers limited or denied by action of the State legislature (1970 Constitution, Article VII, Sectons 6(g) & (h)). There are numerous functions performed by local units, however, which are permitted rather than mandated, and it is necessary to distinguish among these so as to avoid falling into the belief that there are no options available to local units.

Table 17-4 illustrates four general patterns of administrative relationship between the State and local units of government. These are based on the degree to which the State mandates or permits an activity by a local unit and the extent of financial support provided by each level of government. The table is selective, using a limited number of examples to illustrate each category. It does not include those governmental activities in which, by law, the State enables a local unit to engage in an activity and receive federal funds (public housing, urban renewal).

State Mandate-Local Funding One of the clearest examples of a State-mandated function with the local unit providing funding is the operation of the county sheriff's office. The office is established by Constitution (Article VII, Section 4(c)), general duties are set forth in law (Illinois Revised Statutes, Chapter 125, Section 15), and the county is directed to pay the sheriff a salary within a range stipulated by law (*IRS,* Chapter 53, Section 37a) and to defray expenses related to performance of duties. The State does not provide funding for the office, although many of the duties performed relate to enforcement of State law and providing service to the courts.

State Mandate-Shared Funding Article X, Section 1 of the Illinois Constitution states that "Education in public schools through the secondary level shall be free." This provision, which has been in effect in modified form for more than a century, has resulted in a complex system of State-local relations, both in terms of administration and funding. Although an elected State Board of Education, an appointed chief State educational officer and an office of education have replaced the elected Superintendent of Public Instruction, the primary role of the State in public education relates to policy and money. The State promulgates rules and regulations providing for teacher certification, minimum content of curriculum and various other aspects of education, but locally elected or appointed boards of education oversee the actual delivery of public schooling. Funding is through a combination of local property taxes and State aid. State aid is allocated inversely to the assessed value of taxable property per pupil within the local school district.

Other mandated functions in which the State provides substantial funding include the county office of State's Attorney, the Circuit Court with at least one judge elected from each county, and the adult and juvenile probation offices. All are imposed by State law or constitution, but substantial State funds are provided. For example, two-thirds of the State's Attorney's salary is paid by the State (*IRS,* Chapter 53, Section 7). Judges and probation officers are also paid in part by the state.

State Permits-Shared Funding There are few activities where the State both permits the local unit to provide a service and supplies substantial funds to support it. One important function is the provision of nursing home care for indigent persons, especially the elderly. Creation of such facilities is optional for counties (*IRS,* Chapter 34, Section 5361 *et seq.*). Once created, however, most of the costs of maintaining indigent residents in such homes are borne by the State through support payments from the Illinois Department of Public Aid. The same is true in the case of sheltered care facilities, which are authorized by the same law. Policy in these programs is heavily influenced by the availability of federal funding.

State Permits-Local Funding The majority of functions performed by local units of government are permitted by State law and no funds are directly allocated for their support. These functions include municipal police services, waste disposal, fire protection and a wide variety of other services provided by both general and limited purpose governments. In most cases these are funded from local property taxes, user fees, licenses, sales taxes and other revenues available to local units. Some State funding is provided in the form of shared income tax but, as shown in Table 17-2 this constitutes a small part of the total revenue of counties and municipalities. It is not available to other local units.

Conclusion

Local units of government in Illinois perform important functions and provide vital services to their citizens. In some cases (police protection, waste disposal) the local unit is completely responsible for funding and performance, while in others (courts, education) there is a sharing of financial and administrative responsibility between the State and the local unit. It is clear, therefore, that local units in Illinois are essential to the accomplishment of public goals within the existing framework of government. Moreover, the strong tradition of local governance which evolved in America militates in favor of the continuation of local citizen involvement in policy-making and implementation. It is equally clear, however, that the State often imposes a heavy burden of local responsibility without providing adequate financial support. The rule of Justice Dillon continues to hang heavy over local governments in Illinois, and its onerous effects are only partially mitigated by the 1970 Constitution. Local government remains, as a theory of national or state sovereignty demands it must, subject to the ultimate control and direction of the superior jurisdiction.

NOTES

[1]United States, Department of Commerce, Bureau of the Census, *Census of Governments, 1977* (Washington, D.C.: U.S. Government Printing Office, 1977).

[2]See, for instance, Alice L. Ebel, "Local Government Outside Cook County," in *Con-Con: Issues for the Illinois Constitutional Convention,* ed. by Samuel K. Gove and Victoria Ranney (Urbana: University of Illinois Press, 1970), pp. 203–227. See also David Kenney, *Basic Illinois Government* (Carbondale: Southern Illinois University Press, 1970), p. 245.

[3]Harold F. Alderfer, *American Local Government and Administration* (New York: The Macmillan Co., 1956), p. 2–3.

[4]Donald Foster Stetzer, "*Special Districts in Cook County: Toward a Geography of Local Government,*" Department of Geography Research Paper No. 169, University of Chicago, 1975, pp. 12–13. Stetzer provides a survey of the history of special district government as a prelude to a case analysis of Cook County.

[5]*Ibid.*, p. 14.

[6]United States, Department of Commerce, Bureau of the Census, *op. cit.*, Vol. 1, Governmental Organization.

[7]See, for instance, Committee for Economic Development, *Modernizing Local Government* (The Committee, 1966); National Commission on Urban Problems, *Building the American City* (Washington, D.C.: U.S. Government Printing Office, 1968); Advisory Commission on Intergovernmental Relations, *Regional Decision-Making: New Strategies for Substate Districts* (Washington, D.C.: U.S. Government Printing Office, 1973).

[8]Commission on Urban Area Government, "Legislative Recommendations for Structural Modernization of Local Government," staff paper prepared January, 1971 for the Governor and General Assembly of the State of Illinois.

[9]For a thorough discussion of Jefferson's concept of local government, see Anwar Syed, *The Political Theory of American Local Government* (New York: Random House, 1968), especially ch. 3.

[10]*Ibid.*, p. 19.

[11]For further information on the corruption in local governance during the last half of the nineteenth century, see Alexander B. Callow, *The Tweed Ring* (New York: Oxford University Press, 1970); Lincoln Steffens, *The Shame of the Cities* (New York: Hill and Wang, 1957), and for an alternate perspective, William L. Riordan, *Plunkitt of Tammany Hall: A Series of Very Plain Talks on Very Practical Politics* (New York: A.A. Knopf, 1948).

[12]Constitution of the State of Illinois (1870), p. 9.

[13]Illinois Revised Statutes (1977), Ch. 24, Art. 4-1-1, *et seq* and Art. 5-1-1, *et seq.* Article and section numbers do not indicate the time when these forms were first provided in law because the statutes relating to municipal government were codified and reenacted as The Illinois Municipal Code in 1961. Although the provisions for council-manager government are found in Article 5, this form was not made available until the 1950's.

[14]*Ibid.*, Ch. 24, Art. 6-1-1, *et seq.*

[15]*1870 Illinois Constitution*, Art. X, sec. 8.

[16]Stetzer, *op. cit.*, at p. 50, provides a partial listing of the types of special districts and the date of passage of enabling legislation authorizing their creation. Almost one-half of the approximately twenty types of districts and authorities have been authorized since World War II.

[17]Syed, *op. cit.*, at ch. 3, offers a thorough discussion of the emergence of the case law which was summarized and published by Dillon. His *Commentaries* set forth the doctrine which became known as "Dillon's rule."

[18]*Rylands v. Clark*, 278 Ill. 44–45 (1917).

[19]United States, Depart. of Commerce, Bureau of the Census, *Census of the Population: 1970*, Vol. 1, Part 15, Illinois (Washington D.C.: U.S. Government Printing Office, 1971), Sec. 1, Table 3.

[20]The Illinois sales tax, or Retail Occupation Excise (*Illinois Revised Statutes*, Ch. 120, sec. 440 *et seq*) is imposed on purchases at retail, including food, clothing, and other essentials which must be purchased by all persons, regardless of socioeconomic status. The result is that low-income persons pay a disproportionate part of their income in sales taxes. The sales and property taxes, either directly or indirectly, are imposed on all consumers of retail goods and housing within the state.

[21]The Comptroller of the State of Illinois compiles annual reports on revenues collected, by source, and expenditures by units of local government throughout the state. These reports are issued under the title *1976 (etc.) Statewide Summary of (type of government) Finance in Illinois*.

[22]General obligation debt is that which is incurred against all taxable real and personal property within a jurisdiction and constitutes a claim against taxes paid by owners of such property. This is in contrast to revenue debt, which is an obligation against receipts from the sale of public goods or services such as municipally distributed water, electric power, or sewerage collection and disposal.

[23]For example, the Chicago Metropolitan Sanitary District may incur debt up to five percent of the assessed value of all property within its jurisdiction (*Illinois Revised Statutes*, Ch. 42, sec. 328), park districts up to two and one-half percent (Ch. 105, sec. 6-2), tuberculosis sanitarium districts up to one-half of one percent (Ch. 34, sec. 5216), and so on for the approximately twenty types of special districts authorized by Illinois law.

[24]The appointment of officers of special districts by the judiciary was not unique to Illinois. By 1970 the number of such appointments had become a significant burden on the courts, and one unrelated to their primary function. The Local Government Committee of the Sixth Illinois Constitutional Convention proposed and saw adopted an alternative which prohibited appointments by the judiciary. The General Assembly has since provided by law for appointment of most special district officers by chairmen of boards of counties in which the districts are located, subject to approval by the appropriate county boards.

[25]United States, Department of Commerce, Bureau of the Census, *Census of Governments, 1977, op. cit.*, Vol. 6, No. 4, Historical Statistics on Governmental Finance and Employment, p. 60.

[26]Thomas Vocino, *Professional, Administrative and Technical Manpower in Illinois Local Government* (Carbondale: Public Affairs Research Bureau, Southern Illinois University, 1969), at ch. 4. See also Table 20, Vol. 6, No. 4 of United States, Department of Commerce, Bureau of the Census, *op. cit.*, which illustrates that the proportion of persons serving in professional and technical capacities (social welfare, health and hospitals, education) increased from about fifty-three percent of public employees in the state in 1953 to sixty-three percent in 1972. Employment in education doubled, that in social welfare increased more than three-fold, and in health and hospitals it more than doubled.

[27]As of 1979 Lake, McLean, Peoria and St. Clair Counties are known to have created an office of county board secretary, assistant, or administrator under authority found in Article VII, Section 4(c) of the *1970 Illinois Constitution*.

[28]House Bill 777, introduced in the First Session, 81st General Assembly (1979) would create the elective office of Multi-Township Assessor and require pre-election qualifications for candidates.

[29]Samuel K. Gove and Thomas R. Kitsos, *Revision Success: The Sixth Illinois Constitutional Convention* (New York: National Municipal League, 1974), pp. 46–47. Gove and Kitsos are among a number of authors who have analyzed the product of the 1970 Convention and found it to be innovative in many areas but not a radical reconstitution of Illinois state or local government.

[30]David R. Beam, *et al*, eds., *County Home Rule in Illinois* (DeKalb: Center for Governmental Studies, Northern Illinois University, 1977), p. iii. This collection of essays is a brief but lucid analysis of the efforts of counties to adopt home rule by referendum since passage of the 1970 Constitution.

[31]Data is from *Home Rule Newsletter* (Champaign: Institute of Government and Public Affairs, University of Illinois), a periodic commentary published between November, 1972 and Fall, 1974.

[32]*Ibid.*

[33]*Ibid.*, No. 2, p. 2.

[34]Downstate counties (those outside the Chicago SMSA) known to have established administrative offices include McLean, Peoria and St. Clair counties. Other counties are either considering creation of a similar office or are using persons from other areas for liaison functions (personal observations from attendance at meetings of the Urban Counties Council of Illinois, 1979).

[35]Gove and Kitsos, *op. cit.*, p. 156.

[36]Numerous examples of intergovernmental cooperation are discussed in a handbook on *Intergovernmental Cooperation In Illinois*, prepared jointly by the Department of Local Government Affairs and the Northeastern Illinois Planning Commission and issued by the State of Illinois in March, 1976.

[37]Louis Ancel and Stewart H. Diamond, *Illinois Municipal Handbook* (1976–77 ed.; Springfield: Illinois Municipal League), p. 4.

[38]Robert A. Weidaw and James M. Banovetz, *City Management in Illinois* (Illinois City Management Association, 1978), p. 5.

[39]*Board of Proceedings of the 6th Illinois Constitutional Convention*, August 6, 1970, and September 3, 1970, John Lewis, Secretary of State, pp. 3242–3243 and 3303–3304.

[40]Chicago Home Rule Commission, *Chicago's Government*, 1954. The report was also published under the title *Modernizing a City Government* by the University of Chicago Press.

[41]League of Women Voters, *The Key to Our Local Government* (Chicago: Citizens' Information Service of Illinois, 1978), pp. 53–56.

[42]The council may, however, pass ordinances over a mayoral veto by a two-thirds vote.

[43]There have been many book-length treatments of the power of Mayor Daley over Chicago's government. The best treatments are: Bill Gleason, *Daley of Chicago* (New York: Simon and Schuster, 1970) and Milton Rakove, *Don't Make No Waves—Don't Back No Losers* (Bloomington: Indiana University Press, 1975); and *Don't Send Nobody Nobody Sent* (1979).

[44]The League of Women Voters, *op. cit.*, pp. 56–57.

[45]James M. Banovetz, "County Home Rule in Illinois: A Status Report and Perspective on the Future in *County Home Rule in Illinois*, ed. by David R. Beam, *et al.* (Northern Illinois University, Center for Government Studies, 1977), pp. 95–128. See especially the discussion at pp. 101–103.

[46]The reference here to money does not necessarily mean bribery or other forms of corruption, although corruption is likely to occur in these circumstances. Money is more frequently spent on legitimate purposes, such as the employment of lawyers, consultants and other experts.

ADDITIONAL REFERENCES

Banovetz, James M., "Modernizing County Government Without Home Rule," *Policy Issues* 3:4 (Summer, 1978).

Beam, David R., *et al.*, eds. *County Home Rule in Illinois*. DeKalb: Center for Governmental Studies, Northern Illinois University, 1977.

Cole, Stephanie. *Home Rule Handbook for Illinois Local Officials*. Urbana: Institute of Government and Public Affairs, University of Illinois, 1975.

Cole, Stephanie, ed. *The Local Government Committee Reconvenes: Home Rule and Intergovernmental Cooperation in Illinois*. Urbana: Institute of Government and Public Affairs, University of Illinois, 1975.

Duncombe, Herbert Sydney. *Modern County Government*. Washington, D.C. National Association of Counties, 1977.

Gove, Samuel K. and Thomas R. Kitsos. *Revision Success: The Sixth Illinois Constitutional Convention.* New York: National Municipal League, 1974.

Home Rule: An Annotated Bibliography with Emphasis on Illinois. Urbana: Institute of Government and Public Affairs, University of Illinois, 1974.

Illinois. *Intergovernmental Cooperation in Illinois,* Report prepared by the Department of Local Government Affairs and The Northeastern Illinois Planning Commission, March, 1976.

Judson, Harry Pratt. *The Government of Illinois.* New York: Manard, Merrill, & Co., 1900.

Pelekoudas, Lois M., ed. *Illinois Local Government.* Final Report and Background Papers, Assembly on Illinois Local Government. Urbana: University of Illinois, Bulletin Vol. 58, No. 67, May, 1961.

Research and Policy Committee. *Modernizing Local Government.* New York: Committee for Economic Development, July, 1966.

Research and Policy Committee. *Reshaping Government in Metropolitan Areas.* New York: Committee for Economic Development, February, 1970.

Stetzer, Donald Foster. *Special Districts in Cook County: Toward a Geography of Local Government.* Chicago: University of Chicago, Department of Geography Research Paper No. 169, 1975.

Syed, Anwar. *The Political Theory of American Local Government.* New York: Random House, 1966.

Torrence, Susan Walker. *Grass Roots Government: The County in American Politics.* Washington-New York: Robert B. Luce, Inc., 1974.

Vocino, Thomas. *Professional, Administrative and Technical Manpower in Illinois Local Government.* Carbondale: Public Affairs Research Bureau, Southern Illinois University, 1969.

Weidaw, Robert A. and James M. Banovetz. *City Management in Illinois.* Illinois City Management Association. (Undated mimeograph.)

Wilson, Thomas D. *Illinois County Government: An Introduction and Guide to Resources.* Prepared for the Urban Counties Council of Illinois, 105 West Adams Street, Chicago, Illinois, February, 1979. (Mimeograph.)

Wilson, Thomas D. *Illinois Local Government Under the 1970 Constitution.* Normal: Division of Continuing Education and Public Service, Illinois State University, February, 1975. (Mimeograph.)

CHAPTER **18**

Chicago Politics and Government

Dick Simpson

Chicago's government is so fragmented that we might rightly expect the City and metropolitan region to be ungovernable under such a system. Three million people live in the City and more than seven million people live in the region. When we recall that this is larger than the population of many small nations, the dysfunctional structures of local government become even more incomprehensible. Added to general population pressures are profound social and economic problems—ghettoes where thousands of poor people struggle desperately to survive harsh conditions; widening racial and economic barriers between rich and poor; dozens of warring ethnic groups; and many elderly living on fixed income, many illiterates and the sick. Who can hope to govern this cauldron of humanity, solve these deep social and economic problems, provide needed government services and maintain law and order? How can it be done?

To answer this question we need to consider at least six aspects of Chicago politics and government: 1) Chicago and Cook County's fragmented governmental framework, 2) its unified political structure despite voices of dissent, 3) the informal power structure which controls much of its government and politics, 4) the balance of power between ethnic and racial groups, 5) political and governmental decision-making processes and 6) the level of citizen participation. In a more complete analysis we also would have to consider social and economic conditions in depth. However, we will focus in this chapter on aspects of politics and government in order to answer only who can rule, who does rule and what are the effects of their rule?

A Fragmented Governmental Framework

Chicago and its metropolitan region are not governed by a single government but by hundreds of local units of government of different sizes, structures, rules and powers. It is a governmental jigsaw puzzle built ad hoc over the last 150 years to meet continual emergencies caused by previously inadequate government unable to cope with the problems of a growing region.

Briefly the governmental history of Chicago is as follows.[1] Illinois became a state in 1818. Chicago first incorporated as a village in 1833 and then as a city in 1837. By 1871, when Chicago was mostly destroyed by the great fire, more than 300,000 people resided there. One hundred years later in 1970 3.3 million people resided in Chicago, 5.5 million in Cook County, and 7.6 million in the six counties of Northeastern Illinois and two counties of Northern Indiana. Since 1970, population in the City of Chicago has dropped by an average of 60,000 people a year. Thus, by 1980 less than 3 million will still live in the city. In contrast, the metropolitan region as a whole has maintained a more or less constant population.

As Chicago mushroomed into the second largest city in the nation and the metropolitan region became one of the major industrial and transportation centers of the country, the original structures of village and even city government were insufficient to cope with the problems created by this population growth. The 1870 State Constitution explicitly "forbade any local government unit from incurring indebtedness amounting to more than 5 percent of the assessed valuation of the property within it."[2] Furthermore, nearly all non-property taxes could be levied only with the expressed consent of the State Legislature. Thus, when the financial limits of one unit of local government were reached it became easier to create a new special district with its own property tax or special taxes than to have the original governmental units incur additional debts.

The end result was a governmental nightmare of unconnected and frequently dysfunctional units. By 1972 there were 129 cities and autonomous villages with their own laws within the boundaries of Cook County and a total of 520 local government units with the power to levy taxes.[3] Today instead of a rational governmental structure built around general purpose local governments, there are hundreds of separate bodies with unrelated structures, overlapping duties and separate taxing powers. These multiple governments are now very difficult to eliminate or consolidate. There are too many vested interests supporting the current system, too many elected officials who would lose their offices and prestige, too much uncertainty about the political effects of creating a more rational metropolitan form of government.

The impact is clearly evident in the property tax bill of individual taxpayers. All Chicagoans pay property taxes to at least seven governments: 1) City of Chicago, 2) Cook County, 3) Cook County Forest Preserve District, 4) Chicago Park District, 5) Chicago Board of Education, 6) Chicago Junior College District and 7) Metropolitan Sanitary District. In addition, many Chicagoans also pay some property tax levies either to the Cook County Mosquito Abatement District or to special assessment districts for Chicago Transit Authority improvements. Naturally, all citizens also are taxed by the State and federal government. Yet even these tax bills are simple compared to those of many citizens in the suburban areas of Cook County who pay property taxes to as many as thirteen taxing bodies. To some extent, this duplication in governmental agencies and administrative overhead expenses also brings higher taxes.

The problem of multiple governments is not just one of neatness or esthtic, tidy structures. The plethora of local governments inhibit accountability, efficiency, effectiveness and coordination. Suppose citizens are angry about high property taxes. There is not just one taxing agency that they must confront but at least seven. Moreover, some tax regulations can be changed only by the State government. On the other hand, if citizens are disturbed just about their personal taxes it may not be the fault of the taxing agencies of the State Legislature but of the county assessor who appraises the value of the property for which they are being taxed. If they don't like the payment schedules, that may be the fault of the State Legislature, Cook County Board or the County Treasurer. Because so many government agencies are responsible for different aspects of property taxes there is no one official that a citizen can blame, confront or defeat at the next election. There is not even a single agency before which the citizens can appear to testify on behalf of changes in the law. Laws governing taxation, by being made complicated, are hidden and made inaccessible to citizens. Passing petitions, writing letters to the editor, complaining to individual public officials or even voting for advisory referendums will not change property taxes significantly.

Fragmented government has similar effects on other issues. Suppose a citizen organization in a neighborhood wants more recreation facilities. Do they go to the Chicago Park District or the Cook County Forest Preserve District? Suppose both agencies tell them they have exhausted their property tax funds and cannot build additional recreational facilities. Then the citizen organization will have to appear at City of Chicago or Cook County hearings on the use of their federally funded Community Development Program to request that federal funds be spent to build the facility. If these funds are spent on other programs, then an appeal can be made to the State Department of Conservation to obtain State funds to at least purchase the park land but this will require an official request to the State agency from the Park District or Forest Preserve District. Thus, even the simplest proposal for a small additional playlot in a community can easily be entagled in a structural maze.

Many of the projects which citizens want government to undertake, from small playlots to big super highways, require large sums of money which are not available in the operating budgets of local governments. Before 1970 the 520 local government units which could tax within Cook County could also borrow money, generally in the form of government bonds to be paid back over 20 to 40 years, much like an individual citizen would take out a mortgage for a home. However, before the 1970 Constitution nearly all of these bonds could be issued only if approved by direct referendum of all the voters within the boundaries of the local government unit. Frequently, these bond issues were voted down and governmental planning was considerably hampered even though governmental indebtedness was restricted to reasonable limits. Since the adoption of the new State Constitution of 1970, the large general local governments such as the City of Chicago and Cook County Government have been made "Home Rule Units." They can now issue general obligation bonds without referendum.[4] This has enhanced the financial strength of the general units of government, and allowed them to borrow without direct citizen approval. It may encourage future consolidation of the smaller, special local government districts into larger, more comprehensive governmental units.

Since 1972 the federal government has begun to share revenue from the federal income tax with local units of government—but only with the general units like the city and county governments, not the special districts. Since these funds are often as much as 100 million dollars a year and would be increased by merger into comprehensive units like the City of Chicago, revenue sharing also tends to promote general rather than specialized government.

Centralized Political Control

Just as Chicago *government* has been incredibly decentralized and fragmented, Chicago *politics* which controls general City and county government has been incredibly centralized and monolithic. Politics within the several hundred towns and suburbs is more fragemented but much less critical to the overall government of the metropolitan region. Some political scientists argue that Chicago and Cook County politics has to be centralized and tightly controlled in order to make the fragmented governmental system work at all. Banfield in his book *Political Influence* suggests that a poltitical head or party boss is needed in Chicago to concert the action of diverse and fragmented centers of power and government. A boss controls directly through his party position and indirectly through other leaders in the City who seek his favors and support for their own schemes and projects.[5]

Even if we accept the premise that the political parties provide unity and centralized control which is missing in the governmental structures of Chicago and Cook County, we are still left with the question: Does the party have to be a "political machine" based upon patronage, pay-offs and ethnicity in order to provide coherent government?

The most frequent reason given for the existence of the Chicago Machine, and political machines in most of the major cities of America during the last century, is the machine's help for the millions of immigrants who swelled the urban population. It got them jobs and city services, trained them in American politics and provided a ladder of success out of the ghetto for many. More recent studies of other cities have suggested that this explanation is only half the story; that business elites and wealthier elements of society also benefited from and supported machine rule.[6]

In Chicago there was never really an alternative to machine politics whether poor immigrants, or wealthy businessmen, or both are the cause. A machine has always run Chicago. This historical and cultural tradition of machine politics provides the prerequisite for the continuation of the political machine.

Machine politics grew with the City. The first political machine was born with the rebirth of the City after the Chicago fire of 1871:

> The first recognizable boss was Michael Cassius McDonald, who came on stage early and stayed late. McDonald, a gambler-saloon-keeper by profession, was the first to detect the common bonds of interests of the ciminal element and politicians and introduce one group to the other. He went to work as matchmaker shortly after the fire of 1871, prospered, and lasted until 1907 . . . [The *Chicago News* gave] McDonald credit for electing aldermen who lorded it in city council and county commissioners who stole everything in sight, and for providing contracts for public works that had "thievery written between the lines."[7]

Through the early years of the twentieth century the alliance between gamblers, saloonkeepers and politicians produced a series of legendary local bosses like Hinky Dink Kenna and Bathhouse John Coughlin.[8] They flourished until Prohibition and old age combined to put a halt to this particular alliance as the base of machine politics.

As most current analysts of machine politics point out, the first genuine citywide machine to amalgamate all ethnic groups and wards into a single organization was built by Anton Cermak in 1931.[9] After Cermak's assassination in 1933, the Chicago Democratic Machine contined under Kelly, Nash and Arvey. It was then consolidated, expanded and perfected under Richard J. Daley from 1953 to 1976. Since Daley's death, power within the machine fragmented somewhat, but it continued its absolute domination of Chicago and Cook County politics more than a century after the Chicago fire. Now that Daley's successor, Michael Bilandic, has been defeated at the polls in a surprise upset by Jane Byrne, power has fragmented even further. But machine dominance remains.

To fully understand machine politics and its tenacity, it is important to recognize that this century has seen both Republican and Democratic Party machines, Republican and Democratic bosses. Republican ward bosses were as frequently in power before the Great Depression as Democratic ward bosses have been since the Depression. And machine principles continue to guide both political parties today. While reformers, both party reformers and Independents, have also existed and been elected to office in Chicago since the great fire, they have never gained control of either political party or weened it from its machine principles of patronage and payoffs.

To better understand why the Party Machine has survived and flourished in Chicago for the last hundred years requires a study of the principles upon which the Machine is built. Milton Rakove in his book *Don't Make No Waves, Don't Back No Losers* begins with this proposition:

> The machine believes with Machiavelli that men in politics are greedy, emotional, and passionate, and are not governed by reason, morality, or concern for their fellow man. It believes that men can be co-opted, bought, persuaded, or frightened into subservience to or cooperation with the machine. Every man has his price, according to the machine, and the major problems are finding out what that price is and whether it is worth paying. Those unwilling to be bought must be persuaded or, if necessary, dealt with by force.[10]

From the first proposition comes its corollary:

> . . . the machine has governed the city, retained power, and pacified the citizenry by striking a balance between providing good technical services for the majority of the citizenry; making concessions to every powerful, organized interest group on matters of concern to each group; resisting reform' and providing for the political and economic interests of the machine's leaders.[11]

Thus, a simple exchange has been worked out. The Machine provides certain goods and services to satisfy the economic self-interest of both individuals and interest groups in return for their votes. These votes and monetary contributions from individuals and interest groups elect Machine men (and now occasionally machine women in liberal districts) to office, which gives them control of the patronage jobs necessary to produce Machine precinct workers, who canvass the precincts to produce still more Machine votes in the next election based upon the same exchange of favors and votes.

Obviously, then, the Machine depends not only upon a generalized exchange of favors and votes but particularly upon patronage jobs. As Senator Plunkitt of Tammany Hall in New York said in words which the party bosses of Chicago would echo:

> We stood as we have always stood for rewardin' the men that won the victory. They call that the spoils system. All right; Tammany is for the spoils system, and when we go in we fire every anti-Tammany man from office that can be fired under the law.[12]
>
> . . . you can't keep an organization together without patronage. Men ain't in politics for nothin'. They want to get somethin' out of it.[13]

The most revealing information about Chicago's patronage system today is to be found in depositions in a pending court cast *Michael L. Shakman and Paul M. Lurie, et. al. vs. The Democratic Organization of Cook County et al.* Several years ago Shakman won a consent decree in federal court to which the leaders of both political parties and the chief executives of State and local governments agreed. In the consent decree these officials pledged not to fire current government employees for failing to do political precinct work. Shakman is now suing to prevent patronage hiring. Already, in depositions in the case the Cook County Democratic Central

Committee and the City of Chicago have admitted the following:

1. That the "City of Chicago gives preference in hiring for many City jobs to persons who are politically sponsored by Democratic ward committeemen or other Democratic regular organizations officials. For some of these City jobs persons normally can be hired only with Democratic political sponsorship . . ."[14]
2. That "[a]bout one-half of the people hired by the City in recent years other than police and fire officers were for jobs for which preference was given to applicants with Democratic Party sponsorship."[15]
3. That "usually persons do obtain sponsorship from a Democratic party official for either having done or upon expectation that they will do precinct political work."[16]
4. The "political precinct work helps elect candidates . . ." which "is one of the purposes for giving preference in hiring."[17]

In short, patronage is alive and well in Chicago. Government employees are still hired as a reward for past political work and in the expectation that they will continue to work precincts for the party in the future. Since Jane Byrne has began her term as Mayor the issue has not been whether there will be patronage jobs but who will control those jobs and how they should be distributed among the ward organizations.

Estimates of the total number of patronage workers controlled by the Democratic Party through local, State or federal jobs vary from as few as 15,000 to as many as 35,000. Since there are 3,000 precincts in Chicago (and 5,000 in the county), this results in an average from 5–10 paid party precinct captains in every City precinct and a fair number of precinct workers scattered in different townships in the county. There is, of course, a public cost of patronage. Overstaffing makes City services less efficient and more costly. In 1974 the Better Government Association and the *Chicago Tribune* discovered that it cost $34.48 per ton for refuse collection in Chicago and only $30.84 per ton in Milwaukee or $23.70 in Kansas City. By 1978 Chicago would be spending $43.28 per ton while Baltimore would spend only $22.35 and Philadelphia $33.06.[18]

Neither the Republican Party, which has lost most of its patronage jobs over the many years since the Depression, nor individual Independent candidates, who must depend upon volunteers, can match the Democratic Party army citywide. At best, Republicans and Independents within the city can regularly win elections only in individual wards and districts for Alderman or State Legislature.

Jane Byrne defeated Michael Bilandic in the 1979 Democratic Primary for Mayor without precinct workers. She was elected in large measure because of the City government's inept handling of snow removal after the largest blizzard in Chicago's history. While her election proved that a former regular Democrat can, in special circumstances, be elected without party backing and demonstrated the level of citizen unhappiness with City government, fundamental political change will not come to Chicago until the Machine can be defeated regularly in the precincts. That time, if it is coming, is still years away.

The county political situation, like the most recent mayoral campaign, also differs somewhat from the norm of Machine control. Because of the heavy predominance of Republicans in the suburbs, County and State Republican candidates such as County State's Attorney Carey and Governor Thompson can be elected. Thus, qualified Republican candidates with strong issues can be elected at the county and State level despite the opposition of the Democratic Machine in Chicago. But suburban Republicans and dissident Democrats remain too disorganized to take over county government or provide much of a counter to the Machine.

It has been frequently charged that Machine dominance in Chicago is maintained not only by historical traditions and by patronage, but by corruption as well. Reform movements such as the Municipal Voters' League have fought hard against corruption ever since the turn of the century. However, corruption persists despite all reform efforts.

Evidence of current corruption comes from both federal government prosecutions of party and government officials and from investigations by the Better Government Association and the news media. Gardiner and Lyman in their new book *Decisions for Sale* provide the following examples of corruption in land and zoning deals:

1. Alderman Joseph Jambrone was convicted of accepting a $4,000 bribe from a real estate representative of Humble Oil Co. to rezone property for them. He was sentenced to two years in prison and fined $15,000.[19]
2. Alderman Thomas E. Keane "was convicted on mail fraud charges related to acquisition of tax delinquent properties, cancellation of tax liens, and subsequent sale of land to city agencies." Keane was sentenced to five years in prison and forced to vacate his Aldermanic position.[20]
3. Clerk of the Circuit Court of Cook County, Matt Danaher, was indicted "on charges of conspiracy to defraud the government and to receive illegal payments relating to rezoning and building permits . . ."[21] Danaher got the zoning and permits for a housing development, and his brother-in-law, who was President of Evergreen Savings and Loan Association, loaned the developers $3,600,000. In return Danaher and his brother-in-law received over $400,000 in real estate commissions.
4. Alderman Paul Wigoda rezoned the Edgewater Golf Course for developers who ended up selling it to the State. "Before rezoning was approved, the developers estimated that they might be able to sell the land (purchased for $7.6 million) to the state for $9.5 million; after the rezoning the land was sold for $18.3 million."[22] He was sentenced to prison for one year and disbarred as a lawyer.

Over the last four or five years more than 200 hundred elected and appointed Chicago government officials have been convicted of similar crimes. And highly placed elected officials are not the only ones to engage in corruption. In 1977, in order to determine the corruption and payoffs which occur at this level, the Better Government Association and the *Chicago Sun-Times* bought a tavern, which they named the Mirage. As Gardiner and Lyman conclude:

> The findings of the Mirage investigators provided front-page news in the *Chicago Sun-Times* for a month. Skimming income and sales taxes. Juggled records. Vending machine salesmen who offered illegal kickbacks. With twelve city and state inspectors; six taking bribes and six being negligent at no charge—over four months, the Mirage *never* was subjected to a competent inspection. A precinct captain expedited city approval of the tavern license. City trash collectors who took $15 to clean up the Mirage's garbage (only private scavengers are supposed to service commercial establishments). Firemen selling (while on duty) tickets for a charity intended to aid widows and orphans of firemen; proceeds actually supporting the Fire Department band. . . . Fourteen city and state employees who took payoffs at the tavern were suspended.[23]

The zoning deals, the petty corruption with building inspections, are part and parcel of machine politics. The Machine itself works as a private economic exchange in which favors are exchanged for votes. The participants in the Machine who are required to participate in that fundamental economic exchange find it hard to tell the moral difference between the exchange and graft. Thus, corruption is as natural a result of Machine politics as patronage. Both are spawned by the need for a powerful political machine which can overcome the structural fragmentation and natural inefficiency of Chicago government. Patronage, corruption and political control by a small elite is the high cost of machine politics which citizens pay.

The public costs of patronage and corruption are several. The cost of services is higher which is reflected in higher tax bills. Gardiner and Lyman also conclude:

> In Chicago corruption in the rezoning process doubled the price paid for parkland; corruption in inspections led to approval of buildings with major fire, health, and safety hazards, and widespread 'skimming' of tax revenues. . . .
>
> Corruption is developments where people don't want them or where communities aren't ready for them. It is shoddy construction which must be immediately redone or which becomes rapidly obsolete. It is tax dollars used to fund inflated contracts or to replace skimmed revenues. It is old or new buildings which threaten the health and safety of their occupants and neighbors. It is something we all pay for.[24]

The Chicago Power Structure

The power structure in Chicago is built upon the exchange of favors and the concerting of resources by its members to achieve goals for each of them. The Chicago power structure is fundamentally an alliance of powerful private groups, each with their own leaders and spokesmen, each with their own interests, each with their own internal politics, but with a shared interest in continuing the status quo and in undertaking certain governmental projects from which they can benefit at public expense.[25]

The principal members of importance in the Chicago power structure seem to be: 1) the political Machine or Regular Democratic Party, 2) big business, 3) the labor movement, 4) major institutions such as universities and hospitals, 5) ethnic groups, 6) the churches (especially the Catholic Church), 7) civic groups, and 8) the mass media. These various groups are not always a cohesive force—there are different interests among different big businesses in the city: ethnic groups are more of a self-identification than an organization; and the members of news media may differ in their positions on different public issues. Likewise, other non-elite groups and leaders may count in decisions about specialized issues. However, the leaders of the eight groups listed above seem to count most in the major decisions affecting Chicago. That is to say, most governmental decisions seem to be the outcome of bargaining, or conflict, among these eight groups. This means Independents, Republicans, reform Democrats, non-Catholics, the poor, less powerful interest groups and the general public are excluded from decision making.

The power structure in Chicago probably most differs from other major cities in the country in the dominant role of the political party in determining the final governmental outcome. In other American cities, other elites such as the local business elite may be much more dominant. This is not to say that the political Machine makes every decision itself in Chicago and imposes these decisions upon other groups in the power structure. However, the political Machine, as we have already seen, controls the decentralized governmental machinery necessary for official governmental actions and the governmental resources necessary for many projects which members of the power structure want.

Banfield in his book *Political Influence* describes the normal process for most decisions involving the Chicago power structure as follows:

> Civic controversies in Chicago arise out of maintenance and enhancement needs of large formal organizations. The heads of an organization see some advantage to be gained by changing the situation. They propose changes. Other large organizations are threatened. They oppose, and a civic controversy takes place. . . .
>
> The political heads are slow to take up on issues presented to them by the "civic leaders." They know from experience that what one organization wants is almost certain to be opposed by others. . . . According to the Chicago view, a policy ought to be framed by the interests affected, not by the political head or his agents. In this view, the affected interests should work out for themselves the "best" solution of the matter (usually a compromise). . . . The political head will ratify almost any proposal upon which the principally affected interests agree, and they will postpone as long as they can a decision upon any proposal about which they are not agreed.[26]

Milton Rakove uses a similar description of Daley's method for dealing with most City problems:

> His normal method for dealing with a problem in his city is to get it on his desk, then move it out to those in the community whose interests are most deeply affected by the

> problem. If they cannot arrive at a solution, he will use all of his authority as mayor to induce them to move in that direction. But he will normally not use his power and authority as mayor of Chicago to force on any side in a dispute a solution which that side is not willing to agree to and abide by. However, if the parties to a dispute can agree on a solution, he will put the city's authority behind it, and do everything in his power to implement and expedite the matter.[27]

The process described by Banfield and Rakove concerns decisions to use governmental resources to construct new projects wanted by various members of the power structure. Other decisions regarding the distribution of power, or crisis decisions such as how to handle a race riot, are handled entirely differently; as yet there has been no thorough study of this type of decision-making in Chicago.

There are, of course, many groups which are not members of the power structure, yet would like to have governmental support for their projects. In general, they are out of luck. They must begin by demonstrating at least some potential power (most often, the votes they control) before they will have access to the head of the political Machine to get their project considered. Thus, for instance, while ethnic groups *can* be important, Latinos are unable to get any support from the political Machine—*they* don't have much money and *they* do not have a carefully controlled vote in elections, which they can barter for power. So there are virtually no Latino elected officials, only 2.6% of the City employees are Latino, and there are few major projects in the Latino community by City government. They have not yet been able to enter the power structure successfully. The same is true of many non-ethnic groups in Chicago such as women, youth and homosexuals.

The members of the power structure do more for each other than simply approve governmental projects. Peter Knauss in his book, *Chicago: A One-Party State* sumarizes the role of the political machine in supporting big business as follows:

> A final logical integration of politics and big business was the consolidation of a covert alliance between the city machine and the corporation. The machine, I suspect was permitted a virtual free rein so long as it served the ruling elite with these crucial functions:
>
> 1. control of the franchise by trivalizing the meaning of the ballot;
> 2. socialize immigrants into passive, quiescent, and obedient Americans by giving them proper "citizenship training" about American political practice;
> 3. replace the outnumbered, overrun WASP gentry with men who were reliable models of ethnic success and fit objects of emulation by large elements of the immigrant population.[28]

Thus, the exchange of favors and the concerting of influence by elite groups within the power structure occurs at general levels of support as well as in terms of trade-offs on particular issues and projects.

A series of recent City government decisions further illustrates how governmental decisions help to maintain the existing Chicago power structure by providing different benefits for different members:

1. When the federal government withheld nearly $150 million in Revenue Sharing Funds because the City of Chicago was found guilty of discriminating in the hiring and promotion of minorities in the Chicago Police Department, the large downtown banks on December 31, 1975 lent $55 million to keep the city government afloat.
2. In return for help of the banks in the Revenue Sharing fight the Mayor and the City Council voted on July 8, 1976 to allow Community Bank Offices in order to allow banks to get around state restrictions prohibiting branch banking. This ordinance was later ruled to be unconstitutional by the courts.
3. Each year the City of Chicago refuses to grant a contract to its employees. However, it pays its union tradesmen the so-called "prevailing wage" which is 30% or more higher than the yearly salary of most construction workers. In addition, the Mayor appoints and the City Council approves the appointment of union leaders to the School Board, Park District Board, and most boards and commissions in the city.
4. The mayor and the City Council regularly provide the necessary planned unit development zoning and often urban renewal subsidized land for the major university and hospital expansion programs in Chicago.
5. The County Assessor regularly underassesses the value of the land owned by the major newspapers and television stations in Chicago.
6. To help the downtown business community the City of Chicago undertook the construction of the new State Street Mall which it was able to build in large measure with federal grants which the city was able to obtain.
7. The Mayor and City Council in 1977 approved a privately financed housing development called Dearborn Park Project to build hundreds of units of upper middle class housing just south of the Chicago Loop business district.

This list of exchanged favors and joint projects between members of the Chicago power structure could be extended to cover hundreds of governmental decisions—large and small—over the last four or five years. But even this short list demonstrates the kind of governmental decisions with which the members of the power structure are concerned. The Party wants to continue discrimination, the banks want branch banking and City government deposits, unions want high wages, universities and hospitals want to expand their empires, the media want lower taxes, big businesses want expensive government services, subsidies and support for their projects.

Chicago is not unique in having an elite, but it may be unique in the total control which members of the elite are able to exercise over decisions that concern them. The power structure is often challenged in these decisions, but the power structure during the last several decades has usually been defeated only when the courts or the State and federal government opposed them directly.

Other battles the power structure has won. One consequence of the strength of the power structure is that the dominant political party—the Chicago Democratic Machine—as a full, if not the principal partner in the power structure, gains part of its permanence and stability from the loyal support offered by the other members of the power structure who are themselves appropriately rewarded with favorable governmental decisions which the Machine controls. And when changes occur inside the political Machine, such as the succession of Mayors Bilandic and Byrne after Daley's death, the other members of the power structure are quick to reestablish connections with the new political and governmental leaders. In this way the basic alliances upon which the power structure is founded are quickly reconstituted and the power structure continues despite internal changes within any partner interest group.

Control of the Chicago City Council

No discussion of the politics and government of Chicago would be complete without considering Chicago's legendary City Council. By law, Chicago has a strong-council form of local government. The fifty members of the City Council make the laws which govern Chicago, approve all major appointments by the Mayor, and, theoretically at least, control by a line item budget virtually every penny spent by the City government. In earlier eras when men like Bathhouse John Coughlin and Hinky Dink Kenna served in the City Council, these "grey wolves" (as the press called them) plundered the City and divided the spoils amongst themselves. In those days Aldermen were, in fact, all powerful.

More recently, particularly during the reign of Mayor Richard J. Daley, the Mayor became dominant over the Council. Daley used his combined powers as Mayor and Democratic Party Boss to control the vast majority of votes in the City Council and thus forced Aldermen to rubber stamp *his* program, *his* ordinances, *his* appointments and *his* budget. This pattern continued after Daley's death despite the fact that Mayor Bilandic was not as all-powerful as Daley because of splits and divisions within the Democratic Party. It still continues under Mayor Byrne so far.

Former Alderman Ross Lathrop (5th Ward) in his recent study of City Council voting found the following patterns:

> During 1977, Mayor Bilandic's first full year in office, none of the Mayor's 169 pieces of substantial legislation failed! 145 or 85.8% passed and 24 or 14.2% were still pending at the end of the period of analysis. . . . Legislation introduced by Aldermen suffered a quite different fate, however. Only 22.2% of all Aldermanic legislation whether sponsored by administration Aldermen, independents, or jointly had passed by April, 1978; 30.9% had failed and 46.9% was still pending.[29]

In short, the Mayor proposes most of the major legislation which becomes law. The Aldermen propose and pass very little of their own legislation.

The pattern of executive and party control over the Council is also clear in the votes which are cast by the Aldermen. The Lathrop study confirmed my own findings regarding the 1971 City Council:

> [The Table displaying all the] controversial roll call votes for 1971 shows clearly that majority aldermen [who support the city administration] were almost never persuaded by argument. In 58 key votes (which included every major piece of legislation on which there was a divided vote regarding its passage, many key procedural votes, and a number of important amendments) *there were only three votes in which any majority aldermen voted with the minority*. . . . On all other issues the majority remained absolutely monolithic.[30]

As former Alderman Lathrop concluded: "The city administration permits few exceptions to absolute obedience on final votes on substantial legislation."[31] It does not matter what an Alderman's constituents might think about the issue. It does not matter what an Alderman may believe to be the merits of an issue. What matters is the loyalty of the Aldermen to the party which elected them in the first place and which can reelect *or* defeat them at the next election. It remains to be seen if the City Council will be any different under Mayor Byrne. In the several City Council meetings since her April 16th inauguration the older patterns have remained unchanged. However, the balance of power in the City government is still fragile, and change could yet occur during the Byrne Administration.

This rigid voting pattern is not confined only to the Chicago City Council. Indeed party and executive branch control, as well as ideological conflict between Machine supporters and Reformers, extends to all units of local government on which Reformers have been able to obtain representation but remain in the minority. For instance, Paul Peterson in his study of the Chicago School Board found that ideological conflict prevailed there in the 1940's, that this conflict abated somewhat during the 1950's when the "consensus which marked national politics under Dwight Eisenhower seems also to have prevailed locally."[32] Then in the 1960's and since, "the pattern of cleavage became more firmly delineated than ever before."[33] As Peterson concluded on the current condition of the school board, "Because of two distinct ideological perspectives [Machine and racial Status Quo vs. Reform and Integration] were well represented on the board, the members tended to polarize into two groups and found themselves voting with the same allies on a large number of issues."[34] Just as in the City Council, the result is that the supporters of the City Administration have consistently been able to out-vote the reformers and to maintain control although they have later adopted some reform proposals as their own and thus modified the school system slowly to meet new challenges.

Bargaining becomes ideological when each issue must be resolved, not simply on its own terms, but as part of a much wider set of interrelated issues. By this definition, the Machine is ideological: issues are decided, not on their own merits, but according to how they affect political power and the level of political controversy. While in many ways the local ideologies of the Machine and Independents may not seem to possess the same scope as international ideologies such as Democracy, Fascism and Communism, they do provide a consistent position on local issues which makes the votes of Aldermen, School Board Members and other governmental officials far from trivial and causes the legislative process in all these units of local government to be one of enduring cleavages and conflict rather than compromise and consensus which characterizes many local governments in America. As Paul Peterson describes this form of Chicago politics based upon ideological bargaining and conflict, it has four characteristics which are manifested in the City Council, the School Board and other local government bodies:

> . . . (1) participants in the policy-making process will include groups committed to broad-gauge objectives who become involved in a range of policy questions; (2) such groups will find similar allies and similar enemies across a range of policy questions; (3) enduring and significant linkages between inclusive social groups and important political factions will occur; and (4) groups will find defeat of the opposition preferable to "reasonable" compromise.[35]

Thus, the view of Chicago politics as a monolithic power structure in which elite groups bargain and concert their efforts to undertake profitable projects for themselves must be set against the other aspect of Chicago politics as a continual ideological war in which neither Machine nor power elite dominance goes unchallenged, but in which, ideology is denied (see below). The battlelines are public and clearly drawn. The war continues inside as well as outside Chicago government. There are also constraints upon Chicago City government by federal and State governments, by the courts, and by public opinion. Both reformers and the Machine make appeals to these outside forces to help them win the local ideological war.

Chicago government has more aspects, however, than just law making. Aldermen in Chicago have more than a legislative function, both in their own eyes and in the expectations of their constituents. They are the closest that Chicago comes to having an Ombudsman. They and their constituents believe that they have an obligation to make sure that City services are provided to citizens in the ward which they represent. If a tree needs trimming, a curb fixing, a street repairing, a constituent a welfare check, or an unemployed person a job, they go first to their Alderman (who is also likely to be their Democratic Party Ward Committeeman). By letter, phone and personal contact the Alderman reports these constituent needs and demands to the appropriate City employees among the 45,000 who work at City Hall. By the magic of an Alderman's "clout" or simply by getting the right information to the right employee in the intricate service delivery system, the government service is provided. Those Aldermen who work hard at providing services, be they Administration supporters or Independents, obtain many different services for their constituents.

In 1973 my Aldermanic Service Office handled 1486 major service requests, not counting hundreds of requests only for information or major community and legislative projects. The most frequent requests were to remove abandoned autos, to get garbage picked up by the sanitation department, to get buildings in need of repair inspected or torn down and to repair broken streets, sidewalks and curbs. But citizen complaints also included crime problems, reports on street gangs, zoning cases and traffic congestion problems which could not be solved as easily as getting the garbage picked up in a particular alley. Moreover, social service agencies wanted help in getting funding, and community groups wanted major community improvements like new parks and housing renovation programs. As evidenced from all these demands and the services provided by my Aldermanic Office, an Alderman in the City of Chicago, like most elected representatives in American government, is expected not only to represent constituents by votes in the City Council but by providing better access to and better services from the City government.

Some pro-Administration Aldermen maintain that they have to give their vote in the City Council unequivocably and unquestioningly to the Mayor and the Democratic Party in order to get as political favors the services their communities need. This is, at best, a half truth. Most City services must meet minimal standards or the Mayor and all his Party supporters would get kicked out of office by irate constituents. The story is told that long ago the Machine wanted to punish a Republican Alderman representing a southside ward. They stopped delivering City services like garbage collection efficiently. As the story goes the constituents got so mad that they elected a number of Republican state legislators in retaliation at the next election. In any case, the Machine has never in recent years tried to cut off basic services to any ward.

The most recent example of the reaction to the Administration's failure to deliver on service expectations was the Mayoral and Aldermanic elections of 1979. Because citizens believed that Mayor Bilandic had failed to get the snow removed from their streets and sidewalks after the Blizzard of '79, they elected Jane Byrne and eight Independent Aldermen instead of the Regular Party candidates.

In addition to ideological battles over major legislation with city-wide impact and in addition to individual constituent services which Aldermen provide, the City Council is a major center for grading favors and adopting the routine traffic, zoning and service legislation which are critical to the livelihood and quality of neighborhood life for most Chicagoans. Presumably members of the Chicago power structure make their trades for favors and consideration directly with the Mayor and the Party bosses. The City then ratifies those decisions even after ideological debate and conflict. But those Chicago citizens who are outside the power structure and not represented by big business, big labor or large interest groups must get their needs met through contact with their Alderman. Thus, the City Council provides not only a legislative rubber stamp for the Mayor's programs but a place for the secondary level of the politics of political favors which is uniquely Chicago's style of politics.

Proposals to reform the Chicago City Council so as to make it a more genuine legislative body, a more representative and democratic body, and a more efficient agency for providing services have persisted for many years. Since 1954 two "Home Rule Commissions" have offered formal proposals for improving the composition, structure and legislative process.[36] Thus far, however, any improvements in the City Council have been very limited and the Home rule Commission proposals, other than those for an executive controlled City Budget and new taxes, go unadopted. In many ways the City Council rules are more restrictive today then they were a decade ago. As one infamous Alderman, Paddy Bauler of the 43rd Ward, summarized the situation years ago, "Chicago ain't ready for reform."

Citizen Participation in Chicago Politics

If democracy consists of "government of the people, by the people, for the people," Chicago is no democracy. It is true that elections are held, but those are too controlled by the Democratic Machine to represent accurately the opinion of the voters. For example, in the 1979 Aldermanic elections no opponent even ran against the Machine candidate in twenty Chicago wards—the cause was simply too hopeless and, perhaps, too dangerous. In another eight of the fifty wards, Machine Aldermen were reelected to the City Council by at least 60% of the vote and many of them by 70–80%. In these wards there might as well have been no opponent. Thus, the Democratic Party in practice has majority control of the Chicago City Council even before the election is held.

Yet, the demand for citizen participation—in short, the demand for democracy—is as old a tradition as Machine control in Chicago. At the end of the 19th century groups like the Municipal Voters' League were formed. By exposing the corrupt deeds of incumbent Aldermen, the League was able to defeat some and replace them with reformers. Large public rallies were held and eagerly covered by the newspapers of the time to decry the graft, boodle and corruption of Chicago government. Indeed, in 1894 the Leagues sought to defeat 23 Aldermen and actually succeeded in beating 18.[37]

Along with the Municipal Voters' League, a variety of civic and good government groups were founded to reform the City. The Civic Federation, which was born in this era, not only worked to elect better Aldermen but attacked problems like joblessness directly.[38]

Civic groups like the Civic Federation have survived from the turn of the century to the present day. Others were dismantled and replaced with new civic groups. They were joined in the late 1930's by an entirely different type of organization, however. Saul Alinsky began to organize community organizations like Back of the Yards, The Woodlawn Organization (TWO) and the Northwest Community Organization (NCO) and to train community organizers to create others throughout Chicago and the country. In general, community organizations avoided a direct challenge to the Machine over elections to public office. However, they mobilized thousands of citizens around concrete issues and grievances in conflict with the major corporations which were part of the Chicago power structure. At other times they applied pressure directly on the Mayor and the Aldermen to meet the needs of people in the local communities. Over the years they won many important battles and, equally importantly, provided an avenue for thousands of Chicagoans to have an impact on the destiny of their own community which the political system did not offer directly.[39]

Around the time of World War II opposition to the Machine began to take an explicitly political form. A group known as the Voters for the Victory during the war period later became the Independent Voters of Illinois (IVI), an affiliate of the Americans for Democratic Action. At first, IVI simply endorsed the best candidates of either party, but soon it began running its own "Independent" candidates in Aldermanic and other local elections. IVI thus grew into an alternative political organization outside the existing political parties. While IVI continued its outside attacks against the Machine, a party reform group, the Democratic Federation of Illinois (DFI) was created in 1957 to push for reform within the Democratic Party. In addition to fighting on issues, these organizations fought the Machine directly in the electoral arena.[40]

By 1968, reform groups proliferated in Chicago like wildflowers. Civic groups, community organizations, the civil rights movement, political reform efforts and newer public interest groups grew in both numbers and power. They were fueled by powerful issues—civil rights, the War in Vietnam, and citizen participation. The conflict with the Democratic Machine came to a head in the clashes both inside and outside the 1968 Democratic National Convention. The struggle in the streets of Chicago was later labeled a "police riot" by the commission which investigated it.[41] The struggle in the Democratic Convention itself led to a fracture within the party and to its eventual defeat in the 1968 presidential election. It sparked the proliferation of reform efforts for the next decade.

The 1968 battles led to the formation of still newer reform groups such as the Independent Precinct Organization which brought Independent politics to the north side of Chicago. In the following decade IPO was able to elect to public office more than a dozen reformers, who, working with the civic and community organizations, were able to get passed major laws both in the State Legislature and in the Chicago City Council. Moreover, Independents elected from throughout the State held the balance of power between Democrats and Republicans in drafting the new State Constitution in 1970 and were able to make the final document one of the most progressive in the nation. (See the chapters by Lousin and Kenney.) IPO in 1978 merged with IVI to create a new state political organization, IVI–IPO.

Despite the surge of reform activity since 1968, the basically fragmented structure of local government, Machine-dominated politics and more or less stable Chicago power structure have persisted intact. While some gains in reforming the process, encouraging citizen participation and improving Chicago government have been made, the Chicago system of politics and government still remains. During the 1970's the Republican Party has weakened to a mere shell of opposition to the Democratic Party Machine, not only in Chicago but within Cook County as well. Long before, Republican officials on the west side of Chicago were widely recognized as part of the network of corruption and favor-trading; they hardly could be said to represent the opposition! Independent politics has also had difficulty fulfilling the role of the "loyal opposition" and providing an alternative to Machine politics, because the economic recession nationally has made people more self-centered and job conscious, therefore less willing to serve as volunteers in the precincts. The older issues of civil rights and the Vietnam War have waned and no new issue has rekindled the passions aroused in the late 1960's. Mayor Daley has died and no longer serves as a rallying symbol for those who would oppose the Machine. Thus, the reform movement began to recede. However, with the election of Mayor Byrne and eight Independent Aldermen in the 1979 City elections, the momentum for change has surged again. At a minimum, major changes within the Machine itself can be expected in the years ahead, and these will have a major impact on Chicago's future.

Chicago's Future

In the last decades of the Twentieth Century, Chicago faces three major challenges. First, it continues to be one of the most racially segregated cities in America. Second, it continues to decline economically with an ever growing unemployment rate, as industries flee to the suburbs and other parts of the country. Third, it continues to have outmoded political and governmental structures inadequate to cope with the social, economic and political problems which it faces.[42]

It may be argued that Machine politics will survive these challenges and continue to dominate Chicago. I believe, however, that our politics and government must change if Chicago is to end discrimination and alleviate the misery of poverty, if Chicago's economy is to become more diversified and modern, if we are to reunite the city and its suburbs, and if we are to have a modern politics and government of citizen participation. I argue that our fragmented local government and Machine style politics grew up over a century ago within the restraints of an old State Constitution and an immigrant society which has since evolved. In short, I argue that our fragmented government and Machine style politics are simply inadequate to meet our current needs or to overcome the challenges facing our city. Therefore, I believe that our government and our politics will evolve accordingly.

It may be perfectly true that Chicago is better off financially than New York City, or Cleveland or Detroit. The real issue is not the plight of other American cities but the plight of Chicago. We need to seek a better politics and a better government than we have had in the past and than other cities now enjoy. As indicated earlier, Chicago city government is almost entirely mismatched with the mounting social and economic problems with which it is faced. On the one hand, the governmental bodies which are forced to cope with a city of three million people and a larger county of five million are so large and complex as to be remote from the citizens. Even the Aldermen represent over 60,000 constituents each. On the other hand, local units of government are too small, fragmented and uncoordinated to handle regional economic problems and have too little money to meet the massive social needs of their populations.

The governmental solution requires, on the one hand, the expansion of the scope and power of local government so that it can govern effectively the entire metropolitan region and cope with the serious social and economic problems. On the other hand, government must simultaneously be made smaller and brought close enough to the citizens that they can understand the problems and participate directly in their solution. The dual structural solution to the governmental mismatch is thus to form "neighborhood governments" in the wards of the City and in the suburban townships under the broader umbrella of a strong "metropolitan government." These two new units of government would in time replace the existing City, township, county, district and special purpose governments. Clearly such changes would require major state legislative action.

Neighborhood government is especially important to any governmental reformation because it allows for citizen participation in a government which both locally and nationally has become remote. With neighborhood government citizens can know that their views and opinions count. Dependence upon the mass media to provide information about the government and dependence upon patronage party precinct captains to organize voters would be lessened. Moreover, with local public assemblies which neighborhood government provides, elected representatives to the metropolitan governmental level can be held fully accountable to the voters whom they represent. And key decisions which affect the local community can even be made directly by citizens themselves in their neighborhood meetings.

Neighborhood government is not just abstract political theory. Since 1972 in Chicago's 44th Ward there have been experiments in neighborhood government, including a Ward Assembly with elected delegates from each precinct and community organization. These delegates, by their deliberations, mandate their Alderman's vote in City Council. Ward Assembly delegates also propose new legislation which their Alderman introduces as well as projects to be undertaken in the Ward without official City approval. A Community Zoning Board and a Traffic Review Commission have also served in the 44th

Ward to allow citizens to participate directly in important governmental decisions which affect their lives. Similar experiments have been undertaken in six other Chicago wards and in some 40 other cities throughout the country, suggesting broad applicability.

Based upon neighborhood government in the City and local government in the suburbs, a successful metropolitan government should also be possible. Many of the current intermediate governments such as the Park District, Metropolitan Sanitary District and County government would become departments within this new government. Metropolitan government is needed in addition to neighborhood government in order to allow for planning and delivering services which are essentially regional in scope, to create an authority able to handle Chicago's massive economic and social problems and to create a tax base broad enough to pay the costs of local government. Already metropolitan or regional government has begun in a small way with the creation of service districts such as the Metropolitan Sanitary District and the Regional Transportation Authority (RTA) and with the creation of planning units such as the Northeastern Illinois Planning Commission (NIPC).

The principal component of this new Metropolitan Government would be a legislative branch composed of at least 100 legislators (or Aldermen) representing neighborhoods and townships of 50–60,000 people each. Approximately half of the legislators would represent the City neighborhoods and half suburban. In addition to the legislative branch there would need to be a chief executive—but one without party clout of past Chicago Mayors. Finally, there should be a local judicial branch chosen by merit selection instead of the current bedsheet ballots by which we elect and retain local judges now under the control of the political parties.

Neither neighborhood nor metropolitan government is likely if the political parties remain unchanged. Significant governmental reform is impossible without political reform in Chicago. The dominant Democratic Party and its Republican Party counterpart are not prepared to make government more participatory, to espouse and push racial integration, or to create new governmental units they might not control. While the election of Jane Byrne has not brought a new political movement or organization to power, she has broken some of the power and many of the myths which sustain the Machine oriented political parties.

What will be required eventually will be either reformed political parties or new political organizations which perform the traditional party functions differently. Political campaigns will have to be based upon citizen volunteers rather than paid, patronage precinct captains. Political candidates will have to be selected publicly by the volunteers rather than by closed-door party slatemaking sessions. Elected officials will have to be held accountable both to the volunteers who worked on their behalf and to the voters who elected them. Volunteers will be rewarded with the psychological rewards such as a fulfilled sense of citizen duty and the advancement of candidates and causes they favor, rather than economic payoffs which inevitably lead to both political control and corruption. Altogether it can be said that citizens will first have to be able to participate effectively and control for themselves the political process before they can participate and control their government.

For a reform movement favoring participatory politics to succeed in overturning the Machine in Chicago will require a fundamental change in citizen attitudes. As long as Chicagoans follow Royko's version of the City slogan, "*Ubi Est Mea?*" which means "Where's mine?"[43] as long as Chicagoans seek favors instead of rights, as long as Chicagoans are willing to increase private profits at public expense or at least allow others to do so, the cultural basis of Machine politics is intact. When Chicagoans become concerned about public service and public interest, when they focus upon important issues of public policy instead of private profit, then a new politics will be born. David Protess in an article several years ago put the matter this way:

> *Regime stability* in a machine city is maintained as long as the logrolling coalition of disparate interests *remains* nonideological, that is, continues to be concerned only with the distribution of tangible incentives to the wards. Under distributively perceived conditions, politics is quiescent and a machine will thrive.
>
> *Regime transformation* in a machine city will occur when key economic and social policy questions (e.g., civil rights, the tax structure, control over education and police, and the like) that have been distributively perceived become regulatively and redistributively perceived. When such a change in the perceptions of local political actors occurs, politics becomes ideological and logrolling breaks down.[44]

In a variety of elections since 1968 there have been indications of such changes beginning. In analyzing the 1972 election Protess concluded:

> Perhaps the most important departure from the past in Chicago's 1972 election was the widespread ticket splitting that occurred. The city's black wards overwhelmingly supported Democratic candidates for President and Governor. Yet in the state's attorney's race, ten of the fourteen predominantly black wards were carried by Republican Bernard Carey.[45]

The 1979 Mayoral and Aldermanic elections again evinced a shift in mood among the electorate. What remains unanswered is whether fundamental, ideological, public issues will remain dominant over private interests in future elections.

As in the case of neighborhood government, a more participatory politics is not abstract theory. Historically, efforts to gain citizen participation and civil and political reform began in Chicago almost as early as Machine politics. Currently "independent politics" as practiced by the newly merged IVI–IPO provides a model for a future participatory politics in Chicago. Its decisions are controlled by its voluntary members by a ⅔ vote at local chapter meetings. It is concerned with issues rather than with power for its own sake. It has an agenda for change which includes integration, economic development and citizen participation.

But there are dangers inherent in the attempt to bring a more participatory politics to Chicago as well. Michels in his book, *Political Parties,* published more than 60 years ago proposed the "iron law of oligarchy."[46] He maintained that all institutions become oligarchical no matter how democratic their ideals, how devoted their leaders, or how well educated their members. As any organization, even a political organization dedicated to participatory politics, grows stronger, becomes larger and hires the necessary professional staff, oligarchy increases. Machine politics may be reformed, corruption curbed and patronage eliminated, but oligarchy rather than a democracy of citizen participation will still reign.

James Wilson in a later book, *Amateur Democrat,* studied party reform efforts including Chicago's Independent Voters of Illinois.[47] He found that these reformers were mostly middle class in origin and concluded that "If the center of gravity in the Democratic party moves toward the middle-class intellectual clubs, then the party will cease to be a device for the socialization of the lower classes and the excluded minority groups."[48] Thus, to Wilson, participatory politics really means participation for the upper middle-class and the exclusion of the working class and poor Chicagoans.

Finally, Wilson argues that even if greater participation were possible in politics, it would be undesirable. Wilson believes that government is not necessarily "more democratic if as many people as possible can participate in the choice of . . . [party] candidates and the writing of . . . [party] platforms."[49] He sees democracy differently:

> An alternative theory of democracy rejects the participatory view as unrealistic. This second theory takes into account the fact that people have many fundamental disagreements which cannot be reduced to two simple choices no matter how elaborate the party system may be; that these people are by and large uninformed on all but the most dramatic and fundamental issues; that many of the politically relevant views of people are emotional and even irrational; and that therefore there is no way—and there should not be any way—to arrive at decisions on all important matters or at some conception of the common good by algebraically adding the likes and dislikes of the voters. The implication of this view is that, far from increasing public participation in the choice of candidates and issues, democracy is best served by reducing and simplifying those choices to a single elemental choice—that of the principal elective officials.[50]

These complaints are valid concerns about reform efforts in Chicago. Special precautions must be taken to prevent or at least to lessen oligarchy in reform organizations. The platform of reform must include issues of concern to the poor and the minorities and must offer avenues for their participation as well as for the participation of the better educated and wealthier Chicagoans. Finally, the goals must not be absolute participation by every citizen on every public issue without benefit of any system of representation. The goal is for *more* citizen participation in candidate selection, platform formation and government. If the Machine can be defeated consistently in elections, this is a practical and reasonable goal.

Participatory politics will not prevail easily in Chicago with its long history of Machine control. Participatory politics, like democracy of old, can be established only by the choice of citizens. Thus, reforming or replacing political parties, creating neighborhood and metropolitan government, and assuming, once again, responsibility for our destiny as a people can be achieved only by our own free choice. Only citizens can reestablish democracy in Chicago.

Conclusion

Finally, then, the greatest issue facing Chicago is the question of our future. Is neighborhood and metropolitan government based upon participatory politics possible in Chicago or is Chicago destined by its political culture, historical tradition and human limitations to continue its fragmented local government structures and Machine politics during America's third century? This is not a question whose answer is entirely predetermined. To a large extent it depends upon the choices of individual citizens and political leaders. To determine Chicago's political and governmental future we must first ask, "What future do we want?" Then we must determine whether the current social and economic conditions both in Chicago and nationally would support the politics we prefer. Finally, we must ask, in order to change from our current system to the system we would prefer, what resources in time, work, leadership, money and organization are required, and are these resources available to those who favor change? Predicting Chicago's future is made more difficult because fundamental reform, although a product of gradual changes over many years, often occurs quickly when a major crisis or issue triggers the change.

Thus, for instance, the election of Mayor Byrne came suddenly. It surprised all students of Chicago politics. On the other hand, the fact that she was elected without the benefit of a precinct army limits the degree of change which her election can bring. Most students of Chicago politics believe that the Byrne Administration will prove transitional. They disagree on the nature of the transition. Whether the Byrne Administration will have the effect of modernizing Machine government, or of providing the opportunity for the emergence of a new Party boss in the Daley tradition, or of laying the foundation for the election of a future reform administration is the question. Change is certainly coming in Chicago politics. The Byrne election signals that much. What citizens and political leaders do in the years immediately ahead will determine the direction of change in Chicago politics and government for decades to come.

Unresolved Issues and Further Research Opportunities

This chapter has presented the most plausible hypotheses and theories about Chicago politics and government and my own prescription for Chicago's political future. The best way to end may be by making these hypotheses upon which my analysis depends more explicit and by indicating the further research which would be necessary to support or disprove them.

First, I have asserted that the fragmented structure of Chicago's government is due to three factors: 1) rapid population growth since 1833, 2) unrealistic taxing restrictions in the 1870 State Constitution and later State legislation and 3) political advantages to a party political machine which is able to overcome this governmental fragmentation. It would be worthwhile in testing these hypotheses to have a definitive and exhaustive historical analysis of the creation of each of the separate governmental units based upon legal documents of incorporation, legislative debates, memoirs of significant political figures, newspaper accounts and oral histories. No such study has yet been made. In addition to the historical study, it would be very useful to have a current political study made which would analyze the extent to which the dominant political party actually controls decisions of each local unit of government (not just major bodies like the City Council and School Board). By interviews and decision-making analysis it should be possible to determine to what extent party leaders are actually informed about and direct specific governmental decisions in different local agencies. Some decisions seem to be made with some autonomy by each agency and its leadership. Other decisions seem to result from contacts between party leaders at one agency with those at another. The degree of local autonomy and centralized control has never been accurately measured.

Second, I have asserted that for the last hundred years political control has been centralized in a political party machine based upon patronage and other economic rewards for party supporters which has, in turn, resulted in a high level of corruption in local government as one of the unintended but inevitable consequences. Despite the many colorful accounts which have been written over the years by journalists, reformers and scholars of the Chicago Machine and of party machines in other American cities, we have surprisingly little evidence in support of the most fundamental hypotheses about Machine politics. These studies have not been able to answer definitively the following questions:

1. What is the precise effect of party precinct workers in a given election? Under what conditions do they swing voters to support party candidates and how many votes can they control per precinct?
2. How much effect does the patronage system have on electoral outcomes in Chicago? How many people in Chicago vote a straight party ticket because they or a relative have a job? We do not even know, despite the pending court case, exactly how many patronage precinct workers there are in Chicago.
3. How many votes are actually stolen in Chicago elections by vote fraud?
4. How much graft and corruption is there in Chicago? Does machine politics inevitably lead to corruption or can some governmental safeguards prevent and limit corruption? What are the attitudinal factors which link Machine politics, patronage, and corruption? How can these attitudes be modified?
5. What is the public impact of patronage and corruption upon the City as a whole?

These questions can only be answered by in-depth interviews with party leaders, sample surveys of both voters and party activists, election statistics and court depositions. However, from carefully designed empirical studies, we ought to be able to make the conditions under which Machine politics flourishes and has evolved more explicit. Only then will we begin to have the foundation necessary for any adequate explanation of the actual operation of Chicago politics.

Third, I have asserted that there is a Chicago power structure composed of a few member groups whose leaders work together to control governmental decisions in ways beneficial to themselves. Despite Banfield's study of Chicago's process of political influence, no empirical method has yet been developed to determine specifically who is and who is not a member of the power structure. Nor has any clear definition or method of measuring the exchange of favors been invented. As appealing as the concept of a Chicago power structure may be in explaining the results of Chicago politics, it has yet to be proven that such a structure actually exists.

Fourth, while executive and party control over the Chicago City Council can be demonstrated by a roll call vote analysis, these voting patterns raise three important questions of political philosophy: 1) Is the Chicago City Council representative? 2) Is it democratic? 3) Is it effective? The paradoxical nature of the answers to these questions should serve to deepen our understanding of democratic politics and government. For instance, it is easy to show that in their absolute and unwavering party loyalty pro-Administration Aldermen cast at least some votes against the strong views and direct interests of their constituents and the community they "represent." Yet these same Aldermen and the Mayor are easily reelected by large majorities every four years in those wards. Are they reelected because opposition party and opposition political organizations are too weak to offer real alternatives? Or do citizens actually calculate that, on balance, the Democratic Machine does a better job of running the City and providing basic City services, protection and civic stability than their opponents; and that this outweighs occasional votes by Aldermen with which they do not agree? To answer the fundamental questions about the Chicago City Council we must first define the goals of democracy, representation and effectiveness and then determine by empirical studies how closely, if at all, Chicago government comes to meeting them. No such study combining political philosophy and political analysis has yet been made.

Fifth, other than Paul Peterson's study of the Chicago School Board, the politics of ideological bargaining as it occurs throughout Chicago government has been little understood. Since the Democratic Machine is usually portrayed as "pragmatic" rather than as "ideological" there is considerable terminological confusion in trying to describe Chicago politics with labels like "ideological bargaining." Obviously, the principal ideological split is between various reformers who want to end Machine politics and to promote policy goals such as racial desegregation and Machine supporters who wish to continue the existing political system with little policy change. But, to analyze ideological bargaining in Chicago fully, it will be necessary to analyze the goals of the Machine and its opponents in various governmental bodies, determine which governmental decisions are the result of ideological bargaining and which of other political processes and discover how decisions for each group are made. Once the extent of ideological bargaining is determined, then we must attempt to determine its consequences. Does ideological warfare in Chicago government result in rigidity, a lack of legislative improvement and, therefore, poor laws *or* does the lack of a need to compromise allow for stronger legislation? Finally, we must fit this model of ideological bargaining within the general pluralist model of American politics and within the elite decision-making model based upon the informal power structure in Chicago. The pluralist, ideological and elite forms of politics seem to coexist in Chicago and a full description of Chicago politics and government would need to assign a place for each.

Sixth, I have asserted some of the reasons for the stability and durability of Machine politics and government, despite its disappearance from most other major American cities. Milton Rakove has explored this issue further elsewhere. However, both his explanation and mine have yet to be empirically verified. Presumably, these hypotheses can be tested only by comparative studies with other American cities which share similar demographic, cultural and historical characteristics.

NOTES

[1]This history is taken primarily from The League of Women Voters: *The Key to Our Local Government,* (4th ed.; Chicago: Citizens Information Service, 1978), pp. 1–5. Also a discussion of population growth and the general governmental structural inadequacies are to be found in Dick Simpson, ed., *Chicago's Future: An Anthology of Reports, Speeches, and Scholarship Providing an Agenda for Change* (Champaign, Ill.: Stipes, 1976).

[2]The Illinois State Constitution of 1870. Also cited in *The League of Women Voters, op. cit.,* p. 9.

[3]*Ibid.,* pp. 8–9.

[4]*Ibid.,* pp. 11–12. There are grave fiscal dangers to open-ended borrowing by local government without referendum. When I served as 44th Ward Alderman in the Chicago City Council, I offered amendments to the Municipal Code which would have limited the amount of bonds which Chicago could issue in a single year without voter approval.

[5]See especially, Edward Banfield, *Political Influence* (New York: The Free Press of Glencoe, 1961) and Milton Rakove, *Don't Make No Waves, Don't Back No Losers* (Bloomington: Indiana University Press, 1975).

[6]Martin Shefter, "The Emergence of the Political Machine: An Alternative View" in *Theoretical Perspectives on Urban Politics,* ed. by Willis Hawley, *et al* (Englewood Cliffs, N.J.: Prentice-Hall, 1976), pp. 14–44.

[7]Len O'Connor, *Clout: Mayor Daley and His City* (Chicago: Regnery, 1975), p. 9.

[8]For the best description of these ward bosses and this era see Lloyd Wendt and Herman Kogan, *Bosses in Lusty Chicago* (Bloomington: Indiana University Press, 1967), originally published under the title *Lords of the Levee* by Bobbs-Merrill in 1943.

[9]See especially Len O'Connor, *op. cit.,* pp. 10–11 and Alex Gottfried, *Boss Cermak of Chicago* (Seattle: University of Washington Press, 1962).

[10]Milton Rakove, *op. cit.,* p. 4.

[11]*Ibid.,* p. 14.

[12]William Riordon, *Plunkitt of Tammany Hall* (New York: Dutton, 1963), p. 12.

[13]*Ibid.,* p. 37.

[14]*Michael L. Shakman and Paul M. Lurie, et al. vs. The Democratic Organization of Cook County et al.,* Case No. 69 C2145 in U.S. District Court. Deposition by William R. Quinlan, Corporation Counsel and Attorney for the Defendant City of Chicago, p. 1.

[15]*Ibid.,* p. 2.

[16]*Ibid.,* pp. 2–3.

[17]*Ibid.,* p. 4.

[18]A summary of the entire study is to be found in Better Government Association, "Better Government Association 1974 Annual Report," reprinted in Simpson, ed., *Chicago's Future,* pp. 375–384. The later budget study is by Aldermen Oberman, Simpson and Lathrop "The Case for Property Tax Reduction in This Year's City Budget," mimeographed document, November 1979, 27 pp.

[19]John Gardiner and Theodore Lyman, *Decisions for Sale* (New York: Praeger, 1978).

[20]*Ibid.,* p. 75.

[21]*Ibid.,* p. 77.

[22]*Ibid.,* p. 80.

[23]*Ibid.,* p. 82.

[24]*Ibid.,* p. 202.

[25]Some of my description of the Chicago power structure, its components and its exchange of favors is based upon research which Peter Knauss is undertaking on a new book on Chicago politics which we have discussed at length. While it is not yet possible to cite specific pages in that book, I am indebted to him for his contribution to this section.

[26]Edward Banfield, *op. cit.,* pp. 263 and 270–72.

[27]Milton Rakove, *op. cit.,* p. 83.

[28]Peter Knauss, *Chicago: A One-Party State* (Champaign, Ill.: Stipes, 1972), p. 9.

[29]Ross Lathrop, "Improving the City Council," published both in *Focus/Midwest Magazine* 13:79 (January/February 1978) and in *The Future of Chicago,* No. 3, 1978, a series of speeches and articles published by the University of Illinois at Chicago Circle.

[30]Dick Simpson, "Neighborhood Government and City Council Reform" in Simpson, *op. cit.,* p. 204.

[31]Lathrop, *op. cit.*

[32]Paul Peterson, *School Politics Chicago Style* (Chicago: University of Chicago Press, 1976), p. 65.

[33]*Ibid.*

[34]*Ibid.,* p. 78.

[35]*Ibid.,* p. 51.

[36]The 1954 Chicago Home Rule Commission, *Chicago's Government: Its Structural Modernization and Home Rule Problems* (Chicago: University of Chicago Press, 1954), and The 1972 Home Rule Commission, *The Chicago Home Commission Report and Recommendations* (Chicago: University of Illinois at Chicago Circle, 1972). The key proposals from both these reports and those by critics are contained in Simpson, *op. cit.,* pp. 131–240.

[37]Lloyd Wendt and Herman Rogan, *op. cit.,* pp. 144–49.

[38]*Ibid.,* pp. 91–96.

[39]For more on Saul Alinsky, community organizing, and community organizations in Chicago see Saul Alinsky, *Reveille for Radicals* (New York: Random House, 1969), originally published in 1946; and Saul Alinsky, *Rules for Radicals* (New York: Random House, 1971).

[40]For a brief description of the formation of IVI see Mary Herrick, "The Roots of IVI" in the Appendix to *Strategies for Change,* by Dick Simpson and George Beam (Chicago: Swallow Press, 1976). For an analysis of IVI and DFI see James Q. Wilson, *The Amateur Democrat* (Chicago: University of Chicago Press, 1962).

[41]Dan Walker, *Rights in Conflict: The Violent Confrontation of Demonstrators and Police in the Parks and Streets of Chicago During the Week of the Democratic Convention in 1968*. Report to the National Commission on the Causes and Prevention of Violence (New York: Bantam, 1968).

[42]This general analysis of Chicago's future is taken from an earlier article of mine entitled, "Chicago's Future: A Blueprint for Political Change," which appears in slightly different versions in *Focus/Midwest Magazine* 4:73 (December 1976/January 1977), 16–22; *The Future of Chicago,* No. 2 (Summer 1977); and Dick Simpson, Judy Stevens and Rick Kohnen, eds., *Neighborhood Government in Chicago's 44th Ward* (Champaign, Ill.: Stipes, 1979), pp. 216–24. Some of the following prescription in this chapter is taken from this article and revised without the use of quotation marks to indicate the passages which remain unchanged.

[43]Mike Royko, *Boss* (New York, Dutton, 1971), p. 67.

[44]David Protess, "Banfield's Chicago Revisited: The Conditions for and Social Policy Implications of the Transformation of a Political Machine," *The Social Service Review* 48:2 (June 1974), 196.

[45]*Ibid.*

[46]Robert Michaels, *Political Parties: A Sociological Study of the Oligarchical Tendencies of Modern Democracy* (New York: Dover Publications, 1959), first published in English in 1915.

[47]Wilson, *op. cit.*

[48]*Ibid.*, p. 354.

[49]*Ibid.*, p. 342.

[50]*Ibid.*, pp. 342–43.

CHAPTER **19**

Politics in Suburban Chicago: Fragmentation, Cooperation and the Problem of Accountability

John A. Williams

Suburban Chicago is growing in population, problems, and political power. While the City of Chicago loses population, the balance of Cook County and the five "collar counties" surrounding it gain. The result has been a steady erosion of Chicago's political power at the State and national levels. At the State level, legislative reapportionment was widely expected to benefit the cities, which were underrepresented in comparison to rural areas. What resulted was a political windfall for the fast-growing suburban areas, whose legislators could team up with their rural counterparts to oppose legislation benefiting the central City.[1] At the national level, Presidential candidates need to win the popular election in the State to win Illinois' electoral votes. If this is to continue, Democratic candidates can no longer afford to build up a large majority by concentrating on the City of Chicago and try to coast to a statewide victory. The suburban areas of Chicago have become decisive in presidential elections, and candidates who hope to win will be seen more frequently outside the City of Chicago than in the past.[2] Truly, suburban Chicago is the new political force in Illinois.

But to speak of "the suburbs" is to speak of a complex reality. Suburban towns differ greatly from one another, and there are other governmental forms. Yet various governmental units cooperate with one another to a remarkable extent. This chapter discusses the different kinds of governments in suburban Chicago, their similarities and differences, their problems and their relations with one another, with the city of Chicago, and with the State and Federal governments.

Governmental Units: Proliferation, Change and the Problem of Accountability

The types of governmental units found in metropolitan Chicago are four: cities, counties, townships, and special districts. The first three are general-purpose organizations that perform a variety of functions. The special districts, as the name implies, are established to carry out some special function, such as education, recreation or sanitation. All levy taxes. All spend money—sometimes a lot of it. And all affect the quality of life of the residents of the region.

Although Chicago is sometimes referred to as the "second city," metropolitan Chicago is in undisputed first place with respect to the number of governments in any metropolitan region. The Chicago area[3] leads the nation with a whopping 1172 separate governmental units. The Philadelphia region is second with 852, Pittsburgh third with 698 and New York fourth with "only" 538.[4] Clearly government is not an endangered species in the area. The result of this proliferation has been a "crazy quilt" pattern of governments superimposed on one another and the near impossibility of any citizen keeping up with what each unit is doing. The cause of this embarrassment of riches is the 1870 Illinois State Constitution. That document limited the ability of local governments to go into debt beyond five percent of the assessed value of its property. The result was the creation of numerous separate governmental units, each of which could go into debt.[5] A particular piece of property could be located simultaneously in a county, a township, a city and several special districts, each of which could count the value of the property in establishing its debt limit—tricky, these Midwesterners!

Counties

The area we are concerned with in this chapter is that portion of Cook County outside the city limits of Chicago (about 39 percent of the population of the county is not in the City of Chicago) plus the five "collar counties" surrounding Cook County: Lake, McHenry, Kane, DuPage and Will Counties. These six counties comprise something called the Chicago Standard Metropolitan Statistical Area (or SMSA), concerning which the U.S. Census Bureau gathers truckloads of statistics. Chicago itself, which lost more than five percent of its population during the 1960's, had by 1970 about 48 percent of the population of the SMSA, and 30 percent of the State of Illinois.[6] As an indication of change, Chicago had in 1950 about 70 percent of the population of the SMSA.[7]

As might be expected, the counties differ among themselves in ways other than location. One of the most important differences, and one which creates other differences, is economic status. Income per person varied significantly among the counties. DuPage County residens are, on the whole, the wealthiest, with a per capita income of $6,210. Lake County residents earned $6,032 per person; Cook County $5,324; Kane County $5,215; McHenry County $5,189; and Will County $4,834.[8]

Townships

All of the counties in question are further divided into townships, which include the entire area *outside* of the City of Chicago. Township functions, which were once extensive, have diminished in the last several years and now include such things as making temporary welfare payments, giving tax advice, dog-catching, and running various social programs such as senior citizens' centers. Rural townships still retain some road maintenance responsibilities. Cook County townships alone get more than $5 million per year of federal revenue-sharing—from twenty to fifty percent of their budgets.[9] Some people feel that townships are no longer necessary, since more and more of their functions are being performed by counties and cities.[10] And with the increasing urbanization of the region, cities are expanding at the expense of both counties and townships.

Townships are kept afloat by federal revenue sharing and tax increases, increases which averaged 52 percent for the Cook County townships from 1972 to 1976—higher than those for Cook County or the average city in Illinois. Indeed, Hanover Township's property tax levies increased by a phenomenal 226 percent during the period.[11] One explanation of the continued popularity of townships is the support of the Republican Party, which generally controls them and benefits from the patronage opportunities thereby presented. There is a provision in the 1970 Constitution for holding referendums to abolish townships, but Republican political opposition to such a move has been intense. We may see Chicago wards abolished before the suburban townships are!

Cities

Like townships and counties, cities in metropolitan Chicago differ greatly from one another. It is meaningless to speak of the "average" suburb. Barrington Hills, probably the wealthiest one, has a median family income of $42,250. This means that half of the families living there make *more* than that. The median home value is $129,500, and 92.4 percent of the families make more than $25,000 per year.[12] Compare these figures to those for Robbins, a much poorer city to the south of Chicago. There the median family income is $13,360, the median home value is $18,500, and the percent of families earning over $25,000 per year is 6.4.[13] Other suburbs fall in between these extremes, but the range of possibilities is clear—the myth of uniform suburban affluence is far from accurate.

Despite the fact of heterogeneity among suburban cities, the cities themselves often tend to be homogeneous internally. That is, people of a similar income level tend to live near one another and in the same city. The result is a system of "enclaves," where people live in the best circumstances they can afford and use various strategies to keep out the less privileged. Among the tools for doing this are restrictive zoning laws preventing multi-family dwellings or requiring very large lots for new construction, preventing the building of additional streets and sewers to handle new construction, and unwritten—and often illegal—"understandings" among home sellers concerning who should be permitted to buy into a community. Attempts to open up suburbs to subsidized housing and the resultant inflow of lower socio-economic status persons have been frustrating. Economic and even racial discrimination is still very much with us.

One way in which to categorize communities is by the ratio of jobs available in the community to the number of workers living there. *Employing towns* have at least 16 percent more jobs than workers. *Residential* or *dormitory* towns have fewer than 85 percent of the jobs needed by workers living in them. The other towns, not surprisingly, are called *balanced*.[14]

While it is dangerous to make generalizations about such disparate units as cities in suburban Chicago, residents of the region frequently speak of the suburbs of the "north shore" or "south" or "northwest" as if there were certain similarities among them. There is enough truth in such assumptions to make them worth repeating here. North shore suburbs are generally upper middle and upper class, with high economic levels. People living there tend to be more affluent managerial types, who frequently commute a fair distance to get into Chicago for work. The largest suburb of the SMSA, Evanston, is an interesting exception to this. Evanston is more culturally, ethnically, and economically diverse than any other Chicago suburb, with the possible exception of Oak Park. The northwestern cities are newer, with a more recent housing stock and a younger, more mobile population. This area is growing very rapidly, and is generally populated by middle class people in white-collar jobs. Many Chicagoans move to the suburbs, particularly the northwestern ones. Some of these cities have developed an industrial base, such as Elk Grove Village. Other cities in the area profit from the proximity to O'Hare Airport. The near west suburbs are older, ethnic, blue-collar cities. Middle class blacks have moved in significant numbers to such places as Oak Park, but have not significantly integrated several white ethnic bastions such as Cicero, the location of an integration march by Martin Luther King in 1965. The far west suburbs with some notable exceptions in the Fox Valley, are rather similar to those of the northwest: young population, relatively inexpensive land and new housing stock. The south and southwest suburbs are, with a few dramatic exceptions such as Flossmoor and Homewood, generally of a lower socio-economic level. It is in the south that the really poor suburbs are to be found, such as Robbins, mentioned above, and East Chicago Heights.

Under the 1970 Illinois State Constitution, cities have a great deal of discretion in how they conduct their affairs, perhaps more than in any other state. Cities in general are creatures of the state, which sets the conditions for incorporation, grants and withholds powers, and even dissolves municipal corporations on rare occasions.[15] The extensive "home rule" powers given automatically in Illinois to any city with more than 25,000 people and to any other city after a referendum mean, in effect, that cities may do as they please so long as they do not contravene state law. As cities expand into previously unincorporated territory, the powers of the counties and townships directly affected are reduced. The cities begin to perform many of the law-enforcement, taxing and zoning functions previously performed by the counties or the townships.[16]

Special Districts

The great proliferation of governmental units in the Chicago area is due largely to the number of special districts. Unlike general-purpose governments, these districts are established for some particular purpose. Each district has some function to perform, such as education, sewage treatment and even mosquito abatement.[17] These special districts are not always merely a way to circumvent Constitutionally-imposed bonding limitations; they frequently perform services that would be very difficult or even impossible for one of the other types of government to perform. The system of forest preserves is maintained by such a district, and both the Metropolitan Sanitary District and the Regional Transportation Authority confront area-wide problems that do not stop at city or county lines. The problem with the large number of special districts is that it is very difficult to remain abreast of what they are doing. This is the problem of accountability. For now we note that the tax rate of the Metropolitan Sanitary District increased 171 percent from 1970 to 1977; this was done very quietly and without any public referendum.[18] These governments may seem invisible, but they are not inexpensive.

Change

The dynamics of suburban change are well understood. Suburbs were made feasible through the development of improved transportation: first trolleys, then railroads and expressways. Federal government policies granting loans for new homes in the suburbs and tax reductions for interest paid on home mortgages caused the suburbs to be very attractive economically as well as esthetically. Extensive zoning and taxing powers permitted suburbs to exclude those developments which cost the city more than they bring in revenue. For example, most cities like to have shopping centers just inside their borders. They would get all of the tax revenue, about half of the increased traffic flow, and no additional children to educate as a result. On the other hand, most cities try to avoid large public housing projects. In addition to possible racial antipathy, citizens fear that an influx of lower socio-economic status people might mean more children in the schools, more need for law enforcement expenditures and insufficient additional tax revenue to pay for these things.

The "specialized" suburbs consist of various business and residential units that have chosen for some reason to be there.[19] These groups all make their locational choices, in the words of Oliver P. Williams, "not only to increase the ease of exchanging rewarding messages, but also to minimize unrewarding and unwanted messages. . . ." A middle class family chooses a suburb which will also reduce unpleasant message exchanges from lower class persons in the form of muggings, fistfights and uncouth syntax."[20] Zoning is basically a device for reducing the incidence of incompatible adjacent activities. If some noxious element, such as a factory, cannot be zoned out of a community—or is wanted in the community for economic reasons—it can still be forced to locate in an area of the locality's choosing if it wishes to come into the community.

This tendency toward homogeneity and specialization conflicts with recent attempts of racial and economic groups to "open up" the suburbs. There is some evidence that homogeneity is still winning out. A statistical analysis of changes in Philadelphia suburbs may well apply to the Chicago area.[21] The "index of dissimilarity" between white collar and blue collar workers, defined roughly as the percent of such workers who would have to move in order for the distribution to be completely uniform, increased from 17.5 in 1950 to 23.5 in 1960 to 27.0 in 1970. For college educated versus elementary educated people the index increased from 29.0 to 35.0 to 39.0 during the same time periods. We have no reason to think that the Chicago area findings would differ significantly from these, although a report of the Northeastern Illinois Planning Commission did suggest that, "among suburban communities . . . income disparities seem to be decreasing slightly."[22]

Intergovernmental Relations: Limited Cooperation Among Semi-Sovereign Entities

Governments in the region do not exist in a vacuum. Despite home rule, cities are still the creatures of the State, subject to State regulations and in need of State financial aid. And since the mid-1960's the federal government has increasingly dealt directly with cities in its grant programs. Counties, townships, and special districts relate similarly to both the State and federal governments. These are examples of "vertical" intergovernmental relations, among governmental units at different levels. It is most useful to think of cities, townships and counties as if they were all at the same level, even though a county would contain several townships and even more cities. All deal directly with the State, and all deal directly with one another more or less as semi-sovereign entities. Relationships among governmental units at the same level are referred to as "horizontal" intergovernmental relations.

Intergovernmental cooperation in the Chicago area has been greatly facilitated by Article VII, Section 10 of the 1970 Illinois Constitution, and the Illinois Intergovernmental Cooperation Act of 1973. As a result of these documents, "almost anything local governments can do, they can do cooperatively."[23] There are several factors that impel governments in the area to cooperate with one another.[24] Economies of scale arise when service areas are combined, existing facilities can be used more efficiently, and the problem of overlapping jurisdictions can be overcome.[25] The following are the types of cooperative agreements commonly entered into:[26] General Administrative Services and Facilities; Transportation and

Public Works; Recreation and Culture; Community Development; Health, Fire Protection, and Emergency Services; and Law Enforcement and the Courts.

Specific examples of agreements entered into include the very important City of Chicago/Suburban Cook County Water Supply Service, through which Chicago supplies water at its city limits to suburban cities willing to build the connections. The North Suburban Library System links the resources of the libraries of north and northwest suburban libraries. The Aurora-Naperville Boundary Agreement reduces unseemly competition between the two cities over the unincorporated area between them. The Evanston North Shore Health Department permits Winnetka, Glencoe, and an unincorporated part of New Trier Township to use the facilities of the Evanston Health Department. And there are a large number of mutual aid pacts for fire and rescue services.[27]

Many kinds of intergovernmental agreements are possible in principle, but in fact certain types are less likely. These concern the functions central to the "life style" of a community, such as schools, housing and urban renewal.[28] It is fairly easy to get agreements on police radio frequencies, but much more difficult to get agreement on consolidating school districts. One researcher has suggested that these difficult agreements are more likely among communities similar in social rank.[29] Nevertheless two elementary school districts in Highland Park were unable to agree on a merger, even though one of the districts subsequently had to close two schools. As the superintendent of a nearby elementary school district commented, "People feel that their school district has a unique set of values that it is imparting to their children."[30] The ultimate step of combining to form one city was rejected by Park Forest and Park Forest South, despite projected savings over the years of hundreds of thousands of dollars.[31] Two institutions of particular importance in facilitating intergovernmental cooperation are metropolitan councils of government ("COGS") such as the Cook County Council of Governments, a voluntary organization formed in 1967 to consider common problems and their solutions, and the Northeastern Illinois Planning Commission (NIPC), which is discussed in greater detail below.[32] Other examples are the Northwest Suburban Council, the Southwest, and the DuPage Mayors' and Managers Conference.

As expected, there are numerous areas of potential conflict among suburban governments. Suburbs compete to develop and incorporate areas that will be a net gain economically or socially. Schaumburg succeeded in getting a huge shopping mall, so it gets all of the property taxes thereby generated. Neighboring areas in nearby suburbs share the increased traffic—but not the tax revenues. Affluent Oak Brook has about $350 million in non-polluting facilities such as shopping centers, offices, and hotels, but has provided no low-cost housing. A planning commission member commented, "we are sympathetic to the achievers and the underprivileged. . . . We have provided for the achievers, however."[33]

Toward a Quasi-Metropolitan Government: Functional Cooperation Amidst Heterogeneity

One solution to the patchwork arrangement of governments in the region is to combine them in an areawide metropolitan government. In fact, for reasons known only to himself, the Republican candidate for Mayor of Chicago made a similar suggestion in the 1979 campaign. The political ramifications of the suggestion were mainly negative, but the idea is not without advantages. The tax burden would be equalized, and resources would no longer be able to "hide" in low-problem, low-tax areas. Funds available could be spent on alleviating severe hardships rather than increasing the level of amenities in places that are already well-off. Services would be standardized, and significant economies of scale would be expected. Suburbs could no longer avoid taking their fair share of public housing projects. Schools could be more effectively integrated if the primarily white schools outside the city of Chicago were included in the plan.

But there would be some real costs involved. Smaller, homogeneous cities can spend their limited resources on services of interest to the people who live there. A large metropolitan government might not be responsive to citizen preferences and needs, but be propelled by bureaucratic or political considerations. As the Executive Director of the Northeastern Illinois Planning Commission noted,[34]

> . . . it is necessary to perform a difficult balancing act between the need to solve areawide problems and reduce the cost of government, and the ideal of maintaining healthy local governments at a small scale where the individual citizen can be directly involved and have his preferences accounted for.

Metropolitan government has the potential of reducing the influence of central city minorities, since their newly-won political power would be severely diluted if the city were combined with the largely white suburbs.[35]

Whatever the theoretical costs or benefits of metropolitan government, no groundswell of support for the idea is emerging. The idea has been around for a long time without much being done about it. The best explanation for this is that there are no powerful political groups who feel they would gain from such a change. Suburban leaders don't want to see their tax revenues go back to Chicago or to less wealthy suburban areas, or to lose control over their "life style" functions. If they are unwilling to merge school districts, consider how much less likely they are to approve merging all governmental functions into a political structure they probably could not personally control. City political leaders are comfortable with their own political arrangements, and would hesitate to get enmeshed in a metropolitan government dominated by Republicans. The voting strength of inner-city Black and Hispanic groups could be severely curtailed in such an arrangement, even though these groups stand to gain the most from access to suburban wealth.

What has evolved as a substitute for metropolitan government is the maze of special districts, intergovernmental agreements and planning agencies referred to in Dick Simpson's chapter. The area is decentralized to preserve the life style values of its residents. Vital services, such as transportation and waste disposal, are centralized when feasible through special districts. Intergovernmental agreements cover a wide range of problem areas. And the various planning agencies are coordinated at least somewhat by the Northeastern Illinois Planning Commission. It's not metropolitan government. But it's as close to it as the area is likely to get in the forseeable future.

Conclusion: Toward the Year 2000

The future of the region is likely to be an extrapolation of present trends, modified by outside forces such as the restricted availability of fossil fuels or by some unforeseen catastrophe. We may expect the political power of the suburbs to increase relative to the city of Chicago. Suburbanites will continue to resist encroachment on their fiefdoms, particularly by those less affluent than themselves, but the pressure to "open up" the suburbs to the less well-off will result in some demographic changes. The primary basis of exclusion will continue to be economic and only indirectly racial. Some gradual sharing of wealth may occur, but it is likely to be due to action at the state or national level. A major uncertainty is whether court decisions will force redistributive policies that are most unlikely if the residents of the region are left to themselves. Rising costs and increased voter sensitivity to tax rates will force suburban governments to economize, which will result in more areas of intergovernmental cooperation. These areas may include life-style functions, but such agreements are likely to be between governments of similar social rank. A long-term restriction in gasoline supplies will result in increased demands for service upon the Regional Transportation Authority. We can also expect demands for housing closer to job locations, and for job opportunities near where people now live.

Probably the most important factors shaping the future of metropolitan Chicago are the values that citizens and policy makers bring to the political process. Will the wealthy suburbs be permitted such autonomy that they can exclude poorer people and prevent the construction of public housing facilities? Will the traditional American value of rewarding achievement take precedence over other American values, such as equality. Is freedom to be defined as freedom from governmental interference in private lives or freedom to move into better surroundings? Will American notions of fair play and governmental accountability cause the better supervision or even consolidation of the multiplicity of special districts?

Our prediction of continuity in the politics of the region does not mean that there will be no change. As this chapter is written there are movements afoot to abolish the townships[36] and most of the special districts.[37] These attempts will probably fail, but the current citizens' "tax revolt" will be with us for a while. This will cause the rate of governmental growth to slow, although we do not expect much reduction in governmental size. There are many problems in the metropolitan region that can be addressed only by government. Governments may reorganize and cooperate in ways that will make them at once more effective in the delivery of services and more efficient in the expenditure of public funds. Citizens may work more actively to ensure that governments attack the serious problems affecting the whole region. The resources are there—Whether the will to act is there remains to be seen.

NOTES

[1] Alan Shank and Ralph W. Conant, *Urban Perspectives: Politics and Policies* (Boston: Holbrook Press, 1975), p. 106.

[2] Peter W. Colby and Paul Michael Green, "Vote Power: Suburbs Up, Cities Down," *Illinois Issues* 4:11 (November 1978), 21.

[3] By metropolitan region we mean the Standard Metropolitan Statistical Area (SMSA), defined by the U.S. Bureau of the Census in the case of Chicago as the city of Chicago plus the balance of Cook County and the five adjoining "collar counties": Lake, McHenry, Kane, Du Page, and Will.

[4] Robert L. Lineberry and Ira Sharkansky, *Urban Politics and Public Policy* (New York: Harper and Row, 1978), p. 70.

[5] Illinois Department of Local Governmental Affairs and the Northeastern Illinois Planning Commission, *Intergovernmental Cooperation in Illinois* (Springfield: State of Illinois, 1976), p. 3.

[6] Colby and Green, *op. cit.*, p. 21.

[7] Lineberry and Sharkansky, *op. cit.*, p. 58.

[8] *Chicago Tribune*, March 23, 1978. The income figures are for 1974.

[9] *Chicago Tribune*, September 1, 1977.

[10] David Kenney, *Basic Illinois Government: Systematic Explanation* (Carbondale: Southern Illinois University Press, 1970), p. 245.

[11] *Chicago Tribune*, September 1, 1977.

[12] *Chicago Tribune*, September 28, 1977. Data were reported by Pierre de Vise.

[13] *Ibid.*

[14] International City Management Association, *Municipal Yearbook, 1967* (Washington: ICMA, 1968), p. 36. Cited in Thomas P. Murphy and John Rehfuss, *Urban Politics in the Suburban Era* (Homewood: The Dorsey Press, 1976), p. 74.

[15] This is called "Dillon's Rule," after Iowa State Supreme Court Judge John Dillon, who first formulated it in an 1868 case. See Murphy and Rehfuss, *op. cit.*, pp. 167–8.

[16] Theodore Lowi and Benjamin Ginsberg, *Poliscide* (New York: Macmillan, 1976), p. 182.

[17] Kenney, *op. cit.*, p. 245.

[18] *Chicago Tribune*, May 3, 1979.

[19] This distinction is made very clearly by Oliver P. Williams. The discussion in this section relies on Oliver P. Williams, "Life Style Values and Political Decentralization in Metropolitan Areas," in *Community Structure and Decision-Making: Comparative Analyses*, ed. by Terry N. Clark (Scranton: Chandler Publishing Company, 1968), pp. 427–440. For an extended theoretical treatment of the dynamics of urbanism, see Oliver P. Williams, *Metropolitan Political Analysis: A Social Access Approach* (New York: The Free Press, 1971).

[20] Williams, "Life Style Values . . .," *op. cit.*, p. 431.

[21] Data were collected and the statistical technique suggested by Oliver P. Williams. Indices of segregation and dissimilarity are explained in Otis Dudley Duncan and Beverly Duncan, "Residential Distribution and Occupational Stratification," *The American Journal of Sociology* 60 (March 1955).

[22] *Chicago Tribune*, March 23, 1978.

[23] *Intergovernmental Cooperation in Illinois*, p. 6.

[24] Williams, "Life Style Values . . .," *op. cit.*, p. 433.

[25]*Intergovernmental Cooperation in Illinois,* p. 4.

[26]*Ibid.,* p. vi.

[27]*Ibid., passim.*

[28]Williams, "Life Style Values . . .," *op. cit.,* pp. 434–36.

[29]James V. Toscano, "Transaction Flow Analysis in Metropolitan Areas: Some Preliminary Explorations," in *The Integration of Political Communities* Philip E. Jacob and James V. Toscano (Philadelphia: Lippincott, 1964), p. 117.

[30]*Suburban Trib,* April 25, 1979.

[31]Northeastern Illinois Planning Commission, *Planning in Northeastern Illinois* 20:6 (Spring 1979), 1.

[32]The League of Women Voters, *The Key to Our Local Government: Chicago Cook County Metropolitan Area* (3d ed.; Chicago: Citizens Information Service of Illinois, 1972), pp. 203–4.

[33]Michael N. Danielson, *The Politics of Exclusion* (New York: Columbia University Press, 1976), p. 41.

[34]Northeastern Illinois Planning Commission, *op. cit.,* p. 4.

[35]John J. Harrigan, *Political Change in the Metropolis* (Boston: Little, Brown, 1976), p. 238.

[36]*Chicago Tribune,* September 1, 1977.

[37]*Chicago Tribune,* May 1, 1979.

CHAPTER **20**

Taking Over City Hall —and Losing It

William K. Hall

This is a case study with tall ambitions. It examines the historical and political background of the decision of one Illinois city (Peoria) to try to undertake a major urban renewal effort—carried out with *local* funding. The decision to make use of local funding provoked a strong public response, affected municipal elections and led to the birth and political debut of a special citizens' political organization. That organization grew out of opposition to the City's urban renewal funding plans. The organization fielded candidates of its own in the 1969 municipal elections.

Many important questions, problems, currents and cross-currents are evident in this case study. Among these: the role of citizens' political organizations,[1] the nature of the process of recruiting public officials,[2] and the role of public opinion in the formulation of public policy.[3] Cross-currents contributing to the befogging of the specific issue of urban renewal and the means of funding included the overtones of race (urban renewal programs were often portrayed incorrectly as benefitting blacks exclusively), the ideological underpinnings of the citizens' political organization and its members and candidates, and the fact that the "establishment" had lost control of the local reins for the first time since the end of the Korean War.

Peoria and Urban Renewal

Like many cities its size, Peoria had been concerned about the problems of deteriorating housing conditions for some time. Urban renewal had roots in Peoria extending as far back as 1955 when groups called on the City to create a planning office. The first real step toward a viable urban renewal proposal was the bond referendum submitted to voters in 1960. They rejected the bond proposal and urban renewal foundered for much of the rest of the decade. The concept was sustained by the hope of obtaining federal funds from various Great Society programs. In the late 1960's, the demand for federal urban renewal funds outstripped the supply. By the end of the Johnson Administration, the waiting-list had lengthened to four years.

Late in 1967, members of the Peoria City Council decided that the four-year waiting list for federal funds prevented that avenue from being considered as a viable solution to the housing problem. Several other alternatives were considered, based on the experiences of other Illinois communities. The wheel tax did not appear to be a workable alternative; the issuance of bonds required a public referendum, and such an idea had earlier met with public disfavor. The property tax—an already overused form of taxation—was simply out of the question. The utility tax seemed to be the only remaining alternative as a locally-funded solution to the housing problem. A number of other cities in Illinois had used the utility tax, though not usually for urban renewal.

In December 1967, the utility tax proposal was presented on the floor of the Council by Alderman John Radley (R-5) for the first time. Basically the proposal was simple. A 5 percent tax would be levied on all utility bills (gas, phone, electricity and water), with the money going exclusively to urban renewal. The tax would remain in effect for a period of four years, and according to projections the tax could be expected to raise approximately \$6 million.

There was little immediate public reaction to the tax proposal. Even so, the Council delayed in taking up consideration of the proposal until February 6, 1968. By that time, an outcry was heard from some segments of the community. On the night of February 6, a number of concerned citizens appeared at the Council meeting in opposition to the utility tax. Those citizens presented petitions bearing nearly 9,000 signatures of Peoria residents opposed to the imposition of the tax.[4] Members of the City Council were attentive but voted 8 to 2 later in the meeting to impose such a tax with an effective date of July 1, 1968.[5]

In 1968, Peoria was a council/manager city. The City had converted to that form of government in 1952. The Mayor (a part-time position) was elected from the entire City. The ten members of the City Council were elected from wards. The Mayor was limited in his dealings with the Council by having voting privileges only in case of a tie and had only minimal veto power.

All members were elected for four-year terms on a partisan ballot. The same was true of the Mayor. Elections were scheduled not to coincide with other elections on the State or national levels. All members of the Council as well as the Mayor were elected at the same time. There were no staggered terms. Municipal elections were scheduled for the spring of 1969. The primary was set for February and the general election for April.

Peoria, which is the timeless measure of middle Americandom (e.g., "Will it play in Peoria?") was a

TABLE 20-1
Selected Demographic Characteristics
City of Peoria

Ward	Population	Non-White	Education 0-8 Years	Education 12+ Years	Median Income Below $5,000	Median Income Above $15,000
First	11,341	—	51.9%	5.2%	39.1%	3.0%
Second	17,399	30.1%	57.5%	3.4%	47.6%	—
Third	17,421	22.9%	55.4%	6.7%	58.4%	1.2%
Fourth	11,126	1.9%	29.9%	20.8%	32.1%	4.1%
Fifth	12,723	—	19.9%	30.4%	26.8%	7.5%
Sixth	11,458	—	40.6%	13.4%	29.6%	5.1%
Seventh	8,798	—	29.6%	19.1%	27.4%	3.4%
Eighth	10,346	—	23.8%	31.0%	16.7%	14.7%
Ninth	12,047	—	17.2%	28.0%	12.8%	6.9%
Tenth	10,273	3.8%	21.5%	34.8%	12.4%	18.3%
	122,932					

Source: 1970 U.S. Census

typical mid-sized American city. Selected demographics of the city are presented in Table 20-1.

The controversy over the utility tax and urban renewal occurred a full year prior to the municipal elections. In fact, the citizens would already have been paying the tax for eight months by the time the primary election was held. Members of the City Council must have concluded that the furor would subside by the time of the primary election. Members of the Council apparently felt the noise caused by vocal opponents of the utility tax was not a true indication of the opinion of most of the citizens of Peoria.

Those assumptions proved to be grave and politically expensive miscalculations. The vehemence of those who opposed the tax and/or urban renewal did not fade. Rather, the noise level increased. A major factor contributing to the increased din was public knowledge of the link between the utility tax and urban renewal.

A number of citizens appeared at the April 22, 1968, meeting of the City Council, this time bearing petitions containing 17,000 signatures,[6] asking the City Council to rescind the action taken at the February 6 meeting (the tax had not yet gone into effect). The Council, however, refused to reverse its previous position and the battlelines were drawn.

Turnover at City Hall

The local funding of urban renewal through a utility tax provoked some Peorians to create a new citizens' organization which contested for control of the City government in the primary and general elections of 1969.

The Birth of the Citizens for Representative Government

Political organizations do not simply spring into existence without some political ancestry. Usually there are one or more forces responsible for creating a climate in which a new political organization can take root. Such was the case in Peoria in the late 1960's. Peoria had known other citizens' organizations and third parties in the recent past, but none had been as successful as the Citizens for Representative Government (CFRG) would prove to be. The CFRG traced its origins to several of the earlier groups.

In 1960, a referendum had been held on the question of changing the representational system in the City from at-large aldermanic election to aldermanic election by ward. An organization of those who favored the change to ward representation (Peorians for Representative Government) won a narrow victory. Activists in the Peorians for Representative Government went on in the 1961 municipal elections to win four of the eight council seats. In 1965, that same organization presented petitions and had placed on the ballot a referendum question on changing Peoria's basic form of government from the "city manager/council" form back to the "strong mayor/council" form. The proposed change was crushed by a two-to-one margin. In addition, the four Council seats won in 1961 were lost.[7]

In 1964, a new organization known as VOTE (Voice of the Electorate) came into existence. Partially an outgrowth of the Goldwater phenomenon and candidacy, VOTE was the focal point for the community's conservatives. Some members of VOTE were also members of the John Birch Society; many in the organization opposed the War on Poverty, and it became basically a conservatively-oriented ideological organization for purists.

Mayor Robert Lehnhausen (1965–1969) characterized VOTE as having a membership which was " 'anti-black, anti-poor, anti-renter and who felt that, unless you own property, you shouldn't have a voice in what happens in your community.' "[8] He went on to note that the Citizens for Representative Government was "much like VOTE."

Citizens for Representative Government came into existence officially in the early months for 1968, approximately two months after the passage of the utility tax. CFRG was founded by Dan Thurman and Ray

Swearinger, both of whom were later to stand as aldermanic candidates. The organization had been formed "to give voice to citizen opposition concerning a five percent utility tax by the City Council to fund Peoria's urban renewal endeavor,"[9] and as was to be expected, many of the angry citizens who had appeared at Council sessions to protest the tax were among the founders of CFRG.

To illustrate how critical the utility tax was to the formation of CFRG, its state-chartered constitution had as its first section a pledge to work for the repeal of the utility tax. CFRG attracted a much broader spectrum of people than had previous Peoria citizens' groups. Less ideologically-oriented than VOTE, CFRG presented to the residents of Peoria a vehicle to fight the common enemy—the utility tax.

Like most political organizations, CFRG based its structure on the electoral units of the political system. Besides the mass membership, ward captains were elected from each of the ten wards in the city. Those ten ward captains and the president made up the Board of Directors of the Citizens for Representative Government. The ward captains and the president were nominated by a nominating committee and ratified by CFRG membership. The organization published what began as an in-house newspaper, with individuals (often ward captains) presenting their views to the general membership. Two of those most active in the CFRG at its inception—Dan Thurman, the first president and John Carver, his successor (who had been a member of VOTE)—estimated that within a year of its creation, dues-paying membership was somewhere in the general neighborhood of 600 to 1,000,[10] with Republican/Democratic ratios in CFRG at 2 to 1 or 3 to 1.

The question of whether the CFRG was a citizens' interest group or a political party was never settled. However, the debate might be moot as J. Leiper Freeman has noted: ". . . any such association which backs candidates, raises money for and conducts a campaign, and espouses a platform functions as a party in the local political arena."[1]

The February Primary Election

By organizing in the early months of 1968, CFRG had approximately a year to prepare for the upcoming municipal elections. Unlike many cities utilizing the council/manager form of government, municipal elections in Peoria were conducted with party labels on the ballot. With opposition to the utility tax as its symbol, CFRG began to look about for candidates who supported the utility tax position endorsed by the organization. Candidates sponsored by (or who were membes of) CFRG would not be on the ballot as members of the organization, but would wear either the Republican or the Democratic label.

In many instances, the Citizens for Representative Government solicited candidacies. In other instances, such solicitation was unnecessary. Candidates who were endorsed by the CFRG were endorsed first by a majority of the board of directors, to be ratified later by the organization's membership.[12]

As Table 20-2 indicates, in each of the wards there were several candidates competing for aldermanic seats who opposed the utility tax. Of the 49 candidates (including 7 incumbents) who announced for positions on the Council, 27 declared themselves in favor of repealing the utility tax. Eleven aldermanic candidates opposed repeal and eleven remained publicly noncommittal. Of the five candidates seeking the office of Mayor, only the incumbent came out in favor of the utility tax while the other four candidates favored repeal.

To the casual observer, the primary election to nominate candidates for Mayor and positions on the Peoria City Council looked like most municipal elections in most cities in the nation. There appeared to be very little drama in the offing. All but three of the ten members of the City Council had decided to seek re-election.

The incumbent Mayor, Republican Robert Lehnhausen had also decided to seek re-election—not a common occurrence in Peoria municipal politics. Lehnhausen was the first Mayor to seek re-election since the council/manager form of government had been adopted in 1952. No mayor had successfully won re-election since 1927.

The Mayor was an established member of the ruling group of interests which had dominated Peoria poltics since the end of the Korean War, and he was widely expected to win re-election. The group which held the reins of local political power in 1969 was comprised of banking interests and major officers of Caterpillar, local construction firms, businesses and, of course, Lehnhausen himself. As an active member of Peorians for City Manager, Lehnhausen had been one of those who took the lead in successfully changing Peoria's structure of government in the early 1950's from the strong mayor form to the city manager form.

The campaign for the various positions on the Council and for the office of Mayor were fought almost entirely around the issue of the utility tax. A review of the speaking appearances of the 54 candidates seeking nomination indicated that only infrequently did these candidates deal with other subjects. The utility tax as an issue was of such paramount importance that candidates were basing their entire campaigns on opposition to the utility tax. Incumbents (notably the Mayor) spent most of their time during that campaign defending the utility tax.

Yet, to say that the campaign was "fought" at all may be inappropriate. Neither those behind-the-scenes individuals who had held political control in recent years, the incumbents, nor the Peoria "liberals" took the challenge of CFRG very seriously. They mounted no counteroffensive and surfaced no alternative issues. They had every reason to expect easy victory. Further, to have attacked CFRG directly might have been perceived as giving credence to their position.

On February 11, 1969, the primary election was held. A meager 26 percent of the registered voters turned out to vote, down from a 35 percent turnout in 1965. This was a surprisingly low showing for an election in which the campaign rhetoric had been both loud and bitter. It seems likely, in retrospect, that the low turnout did not

TABLE 20-2
1969 Primary Election Results

	Candidate	Utility Tax Position	CFRG Endorsement	Party Affiliation	Number of Votes	Percent of Votes
Mayor						
	E. Michael O'Brien	Opposed	Yes	D	2,728	100%
	Robert Lehnhausen*	Favored		R	6,531	52%
	William Buob	Opposed		R	4,783	38%
	Carolyle Charvat	Opposed		R	501	4%
	Ralph H. Goodwin	Opposed		R	677	5%
First Ward						
	James Lavin*	Favored		D	247	33%
	Joseph Mudd	Opposed	Yes	D	407	54%
	Robert Hall	?		D	10	1%
	William Tripp	Opposed		D	92	12%
	Raymond Landis	?		R	228	50%
	John C. Aiello (write-in)	?		R	229	50%
Second Ward						
	Thomas Dunne*	Favored		D	280	59%
	Lyle Ball	Opposed		D	51	11%
	Harry Sephus	Opposed	Yes	D	140	30%
	James K. Polk	?		R	174	100%
Third Ward						
	William Wilson	?		D	21	7%
	Ralph Metts*	Favored		D	193	63%
	Herman Carter	?		D	55	17%
	George Goins	?		D	38	12%
	William O'Brien	Opposed	Yes	R	278	100%
Fourth Ward						
	Charles Duke (write-in)	?		D	1	100%
	Gerald Bibo*	Favored		R	451	43%
	James Stickelmaier	Opposed	Yes	R	592	57%
Fifth Ward						
	Dallas D'Hondt	?		D	153	100%
	John Radley*	Favored		R	480	46%
	James Ardis, Jr.	Opposed	Yes	R	574	54%
Sixth Ward						
	Verne E. Milloy	Opposed		D	67	17%
	David Mitchell	?		D	112	28%
	Richard VanNorman	Opposed		D	212	54%
	Gary Stella	Opposed	Yes	R	500	42%
	Thomas A. Butler, Jr.	?		R	285	24%
	Bruce G. Watt	?		R	418	35%
Seventh Ward						
	Charles Adkins	Opposed	Yes	D	124	63%
	Charles Layne	Opposed		D	73	37%
	Sam Arnold*	Favored++		R	511	34%
	John V. Feger	Favored		R	266	18%
	Dan Thurman	Opposed	Yes	R	746	49%
Eighth Ward						
	Frank Beall (write-in)	Opposed	Yes	D		
	Arthur Greenberg	Favored		R	616	35%
	Robert Janssen*	Opposed	Yes	R	1,162	65%
Ninth Ward						
	Ray C. Swearinger	Opposed	Yes	D	204	100%
	Louis E. Carr	Opposed	Yes	R	897	43%
	James E. Christopher	?		R	767	37%
	Donald W. Doyle	?		R	413	20%
Tenth Ward						
	Arthur Bader (write-in)	?		D		
	Robert G. Miller	Favored		R	133	6%
	Daniel L. Stull	Favored		R	252	11%
	Richard Carver	?		R	998	42%
	Robert Doubet	?		R	818	35%
	Harold Lindholm	Favored		R	172	7%

*Incumbent
++Favored the utility tax, but had not voted for it on February 6, 1968.

indicate satisfaction with the manner of governance, but rather was low because only a minority of the voters had a very high level of political interest in the urban renewal dispute.[13] The turnout in the wards varied from a low of 14 percent (Second Ward) to a high of 34 percent (Tenth Ward). By comparison, three months earlier in the 1968 presidential election, 82 percent of the registered voters had cast ballots. The turnout was so low that one incumbent alderman was toppled when his opponent polled 407 votes. In fact, the four candidates who defeated incumbent aldermen had only 2,319 *total* votes!

When the votes were tallied that evening, several things became quite clear (see Table 20-2). Although Mayor Lehnhausen was renominated, his total from among four Republican candidates was only 52 percent. Other warning signs were present. Of the seven aldermen who ran for renomination, five had voted for imposing the utility tax. Three of those five went down to defeat in the primary election. Two of the aldermen who had voted for the utility tax were renominated in wards which would directly benefit from urban renewal (Second and Third Wards). All three incumbent aldermen (Lavin, Radley and Bibo) who supported the utility tax and who represented wards which wouldn't directly benefit from urban renewal were defeated by CFRG-endorsed candidates. The citizens' organization had passed its first electoral test with flying colors.

The role of the media in this campaign, especially the role of the City's only daily newspaper the *Journal Star* was most curious. The *Journal Star* had been aligned with the ruling group of interests since the early 1950's. During the course of the election, it carried dozens of articles on various facets of the campaign, on the appearances of candidates before civic organizations and on the problems and plans for urban renewal in Peoria. The paper did not endorse any candidates for any office in the primary election. This was curious in light of the strong disagreement between the position taken by many of the candidates on the utility tax and the position taken editorially by the paper.

The *Peoria Journal Star* seemed to miss the point of the primary election contest not only during the primary itself but even after the results of the election became known. In a post-primary editorial the paper noted:

> . . . it is obvious that whatever individual appeal each candidate had Tuesday, his totals were swelled in many cases . . . by those embittered by such things as the utility tax.
>
> Yet the light vote demonstrates that there is nothing even faintly resembling a tidal wave of opposition to urban renewal and the funds to get something going. Most people were content to let things ride and didn't even go to the polls.
>
> Indeed, overall those who did turn out voted the strongest support of the whole election to Mayor Robert Lehnhausen.[14]

These editorial statements were made in spite of the fact that four of the incumbent aldermen seeking renomination supporting the tax went down to defeat, and the incumbent Mayor polled only 52 percent of his party's votes. Although this issue divided the community as few issues have in recent years, the ruling group of interests in office for twenty years had apparently grown lazy and deaf to the loud public outcry.

The April General Election

As the two-month general campaign got underway, some implications of the CFRG strategy became clear. First, as many electorial studies show, although voters tend to vote against something, a totally negative campaign runs a grave risk of backfiring. The CFRG candidates had taken an essentially negative position with their opposition to the utility tax for the funding of urban renewal. In order to balance such a negative posture, most of the candidates endorsed by the organization stated publicly that although they opposed the imposition of the utility tax they were not opposed to urban renewal for Peoria.

Many of the CFRG candidates also stated publicly that although they opposed the utility tax as such, their opposition was in reality only opposition in principle. The utility tax had not been submitted to the people in a referendum. Most CFRG candidates stated that they would vote to submit the future of the utility tax to a public referendum.

The CFRG ran its group of candidates as a slate. According to the CFRG spokesmen, in excess of 20,000 flyers supporting the entire slate were distributed during the general election campaign. This slate included candidates for Mayor and at least one candidate in every ward race except in the Second and Tenth Wards. In the Seventh, Eighth, and Ninth Wards the CFRG endorsed *both* candidates. In addition, the CFRG vigorously supported two candidates seeking election to the Peoria District #150 school board. One of the major issues of the school board race was busing.

The strategy employed by those who favored the utility tax or who at least were not endorsed by the CFRG was also interesting to observe. These candidates were confronted with two problems. On the one hand, there was the problem of increasing the turnout at the general election. Several incumbents had been upset in the primaries by opponents who polled only a few hundred votes. On the other hand, those candidates also had to grapple with the question of what public stand to take on the dominant issue of the election. Of the twenty-two aldermanic and mayoral candidates who survived the primary, only 7 opposed the repeal of the utility tax. Those candidates not supported by CFRG were not a cohesive unit. They ran separate, unrelated campaigns. There seemed to be little, if any, effort to coordinate their activities or candidacies.

The general election campaign was a rough one. Charges of racism were flung about. Candidates' credentials as conservatives were challenged. In the Fifth Ward, for example, supporters of the CFRG-sponsored candidate mailed out postcards noting: "Jim Ardis will make a *fine* Alderman. He is *not* a member of the Americans for Democratic Action or any other 'leftist' or radical *tax-us-to-death* group. Jim Ardis is a fine, upright neighbor—a good citizen.''[15]

Questions were raised about the ability of some candidates to accurately and literally ''represent'' the people. All of these charges, counter-charges, challenges, retorts and character assassinations stemmed from the unseen presence on the ballot of the issue of whether the City of Peoria should use utility tax funds for urban renewal. The decision of almost all CFRG-endorsed candidates to express a willingness to keep the utility tax for urban renewal if the tax were approved in a public referendum put other candidates in a corner. CFRG candidates looked to be true democrats, true champions of the public's right to participate in the decision-making process.

Although the election was of obvious importance to various community groups and elements, there seemed to be little worry by those who had run the City since the early 1950's. During the general election, the *Peoria Journal Star* did break its primary election endorsement silence when it endorsed the incumbent Mayor. The paper made no endorsements in any of the aldermanic races.[16]

The general election campaign was as loud as it was bitter. It was divisive and it was a single-issue struggle. Just before election day, William Buob—the Republican candidate for Mayor who had run second to Lehnhausen in the primary—endorsed the Democratic candidate E. Michael O'Brien. It was a critical election in many ways, but many citizens decided to sit it out. The turnout was improved compared to the primary election, but was still less than the norm for recent municipal elections in Peoria. Forty-eight percent of the registered voters turned out to cast ballots and to deny a second term to Mayor Robert Lehnhausen. He went down to defeat by a substantial margin. His Democratic opponent, E. Michael O'Brien, polled 61 percent of the vote, becoming the first Democratic mayor since 1949. O'Brien ran ahead of the Democratic ticket in all ten wards while Lehnhausen ran behind the Republican ticket in all ten wards, an illustration of the salience of the utility tax as a campaign issue. In fact, 49.9 percent of all the votes Lehnhausen received came from 5,443 individuals who voted ''straight ticket Republican'' for Mayor, Alderman, City Clerk and City Treasurer, etc.

CFRG-endorsed candidates won victories in the First, Fourth, Fifth, Sixth, Seventh, Eighth and Ninth Wards and narrowly missed being successful in unseating the incumbent who had voted for the utility tax from the Third Ward. The CFRG candidate in that ward polled 49.3 percent of the vote (losing by 21 votes). Table 20-3 shows the general election results.

As a neophyte political organization, the CFRG had met with nearly unparalleled success in defeating those interest which had been regularly electing individuals to office in Peoria since the early 1950's. The organization's attention now shifted from the problems of gaining power to the problems of making the most effective use of that power.

TABLE 20-3
1969 General Election Results

Ward	Candidate	Vote (%)	Vote for Mayor (%)
First	Joseph Mudd (D)	64	84
	John Aiello (R)	36	16
Second	Thomas Dunne (D)*	65	71
	James K. Polk (R)	35	29
Third	Ralph Metts (D)*	51	71
	William O'Brien (R)	49	29
Fourth	Charles Duke (D)	28%	58%
	James Stickelmaier (R)	72%	42%
Fifth	Dallas D'Hondt (D)	36%	50%
	James Ardis, Jr. (R)	64%	50%
Sixth	Richard VanNorman (D)	46%	70%
	Gary Stella (R)	54	30
Seventh	Charles Adkins (D)	31	60
	Dan Thurman (R)	69	40
Eighth	Frank Beall (D)	36	53
	Robert Janssen (R)*	64	47
Ninth	Ray Swearinger (D)	39	62
	Louis Carr (R)	61	38
Tenth	Arthur Bader (D)	25	46
	Richard Carver (R)	75	54

*Incumbent

The New City Government

The municipal elections were over. Although they knew there were many problems and challenges facing their City, Peorians knew little of those who were about to seize the reins of government. They knew only that many of those elected to the City Council had expressed opposition to the utility tax for urban renewal.

Of the ten members-elect of the City Council, all were men (there had not even been any women running in the primary), three were incumbents (two of whom represented wards likely to directly benefit from urban renewal and who had voted for the tax, and one incumbent who had opposed it), and seven councilmen-elect who had been endorsed by the Citizens for Representative Government. That total includes the incumbent (Janssen) who had voted against the utility tax. The CFRG ''had'' to endorse him since he had voted right on the utility tax issue even though they really hoped to elect his Democratic opponent.

Of the ten incumbent councilmen (prior to May, 1969), seven had sought re-election but only three had survived. All four incumbents who had lost their seats had been defeated in the primary. The CFRG did come within 21 votes of defeating another incumbent in the general election, but that was all. An incumbent mayor had been seriously challenged in the primay and had been overwhelmed by his Democratic opponent in the general election. This situation where four of seven incumbents were defeated is certainly different from Prewitt's study of 82 California cities where he found the success rate for aldermen in these cities to be around 80 percent over a ten-year period.[17]

The seven new members-elect of the Council had had little political experience before winning seats on the Council. Four had held partisan precinct committeeman positions and two had served on appointed city boards and commissions. Only one had sought public office (school board) before 1969. That attempt had been unsuccessful.

The Mayor-elect had lived in Peoria only four years and had been unopposed in his party's primary. That was probably a result of the early speculation that the incumbent seemed to have such a firm grip on the office. The Mayor-elect had not eagerly sought the office. Rather, he seriously considered seeking a Council seat from the 9th Ward. As he later explained to the author's classes: "I was asked to run for Mayor. I did so. Then the people turned on me—and elected me!"

The one factor about the new City Council which had not changed was the fact that the party ratio remained at seven Republicans and three Democrats. The Democrats continued to control only Wards 1, 2, and 3. Party affiliation, however, had not been a major (or even minor) factor in the behavior of previous Councils since the City had changed to council/manager government. Party affiliation would not be a factor in the deliberations and activities of the Council elected for the period 1969–1973.

It appeared to those Council observers watching the Council-elect that for the first time in many years, the majority of the Council were endorsees (or members) of an ideologically narrow, single-issue political organization. Six of the ten members-elect had been CFRG candidates (Ardis, R-5, Carr, R-9, Mudd, D-1, Stella, R-6, Stickelmaier, R-4, and Thurman, R-7) as was the Mayor-elect. It appeared to be the dawning of a new day for Peoria politics.

Peoria in 1969

There were a variety of problems (or issues) which were hanging in the balance as a result of the election returns. The two most glaring problems were urban renewal and its base of funding—the now famous utility tax. Would urban renewal move ahead under the new Council? How would it be funded? Would the utility tax be repealed? Would it be submitted to the public in a referendum?

What of the future of the professionals who operated the City on a day-to-day basis? Would the City Manager who had been hired by the outgoing City Council be retained? What of those who worked under him? There was widespread concern expressed before and during the new Council's term that some members actually opposed the council/manager form of government and wanted to return to the strong mayor system.[18]

What of the other programs involving race relations in Peoria? What would happen to such programs as T.I.P. (Together In Peoria) a sensitivity-group effort in police-community relations to ease racial difficulties? The concern for racial problems was widened by the fact that the Peoria school district (District#150) was in the process of formulating and effecting a system-wide court-mandated integration plan.

Of course, there were many other—seemingly mundane—problems involving such varied concerns as zoning, mass transit, and garbage collection contracts. The new Council would have to wait, however, to make its imprint on the budget until 1970 since the budget for Fiscal Year 1969 would have been approved before the new Council was sworn in.

The New Council Takes Office

As might be expected, the first six months brought a number of surprises. Two major items stand out. First, the new Council divided itself into two factions on many major issues. One faction generally consisted of CFRG stalwarts—Aldermen Ardis, R-5, Mudd, D-1, Stella, R-6, Stickelmaier, R-4, and Thurman, R-7. Thurman generally acted as the leader of this faction. He was an active floor debater and manager. The other faction was made up of Aldermen Carr, R-9, Carver, R-10, Dunne, D-2, Janssen, R-8, and often Metts, D-3. This faction included all three holdovers from the previous Council as well as two new members from the northern parts of the city—the Ninth and Tenth Wards.

Alderman Janssen, although endorsed by CFRG, had no real ties to the organization. On the one hand CFRG had preferred his primary opponent, but had been forced by the situation to endorse him—he had voted against the utility tax. On the other, Janssen had neither needed nor welcomed the CFRG endorsement, but he could not afford to disavow it. Now, with several CFRG Aldermen on the Council, Janssen remained independent of the organization which had endorsed him.

Alderman Carr sided with the non-CFRG faction not long after taking office. His break with Citizens for Representative Government began shortly after he voted with the CFRG aldermen to repeal the utility tax. It was not that Louis Carr had been a member of the CFRG and run with their endorsement with the intent to deceive. His membership indicated an agreement on many policy positions. Once in office, however, he concluded the group's aims were much different from his. A man willing to go the distance alone if necessary, Carr decided to break with the CFRG. Not only did he break with them, he took special aim at many of their proposals. Debate between Alderman Carr and CFRG Councilmen was often both personal and bitter. There was rancor aplenty.

The other interesting breakaway from the CFRG camp was the defection of Mayor E. Michael O'Brien. Again, it did not seem to be a matter of the candidate attempting to deceive. Rather, it appeared that the Mayor was won away from the CFRG by his job. He came to oppose the organization's stands on various issues on the merits of these issues and often he came down on the opposite side of the CFRG faction.

A somewhat volatile situation had quickly become an extremely volatile one. The City Council which took office May 6, 1969 was certainly different from its predecessors. It was more active, more combative, more divided and divisive, and certainly more controversial.

The First Year

The new Council took office amid much anticipation of change. On the one hand those who had lost control of the Council anticipated the worst. Their expectations were that many programs would be discontinued and others in the various planning stages halted. On the other hand, those who had long been on the outside looking in anticipated gaining control of the levers and positions they had long criticized from afar.

One word about the mechanics of City Council voting before exploring the Council's first year. Councilmen vote by voice in alphabetical order. The seating was arranged correspondingly with five aldermen on one side of the room and five on the other side facing them. The Mayor's chair was at the head of the room with one row of aldermen on the left and the other on the right.

As the new members of the Council soon learned, to merely seize the policy-making apparatus was not enough. It is also necessary to control the machinery charged with the implementation of policy. In a council/manager city, however, only the manager owed his job to the City Council. Department heads were hired and fired only by the City Manager. The CFRG faction began almost immediately to put pressure on the City Manager to replace a variety of staff members. Among the officials singled out were the Traffic Engineer and the Director of Inspections.[19]

The City Manager of Peoria since 1964 had been Leonard Caro. The CFRG aldermen charged that Caro was aligned with the political elements they had defeated. Caro denied that he was aligned with any segment of the Council, or any faction in the City. He went on to add, however, that he found it embarrassing to have his professional experience "so easily challenged by persons unskilled, untrained, with no long period of community service and political background, who had developed in six short months the insight to perceive all our community's problems and to have the knowledge that all we have to do to correct them is to change the existing structure and personnel."[20] Whatever was uncertain, one thing was certain—City Manager Caro and many other figures in the administration had indeed played a part in many of the programs the CFRG had criticized.

The criticism of Caro mounted during the early months of the new Council's term. In late October, members of the Council gave Caro a 7 to 3 "vote of confidence" when they rejected a motion to fire him.[21] This vote had followed a closed-door meeting of the Council and the City Manager sought by Caro. The meeting had lasted 3½ hours.[22] Most meeting participants were tight-lipped, but it was felt that the meeting had been a productive one and had done much to clear the air.

The vote of confidence was a hollow one. At least two of those voting "confidence" had been very vocal in their criticism of the City Manager. On November 14, 1969, City Manager Caro surprised nearly everyone by tendering his resignation. At the following Tuesday City Council session, a motion was offered to reject the resignation. The motion was deferred for three days and in an extraordinary Friday evening session, the members of the two factions on the Council took off the gloves. After "one of the bitterest council meetings in years"[23] the Council voted 6 to 5 to reject the Manager's resignation. The Mayor broke the tie by casting his vote with Aldermen Ardis, Carr, Carver, Dunne and Janssen. Although Ardis was one of the CFRG aldermen, he voted to retain the City Manager. The votes against Caro came from Metts, Mudd, Stella, Stickelmaier and Thurman.

Caro, in light of the razor-thin margin of his "win," refused to withdraw his resignation. His resignation took effect December 12, 1969. Plans were underway immediately to name an interim manager. One important difference between a City Manager and an interim City Manager was that the latter could hire or fire department heads only with the approval of the City Council. The Council had moved to strengthen its grip on the machinery. Peoria would not see a new City Manager take office until 1971.

Thus, the last of the major administration figures was gone. City Corporation Counsel (city attorney) Max Lipkin and Director of Public Safety (combined fire and police chief) Bernard Kennedy had resigned, publicly stating they could not work with a majority of the new Council.[24]

The resignation of these three major administrators and the resignation of several others at lower levels (Administrative Assistant to the City Manager and the Intergovernmental Affairs Officer) resulted largely from the Council trying to run the administrative machinery of the City. Professionals trained in the art of management resented the intrusion. In time, the Council would admit to its excess, but many professionals were gone by then. It was not surprising that the line between policy-making and administration (never a very clear line) would be violated by a group new to power.

On other matters, the City Council showed that many of those who won seats were true to their campaign promises. Members of the new Council had been sworn in at the end of the meeting on May 6, 1969. The May 13 meeting, therefore, was the first official meeting of the new Council. At the May 13 meeting, the Council voted 6 to 4 to repeal the utility tax.[25] Voting to repeal were Aldermen Ardis, Carr, Mudd, Stella, Stickelmaier and Thurman. Voting to retain the utility tax as a source of funding for the urban renewal programs were Aldermen Carver, Dunne, Janssen and Metts.

In early 1970, an attempt was made to revive the much-discussed utility tax but this time with the aim of producing revenue for a new fire-police station and a new City Hall, as well as for urban renewal projects. The question was whether the City Council should authorize a referendum on the imposition of the utility tax for five years.[26] Interestingly, the effort to revive the tax was made by Alderman Carr, one of those who had voted 9 months before to repeal the tax. As soon as the motion was offered by Carr, a motion to table Carr's motion was offered. The motion to table was approved by a vote of 6 (Aldermen Ardis, Carver, Mudd, Stella, Stickelmaier, and Thurman) to 4 (Aldermen Carr,

Dunne, Janssen, and Metts). Five of those voting in favor of tabling the motion on holding a referendum had publicly supported such a referendum on the utility tax during the 1969 campaign!

The Coalescing of Factions on the Council

As noted above, the Council divided itself into factions almost immediately upon being sworn into office. There was very little trafficking between the two factions. At times, there was great personal bitterness between members of the two different factions. There was constant policy friction between the two camps.

One of the coalitions was formed by those CFRG candidates elected to office who continued to support the group's interests. This faction generally included (in varying degrees of faithfulness) Aldermen Ardis, Mudd, Stella, Stickelmaier and Thurman. The other faction was largely a result of reaction to the first faction. There was little in the way of cohesiveness except as it stemmed from that reaction. This faction generally included Aldermen Carr, Carver, Dunne, Janssen and Metts.

Actually, those factional characterizations are probably too over-simplified. As the following tables will indicate, the factions shifted from year to year. The shifting coalitions were studied only for the Council years 1969–1970, 1970–1971, and 1971–1972. At the conclusion of the Council's third year (May 1972), Alderman Janssen resigned. For that reason and others, the factions were not studied during the fourth year of the Council's term.

A careful examination was made of *all* roll call votes for each of three years 1969–1972. All Council votes which were 7 to 3, 6 to 4, or 5 to 5, were selected for the cluster-bloc analysis. It was decided that unless at least 30 percent (3 members) of the Council voted in opposition to the remainder of the members, there was little controversy. It should be noted that most roll calls (probably 90 percent) were 8 to 2, 9 to 1, or 10 to 0. The focus here is only on the more controversial questions. All roll calls showing at least some division on the Council were further analyzed from the standpoint of who voted with whom on each issue. The aim was to see whether such an analysis indicated the existence of identifiable voting blocs on the Peoria City Council.

In any effort at cluster-bloc analysis, the question is always what level of agreement is considered a "high level of agreement."[2] After reviewing the available literature on the subject the author decided to do what other researchers had done—that is, to set his own level of agreement. That level was a minimum agreement of at least 65 percent. If two aldermen did not vote together at least 65 percent of the time (on the votes as described above) the level of agreement was not considered significant. It should be noted that all of the clusters and vote pairings are significant at least at the .05 level of statistical significance. Tables 20-4, 20-5 and 20-6 show the blocs year by year.

Table 4 is for 1969–1970 (May to May) and shows the existence of two distinct voting blocs. Each bloc had four "members." The CFRG bloc had one sympathizer (Ardis) who voted frequently with bloc members. The other major grouping was the bloc which formed as a reaction to the CFRG bloc. This bloc also had four "members" but an additional fragmenting of the block's solidarity is evident in a smaller, three-aldermen (Janssen, Carver and Carr) bloc. The levels of agreement are generally higher in the CFRG bloc.

Table 4, for example, shows that Aldermen Mudd voted with Alderman Stickelmaier 87 percent of the time on these 38 roll calls, whereas Stella voted with Mudd 82 percent of the time and with Stickelmaier 79 percent of the time. Where no figures of agreement appear, agreement was less than 35 percent.

During 1969–1970, the Mayor cast votes on 12 of these 38 roll calls—10 of his votes being cast against the position taken by the CFRG faction. In other words, approximately one of every 4 controversial votes ended in a tie vote bringing the Mayor into the fray.

The second year of the Council (1970–1971) saw two major changes in the factions. In the CFRG bloc, Ardis became a full-fledged partner but Stickelmaier moved out of the bloc to the position of part-time supporter. He voted at a high level of agreement only with Alderman Thurman. The second year also saw the strongest levels of agreement among the anti-CFRG bloc. Carr moved into the bloc and with the exception of Aldermen Janssen and Metts, all levels of agreement were very high. Thirty-two roll calls made up the votes for the second year. The Mayor voted on exactly half of those roll calls. He voted ten of those 16 times against the CFRG bloc's position.

The third year (1971–1972) as reflected in Table 21-6 shows some interesting changes. For the CFRG, Stickelmaier remained outside but now agreed often not only with Thurman but also with Alderman Stella. Notice the overall lowering of agreement scores. The anti-CFRGers fell apart and became two disassociated clusters. One cluster included only Aldermen Metts and Dunne and the other cluster consisted of Janssen, Carr, and Carver. Gone was the unity of 1970–1971. Interestingly, the number of roll call votes doubled to 68. The Mayor voted to break ties 24 times during the year.

The CFRG blocs remained relatively strong throughout the three years. There were always at least four members in the bloc, with one camp follower. Those who banded together in reaction, however, were less successful in staying together. The first two years were good for the reaction bloc but the third year exposed the bloc's weaknesses. In fact, by 1971–1972, one bloc had divided itself into two.

In interpreting these patterns it is not enough to point out that there were many close votes each of the first three years and to note that blocs of aldermen were in

TABLE 20-4
Peoria City Council Voting Blocs, 1969–1970
(In percent)

	Mudd	Stickelmaier	Stella	Thurman	Ardis		Carver	Janssen	Metts	Dunne
Mudd		87	82	76	66					
Stickelmaier	87		79	84	74					
Stella	82	79		79						
Thurman	76	84	79							
Ardis	66	74								
Carr							72	76		
Carver						72		86	67	66
Janssen						76	86		70	73
Metts							67	70		76
Dunne							66	73	76	

Source: *Official Proceedings of the City Council of Peoria, 1969–1970*
N = 38 roll calls

TABLE 20-5
Peoria City Council Voting Blocs, 1970–1971
(In percent)

	Mudd	Ardis	Stella	Thurman	Stickelmaier	Carver	Janssen	Carr	Dunne	Metts
Mudd		89	89	76						
Ardis	89		90	74						
Stella	89	90		74						
Thurman	76	74	74		75					
Stickelmaier				75						
Carver							90	86	77	82
Janssen						90		83	71	62
Carr						86	83		84	79
Dunne						77	71	84		93
Metts						82	62	79	93	

Source: *Official Proceedings of the City Council of Peoria, 1970–1971*
N = 32 roll calls

TABLE 20-6
Peoria City Council Voting Blocs, 1971–1972
(In percent)

	Mudd	Ardis	Thurman	Stella	Stickelmaier	Metts	Dunne	Janssen	Carr	Carver
Mudd		78	73	69						
Ardis	78		65	65						
Thurman	73	65		67	77					
Stella	69	65	67		70					
Stickelmaier			77	70						
Metts							73			
Dunne						73		71		
Janssen							71		77	81
Carr								77		69
Carver								81	69	

Source: *Official Proceedings of the City Council of Peoria, 1971–1972*
N = 68 roll calls

TABLE 20-7
Cluster-Bloc Votes by Issue Area

Issue Area	1969-1970	1970-1971	1971-1972
Personnel and Administration	26%	6%	4%
Race Relations	13%	16%	—
Urban Renewal	3%	34%	9%
Utility Tax	13%	—	—
Mass Transit	11%	—	—
Cable Television	—	13%	22%
Garbage Collection	13%	—	—
Zoning Matters	11%	6%	32%
Council Matters	3%	9%	7%
Traffic	3%	—	7%
Purchases	—	—	9%
Budget Decisions	—	—	3%
Miscellaneous	5%	15%	6%
	N = 38	N = 32	N = 68

Note: The breakdowns of issue categories includes only those votes which occasioned (7 to 3, 6 to 4, or 5 to 5) divisions.

evidence on those close votes. Table 20-7 shows year by year what issues are included.

During the Council's first year, the biggest areas of concern had been personnel, race relations, the City's garbage contract, the utility tax, and zoning matters. In the second year, the major areas were urban renewal, race relations and consideration of a cable television franchise. The third year saw cable television and zoning matters taking up the majority of the Council's time.

Two features are striking. The first is the observation that as each year passed, issues such as personnel matters were less easily characterized by CFRG or anti-CFRG stands. The other striking feature is the consistent non-controversial nature of budgetary decisions. During the Council years 1969–1970 and 1970–1971, no close votes were recorded on budget decisions. Most votes were, in fact, unanimous—strange behavior from a Council able to broadly agree on few other matters! In the third year, only two votes on the budget caused major differences of opinion.

There are two possible explanations for this. One is that the budget, prepared by the professionals in City Hall, was presented in such a way as to preclude any substantive budget changes by the legislative branch. This is not to imply anything unusual—in fact, this would be the norm for legislative bodies from Congress on down. A second explanation could be that the CFRG aldermen did not see the budget as an instrument of policy-making and therefore did not attempt to alter budget proposals. The budget was finished for 1969–1970 by the time they came on board, but that was not true for the other two years.

The Beginning of the End of the CFRG

By the end of the third year, things were beginning to go against the CFRG—the evidence was everywhere. Public support of CFRG and its endorsed office-holders was cooling. Racial problems which flared up in the public schools were exacerbated by CFRG Alderman Joe Mudd when he went on television and urged students to boycott an integrated grade school.[28] The school board pondered taking legal action against the alderman, but decided not to do so.

In March, 1970, the CFRG candidate for the District #150 school board was soundly defeated in an election marked by attacks on the organization by Mayor O'Brien. The Mayor noted that the success of the CFRG candidate would be " 'a detriment to the social health of this community.' "[29]

In March, 1971, the Peoria Human Relations Commission issued a report which noted the City Council had contributed significantly to the racial tensions which existed in Peoria. The Commission's "Tension Report" noted:

> . . . it must be admitted that the present City Council has a negative image with large segments of the community. Within the first few months in office, the Council has repealed the Utility Tax and promised it would seek Federal funding for Urban Renewal. Yet, the effect has been to halt Urban Renewal for two years. In addition, the persistent attacks by some aldermen on the T.I.P. program, which was aimed at improving the Human Relations skills of the police, resulted in greater disunity, and made the private funding of the program virtually impossible. Further, within their first year as aldermen, many professional administrators either resigned under pressure or were fired. . . . These actions contributed to the lack of trust in the Council on the part of many.
>
> Further, the actions of individual aldermen outside of Council Chambers have done little to improve the sense of trust. When alderman Thurman accuses the Commission on Human Relations of being discriminatory, without reference to facts, citizens wonder how sincerely he wants to improve the climate of human relations in Peoria. When Alderman Mudd uses a television appearance to call for a boycott of the schools, or when Alderman Stella is involved in an alleged "hit and run" accident, some in the community won-

der if these members of the Council are for "law and order" or "above" the law. The result has been a widespread lack of confidence in the Council and its ability to deal responsibly with the inevitable crises that confront the community.[30]

One alderman took written exception to the Commission's report. He produced his own reply:

> The assumption that the present City Council has a negative image with *"large segments"* of the community is partially true. It is true in the sense that those seeking "something for nothing" have met with stiff resistence from many members of the council. . . . It is also true in the sense that those that fail to closely examine our activities, and instead rely on certain segments of the local news media, will be led to believe that the council has done little that is positive. This is related to a deliberate campaign on the part of a portion of the media, *not all,* to accent the negative and ignore the positive.[31]

Alderman Stella concluded his "Authenticity Report" with this statement: "The only sound recommendation is the abolishment of the Peoria Commission on Human Relations."[32]

Members of the former ruling clique, who were the "outs" at the moment, successfully (via petitions) pushed for a change in the representational system used to select members of the City Council. Instead of electing ten aldermen from wards, the new system provided for nonpartisan staggered elections. Three at-large aldermen would be elected, followed two years later by five ward representatives and the Mayor. This staggering of terms would avoid a complete Council turnover, as had nearly occurred in 1969.

Such a change in the representational system required that the matter be placed before the voters. In April, 1972, Peorians approved the change by a narrow margin of 682 votes (7,876 for and 7,194 against). The City Council had unsuccessfully opposed the referendum, and it was not through yet. An ordinance was adopted requiring the same issue to be placed on the November, 1972 general election ballot. The matter was taken to court but the petitioners lost and the question was again placed on the ballot. A second election was held in November and the proposal to change the system of electing council representatives was again approved but this time by a larger margin of 60 percent to 40 percent.[33] Thus, the municipal elections of 1973 would be fought on a different basis than the 1969 elections. Candidates would contest for the three at-large aldermanic seats for two-year terms, as well as for five ward aldermanic seats and the position of Mayor, all for four-year terms.

Item: When the elections of 1973 rolled around, CFRG candidates found the going much tougher than in 1969. They were not overlooked by the "establishment" this time. In the primary, Alderman Ardis was defeated in a bid for one of the three at-large seats. In the general election, Alderman Stella was defeated in the newly-drawn Third Ward. In addition, Alderman Thurman was soundly defeated (64 percent to 36 percent) by Alderman Carver in the race for Mayor. Alderman Mudd was the only CFRG alderman to be re-elected and Alderman Dunne the only non-CFRG alderman to be returned to office. Turnout in the 1973 primary election rose to 42 percent (up from 26 percent four years earlier) although the general election turnout only equaled the 48 percent of 1969.

Thus, time ran out on the Citizens for Representative Government. Following the losses suffered in the election of 1973, the organization was obviously in trouble. It ceased to exist within two years. Two CFRG aldermen did go on to other elective offices. Alderman Stella was appointed and then elected to a position on the county board and Alderman Mudd was elected to the Illinois House of Representatives in 1974. None of the others were successful in obtaining other elective positions.

Subsequently Richard Carver, the Alderman during these CFRG years, who had been elected Mayor, changed the fifty-year pattern in which no Mayor had succeeded himself, by winning re-election in 1977.

Conclusions

There is always a certain amount of danger in generalizing from a single case study. Nonetheless, in reviewing the literature and in analyzing this case study, several conclusions do seem to be in order.

Many local citizens' organizations spring into being, but very few of these organizations are ever able to influence electoral and/or policy outcomes. The difficulties of defeating incumbents, finding an issue to rally around and being able to mobilize citizen support are usually more than most groups can overcome. Those groups which do spring up are usually built on the skeletal remains of previous similar organizations.

In order for a citizens' organization to be effective, several ingredients must be present: (1) there must be an issue which is salient—in varying degrees—to all segments of the community; (2) the issue must be of such a nature as to polarize a community; (3) the organization must be able to become clearly identified with only one side of the divisive issue; (4) the organization must have the time to organize, to structure itself, and to recruit candidates sympathetic to its cause; (5) in order for an organization to be electorally successful, it is helpful (though not necessary) if the local "regular" parties and ruling cliques (if they exist in a locality) perceive the threat from the organization as minimal and that party's chances for success unlikely.

Because members/supporters of such organizations are usually in office for a short period of time, they find it difficult to familiarize themselves with the machinery of government and how to operate that machinery.

Local organizations which manage to be successful at the polls will have serious problems in holding elected officials to the "party line," just as is the case with the Republican and Democratic organizations. The homogeneity of the organization candidates elected to office will vary according to the broadness of the party's ideological spectrum as well as the applicability of ideological solutions to local problems.

The longevity of an organization will depend upon the breadth of the issues seized upon by the party (upon which the party may take a *unified* position) and which are salient to the public. The greater the breadth, the less likely the unity in the party's position, but the greater the mass appeal. In order for a citizens' organization to survive the issue which it used to get into office, it must find other issues which allow it to retain the group's earlier adherents or replace them in approximately equal numbers.

If an organization is successful at the polls at one election, losses at later elections will loom large. An organization will not remain in existence long if the electoral losses are severe. This is true because it has no other electoral base to fall back on.

The rise and fall of the Citizens for Representative Government presents an interesting panorama of municipal politics. In the end, the panoply of problems which would likely beset any novice organization, coupled with the strong reactions by several segments of the community, proved to be enough to overcome the CFRG. It had risen out of the tensions and problems of urban America in the late 1960's. It would disappear before these problems were solved. These problems remain largely unsolved today. As this case study indicates, the difficulty in resolving such problems stems, in part, from the politicalness of the issues and the community divisions these issues can reflect or provoke.

Suggestions for Further Research

This case study of the divisiveness of community politics would seem to be an excellent launching pad for a variety of additional research forays.

First, what of these citizens groups/political organizations which spring up in nearly every metropolitan area? Are there common features which lead to the birthing of such organizations? What of their demise? When these organizations which are based—in part—on ideology confront non-ideological questions and problems, does that usually lead to the organization's break-up?

Second, have we studied the voting patterns of city councils over an extended period of time? This would seem especially crucial following major council personnel turnover. How are voting blocs formed? Does the existence of blocs vary according to the type of city government (council/manager vis-a-vis strong mayor)?

Third, what are the separations of "politics" and "administration"? Are they very clear? Does the existence of voting blocs invalidate the distinction between those who make the decisions and those who carry out the decisions? What implications does this have for the council-manager form of government, which is based on that distinction?

Finally, what are the long-range effects of the existence and success of political organizations such as the CFRG? Are they able to alter the direction a city is taking or do they merely force a detour, an interruption?

NOTES

[1]See such articles as: Gordon S. Black, "Conflicts in the Community: A Theory of the Effects of Community Size," *American Political Science Review* 68 (September 1974), 1245–62; James S. Coleman, *Community Conflict Politics and Public Policy* (New York: John Wiley & Sons, Inc., 1968); Betty Zisk, *Local Interest Politics* (Indianapolis: Bobbs-Merrill, 1973).

[2]See such references as: A. Lee Hunt and Robert E. Pendley, "Community Gatekeepers: An Examination of Political Recruiters," *American Journal of Political Science* 16 (August, 1972) 441–438; Kenneth Prewitt, *The Recruitment of Political Leaders: A Study of Citizen-Politicians* (Indianapolis: Bobbs-Merrill Co., Inc., 1970); Kenneth Prewitt and Heinz Eulau, "Social Bias in Leadership Selection, Political Recruitment, and Electoral Context," *Midwest Journal of Political Science* 33 (May 1971), 293–315.

[3]See Robert J. Huckshorn and Charles E. Young, "Study of Voting Splits on City Councils in Los Angeles County," *Western Political Quarterly* 13 (June 1960), 479–97; Albert K. Karnig, " 'Private Regarding' Policy, Civil Rights Groups, and the Mediating Impact of Municipal Reforms," *American Journal of Political Science* 19 (February, 1975), 91–106; Robert Lineberry and Ira Sharkansky, *Urban Politics and Public Policy* (New York: Harper & Row, 1971); David Morgan and Samuel A. Kirkpatrick, eds., *Urban Political Analysis: A Systems Approach* (New York: The Free press, 1972); James Q. Wilson and Edward C. Banfield, "Public Regardingness as a Value Premise in Voting Behavior," *American Political Science Review* 58 (December 1964), 876–87; James Q. Wilson, ed., *Urban Renewal: The Record and the Controversy* (Cambridge: The M.I.T. Press, 1966).

[4]Jim Mansfield, "Urban Renewal Levy Becomes Effective July 1," *Peoria Journal Star,* February 7, 1968, pp. 1f.

[5]*Official Proceedings of the City Council of Peoria,* February 6, 1968.

[6]Jim Mansfield, "Council Receives Anti-Utility Tax Petitions," *Peoria Journal Star,* April 24, 1968, p. C-10.

[7]The story of these events is told by John Bartlow Martin in "The Town That Reformed," in *Public Administration: Concepts and Cases,* ed. by Richard J. Stillman II (Boston: Houghton Mifflin Company, 1976), pp. 283–89.

[8]Edward M. Lembech, "250–300 Organize, List VOTE Beliefs, Objectives," *Peoria Journal Star,* January 17, 1965, p. D-20.

[9]*Peoria Journal Star,* March 7, 1968, p. 5.

[10]Dan Thurman and John Carver, private interviews held during July, 1970.

[11]J. Leiper Freeman, "Local Party Systems: Theoretical Considerations and a Case Analysis," *American Journal of Sociology* 64 (November 1958), p. 283.

[12]Thurman and Carver, *op. cit.*

[13]Robert R. Alford and Eugene C. Lee, "Voting Turnout in American Cities," *American Political Science Review* 62 (September 1968), 796–813; and Kenneth Prewitt and Heinz Eulau, "Social Bias in Leadership Selection, Political Recruitment, and Electoral Context," *Midwest Journal of Political Science* 33 (May 1971), pp. 293–315.

[14]Editorial, *Peoria Journal Star,* February 13, 1969, 4A.

[15]Postcard used in Fifth Ward aldermanic elections, 1969.

[16]Editorial, *Peoria Journal Star,* March 29, 1969, 4A; Editorial, *Peoria Journal Star,* March 30, 1969, 8A.

[17]Kenneth Prewitt, "Political Ambitions, Volunteerism and Electoral Accountability," *American Political Science Review* 64 (March, 1970), pp. 5–17.

[18]Editorial, *Peoria Journal Star,* July 15, 1970, 6A.

[19]Fred Filip, "Anti-Caro Faction Believed Seeking Ouster Before 1970," *Peoria Journal Star,* October 28, 1969, 14B.

[20]Fred Filip, "Caro Denies Teaming with Some Political Units," *Peoria Journal Star,* October 29, 1969, p. B-18.

[21]Fred Filip, "Attempt by Mudd to Fire City Manager Caro Fails by 7–3 Vote of Council," *Peoria Journal Star,* October 22, 1969, 12E.

[22]Fred Filip, "Council, Caro Executive Meet, May Have Improved Relations," *Peoria, Journal Star,* November 13, 1969, 18D.

[23]Fred Filip, "Caro Declines Bid to Stay with City," *Peoria Journal Star,* November 22, 1969, pp. 1+.

[24]*Ibid.*

[25]*Official Proceedings of the City Council of Peoria,* May 13, 1969.

[26]*Ibid.,* February 3, 1970.

[27]Peter Willetts, "Cluster-Bloc Analysis and Statisticaly Inference," *American Political Science Review,* 66 (June 1972), pp. 569–81.

[28]Barb Proctor Mantz, "School Board Discusses Suit Over Boycott Plea," *Peoria Journal Star,* October 21, 1969, pp. 1B+.

[29]John Barrette, "Ald. Mudd Assails Mayor for Labeling of Candidate," *Peoria Journal Star,* March 16, 1970, p. B-14.

[30]Peoria Commission on Human Relations, "Tension Report," March 1, 1971, pp. 3–4. (Mimeographed.)

[31]Gary Stella, "Authenticity Report," March, 1971, pp. 1, 5. (Mimeographed.)

[32]*Ibid.,* p. 5.

[33]"Election Returns," *Peoria Journal Star,* November 9, 1972, p. B-4.

SUPPLEMENTAL READINGS

Coleman, James S., *Community Conflict*. New York: The Free Press of Glencoe, 1957.

Eulau, Heinz and Kenneth Prewitt. *The Labyrinths of Democracy*. Indianapolis: The Bobbs-Merrill Co., Inc., 1973.

Eyestone, Robert. *The Threads of Public Policy*. Indianapolis: The Bobbs-Merrill Co., Inc., 1971.

Lineberry, Robert and Ira Sharkansky. *Urban Politics and Public Policy*. New York: Harper & Row, 1971.

Loveridge, Robert O. *City Managers in Legislative Politics*. Indianapolis: The Bobbs-Merrill Co., Inc., 1971.

Prewitt, Kenneth. *The Recruitment of Political Leaders: A Study of Citizen-Politicians*. Indianapolis: The Bobbs-Merrill Co., Inc., 1970.

Wilson, James Q., ed. *City Politics and Public Policy*. New York: John Wiley & Sons, Inc., 1968.

———, ed. *Urban Renewal: The Record and the Controversy*. Cambridge: The M.I.T. Press, 1966.

Zisk, Betty. *Local Interest Politics*. Indianapolis: The Bobbs-Merrill Co., Inc., 1973.

PART V

THE POLITICAL ECONOMY OF ILLINOIS

CHAPTER **21**

How Big Is State Government? (And Is it Getting Bigger?)

Richard Kolhauser

In 1978 Caterpillar Tractor, the largest manufacturer in Illinois and the twenty-fourth largest firm in the Fortune 500 list, reported worldwide sales of just over $7.2 billion. In that same year, Illinois State government spent $8.8 billion, about $2,340 for every household in the State.[1] The comparison suggests that State government is very large and that Illinois taxpayers may have reason to question the size and growth of State government just as taxpayers nationwide have voiced concern.

This chapter seeks to establish an approach that can be used to help answer the question—how big is Illinois State government?—by comparing State government spending with the income received by Illinois taxpayers. Based upon this approach, changes in the size of State government are traced over the last two decades and observations are made regarding the growth of Illinois State government in future years.[2]

The current interest in government spending is also timely from another perspective. Important arguments based upon rapidly growing populations, used since the 1960's to justify higher spending, are no longer relevant. For example, the number of young persons to be educated (Illinois' largest spending program) has declined each year since 1971, after years of steady increases. The number of families receiving public assistance (the second largest program) has also trended downward since 1976, following years of near spectacular growth. The declining size of both population groups is projected to continue, although the size of the public assistance population will remain contingent upon the strength of the State's economy.

Admittedly, the answer to how much government spending is too much will depend upon individual philosophies of government, perceptions of the need for government services and the willingness of individuals to pay for government activities. However, the perspective on government spending relative to income growth which this chapter seeks to portray can also provide a useful framework for assessing these larger policy issues.[3]

State Employment and Financial Data Depict State Government's Size

Every working day State government spends about $38 million.[4] Over the course of 1979 spending will reach about $9.4 billion. There are over 225 major spending units including State agencies, boards, commissions and universities. These agencies fall broadly into eight categories: education, human services, transportation, business regulation, economic and community development, natural resources, public health and safety, and central administration. The hundreds of programs managed by these agencies range from ensuring nuclear safety, inspecting restaurants, providing babysitters or housecleaning services and subsidizing medical care to repairing roads, sheltering the aged and educating Illinois residents. To provide these services, State government has a work force of over 115,000 persons, including 38,000 who are employed by the ten State universities.

State programs are financed by over 1,000 different revenue sources. These include the State income and sales taxes, each yielding well over $2 billion, as well as consumption taxes on cigarettes and liquor, user fees such as motor fuel tax and hunting and fishing permits, regulatory charges such as examination and license fees paid by the financial community and pari-mutuel wagering.

The State's bookkeeper, the Comptroller, records daily the expenditures, receipt of revenues and transactions among funds. This elected official (along with 350 employees and two computers) pays the State's bills, writing nearly 14 million checks each year. These include over 400,000 checks to the elderly for tax relief, four million checks to low-income families, three and one-half million checks to State employees and pensioners and three million refund checks to persons who overpaid their State income tax.

These financial and employment statistics only partially describe the size of Illinois State government. The measure used most frequently by State officials and the news media to define the size of State government is State spending from appropriations which have been approved by the Illinois General Assembly.

State Spending Increases Eightfold: 1960–1979

In 1960, State spending totaled $1.2 billion ($387 per Illinois household). Two decades later, State spending will have increased nearly eightfold, reaching an estimated $9.4 billion in 1979 ($2,520 per Illinois household). Chart 21-1 traces the path of State spending from 1960 through 1979.[5]

Each year, State spending increases over the prior year's level. Spending grew at an average annual rate of 10 percent in the 1960's and 12 percent during the 1970's. The smallest annual percentage increase in spending occurred in 1978 (2 percent) and the largest in 1970 (29 percent). The extreme low was the result of a successful effort to avoid new taxes while the extreme high occurred in the first year of the State income tax. By then it was necessary to catch up in a number of areas.

During both decades, the average annual growth in spending exceeded the rate of inflation as measured by the Consumer Price Index (CPI). In 1978 and 1979, however, spending has grown at a slower rate than inflation. Table 21-1 compares the growth in State government spending with the inflation rate.

Annual Spending Increases Are Financed by Annual Revenue Increases

The annual increase in State spending due to inflation, new programs and expansion of old programs must be financed by higher annual revenue yields. Revenues to the State increase with planned expansion of either the tax base or tax rates for existing taxes, the addition of new tax sources and increases in federal aid.[6] Revenues from State sources also grow "automatically" as real economic growth and inflation expand the State's tax bases.

TABLE 21-1
Comparison of State Spending and Inflation

	Two Decades Average Annual Growth		Year's Growth Over Prior Year				
	1960-1969	1970-1979	1975	1976	1977	1978	1979
State Spending*	10%	12%	17%	14%	6%	2%	8%
CPI	2%	7%	11%	7%	6%	7%	9%

*Spending from all appropriated funds.

Chart 21-1

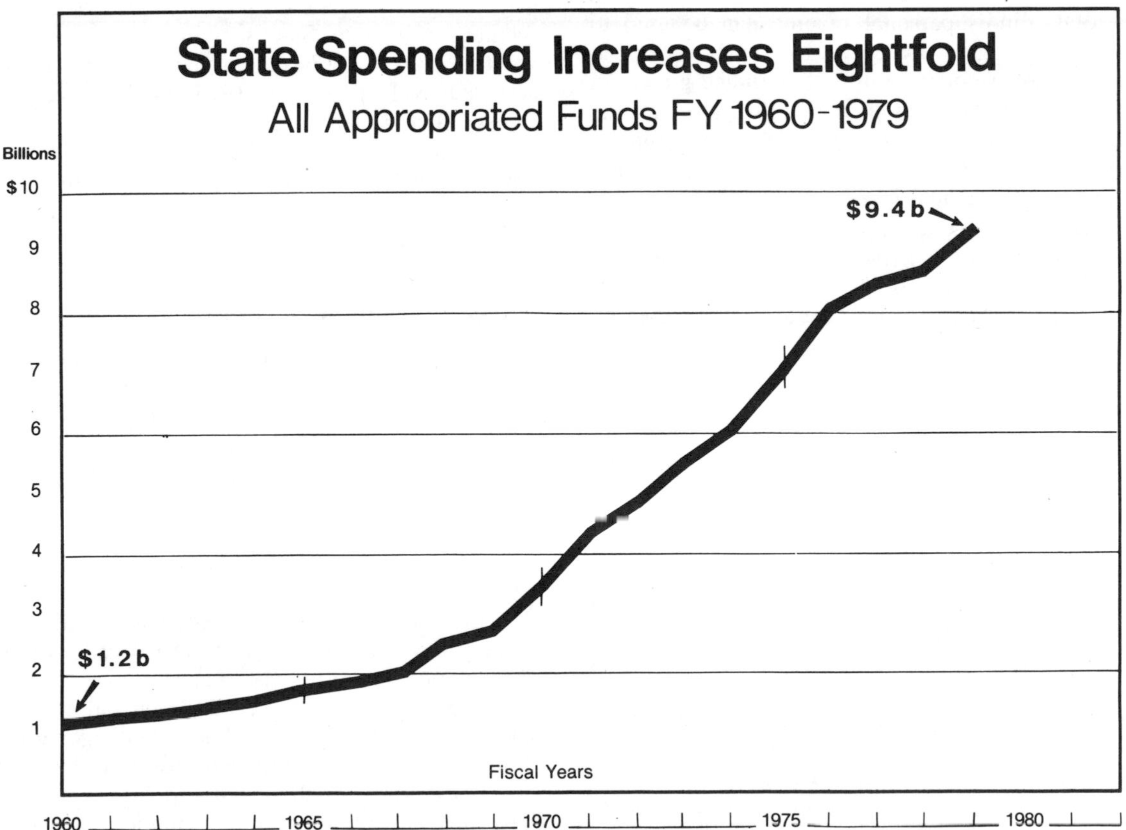

The data in Chart 21-2 shows that State revenues have increased steadily from $1.2 billion in 1960 to $9.6 billion in 1979.

The "automatic" growth in revenues through 1972 was greatly supplemented by new revenues from several State tax increases including the introduction of the income tax in 1970.[7] Since that time, there have been no expansions of the State's tax structure. In recent years, most of the annual growth in State revenues has come from inflation. For example, as inflation increases the price of automobiles, energy, food, clothing and appliances, the receipts from the State sales and public utilities taxes also increase.

As State spending has increased in the last twenty years, Illinois taxpayers have provided billions more in State revenues to support the additional spending. Steadily increasing taxes would, at some point, become intolerable if the income received by Illinois taxpayers were not also increasing along with the increasing tax level.

Illinois Personal Income Increases Fourfold: 1960–1979

Illinois personal income is reported by the Bureau of Economic Analysis, United States Department of Commerce and includes wages and salaries (65 percent), investment income (14 percent), income from small businesses (6 percent) and other varied sources. Although the income of individual Illinois taxpayers varies widely, total Illinois personal income can be used to measure the aggregate ability of Illinois taxpayers to support State government. Without continued growth in Illinois personal income, both the willingness and the ability of Illinois taxpayers to support State government would decline over time. Chart 21-3 shows the steady growth in Illinois personal income since 1960.

The combined income of all Illinois taxpayers increased approximately fourfold in the last two decades from $26 billion in 1960 to $102 billion in 1979. Yet, during the same period, government spending increased eightfold.

State Government Doubles in Size: 1960–1979

Government "expands" when the growth in spending and revenues outstrips the growth in income received by Illinois taxpayers. This relationship is best explained by the ratio of State spending to Illinois personal income expressed as a percentage. For example, the $9.4 billion State spending anticipated in 1979 is 9.2 percent of the $102 billion income received by Illinois residents. Put another way, State spending represents about 9.2 cents of each dollar of Illinois income.

Annual changes in State spending as a percentage of Illinois personal income indicate whether or not spending is growing faster than personal income. Viewed over time, the annual ratio of State spending to personal income will readily identify significant changes in the relative size of State government. Chart 21-4 shows how State government has doubled in size. State spending represented 4.6 percent of Illinois personal income in 1960 to 9.3 percent of personal income in 1979.

The growth from 4.6 percent to 9.3 percent seems to confirm the widespread feeling that government is continually getting bigger. Closer examination of the chart, however, also shows that State government has "lived within its means" and has not gotten any larger in the last decade.

Four distinct periods are depicted in Chart A. Two reference lines drawn in Chart 21-4, one at the 5 percent level and another at 9 percent, help to define these periods. From 1962 through 1967, State spending as a percentage of Illinois income remained roughly constant at about the 5 percent level. During this period political problems prevented tax increases required to meet growing service demands.

Thereafter began a period of extraordinary growth in State government. State spending increased 25 percent in 1968, 29 percent in 1970 and 25 percent in 1971. In contrast, Illinois personal income grew only 6 percent, 5 percent and 7 percent in the same years. Sharply higher spending was supported by revenues from a tax increase in 1967 and a new income tax in 1970. At the end of the last decade, State government jumped in size from about the 6 percent level to the current 9 percent level.

The chart shows that State spending growth exceeded income growth again during the mid 1970's.[8] As a percentage of income, State spending jumped from 9.2 percent in 1974 to 10.3 percent in 1976. State spending increased by 17 percent in 1975 and 14 percent in 1976, when Illinois income grew by only about 9 percent in each year. This time, rather than a tax increase, higher spending was financed by drawing down the balances in the State treasury to crisis levels, causing, at times, significant delay in payment of the State's bills.

Slower Growth in Government Spending

The growth in State spending was cut back beginning in 1977 so that new taxes or tax increases could be avoided. State spending increased 6 percent in 1977 and only 2 percent in 1978—well below the 9 percent in Illinois income. Spending growth will also be less than income growth in 1979. In consequence, the "size of government line" in Chart 21-4 bends downward each year after 1976, bringing the current size of Illinois government back to roughly 9 percent of Illinois personal income. State government then, has remained approximately the same size over the last decade, except for a brief period in the mid 1970's.

Timely updating of Chart 21-4 can help predict future increases in the size of Illinois State government. In time, new State taxes will be necessary if the chart shows that spending growth is outstripping personal income growth. Depending upon the condition of other detailed features of State finance (such as State treasury balances

Chart 21-2

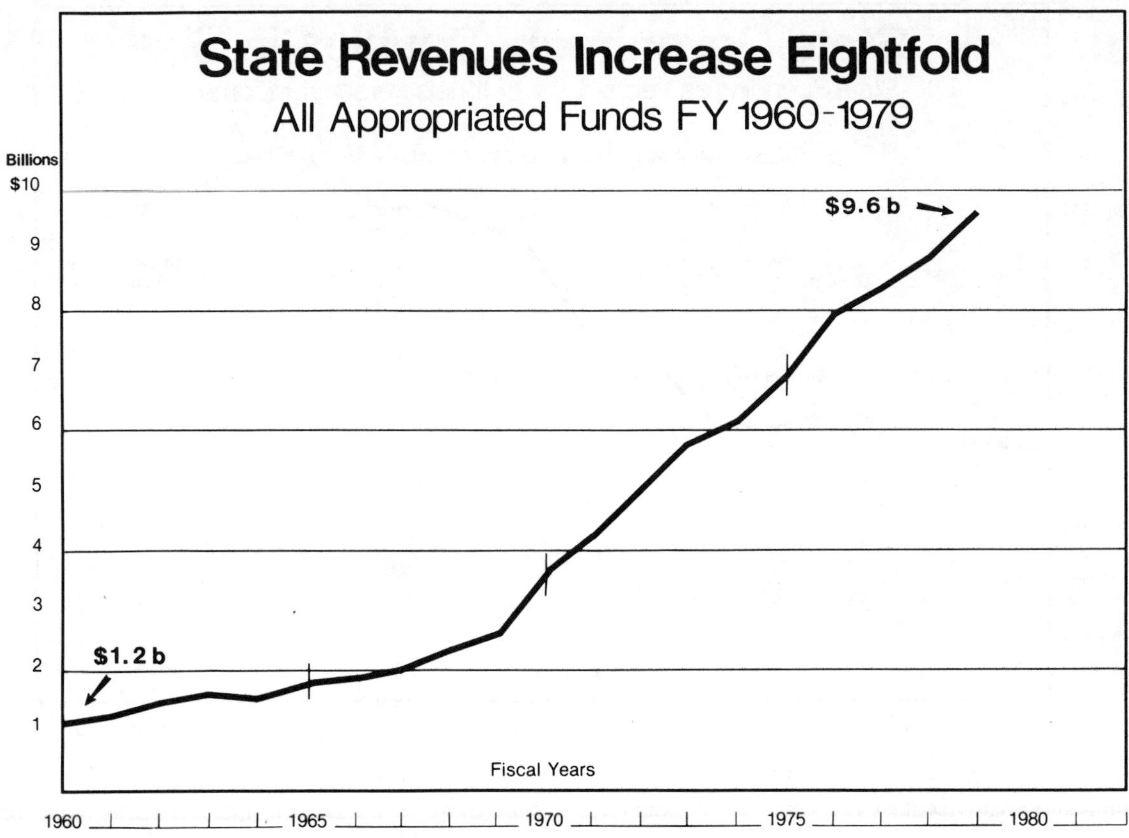

Chart 21-3

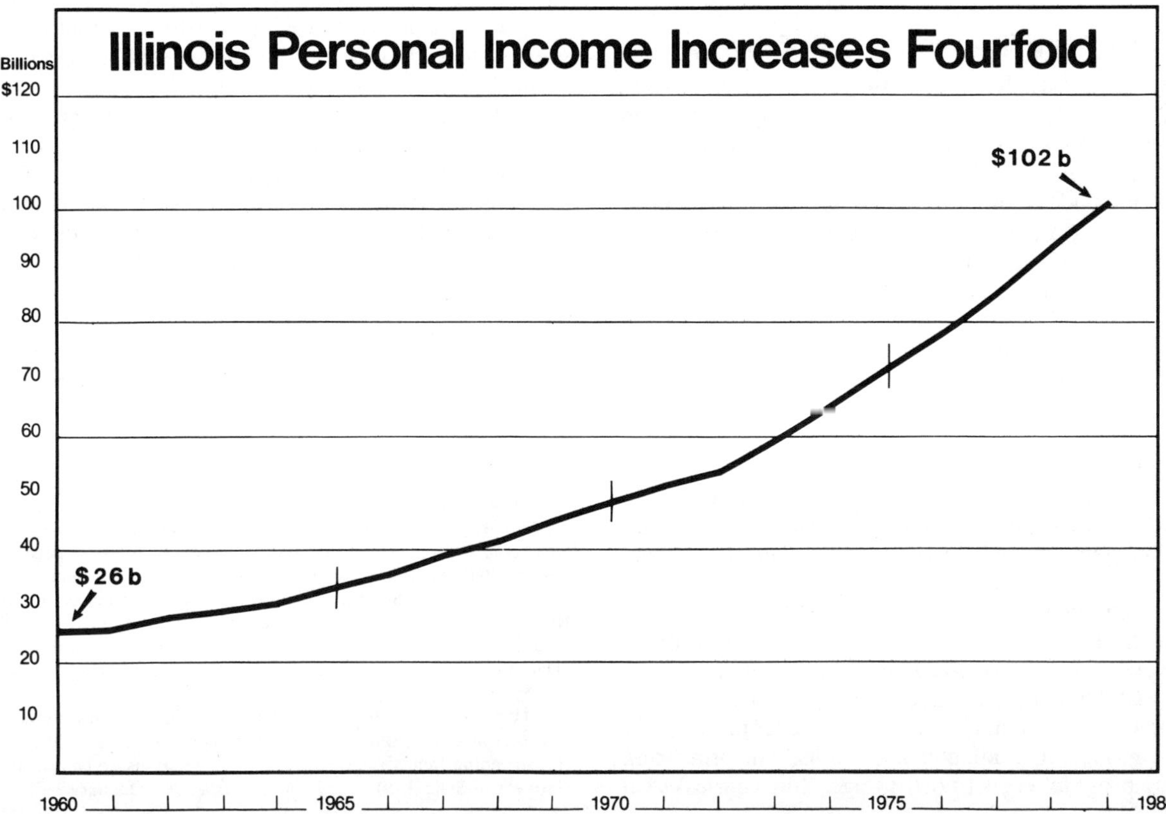

Chart 21-4

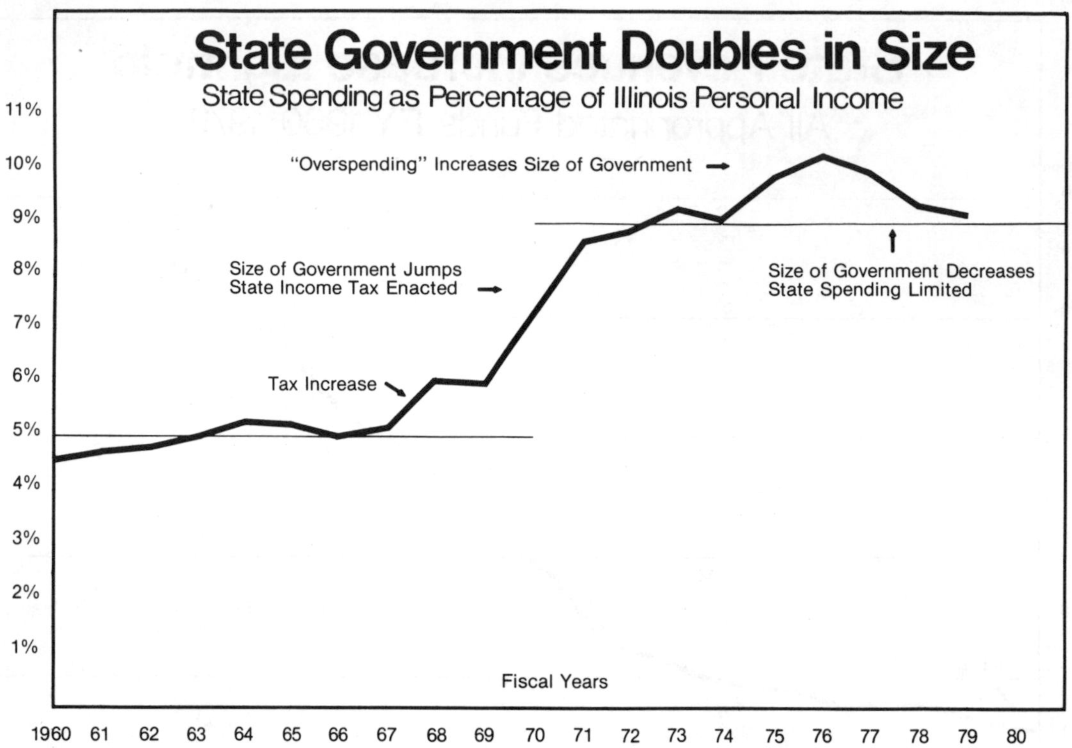

and the magnitude of budget deficits), this method can be used to help anticipate new taxes. There may, of course, be no advance warning if taxes are raised solely in anticipation of future spending.

The Size of State Government in the Future

Following the trend of the last twenty years (Chart 21-1), State spending will very likely continue to increase, producing a "record budget" each year. Even if there are no new State programs and existing programs are not expanded, inflation pressures alone will push State spending higher. However, only when the *rate of increase* in State spending exceeds, for a time, the *rate of increase* in Illinois income will State government expand in the sense that irritates many taxpayers: more of each dollar earned going to support government.

Will the relative size of Illinois State government as depicted in Chart 21-4 continue to decline as it has since 1977? It seems unlikely. State spending grew more slowly than personal income in 1977, 1978 and 1979 because the financial problems which plagued the State in the mid-1970's—"overspending", cash shortages, and deficit budgets—were resolved by tight controls on State spending.

It was possible to sharply limit spending growth for a time because the severity of the state's financial problems were widely recognized. Now, as elected officials report that State finances are once again in order, the pressures for additional spending have become intense. Interest groups, including labor unions, are pressuring for State program costs (mostly wages and salaries) to at least keep pace with inflation and in many cases to expand State programs. The pressure will likely result in State government spending nearly all the available revenues each year. However the intensity of the tax revolt will probably prevent elected officials from raising taxes. Therefore, since State revenues grow at about the same rate as the economy, the relative size of Illinois government will likely remain at about 9%.

In the longer run, the relative size of State government in Illinois will depend upon taxpayer willingness and ability to pay for State programs and changes in the need for State programs. Ability to pay is dependent upon the state of the economy. Ability to pay will be increased if the economy grows and real incomes increase. Should economic growth stall, perhaps due to an energy crisis or uncontrolled inflation, then Illinois taxpayers (as well as taxpayers in other states) will be reluctant to share more of each dollar of their income with State government.

NOTES

[1]Most of the spending was for education (elementary, high school, and university), income assistance and health services to the poor, and road construction and maintenance. The spending was largely paid for by the State income and sales taxes, road taxes and federal monies.

[2]Unless noted otherwise, all years shown will represent the State's fiscal year. A fiscal year covers the period July 1 through June 30. For example, July 1, 1977 through June 30, 1978 defines fiscal year 1978. Data for 1979 (fiscal year) are estimated by the Illinois Bureau of the Budget.

[3]The objective is limited to defining and describing the size and changes in size of Illinois state government. A detailed discussion of the spending trends for specific state programs is contained in "The Growth in State Spending," *Illinois Issues* 5:1 (January 1979).

[4]For perspective, daily spending of $38 million represents the combined annual income of over 2,500 Illinois families each earning $15,000 a year.

[5]Spending is from *all* appropriated funds including the general funds, highway funds, bond-financed funds, debt service funds, special State funds, revolving funds and university funds.

[6]The proportion of federal aid to total revenues received in the state's appropriated funds has declined moderately over the last twenty years. Federal aid was 27 percent of total revenues in 1960 ($337 million) and 24 percent in 1979 ($2.3 billion).

[7]Recent tax increases by specific source and the calendar year enacted are: Sales tax—1959, 1961, 1967; public utility tax—1965, 1967; cigarette tax—1961, 1965, 1967, 1969; liquor tax—1969; horse racing—1964, 1965, 1969; motor fuel tax—1967, 1969. The income tax became effective August, 1969 (fiscal year 1970), but the full potential was not realized until fiscal year 1972. The State lottery was established in 1975. The lottery amounts to only 4/10 of 1 percent of total State revenues.

[8]Reasons for the "overspending" include funding for a new school aid formula for elementary and secondary education, recession-induced increases in public aid spending, and two new State programs—subsidy to the RTA and tax relief for the elderly.

CHAPTER **22**

Government and Economic Growth in Illinois

A. James Heins

The purpose of this chapter is to discuss the impact of political institutions on the course of the Illinois economy. The State spends for public services that enhance the economic attractiveness of Illinois. The State also collects taxes to pay for those services, and the institutions used to collect those taxes have their effect on economic activity.

Beyond the provision of public services and collection of taxes, the State regulates business activity. These regulations may be broad as in workmen's compensation, which affects all firms, or narrow as in the regulation of horse racing. The State also has a public relations function under which it attempts to assist firms that may wish to locate in Illinois. As part of this "PR" function, the State also attempts to sell the economic advantages and product of the State generally.

An accurate assessment of the success or failure of any policy requires firm grounding in an understanding of the differences that policy can make. Therefore, it is important to emphasize at the outset that state promotional efforts have at best a modest impact on economic growth in any state—considerably less than a number of other state government activities.

The Illinois Economy

Illinois is a major factor in all areas of the United States economy. The State ranks among the leaders in agriculture, manufacturing, commerce and finance. Because of its importance in the area of agri-business, Illinois always ranks in the top three states in shipments into international markets.[1] Its location in the heartland has given it a particular advantage in transportation; Chicago is the rail capital of the nation, and O'Hare is the world's busiest airport.

Because of its diversity, Illinois has traditionally had a stable economy. It has tended to experience smaller swings in economic performance than states that have a less diverse industrial and agricultural base. And, until very recently, its unemployment rate has been well below the national average.

Despite these advantages, the Illinois economy has grown more slowly than that of the nation. Table 22-1 shows aggregate and per capita income figures for Illinois and their relationship to U.S. figures for selected years 1947 to 1977. In 1947, Illinois generated 7.2 percent of aggregate U.S. personal income. In 1977 it generated only 5.8 percent of total U.S. income.

TABLE 22-1
Aggregate and Per Capita Income in Illinois, 1947–1977

	Total Illinois Personal Income (Billions)	Percent of U.S. Total	Illinois Per Capita Income	Percent of U.S. Per Capita
1947	$13.6	7.2%	$1,624	123%
1950	15.3	7.0	1.752	122
1955	21.0	6.8	2,251	121
1960	26.4	6.6	2,613	118
1965	39.4	6.6	3,280	119
1970	50.1	6.3	4,501	115
1975	75.7	6.0	6,792	115
1977	87.3	5.8	7,768	111

Source: U.S. Department of Commerce.

A similar picture is drawn by changes in per capita income. The $1,624 generated by the average Illinois resident in 1947 represented 123 percent of the national average. By 1977, the $7,768 income per capita in Illinois had declined to 111 percent of the U.S. average.

While the picture is similar, the explanation for relative changes in total and per capita income figures is different. The narrowing of per capita income differential in the State reflects a "catching up" process by the poorer states. There is little doubt that it has been caused by population mobility in search of a better livelihood as well as the mobility of business in search of lower wages. Federal policies of geographical redistribution have reinforced the narrowing of per capita income differential between the states.

The relative decline of the Illinois economy reflected in its decreasing share of total income presents a different problem. This change has resulted from a relative flight of capital in the post-war years to the South and West. In some part the capital flight from Illinois can be explained by lower wages elsewhere, but undoubtedly the larger part of the explanation lay elsewhere. The question posed here is: could the policies of government in Illinois have slowed its relative economic decline?

Government and Economic Growth in Illinois

By and large the course of economic events in any state in the United States is determined by factors beyond the control of the body politic of that state. Business prefers to locate close to its raw materials and its markets. Transportation advantages—seaports, rivers and flat terrain—draw business activity and that activity draws people.

Climate plays an important role. It was no accident that people migrated to California in the current century. California has a marvelous climate, and people enjoy living there. It is no accident that Florida attracts retirement villages and North Dakota does not. People go where the living is pleasant. And business follows people.

Midwesterners and Easterners have become painfully aware of the "sunbelt state" syndrome. States in the sunbelt, the South and Southwest, have recently experienced more economic growth than the northern tier of states. The effect on Illinois was previously shown in Table 1. In a multivariate study of the economic performance of 28 states over the period 1947–1974, climate variables explained almost 50 percent of the differential in growth among the states.[2]

Other factors surely explain much of the remaining growth differential between the states. Resources are particularly important. Those states that have abundant energy sources will tend to do well in the energy short years ahead. Decisions made in Washington—highways, energy policy defense spending—play their role in directing the pattern of development across the states. And, there is precious little any state can do to make substantive changes in national policy to its own economic benefit.

The upshot of all this is that the body politic in a state has relatively little room to direct the course of its own economy. But, it does have *some* room, and that is what this chapter is all about.

With respect to the effect of government on the performance of the Illinois economy over the period, 1947–74, the multivariate analysis described earlier suggests that the Illinois economy fared about as expected. Income grew at a rate of 6.27 percent per year during that period compared with the 6.22 percent growth rate that could have been expected in Illinois given its climate and resource base. The conclusion is that if government failed to adopt policies that substantially off-set the economic decline, neither did its policies create a positive economic drag. But, that may change in the future.

In the main, the economic impact of government is dictated by its policies for the collection of taxes and the provision of public services. If government provides public services people want at a tax price they are willing to pay, the economy of the State will perform up to its potential. If not, it will not. The sections that follow discuss spending and tax policy in Illinois and judge its impact on the economy.

The Provision of Public Services

While government provides some public services directly to business, the principal impact of government is felt indirectly through its effect on the quality of life and on the labor pool. Government is the principal provider of education, welfare and other social services; roads; and police and fire protection. It is also a major provider of health services. Putting welfare aside for the moment, each of these services enhances the quality of life and affords a cheaper labor pool to business.

Education

The effect of education on economic performance in any state is obvious. It trains the workers whom business firms hire and improves the quality of family life. The economic impact of education has been estimated through regression analysis. The findings confirmed the obvious hypothesis that educational services enhance economic performance. States that spent more on education generated higher rates of economic growth than states spending less.[3]

In 1978 Illinois governments spent an estimated $437 per capita on its elementary and secondary public schools. The level of spending ranked sixth among the 50 states in public school spending. That $437 represented an estimated 5.36 percent of the income of the average Illinois resident. This compares with the 5.06 percent of income spent in the average state. In terms of both absolute and relative effort. Illinois has done well for its elementary and secondary schools.

In the area of higher education, spending by the State government lags well behind other states. In 1977 Illinois spent $78.30 on its colleges and universities. This gives Illinois a ranking of 42nd in this regard, and represents a spending of only one percent of its income for this purpose. The average state spent two percent of its income on higher education. In some part this may reflect the quality of private colleges in Illinois and attendance at colleges in other states. But, it may also reflect lost opportunities for economic advancement in Illinois through an improved system of higher education.

Welfare

Theoretically the effect of welfare spending on economic performance is ambiguous. While a good welfare system is capable of improving the quality of life, an overly endowed system can create economic drag by enticing people into a life of idleness. Business competes with the welfare system, and higher levels of benefit for idleness require higher wage inducements.

The aforementioned regression analysis indicates that the overall impact of welfare spending on economic growth has been negative. States that spent more on welfare experienced slower rates of income growth than states spending less.[4] On balance the welfare system appeared to be a drag on the economy of a state.

In 1977 the Illinois State government—the State accounts for the bulk of all welfare spending—spent $187.89 per capita on its public welfare program. This represents 2.56 percent of its personal income compared with a spending level of 2.40 percent of income in the average state. Illinois ranks 11th among the 50 states in welfare effort.

These figures are somewhat misleading, however. Of that $187.89 spent on welfare, only $85.78 comes from the federal government, leaving $102.11 per capita to be raised from Illinois sources or 54 percent of total welfare spending. Of the $152.01 per capita spent in the average state, the federal government picks up $86.82 leaving the average state with only $65.19 or 43 percent to be raised from state sources. In terms of per capita spending on welfare from its own sources, Illinois ranks sixth in the nation.[5] However, the State share is not entirely voluntary—federal alloction formulas favor states with low per capita income.

Other Services

Among the other services provided by government, roads and streets have the most direct connection with the economy of the State. Since this public service is tied to particular revenue sources, the gas tax and vehicle and driver fees, it is discussed below where spending for roads and corresponding revenues can be considered together.

Among the remaining public services health care is the most significant. In 1976 all units of Illinois government spent $73 per capita on health care and hospitals. This compares with a national average of $96 and leaves Illinois with a ranking of 34 among the fifty states. It is clear that Illinois governments subsidize health care provisions well below the level of the average state, but the economic impact of this discrepancy cannot be addressed here. Research is needed.

Table 22-2 summarizes spending by the State government in Illinois for a variety of other services in 1977.[6] It is evident that Illinois spends an amount well below that of the typical state in every case.

TABLE 22-2
Per Capita State Spending by Service Area, 1977

	Illinois	U.S. Average	Illinois Ranking
Natural Resources	$10.87	$20.26	46
Corrections	9.77	13.37	37
Financial Administration	8.02	10.39	40
Employment Security Administration	6.50	7.88	41
General Control	8.01	8.62	33

Source: U.S. Bureau of the Census, *State Government Finances*, 1977.

Were these figures to represent costs for the provision of a given level of services, Illinois clearly would be doing well. It is more likely, however, that these figures demonstrate that Illinois is offering fewer public services in these areas. The corrections figure is particularly revealing because of the general knowledge that the Illinois corrections system lags in overall capability. The economic impact of Illinois spending for these services is impossible to judge at this point, but a question might be raised about lost economic opportunities attributable to underfunding of some public services. Greater expenditures for natural resource development—for example, coal gasification—could have positive economic impact.

General Taxation

Few states offer a general tax structure that is more conducive to economic expansion than that of the State of Illinois. The individual income tax is flat rate, the sales tax is broad and the corporate income tax constitutionally limited to eight-fifths the flat rate of the individual income tax. If there is a tax problem in Illinois, the problem would seem to rest in taxes for the unemployment compensation program and insurance fees required under the State's workmen's compensation program. Beyond that, assessment practices for the property tax may pose some problems.

The Level of Taxes in Illinois

In the main, Illinois has been a relatively low tax state as measured by the proportion of income taken off by taxes. In 1976, the general revenue raised by all units of Illinois government totalled $10.4 billion. That amounts to $930 per capita compared with $880 in the median state, giving Illinois a rank of 19 among the 50 states. But since Illinois is among the wealthiest states, that $930 amounts to only 13.8 percent of the income of the average resident compared with 15.5 percent in the median state, giving Illinois a rank of 42 in terms of tax burden relative to income.

Of the $930 collected from the average person in 1977, $489, or 52.6 percent, was collected by the State government, local units collecting the remainder. Illinois is about average in terms of the percentage of revenue collected by State and local units of government. By way of polar comparisons, 78.5 and 41.2 percent of revenues are collected by the state governments in New Mexico and New Jersey respectively.

The Structure of General State Taxes

Perhaps no governmental policy is as important to the economic climate as the general tax structure of the state. Taxes that lie too heavily on the business community tend to push business to other states. On the other hand, taxes laid too unevenly on the laboring classes tend to dampen the labor pool, and the economy similarly suffers. Balance is required. Needless to say, there is dispute about where the balance may lie.

Tax predictability is also an important attribute of the tax structure. Nothing is more of an anathema to business than uncertainty about the future structure of taxes. In general, business likes a climate of known variables. This is the principal source of concern for the recent controversy over the replacement of the corporate personal property tax mandated by the 1970 constitution. Uncertainty about the nature of a replacement tax continued for a decade.

On both counts, balance and certainty, Illinois ranks high among the states in its general state tax structure. Since the income tax was adopted in 1969, there has been no substantive change in the rate or structure of any major State tax. On the side of balance, the general funds of Illinois derive about one-third of their revenues from the income tax, one-third from the sales tax, and one-

TABLE 22-3
State Taxes Paid into the Illinois General Fund, 1978

Tax	Year Adopted	Latest Rate Change	Current Rate	1978 Revenues (Millions)	Percent of Total
Personal Income Tax	1969	1969	2.5%	$1,662	26.7%
Corporate Income Tax	1969	1969	4.0%	455	7.3
Sales Tax	1933	1970	4.0%[a]	2,003	32.2
Public Utility Taxes	1937	1968	5.0%	371	6.0
Cigarette Tax	1941	1970	12¢	180	2.9
Liquor Tax	1934	1970	VAR	76	1.2
Insurance Tax	1937	1937	2.0%	95	1.5
Inheritance Tax	1895	1921	2–14%[b]	115	1.8
Other State Sources	—	—	—	186	3.0
Federal Aid	—	—	—	1,085	17.4
Totals				$6,228	100.0%

[a]For the most part municipalities or counties add one percent making the total tax five percent on sales.
[b]For close relatives. The rate is 10–30% for the unrelated.

third from all other sources of revenue. Beyond this balance, the broadness of the sales tax and the flat rate income tax provide for year after year stability in tax revenue not present in other states with narrower sales taxes and more progressive income taxes.

Table 22-3 provides details about the major State taxes funneling into the general fund, including years of adoption and most recent rate change, current rate, revenues realized in 1978 and percent of the total revenues.

Local Taxes–The Property Tax

The property tax provides about 65 percent of the revenues which local units of government derive from their own sources. The remainder comes principally from the piggy-back sales tax, utility taxes and license fees.

The property tax is the general tax of greatest concern to business. It is the largest single State or local tax paid by business, by far. And it offers the greatest degree of tax uncertainty because of the vagaries of assessment practices. Some of the uncertainty will be resolved when the issue of corporate personal property tax replacement is finally laid to rest.

The agriculture community has a special case against the property tax. It generates by far the biggest tax bite on farmers, and inconsistent assessment practices bedevil agriculture. A problem has arisen recently with the rapid escalation of farm land values. Five fold increases in the price of acreage in the 1970's tended to increase the relative burden of the property tax on agriculture. The merits are, of course, in dispute, but the Illinois Legislature took action in 1978 to change the basis of firm property taxes from property value to cash flow. It is much too early to evaluate the effect of this change in the property tax.

In terms of property tax levels, Illinois is an average tax state. In the latest year for which complete data are currently available, 1976, Illinois collected $284 in property taxes from the average resident. This compares with the national average of $266 and gives Illinois a ranking of 18th among the 50 states. Noting the relative wealth of Illinois, tht $284 represents 4.0 percent of the income of Illinois taxpayers, compared with the 4.3 percent taken nationally. By this measure, property taxes are relatively low in Illinois.

Property tax growth has also leveled off in Illinois. In 1967, property taxes were just over 4.0 percent of income, slightly higher than current figures, and, most interestingly, total property taxes collected in Illinois actually declined from 1974 to 1976. These seem to be little known facts. With the abolition of the personal property tax, figures for 1980 will reflect even greater declines in property tax revenues.

In terms of the economic impact on the economy, the division of burden of property taxes between business and residential property owners would be a crucial variable. At this point, little is known about this division because of the lack of data, and no firm conclusions can be drawn. Beyond that, the practices followed in specific areas of the State are probably more important than any practices revealed by statewide averages (see the Kenney discussion of Chicago practices).

Highways in Illinois

Save education, no public service is more important to economic growth in any state than the system of highways and streets. Highways bring goods to market and labor to the place of business. Funding of roads at a level that creates inefficiencies in these areas takes its toll on the economy of any state. Recently there has been feeling in Illinois that highways are already at an inefficiently low level.

A study sponsored by the Illinois State Chamber of Commerce evaluated the economic effects of highway investment and finance on economic growth in 28 states over the period 1957–1976. The procedures followed in that study were refined for further publication as a scholarly effort to determine the economic effect of highways as a social investment.[7] The effect of the highway program can be divided into two components, level of investment or spending and the method of finance.

Highway Investment

The basic theory of highway investment is simple. Some highways are necessary even to stand still economically. Beyond that level of spending, additional highway investment will enhance economic growth until investment reaches the point at which additional dollars spent on highways are not worth the tax cost—the "point of diminishing returns". The experience of 28 states from 1957 to 1976 confirms that notion with a high degree of statistical significance.[8]

When the findings of this study were fit to the Illinois situation they revealed the relationship shown in Figure 22-1.[9] That figure shows that Illinois spent 1.93 percent of its personal income on highways in the period 1957 to 1976 and realized an annual growth rate of real income of 2.75 percent per year. The multivariate procedures used in the analysis estimate that had Illinois spent 3.27 percent on highways—the average of the 28 states was 2.83 percent—the income growth rate in that period would have been 3.96 percent annually. This shortfall in highway investment was greater in Illinois than any other state. Indeed, five of the 28 states actually spent more than the maximum effective amount.

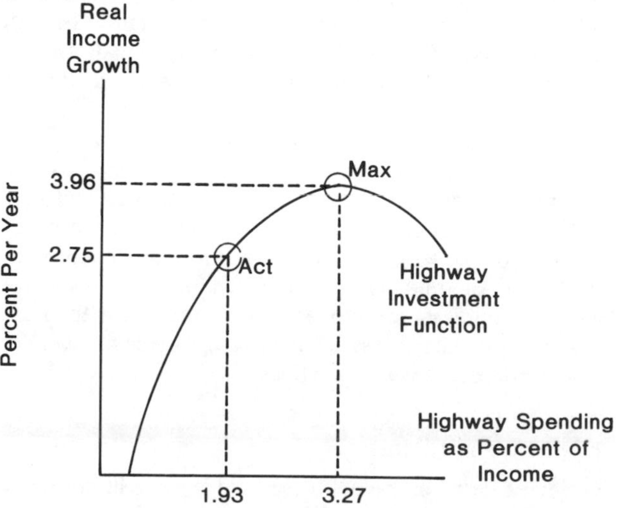

Figure 22-1. INCOME AS A FUNCTION OF HIGHWAY SPENDING

The road funds in Illinois are currently at a level that will permit no new construction or major refurbishing of Illinois highways in the years ahead unless motor fuel taxes and road fees are increased or the State resorts to borrowing. Illinois road revenues come from taxes and fees that are not ad-valorem (based on value of sales), and those revenues have leveled off in recent years. Combined with the added costs posed by escalating inflation, the shortfall in real highway spending has widened. As a result, the economy of Illinois is probably suffering.

Highway Revenues

Traditional economic theories would argue that economic growth is fostered by pricing schemes that put the cost of public services on the beneficiaries of those services. When the costs are levied against non-users, and users get a cheap ride thereby, resources are not used efficiently. This notion suggests that efficient highway finance would rely on motor fuel taxes and fees rather than general revenue funds. These notions were borne out rather remarkably in an Illinois highway study, gas taxes being the preferred method and vehicle fees next.[10]

By these criteria, Illinois does better than the typical state in one regard; it raised 72.5 percent of its highway money directly from road users in the 1957–1976 period compared with the average of 71.5 percent. But, within the road user category, Illinois relied less heavily on motor fuel taxes than the average state, 55.3 percent to 62.0 percent, and correspondingly more heavily on vehicle fees. In this regard Illinois might have done better.

Illinois' heavy reliance on vehicle fees derives from the fact that it has far and away the highest truck fees in the nation. Beyond the general inefficiency of using fees rather than fuel taxes, pushing a higher percentage of road costs onto trucks may pose an economic problem. While the problem of joint costs leaves us with no unambiguous theory of efficient pricing as between cars and trucks, there is some evidence that high truck fees may limit economic growth.[11] Since Illinois derived 46.5 percent of its fees from trucks, the highest percentage of the states studied, caution should be exercised in relying on higher truck fees to finance the increase in highway spending that will be required in the years ahead.

A current issue in the politics of highway finance surrounds the question of "diversion": the use of road funds to pay administrative costs in the Secretary of State's Office and the State Police. But these State services are highway related for the most part, and it is not clear that using road funds for these purposes constitutes "diversion." In any event, taking road funds away from Secretary of State and Police for road construction would require other non-road funds to make up the difference, and that would be tantamount to financing highway construction from sources other than road users. Such a method of resolving the highway finance problem in Illinois would appear to be inefficient.

Current Economic Issues in Illinois

This section discusses a few of the economic issues of current concern in Illinois and emphasizes the need for more research on the Illinois economy. Research generates knowledge, and knowledge offers hope of finding sensible answers to multidimensional social and economic problems.

In its report to Governor Thompson in January, 1979, the Illinois Commission for Economic Development points to the following issues: (1) development of international markets for Illinois manufacturing and agriculture; (2) the escalating costs to employers of the workmen's compensation (WC) and unemployment compensation (UC) programs; (3) the relationship between federal grants to Illinois governments and federal taxes paid by Illinois residents; (4) the tax climate and interstate competition for industrial development; (5) improvements in highways, waterways, airports, and railroads; and (6) promotion of tourism in Illinois.[12]

I would add the following to the list of significant economic issues with which Illinois government will deal in the years ahead: (1) "lifeline" pricing of utility services; (2) implementation of federal environmental standards, including those concerning disposition of hazardous materials; (3) collective bargaining for public employees; (4) resolution of the problem of personal property tax abolition; and (5) energy development in Illinois. Transportation has been discussed in an earlier section; and the issues of developing exports and tourism and improving the relationship between federal grants relative to federal taxes are sufficiently obvious as to eliminate the need for further discussion. Taking the other issues in turn:

Workmen's and Unemployment Compensation

The WC/UC programs in Illinois have been a principal rallying point for the opposition of the Illinois business community to the actions of the Illinois Legislature. It is alleged that legislation adopted in 1975 has significantly damaged the Illinois business climate by dramatically increasing the employment costs of these programs, by some estimates already the highest in the nation. The Illinois Fiscal Commission has concluded that the cost of the Illinois WC program was highest among the 33 states studied, including all of the major industrial states.[13]

In a report to the Conference of State Manufacturers Associations (COSMA—not an Illinois association), Alexander Grant and Company cite federal data that shows Illinois to rank 34th among the states, and higher than all but Michigan and Ohio in the midwest, in terms of WC costs.[14] The same report shows Illinois to rank 43rd in unemployment benefits paid, making that program more costly to Illinois employers than any other state in the midwest.

The specific business concerns about the WC/UC programs in Illinois surround the question of eligibility for benefits under these programs. For example, it is too easy for people to get WC benefits for illness that is not job related; unemployment is paid after five weeks to those who voluntarily quit jobs. Such liberal eligibility for benefits increases employment costs of business under the WC/UC programs. This situation has led the Commission for Economic Development to recommend: ". . . that the Illinois General Assembly enact changes in the Workmen's Compensation and Unemployment Compensation Insurance laws that will tighten eligibility standards and stabilize or reduce rates."[15]

From the vantage point of labor, the 1975 legislation makes Illinois an attractive place to work, and those legislative victories will not be given back easily. One could argue that other employment costs to business are lowered because of the attractiveness of legislatively mandated insurance programs, and that the net impact on employment by Illinois business is not clear. This, of course, is a researchable question.

Lifeline Utility Pricing

The last three winters in Illinois have been, in tandem, the coldest on record; and cold weather means high energy use. This fact combined with a doubling of energy prices in the last five years has worked significant hardship on lower income groups as they struggle to fit the cost of utility services into their budgets. The concern for low income people and the interest of environmental groups for energy conservation has fueled the political drive for a change in utility pricing practices to that of the "lifeline."

Lifeline, in contrast to the current practice of pricing utility services on a "cost-of-service basis," calls for a reduction in rates to small residential users and an increase in rates on large users and industrial users of power to make up the revenue difference to utilities. Adherents claim tht lifeline will ease the undue pressures of the energy crunch on low income people and induce large users and business to conserve energy because of higher prices. One proponent has even claimed that "lifeline will save jobs in Illinois."[16]

In general, utilities and the business community resist a change from the cost-of-service pricing basis that calls for declining rates with larger blocks of energy use and a different price basis for industrial and residential users. They contend that under current practices followed by the Illinois Commerce Commission and other State regultory bodies, industrial users already pay rates that subsidize residential users, and lifeline would worsen already inefficient pricing arrangements.[17] It is also claimed that problems of equity attributable to the energy crunch would be better dealt with under existing welfare programs.

These are questions that beg for research. Among other aspects of this problem, it is clear that increasing energy prices paid by business will pose costs that fall ultimately on consumers. Will they be the same consumers paying lower utility bills? Will energy conservation result? Or, will business merely turn to more costly forms of on-site energy production?

The Tax Climate and Tax Limits

Taxes in Illinois are below average in terms of the bite they take out of income in Illinois. Nonetheless there has been interest in limiting future tax growth in Illinois, though that interest is clearly less than in the Proposition 13 state, California.[18]

The specific proposal receiving the most press in Illinois has been that introduced by Representative Donald Totten. His proposal calls for a State revenue limit of eight percent of personal income, a stabilization fund for contingencies and a three percent limit on the rate of increase in the revenues of any local governmental unit without a referendum. In the 1979 legislative session, this proposal was in its second legislative go around and had significant support.

Prodded by the three-to-one passage of his tax limit advisory referendum in the general election of November, 1978, Governor Thompson has come forward with a proposal that would similarly restrict both State and local revenue growth to the rate of increase in personal income.

A substantially different proposal was introduced by Senator Prescott Bloom with the endorsement of the Illinois State Chamber of Commerce. This proposal would focus only on the general funds of the State, and would call for an annual resetting of income tax rates so as to limit revenue growth to the pace of inflation. Increases in tax rates beyond this point would require a three-fifths majority of both houses of the Legislature.

Tax limits are new in the United States, and there is little knowledge about their impact on the provision of public services. Research is needed on this question. In the meantime, it can be expected that political pressures will force action which may or may not be supported by subsequent research.

Enhancing the Environment

The federal government has mandated that states design and implement programs to enhance the quality of the environment. These programs are mandated by such legislation as the *Clean Air Act, Water Pollution Control Act, Resource Conservation and Recovery Act,* and the *Toxic Substances Act*. The Illinois Pollution Control Board (IPCB) is responsible for drafting the rules, with implementation by the Illinois Environmental Protection Agency (EPA). It is patently obvious that pollution control standards will have an important and direct effect on the course of the Illinois economy.

Examples of the production activities affected by pollution standards are hydrocarbon emissions associated with steel production, road construction, painting, dry cleaning, operation of conveyers and the maintenance of storage piles. In each of these activities business will have to incur costs to keep emissions within the standard for clean air laid down by EPA. The amount of those costs, directly related to the stringency of the standards, will have a direct impact in Illinois. Of course, other states labor under the oar of complying with the same federal pollution standards. The Annual Survey of Manufactures, 1976, from the U.S. Department of Commerce, shows Illinois manufacturers to have spent an amount equal to 0.31 percent of shipment value on pollution abatement. This figure gives it a rank of 24 among the 48 contiguous states, quite an average level at this point.

A recent headline maker in Illinois has been the problem of dealing with nuclear waste materials.[19] Illinois has provided the nation with its largest dumping ground. There is not only the difficulty of storing wastes once on location; those wastes come to Illinois by truck and rail, and the risk of accident at the point of transportation is real. But, the production of nuclear power and storage of wastes has become big business in Illinois. Reversing that trend, whatever the desirable consequences for the quality of the Illinois environment, will have an effect on the economy.

Energy—Illinois Coal

Illinois sits on the nation's largest bed of coal. Unfortunately, that coal is not very usable under current environmental standards because of its high sulfur content. Innovation—coal gasification, perhaps—that would make Illinois coal cheaper to use could provide an important boost to the economy, directly in the southern coal region of the State and indirectly elsewhere, through cheaper energy and added tax revenues.

A coal boom in the south of Illinois may be a mixed blessing.[20] Coal mining is hazardous, and mined land is difficult to reclaim. The environment in the area of a coal mining boom tends to be less than optimal. Nevertheless, development of Illinois coal reserves would stimulate the economy of the State.

The newly created Illinois Institute of Natural Resources has been charged with supplementing efforts to improve the technology of using high sulfur coal. Under the *Illinois Coal and Energy Development Act of 1974*, the State is authorized to issue $65 million in funds, the proceeds of which can be used to subsidize proposals that would develop this technology. Coal gasification is one of the highest hopes (see the Schneiderman Chapter). Other proposals have been introduced into the Illinois Legislature. The questions are: should more money be spent? And, what would be the impact of these efforts on the economy and the environment?

Other Problem Areas

Illinois Government will make a host of other decisions in the years ahead that will have a significant impact on the course of the economy. A particularly hot current issue is the replacement of the personal property tax.

Under the old personal property tax, local units of government received tax revenues from business on the basis of their personal property, including the so-called Capital Stock Tax. Because firms paying this tax were entitled to elect the office at which the tax applied, a few relatively small units of government were disproportionate beneficiaries of these revenues. The 1970 Constitution mandated an end to this tax by 1979, requiring a new tax on the same class of taxpayers, business, to "replace" the lost revenues.

Initially, the difficulty was finding the replacement tax. It seems clear now that the biggest difficulty was finding the distribution formula designed to "replace" the lost local revenues. If the replacement tax collects money from business generally and channels it into a few local districts to replace special revenues that entitled property owners in these districts to abnormally low real property tax rates, resentment will surface. No matter which way the State turns to solve this problem, difficulties will abound.

The issue of collective bargaining for public employees in Illinois may be a thorny one.[21] Until this point, the desire of Chicago political leaders to use informal procedures in dealing with labor has prevented adoption of a statewide law that would, of necessity, formalize bargaining procedures. A change in Chicago's leadership may bode a new collective bargaining law for State and local government employees.

The economic impact of State politics and policies in this area can be too casually dismissed. Such a law may bid up the cost of government services. It may generate instability in the offering of public services. Note the economic impact of the police strike in New Orleans during the 1979 Mardi Gras festival. Perhaps these questions call for a close look at the economic effects of collective bargaining laws in effect in some 40 states.

Conclusion

In closing this discussion, it is appropriate to note the efforts of some 150 volunteers from all walks of Illinois life working under the auspices of the Illinois State Chamber of Commerce through its Illinois 2000 Foundation. In its preliminary report, *Alternative Economic Futures for Illinois,* Illinois 2000 points out the general problem faced by labor, business and government.[22] Natural climatic and resource disadvantages pose a threat to the Illinois economy. Illinois' share of national employment and income have fallen steadily since 1950. Continued economic erosion poses a problem for those of us who are committed to Illinois as a home. The main task of government in Illinois is to find policies that deal with the problem of energy, the environment, welfare and education, but, in the process, minimize the drag placed on the Illinois economy.

NOTES

[1]*Foreign Trade and the Illinois Economy* (Chicago: Illinois State Chamber of Commerce, September 1978).

[2]A. James Heins, *Illinois Economic Growth Study* (Chicago: Illinois State Chamber of Commerce, 1976).

[3]*Ibid.*, p. 19. T-ratios from the regression analysis were always positive and ranged from 1.23 to 1.85. Of course, others have argued the opposite—educational expenses are a function of wealth.

[4]*Ibid.* T-ratios ranged from −1.67 to −1.90.

[5]It is worth noting that of the $247.20 per capita spent on welfare in New York State, some $159.64 or 64 percent comes from the federal government. We should send emissaries to New York to learn how to do it.

[6]State government spending is highlighted here because of the absence of up-to-date data by these categories for combined units of government in the various states. In any event, consideration of government structure washed out by the process of combining spending figures are less important here because of the dominance of the state government in spending for these purposes.

[7]A. James Heins and John Graham, *Illinois Highways and Economic Growth,* Illinois State Chamber of Commerce, 1976, and John Graham and A. James Heins, "A Highway Investment Function," University of Illinois, Urbana-Champaign, mimeograph, n.d.

[8]The precise function fit to estimate this relationship was parabolic. In all variants of the regression T-ratios on the linear term ranged from 2.5 to 4.0. T-ratios on the squared term ranged from −2.0 to −3.5.

[9]These precise results were taken from the revised procedures reported in "A Highway Investment Function." In the original study, *Illinois Highways and Economic Growth,* the maximum effective level of spending was 4.03 percent of income and corresponding income growth rate 4.55 percent per year.

[10]T-ratios or variables that implemented these relationships ranged from 1.48 to 3.30.

[11]From the highway studies noted earlier, T-ratios in the truck-car fee variable ranged from 1.30 to 2.09 in the variants of the basic regression analysis.

[12]State of Illinois, Commission for Economic Development, *Report and Recommendations to Governor James R. Thompson and the 81st General Assembly,* January 1979.

[13]Illinois Fiscal Commission, *Report on Economic and Fiscal Trends in the State of Illinois,* December 1977.

[14]Alexander Grant & Co., *A Study of Business Climates of the Forty-eight Contiguous States of America,* a report to the Conference of State Manufacturers Associations.

[15]Commission for Economic Development, *Report,* January 1979, p. 18.

[16]Gregory Palast, "Testimony Before the House Utility Committee: Lifeline Electricity Rates," February 23, 1977.

[17]Electricity Consumers Research Council, *Profiles in Electricity Issues,* Washington, D.C., Vol. 1, No. 1, February 1977. Beyond the research work of this council see the testimony of any representative of industry or the utilities before the Illinois Commerce Commission.

[18]For a discussion of tax limits in other states see Gary E. Schmitz, "Tax and Spending Limits: What Other States are Trying," *Illinois Issues* (March 1979).

[19]Catherine Quigg and Cordell Reed, "Should Com Ed Increase Spent Fuel Storage at the Zion Nuclear Station," *Illinois Issues* (April 1979), and "Illinois Babysits Nuclear Wastes," Staff report, *Illinois Issues* (September 1977).

[20]Jessica C. Weber, "Illinois South Project Takes on the Coal Industry," *Illinois Issues* (May 1979).

[21]John Rehfuss, "Is Collective Bargaining a Good Bargain?" *Illinois Issues* (April 1978).

[22]Illinois 2000 Foundation, 20 North Wacker Drive, Chicago, Illinois 60606.

SUPPLEMENTAL READINGS

Commission for Economic Development. *Report and Recommendations to Governor James R. Thompson and the 81st General Assembly*. January 1979.

Elsass, Dan. "The Industrial Sweepstakes." *Illinois Issues,* December 1978.

Fisher, Glenn W. *Financing Illinois Government*. Urbana: University of Illinois Press, 1960.

Heins, A. James. *Illinois Economic Growth Study*. Chicago: Illinois State Chamber of Commerce, 1976.

Heins, A. James, and John Graham. *Illinois Highways and Economic Growth*. Illinois State Chamber of Commerce, 1979.

Illinois Economic and Fiscal Commission. *A Hearing on the Business Climate in Illinois,* March 1978.

Illinois Environmental Protection Agency. *Clean Water Horizons,* January 1979.

Illinois Fiscal Commission. *Report on Economic and Fiscal Trends in Illinois*. December 1977.

Illinois, State of. *Report of the Commission on Revenue*. 1963.

Illinois, State of. *Report of the Governor's Revenue Study Committee, 1968–69*. 1969.

Jusenius, C. L., and L. C. Ledebur. *A Myth in the Making: The Southern Economic Challenge and Northern Economic Decline*. Economic Development Administration, U.S. Department of Commerce, November 1976.

Minert. "Illinois Tax Revolt—The 8% Solution." *Illinois Issues* 4:12 (December 1978).

Quigg, Catherine, and Cordell Reed. "Should Com Ed Increase Spent Fuel Storage at the Zion Nuclear Station?" *Illinois Issues* 5:4 (April 1979).

Rowell, Phillip M. "Product Liability Insurance." *Illinois Issues* 4:7 (July 1978).

Schmitz, Gary E. "Tax and Spending Limits: What Other States are Trying." *Illinois Issues* 5:3 (March 1979).

CHAPTER **23**

The Legislative Appropriations Process: Selective Use of Authority and Tools

*Raymond F. Coyne**

Political considerations determine how and why authority is used. They are particularly important in understanding the selective formal and informal uses of authority by the Illinois General Assembly in making revenue and expenditure decisions. This chapter examines how the legislative "power of the purse" is used or not used and the possible political considerations involved. In that context, the evolving legislative tools for managing the appropriations process and making fiscal decisions are examined. Suggestions for reform in various areas are reviewed and critiqued.

Politics of the Appropriations Process: Power in Action

Any attempt to understand the legislative appropriations process will be severely limited unless it comes to grips with the need for a clear distinction between power and authority. This section attacks the problem by proceeding from observations at the gut level to a more rigorous conceptual analysis.

Fundamental Political Realities: The Basis of Incremental Budgeting

The actual uses of authority are visible, but the mobilizations of power to bring about those uses of authority are less visible, and the value judgements which lead to these mobilizations of power are the least visible. While the votes of individual legislators are recorded and the groups comprising the majorities can be identified, the reasons why a majority of legislators collectively exercised their respective individual authority in a particular fashion are not always clear. Nevertheless, *how* authority is used gives clues as to *why* it is used.

One of the drawbacks of looking only at public actions such as roll call votes is that many opportunities for exercising legislative authority never find their way into the formal agenda. The General Assembly has many formal and informal opportunities to exercise its authority. It can approve, reject, or modify every word and every dollar amount in appropriation bills. The record indicates greater legislative revision of executive requests, particularly by appropriations committees, in recent years.[1] But the frequent use of authority is not necessarily a manifestation of power—it may even suggest the user's powerlessness.

Political gains and losses are frequently achieved through the use or disuse of authority. These uses take on greater meaning when viewed in the light of political questions, such as: does the Governor invite conflict with the General Assembly or does he require their support? Does the Legislature balance appropriations and resources or does it leave that task to the Governor's veto pen and his impoundment controls? What does the Legislature have to gain by balancing the budget? What does it cost the General Assembly to balance the budget? What does the Governor have to gain by announcing before a battery of television cameras that he has taken the responsible course of vetoing the Legislature's "irresponsible overspending" in order to avoid a tax increase? What does a Governor have to gain by balancing the budget through vetoes and impoundments? Why would the Legislature assert spending priorities contrary to those proposed by the Governor? Why does or does not the Legislature defer to the Governor? Does its deference occur voluntarily or involuntarily? Why does it act incrementally or nonincrementally.**

The Governor usually obtains the support or acquiescence of a majority of legislators in the majority of financial decisions. The usual pattern of what appears to be gubernatorial domination occurs because of political, and not institutional or legal, reasons. How the Governor obtains support or acquiescence, on which issues and at what cost are beyond this effort. This chapter is about the way in which the Illinois General Assembly formally exercises its authority with respect to financial decisions. It stresses that reasons guide the Legislature's uses of its tools—political considerations, broadly construed, play a role in determining whether authority will be exercised, how it will be exercised and whether the Legislature's use of authority will prevail.

Observing this pattern of power in action is somewhat difficult because the use of power is not always visible and the distribution of power is uncertain. All too frequently, discussions of legislative financial decision-making fail to appreciate the distinction between authority and power. They suggest that the Executive's tendency to get what he wants from the process comes at the

*Portions of this paper have been derived from the Illinois Economic and Fiscal Commission's *Legislative Control of State Finance*. The opinions and conclusions contained in this chapter are solely those of the author and do not necessarily reflect the views of the Commission. The author would like to acknowledge the comments made by Marshall Lanberg and Walter Kesselman.

**Incremental changes are small in magnitude and do not reflect major policy changes.

expense of the legislative branch. They neglect to consider that while the authority relationship outlined in constitutions calls for coequal partners, power relationships between a particular Governor and a particular Legislature need to be included in any complete explanation. While frequently there are appeals for greater legislative involvement in the budget process, there are never appeals for greater Democratic or Republican involvement! In short, much of the literature fails to view one of the more consumately political processes in terms of political costs and benefits, especially partisan ones. The public finance literature pushes for a nice, straightforward rational budgeting process without politics.

Second, very little attention has been given to the role of legislatures,[2] and that has been primarily reformist in orientation: a legislature should exercise the independent judgment of a coequal branch.[3] The reformist literature finds the prevalance of executive domination of the resource allocation process and explains it as a result of superior access to professional staff and year round consideration of financial matters, in contrast to understaffed, part-time legislatures reviewing appropriation requests during relatively short periods.[4]

Much of Anton's *The Politics of State Expenditure in Illinois*[5] is concerned with themes flowing from the reformist literature: balancing appropriations against expected revenues, devoting sufficient time, promoting rationality and responsibility, obtaining adequate information and exercising formal authority. Fisher's short discussion of the appropriations process in *Taxes and Politics: A Study of Illinois Public Finance*[5] is similarly concerned with the ascendancy of political considerations over "economic and fiscal analysis." Neither demonstrates an adequate comprehension of the reasons for variation in application of legislative authority over financial matters.

The basic failure of the reformist literature is that it points to inadequate *application* of resources (in the narrow sense) as the problem to be solved instead of concerning itself with the legislature's differential *willingness* to apply resources. Gubernatorial dominance can occur even when a full-time legislature uses adequate staff resources. A legislature with overwhelming political and institutional resources may allow the gubernatorial budget proposal to emerge unscathed from the legislative process, but that is certainly not what one would expect from reading the reformist literature. Having the will to apply institutional resources is even more important than the mere possession of those resources.[6]

In addition to the "politics is distasteful" emphasis, there is the "politics is superfluous" school of thought. In other words, "politics does not make a difference," except perhaps trivially at the margins. Not all incrementalists concur with such assumptions, but some of their conclusions can be used to support them. Their basic point is that financial decisions are the product of the past and that both governors and legislatures only incrementally affect contemporary financial parameters.[7] For example, Wildavsky, Sharkansky and others have noted the popularity of incremental patterns of budgetary decisions. Incrementalism limits the number of conflicts, whereas a "rational budgeting approach" would require a comprehensive assessment of every item in the entire budget, including those items which were included in the past only after the resolution of differences. Incrementalism, in contrast, does not encourage "the opening of old wounds." Incrementalists recognize that last year's budget comprises a set of commitments which are impossible, or at least costly, to renege on or retrench. For example, pension benefits contracted for last year must be maintained this year and for years to come. A building or road started last year, on the other hand, can be left unfinished. Politically it is hazardous to terminate large numbers of current employees or major public services, but beyond that, a majority recognize that for the most part the activities which government funded last year were legitimate.[8]

Illinois legislators often think in such terms: the cost of maintaining current activities (the base), the cost of updating the base for uncontrollable factors (e.g., Social Security tax increases), the cost of previously agreed upon policies (e.g., step and merit increases) and the cost of changes in the scope of agency activities (the increment). While the activities which comprise the base can be changed and previous commitments can be discontinued or altered, legislators generally do not want to reopen previously resolved conflicts about the proper activities of an agency. Once it has been decided that an agency is to pursue a particular purpose, most legislators believe they should support whatever funding is "needed." While most of the emphasis is clearly on the margins, the Illinois General Assembly has occasionally redefined the base, temporarily suspended commitments of previous General Assemblies, altered many and reversed some previous commitments and even refused to fund entire agencies. Incrementalism, then, is common, but it is not a universal or a blind incrementalism where only trivial changes are considered.[9]

The General Assembly is motivated by political considerations, broadly construed, when it acts nonincrementally. But denying the legitimacy of an agency's base is nonincremental, as is reversing a commitment made by a prior General Assembly. The political forces most commonly at work in the Illinois environment also help explain why legislative and executive branches generally act incrementally and why the Legislature tends to act incrementally upon the Governor's proposal. These forces usually produce a situation where the best mix of political costs and benefits flows from an incremental course of action—it helps keep the consequences both predictable and manageable.

The Distinction between Power and Authority

Authority is formally conveyed to institutions by constitution or statute, but political action occurs only when authority is joined by power.

Power is a variable which measures the ability to see one's will actualized, usually in the face of conflicting wills. Political power is the ability to cause others to perform requisite actions, including the exercise of formal authority in accordance with one's will.[10]

The distinction between power and authority suggests that the question of whether the governor or the legislature prevails should be examined simultaneously with the questions whether the legislature and the governor agree on who should get what, when, and under what conditions and whether agreement is forced or willing. What looks like gubernatorial domination of a full-time professionally staffed legislature may occur when the governor's views coincide with or anticipate theirs. If gubernatorial domination exists it may be the product of a lack of legislative resources—informational or political—or a conscious deference to the governor's decisions, voluntarily or unvoluntarily. On the other hand, agreement may indicate anticipation of legislative wishes by the governor. His relationship with the legislature determines whether his proposals are disposed of, modified, or approved; and the extent to which his proposals reflect anticipation of their choices.

Executive and legislative branches operate in a political environment. Formal authority is distributed between the branches by the constitution and the statutes, and among parties and factions by the electorate. But it is misleading to look at the legislative role in financial decisions without considering who controls the two branches. Is the governor's party in control of one or more chambers? Are the parties cohesive or splintered? Are the majorities firm or can a governor "pick off" the needed votes? These and other less formal power considerations are more important than the simple consideration of formal authority.

Just because legislators use their authority to pass appropriation bills which reflect the governor's budget proposal does not mean that the governor has political power over their actions. "His" proposals may not reflect his choices, but rather theirs. The expenditure plan composed so it will be passed without alteration probably is different from the one which he would select if it did not have to go through the legislative process. This crucial anticipation factor is too often ignored by outside observers.

In this context of informal power bases and anticipatory action, Aaron Wildavsky's discussion of political costs is useful for understanding the politics of the Illinois allocation process.[11] Frequently a leader incurs "exchange" costs in order to obtain support for the adoption of a policy. These costs take a variety of forms, depending upon those which the leader has or for which he can obtain credit. Sometimes a governor can threaten a legislator with the loss of his patronage. Sometimes a governor can promise that a portion of the additional bonding authority he desires will be used for projects in a particular area. Sometimes a governor needs to accept changes in some of the specifics of his proposal in order to obtain passage. For example, Governor Ogilvie accepted the eight to five ratio for corporate to personal income tax rates instead of the one to one ratio he desired, in return for the Democratic votes he needed for passage. Some may be antagonized because of the policy being supported or by the tactics used to obtain support—these antagonists may retaliate either upon those who influenced or those who are influenced. Such conflict may alter the probability of success at the polls for the leader, his allies and his antagonists; it may also alter the governor's ability to obtain approval of other proposals.[12]

Whose will is actualized in the process of determining appropriations? Who gets their way? At what cost? Could the "cost" of getting one's way be higher than the "value" of getting one's way? Is it always clear whose way has prevailed? Could one branch quietly accede to the wishes of another, knowing full well that while those wishes are anathema, they are preferable to the costs of conflict or the shame of defeat? What does the Governor need to do to have the General Assembly pass appropriations which conform to his request? Is the Governor so weak that no matter what he does the Legislature will ignore him? What will it cost the Governor to change the mind of the Legislature? What will it cost the Legislature to fight the Governor over the budget? What will the Legislature gain if it wins? What is victory worth if the Governor has the power to decide how much of an appropriation to spend? What will the benefits be to those individuals who potentially comprise the majorities for appropriation questions? What will be the costs of organizing these appropriation majorities? Can the Governor change the number of participants in a conflict by appealing through the media in order to bring public pressure? What benefits and costs flow from appropriating more than the Governor's request? What costs are incurred in overriding gubernatorial appropriation vetoes? Can either branch increase or reduce these costs? These benefits?

The Illinois General Assembly has the authority to reject the Goveror's budget and develop its own from scratch. Yet it has not done so. The explanation lies not in any principled unwillingness to use its authority in that manner, but in the balance of political benefits to be gained and costs to be incurred.

The costs of formulating a legislative budget are enormous when the Governor would prefer his own and when the Governor has sufficient legislative allies, whether permanently or for allocation decisions, to resist with at least a fair chance of prevailing. First, assuming the Legislature does not want to propose an increase in taxes, the budget balancing process is a constant-sum proposition. In order to reallocate within a certain sum, the amount by which each part is increased is the amount which must be reduced elsewhere in the budget. Secondly, the Governor's budget is usually presented with some statement to the effect that the allocations within his budget provide each department with the minimum amount necessary to run that department in an efficient and effective manner. Taking from one department to give to another is fought by the Governor on the grounds that this underfunds one department's requirements and overfunds another's. The Governor is not necessarily right; however, agencies will agree publicly with his assessment of agency need. If those who are perceived as knowing most about the needs of their agency say the Governor's assessment of their need is correct, then anyone who proposes a different amount appears to be in public disagreement with the actual spenders of the funds about what their needs are. Consequently, a legislative budget would carry a price tag which includes the cost of selling a need assessment which disagrees with the agency's. Since the Governor's budget is probably only incrementally different from the one the General Assembly passed last year, a legislative budget which was significantly different from the Governor's would to a certain extent reopen the conflicts resolved last year and during other prior General Assemblies. In other words, using the authority to propose a budget usually does not occur because the political benefits do not outweight the costs. Reformist proposals often fail to come to grips with this reality.

The Tools of Power

The General Assembly has the authority to exercise its "power of the purse." It uses this authority to achieve the complex political purposes of a multitude of political actors. It is necessary to understand the evolving set of tools and processes made available by the legislative institution, for it is through them that these purposes are achieved. This section examines tools and procedures employed in each element of the budget cycle: the content and format of the budget documents and appropriations bills which are the formal vehicles of executive and legislative action; the manner in which the timing of budget action and legislative access to information is structured; the major outlines of appropriation decisions; legislative and executive opportunities for limiting the availability of funds through allotment or impoundment, despite their appropriation or incorporation in statutory formulas; and the emerging tools of legislative oversight and expenditure review during the implementation process.

Budget Action: Timing and Access to Information

One reformist concern is with the timing of budget actions. This section examines three major issues related to the timing of the Governor's budget presentation to the General Assembly: First, whether the Legislature has sufficient time or information for its budget authorizing actions; second, the dates of the State's fiscal year, which runs from July 1 to June 30 (the federal government has changed to an October-to-September fiscal year); third, the issue of annual versus biennial budgeting. The first and third questions revolve around the adequacy of legislative opportunities for action regarding budget matters, while the second centers upon the problem of making allocation decisions with less than total information.

Budget Presentation The Governor's power to present the budget has been called the most important of his powers.[13] In theory an executive budget centralizes power in the Office of the Governor. In practice, this power is "formally diluted by a variety of statutory limitations and informally by political facts of life."[14] The formal limitations consist primarily of the necessary Legislative authorization of appropriations and the unnecessary practice of earmarking revenues. The informal constraints include the reluctance of the Governor, often borne of political realism, to exert his influence upon the budgets of the other independently elected executive officers, and sometimes "sacred" higher education requests. Nevertheless the presentation of an executive budget does permit a gubernatorial agenda with which the Legislature may begin if it so desires. In Illinois the General Assembly could begin its own budget considerations prior to the gubernatorial unveiling but it chooses not to do so.

Not only does the Governor's presentation provide an agenda for the General Assembly to start with, but it provides all the actors with an important set of reference points. The presentation sets forth the Governor's position and somewhat establishes the stakes of the game. Richard Neustadt's classic analysis of the difference between a President's authority and his power reflects on the interaction of the budget presentation and political considerations:

> A budget presentation is among the cardinal services the President-as-clerk performs for Congressmen and bureaucrats and lobbyists, alike. Without it they would be hard put to do their jobs. Its money estimates and legislative program are the nearest things available to an agenda for their struggle over scope and shape of government. By fixing the position of a chief participant, it gives the rest a reference point in judging their own interests, risks, and tactics. As a device for organizing struggle and for giving strugglers something to respond to or react against, this agenda is perhaps the biggest labor-saver known to Washington. In the degree to which it saves their labor, those who use it are dependent on the President who makes it. In the degree to which his own endorsement helps or hurts their causes, they depend upon his choice of what to ask. In the degree that they gain protection or publicity by helping (or opposing) him, they depend on his asking. As always, *their* dependence means some leverage for *him*. His clerkship may be onerous, but services like these yield bargaining advantages to him. However, the advantage in this instance turns upon one working premise: that the presidential budget is the President's; that what he says he wants will be supported, within reason, by his "powers" and his influence so long as it is asked. Unless this premise works in practice nobody is served, there is no labor saved, dependence vanishes, the leverage is lost. (Emphasis in the original).[15]

In short, the budget presentation may be the start of a series of interactions which not only reflect the current power but also affect the future power of the chief executive and legislators.

The 1870 Constitution required the Governor to inform the Legislature of the State's income and expenditures and to give the General Assembly estimates of the resources needed to continue the State's functions and activities. (1870, Art. V, Sec. 7)[16] Under the two previous constitutions, there were no sections which stated or implied authority for a State budget. However Article V, Section 7 of the 1870 Constitution at least implied if it did not in fact authorize an executive budget.[17]

In the years immediately preceding World War I, reformers throughout the country advocated "economy and efficiency" and Illinois was no exception.[18] The rapid proliferation of State agencies and the near doubling of appropriations combined with the public's suspicions about duplication and inefficiency in government—corroborated by the Economy and Efficiency Committee—to pave the way to reform.[19] Under the circumstances reform meant replacing a "legislative" budget with an "executive" budget.

Despite the constitutional requirements of 1870, not until 1915 did any Governor present an estimate of the taxes necessary to support the operations of the State. Prior to 1915 each state agency negotiated with the General Assembly for its own appropriation. The task of collecting and summarizing all appropriation requests was given in 1915 to the Legislative Reference Bureau.[20]

Change came with the election of Colonel Frank Lowden who brought about the Reorganization Act of 1917, sometimes referred to as the Civil Administrative Code of 1917.[21] This law eliminated scores of agencies and commissions (there were over 100) and replaced them with just nine code departments, each controlled by a director, appointed by and accountable to the Governor. One new code department, Finance, was given extensive powers over State revenues and expenditures, virtually centralizing the control of State spending. It was "the capstone of the Governor's administrative organization," the "staff agency" that assisted the Governor in managing the State and the primary agent through which the Governor exercised control over the code departments and other State agencies.[22] Most importantly, it was assigned the duty of developing a budget for the Governor.

The early history of budget power in Illinois centers more upon the gubernatorial assumption of the opportunity of presenting a budget, a task rendered politically desirable by the climate of economy and efficiency, than it does the Legislature's utilization of its authority. However, while the Governor had the authority to impose his values on State spending he did not always use it. When the political climate changed and supported gubernatorial usage, he began to do so.

In 1937, following open conflict between Governor Henry Horner and his fellow Democrats in the Legislature, the Budgetary Commission was created to act as an intermediary between the Legislature, especially its leadership, and the Governor.[23] This new institution was given authority because the usual method of reconciling differences had failed.

Its initial membership included the Governor and legislative leaders from both houses; later only legislators were members. Historically, its role varied in importance and scope. Its authority regarding appropriations extended only to making recommendations to the Governor and the General Assembly.[24] Its power was dependent upon the role it was allowed to play, the weight given its recommendations, and the amount of information known by other participants in the budgetary process about its behavior.[25] The point at which—or whether—the Budgetary Commission entered the picture varied over the years depending upon the decision of the Governor.[26] At times the Commission acted after the Department of Finance held hearings. However at other times Finance held no hearings and served merely as an information conduit for the Commission. The Commission often served as a way of getting prior approval of the budget from the Legislature even before it was submitted. However, it also frequently served as an important vehicle for discussions about the respective wishes of *both* branches.[27]

Access to Budget Information. Before 1969, the General Assembly's Budgetary Commission, whose members were drawn from the leadership of both houses, had access to departmental budget documents months before the Governor submitted his budget. In most years the Commission reviewed agency budget requests and informed the Governor of their preferences prior to the announcement of his budget proposal. Since the Budgetary Commission membership was composed of politically influential legislators, their preferences were usually respected. Consequently, the Governor's April 1 budget was likely to reflect a series of compromises with the Legislature. Depending upon the political positions of the two branches the Commission was a tool for reaching agreement, a forum for revealing preferences and a means of obtaining early access to information useful in making appropriation decisions.

Since the creation of the Bureau of the Budget (BoB) in 1969 and the change to an executive budget, the Legislature has not received the budget until the Governor's message. Generally having an executive budget means it is formulated exclusively by the executive branch. Some members of the General Assembly may be able through informal mechanisms to have the executive budget reflect their wishes and the Governor's. The Chief Executive's preannouncement input from the General Assembly may or may not be reflected in his budget, depending to a certain extent on his agreement with their wishes and his need to engender support within the legislative branch. His budget may include items which he himself would not support but on which he can not afford to appear to lose. If he endorses the item it appears as his proposal regardless of the fact he may have been forced into it. Ever since 1969 the Governor's budget has been a purely executive proposal, although it is impossible to tell how many of his proposals were really someone else's.

When the budget became an executive production, the Governor's statutory deadline for submitting the budget was changed from April 1 to the first Wednesday in March. The Legislature's deadline (effectively June 30, the end of the fiscal year) has not changed. In almost every other state, the Legislature receives the Governor's budget before March. Two-thirds of state legislatures receive their budgets by the end of January. However, many other state legislatures operate under different constraints than Illinois. The legislature in New York, for example, which receives the budget in mid-February, must complete its requisite actions by April 1, the beginning of its fiscal year. Many states, like neighboring Wisconsin, still use biennial budgets. Furthermore, most state legislatures choose to use fewer bills and not to appropriate in detail as is done in Illinois. They give the executive broad discretion in the means to implement programs. By the time the Illinois General Assembly completes its review of veto action, as long as nine months may have elapsed since the unveiling of the Governor's budget and as few as three months may be left before the next budget presentation. Supplemental appropriations can be introduced at any time, so the General Assembly is concerned continually with budget matters, like most other big-state legislatures.

After the Governor submits his budget, there is generally some delay before bills are introduced in the Legislature. As shown in Table 23-1, most of the 104 budget bills in 1975 were not introduced until late March or early April. The table includes only those appropriations bills needed to enact the Governor's Budget—numerous lesser appropriations bills are introduced independently.

TABLE 23-1
Date of Introduction of
Budgeted Appropriations Bills, FY 1976

Dates	Number of Senate Bills	Number of House Bills	Total
Before March 1	1	2	3
March 1–15[a]	11	11	22
March 16–31	17	20	37
April 1–15	19	17	36
April 16–30	0	3	3
After April 30	1	2	3
Totals	49	55	104

[a]Governor's message delivered March 5.
Source: Legislative Information Systems; Legislative Reference Bueau.

Some legislators and staff believe more time is needed for the General Assembly to consider the bills as a coherent State fiscal program. However, the time available under the current schedule is not used as intensively as it could be: except for some legislative initiatives in this area in 1976, the General Assembly does not immediately and independently transform the Governor's budget documents into appropriations bills in order to lengthen the time available for consideration; instead it awaits the Bureau of the Budget's drafts of these bills; it also cooperates with the Governor's preferences over the chamber in which a bill will originate.

Moreover executive officials argue that earlier submission of budget information would result in less accurate projections of needs and resources. They assert that the Legislature would not use the additional time productively, claiming that the last-minute rush of floor action will occur regardless of when the budget is submitted.

Earlier access to the budget might allow staffs of both appropriations committees more time for analysis and might permit earlier scheduling of hearings, but it is not necessary to await the arrival of appropriations bills to analyze and evaluate State spending. Legislative staff follow agency spending the year round. Legislative members do not need budget bills to assess whether an agency's spending is legal, effective, efficient or in conformance with the policies of the General Assembly. If legislators were not oriented primarily toward appropriations bills, they could review agency spending prior to the Governor's budget proposal. The Legislature sometimes completes its review of gubernatorial veto action on appropriations as late as mid-December, almost the midpoint in the fiscal year. Thus the Legislature devotes extensive portions of every year to the Governor's proposed budget; and within the current framework it could conduct a more intensive and independent review if legislators so desired.

From the Governor's point of view, the current schedule may actually present a more serious problem: how a new Governor is to "put his mark" on the State's budget by mid-February. As it is now, a newly elected Governor inherits his predecessor's budget and can make only marginal changes. Although provisions are made for financing transition workers after the election, it is unlikely a newly elected Governor would be able to spend much time on the budget before his inauguration.

Changing the State's Fiscal Year Related to the issues of sufficient time and information for legislative budget decisions are (1) when the Legislature obtains access to the Governor's proposals and (2) how the timing of federal budget decisions affects the flow of information on federal aid which the State will receive.

Under the 1974 Congressional Budget and Impoundment Control Act (PL 93-344), the federal government changed its fiscal year from the July 1–June 30 cycle it shared with Illinois to an October 1–September 30 period. Federal spending has a large impact on State expenditure plans, but the Illinois fiscal year need not be identical. In FY 1976, about $2.5 billion—or 23 percent of all receipts into the State Treasury—came from the federal government. While it might be desirable for Illinois to know how much federal money will be available before planning State expenditures, changing the dates of the State's fiscal year will not necessarily provide better information on the exact amounts for various purposes.

If State and federal fiscal years began on October 1, and if the General Assembly waited for final Congressional action, then the State budget might not be completed until October 1. Furthermore, there is no guarantee that Congress can complete the budget process by the October 1st deadline: very few major federal appropriations bills were passed before the next fiscal year began for the five fiscal years preceding the federal change; in the "trial" year, several major bills were still unfinished by mid-November; and in 1978, an election year, several agencies did not have appropriations by October 1.

Even if federal budget action were completed by October 1st, the State would not necessarily know precisely how much federal money it would receive, because of the federal bureaucracy's subsequent role in the process. Its calculation of the exact allocations for the major formula grant programs takes several months. Furthermore, a large part of the marginal changes in federal funding takes place late in the year, long after Congress has completed its role.

A substantial proportion of federal aid does not even depend directly on the annual federal authorization and appropriation processes. For example, in Fy 1977, about 43 percent of federal aid to Illinois was for public aid. Under these programs, such as Aid to Families of Dependent Children and Medicaid, the federal government pays a percentage of cost, and the State knows these percentages well in advance—they are basically unchanging from year to year. While Congress must appropriate these funds annually, State decisions about Public Aid expenditure do not need to await Congressional action.

Annual versus Biennial Budgeting The change to annual budgeting is advocated because of the more frequent opportunities given the General Assembly to exercise its authority over the budget process.

The 1970 Constitution's requirement of annual budgets means that a Governor will no longer be halfway through his term before he can introduce a budget which he can truly call his own. This requirement gives him more opportunities to submit a budget and, hence, more opportunities to attempt to impose his values upon the activities of the State. It also gives General Assembly additional opportunities to attempt to impose its will regarding appropriations.

Legislative control is enhanced under annual budgeting by the requirement that each agency must justify its activities every year. Annual budgets provide annual opportunities for the Legislature to review agency spending behavior and to reexamine priorities. Finally, annual budgets enable the same group of legislators at least one opportunity to compare an agency's spending plans with the execution of those plans. Reviewing budgets is facilitated by intimate knowledge of the expectations which existed when the appropriation was passed and of the agencies' use of those funds. Biennial budgets make it virtually impossible for the same group of legislators to hear the initial justifications and explanations and to compare them to actual performance before passing the appropriation for the next fiscal period. A legislator whose personal expectations of agency behavior have been unfulfilled is more likely to perform oversight responsibilities well.

Illinois operated under biennial budgets until July 1, 1969. Some critics of annual budgeting argue that the change to annual budgeting has had some unintended adverse effects, notably increased spending. One official explained it this way: "The lobbyists and special interest groups get twice as many shots at the Legislature, and so more money gets appropriated."

The effect of annual and biennial budgeting on appropriations and expenditures is examined in Table 23-2 and Table 23-3. By themselves annual budgets do not seem to have major effects. The numbers do not completely rule out such effects, but it seems likely that other factors—notably the enactment of the income tax in 1969 and the appropriation of federally generated resources—have been more important in contributing to the increase in State spending. (See the Kolhauser chapter.) A dollar increase in welfare spending costs the State only fifty cents whereas a dollar spent for most other purposes costs the State a dollar. The bulk of the welfare "explosion" occurred in the same biennium as the introduction of the income tax, producing appropriation and expenditure growth which required only half as much State supplied revenue as normal spending at the same time as State revenues were increased tremendously by the income tax. Changing the amount of resources available for spending is likely to be followed by an increase in spending. Although not reflected in the tables, during the annual budgeting years the State began using non-referendum general obligation bond financing, a tool which has dramatically increased appropriations.

The budget period does seem to make some difference in terms of expenditure projections. Economic condi-

TABLE 23-2
Appropriations to General Revenue and Common School Funds
Illinois, Biennia (Dollars in Millions)

Years	Appropriations	Increase From Previous Biennium	Appropriations in Constant 1972 Dollars[a]	Increase From Previous Biennium
1958–59	$ 1,188	—	$2,362	—
1960–61	1,501	26%	2,647	12%
1962–63	1,768	18	2,942	11
1964–65	2,007	14	3,171	8
1966–67	2,581	29	3,768	19
1968–69	3,836	49	4,982	32
1970–71	7,041	84	7,974	60
1972–73	7,886	12	7,855	−1.5
1974–75	9,294	18	7,843	− .2
1976–77	10,960	18	7,913	.9
1978–79	12,506	14	7,391	−6.5

[a]The U.S. Department of Commerce's Index of State and Local Government Purchase of Goods and Services was used to convert current dollars into constant dollars.
Source: Comptroller, *Illinois Annual Reports*.

TABLE 23-3
Expenditures from General Revenue and Common School Funds
Illinois, Biennia (Dollars in Millions)

Years	Expenditures	Increase From Previous Biennium	Expenditures in Constant 1972 Dollars[a]	Increase From Previous Biennium
1958–59	$ 1,146	—	$2,278	—
1960–61	1,418	24%	2,501	10%
1962–63	1,690	19	2,812	12
1964–65	1,929	14	3,047	8
1966–67	2,457	27	3,587	18
1968–69	3,508	43	4,556	27
1970–71	5,549	58	6,284	38
1972–73	7,438	34	7,408	18
1974–75	9,063	22	7,648	3
1976–77	13,143	45	9,055	18

[a]The U.S. Department of Commerce's Index of State and Local Government Purchase of Goods and Services was used to convert current dollars into constant dollrs.
Source: Comptroller, *Illinois Annual Reports.*

tions change so rapidly that biennial revenue and expenditure estimates would be less reliable than annual ones. In Illinois, the change from biennial to annual budgets has reduced the amount of supplemental appropriations as a percentage of total appropriations.[28] In the last year of biennial budgets, supplemental appropriations were 4.3 percent of total appropriations. The average for the first seven years of annual budgets was 2.9 percent, suggesting some improvement in the accuracy of expenditure estimates. These percentages would be less, particularly for the annual budget years, if the Department of Public Aid did not receive such large supplementals so frequently.

In terms of actual budget preparation costs, most executive agencies reported that changing to biennial budgets would make little difference. No official interviewed said that his agency's budget staff could be reduced. Most said that budget staff would be diverted to analysis and evaluation functions during the nonbudget year.

While spending has increased under annual budgeting, there is no evidence that annual budgeting itself is the primary cause of the increase. Economic growth and inflation have significantly increased State revenues. Annual budgeting contributes to more accurate revenue and expenditure estimates. A return to biennial budgets would permit no savings in overhead costs, such as less staff or less paper work. There is no convincing evidence that changing to biennial budgeting would lead to better control or less cost. There are even some reasons that suggest it would give the Legislature less control.

This section has covered the time frame of the General Assembly appropriations process. The next sections examine some of the activities which take place during that process: the transformation and modification of the Governor's spending plans into laws which reflect the priorities of the General Assembly.

Budget Documents and Appropriations Bills: the Vehicles For Action

This section analyzes how executive budget documents and legislative appropriations bills reflect two conflicting orientations toward State finance: "executive flexibility" and "legislative control." Each view implies a different approach to appropriations. These two views are reflected in the documents of the budget process—the budget books, the forms used by the appropriations committees staffs, and the appropriations bills.

The budget process requires information. The sources of this information are the budget books submitted by the Governor, the appropriation bills introduced in the General Assembly and expenditure data. Budget books reflect the Governor's proposed spending plan. Appropriations bills define what portion of the plan is approved, and expenditure data reveal the costs of executing last year's plan.

The Budget Books The Bureau of the Budget compiles program information from each code agency—objectives, measurements and costs by which to judge program efficiency and effectiveness. This information is assembled into a budget which reflects the Governor's recommendations and is then presented to the Legislature in the form of budget books.

The budget is contained in three books: *The Budget Narrative,* a description of the functions and activities of all agencies including comparative performance data on the various functions and activities; *The Budget Appendix,* a line item budget for each function and activity; and *The Personnel Detail,* a list of all State employees tabulated by position, title and salary for each agency.

The Budget Narrative contains some of the comparative performance data required by statute. However, in many cases, the data for various activities and functions are not shown. Often the data are measures of workload, such as so many tests given and so many licenses issued.

The budget books do not fulfill all of the statutory requirements, even though program information collected by BoB might contain some of the comparative performance data required by statute. The costs of individual programs are not shown in any systematic fashion. For example, the cost of community-based mental health care is given, but not the cost of inpatient or outpatient care at State institutions.

Program effectiveness data are also presented inconsistently in the *Budget Narrative*. The Department of Vocational Rehabilitation, for example, set as an objective for FY 1975 to service 6,000 cases under the Disabled Public Offenders Program. The FY 1976 *Budget Narrative* estimated that with four months left in FY 1975, the department would serve 4,800 cases, a decline of 20 percent from the previous estimate. A new objective of 6,300 cases served was listed for FY 1976, an objective which exceeds only slightly the FY 1975 goal which the Department could not achieve. This is only one of numerous examples of how data are not presented in a systematic fashion so the Legislature and the public can readily discover if the agencies are meeting their own goals.

Some states have budget documents which integrate line item and program data. This is not a new idea in Illinois. The budget submitted by Governor Kerner for FY 1968–1969 was contained in one book. Each section dealing with a department or agency started with a narrative about its operations. Under each institution and administrative division, proposed line item appropriations were made by division and fund, allocations were shown by programs and line item expenditures were allocated to each program. The program categories were very broad, sometimes as broad as a division. Nevertheless, these categories did provide some idea of the relative allocation of resources to programs at specific institutions. For example, in the Department of Mental Health, at Dixon State School, $26.5 million were allocated among six broad functions which were never defined:

Administration	$ 770,903
Operations, Maintenance, and Institutional Service	6,139,164
Dietary Services	5,007,032
Medical, Nursing, and Residential Care	12,623,960
Education and Therapy	1,676,035
Training and Education	383,570

Another example was the Parks and Memorials Division of the Department of Conservation where $9.3 million were allocated among three areas:

Administration	$ 653,018
Parks Operation	8,331,515
Memorials	825,619

Sometimes, as in the case of the $10.6 million appropriation for the Management Information Division of the Department of Finance, there were no program specifications.

Governor Ogilvie's budget document for FY 1973 contained some allocations of current year spending authority and budget year recommendations by budgetary activity, a category somewhat more inclusive than Governor Kerner's program classifications. The heading, "Budgetary Activities," used in the Department of Mental Health's FY 1973 budget, encompassed items that can be classified as programs, as target population or as activities, such as administration, which presumably cut across all of the other items. Furthermore, since Budgetary Activities were not the categories used in appropriations bills, presentations under these headings were not binding. Narrative descriptions could not be compared with dollar recommendations to see if they were reflected in the resource allocations for a division or institution, nor could actual expenditure data confirm whether actual spending conformed to the proposed plan. It was impossible to discover, using the budget document, the relative emphasis a particular program received at a particular institution. These drawbacks inhibit the use of programmatic appropriation language. The current budget books allow the Executive to make promises which are frequently unspecific or unquantifiable, knowing full well that it will be difficult to hold him accountable for failing to live up to those promises.

Starting with the FY 1981 budget the Governor is statutorily required to present five year comparisons of departmental objectives and achievements. These five years will include three completed years (FY 1977, 1978, 1979) the current year (FY 1980) and the budget year (FY 1918). This data will help to enable legislators, the press and the public to evaluate the ability of State agencies to attain their goals. After several years it should be interesting to examine whether agency goals are self-fulfilling prophecies, generally always achieved, or generally never reached. Since the publication of this kind of information in a convenient accessible format facilitates criticism of agencies and those individuals held accountable to the people for agency performance, it should not be too surprising if the Governor's Bureau of the Budget spends as much time negotiating what information is to be presented in the budget book narrative as it does negotiating the budget allocations. In 1974 the State of Michigan attempted something similar and found it so difficult to live with the implications of the data and with skepticism about their validity, that they were withdrawn from the documents.

Legislative Budget Forms After the Legislature receives the budget, the two partisan appropriations committee staffs in each chamber collect information from agencies in preparation for committee hearings. This information is meant to supplement the budget books. Early in the development of legislative staffing, each of the four staffs required separate forms from the agencies. In recent years, the two House staffs and the two Senate staffs respectively have circulated joint forms.

The House and Senate forms differ, because each chamber has different views about the kinds of information it needs. For FY 1976, only three pages in the 13-page Senate forms requested information not in the 24-page House forms. These three pages concerned transfers, funds for external agencies and a summary of receipts. On the basis of one year's behavior, an outsider might observe that the two houses have similar information needs and therefore the forms should be combined. But for FY 1977 the Senate forms were 15 pages, and the House forms were 44 pages. Information requested by the individual chambers was different for FY 1977 as reflected in the page disparities. This reflected differences in values and perspectives.

Consolidating forms might make it easier for agencies to disguise expenditure patterns, since it is difficult to calculate the cost of programs by line item expenditure. Different forms do permit budget staffs from each chamber to ask different kinds of questions. They increase the likelihood that information about costs is accurate and useful. Different forms also permit relatively quick assessments of agency veracity and competence.

Appropriations Bills The Legislature uses appropriation bills to authorize expenditures and thereby determine who benefits from government. While the budget books are politically useful, these bills are legally necessary before any money can be spent. Without these products of the use of legislative authority, the day-to-day activities of government cannot occur. In order to be explicit about some of the beneficiaries and some of the benefits, the Illinois General Assembly usually is very generous in the use of specific language when it provides for funding of capital and road projects, except that the allocation of sewer funds provides no restrictive language as to location. ''Pork'' (as in ''pork-barrel'') is important, just as is the credit for obtaining it. Even when the administration has already promised a project, sometimes specific language is included in bills just so one or more legislators can claim credit. Without using their authority in this fashion to specify projects, the administration might use the spending authorization for some other purpose than the one which was used as justification when the bill went through the appropriation process.

Much of the budgetary literature focuses on material from executive budget documents. Yet Budget documents are only plans. The expectations they create may not be fulfilled, as they do not prevent the Executive or agencies from deviating from the budget books. In contrast appropriations are laws which impose restrictions on agencies and reduce their discretion.

What good is an elaborate presentation which has very little corrspondence to the actual activities which are financed by the legislature and subsequently implemented? No matter how extensive the budget book material, appropriations bills are used by the General Assembly to insure that agencies comply with legislative decisions. If the General Assembly seems to have an obsession with line item controls, this does not reflect an antipathy to programmatic considerations—only that legislators have discovered many of the promises contained in budget books are never fulfilled!

The dominant legislative view is that exeuctive agencies have too much flexibility. Legislators and appropriations staffs worry about the ability of agencies to hide programs and activities in appropriations bills. They have experienced too many examples of executive discretion which conflicted with legislative expectations. Thus, the General Assembly tries to insure closer legislative control by providing for more line items. A line item budget tells agencies how much they can spend on hiring personnel but places no restrictions on the duties the employees perform. Nevertheless, there is a legislative expectation that the employees conform in large part to the manpower utilization plans of the *Personnel Detail*. While the Legislature does not restrict departments to specific numbers of particular job titles as do some jurisdictions (e.g., Chicago), the General Assembly is not pleased by deviations from the *Personnel Detail*. Agencies where this is a chronic problem may well experience future budget problems.

The Legislature does not specifically appropriate by each ''detail object'' (e.g., legal fees and postage in the Contractual Services line) which is subsumed in each ''line item,'' but decisions are frequently made about the magnitude of the line items by examining the proposed use of funds at the detail object level. Legislators frequently question in advance how much supporting information about Contractual Services reveals about proposed spending on legal fees, while they usually leave unquestioned the amount for postage. However, the General Assembly is not pleased when it later learns that dollars justified for postage are used instead for legal fees or consultants. Legislative action on such problems is not automatic, however—it depends on numerous other considerations.

Occasionally, the Legislature concludes the executive branch abused its flexibility and acted contrary to legislative expectations. The General Assembly has responded either by making some appropriations nontransferable, or by appropriating at the detail object level.[29]

The General Assembly is concerned not only with what programs the State undertakes, but also how it undertakes them. The Legislature wants to know whether the personnel at a State institution are on a State payroll or if they are paid by an outside contractor. Legislators are interested in whether the State has to pay the contractor now so he can arrange for retirement benefits, whereas with most programs the State makes a conscious choice to defer funding of the pension liabilities attributable to these employees. The potential political concern about who gets what is obvious.

The General Assembly may also express displeasure with the way agencies execute their responsibilities or with the relative emphasis they give to their duties. In 1975 some of the members of the General Assembly opposed all of the large percentage increase recommended by the Governor for the Registration Division of the Department of Registration and Education except that portion intended for regulation of the real estate industry. The next spring, the same group of legislators used the appropriation process to limit the Department's ability to let new people into the real estate occupation and enhance its ability to regulate those already licensed. While the General Assembly cannot make or amend substantive law in an appropriation bill, as Congress does, the Legislature can and does use appropriation bills to rein in wayward agencies and to encourage new emphases in other agencies. It often uses the opportunities of the appropriation process where legislative authorization activity is required to express, and occasionally impose, its views on the activities of State government.

Proposed funding from each revenue source is usually listed by line item for each agency, division, or institution in appropriation bills which mostly but not exclusively follow a line item format. There are some examples of budgeting by programs in the form of lump-sum appropriations, but use of lump sums has diminished rapidly. Programmatic language, with line items underneath, occasionally has replaced lump sums. Construction and road projects are often appropriated as individual line items.

Of course, the itemization of projects within the Governor's budget totals is a constant-sum game. For someone to be allocated more than they would under the Governor's proposal someone else must be allocated less. The Legislature tends to ignore this—there is a tendency for capital projects which are "line-itemed" to total more than the amount proposed by the Governor. That is, the General Assembly sometimes treats construction and road projects as if it were not a constant-sum game. These appropriations are not mandates but only authorizations to spend. Because of the control of the Governor over the expenditure of these funds, it is recognized that the mere appropriation of a specific project does not guarantee its initiation even if the Governor chooses not to veto it.

When sponsors appeal for the inclusion of an unbudgeted item, particular of a capital project such as a building, road or dam, they sometimes argue that they want to give the Governor an opportunity to change his mind and approve a project not originally included in his proposal. Furthermore, because these projects are funded with bond resources and not current tax dollars, the normal sort of short-term budget balancing does not apply.

The Omnibus Appropriation Bill. The General Assembly uses many separate appropriation bills in authorizing spending, usually one bill per agency. This practice necessitates many separate authorizing actions by the General Assembly. In the Spring of 1976, there was an experiment which received mixed legislative reaction. A massive $6.7 billion, 575-page omnibus bill covering executive branch agencies was introduced along with ten companion bills covering the rest of State government, including one for $2.8 billion which encompassed primary, secondary and higher education. These bills were drafted by legislative staffs rather than by the Bureau of the Budget. They used the same language found in the FY 1976 appropriations bills and replaced the FY 1976 amounts with those proposed by the Governor in FY 1977. Unlike omnibus bills in other states, these bills used the customary appropriation language and line item detail with which the Illinois General Asssembly controls the specifics of spending.

Ultimately, the experiment was abandoned, because there was almost universal resistance to the idea of an entire budget presented in a handful of bills. The Legislature's insistence on control over the specifics of State spending is one reason why Illinois has not adopted the relatively undetailed appropriations bills used by other states. Part of the reason that the omnibus appropriation bill approach was rejected in Illinois is that the politics of bill passage is changed when questions about government spending are not treated on an agency-by-agency basis. Forming majorities is a task which varies depending upon the bill's content. If there are many interests to reconcile, it is a more complicated process than when there are only a few.

Congressional experience casts additional light on the problems of omnibus appropriations bills. Shortly after World War II, Congress experimented with a single omnibus appropriation bill to facilitate the balancing of expenditures against revenues. Congress abandoned the omnibus bill approach primarily because it caused casual consideration of important details. The President thought the approach unpalatable because it forced him to accept or veto the entire bill. Of course, the Governor's line item and reduction veto authority would permit him to avoid this "all or nothing choice" which faced President Truman.[30]

Although Illinois uses a large number of appropriations bills, the General Assembly and the Governor do not devote equal time and scrutiny to all bills. Consolidating departments into one appropriation bill may allow an unwanted or unnecessary appropriation to be carried along by the other components of the bill, permit a new program to go unnoticed, or delay a number of uncontroversial appropriations because of one objectionable component.

According to a 1975 survey by the Council of State Governments, there are twenty-five states where there is normally only one budget bill, while in twelve other states there are from two to ten appropriations bills. Thus, in almost three-fourths of the states there are usually ten or fewer budget bills. In only six states are there one hundred budget bills. Only two states (Arkansas and Mississippi) usually have more bills than Illinois. An examination of appropriations bills from other states reveals that most legislatures have much less detail in their appropriations bills.

Some of the reasons other states have fewer bills include:

—Other legislatures rely less on appropriations bills as devices for legislative control of the specifics of State spending authorizations;
—The governor's budget may be contained in a single bill;
—"Unbudgeted" items must be introduced as amendments to budget bills rather than separately;
—All supplemental appropriations may be consolidated into a single bill; and
—Transfers may be accomplished without legislative action.

The shortcomings of the consolidated bill approach are particularly noticeable in the area of deficiency appropriations and transfers. Agencies request deficiencies or transfer authorizations from the General Assembly when they need additional spending authority to complete the fiscal year. Transfers are made possible by underusing authority in order to reallocate within a constant sum. Deficiencies and transfers constitute deviations from spending plans approved by the Legislature. Most deficiencies which result from factors outside the control of the departments pass without any great debate. Some uncontrollable deficiencies, such as the Department of Public Aid's, are anticipated, generate a few days of debate and pass. Sometimes, however, departments have blatantly spent at deficiency rates in defiance of legislative expectations. Deficiencies which exist because of collective bargaining agreements signed at mid-year also pose problems legislators want to deal with separately. The fact that these deficiencies are treated individually and not in groups often enables legislative committees to learn more about a particular department than they could discover during consideration of the department's regular appropriation bill. Furthermore, since deficiencies indicate areas which probably need legislative oversight, reducing the number of deficiency bills minimizes specific occasions for detailed review of department operations.

Clearly, there are tremendous differences between deficiencies caused by agencies which cannot process their vouchers in a timely fashion, Public Aid deficiencies, and personnel headcount overruns. It has been the judgment of the General Assembly that each should be treated separately. An agency which is considered to have purposely deviated from its approved spending plan is potentially a living reminder to every other agency that you can ignore, and perhaps even defy, the wishes of the General Assembly without impunity. An example is the Department of Mental Health at the close of the Kerner Administration (1967). It became evident the DMH was increasing its expenditures at the end of each fiscal year to create a momentum for future budget increases. The Director was called before the Budgetary Commission and the practice was halted. If the authority applications of the General Assembly will not "stick," then policy will not reflect the values of the Legislature.

Program Appropriations. A program budget might not tell an agency specifically how much money to spend on Equipment as opposed to Travel, Personal Services, or Contractual Services, but theoretically it would restrict the use of the equipment to a specific program or activity. Unfortunately, lack of program definitions and the necessary arbitrary (in the absence of program accounting systems) allocations of expenses to programs, instead of to organizational units, gives the Executive a virtual free hand in deciding how to use a program's fund. Popular and useful programs could obtain equipment and commodities which could be used the following year for less commendable purposes, even though they might not obtain legislative approval on their merits. What prevents film equipment purchased with federal funds for the Governor's Traffic Safety Coordinating Committee from being used the following year for some purpose other than Driver Safety Education?

Program budget appropriations can be totally flexible as in the State of Washington. There the detailed budget books contain program data, and appropriation acts are written with few specifics. The Washington budget book states the amount from each fund for each program, while program descriptions in its appropriation acts are two or three words long. "Seventy-one million dollars for Developmental Disabilities Program" is not much restriction at all. How does this allow the Legislature to control activities and programs? How can it influence emphasis at the subprogram level? Clearly the Washington Legislature does not fully use this opportunity to promote its own values although its involvement is constitutionally required.

To the extent they have been used, programmatic appropriation restrictions have not constrained executive discretion in Illinois. In those cases where legislative expectations are not realized, agencies are again made subject to line item appropriations to prevent any recurrence. Program budgeting probably would make it easier for any executive to legally fund activities specifically denied appropriations by the General Assembly. During the Walker Administration, the program budget for Food Stamp Program Administration funded activities and equipment purchases beyond what common sense would attribute to Food Stamp Administration.[31] The Governor used the food stamp resources, arguing that this program should bear part of the cost of developing the State's film production facilities. The Legislature imposed line items on this program budget for FY 1977 so that it would be difficult, if not impossible, to purchase more color television production equipment with Food Stamp Administration funds.

Program budgeting makes it politically more difficult for the General Assembly to reduce appropriations, and thus may be conducive to increased expenditures. It is easier for the General Assembly to justify cutting Personal Services or Travel than it is to reduce appropriations for child abuse detection services and programs for the mentally ill. It is easy to oppose bureaucrats and junketing, but it is hard to be responsible about program funding since every program has merits and advocates. It is easier for legislators to defend themselves against charges of meddling with administrative details than it is to explain that they really have not destroyed a useful program. Programs have constituents but line items generally do not. An important exception is the personal services line item, which is followed very closely by public employee groups.

Successful program budgeting requires accurate cost figures compiled by program, as well as output and effectiveness measures. At present, these conditions are not met in Illinois. Programmatic measures are expensive to generate, difficult to maintain consistently, and complicated to interpret. The State's accounting system is set up by divisions and designed so that clerical help routinely can attribute expenditures to the proper division with a high degree of reliability and replicability. It facilitates instantaneous access to an agency's expenditure patterns at any point in the accounting period. But it is important to remember that legislative control over expenditures is limited to the restrictions imposed by the language and dollar amounts of appropriations bills and the relatively more permanent context of control. Important aspects of the permanent context, such as the Finance Act, and specific appropriation controls are often evaded or stretched as agencies administer programs.

Information For Appropriations Decisions

This section examines the quality of information available to the General Assembly for its appropriations decisons and the criteria used in the appropriations process to determine funding levels. The content of the information available affects which political considerations come into play and which will take precedence. Conversely the relative importance of available information varies from year to year as the political impact of conflicting values changes. There are four analytical factors which seem to be important in appropriations decisions: (1) The Constitutional requirement that total appropriations not exceed anticipated resources; (2) The change in each agency's budget from the prior year; (3) The agency's efficiency and effectiveness; and (4) The future fiscal impact of current budget requests.

Balancing Appropriations and Resources The reformist stance is that revenue and expenditure decisions should be simultaneously considered. There have been frequent attempts in Congress to require comprehensive consideration of taxing and spending decisions. In 1946, the revenue and appropriations committees jointly considered the budget. In 1950, Congress used a consolidated omnibus appropriations bill for all departments.[32] The 1974 Congressional Budget Reform Act revived these earlier attempts at linking revenue and expenditure decisions. The Congressional Budget Office was created in part because the Democratic-controlled Congress did not want a Republican President to dominate the budget process.[33] Congress prescribed formal procedures for simultaneous consideration of revenues and expenditures through budget comittees in each chamber with responsibility for proposing spending priorities.

A secondary impetus for the Congressional Budget Reform Act was the desire of the fiscal committees (mostly Appropriations, but also Finance and Ways and Means) to recapture control over spending from the subject matter committees. The growth of spending not subject to the appropriations process, called "backdoor spending," and the pressure for "full funding" of programs which do go through the appropriations process, but which have their authorizations set by substantive committees, combined to erode the controls which the fiscal committees could exercise over spending.[34] In short Congress established mechanisms to exert its budget authority in the light of available revenues because it believed its values were inadequately reflected.

Illinois, in contrast, does not permit backdoor spending of State funds. All authority to spend State funds must pass through the appropriations process. Even the formula laws which allocate funds have pro rata clauses, so that in the event insufficient funds are appropriated, the appropriation governs, not the substantive formula legislation.

While the General Assembly lacks formally prescribed methods to coordinate revenue and expenditure considerations, nevertheless it is aware of potential deficits and surpluses. Allowing proposed expenditures to exceed revenues is in essence a calculation that either revenues are likely to grow more rapidly than expenditures or additional revenue can be obtained in the future at less political cost. Recently most gubernatorial revenue forecasts have been too low.

Throughout the process the question is asked how a particular item compares with the detail in the Governor's budget. In other words, "if we want to appropriate $X + $Y when the budget recommends $X, what does $Y do to the budget balance?" There is also appreciation of the fact that if an item is not included in the Governor's proposal and the item is approved, in order for it to be actually spent, the Governor must either maintain lower than anticipated treasury balances or reduce spending elsewhere.

Given the Governor's veto powers for balancing total expenditures and revenues, as long as reallocations are made within those totals the budget remains balanced. Of course, the General Assembly's reallocation attempts are usually met with gubernatorial pronouncements that the budget can not be reduced in any area because every area has been "cut to the bone" and that any further reduction would drastically impair the ability of the affected agency to fulfill its mission. Agencies benefitting from such reallocations publicly make solemn pronouncements as to how this add-on is not needed.

A variety of factors complicates the problem of balancing spending and resources. Foremost is the fact that not all of the appropriations approved are ever spent; depending upon the item involved this amount can be significant or inconsequential. Capital items are the major contributor to this pattern. With capital items the entire cost of a project is appropriated at the beginning to reflect what the State's commitment will be if the project is carried through to fruition, regardless of the probability that very little of the appropriation will be spent in the first year or two following the initial appropriation. With capital items which are funded with bond derived resources, the commitment of this year's marginal growth in revenues is minimal, even though the cost of the project will be borne for years to come.

Combining these last two factors allows the creation of a commitment for a project with a very minimal current utilization of resources. For example, assuming flat payments on twenty-five year bonds and ten percent planning costs, only about $600,000 in current General Fund resources are needed to start a $100 million project. If all that occurs is the extension of the commitment, the current year cost is zero.

Changes in Agency Budgets The most prevalent authority applications flow from judgments made about increments. In most cases the question before the Legislature is not whether funding will be granted but rather how much additional is needed. Frequently, next year's need is judged to be what the agency received last year—however, the General Assembly is hampered in making its decision about what is needed for the budget year, because information is not readily available about exactly how the agency spent its prior year's appropriation. This is understandable since the Legislature makes appropriations for the budget year before expenditures are complete for the current year and frequently before it knows the amount of supplemental and deficiency appropriations.

Another factor complicating appropriations decisions is a change of administration. An outgoing administration can obligate extraordinarily large sums for Contractual Services, Commodities and Equipment. On the other hand, a newly arrived administration can speed up spending in some areas and retrench in others. In any case, there seems to be a temporary slowdown in agency activity as one set of officials leaves and the other arrives.

Efficiency and Effectiveness The General Assembly is increasingly concerned about the efficiency and effectiveness with which agencies operate their programs. Some simple efficiency measures are included in the *Budget Narrative,* but they consist mostly of crude workload measures. Unfortunately, as noted, these kinds of data are not yet useful for decision making.

Legislators are discovering that important questions remain unanswered by simple financial reports. As the advantage of addressing questions of efficiency and effectiveness become clear, more legislative officials in Illinois, as in other states, will support efforts to gather information. The assignment of a program audit responsibility to the Office of the Auditor General and the impact of the Illinois Economic and Fiscal Commission's evaluation studies are evidence of this trend.

The first step toward the development of measures of effectiveness was taken in 1975 when the General Assembly passed the Illinois Welfare and Rehabilitation Services Planning Act. It specified that plans should set "a perspective for the current year's actions, setting forth goals and intentions and issues and recommendations for future actions, within the two years following the next fiscal year."

The General Assembly chose to concentrate in the area of human service planning, an area of special interest due to forecasting difficulties, instead of initiating an across-the-board conversion to effectiveness data. The Legislature chose a high priority spending area, perhaps assuming that if measures of effectiveness can be developed in these areas and their utility demonstrated to individual legislators, then it is more likely the Legislature will expand this approach to include additional areas of governmental activity. On the other hand, a greater risk of failure is present as a result of this selection.

Earlier, in the section on budget books, there is a discussion of the requirement that the Governor's budget beginning with FY 1981 contain five year comparisons of departmental objectives and achievements. Exactly how this information might be used by legislators is uncertain. . . .

Estimating Future Fiscal Impacts The experience of the past two decades has been one of dramatically increased expenditure demands. Legislatures have sometimes failed to forecast the true fiscal impact of new programs, such as the medicaid program introduced in 1965. The General Assembly has learned from this painful experience. It has made some important changes in its approach to estimating future fiscal impacts, and it has identified some potential future problem areas.

Methods of Estimation—Fiscal Notes and Capital Authorization. Future fiscal impact information is included in "fiscal notes" prepared for every substantive bill, "the purpose or effect of which is to expend any State funds or to increase or decrease the revenue of the State." A bill's sponsor must have a fiscal note prepared prior to second reading of the bill in the house of introduction. The fiscal note is to provide both immediate and long-range cost estimates for the new activity.

Since July 1977, the Fiscal Note Act has required the Bureau of the Budget to specify future year principal and interest payments for all capital authorization legislation, including appropriations. Future year cost implications are significant in capital projects and bond funded initiatives even though they are created or expanded through changing "only a line or two" in an appropriations bill.

Identifying Potential Problem Areas: Pensions and Federal Funds. While agencies may make honest efforts to provide accurate future cost estimates, for many programs it is virtually impossible to be very accurate. However, in one program accurate future year cost estimates are available. This is an all too often neglected aspect of State finance—the State pension system. The Illinois State Budget for FY 1977 lists estimates of Investment Income, State and Member Contributions, and Payout and Assets for the end of FY 1976, but there is no mention of actuarial liabilities. Actuaries have developed some relatively straightforward estimates of future year pension costs and the level of current contributions needed to fund future year pension costs. Starting with the FY 1981 budget, the Governor must include in his budget book statements showing pension fund liabilities and assets. Prior to 1977, the Pension Impact Note Act stated that the Public Employees Pension Laws Commission "*may* (italics added) prepare a written pension system impact note in relation to any bill introduced in either house," or whenever any committee of either house reports any bill with an amendment, or whenever any bill is amended on the floor. It "*shall* (italics added) prepare notes in these circumstances if requested by a member of the General Assembly." The Act was strengthened in 1977 to require that all pension legislation go through the Pension Laws Commission and that such bills cannot be moved beyond "second reading" until the impact note is received.

The bulk of federal funds provided to the State are for public aid and road reimbursements. Recently legislatures across the country have recognized the importance of asserting their prerogative over the pursestrings of state government, even when federal funds are involved. Too often programs start with 100 percent federal financing and without state legislative authorization, and then, when federal funding is decreased or terminated, the legislature must decide whether to finance the program with state money. Very often, the program has developed client and provider groups which support its continuation. Shutting off funds to an ongoing program is much more difficult than denying funds to a program which has never received any before. Many governors across the country disagree with this approach to state finance. Interestingly enough, when Pennsylvania Governor Schapp took his challenge of the legislative requirement that federal funds be appropriated to the United States Supreme Court, he was supported by the American Association of State Colleges and Universities and a number of civil rights groups.

Executive Impoundment and Allotment

Although the General Assembly is involved in authorizing appropriations, once the appropriations are made, the Legislature may or may not be able to influence whether the expenditures are actually made. The Illinois constitution requires obligations or payments from public funds to be "authorized by law or ordinance" and establishes procedures for the General Assembly to make appropriations. There are no provisions, however, for cases where the Legislature appropriates funds and the Governor refuses to spend the money and "impounds" the funds.

The problems of executive impoundment at the federal level are not analogous to the situation in Illinois, due to differences in the way the two legislative bodies appropriate funds. Illinois' appropriation language states explicitly that the General Assembly is granting agencies the ability to spend particular amounts "or so much thereof as may be necessary." Congress, in contrast, authorizes agencies to spend up to a certain amount in a particular period in pursuit of various objectives. It then appropriates funds. In contrast to Illinois appropriations, federal appropriations often are carried over into succeeding years.[35]

Federal appropriations are closer to actual disbursements from the treasury. Many federal agencies accumulate and use appropriation authority from earlier years. When unused federal appropriation authority expires, it is closer to the truth to say, "The funds have been returned to the treasury." When unused State appropriation authority lapses, the funds do not return to the Treasury because the funds have never left. State appropriations are ceilings on spending, whereas federal appropriations are closer to spending allowances agencies can use now or save for future years.

Money is appropriated by Congress for particular programs. If the President proposes to rescind expenditure authority for a program and Congress turns down the proposal, then the funds must be spent on that program. In Illinois, operating funds usually are appropriated by items of expenditure, although some programs are occasionally appropriated in lump sums.

The Congressional Budget and Impoundment Control Act of 1974 (PL 93-344) established procedures to prevent the President from impounding appropriated funds without the consent of Congress. When the President wants to rescind or defer part or all of the expenditure authority for a particular program, he must submit a message to Congress. If Congress refuses to approve the impoundment, the funds must be released. If the President tries to impound funds without notifying Congress, the Comptroller General may send deferral or rescission messages to Congress. These messages are then treated as if they came from the President, and Congress can approve or reject them. The Comptroller General may also bring civil actions to require that funds be released when Congress has refused presidential impoundment requests.

A bill establishing an Illinois Impoundment Control Act (HB 518), closely modeled on the impoundment section of the federal law, was introduced during the 1975 Legislative Session but never passed. Because it was not adopted, Illinois appropriations are spending ceilings and not mandates to spend.

About half of the State budget involves funds allotted periodically by statutory formula. However, not all formulas are always fully funded. The school formula has occasionally been a prominent example of an underfunded formula. The School Code contains a *pro rata* provision to adjust distribution when an appropriation is insufficient to meet formula claims. An example of a formula successfully defended against underfunding is the Local Government Distributive Fund which distributes to local governments their share of the income tax. The General Assembly rejected Governor Walker's proposed underfunding of the Distributive Fund so that these resources could be used elsewhere. It refused to alter the 1969 decision which allocated to local government a fixed percentage of income tax proceeds. In all likelihood this demonstrates the continuing political strength of local government, rather than any legislative commitment to old promises.

The General Assembly and the Governor can decide to authorize an appropriation at a less than fully funded level. While it is clear in the case of schools that the amount of underfunding is not "owed" to the local school districts, it is not clear whether the State would owe local governments for their share of the income tax. Most likely, the distribution of the locals' share would be deferred until additional appropriations are passed.

Another kind of allotment control is used by the executive Bureau of the Budget (BoB) for the operating budgets of code departments. Each agency submits a quarterly allotment plan which ostensibly controls cash flow and avoids deficiencies. These plans must be approved by BoB. The purpose of the allotment system is to call to the attention of BoB and the Governor "any appropriations that should not be spent because of changed circumstances or low priority programs." If such appropriations are identified, there is nothing in the statutes to prevent the Governor from impounding the funds.

Legislative staffs can review allotments to see whether impoundments are in effect, although the reported allotments can indicate a higher proposed expenditure than the executive planned. The staffs can monitor agency spending during the year through information provided in the Comptroller's Unified Statewide Accounting System. However, there are many delays which may make it difficult to determine whether actual spending corresponds to reported allotments.

A third form of allotment control is used by the General Assembly. The language of the appropriations bills for FY 1977 and FY 1979 limited the timing of contracts, obligations and expenditures to the first half of the fiscal year. This control had been used under biennial budgeting to prevent agencies from running out of funds before the return of the Legislature eighteen months later. This legislative action was an attempt to prevent deficiencies and to smooth out cash flow in a fashion similar to the Governor's allotment system. Since these legislative allotments were statutory, they were enforced by the Comptroller.

Expenditure Review

The budget process is cyclical, with judgments about the aftermath of General Assembly action informing its future actions. After funds are appropriated, it is necessary to verify that the money was spent for the goods and services the Legislature intended and that the results are worth the costs. This process — called expenditure review—is performed in systematic fashion by two legislative agencies, the Office of the Auditor General and the Economic and Fiscal Commission. It is also carried out informally by legislators, committees and legislative staffs. This section examines the main types of expenditure reveiw and describes the structure and functions of legislative review agencies in Illinois.

Types of Expenditure Review Expenditure review involves four types of considerations: (1) *Legality*. Was money spent on the items for which it was appropriated? Were expenditures made in accordance with State laws? Were they recorded properly? (2) *Efficiency*. Was the program operated as efficiently as possible? (3) *Policy conformance*. Did the policies, administrative actions, and expenditures carried out by an agency conform to the expectations of the General Assembly?; and (4) *Effectiveness*. Did the program achieve the results desired by the General Assembly and the Governor?

Each of these questions involves a different kind of review, but all four are necessary. For example, serious inefficiency should not be tolerated even though a program is effective. It is equally unacceptable to operate a program without beneficial results even if it is operated efficiently.[36]

Legality. The first type of review, called financial or compliance auditing, investigates whether obligations and expenditures are legal and proper. The statutes require biennial audits of this type for all State agencies. In addition, the larger executive agencies also undergo internal audits to certify expenditures.

Efficiency. The second type of review is the efficiency, management or operational audit, which examines an agency's processes to determine whether work is being done simply, efficiently and economically.

Policy conformance. This review verifies that policy objectives are accomplished and that the means employed are consistent with the expectations of the General Assembly. For example, Illinois sent wards of the Department of Children and Family Services to out-of-state institutions, with mixed results. General reaction to that policy was unfavorable. The practice was changed because the means were unacceptable, not because alternative means would produce better results.

Other examples of policies which do not conform to legislative mandate flow from some uses of the two percent transfer provision which was enacted originally to eliminate the need for small supplemental appropriations and the "Contingencies" line item. It was *not* enacted to allow agencies to make major reallocations after their appropriations passed. The Department of Mental Health and Developmental Disabilities had an FY 1977 General Revenue transfer potential of more than $5.8 million. This could be used for 500 additional jobs for one year, for legal fees, or for any of the other myriad activities within the scope of that department. Another example is the University of Illinois, which has a transfer potential of $4.5 million from General Revenue and $575,800 from the Income Fund.

As a rule, policy nonconformance is not easily detected in the systematic expenditure review carried out by the Auditor General and the Illinois Economic and Fiscal Commission. Systematic expenditure review tends to consist of checks for legality, efficiency and effectiveness, but nonconforming policies can be legal to the letter of the law, efficient and effective. In addition, it is difficult to discover specific expressions of legislative intent with respect to means. The General Assembly does express some concern for means in its use of line items instead of broad program categories. Nevertheless, the importance of *how* government does things requires that executive policies and administrative actions be checked for policy conformance. Those policies and actions which deviate significantly from legislative expectations will probably surface as a result of legislative oversight.

Legislative oversight and expenditure controls represent the most effective legislative controls over the executive. Legislative oversight activities are undergirded by that sense of institutional rivalry which most legislators bear toward the executive branch. To be sure, party ties with the Governor or alliances of mutual interest with particular administrative agencies mitigate and blunt legislative-executive antagonism. Many legislators perceive the oversight task as predominantly a negative or checking activity, but oversight also provides agencies with an appreciation of legislative expectations about various matters.

Appropriations committee members use both statutory and nonstatutory oversight techniques. The most obvious kind of statutory control flows from appropriations decisions. Appropriation levels control agency activity. If an agency or part of an agency is suspected of not using funds in accordance with the General Assembly's wishes, the Legislature can exert financial leverage to insure compliance. The Legislature has inserted language in appropriations bills specifying the conditions under which money can be obligated. In one case, the Legislature tried to "limit" the use of funds by stating that "no part of their appropriation shall be expended for (a specified activity)." Or the General Assembly may fix the length of time over which the money can be obligated, usually for a single fiscal year but sometimes less.

The Legislature can also pursue its oversight tasks in nonstatutory ways. Hearings are held each year to examine agency budget requests and to question agency officials. Opportunity exists, both "on and off the record," to scrutinize agency behavior and to communicate legislative preferences to the appropriate agency officials. Another nonstatutory means of oversight involves the informal contact, face-to-face or written, between the individual legislators and staff on the one hand and the agency director and budget officers of executive agencies on the other. The influence of the Appropriations Committee can be wielded through fairly continuous personal communication with executive agency personnel.

The importance of legislative oversight derives not only from the fact that the General Assembly holds the power of the purse, but also from the frequency of opportunity for control. Since appropriations decisions are made annually, the Legislature can be continuously watchful. The same Legislators who make the original decisions are there to check on agency compliance. Informal oversight activity surrounds appropriations hearings, and formal oversight activity takes root there.

Effectivess. The fourth type of review is "program audit" or "program evaluation," which focuses on the results of programs rather than on means. It examines whether intended or assumed objectives are accomplished. For example, in a manpower training program an evaluation might determine whether the people enrolled acquired any occupational skills, whether they were placed in jobs and whether the results justified public investment.

One major problem in program evaluation is determining the intended consequences of a program. The fact that most governmental functions have multiple purposes complicates the problem of specifying goals. Furthermore, it may not be possible to develop a consensus about a particular agency's objectives. Is the purpose of the Department of Corrections incarceration, rehabilitation or punishment?

The powers and duties of agencies are enumerated in the statutes, but these do not specify the relative emphasis which agencies are to give each program. In one sense, dollar amounts are indications of the General Assembly's priorities, but in many instances appropriations are made to divisions which have more than one program or goal. While it may be possible to evaluate progress toward explicit program goals, comparing programs is more difficult because priorities are not expressed explicitly in appropriations bills.

Another major problem with program evaluation is measurement. While financial data are abundant, the assumptions necessary for governmental cost accounting raise questions about its value. "Social indicators" and "social accounts" have been developed to some extent, but there is still considerable debate over what to measure and the appropriate levels of measurement. Since most agencies do not keep records which spotlight inefficiency or ineffectiveness, the analyst or evaluator must actually "set up the books." He or she must decide what data to compile and examine (and often he must collect the data himself). The adoption of regular performance reporting data are also relatively expensive to accumulate regardless of their reliability. Finally, there is the intricate problem of interpreting the assessment of costs and benefits — which is not easy even if there *are* reliable indicators of costs and benefits.

However, the Comptroller's Uniform Statewide Accounting System (CUSAS) in its present or even a revised form cannot be expected to provide such program cost data except where agency divisions correspond exactly to programs. When a unit of an agency, such as a mental health institution, provides a variety of programmatic services, only the agency can design and maintain a meaningful cost accounting system.[37]

Systematic Expenditure Review Systematic expenditure review for the Illinois Legislature is conducted by the Office of the Auditor General and the Illinois Economic and Fiscal Commission (IEFC). The Office of the Auditor General was made part of the legislative branch in 1973. Before that time, the Office was lodged in a Department of Audits, nominally in the executive branch but responsible to a legislative commission. The 1973 State Auditing Act enlarged the scope of activities from a narrow focus on financial audits to a broader responsibility encompassing management, efficiency and program effectiveness audits.

The IEFC, successor to the Illinois Budgetary Commission, was established July 1, 1972. It was assigned three main responsibilities: to prepare an annual revenue estimate and economic forecast; to provide the General Assembly with the most reliable and authoritative information possible about the operations of State government and economic developments and trends in Illinois; and to conduct studies and to make recommendations "intended to improve the functioning of State government including program evaluation studies." For a time the IEFC conducted in-depth evaluations, but since 1976 the General Assembly has assigned its evaluation requests to the Auditor General, freeing the IEFC staff to conduct fiscal studies.

Conclusion

Studying the role of the Illinois Legislature in the budgetary process is most successful when the application of authority is viewed in the light of the participants' power resources and their willingness to use them. While the General Assembly's role in the process may appear to inexperienced observers as a series of unrelated actions accompanied by many opportunities where legislative authority could have been applied but was not, sensitive spectators will look for the reasons legislative authority was exercised the way it was. Further research in this area could expand our shared understanding well beyond the existing literature.

There are many ways the General Assembly can utilize its authority. The way in which it is used does not usually take place by accident, but rather by a design influenced by the pattern of power in action. Attempting to understand why the General Assembly used its authority in a particular fashion without looking at political factors is an endeavor doomed to failure. Authority is never used in a vacuum; it is used only in an atmosphere of power.

NOTES

[1]Samuel K. Gove, Richard W. Carlson and Richard J. Carlson, in *The Illinois Legislature: Structure and Process* (Urbana: University of Illinois Press, 1976), pp. 102–103, cite Donald S. Glickman's comparison of committee action on appropriation bills during 1963 and 1973. Glickman reported that there was a greater propensity to amend bills and to "kill" them in 1973 than there was in 1963.

[2]Eli B. Silverman, "Public Budgeting and Public Administration: Enter the Legislature," *Public Finance Quarterly* 2 (1974), pp. 472–484. Another enlightened exception besides Wildavsky's works is Robert D. Lee, Jr. and Ronald W. Johnson, "Budget Approval: Role of the Legislature," *Public Budgeting Systems* (2d ed.; Baltimore: University Park Press, 1977), pp. 175–207; also S. Kenneth Howard, *Changing State Budgeting* (Lexington, Ky.: Council of State Governments, 1973).

[3]See Aaron Wildavsky, *The Politics of the Budgetary Process* (New York: Little, Brown and Company, 1964), at pp. 127, 133, and elsewhere. Also see his "Budgeting as Political Process," in *The Revolt Against the Masses: and other essays on Politics and Public Policy* (New York: Basic Books, Inc., Publishers, 1971), p. 339.

[4]See the Citizens Conference on State Legislatures, *The Sometimes Governments: A Critical Study of the 50 American Legislatures* (New York: Bantam Books, 1971).

[5]Thomas J. Anton, *The Politics of State Expenditure in Illinois* (Urbana: University of Illinois Press, 1966); and Glenn W. Fisher, *Taxes and Politics: A Study of Illinois Public Finance* (Urbana: University of Illinois Press, 1969), pp. 182–183.

[6]An important exception is Alan Rosenthal, *Legislative Performance in the States* (NY: Free Press, 1974).

[7]See Ira Sharkansky, *The Routines of Politics* (New York: Van Nostrand Reinhold Company, 1970).

[8]See Ira Sharkansky, *Public Administration: Policy Making in Government Agencies* (Chicago: Markham Publishing Company, 1970), pp. 222–233.

[9]For a similar argument on the federal level see John R. Gist, " 'Increment' and 'Base' in the Appropriations Porcess," *American Journal of Political Science* 21 (1977), 341–352.

[10]See Edward C. Banfield, *Political Influence: A New Theory of Urban Politics* (New York: Free Press, 1961), pp. 309, 348; Robert A. Dahl, "The Concept of Power," *Behavioral Science* 2 (1957), 202–203; and Karl W. Deutsch, *The Nerves of Government: Models of Political Communication and Control* (New York: Free Press, 1966), p. 111.

[11]Aaron Wildavsky, "The Political Economy of Efficiency: Cost Benefit Analysis, Systems Analysis, and Program Budgeting," in *Revolt Against the Masses*, pp. 205–206.

[12]See Wildavsky, *The Politics of the Budgetary Process*, pp. 158–159.

[13]William J. Keefe and Morris S. Ogul, *The American Legislative Process: Congress and the States* (Englewood Cliffs, New Jersey: Prentice-Hall, Inc., 1964), p. 375, attribute this evaluation to Lynton K. Caldwell, *The Government and Administration of New York* (New York: Thomas Y. Crowell Company, 1954), pp. 86–87.

[14]Alan Evan Schenker, "When Governors Change: The Case of the California Budget" (unpublished Ph.D. dissertation, University of California at Davis, 1969), p. 98.

[15]Richard E. Neustadt, *Presidential Power: The Politics of Leadership* (New York: Mentor Books, 1964), pp. 110–111.

[16]Illinois, Constitution (1870), Article V, Section 7: "The Governor shall, at the commencement of each session, and at the close of his term of office, give to the General Assembly information, by message, of the condition of the State, and shall recommend such measures as he shall deem expedient. He shall account to the General Assembly, and paid out by him from funds subject to his order, with vouchers, and at the commencement of each regular session present estimates of money required to be raised by taxation for all purposes."

[17]Dawn Clark Netsch, "The Executive," in *Con-Con: Issues for the Illinois Constitutional Convention,* Papers Prepared by the Constitutional Research Group, Victoria Ranney, ed. (Urbana: University of Illinois Press, 1970), pp. 169–170. Netsch held that Article V, Section 7 of the 1870 Constitution "authorizes" while Glen Fisher in . . . *Public Finance*, p. 322, held "Section 7 'implies' an executive budget." A contrary view was held by Shontz: "Budgeting as practiced in the Illinois State Government today is undergirded only by statutory provisions. The 1870 Constitution, . . ., did not envision any formal budgetory procedures." Vernon L. Shontz, Jr., "Budget Making in Illinois State Government" (unpublished M.A. thesis, University of Illinois at Urbana, 1957), p. 1.

[18]In 1913, at the suggestion of Governor Dunne, a legislative Efficiency and Economy Committee was created which recommended a total reorganization of Illinois government. This report was summarily rejected by that session of the legislature to which it was presented. It apparently was presented late in that session. See W.F. Dodd, "Legislative Notes and Reviews: The Illinois Legislature of 1917," *American Political Science Review* 11 (1917), pp. 711–17; *Report of the Efficiency and Economy Committee* (Chicago: Windemere Press, 1915); Daniel J. Elazar, "The Office of Governor in Illinois: 1818–1933," in *Office of the Governor*, pp. 27–28; Horace E. Flack, "Efficiency and Economy in State Government," *American Political Science Review* 8 (1914), pp. 63–64; C.C. Waters, "Legislative Notes and Review: Economy and Efficiency Commissions," *American Political Science Reveiw* 10 (1916), pp. 96–97; P. Orman Ray, "Legislative Notes and Review: Economy and Efficiency," *American Political Science Review* 11 (1917), pp. 115–16; and J.M. Mathews, "State Administration Work of Efficiency and Economy Commissions," *American Political Science Review* 12 (1918), pp. 510–14.

[19]Anton, *op. cit.*, p. 11, notes "Between 1909 and 1913, thirty-four new state agencies were created and biennial appropriations rose from $19.8 million to $37.9 million."

[20]For further details see Finley F. Bell, "The Illinois Budget," *The Annals* 62 (November 1915), pp. 73–84; J.E. Fairlie, "Budget Methods in Illinois," *ibid.*, pp. 85–90; and Frank A. Updyke, "Legislative Notes and Review: State Budgets," *American Political Science Review* 8 (1914), p. 60.

[21]Elazar declared that it was the first of its kind in the United States. See *The Office of the Governor*. See also W.F. Dodd, "Legislative Notes and Reviews: The Illinois Legislature of 1917," *American Political Science Review* 11 (1917), pp. 711–17.

[22]Neil F. Garvey, *The Government and Administration of Illinois,* Vol. 11 of *The American Commonwealth Series,* ed. by W. Brooke Graves (New York: Thomas Y. Crowell Company, 1958), p. 138.

[23]Anton, *op. cit.*, p. 77.

[24]*Ibid.*, p. 85.

[25]*Ibid.*, p. 111.

[26]See Gilbert K. Steiner and Samuel K. Gove, *Legislative Politics in Illinois* (Urbana: Univerity of Illinois Press, 1960), p. 42.

[27]See Shontz, "Budget Making in Illinois State Government," pp. 47–50, and Anton, *The Politics of State Expenditure in Illinois,* pp. 78–85.

[28]A supplemental appropriation is made when the purpose of a regular appropriation has been expanded or when the funds for a particular purpose have been exhausted before the end of the fiscal year.

[29]For examples of Congressional reaction to federal transfers, see Louis Fisher, *Presidential Spending Power* (Princeton, New Jersey: Princeton University Press, 1975), pp. 99–122.

[30]See Robert Ash Wallace, *Congressional Control of Federal Spending* (Detroit: Wayne State University Press, 1960).

[31]Better Government Association, *A Report on the Funding of a Color TV Studio and Equipment for the Illinois Information Service.*

[32]Wallace, *Congressional Control of Federal Spending,* pp. 131–136.

[33]See "Interview with Alice M. Rivlin: A Guide to the Congressional Budget Process," *Challenge* (July/August, 1975) and James A. Thurber, "Congressional Budget Reform and New Demand for Policy Analysis," *Policy Analysis* 2 (1976), p. 201.

[34]Roger H. Davidson, "Congressional Committees: The Toughest Customers," *Policy Analysis* 2 (1976), pp. 318–319.

[35]See Fisher, *op. cit.*

[36]S. Kenneth Howard, *Changing State Budgeting* (Lexington, Ky.: Council of State Governments, 1973), pp. 290–293.

[37]*Ibid.,* pp. 297–304.

PART **VI**

MAKING GOVERNMENT WORK: INPUTS TO POLICY AND ADMINISTRATION

CHAPTER **24**

Administrative Reorganization in Illinois

Samuel K. Gove and Richard J. Carlson

"It must be remembered that there is nothing more difficult to plan, more doubtful of success, nor more dangerous to manage, than the creation of a new system. For the initiator has the enmity of all who would profit by the preservation of the old institutions and merely lukewarm defenders in those who would gain by the new ones."

—Machiavelli

(He must have been in charge of reorganization . . .)

Strengthening state government through administrative reorganization has been a "good government" goal in most states since early in this century. Reorganization has often been put in the "motherhood" category. The political payoff of reorganization is shown by the number of governors either recommending or implementing reorganization who have become presidential candidates. The most recent wave of reorganization activities began with the comprehensive restructuring of Michigan's executive branch in 1965. Since then 21 states have undergone major reorganizations.[1] Illinois has had more than its share of reorganization studies. In fact, the comprehensive reorganization implemented by Governor Frank Lowden in 1917 initiated the state reorganization movement nationally. Since then there have been other attempts to reorganize the State's executive branch but none have met with the success of the 1917 effort.

Illinois, like most states, has a complex governmental structure. A 1976 study identified 65 major agencies and nearly 250 smaller boards and commissions whose memberships require more than 2,000 appointments by the Governor.[2] The complexity of this structure has been the central issue in periodic calls for "simplifying" State government through reorganization, primarily by reducing the number of agencies reporting to the Governor through consolidation around broad functional areas such as energy or environment.

The strong tendency toward the proliferation of organizational units in State government has a variety of causes, many of them political in origin. And it is the strong political base which underlies the structure of government that makes reorganization efforts difficult and only occasionally successful.

Government structure is often perceived as reflecting the priorities of the political system. The creation of agencies representing specific issues or interests has a strong symbolic appeal to groups which advocate those same issues and interests. Thus the creation of "interest-specific" agencies is often pursued by interest groups because it provides status and recognition to the causes they espouse. Their creation also has practical significance: such agencies can give interest groups greater leverage in the administration of programs that affect them most directly. Agencies, in effect, become advocates for the client groups they serve. This is evident, for example, in the creation of the Department of Children and Family Services in 1963 and the Department on Aging in 1973. Both had been divisions within what is now the Illinois Department of Public Aid. The creation of separate agencies was intended to give greater emphasis and visibility to programs for the aged and for children—in response to interest group and legislative pressures.

New agencies are sometimes created in response to new social and political problems. The Illinois Environmental Protection Agency created in 1970 was modeled after the federal Environmental Protection Agency and paralleled the creation of similar "little EPAs" in other states in the late 1960s. The new agency not only successfully consolidated Illinois' fragmented pollution control system in a single agency but also symbolized the State's new commitment to dealing with the emerging issue of environmental protection.

In some instances federal statutes and regulations impose organizational requirements on state governments that add to the proliferation phenomenon. Federal programs invariably require advisory groups to provide various kinds of representation to the public at large as well as specific interests. Such bodies typically have only advisory responsibilities but occasionally have major planning and coordination roles. An example is the Illinois Employment and Training Council, created under the Comprehensive Employment and Training Act of 1973. Some federal statutes go as far as to mandate specific organizational requirements for administering federal programs, such as requiring administration of a program or set of programs by a "single state agency." For example, when Congress reauthorized the vocational rehabilitation (VR) program in 1973, it responded to the increasing trend at the State level to consolidate human services programs into comprehensive "umbrella" agencies. Out of concern that the VR program might get lost among "welfare" programs, and to give it added visibility, Congress required that where VR is in an umbrella agency, it must be administered by a single organizational unit: a self-contained agency within the

An earlier version of this paper prepared by Samuel K. Gove was presented at the Symposium on Administrative Reform, University of Nebraska, on April 13, 1978, under the title "Administrative Reorganization: The Illinois Case."

larger structure. This requirement works directly against the objective of an umbrella human services agency to "integrate" the delivery of services to citizens. Many of the clientele have more than one problem and thus require the services of more than one program. The integrated service system attempts to respond to the multiple needs of the whole person not the effects of a single problem. This is accomplished by bringing together, under one organizational roof, programs such as services to the elderly, handicapped, families, cash assistance, health and related medical services. Then, at the point where a client attempts to avail himself of one program, there will be greater opportunity to use other related programs in order to maximize services while minimizing the bureaucratic maze.

Attempts by the State of Florida to develop an integrated social service system under its Department of Health and Rehabilitative Services ran afoul of the federal VR Act in 1976. After lengthy litigation, the Supreme Court on April 27, 1979, refused to hear a lower court decision upholding HEW's refusal to fund Florida's VR program unless the single organizational unit requirement was respected.

The creation of separate organizational units is often attributable to a concern for isolating certain kinds of decisions from politics, usually by making agencies independent of the Governor through multi-member boards or commissions that represent a mix of political party and other interests. This is particularly true of functions that involve quasi-judicial decision-making, such as workmen's compensation (Illinois Industrial Commission) or utility rate setting (Illinois Commerce Commission). The use of a multi-member body in such cases also reflects the long tradition in Anglo-Saxon jurisprudence that, where laws are to be applied to situations that affect an individual's rights or privileges, a decision made by a number of people is less likely to be arbitrary and capricious than the decision of a single individual.

State administrative reorganization is addressed to the problems that can arise in a structure with many separate organizational units reporting to a single elected chief executive. Solutions to these problems are generally found in the principles of reorganization that date back to early public administration students, for whom span of control, accountability, responsiveness, efficiency and economy were key words. Even present-day reorganization reports contain similar statements of principle.

The common theme behind the "principles" in all the Illinois reorganization studies is the need to strengthen the Office of Governor, even though the Illinois' chief executive is among the most powerful in the nation. On Schlesinger's scale of constitutional gubernatorial power, he is ranked either first or second.[3] No study has suggested that governors in general are too strong, and that the separation of powers concept may be out of balance. Very seldom is the concept of a strong governor even questioned.[4]

When it comes to implementing the reorganization proposals in each State report, no one openly reflects in the administrative reorganization literature on a recent observation by Garnett and Levine: "Why does reorganization occur? It occurs because of political action by political actors with largely political motives."[5] In fact, many recommendations seem to be directed at taking administration out of politics, usually repeating the traditional public administration principles mentioned above. A recent example, the latest proposal for a major Illinois reorganization, was prepared by the Task Force on Governmental Reorganization for the 1976 gubernatorial candidates. Entitled *Orderly Government,* the report sets out familiar "basic principles and organizational criteria": (1) achieving some *simplification* of the complex structure of the Illinois executive branch, thereby improving the managerial capacity of the Governor; (2) improving *accountability* for the operation, success, or failure of Illinois programs and policies; (3) improving *accessibility* to services or programs provided by Illinois State government so that these programs affect Illinois citizens in an equitable manner; (4) maintaining the *separation of powers* between the legislative, judicial and executive branches of Illinois government; (5) reducing the *span of control* which the Governor exercises over executive branch agencies in Illinois; and (6) achieving *economy of operation* and improved *efficiency* and *effectiveness* in the delivery of services or operation of Illinois programs.[6]

While reorganization initiatives may be stimulated by political considerations and shaped around traditional principles of public administration, the process of reorganization can be used effectively to address basic management issues in State government. From the standpoint of the Governor, a structure which includes a large number of agencies, many of which represent narrow functional interests, impedes strong central management and control over policy development and can inhibit the creation of effective service delivery systems. Illinois State government is a highly decentralized system that is subject to few central control mechanisms. The most important of these is the budget process. Yet there are many issues and concerns that cannot—or should not—be dealt with solely on the basis of revenue and expenditure considerations.

The Governor is held accountable for all of the programs and activities of the agencies under his jurisdiction, even those multi-member boards and commissions that are ostensibly "independent," but he is hard-pressed to monitor, much less directly influence, the plethora of agencies in the executive branch on more than a highly selective basis.

The resultant fragmentation of program responsibility results in the need for a great deal of inter-agency consultation and coordination. The press of day-to-day business frequently inhibits agencies from devoting the necessary time to this process. The result is duplication, inconsistency and sometimes conflict among agencies. For the clients of State government programs, program fragmentation can mean bad service. Individuals with a problem will receive different handling by the State depending upon the nearly random event of where they choose to enter the system. Some problems will not be dealt with because no one feels responsible for them. A government with a large number of narrowly defined and independent functions has more possibility for clients to "fall through the cracks" than one with a small number of broadly defined functions.

Government will never be totally subject to the concept of management prevalent in the private sector. The goals of government are political and therefore measured by political criteria and not necessarily by objective measures of program performance. Yet, since government does provide services that affect the health and welfare of the citizency on a broad scale, the effectiveness with which these services are provided is a significant issue of public policy. Moves to reorganize are couched in terms of better management of public services, and structural reform can be the key to better public management. To achieve this, however, political leaders must resist the tendency to solve problems by doing nothing more than creating new organizational units or simply "moving the boxes around." Organizational structure should be viewed and used simultaneously as a tool of political power and as a tool of management, just like planning and budgeting. If utilized properly, the reorganization process can provide a strong framework for effective management of public programs—unfortunately, experience suggests that Illinois political styles present serious barriers which can only be overcome by strong political leadership.

The large number of agencies does not allow for an institutionalized mechanism for bringing major issues to the Governor's attention and resolving them. Cabinet meetings are unmanageable for anything but limited informational briefings. In practice, director access to the Governor can be limited or non-existent. In addition to creating a morale problem, this encourages undue attention to crisis situations and an ad hoc approach to problem solving. With no systematic method for establishing gubernatorial policy on a comprehensive basis (outside of the budget process), agencies are often left to either formulate their own policies or continue ones previously in existence. This encourages agencies to act as advocates for certain interest groups rather than as administrators of legislative and gubernatorial policy. The existence of many agencies results in parochial perspectives on policy development. Consequently, agency personnel often tend to view emerging problems or programs from the viewpoint of a narrowly defined agency mission, client group or work activity. This serves as an obstacle to broad-based policy making.

History

The first significant reorganization in Illinois came in 1917, when Frank O. Lowden was Governor.[7] The inspiration for the reform was a 1915 Efficiency and Economy Report that was given impetus in turn, by President Taft's reorganization efforts at the national level in 1911. These tandem federal-State efforts at reorganization were to be repeated in later years. Although the Efficiency and Economy Committee of the Legislature did its work during Governor Edward F. Dunne's Administration (1912–16), implementing the modified recommendations came about through the efforts of the new Governor.

The reform committee recommended that the then one hundred separate and more or less independent agencies be regrouped into nine "code" departments under the Civil Administrative Code. Each code department was to be headed by a single director appointed by the Governor. The model used for this reorganization was the organization of the executive branch at the national level. The final code organization adopted was modified from that recommended by the 1915 committee.

That the purpose of the 1917 reorganization was economy and that this had been achieved was made clear later by Governor Lowden. He said that the reorganization was very successful in terms of State finances, citing the fact that appropriations for the biennium ending June 30, 1921, exceeded appropriations for the biennium ending June 30, 1917, by only 36 percent. Comparable State appropriations for the same period for Massachusetts, Michigan, New York, Ohio and Wisconsin increased an average of 76 percent. In large part because of his success in passing the Civil Administrative Code, Governor Lowden captured the public's imagination throughout the country as a vigorous State executive. He was a prominent contender for the Republican nomination for President in 1920, when a split convention nominated dark horse Warren G. Harding.

The next significant reorganization study started in 1949 under the administration of Governor Adlai E. Stevenson II. This study also followed a national reorganization study, one conducted by a commission headed by former President Herbert Hoover. In fact, the Illinois commission and its counterparts in other states became known as "little Hoover" commissions. The Illinois little Hoover commission was created by the Legislature; it included representatives of the public appointed by the Executive and the Legislature. The chairman was Walter V. Schaefer, a former member of Governor Stevenson's staff and subsequently a well-respected member of the State Supreme Court.

The commission did not recommend a major restructuring of State government comparable to that of the 1915 committee, primarily because the action taken as a result of the latter's work had established a solid organizational base. Only one department (the small Aeronautics Department) was recommended out of existence. The other major recommendations would have reshaped several departments, resulting in departments with new names but with functions reassigned from existing departments. New departments of administration, natural resources and highways would have been created. The commission also recommended combining many independent boards and commissions into existing code departments. The total number of agencies in State government would have been reduced from seventy-nine to forty-nine. There were many other recommendations for reorganizations within agencies, such as coordination within the Department of Labor of its unemployment compensation and employment service responsibilities. The commission also recommended that the Governor's office be strengthened—a recurring theme in State administrative reorganization.

Given the partisan conflict, not unexpectedly the Republican Legislature which received the report took no action to help the Democratic Governor Stevenson's image. The only significant recommendation to be adopted was the transfer of the Division of Parks and Memorials to the Department of Conservation.[8] Governor Stevenson went on to be the Democratic presidential candidate in 1952. Although his reorganization efforts did not play as prominent a role as those of Governor Lowden in 1920, they were mentioned by supporters of his candidacy.

Sporadic efforts for further administrative reorganization were made, beginning in 1953. Republican Governor William G. Stratton proposed a package that was put together with little fanfare and did not receive much support. In 1956 there was a major scandal involving the Auditor of Public Accounts, and as a result the organization for auditing State funds and regulating banks and other financial institutions was revamped.

The next significant effort came in 1965, when many attempts at reform in State government grew out of the "at-large" election of House members. (The election had been conducted this way because of the failure of the Legislature and the Governor to reapportion the General Assembly.) In 1965 legislative commissions were established to study not only the executive branch, but also the legislative branch and the State Constitution. Like the 1949 little Hoover commission, the 1965 commission was composed of public members appointed by the Governor and the Legislature. The chairman of the Commission on State Government—Illinois (COSGI) had been staff director for the 1950 commission.

Since 1949 there had been a marked increase in the number of State agencies, a characteristic common to most State governments and one that reorganizers try to slow down. COSGI found that by 1965 the number of code departments had increased to eighteen from thirteen in 1950 and nine in 1917. In addition to the eighteen departments, there were approximately seventy other autonomous units with administrative functions.

While the study was being conducted by COSGI, under newspaper pressure the Governor created a separate business management study group that somewhat duplicated the statutory commission. Although all parties denied duplication, the two studies covered many of the same areas. However, when the Governor formulated his legislative program in 1967, he rather clearly leaned more heavily on the business study than on COSGI.

The COSGI report contained 385 numbered recommendations, most relatively minor. Several, however, would have rearranged the code department structure, with no fewer than eight of the then-existing code departments undergoing basic changes. Some of the recommendations were adopted, some in modified form. No major restructuring of the code department organization took place.

The commission followed the format and procedures of its 1949 counterpart. The results were not too much different, although this time the commission was reestablished to review the process of implementation of its recommendations. Two of the commission members Mrs. Netsch and Mr. Gove, in frustration critiqued the approach of detailed agency review and the absence of a broader overview of State government, its programs and its role in the evolving federal system. They submitted a supplementary statement for inclusion in the report that said in part:

> From the time of our appointment to this Commission, we have been concerned with the approach which the Commission took toward its studies. At this moment in history, when state government has never had more to do and yet is under vigorous attack, we felt that a commission such as this should concern itself with the scope and nature of the role it is to play, not with the minutiae of operations. That is not to say that a periodic—in fact, a continuous—review of effective organization and performance of those functions which are performed should not be undertaken. We underscore that this process should be continuous and not left to a decennial legislative commission. . . .
>
> Foremost among these weaknesses is the inability to come to terms with the increasing complexity and interdependence of federal, state and local government—some of it due to the state's failure in the past to respond to responsibility—and to attempt to evolve a concept of state action in the future. In what program areas can the job be more effectively done at the federal or at the local governmental level with perhaps minimum participion of the state? In what areas can the state make a major contribution to programs if it would assume a role of leader and innovator in new administrative techniques as well as in programs? . . .
>
> We believe that only a more vital state government can bring to bear on these and other difficult questions the insight and techniques which will permit of their identification, let alone solution. It is inescapable that the Governor must be the central figure in this reexamination; yet historically we have starved the chief executive. He must be given means for acquiring adequate professional staff with some time free of administrative detail, fiscal planning instead of bookkeeping, creative personnel in all programs and resources for long range planning for the citizens and the cities.[9]

They wanted the Governor to concentrate efforts on the overall situation, being unconvinced that detailed restructuring alone would bring this result.

Recent Developments

Two other, more recent reorganization reports should be considered to complete the Illinois story. In addition, the roles of the new Constitution and executive reorganization need to be mentioned.

Beyond Bureaucracy was the next major reorganization study to surface in Illinois. Unlike the other studies mentioned here, this one was the work of primarily one person, John Briggs who had served as director of a code department and had other assignments in Republican Governor Richard B. Ogilvie's Administration. Late in Ogilvie's tenure, Briggs was designated coordinator for executive reorganization. He was given a free hand to develop a reorganization plan for the Governor to consider in his second term, a term that did not materialize (Ogilvie was defeated in 1972). The report was rushed to completion in Ogilvie's last month of office, but not unexpectedly received little public attention.

Recommendations of the Briggs report were more far reaching and would have resulted in more restructuring than either the 1951 or the 1967 reports, which came from legislative committees. The Briggs report noted that there was a "need for reducing the internal self-serving bureaucracy which tends to divide rather than unify effort." Like its predecessors, the study found State government to be composed of a multiplicity of agencies that were quite independent of each other. The number of State agencies was now twenty-four code departments (up from eighteen in 1967): thirty-six other budgeted agencies also existed. The solution again was to revamp the code department structure, bringing it down from the twenty-four departments to ten. More so than other reports, this one was filed and soon forgotten. Even some of the Ogilvie people disowned it as Administration policy.

Executive Reorganization Under the 1970 Constitution

A new approach to administrative reorganization came on the scene in 1970. In 1968, for the first time since the 1920s, Illinois voters had approved the call for a State Constitutional Convention. The Convention convened in late 1969 and sat during most of 1970. Like similar bodies, the convention did most of its work in committees including one on the executive branch. Unlike many conventions in other states, the Illinois convention's product was approved by the voters (in a referendum in November 1970).

The Executive Committee addressed most aspects of State government affecting the executive.[10] These included reducing the number of elective officers in the executive branch of State government, a matter not considered seriously in the reorganization studies. The Committee and Convention, however, could agree only on a slight reshuffling, and effectively eliminated only one office, the Superintendent of Public Instruction. The Committee and the Convention did agree on an expansion of the veto powers given the Governor.[11]

The new Constitution provides, "The Governor, by Executive Order, may reassign functions among or reorganize executive agencies which are directly responsible to him. If such a reassignment or reorganization would contravene a statute, the Executive Order shall be delivered to the General Assembly. . . ." The Constitution provides for a legislative veto.[12] The first two Governors to whom this new authority was available Ogilvie and Democrat Dan Walker, did not use it.

The most recent, major, and far-reaching reorganization study was tied into the 1976 campaign for Governor. Early in the campaign, Republican James Thompson had announced the formation of a nonpartisan volunteer task force to undertake a review of State government. "The group will take a massive and sweeping look at current policies and programs of government from a fresh perspective and examine the very foundations on which our governmental structure is built," said Thompson. Later, Thompson's opponent, Michael Howlett, proposed a similar commission to study State government. Subsequently, in an unusual move, the candidates agreed to combine efforts, and the bipartisan Illinois Task Force on Governmental Reorganization was formed and charged with developing recommendations for reorganizing the executive branch of State government.

The four-person task force included new members not involved previously in reorganization in Illinois and it turned to an out-of-state consulting firm. Unlike most of the earlier studies, funding came, not from public sources, but from donations from Illinois businesses and labor unions. The 344-page document, entitled *Orderly Government—Organizing for Responsibility,* was given to Governor-elect Thompson with a November 3, 1976, date.

The task force report, like its predecessors, was critical of the structure of State government: "The fact that no single source could produce a complete organization chart or a listing of all Illinois agencies, boards, and commissions is but one measure of the chaotic and complex organization faced by Illinois Governors." In contrast to former documents, the report was designed to be useful beyond the immediate point in time.

The task force noted, quite realistically,

> The Governor's decision about whether or not to reorganize Illinois government will hinge on consideration of his own policy priorities, intensity of other pressing problems in Illinois, the political climate, and his judgment of the practicability of reorganization. The Task Force does not presume to make such judgments for the Governor, but it does feel it is necessary to set forth the potential advantage of reorganization in order to give the Governor the full understanding of the assets to be balanced with these other considerations.

The task force developed a set of guiding principles, listed in the introduction of this chapter. Using these principles, the functions of State government were to be reorganized into fourteen departments (see Figure 24-1), similar in number, though different in nature from those recommended in some of the earlier reports. The report went beyond the others into the no-man's-land of higher education to commend that intermediate boards of the university and community college systems be replaced by individual institutional boards. Thus each board would supervise one institution, whether single- or multicampus.

The new Governor was now the recipient of an impressive reorganization document. However, several problems prevented early action. One was the Democra-

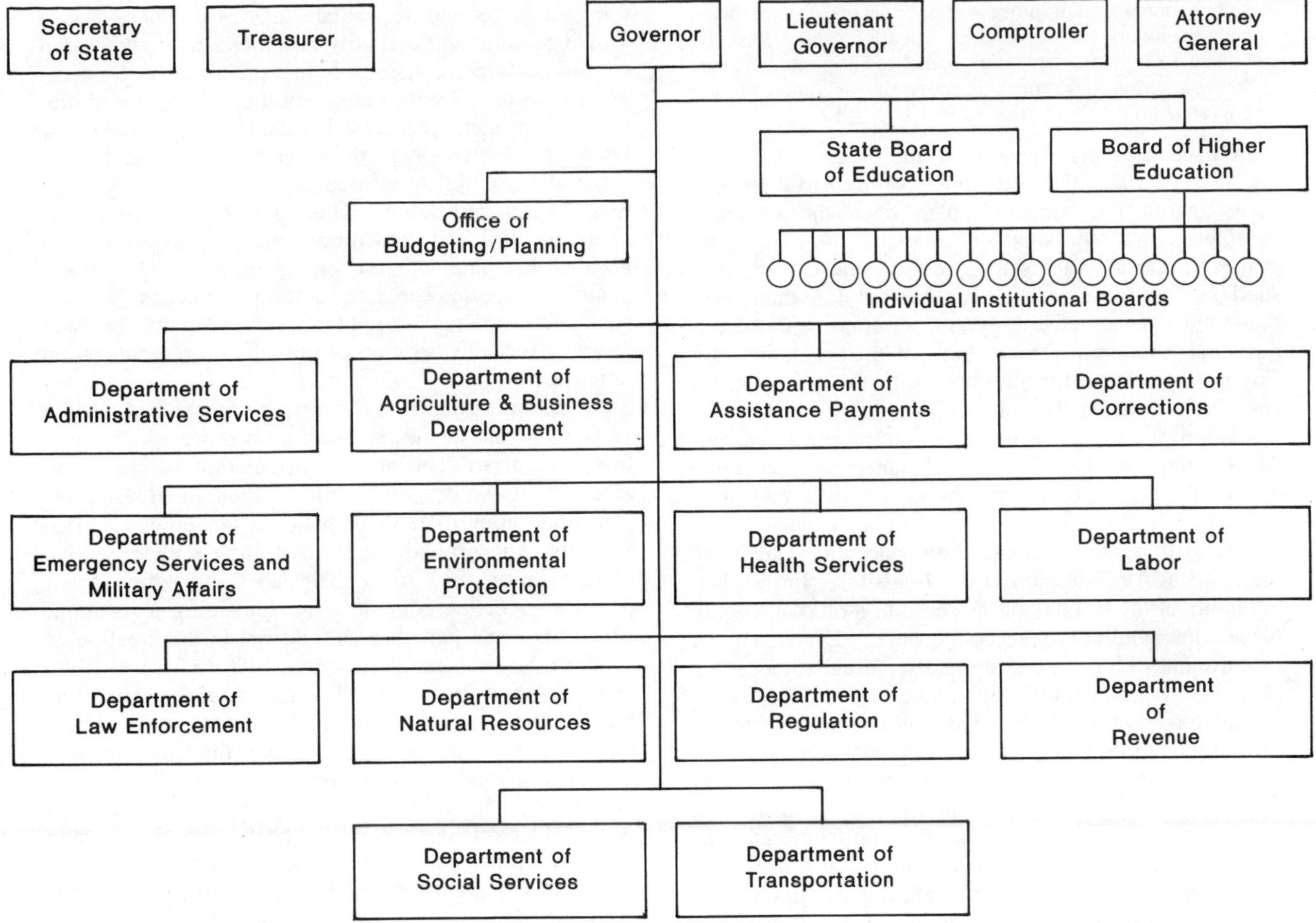

Figure 24-1

tic control of the Legislature; another, a two- rather than four-year term.[13] With all the other problems of a new Governor in a major state, Thompson took the advice of the task force and put off any broad-sweeping action. He did create a panel to listen to public sentiment, which held hearings at nine locations throughout the State. Most of the witnesses were concerned with how the reorganization proposal would affect their limited areas of concern. As noted in the summary of the hearings: "The most vociferous opposition came from those persons advocating for specific target populations, such as senior citizens, children, and the handicapped. They felt that these groups have unique needs which specialized training and an *identifiable agency which can advocate for them*" (emphasis added). The senior citizens were particularly vocal in defending the Department on Aging.

Thompson has used the executive reorganization power to implement reorganization plans, not necessarily in full agreement with *Orderly Government*. In the 1977 legislative session, his first, he introduced two proposals for relatively minor reorganizations by executive order. Unsure about how to handle the new authority, the Legislature introduced conforming legislation so it would have a vehicle to amend the Governor's proposal. (Con-con had intended that the Legislature only accept or reject, not amend, executive branch reorganization.) The majority Democrats used this amendatory power, changing the Governor's proposals that provided for a consolidated Department of Law Enforcement to include the independent Illinois Bureau of Investigation, but adding an independent Office of State Fire Marshall. The other proposal that was adopted created a new Department of Administrative Services, absorbing the earlier Department of General Services and the Department of Finance. This was not amended.

The conflict between the Governor and the Legislature had political overtones, but it also was the more classic executive-legislative conflict, as illustrated by a post-session Republican staff document that said:

> After deliberation, the General Assembly agreed that the executive orders were to be accepted and implementing legislation enacted. The legislation was enacted for several reasons. First, to clarify any ambiguities in the orders. Secondly, to correct provisions that the General Assembly felt to be outside the scope of the power of the executive order, namely the creation of new agencies and new powers. Thirdly, to provide a vehicle in the statutes to make later organizational changes. Finally, to establish a precedent [for] the passage of implementing legislation as a means to amend the provisions of an executive order.

> The reorganization process was a system of compromise and teamwork between the executive and legislative branches of government. Both branches confronted the matter in a serious attempt to improve the operation of state government.[14]

In a special energy message to the General Assembly on April 7, 1977, the Governor promised to develop a State energy reorganization plan once the President completed his reorganization of federal energy programs. In the 1978 legislative session, the Governor issued his third reorganization executive order which combined the Division of Energy in the Department of Business and Economic Development with the Institute for Environmental Quality into a new Institute for Energy and Environmental Resources. The purpose of the consolidation, the Governor noted, was to provide an identifiable energy agency that can "balance the competing demands of environmental protection and economic growth."

Energy reorganization had already been an issue in the prior Spring 1977 session of the Legislture. In the closing hours of the last day of the session, a bill was hastily passed that would have placed the Energy Division in the Department of Mines and minerals, an agency devoted primarily to mine safety regulation. The bill was later amendatorily vetoed by the Governor, who objected to certain provisions that would have changed the composition of the State Mining Board. By the time the amendatory veto was considered in the following fall session, a substantial amount of legislative opposition had been generated against the bill, opposition which had not had time to surface in the confusion that prevailed in the waning moments of the previous session. The bill was then killed by the Legislature, giving the Governor and his staff time to prepare their own proposal.

As in the consideration of his first two executive orders, the House took an active role in dealing with the Governor's energy reorganization proposal. During the course of hearings by the House Select Committee on Government Organization, the Committee suggested modifying the Governor's proposal to include the State's three scientific surveys in the Department of Registration and Education. Over the years the Natural History, Water and Geological Surveys, headquartered on the campus of the University of Illinois at Urbana-Champaign, had developed national and international reputations for scientific research on a wide variety of natural resource issues—functions quite different from Registration and Education's occupational licensing responsibilities, but quite compatible with the research and policy responsibilities of the Energy Division and the Institute for Environmental Quality. The Governor agreed to the suggestion and a compromie bill was developed creating the Institute of Natural Resources, integrating the surveys into the Governor's original proposal. This time the legislative vehicle was a Senate bill introduced by the Administration under Republican sponsorship to implement the provisions of the executive order.

Creation of the Institute helped to further institutionalize the procedure for consideration of executive orders reorganizing State agencies. There was a growing—although certainly not universal—recognition within the General Assembly that the initiative for reorganization rested with the Governor and that the initiative was properly expressed through executive orders. On the Executive's part, there was a recognition that the General Assembly preferred to implement reorganization through legislation. Thus, for the first time, the Governor initiated the introduction of implementing legislation along with the order. Both the House and Senate had created separate committees to consider reorganization orders, providing a single point in each chamber for consideration of virtually all reorganization proposals.

From the beginning, however, the House had taken a greater interest in the reorganization process. This was first evident in legislative consideration of the Governor's first two executive orders, when the House reorganization committee dealt with the Governor's Office in setting the ground rules for dealing with executive reorganization and took the lead in reaching compromises over the content of implementing legislation. Much the same pattern was followed in the creation of the Institute of Natural Resources. The active involvement of the House Committee had several positive effects on the Governor's reorganization efforts. It, in effect, created a small legislative constituency that was generally favorable toward reorganization as a process even though the Committee might disagree on the substance of a particular proposal. The working relationship that evolved between the Committee and the Governor's Office also helped to establish a bi-partisan basis for reorganization, since the Committee, like both houses, was controlled by the Democrats. The Republican Governor clearly needed Democratic support to pass his reorganization plans.

In addition, the House, by rule, developed a separate procedure for handling executive orders, providing, for example, that any Committee bills implementing executive orders were exempt from the deadlines applying to other bills. Both the executive and legislative branches were becoming more comfortable with the process, if not the substance, of reorganization under the 1970 Constitution.

In Governor Thompson's State of the State Message of March 1979, he again announced his intention to introduce reorganization proposals to the General Assembly, this time in two areas likely to be quite controversial: economic and community development and civil rights. The first proposal was Executive Order Number 3 creating a Department of Commerce and Community Affairs, combining the departments of Business and Economic Development, Local Government Affairs and the Governor's Office of Manpower and Human Development. The second was a bill creating a Department of Human Rights, combining the Fair Employment Practices Commission, the Commission on Human Relations and the Department of Equal Employment Opportunity.

The human rights proposal was introduced as legislation because it not only combined the State's anti-discrimination programs into a single enforcement agency but also expanded coverage of the existing laws to include new jurisdictions such as public accommodations. The Governor's power to reorganize by executive order does not include the power to create new substantive powers or functions. The Department of Commerce and Community Affairs was a proposal to transfer functions only and thus subject to the executive order process under the Consitution.

Subsequent legislative consideration of the proposal to create a Department of Commerce and Community Affairs illustrates how the use of executive orders can create certain tactical advantages for the Governor's Office. Introduction of the Governor's executive order had generated opposition from both business and labor. Business groups wanted the new agency to emphasize only promotion and industrial development activities, while labor objected to the inclusion of the Governor's Office of Manpower, which administers the Comprehensive Employment and Training Act, preferring that it be part of the Department of Labor. Since executive orders cannot be amended, attention shifted to compromise over implementing legislation in the House. Changes were made at the amending stage and the bill was moved to third reading ready for a final House vote. Under House rules, all House bills had to be acted upon by May 25 or they automatically died. The compromise bill was not called by the Speaker, who along with other Democrats had argued strongly for keeping a separate department for local government affairs. Meanwhile the constitutional deadline for legislative consideration of executive orders—60 calendar days from the date of delivery to the General Assembly, or April 29 in this case—was growing near. If neither chamber disapproved the order by that date, it automatically became law. Both Houses adjourned on May 25 for a long Memorial Day weekend. Only the Senate was scheduled to be in session on Tuesday, May 29, the last day of the 60 day period. When legislators began arriving in Springfield on Tuesday morning it became clear that the Governor's order would become law unless the Senate voted it down. A motion to disapprove the order fell four votes short of the necessary 30 votes that afternoon, primarily because of Democratic absentees in what was a close partisan vote; the order then became law.[15]

The experience with Executive Order Number 3 stemmed from confusion over the exact date on which the 60 day deadline was to occur and an understandable legislative tendency to concentrate on the more familiar implementing legislation rather than the order itself. The constitutional provision for executive reorganization clearly gives the Governor a strong mechanism for initiating reorganization proposals and gives him a substantial amount of leverage in getting legislative approval.

The House bill was subsequently resurrected and passed in the House but failed in the Senate, leaving the executive order unchanged. The Department of Human Rights, however, failed to receive full legislative approval by the time the General Assembly adjourned on July 1.

Based upon Governor Thompson's reorganization efforts during his first three years in office, it appears that an across-the-board reorganization will not occur, but that the Governor will attempt to reorganize on a selective basis in each annual legislative session. One of the major consequences of Thompson's use of the executive order process has been the establishment of precedent and procedure for the consideration and implementation of executive reorganization orders. To formalize legislative consideration of executive orders, the General Assembly passed the "Executive Reorganization Implementation Act" in the 1979 Session. The bill provides a set of ground rules for considering orders, including a specific procedure for determining the expiration of the 60-day deadline. It also directs the Legislative Reference Bureau to draft revisory legislation to implement executive orders.

Reflections

From this brief summary of efforts for executive reorganization, it is clear that administrative reform of any magnitude does not come easy in Illinois. The State is probably not atypical in this regard. The pattern is for the Executive and Legislature to attack relatively narrow problems (e.g., energy or the environment) with solutions that result in the creation of new agencies, generally increasing the number of agencies, seldom abolishing or consolidating them. Every function and group wants its "own" agency.

At the federal level, Herbert Kaufman has shown that agencies have great ability to survive. Those with strong constituencies tend to become immortal. More volnerable are staff agencies that do not have natural constituencies. Thus, reorganization tends to involve such agencies, as illustrated by the creation in 1977 of the Illinois Department of Administrative Services from the merger of the departments of general services and finance—an event that generated little controversy. But in general the total number of agencies tends to increase gradually in both the federal government and in the states.[16]

For those interested in administrative reorganization, one major question is whether it is better to try across-the board reorganization or to focus on a smaller area of concern. Former Governor Jimmy Carter thought we should attack the big scene. His reasoning was:

> The most difficult thing is to reorganize incrementally. If you do it one tiny little phase at a time, then all those who see their influence threatened will combine their efforts in a sort of secretive way. They come out of the rat holes and they'll concentrate on undoing what you're trying to do. But if you can have a bold enough, comprehensive enough proposal to rally the interest and support of the general electorate, then you can overcome that special interest type lobbying pressure.[17]

But, in Illinois at least, across-the-board reorganizations have little chance of success for the same reasons that Joseph Califano described with regard to the national scene:

> Reorganizations are enormously difficult to achieve politically. In the Congress, committee members covet their jurisdictions as bees protect their hives: taking away any honey without being stung is not a task for political amateurs. They have potent allies among their parochial cohorts in the legislative branch, the executive bureaucracy, and the special interests that are aroused by any attempt to disturb existing cozy relationships.[18]

State legislative committees, in Illinois at least, are not quite as strong as congressional committees, but still the State Legislature as an institution is a hindrance that should not be disregarded. This was most recently illustrated in Illinois by the insistance of the Legislature in 1977 that there be a separate Office of State Fire Marshall when the consolidated Department of Law Enforcement was created by the Governor's executive order. Also, the legislature insisted on putting the executive order into statutory language.

Further, the role of the bureaucracy as a negative force should not be disregarded, particularly as the bureaucracies become unionized.[19] Reform by definition challenges bureaucratic routines and the personal security these routines offer many individuals.

Why have broad-based reorganizations in Illinois met with little success for the past half century? There are many reasons. One is the national inclination to resist change at all levels of government. The unknown impacts of reorganization are a problem for many people, especially for those who might be losers. The number of proposals for restructuring local governments that lose in referenda illustrate the wide concern of the unknown future.

Second, reorganization proposals are usually made in a sort of vacuum, with actual goals unclear. Efficiency and economy alone do not get very many supporters, especially when someone's agency is to be dismantled. This is so even if the proposed change is really little more than a symbolic act.

Other reasons for lack of success are political. As Garnett and Levine say, reorganization is a political act. There are winners and losers. Far-reaching reorganization is usually proposed in abstract situations. It discounts the concerned interest groups. It also discounts the bureaucracy as a pressure group to maintain the status quo.

The Legislature will continue to be a negative force to reorganization, especially if it would help the Executive of another party. In the last few years state legislatures have been "strengthened" in states such as Illinois, and they insist upon their prerogatives. They will resist reorganization by executive order unless their role includes more than approval or veto. In a sharply divided state such as Illinois, there is considerable legislative distrust of anything resembling an executive power grab—a category that can include any broad-based reorganization.

There will always be strong support for the status quo. Many feel that they know what they have and do not care to risk change.

Conclusion

Illinois, the leader in state reorganization in 1917, has had few rar-reaching reorganizations since then, and probably will not in the future. The tendency will be for more agencies to be created, as in the past, with some relatively minor reorganization taking place. It is possible that "sunset" legislation will be adopted in Illinois, but it is doubtful if it will have any major effects other than to eliminate some minor licensing or regulatory functions. In general, too many forces work against broad-based reorganization for it to succeed—political pressures, bureaucracy pressures, interest group pressures and legislative pressures.

The policy implications of extensive reorganization are very few, because there have been very few reorganizations. Policy implications come about from new programs or new agencies, such as in the energy and environment fields.

It is very likely that actions of the federal government will have more policy implications for the states than will administrative reorganization. And on the organization charts of most state governments there is no place for the federal government. This is unfortunate and unrealistic. Hopefully future reorganization efforts, no matter how selective they may be, will pay more attention to the crucial dimension of intergovernmental relations which affects nearly every state agency.

NOTES

[1]Judith Nicholson, "State Administrative Organization Activities, 1976–1977," *The Book of the States 1978–79* (Lexington, Kentucky: The Council of State Governments, 1978), p. 105.

[2]*Orderly Government: Organizing for Manageability,* Report of the Illinois Task Force on Governmental Reorganization, (November 3, 1976).

[3]Joseph A. Schlesinger, "The Politics of the Executive," in *Politics in the American States,* ed. by Herbert Jacob and Kenneth N. Vines (Boston: Little, Brown, 1965), p. 229.

[4]One paper that did was Samuel K. Gove, "Why Strong Governors?" in *National Civic Review* 53 (March 1964) pp. 131–136.

[5]James L. Garnett and Charles H. Levine, "State Executive Branch Reorganization: Patterns and Performance," paper prepared for the 1977 Annual Meeting, American Political Science Association, Washington, D.C., p. 22.

[6]*Orderly Government, op. cit.,* pp. 3–4.

[7]The source for much of the material between 1917 and 1967 is Arvid Hammers, "Three Executive Branch Reorganizations in Illinois," unpublished Masters Thesis, Southern Illinois University, Carbondale, June 1971.

[8]In a 1953 article, I termed the action on the recommendations "moderately successful." See Gove, "Reorganization in Illinois," *National Municipal Review* 42 (1953) pp. 502–06, 511.

[9]*Management, Organization, and Functioning in the Executive Branch,* report of the Commission on State Government—Illinois (January 1967), p. 131.

[10]Interestingly, the executive committee staff director had been staff director of the 1949 commission and chairman of the 1965 commission.

[11]The convention wisely did not attempt to limit the number of departments that could be established, as has been done in other states.

[12]Illinois Constitution, 1970, Art. V, sec. 11. In explaining this action, the convention's executive committee said: "The effect of the section here proposed is to emphasize that the Governor has responsibility for formulating reorganization plans, comprehensive or selective, for the agencies under his discretion. His initiative should replace the common inertia, so that carefully thought out changes will, periodically, be placed before the General Assembly. . . ."

[13]The new constitution provided a two-year term to get Illinois on a schedule of electing Governors and other State officials in the off-year nonpresidential elections. Candidates elected in 1978 and thereafter serve four-year terms.

[14]"Reorganization and Review," House Republican committee staff report (August 1977), p. 5.

[15]Basil Talbott, Jr., "Dems Loss to Thompson Lob," Chicago *Sun-Times,* June 7, 1979.

[16]See Herbert Kaufman, *Are Government Organizations Immortal?* (Washington, D.C.: The Brookings Institution, 1976).

[17]Neal Peirce, "Structural Reform of Bureaucracy Grows Rapidly," *National Journal* 7, no. 14 (April 5, 1975), pp. 502–508.

[18]Joseph A. Califano, Jr., *A Presidential Nation* (New York: W.W. Norton, 1975), p. 27.

[19]For an excellent example of the bureaucracy fighting a reorganization proposal in the federal government and its implications to broader reorganizations, see Michael P. Balzano, *Reorganizing the Federal Bureaucracy: The Rhetoric and the Reality* (Washington, D.C.: American Enterprise Institute, 1977).

CHAPTER **25**

Implementing Public Policy: Government Without Glamor

Paula Wolff

Implementing public policy is typically not mentioned in discussion of political genius. Making government do what must be done to reach an objective is a thankless and frustrating job; yet it is the reason government exists.

In state government, the process of implementation is also typically overlooked as a significant determinant in the success or failure of any elected official. Yet, if policy is not implemented, a politician will appear inept in "keeping his word" on policy pronouncements. On the other hand, an elected official whose implementation is good will often not get political credit for this, since the public is rarely made aware of a policy or program when it is working well, only when it is working badly or not at all. Why learn about a frustrating and unacknowledged dimension of public policy? Because it is the source of government activity; it is law in action.

Using examples of policy implementation from Governor Thompson's administration, this chapter will describe various types of implementation and demonstrate its importance.

What Constitutes Implementation?

In Illinois government, policy can be implemented in a number of ways. The four most obvious are: through legislation, through court order, through the budget process, through administrative action in the bureaucracy—and through various combinations of all four. Until recently it was common for public administrators to advocate a dichotomy between "politics" and "administration" and with it the principle that only a "neutrally competent" administrative route to implementation was suited to modern government. Those wishing to adhere to this principle would be particularly frustrated by the implementation experience in Illinois government.

When policy is implemented by either detailed legislation or court order, it is usually viewed as an inappropriate method: it is said to violate the doctrine of separation of powers. Courts and the Legislature—according to some text books and constitutions — should articulate policy, but not try to implement it. They are to paint with the broad brush. The Legislature can say: citizens should have access to all rules of operation made by an agency, but a law should not be passed outlining each step which must be taken in order to make rules accessible. The Legislature, it is said, should not be part of the implementation process — implementation should be done by those responsible for the execution of the law, the executive branch.

Legislative Implementation

There are many fine examples of how the Legislature violates this theory and paints like an impressionist with hundreds of small dots and no broad strokes. One example can illustrate the point.

The Illinois Legislature tried for many years to pass and to have a governor sign an Administrative Procedures Act, similar to the federal one.[1] Finally in 1977 one was passed and signed by Governor Thompson. At the time, he indicated the importance of opening the agency rule-making process to public scrutiny. For the first time, Illinois citizens would be able formally to comment on the rules of government which could dramatically affect their lives.[2]

The new law was 21 sections long and contained provisions of great detail about how the process was to work.[3] The act set up a Joint Committee of 16 legislators to "oversee" the Administrative Procedures Act implementation process. In its first year, the Joint Committee had an appropriation of $250,000 and 6 staff members. In its second year the staff was 20 and the appropriation $381,500. Going into its third year, the requested appropriation is $598,000.[4]

The Administrative Procedures Act prescribes the process for drafting and certifying rules in great detail. The Joint Committee makes sure it happens. After one year of operation, the Joint Committee published its annual report,[5] indicating its involvement in the rule-making process. It appears that the legislators and their staff are an integral part of the implementation of rule-making, particularly through the Commission's right to object to rules. Agencies of State government published 507 sets of rules for public/legislative review in 1978. Of those 72 were formally objected to by the Joint Committee. A total of 185 had, according to the Committee, "serious problems."[6] The basis for objection to the rules fall into two main categories: (1) the agency is making rules in an area in which it has no statutory authority to do so and (2) the agency is making rules that are too vague.

The second category was used to open a door that puts the Joint Committee foresquare in the process of implementation of agency rule-making. The objections are that the agency has not articulated to the Joint Committee the public policy grounds or the objectives of its actions. In other words, the Joint Committee has moved from a body which oversees or monitors the rule-making process (e.g., being sure that the *form* of the Administrative Procedures Act is followed, thereby allowing adequate public participation, etc.) to a body which objects to rules because those rules do not follow from a policy or objective, the "substance" of which should be available for scrutiny by the Joint Committee, under its broad definition of "rule." A law designed to allow the Legislature to oversee the rule-making process has resulted in creation of a strong legislative body which monitors and participates in the implementation of policy through agency rule-making.[7]

Of course, agency directors do not have to do what the legislators suggest in their "oversight" capacity; but in practice legislators exert considerable leverage because in other capacities they pass appropriation bills to fund the agencies and legislate the mission for the agencies. The Legislature is now deeply involved in "Executive" rule-making and implementation of public policy. As one director put it, "Signing the bill may have been the biggest 'oversight' of them all," from the viewpoint of the bureaucracy.

Judicial Implementation

The courts are also prone to be involved in implementation. One example of this is the Lake Michigan water diversion case. This is a situation in which the court is doing the hard job of implementing a program for which—a cynic might say—no other branch of government wants to have responsibility. It is a program to dispense water among needy communities, making no one happy, because every community thinks it deserves more.

The issue can be traced back to 1913, when water was diverted from Lake Michigan to maintain sanitary conditions in waterways between Lake Michigan and Lockport.[8] There were court decrees concerning diversion in 1930, 1938 and 1967; each entailed litigation which lasted for many years. The decree in 1930 specified that the Supreme Court would retain jurisdiction, which it does up to this day.

How broad are the brush strokes of implementation by the Court? The decrees specify in long tables, for many communities, the maximum number of cubic feet of water which can be diverted and for what purposes. Even the accounting procedures used to measure diversion are approved by the Court. On April 23, 1979, the Supreme Court entered an order appointing a Special Master for diversion. In this case, the judiciary is deeply involved in the technical elements of implementing the policy to divert Lake Michigan water for public use.[9]

Implementation by the Budget Process

The budget process is another method of implementing policy. Since 1969, with the creation of the Bureau of the Budget, this has been one of the strongest management tools available to the Governor. Not only is policy given life through the process; but the Governor can use the budgeting system to retain control over a program as it is being implemented.

The first point is obvious: no money, no program. The Governor can announce creative initiatives to his heart's content, but until money is appropriated or diverted from another activity, no new services can be delivered.

There is a good example of this. In 1978, the Capital Development Board (CDB), the State's agency for designing and contracting for building of public facilities and capital works, issued a report on how to "revitalize" East St. Louis through capital projects.[10] The report outlined various capital construction projects to restore the area. While no specific dollar amount was indicated in the report, the price tag on the revitalization would have been hundreds of millions of dollars.

Funding for these projects has not been made available except for railroad relocation, sewers and some port design. The CDB report, the blueprint for revitalization, a complete and well-documented analysis with a noble object, sits on a shelf, unimplemented. In a time when most State agencies are expected to continue to deliver services while being funded with budget percentage increases lower than the inflation rate, a monumental program such as the East St. Louis one is simply not fundable and, therefore, not implemented.

The use of the budgeting process to *control* implementation is a very effective administrative device. A good example of this is a 1978 law[11] establishing a "Home Health Care" service. The intent of the law was to keep people who need health care—but not 24-hour supervision—from being unnecessarily removed from their homes and placed in costly and impersonal institutions; they could receive needed services in their homes.

The concept, consistent with one of Governor Thompson's major human services priorities, deinstitutionalization, was seen as superb. The major problem was one of implementation. No state had undertaken such a program, made available on a statewide basis, so it was virtually impossible to anticipate how extensive the demand for it would be or how much it would cost. In making the decision to sign the bill, Governor Thompson also had to assess how the cost could be held to a reasonable and predetermined level—to avoid creating a "budget overrun." Some advisors were arguing that such a law could—and would—"break the bank," because of its broad applicability. Illinois in 1978 was just beginning to rebuild its State budget surplus. The savings account in the bank was being built up, but could not be dipped into very far for new programs. Cost estimates for the program were as high as $200 million per year; this was almost half of the new "savings account."

At meetings with the Governor, the cost of implementation was the central focus of arguments about signing the bill. The Governor made the decision to sign the bill, to have the program run on a trial basis and to budget $6 million for one year. The entire first stage of implementation centered on the creation of a system under which some budgetary control could be exerted so that no more than $6 million would be spent. The Department of Public Aid, with the Governor's Office program staff and the Bureau of the Budget, reviewed possible methods to control costs yet make the program widely available. Eventually, a process was designed which would screen people for the service; that system was based on the financial need of those applying. The implementation of the new home health care program rested on the development of the fiscal evaluation system. Not one cent of the appropriation was spent until the fiscal controls were in place. The budget controls were the heart of implementation.

After the fiscal control system was designed, procedures were established to translate the system into activities to provide home health care to those in need of it. Case workers interviewed people for the program, and Department personel contracted with health care specialists to provide the services.

Implementation through Executive Administrative Action

Administrative action accounts by far for the largest proportion of implementation. Administrative action for implementation can, for theoretical purposes, be divided into two categories: (1) the creation of implementation procedures by which a program will be administered and (2) the "hands-on" implementation which actually provides the activity which "creates" the program, e.g., service delivery of foster care, building highways. One example of this can illustrate how the implementation process can work. This is the story of the Donated Funds Initiative. It is a complicated story; but it illustrates how politics, policy, federal bureaucracy and public pressure all come together in the implementation of a program. A most complex project was launched and implemented in eight months, under the close scrutiny of an election campaign. The implementation of the Donated Funds Initiative, while primarily an example of implementation by administrative action, also included legislative and budget involvement.

There were two strong motivations for the Donated Funds Initiative (DFI): one was the private sector people involved in delivering social services in Illinois, the other was a fiscal or budget problem. The human problem had a number of dimensions. In 1975, 1976 and 1977, Governor Thompson discovered while campaigning and serving as Governor that the State was providing some human services which various communities did not want. At the same time, he learned that some citizens and communities were not getting services they needed. The Governor also discovered one set of extremely disgruntled organizations in the State, the human service providers. These are people who work in the "voluntary sector" to provide human services—foster care homes, day care, ex-convict job training, meals on wheels to the aged, etc. Under the administration of Governor Walker, many of these groups felt that it had been difficult to work with State agencies. Contracts were not signed promptly, if at all; rates had been frozen for years; confrontation was the modus operandi.

The budget problem was a more technical one. Under the federal Social Security Act, Title XX,[12] the states were asked to develop a plan of services to be available to poor people and to document that poor people utilized these services. For appropriate services and usage, the federal government would reimburse 50 cents of every dollar spent. Unfortunately by 1976, under the prior administration, $239 million had been spent for services in anticipation of federal reimbursement, but only $136 million or 57 percent over a 2 year period had been reimbursed (at the 50 percent rate) as having been spent appropriately. A total of $132 million for a four year period was in dispute—the State saying it had been rightfully spent, the federal government saying it had not. The upshot of the argument was, however, that millions of dollars had been spent in Illinois in anticipation of half of it being reimbursed; yet no reimbursement was forthcoming. In addition, the federal government had established a "ceiling" for reimbursements for Title XX services for each state, based on the state's population of people under the poverty line. Illinois could have claimed up to $142.4 million under its federal fiscal year 1977 ceiling; yet the State was going to claim only $120.5 million for its services—$22.1 million short of its (maximum) entitlement. Some money had been expended under the assumption that it would be reimbursed; yet it was not. Thompson as a candidate had criticized the prior administration for not "reaching the Title XX ceiling." As soon as he was elected, he was confronted with the problem of reaching that ceiling himself. In fairness to Walker, many states had experienced similar or worse problems—and HEW had also given Ogilvie problems with reimbursement—this is a generic, continuing problem in intergovernmental relations.

To provide needed services and to "reach the ceiling," the Governor decided in August 1977 to launch the Donated Funds Initiative. On September 10, 1977, at the United Way Governor's Social Services Breakfast for human service providers he announced a new program:

> In order to improve the cooperation between state government and private human service agencies, I am today announcing an expansion of up to $10 million in community-based social services predicated on your ability to "match" Title XX funding. This means that for every 1 dollar raised on the local level we will add 3 federal dollars from those allocated to the State of Illinois. Under current projections, we anticipate the total amount available under this program will grow to $20 million in the following year, Fiscal '79.

The object of the program was to permit local decision-making, so that communities could "buy" human services which those communities felt were needed, rather than having the State or federal government provide services unsuited for that community. In addition, local organizations would put up their money to get federal money back. Ten million dollars of new money for the ceiling would be there, eligible and claimable if a sound system were established. With the announcement of the program came the first—and easy—step of implementation. The hard work of designing the process and putting it into action followed.

The first phase of implementation, the design of the process, entailed using the Governor's Human Services Subcabinet to make policy decisions about how the program would look: what agency would run it, how local groups would be involved, who would choose the groups, what organization would put up the local money to "match" the federal dollars, etc. Answering all of these policy questions was the "discretionary element" of implementation. While the major policy decision had been made by the Governor (i.e., There will be a Donated Funds Program), a series of less significant questions which lie between policy and implementation ("impolmentation") had to be answered.

The result of these decisions was, among other things, a determination that legislation outlining the proposal had to be drafted and that a separate, special account for the appropriation had to be set up. The Governor's Program staff, the Bureau of the Budget, and the Department of Public Aid, along with the twenty human service "allied agencies" serviced under Title XX worked together to reach agreement on the system.

The "hands-on" side of implementation began on several fronts. The legislation was drafted. The local voluntary sector groups and social service clients throughout the State were mobilized to help pass the legislation. Never has such a large appropriation for a social service program of this innovative nature, and requiring such statewide teamwork, passed the General Assembly.

The next step of the "hands-on" implementation process included the actual activities which would cause money to flow from the federal government, through the State process (dotting all the "i's" and crossing all the "t's" so that the federal government would not disallow the money) to the local human service groups. These steps involved having twenty State agencies solicit proposals from local groups throughout the State. The United Way of Illinois set up a system for donating the local share of funds and for insuring that the services would be paid for even if the federal government disallowed the money. The local agencies submitted proposals that went through a review process by the appropriate human service agency (e.g., Mental Health for a proposal for the developmentally disabled) and then by a team from the Governor's program staff, the Department of Public Aid and the Bureau of the Budget. A tight and complicated contract system to pass $10 million through governments to local units was also set up and implemented.

Finally, by August 1978, human beings other than State employees began to benefit from the process. Over fifty proposals had been funded under the donated funds initiative. Services were being provided by neighborhood groups to their local citizens. State government—against the time-honored bureaucratic tradition—actually was asking citizens to tell government what services they wanted and needed and then *not* creating a bureaucracy to provide the services, but rather, permitting existing groups to provide the services. And in his debate on human services, conducted as part of the 1978 reelection campaign, Governor Thompson could reply to the criticism that the State had not reached the ceiling in that year. Illinois would reach the Title XX ceiling in 1978, he noted, based in part on the services delivered under the Donated Funds Initiative. Furthermore, wherever the Governor went in the State, there were Donated Funds Initiative projects—for battered wives, for ex-offenders, for abused children. . . .

Conclusion

If you are still reading this chapter, you have learned the most significant point about implementation—it can be beastly tedious! There is not much sex-appeal to setting up guidelines or establishing contractual language. Were there not implementation, however, there would not be government. There would be laws on the books; but there would be no services delivered to citizens, no taxes levied and no inspections made of hospitals. On the other side of the coin, however, without implementation in Illinois there would also be nor horse-shoer certification, no peach-seller inspection, no cosmotologist licensing. Implementation makes both the grand and the tawdry programs of government live. Doubtless future Governors, Legislatures, and managers will gnash their teeth over programs implemented by the Thompson Administration, but rendered obsolete by changing conditions. . . . The challenge is to devise ways of making it as easy to terminate such activities as it was to initiate them when it was timely!

But for now all we can observe is that, between 1977 and 1979, the Thompson Administration has rarely been cited for failing to carry through its projects. In that two year period, implemented projects have ranged from water conservation demonstrations, launched by the Natural Resources Subcabinet in two communities and costing less than $50,000 to a massive $360 million road program. In between these ends of the continuum, there is a $500,000 welfare/work demonstration project, estimated to save the State over $2 million a year; it keeps or takes off welfare over 100 persons a month. There is a pilot immunization project in Rockford and East St. Louis under which local McDonald's restaurants give free hamburgers to children showing proof of immunization. There is a statewide clean air and clean water program, for the first time setting standards and enforcement procedures for sulfur dioxide pollution or sediment erosion under which steel mills and farmers alike are working with the State to guarantee a healthy environment. The Department of Transportation is now mowing strips beside some highways because the Department of Conservation wants to increase Illinois's wildlife habitat. The two new prisons will be partially serviced by solar energy. Tickets are issued to those unentitled to park in spaces reserved for the handicapped.

Each of these activities, big and small, started as an idea and ended up as government in your life—only because of implementation: the frustrating, unheralded heart of public policy.

NOTES

[1]Cf., Veto message to House Bill 1706 by Richard B. Ogilvie, which says, *inter alai* ". . . insufficient legislative consideration has been given to the exact ramification the bill would have for many diverse types of State agencies . . ."

[2]September 1977, Public Act 80-1035.

[3]*Illinois Revised Statutes* Chapter 127, § 1001; Public Law 80-1035, 1978.

[4]House Bill 1497, 1979.

[5]*Annual Report, Joint Committee on Administrative Rules,* February 1979, 259 pages.

[6]The objections in about 50 percent of the cases result in modification of the rule; in about 20 percent of the cases; the rules are withdrawn.

[7]This analysis is based on a report by Vivien Ravdin to the Governor's Administrative Rules Commission, July 13, 1979.

[8]At this time a permit was issued by the Secretary of War which became the legal basis of the suit.

[9]*Wisconsin et. al., v. Illinois et. al.,* 388 U.S. 426, October Term, 1967.

[10]*The East St. Louis Area: An Overview of State Capital Projects and Policies,* July 1977.

[11]Public Act 80-1411; HB 2691, signed August 30, 1979.

[12]Title XX, Grants to States for Services; Social Security Act, 42 U.S.C. § 1397; Public Law 93-647; United States House of Representatives Document 93-117. For a full account of an earlier episode with federal funding of social services see Martha Derthick *Uncontrolled Spending* (Washington, D.C.: Brookings, 1974).

CHAPTER **26**

Illinois as Technocracy: Governing Big Science and Technology at the State Level

Boyd Keenan

In an era of space laboratories and inter-continental nuclear missiles, why focus on state government as an element in the governance of science and technology? The response to the nation's first major nuclear power plant accident near Harrisburg, Pennsylvania, on March 28, 1979 offers an emphatic answer to such a question. Pennsylvania's Governor was at the center of crisis management during the actual episode. And Pennsylvania State government will be closely tied to the examination of the cause of that accident for many years to come. Though the handling of technology is almost always viewed as the task of the national government, an emergency situation such as that at the Three Mile Island power plant inevitably alerts us to the reality that the individual state remains a vital element in managing big science and technology. Where the state role is weak, the public will pay the price.

In our federal system, there is simply no way to avoid the recognition that states—at least the large industrial states—are "technocracies" in their own right. Major signals may come from Washington, but certain large states have functioned for many years as technological sub-systems within our federal establishment.

By some measures, the State of Illinois is as massive a technocracy as any state in the union. The claim by Illinois chambers of commerce and other "boosters" that the State is the birthplace of more significant scientific and technological developments than any other state is not entirely chauvinistic. Indeed, the roots of many such achievements—including nuclear power—are buried in Illinois soil.

The purpose of this chapter is to give the reader some notion of how State government in Illinois has become deeply involved in the politics and governance of what are sometimes called "big science" and "big technology." The extent to which the states have become subtle but integral components in the management of such enterprises is known by few. Perhaps as much as any other state, Illinois has become a partner—with the federal government, universities and the private sector—both in stimulating the creation of these massive entities and in their operation.

It is unusual to lump "science" and "technology" together as is done in this chapter. More often, an effort is made to define science as a pure research activity, define technology as an applied activity and then move towards distinct discussions of the two. Such definitions contribute little towards an understanding of how government and politics are embedded in the effort to handle massive scientific and technological problems.

Science and Government: Early Prominence of the Private Sector

In Illinois and the nation the private sector has until recently taken the lead in scientific developments and technological applications. The state role emerged slowly under the impetus of the public implications of centralized generation of electric power. The implications were clear in dynamos on display at the Chicago World's Columbian Exhibition of 1893, but it was not until 1914 that the Legislature created an energy regulatory agency, the Public Utility Commission. Significantly, this was done at the urging of the utility industry, which feared that government take-over was the alternative.

While Illinois achieved spectacular success as an agricultural producer and industrial giant, the role of state government was limited to the important research and development activities of the land grant universities, including the well-known water, geological and "natural history" surveys as well as growing science and engineering laboratories. The major scientific, technological and educational institutions remained in the private sector.

The early history of nuclear power illustrates the growing role of the federal government in promoting and conducting scientific "R and D". Under the impetus of World War II the first nuclear chain reaction was conducted at the University of Chicago Metalurgical Laboratory. At the war's end the future of government laboratories became a major problem, and without state involvement the Chicago activities were transferred to Argonne Laboratory in 1947, under the jurisdiction of the U.S. Atomic Energy Commission.

Some of the world's most pioneering research on the possibilities for nuclear generation of electric power has been carried on at the Argonne National Laboratory in the intervening years. Commonwealth Edison Company, the electric utility which serves Chicago and much of Northern Illinois, was among the first utilities in the country to cooperate with scientists at Argonne. Such cooperation was partially responsible for this firm's success in placing the world's first large-scale privately-owned nuclear reactor into operation at Dresden, Illinois near Morris, in 1960.

Science and Government: A New Beginning in 1960

The year of 1960 is also a convenient one for beginning a review of the conscious effort of Illinois leaders to guide the State's involvement in mushrooming science and technology. In November of 1960, Illinois voters elected Otto Kerner of Chicago as their Governor and John F. Kennedy was the nation's choice to become President. In a real sense technological marvels gave both Kennedy and Kerner the chance to hold high office. Without the airplane and television, neither would likely have been able to wage successful campaigns. The presidential experience with science leadership presents strong parallels with the experience of Illinois governors. Also the federal government has had a major influence on the state role.

In 1979, midst the fear of nuclear accidents, possible disruption of oil supplies from the Middle East and other technologically-related concerns, it is difficult to recapture the optimism of 1961. Much of the hopefulness of President Kennedy's inaugural address in January of 1961 was derived from his conviction that science provided our nation with vast powers of good. He summed up his feelings this way: "Let both sides seek to invoke the wonders of science instead of its terrors. Together let us explore the stars, conquer the deserts, eradicate disease, tap the ocean depths and encourage the arts and commerce."[1]

The other "side" to which President Kennedy alluded of course, was the Soviet Union. In October of 1957, barely three years before Kennedy's election, the Soviet had launched its space satellite, Sputnik, and the United States was shocked into a thorough re-examination of its scientific activities. During the early years of the Eisenhower administration prior to Sputnik, there had been little effort to place scientific advisors close to the President in the White House. However, after the Soviet launching, the long-standing Presidential Science Advisory Committee (PSAC) was moved directly into the White House, where it was to become a much more active and effective device for assisting the President. At the same time, the post of Special Assistant for Science and Technology was created to provide a means for matching the activities of PSAC to the needs of the President. But the popular consensus was that President Eisenhower had not been able to create a sense of excitement surrounding the scientific and technological challenges of the day.

Kennedy thus used his presidential campaign, his inauguration address and other opportunities to call attention to Russia's apparent superiority in space and a growing number of other scientific fields. Early in his administration, the President initiated a national program to strengthen civilian technology, including the appointment of an Assistant Secretary of Commerce for Science and Technology. On many occasions Kennedy urged state governors to follow his lead in seeking ways of applying modern science and technology to the solving of social problems. He also urged the governors to study the federal organizational attempts to bring science into a central position in the White House. He quickly strengthened the arrangements initiated by Eisenhower and established a new Office of Science and Technology in the Executive Office of the President. Alert governors around the country were seeking ways to create similar mechanisms in the state capitals.

Governor Kerner was among such governors. By Executive Order he established the Governor's Science Advisory Council in 1964. Probably no governor in the nation was as successful as Kerner in initially persuading outstanding scientists and engineers to serve on his Science Advisory Council. Its first chairman was Dr. Frederick Seitz, distinguished physicist, dean of the University of Illinois Graduate School and soon to be elected to the presidency of the National Academy of Sciences. In mid-1965, Dr. Seitz described Governor Kerner's advisory group as follows:

> About a year and a half ago, Governor Kerner asked me to assist him in the creation of a science advisory council which would help him and our State to review matters of pure and applied science relevant to the welfare of the State of Illinois in order that our State would be better prepared to deal with many of the problems which our community faces in these days of shifting science and technology.[2]

Dr. Seitz included this comment in a letter to a leader in the Illinois State Senate. The purpose of the letter was to solicit the support of this Senator in passage of legislation which would give the Governor's Science Advisory Committee a statutory foundation. According to Dr. Seitz, a law creating such a body "would place the work of the Council on a much more firm foundation and would expedite its role in providing increased communication between the scientists and engineers in Illinois and the Legislative and Executive Branches of our State Government."[3]

In 1965 the Illinois General Assembly did create such a statutory Science Advisory Council, and Dr. Seitz continued to chair the new group. Ironically, by the time the statutory body was established, the State of Illinois was involved in a nuclear activity which created many more headlines in Illinois than had the secret Manhattan Project nearly twenty-five years earlier.

A nation-wide competition had begun in 1965 among almost all the states to determine which would become the site of the world's largest accelerator or—as popularly known—"atom smasher." The story of how this "prize" accelerator was won by Illinois reveals graphically both how national science policy was made in the sixties and how states became involved in Federal decision-making.

Those people who deal with atom smashers are specialists in particle physics, or high-energy physics. In experiments, sub-atomic particles are bombarded by other particles at an incredibly high energy or velocity. These particles are the fundamental building blocks of matter. In 1965 physicists in this field had great hope that they were close to discovering the basic secrets of matter. They transmitted this hope to political decision-makers of the United States and persuaded the latter to finance the construction of the world's largest proton accelerator. It would become the most expensive and complex scientific machine ever built by man.

Physicists at the University of California's Lawrence Radiation Laboratory were then viewed as the giants of particle physics. They were already designing what was to become the world's largest accelerator. Most knowledgeable observers felt that a California site accessible to these physicists was almost a certainty. Among professional physicists, the proposed gigantic machine was known as the 200 billion-electron-volt (BEV) accelerator.

However, an announcement by the United States Atomic Energy Commission (AEC)—the agency which would fund the installation—indicated in 1965 that the site had not been determined. This announcement signaled the beginning of a high-energy scientific and political "civil war" between the states, probably unprecedented in the nation's history. In its early months this war was to be waged subtly by scientists. Later, in various state campaigns, virtually every level of government and many social and economic sectors were to become involved in almost-vicious battles.

Illinois in the Midst of High-Energy Politics

As noted above, when the Democratic Kerner Administration moved into Springfield in 1961, it was influenced by the emphasis upon science as articulated by President Kennedy. But ranking even higher than science and technology with Kerner and his associates was economic development. During his first three years in office, Governor Kerner attempted to persuade the General Assembly to establish a code department with responsibility for economic development. Finally, in 1964, legislators approved a bill creating the Department of Business and Economic Development (BED). The first director of the new department, named immediately by Kerner, was Gene Graves, former director of the Community Development Department of Southern Illinois University at Edwardsville.

Leadership demonstrated by Governor Kerner and Director Graves in orchestrating the effort to persuade Federal decision-makers to locate the 200-BEV accelerator in Illinois is probably the most dramatic success-story in the political history of Illinois science and technology. Many individuals who had been appointed to the Illinois Science Advisory Council, described above, were active in the campaign to bring this facility to Illinois.

Apparently Graves, in his capacity as director of the Department of Business and Economic Development, first heard about the accelerator when he received a telephone call from the Washington Office of Representative Melvin Price of Illinois, then chairman of the Subcommittee on Research, Development and Radiation of the Joint Committee on Atomic Energy (JCAE).[4] Of course the late Governor Kerner cannot offer his opinion on who contributed most to the spectacular success of Illinois in capturing what was often called the "scientific prize of the century." But Graves hands that honor to Rep. Price:

> The man that was probably the most important in this whole operation was Melvin Price. He was my mentor. I called on him constantly. I did exactly what he told me to do in terms of giving the leadership and the knowledge and so on. I relied on him almost exclusively, as did the governor. He was more influential than anybody else.[5]

One scholar of the accelerator site selection process, Professor Anton G. Jachim, characterizes the initial sequence of events planned by Graves and Kerner as "dazzling."[6] Chicago bank presidents, officers in the city's Association of Commerce and Industry and a host of other influential Illinois leaders were brought into the campaign early and remained dedicated to the effort for many months.

The success of the attempt to bring the accelerator to Illinois assumes greater relevance in 1979. Now, of course, another State administration and Legislature are striving to devise strategies to attract energy installations, particularly coal liquefacation and gasification facilities, to the State.

Writing of the style of the Department of Business and Economic Development, Jachim argues that "to a great extent one can attribute Illinois' success to the discrete approaches taken by the department with regard to the use of the mass media."[7] According to him, a "soft sell" seemed to pay dividends throughout the campaign. He also asserts that an elaborate "series of information and feedback loops" was used. The strategy included having Mayor Daley of Chicago talk with President Lyndon Johnson. Scientists at universities in the state were encouraged to apprise scientific leaders in Washington of the advantages of an Illinois site for the accelerator.

Apparently never before, nor since, has the entire State government bureaucracy been so mobilized to help in promoting Illinois as a site for a scientific or technological installation. Such mobilization did not cease at the State line. Graves, other state leaders and educators at research-oriented universities persuaded various Midwestern groups—including units of the Midwestern Governors Conference—to jointly lobby for a Midwest laboratory site. Though two other Midwestern states—Michigan and Wisconsin—were eventually included among the list of six finalists, the early regional discussions certainly helped Illinois leaders to successfully discourage the AEC from turning to competing sites on both coasts.

Space does not allow a full account of the fascinating events which both preceded and followed the AEC's announcement on December 16, 1966 that a 6800-acre site near Batavia, more than thirty miles west of Chicago had been chosen for the accelerator. The episode is of significance here for two reasons. First, it illustrates that the executive branch of State government can hurriedly and successfully develop a broad-ranging strategy to help capture a massive installation within a nationwide competition.

Secondly, it reveals that a site selection process for an incredibly-complex scientific machine apparently cannot avoid being embroiled in what is popularly known within our Federal system as "pork barrel" politics.[8] In such politics, of course, congressmen negotiate among themselves over costly public works projects which will benefit their constituents back home. The role of Rep. Price has already been cited. But the most dramatic statement about the modus operandi of the pork barrel process during the nuclear accelerator site selection process was made by the late U.S. Senator Everett Dirksen, when Eastern Seaboard senators challenged the decision to place the installation in his state. When the Eastern senators argued that Illinois' legislative record on open housing and other civil rights issues should disqualify an Illinois site, Sen. Dirksen threatened to take action to terminate pork barrel politics in the U.S. Congress.

As Professor Theodore Lowi and his colleagues have noted, ". . . it took only one utterance from one senator to remind them that the application of policy conditions to a pork barrel allocation would put an end to the pork barrel process." Implications of the pork barrel approach for future technological projects are addressed later in this chapter.

Now, thirteen years after the AEC announced its choice for the accelerator, most scientists seem to judge the entire project a success. Known officially as the Fermi National Accelerator Laboratory, its original 200-BEV capability has been elevated to 500 BEVs as a result of the innovative work of the first laboratory director, Robert Wilson. But in 1978 Wilson resigned his post in protest against what he felt was inadequate funding provided by the federal government—total construction costs for the Fermi Laboratory are estimated at about $250 million, and the facility operates with an annual budget of approximately $60 million.

Unlike the Argonne National Laboratory, the Fermi Laboratory is devoted entirely to pure or fundamental research. And there are still critics who argue that the State of Illinois paid dearly by sacrificing 6800 acres of prime farm land when it persuaded the Federal government to place its prize atom smasher near the town of Batavia. But there are many other citizens of the State who would laud the fact that no other state—and few countries—can claim two such massive research centers as the Argonne National Laboratory and the Fermi National Accelerator Laboratory.

Ironically, the State of Illinois had almost nothing to do with the location of the Argonne facility Southwest of Chicago following World War II. Now, however, that Laboratory carries out considerable research for the State on a contract basis. The Fermi Laboratory, for which the State fought so vigorously, was never expected to engage in applied research which could be utilized either by the State or the federal government. Its purpose from the beginning was to provide a center where pure scientists could explore the nature of matter for the sake of advancing the frontiers of sub-atomic knowledge. The claims of Governor Kerner and others that the location of the Fermi Laboratory on the Western fringe of Chicago would serve as a magnet to bring scores of research-oriented installations to the area have not been realized, though a limited number of such facilities have been constructed in the region.

Though the AEC's choice of Illinois for the accelerator had been announced in December 1966, the matter was not finally resolved until July 12, 1967, when the U.S. Senate—after a bitter floor debate—approved initial funding for the project. Immediately Governor Kerner signed an Illinois appropriation bill for $30 million to purchase the 6800 acres of land that made up the site. He proclaimed the site selection "a scientific breakthrough for Illinois" but within a few days he was to become involved in a far different kind of national drama.

Protests and Environmental Awakening

The summer of 1967 brought racial disorders to American cities, and with them shock, fear and bewilderment. Particularly serious violence came during a two-week period in July, first in Newark and then in Detriot. Social chain reactions were set off in communities around the country. On July 28, 1967, Governor Kerner accepted President Lyndon Johnson's invitation to become chairman of the National Advisory Commission on Civil Disorders. Governor Kerner's abrupt switch from preoccupation with matters of science to an examination of civil disorders symbolized the changing mood of the nation.

A "golden" decade of enthusiastic state and national funding for all manner of science and technology was drawing to a close. The period had begun with the launching of Sputnik by the Russians and was closing with social protests centered around racial injustices and U.S. involvement in Vietnam.

In Illinois, Governor Kerner resigned as Governor in February, 1968, and was shortly afterward appointed to the U.S. 7th Circuit Court of Appeals. His Lieutenant Governor, Samuel Shapiro, served as Governor for nearly a year but was defeated by Republican Richard B. Ogilvie in November of 1968. In the same election, of course, Richard M. Nixon was elected to the Presidency of the United States.

Republicans Nixon and Ogilvie inherited an array of science and technology-related programs from their Democratic predecessors. Ideologically, both might have been expected to scrap many such programs. Indeed they did discontinue some, but a cause was gaining momentum across the country that forced them and other political leaders to revamp conventional attitudes. This was the environmental movement.

Ogilvie's experience as a lawyer, Cook County sheriff, and President of the County Board of Commissioners had not acquainted him with science or the environment in State government. Yet he soon urged his new appointees to suggest options for action in these fields.

He discovered that the Illinois Science Advisory Council had become inactive with the departure of Dr. John A. Cooper, dean of science of Northwestern University, who moved to Washington to become president of the Association of American Medical Colleges.

Late in 1969, the author of this article—a University of Illinois political scientist—was invited by Governor Ogilvie to become interim chairman of the Council. Among my directives from Governor Ogilvie was that of exploring the meaning for State government in the conflict already arising between environmentalists and proponents of economic development. Another charge was that of seeking recommendations from the Science Advisory Council itself as to its most appropriate future.

At a session of the Science Advisory Council convened on May 15, 1970, members present unanimously adopted a motion to apprise Governor Ogilvie of the consensus in regard to its future activities and usefulness to the State of Illinois. The adopted motion expressed the Council's consensus that *no* volunteer council of "high level" personnel is every effective without the following conditions: (1) high administrative support by someone at the Governor's level who strongly desires the Council to exist as a close advisor; (2) a definite and adequate budget; (3) a staff headed by a high-level individual who could prepare action papers involving a doctrine of "completed action" upon which an advisory committee could give approval, disapproval or suggested modifications; and (4) close liaison with members of State government who would have the power to *translate* recommendations into action.

Council members further expressed the feeling that unless they could be supported under the above conditions the law creating the Council should be repealed and the body discharged.

Governor Ogilvie publicly acknowledged the motion several months later but took no official action. The acknowledgement came in an address delivered at a fifteen-state Midwest Regional Conference on Science, Technology, and State Government. The theme of the event, held in November of 1970 under co-sponsorship of the State of Illinois, the National Science Foundation, and the U.S. Department of Health, Education, and Welfare was "Achieving Environmental Quality in a Developing Economy." In reference to the communication, Governor Ogilvie declared:

> Our Science Advisory Council, under the leadership of Dr. Boyd Keenan, has recommended a reorganization of our science-oriented agencies which will provide a more direct line of scientific communication with the governor of Illinois. Those recommendations are now receiving my careful study and consideration.[9]

Ogilvie As Prophet: Science Advice

Governor Ogilvie's recognition of the possible need for a "more direct line of scientific communication with the governor" has a prophetic tone when it is realized that these words were uttered nearly a decade before the Three Mile Island nuclear accident near Harrisburg, Pennsylvania:

> We are waking up to the fact that scientific and technological problems are probably the least responsive—of any we face—to solution on a state-by-state basis . . . We must understand that our vast array of problems are not encompassed by a single academic discipline, for they span the great spectrum of the human experience. To deal with the urban crisis, for example, will require not only the principles of civil engineering, economics and architecture, but also the chemistry of air sheds, the biology of water systems, and the ecology of the domestic rat and cockroach.[10]

More than 250 participants from all fifteen states also heard a debate between two young public figures who have since become even more prominent spokesmen, respectively, for economic growth and environmental protection. They were Albert H. Cox, Jr., executive vice-president and chief economist of the Lionel D. Edie Company, and Ralph Nader, then establishing himself as a consumer advocate. The latter chided leaders of Illinois and other states for listening to economists rather than scientists—physiologists, geneticists, and biologists. Nader spoke of the "horror" of possible nuclear and other environmental accidents of which many such scholars would speak only privately. Again—nine years later—the recent memory of Three Mile Island adds meaning to the debate.

Science advisors of the governors met following the conference and agreed to recommend to their chief executives that Midwestern mechanisms be developed to address the problems of science and technology on a regional level. The conference director, Dr. Stephen J. Gage, then a nuclear engineer and in 1979 Assistant Administrator for Research and Development of the U.S. Environmental Protection Agency, captured the spirit of the closing session of the conference in the Preface to the Proceedings:

> As a native Midwesterner, I was excited by the prospects of the great slumbering giant nestled in the midlands of America rising, shaking off his sleep, and making his bid for leadership in the seventies and eighties.[11]

The pressures associated with such problems as welfare, taxation, school funding and correctional systems apparently prevented Governor Ogilvie from responding formally to the requests of the Science Advisory Council. Many of his supporters in scientific and engineering circles felt that he would do so in a second term. But he was not afforded such an opportunity inasmuch as he was defeated in his bid for re-election by Daniel Walker in the gubernatorial election of November, 1972.

However, environmentalists around the country generally concede that Ogilvie was one of the most innovative governors in office at the time the American people became aware of ecological problems. Early in his administration his aides had proposed several environmental measures which found favor in the General Assembly and on June 29, 1970, the Governor signed them into law as the State's first Environmental Protection Act.

Three new agencies were created by this legislation: (1) the Pollution Control Board; (2) the Illinois Environmental Protection Agency; and (3) the Illinois Institute for Environmental Quality. At a time when environmentalists across the country were demanding reorganization of state government to meet ecological challenges, the legislation was hailed by Illinois environmentalists. Industrialists were less enthusiastic, and the past nine years witnessed many efforts, some successful, to weaken the elements of the Act.

After Walker's election, the Science Advisory Committee chairman made several efforts before the new governor's inauguration to achieve a reactivation of the Council, which still remained a statutory body. There were several informational reports prepared for the Governor's Transition Task Force, and at least one meeting was held with members of the Governor's staff to determine if some mechanism might be devised to provide Council advice on science and technology to the Governor and his immediate staff.

The author resigned as chairman of the Council in July of 1975. Neither Walker nor his successor (the incumbent, James R. Thompson), have appointed members to the Council, though it still remains a statutory body.

Technological Crises Faced by Walker

It would be unfair to emphasize Governor Walker's failure to utilize the Science Advisory Council while ignoring his Administration's efforts to meet the technological challenges of his term of office from 1973 to 1977. By most measures, these challenges were more crisis-oriented and less foresight-oriented than those of Governor Walker's two immediate predecessors. He had been in office only a few months when the Arab oil embargo of 1973 signaled the end of cheap fuel for the Western world, and he was forced to act without any precedents whatever to follow.

In the fall of 1973, when Arab nations cut the supply of crude oil delivered to the U.S., Illinois, like other states, responded on an emergency basis. The Illinois Department of Agriculture set up a "hot line" and personnel there began assisting not only farmers in need of fuel, but also industries, independent gasoline dealers and even large oil companies. Governor Walker created several temporary offices to meet other energy-related problems.

On April 1, 1975, Walker centralized many energy activities in a new Division of Energy within the state Department of Business and Economic Development. One of the most taxing tasks of this unit was to consider how the State might best develop its vast coal reserves.

Geologists have long known that Illinois possesses the largest bituminous (soft) coal reserves of any state, estimated at between 140 and 150 billion tons. It has often been argued that as much potential energy is locked in Illinois coal as is contained in the oil reserves of the Middle East. Ironically, much of the coal in Illinois and several neighboring states was being declared unacceptable for use by environmentalists during the period just discussed. It was argued by some that the high sulfur content of most Illinois coal constituted a health hazard when burned in utility boilers or by other industries.

As early as 1969 lawmakers in Congress and in the Illinois General Assembly had enacted legislation which discouraged burning Illinois coal for generating electricity or other purposes. For example, power plants in Chicago were ordered to discontinue their use of Illinois coal. Thus, in the early 1970's many public utilities and other industries which had depended upon Illinois coal either made expensive conversions to oil and/or natural gas burners or began transporting low-sulfur coal from western states. Costs of transportation in moving such coal to Illinois became a burden on both public utilities and consumers. Of the coal burned by electric utilities in Illinois, western coal's share was estimated to have increased from 3.7 percent in 1970 to nearly 25 percent in 1974.

With only a few months in office behind him, Governor Walker became aware of these conditions—but he also discovered that recognition of the country's growing dependence upon foreign oil had led Congress to direct the new Energy Research and Development Administration (ERDA) (which absorbed the old AEC) to partially fund coal liquefaction and gasification demonstrations which might encourage safe utilization of high-sulfur coal such as that available in abundance in Illinois.

In his second annual State of State Message in January of 1974, Walker offered sweeping proposals for energy legislation, including a plan to develop ways to use Illinois' vast soft coal reserves. Five months later, in June, the General Assembly passed legislation in the form of four specific energy bills, which he signed into law on August 19, 1974. Among them was Senate Bill 1659, which authorized the sale of $70 million in State bonds to be used for coal development projects. Under this provision, BED was to administer the bonding authority. Another law, House Bill 2651, established the Illinois Energy Resources Commission, composed of ten legislators and eight public members. Before BED could fund projects through its bonding authority the Commission would be required to give its approval. Still another measure, Senate Bill 1667, allowed BED to utilize the right of eminent domain in acquiring or using land for coal development.

The Legislature's efforts to provide checks and balances in the management of Illinois coal development resulted in two major rival entities. One, the BED's Division of Energy, would be the spokesman for the executive branch of Illinois government. The other, the Energy Resources Commission, would mainly reflect the attitudes of the legislators. The latter condition rests on the provision that all appointments to the commission, including the eight public members, are made by the legislative leaders of both parties.

About the same time, it was clear that massive new industrial consortia—powerful energy corporations fortified with multimillion-dollar federal grants—would be seeking funds from the available $70 million. It also soon became evident that the BED and the legislatively-oriented Commission would be pitted against each other. Coal politics has always been "winning" politics in Illinois, and both officials of the executive branch and legislators, irrespective of party, were certain to battle for credit in bringing coal development projects to Illinois.

On November 17, 1975, ERDA—soon to be replaced by the U.S. Department of Energy—announced that an Illinois site was its choice for the location of the nation's first major demonstration coal conversion plant. For a time, at least, there was enough credit to be spread around both the executive and legislative branches. The proposed $237 million facility was to convert sulfur-tainted coal into substitute gas and fuel oil. The plant was slated for construction by the Coalcon Corporation of New York City, on a 2,000-acre site just east of New Athens, twenty-five miles southeast of East St. Louis.

The proposed Coalcon facility at New Athens was only the largest of several synthetic fuel projects which the Walker administration had developed in cooperation with the Federal government and private industry. After the ERDA announcement that Illinois had defeated several other states in this competition, a sense of euphoria was pervasive both among Walker's energy planners and in Southern Illinois coal circles. It seemed for a time that Illinois was destined to become the synthetic fuel center of the nation.

This euphoria faded, however, as nagging rumors originating in Washington suggested that the technology to be utilized in the Coalcon process was inadequate for the job. As these rumors persisted, the Walker Administration faced severe difficulties on the political front in Illinois. Democratic Secretary of State Michael J. Howlett defeated Governor Walker in the 1976 gubernatorial primary. In turn, Illinois voters chose the Republican nominee, former U.S. attorney from Northern Illinois James R. Thompson over Howlett for Governor in the 1976 fall general election.

Governor Thompson In Unusual Situation

When Thompson was inaugurated in January of 1977, he faced an unusual set of circumstances, both in planning relating to energy developments and in broader matters. Principal among these was the prospect of being elected for only a two-year term. A new Illinois Constitution ratified by voters in December of 1970 had provided that the Governor elected in 1976 serve for only two years so that future gubernatorial elections would henceforth occur in non-presidential election years.

On the energy front, Thompson was confronted with complex problems stemming chiefly from the difficulties experienced by the federal government in devising a national energy policy. Officials of both Republican and Democratic administrations in Washington had espoused massive plans for the conversion of high sulfur coal into synthetic oil and gas. But virtually every project had failed to materialize. It seemed almost certain early in 1977 that none of the much-heralded joint projects involving Illinois and the federal government would come to fruition.

Thompson and his staff were well aware that cancellation of these projects during his short term could be misconstrued by the public. Actually, of course, blame for such cancellation could be attached to neither the Walker nor the Thompson Administrations. The complexity of the challenge was simply such that the federal government's capabilities could not match its earlier aspirations for putting pilot coal conversion plants on line. As expected, the Union Carbide Corporation, the major corporation involved in the Coalcon consortium, announced that the group was formally disbanding effective September 30, 1977. The much-publicized proposed facility near East St. Louis was dead as were most of the other similar proposals. However, despite disenchantment among certain coal interests over this and other energy-related interests as discussed below, Governor Thompson won election to a full four-year term in November of 1978, defeating Democrat Michael J. Bakalis.

Thompson's most serious difficulties in the energy field originated in the signing by President Carter of the U.S. Clean Air Amendments in August of 1977. This legislation signaled even more stringent standards for the burning of high-sulfur coal in electric power plants. Often described as the most complex law ever passed by the Congress, one effect of the measure was to encourage utilities operating such plants in Illinois and other Midwestern states to import out-of-state low-sulfur coal.

Two years earlier, in December of 1975, the Illinois Environmental Protection Agency had consented to permit Commonwealth Edison to burn high sulfur Illinois coal rather than low sulfur, high ash Western coal because of the economic benefits to the State. But by the Spring of 1978 the utility announced that the need to comply with the Clean Air Amendments by 1979 would force it to switch to out-of-state coal. Thompson called a series of public hearings, expressing concern at the prospects that Illinois miners could be deprived of jobs and that other serious economic disruptions could occurs in the State. He also reported he was considering exercising authority under Section 125 of the Clean Air Act to request the President to order Commonwealth Edison to continue using locally-available coal.

After a year of complex controversy—including miners' protests and calls by environmentalists for Thompson to cease his challenges to the Federal legislation—Thompson issued a statement on the situation on March 26, 1979. At that time he charged that confusing and conflicting federal energy and environmental policies were at the root of Illinois coal marketing problems. He asked President Carter to conduct special hearings on a regional or national scale to probe the possibility of economic disruption resulting from federal policies. Thompson also contended that his authority to halt the Commonwealth Edison switch from Illinois to Western coal at the Powerton plant was cancelled by the Federal government on November 9, 1978. Finally he argued that the policies of the Federal government were fostering a destructive energy competition between states and regions. Within a week of this statement, Thompson joined another Republican governor from a high-sulfur coal producing state, James Rhodes of Ohio, in attacking President Carter's coal policies in a televised news conference. As of this writing (early July, 1979) Commonwealth Edison's Powerton power plant operators are apparently preparing to switch major boilers to western coal.

Illinois and the Nuclear Dilemma

Yet as significant as the coal burning issue seemed to the parties affected in the Spring of 1979, a more serious technological and political dilemma for Governor Thompson and Illinois citizens burst on the scene on March 28, 1979. A nuclear accident at Metropolitan Edison's Three Mile Island plant near Harrisburg, Pennsylvania, was probably felt with more impact in Illinois than in any other state. The Commonwealth Ediscon Company, which provides electric power to Chicago and surrounding areas of the State, had been boasting for weeks that about one-half of its total electric power through the last three severe winters had been generated by nuclear energy. Commonwealth Edison is by far the nation's largest producer of nuclear-generated electricity. The nuclear capability of that utility so dominates the Illinois scene that it was estimated that one-third of the state's electric power was dependent on nuclear facilities.

Overnight two burning questions troubled Illinois residents: (1) Was an accident similar to that at Three Mile Island possible at Commonwealth Edison's seven plants? (2) Would Illinois be as ill-prepared for such an episode as Pennsylvania? At this writing, answers are available to neither of those questions. Both Governor Thompson and Commonwealth Edison have appointed technical safety review panels to examine the nuclear scene in the State.

Among those appointed by the Governor to his review committee was a representative of the Illinois Commission on Atomic Energy, a body first established by the General Assembly in 1955 but little known to the rank and file of Illinois citizens. To its credit, this agency has maintained close contacts through the years with state and federal civil defense officials. But there is no way from available literature to determine the Commission's overall capability. The degree of preparedness of this body for possible emergency situations and the effectiveness of its linkages with other state agencies is really unknown. One can only guess that chaos matching or exceeding that at Harrisburg, Pennsylvania, would prevail if a nuclear accident occurred within the borders of Illinois.

Of course, the concerns of Illinois citizens are not limited to accidents at nuclear power plants. Some contend that the use of Illinois as a burial ground for nuclear wastes and other toxic substances exceeds that of any other state. Certain officials, notably Attorney General William Scott, have argued for years that such dangers are underestimated by the vast majority of the States' citizens. Targets of Scott and others have been two locations: (1) a site near Sheffield, about 100 miles southwest of Chicago in Bureau County, where low-level radioactive wastes and other explosives and chemicals have been dumped since 1963; and (2) a site near Morris, Grundy County, where high-level wastes from Commonwealth Edison's Dresden reactors are stored.

Both sites have been operated since their opening by private corporations. Operator of the Sheffield plant is the Nuclear Engineering Corporation, which Scott claims has been functioning without a license since 1968. The General Electric Corporation originally designed the Morris installation to serve as a reprocessing plant, but the technology was unsuccessful. Despite the expenditure of many millions of dollars to correct its flaws, the GE facility has been destined to remain merely a storage site. In February of 1978, the Illinois Atomic Energy Commission's Subcommittee on Radioactive Waste Management reported at a public meeting that both sites can be operated safely until the 1980's when the federal government is expected to develop a national atomic waste-disposal policy. The report stated that both nuclear dumps are operating "within the limits set by existing regulations and standards for protection of the public health and safety and due regard has been given to environmental protection."

As this is written in July of 1979, Attorney General Scott continues his efforts to close both nuclear dumps. Spurred by the accident at Three Mile Island, a number of legislators in the Illinois General Assembly introduced measures relating to all aspects of nuclear energy during the fading days of the 1978 session. But bills banning new nuclear power plants and the more stringent proposals on nuclear waste had failed when the Legislature adjourned at the end of June. One bill that did reach Governor Thompson's desk is a plan he requested for an instant warning system for nuclear power station accidents and similar statewide disaster situations.

Executive Reorganization and Innovations by the Thompson Administration

Since the Arab embargo brought the various dilemmas of energy management to the attention of the states, students of government have often marveled at the variety of organizational approaches among the states. Slowly most governors have come to the recognition that energy and environmental challenges cannot be separated at the state level. Following such recognition, reorganization has often followed. In March of 1978, Governor Thompson declared:

> There is an inescapable connection between energy and the environment. One of the most important issues state government faces today is establishing a workable relationship between our demands for energy and our need to care for the environment. It would serve no one to let the issue deteriorate into either a standoff or a war between those who would ignore environmental standards and those who would impose such exacting standards as to make it impossible to use the energy we have or develop new sources.

To provide such a "workable relationship" Governor Thompson announced a plan to consolidate the Institute for Environmental Quality and the Division of Energy of the Department of Business and Economic Development (BED). He hoped such a merger would bring together the State's energy and environmental efforts into a working organization. The Governor started the process with an executive order, which was expanded upon by the General Assembly. After weeks of negotiations a bill was passed creating an Institute of Natural Resources on July 1, 1978 (see the Schneiderman chapter).

Gov. Thompson's new Institute of Natural Resources has followed the BED's precedent of seeking funds from the Coal Development Bond Fund to encourage the siting of synthetic fuel demonstration plants which would utilize high-sulfur Illinois coal. In January of 1979, the Governor, on the recommendation of the Institute, proposed that $18 million in bond funds be made available towards construction of a $100 million coal gasification demonstration plant near Wood River, Illinois. The Illinois Energy Resources Commission soon approved the allocation.

The process for the Wood River plant, developed by the Allis-Chalmers Corporation, is known as the KIL^{n}GAS process and will convert up to 675 tons per day of high-sulfur Illinois coal to low-Btu gas that will fire a boiler producing electricity at Illinois Power Company's Wood River generating station. The boiler now burns oil. Construction is expected to begin early in 1980 and will be completed by late 1982. A total of thirteen Eastern and Midwestern utilities are participating in the program.

As noted previously, such projects are felt to offer the potential of converting high-sulfur Illinois coal to a clean fuel for power generation, thus reducing imports of low-sulfur coal to the State. Though Illinois' efforts to bring coal conversion facilities to Illinois have disappointed many leaders, a number of proposals are still in the "active" stage. Among them is a project of a group known as the Illinois Coal Gasification Group (ICGG) to design a demonstration plant that would transform coal into synthetic pipeline gas. Under contracts from the U.S. Department of Energy (DOE), the ICGG is proceeding with a detailed design of a demonstration plant, to be located in Perry County, Illinois, near Cutler. The plant hopefully would convert 2,200 tons of coal per day into 18 million cubic feet of gas and 2,400 barrels of heavy coal liquids. The overall project would be co-funded by DOE and a consortium consisting of five Illinois-based utilities.

To this point (July 1979), Governor Thompson has, with one exception, chosen to rely upon his administrative appointees for science and technology advice rather than an external body such as the inoperative Science Advisory Council. The one exception is a Governor's Science and Technology Task Force, appointed in November of 1977. Its purpose was to address the following issues: 1) historical and current scientific, engineering, and technological (SET) information mechanisms of the Illinois executive branch; 2) the potential for Illinois universities to play a more active role in solving executive agency research needs; and 3) ways in which State government could effectively manage its research priorities.

Task Force members included representatives of public and private universities, a federal laboratory, a technical society, and present and past members of the legislative and executive branches of Illinois State government. The Task Force's activities were supported in part by a National Science Foundation grant to the now-defunct Illinois Institute for Environmental Quality. A report submitted to the Governor in December of 1978 acknowledges that the Task Force played a role in the reorganization creating the Institute of Natural Resources in 1978. Recommendations contained in the Task Force report follow: (1) Initiate a series of Science, Engineering and Technology Task Forces to focus SET resources on immediate and pressing problems faced by State government; (2) Use the Natural Resources Sub-Cabinet to comprehensively identify State SET research needs; (3) Institute personnel exchange and recruiting programs to enhance cooperation between State government and the academic community; (4) Improve salary structure, hiring practices and personnel procedures to attract trained, professional scientists. (5) Enhance inter-agency communication by collection and disseminating information regarding on-going SET research in Illinois; (6) Develop SET expertise in the budget process; and (7) Develop an SET inter-governmental brokerage system to transfer Federal and State SET research expertise.[12]

Theoretical Challenges to the Illinois Technocracy

In keeping with the objectives of this book, this chapter is entitled "Illinois as Technocracy." Such a title should not be allowed to hide the reality that no state can function alone in today's world. Illinois' technological problems are those of the nation and the world. Likewise the chapter's emphasis upon the State's energy problems is not meant to imply that it does not face other difficult challenges. But in 1979 energy dilemmas dominate government at every level.

Too often attention to structure and process in government obscures emerging theoretical considerations. Presently instability in the Middle East and the post Three Mile Island attitude pose questions with theoretical elements of a sort not confronted before in the American federal system. Many such elements focus on Illinois. For example, as this volume goes to press President Carter is promising a national blueprint to allow development of a gigantic new synthetic fuel industry. Similar talk occurred immediately after the Arab oil embargo of 1973–74, but, as this chapter outlines, little progress was made. However, Illinois will be dramatically affected if such an industry is established.

The short-lived, post-embargo competition among coal-producing states for synthetic fuel demonstration plants and the "sweepstakes" atmosphere of the contest which resulted in the selection of the Illinois site for the

Fermi accelerator offer cause for concern. Some of us who watched those proceedings wonder if the American federal system will be capable of withstanding the "pork barrel" politics almost certain to be associated with such a massive public works efforts as are being projected by some for the synthetic fuel industry. We already have hints of how developers in coal-producing states will expect their congressmen to "bring home" billion-dollar installations if the industry is indeed launched.

Professor Theodore Lowi, identified earlier in connection with the Fermi Laboratory site selection, has noted that "public works projects . . . are part of a larger system of modern irresponsibility."[13] According to him and other scholars of pork barrel public works politics, the process is distinguished by decisions that embody no rule of conduct and no conditions or standards that tie together various discrete units of government. Our energy problems already derive in part from a "Balkanization" of the country. One can hardly imagine a development with greater potential for further Balkanization than a massive government-sponsored synthetic fuel industry. If such should indeed be developed, it would have major significance for Illinois as "technocracy."

The task of educating a generation to the technological challenges of a magnitude never known before must fall to the states. Academic leaders must share this responsibility with office holders in both the executive and legislative branches. Politicians at the state level must learn to resist the fickle public which at times is unable to take the long view in a technologically-oriented society. Failure of the State of Illinois to somehow learn from such episodes as Three Mile Island and other less-frightening technologically-induced episodes would be shameful if not potentially disastrous.

In a fast-moving technocracy, whether we view the states separately or the nation as a whole, we slip easily from one administration to another. We increasingly dismiss pronouncements of presidents and governors in inaugural addresses and similar ceremonial speeches as political rhetoric. Early in this paper we discussed a fifteen-state conference on science and state government held in the Chicago area in 1970 and noted a quotation by Stephen Gage, director of that conference, on the possibility of Midwestern states providing much-needed leadership. More recently, in making reference to that conference, Gage, now a top Federal official, had this to say:

> But curiously enough, the new ideas, conclusions, and recommendations originating from that conference seemed to go underground. This was a very strange phenomenon in the early part of the 1970's, when so much of the intellectual ferment which had come out of the 1960's was beginning to crystallize and was beginning to move into conceptual form. It was simply buried, and only now do I find it beginning to emerge.[14]

If such intellectual ferment is to emerge in the country, replacing the despair and hopelessness surrounding our technocratic machines, it will likely begin with the hope—if not the faith—that science and technology can somehow be controlled. States like Illinois, which have great educational institutions capable of "planting" the ideas to fulfill such hope, bear a major responsibility to begin such a planting process anew. On October 22, 1963, a month to the day before his tragic death in Texas, President Kennedy appeared before the National Academy of Sciences and talked of the need to consciously plant ideas in the scientific setting.

He concluded his talk with an anecdote that revealed the strength of his own conviction about the importance of science to the country's future: "The great French Marshal Lyautey once said to his gardener: 'Plant a tree tomorrow.' And the gardener said, 'It won't bear fruit for a hundred years.' 'In that case,' said Lyatey to the gardener, 'plant it this afternoon.' This is how I feel about your work," said the President.[15]

If state government is as important to the preservation of our free political system as we claim it to be, we should plant some new ideas about science, technology and state government "this afternoon."

NOTES

[1]Jerome B. Wiesner, *Where Science and Politics Meet* (New York: McGraw-Hill Book Company, 1965), p. 5.

[2]Letter from Frederick Seitz to Thomas A. McGloon, dated June 18, 1965.

[3]*Ibid.*

[4]See Anton G. Jackim, *Science Policy Making in the United States and the Batavia Accelerator* (Carbondale and Edwardsville: Southern Illinois University Press, 1975), p. 110.

[5]*Ibid.*, p. 118.

[6]*Ibid.*

[7]*Ibid.*, p. 120.

[8]For a severe critique of the selection process and the involvement of both state and federal officials, see Theodore Lowi, *et al.*, *Poliscide* (New York: Macmillan Publishing Co., Inc., 1976), p. 292.

[9]Conference Proceedings; *Midwest Regional Conference on Science, Technology and State Government,* Arlington Heights, Illinois, November 17–19, 1970 p. A-3.

[10]*Ibid.*, p. A-2.

[11]*Ibid.*, Preface.

[12]State of Illinois Governor's Science and Technology Task Force, *Report to the Governor,* December, 1978.

[13]Theodore J. Lowi, *et al.*, *Poliscide* (New York Macmillan Publishing Co., Inc., 1976), p. 288.

[14]Stephen J. Gage, "A New Environmental View of the Ohio River Valley," in *Energy and Environment An Intergovernmental Perspective,* Boyd R. Keenan, ed. (Urbana: University of Illinois, 1978), p. 119.

[15]This incident is related by Jerome B. Wiesner, who was science advisor to President Kennedy, in his book, *Where Science and Politics Meet* (New York: McGraw-Hill Book Company, 1965), p. 7.

CHAPTER **27**

Scientific and Technical Information for Legislative Decisions

John W. Ahlen

This chapter is written to introduce the reader to a relatively new capability of state legislatures in general and the Illinois General Assembly in particular. The capability involves directly tapping sources of scientific and technical information and focusing that knowledge on specific issues of interest to legislative policymakers. The development of this ability in state legislatures is recent, having first begun in 1969 in California. The history, therefore, is rather limited, but significant.

Illinois was the third state, after California and New York, to add a science capacity to its legislative staff. The unique characteristics of the Illinois effort were that the science staff was added to an existing legislative service agency, the Legislative Council, instead of being established as a separate organization, and that, unlike California and New York, the Illinois science capacity was intended to serve both houses of the Legislature. The Legislative Council's science staff formally began to function in January 1973, and since then its operation has been continuous. With its initial establishment and subsequent support of the Council's science staff, the Illinois General Assembly has demonstrated its national leadership in providing scientific and technical information for legislative decisions.

Decisions Involving Science and Technology

It is essential to remember that the business of the Legislature is a complex totality. In examining a single element of the Legislature's work, it is sometimes easy to lose sight of where or how that element fits into the whole. It is also possible to attach more or less importance to a single element when it is being examined alone than it would receive when seen in a larger framework. The structural components of the Legislature are discussed elsewhere in this volume, and the reader is encouraged to use those contributions to construct a framework within which to place the scientific, engineering and technical elements.

The range of subjects that come before the Legislature of a major agricultural and industrial state like Illinois is impressive. Topics include abortion, banking, criminal justice, education, pensions, social services and transportation, among many others. The number of matters that formally receive the attention of the Legislature is largely, but not completely, measured by bills which are introduced. However, the number of bills alone represents a potentially awesome workload: for instance, the 80th Illinois General Assembly (1977–1978) considered over 5300 bills.

Given the breadth of subjects and the number of bills considered by the Legislature, and further given the ubiquity of technology in society, it should be expected that some portion of the Legislature's workload will involve either technology at some level of development or the precursors of technology—the fundamental knowledge of science and the applied knowledge of engineering. Examining the content of bills verifies the expectation. Consider for example the bills dealing with the following subjects: chlorinated biphenyls, hazardous refuse, nuclear power plants, ozone layer protection, sulfur dioxide emissions, solar energy, thermal infrared overflight scanning, the use of the compound laetrile by cancer patients, substitution of generic drugs by pharmacists and recombinant DNA research.

National attempts to determine the percentage of bills that address sicentific and technical issues have shown that as much as 17 percent of the bills passed by state legislatures have science or technology components.[1] Surveys of introduced bills in the 79th and 80th Illinois General Assemblies indicate that one bill in 16, about 6 percent, has obvious relevance to science or technology.

There are implications which accompany the fact that legislatures are concerned with and consider bills of technical import. One implication is that legislatures require a different kind of information than they have traditionally used: information rich in science and technology. Another implication is that in order to get that information, legislatures will need to use sources of information with which they probably have had little experience.

Sources of Technical Information

Specific sources for scientific and technical information are numerous and of various description. There are at least three general types of public and private sources for technical information to which a legislature might at first turn: (1) State supported institutions, including State agencies, boards, and commissions which have specific missions that involve science or engineering, and State universities that have technical expertise in departments and centers and substantial collections of information in scientific libraries, (2) Federal agencies that have broad missions and specific programs which are based on solid scientific and technical foundations are other sources of information—of particular significance are: specific programs that require the use of high level technology, federal laboratories that are actively engaged in basic and applied research and federally supported research reports and abstracts; (3) private organizations provide yet another source—these include private universities; corporations involved in the research, development and marketing of products that require technological sophistication; national trade associations that represent the interests of industries which use technology; professional societies that represent professionals who have technical or scientific expertise; and public interest groups which have special concerns that involve elements of science or technology.

Information Transfer

Once the source for information has been identified, the task still remaining is to transfer the information from the source to the end user, in this case legislators. Where special interests are involved, information needs of the legislature may be obvious to, and the transfer actively sought by, representatives of the special interest. The transfer mechanism is pretty well defined in these cases.

If a legislator or group of legislators recognizes the need for technical information, and if they are able to identify a source for the information, then it probably will be discovered that the information is in the language and format that facilitates its transfer to other scientists, not to the legislators who need it. This is an obvious disincentive for legislators to use technical information. Measures were begun in the late 1960s to correct this situation, when legislatures started to demand that they have ready access to the technical information required for their deliberations.

The Role of the National Science Foundation

One of the earliest signs of National Science Foundation (NSF) interest in state science activities was a 1954 study of state expenditures for science and technology. The study[2] found that in the six states under review there was little scientific activity outside of line agencies; that communication of scientific information to those not in the scientific community was a problem; and that utilization of scientific resources by policymakers would strengthen policy-making institutions. This 1954 study is significant in that it is the first clear indication that the federal government had some interest in state governments' scientific capacity.

Through the years since the 1954 study, the NSF has been a force helping legislatures move toward science and technology self-sufficiency and a financial supporter of science and technology capacity building. NSF was involved in the efforts to establish science and technology mechanisms for the legislatures in many states, including California, New York and Illinois.

Models for Developing a Legislative Capability

In 1973, Menzel, Friedman and Feller published their analysis of the development of a science and technology capability in state legislatures.[3] The study was funded by the National Science Foundation and followed several efforts by states to develop such capability. One part of their analysis offered six models that state legislatures might use as mechanisms to secure information in areas of science and technology and bring this kind of information into their decision making processes: (1) the Personal Research Model: Individual legislators, through their personal efforts, can be the information transfer mechanism; (2) the Science and Technology Committee Model: Legislative committees can bring science and technology information to the attention of legislators; (3) the Task Force Model: A temporary or continuing task force is another way to gather information, especially on specific technical issues; (4) the Expert Consultant Model: This model uses individual expert consultants for providing scientific and technical information; (5) the Intern Staff Model: Science interns assigned to legislative staff or individual legislators can bring scientific information into legislative activities. (6) the Professional Staff Model: Legislators can hire scientists and engineers onto legislative staff and rely on such personnel for scientific and technical information.

Other States' Activities

Before discussing the Illinois efforts to establish a science and technology mechanism, it is instructive to examine early efforts in the two states which preceded Illinois in creating such a capacity.

The California Assembly Science and Technology Advisory Council (ASTAC) was authorized by Assembly resolution in 1969. ASTAC was similar to the U.S. President's Science Advisory Committee. Seventeen members were appointed to ASTAC in 1970. The Council was set up to respond to requests on issues of both short- and long-term interest. The "state of the art" technical reports were prepared by either ASTAC staff or Assembly Office of Research staff and usually addressed problems of short-term interest. Long-term projects were referred to ASTAC's technical panels, of which there were five: (1) population; (2) solid waste management; (3) health care; (4) scientific and technical employment; and (5) telecommunications. There was also a committee on environmental issues.[4]

The New York Assembly Scientific Staff was created by the Speaker of the Assembly in 1971. Its primary function was to bring scientific and technical expertise and perspective into the legislative process. This was done by creating a separate staff whose major duties were to: (1) respond to questions ranging from simple to complex; (2) comment on bills and assist in the preparation of bills; (3) formulate directly or indirectly the technical aspects of legislative policy; (4) administer public service legislative studies; (5) interact with professional societies; and (6) assist other states in building their scientific capacity.[5]

The science advisory mechanisms in both California and New York are different now from when they were first created. ASTAC was dismantled in the mid-70s and is no longer functioning,[6] partly because the individual members of the Council were too removed from legislative activities. The New York Assembly Scientific Staff survived a change in party leadership in 1974. After the death of the first staff director in 1976, the Assembly Scientific Staff evolved into a more politically involved Assembly Science and Technology Staff. This staff was reorganized out of existence after failing to weather a change of leadership in the Assembly's majority party. It is expected that it will be resurrected to serve a joint science and technology committee later in 1979.

Illinois

Illinois State government has made a number of attempts to establish and perpetuate formal science and technology advisory mechanisms.[7] The first significant effort was in 1964 when Governor Otto Kerner created the Science Advisory Council of Illinois by executive order. In 1967, the General Assembly established the Science Advisory Council of Illinois by law.[8] Research has uncovered only one undated Council report, submitted to Governor Ogilvie and the 76th General Assembly (and probably prepared in 1970). Since 1972, the Science Advisory Council has been totally abandoned by both the legislative and executive branches.

The 74th Illinois General Assembly created[9] the Commission on Automation and Technological Study in 1965. The Commission was given a two year period to study all areas of automation and technological changes and their existing and potential effects on Illinois. The Commission was recreated[10] for another two years in 1967 and again in 1969, although the name was changed to the Commission on Technological Progress. During its six year existence, the Commission was especially active in studying the scientific and technological base in the State and was responsible for holding the Midwest Regional Conference on Science, Technology and State Government in November 1970. The Commission's work is significant in a number of respects. It undoubtly exposed the General Assembly to scientific and technical information and stressed the importance of science and technology in the State. This probably prepared the Legislature to easily accept the notion that it could benefit from the existence of a legislative science staff. One of the final recommendations of the Commission on Technological Progress, before it passed out of existence in 1971, was that the Illinois Commission on Technological Progress and the Illinois Science Advisory Council be consolidated into a single body serving in a science advisory capacity for the General Assembly, the Governor and other State agencies.[11]

Illinois: The Legislative Council

The Illinois Legislative Council was created by statute in 1937 and serves as the Legislature's research agency. Presently, Council membership numbers twenty legislators; four legislative leaders ex-officio, and eight members of each house appointed by the presiding officers. Membership is bipartisan, to be roughly in proportion to party membership in each house but with the majority party to hold no more than two-thirds of the membership from either house. The Council selects a director of research who is responsible for hiring staff for the Council.[12]

The research department provides a governmental research service on a nonpartisan basis to individual legislators and committees and commissions of the General Assembly. This service is keyed to needs of individual legislators and obviously emphasizes legislative research. The staff has traditionally been composed of persons with extensive training or experience in social sciences, law or journalism. In recent years, the need of legislators for quickly provided information has become the focal point of Council staff research work, and responding to such requests with written reports form the bulk of staff writing. However, as time and the Council permit, the staff undertakes more extensive, detailed research. Approximately 2,000 items of recorded research and an uncounted but substantial number of minor research tasks are now produced during a biennium.

Research reports provide factual background information but do not make recommendations for legislative policy. When it is appropriate, a research report may indicate pros and cons of governmental programs and policies and may indicate suggested legislative alternatives with corresponding advantages and disadvantages.

Science Staff

The idea of adding scientifically trained persons to the Council staff resulted directly from a complaint by a freshman legislator. The legislator represented a district in which abandoned strip mines presented major problems. When he came to the Legislature in 1969, one big concern of his was strip mine reclamation. Where did he turn for technical information? He asked the Legislative Council for information on strip mine reclamation and receive a report[13] detailing the kinds of laws other state legislatures had enacted. But from a scientific and technical point of view, the Council's information was inadequate. (Coincidentally, this legislator's freshman term was the same as the final two year existence of the Commission on Technological Progress.) The informational "blind spot" was recognized, and, after several false starts, the proposal by the Council's director of research for adding scientific personnel to the Legislative Council staff was supported.[14]

The Illinois General Assembly, in 1972, appropriated $25,000 to be used by the Council in a cooperative, jointly funded project with Sangamon State University and the National Science Foundation. The project involved bringing a National Science Foundation scientist to Illinois for 18 months. The scientist was to develop ways for the Illinois General Assembly to use science and technology information and to promote science in public affairs at Sangamon State University.[15]

During this 18 month period, the legislative staff scientist engaged in four principal activities for the Legislative Council: (1) promoting science and technology related services of the Legislative Council: (2) performing research and providing information in response to legislator's requests; (3) identifying science and technology resources within the State; and (4) building a science and technology capacity for the Legislature and developing programs for its continued operation.

Science Internship

In 1962, the Legislative Council began a legislative staff internship program with support supplied by the Ford Foundation. The University of Illinois coordinated the internship program for the Legislative Council from the beginning of the program until 1972. In that year, Sangamon State became the coordinating university. There were then 16 legislative staff interns serving 9½ month internships beginning in October. Four interns were assigned to each of the leadership staffs in the General Assembly. In 1973, a Sangamon State University faculty member proposed to add a seventeenth intern with educational training in engineering or natural sciences. The seventeenth intern would be supported by the National Science Foundation for one year and would spend his internship with the staff of the Legislative Council and work directly with the legislative staff scientist.

The proposed responsibilities of the science intern would be: (1) to develop liaison with agencies and organizations both inside Illinois and elsewhere in the country; (2) to submit reports to the Illinois Legislative Council applying the results of the liaison work to State problems; (3) to visit organizations engaging in science and technology activities in other states and to apply the knowledge gained to efforts in Illinois; and (4) to participate in the academic segment of the Legislative Staff Internship Program along with the 16 graduate students who were assigned to the leadership staffs.[16]

In retrospect, the experiment with a science intern in Illinois can be assessed as very successful. The General Assembly has assumed full financial support for the internship as part of its annual appropriation to the Legislative Council for the Legislative Staff Internship Program. Science interns have gone on in their individual careers to make professional contributions in state government. Of the six former interns, three are employed on legislative science staffs, two in Illinois (including this author) and one in Minnesota. Another finished a masters degree in environmental engineering and is on the staff of the Washington State Energy Office. Two others are continuing their educations full time in law and respiratory therapy.

Routine Research

Three broad subjects dominate research requests: (1) environment and ecology, (2) energy and (3) health, medicine and safety. Most of the requests came from members of the House (60 percent), with requests from members of the Senate, legislative staff and other states about equal (at 10 percent). The two typical formats for responses are letters and memoranda. Letters average 2.2 pages of information and require about three weeks on the average to prepare. Memoranda are about 7.3 pages in length and take roughly six weeks to complete. The general sources for information, determined from an analysis of footnotes, in rank order, include: other state statutes; special interest publications; telephone conversations; scientific journals, federal agency publications; Illinois agency publications; books and reference works; other sources (miscellaneous); Illinois statutes; agency publications from other states; newspapers and news magazines; corporate publications; court cases; and federal statutes.

Special Projects

Besides the routine research tasks, the Council's science staff also takes part in special projects to support legislative activities. These special projects include: (1) developing the science internship; (2) experimenting with contracted studies to obtain scientific and technical information for legislators; (3) arranging for and coordinating seminars for legislators and legislative staff on energy related topics; (4) arranging for less formal workshops for legislators; (5) conducting special, long term research projects for the Legislative Council or other legislative committees, or subcommittees; (6) testing the feasibility of having a visiting staff scientist on temporary assignment from another organization; and (7) developing university resources.

State Science, Engineering, and Technology Project

The most recent development in Illinois legislative science activities is the National Science Foundation's State Science, Engineering, and Technology (SSET) Program. This program was specifically authorized by Congress in its joint explanatory statement of the committee of conference on Public Law 94-471; the 1977 National Science Foundation Authorization Act. Of particular interest is the $50,000 which was earmarked for each state, $25,000 for the legislature and $25,000 for the governor, "to identify and analyze potentially useful ways in which States and local governments can increase their capabilities for using science, engineering and technology in meeting the needs of their citizens, including consideration of the establishment of science and technology policy offices within both the Executive and Legislative Branches."[17]

Governors in 49 states and legislatures in 42 states participated in the SSET Program, including executive and legislative branch projects in Illinois. The Legislative Council was the performing organization for the legislature's effort and its final report[18] was published in April 1979. (The executive branch project report[19] was released in December 1978.)

Space does not permit a detailed review of the Council's SSET report, but two chapters may be of special interest to readers of this book. Illinois now has over six years of continuous science staff activity, and these chapters analyze the special and routine research projects carried out by the science staff from its beginning in Janury 1973 through May 1978.

The Next Decade

The history of legislative science mechanisms is limited. In the first decade of serious effort, beginning in 1969, state legislatures have moved consistantly forward; from California in 1969, to three states in 1973, to more than a dozen operating legislative science and technology mechanisms (and 42 legislatures participating in thc State Science, Engineering, and Technology Program) in 1979.

What kind of changes will be made in legislative science mechanisms during the next decade? There are two trends that might yield a clue as to future development: (1) legislatures will see more science and technology (S&T) issues and require that more sophisticated data be available to them; and (2) more states will be involved in legislative S&T efforts on a continuing basis.

Better contacts with, and use of, university based scientists might evolve, perhaps even including state legislative offices on university campuses. This would facilitate involving faculty in two distinct kinds of projects. The first is the traditional project with a quick response to a specific query. The second is a more modern response to anticipated questions involving emerging issues. Precision forecasting will be needed so that the information which is developed will be applied by the legislature soon after the data are compiled. If the information is developed too early, complaints might be made that science is attempting to set the public policy agenda. Perfect timing would have the anticipated response ready the day before the legislature makes its inquiry because much legislative information is needed "yesterday."

More scientists might be involved in preparing preliminary drafts of bills. Some of this work might be supported by the federal government through state legislative planning and development grants.

More legislators will probably have scientific or engineering training and legislatures might have science and technology committees to deal with emerging technical issues. These committees will be staffed by a new breed of public service scientist.

NOTES

[1]Council of State Governments, *Power to the States* (Lexington, Ky.: Council of State Governments, 1972), pp. 18–22.

[2]Frederic N. Cleveland, *Science and State Government* (Chapel Hill: University of North Carolina Press, 1959).

[3]Donald C. Menzel, *et al., Development of a Science and Technology Capability in State Legislatures: Analysis and Recommendations* (University Park: The Center for the Study of Science Policy, Institute for Research on Human Resources, Pennsylvania State University, 1973).

[4]Carol Bursik and Stephen J. Larson, "A Model for Utilizing Scientific Expertise," in *Meeting the Challenge,* ed. by Edward L. Helminski and Ralph J. Marceli (Lexington, Ky.: Council of State Governments, 1975), pp. 21–30.

[5]Seville Chapman, "Scientific Staff for a Legislature," in Helminski and Marcelli, *op. cit.,* pp. 37–42.

[6]James O. Gollub, *et al., Increasing the Capacity of State Governments to Access and Use Scientific, Engineering, and Technical Resources* (Menlo Park, California: SRI International 1979).

[7]Richard W. Sames, "Past Scientific Mechanisms for the Executive Branch," in *State of Illinois Governor's Science and Technology Task Force Report to the Governor* (Chicago: Institute of Natural Resources, 1978), pp. 36–72.

[8]Laws of the State of Illinois, 1967 Session, p. 4242.

[9]Laws of the State of Illinois, 1965 Session, p. 3109.

[10]Laws of the State of Illinois, 1967 Session, p. 4232; and Laws of the State of Illinois, 1969 Sessions, Public Act 76-751.

[11]Illinois Commission on Technological Progress, Report Submitted to the Governor and Members of the 77th General Assembly, n.d. [1971].

[12]Illinois Revised Statutes, 1977, ch. 63, secs. 33 through 41.10.

[13]James T. Mooney, "Leading State Strip Mine Laws," Illinois Legislative Council File 7-026, Springfield, 1969.

[14]William L. Day, "Illinois Science and Technology Effort Corrects Information 'Blind Spot,' " *The American Legislator* 3:5 (December 1973), pp. 4–5.

[15]J.C. Kellett, Jr., *Science and the Illinois General Assembly* (Springfield: Illinois Legislative Council, 1974).

[16]"Request to the National Science Foundation for Initiation of the Illinois Legislative Science Intern Program," n.d., funded as National Science Foundation Grant GT-40964, effective November 1, 1973.

[17]"House Conference Report No. 94-1689," *United States Code Congressional and Administrative News 94th Congress-Second Session 1976,* Vol. 4 (St. Paul: West Publishing Company, 1977), p. 4657.

[18]Margaret M. Cetera, *et al.,* "Science Staff Services in the Illinois Legislative Council," Illinois Legislative Council File 9-000, Springfield, 1979.

[19]*State of Illinois Governor's Science and Technology Task Force Report to the Governor,* The State Science, Engineering, and Technology Plan for the Illinois Executive Branch, 1978.

PART **VII**

SELECTED POLICY ISSUES

CHAPTER **28**

Major Issues Influencing Development: Energy and Environment— the Big Trade-Off

Illinois 2000 Foundation

With the Keenan and Schneiderman chapters as background, this chapter on alternative energy and environmental scenarios may be read as an exercise in state planning, analysis and policy-making: what alternatives does Illinois face in this area? What are the consequences of each? What choices might the reader prefer? What are the major interest alignments? How are the political process and governmental institutions likely to deal with these issues? What are the implications for achieving an appropriate balance between politics and planning in Illinois government?

Energy

Issues

1. Levels of energy demand and sources of supply in the year 2000.
2. Sufficiency of capital to meet energy supply/demand needs.
3. Effects of regulatory constraints on the energy industry's capacity to meet supply/demand needs.
4. The effect of energy prices on sources of energy supply in Illinois.

Major Trends and Indicators

1. Energy growth scenario for the year 2000.
   A. Based on analysis of various national energy scenarios, Illinois 2000 adopted a probable trend which projects an increase in energy use from 70.6 quadrillion BTU's (quads) in 1975 to 135.1 quads in 2000. (Chart VII)
   B. For Illinois, assuming its share of energy consumption would remain at 4.9% of U.S. consumption, energy use would almost double from 3.54 quads to 6.62. The compound annual growth rate is 2.63%, as opposed to 3.5% in the post-war era.
   C. Like all other projections, this is subject to a wide range of possible variations and shifts for energy mix, conservation, and supply restrictions.
2. Sources of energy supply for Illinois—implications of the scenario.
   A. Coal represents Illinois' primary energy supply resource. With estimated reserves of 160 billion tons, Illinois could supply itself and much of the nation with coal for hundreds of years. Currently, environment, productivity, transportation, cost, and price constraints limit the use of coal. The probable trend projects doubling coal use for electric power generation in Illinois by the year 2000. The question is whether this will be Illinois or western coal. Illinois coal also has great potential as an alternative fuel source as petroleum and natural gas prices increase between now and the year 2000.
   B. Nuclear power had its commercial start in Illinois. Today, the state has seven operating plants totaling more than 5,000 megawatts of electrical capacity, representing over 25% of the state's total production. Energy utility plans indi-

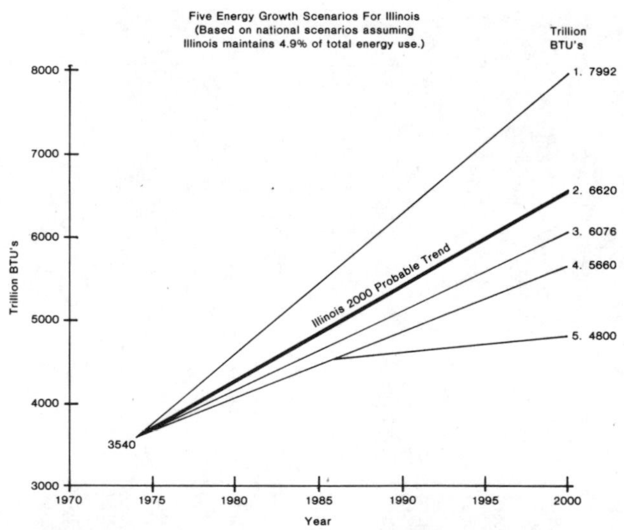

Major Assumptions

1. Bureau of Mines: 3.2% growth rate, historical trends continue, no supply problems.
2. Illinois 2000: Based on Standard Oil of Indiana scenario, 2.6% growth rate, conservation by industry and residences, supplies respond to price increases.
3. Carter Administration National Energy Plan: 2.0% growth rate by 1985, response to restrictions on oil and natural gas use, strong conservation program.
4. Ford Foundation Technological Fix: 1.9% growth rate, strong conservation from shifts to service-oriented economy, increased home insulation, energy-efficient appliances, large reductions in petroleum use.
5. Ford Foundation Zero Energy Growth: reduction in growth rate to zero by 2000, strong tax policies reduce energy use, causing major employment shifts to government and service sector jobs, heavy reliance on mass transit, reduction of conventional energy inputs.

The editor thanks the Illinois 2000 Foundation for permission to publish the following excerpts from *Alternative Economic Futures for Illinois: Executive Summary* (December, 1978), pp. 19–24.

cate that nuclear power will provide almost 50% of the state's electric power by the year 2000. Although Illinois' experience with nuclear power has demonstrated significant cost savings to consumers over other alternatives, regulatory issues are increasing capital and operating costs. Increased use of nuclear power in the state and nationally will depend in part on the federal government's ability to resolve long-term waste storage and fuel recycling issues.

C. Natural gas and petroleum contributed 35% and 33%, respectively, of Illinois' energy consumption in 1974. In the state, natural gas is used primarily for home heating and industrial uses; petroleum is used primarily for transportation. The future of both these critical fuels, in terms of price and supply, will be determined by forthcoming national energy policies and pricing patterns.

D. After the year 2000, alternative and renewable sources of energy, such as solar, wind, and waste combustion, could play an increasingly important but relatively small role in power generation as non-renewable sources decline. This will depend on technological and cost breakthroughs. Solar heating and cooling for homes and buildings are already increasing throughout the country. Solar installations will eventually have lower environmental and energy input costs and will be more decentralized. Illinois also has the potential for national leadership in production of alcohol for fuel from grains.

E. Conservation represents a major "source" for solving future energy problems. Increased conservation has already led to a downward revision in long-term energy projections, as reflected in the Illinois 2000 probable trend. Savings can be effected through adoption of energy-efficient production techniques and implementation of new design and thermal standards for all buildings.

F. Petrochemical companies and energy producers will compete for petroleum and natural gas as stocks of these resources decline. Eventual production of liquid fuels from coal and agricultural products would insure the continued availability of petroleum feed stocks for the petro-chemical industry.

3. Capital availability.

   A. Capital requirements in the energy industry grew by 15% per year from 1965 to 1973, while energy use rose at 3.6% per year. In addition, energy increased its share of national capital needed from 23% to 34%.

   B. This dramatic rise in capital needs was accompanied by a shift in capital generation mechanisms, in which internally-generated capital dropped from 60% to 40% of total capital.

   C. Based on the probable trend and these growth rates, long-term national energy capital needs will increase from $.325 billion/quad in 1985 to $2.71 billion/quad in the year 2000.

   D. The energy industry in Illinois and other states will be hard-pressed to meet these staggering capital needs, particularly in light of the intense competition from other sectors, long lead times for installations, and increasing environmental and safety costs. Changes in the above patterns, plus increased conservation and energy efficiency, will affect total capital needs.

4. Regulatory policy and energy planning.

   A. There are no uniform, agreed-upon goals for state energy policy. The conflicts among energy interest groups in Illinois provide no unified voice on proposed federal laws and regulations. Therefore, regulations may be adopted which are not in the state's best economic interest.

   B. The combination of overlapping authorities for the administration of energy and energy-related environmental regulations severely hampers state-directed development of its energy resources. This is particularly true of coal development. In addition, the confusing number of permits necessary for energy site development cause costly major delays in construction.

   C. Although the state has a mechanism for assessing the economic effects of environmental regulations, there is now no means of extending that process to the effects of regulations on meeting energy needs.

5. Energy pricing.

   A. Energy price increases are an important element in increased coal production, accelerated development of alternative energy sources, and further expansion of domestic natural gas and petroleum supplies. The state must await federal decisions as to what extent the market will be permitted to shape future energy prices.

   B. Price increases may increase conservation, particularly in transportation. However, technological changes in automobiles and public transit will also conserve fuel.

   C. Price increases will tend to cause social and economic disruptions because many capital structures and land use patterns have been set by low energy prices. Further, low income citizens will be most severely affected.

   D. Until the early 1970's, electric rates had been declining. With increased fuel prices, environmental costs, and interest charges, rates have risen in line with other prices. The utilities and the Illinois Commerce Commission face major options concerning alternative pricing policies that will affect total energy use and peak loads.

Alternatives

I. Business as usual (no change for current policies and programs)

Lacking any national energy policy, Illinois takes no significant action to insure that its energy needs for the year 2000 will be met. As a result, national shortages of petroleum and natural gas caused by continued price controls, accompanied by cyclical capital shortages for energy development, lead to an uncertain energy supply, slow erosion in economic growth, and loss of jobs in the state.

Energy industries are obliged to plan around capital availability rather than energy need. Although the state's role in energy policy increases, uncoordinated implementation of federal environmental regulations and lack of consensus among interest groups cause further delays in state energy development. This boosts costs for design and construction of new coal and nuclear installations. These must double output to meet projected needs by the year 2000. But the problems detailed above cause some serious delays.

Illinois coal development will increase as petroleum prices climb, but full development will be hindered by uncoordinated environmental and safety regulations.

II. Aggressive initiatives instituted to overcome problems

At the national level, consensus is finally reached on a national energy policy permitting domestically produced oil to seek world price levels and allowing deregulation of natural gas by 1985. The effects of these crucial steps are felt in Illinois and the nation as coal becomes more competitive with oil for electricity generation.

This increases Illinois coal production and use. Alternative sources, such as solar and wind, may become more economically justifiable. Increased energy efficiency is realized in transportation, industrial production, and building. National policy makers also recognize that social and income problems must be solved separately from energy policy. One option proposed is an "energy" stamps program for low and fixed income citizens.

In Illinois, the state, industry, and public interest groups agree to develop a state energy policy consistent with a projected 87% increase in energy use, yet meeting basic environmental and social goals. Based on these goals, a cost/benefit analysis of new energy regulations is undertaken.

Regulatory authority is unified at the state level for each energy source. The state adopts special policies to speed up the site selection and construction process in order to remove uncertainties from capital investments in energy. The Illinois Commerce Commission acts flexibly to shape electric utility rates compatible with actual investment costs, including environmental costs. Interim rate relief is allowed to permit utilities to keep pace with inflation. These and other steps signal the state's commitment to economic growth and result in increased state competitiveness for plant creation and expansion. This is further enhanced in the 1990's by Illinois' expansion as a center for alternative fuels from coal and agricultural products.

Policies:

1. Increasing involvement at the state level.
   A. Establishment of a limited-risk corporation through initial state guarantees (similar to COMSAT) for development of alternative energy sources:
   B. ICC could consider allowing construction work in progress into the rate base, to aid in financing energy supply growth.
   C. Legislative action to reduce regulatory lag in rate hearings.
   D. State agency action to reduce lead times for new energy installations.
   E. State agency action to avoid changing environmental controls after a project is under construction.
2. State regulatory and planning policy.
   A. Development of a public/private energy forum to set uniform state energy goals as the basis for balancing environmental, energy, and economic issues. This may be difficult to do, given current disagreements over energy goals among major state and private agencies.
   B. State adopts a policy of unifying regulatory authority for each source within one agency and at the appropriate level of applicability.
   C. State, industry, and interest groups agree on simplified siting legislation.
   D. State presses for a national clearninghouse on emergency energy allocations and then ties state allocations plan to it.
3. Pricing policies for state action.
   A. ICC and utilities design new electric pricing structures which accurately reflect the costs of service. This should encourage conservation.
   B. ICC and utilities institute studies of "time of day," cogeneration, and "assist" energy pricing. (The latter refers to combined central station and alternative energy generation.)

III. Affirmative rejection of energy problems; resources shifted to other sectors

Society at national and state levels decides that the price for energy sufficiency, as projected by the energy industry, is too great to pay. Past rapid increases in energy capital costs are seen as excessive, and steps are taken to reduce the energy industry's future ability to raise capital. Further, at the national level, prices are kept under strict political control on the theory that supplies will be developed in response to continuing demand. Also, the disruption of other sectors of the economy would be too serious to risk. Thus, there is no incentive to conserve petroleum and natural gas.

In Illinois, the rejection of utility rate increases, based on strong consumer pressure, coupled with strict enforcement of environmental regulations and extended delays in energy site approval, lead to a rapid decline in industry confidence in future energy supplies. Coal development is stifled by lack of competition and continuing environmental regulations.

Unforeseen national fuel shortages during severe winters accelerate departure of industries dependent on natural gas to areas with intrastate supplies. Combined state and national shortages lead to economic decline.

Policies:

1. Federal policies to reduce investment tax credit rates, disallowal of deferred tax on accelerated depreciation, changes in amortization rates.
2. State policies to reduce allowable rates of return, elimination of lower cost bonding, and strict and accelerating enforcement of environmental regulations.

Environment

Issues

1. Illinois' capacity to achieve national environmental standards set to improve public health and general welfare.
2. Lack of public awareness of the costs, benefits, or trade-offs of present and future environmental control activities.
3. Management of pollution control programs as a major determinant of growth patterns.
4. Increased decision-making and the design of implementation policies at the federal level. This exists in the absence of clear state objectives and an effective state administrative unit for environmental management.
5. Effectiveness of the enforcement approach in controlling non-point sources of pollution and non-traditional pollutants and in dealing with more complex and costly pollution issues.

Major Trends and Indicators

1. Costs of achieving additional reductions in pollution will increase for existing plants, but total costs cannot be accurately predicted on a statewide basis.
2. Government, industry, and environmentalists generally agree that the goal of zero pollution is unattainable and undefinable.
3. Physical and monetary limitations will produce a leveling-off in improvements of environmental quality in respect to "traditional" pollutants.
4. The federal government will continue to rely on technology-forcing regulations to meet environmental goals.
5. As we move toward the year 2000, emphasis in environmental management will shift from control of point to control of non-point sources of pollution.
6. The nature of pollution will change in terms of types of pollutants and estimates of impact on health.
7. Management of environmental programs will develop along two basic paths:
   A. Setting of goals and standards will be focused at the federal level.
   B. The federal government will increase its use of financial sanctions and other incentives to increase the role of the state and local governments as implementers and enforcers of federal law.

Alternatives

I. National environmental goals are achieved by the year 2000 through significant lifestyle changes and advances in technology

Simpler lifestyles, brought on by high costs and education programs about the effects of pollution and technological advances in pollution control and energy generation, enable the country to achieve its environmental goals. Focus on implementation in the 1980's is on the local and neighborhood levels, particularly for development of non-polluting industries. Strict limitations and high user fees on water supply and waste treatment permit water treatment plants to use excess capacity to treat storm run-off, a major cause of non-point water pollution.

Pollution from traditional energy production is reduced through increased application of stack gas control techniques, together with the use of nuclear energy and the advent of solar heating and cooling units in many Illinois homes and buildings.

Under pressure from high capital costs for farm inputs, agriculture shifts to labor intensive cultivation methods which emphasize soil conservation, use of organic fertilizers, and integrated pest management. These practices nearly solve the agricultural erosion and run-off problems by the year 2000. Hazardous wastes and toxic substances are greatly reduced as businesses respond to public pressure and to legislation to remove all such wastes from production.

The citizens learn to live more frugally, on a smaller scale, and in a slower growing economy. However, the increase in labor intensive activity and recycling industries increases job opportunities and keep unemployment at low levels.

II. By the year 2000, national environmental goals are achieved through major advances in pollution control technology, large capital investments, and some changes in lifestyle

The next decade proves difficult for commerce and industry as they struggle to meet new federal environmental standards with inadequate technologies. Major outlays for air and water pollution control, control over industrial siting, and restrictions on auto use to reduce non-point pollution lead to increased inflation, slowed growth in urban areas, and shifting lifestyles as higher costs force citizens to conserve.

By the middle of the 1980's, however, the investments in new technologies begin to yield benefits in terms of reduced pollution and installation costs. Fossil-fueled automobiles with cleaner emission systems, combined with electric cars, remove the major urban source of non-point air pollution, permitting a relaxation of land use controls and transportation controls. Newer, quieter aircraft permit removal of operations restrictions on airports which had caused severe economic hardship. In spite of these advances, however, new pollutants challenge industry to develop more sophisticated control technologies.

Benefits from these programs also become evident in reduced damage to exposed materials, reduced health costs from respiratory diseases, improved urban environments for tourism and recreation, and increased use of Illinois coal.

New recycling industries emerge in response to higher costs and legislation. Agricultural policies for land preservation and prevention of erosion and run-off through improved cultivation and fertilization practices succeed in eliminating the major rural non-point source of water pollution.

Federal standards for environmental protection prevail nationally, with state serving as primary implementer of the programs. The federal government maintains control of toxic substance regulation, pressing producers to determine the environmental effects of new products in advance.

In sum, this federal, state and private partnership, aided by technological breakthroughs and significant changes in public awareness, permits higher environmental quality than anticipated, while still maintaining a strong economy.

III. National environmental goals are selectively revised and partially attained

During the 1980's and 1990's, federal environmental standards become a mixture of stricter standards for some pollutants and relaxation for others. Lack of technical progress in management of auto emissions and other non-point sources of air and water pollution leads to more severe and costly controls for industrial and municipal point sources. Restrictions on growth in urban areas, caused by the continuing inability of Illinois' major cities to meet ozone and hydrocarbon standards, cause citizens and industry to seek a more flexible relationship with the federal Environmental Protection Agency.

Under this new approach, based on a consensus among the major interest groups, the state still conducts its program within the envelope of federal standards. However, simpler plans for implementation, increased flexibility in designation of "economic development areas" under the Clean Air Act, and greater consideration of economic and social goals permit industrial expansion in the urban areas at the expense of some increased pollution.

IEPA administration is strengthened to handle industrial needs for timely processing of permits and the development of creative incentive and cost-sharing plans for pollution control. In the area of airport noise abatement, the federal government assumes complete control over regulations, eliminating the complex of conflicting local restrictions.

In agriculture, cultivation, pest control, and fertilizer use continue along traditional lines, thus delaying attempts to control farmland erosion and run-off. As international resource prices rise, resource recovery and energy conservation become more widespread. Efforts to control toxic substances and hazardous wastes make little progress, except in crisis situations. No long-term solution is found for disposing of nuclear wastes.

This flexible and creative environmental control program which Illinois adopts in the 1980's permits the state to grow economically while adjusting to stronger federal environmental controls.

IV. Environmental standards are generally frozen at 1980 levels with some relaxations in air quality standards

The lack of technical advances in auto emission control, accompanied by increasing capital shortages for pollution abatement, forces the federal government to relax its increasingly strict environmental standards.

Although point source control is achieved, non-point source control proves unattainable because of the complexities of implementation. As a result, the urban environment does not improve.

Continued economic growth necessitates greater energy production, leading to development of coal and nuclear energy parks and increased production of Illinois coal. With concentration of jobs in the city, urban sprawl decreases, although more agricultural land is lost to strip mining. Agricultural run-off and heavy use of chemical pesticides continue to pose problems for stream and ground water quality. The problems of disposal of toxic substances, hazardous and nuclear wastes, and solid wastes multiply as existing facilities become overloaded in the 1980's.

The inability of government, business, and environmental groups to develop cooperative means of reaching environmental goals leads to a steadily deteriorating environment, despite continued economic growth.

CHAPTER **29**

Environment and Natural Resources

Michael Schneiderman

This Chapter covers governmental programs and issues commonly grouped under the headings "environment," "natural resources," and "conservation." The topics traditionally thought of when those terms are used include: (1) pollution control; (2) surface mining regulation; and (3) management of open space, recreation, water, soil, fuels and energy.

Pollution Control

Constitutional Right

The 1970 Illinois Constitution explicitly provides for environmental protection.[1] The Convention met in 1970, at the height of public and political environmental awareness; its sessions surrounded the first "Earth Day" national environmental demonstration. It is not surprising that a constitution drafted in that atmosphere addresses this subject. However, the "Environment" Article in the new Constitution is more limited in its objectives than Earth Day was. It provides:

> The public policy of the State and the duty of each person is to provide and maintain a healthful environment for the benefit of this and future generations. The General Assembly shall provide by law for the implementation and enforcement of this public policy.
>
> Each person has the right to a healthful environment. Each person may enforce this right against any party, governmental or private, through appropriate legal proceedings subject to reasonable limitation and regulation as the General Assembly may provide by law.

The principal spokespersons for this Article at the Constitutional Convention made clear that this is a pollution control provision; it does not deal with other environmental concerns.

The right created by the Environment Article is limited to effects of pollution on human health. The meaning of the phrase "healthful environment" was debated at length. One of the drafters explained:

> We were concerned, really, with the essence of what people were complaining about, and that was damage to their health and damage to the health of future generations.[2]

The Convention apparently intended to cover "those things that might adversely affect the mental healthful [sic] environment as well as the physical."[3] It did not intend to cover "esthetics,"[4] or property damage,[5] or "sight pollution" (such as roadside signs).[6] According to one court which has ruled on the scope of this consitutional right, the recreational interest of a hunter in a healthy supply of game is not protected by the Environmental Article.[7]

The limitation of the Environment Article to pollution was in part a result of the committee's allocation of "conservation" to another proposed article, which it had also drafted.[8] The "Conservation Article" was presented to the Convention, and extensively debated by it, but was not adopted.[9]

The limitation of the Article was also a result of compromise among various views at the Convention. Although public interest in environmental protection was substantial in 1970, some Convention delegates were concerned about the effect of aggressive pollution control regulation on business and economic development, and about preserving local prerogatives to regulate such matters as local pollution. Others feared government interference in private affairs. This coalition of interests managed to get the provision pared down to a protection against damage to human health. The principal spokesperson for the Article said:

> Well, to put the cards on the table, this was the most we could get through the committee and thought we could get through the Convention. The majority of the committee just simply didn't feel that words like recreational, esthetic, pleasant, clean, et cetera, would make it through the committee or through the Convention.[10]

The State Program

The major focus of government environmental programs since 1970 has been pollution control. Of all environmental initiatives in the decade following Earth Day, pollution control commands the broadest political support. The Illinois program adopted in 1970 has weathered years of determined attack essentially unchanged.

What is Pollution? Pollutants are materials present in the environment which for one reason or another people do not want there. Technical definitions reflecting this common understanding appear in State law. They speak in terms of the harm caused. For example:

> "Air pollution" is the presence in the atmosphere of one or more contaminants in sufficient quantities and of such characteristics and duration as to be injurious to human, plant, or animal life, to health, or to property, or to unreasonably interefere with the enjoyment of life or property.[11]

Water pollution is similarly defined in State law.[12] To "prevent the pollution or misuse of land," State law controls disposal of wastes on land.[13] The State's "noise pollution" program is designed to control noise that "unreasonably intereferes with the enjoyment of life or with any lawful business or activity."[14]

As these definitions make clear—through their use of such terms as "sufficient quantities" and "unreasonably interfere"—not all new contributions to the air and water are pollution for purposes of law enforcement. On the other hand, some materials which might appear harmless, can be pollutants—for example, hot water discharged to a river, and emissions of materials already naturally present. In each case, the test is framed in terms of the harm which the emissions cause.

These legislative notions of pollution are broader than the Constitutional Convention's health-related concept. When the State's current pollution control law was proposed, the Governor made that clear.

> The present narrow conception of environmental protection as a mere incident of public health is no longer adequate. Degradation of the environment is often a serious health problem. It may adversely, however, effect recreational, esthetic, industrial, agricultural and commercial interests.[15]

State Administrative Program One law, and three closely related agencies created by that law, administer the Illinois program. The law is the Environmental Protection Act;[16] the agencies are the Environmental Protection Agency (EPA), the Pollution Control Board (PCB) and the Institute of Natural Resources (INR).[17] Such centralized management of all pollutants, regardless of whether they are discharged into the air or water, or on land, is now characteristic of programs in other states, and of local and federal programs.

The view of pollution as a single problem requiring co-ordinated attention is relatively recent. Historically, pollution was perceived in government in terms of what was polluted: generally, air, water or land. The attention of government was drawn to these problems at different times, and produced separate programs, each assigned to its own agency. In Illinois and the federal government, three essentially separate administrations dealt with air, water and solid waste.

In 1970, Illinois reorganized pollution control into a single program. The federal government and many other states, including all of the major industrial states, reorganized their environmental administrations at about the same time.[18] All of this sudden activity responded to the political fact that environmental protection had become a "hot" issue. Reorganization is one classic way that people in political life attempt to demonstrate attentiveness to such an issue. The Governor's explanation relied on well-established ideas:

> [A]uthority is fragmented among various agencies according to artificial subject-matter distinctions: Air-pollution is lodged in the Air Pollution Control Board, water-pollution control in the Sanitary Water Board, solid-waste management in the Department of Public Health. Communications are facilitated by the expedient of having three staffs with a single head, but decision making authority is parceled out to three theoretically independent agencies.
>
> Environmental protection cannot with safety be so artificially categorized. What is done to the air may affect the water. Disposal of solid wastes may cause air and water pollution problems. Care *must* be taken so that efforts to improve one resource do not worsen another. We live in one unified environment and we need one unified program.[19]

One effect of the reorganization was to remove this whole subject from the Department of Public Health, which was left primarily with control of diseases caused by micro-organisms. While consolidating previously scattered functions, the Act also added new powers with respect to noise and radioactivity.[20]

Any pollution control program must perform the following functions: make detailed rules specifying the amounts of pollutants that may be emitted, the acceptable conditions of the receiving medium, and the practices of polluters; inspect for pollution and for violaters of the Act and the rules; issue administrative orders and prosecute violaters; hold hearings and decide cases involving alleged pollution and grant permission to violate the rules (variances); order remedial and abatement action and impose penalties; and conduct research into the causes and effects of pollution, the impact of pollution control, and the technology of abatement. In Illinois, the Environmental Protection Agency investigates, inspects, and enforces; the Pollution Control Board makes rules, hears cases, issues orders to abate pollution, and levies civil penalties; the Institute of Natural Resources does research. The Directors of the EPA and INR, and the five PCB members are appointed by the Governor, with the advice and consent of the Senate.

The Illinois three-agency arrangement is unique. It is "an atypical response to common problems that have led various other states to reorganize."[21] In most states, and in the federal government, all of the major functions of a pollution control program are centralized in a single agency under a single director. The unusual Illinois approach was motivated in part by administrative theory, and in part by practical considerations thought to be important at the time.

Separation of enforcement activity from hearings avoids the situation in which the "staff becomes in substance both prosecutor and judge—a situation not consistent with the impartiality expected of an arbiter under the rule of law."[22] Under the old system, a polluter would be charged with a violation by the same official who controlled the decision of whether he was guilty. Such combinations are common in government, particularly in federal administrative agencies.[23] However, it is reasonable to doubt the fairness of a hearing conducted within the prosecuting agency; conversely, how can a prosecutor zealously do his job if he must maintain the appearance (as well as the fact) of impartiality at the hearings on the charge he has brought. Such difficulties can be avoided by committing all decision-making to the courts, which is common elsewhere. However, the drafters of the Act thought that an administrative tribunal would develop expertise which would make it peculiarly competent to try pollution cases.

The assignment of rulemaking to an independent PCB resulted from political considerations. One of the drafters of the Act explained this decision as follows:

> Rulemaking authority was given to the Board, not so much out of abstract public-administration principles as to assure that the authority would be exercised vigorously; it was known in the drafting stage that the Agency would necessarily be manned largely by the staffs of the previous agencies and headed by the longtime chief of staff to the old air and water boards, while the new Board would be chosen afresh by the Governor.[24]

The promise to staff the new EPA with old enforcement agency staff was thought by the Governor's staff to be a political necessity to get votes for the proposed Act. It was designed to calm fears in some quarters that the new program would be a radical departure from the past. The impact of that commitment was reduced by the expedient of giving the PCB, with its new personnel, as much power as possible under the new law.

Rulemaking usually involves policy choices. How clean should the air or water be in light of the costs and technology of pollution control? Should some polluters be excused? How fast must offending pollution be stopped? Because such decisions are made by the independent PCB, some pollution control policy in Illinois is beyond the direct control of the Governor and the EPA. Such independence may be both blessing and curse for the Governor. The notorious example is the PCB's September, 1971 Statewide ban on burning autumn leaves. In July, 1972, in the midst of the Governor's re-election campaign, the EPA suggested to the PCB that the ban be relaxed. In late November, after the election, the PCB complied.

Leaf burning was a campaign issue. The new Governor's EPA head said later:

> Walking through the state, Walker (the new Governor) was literally accosted by farmers and residents of small towns bitterly assailing the (previous) administration for a variety of regulations beginning with leaf burning.[25]

The new Governor promised he would end the leaf burning ban.[26] But the real relaxation of such regulation was the product not of the independent PCB, but the General Assembly, which amended the Act.[27]

Practically everywhere except in Illinois, rulemaking is the job of the enforcing agency. This is plainly more efficient. The cumbersome PCB procedures can drag on for years. Reasonably prompt response to regulatory errors and needs for change is practically impossible.

The separation of research from enforcement and rulemaking, which the Illinois scheme provides, is also unusual. The drafters' rationale was that "staff experts cannot be freed from immediate enforcement duties" to attend to research on longer range problems.[28] At the time, the drafters had in mind the complex planing required to clean the air in Chicago, which included rules affecting the location of new industry. The Act requires the INR to provide "expert advice" to the other two agencies. It does not specify what the EPA and the PCB are to do if the INR will not, or cannot, respond.

When the Act was passed, some people were concerned about the potential for inefficiency in the three-headed system. The first Chairman of the PCB has said:

> I acknowledge that there were times when as Chairman of the Board I wished I had power to file complaints or to undertake extensive studies looking toward the development of regulations, but efficiency is not the only concern in devising government institutions.[29]

A careful analyst of environmental programs in many states reached this conclusion:

> The interdependence of the three organizations, without a formal coordinating mechanism, has created the main problems in the Illinois system.[30]

More or less voluntary efforts to coordinate the activities of the three agencies have characterized the system since 1970, largely based on the personal efforts of the EPA and INR directors and the PCB's chairman. But the process has its frictions. The PCB has been known to blame INR for delaying rules by producing studies too slowly. EPA directors have complained that the PCB takes too long to adopt rules. The PCB has charged that the EPA processes certain kinds of cases too slowly. Such finger pointing is inevitable; however, it is overshadowed by the public benefits from a decade of interagency support and coordination.

Other Players Local governments, the Attorney General, and private citizens are independent pollution controllers. In 1970, when the Act was being considered, some people wanted to pre-empt such separate powers. The Governor's spokesman opposed preemption.

> The Attorney General and the cities have done some of our most effective work in this field; it is no wonder that polluters want to get rid of them.
>
> The State is in no position to put other pollution fighters out of business since it has never had an adequate program of its own. The mere passage of a new law, however promising, is not enough to establish that the State will do its full share.[31]

Preserving the Attorney General's powers was consistent with the program. Because of his influence with some members of the General Assembly, it was also a political necessity to get the votes to pass the Act.

Citizens can bring enforcement actions before the PCB or file common law nuisance cases in the courts. The Attorney General can file proceedings before the PCB *or* bring independent actions under other laws in the courts. Cities and counties can operate their own pollution control administrative efforts, and many do. A factory in Chicago may be subject to State, Cook County and City of Chicago authorities, and may have to defend litigation brought by the Attorney General or a private citizen.

All of this potential for action breeds competition for visibility and public approval. This was part of the design.

> [T]he Illinois approach is grounded in the belief that some duplication of responsibilities promotes a healthy competition that will maximize action against pollution. It assumes that interacting and overlapping organizations, with an involved citizenry, will "check and balance" inadequate or arbitrary action by any one organization.[32]

The players have competed. Citizen suits have been brought, with the petitions sometimes suggesting that the EPA has not done its job.[33] The Attorney General has sued on his own, and as the EPA's lawyer. He has sued to close a land fill which had received an EPA permit.[34] A battle was waged for years between the EPA and the Attorney General, trading charges about their zeal.[35]

Citizens rarely file formal complaints against polluters. In more than eight years, an average of 18 citizen complaints have been filed each year.[36] Industry feared a flood of citizen suits, but none has occured. The reasons are unclear. The PCB's first Chairman has said:

> The responsibility for providing one's case seems to be sobering one, to the point that, in my opinion, too few citizen complaints are being filed.[37]

Other possible reasons are the cost of suit, the fear of being charged with attorney's fees if the suit is unsuccessful and the effectiveness of the efforts of the EPA and the Attorney General in controlling pollution.

Federal Presence Illinois pollution control efforts, like those in most states, follow a federal recipe. In many cases, the State does little more than administer a federal program.

Federal control is designed to protect everybody in the country from certain hazards, even if they, or their state governments, are unconcerned. A decade ago, when the movement to strengthen federal pollution laws was gaining momentum, Illinois had relatively good pollution control programs. Many other states did not, and Congress wanted to fill the gaps.

> The promulgation of Federal emission standards for new sources . . . will preclude efforts on the part of States to compete with each other in trying to attract new plants and facilities without assuring adequate control of extra-hazardous or large-scale emissions therefrom.[38]

Similar arguments were made in connection with recent amendments to federal water pollution control legislation.

Federal control is not subtle. Laws dealing with air and water pollution and with solid waste subject the whole country to uniform requirements.[39] These laws, and massive regulations under them, set standards, establish deadlines, and provide procedures. They apply everywhere, either through state or federal officials.

A state may administer a program if it persuades the United States Environmental Protection Agency (USEPA) that it has the legal, administrative and fiscal resources to do the job. Once a state program is approved, USEPA checks periodically to see if it is being implemented. Federal approval can be revoked. In the absence of an effective state program, the federal government is supposed to do the job in the state itself.

States generally want to administer these federal programs. Virtually all states do so. Polluters exercise their political influences to persuade states to take over such control because they prefer to deal with state enforcement personnel and the somewhat more accessible state government. State governments want to control pollution, to the extent they can within federal rules, according to their own political priorities.[40] Under federal pollution control laws, states receive federal subsidies for part of their administrative costs. If a state is going to be in the pollution control business anyway, it costs fewer state tax dollars to do it as part of an approved federal program.[41] These various incentives make state participation in federal pollution programs a political and fiscal necessity.

The result is pervasive federal presence in the Illinois pollution effort. The Illinois EPA's *Annual Report* displays the strength of the federal grasp. Messages from two federal officials open the *Report* and occupy the most prominent place in it—ahead of any hint that state officials even exist. The EPA's Director focuses repeatedly on federal requirements in his message.[42]

As federal programs have developed, Illinois has tried to modify its pre-existing pollution control programs to conform, not always successfully. As federal demands have increased, Illinois has not always been able or willing to comply. For example, controls on automobile emissions, and requirements to limit driving or inspect vehicles to achieve clean air goals, have been particular sore points because of their political volatility. As in many states, Illinois has resisted such federal instructions, often successfully. The USEPA and Congress are reluctant to resort to Draconian measures to force state compliance. Although Illinois generally dances to the federal tune, some federal demands will not be implemented.

Issues

Among the major issues concerning pollution control are these: (1) regulation in the face of scientific uncertainty, (2) balancing costs of pollution control against benefits, and (3) the role of local government.

Scientific Uncertainty Political support for pollution control is rooted in the desire to prevent the damage pollutants cause. Although the general proposition that pollution causes harm is plainly true, the difficulty is that the effects of particular pollutants are frequently unknown. In the rush to regulate, ignited by public clamor, the scientific method is sometimes forgotten. As a result, public policy sometimes is made on a base of scientific uncertainty. For example, the effects of such air pollutants as sulfur dioxide and carbon monoxide in the concentrations commonly found are not fully known. The same is true for trace metals in the atmosphere, such as beryllium and lead. It is possible, but not clear, that such materials even in low concentrations cause very serious illnesses.

Congress has declared that regulation must proceed, even when knowledge is imperfect.

> The Committee is aware that there are many gaps in the available scientific knowledge of the welfare and other environmental effects of air pollution agents. . . . A great deal of basic research will be needed to determine the long-term air quality goals which are required to protect the public health and welfare from any potential effects of air pollution. In the meantime, the Secretary will be expected to establish such national goals on the basis of the best information available to him.[43]

Regulatory action without a firm scientific base is both defended and criticized. One regulator defends it as follows:

> Obtaining good epidemiological data that can resolve certain issues will require 20 years or so. To wait for such resolution may expose humans to potential hazards that can lead to even greater burdens and health care costs.
>
> In many instances, current data are sufficiently strong to warrant policies for regulatory intervention. In these cases, the economic and social costs of waiting for more definitive scientific answers outweight the costs of preventive policies that limit exposure to suspected health hazards.[44]

Here is the opposing view:

> Obviously, policy-makers will never have enough data; however, 'bad science' severely compounds the problem, and premature regulation can have many disbenefits, including the foreclosure of research. . . . Increased industrial costs and inefficiencies [resulting from environmental controls] mean increased poverty and decreased health which has to be balanced against the health effects avoided in the first place.[45]

How much proof of harm should be required before regulatory action may be taken? Must industry prove absolutely the absence of harm? May regulators prove only that a reasonable likelihood of harm exists? "The whole delicate framework of toxic substances regulation rests on the fragile premise that it is possible to identify which chemicals are hazardous and should be regulated and which are safe and can be ignored."[46]

It is easy to say that all risk should be avoided, and that any reasonable evidence of possible harm should trigger control. A substantial political constituency exists for views at that end of the spectrum of regulatory possibilities. But regulation and pollution control are not free.

> The point underscored is that chemicals are ubiquitous in the environment and that some of them are dangerous. Chemicals also contribute significantly to American living standards, and regulating them involves substantial economic consequences.[47]

In politics, the existence of scientific uncertainty is sometimes overlooked. Preliminary findings, tentative conclusions and credible hypotheses may be treated as if they are facts. Suspected risks may be represented as unavoidable hazards. Government officials may prefer to listen to the scientists who speak in readily comprehended, unequivocal phrases. An experienced observer of the politics of the environment says: "The public does not understand the need for scientists to equivocate."[48]

Scientific uncertainty produces political and policy difficulties. No clear procedure has been developed for weighing such risks.

> The matter boils down to some determination of society's acceptance of the risk implied by the estimated uncertainties. This judgment can only be properly made by the decision-makers who have been politically designated by society and entrusted with the power to decide for it.[49]

The Illinois Constitution grants each person "the right to a healthful environment." If an environmental danger to health is possible, but not scientifically certain, what does the Constitution require? Does the answer depend on whether there is (1) a slight chance of a great harm, or (2) a great chance of a minor injury? If the degree of the danger is simply unknowable, what should government do? If elimination of a hypothetical, but unproved, injury is very costly, how should the absolute certainty of the cost of prevention be weighed against the theoretical harm? Should such choices be left to the legislature? Should a referendum be held to determine how much uncertainty the public will tolerate? In the absence of clear answers from science, we rely upon the political process to answer, or avoid answering, these questions at any given time.

Costs and Benefits Pollution control is expensive. Is it worth the price? The General Accounting Office of Congress concludes that government is not equipped to decide that question intelligently.

> One shortcoming we noted throughout our review was that the primitive state of cost/benefit analysis generally precluded Federal decisionmakers from comparing air and water pollution control costs with benefits. Existing environmental controls were generally established in response to public pressure and concern over the seriousness of the pollution problem. Now, however, there is increasing concern in the private and public sectors about whether the economic and social costs of achieving current environmental protection standards and requirements are worth the degree that the environmental quality is improved.[50]

Costs of pollution control generally can be measured with reasonable certainty in dollars. The cost of installation, operation and maintenance of equipment is known. However, some costs remain speculative. If an industrial facility cannot comply with standards and goes out of business, the resulting social and economic costs may be hard to quantify. Interstate and international competitive costs are difficult to determine.

Benefits are far more difficult to estimate.

> [B]enefits of controlling environmental pollution arise from the reduction of damages caused by pollution. As such, the measurement of benefits is based on the costs of damages

> that would be incurred if there were no pollution reduction. Economists prefer to evaluate benefits in monetary terms, because it provides a common unit of measure for all the categories of benefits and all the types of costs.[51]

Many damages cannot be stated in terms of money, such as those related to aesthetics and behavior. It is difficult to value in dollars the pleasure people experience from clean water or spectacular views. No objective way exists to measure in money the psychological damages resulting from noise or dirt.

Illinois law requires the Institute of Natural Resources to make a cost and benefit analysis for proposed pollution control regulations. Such "economic impact studies" must include, among other things:

> An evaluation of the environmental costs, and benefits of the rules and regulations to the people of the State of Illinois, including the health, welfare and social costs and benefits.[52]

Complete studies generally reveal frustration with the "benefits" part of this analysis.[53]

Even if regulations are adopted, application of them to particular cases requires consideration of the economic impact of the emissions and the cost of their control. On the basis of such an analysis, some pollution has been held to be "reasonable" and therefore permissible.[54]

In recent years, the political process has become increasingly sensitive to the money costs of pollution control. The 1975 law which requires economic impact studies was an industry proposal for which industry fought hard. The law's long prescription for the studies concentrates on costs of regulation. Similar requirements have been imposed by Congress recently. These efforts may be viewed as counterattack to the assumption built into many pollution control laws that pollution control is a desirable social good even at extremely high costs.

How should costs be balanced against benefits? Do small groups of seriously affected people have a right to be protected at any cost? Should a majority be allowed to decide that protection of a vulnerable minority (for example, the elderly and the ill) is not justified in light of the cost? Who should balance the harms resulting from closing a hopelessly polluting factory against the harms resulting from its pollution? What principles of decision should apply? Once again, in the absence of technically derived answers, we turn to the political process and the administrative devices created by the Legislature.

Local Control State government has broad pollution control power. What, if anything, should local governments be allowed to do about pollution? It is clear that they can enforce State standards concurrently with the State. However, some local governments have adopted requirements which exceed State standards. The Illinois courts have held that some local enforcement is preempted by State law.

Uniformity in pollution control makes some sense. The Environmental Protection Act states "that because environmental damage does not respect political boundaries, it is necessary to establish a unified state-wide program for environmental protection."[55] That is an argument for uniform minimum standards; polluters in a lenient community should not be allowed to foul other communities' air and water. But it is not clear why communities should not be allowed to impose additional standards which do not conflict with State rules, in the way that federal pollution control laws allow states to establish more stringent requirements. That would let local governments protect their people from unusual local effects of pollution.

One reason commonly given for exclusive State jurisdiction is that polluters are entitled to uniform requirements regardless of location to avoid competitive disadvantage. Furthermore, it is argued that State pre-emption may be essential if facilities such as sanitary landfills are to exist at all. Everybody depends on landfills to absorb their garbage, but nobody wants one nearby. In theory, unless the State can override local objections to such facilities, all communities could exclude them. Twice the Illinois Supreme Court ruled by narrow majorities that a local government cannot exclude a landfill which has been approved by the State.[56]

Despite its emphatic statement of exclusive State control in a 1972 case, the Court held in 1979 that home rule units may use their zoning powers to prohibit at least some landfills approved by the State.[57]

The Supreme Court has also ruled by a narrow majority that a community may not use its constitutional home rule powers to enforce its noise control ordinance against a railroad. The Court reached its result on the surprising ground that noise pollution "is not an environmental problem of local concern" and therefore is not within the permissible home rule powers of the city under the Illinois Constitution.[58] An appellate court has voided a local attempt to regulate air pollution.[59]

How much pollution control power should local governments have? How can a local government enforce rational zoning if the State can pre-empt it for land fills? Where should land fills be located if every local community bans them? Who should decide? How? Where will the garbage go? In the railroad noise case, locomotives imposed a peculiarly local harm. The court said the city cannot stop it. If the State will not do so, what should irritated residents do? Petition the General Assembly? Sue to enforce their constitutional rights to a healthful environment? Buy ear muffs?[60] Issues like these are likely to remain with us, unresolved, for some time.

Surface Mining

The first commercial surface mine in the nation opened near Danville, Illinois in 1866. Since then, more than 197,000 Illinois acres have been stripped (twelve counties are smaller than that).[61] Some land has been put to good use since the miners left, some not. Government pressure to reclaim land began in earnest in Illinois in 1962. Today surface mined land reclamation is a major environmental program at both the State and federal levels.

The Surface Mining Problem

When coal lies deep—hundreds of feet below the surface—men and machines go underground to mine it. Slightly more than half of the coal mined in Illinois is mined in deep mines.[62] Such mines leave traces on the surface: refuse piles, abandoned shafts, and sinking of the surface over the empty caverns below (subsidence).

The other half of coal mining injures the surface even more. Where coal is near the surface—within 150 feet—earth and rock above it are scraped away and the coal is scooped out with enormous shovels. When these shovels leave, the land is generally useless unless something is done to restore it.

The United States Department of Interior has noted other environmental impacts. "Surface mining of coal completely eliminates existing vegetation, disrupts natural soil structure, destroys the genetic soil profile, displaces and (or) destroys wildlife and habitat, degrades air quality in an area, alters current land uses, and to some extent changes the general topography of the area being mined."[63] Streams may be polluted with acid and sediment, and drinking water may be contaminated. Ground water levels may go down. The countryside is dramatically changed: high walls, spoil piles, and barren acres replace rolling land. Reductions in the tax base can occur.[64]

All that damage suggests an easy political issue. But surface mining control is a classic confronttion between environmental values and economic values. Where productive farmland is stripped, the contest is between two interests, each cloaked in economic need. Stripped coal is a necessary national resource; without surface mining it can never be used. Stripping is efficient and relatively more safe for miners than deep mining. Land reclamation is never inexpensive, and its cost raises the cost of coal.

Historically, much stripped land was left without reclamation. In 1961, before the first effective Illinois law requiring reclamation, about 109,000 acres had been disturbed by surface mining. About one-third of that land is now used for pasture or other agricultural purposes, including small amounts for orchards and tilled crops. Another third is devoted to land and water recreation.[66] The remaining land is unreclaimed and unused—in the language of politics, it is "orphan" or "pre-law" land.

State Government Program

Illinois law first required reclamation in 1962.[67] Although that law (and its successors) did nothing for the orphan land, it forced miners to repair newly-mined land. That first law responded largely to rural agricultural interests. "Much of the thrust for existing mining laws came from the northwestern [Illinois] surface-mining area, which is the heart of the nation's row-crop producing region."[68] That part of the State has a history of attempts to control and prevent surface mining.[69] The law was strengthened in 1963, and again in 1968.[70]

By 1970, surface mining was no longer a rural agriculture issue. The broadened environmental constituency provided political support for new and stronger surface mine controls. In 1971, another surface mine law was adopted. It raised standards and involved county governments in the reclamation planning. Again, the initial pressure for reform came from Northwestern Illinois when a legislator from Stark County and a County Board member from Henry County persuaded the Governor that a new law was needed.[71] The broader interest in surface mining in Illinois was part of a national trend.[72]

Illinois further strengthened its law in 1975.[73] A new federal law, imposing nationwide minimum standards was passed in 1977.[74] To bring the State into compliance with it, the General Assembly adopted interim amendments to the State law in 1978,[75] and a wholly new law in 1979 to comply with the federal law.[76]

Standards are enforced largely through a permit system, which works well because surface mining is so easy to spot. Without a permit, mining is not allowed. Miners must prepare a reclamation plan which proposes post-mining land uses and shows how all requirements (such as control of acid drainage and grading of the land) will be achieved "by feasible and available means."[77] The law states:

> The Department shall approve a conservation and reclamation plan if, and only if, the plan complies with this Act and completion of the plan will in fact achieve every duty of the operator required by this Act.[78]

Among the operator's duties are compliance with the Environmental Protection Act.[79]

The power of local governments to influence land use has been a recurring issue. The Illinois Supreme Court has held that a county cannot generally exclude or regulate surface mining.[80] The 1971 law gave county boards a voice in the post-mining land use decision. Although not binding, the law requires consideration of such local views.[81]

Until 1971, the law was administered by the Department of Conservation. Much of its expertise — particularly that related to vegetation and wildlife—is relevant to reclamation. Among the trades made with coal industry representatives to get the 1971 law passed, the General Assembly transferred administration of the law to the Department of Mines and Minerals. At the time, this shift was perceived as a shift from an agency with a clear reclamation point-of-view to an industry-oriented agency. Conservation directors have tended to be conservationists and duck hunters; the Director of Mines and Minerals is by law a miner. The agency change caused some observers to worry about the future of vigorous surface mining administration.[82]

The shift in departments was designed by its sponsors to make a difference in administration of the law. It is difficult to tell whether a change occurred. The same staff administered the program before and after the shift; it was simply transferred from one agency to the other. A significant number of permits are rejected each year because proposed reclamation plans are inadequate.[83]

Federal Presence

Until 1977, surface mine regulation was a matter for the states. Some states, such as Illinois, had effective reclamation programs. Others had none. This regulatory patchwork attracted the attention of Congress.

> While a number of States do have surface mining reclamation programs, regulation of surface coal mining is not uniform, and in many instances is inadequate. . . .[84]

The new federal mining law follows the model of the federal pollution laws. The Act provides for Federal regulation of surface mining and reclamation operations in any State which proves unwilling or unable to do the job itself.[85] Federal subsidies are available for an approved State program.

Federal law allows Illinois to continue to enforce reclamation requirements which are ''more stringent'' than those in the Federal law.[86] The State will exercise this option with respect to agricultural lands not protected by federal standards for ''prime farmland.'' The agricultural interests which have put their stamp on the Illinois program for many years have done so again. In the extensive negotiations on the 1979 Illinois law, the retention of the more demanding Illinois requirements for certain agricultural land was one of a small number of significant issues.

With such exceptions, Illinois will copy much of the more than 150 pages of federal regulations under the new law, enforce the new federal requirements and collect its federal subsidy check.[87]

Issues

Most major surface mining issues have now been decided by the new federal law. Illinois has choices under that law: (1) Should Illinois enforce standards more stringent than federal standards? (2) Should surface mining be completely banned anywhere in Illinois? and, (3) How should the use of reclaimed land be decided?

Answers depend in large part on how the tension between the need for coal and the environmental costs from coal mining is resolved. The new federal law imposes substantial new costs on surface mining and makes some coal entirely unavailable. How badly do we want coal? What are we willing to sacrifice to obtain the energy coal produces?

The more stringent Illinois standards mostly deal with reclamation of land suitable for row crop agriculture. Federal law requires restoration of ''prime farmland.'' But such land is defined by the federal law in a way as to include less agricultural land than would be subject to special reclamation requirements under current Illinois law. Should these special Illinois standards be retained? It is a contest between the needs for coal and long-term agricultural productivity.

Under the federal law, citizens may ask the State to declare some lands ''unsuitable'' for surface mining because it is fragile, significant for historical or other reasons, important to food or water supply, or hazardous to mine.[88] If the State agrees, the land is off limits. The process for designation of unsuitability must be ''integrated as closely as possible with present and future land use planning and regulation processes.'' But the decision is discretionary. Lands which qualify for designation need not be designated by the State. How are decisions to be made? How are coal mining and other values to be tested against each other? The federal law does not say.

Finally, somebody must decide the future use of mined land. Generally the mine operator decides, subject to reclamation requirements. Most land use decisions historically have been made by local governments; but the effect of current surface mining law is to make the State a master planner for mined lands. Local input must be heard, but need not be followed. Should the State make such decisions? How?

Natural Resources Management

Government plays two major roles in natural resources management: development and preservation. Sometimes they collide. First, State government tries to increase the supply and use of some resources. It grows fish, game and trees. It stores and channels water to make more of it available for recreation. It promotes increased use of some natural resources, as when it sponsors coal development. Second, government also tries to preserve resources. Natural areas, endangered species, unique historical and archeological sites, and farm soil are targets of State programs to save a resource from permanent loss.

Both kinds of programs are sometimes called ''conservation'' or ''natural resource'' programs. But only a few ''conservation'' programs are managed by the Department of Conservation. Some ''conservation'' programs only prepare resources for consumption. Some ''natural resources'' are anything but natural.

Keep an eye on how government groups programs. This is not like pollution control, for which the General Assembly created the program and the administering agencies in one integrated law. Here there are dozens of laws, some minor, allocated among several agencies. They were passed at different times—decades apart in some cases—with little thought to how they relate to one another. Each time the General Assembly created one of these programs, it chose an existing agency to run it. How did it choose?

Parks and Wildlife

''Conservation'' in the public mind traditionally referred to the programs found today in Illinois in the Department of Conservation: parks, outdoor recreation, forestry, wildlife, fish, historical sites, and nature preserves.[89] What do these programs have in common? What distinguishes them from other natural resources programs?

One obvious similarity: the programs largely involve resources which are enjoyed in leisure time. In political terms, some see them as secondary to the life-and-death matters which are a main concern of government such as public health, safety, morals, and the economy. Of all "environmental" matters, these programs often seem to mirror themselves: they are off the beaten track.[90]

Within this group, some programs may be more potent politically than others. Hunters and fishermen command the attention of the political system more than other conservation constituencies. A committee of the 1970 Constitutional Convention formally reported that "fish, game and wildlife" are "the area of primary concern to the People of the State" when it comes to conservation.[91] That leaves out a lot. The committee's proposal to create a separate commission to administer these programs barely died on the convention floor amid complaints that too much was missing.[92] No other "conservation" interest even made it to the floor.

The Department of Conservation manages more than 300,000 acres of land and water. The United States Forest Service and the U.S. Army Corps of Engineers control approximately 600,000 acres; local governments provide another 200,000 acres, about half of which is in forest preserve districts. Although much new land was purchased between 1969 and 1979, Illinois continues to rank among the lowest states in available acres per capita. It has no national parks. The State estimates continued growth in demand for open space.[93]

The demand is unlikely to be where the land is. Most of the people are in northeastern Illinois, and most of the public open space is downstate. The trend is almost certain to continue. The Department has explained why:

> The land acquisition process is increasingly complex because of price escalation, competition for available acres, required services for those who must be relocated, and the many documented justifications required by both state and federal agencies who share responsibilities with the Department of Conservation.[94]

Land costs tend to be higher where population is most dense. More open space is needed in these areas and more is consumed there by housing, employment centers and support facilities. Land development and cities are largely inconsistent with acquisition of large tracts of open land for conservation.

The cost per acre of public open space increased more than 500% between 1968 and 1977 in one Chicago-area county; in another nearby county the increase exceeded 450% percent.[95] In times of government austerity, little land will be purchased. Annual land acquisition in Illinois has declined to a fraction of what it was in 1970, just after the new income tax provided relatively plentiful funds.

Open space conservation is not so universally loved that it is possible without large expenditures. A long, often bitter, fight over scenic rivers legislation shows that. Bills have been introduced several times to preserve stretches of rivers through State zoning. They have repeatedly failed. Landowners lined up on one side; "conservationists" on the other. One newspaper reporter characterized the controversy—and how the battle was going—with this report on a downstate legislative hearing:

> But Saturday was unquestionably the opposition's day. One look at the corn-fringed parking lot explained why: the pickups outnumbered the cars with canoe carriers 5 to 1.[96]

Zoning controls land use without cost to government. The State wanted to preserve scenic river banks without buying them, in much the same way as cities and counties control the location of factories and apartment buildings through zoning ordinances—although the State has the power to purchase scenic river stretches, through negotiated sales or its power of eminent domain. But it cannot afford to. Farmers and other landowners object to control of the use of their land without payment.[97]

When the State controls public open space it faces conflicts among segments of the public. People interested in parks often appear to be a single constituency; sometimes they act as one. But competition for limited resources can break that coalition. One State study concludes:

> A problem area is conflict and prejudice among various wildlife interest groups and between the public and government. Each group tries to enhance its own activities and many attempt to malign other interest groups. There is a need for a joint wildlife conservation "program" formulated by sportsmen, non-consumptive nature enthusiasts, landowners, scientists, government, and the general public.[98]

Claims on open space often conflict. Hunters cannot hunt where other people are doing other things. Snowmobiles and cross country skiing are incompatible. Heavy use of fragile natural areas destroys them, turning nature trails and remote campsites into dust bowls. Motorboats and sailboats trouble waters for swimmers and fishermen. The Department must sort out these competing claims in a politically volatile area without guidance from law.[99]

The Department not only conserves natural resoures; it grows them. Natural resources protection often means development for exploitation. In 1978, the Department grew over six million tree and shrub seedlings, 137,500 pheasant chicks, and millions of fish.[100] Are these "natural resources?"

> Illinois contains nearly 282,000 surface acres of lakes (not including Lake Michigan and the 2 Army Corps of Engineers' reservoirs). The majority of these lakes are artificial or manmade. No natural fish population or balance exists so good fishing must be developed through proper management.[101]

The Department also develops and protects wildlife habitat, administers laws to protect endangered plant and animal species, and preserves natural areas. It surveys and, in some cases owns and operates, archeological, historical and other unique resources. It also acts as an advocate—something of a spokesman for the fish, wildlife and trees. The record on a typical highway or river dam proposal may contain the objections and suggestions of the Department. It may even find itself opposed to other "conservation" agencies in the process.

Economically Significant Natural Resources

The Department of Conservation describes its mission as "protecting all of Illinois' natural resources."[102] That mission far exceeds the Department's powers. Responsibility for most economically important natural resources lies elsewhere in State government. Water, soil, minerals, fuels and energy are conserved, if at all, by other agencies. Some natural resources are not protected. They are developed and exploited.

Many natural resources are economic building blocks. For such resources the Department of Conservation has virtually no authority. Soil and water conservation is a program in the Department of Agriculture. Oil and gas conservation are administered by the coal miners in the Department of Mines and Minerals. Energy conservation was, until 1978, assigned to the Department of Business and Economic Development.

While it cannot be concluded that these programs would be differently administered in one department rather than another, the General Assembly must have attached some significance to the allocation among agencies. Natural resources which directly affect the economy are housed in agencies whose principal mission is not conservation.[103]

Farmland Agriculture depends on land. Illinois farmland is being lost to soil erosion and land development. About half the farmland in Illinois suffers signficiant soil erosion. Since soil is a prerequisite for agricultural productivity, erosion control is necessary to preserve the long-term ability of land to produce. Erosion causes other damage, as well, such as the siltation of lakes. Regaining lost capacity in Illinois lakes due to erosion would cost Illinois citizens more than 120 million annually.[104]

Some of these consequences can be controlled. Technology for doing so has long been known. But soil conservation practices may require current sacrifices by farmers.

> The economic benefits of a soil conservation program are related primarily to the long-term preservation of the land's agricultural productivity. However, such long-term benefits are difficult to balance against the immediate high cost to the farmer of implementing a practice. The incentive for private, voluntary expenditures for [best management practices] is further reduced by land ownership patterns in the region. It is common for agricultural land to be farmed by someone other than the owner. The farmer who rents or share-crops land has a limited stake in the long-term productivity of its soil. It is unrealistic to expect him to increase his production costs to preserve productivity in the future.[105]

The cost of erosion control is very high. One State report concludes that "clearly, there are no immediate financial incentives for farmers to reduce fertilizer use or harvested acreage, in voluntary compliance with a soil erosion and sedimentation program."[106]

This is the sort of problem that often leads to State regulation. Loss of agricultural productivity to surface mining has resulted in strict State and federal requirements for reclamation, even if the owner of the land neither wants reclamation nor wants to pay its substantial cost. Illinois has erosion control programs. But they lack the bite of the surface mining programs.

Several subsidies are available to encourage erosion control. Cash payments, technical assistance, low interest loans, and income tax credits are available from the federal government. It has been proposed that these be expanded, on the one hand, and that other agricultural subsidies be contingent on good soil management practices on the other.[107]

The prinicpal State soil conservation program is supervised by the Department of Agriculture, which generally describes itself as "a major advocate for the concerns of farmers and farm-related businesses . . ."[108] Most of the program is administered through 98 separate local soil and water conservation districts created by referendum. State law empowers these districts to impose land use regulations and other controls on farming practices.[109] However, districts are often controlled by people involved in agriculture who are understandably unlikely to take steps which would interfere with current farm productivity. They are assisted by the Department of Agriculture, which in turn is aided by a statutory advisory board composed by law entirely of farmers.[110] The resulting erosion control program consists largely of education and persuasion.

A new Illinois law, effective in 1978, was adopted in light of new federal pollution control requirement.[111] It requires each District to adopt "a soil erosion and sediment control program and standards that are technically feasible, economically reasonable" and consistent with Department programs and guidelines.[112] But the law retains the voluntary approach. Although it contains procedures for complaints, notices of violation, and hearings, nothing happens to violators, except publicity.[113]

Soil erosion control ultimately may become mandatory—not as a "conservation" program, but as a pollution control program. Unlike erosion control programs administered by federal and State departments of agriculture, pollution control programs administered by the federal and State environmental protection agencies must achieve stated goals. Eroded soil is a major water pollutant. Although programs now proposed are voluntary, they may someday have the teeth usually associated with pollution control regulation.

In addition to soil erosion, farm land is lost to development. Major competitors for land are industrial and residential development, power plant construction, and recreational development. More than two million acres of Illinois farm land will be converted to non-farm uses by the year 2000 if present trends continue.[114] The State does little to slow this trend. Should it? Some counties have utilized zoning power to protect such land. See the Esseks chapter for an assessment of one such effort.

Water Illinois is rich in water. In contrast to arid states, with their extensive water management programs, Illinois makes few governmental attempts to conserve water. The important programs deal with (1) special situations where scarcity exists, and (2) projects requiring major capital investment.

Available Lake Michigan water is insufficient to meet demands for it. Other Great Lakes states persuaded the United States Supreme Court to restrict the amount of water Illinois can take from the Lake.[115] Demand for this relatively pure and readily available water in the Chicago region now exceeds the limit set by the Court.

The Illinois Department of Transportation controls conservation and apportionment of this water.[116] Municipalities, sanitary districts and others apply to the Department for water. Allocations are then made in complex, extended legal proceedings. Among the information which the Department considers are other sources of water in the area, the need for an allocation of Lake water, and "the purpose or use to be made of the water."[117]

Scarcity focuses attention on conservation. The law requires water conservation for users of Lake Michigan water:

> The Department shall require that all feasible means reasonably available to the State and its municipalities, political subdivisions, agencies and instrumentalities have been employed to conserve and manage the water resources of the region and the use of water therein in accordance with the best modern scientific knowledge and engineering practice.[118]

Nowhere else in the State can State government allocate scarce water, or impose water conservation.

Until recently, the State showed little interest in water conservation.

> Until late 1977 there had been at both the state and local level a lack of active concern for water conservation efforts. Illustrating this point is the fact that during the early stages of the 1976–77 drought in Illinois, most responses were restricted to finding new or supplementary sources of water. . . . Unfortunately, in many instances, this search for new supplies preceded rather than followed efforts to better conserve existing supplies of water.[119] Since then, the State has improved its co-ordination of technical assistance to local governments in developing and implementing water conservation measures.[120]

Water can be "conserved" by storage in times of high flow. The State participates in projects to build dams and reservoirs to improve water supplies, and for recreation, flood control, navigation, and sewage disposal.[121] State law also allows creation of river conservancy districts at the local level to provide such projects.[122]

Allocation and mandatory conservation of water, and construction of water storage projects, involve government choices between competing interests. Award of Lake Michigan water to one community, leaves another to invest in expensive facilities and use lower quality water. Communities with adequate water supplies, have greater development potential than others. Creation of a new reservoir lake destroys wildlife habitat and freeflowing streams. Sorting out these interests is a classic political function.

Minerals and Fuels Most State attention to minerals and fuels protects employee safety and other natural resources. Modest efforts are made to expand markets for Illinois coal. No effort is made to conserve these resources for future use.

Sand and gravel quarries are subject to land reclamation requirements similar to those applicable to coal. Those regulations conserve land, not minerals. The principal State involvement is as a customer; road building consumes a signficant share of quarried materials.

Oil and gas are regulated under a law which looks as if it might be about conservation. That law flatly prohibits "waste."[123] But the concept of waste is technical. The law deals more with the dangers of drilling, and impacts on other resources such as water. To insure that an aggressive government does not misunderstand the limited purposes of the law, the General Assembly provided:

> No power herein granted to prevent waste shall be interpreted or construed as authorizing limitation of production of any well, wells, lease, leases, pool, field or properties to prevent or control economic waste or limit production to market demand.[124]

The drafters of this law were careful to avoid too much conservation.

These laws are administered by representatives of the extraction industries, generally coal. The Mining Board regulates coal, oil and gas; its public members by law consist entirely of coal mine operators and their employees (except for the Director of Mines and Minerals).[125] They are advised on oil and gas matters by the Oil and Gas Board, the membership of which is not specified by law,[126] but which in practice consists of representatives of that industry.

The Director of Mines and Minerals, under whose jurisdiction all of these laws fall, by law must be a person "thoroughly conversant with the theory and practice of mining," and must hold a certificate issued by a board composed by law of coal miners.[127] The Department's assistant directors are, by law, coal industry people. Given the important responsibility of the Department to insure coal mine safety, such requirements make sense.

Coal mining is extensively regulated for safety; it is also subject to land reclamation requirements of federal and State law. To avoid repeated disruption of land, surface mining laws require maximum extraction of coal in a single mining operation.[128]

The central problem for Illinois coal is not conservation, but development. Much of the State looks to a healthly coal industry for economic vitality. However, substantial parts of Illinois coal reserves cannot be used commercially without expensive pollution control equipment. Surface mining regulation increases the cost of coal. Illinois has made $65,000,000 in bonding authority available for the "capital development of coal resources."[129] This has generally meant projects to convert coal into clean-burning gas to expand the markets for Illinois coal.

Energy[130] Energy development and conservation are commonly treated as natural resources programs. Because energy production consumes natural resources in various ways, this is understandable. Energy conservation efforts are administered by the Institute of Natural Resources, a research and program development agency which has few regulatory or operating responsibilities.[131]

The underlying hard fact about energy conservation is that fuels are becoming scarce, that alterantives must be found, and that consumption must be limited.[132] State government interest in these problems derives almost entirely from the fact that the federal government has provided incentives for State energy conservation programs.[133]

Energy conservation and development were originally housed in the Department of Business and Economic Development. In the fuel shortage years in the mid-1970's, one important State energy conservation program dealt with allocation of scarce fuel among users. That was a program with immediate economic significance to business; it was administered then by a business agency rather than a conservation agency. The transfer to the Institute occurred in 1978, after allocation appeared to be of little concern.[134] Ironically, such recent events as long lines at gasoline stations have placed this relatively uncontroversial research agency in the thick of administering the State's critical fuel allocation program. Most energy consumption is regulated by the Illinois Commerce Commission, which has general jurisdiction over public utilities. Automobile fuel use is not regulated by the state, except perhaps in an emergency.

Key natural resources questions raised by energy use relate to resources other than fuels. A nuclear-fired electric generating station uses many acres of land, frequently prime farmland. Surface mining for coal consumes land and can cause lasting environmental damage. Coal gasification requires large amounts of water.[135]

No clear method for balancing increased energy demand against other values exists. One result is frequent political confrontation between energy producers and their customers, and some conversation interests. Use of alternate energy sources, such as the sun, and energy conservation through reduced use, would relieve some of this pressure. Indirectly, a strong program for energy conservation is also a program for preservation of open land, and other natural resources.

Issues

Major issues affecting natural resources can be framed in terms of competing values. They pose choices among things society needs, and between things it needs and things it wants. How are such hard choices to be made? Are any of them inappropriate for the political process, with its principle of majority rule? If choices are to be made politically, who speaks and votes for future generations.?

Co-ordination, Policy-Making and Program Development

State government needs comprehensive natural resources and environmental planning, policy-making and program development. The environmental work of many scattered agencies should be coordinated. Environmental impacts of the activities of all agencies should be evaluated. When environmental values and other values, such as economic development values, conflict, the conflicts must be resolved; a broad overview of the environment and natural resources improves such decisions.[136]

No single Illinois agency has primary responsibility for such a broad overview. This is a symptom found everywhere in government. The Task Force on the Future of Illinois suggests that Illinois has neither a coordinated approach to providing government services, nor a way to define overall State goals.[137] No clear natural resources policy exists for Illinois; no single theme runs through the State's programs described in this chapter.

Organization

Proposals have been made, and many experiments have been tried, to provide Illinois government with some sort of comprehensive overview of environmental and natural resources issues.[138] The underlying goal is coordination of programs, guided by a central plan and policy. Such a process can help make choices such as these: between (a) a new airport, and (b) the farm land it will consume, and the peace and quiet it will invade;[139] between (a) a nuclear power plant, and (b) the farm land it will consume and the radiation risks it may produce;[140] between (a) surface mining and the energy and jobs it produces, and (b) agricultural productivity or a unique natural area;[141] between (a) a water supply reservoir with needed recreational facilities, and (b) the free-flowing stream and fish habitat it will replace;[142] between (a) completely fishable and swimmable rivers at high cost to taxpayers, and (b) lower water quality in some streams at lower cost;[143] between (a) requiring existing industrial facilities to install costly pollution control equipment, and (b) limiting growth in an area which has used up its limited clean air quota.[144]

Such choices must be made by government. A study for the Council of State Governments concludes:

> [T]he pursuit of integration [of government programs] and coordination, while essentially an administrative function, has definite political implications. This is due, in part, to the fact that coordination frequently involves the reconciliation of programs with fundamentally different objectives, such as pollution abatement and economic development. These are basically political choices, even though the established political institutions of state government may seek to avoid making such choices by delegating broad decision-making responsibility to the executive branch. Ultimately, decisions of this sort are always subject to final review in the political arena.[145]

Although the decisions are political, state government ought to have a better procedure for making them. There are two kinds of basic functions to be performed: (a) assessment of the environmental impacts of proposed action (or inaction), and (b) policy-making and decision. The second depends on the first.

In the last decade, enormous resources have been poured into environmental impact assessment. The National Environmental Policy Act of 1969 requires environmental impact studies to be performed before major federal action goes forward. Such an assessment process is politically neutral. By making clearer the consequences of proposed actions, it provides an opportunity for political constituencies to form and seek political action.[146] If not implemented carefully, however, it may direct resources from administrative change to paper pushing.

Evaluation of environmental impact requires single-purpose agencies to reach beyond their expertise and limited interests. Because conflicts between environmental and other values must also be resolved outside the single-purpose agency, it is sensible to coordinate programs and make major policy outside the administering agencies, and above them. The principle debate among reorganizers is whether that should be done by the governor's office or by a superagency which has within it the major competing programs and points-of-view.

A major study on government reorganization prepared for the incoming Illinois Governor in 1977 discusses the options.

> Emphasis upon the comprehensive [natural resources] plan does not necessarily imply that all natural resources agencies should be joined in a single department. In South Dakota, where this and related questions were given a great deal of attention, the Reorganization Commission finally concluded that natural resources functions should be spread across three separate departments guided by three distinct sets of goals and objectives. Conflict, it decided, should not be internalized by the bureaucracy, but should be exposed to political processes. Each of the three departments submits a long-range plan to the State Planning Bureau located within the Office of the Governor, where conflicts are identified and resolved under gubernatorial direction. North Carolina represents another extreme in that most natural resources activities are located within a Department of Natural Resources that is theoretically capable of producing a comprehensive and integrated approach to the solution of most of the state's natural resource problems.[147]

Even with an all-inclusive natural resources agency, which includes pollution control, parks and wildlife, and water conservation, conflicts with other interests outside those fields will arise. These must be resolved by the governor. Studies of state government conclude that combination of many functions in one agency produces relatively little co-ordination, and does not materially improve comprehensive planning and policy-making.[148] Proposals for a broad department of natural resources have been made in Illinois, but none has been seriously considered.

Most observers who have studied this problem suggest that the office of the governor should be responsible for co-ordination, environmental policy-making, and planning.

> The advantage of the governor's office as the locus for environmental planning and impact adjudication is that this office is supposed to have a broad view of the entire executive branch, and also the highest decision-making power needed to settle interagency disputes. . . . The governor can be held directly accountable to the voters, and thus is more likely to be responsive to the full range of individual preferences in society. The governor should not be shielded from the clash of environmental and other state objectives, such as economic development. These clashes are some of the most significant statewide issues today.[149]

To perform these functions well, a governor needs help. Given the pre-occupation of the administering agencies, and the fact that they are part of the problem, he cannot rely on them entirely for a solution. He needs adequate staff and other resources to do the job.

However, a focus on the governor should not overlook the importance of the legislature. It plays a central role in policy-making through passage of laws and investigation. But one student of state environmental policy-making notes:

> State legislatures, even more than the U.S. Congress, have increasingly abdicated many significant powers to the executive branches of government. Now, with the creation of streamlined and aggressive administrative environmental agencies, the domination of the state legislatures [by the executive branch] will increase unless these bodies take steps to reassert their authority.[150]

Illinois

Policies are made, programs are developed, and activities are coordinated in Illinois government in many places. The most important are the federal government, the Governor and General Assembly, and the Institute of Natural Resources.

Federal Government The shape of State pollution control and surface mining reclamation programs makes clear that important Illinois environmental policy and program development occurs in Washington. When the federal government takes an interest, it sets Illinois priorities, designs Illinois programs and makes Illinois policy. If there is close program coordination, it is prescribed in federal law. If programs only grudgingly coexist or engage in open hostilities, blame Congress. The major policy decision left to the State is whether or not to participate in a federal program.

Less visible is the federal government's influence on State environmental and natural resources planning. Illinois does extensive environmental planning to comply with federal law. Requirements for detailed plans are now routine as conditions for federal grants and as part of regulatory programs. The lure of grant money, and of federal subsidies for the planning process itself, result in such State planning efforts.

Before Illinois can receive federal funds for parks, The Department of Conservation must prepare a Statewide Comprehensive Outdoor Recreation Plan (SCORP). The Department thus plans for its own programs; it suggests the policies which should control. To be eligible for grants for sewage treatment plan construction, a state must have waste treatment management plans. The Environmental Protection Agency, whose programs are the subject of planning, supervises the planning and makes the policies. Other federally mandated plans are parts of regulatory programs.[152]

Such plans insure order in state use of federal funds and help attain federal regulatory goals. However they also influence the way Illinois approaches long range policy-making on environmental and natural resources issues. These federally-sponsored plans deal with one problem at a time. Some directly affect government capital investment; others directly affect land use through regulation; most have long term effects. All are prepared by single-purpose agencies. Such planning guarantees that essential elements of what should be a long-range State environmental policy and program will be formulated on a single-purpose, largely uncoordinated, basis.

Virtually all federally-sponsored state planning requires state contributions to the cost of the plan. This consumes most of the relatively small part of the State's total resources which it is willing to spend on planning. Little is left for comprehensive policy-making and program coordination. Because single-purpose planning accomplishes none of the goals of comprehensive policy analysis, the federally-sponsored planning efforts effectively obstruct broader State analyses.

Some federal funds are available for comprehensive planning. Such a grant supported a major State report on comprehensive growth and resource conservation policies.[153] Without that grant, such long range thinking might not have occurred in State government. However, such a study cannot overcome the influence of the single-purpose plans which directly influence major capital investment and regulatory policy.

The Governor and the General Assembly Illinois environmental and natural resources programs are scattered. Only the Governor has the power to coordinate them. Only the Governor can make major policy that involves interests of more than one agency if disputes arise.

Illinois Governors have used a variety of devices. A subcabinet is used by Governor Thompson. It is composed of cabinet officers with responsibilities for natural resources and environmental programs and includes those whose programs can affect the environment (such as highway construction and business development). The Governor's staff supplies administrative support. The Institute of Natural Resources has provided research and program development support. Sub-cabinet groups such as this appear to be in use in about 20 states.[154] Illinois sub cabinets have successfully cut across agency lines on some issues, and have provided coordination between some programs. Their usefulness in policy-making has varied, depending on the Governor's interests. Such modest success is typical of other states.[155]

Illinois law creates a vast array of interagency committees which deal with narrow aspects of natural resources management. The Natural Resources Development Board, despite its grand name, has statutory responsibility only for reviewing water resources.[156] Although it once was active as the coordinator of state efforts for major reservoir construction projects, it no longer meets. Other interagency committees exists to deal with pesticides and surface mining. Governor Thompson has created a Rural Development Planning Council, an advisory committee to aid in water quality planning, an Interagency Water Management Conservation Committee, and an advisory board to provide environmental information to the Illinois Department of Transportation. These groups have coordinated agency participation and expertise on narrowly focused issues and projects.

The General Assembly also has created numerous commissions and committees for itself to deal with natural resources problems. Many legislative commissions have appropriations sufficient to hire staff and undertake investigations. An example is the Energy Resources Commission, which studies energy and coal issues, recommends legislation and plays a role in the allocation of coal development bonds.[157] The Commission on Atomic Energy is concerned with a variety of nuclear energy issues, and has been used to study the risks associated with nuclear power generating facilities.[158] These commissions often have public members, unaffiliated with the legislative or executive branch.

Major environmental legislation has generally been a product of the executive branch. Although much of the work has been done at the agency level, the Governor's Office has usually played a major role. The Environmental Protection Act was drafted in the Governor's Office. The surface mining laws were Governor's initiatives.

Institute of Natural Resources In its use of the Institute of Natural Resources (INR), Illinois is unique among state governments. It has successfully improved long-range planning and policy-making for natural resources and environmental issues. INR was created in 1970 as one of three environmental agencies under the Environmental Protection Act. Unlike its sisters (the Illinois Environmental Protection Agency and the Pollution Control Board), its responsibility is not limited to pollution control. The law currently says:

> It shall be the duty of the Institute to investigate practical problems, implement studies, conduct research and provide assistance, information and data relating to the technology and administration of environmental protection; energy; the natural history, entomology, zoology and botany of this State; the geology and natural resources of this State; the water resources and weather of this State; and the archeological and cultural history of this State. The Institute shall obtain, store, and process relevant data; [and] recommend technological, administrative, and legislative changes and developments . . .[159]

The Act also directs INR to seek interdisciplinary approaches to environmental problems, and to participate in environmental education. In 1978, INR's authority was substantially expanded to include energy conservation.

Using this broad mandate, INR is the major creative and coordinating force in Illinois government for natural resources and environmental programs. It routinely works on new program initiatives, policy-making, coordination among agencies, resolution of conflicts within the government and data collection. It provides research and information for other agencies and the Governor. The Governor can turn to INR for staff work on natural resources problems; he has no similar option on other kinds of problems.[160]

INR has worked on interagency problems such as power plant siting, coal development, agricultural pollution and sedimentation in the Kankakee River. It has created and coordinated large parts of the surface mining program by preparing new laws, collecting data on abandoned lands, running a task force on reclamation and sponsoring projects on abandoned mined lands to demonstrate and test reclamation technology.

According to INR, its ability to succeed at such tasks results from a combination of factors:

- *Independence:* Without a vested program interest, the Institute is free to scrutinize all programs. Unencumbered by parochial concern for the survival of the programs it reviews, the Institute can worry about achievement by State government as a whole of short- and long-range program goals.
- *Time and Concentration:* Pursuit of the Institute's missions is all that the Institute does. This work does not compete for attention and resources with more immediate operational activities. The kind of work the Institute does is done best when somebody pays full attention to it; that is impossible if it shares management time with crisis.
- *Powerlessness:* The Institute has no power to do anything to anybody. It cannot issue orders, adopt standards, or direct action. All it can do is persuade. Because it poses no direct threat to the exercise of power, it has access to agencies and private parties which an enforcement agency cannot have. Wherever research is housed with enforcement, research suffers.[161]

INR's plea of "powerlessness" is overstated. Information, properly used, is powerful. Furthermore, two of INR's three directors have served simultaneously as assistants to the Governor for natural resources and environment, combining INR's resources with the authority of the Governor. Finally, INR has a substantial appropriation and can pursue its duties without having to beg funds from the agencies it is trying to co-ordinate.

Students of government organization think that the Governor should perform the co-ordinating and policy-making functions for natural resources and environment. They also say that governors can perform those functions effectively only if properly staffed—INR is the response.

Conclusion

Natural resources programs in Illinois government lack a unifying theme or policy. But the difficulty may lie not with government, but with our expectations. Although it is common to lump the programs reviewed in this Chapter under a single heading, it does not follow that government treats them as a single topic. The evidence shows that natural resources programs are separately administered, with little coordination between them. Each administering agency's constituency may have more to do with policy making and implementation than orders from the Governor.

These programs are grouped together under one tent because of a perception about the origins of the resources—they are all in some way thought to be "natural." Although it might make sense to adopt an integrated approach to avoid conflicting policies, the same can be said of all of government. The lack of coordination of natural resources programs is typical of a broader failure of government to relate programs to one another. Failure to coordinate one natural resources program with another is as troublesome as failures to coordinate natural resources programs with human resources and economic development programs.

How can coordination be achieved? Who should do it? Is there a better way than the existing push and pull of the political process? Would the process be improved by better collection, analysis and public availability of basic data? Although scholars commonly say that State government lacks planning, what goes wrong without planning? What mistakes are made? Which of the programs discussed in this Chapter would be improved by improved coordination with other activities of Government?

NOTES

[1]Illinois Constitution of 1970, Art. XI.

[2]Transcript of Debates, Sixth Constitutional Convention (referred to in this Chapter as "Debates"), p. 2997.

[3]Debates, p. 2998.

[4]*Ibid.*

[5]*Ibid.*, p. 2997.

[6]*Ibid.*

[7]*Scattering Fork Drainage District* v. *Ogilvie,* 19 Ill. App. 3d 386, 395 (1974).

[8]Report No. 17, General Government Committee, proposing a "Conservation Article."

[9]Debates, p. 3480–3512, 3927–31, 4509–14, 4549–50.

[10]Debates, p. 2995.

[11]Illinois Environmental Protection Act, §3(b) (referred to in this Chapter as the "Act"); Ill. Rev. Stat. (1977) ch. 111-½, §1003(b).

[12]Act, §3(n); Ill. Rev. Stat. (1977) ch. 111-½, §1003(n).

[13]Act, §20; Ill. Rev. Stat. (1977) ch. 111-⅜, §1020.

[14]Act, §24; Ill. Rev. State. (1977) ch. 111-½, §1024. Illinois State Budget, Fiscal Year 1978, 111.

[15]R.B. Ogilvie, "Special Message on the Environment," April 23, 1970, 2.

[16]Ill. Rev. Stat. (1977) ch. 111-½, §§1001–1051.

[17]The Institute was named the "Institute for Environmental Quality" in the Act. Ill. Rev. Stat. (1971) ch. 111-½, §1006. In 1978, first by executive order and then by statute, the Institute's responsibilities were greatly increased. Its name was changed to the Institute of Natural Resources. A discussion of the Institute in its present form appears later in this Chapter.

[18]Major early reorganizations were in Wisconsin (1966), Minnesota (1967), Washington (1970) and New York (1970). These are described and analyzed with the Illinois reorganization in E.H. Haskell and V.S. Price, *State Environmental Management: Case Studies of Nine States* (1973). This study is a basic source on State environmental management. Among the other states undertaking such reorganizations were Arkansas, California, Delaware, Massachusetts, New Jersey, Oregon, Pennsylvania and Vermont.

[19]Ogilvie, *op. cit.*, p. 2 On the questions of pollution created by pollution control see Comptroller General, *Report to Congress: 16 Air and Water Pollution Issues Facing the Nation. Appendix III* (1978).

[20]The powers relating to radioactivity were subsequently held to have been pre-empted by federal law.

[21]Council on Environmental Quality, *Environmental Quality* (1971), p. 52.

[22]Ogilvie, *op. cit.* n. 15, p. 2.

[23]See *Texaco, Inc.* v. *FTC*, 336 F.2d 754 (D.C. Cir. 1964), *vacated and remanded on other grounds*, 381 U.S. 739 (1965); *Cinderalla Career and Finishing Schools, Inc.* v. *FTC*, 425 F.2d 583 (D.C. Cir. 1970); *Association of National Advertisers, Inc.* v. *FTC*, 460 F. Supp. 996 (1978).

[24]D.P. Currie, "Rulemaking Under the Illinois Pollution Law," *University of Chicago Law Review*, 42 (1975), 457.

[25]M.L. Leahy, "Illinois Environmental Backlash," *Chicago Guide* (January 1974), 137.

[26]*Ibid.* The Agency's Acting Director said: "I can recall so vividly in Governor Walker's state of the state speech in January when he said he would end the leaf burning bans and both sides of the legislative aisle jumped to their feet to applaud in unison with others sitting in the balconies."

[27]A brief review of this history appears in Kohn, "The Economics of Proposed Regulation R73-5 on Leaf Burning and a Benefit-Cost Analysis of an Alternative Approach Based on Population Size EXKm," Illinois Institute for Environmental Quality Document, No. 76/27 (1976), pp. 1–5.

[28]Ogilvie, *op.cit.*, p. 2

[29]Currie, *op.cit.*, p. 458, n. 2.

[30]Haskell, and Price, *op.cit.*, p. 35.

[31]Testimony of David P. Currie Before a Subcommittee of the Executive Committee of the Illinois Senate, on H.B. 3788 and Related Bills: The Environmental Protection Act, May 25, 1970.

[32]Council on Environmental Quality, *Environmental Quality* (1971), p. 54.

[33]Se *Landfill, Inc.* v. *Pollution Control Board,* 74 Ill. 2d 541 (1979), in which citizen intervenors attempted to treat the Agency as a "person violating the Act." The Court held that the citizen suit provisions could not properly be used directly against the Agency. "Prosecution under the Act . . . is against polluters, not the Agency." 74 Ill.2d at 556.

[34]*People of the State of Illinois v. Earthline Corp.*, Circuit Court for the Seventh Judicial Circuit, No. 77-CH-13 (consolidated with 77-CH-10).

[35]W. Lambrecht, "Pollution Control Board," *Illinois Issues* 2:2 (February 1977), 7. This article describes the Attorney General's relationship with the EPA as "a running battle," and describes litigation in which the Attorney General's position has differed from that of the EPA and the PCB on substantive issues. The Attorney General is quoted as saying: "[T]he EPA has been arbitrary and making bureaucratic decisions we don't think they have a legal obligation for making." The EPA's current view is cautiously optimistic: "Significant advances have been made in the working relationship between the Agency and the Attorney General's Office." Illinois Environmental Protection Agency, *Illinois Environmental Progress, Annual Report Issues* 4 (1979), p. 14.

[36]Pollution Control Board, "Eighth Year Annual Report," Appendix B, appearing in *Environmental Register* No. 183, (November 14, 1978), 10.

[37]Pollution Control Board, "Second Report," p. 11, appearing in *Pollution Control Board Newsletter* No. 25 (June 30, 1971).

[38]United States House of Representatives Committee on Interstate and Foreign Commerce, *Report No. 91-1146,* 91st Cong., 2d Sess. (1970), p. 3.

[39]Clean Air Act, 42 U.S.C. §§7401-7626; Federal Water Pollution Control Act (Clean Water Act), 33 U.S.C. §§1251-1281; Solid Waste Disposal Act, 42 U.S.C. §§6901-6987.

[40]Federal laws generally do not pre-empt parallel state regulation, even if direct federal enforcement is in effect. E.g., Clean Air Act, 42 U.S.C. §7416 (however, certain state regulation of moving sources such as automobiles is pre-empted); Solid Waste Disposal Act, 42 U.S.C. §6929. One State official who read a draft of this Chapter commented that state acceptance of these federal programs is no longer automatic and that the nuisance of dealing with the "feds" may some day outweigh the attractiveness of obtaining federal approval of a state program.

[41]For FY1978, USEPA provided approximately 41% of the cost of the Illinois pollution control program (excluding grants for construction of treatment works). Illinois Environmental Protection Agency, *op.cit.*, P. 13.

[42]*Ibid.*, pp. 4, 5, 7. And see *Illinois State Budget, FY 1980,* p. 104.

[43]United States Senate Committee on Public Works, *Report No. 91-1196,* 91st Congress, 2d Session (1970), p. 11.

[44]D.L. Davis, "Science and Regulatory Policy" (Letter), *Science* 203:7 (January 5, 1979).

[45]C.L. Comar, *Ibid.* See also C.L. Comar, "Bad Science and Social Penalties," *Science* 200. (June 16, 1978), 1225; C.L. Comar, "Environmental Assessment: A Pragmatic View," *Science,* 198 (November 11, 1977), 567.

[46]T.H. Maugh, II, "Chemical Carcinogens: The Scientific Basis for Regulation," *Science* 201 (September 29, 1978), 1200.

[47]J. Walsh, "FPA and Toxic Substances Law: Dealing With Uncertainty," *Science* 202 (November 10, 1978), 598.

[48]M. Eisenbud, *Environment, Technology and Health: Human Ecology in Historical Perspective* (1978).

[49]Governors State University Environmental Management Program, "A Preliminary Guide for Benefit Consideration in Economic Impact Studies," IIEQ Document No. 76/12 (1976), p. 29.

[50]Comptroller General, *Report to Congress: 16 Air and Water Pollution Issues Facing the Nation* (1978), p. 91. In response, "EPA agreed that more research is needed but that it would be a long time before cost/benefit analysis can be used by decisionmakers." *Ibid.* p. 97.

[51]Governors State University Environmental Management Program, *op.cit.*, p. 26.

[52]Ill. Rev. Stat. (1977) ch. 96-1/2, §7404.

[53]"The types of benefits to be expected are easy to identify. They are a good deal more difficult to measure, and the question is sometimes raised of whether they are inherently quantifiable and have economic content." Task Force on Noise, "Economic Impact Study of the Proposed Motor Vehicle (In-Use) Noise Regulations," IIEQ Document No. 76/10 (1976), p. 100. "The evaluation of benefits is a difficult task indeed." ETA, Inc., "Economic Impact Study on the Proposed Illinois Regulation of Toxic Substances," IIEQ Document no. 76/29 (1976), p. 43. The United States Comptroller General has praised this Illinois requirement, and its implementation, as helpful models for cost/benefit analysis. Comptroller General, *op.cit.*, pp. 95–96.

[54]Ill. Rev. Stat. (1977) ch. 111 1/2, §1033(c). *Wells Manufacturing Co.* v. *Pollution Control Board,* 73 Ill.2d 226 (1978).

[55]Ill. Rev. Stat. (1977) ch. 111 1/2, §1002(a) (ii).

[56]*O'Connor* v. *City of Rockford,* 52 Ill. 2d 360, 367 (1972). The same result was reached in *Carson* v. *Village of Worth,* 62 Ill. 3d 406 (1976). A contrary result was reached in *Carlson* v. *County of Cook,* 61 Ill. App. 3d 247 (1978). As this is written, the case is pending before the Supreme Court.

[57]*County of Cook* v. *John Sexton Contractors Co.*, —— Ill.2d —— (1979).

[58]*City of Des Plaines* v. *Chicago and North Western Railway Company,* 65 Ill. 2d 1 (1976).

[59]*Village of Union* v. *Southern California Chemical Co.,* 69 Ill. App. 3d 373 (1978).

[60]A discussion of the legal issues involved in the State pre-emption question appears in W.L. Niro, "Illinois Environmental Law—State Preemption of Local Governmental Regulation of Pollution Related Activities," *Illinois Bar Journal* (October 1978), pp. 118–126, 137.

[61]Department of Mines and Minerals, *1977 Annual Coal, Oil and Gas Report (Land Reclamation Division)* (1978), p. 24.

[62]C.G. Treworgy, L.E. Bengal and A.G. Dingwell, "Reserves and Resources of Surface-Minable Coal in Illinois," Illinois State Geological Survey Circular 504 (1978), p. 1.

[63]United States, Department of the Interior, *Permanent Regulatory Program Implementing Section 501(b) of the Surface Mining Control and Reclamation Act of 1977: Draft Environmental Statement* (1978), p. EII–55. See also, Illinois Institute for Environmental Quality, *Strip Mine Reclamation in Illinois* (Prepared by Argonne National Laboratory) (1973), pp. 35–47.

[64]W.D. Seitz, "An Analysis of Strip-Mining and Local Taxation Practices," *Illinois Agricultural Economics* (January 1972), p. 23, 29.

[65]Illinois Institute for Environmental Quality, *op. cit.*, n. 63, pp. 53–92.

[66]*Ibid.*, pp. 28, 37. The basic research on pre-law land in Illinois is reported in W.D. Klimstra, R.J. Haynes and S.R. Jewell, *A Survey of Lands Surface Mined for Coal in Illinois* (1973).

[67]Open Cut Lard Reclamation Act, Ill.Rev.Stat. (1961) ch. 93, §§ 180. 1-180.13. All subsequent laws (through 1978) have retained the format of this Act.

[68]United States, Department of the Interior, *op. cit.* n. 63, p. 35.

[69]See *Midland Coal Corp.* v. *County of Knox*, 1 Ill. 2d 200 (1953); *American Smelting & Refining Co.* v. *County of Knox and County of Peoria*, 60 Ill. 2d 133 (1975).

[70]Ill. Rev. Stat. (1963) and (1969), ch. 93, §§180.1 et seq.

[71]Surface Mined Land Conservation and Reclamation Act, Ill. Rev. Stat. (1971) ch. 93 §§201–216. The Governor sent these two officials to the Institute for Environmental Quality, and directed it to draft amendments to the law which would satisfy their requests. In the period covered by the Department of Mines and Mineral *1977 Annual Coal, Oil and Gas Report (Land Reclamation Division)*, the 11 hearings requested by county boards on applications for surface mining permits, 9 were from northwestern Illinois counties. p. 44.

[72]E.A. Imhoff, T.O. Friz and J.R. LaFevers, "A Guide to State Programs for the Reclamation of Surface Mined Areas," U.S. Geological Survey Circular 731, (1976), p. 28.

[73]Ill. Rev. Stat. (1975) ch. 93, §§201–216.

[74]Surface Mining Control and Reclamation Act of 1977, Public Law 95–87, 30 U.S.C. §§1201–1328.

[75]Public Act 80-1342. The codification of the Act now appears at Ill. Rev. Stat. (1977) ch. 96-1/2, §§4501–4520.

[76]P.A. 81—The federal law gives each state the choice of administering the program itself, in strict accordance with federal standards, or direct federal administration without substantial state participation.

[77]Ill. Rev. Stat. ch. 96-1/2, §§4506(e) (¶ 14) (i).

[78]*Ibid.*, §4506(g).

[79]*Ibid.*, §4507(g).

[80]See n. 69 above.

[81]Ill. Rev. Stat. (1977) ch. 96-1/2, §4506(g).

[82]"[T]he Legislature placed enforcement of the new law under the industry-oriented Department of Mines and Minerals, rather than under the Department of Conservation, where it belonged. The test of enforcement is therefore still to come." Editorial, *Chicago Sub-Times*, September 22, 1971.

[83]Department of Mines and Minerals, *op. cit.* n. 61, pp. 18, 44.

[84]United States Senate Committee on Energy and Natural Resources, *Report No. 95-128*, 95th Congress, 1st Session (1977), pp. 49, 52.

[85]*Ibid.*, p. 72.

[86]30 U.S.C. §1255.

[87]44 *Federal Register* 15311–15463. Since a typical page in the Federal Register contains about 1200 words, these regulations consume more than 186,000 words. The explanation of these regulations takes almost 500,000 words, about twice the length of this book. 44 *Federal Register* 14901–15309.

[88]30 U.S.C. §1272.

[89]The Department administers at least 11 major laws, including: Boat Registration and Safety Act, Endangered Species Protection Act, Fish Code, Game Code, the laws with respect to the Nature Preserves Commission, Open Space Lands Acquisition Act, Snowmobile Registration and Safety Act, State Forests Act, the laws with respect to State parks and nature preserves, Timber Buyers Licensing Act, and the laws with respect to wild or scenic rivers.

[90]The Illinois 2000 Foundation, an affiliate of the Illinois State Chamber of Commerce, is studying the economic future of Illinois. In a report, it considered virtually every aspect of life and government except parks and recreation, as to which it said nothing at all. *Illinois 2000, Alternative Economic Futures for Illinois* (1978). The results of a University of Illinois survey of attitudes are ambiguous on this point. That survey showed "pollution and littering" as the fifth most serious "community problem," and "recreation services" as the eighth. Both are above "education," "health services," and other issues on the list of 13 problems. University of Illinois, *Illinois: Today and Tomorrow—Final Statewide Results* (1978). Such conservation issues as wildlife and natural areas preservation do not appear on the list at all. Failure to perceive parks, wildlife and recreation as important economic issues may be a mistake. Some evidence exists that such amenities are important in decisions by business on locations for new or expanded facilities. See Joint Economic Committee of the Congress of the United States, *Central City Businesses—Plans and Problems* (1979), pp. 4, 23–24; J.G. Udell, *Rockford, Illinois* (Reprint of articles in the Rockford *Register-Star*) (1978), pp. 4–10. Outdoor recreation planning was assigned by law to both the Department of Conservation and the Department of Business and Economic Development (BED). Ill. Rev. Stat. ch. 105, §532. The BED role probably was based on its responsibility for tourism. In 1971, by executive order, the Department of Conservation was given exclusive responsibility for such planning.

[91]Proposal No. 17, General Government Committee, p. 6 (reprinted at Sixth Constitutional Convention Proceedings, Committee Proposals, p. 732.)

[92]Debates at 3480, 3483, 3485, 3490–92, 3497, 3501.

[93]Task Force on the Future of Illinois, *A Working Paper on the Future of Illinois* (referred to in this Chapter as *"Working Paper"*) p. 81; Illinois Department of Conservation, *Outdoor Recreation in Illinois* (1978), pp. 55, 56–57.

[94]Illinois Department of Conservation, *FY 1978 Annual Report*, p. 22.

[95]Estimate by Open Lands Project, reported in *Working Paper*, pp. 81–82.

[96]B. Ingersoll, "Scenic Rivers Bill blasted by farmers at first hearing," *Chicago Sun-Times* (August 4, 1971), p. 42.

[97]They might have objected to a proposed purchase as well. Many of the arguments against the scenic rivers legislation dealt with a feared influx of canoers and others using the river, and trespassing on privately-held river banks.

[98]Illinois Department of Local Government Affairs and the Illinois Bureau of the Budget, *Conservation Growth and Resource Conservation Policies: Natural Resources* (1978) (referred to in this Chapter as *"Growth and Resources Report"*) p. 102.

[99]Illinois Department of Conservation, *Outdoor Recreation in Illinois* (1978), pp. 134, 141, 145, 148, 151, 159, 161.

[100]Illinois Department of Conservation, *FY 1978 Annual Report*, pp. 9, 12, 16.

[101]*Ibid.*, p. 14.

[102]*Ibid.*, p. 24. Such references appear throughout this *Report*. See pp. 3, 8. The statutory statement of the Department's powers uses the broad term "natural resources" only in connection with the Department's land acquisition powers. Ill. Rev. Stat. ch. 127, §63a19.

[103]The labels used in government give some idea of the way agencies are perceived. The Governor's annual budget sorts agencies into several major categories. The Department of Conservation is listed under "Environment and Natural Resources" with the pollution control agencies; the Departments of Agriculture and Business and Economic Development are under "Economic and Community Development;" the Department of Mines and Minerals, despite its surface mine reclamation responsibilities, appears under such headings as "Services for Working People" or "Employment Opportunities," a result of its mine safety programs. See *Illinois State Budget* for Fiscal Years 1978, 1979 and 1980.

[104]Illinois Environmental Protection Agency, *Water Quality Management Plan,* Vol. III (1979), p. 5.

[105]Northeastern Illinois Planning Commission, "Areawide Water Quality Management Plan," Public Hearing Draft, 1977, p. 6–52. This document contains a clear, politically sensitive analysis of the problem of agricultural erosion control. *Ibid.*, pp. 6–40—6–55.

[106]*Growth and Resources Report, op. cit.* n. 98, p. 82.

[107]Illinois Environmental Protection Agency, *Water Quality Management Plan,* Vol. III, 1979, pp. 152–55.

[108]*Illinois State Budget, Fiscal Year 1980,* p. 128.

[109]Ill. Rev. Stat. (1977) ch. 5, §§128, 129.

[110]Ill. Rev. Stat. (1977) ch. 5, §109.

[111]P.A. 80–159.

[112]Ill. Rev. Stat. (1977) ch. 5, §38.

[113]Ill. Rev. Stat. (1977) ch. 5, §41.

[114]*Working Paper, op. cit.* n. 93, p. 61.

[115]*Wisconsin* v. *Illinois,* 388 U.S. 426 (1967). This is the latest such Supreme Court decree. See 281 U.S. 696 (1930) and 289 U.S. 395 (1933). The Court decreed that the State would make allocations. 388 U.S. at 427-28.

[116]The law under which this program is administered is usually referred to as the "Levels of Lake Michigan Act." Ill. Rev. Stat. (1977) ch. 19, §§119–120.11.

[117]Ill. Rev. Stat. (1977) ch. 19, §120.3. See Illinois Department of Transportation, *Rules and Regulations Regarding Allocation of Water from Lake Michigan,* 1976, Rule 303.

[118]*Ibid.;* see Illinois Department of Transportation, *Rules and Regulations Regarding Allocation of Water from Lake Michigan,* 1976, Rule 304. And see *In the Matter of Lake Michigan Water Allocation, Opinion and Order,* LMO 77-1, LMO 77-2 (1978).

[119]*Growth and Resources Report, op. cit.* n. 98, p. 10.

[120]*Ibid.*, p. 12.

[121]Ill. Rev. Stat. (1977) ch. 19, §§126a–126h.

[122]Ill. Rev. Stat. (1977) ch. 42 §§383–410a.

[123]Ill. Rev. Stat. (1977) ch. 96-1/2, §5402.

[124]*Ibid.*, §5455. Despite this injunction, the Department attempts to insure that wells are properly spaced. If too many wells draw from the same pool, none will be sufficiently profitable to support the investment necessary to drill. Some statutory authority exists to regulate well spacing, although not clearly for this purpose. *Ibid.*, §5409(9).

[125]Ill. Rev. Stat. (1977) ch. 127, §5.04.

[126]Ill. Rev. Stat. (1977) ch. 127, §6.11.

[127]Ill. Rev. Stat. (1977) ch. 127, §7.02.

[128]30 U.S.C. §1265(b). Mining and reclamation operations are required to "maximize the utilization and conservation of the solid fuel resource being recovered so that reaffecting the land in the future through surface coal mining can be minimized."

[129]Ill. Rev. Stat. (1977) ch. 96-1/2, §4107.

[130]This brief foray into one of the critical issues of our time is inadequate. Energy deserves a full chapter of its own. It is not fully treated in this Chapter because (1) energy (like transportation), while involving natural resources issues, is so important that it commands separate attention, and (2) the State has almost nothing to do with energy questions (which are in the hands of various federal and foreign potentates).

[131]P.A. 80-1218; Ill. Rev. Stat. (1977) ch. 96 1/2, §§7401–7407.

[132]Illinois Department of Business and Economic Development, Division of Energy, *Illinois Energy Conservation Feasibility Report* (1976); *Working Paper, op. cit.* n. 93, pp. 37–46.

[133]Energy Policy and Conservation Act, P.L. 94–163, codified primarily at 42 U.S.C. §§6201–6422.

[134]P.A. 80-1218; Ill. Rev. Stat. (1977) ch. 96-1/2, §§4103, 7303–7316.

[135]B.M. Hoglund and J.G. Asbury, "Potential Sites for Coal Conversion Facilities in Illinois," Illinois Institute for Environmental Quality Document no. 74-60, 1974, pp. 20–23.

[136]*Haskell and Price, op. cit.* n. 18, pp. 104, 259–62.

[137]*Working Paper, op. cit.* n. 93, p. 7.

[138]E.g., Illinois Task Force on Governmental Reorganization, *Orderly Government: Organizing for Manageability* (1976), pp. 150–163.

[139]See the Environmental Impact Statement prepared by the St. Louis Metropolitan Area Airport Authority for the proposed new airport near Columbia and Waterloo, Illinois.

[140]See the Environmental Impact Statement for proposed Commonwealth Edison LaSalle County Nuclear Station.

[141]Such choices are required by the new federal surface mining law.

[142]See Natural Resources Development Board, *Priority and Planning Elements for Developing Illinois Resources,* (1970); Committee on Allerton Park, *Battle for the Sangamon* (1971).

[143]See Northeastern Illinois Planning Commission, "Areawide Water Quality Management Plan," Public Hearing Draft, 1978; Illinois Environmental Protection Agency, *Water Quality Management Plan* (1979).

[144]Such choices are required under the Clean Air act. 42 U.S.C. §7410.

[145]Council of State Governments, *Integration and Coordination of State Environmental Programs* (Lexington, KY: the Council,) (1975), p. 96.

[146]For another view, see S.K. Fairfax, "A Disaster in the Environmental Movement," *Science* 199 (February 17, 1978), 743. The argument is that environmental impact analysis diverts resources from administrative change to paper pushing.

[147]Illinois Task Force on Governmental Reorganization, *op. cit.* n. 138, p. 149.

[148]Haskell and Price, *op. cit.* n. 18, pp. 59, 128, 160; Council of State Governments, *op. cit.* n. 145, p. 90.

[149]Haskell and Price, *op. cit.* n. 18, p. 260.

[150]*Ibid.*, p. 263.

[151]33 U.S.C. §1284(a) (1).

[152]E.g., Clean Air Act, 42 U.S.C. §7410.

[153]*Growth and Resources Report,* financed in part by a grant from the federal Department of Housing and Urban Development.

[154]See Council of State Governments, *op. cit.* n. 145, pp. 67–69.

[155]*Ibid.*, p. 69.

[156]Ill. Rev. Stat. (1977) ch. 19, §§1071–1077.13.

[157]Ill. Rev. Stat. (1977) ch. 96 1/2, §§101–108.

[158]Ill. Rev. Stat. (1977) ch. 127, §§541–543.

[159]Ill. Rev. Stat. (1977) ch. 96 1/2, §7401. This current language is somewhat broader than the statement of the Institute's powers in the original Environmental Protection Act, as adopted in 1970. See n. 17, above.

[160]In 1970, Illinois had an Institute of Social Policy, which had responsibilities similar to those of INR in the human resources areas of government. That institute no longer exists.

[161]Illinois Institute for Environmental Quality, *Annual Report 1972,* p. 8. This *Report* explores the Institute's role in government at length.

ADDITIONAL READINGS

Comptroller General. *Report to Congress: 16 Air and Water Pollution Issues Facing the Nation, Appendix III* (1978).

Council of State Governments, *Integration and Coordination of State Environmental Programs* (Lexington, Ky.: The Council, 1975).

Eisenbud, M. *Environment, Technology and Health: Human Ecology in Historical Perspective* (1978).

Haskell, E.H., and V.S. Price. *State Environmental Management: Case Studies of Nine States* (1973).

Illinois Department of Business and Economic Development, Division of Energy. *Illinois Energy Conservation Feasibility Report* (1976).

Illinois Department of Local Government Affairs and the Illinois Bureau of the Budget. *Comprehensive Growth and Resource Conservation Policies* (1978).

Illinois Institute for Environmental Quality. *Annual Report 1972.*

Illinois Institute for Environmental Quality. *Strip Mine Reclamation in Illinois* (prepared by Argonne National Laboratory) (1973).

Illinois Task Force on Governmental Reorganization. *Orderly Government: Organizing for Manageability* (1976).

Task Force on the Future of Illinois. *A Working Paper on the Future of Illinois* (1978).

CHAPTER **30**

Zoning to Curb Residential Sprawl onto Rich Farmland: The Case of Illinois' DeKalb County

J. Dixon Esseks

COUNTRY LIVING LOTS–One or two acres. Only ten minutes from shopping, schools. Priced to sell. Call . . .

"Country living" has great appeal to the many Americans seeking to flee the high real estate taxes, traffic congestion, air pollution, and other problems of our cities and suburbs. Networks of good state, county, and local roads put large areas of rural land within work-commuting distance. Rising gasoline prices may not significantly reduce the attraction of homesites four or more miles from the nearest shopping or 20 or more miles from work, so high a priority do many Americans place on escaping urban-suburban environments.[1]

In Illinois and other Corn Belt states, however, much or most of rural residential development takes place at the expense of productive cropland. According to United States Department of Agriculture estimates, arable land comprises about 68 percent of Illinois' total land surface (24.4 million out of 35.8 million acres).[2] And approximately 86 percent of the farmable acres (21 million out of 24.4 million) is prime farmland, that is, land with the "soil quality, growing season, and moisture supply needed to produce sustained high yields of crops economically. . . ."[3] Therefore, in Illinois there is a high probability, close to 6 in 10 (.68 × .86) that any new residential development will occur on good if not excellent land.

"So what?" may be asked. Does not this country have enough good cropland to meet its present and foreseeable-future needs for food and fiber, both for domestic consumption and for export? This question has yet to be resolved. Groups within both Congress and the federal executive branch, especially in the United States Department of Agriculture (USDA) and the Council on Environmental Quality, are currently (May 1979) seeking to establish a national study committee to investigate, among other questions, whether the continued (a) conversion of good farmland permanently out of agriculture, such as into housing, roads and reservoirs, and (b) degradation of other cropland through soil erosion, strip mining and other forces will not cumulate into a serious land-supply constraint for our agricultural sector.[4]

Another important question for study is whether the nation can afford, in terms of energy costs, the removal from production or the degradation of cropland which is energy-efficient. The relatively flat, open land, with normally adequate moisture, and with soils of high organic content which comprise the typical prime farmland of the Corn Belt, can produce high yields with comparatively low energy inputs. Petroleum—based fertilizers need not be applied as heavily as on lower-grade land; fuel consumption for cultivating and harvesting machinery tends to be less than on hilly and/or small-sized parcels; and irrigation, with its pumping energy costs, should normally not be necessary. Another important energy saving which could result from discouraging "country living" on prime cropland can be in reduced use of gasoline by private cars. In comparison to in-town dwellers, the residents of rural subdivisions tend to consume considerably more gasoline per capita. Their average trips to work, school, shopping, church, etc. are longer; and they have less opportunity to walk or bike to destinations rather than driving.

A third question for study is whether in-town taxpayers subsidize residential sprawl occurring in rural areas. The distance factor tends to make school busing, police patrolling, snow plowing and providing electricity and other services more costly than if the same subdivisions were located within or adjacent to towns. Yet country residents pay for those services at the same tax rates as do town dwellers; and their electricity and other utility rates are typically also the same, despite the greater costs attributable to distance.

Doubts about zoning's effectiveness have led a number of agriculturally rich counties to adopt or consider other techniques for curbing sprawl. New York's Suffolk County (Long Island), for example, in 1976 launched a program under which the county government was to purchase eventually a total of about 11,000 acres worth of "development rights—farmland owners were voluntarily to transfer to the county the right to develop their land in exchange for sums supposedly equal to the difference between its market value for development and its value in farming.[5] The per acre cost of development rights purchased by Suffolk through mid-1979 averaged close to $3,000.

Relatively few farming counties have the kind of tax base for underwriting development-rights or related schemes that Suffolk has. Another technique, being considered in New Jersey and elsewhere, is "transfer of development rights," whereby, through a complex process, farmland owners in a "preservation zone" could sell their development rights to private parties seeking to develop intensively parcels of land located elsewhere in the same jurisdiction and designated for residential use.[6] By this means they could be compensated for the resulting productivity losses and ultimate loss of agricultural use.

The high costs and /or legal-political complexities of the preservation techniques which rival zoning suggest a closer look at the latter's viability. It has apparently worked in Wisconsin's Walworth County (near Milwaukee). Planning officials there reported in 1977 success in administering a zoning ordinance which balanced "the need to accommodate urban and recreation growth in the county, with the need to preserve the rich agricultural resource base and to protect its natural beauty."[7] In the same year their counterparts in Black Hawk County, Iowa, with a population of 111,000 claimed that restrictive zoning had since 1973 diverted residential growth away from prime farmland onto property which had both poorer agricultural soils and "desirable properties for building."[8]

Who is right—the advocates of restrictive zoning or the critics? Probably, both are in the sense that in some jurisdictions this regulatory tool will largely succeed while in others it will fail. DeKalb County, Illinois, has had experience with zoning since 1972. That experience can help identify conditions for success and failure. The DeKalb record is well documented: complete transcripts or tape recordings of the Zoning Board of Appeals' deliberations on each case; minutes of the County Board's consideration of each case, both in the committee stage and before the whole Board; and soil maps and other physical data on each case. These sources enable us to determine (1) the extent to which the county followed its growth management plan of concentrating development in designated areas, (2) the extent to which zoning decisions actually curbed sprawl and protected farmland, and (3) what are the likely conditions for success and failure when this approach to curbing growth is employed. The contemporary decision-making records (transcripts, tapes, minutes), are useful for identifying likely causes of decisions. For example, does the record indicate that zoning authorities explicitly considered the plan's designation for parcels proposed for rezoning, or was the plan largely ignored? Does the record reveal whether those authorities took into account the land's soil quality and other dimensions of farmability? Were they really concerned about sprawl, such as by inquiring into the land uses surrounding the subject property; or were they, as far as the record shows, indifferent to whether the proposed development was to be located near existing housing or on a cornfield far from existing residential development?

The DeKalb County Case

The government of Illinois' agriculturally rich DeKalb County has formally committed itself to managing residential growth so as to protect good farmland and to economize on public service costs. The county presently has about 71,000 people and is situated immediately adjacent to two metropolitan areas (Chicago's and Rockford's) in northern Illinois. According to the Department of Commerce's 1974 *Census of Agriculture,* DeKalb had 93 percent of its land surface in farms;[9] and according to USDA estimates about 97 percent of the approximately 369,000 acres in farms was prime farmland.[10] In 1974 DeKalb was the State's richest county in terms of the market value of agricultural products sold per farm, an average of $73,420, as opposed to the statewide average of $42,012 and the national mean of $35,234.[11]

DeKalb County's main tool for growth management has been restrictive zoning. In 1972 the county adopted a comprehensive plan which assigned, by means of a land-use map, about 10 percent of the county's land area to urbanization and the remaining 90 percent to agricultural use and to open space.[12] New residential development to the year 2000 was to be concentrated in designated growth zones (collectively adding up to the 10 percent) located around the county's 12 municipalities, with a continuous growth area stretching about 18 miles from the county's largest city to the third largest. While the municipalities zoned within their own jurisdictions, the county's incorporated areas comprised only 2 percent of the total land surface. Therefore, the main zoning authority was the County Board, advised by a Zoning Board of Appeals. The County Board's stated objective, as expressed in the new plan was.[13]

> To preserve the land best suited for farming and other agricultural pursuits, and to protect these areas from the encroachment of residential, commercial and industrial development by:
> a. Encouraging growth to occur in and adjacent to existing municipalities where services can be extended most economically.
> b. Establishing adequate protection through modern zoning regulations and development standards.

This chapter evaluates DeKalb County's experience since 1972 in using its zoning power to curb residential sprawl onto farming areas. Such inquiry has importance for Illinois and other farming states, because zoning's effectiveness for this policy purpose is a matter of considerable controversy. Land-use regulatory authorities seeking to protect farmland in Maryland, Massachusetts, New Jersey and New York have explicitly rejected zoning, largely from the belief that the "taking" issue poses an insurmountable obstacle.[14] Other critics argue that local zoning tends to be a politically unreliable tool for preserving prime farmland. The "taking" issue revolves around the Fifth Amendment prohibition against taking of property without fair compensation. If denied by zoning authorities the opportunity to develop their land, affected farmland owners may challenge the denials in court, claiming uncompensated losses of potential income (rents, capital gains).[15] The unreliability arguments against local zoning include skepticism about the capacity of zoning authorities to resist pressures from local developers (some of them farmer-developers), realtors, retailers and others expecting to benefit from growth.[16]

Congruence of DeKalb's Zoning Decisions with the Comprehensive Plan

The congruence of zoning decisions with the plan's land-use map is judged simply by identifying, from the records for each case, the subject parcels' locations and then plotting them on the map. In DeKalb County between March 1972, when the new plan and an accompanying zoning ordinance were adopted, and the end of 1978, the county acted on 56 petitions for rezoning land from agricultural to residential uses. Twenty-five of those involved parcels located in areas designated by the plan for residential growth, and 24 of those 25 were approved by the County Board. The remaining 31 petitions involved land planned for agricultural use or for parks/open space. The County Board rejected nine of them but granted rezoning for 22.

Why did the Board deviate from the plan? A prior question, however, is whether the zoning authorities of this county were aware of the plan's designations for parcels proposed for development. The land-use plan may have never or only rarely entered into their deliberations. The contemporary record suggests the contrary. In 48 of the 56 cases, the Zoning Board of Appeals' transcripts/tapes show a formal finding, by the county planner or an assistant state's attorney and communicated verbally to the Board's members, as to whether the proposed land use conformed to the plan. Those 48 cases include 18 of the 22 instances where the county granted rezoning contrary to the plan and eight of the nine petitioners where rezoning was denied, in accordance with the plan. The Zoning Board of Appeals was the principal fact-finding body for zoning decisions, and its recommendations to the County Board whether to grant or deny petition were rarely rejected—in only four of the 56 cases.

While zoning authorities were aware of the plan's use designations, why in 23 cases did they not follow them? The contemporary record indicates four types of justifications for deviating from the plan: the subject property was immediately bordering on a growth zone (in three cases which were approved for rezoning), the land was marginal for farming (16 petitions), the parcel's soils were too wet for residential building (one case of denial), and/or the land was in an area already containing substantial housing development or where the "trend" was towards such development (a "finding" for nine of the approved petitions).

The Zoning Board of Appeals' deliberations (in transcript or tape form) and the County Board's minutes (including those of its Planning and Zoning Committee) for each case were content-coded for evaluative findings by members of those decision-making bodies on dimensions considered important in the literature on zoning: congruence with the plan; compatibility with land uses of adjoining parcels; trend of development in the area; the soils' suitability for residential building (i.e., for spetic tanks, for homes with basements) the land's farmability; the difficulty of serving the area with fire, police and other services; and the attitudes of neighboring landowners towards the petition, among other dimensions.[17] The purpose of coding was to identify likely reasons for approving/denying petitions. While few decision-makers reveal all of their motives in public deliberations, some or many gunuine reasons should surface, particularly in the context of zoning where land values may be substantially affected (inflated or repressed) as the result of local officials' decisions. A public record of no reasons for decisions or of apparently specious ones invites court challenges and/or political backlash.

In the single DeKalb case where the comprehensive plan permitted residential development but the County Board denied the petition, the record indicates only one reason, but a suitable one. Both the County Health Board and the Soil and Water Conservation District (SCWD) reported that the subject parcel's soils were undesirable for residential development. Wetness problems made septic systems unadvisable, and the area was not expected to be served by a municipal sewer system. In all 56 cases, the deliberations of the Zoning Board of Appeals (ZBA) included consideration of the soils-suitability dimension; and beginning in 1975 almost all of the ZBA's "Findings of Fact" submitted to the County Board contained statements on that dimension.

Another physical dimension frequently evaluated in the DeKalb County cases, 1972–78, was the subject parcel's farmability. In 51 of the 56 cases the record shows such evaluations by the petitioner, his attorney, or some zoning official(s), with the petitioner's side usually claiming that the land was poor for farming, so as to justify conversion out of agriculture. In 38 cases, the county planner and/or the ZBA as a whole made findings as to farmability; and beginning in 1975, the ZBA regularly included them in its reports to the County Board. Those findings were based in large part on a "Natural Resources Report" prepared by the SCWD on each parcel proposed for conversion out of agriculture. Such reports had been made since 1972, but beginning in 1976 they included productivity indexes, in terms of likely yields, for each of the soil types found on the subject property. SCWD staff had access to detailed USDA soil maps for the county.

Other less satisfactory bases for evaluating farmability were petitioners' claims about the parcel's poor drainage, small size and/or awkward shape for efficient farming. In judging the validity of such claims, the ZBA and County Board had little to go on besides the largely subjective opinions of farmer-members of both boards. The county planner stayed out of the debate since he lacked a background in farming. The SCWD reports could not help overcome subjectivity on these dimensions since they were limited to analyzing soils and vegetation. However, those reports could be expanded, with the additional financial costs of gathering data on size/shape drainage conditions (and relating them to such factors as the crops grown and the machinery typically used) charged to the persons(s) seeking rezoning. The Natural Resources Reports in their present form are paid for by the petitioners.

Poorly documented findings regarding farmability may contribute to the county losing in court when rezoning denials are challenged. This happened to DeKalb County in 1978, when it lost at the appeals court level (State) in part because its brief failed to satisfy the court that the 80 acres at issue were economic for farming. The developer claimed that they were not, and the justices found his evidence more persuasive.[18]

The farmability dimension appears to have helped to shape county decisions to approve petitions for rezoning on land *not* designated by the plan for development. There were 22 cases; and in 18 of them there was an explicit finding by the ZBA (14 cases) or by the county Planning Department (four cases) that the soils were poor, the parcel too small or otherwise uneconomical for farming. The policy implication was that, where land was unsuitable for farming, the county should not prevent the owner from converting it to a profitable use (housing), whatever the plan's designation. The county formalized this policy in a new zoning district, the "Rural Residence District", established by ordinance in September 1977. The ordinance reads in part:[19]

> The Board of Appeals shall not recommend a rezoning to this zone district classification unless the applicant shall present clear and convincing evidence to the Board of Appeals that the property sought to be rezoned is not suitable for agricultural use.

The ordinance mandated, further, that "in determing suitability of property for agriculture", the ZBA should consider soil types, topography, vegetation cover and "man-made and physical features which may serve as barriers."

Another justification for deviating from the plan was, in three cases, that the subject parcel immediately bordered on a growth zone and that, since the map had not been drawn with precision, it was unfair to deny rezoning just on the grounds of falling marginally outside a zone. Moreover, in all three cases the land was evaluated to be poor for farming; and in two of the three there was the additional finding of a trend in the area around the subject parcel towards residential development.

A close cousin to a "trend" finding was one of substantial residential development already existing in the area. These two types of justifications for deviating from the plan were present in the records of nine of the 22 cases. How could substantial development or a trend occur in areas outside designated growth zones? The lots may have been recorded before enactment of the zoning ordinance; hence, rezoning was not needed, only a building permit. The county may have permitted some rezoning in the area since 1972. And up to April 1974 homes could be built on agriculturally zoned land if the parcel was at least five acres in size. In 1974 the county increased the minimum lot size from five to 40 acres, expecting that few persons seeking rural home sites and unwilling (or unable) to secure rezoning would bother to burden themselves with the cost of acquiring at least 40 acres.

In rezoning where substantial development had already occurred, the county would simply recognize, with a change in zoning classification, the accomplished fact of changes in land use. Moreover, farmland preservation may become unfeasible as a policy goal where considerable land has already been converted to housing. The remaining land tends to fall into the hands of non-farmers who, waiting to resell or develop the land themselves, do not carry out the investments necessary to maintain its productivity in agriculture. In addition, the remaining fields may be too small, have drainage problems due to adjacent development, and otherwise have seriously declined in farmability. However, where the existing development is still scattered, agriculture may still be viable in the area. And a county decision to rezone a parcel may help to push the balance against agriculture, since one new rezoning provides a precedent for additional petitions being granted in that area. For most of the nine cases under review, the record suggests that the development prior to rezoning was in fact scattered. Seven of the nine subject properties either had no residential development immediately adjacent to them or had it only to one side. If we use a radius of one-half mile, six had some housing in two directions, but only one had it in three. While the contemporary record may understate the degree of housing development in those areas, it does indicate that, when the zoning authorities made evaluations on that dimension, they did so unsystematically. There were no guidelines similar to those for the farmability dimension (i.e., the 1977 ordinance on Rural Residences), and that lack of guidelines showed up in the frequent vagueness and variability of the evaluations: "several single-family residences close to the subject property," "four new homes built in the area in the last few years," "a trend toward building some single-family homes in the area," etc.

The record for the ten cases of rezoning *denials* reveals rather well-based evaluative findings on two dimensions—conformity to the plan and suitability of soils for residential development—but vagueness or subjectiveness on farmability, trend of development and degree of remoteness (distance to fire stations, access to all-weather roads). Lack of precision and documentation is particularly serious in denials, since the frustrated developer may sue to overthrow the county's decision, and, where the county's reasons for rejection are vague and/or lacking in evidence, the suit is much more likely to succeed. The record indicates that two petitions were turned down because of wet soils, with the problem situation documented by soil maps. In two other cases, however, the main issue appears to have been farmability, particularly the adequacy of parcel size, with the issue resolved largely on the basis of County Board members' subjective judgments. In the other six cases, the major issue appears from the record to have been the remoteness of the sites, compounded in five instances by the relatively large sizes of the proposed developments. They averaged 2.5 miles from the edge of the nearest municipality; and the five large ones ranged from 31 to 90 proposed dwelling units. At the Zoning Board of Appeals hearings, the six were criticized as being too far from the sources of public services (especially for fire protection), located on roads inadequate to the traffic likely to be generated by the proposed development and in other ways unacceptable because of the distance factor. However, these criticisms tended to lack precision. They were vague, for example, about the levels of risk to public safety in locating a subdivision 2.5 miles or more from town and about the costs to in-town taxpayers of providing school busing and other services to remote subdivisions. Therefore, when one frustrated developer challenged the county's denial of his petition (the same case mentioned above), the county lost in part because it failed to prove that there was a public gain (e.g., economizing on public service costs) to offset "the hardship imposed upon the individual property owners."[20] Subsequent to this court defeat, the county's Planning Department began to acquire the capability to estimate the likely costs and revenues generated by proposed residential developments.

Sprawl Curbed? Farmland Protected?

DeKalb's growth management efforts saved farmland from being converted in two ways. Nine zoning denials kept specific acreage from being developed (the tenth denial involved land not in farming but covered with trees), and those rejections established precedents which apparently discouraged would-be developers from seeking rezonings for comparable cases, that is, ones for sites outside growth zones and relatively large by DeKalb standards (more than a dozen dwelling units), particularly where the land was good for farming. No such development proposal was brought to the County Board after 1975, although several relatively large ones for sites *within* growth zones were proposed and passed. The current County Planner reports that since 1976 he has been discouraging people coming into his office with rezoning proposals affecting land outside growth zones, unless the land was likely to be found unsuitable for farming.

Being *in* a growth zone has tended to eliminate farmability as a grounds for denial. For example, there was a 1977 case which, except for its according-to-plan location, was ideal for rejection. Several township officials and many other local residents strongly opposed the petition at the public hearing, the soils were largely good for farming and the Zoning Board of Appeals voted against it. However, the county planner argued successfully to the County Board that, since the petition satisfied both the plan and other county regulations, the county was legally bound to grant it.

The plan was a double-edged sword also in terms of curbing sprawl. While it helped to block development outside the growth zones, it legitimized sprawl within the ten percent of the county designated for development. Population growth slowed, and not all that land originally zoned for development was needed. In fact, most of the new developments resulting from rezoning approvals in growth zones were residential islands or appendages to existing small islands or strips of housing. Six of the 24 had no residential development adjacent to them on any side. Four had some in one direction, and five, on two sides. In 1978 the county Planning Department began developing a new land-use plan with considerably less acreage designated for growth and with the major purpose of the reduction being to lessen the sprawl permissable under the plan.

Factors for Success and Failure in Using Restrictive Zoning

The factors for failure suggested by the DeKalb experience since 1972 include overgenerous estimates of population increase, so that the growth zones on the land-use map are too large and end up promoting sprawl. Another factor may be the lack of adequate documentation on which to base judgments as to farmability and as to the public costs/inconvenience/risk in locating subdivisions in remote rural areas. (De Kalb lost a court challenge at the appellate level because its brief on these two dimensions was unpersuasive.) A third factor suggested by the DeKalb case may be insufficient information on which to judge whether the trend in an area's land use is towards residential. A wrong judgment, leading to rezoning, can help to cause such a trend rather than simply acknowledge it.

An important factor for success suggested by the DeKalb case is an energetic and politically adroit planning department. DeKalb's department consistently advocated, before the ZBA and County Board, that the comprehensive plan be followed or, if not, amending legislation be enacted. That department drafted and shepherded through the new Rural Residence District, lobbied the Soil and Water Conservation District to provide better data on farmability (e.g., the productivity indexes) and arranged for a study of the fiscal costs of sprawl.

Probably the most critical factor for the success of restrictive zoning as a technique for farmland preservation is the degree of its acceptance by local farmers. In agriculturally rich counties faced with significant development pressures, farmers may have substantial direct representation on land-use regulatory bodies (Planning Commissions, Zoning Boards of Appeals, etc.). Further even where farmers are in a small minority, the majority is likely to defer to their opposition to zoning, if only out of a sense of fair play (i.e., "It's their land that's at stake"). In DeKalb much of the farming community has supported the use of zoning to protect agriculture. For example, the county's influential Farm Bureau in December 1978 endorsed the principle of "keep[ing residential] expansion in a narrow band around each city," especially "if we keep this expansion in wooded or more erosion-prone, less productive areas."[21] Among the supporters of zoning decisions in compliance with the comprehensive plan and with the 1977 Rural Residence District amendment have been farm operator-owners on the Zoning Board of Appeals (four out of the seven members in 1978) and on the County Board (eight out of 24). And their farmland was not all in the growth zones, so that they were free to sell to developers while others, whose petitions they judged, were not. All four of the ZBA farmer-members and seven of the eight on the County Board had cropland in the preservation zone.

In much, perhaps even most, of the United States, however, farmers tend to oppose restrictive agricultural zoning. They cherish the freedom to sell their land when and to whom they wish.[22] What accounts for the political acceptability of restrictive zoning among DeKalb farmers? It derives in part from perceptions that the DeKalb program is fair to cropland owners in the important sense of allowing rezoning on poor land, even though it is in the preservation zone. Under the Rural Residence District ordinance, farmers need not be stuck with marginal land and no alternative use to which to put it. A second, complementary perception is that DeKalb is still a good place in which to farm. In contrast to other counties closer to Chicago, where higher rates of urbanization have reduced/eliminated the viability of agriculture, DeKalb still has the conditions for profitable farming: a good infrastructure of credit institutions, seed and fertilizer suppliers, farm-machinery dealers and other essential services; levels of traffic on county and township roads which do not seriously hinder access by farm vehicles; adequate-sized farming units, i.e., urbanization has not yet cut up many parcels into uneconomic units. Yet another important, if not essential, perception held by apparently many DeKalb farmers is that relatively few of them stand to be financially hurt by the restrictions on growth. Residential development in rural areas of the county has historically been at a modest pace, so that not many farmland owners can expect developers or speculators to bid for their land, at least not in the foreseeable future. Moreover, if they were to acquiesce in rezonings for the few, they—the majority of farmers—would likely be burdened with some of the consequences: higher tax rates to fund services for rural subdivisions, increased traffic on roads used for farming purposes, and perhaps more nuisance complaints (including in court) from non-farmer residents against farm odors, dust, and noise (e.g., early-morning or late-night cultivating).

Donn Derr and colleagues at Rutgers University suggest that zoning can work as a preservation tool only in such counties as DeKalb, where "urban pressures are still minor" and the financial stakes in being denied rezoning are relatively modest.[23] However, recent demographic research suggests that there are many such counties like DeKalb, with slow but significant growth resulting from decisions by large numbers of Americans to flee cities and suburbia or to remain in the rural environments where they were born rather than emigrate to metropolitan areas.[24] In each such modest-growth county, zoning may protect from conversion only a few hundred acres per year. But, if a number of urban-fringe counties like DeKalb simultaneously used zoning to protect their agricultural sectors, the collective and cumulative effect could be large nation-wide.

NOTES

[1]Calvin L. Beale, "Internal Migration in the United States since 1970," statement before the House Select Committee on Population, February 9, 1978, Washington, D.C., p. 6.

[2]Letter to author from the Soil Conservation Service, U.S. Department of Agriculture, Champaign, Illinois, February 28, 1977.

[3]*Ibid.*; and Daniel E. Holmes, State Conservationist, Soil Conservation Service, United States Department of Agriculture, Champaign, Illinois, "Land Inventory and Monitoring Memorandum . . . Prime and Unique Farmlands," July 14, 1976, p. 2.

[4]Representative James Jeffords of Vermont introduced on March 1, 1979 on behalf of himself and 41 other Congressmen the "Agricultural Land Protection Act" (H.R. 2551), which would authorize a national study into these and related questions. In the same month a parallel initiative for a similar study emerged from USDA and the Council on Environmental Quality.

[5]John V.N. Klein (Suffolk's County Executive), "Preserving Farmland on Long Island," *Environmental Comment,* January 1978, pp. 11–13.

[6]See "Transfer Development Rights Concept," pp. 7, 30.

[7]Harold Kolb and James A. Johnson, "Preserving environmental resources: The Walworth County, Wisconsin, Story," in *Land Use: Tough Choices in Today's World* (Ankeny, Iowa: Soil Conservation Society of America, 1977), p. 317.

[8]Janice M. Clark, "Agricultural Zoning in Black Hawk, County, Iowa," in *Land use: Tough Choices, op. cit.,* p. 154.

[9]United States, Department of Commerce, Bureau of the Census, *1974 Census of Agriculture,* Vol. 1. Part 13, Illinois: State andCounty Data (Washington, D.C., 1977).

[10]United States, Department of Agriculture, Soil Conservation Service, "Prime Farmland in DeKalb County: By Soil Types and Mapping Units" (DeKalb, Illinois, 1977).

[11]United States, Department of Commerce, Bureau of the Census, *op. cit.,* Parts 13 and 51.

[12]William S. Lawrence and Associates, Inc. *A Comprehensive Plan: DeKalb County* (Chicago, Ill., 1971), p. 90.

[13]*Ibid.*, p. 73.

[14]See Fred Bosselman, David Callies and John Banta, *The Taking Issue: An Analysis of the Constitutional Limits of Land-Use Control* (Washington, D.C.: Council on Environmental Quality, 1973).

[15]See the arguments against restrictive zoning given by New Jersey Assemblywoman Rosemarie Totaro in "The Transfer Development Rights Concept as a Preservation Tool," *New Jersey Municipalities,* 52 (November 1975), 7; and by the Presiding Officer of the Suffolk County (New York) Legislature, Floyd Linton, in *Pennysaver News,* July 12, 1976.

[16]William Ellingson, "Differential Assessment and Local Governmental Controls to Preserve Agricultural Lands," *South Dakota Law Review,* 20 (Summer 1975), 570–71.

[17]Richard Babcock, *The Zoning Game: Municipal Practices and Policies* (Madison, Wisconsin: The University of Wisconsin Press, 1966); Marion Clawson, *Suburban Land Conversion in the United States: An Economic and Governmental Process* (Baltimore Maryland: The Johns Hopkins Press, 1971); William J. Block, *Rural Zoning: People, Property, and Public Policy,* Extension Bulletin 600, reprinted January 1974, Cooperative Extension, Washington State University.

[18]*Gary Pettee vs. County of KeKalb and the DeKalb County Zoning Board of Appeals,* Appellate Court, 2nd District, Illinois, May 17, 1978.

[19]Ordinance 76-22, DeKalb County, adopted September 21, 1977.

[20]From the *Pettee vs. DeKalb County* opinion cited in note 18 above.

[21]From a statement by Allan Aves, President of the DeKalb County Farm Bureau, to the Planning and Zoning Committee of the DeKalb County Board, December 27, 1978.

[22]William D. Anderson, Gregory C. Gustafson and Robert F. Boxley, "Perspectives on Agricultural Land Policy," *Journal of Soil and Water Conservation* 30 (January/February 1975), 41; James W. Giltmier, "Review," in *Perspectives on Prime Lands: Background Papers for Seminar on Retention of Prime Lands* (U.S. Department of Agriculture, 1975).

[23]Donn Derr, Leslie Small and Pritam Dhillon, "Criteria and Strategies for Maintaining Agriculture at the Local Level," *Journal of Soil and Water Conservation* 32 (May/June 1977), 122.

[24]Beale, *op. cit.*, pp. 1–3.

CHAPTER **31**

Politics and Policies of Elementary and Secondary Education

Martin Burlingame

This chapter examines three major themes of politics and policies of elementary and secondary education in Illinois. First, it highlights some of the issues surrounding governance and policymaking for public schools. While education is clearly the responsibility of the State, the educational governance structure involves not only State but also local and regional officials and agencies. Conflicts abound over what governmental levels do or what ought to have sole, major or limited responsibility over topics such as taxation for, regulation of, or assistance to educational enterprises. Equally, the formal governing structure is surrounded by what seem hosts of interest groups, covering a wide range of concerns. It begins with a brief description and analysis of the governance and policymaking structure of Illinois elementary and secondary schools from the end of World War II to the present. Of particular importance in this account are the development of the School Problems Commission in the late 1940's and the new 1970 State Constitution which created a State Board of Education and an appointed State Superintendent of Schools.

Second, the chapter reflects the influences of changes in societal factors such as numbers of students or the overall state of the economy on public concerns about education. Sheer numbers, be they dollars or students, provide the baseline of conditions and the stuff of problems in education.

Finally, the chapter underscores the number of actors involved in making educational policy. A broad range of participants seek to shape not only the contents of policy decisions but also the very processes of policymaking itself. Both substantive and procedural issues influence policy outcomes about schools. This analysis seeks deliberately to bare linkages among the governance structure, the conditions of education and the policy system. It concludes with suggestions for further examination of the politics and policies of the Illinois common schools.

The Governance of Elementary and Secondary Education

This section examines the governance of elementary and secondary education from the end of WW II to the present. This thirty-year period witnessed the development of two major structures of governance: the School Problems Commission and the State Board of Education.

The School Problems Commission

As fighting in Europe ended with the fall of Berlin, and the attention of the nation turned to the defeat of Japan, the General Assembly of the State of Illinois created a Postwar Planning Commission to study and report on conditions of education in the State. This action reaffirmed two constants in the governance of Illinois education: first, the General Assembly had always played the preeminent role in governing the schools. The General Assembly dealt with topics such as distributions of school funds, structures of county and local school districts, and education and training of handicapped children. Second, the General Assembly had often created special commissions involving legislators, educators, members of special interest groups and citizens to make recommendations about needed legislative actions. Between 1900 and 1945, commissions were created nine times (1907, 1921, 1923, 1931, February 1935, July 1935, 1938, 1939, 1941).

As this Commission began its work, the governance structure of education consisted of agencies at the State, county and local levels. The State level included the General Assembly and the Office of the Superintendent of Public Instruction (OSPI). The 1870 State Constitution required that: "The General Assembly shall provide a thorough and efficient system of free schools whereby all children of this State may receive a good common school education." (Article VIII, Section I) The General Assembly delegated much of this responsibility to village and township school districts while vesting State policy making to standing committees on education in both the House and Senate.

The 1870 Constitution also created the elected position of Superintendent of Public Instruction. The office had a four-year term, and candidates ran as members of political parties (partisan). The Superintendent ran the Office of the Superintendent of Public Instruction (OSPI), a small agency in Springfield whose primary task involved the enforcement of regulations concerning schooling. These regulations generally established minimum standards and the rules necessary to carry them out. The OSPI also heard complaints and settled disputes, as well as producing statistical information about the schools of the state.

At the county level, the Office of the County Superintendent of Schools carried out a number of administrative and supervisory jobs. These county superintendents were elected on partisan slates of candidates, and in the more populous counties two or three superintendents were elected to districts. The superintendents also worked with county boards of education who dealt primarily with boundary disputes and other special hearings.

In 1944–45, the State of Illinois had 11,955 local school districts. Of this total, 99 were unit districts (grades 1–12), 646 were secondary districts (grades 9–12), and a whopping 10,610 were elementary districts (grades 1–8). The vast majority of these elementary districts were one room township schools. Each of these some 12,000 districts were governed by a local board, in all cases except Chicago elected by the voting citizens of the district. The local school board hired school personnel, prepared the local school budget, conducted elections for approval of operating and capital development tax referendums, and approved local school operations in areas such as curriculum and course offerings when they exceeded the state's requirements. These local boards were supervised by the county superintendent, who provided services many single small districts could not afford themselves. County cooperative services in areas such as education for handicapped children were common.

The 1945 Commission faced not only new challenges created by the war but also older issues about the governing of the common schools. The State's schools faced a shortage of teachers which many called desperate, an increasing birth rate which threatened to become a baby boom and major problems about school funds. Teachers were poorly paid, local property taxes seemed too high and the State lacked sufficient monies for the local schools. These problems constituted a crisis in education.

Other earlier commissions had faced similar crisis conditions. In general, these earlier groups had recommended that: (1) the State create a non-political State board of education which appointed a professionally trained state superintendent; (2) the State create larger local school districts; (3) the State provide more and more funds for local districts without concomitantly increasing State regulation; and (4) local tax machinery including assessment procedures be made more equitable across the districts and counties.

The *Report and Recommendations* of the Illinois Postwar Planning Commission, 1945, offered few surprises. The report pressed for extention of State support for funding, greater attention to the welfare of public educators and uniform and fairer property assessments. While the General Assembly discussed the report, it took no immediate action.

But the crisis did not vanish. In 1947, the General Assembly created another study group, the School Finance and Tax Commission. Its report did influence the General Assembly so that they increased the dollar amount of the basic (''foundation'') State aid per pupil. In 1949, Governor Adlai E. Stevenson created by executive order still another commission, the Advisory Commission on Education. The perplexing post-war problems in education simply hung on the coattails of the Legislature, and the leadership of the State seemed constantly pressed to deal with on-going, and seemingly unsolvable, problems.

The 1949 Advisory Commission on Education repeated many of the earlier problems and solutions, but did offer one major new recommendation. The Commission recommended the General Assembly establish a *continuing* commission to work full time studying the problems of the common schools. The 1949 General Assembly moved on this proposal, creating the School Problems Commission (SPC). The SPC, in 1949, was to be composed of thirteen members: five members appointed by the Governor, three Senators, three Representatives, the Director of Finance and the State Superintendent of Public Instruction. The SPC members were to serve until July 1, 1951, at which time the Commission was to expire. But the General Assembly did not permit the SPC to die: between 1951 and 1957 three additional SPC's were created. Finally, in July, 1957, the General Assembly made the SPC a continuing agency of the state.

The SPC became the major vehicle for setting educational policies in Illinois. While the General Assembly retained its power, over 90% of all bills recommended by the SPC were approved. The SPC's success rested upon three major factors: bipartisan composition, consultative procedures, and diplomatic relations with other governmental agencies.

The SPC provided a place where those with deep interests and important stakes in education could meet, discuss various alternative solutions and strike bargains. By 1957, the SPC had grown to seventeen members. Five of these members were appointed by the Governor. Traditionally, those appointments included: a representative of the Illinois Education Association, the state's largest teacher association; a representative of the Illinois Association of School Boards; a member of the City of Chicago Board of Education; and one ''wild card'' selection of the Governor, often a member of the Illinois Chamber of Commerce. Ten members of the SPC were from the General Assembly. The House and Senate each appointed five members, with three from each chamber from the majority party. Traditionally, the chairmen of the standing committees on education were appointed, as well as other members of these committees. The appointments also took into account the geographical politics of the state: a Cook County Democrat, a downstate Democrat, a suburban Republican and a downstate Republican appeared on both House and Senate delegations. Finally, the elected State Superintendent of Public Instruction and the State Director of Finance served as ex officio members. The State Director of Finance, a Governor's appointee, was responsible for estimates of the State's revenue and expenditures for the Chief Executive.

The composition of the SPC thus provided an opportunity for the major interests in education to have their say, for legislators to weigh these interests against party and regional concerns and for these interests and concerns to be compared to the financial conditions of the state. These deliberations were enhanced by the work of an appointed research director and staff.

Hence, the SPC existed as the only continuing legislative commission in the United States dealing exclusively with education. In most states, legislatures dealt with state superintendents of schools and state boards of educations. Whether elected or appointed, these superintendents and state boards stood apart from the legislative and executive branches of government. But in Illinois, the concerns of the General Assembly over the control of education and over the opportunities for patronage jobs were so deep and abiding that the Assembly deliberately tied education deliberations directly to the Legislature and to the Executive Branch. These legislative deliberations were enriched by the on-going presence of major educational interests. The SPC stood alone among the states as a uniquely created and maintained forum for bargaining about the role of a state in organizing and financing its schools.

The procedures of the SPC became the mechanisms for consensus. The SPC membership reached consensus by being conscious of the problems it sought to solve, of the manner in which solutions were created and of the need to get SPC proposals to the floor of the General Assembly.

The SPC maintained as its first priority solutions to problems of school funding. The SPC devoted considerable time and energy dealing with the role of the State in financially supporting schools. These efforts rested upon the belief that more money would help the schools, but that how much more money would have to be resolved politically. These negotiations about dollars were enhanced by the composition of the SPC.

While finance predominated, the SPC also dealt with topics directly assigned to it on occasion by the General Assembly, with issues raised by formal communications with interest groups in education and with problems brought to open hearings or in private communications with members. While topics covered a wide range of educational issues, the SPC carefully avoided a series of problems. First, the SPC did not deal with problems of a single school district or of a small geographical cluster of districts. Second, the SPC avoided topics its members believed to be so controversial as to be incapable of solution at that moment. Third, the SPC avoided the issues of teacher welfare, racial desegregation or religious problems. Finally, the SPC avoided those problems which might have lead to conflicts with the general prerogative of the General Assembly to run the public schools.

Much of the work of the SPC was done using subcommittees and open public hearings. These mechanisms allowed committee members to become experts in various areas of education as well as letting all who were interested have an opportunity to express their viewpoints. Both mechanisms strengthened the internal procedures of the SPC and enhanced its reputation as a problem-solving commission.

The result of all these hearings, sub-committee and commission meetings was a package of legislation for the General Assembly. The SPC not only provided recommendations, but also went so far as to draft the legislation itself. This process involved the SPC membership and members of affected interest groups. In these meetings, bargains were struck about what topics would receive highest priority. Once priorities were set, SPC members and special interest group members drafted the actual bills, and SPC legislative members became their sponsors in the General Assembly.

The procedures of the SPC accentuated the process of political bargaining. Members of the SPC were pragmatic in orientation, seeking incremental changes in the financing and organization of the common schools. "Hot" or potentially controversial topics were avoided in proceedings which stressed openness and compromise.

The SPC's composition and procedures enhanced its standing with other governmental agencies as well as special interest groups. For members of the General Assembly, the SPC provided a "filter" for educational topics. The SPC processes of bargaining and accomodation meant that legislators had at hand "experts" who could supply answers to constituent demands as to why this or that had happened. Either the SPC became the scapegoat or else legislators could take some credit because of the wisdom of colleagues on the SPC. The SPC, thus, became a trusted advisor to the General Assembly, providing guidance on important issues such as school finance, but never trespassing to control education. Overall, consensus built by the SPC meant that legislators faced far fewer controversies about public school issues.

The Governor, who controls the State's purse strings, had direct access to the SPC deliberations about school funding through his appointments. The procedure generally followed by the SPC was to make a preliminary estimate of school financial needs before the General Assembly met. The Director of Finance and other SPC leaders then consulted with the Governor. In turn, the Governor then met with his financial and political advisors and informed the SPC of estimated school expenditures. The SPC then revised its original estimate to coincide with the Governor's estimate. Hence, while the SPC could not act without the Governor, most Governors found the SPC to be of benefit.

The SPC dealt with State education groups in three ways. First, the SPC "carried" many technical bills for the elected State Superintendent and the Office of the Superintendent of Public Instruction to make their work easier through minor adjustments in the organization and regulation of common schools. These bills, often the majority of the SPC's legislative agenda, provided few drastic changes but helped those running the system by clarifying or changing minor technical problems. These bills keep the educational system "tuned up" the same way new spark plugs tune up a car.

Second, the SPC became the formal avenue for State education interest groups to influence State policies. Leaders of the Illinois teacher, administrator and school board associations used their seats on the SPC to work toward their ends. As the SPC flourished, the General Assembly's tolerance for special bills carried by single special interest groups diminished. On the other hand, if hard work on the SPC did produce a bill carrying the SPC stamp, approval by the Legislature was almost certain.

Finally, the SPC had little to do with the Chicago school system. An uneasy truce existed between the State's largest school system, the remainder of the State's schools and the SPC. The Chicago public school system had a special grant of authority from the General Assembly. This grant literally made the Chicago schools a separate entity. The SPC and other education groups did not deal directly with the Chicago school system bureaucracy, but with a bloc of Cook County legislators, mostly Democrats, who were controlled by the Democratic machine of Cook County. This group of legislators bargained over Statewide initiatives with the SPC, protecting the special interests of Chicago while supporting measures which helped the State's schools generally. However, the Cook County legislators always keep a watchful eye on any legislation which might harm Chicago's interests—and were quick to upset this quid pro quo if their City schools were disadvantaged by SPC recommendations.

Hence, the SPC was in the 1950's and 1960's a unique body in American educational governance. No other state created such a standing committee of the legislature—a committee whose composition, procedures and linkages to other groups made it the chief policymaking group for the state. The support of a proposal or the rejection of alternatives by the SPC sealed its fate with the General Assembly.[1]

Nonetheless, the SPC's relationship to the governance and policymaking of education in the late 1970's has been clouded by the 1970 State Constitution. That document created a State Board of Education, appointed by the Governor, with the power to select a State Superintendent of Education. Before examining that new policy-making and governance structure, the history of the SPC in the late 1960's must be sketched. This portrait suggests that the SPC increasingly was beleaguered by the press of three issues—desires of professional educators to have a state board of education, demands of groups such as racial minorities and teachers to become involved in policymaking activities and growing efforts to use school finance as a way to achieve equity and educational reform.

Every major school commission from 1907 to 1945 recommended a State board of education with the legal authority to appoint the State superintendent. In 1963 the SPC continued this tradition when it recommended that the Legislature create a state board and then propose a constitutional amendment which would end the elected superintendent and have the new board appoint one. In 1966 the Illinois Task Force on Education, a group appointed by the Governor, State Superintendent and SPC, once again recommended a State board. In 1969 the SPC urged the pending Constitutional Convention to face and solve this issue.

It seems to be a tenet of faith among professional educators that school superintendents, at the local county or state level, should be appointed to office by an elected board of citizens. This model of governance provides for the general setting of policy by the citizens, with informed professional advice offered by the superintendent. Once the policy is established, the superintendent is responsible for its implementation. The blatantly political character of the elected state and county superintendent in Illinois ran counter to this image. This overt partisanship reduced the differences many educators believed existed between education and all other government functions. Education was to be set apart from the dirty partisan and patronage politics of other government services. Professional educators particularly feared that partisan politics in education meant teachers would become patronage appointments and that school districts would offer lucrative contracts, such as food, construction or transportation, to political cronies.

The SPC in the late 1960's also faced increasing demands from minority and teacher groups for their involvement in educational policy making. Since the Supreme Court's decisions in 1954 and 1955, the black community had pressed for the integration of schools. In 1965, the Elementary and Secondary Education Act had channeled federal funds to children of low income families—many of them black. Combined with the social unrest of this period, particularly in urban areas, the SPC was pressed to involve members of minority groups in their deliberations, and to make efforts to channel funds to those who might be economically and socially disadvantaged.

Beginning in 1960–61 with strikes in New York City, teachers became more militant in their demands not only for improved welfare benefits but also for participation in making decisions. By the late 1960's teacher strikes, conflicts between the National Education Association and the American Federation of Teachers over representation of teachers and collective negotiations between teacher associations and local school districts were common. The growing activism of these teacher associations meant that older accommodations among educational interests and other members of the SPC were strained. No longer did education present a solid front—in fact it appeared fractionated.

Finally, in the late 1960's the SPC faced a new movement in the area of school finance. The more traditional school finance specialists had concentrated their attention upon the creation of a funding formula, the efficient organization of school districts and the development of equitable taxing and assessment procedures. This strategy relied upon several important understandings: taxpayers believed that education was an important service; parents and teachers collaborated in supporting increased funding; urban, suburban and rural interests could resolve differences amicably; and those who supported education in general also supported funds for special needs, such as handicapped students.

By the late 1960's not only had many of these understandings collapsed, but also reformers in school finance were using the courts to challenge State financing of education. In general, these cases pitted reformers against traditional school finance practitioners. Reformers generally sought to equalize educational opportunities by concentrating on differences between ''rich'' and ''poor'' districts. This reform pressure from the courts created major changes in a number of states, including Illinois. The upshot of this movement was that the unanamity which had existed about the problems and solutions of school finance was shattered. The older consensus was gone—in its place stood conflicts between traditionalists and reformers. Also gone were many tacit understandings which made possible compromises among diverse interests. In contrast to the general sense of bargaining which permeated the SPC, the 1960's were marked by adversary proceedings. The courts, not political compromise, predominated.

The State Board of Education

Convening in December 1969, the Sixth Illinois Constitutional Convention produced major changes in the governance structure of education. In Section 2 of Article X, the new Constitution created a State Board of Education, provided an overview of the Board's duties and powers and required the Board to appoint a chief state educational officer.

The convention could not reach accord on whether the new State Board should be elected or appointed. While it was clear that the Board would have to represent regions of the State, when disagreement emerged over election or appointment the Convention simply passed the buck to the General Assembly. As the Convention decided: ''The number of members, their qualifications, terms of office and manner of election or selection shall be provided by law.'' [Article X, Section 2(a)] In its wisdom the General Assembly decided that the State Board of Education should be appointed by the Governor and confirmed by the Senate. The seventeen members were appointed on a regional basis: eight from the First Judicial District (all of Cook County), two each from the four downstate judicial districts and one at-large member. Terms were staggered.

The Constitution provided a broad overview of the responsibilities of the new Board. ''The Board, except as limited by law, may establish goals, determine policies, provide for planning and evaluating education programs and recommend financing. The Board shall have such other duties and powers as provided by law.'' [Article X, Section 2(a)] While clearly accountable to the General Assembly, since by law the Assembly could deny responsibilities, the Board appeared to assume the duties of the Office of the Superintendent of Public Instruction. To these duties was added one new responsibility—recommending financing. Whether deliberately or inadvertently, the inclusion of this duty and power to ''recommend financing'' created a potential conflict between the State Board and the School Problems Commission. (This issue will be examined in the final section of the chapter.)

In 1973, the General Assembly sought to elaborate the duties of the State Board.

> The duties of the State Board of Education shall encompass all duties currently delegated to the Office of the Superintendent of Public Instruction and such other duties as the General Assembly shall designate. The Board shall be responsible for educational policies and guidelines for public and private schools, pre-school through grade 12, and Vocational Education in the State of Illinois. The Board shall analyze the present and future aims, needs and requirements of education in the State of Illinois and recommend to the General Assembly the powers which would be exercised by the Board.

This elaboration made clear that the new Board did ''take over'' the OSPI and did have responsibility for policy making. It underscored that the Board was a servant of the General Assembly.

As the new Board came into existence, the general character of the governance structure at county and local levels remained the same—but with one important difference. Beginning in 1945, the General Assembly had changed regulations concerning both county superintendents and school districts. The Assembly reduced the number of county superintendents by requiring they service a certain number of the general population. This meant that in sparsely settled regions, consolidation of two or more counties occurred. Even more dramatically, the General Assembly slashed the numbers of school districts. For instance, in 1945–46 there were 11,784 districts; in 1955–56 there were 2,212 districts; and, in 1965–66 there were 1,353 districts. The chief victim was the one-room school—destroyed by professional consensus and the General Assembly requirement that each school provide one teacher for each grade in the school.

The new State Board of Education officially assumed its duties on January 13, 1975, with the end of the term of the last elected Superintendent of Public Instruction. But the Board, assisted by Deane Wiley of Southern Illinois University, had been meeting informally since 1974, concentrating most attention on the selection of a new State Superintendent. To this end, the Board selected Carl Marlburger (a former chief state school officer) and Robert Green of Michigan State University to screen candidates. On November 23, 1974, the Board appointed Joseph Cronin as Superintendent of Education.

Cronin, a native of Massachusetts, had served as a Professor and Associate Dean at Harvard University and as State Secretary of Educational Affairs in Massachusetts prior to coming to Illinois. Working with the State Board, Cronin now faced the task of helping to shape Illinois educational policy. In April 1975, the Board and Superintendent met in Itasca to discuss the development of goals. This first retreat developed a list of topics for consideration as possible goal statements. This list underwent public comment and several revisions. On November 13, 1975, the State Board adopted a list of twenty-one goal statements.

These statements dealt not only with topics but also with the relations between the Board and the State agency. While not listed in order of priority, the Board made clear its deep interest in, and de facto assigned its highest priority to, the provision of quality, integrated education. To achieve this goal, the Board formally adopted on February 12, 1976 (Lincoln's birthday) regulations which required district action plans for all schools with racial minorities in excess of 15 percent above or below the districtwide average.

The November goals also dealt with the general relations between Board and staff of the State agency.

> The Illinois Board of Education shall set policy and direction for education in the State of Illinois. The Board shall have as its administrative body the Illinois Office of Education which shall function as the agency for implementation and technical assistance.
>
> In order to determine adequately policies and to stay alert to public needs, the Board shall set hearings, use questionnaires, and create other ways in which to ascertain the educational requests and needs of the citizens of Illinois.

The older Office of the Superintendent of Public Instruction was renamed the Illinois Office of Education (IOE). The IOE now served as the implementing and administrative agency for the policy-making State Board of Education (SBE).

The SBE and IOE have worked diligently to improve their policymaking skills. In 1976, at the second Itasca retreat the Board evaluated its own internal operations—how well its committee structure was working, how well the process of policy development was working, and how the Board should evaluate the Superintendent. In June 1977, at Itasca III, the Board reviewed not only the policy development process but also raised questions about revision, expansion and establishing new priorities and goals.

As the SBE felt its way along, two points emerged. First, the SBE's relationship with the General Assembly remains generally clear, but murky in detail. The SBE has the power to recommend to the General Assembly. On the other hand, the Board has made policy directed at local districts and IOE internal operations: desegregation, truancy, affirmative action within the IOE and metric education, for example. In most of these cases, the SBE has had clear legislative intent supporting its rules and regulations or has argued that the legislative intent can be reasonably interpreted to support the SBE position. However, in metric education the SBE created a mandate independently of the General Assembly when a metric education bill languished in a legislative committee.

Second, the SBE has been forced to limit its attention to fewer items than many Board members or constituents might have wished. For instance, in early 1977 IOE staff created a list of about 40 topics for SBE review. No board has the time to undertake this quantity of tasks. The SBE has created a procedure for screening issues, linking staff and other resources to the deliberations surrounding selected issues, and providing definite times when specific issues will be acted upon by the SBE.

Hence, the new State Board of Education, State Superintendent and Illinois Office of Education are in the process of working out what the 1970 Constitution and 1973 General Assembly meant by "educational policies and guidelines." In contrast to the School Problems Commission, the State Board had to create its own linkages with the General Assembly, the educational interest groups, the Governor and the State's Director of Finance.

The Conditions of Illinois Education[1]

This section examines three major conditions of education in Illinois today which influence politics and policies. These conditions are: declining student enrollments, increased levels of funding for schools and declining scores on standardized tests aimed at finding out what students have learned in schools. These conditions generate opportunities for conflict and consensus about what should be done. For example, why are test scores declining when the citizens of Illinois are spending more and more money on fewer and fewer students? By themselves, and in combination with the other conditions, these themes dominate the agendas of those who govern and who think about policies for Illinois common schools.

Declining enrollments

Enrollments in Illinois public and nonpublic schools peaked in the 1971–72 school year at nearly 2.8 million students.

TABLE 31-1
Number of Public School Districts and Public and Nonpublic K-12 Enrollments, 1967–68 to 1977–78*

Year	Total Districts	Public	Nonpublic	Total
1977–78**	1,013	2,183,736	368,007	2,551,743
1975–76	1,028	2,252,000	364,000	2,616,000
1973–74	1,060	2,311,916	389,269	2,701,180
1971–72	1,146	2,373,776	420,155	2,793,931
1969–70	1,227	2,324,516	453,356	2,777,872
1967–68	1,315	2,215,328	528,014	2,743,342

*Source: Illinois Board of Education, *State, Local, and Federal Financing for Illinois Public Schools, 1975*–76, Circular Series A, Number 349 (Springfield, Illinois: Illinois Office of Education, Revised December 1975), p. 6.

**Source: Illinois State Board of Education, *Educational Statistics for Illinois Elementary and Secondary Schools, 1978* (Springfield, Illinois: Office of Education, n.d.), n.p.

As Table 31-1 demonstrates, from 1967–68 to 1971–72 total school enrollments was stable at 2.7 million students, although enrollments in nonpublic schools declined. From 1971–72 on, total enrollments have declined steadily, so that by 1977–78 the loss from 1971–72 was one-quarter of a million students.

The key factor has been the sharp decline in the annual number of live births in Illinois. Table 31-2 illustrates not only this decline, but also its effects on public school enrollment. In terms of live births, since 1959 there has been steady decrease—the 1975 live birth figure represents a nearly thirty percent decline from 1959. When translated into school enrollment projections, this decrease in live births suggests that by 1985–86 public school enrollments will decline by over twenty percent from 1971–72. Projecting from live birth statistics suggest that by the mid-1990's the decline in enrollments could continue, reaching almost thirty percent. Such long range projections, nonetheless, can be misleading.

The magnitude of this decline has profound effects on two major components of schooling—courses and teachers. For instance, the decline in the number of students influences the course offerings of schools. Table 31-3 reflects this decline in a single high school. In less than a

TABLE 31-2
Annual Number of Illinois Resident Live Births and Projections for Public School Enrollments, 1947 to 1985–86*

Year	Number of Live Births	Index of Live Births (1959—100.0)	Year	Total Enrollment	Birth Year of Grade 12 Students (18 Years of Age)	%Change from Peak Year (1971—72)
1947	196,007	81.7				
1949	189,313	78.9				
1951	201,082	83.8				
1953	206,813	86.2				
1955	220,541	91.9				
1957	238,579	99.5				
1959	239,871	100.0				
1961	237,051	98.8				
1963	224,787	93.7				
1965	208,063	86.6				
1967	195,644	81.6				
1969	195,699	81.5				
1971	195,311	81.4	1971–72	2,373,659	1953	
1973	168,992	70.5	1973–74	2,311,797	1955	− 2.6%
1975**	169,248	70.6	1975–76	2,256,336	1957	− 4.9%
1977	177,148	73.9	1977–78	2,167,459	1959	− 8.7%
Projections			1979–80	2,050,535	1961	−13.6%
			1981–82	1,959,529	1963	−17.4%
			1983–84	1,899,000	1965	−20.0%
			1985–86	1,871,000	1967	−21.2%

*Source: Illinois State Board of Education, *Report of the Illinois Task Force on Declining Enrollments in Public Schools* (Springfield, Illinois: State Board of Education, December 1975), p. 3 and 10 (revised). All projections are based on the rate of 68.5 live births per 1,000 females ages 15 through 44.
**Source: Illinois Board of Education, *Illinois Public School Enrollment: Projections and Analysis* (Springfield, Illinois: Illinois Office of Education, August 1978), Table 3.

TABLE 31-3
Total Course Offerings in a High School by Subject Area and Reflecting Declining Enrollment*

		Subject Area										
Year	Enroll-ment	Art	Bus. Ed.	Eng-lish	Foreign Lang.	Home Econ.	Math	Indust. Ed.	Sci-ence	Social Science	Total++	Percent of 1977–78***
1978–79	2,125	6	13	33	14	9	14	22	15	20	146	97.3
1979–80	1,970	6	13	32	13	9	14	22	15	18	142	94.7
1980–81	1,805	6	13	29	13	8	14	22	15	18	138	92.0
1981–82	1,670	5	13	28	12	7	14	18	15	14	126	84.0
1982–83	1,535	4	11	26	10	7	13	12	13	11	107	71.3
1983–84	1,460	4	11	26	9	7	12	11	13	11	104	69.3
1984–85	1,420	4	11	26	9	7	11	11	12	11	102	68.0
1985–86	1,340	4	10	25	9	6	10	11	12	11	98	65.3

*Source: Administration, "Declining Enrollments in District 214: A Discussion Paper for Board of Education Consideration," Mt. Prospect, Illinois, February 27, 1978, Table 3 (revised), (mimeographed).
**Excludes Music and Physical Education.
***In 1977–78 there were 150 courses offered in these academic areas.

ten year period, this high school's enrollment will decline by nearly eight hundred students and the total number of course offerings will decrease by one-third. Such a decline means not only that fewer teachers will be needed but also in all likelihood that some elective courses will no longer be offered.

The influence on the total teaching force of declining enrollments is twofold. First, overall the State will need fewer teachers. Those who seek positions as teachers in elementary or secondary schools may have fewer and fewer opportunities. Table 31-4 suggests the influence of this declining market for teachers. In only a five year period, the total number of Illinois college graduates preparing for standard teaching certificates has declined nearly forty two percent. The decline has been steep in those preparing for secondary teaching certificates.

TABLE 31-4
Numbers of Illinois Graduates Preparing for Standard Teaching Certificates, 1972–76*

Year	Elementary	Secondary	Total Teachers
1976 (Estimated)	4,088	6,283	10,371
1975	4,636	6,781	11,417
1974	5,935	8,119	14,054
1973	6,644	9,231	15,875
1972	6,801	10,967	17,768

*Source: Illinois State Board of Education, *Illinois Teacher Supply and Demand, 1975–1976* (Springfield, Illinois: Illinois Office of Education, Fall, 1976, revised), p. 16.

Second, the decline not only limits new opportunities but also suggestions that the teaching force will become older and more experienced. With fewer opportunities for new teachers to capture positions, the remaining force may stay in place. Table 31-5 lends some credence to this line of reasoning. The rapid growth in student population from the end of WW II to 1971 not only tripled the teaching force but also stood the ratio of experienced to less experienced teachers on its head. Whereas in 1951, two of three Illinois teachers had ten or more years of experience, by 1971 these figures were reversed. These changes mean that students now are taught by less experienced teachers and that recent college graduates are competing for positions with individuals who are nowhere near retirement age. In the 1980's prospects are that teachers may have little opportunity to move from district to district because of the loss of job security. As they gain experience, more and more teachers will earn higher salaries—another incentive for remaining on the job in the same district.

Finally, declining student enrollments create numerous other problems including teacher/pupil ratio, number of school buildings and school districts needed, and increasing numbers of parents with no children in schools. Enrollment decline creates problems about the numbers of students which teachers would teach in class (teacher/pupil ratio). For instance, if a district of three

TABLE 31-5
Total Numbers and Percentage of Teachers with Years of Experience in Illinois, Excluding City of Chicago, 1951–1977*

Year	Years of Experience in Illinois 0—9	10 or more	Total Number of Teachers
1977	63%	37%	105,316
1971	65	34	96,052
1967	61	40	76,809
1961	52	48	56,466
1957	45	55	40,966
1951	36	64	37,518

*Source: Compiled from selected years, *Report of Examination: Public Employees' Pension Funds* (Springfield, Illinois: Department of Insurance).

hundred students has one teacher for every thirty pupils, the district needs ten teachers. If the same district had a ratio of one teacher to every fifteen pupils, the district would need twenty teachers. Discussion of teacher/pupil ratio involves not only educational issues of the best ratio for optimum student learning but also financial discussions about the total number of teachers a district can afford.

Declining enrollments create tensions about school closings and district consolidations. Both of these events are politically volatile situations. Many people rented their apartments or purchased their homes close to their neighborhood schools. They fear the loss of their school will mean the destruction of their neighborhood. In smaller communities, schools are sources of entertainment and athletic events as well as visible symbols of the community. Closing schools or consolidating smaller districts into larger districts often creates "winners" (who keep their school) and "losers," thus disrupting the social fabric of the community and producing sharp conflicts between local desires and mandated State regulations concerning necessary course offerings or teacher preparation requirements.

Declining numbers of students in schools means that more and more parents no longer have their children in school. With sighs of relief, they either see their children move into the world of work and the creation of their own families, or with groans about costs, they support further education of their sons and daughters. In either case, their interests in the elementary and secondary schools decline and their general willingness to support increases in funding for schools also decreases. Other concerns, such as health care or retirement planning, not only capture their attention but also appear more important places to invest their tax dollars. For parents whose children are no longer in elementary or secondary schools, the ranking of education as a major priority for tax dollars slips.

In sum, declining elementary and secondary school enrollments create numberous problems. Issues surrounding the management of this decline entangle administrators, teachers, parents, and local and state representatives and government officials in controversy.

Funding

Funding of the elementary and secondary schools of Illinois is similar to funding in most American states. First, the school funding formula basically allocates money in terms of the number of students in a school district. Second, monies to school districts come from local, State and federal revenues. Third, over half of a district's money goes to instructional purposes. Finally, since a series of so-called school reform cases in the early 1970's, states have made efforts to equalize expenditures between districts with high property values ("rich") and with lower property values ("poor"). This equalization movement has frequently involved an increase in funds provided by the state to local districts.

Illinois uses two general State aid formulas for school districts.[2] The "Strayer-Haig" formula guarantees to a district a basic level of support for pupils. In 1976 this foundation level was $520. However, the actual number of students does not solely determine State aid—a series of weightings which represent estimates of educational costs are used to calculate aid. For instance, grade 1–8 pupils are weighted 1.0, while grade 9–12 students are weighted at 1.25. These weightings are calculated to provide weighted average daily attendance (WADA). State foundation aid is calculated by multiplying $520 by the WADA. Thus, 100 elementary pupils would produce $52,000 for a district (1.0 × 100 × $520) while 100 secondary pupils would produce $65,000 (1.25 × 100 × $520). On top of this State foundation, districts are able to generate their own local contribution by local tax levies.

The second formula is the "resource equalizer" formula. This formula provides for each district a guaranteed level of wealth as measured by the district's assessed valuation. Passed during the 1973 legislative session, this formula assures a school district that the State will provide funds equal to what its tax rate would raise if that district's assessed valuation was equal to an assessed evaluation figure guaranteed in the law. These guarantees in 1976 were: $66,300 in elementary districts, $120,000 in high school districts and $43,500 in unit districts. To determine State aid, districts multiply their tax rates, which must exceed a minimum level set by the Legislature, by their per pupil assessed valuation. If the district's tax rate multiplied by the district's valuation is below the district's tax rate multiplied by the State's guaranteed assessed valuations (GAV), the difference will be made up by State funds. Hence, for districts of equal tax rates, those with lower assessed valuations ("poor") generally receive more State funds than districts with high assessed valuations ("rich"). For instance, if two unit districts had similar tax rates and also had 500 students each, but one had an assessed valuation per pupil of $43,500 and the other $21,750, the poorer district would be "guaranteed" an additional $21,750 per pupil by the State resource equalizer formula.

The resource equalizer also includes a weighting factor for children from lower income homes (Title I, Elementary and Secondary Education Act of 1965). As the number of Title I children increases, the formula increases weightings. Hence, districts which have low assessed valuation of property and larger numbers of low income families receive more State aid than districts with high assessed valuation and few low income families.

Both of these formulas—Strayer-Haig and resource equalizer—are affected by declining enrollments. As the number of pupils decrese in the Strayer-Haig formula, the State's level of support declines. For example, the high school examined in Table 31-3 enrolled 2,125 students in 1978–79, but in 1979–80 would enroll 1,970 student. This loss of one hundred fifty-five students could mean a loss of $100,750 in just one year (1978–79, 2125 × 1.25 × $520 = $1,381,250; 1979–80, 1970 × 1.25 × $520 = $1,280,500). In the resource equalizer formula, the change in student numbers affects the assessed valuation calculation. For example, suppose the Table 31-3 high school district had an assessed valuation of $212,500,000. In 1978–79, the State would increase funds to insure that the guaranteed assessed valuation (GAV) of $120,000 was reached [$120,000 GAV — ($212,500,000 ÷ 2125 = $100,000)]—in this case, $20,000 per pupil. Just one year later, however, the State would be responsible for $12,132 less [$120,000 GAV — ($212,500,000 ÷ 1970 = $107,868)]. As the number of students declines, the assessed valuation calculated for the formula increases. This means the State will provide fewer dollars to "equalize" the discrepancies between this "poor" district and its "richer" neighbors.

Hence, declining enrollments often mean that local districts recieve fewer funds from the State. This loss in State revenues suggests that districts must increase their local levies to support the educational programs they currently operate. Many districts are unable to increase local support, therefore are seeking to reduce the costs of programs by measures such as reducing staff, eliminating some programs and closing school buildings. For the time being districts in Illinois have the option of selecting the formula which provides the greater amounts of funds. More than seventy-five percent choose the resource equalizer. From the standpoint of the State, therefore, the resource equalizer formula has shifted more of the burden of supporting schools to the State level.

Table 31-6 illustrates the amounts and shifting percentages of the sources of school funding. In the past decade the State's involvement has incresed sharply—twenty-seven to forty-four percent—while local contributions have decreased over twenty percent. In terms of dollars, in the last ten years the State's dollars have increased over four hundred percent while local dollars have increased one hundred seventy percent. The sharpest increases in State dollars occured after the resource equalizer formula was passed.

The monies that districts receive have been spent in a consistent manner for the last few years. An examination of Table 31-7 shows that amounts in the seven major expenditure categories have varied little. The costs of

TABLE 31-6
Sources of Funding for Schools
1967–68 to 1975–76 ($ in millions)*

Year	State	Percent State	Local	Percent Local	Federal	Percent Federal	Total
1977–78[a]	$2,040,9	44.65	$2,100.0	45.95	$429.8	9.40	$4,570.7
1975–76	1,988.1	48.36	1,856.8	45.16	266.5	6.48	4,111.4
1973–74	1,325.8	38.10	1,962.5	56.39	191.8	5.51	3,480.1
1971–72	995.7	37.42	1,508.6	56.70	156.5	5.88	2,660.8
1969–70	787.0	30.74	1,651.4	64.51	121.6	4.75	2,560.0
1967–68	491.9	27.13	1,230.0	67.84	91.1	5.03	1,813.0

[a]Estimate
*Source: Illinois State Board of Education, *State, Local, and Federal Financing for Illinois Public Schools, 1977–78* (Springfield, Illinois: Illinois Office of Education, Revised November 1977), p. 4, revised.

TABLE 31-7
Percentage Distribution of Expenditures for
Illinois Public School Districts,
1970–71 to 1974–75*

Expenditures	1970—71	1971—72	1972—73	1973—74	1974—75
Administration	3.4%	3.4%	3.4%	3.3%	3.2%
Instruction	56.3	56.7	56.2	55.9	54.4
Student and Community Services	6.8	6.9	7.1	6.7	6.4
Operations, Maintenance and Fixed Charges	18.5	19.0	19.9	20.7	20.8
Bond Principal Retired	4.6	4.6	4.5	4.3	3.8
Capital Outlay	9.2	8.1	7.6	7.9	9.8
Other Expenditures	1.1	1.2	1.3	1.3	1.6

*Source: Illinois State Board of Education, *Illinois Public School Financial Statistics, 1974-1975 School Year*, Circular Series A, Number 357 (Springfield, Illinois: Illinois Office of Education, n.d.), n.p. revised.

instruction, administration and student and community services consume some sixty-five percent of operational expenditures. Whether this pattern will continue into the 1980's is a matter of some discussion, with many suggesting that operational costs will increase because of the energy crisis and that maintenance costs will increase as buildings are renovated in preference to new construction.

While these increases in dollars seem staggering, Table 31-8 suggests that real expenditures have increased much less than inflation rates. Between 1963–64 and 1972, the current operating expenditure rate in current dollars tripled, while in adjusted dollars the rate did not even double. What must be remembered is that these figures represent inflation problems prior to the major impact of the oil embargo and energy cost increases. Regardless of this caution, the costs of education are rising—and even more rapidly in terms of current inflated dollar figures.

One of the major reasons for this actual increase in real dollars has been efforts by states to equalize educational opportunities. In a series of court cases in the early 1970's, state courts held that state constitutions prohibited differences in the wealth of school districts. In *Serrano v. Priest* (California), *Van Dusartz v. Hatfield* (Minnesota) and *Robinson v. Cahill* (New Jersey), for example, courts struck down state financing plans which discriminated against poorer districts and claimed the wealth of the state must be used to educate all children. These general arguments about the fiscal neutrality of the State formed the background for the enactment in 1973 of the resource equalizer formula by the Illinois General Assembly.

TABLE 31-8
Operating Expenditure Per Pupil,
1963–69 to 1972–73, in Current and
Real Dollars (1967 = 100)*

Year	Operating Expenditure Per Pupil, Current Dollars	Real Operating Expenditure Per Pupil (1967 = 100)
1963–64	$ 481	$521
1965–66	610	637
1967–68	738	724
1969–70	931	823
1971–72	1,122	910
1972	1,228	958

*Source: Illinois State Board of Education, *Illinois Education in 1975/Progress and Problems* (Springfield, Illinois: Illinois Office of Education, 1975), Appendix E, revised. Expenditure divided by average daily attendance for the year.

It is clear that in Illinois, as in most states, there are richer and poorer regions, counties and school districts. As illustrated in Table 31-9, in 1974 there were great differences in the assessed valuation per pupil. These distributions suggest enormous differences between the very richest and very poorest districts. For example, the richest elementary district was fifty-seven times as wealthy as the poorest district. For every one dollar of assessed valuation St. David had, McCauley had fifty-seven dollars. To produce the same amount of revenue for a pupil, St. David had to tax its residents fifty-seven times greater than McCauley.

These disparities in assessed valuation also correlated with the number of lower income families in districts, although not perfectly. Some districts with industrial properties have high assessed valuations, but few lower income residents. In general, however, the resource equalizer required the State to supply additional funds to districts which had lower assessed valuations, and even more funds to districts which had low valuations and high incidence of lower income families. As demonstrated in Table 31-10, in general, more State aid went to counties with lower assessed valuation and more low income families. For example, although Tazewell and Peoria have similar assessed valuations, Peoria has the higher percentage of Title I students and poor families, hence it receives more State aid per pupil. Counties such as Saline or Williamson receive far more aid than DeWitt or LaSalle.

In sum, the funding of elementary and secondary education links dollars to numbers of students in the districts, relies on a growing percent of resources from the State Treasury, carries a number of relatively fixed expenditure categories increasingly spending more real and inflated dollars, and illustrates a growing effort to equalize expenditures between rich and poor districts.

Test Scores

In contrast to the issues surrounding declining enrollments and funding, those surrounding declining scores on standardized tests are less clear cut. Yet the debate in Illinois over testing in schools has grown in volume in the last two or three years. A part of this debate is generated by national movements, but the discussions also carry a unique Illinois flavor.

One cannot overlook the impact of the Watergate scandal on any public institution, including education. Parents and others simply want to know what is going on in public schools. They believe they have every right to know. Equally, the general public has grown in its distrust of public servants—and teachers are no exception. Many believe that the increased militancy of teachers has had little impact on improving teacher performance while greatly increasing teacher salaries. Finally, the late 1960's saw a spate of educational criticism and reform. There is a lingering legacy of doubt about what public schools are doing, what they ought to be doing and whether or not schools are powerful instruments for reforming society. Friends and foes of public education on the national level provide powerful arguments for useful monitoring of schools.

In Illinois, the press for testing has been translated into a cautious, step-by-step process. Lead by Senator John Nimrod (Republican, Park Ridge), the Legislature and State Board of Education are studying what program best fits the schools of the State. The study, being conducted

TABLE 31-9
1974 Assessed Valuation Per Pupil*

Rank	District Name	Assessed Valuation Per Pupil
	Elementary (n = 464)	
1	McCauley School District 27	$504,956.64
116	Community Consolidated School District 59	53,150.90
232	Addison School District 4	33,570.07
348	Darien School District 61	23,517.14
464	St. David School District 87	8,871.38
	Secondary (n = 134)	
Rank	**District Name**	**Assessed Valuation Per Pupil**
1	Joppa Community H.S. District 21	$261,592.26
34	Reavis Township H.S. District 220	92,821.76
67	New Trier Township H.S. District 203	72,577.47
100	North Chicago Community H.S. District 123	54,393.63
134	Christopher Community H.S. District 38	25,057.14
	Unit (n = 444)	
Rank	**District Name**	**Assessed Valuation Per Pupil**
1	Monticello C.U. School District 25	$110,905.33
111	Hutsonville C.U. School District 1	33,028.67
222	Mid County C.U. School District 4	25,349.69
333	Cuba C.U. School District 3	19,091.33
444	Brookport Unit School District 38	2,882.80

*Source: Illinois State Board of Education, *Assessed Valuation and Tax Rates, Descending Order, 1974,* Circular Series A, Number 352 (Springfield, Illinois: Illinois Office of Education, October 1975).

TABLE 31-10
State Aid, Assessed Evaluation, Title I Eligibles,*
and Percentage Families Below Poverty Level Income**

County	State aid, Best Six Months, Average Daily Attendance 1974–75	Assessed Valuation, 1973 ($ in millions)	Title I Eligibles, 1974–75	Percentage of Families Below Poverty Level Income, 1970
Adams	$433.84	$ 328.4	1,752	9.3
Champaign	484.27	776.0	3,929	7.2
Cook (including City of Chicago)	652.90	33,563.2	246,625	7.6
DeWitt	328.61	113.8	321	7.2
Gallatin	647.30	34.4	428	16.3
Jasper	527.52	51.4	459	14.1
LaSalle	328.99	1,171.2	1,811	6.7
Marion	680.01	243.1	1,715	13.7
Mercer	567.30	85.4	525	10.8
Peoria	393.92	1,135.7	5,192	6.5
Richland	572.48	65.0	608	12.4
Saline	882.80	75.3	1,258	19.2
Tazewell	366.67	1,132.6	1,590	4.4
Williamson	792.16	126.0	1,904	14.1

*Source: Illinois Board of Education, *Annual State Aid Claim Statistics, Illinois Public Schools, 1975–1976,* Circular Series A, Number 348 (Springfield, Illinois: Illinois Office of Education, October 1975), n.p.

**Source: Illinois Department of Commerce, Bureau of the Census, *General Social and Economic Characteristics (Illinois)* (Springfield: Illinois Department of Commerce), Table 124, 1970, pp. 753–61 revised.

by the Illinois Office of Education, explores such questions as whether there should be a single test for all districts in the State. Proponents and opponents of testing have taken opportunities to debate this and other issues at most of the major educational association meetings around the State. In the next few pages we shall examine the outline of the testing controversy. This debate revolves around three poles: (1) what is the place of testing in general schooling? (2) what standardized tests and what results are to be believed? (3) what is the role of testing in assessing American schools?

There can be little doubt that in the minds of the general public tests are an important part of schooling. The 10th Annual Gallup Poll of the Public's Attitude Toward Public Schools reports that 68 percent of those sampled believed that children should be promoted from grade to grade *only* if they can pass an examination. This same sample believed that failure on these tests should lead to students taking special remedial classes (81 percent). If such tests were used, there were differences of opinion about whether they should be prepared at the local level (37 percent), by the state (25 percent) or prepared at the national level (28 percent). There was, however, little disagreement that high school graduation tests should cover certain specified skills, especially for those who do not plan to attend college. Rated as *very important* were items such as the ability to write a letter or recommendation with correct grammar and spelling (90 percent), ability to read an appliance instruction manual (86 percent), knowledge of enough mathematics to calculate the square feet in a room (84 percent), knowledge of the health hazards of alcohol, smoking and drugs (83 percent), and having a salable vocational skill, such as typing or auto mechanics (79 percent).

The Gallup Poll also produced evidence of a drop in the public's rating of the schools. While in 1974 48 percent of the sample gave schools either an A or B rating, in 1978 this rating of A or B was given by only 36 percent. Those giving grades of D or F increased from 11 percent in 1974 to 19 percent in 1978. Analyses of these grades indicated that Northern blacks in large communities rated the schools the lowest of any group (D–F of 43 percent).[3]

Hence, tests of some sort appear to be an important part of education, according to public opinion. These tests should be used to assure parents and others that children have certain basic skills before they are promoted or allowed to graduate from high school. There seems to be less certainty over the consequences of where these tests are prepared. If students do poorly on these tests, most believe they should be required to do remedial work. If schools do not achieve goals such as these, they are seen by most people as "failing."

Despite this interest in testing, the results obtained from nationally administered standardized tests about what is happening in schools are mixed. The most visible symbol of decline has been in the scores of applicants for college admission on the Scholastic Aptitude Test (SAT) of the College Entrance Examination Board. In 1962–63 the mean verbal score was 478 and the mean mathematics score was 502. In 1974–75 the mean verbal score was 437 (a decline of 41) and the mean mathematical scores was 473 (a decline of 29). These declines have been the subject of much scholarly and public debate. Did the tests get harder? No. Did more lower-ability students take these tests for college admissions? Yes. Is there less pressure for higher scores? Yes. Is school achievement lower? Yes. Are the American youth of the

TABLE 31-11
Reading Performance on Specified Practical Exercises: 1974*

Population Characteristics	Percent Correct on Job Application	Percent Correct on Traffic Ticket
Superior readers[a]	100.0[b]	100.0[b]
National total	81.7	77.7
Region		
Southeast	79.6	70.2
West	77.2	77.3
Central	83.4	85.7
Northeast	84.9	74.7
Sex		
Male	79.3	77.8
Female	89.5	77.5
Race		
Black	68.4	45.8
White	83.6	85.3
Parental Education		
No high school	79.3	50.0
Some high school	85.8	71.3
Graduated high school	80.0	76.8
Post high school	84.5	85.2
Size and type of community		
Low metro	86.2	60.2
Extreme rural	82.6	85.2
Small place	77.4	73.7
Medium city	71.4	81.5
Main big city	87.7	84.2
Urban fringe	89.9	76.2
High metro	92.1	97.5

*Source: National Center for Education Statistics, *The Condition of Education: 1976 Edition,* NCES 76-400 (Washington, D.C.: U.S. Government Printing Office, 1976), p. 209, Table 3.9, abridged.
[a]Sample of students attaining at least 95th percentile on the College Entrance Examination verbal test or an equivalent standardized reading test.
[b]Scores are adjusted so that superior readers equal 100% correct; all other groups are then compared to this superior reader standard.

1970's different from the youth of the 1960's? Yes. The debate still rages.

Other standardized testing programs do not reveal such markedly gloomy results. Tests by organizations such as the National Assessment of Education Progress (NAEP) display a pattern in which factors such as differing regions of the country, racial background, size and type of community and parental education strongly influence test results. For example, as illustrated in Table 31-11, the percent of correct responses differed among the regions, with the Central region including Illinois, the highest. Other factors, such as sex, race, parental education and size and type of community, illustrate differences—differences which suggests a complex picture of what goes on in schools.

Beginning in 1976, the Illinois Office of Education has conducted the annual Illinois Inventory of Educational Progress (IIEP). This program tests a random sample of fourth, eighth and eleventh grade level students. The tests in 1976 examined student performances in mathematics and reading while those in 1977 examined science and, for grades 8 and 11 only, citizenship. In 1978, mathematics and reading will be reassessed for all grade levels, and citizenship for grades 8 and 11. The 1978 report will allow comparisons to be made against the results of 1976 and 1977.

The tests were created by committees of educators from Illinois. These committees developed objectives for the subject matter areas chosen for assessment. In turn, test questions were developed and then field tested on several representative districts. The results of these field tests were used to determine which questions would be used in the IIEP. The completed tests are then given to a random sample of approximately 340 schools across the state. The final sample of students involves about 8,500 students at the fourth, eighth and eleventh grades.

Results are then reported by the Illinois Office of Education. The results indicate the subject matter area, the particular objective to be assessed, the question asked and the percent of students responding correctly. For example, on the eighth grade level of mathematics, students were examined about percentages. The question asked was: What is 45% of 180? Some 25% of the students marked the correct answer of 81. When the objective was the calculation of earnings, 73% of the eighth graders tested produced the correct answer to the question: Sue charges 74 cents per hour to baby-sit. Last week she baby-sat three hours on Tuesday, two hours on

Thursday, and four hours on Saturday. How much money did Sue earn last week? ($6.75). The results of such questions provide information on what students are currently learning in schools as well as permit the measuring of trends (growth or decline) in educational achievement in Illinois.

Thus, several different types of standardized tests which could measure the progress of students do exist. The results of these tests provide evidence for some to conclude that student achievement in schools is declining. Others find that student achievement is strongly related to factors such as parental background. Within a year or so, the Illinois Office of Education program to assess achievement in the schools may make available information on trends in the State.

While many different standardized tests exist, and a multitude of interpretations surround their results, a small band of scholars believe these tests to be of limited or no value. Their criticisms may be consolidated into seven major theses.[4]

1. Standardized tests may not "fit" or "overlap" program objectives of course offerings. For example, a standardized test in U.S. History may concern itself primarily with major political parties and the presidency while the actual course taught by the instructor dealt with the life of everyday Americans at various times in our history.
2. Standardized tests often require skills and knowledge which are not described by the test's title and description. For example, many tests of mathematics require the ability to read the directions before proceeding to work problems.
3. Standardized tests are built so that differences near the top ("ceiling") or bottom ("cellar") scores are extreme, but differences near the average of the test are small. Thus, if a test had 100 points, and the average score was 50, differences between a 10 and an 11 score or a 96 and a 97 score might be very great. The differences between a 49 and a 50 or a 50 and a 51 might be small. The intervals between test scores are simply not equal.
4. Standardized tests often have directions or instructions which may confuse the test-taker. Equally, the directions for marking answers may be confusing.
5. Often the reading or interpretation of test instructions are inconsistent from one test supervisor to another.
6. Standardized tests may contain systematic biases because of the cultural backgrounds of students. Children in southern Illinois, for instance, might be confused by questions about surfing while children in southern California might be confused by questions about wind chill factor.
7. Standardized test measure only a limited range of the spectrum of educational goals. To take this small slice of what children learn and to act as if it measured the entire process is a dangerous and misleading indicator of what is happening in schools.

Hence, there exist not only a number of tests, and their results, but also a lively dabate about what tests do or do not measure. Many tests claiming to be standardized (and national) in scope are seen by test experts as flawed. Tests created by teachers, local districts or state agencies would be examined just as minutely by these same experts to ascertain their validity.

At another level, the discussions about testing raise the issue of whether or not testing provides an accurate assessment of what is happening in our schools.[5] Those who support standardized testing, and who push for the development of tests with greater validity, believe that education in America has adopted the wrong philosophy, espoused the wrong goals and become the province of administrators and teachers who desire not freedom but license.

Those who support rigorous testing programs believe that our current educational philosophies embrace too strongly the notions that by nature humans are good and that the imposition of external authority and control is wrong. In place of the false idols of a "fuzzy" humanism, these advocates believe that schools should stress cognitive competence. This competence is *not* developed by the natural tendencies of human beings and must be imposed on and assimilated by students.

The goals of contemporary schooling, proponents of testing assert, have gone awry. Instead of stressing cognitive competence as their goals, schools stress immediate social concerns. The broadening of the curriculum to include electives and courses dealing with immediate social problems ensures that students will be involved in social concerns, but may have limited intellectual competence.

Finally, those who support testing believe educators do not wish to be accountable to the public. While sensitive to fears by teachers and administrators that tests may be misinterpreted, proponents also see a large amount of self-serving in educators' critiques of testing. If educators were honest, they suggest, testing would disclose not only some success but also a good deal of failure in schools.

Opponents of these testing arguments counter that verbal knowledge is simply not an adequate definition of an "educated" American, that the goals of American education are multiple and that the data educators use to assess pupils includes much more than a few test scores.

The development of the youth of America need not rest on the single standard of the imposition of cognitive competence. When students do learn such basic skills as reading, writing or calculating, these learnings are about *something*. Students, for example, rarely read about how to read. By asking students to read about social concerns, teachers not only teach reading but also are making the stuff of schooling relevant to the realities of everyday life. In this way, relevance may enhance the learnings of cognitive skills.

Schools do many things to and for students. One of the key processes is instruction, but they also provide to students opportunities to become involved in governing and leadership experiences, to try their hand at the creative arts, to experience "the joy of victory and the agony of defeat" in intramural and inter-school athletic events, to learn to live with and to value individuals from different social, ethnic and racial groups, to underscore the joyful differences between boys and girls, and on and on. In America, schools are multiple purpose activities, centered around cognitive competence, but maintaining a wide spectrum of activities important for the development of citizens in American society.

Finally, tests provide only a small part of the evaluations and assessments of youth in schools. While much of what happens in schools is planned, a significant part of schooling depends upon the capacity of teachers to capture the interests of students in an immediate experience. In these moments, be they on the playground, in the classroom, on the stage or basketball court, important goals of schooling are achieved which cannot be captured by standardized tests. The subjective information may contrast sharply with numbers produced by standardized tests, but this "soft" information may be the more important in understanding the effects of schooling on children. Many of the critical outcomes of schooling appear as long-term changes in the future lives of current students—a dimension standardized tests omit completely.

Thus, the discussion of test score decline ebbs and flows around the public's desire to have some kind of marker to insure that students possess some minimum level of reading, writing and calculating skills; the ability of standardized tests to measure in some adequate way what students have learned; and the usefulness of tests to assess what schools are doing to and for their students.

One last note on testing. While Illinois has moved cautiously toward testing programs, a number of states such as Florida and Oregon have moved quickly to state-wide mandated tests. These competency tests have resulted in Florida, at least, in a series of law suits which charge that tests are racially biased and that schools fail to offer enough remedial work. These court cases will undoubtedly explore issues surrounding testing. Many in Illinois are watching what is happening in these other states.

Making Educational Policy in Illinois

The earlier two sections described the governance of the common schools since WWII and current conditions affecting Illinois education. This concluding section deals with some of the major problems generated by interactions of these two factors. These interactions will be explored by examining key issues and actors. This exploration begins with the topic of funding the schools, turns to questions about the overall performance of the educational system noting conflicts over both goals and means of assessment, and concludes with conflicts about the governance of education.

Funding the Schools

No single issue has occupied the attention of policymakers and politicians interested in education more than the funding of schools. In good part, the creation of the School Problems Commission was the General Assembly's answer to the perplexing problem of how to deal with funds for schools. Why has so much time and energy been spent on this single issue?

At least one part of an answer is that the State of Illinois has the responsibility for providing a system of public education for the children of the State. In fact, education is the largest single activity of Illinois State Government. The Governor, the General Assembly and the elected, now appointed, State Superintendent are required to provide, maintain and guarantee a minimum level of schooling. With the rapid expansion of students following World War II, no responsible official of the State could ignore educational needs. And, even had they tried, the expansion in students was paralleled by more interested parents and greater numbers of educational workers—vocal constituencies demanding attention. Overall, the increased number of students suggested to most politicians and policymakers a course of pragmatic reasonableness. It seemed reasonable to argue for constant increases in dollars going to schools and maintenance of funding formulas that linked closely the number of dollars to the number of students.

In return for increased dollars, State officials expected that local communities would accept the cost burdens of increasing the quality of education and that State regulation and local pressures would produce efficiently run local districts. State dollars were to be the floor ("foundation") on which all Illinois education rested—anything beyond that minimum level of requirements would have to come from local tax levies. Equally, the State would press for the efficient organization and management of schools, augmenting local taxpayers who watched closely how efficiently local tax dollars were spent.

In this post WW II atmosphere, then, the SPC was a powerful device for creating coalitions which kept more dollars flowing to schools while pressing for increased educational efficiency. But two major events upset this consensus. First, reformers attacked this agreement as discriminattory. Second, the constant increase in students stopped, and a decline in numbers has begun.

The reformers not only suggested that the State's foundation discriminated against students in poor districts but also they challenged the notion that more dollars alone meant better education. The resource equalizer formula shifted the earlier notion of foundation from one in which all students received the same amount to one in which students in different districts received different amounts of State aid. Students in poor districts would be receiving more State dollars for their education than students in rich districts.

The reformers argued that students in poor districts were more likely to have come from lower income families and minority backgrounds. This constellation of factors mean that such students needed more resources, including special programs and staff, to profit from schooling. Reformers pressed the point that additional State monies should be given to districts with clear directions to use these funds to help disadvantaged children. These State funds would reinforce the federal monies provided by Title I of ESEA. Simply, the reformers argued that spending exactly the same amount of money on each student did not promote equality of opportunity. Equality was to be gained by spending more on children who were disadvantaged because of social or economic backgrounds. The federal dollars and State support were to be used by local districts for a specific—and the reformers believed a just—end.

The reformers' line of argument challenged the notion that districts could spend their money as they saw fit so long as local districts met the State minimum requirements. This challenge raised not only the problems of control but also more importantly pressed districts to link educational outcomes to educational expenditures. If districts could prove they were doing a good job for disadvantaged students with their normal programs, then why should they put State and federal dollars on these students when they needed no special assistance? Could not local districts with efficient programs for helping the disadvantaged take State or federal funds and spend them on other local priorities?

The answer seemed to be obvious to most. If districts could prove they were succeeding, then the money should be theirs to keep and use. But local districts now faced the task of proving that they were succeeding. In this effort, local districts received scant support from the findings of social science research on education in the 1960's. In the largest study conducted during this period, *Equality of Educational Opportunity,* the authors found evidence that schools across the country failed miserably to improve the achievement of disadvantaged students. Local districts floundered in their attempts to prove educational success.

The nub of the problem was precisely linking expenditures to schooling outcomes. Almost immediately this issue subdivided into two thorny problems: (1) what is the relationship of dollars to student achievement in the *outputs* of schooling? (2) What is the relationship of dollars to student achievement in the *impact* of schooling? The first question fixed attention on immediate consequences and educational production processes, while the second raised the issue of long-range outcomes and the effects of influences beyond the control of the schools.

Imagine, for the moment, that dollars spent for schooling are closely tied to the amount of student learning that occurs. At first blush, the argument would be that for every dollar spent, learning increased one unit. For example, if the relationship between dollars and learning is *linear* and *additive,* each new interval of dollars ($500) buys one additional unit of learning. So, if a district expends $1,000 the district buys two units. If the same district buys $1,500, it has purchased three units. Under these conditions, increases in dollars guarantee increases in learning.

What is clear on a moment's reflection is that, while buying bologna by the pound may be linear and additive, the purchase of education is not. A host of factors, including skills of the teacher, abilities of individual students, family background of students, peers of the student, courses offered and school facilities available, impinge upon and disturb the relationship of dollars to learning. Some of these factors may either reduce or enhance the relationship, e.g., family need may dictate that students reduce study time to produce income or family pressure may result in students over-achieving. Hence, the linkage between dollars spent and education attainment purchases seems neither linear nor additive. Dollars do not buy the same units nor do these dollars always make purchases which add up to more educational achievement.

Then what of the purchases of long-range benefits of education? What are to be the outcomes for those who are products of the schooling process over their lifetimes? Some of the general categories seem evident: good citizens; intelligent consumers; capable workers; decent parents; and, wholesome human beings. But again, we are not purchasing bologna. How are these long-range outcomes to be measured? When are they measured—every ten years similar to the U.S. Census, for instance? And, once these measurements are accomplished, how is this information to be returned to the schools to change and improve performance? These long-range outcome questions become even more complex if we raise questions such as: In which generation should schooling effects be measured—first, second or third? Or, in what ways do school effects *persist* unchanged, *flourish* or *fade* away in the different stages of an individual's life?

The linkage of dollars to education outcomes is not only a technical problem but also a value problem. Even if social scientists and educators were able to tie dollars and achievement together, the issues of which achievements ought to be purchased would persist. Should dollars go to math instead of music, to basketball and not biology, or to history rather than home economics? Is the most desirable long-range outcome of schooling the production of voters, soldiers, workers, consumers or spouses? Reformers' efforts to link dollars to achievement meant not only that more dollars would flow to certain districts and students but also that long-range outcomes might change for these students. In essence, reformers urged that new outcomes, which upset older value preferences, and new processes, which disturbed traditional ways of doing things, become common in local schools.

Traditional ways of settling the issues of process and product such as legislative debate were challenged in the courts. These challenges not only upset state funding systems which treated "rich" and "poor" districts as equal but also expanded the rights of students, required that handicapped students receive educational opportunities equal to all other students, and demanded schools be sensitive to the problems of bilingual students.

The upshot of the reformers' efforts was to upset the older SPC coalition system in Illinois. Pragmatic individuals had long operated out of a system in which some "arbitrary," but considered, number was assigned as a reasonable indicator ("proxy") of the condition of education. These proxies were usually based on the current pattern of expenditures and used such figures as average teachers' salary or average per pupil expenditures as an indicator of how well the system worked. As students increased, dollars increased. The SPC of the 1950's and 1960's was the meeting ground for a network of associations, the Governor's office and General Assembly, where reasonable additions were made to the current patterns. The question was: how much can we afford to add this year to maintain what we are already doing? The answer was a political compromise.

The reformers attacked this system by challenging the grounds of "what was already going on." At the very moment of the peak of their attack, a second change challenged Illinois school funding—declining student enrollments. The effect of decline on school funding is obvious. If formulas are based on number of students, then, the fewer, the worse. The dollars which had naturally come to education because of funding formulas and the use of proxy indicators for the conditions of education now seemed on the verge of drying up. While this reduction in dollars would have been awkward in the era of SPC coalitional politics, it borders on the unmanageable in the next few years because Illinois, and most other states, have weak tools for managing decline.

The major sources of tension surround the general inexperience of government at all levels in dealing with reduction management and the general inexperience of politicians in dealing with setting priorities in education. In sharp contrast to an era of expansion, declining enrollments force government officials and politicians to make sharp policy choices. Expansion generated enough "fat" in the system to "buy-off" various competing interests. The coming of leaner times means little or no fat exists; hence competing interests are forced to positions where some are going to win and others will lose. Winning and losing may now mean the difference between being cut by five percent or by ten percent. Tradeoffs that avert conflict are harder and harder to find.

At this moment, then, three major groups dominate arguments about the funding of education in Illinois. The first, and probably largest, group of individuals—and the most important factor—is the traditional funders of education. These include the General Assembly, the Governor's Office and most who work in education. They are desperately seeking a funding formula which accounts for decline, permits the maintenance of traditional proxies about education and cools rancorous conflicts surrounding education. The second factor is those who hold to reform ideas: they demand that education in Illinois attend to the needs of special populations, funding be closely linked to programs, not to proxies such as average teacher salary, and believe that conflicts are essential because they expose value premises determining which dollars are to be spent where. A third factor is the specter of declining enrollments persisting for at least the next decade. The opportunities for "buying-off" competing interests in an era of tight budgets appear to diminish rapidly in the politics and policies of elementary and secondary education.

Performance of the Educational System

Assessments of the performance of the educational system involve not only objective descriptions but subjective evaluation standards. Since the mid-1960's, assessments have centered on two issues: equality of educational opportunities and testing outcomes.

Those who have favored reform in education have argued that equality of educational opportunity has been systematically denied to groups of students. Those from low-income families, those from ethnically or racially different backgrounds, those who are "handicapped," and those who are female particularly have been denied equality of opportunities. Programs to attack these problems of inequality have been put forward, and funded by private foundations, the federal, state and local governments and private citizens. Some programs concentrated on improving attitudes and capacities of children before they enter schools. Programs such as "Head Start" helped children get ready to go to school, so that schooling was a profitable experience. Other programs focused on providing special assistance and support during the years of schooling. Programs such as "Follow Through" aimed at reducing the disparities in student achievement which were created by artifical barriers. When students graduated from schools, the differences which remained among them were to be the results of differences in student abilities, not in artificially maintained discriminations. Finally, as students left schooling for the larger world, programs aimed at expanding information about employment opportunities, offering funds and special programs for higher education and reducing discrimination in employment opportunities.

This commitment to enhance equality of educational opportunity has meant that funds which could have been spent on other social goods have gone into these particular social and educational programs. As these and other programs have been required ("mandated") by courts, federal or state governments, most were only partially funded, or only funded for their start-up period. Thus, local districts have borne heavy expenses for programs, such as special education, which they did not initiate. These mandated expenses, critics claim, are not similar to the normal state minimum requirements. States not only demand but also fund these minimum programs. On the other hand mandated programs add dollar burdens and social costs not only for programs which many local districts may wish to support, but also for many which districts may not believe are necessary.

These debates about what should or should not be done to achieve equality of opportunity have often shifted to the assessment of educational performance. Those who oppose the aims of reformers often claim reformers have merely thrown money at a problem or that the schools are a very blunt instrument for social reform. These critics argue that declines in standardized test scores indicate that not only have schools failed to meet these new expectations, but also that traditional goals are no longer being met. Such critics' answer to the current mess in schooling has been to reaccentuate the basic skills that schools have always taught—and for those who do not immediately achieve, remedial work.

Reformers counter that education has been an important vehicle for the achievement of our nation's greatness. Schools have been a key place where generations of Americans have not only learned to read and write but also acquired values central to our way of life. Reformers suggest that what some claimed was simply "money thrown at problems" has resulted in major changes in our way of life. Schools are generally desegregated, minorities and women are entering the mainstream of American life, and the price has been right for these and other changes. In fact, other disadvantaged groups, such as the handicapped, the elderly and the very young, now deserve additional attention and funds.

At a time in which declining enrollments threaten funding losses, reformers press for more and more funds linked specifically to aiding disadvantaged groups. They have become a powerful lobby, pressuring the Congress of the United States and the General Assembly of Illinois and other states, to provide funds and to assess educational programs in light of expanded definitions of equality of educational opportunity. Pitted against these reformers are more traditional interests, arguing that these mandated amendments to the educational system cost too much, produce too little and damage the schooling of too many normal students. They urge more traditional measures of education—standardized tests of basic skills.

Hence, those pressures for assessment of the performance of the educational system are contrary. One set of forces seeks the use of wider objective evidence and a set of subjective standards emphasizing expansive conceptions of equality of educational opportunity. Another set of forces demands the use of traditional objective markers of school achievement and more traditional conceptions of equality. These demands for assessment in turn are closely tied to differing conceptions of where educational funds should be invested and what levels of government should control how funds are used.

The Governance of Education

While it is clear that the General Assembly and the Governor are the chief actors in education, they are part of a complex and seemingly confused system which includes other State agencies and many interest groups. Education in Illinois, and across the nation, is an arena that attracts numerous participants. These participants are rarely united on any single goal—policy actors are divided into numerous factions and these factions are fragmented on most issues. While teachers, for instance, want more money for schools, taxpayers groups want not only less money, but also fewer teachers. The points at which decisions are made in this system are diverse and many—local school boards, county superintendents of education, State agencies, the General Assembly and the Governor's Office, to name but a few. Finally, these groups differ in their conceptions of how easy or how difficult it is to improve education. Some believe schools are adaptable; others see them as unbending bureaucratic institutions. The quarrels over what counts as improvement exacerbate further, if that is possible, the amount of noise and conflict which surround the governance of education.

Since the late 1940's the School Problems Commission served as a powerful coalition to link traditional forces in education in reasonable bargains. The SPC served as a filter to the noise and a pacifier to much of the conflict in the policymaking and governance of Illinois schools. But this system was under attack by reform and minority groups and already weakening in the late 1960's when the new State Constitution created a State School Board and appointed Superintendent. Today both the State Board of Education and the School Problems Commission exist as possible coaltion builders.

While it is still too early to forecast precisely what will happen between the SBE and SPC, some hints do exist. First, the SBE early on has taken an aggressive posture which has placed it most frequently in the camp of the reformers. The SBE has been worried about issues of desegregation, equality of opportunity, expanded curriculum programs, such as metric education and responsibility ("citizenship") education, and increased funding of these programs and others in the public schools. The State Board also redefined the roles for the Illinois Office of Education. In contrast to the Office of the Superintendent of Public Instruction, the IOE is to concentrate less on mandating programs and issuing regulations and more on providing both technical assistance to local districts and professional leadership to the State's schools. This posture of aggressive professional leadership stands in marked contrast to both the older OSPI and the SPC's continued concerns for the organization and funding of education.

Second, the SPC and SBE will cooperate in providing funds for special programs which both groups see as important. For instance, increased funding and efficient management of programs for handicapped children has been supported by both groups. Nonetheless, the limits of support for these programs undoubtedly differ. The SBE will press as a matter of educational principle for *maximum* dollars, while the SPC as a matter of legislative reality will seek politically *reasonable* dollars.

Third, the arena of general funding for the schools could produce major conflicts between the SBE and SPC. The SBE Constitutional mandate includes recommending financing, but the General Assembly elaboration in 1973 is silent on that topic. The SBE could move to a position of sharply opposing SPC funding recommendations which the Board sees as "too little," while the SPC could attack an "extravagant" State Board. The potential for such internecine feuds is great at this moment because of the problems of declining enrollments. Both the SBE and SPC are seeking ways of solving those problems by identifying acceptable formulas for funding schools. Because these groups may be starting from two different perspectives—the SPC more traditional, the SBE more reformist—the chances of the formulas looking alike is small.

Tensions between the SPC and the SBE mean that the General Assembly and the Governor now face two proponents of education which may well propose different funding solutions. Not only may these two suggest different dollar amounts and program allocations, but the major education interest groups now may support both proposals, one or the other proposal, or neither the SBE nor SPC proposal. In the latter case, teacher, administrator or school board associations, parental groups and groups advocating special programs may wish to enter these deliberations. In contrast to the days when the SPC put together a legislative package and presented it to the Legislature, everybody may now wish to get into the act by bombarding the Legislature with numerous proposals.

While many in the General Assembly may wish to simply divide the task between the SPC (finance) and SBE (all other actors), most legislators will find this simple division impossible. The vast majority in the General Assembly will have constituencies which include not only traditional but reform interest groups. What the folks back home want will most often not fall neatly into what the SPC or the SBE offers. The system of policymaking and political bargaining looks more and more crowded, noisy and conflict-laden.

Members of the General Assembly will be pressed hardest by the increasingly militant teacher associations. These groups have developed in the last few years a willingness to endorse, provide funds and campaign actively for legislators. Teachers groups have argued convincingly that they know most intimately the needs of the educational system and are important resources for the development of intelligent policy. At the same time, teacher associations are also special interest groups organized to improve the collective welfare of their membership. Traditional groups have generally supported increases for teacher salaries—but at a lower level than most teachers believed necessary. Reformers argue that teachers are the problem, not the solution, in education. Regardless of these varying assessments of the role of teachers, teachers have flexed political muscle since the mid-1960's.

The dual roles of helping to define the general interest on education and the promotion of the special interests of teachers become problematic in times of declining enrollments and dwindling funds. Teachers face tough choices such as those surrounding the retention of more teachers in a school at lower salaries or the retention of fewer, more highly paid teachers. These and other trade-offs may weaken the bargaining posture of teachers. Nonetheless, teachers still possess all the ingredients necessary to be an important political resource—money, time, energy and votes.

Hence, the General Assembly faces conditions much like those which existed at the end of WW II. There is a crisis in education: too much money is being spent, too little money is being provided; too many objectives are sought by schools, too few objectives are sought by schools; and, while everybody speaks for their role in education, no single voice speaks for all of education. In this confusion the General Assembly and the Governor's Office have not stood idle. They have attempted to weigh these claims and counter-claims. In this process both the Legislature and executive branch have greatly increased staff. These staff members are responsible not only for monitoring the external system but also for developing viable alternatives in education.

Above the General Assembly sits the powerful Office of the Governor. With awesome budgetary power, the Governor sets the outlines for the State's expenditures in education. With the SPC in place, the former Governors of the State could precisely determine where the major education groups stood and how much money they wanted. Now the Governor faces the requests of the SPC, the SBE, the political parties in the General Assembly, teachers and groups who seek only the funding of a single program or subject.

It is small wonder then that James R. Thompson, even before his November 1978 re-election to the governship, had called a Conference on Education "for the purpose of developing apporaches and answers to . . . issues confronting our common schools." For the issues of the common schools are intimately linked to the appropriations the Legislature provides for schools. What was so troublesome to the Governor was that increased dollars, decreasing students and declining test scores meant very different things to different groups. Some urged that educational dollars be moved to other categories of social benefits, while others claimed even more education dollars were needed to improve the lot of disadvantaged groups. Few had any answers about declining enrollments while most could describe in vivid detail conflicts created by the closing of schools, the consolidation of districts or the drastic cuts of teachers and courses. Test scores and their multiple interpretations provided mixed evidence about the success or failure of students: overall, the general population has nagging doubts about what is happening in schools. And, last but not least, from the perspective of the executive, there were few guidelines as to which position or which group represented a majority or a consensual position. Illinois education, once again, stood in the midst of a crisis.

Unresolved Issues and Further Research Opportunities

One way to discuss the key issues and actors is to accept those identified by participants in the policymaking system. One asks, simply and forthrightly, what are the most critical (key, timely, important, pressing) issues *and* who (what actors) are likely to help or to confuse the solution? The earlier sections of this chapter took that approach. To continue that approach in this final portion would be to ask questions about the evolution of a funding formula to deal with declining enrollments or the costs associated with the development of testing programs for Illinois students.

A second way, and the way the next paragraphs proceed is to suggest that a series of key tensions dominate the policymaking system in Illinois education. These tensions exist despite the fact that various reasonable solutions can be generated to deal with persistent problems of education. They present us with unresolvable political dilemmas because individuals cannot agree which of the available solutions is correct. Thus the fundamental issues of education persist:

1) What are appropriate measures for assessing the processes and products of schooling?
2) What efforts should be made prior to and during schooling to continue or change the distributions of advantages or disadvantages of different groups?
3) What functions of schooling are most valued by various groups?

The perspective of this chapter underscores the fact that temporary political coalitions accept certain answers to these questions. Question # 1 traditionally is translated into sub-problems and sub-solutions surrounding program finance and evaluation. Question #2 suggests various definitions and strategies for achieving equality of educational opportunity. Question #3 involves issues of the courses offered by schools, the way students are treated in schools and the values overtly and covertly espoused by schools.

Moreover, this perspective highlights the fact that the involvement of many different actors, decision centers conflicting goals and conceptions of change makes unlikely the complete resolution of any issue. The policy system and the political nature of educational governance are such that problems will come and go and that solutions will arrive and depart much the same way that flights come and go at O'Hare Airport. The policy and political system will deal with these problems and solutions one at a time, rarely creating a long-range plan or answer because of sensitivity to the emergencies created by the external environment. Surges in population, economic crises or social unrest drive the policy system to short-term solutions and to stalling in hopes that problems in education either vanish or become so clear that answers are evident to everybody.

Thus, we may wish to study the policymaking and governance of Illinois education in terms of how a single tension or political dilemma is resolved at various times. For example, what has been the fate over the last one hundred years of efforts to change conceptions of equality of educational opportunity. Or we may wish to see if "policy politics" lumps several tensions or dilemmas into a single package, ignoring the uneasy marriage they have created. For example, the solution to the funding problem was to link dollars to students. What happens when the number of students declines, but demands for dollars accelerate? Or we may wish to explore the penchant for certain groups, such as local school boards or the General Assembly, to attack certain tensions and dilemmas and to ignore others. The willingness, for example, of the General Assembly to mandate programs in education may be positively related to the General Assembly's unwillingness to examine whether these programs succeed or fail. These illustrations should suffice.

In sum, the opportunities for describing and analyzing the development of policies and the play of politics in elementary and secondary education are abundant. They range from simple descriptive case studies of how environmental conditions and interest groups act upon legislative actors to full-flown theoretical examinations of how Illinois compares to other states or the federal government in making education policy. Whether one chooses to study declining enrollments or the general characteristics of policy systems in education, Illinois provides fertile opportunities.

NOTES

[1]The account of the School Problems Commission from its inception to the early 1960's drew heavily on Nichols A. Masters, *et al.*, *State Politics and the Public Schools: An Exploratory Analysis* (New York: Alfred A. Knopf, 1964), pp. 99–178.

[2]The following discussion of the Illinois school funding formulas is not technically correct in all details. The outline is adequate only for understanding the general funding mechanisms.

[3]George H. Gallup, "The Tenth Annual Gallup Poll of the Public's Attitude Toward the Public Schools," *Phi Delta Kappan* 60:1 (September 1978), pp. 33–45.

[4]Stephen K. Klein, "Cost-Quality Research Limitations: The Problem of Poor Indices," in *Indeterminacy in Education,* ed. by John E. McDermott (Berkeley: McCutchan, 1976), pp. 33–49.

[5]Much of the literature in the field of education fixes on debates about desirable goals. For those interested in studying politics and policies, the conflict over these goals seems endless. The brief outline provided touches only the highlights of these on-going and varied debates.

SUPPLEMENTAL READINGS

A. General Studies of State Level Politics and Education

Bailey, Stephen K., *et al. Schoolmen and Politics: A Study of Aid to Education in the Northeast.* Syracuse: Syracuse University Press, 1962.

Campbell, Roald R. and T.L. Mazzoni. *State Policy Making for the Public Schools in Twelve States and a Treatment of State Governance Models.* Berkeley: McCutchan, 1976.

Iannaccone, Laurence. *Politics in Education.* New York: Center for the Applied Research in Education, 1967.

Masters, Nichols A., *et al. State Politics and the Public Schools: An Exploratory Analysis.* New York: Alfred A. Knopf, 1964.

B. Funding the Public Schools

Benson, Charles S. *The Economics of Public Education*. 3d ed. Boston: Houghton Mifflin, 1978.

Office of the Supperintendent of Public Instruction. *A Brief History of School Finance in Illinois*. Springfield: The Office, August, 1974.

State Board of Education. *State, Local and Federal Financing for Illinois Public Schools, 1977–78*. Springfield: Illinois Office of Education, November, 1977.

C. Declining Enrollments

Abramowitz, Susan and S. Rosenfeld, eds. *Declining Enrollments: The Challenge of the Coming Decade. Washington, D.C.: National Institute of Education, March, 1978.*

State Board of Education. Report of the Task Force on Declining Enrollments in the Public Schools. Springfield: Illinois Office of Education, December, 1975.

D. Equality of Educational Opportunity

Wise, Arthur E. *Rich Schools, Poor Schools: The Promise of Equal Educational Opportunity*. Chicago: University of Chicago Press, 1968.

E. Testing in Education

McDermott, John E., ed. *Indeterminancy in Education*. Berkeley: McCutchan, 1976.

Phi Delta Kappan 58:2 (December 1976), 306–13.

Phi Delta Kappan 59:9 (May 1978), 585–608.

F. Illinois: Topics of Interest

Buresch, J. G. *A Fundamental Goal: Education for the People of Illinois*. Urbana: Unviersity of Illinois Press, 1975.

State of Illinois School Problems Commission. *Illinois School Problems*. Springfield: School Problems Commission, various numbers and dates.

CHAPTER **32**

Social Services: Unsystematic Approaches to Insoluble Problems

Mary Lee Leahy

Practical experience in managing the social services can quickly disabuse one of the illusion that we now have, or perhaps can ever implement, "integrated delivery systems" or ideal approaches to "policy management" for human resources. It would be more realistic to look at the social services as a constant battleground of conflicting interests in which one clientele group is pitted against another, or against service providers, or vendors of services; agency is pitted against agency; and one level or branch of government is pitted against another. If a given State agency isn't creating issues through advocacy, it is likely to be caught in the cross-fire of conflicting interests.

In this context, this chapter will discuss the problems of agency leadership; the fragmented structure of Illinois social service agencies and the extent to which structural change represents any real solution; and some major common problems which cut across all Illinois social service departments, including (1) the legal right to the least restrictive environment; (2) rate-setting; (3) involuntary commitment; (4) the right to treatment; and (5) maximizing federal reimbursement. Clearly, in the area of social services, legal and financial factors dominate the making and implementation of policy.

The five principle departments which provide social services in Illinois are the Department of Public Aid (DPA), the Department of Public Health (DPH), the Department of Mental Health and Developmental Disabilities (DMH), the Department of Corrections (DOC) and the Department of Children and Family Services (DCFS). Each is a separate department with its own director who reports to the Governor. Under the directors these departments carry out the Governor's responsibility to execute those laws relating to social services. Each department is mandated by statute to render specific social services or to serve particular needs of the citizens of the State.

The Role of the Departmental Director

The appointment of the directors by the Governor is subject to confirmation or approval by the Illinois Senate. Unlike the federal system, the director may begin his or her duties at the time of appointment by the Governor and need not await confirmation. If, at the time the Senate acts, a majority of those elected fail to give approval, the director loses his or her position immediately.

In contrast to the gubernatorial term of four years, directors' terms are two years. Not only must they follow the Governor's direction; they must also take care to avoid offending too many legislators and interest groups affected by their department—that is, if the director wishes to serve an additional term. Other personnel, such as assistant directors, may need Senate confirmation.

Statutes regulating the Governor's appointment power require that the directors of the social service departments have particular qualifications related to their fields. Interest groups may have vital interests in narrowing the field of candidates through specifying certain requirements. This can expand those groups' influence on the actual appointment. During the Ogilvie Administration (1969–1973) at least one director served as Acting Director for two years in order to acquire the two years administrative experience in that field that was required by the statute setting forth qualifications for confirmation in the post. During Governor Don Walker's administration (1973–1977) several appointees were rejected or the actual confirmation was delayed.

The confirmation process involves a number of factors. One is the acceptability of the appointee to the special interest groups and to the political forces in the Senate; another is timing. A director's confirmation may further be tied to efforts to force the Governor to change his position on an unrelated issue.

The Governor who runs on a platform which is opposed by certain special interest groups or established political forces may find his efforts at implementing his platform stymied when he attempts to gain approval of his appointees. This is particularly true when the reasons for rejection do not relate to qualifications for the particular directionship. Mary Lee Leahy, author of the Environmental Article of the 1970 Illinois Constitution, was rejected in 1973 by the Senate as the Director of the Environmental Protection Agency because she had been one of the attorneys who represented in court the challenge delegation which had unseated the Daley delegation in the 1972 Democratic Convention. Veterans organizations mounted a tremendous campaign to prevent the confirmation of Tony Dean as Director of the Department of Conservation due to the fact he had been a conscientious objector during the Vietnam War. Many political observers believed he was confirmed only because he was scheduled on the same day Mary Lee Leahy was rejected; the Senate simply did not believe they should reject two appointees on the same day.

Thus, from the moment of appointment a director is placed in the difficult position of following the direction of the Governor and dealing with political and special interest forces, as well. These pressures are seldom compatible with each other. He or she must deal with such pressures on most changes in legislation and departmental appropriations. Further, the director must deal with them effectively if he or she wishes to continue in position. The Legislative process has been discussed elsewhere, but a few words should be said about the interest groups affected by the social service departments. So many of these groups are affected by the departments where it truly counts: in the pocketbook. To identify just a few such groups, the Department of Public Aid's Medicaid and medical policies and appropriations directly affect hospitals, doctors, pharmacists and nursing homes. The Department of Public Health's regulations affect the entire nuclear industry—and that should not be narrowly defined; new power plants mean construction jobs; nuclear power plants affect the coal industry, both owners and miners. The Departments of Corrections, Mental Health and Developmental Disabilities, and Children and Family Services contract out hundreds of millions of dollars to private or local public agencies for delivery of services. The departments also have the authority to impose standards of care by those agencies. Just as the departments affect the interest groups, the interest groups have a genuine, vital interest in influencing the departments.

The director, whose own position is not secure, is faced with the problem of hiring key employees to implement his or her policies. With very few exceptions, the director inherits the bureaucracy. For example in DCFS, out of nearly 3000 positions, the Director is free to name under ten. If the director is trying to implement new policies, there is often resistence by supervisors at the second and third levels below the director. The resistence is often not readily identifiable. The employee who is directed to promote a particular policy may not overtly resist, but may simply put the matter at the bottom of his or her list of priorities, while producing memos which appear to demonstrate job productivity. The very size of these departments and the scope of the programs may also contribute to the seeming inability or delay in getting top level policies and procedures implemented at the actual service delivery level. Another factor that should be noted is that change in programs and new programs have constantly hit the social service departments over the last ten years.

Thus, the test for a Governor and each of his directors, particularly in the social service departments, is whether he or she can gain control of the departments and the programs—and survive.

Organization of Departments Delivering Social Services

Several years ago the United States Department of Health, Education, and Welfare (HEW), the major source of federal money for human and social services, decided to deal with only one agency in each state for the purpose of funding such programs. Most states responded by establishing a single umbrella social service department.

By the early 1970's Illinois had become the only State to continue separate social service departments for different types of services. In 1976 at a convention of the American Public Welfare Association, Illinois was described as being in the forefront because it was the only state in the nation that had a separate department devoted to child welfare services, namely, the Department of Children and Family Services! A close examination of history would have revealed that Illinois was actually behind the other states, because Illinois had refused to adopt the umbrella agency delivery system. In the field of government reorganization, if one stands still long enough, one is both out in front and behind! Recently other states have considered separating out the various social services into distinct agencies from the umbrella department that they chose partly for convenience in dealing with HEW.

The organization of the State's delivery of social services is under active debate in Illinois. The proponents of the single umbrella social service department argue that people "fall between the cracks" in the delivery of services by separate departments. A single family often simultaneously receives services from several State agencies. This can lead to either duplication of service or a lack of service, with one department assuming that another department is delivering the needed services.

The separate department approach also poses intergovernmental problems as to the relationship of departments to each other and to HEW. The State of Illinois was required to designate one department to represent Illinois in dealing with HEW. It designated the Department of Public Aid. As a result, all the other social service departments receive their federal monies through the Department of Public Aid. HEW holds the Department of Public Aid accountable and responsible for the delivery of social services in Illinois. However, State law holds each separate department accountable and responsible for the services it is mandated to deliver.

This situation poses a thorny bureaucratic issue: is the Department of Public Aid simply a conduit for the passing on of federal funds to other State departments, or does it have a separate responsibility to monitor, audit and evaluate the programs of the other departments? Tension over turf is the inevitable result. The issues surrounding the relationship of the Department of Public Aid and the other social service departments have not been resolved in Illinois.

The proponents of the separate department approach argue that certain social programs would be buried or destroyed in a single umbrella agency. A 1976 HEW study indicated that the status of child welfare services had diminished in many of the states that had converted to the umbrella social service department. Umbrella agencies tend to respond to the most influential constituency groups. Because senior citizens have developed a powerful, vocal and voting constituency that must be dealt with by State government, senior citizen programs have been increasing. Those advocating child welfare services believe that they cannot compete with the popular services to senior citizens within the single umbrella agency. Children do not vote and the families which need services often have little or no political influence. With a separate department the public and the Legislature are forced to concentrate on the different areas of need and the different types of services—with an umbrella department that review might be buried within the department.

The proponents of separate departments also argue that each type of social service requires its own particular type of expertise gained by education, training and experience. In the single umbrella agency the worker may be forced to deal with all types of social services and, thus, may have only limited knowledge in many areas of social service with no well-defined expertise in any one area. All types of social services can suffer. The 1975–76 HEW study of child welfare services confirms this. (See the Gove, Carlson and Schneiderman chapters for differing perspectives on organization).

The problems of duplication of services or lack of services created by the separate departmental organization could be addressed more effectively then they now are by use of the cabinet structure. The directors of all State code departments form the governor's cabinet. Each governor has his own particular style of administration and his own approach to the use of a cabinet structure. To the best of this author's knowledge, use of a cabinet committee composed of the directors of the social service departments as a means to examine the questions of duplication or lack of services has not been used extensively in Illinois. A spin-off of such an approach could be establishment of inter-departmental task forces charged with solving particular problems. Transfer of some services could also be considered. For example, both the Department of Public Aid and the Department of Children and Family Services administer day care programs. A sub-committee of key day care personnel from each department could ensure coordination of those programs—or explore the transfer of all day care to one department.

Some time ago Congress enacted legislation which governs reimbursement by the federal government to the states for social services. The legislation is commonly referred to as Title XX. In order to qualify for funds under Title XX the State must submit to HEW a State plan for delivery of social services. This plan, if taken seriously by the departments, could resolve many of the problems separate departments present; particularly those of duplication of services and lack of services.

As noted above, the debate about the organization and the delivery of social services continues in Illinois. But that debate should focus on the reality of what is. It is not as if Illinois were debating the initial organization of delivery of social services. Massive reorganization may be so disruptive that the delivery of services actually deteriorates. The social service departments have been repeatedly reorganized, each within itself. The result is often chaotic, with each employee worrying about whether a job for him will be found on the new organization chart. Any reorganization, be it transfer of a particular function or massive merging of departments, must be thoughtfully planned with sufficient time and funds for adequate implementation.

As a side comment it should be apparent that the policies of HEW, particularly the funding policies, have a tremendous impact on State social services. "He who pays the piper calls the tune" is an apt description of this phenomenon. With pressure on all State departments to maximize the receipt of federal monies and thereby lessen pressure on State tax dollars, those programs or structures favored by HEW cannot help but be implemented at the State level. For example, in the area of child welfare HEW has put great emphasis on in-home services, and the level of reimbursement is far greater than that for out-of-home services. However, counterpressure from interest groups may result if the particular federal policy conflicts with their vested interests. For example, foster parents and private institutions asserted the need for out-of-home services for children and encouraged the Legislature to fund those services.

Common Problems Cutting Across Social Service Departments

There are several major problems that cut across many or all of the social service departments. These problems range from basic methods and underlying philosophy of service delivery to very practical immediate problems of providing services in a time of inflation and pressure to avoid tax increases.

Right to the Least Restrictive Environment

During the 1970's State programs have moved dramatically away from institutionalization. Initially this change in emphasis was referred to as "deinstitutionalization" but is now commonly called LRE, the "right to the least restrictive environment."

In the late 1960's and early 1970's studies began to reveal the negative longterm effects of extended institutionalization. In 1972 the United States District Court for the Eastern District of Wisconsin noted the effects revealed by such studies. *Lessard v. Schmidt*, 349 F. Supp. 1078 (1972). The Court noted that longterm institutionalization can increase the symptoms that caused the institutional placement and can adversely affect the ability of the person to reintegrate himself into society. Institutionalization carries a certain stigma and can result in the loss of future opportunities. The Court even noted that a person's chances of dying increased during institutionalization in a mental health institution.

Review of Illinois child welfare statistics revealed that chances of a child in placement outside his home returning to his family dramatically decreased if a child was in placement over eighteen months. On the basis of such findings and with increasing frequency, the courts scrutinized State instutional policies and programs and imposed on the State the requirement to institutionalize only those demonstrably in need and the requirement to create alternatives short of institutionalization for others.

In *O'Connor v. Donaldson,* 422 U.S. 563, 95 S. Ct. 2486 (1975), the United States Supreme Court held that a person who was not dangerous to himself or to others could not be held in a state mental health facility against his will. The fact that a person is odd or eccentric does not justify his removal from society against his will. As Mr. Justice Burger noted:

> May the State fence in the harmless mentally ill solely to save its citizens from exposure to those whose ways are different? One might as well ask if the State, to avoid public unease, could incarcerate all who are physically unattractice or socially eccentric. Mere public intolerance or animosity cannot constitutionally justify the deprivation of a person's physical liberty.

In *Morales v. Turman,* 383 F. Supp. 53 (E.D., Tex., 1974), the U.S. District Court in Texas had applied the same doctrine in striking down certain aspects of the Texas program dealing with minors in need of supervision (juveniles who had committed acts that would not be considered crimes were they committed by adults). The Court noted that the "model" institutional person may not be able to adapt to the community after a long period of institutionalization and that the State was under an obligation to create alternatives to institutionalization.

The studies documenting the effects of long-term institutionalization not only had a profound effect on the courts, but led to legislative action on the state and federal levels. Title XX reimbursement policies, favoring less restrictive social services, have already been discussed. Congress also adopted Public Law 94–142, the federal act governing federal reimbursement for public school education, which requires every state to deliver educational services to the

> mentally retarded, hard of hearing, deaf, speech impaired, visually handicapped, seriously emotionally disturbed, orthopedically impaired or other health impaired children, or children with specific learning disabilities . . . . 20 *U.S.C.* 1401.

These services must be delivered in the least restrictive environment (LRE). The delivery of these services by local school districts will profoundly affect social services delivered by various State departments—particularly the Department of Mental Health and the Department of Children and Family Services. Children who used to be automatically referred to the State now must be served in the local school district if at all possible.

As a result of the emphasis on LRE, DCFS noticed a dramatic change in the population at two of the schools the department operated. As local school districts developed programs for the deaf and the blind, children referred to the School for the Deaf and the Illinois Braille and Sight Saving School, both located in Jacksonville, tended to be either older or more difficult than those at the junior high and high school levels who simply could not make it in the local programs, and to have multiple handicaps or emotional problems. This change in the nature of the referrals necessitated programmatic changes and training in new areas.

In 1973, Jerry Miller, a known proponent of deinstitutionalization, was appointed director of DCFS in Illinois. At the time of his appointment, close to 1,000 children who were wards of the State of Illinois were placed in institutions outside the State, hundreds in Texas. Immediate action was taken to return most of those children to the State. Follow-up studies indicated the majority of those children were able to do well in programs short of institutional placement. By January of 1977 out-of-state placement of DCFS wards numbered 57. Most of those children were in one-of-a-kind facilities serving children with unique sets of problems; there also were a small number of children for whom return to Illinois would have been too traumatic for the child. Jerry Miller's deinstitutionalization was viewed by many in the private sector as threatening. His so-called style of confrontation caused controversy. However, he did dramatically shift emphasis and call attention to the very real problems in child welfare that had not received much public attention in prior years.

The LRE movement has been recognized by all three branches of government. The State is now coping with the practical problems of creating quality alternative modes of services. Both the State and the private sector must be willing to adapt and be willing to try new approaches. The need for service of those "deinstitutionalized" in large part remains unmet—the quality of the alternatives still leaves much to be desired.

Rate Setting

Compared to most other states, Illinois relies heavily upon the actual delivery of services by the private rather than the public sector. The private sector is absolutely crucial to the delivery of social services by all of the State Social services departments in Illinois. Thus, the recurring questions: what should the State pay the private sector for delivering those services? What should be the formula for setting rates? Can the State unilaterally set rates? Can the State simply pay whatever the private sector charges? Is the private sector free to raise its salaries, change its program and pass the added cost of this on to the State? That approach would make it virtually impossible for a State department to estimate the funds it will need for the coming year and also make it impossible for that department to live within the appropriation it eventually receives from the General Assembly.

The problem is certainly present in the Medicaid program administered by the Department of Public Aid. That department is constantly struggling with soaring hospital and medical costs. But supposing that Department agrees to pay 95 percent of the actual cost of delivering a particular hospital service. Does—or indeed, should—that 5 percent get passed on to the non-Medicaid patients in that hospital? As in most cases, the Illinois response is an evolving one. Each new administration develops a new twist, but federal regulation has left little flexibility for state action.

Under the Ogilvie Administration DCFS moved to a formula approach, paying private agencies approximately 75 percent of certain recognized costs. In 1975 DCFS moved to pay 100 percent of certain costs for institutional care. In one respect, the significance of that move went relatively unnoticed. Most of the private agencies operating institutions for children were religious or charitable in nature. Yet they asked for and received 100 percent (or close to it) of most of their costs for service. This crystallized the gradual trend from provision of services by charity to provision of services by public tax dollars.

Inevitably a result of the 100 percent funding had to be increased State control. DCFS had to account for the use of its appropriation. Program evaluation and fiscal auditing of the private agencies had to follow, although there was, and still is, much resistance to that type of control by the State. One can wonder if the private sector had, or has, fully thought out the necessary consequences of increased reliance on public dollars.

The move to a percentage of any recognized costs does not resolve all problems. Neither the public nor the private sector can fully control the rise in those recognized costs, so both sectors are faced with the question of whether increases in recognized costs will be paid. The uncertainty of such increases or the commitment to pay them can create havoc with a department's budget.

The following example should illustrate rate problems caused by the fact that there are separate social service departments in Illinois. The Department of Children and Family Services has among its wards children who are developmentally disabled; the Department of Mental Health has a program to provide services to developmentally disabled children who remain under the control of their parents. Wards of DCFS and children of private parents eligible for service financed by DMH may be placed in the same program run by a private agency. In 1975 the Department of Children and Family Services was paying 100 percent of their recognized costs for that program. At the same time the Department of Mental Health had a totally different rate setting formula. What this meant to the private agency running such a program was receiving X amount of dollars for delivering those services to a developmentally disabled ward of DCFS and Y amount of dollars for a child placed in that program by the Department of Mental Health. Yet the actual services performed were identical. It is widely believed that, at a minimum, the private sector should be assured of receiving the same amount of monies for delivering the same services when the bill is being paid by the State.

Rate setting is particularly difficult in a period of inflation when there is also intense public pressure to hold the lid on taxes. On the one hand the providers of services are demanding increased rates; on the other hand the public is resisting increased appropriations. This pressure is particularly intense for the social service departments, for they must provide the services mandated by statute. At this time there is no resolution of these problems.

Involuntary "Commitment"

Many of those who receive social services do so not of their free choice. Those committed to the Department of Corrections arrive there after having been found guilty of a crime before a court of law. The rights of the person standing accused of a crime have long been recognized in Anglo-American law. In recent years courts throughout the country have grappled with the problem of "commitment" to other types of social services. Certainly the results of involuntary "commitment" to the Department of Mental Health or to the Department of Children and Family Services can have as serious, if not more serious, an impact upon the person than commitment to the Department of Corrections.

Courts have begun to extend most of the rights afforded a person accused of a crime to any person whom the State is attempting to commit against his will. The new Mental Health Code mentioned elsewhere in this chapter is the legislative response to increased judicial action in the area of involuntary commitment to mental health institutions.

Extension of procedural rights, long recognized in the criminal area and now recognized in mental health, to the field of child welfare has begun. Parents now have the right to an attorney in any child welfare court proceeding; a guardian *ad litem* is now appointed for the child. What will be next? Be it by judicial edict or legislative enactment, extension of those procedural rights profoundly affects day to day practice on the actual service delivery level. For example, Public Aid must now provide a hearing, if it is desired, before terminating aid. Certainly expansion of these procedural rights into all areas of social service have placed the departments in constantly changing postures. The rules of the game are changing rapidly and the departments are hard-pressed to keep pace.

Right to Treatment

In recent years several courts have recognized the substantive right to treatment. Again, this has primarily affected the Department of Mental Health and the Department of Children and Family Services. In *Welsch v. Likins,* 373 F. Supp. 487 (D. Ct., Minn., 1974), the Court considered the involuntary commitment of six retarded adults. The Court held that the six had a constitutional right to receive treatment that will give a realistic chance of cure or improvement. At the very minimum that requires a humane psychiatric and physical environment with qualified staff in sufficient numbers and individualized treatment plans. The Court added that a person so committed had the right to protection from assaults, the right to reasonable access to exercise and other outdoor activities, and the right to have basic hygiene needs met. The Court outlawed such practices as barren isolation rooms without supervision or strict monitoring, physical restraints without exhausting less restrictive methods of restraining behavior, and the excessive use of tranquilizing drugs to control behavior. The Court held that it could order additional state expenditures to remedy constitutional violations and said

> inadequate resources can never be an adequate justification for depriving any person of his constitutional rights. 373 F. Supp. at 499.

In *Wyatt v. Stickney,* 325 F. Supp. 781 (M.D., Ala., N.D., 1971), the Court reviewed conditions at the Bryce Hospital which housed 5,000 patients, 1,500 of whom were geriatric patients. Finding that the program failed to meet even minimum standards, the Court held such failure could not be justified by lack of funds. On appeal the Fifth Circuit Court of Appeals affirmed the lower court and emphasized that Courts were able to formulate standards of care and to enforce them.

In *Morales v. Turman,* 383 F. Supp. 53 (E.D., 1974), the Court held that many aspects of the programs dealing with juvenile delinquents violated those juveniles' right to treatment or right to have their needs served. The Court placed the entire program for juveniles under his direction and supervision. At the time of writing several courts have placed certain aspects of the programs of the Illinois Department of Corrections under judicial supervision. Many of these decisions have failed to recognize that there may be no known treatment for a particular given condition.

In reading these cases and others in a similar vein one is struck by the necessity of judicial intervention. The State is seriously violating the rights of those committed to its care. Something must be done. But is the judicial system capable of administering part or all of an executive branch of government program? The failure of the executive branch is apparent, but is judicial administration the answer?

An offshoot of the problems created by recognition of the right to treatment is the alleged right to refuse treatment. Chief Justice Burger alluded to that in his concurring opinion in *O'Connor v. Donaldson,* 422 U.S. 563, 95 S. Ct. 2486 (1975). He noted that the case was being returned to the Court of Appeals to reconsider the question of official immunity from liability for monetary damages. (The trial court had found the superintendent of the state hospital liable in monetary damages for the continued involuntary commitment of Donaldson.) He advised the Court of Appeals that, when considering the superintendent's claim he acted in good faith in refusing to release Donaldson, it should take into consideration also the fact Donaldson had consistently refused treatment, claiming he was not mentally ill.

The Courts and legislatures have barely begun to scratch the surface on these issues of the right to treatment and the right to refuse treatment. Judicial and legislative action in these areas will profoundly affect the social service departments and the delivery of services. To cite just one example, if a patient in a DMH institution does well with medication, then suddenly refuses to take the medication, can he be physically forced by DMH employees to take the medication or must the employees seek a court order allowing them to administer the medication against the patient's will? Such practical problems are almost infinite and confront State employees on a daily basis. The potential gap between legal requirements and bureaucratic behavior in these cases boggles the mind. It effectively illustrates the complexity of policy implementation.

Maximizing Federal Reimbursement

Most of the programs administered by the social service departments are eligible for partial federal reimbursement, in various percentages. In recent years Illinois has simply not received its share of federal dollars.

For example, Title XX dollars are allocated nationwide. Illinois is eligible for so many dollars in any given fiscal year. Illinois expenditures in eligible programs have far exceeded the Title XX allocation. Yet Illinois has received far less than its allocation. The main reason: failure of Illinois to meet the federal requirements for obtaining the allocation.

But Illinois may not be solely at fault. This author recalls HEW withholding reimbursement for payments to foster homes for care of wards of DCFS. The funds were withheld because there were children in "foster homes violating licensing regulations." True, there may have been some children in unlicensed foster care homes, but the vast majority of "unlicensed" homes were attributable to the computer. For example, if a home's license had expired and the Department had begun but not yet completed the relicensing process, the computer showed the home unlicensed. A Department legal opinion held the home had a constructive license until the relicensing process had been completed; only if that process resulted in denial of a license was the home considered unlicensed. Yet funds were withheld.

A foster home was also licensed for a particular number of children—e.g. four children. If there were four children there on the first of the month and one left on the 10th of the month and another came on the 20th of the month, the computer would show five children in the home and would show it exceeding licensing capacity, although that capacity was never exceeded on any particular day.

Ironically several states do not license foster homes, but by placement of a child in a foster care home it is considered "approved." Those states would never face the possibility of withholding of federal funds, for all their homes were approved by virtue of placement. But Illinois, requiring licensing for the protection of its children, was being penalized for minor faults and delays within its own licensing system and anomalies of record-keeping.

Given the intense pressure to hold the lid on the spending of State dollars, the social service departments are under enormous pressure to maximize reimbursement even if it results in dramatic changes in actual programs. Paradoxically, some states do better than Illinois in obtaining federal funds without equalling Illinois standards of quality in actual practice. The answer for Illinois is not to substitute gamesmanship for quality, but to make a concerted effort where necessary that will mean using political clout to overcome administrative trivia.[1]

Conclusion

Perhaps the discussion of these problems leaves the impression that the social services departments are in a state of seige. In so many ways that is true. The pressures, so often conflicting, are intense—and they run the complete gamut from funding to method of delivering services. These departments bear close scrutiny, for they face enormous problems and challenges. Will funding be adequate? Will the services be of quality?

Research on the politics, policy and implementation of human resources in Illinois is sadly lacking. In view of the crucial role of the State in the intergovernmental delivery of social services, it is imperative that the skimpy materials now available be expanded.[2] It is also essential that the growing work in a national perspective be applied to Illinois.[3] Is there a way of obtaining the benefits of reorganized integrated social services which meets the objections to "umbrella" social service agencies raised here? What changes in the social service professions and elsewhere would be required to create a real basis for system improvement? Can the common problems which cut across departments ever be "solved," or even reduced to manageable proportions? Or are we destined to enter a long period of expanding legal rights and public expenditures, burdened by the suspicion that, as a society, we lack the scientific knowledge, professional skills, managerial tools and political commitment to deliver a quality product? What are the promises and limitations of expanded purchase of services from non-governmental agencies? In many respects, it appears that Illinois, while committed to major expenditures for its human resources, has done embarrassingly little to come to grips with the problem of quality of service.

FOOTNOTES

[1]For a discussion of efforts under the Ogilvie Administration see Martha Derthick, *Uncontrolled Spending* (Washington, D.C.: Brookings, 1974).

[2]Under Governor Ogilvie, an Institute for Social Policy was created. The results of the research it funded are nowhere to be seen. More recently, see Steve Anderson and Ernest Gullerud, *The Federal Provision for Social Services Through Title XX: The Illinois Experience* (Urbana: University of Illinois, School of Social Work, 1977).

[3]Robert Agranoff (ed.), *Coping With the Demands for Change Within Human Services Administration* (Washington, D.C.: American Society for Public Administration, 1977); Robert Agranoff and Alex Pattakos, *Dimensions of Services Integration* (Rockville, Md. Department of Health, Education and Welfare, Project SHARE Monograph Service, 1979).

PART 

THE FUTURE OF ILLINOIS

CHAPTER **33**

Facing Illinois' Future

Task Force on the Future of Illinois

Illinois Grows Up

Illinois' population is maturing and so is its economy. The Illinois Bureau of the Budget (BOB) projects that by the year 2000, the median age of the population will have shifted from the present 29 years to 36 years. The largest segment of the Illinois population will be in their thirties and forties. We have moved beyond a period of rapid population growth into an era of much slower growth, as both fertility and immigration rates decline.

Our economy, like that of the nation, is moving toward the "post-industrial" age in which growth in jobs to produce services will outstrip those in the production of goods. While Illinois is expected to maintain a diverse economy, including increased jobs in manufacturing, BOB projections show that growth in service sector jobs is expected to outstrip manufacturing jobs two to one.

Maintaining Illinois' Advantages

Illinois' advantages in the past have included a vast transportation network, and ample energy, water, soil and labor supplies. Illinois has maintained the quality and quantity of these resources through substantial investments in all of them. The state has had high standards for transportation availability, state educational institutions, water quality, and wage rates. Major capital investments have been made in energy development and agricultural production.

The level of personal income in Illinois has been and remains high. The Illinois Fiscal Commission notes in its report on the economy of 1977 that in 1976, Illinois per capita income totalled $7,347, ranking the state a very close third behind New Jersey, $7,381, and Connecticut, $7,350. This is well above the national per capita income figure of $6,399. Illinois has also maintained a favorable tax/income ratio. The Illinois tax burden in 1975 was below the median of the 33 largest states in the nation.

Can the state maintain its resources in the future without losing ground in personal income and tax income ratio? This preliminary review of state resources indicates that it's going to be harder. The costs of maintaining quality and quantity are rising. Indications are that costs are rising faster than either population or revenue growth.

The editor thanks the Illinois Futures Task Force for permission to reprint this introductory statement from *A Working Paper on the Future of Illinois* (January, 1979), pp. 4–7.

The demands being placed on most Illinois resources are accelerating faster than population growth and are projected to do so to the year 2000. There is, as a result, an acceleration of the cost to maintain these resources that may exceed the expansion of revenue. For example:

—While population growth is projected by the Illinois Bureau of the Budget at 13% and employment growth at 25% by the year 2000, increased energy demand is projected by the Energy Resources Commission at 60–85%. The capitalization requirements for new plants to meet this demand is estimated by the utility companies to be $132 billion (1977 dollars).

—The sheer amount of wear and tear on our state highways is increasing more rapidly than revenues which maintain them. This is because highway revenues are derived from gas taxes on the assumption that these revenues will grow with vehicle use. However, as cars use less gas per mile and trucks get heavier, the road system is wearing out faster than the maintenance funds are growing.

—Competition for land and water between agricultural and urban development uses is accelerating even though population growth is slowing. The result is that land costs are rising along with the costs of providing water for both uses.

—Demands for varied educational programs remain high; costs of maintaining a large existing capital investment that is increasingly underutilized are also high; wage rates continue to climb. The upshot is that education costs are rising at the same time as school enrollments are declining. Revenues follow enrollments.

—Demands for long-term care for the elderly are expected to increase as the population ages. The Statewide Health Coordinating Council points out that, while there is an excess supply of nursing homes and hospitals beds, there is a shortage of alternative "in home" or "day care" facilities and personnel. Costs of long term care have risen in Illinois from $1 per capita in 1950 to $35 per capita in 1974. Health costs are projected nationally to rise 10% per year to the year 2000. At this rate, state budget expenditures for medicaid payments would rise from a current level of $675 million to $11.6 billion, or from 17 to 31% of state expenditures.* Current national health insurance proposals do not include full coverage of long term nursing care.

If we assume that national economic growth is slowing and that inflation and tax revolt will continue, we cannot look to federal revenue to make up the shortage in local and state revenues. How are we going to maintain the quality and quantity of our resources in the future?

Conserving Our Resources

One important approach will be to examine the possibilities for stretching our uses of existing resources, though various new forms of conservation. More attention is being given to conservation programs for water, energy and soil. There is increasing concern to improve labor productivity. Additional thought is being given to the possibilities of preserving and enhancing existing cities, towns and neighborhoods rather than investing in new buildings, utilities and services. More emphasis is being placed on ways to provide human services without the costs of building, staffing and maintaining new institutions (hospitals, children's homes and the like). Consideration is also being given to services that would meet the needs of more than one group at a time, such as part time employment of older citizens to look after children.

However, current state policies, programs and taxing structures are not well designed for conservation approaches. State policies and taxing respond to physical growth wherever it may occur rather than acting to conserve existing communities. Rehabilitation efforts are hampered by tax assessment practices and clumsy mechanisms for purchase of tax delinquent deteriorating properties. Illinois incorporation and annexation laws encourage separate municipal incorporation and development of services rather than annexation or intergovernmental approaches that would provide the benefits of economies of scale.

*These figures are prior to federal reimbursement which is currently 50%.

In human services, while in many areas there is conscious and effective policy (such as in mental health) to "deinstitutionalize" people, there is question about how effectively the state has been able to assist local communities in providing alternative services. It is difficult to develop approaches that meet the needs of more than one group at a time, as state agencies are designed around the needs of particular people (elderly, children etc.). This leads us to the second point about the state's resources.

Resource Interdependence

An important feature to note about the state's resources is their interdependence. While we discuss each resource separately, it is evident that *state policy toward any one resource has implications for state policy toward many others.* Are our policies for education commensurate with population and employment projections? Approaches to water use will affect transportation, agriculture, community growth. State policies for services to children will affect the family structure, employment patterns, and educational achievement. Environmental regulations will affect economic development.

While it is clear that the state's resources are interrelated, it is also evident that most state programs are designed only around a single purpose: keeping water clean, promoting economic development, promoting education, serving children. How can these programs be engineered to achieve more than one goal at a time?

Do we need mechanisms in the state government for defining overall goals of state programs and seeing that they are implemented across agency lines? Should we consider mechanisms that could enhance cost-efficiency of state government services by coordinating them and eliminating duplication and self-defeating efforts? Can we create mechanisms for providing efficient, coordinated services to the clients of state government? These clients range from a utility company seeking permits for a power plant to an abused child requiring immediate protection *and* a future acceptable home.

CHAPTER **34**

The Future of Illinois: Trends, Problems and Influence

Illinois 2000 Foundation

Trend Highlights

As a prelude to the proposal of long-range goals for Illinois' economic development in 1979, Illinois 2000's volunteer Issue Teams have spent the last year examining major trends and alternatives for the state's economy. Some of the trends of particular importance include:

Jobs/Growth

- The Illinois economy is expected to create 1.2 million new jobs between 1975 and 2000. This increase from 4.7 million jobs to 5.9 million jobs is based on a real growth rate in personal income of 2% per year, compared to a U.S. average of 3% per year.
- Manufacturing employment will grow very slowly and will be bypassed by the service sector as the state's major employer.
- In terms of the business climate, the apparent advantage of the Sun Belt could be considerably diminished in the 1980's as increased growth brings problems long faced by the North.

Workforce

- Almost all funding for training and job placement under the federal Comprehensive Employment and Training Act focuses on public sector jobs in Illinois.
- Workmen's compensation levels in Illinois are the highest among major industrial states.

Agriculture

- Farmland has decreased from 31 million acres to 29 million in the last 20 years. The annual 100,000 acre loss is projected to continue through the year 2000.
- Out-of-state marketings of corn and soybeans will double by the year 2000, necessitating new national and international markets.
- Farm-to-market roads are deteriorating rapidly, due to increased use and delayed maintenance. 15,000 bridges in the system are substandard and require $1.3 billion to repair.

Urban Economic Development

- By the year 2000, the number of urban center dwellers employed in manufacturing will have dropped to 21% of the labor force from 31% in 1970. Employment in the financial sector will increase from 6% to 13% of the labor force, and services from 21% to 24%.

Energy

- Total energy use in Illinois is projected to increase 87% between 1975 and the year 2000.
- Coal use for electric power in Illinois is projected to double by the year 2000.
- Nuclear power will account for nearly 50% of the state's electric power capacity by the year 2000.

Environment

- Government, industry, and environmentalists generally agree that the goal of zero pollution is unattainable and undefinable.
- Physical and monetary limitations will produce a leveling-off in improvement of environmental quality with respect to "traditional" pollutants.

Transportation

- Funds for rail and highway maintenance have been declining in real dollars since 1970, while freight movement has increased.
- Barge traffic on Illinois' waterways continues to increase as lower operating costs allow cheaper transportation rates than rail.
- For Illinois, domestic and international air passenger enplanements have more than doubled since 1963 to 18 million annually in 1977.

Taxes/Revenue

- Compared to other states, Illinois has a moderate state and local tax burden, although it has been increasing since 1969.
- Many pressures, some of which conflict, are gathering to change the tax structure. These include pressure for real property tax relief at the local level that could shift the burden for many services, especially education, to the state level.

Government and Human Resources

- State elementary and secondary school enrollments are declining to a projected level of 1.85 million students by 1985, and higher education enrollments, although they guadrupled between 1957 and 1977, are projected to decline 8% by 1990.

The editor thanks the Illinois 2000 Foundation for permission to reprint this introductory statement from *Alternative Economic Futures For Illinois: Executive Summary* (December, 1978) pp. 2–4.

- State demographic projections indicate a 25% increase in the over-65 population by 2000 and a 7% decrease in persons under 20. They also show a 17% increase in families (51,435) and a 27% increase in unrelated individuals (125,707) below the federal poverty level.

Health

- Health care expenditures, under a projected 11% annual rate increase, could reach $109 billion in Illinois by the year 2000.

Illinois: Economic Leader Today

Population The growth of the population has slowed from the pace recorded in the early 1950's and 1960's and is expected to continue at a slower rate through the year 2000. Nearly 1.4 million additional people are expected to reside in Illinois at that date, up from today's population of 11.3 million.

Personal Income Average Illinois per capita income in 1977 was $7,768 compared with the U.S. average of $7,019. This figure is second only to California among the most populated states.

Industrial Assets Illinois leads all states in the manufacturing of farm machinery, non-electrical machinery, fabricated materials, steel, food products, printing, chemicals, telephones, candy, soap, and appliances. It ranks third among the states in total manufacturing exports.

Agricultural Assets The state has the richest agricultural land in the country, producing more corn and soybeans than any other state. It leads the nation in agricultural exports by value.

Labor Force Illinois' mature, reliable and skilled labor force has been a key to steady economic growth for the state.

Georgaphic Location Illinois' central market location in the Great Lakes region has allowed it to become a major national transportation hub. These prime features are equally important to international trade and travel.

Energy Resources Illinois is considered a "balanced energy" state because of its near-equal reliance on coal, natural gas, and petroleum products. Nuclear power plays an increasing role in electric power generation. Illinois also has the largest bituminous coal reserves of any state.

Financial Center There is a growing acknowledgement of the importance of Illinois' financial institutions to the Midwest, the U.S. and to international capital markets.

A Few Key Problems for the Future

Illinois possesses many advantages, as described above. Yet to take these features for granted without examining key problems which have a growing impact on the economy would be naive. The following provides a synopsis of concerns which evolved from the Illinois 2000 process.

1. Competition from other regions of the U.S. appears to have a negative impact on the state's economy and business activity. Although no firm information is available on business departures due to more favorable climates elsewhere, the perceived displacement must be examined and actions taken to retard such a trend.
2. The environmental constraints posed by the Illinois coal reserves' high sulfur content impinge on the state economy and, more specifically, on the southern and western portions of the state where the reserves exist. The use of Illinois coal, coupled with proper environmental management, could reduce operating costs for business and could allow the state to prepare for potential national energy shortages.
3. Despite the extensive transportation network in Illinois, there are funding problems associated with general maintenance which pose substantial questions.
4. Urban sprawl is complicating the health of cities and adding to the dilemma of supporting public services. People are moving out in search of other housing and living environments. Businesses, too, are departing as the expenses of rehabilitating vintage plants and equipment become too great a burden. This aging manufacturing base must be dealt with: otherwise, it will lead to lower production capabilities and will encourage some businesses to relocate outside the state.

External Influences and the Illinois Economy

The people of Illinois must examine the future in the context of national and international variables over which they have little control. Major concerns such as inflation, energy prices, international corporate and union decisions, and federal regulations and tax policy are all generally beyond the scope of state, public, or private sector action. Yet they must be understood and considered as **Illinois 2000** participants seek policies over which state and local government and the private sector actually have influence. **Illinois 2000** provided the following assumptions in order for the issue teams to standardize the external factors for all teams, while permitting focus on areas of state influence.

1. The organization, role and interrelationships among federal, state and local government will remain essentially the same through the year 2000. The trend of increasing government involvement in private activity will continue.
2. The national economy will continue to grow at moderate rates through the year 2000. And while the postwar cycles of prosperity and recessions will continue, no major booms or depressions are anticipated.

3. The rising price of energy will encourage alternatives to be developed in the next 25 years.
4. Climatic conditions will not vary enough to have a major economic impact between 1978 and the year 2000.
5. The current level of world tension will remain constant, requiring continued outlays for national defense spending at current rates. No major wars are expected.
6. World population will continue to increase at about 2% a year, culminating in a world population of over 6 billion people by the year 2000.

APPENDIX

ILLINOIS STANDING ON SELECTED POLICY INDICATORS

	Illinois/U.S.[1]			Rank		
Indicator	**1960**	**1970**	**1976**	**1960**	**1970**	**1976**
SOCIAL AND ECONOMIC CHARACTERISTICS						
Population (Millions)	10,081	11,114	11,229	4	5	5
	(179,323)	(203,212)	(214,659)			
Blacks as Percent of Total Population	10.3	12.8	13.7	14	13	13
	(10.5)	(11.1)	(11.5)			
Percent High School Graduates	40.4	52.6		33	30	
	(41.1)	(52.3)				
Per Capita Personal Income	2,646	4,507	7,347	8	8	4
	(2,222)	(3,966)	(6,399)			
Percent Persons Below Poverty Level	14.7	10.2	10.5	8	12	28
	(22.1)	(13.7)	(11.4)			
Income Concentration Index	423	342		19	17	
	(433)	(352)				
Percent Urban by State	80.7	83.0		6	7	
	(69.9)	(73.5)				
Per Capita Value Added	1,251	2,038	2,870	6	5	3
POLITICAL AND GOVERNMENTAL FEATURES						
Percent Voting for President	75.5	69.3 (1968)	61.1	12	10	13
	(62.8)	(60.9)	(54.4)			
Percent Democrats in Legislature (1977)	57.7(Sen)	53.1(Hse)		35	38	
	(66.4)	(67.4)				
Apportionment Range of Deviation	1.4(Sen)	1.4(Hse)		9	7	
REVENUE AND EXPENDITURES						
Per Capita State and Local General Revenue	273	658	1,161	28	21	22
	(281)	(643)	(1,193)			
. . . from Own Sources	237	546	930	25	15	19
	(242)	(536)	(934)			
. . . Own Sources, per $1,000 Personal Income	91	132	138	45	36	41
	(109)	(146)	(160)			
State and Local Tax Effort Index		(1971)	(1975)			
	88	102	111	40	15	14
	(100)	(100)	(100)			
Revenue from State Income Tax as Percent of Total State Taxes		25.0	32.0	38	21	23
	(18.8)	(27.0)	(32.2)			
Percent of State and Local General Revenue From Federal Government	13.0	14.2	19.9	38	37	40
	(13.8)	(16.7)	(21.7)			
Per Capita State and Local Direct General Expenditures	287	603	1,176	26	28	21
	(288)	(646)	(1,191)			
. . . per $1,000 Personal Income	110	141	174	47	50	46
	(130)	(176)	(203)			
EDUCATION						
Public Elementary/Secondary Expenditure per Pupil	438	803	1,876	7	18	6
	(375)	(783)	(1,578)			
. . . per $1,000 Personal Income	33.66	42.81	48.80	45	48	39
	(37.91)	(50.31)	(53.82)			
. . . as Percent of Total State and Local Spending	30.7	30.3	28.0	18	21	16
	(29.2)	(28.5)	(26.5)			
Average Annual Salaries for Classroom Teachers	5,725	9,700	14,000	9	4	6
	(5,215)	(8,560)	(12,500)			
Pupil-Teacher Ratio	22.4	22.7	20.3	19	21	31
	(24.2)	(20.4)	(20.3)			
Percent of Draftees Failing	25.9	6.0	4.0	38	37	40

[1] U.S. Figures in parentheses

ILLINOIS STANDING ON SELECTED POLICY INDICATORS

Indicator	Illinois/U.S.[1] 1960	1970	1976	Rank 1960	1970	1976
Selective Service Mental Requirements	(18.8)	(5.7)	(1973) (2.4)			
Percent School Segregation (95–100%	72.4 (61.0)	71.2 (38.2)	76.7 (35.2)	43	49	49
Higher Education per Capita General Expenditure (State)	13.1 (18.1)	67.4 (63.6)	113.9 (113.2)	34	28	30
... per Student (State and Local)	718 (893)	2,377 (2,029)	2,877 (2,751)	42	17	28
... per $1,000 Pesonal Income	5.44 (8.01)	15.82 (17.36)	16.90 (19.33)	43	39	41
... as percent of Total State and Local Spending	5.0 (6.2)	11.2 (9.8)	9.7 (9.5)	38	27	33
FTE State and Local Education Employees per 10,000 population	125.7 (140.8)	203.4 (209.5)	216.5 (233.1)	43	36	42
... non-Educational Employees	153.9 (169.8)	192.7 (210.2)	219.8 (242.4)	34	30	36
PUBLIC WELFARE						
Per Capita State and Local Public Welfare Expenditures	24.39 (24.47)	57.50 (72.24)	164.52 (146.44)	16	19	11
State and Local Public Welfare Spending per $1,000 personal income	9.20 (11.32)	13.50 (19.71)	24.41 (25.00)	38	35	13
Public Welfare Expenditures as a per- cent of Total State and Local Spending	8.5 (8.5)	9.5 (11.2)	14.0 (12.3)	17	19	8
Percent Public Assistance Recipients of Total Population	2.94 (3.53)	5.52 (6.55)	8.09 (7.18)	25	24	11
Average Monthly Family Payments, AFDC	168 (115)	241 (187)	274 (236)	4	7	9
Average Monthly Payment for Old Age Assistance	78 (69)	64(Suppl) (78)	56 (94)	18	30	36
Average Monthly Payment for Aid to the Disabled	83 (68)	41 (97)	67 (146)	16	22	38
Average Monthly Payment for Aid to the Blind	84 (73)	93 (104)	57 NA	16	22	35
Average Weekly Unemployment Benefits	34.10 (32.87)	51.85 (50.31)	91.64 (75.16)	15	11	1
HEALTH AND HOSPITALS						
Per Capita State and Local Expenditures	19.83 (21.09)	39.82 (47.57)	72.64 (96.37)	18	27	34
... Per $1,000 Personal Income	7.59 (9.49)	9.34 (12.98)	10.78 (16.45)	38	38	44
... as Percent of Total State and Local Spending	6.9 (7.3)	6.6 (7.4)	6.2 (8.1)	21	25	37
Infant Death Rates, White	22.2 (22.9)	18.3 (17.8)	15.0 (14.2)	15	28	35
... non-White	39.6 (43.2)	33.6 (30.9)	29.9 (24.2)	22	43	49
HIGHWAYS						
Per Capita State and Local Expenditures	52.92 (52.38)	64.05 (80.84)	127.02 (111.37)	30	44	29
... per $1,000 Personal Income	20.52 (23.56)	15.03 (22.06)	18.85 (19.01)	40	50	38
... percent of Total State and Local Spending	18.5 (18.2)	10.6 (12.5)	10.8 (9.4)	33	43	30
Total Highway Mileage	123.4 (3,546)	129.9 (3,730)	131.5 (3,838)	5	4	4

Source: David R. Morgan, Handbook for State Policy Indicators (3rd ed.; Norman: Bureau of Government Research, University of Oklahoma, 1978).

ILLINOIS STANDING ON SELECTED POLICY INDICATORS

Indicator	Illinois/U.S.[1] 1960	1970	1976	Rank 1960	1970	1976
PUBLIC SAFETY						
Police Protection (Per Capita)	12.05 (10.32)	26.77 (22.11)	52.97 (44.40)	8	7	7
. . . per $1,000 Personal Income	4.61 (4.64)	6.28 (6.04)	7.76 (7.58)	16	9	14
. . . as percent of Total State and Local Spending	4.2 (3.6)	4.4 (3.4)	4.5 (3.7)	5	4	5
Total Crime Rates per 100,000 Population	1,440 (1,038)	2,347 (2,747)	5,055 (5,266)	45	27	32
Property Crime Rate per 100,000 Population	1,169 (902)	1,879 (2,386)	4,586 (4,807)	43	22	30
Violent Crime Rates per 100,000 Population	271.4 (136.0)	468.1 (360.7) (1973)	468.8 459.6)	50	45	40
Inmates per 100,000 Population in State Correctional Facilities	90 (107)	50 (85)		28	36	

[1]U.S. Figures in parentheses

Index